D1047381

FANTASY LITERATURE
FOR CHILDREN
AND YOUNG ADULTS

FANTASY LITERATURE FOR CHILDREN AND YOUNG ADULTS

An Annotated Bibliography

THIRD EDITION

Ruth Nadelman Lynn

R. R. BOWKER
New York

Published by R. R. Bowker Company,
a division of Reed Publishing (USA) Inc.
Copyright © 1989 by Reed Publishing (USA) Inc.
All rights reserved
Printed and bound in the United States of America

Illustration appearing on the cover and title page and
pages 1 and 369 is used courtesy of Delaware Art Museum, Wilmington, Delaware

Library of Congress Cataloging-in-Publication Data

Lynn, Ruth Nadelman, 1948–
    Fantasy literature for children and young adults : an annotated
bibliography / Ruth Nadelman Lynn.—3rd ed.
        p.   cm.
    Rev. ed. of: Fantasy for children. 2nd ed., 1983.
    Includes index.
    ISBN 0-8352-2347-7
    1. Children's literature—Bibliography. 2. Young adult
literature—Bibliography. 3. Fantastic literature—Bibliography.
4. Bibliography—Best books—Children's literature.
5. Bibliography—Best books—Young adult literature.
6. Bibliography—Best books—Fantastic literature. I. Lynn, Ruth
Nadelman, 1948–   Fantasy for children. II. Title.
Z1037.L97 1989
[PN1009.A1]
016.80883'876—dc19   88-8162
                                                                CIP

ISBN 0-8352-2347-7

9 780835 223478

With love to Bruce, to Joshua, and to Noah,
who illuminate my reality with delight
and with joy.

CONTENTS

PREFACE

Fantasy Literature for Children and Young Adults is an annotated bibliography of 3,300 fantasy novels and story collections for children and young adults in grades 3 through 12, as well as a research guide on the authors who write fantasy for children and young adults. The book is intended for use by librarians, teachers, parents, and students in children's and young adult literature courses.

Significant improvements have been made in this, the third edition. Sixteen hundred books have been added to the 1,700 books in the last edition (1983) for a total of 3,300 books in Part One, Annotated Bibliography—a 94 percent increase. The scope has been expanded to include books for young adults in grades 8 through 12. Part Two, Research Guide, which had previously focused on only 75 prominent authors of children's fantasy, now includes critical books, articles, dissertations, interviews, and biographical information on some 600 authors of children's and young adult fantasy literature.

The books in Part One, Annotated Bibliography, are novels and story collections published in English in the United States (including translations) between 1900 and 1988. A few nineteenth-century classics such as Lewis Carroll's *Alice's Adventures in Wonderland* (1865) and Mark Twain's *A Connecticut Yankee in King Arthur's Court* (1889) have also been included. Careful attention has been given to original publication dates and to recommended (by professional review sources discussed later) twentieth-century U.S. editions of these significant works. The same can be said for those works originally published abroad, both in English and in foreign languages that were translated into English. Review citations from professional journals continue to be given in each entry, and only books recommended in two or more sources have been included. Neither science fiction novels nor horror literature has been included, although a number of "science fantasies" with more fantasy elements than science fiction (e.g., McCaffrey's Pern series) and a few short story anthologies containing both fantasy and science fiction or horror will be found.

Part One, Annotated Bibliography

While the genre of children's fantasy is frequently discussed in the professional literature, very little attention has been paid to the burgeoning young adult interest in fantasy. Furthermore, with the exception of a few, necessarily short, book lists published in such journals as *Booklist, English Journal,* and *VOYA,* and one recent nonselective list of paperbacks entitled *Supernatural Fiction for Teens,* there has been until now no comprehensive list of recommended fantasy titles to help middle school, junior high school, high school, and young adult librarians find books for the young people they serve. Therefore, the scope of this bibliography has been expanded to include young adult fantasy and those so-called adult fantasy novels that have found an eager audience in young adults.

The following changes have been made in Part One from the previous edition, including the aforementioned 94 percent increase in titles.

Number of Books per Grade-Level Category. The books can be divided into three broad grade-level categories.

Books written for children in grades 3 through 6 (420 are new to this edition, bringing the total to 1,700).

Books for children and young adults in grades 5 through 8 (430 are new to this edition, bringing the total to 800).

Books for young adults in grades 7 through 12 (750 are new to this edition, bringing the total to 800).

Obviously, the category showing the greatest increase is the young adult category (grades 7 through 12).

Grade-Level Symbols. All books, whether for children or young adults, have been interfiled and arranged in 10 topical chapters, with numerous cross-references. Each entry has been given a specific grade-level designation (for example, Gr. 3–5 or Gr. 8–10). To further aid in accessing a title at a certain grade level, one of three grade-level symbols will be found in the left margin of each entry. These symbols are:

C   Books appropriate for children in grades 3 through 6

C/YA   Books appropriate for those in grades 5 through 8

YA   Books appropriate for young adults in grades 7 through 12

There is an overlap in grades due to the fact that Grade 6 is part of the elementary school (Gr. K–6) in some school systems and part of the middle school (Gr. 6–8) in others.

Reviewing Sources Cited. Seven additional professional reviewing sources have joined the original 17 "Books and Review Journals Cited" (see Abbreviations of Books and Review Journals Cited on p. xvii). All of the books included in this bibliography must have been recommended in at least 2 of these 24 reviewing sources.

Out-of-Print Entries. An ever-growing number of recommended but out-of-print works of fantasy continue to appear in this bibliography. These books still deserve inclusion since many are available in library collections. In this edition unlike the previous edition, all out-of-print entries have a descriptive annotation.

It is discouraging to note how many children's and young adult fantasies are quickly allowed to go out of print in the United States. Some of these outstanding out-of-print works include Andersen's *Seven Tales* (illus. by Sendak), Cresswell's *A Game of Catch* and *Up the Pier*, Curry's *Mindy's Mysterious Miniature* and *The Watchers*, Hale's *The Peterkin Papers*, Harris's *The Moon in the Cloud* trilogy, Ipcar's *The Queen of Spells*,

Jones's *The Ogre Downstairs*, Mayne's *Earthfasts* and *A Grass Rope*, Peyton's *A Pattern of Roses*, and Stolz's *The Cat in the Mirror*.

Many hardcover out-of-print titles are now only available in paperback editions, for example, Aiken's *The Wolves of Willoughby Chase*, Barber's *The Ghosts*, Brown's *The Silver Nutmeg*, Davies's *Conrad's War*, DuBois's *Twenty-One Balloons*, Ende's *The Neverending Story*, Farmer's *Charlotte Sometimes*, Garner's *The Owl Service* and *The Weirdstone of Brisingamen*, Goudge's *The Little White Horse*, Kendall's *The Gammage Cup*, Lively's *The Wild Hunt of the Ghost Hounds*, McKillip's *The Forgotten Beasts of Eld*, Nöstlinger's *Konrad*, Pierce's *The Darkangel*, Raskin's *Figgs and Phantoms*, Sharp's *The Rescuers*, Silverberg's *The Gate of the Worlds*, and Snyder's *Below the Root* and *Black and Blue Magic*.

On the positive side, however, some children's and young adult fantasies have been brought back into print in hardcover editions since the previous edition of this bibliography. These include Boston's *The Children of Green Knowe*, Chase's *The Wicked Pigeon Ladies in the Garden*, Christopher's Winchester trilogy, Dickinson's "Changes" trilogy, Garfield's *Mr. Corbett's Ghost*, Hunter's *Thomas and the Warlock*, Lofting's *The Story of Doctor Dolittle*, Matheson's *Bid Time Return*, Moon's *Knee-Deep in Thunder*, Pearce's *Tom's Midnight Garden*, Preussler's *The Satanic Mill*, Pyle's *The Wonder Clock*, Rawlings's *The Secret River*, Sauer's *Fog Magic*, Stockton's *The Bee-Man of Orn*, and Wrightson's *The Nargun and the Stars*.

Hopefully, enough interest may be generated in other fine out-of-print fantasies to convince publishers to reissue them.

Recommendation Symbols. In this edition, the recommendation symbols [O], outstanding quality recommended in five or more professional review sources or generally regarded as "classics" by librarians who work with children and young adults, and [R], recommended in three to four review sources, have been placed in the left margin of each entry. (The symbol [A], used to denote acceptable quality in the previous edition, has been dropped.) Note that all of the books included in this bibliography have received at least two professional recommendations.

Chapter Title Changes. Chapter 1, "Allegorical Fantasy and Literary Fairy Tales," now combines the "Allegory and Fable" chapter and "Fairy Tale Kingdoms" section of the second edition. Chapter 5, previously entitled "Secondary World Fantasy," has now been retitled "High Fantasy (Heroic or Secondary World Fantasy)."

Other Chapter Changes. Section 5B, "Myth Fantasy," now includes both stories about contemporary protagonists who become entangled in the mythic struggle of good versus evil, as well as retellings of legend and myth, such as Arthurian tales. In the previous editions there was a chapter entitled "Imaginary Beings and Creatures," which listed books in 23 subject categories from angels to unicorns. This made access to specific titles complicated. In the current edition, this chapter has been eliminated and its books have been placed in more appropriate chapters (see the Subject Index under appropriate topical heading, e.g., angels, for location of books about a particular imaginary being).

Sequels. The titles and publication dates of all sequels continue to be given within the main entry annotation. Books with significant sequels have been given expanded annotations, which also include brief plot summaries.

Title Entries for Anthologies. Since it is now commonly accepted library practice to use title entries for anthologies of stories written by many authors and/or compiled by an editor, such anthologies are now listed by title.

Part Two, Research Guide
The following changes have been made in Part Two. Chapter 13, "Teaching Resources," has been added. "Author Studies," Chapter 14, which previously listed information on only 75 prominent authors of children's fantasy, has been expanded to include critical and biographical information on some 600 authors of children's and young adult fantasy literature.

The following sources were used in compiling this Research Guide:

American Writers for Children (*Dictionary of Literary Biography,* Vols. 22, 42, and 52). Detroit: Gale, 1983, 1985, and 1986, respectively.

Cannons, H. G. T. *Bibliography of Library Economy . . . 1876 to 1920.* Chicago: American Library Association, 1927.

Children's Literature, Vols. 1–15. Storrs, CT: Journal of the Modern Language Association, 1972–1974; Philadelphia: Temple University Press, 1975–1978; New Haven, CT: Yale University Press, 1980–1987.

Clareson, Thomas D. *Science Fiction Criticism: An Annotated Checklist.* Kent, OH: Kent State University Press, 1972.

Dictionary of American Children's Fiction, 2 Vols. Westport, CT: Greenwood, 1985 and 1986.

Education Index. New York: Wilson, 1932– .

Hendrickson, Linnea. *Children's Literature: A Guide to the Criticism.* Boston: G. K. Hall, 1987.

Humanities Index. New York: Wilson, 1974– .

International Index. New York: Wilson, 1907–1965.

Junior Book of Authors, 5 Vols. New York: Wilson, 1951–1983.

Leif, Irving P. *Children's Literature: An Historical and Contemporary Bibliography.* Troy, NY: Whitson, 1977.

Library Literature. Chicago: American Library Association, 1921–1934; New York: Wilson, 1935– .

The Oxford Companion to Children's Literature. New York: Oxford University Press, 1984.

Pflieger, Pat, and Hill, Helen M. *A Reference Guide to Modern Fantasy for Children.* Westport, CT: Greenwood, 1984.

Phaedrus: An International Annual of Children's Literature Research. New York: Columbia University School of Library Science, 1973– .

Rahn, Suzanne. *Children's Literature: An Annotated Bibliography of the History and Criticism.* New York: Garland, 1981.

Roginski, Jim. *Newbery and Caldecott Medalists and Honor Book Winners: Bibliography and Resource Materials Through 1977.* Littleton, CO: Libraries Unlimited, 1982.

Science Fiction and Fantasy Reference Index, 1878–1985. Ed. by H. W. Hall. Detroit: Gale, 1987.

Social Science and Humanities Index. New York: Wilson, 1965–1974.

Supernatural Fiction Writers: Fantasy and Horror, 2 Vols. New York: Scribner, 1985.

Survey of Modern Fantasy Literature, 5 Vols. Topsfield, MA: Salem, 1983.

Twentieth Century Children's Writers. New York: St. Martin's, 1983.

Twentieth Century Science Fiction Writers. Chicago: St. James, 1986.

Tymn, Marshall B., and Schlobin, Roger C. *The Year's Scholarship in Science Fiction, Fantasy [and Horror Literature]*, 1972– . (These annual lists are published in the journal *Extrapolation*. Some have also been published as monographs by Kent State University Press, Kent, Ohio. For complete publication information see Chapter 11, "Reference and Bibliography.")

Tymn, Marshall B.; Schlobin, Roger C.; and Currey, L. W. *A Research Guide to Science Fiction Studies*. New York: Garland, 1977.

Writers for Children. New York: Scribner, 1988.

Indexes. A Subject Index has been added to this edition. It includes topical headings on fantasy worlds (e.g., Narnia) and headings on imaginary beings (for example, lilliputians, minnipins, and hobbits). The Subject Index also includes historical periods such as Middle Ages and World War II, and series titles.

Again, I acknowledge the invaluable help of my husband, Bruce, who not only offered loads of encouragement and child care, but spent 13 months of evenings and weekends typing this book! I would also like to thank Simmons College, Boston, and Harvard University, Cambridge, Massachusetts, for allowing me to use their collections for my research.

GUIDE TO USE

Entries in Part One, Annotated Bibliography, contain, where applicable, the following bibliographic information: author's name or pseudonym (the real names of pseudonymous authors are included in parentheses), title, series title in parentheses, suggested grade level, original country of publication other than the United States, and alternate or British title.

Recommendation symbols have been assigned by considering both the number of favorable reviews cited for each title and the degree of recommendation expressed in those reviews. Most entries include a recommendation symbol. If no recommendation symbol appears it is understood that the book received two recommendations from professional reviewing sources. [R] indicates recommended (titles receiving three to four recommendations), and [O] denotes outstanding quality (titles receiving five or more recommendations or those works generally regarded as "classics" by librarians who work with children and young adults).

Following the bibliographic data, annotations provide a brief description of each title. A list of sequels or related works by the same author, including publisher and date, follows the annotation. If the publisher of a series title or related work is the same as that for the main entry title, only the date of publication is given. Sequels or related works judged to be important and significantly different from the main entry have also been given brief descriptive annotations within the main entry.

Each annotation concludes with a notation of any major awards won and a list of review citations. (For a complete list of the review sources used see Abbreviations of Books and Review Journals Cited following this Guide to Use.) Following the annotation, data is provided regarding the illustrator, translator, and adaptor; publisher and date of publication; pagination of the most recent edition; and an o.p. (out of print) designation if applicable.

In cases where a book fits into two or more categories (e.g., time travel and ghost fantasy), it is placed in the chapter that best fits it and a cross-reference is entered in the alternate chapter(s). Cross-references are interfiled alphabetically with the main entries and are listed by author's surname, first name, title of book, and chapter or section reference where the main entry is found.

Each main entry must have been recommended by at least two professional reviewing sources to be considered for inclusion. In addition to the 24 review sources cited (see Abbreviations of Books and Review Journals Cited), publication information has been verified in *American Book Publishing Record, Books in Print 1987–1988, British Books in Print 1986, Cumulative Book Index,* and *National Union Catalog.*

Part Two, Research Guide, is divided into four chapters: Chapter 11, "Reference and Bibliography"; Chapter 12, "History and Criticism"; Chapter 13, "Teaching Resources"; and Chapter 14, "Author Studies." Entries were culled from general periodical indexes, general bibliographies of children's and young adult literature, research lists of adult science fiction and fantasy, and an issue-by-issue search of numerous children's and young adult literature periodicals. A list of the sources used to compile this Research Guide can be found in the Preface. In addition, the specific journals listed in Abbreviations of Books and Review Journals Cited, which follows this Guide to Use, were used.

ABBREVIATIONS OF BOOKS
AND REVIEW JOURNALS CITED

Most journal reviews have been cited by volume and page number. The exceptions are those reviews from *Center for Children's Books, Bulletin* prior to December 1949, *The Horn Book Magazine* prior to 1930, *Library Journal* beginning in 1985, *Times Literary Supplement* for those few years when Roman numerals were used for page numbers, and *VOYA* prior to April 1983. Since these five journals were not given consecutive paging throughout the year, the reviews have been cited by month, year, and page number. For this same reason, all reviews from *Kliatt* and *School Library Journal* have been cited by month, year, and page number.

Seven reviewing sources of children's and young adult literature have been used in this edition for the first time and are preceded by an asterisk (*) below:

BL   *Booklist.* Chicago: American Library Association, 1904– .

* Bookshelf   *The Bookshelf for Boys and Girls.* Edited by Clara W. Hunt, and others. New York: R. R. Bowker, 1918–1935.

CC   *Children's Catalog,* 15th ed. Edited by Richard H. Isaacson, Ferne E. Hillegas, and Juliette Yaakov. New York: H. W. Wilson, 1985; supplements, 1987, 1988.

Ch&Bks   Sutherland, Zena, and Arbuthnot, May Hill. *Children and Books,* 7th ed. Glenview, IL: Scott, Foresman, 1985.

CCBB   *Center for Children's Books, Bulletin.* Chicago: University of Chicago Press, 1948– .

Eakin   Eakin, Mary. *Good Books for Children, 1950–1965,* 3rd ed. Chicago: University of Chicago Press, 1966.

HB   *The Horn Book Magazine.* Boston: Horn Book, 1924– .

JHC   *Junior High School Library Catalog,* 5th ed. Edited by Richard H. Isaacson. New York: H. W. Wilson, 1985; supplements, 1986, 1987.

* Kies   Kies, Cosette. *Supernatural Fiction for Teens.* Littleton, CO: Libraries Unlimited, 1987.

* Kliatt   *Kliatt Young Adult Paperback Book Guide.* Newton, MA: Kliatt Paperback Book Guide, 1966– .

KR   *Kirkus Reviews.* New York: Kirkus Service, 1932– .

LJ   *Library Journal.* New York: R. R. Bowker, 1875–   .

Mahony 1   Mahony, Bertha E. *Books for Boys and Girls: A Suggestive Purchase List.* Boston: Woman's Educational and Industrial Union, Bookshop for Boys and Girls, 1914–1922.

Mahony 2   Mahony, Bertha E., and Whitney, Elinor. *Realms of Gold in Children's Books.* Garden City, NY: Doubleday, 1929.

Mahony 3   Mahony, Bertha E., and Whitney, Elinor. *Five Years of Children's Books: A Supplement to "Realms of Gold."* Garden City, NY: Doubleday, 1936.

Moore   Moore, Anne Carroll. *The Three Owls,* Vol. 3. New York: Macmillan, 1931.

* SHC   *Senior High School Library Catalog,* 13th ed. Edited by Ferne E. Hillegas and Juliette Yaakov. New York: H. W. Wilson, 1987.

SLJ   *School Library Journal.* New York: R. R. Bowker, 1953–   .

Suth   Sutherland, Zena. *The Best in Children's Books, 1966–1972.* Chicago: University of Chicago Press, 1973.

Suth 2   Sutherland, Zena. *The Best in Children's Books, 1973–1978.* Chicago: University of Chicago Press, 1980.

* Suth 3   Sutherland, Zena. *The Best in Children's Books; The University of Chicago Guide to Children's Literature, 1979–1984.* Chicago: University of Chicago Press, 1986.

TLS   [London] *Times Literary Supplement.* London, England: Times Newspapers, Ltd., 1938–   .

* Tymn   Tymn, Marshall B.; Zahorski, Kenneth J.; and Boyer, Robert H. *Fantasy Literature; A Core Collection and Reference Guide.* New York: R. R. Bowker, 1979.

* VOYA   *VOYA: Voice of Youth Advocates.* Metuchen, NJ: Scarecrow Press, 1977–   .

INTRODUCTION

> True fantasy . . . is not so much created as it is distilled and
> interpreted—from impressions that go far back into pre-history,
> impressions that, so far as we can tell from the study of folk tales, are
> common to us all, no matter what our age or nationality. True
> fantasy . . . aims to define the universe. Fantasy offers a system of
> symbols everyone of every age understands; it enriches and simplifies our
> lives and makes them bearable.[1]

These are the words of author and illustrator Natalie Babbitt, whose book, *Tuck Everlasting,* has become a modern fantasy classic.

She and the other authors of contemporary fantasy literature for young people whose work will be discussed here, have created stories that have been called "the most wrenching, depth-provoking kind of fiction available to our children,"[2] in a literary genre that has been described as "the richest and most varied of all of the genres."[3] According to critic Elizabeth Nesbit, "no other type of book has done more to give genuine distinction to children's literature than has fantasy."[4]

"Fantasy literature" is a broad term used to describe books in which magic causes impossible, and often wondrous, events to occur. Fantasy tales can be set in our own everyday world or in a "secondary" world or time somewhat like our own. The existence of the magic cannot be explained. Tales of fantasy should not be confused with science fiction stories, which involve a future made more or less possible by scientific or technological advances.

Paradoxically, imaginative fantasies, especially those written for young people over the past quarter-century or so, often contain the most serious of underlying themes. Such themes as the conflict between good and evil, the struggle to preserve joy and hope in a cruel and frightening world, and the acceptance of the inevitability of death have led some critics to suggest that fantasies may portray a truer version of reality than many or most realistic novels.

For the purposes of this book, "children's" books are those written for children in grades 3 through 6 (about ages 8–12) and "young adult" books are those written for young people in grades 6 through 12 (ages 11–18), as well as those "adult" books that have been adopted by young adult readers. There is an overlap in grade 6 because it is part of the elementary school in some school systems and in the middle school in others.

What is fantasy literature for children and young adults? How does it differ from fantasy written for adults? What is the appeal of fantasy? How does the development of fantasy fit into the development of children's and young adult literature in general? Why do authors write fantasy? Hundreds of articles and books have attempted to answer these questions. This introduction surveys the important critical literature on these topics and contains a historical overview of the outstanding fantasy literature for children and young adults.

Defining Fantasy

The Oxford English Dictionary states that the two forms of the word *fantasy,* spelled "fantasy" and "phantasy," come from the Latin *phantasia* and the Greek φαντραοια, meaning "a making visible." The predominant sense of *fantasy* is described as "caprice, whim, fanciful invention," and that of *phantasy* as "imagination, visionary notion." The 1972 *Supplement* (reprinted 1986) adds that fantasy as a literary composition "deals with things that are not and cannot be."[5]

The Random House Dictionary of the English Language defines fantasy literature as "an imaginative or fanciful work, especially one dealing with supernatural or unnatural events or characters."[6] Literary critics and fantasists have enlarged upon these definitions.

Critical definitions of fantasy vary from the ambiguous, for example, "Fantasy may be almost all things to all men" and "Fantasy . . . is so many different things that attempts to define it seem rather pointless," to the obscure: "[In fantasy] the perspectives enforced by the ground rules of the narrative world must be diametrically contradicted." Between these poles lies a great variety of interpretations.[7]

The two elements of fantastic literature given the greatest weight by critics and fantasists alike are the presence of magic[8] and of the impossible or inexplicable.[9] Critic Jane Mobley has observed that within a fantasy narrative no attempt is made to explain the origin of the magic, it simply exists; and she suggests that the narrative itself is in a sense magical in its ability to enchant readers, drawing them into another world where they demand no explanation as to how they got there.[10]

Many critics have written of fantasy's violation of natural laws,[11] and others give the element of "wonder"[12] prime importance in defining fantasy literature. Still others point to fantasy literature's propensity for pushing past the boundaries of the realities of our own world, the so-called primary world, into secondary otherworlds. Ann Swinfen describes modern fantasy as "a serious form of the modern novel, often characterized by notable literary merit, and concerned both with heightened awareness of the complex nature of primary reality and with the exploration beyond empirical experience into the transcendent reality embodied in imaginative and spiritual otherworlds."[13]

Critic Sheila Egoff and fantasist Eleanor Cameron have pointed out the paradoxes inherent in fantasy. According to Egoff:

Fantasy is a literature of paradox. It is the discovery of the real within the unreal, the credible within the incredible, the believable within the unbelievable. . . . The creators of fantasy may use the most fantastic, weird and bizarre images and happenings but their basic concern is with the wholesomeness of the human soul, or to use a more contemporary term, the integrity of the self. . . . The tenet of the fantasist is "there is another kind of real, one that is truer to the human spirit, demanding a pilgrim's progress to find it."[14]

To Cameron, the paradox of fantasy is that all fantasy that works has a sense of reality; that within the everyday world of the novel there exists a pool of magic possessing a strange but powerful and convincing reality of its own.[15]

It should come as no surprise that fantasists should have their own unique visions of the nature of fantasy. To J. R. R. Tolkien, in *Tree and Leaf* (Houghton, 1965), fantasy is the making or glimpsing of otherworlds. For Jane Langton, fantasy novels are "waking dreams. They make up to us for the sense of loss we feel when we wake up and find our dreams shrinking out of memory. A literary fantasy gives us a dream back to keep." Lloyd Alexander also speaks of dreams, as he succinctly calls attention to the psychological depths that fantasy probes and the fact that even so-called realistic novels are an author's invention: "I suppose you might define realism as fantasy pretending to be true; and fantasy as reality pretending to be a dream." And Mollie Hunter explains that her vision of fantasy comes from her memories of childhood: "as a writer . . . I find that the form of children's literature which best exemplifies both the fascinated terror [of childhood memory] and the yearning [for a sudden glimpse of something strange and wonderful] is what—for lack of a more exact name—we refer to as fantasy."[16]

Fantasy has been variously described as imaginative, fanciful, visionary, strange, otherworldly, supernatural, mysterious, frightening, magical, inexplicable, wondrous, dreamlike, and, paradoxically, realistic. It has been termed an awareness of the inexplicable existence of "magic" in the everyday world, a yearning for a sudden glimpse of something strange and wonderful, and a different and perhaps truer version of reality.

If it is difficult to encapsulate the entire genre of fantasy literature into a single definition, we can, nevertheless, acknowledge the powerful effect that fantasy can have on its readers. As Ursula K. Le Guin asserts:

> [Fantasy] is a different approach to reality, an alternative technique for apprehending and coping with existence. It is not antirational, but pararational; not realistic, but surrealistic, superrealistic; a heightening of reality. . . . Fantasy is nearer to poetry, to mysticism, and to insanity than naturalistic fiction is. . . .
> A fantasy is a journey. It is a journey into the subconscious mind, just as psychoanalysis is. Like psychoanalysis, it can be dangerous; and *it will change you.*[17]

The Purpose of Fantasy

Does fantasy have any function beyond entertainment? Certainly, it can be entertaining. It can also provide the reader with insights into himself or herself through identification with or rejection of a particular character. In these ways it parallels the literature of other genres. But critics and fantasists agree that good fantasy does more. Jane Mobley writes in *Phantasmagoria* (Anchor, 1977) that fantasy's purpose is to evoke wonder and mystery, and Lloyd Alexander tells readers in a *Library Journal* article (December 15, 1966) that its purpose is to refresh the heart through escape or "liberation."

Sheila Egoff and Ursula K. Le Guin have pointed out fantasy's unique way of helping us to better understand our own world. Unlike other genres, which tend to offer either a total escape from or total immersion in reality, fantasy can meet both needs. Egoff puts it this way, "The purpose of fantasy is not to escape reality, but to illuminate it: to transport us to a world different from the real world, yet to demonstrate certain immutable truths that persist even there—and in every possible world."[18]

Critic Swinfen agrees that "the fundamental purpose of serious fantasy is to comment upon the real world and to explore the moral, philosophical and other dilemmas posed by it."[19]

Imagery of Fantasy

Some authors assert that they begin their writing with a mental image, rather than specific characters or a completely developed plot. It is interesting, therefore, to compare the variety of images that some fantasists have used to describe fantasy itself. These images range from onions to soap bubbles.

Alan Garner likens the many layers of meaning found in a serious fantasy to an onion:

> In order to connect, the book must be written for all levels of experience. This means that any given piece of text must work at simple plot level . . . and it must also work for me, and for every stage between. . . . An onion can be peeled down through its layers, but it is always, at every layer, an onion, whole in itself. I try to write onions.[20]

Jane Louise Curry also uses a spherical image in her analogy between the structure of a "visionary" fantasy and that of a pearl:

> The fantasy of the lost "ph" . . . is rarely, if ever, simply a picaresque series of adventures like bright Venetian beads on a string. More often—if it approaches real excellence—it is shaped as a single pearl is shaped: a whole built up around a theme, or person, or place, or relationship.[21]

Susan Cooper compares the ephemeral nature of fantasy to a soap bubble:

> [Fantasy is] the most magnificent bubble I have ever seen, iridescent, gleaming . . . and in the sunlight all the colors in the world were swimming over that gleaming sphere—swirling, glowing, achingly beautiful. Like a dancing rainbow the bubble hung there for a long moment; then it was gone.[22]

French literary scholar Paul Hazard describes the nature of fairy tales as a deep pool: "Fairy tales are like beautiful mirrors of water, so deep and crystal clear! In their depth we sense the mysterious experience of a thousand years. Their contents date from the primeval ages of humanity."[23]

A final example of descriptive imagery comes from the *Green and Burning Tree* (Little, Brown, 1969), in which Eleanor Cameron likens fantasists to wizards, whose imaginative virtuosity allows them to toss up ideas like dazzling brilliantly colored balls; wizards able to juggle past, present, and future with a deftness that almost defies analysis.[24]

Children's and Young Adult Fantasy versus Adult Fantasy

It is obvious that novels for children and young adults can usually be distinguished from novels for adults on the superficial level of format: Children's and young adult novels are often (but not always) shorter and printed in a larger typeface with wider margins. Some children's novels are illustrated. Most, but not all, human protagonists of children's and young adult novels tend to be young people.

Fantasist Natalie Babbitt maintains that although children's literature deals with all of the so-called adult emotions of love, pride, grief, fear of death, violence, and the yearning for success, there is one emotion to be found only in children's books, and that is joy.[25]

Although overt sexuality is usually avoided in books for children and young adults, children's and young adult fantasies can be as complex in terms of plot, theme, and writing style as "adult" fantasies. According to Swinfen: "It is quite clear from any prolonged study of what might be termed 'high fantasy,' that to label them as children's books is grossly misleading. They operate on an adult level of meaning and the issue of deciding the dividing line, if such could ever exist, between worthwhile literature for children and for adults seems to be a futile exercise."[26]

Indeed, Sheila Egoff asserts in *Thursday's Child* that "fantasy written for children is far superior to that written for adults." In the not-too-distant past, however, critical agreement seemed to be quite the opposite. "Adult" literary critics tended to lump children's fantasies under the heading "light entertainment." *Peter Pan* was frequently offered as an example of the frivolousness of fantasy literature for children.[27]

Even librarian Donnarae MacCann, a proponent of children's fantasy, concluded that

The only notable difference in an author's stylistic treatment when he writes for the child audience is the overall tone of gaiety or sympathetic understanding pervading the story. The same writer, perhaps, may allow some bitterness to colour his communications with his peers.[28]

And as recently as 1973, Lin Carter, an author of "adult" fantasy, maintained that "A fantasy is a book or story . . . in which magic really works—not a fairy tale, not a story for children, like *Peter Pan* or *The Wizard of Oz*, but a work of fiction for adults—a story which challenges the mind, which sets it working."[29]

Obviously, Carter was unaware that such powerful "children's" fantasies as William Mayne's *Earthfasts*, Alan Garner's *The Owl Service*, Ursula K. Le Guin's *A Wizard of Earthsea*, and Susan Cooper's *The Dark Is Rising* had already been published. Certainly, none of these "children's" fantasies could be characterized as whimsical, or lighthearted, and it is even more certain that reading any of these novels would "challenge the mind."

What, then, *does* differentiate a "children's" fantasy from an "adult" fantasy, if it is not lightness of tone or the absence of substance? Natalie Babbitt feels that the one tangible difference is that all the children's stories we remember longest and love best have "happy endings."

Not, please . . . a simple "happily ever after," or . . . the kind of contrived final sugar coating that seems to be tacked on . . . but . . . something which goes much deeper, something which turns a story ultimately toward hope rather than resignation and contains within it a difference not only between the two literatures but also between youth and age.[30]

Youth Response versus Adult Response

Other critics and fantasists have turned the question around, proposing that it is not the books that are different, but the level of response to the story that separates adult readers from child readers. "A fantasy," says Sheila Egoff, "may often be read on two levels. It may be only an adventure story for some children; others will have—at once, or on later reflection—the richer experience of sensing the inner truths behind the exciting and entertaining tale."[31]

Critic Neil Philip proposes that children respond to what they read on an emotional level, whereas adults are more analytical. Adults, according to Philip, think like philosophers, using a logical progression of ideas to produce a solution. Whereas children think like poets, gaining insight from a condensation of images, allowing them to experience emotions they may not be able to explain or to completely understand.[32]

Fantasist Susan Cooper feels that children are more open to accepting the fantastic than are adults:

> [It is not] surprising that we [fantasists] should be read, today, mainly by children . . . children are the natural audience for fantasy. They aren't a different species. They're us, a little while ago. It's just that they are still able to accept mystery. . . . They still know the essence of wonder, which is to live without ever being quite sure what to expect. And therefore, quite often, to encounter delight.[33]

According to Ursula K. Le Guin, "Fantasy is the great age-equalizer, if it's good when you're twelve, it's quite likely to be just as good, or better when you're thirty-six."[34]

In the genre of fantasy as a whole, there are great variations in tone and complexity, both in literature written for children and young adults and that written for adults. It seems clear, however, that as in all literature, it is the level of the reader's understanding and his or her willingness to accept the presence of magic and impossibility that determine an individual's choice of reading material.

Classifying Fantasy

In an effort to analyze the many works grouped under the heading Fantasy Literature, the genre has often been subdivided. Fantasies have been categorized by subject matter, by setting, by degree of seriousness of treatment, and by the sex of the author. Psychologist Ravenna Helson, writing in *Horn Book Magazine* (April 1970), feels that fantasies written by men differ from those written by women. Her categories for men's novels are "wish fulfillment and humor," "heroism," and "tender feelings"; and for women's novels, "independence and self-expression," "transformation," and "inner mystery and awe."

In his essay, "On Fairy-Stories," J. R. R. Tolkien separated stories that are set in, or involve, a world other than our own from those tales set in the real world. He called the otherworlds "Secondary Worlds," and our world the "Primary World." Tolkien concluded that only those stories involving secondary worlds were "true" fairy stories. In addition, he outlined four essential elements of a good fairy story: "Fantasy, Recovery, Escape, and Consolation." He described Fantasy as the author's "image-making" or "subcreation"; Recovery as insight or renewal; Escape as a liberation from life's evils, rather than an evasion of reality; and Consolation as a happy ending or "eucatastrophe."

Like Tolkien, critics Tymn, Zahorski, and Boyer, in their *Fantasy Literature* (Bowker, 1979), use setting to distinguish various types of fantasy written for adults. They label those stories set in the real world as Low Fantasy and those set in secondary worlds as High Fantasy. The High Fantasy category includes "myth fantasy" (interpreted retellings of myth), "faery tales," "gothic fantasy" (weird tales with no rational explanation), and "science fantasy" (tales offering a scientific explanation for the existence of the secondary world, but that use magic during the remainder of the story).

Fantasist Jane Louise Curry divides fantasy stories into two categories:

There are excellences and excellences. I would suggest, always with qualifications and reservations in mind, that the two broad types of fantasy differ in focus, tone, technique, and quality of insight in much the same way that fairy tale differs from myth. In one, our attention is focused primarily on the story or action, itself; in the other it is the feeling, the emotional dimension, that holds us.[35]

Although both types of fantasy story can be well written, they appeal to the reader in different ways. For example, Norton's *The Borrowers* and Grahame's *The Wind in the Willows* and *The Reluctant Dragon* "are 'dear' to us," writes Curry, whereas Boston's *Green Knowe* books, Mayne's *Earthfasts,* Lewis's *Chronicles of Narnia,* Tolkien's *Lord of the Rings,* Garner's *Elidor* and *The Owl Service,* and Pearce's *Tom's Midnight Garden*

> are not "dear" to us. It may be nearer the truth to say that they are a power *over* us. . . . Our feeling for them is of quite a different quality. . . . Fantasy offers on one hand entertainment, reassurance, and—yes—escape: on the other, involvement, provocation ideas and insights, consolation, and the intensification of feeling. . . . Whimsical fantasy may give us deep delight, but "visionary" fantasy can give us joy.[36]

The Mythic Element in Contemporary Fantasy

Critics Sheila Egoff and Ralph Lavender have noted that children's novels that relive or reinterpret myth or legend and those that "cast fantasy within the structure of legend" were a notable development of the 1970s.[37] Ursula K. Le Guin, Alan Garner, William Mayne, Susan Cooper, and others, have written fantasies of great seriousness and depth. These books, which usually center around a battle of good versus evil, are of two types. Some involve modern-day characters in dangerous encounters with the mythological past—and a magic that breaks into their everyday world. In others, entirely new mythologies are created. Egoff has observed that

> the mythic element in modern fantasy gives a quasi-religious tone to the narrative; we are persuaded that we are concerned with major moral issues, that the very stability and continuity of our world is at stake. This is in contrast to the magical, almost capricious supernatural efforts of older fantasies [such as *Mary Poppins, Peter Pan,* or E. Nesbit's books].[38]

The Appeal of Fantasy

Fantasy has appeal for adults as well as for children and young adults. Adults find it "a source of marvel and mystery and wonder and joy that [they] find nowhere else." It brings "a sense of the strange, the numinous, the totally Other, . . . [into their lives, as well as something that] cannot be found in any human relationship . . . queer pricklings of delight, excitement and terror . . . magic."[39]

Young people can find adventure, humor, and nonsense in fantasy, while their emotions are being touched and their imaginations stretched. Susan Cooper explains fantasy's appeal for children:

> Very young children, their conscious minds not yet developed, are all feeling and instinct. Closer to the unconscious than they will ever be again, they respond naturally to the archetypes and the deep echoes of fairy story, ritual, and myth. . . . Some children . . . go on seeking out fantasy all their lives, instinc-

tively aware that far from being babyish, it is probably the most complex form of fiction they will ever find.[40]

For fantasist Jane Langton ("The Weak Place . . ."), fantasy "feeds a hunger we didn't know we had," and for critic Jane Mobley (*Phantasmagoria*), it satisfies "the human craving to be carried or enchanted to worlds beyond the one we know, or to have revealed to us here in this world some glimpse of the other."

Fantasy can also provide a fresh perspective on our own world. C. S. Lewis observed that

> fairyland arouses a longing [in the reader] for he knows not what. It stirs and troubles him (to his lifelong enrichment) with the dim sense of something beyond his reach and, far from dulling or emptying the actual world, gives it a new dimension of depth. He does not despise the real woods because he has read of enchanted woods: the reading makes all real woods a little enchanted. This is a special kind of longing.[41]

The concept of time is one aspect of contemporary fantasy that many readers find particularly intriguing. According to Jane Louise Curry: "There is great force in the recognition that today holds yesterday and tomorrow within it: that 'past,' 'present,' and 'future' are not labels to put on isolated pigeonholes . . . [that] the same moment *does* contain the mundane and the marvellous."[42] And Tolkien emphasizes the profound emotional effect great fantasy can have on its readers: "in a serious tale of faerie . . . when the sudden 'turn' comes, we get a piercing glimpse of joy, and heart's desire, that for a moment passes outside the frame, rends indeed the very web of the story, and lets a gleam come through."[43]

Fantasy's direct relationship to our own lives is conveyed by Lloyd Alexander:

> If a work of fantasy delights, refreshes, or gloriously terrifies us, it also encourages us on our own adventures, richer and more exciting than any fiction. . . . [And] whether we're children or grownups, fantasy can move us because it suggests a world where all we value as human beings—courage, justice, love—really work.[44]

The Effect of Fantasy on Children

It seems clear that reading fantasy is beneficial as well as enjoyable for young people. According to Kornei Chukovskii, literary critic and preeminent Soviet children's author:

> Fantasy is the most valuable attribute of the human mind and it should be diligently nurtured from earliest childhood, as one nurtures musical sensitivity—and not crushed. . . . Without imaginative fantasy there would be complete stagnation in both physics and chemistry . . . the value of such tales [is] in developing, strengthening, enriching, and directing children's thinking and emotional responses.[45]

Psychologist Bruno Bettelheim and others have explored the therapeutic value of fairy tales in defusing children's anxieties and resolving their emotional conflicts. And fantasist Lloyd Alexander feels that "Fantasy, by its power to move us so deeply, to dramatize, even melodramatize, morality, can be one of the most effective means of establishing a capacity for adult values."[46]

It is logical to presume that an exposure to fairy tales and fantasy as a child will aid the adult in appreciating more sophisticated literature. Indeed, the lack of exposure to imaginative tales as a child may preclude an adult's interest in epic, allegory, and folklore; at the very least it may make a "suspension of belief" difficult to achieve. Fantasist Penelope Lively contends that fantasy helps children learn about human nature and develop a sense of place and time.

> Children need to sense that we live in a permanent world that reaches away and behind and ahead of us, and that the span of a lifetime is something to be wondered at, and thought about, and that—above all—people evolve during their own lives . . . [They] end up a curious irrational blend of experience and memory. . . . Perhaps books can help, just a little.[47]

Eleanor Cameron finds hope for adult perceptions in children's response to fantasy:

> [Fantasy is] a form of literature which . . . [helps] young children to orient themselves in the surrounding world, that enriches their spiritual development, that enables them to regard themselves as fearless participants in imaginary struggles for justice, goodness, and freedom. . . . I feel that in a child's longing for what cannot be expressed, in his love of what cannot be proved, his cherishing of a vision, there lies a kind of hope. If he guards it and has faith in it, there is nothing more powerful. It may even be the beginning of illumination, and this is to me the precious element in any work of art.[48]

Adverse Criticism of Fantasy Literature

Those critics who feel that fantasy is not an important literary genre often dismiss such works as "escapist." According to Ursula K. Le Guin:

> There is still, in this country, a deep puritanical distrust of fantasy. . . . Fantasy, to [its critics] is escapism. . . . They confuse fantasy, which in the psychological sense is a universal and essential faculty of the human mind, with infantilism and pathological regression. . . . [On the contrary,] fantasy is the natural, the appropriate language for the recounting of the spiritual journey and the struggle of good and evil in the soul.[49]

Donnarae MacCann points out that

> Some adults distrust fantasies as being somehow "unhealthy." They raise the question, "won't these dwarfs and talking beasts encourage unwholesome fantasizing on the part of children or make them withdraw from the real world?" These fears result from a confusion of terms: confusion of the word fantasy when it refers to a *literary form* with fantasy as a *psychological illness.*[50]

Fantasists Alan Garner and Susan Cooper have refuted such suspicions. According to Garner: "Mythology is not an escape, it is not an entertainment. It is an attempt to come to terms with reality, and therefore I would say that fantasy that works is not an escape from life. . . . It is a coming to terms with reality, it is a clarification . . ."; and Cooper contends: "When we depart from our own reality into the reality of the book . . . we're going out of time, out of space, into the unconscious. . . . We aren't escaping out, we're escaping in, without any idea of what we may encounter. Fantasy is the metaphor through which we discover ourselves."[51]

It is interesting to note that two otherwise valuable and scholarly works on children's literature, psychologist Bruno Bettelheim's *The Uses of Enchantment* and French literary critic Isabelle Jan's *On Children's Literature,* disparage contemporary fantasy for young people. Both authors have, it would seem, based their criticisms on an outdated reading of the genre. In 1969 Jan wrote: "Apart from [Kipling and de Ségur] the modern fairy tale has definitely had its day," and proceeds to accuse children's fantasy novels of static settings, a lack of character development, and stereotypical protagonists. She concludes that "Children who are not brought up by nurses in a nursery and for whom [boarding] school lore is something they know only by hearsay or from books, find it difficult to appreciate fantasy. . . . To be successful, children's stories must correspond to real experiences."[52]

That final sentence is most important. "Real experience" always underlies the fantasies written by Alan Garner, William Mayne, Ursula K. Le Guin, Susan Cooper, and Philippa Pearce, to name but a few contemporary children's and young adult fantasists. A reading of even one or two of these authors' novels would demonstrate that such criticisms are unfounded. In spite of their lack of a "nursery upbringing" or a "boarding school education," children and young adults today still read and enjoy fantasy.

A second example of what would appear to be unfounded criticism of modern fantasy is found in Bruno Bettelheim's *The Uses of Enchantment*. Bettelheim devoted only 5 of the 328 pages of his analysis of the effects of fairy tales on children to the thousands of "modern" fantasy novels for children. In these five pages, he makes two questionable judgments. The first is that "Many of these modern tales have sad endings, which fail to provide the escape and consolation which the fearsome events in the fairy tale make necessary, to strengthen the child for meeting the vagaries of his life."[53] Oddly enough, the only "modern" tale Bettelheim mentions by name is *The Blue Bird,* a play written by Maurice Maeterlinck in 1909. A more up-to-date reading of children's fantasy novels would seem warranted. In this light, fantasist Natalie Babbitt's remarks about hope and happy endings are particularly to the point (see notes 30 and 60).

In his second criticism, Bettelheim dismisses "modern" fantasy because "when children are asked to name their favorite fairy tales, hardly any modern tales are among their choices." To back up this statement, he cites a 1958 study in which 264 college students were asked to recall their favorite children's stories. The study found that 59 percent of the women and 30 percent of the men preferred "fairy tales" (including "new tales of magic like *The Wizard of Oz, Brer Rabbit,* and *Little Black Sambo*") to "fiction."[54]

Putting aside the fact that *The Wizard of Oz* is a fantasy novel, not a fairy tale, and that the study's findings do not seem to support Bettelheim's thesis, one obvious question arises: What "modern" tales could students who read children's books before 1950 be expected to mention? A study of adult recollections of books read over 40 years ago could not possibly render relevant information about the reading habits of contemporary children. To dismiss the entire genre of children's fantasy on such a basis is indefensible.

Why Write Fantasy?

Why do writers create fantasy and what makes their work successful? The critical view is expressed by Sheila Egoff, Jane Mobley, and Ann Swinfen. According to Egoff: "Modern fantasists . . . engender a sense of wonder in readers, not so much by making us realize that the fantastic and the real can coexist, as by convincing us that they already do so"; and Mobley says: "The skillful fantasist is the true wizard. Through the magic of naming he makes reality, he calls things into being. As namer, the wonder-storyteller is a poet, and his is the oldest form of poetry: incantation, the making of magic through words."[55] Swinfen writes:

> It is noteworthy that fantasy, which some might expect to be a literature of "withdrawal," since it is so often carelessly dismissed as "escapist," is in reality employed to condemn [the temptation toward violence and withdrawal]. . . . Those views of society which are expressed with such remarkable consistency by so many of the writers of serious modern fantasy arise from a desperate dissatisfaction with contemporary life, a need to break free and realize full human potential. These writers of fantasy are thus amongst the latest voices in the long tradition of liberal humanism in English literature.[56]

Each fantasist has, of course, his or her own answers. According to Andre Norton in *The Book of Andre Norton* (DAW, 1975), "You cannot write fantasy unless you love it, unless you yourself can believe in what you're telling." Helen Cresswell asserts: "I write fantasy . . . because I have always had a very strong sense of the miraculous being about to erupt into the everyday."[57] And Roger W. Drury writes fantasy stories "because they make children creative; because children reared on such stories grow into resourceful adults, who are never bored or cornered. . . . I write such tales because I like them that way. My realism comes naturally with a wide fringe."[58]

In his well-known article "On Three Ways of Writing for Children," C. S. Lewis states that he writes "a children's story because a children's story is the best art-form for something you have to say . . . of course readers who want to hear that will read the story or reread it at any age."[59]

Natalie Babbitt feels that children's fantasists are people who have not settled for compromise in their lives, who have retained their childlike hope that in the end, everything will turn out all right.[60]

Like any artist, a fantasist must draw his or her creations from within, both from his or her conscious experiences and from the unconscious. According to Susan Cooper, "I think those of us who write fantasy are dedicated to making impossible things seem likely, making dreams seem real. . . . Our writing is haunted by those parts of our experience which we do not understand, or even consciously remember."[61] Ursula K. Le Guin carries this one step further. She proposes that writers of fantasy inevitably draw on the "collective unconscious" for their inspiration, whether they intend to or not.

> The artist who goes into himself most deeply—and it is a painful journey—is the artist who touches us most closely, speaks to us most clearly. . . .
> So it would seem that true myth arises only in the process of connecting the conscious and the unconscious realms. . . .
> The writer who draws not upon the works and thoughts of others, but upon his own thoughts and his own deep being, will inevitably hit upon common material. The more original his work, the more imperiously *recognizable* it will be. "Yes, of course!" says the reader, recognizing himself, his dreams, his nightmares.[62]

Mollie Hunter concurs: "no such thing as pure fantasy exists. There is only a succession of folk memories filtered through the storyteller's imagination, and since all mankind shares in these memories, they are the common store on which the modern storyteller must draw in his attempts to create fantasy."[63]

Whether or not a fantasist realizes that his or her works are rooted in "the collective unconscious," good fantasy must have all of the elements of good fiction—unique style, memorable plot and characters, and deep meaning. The additional element needed to ensure the creation of lasting works of fantasy is the author's ability to share his or her wholehearted belief that the impossible is possible.

Patricia Wrightson describes her craft: "What it is that writers do . . . they drop stones into pools: finding a visionary stone, handling and weighing it; dropping it into a pool of another mind; watching for the ripples to spread, and perhaps for the stirred water to give something back."[64]

Women as Fantasists

It should not be necessary to point out that there have been great fantasies written by women as well as by men. Yet it has been asserted that women have not been, and could not be, great fantasists. In an article published in *New Society* in 1962, critic Helen Lourie characterizes Hans Christian Andersen, Lewis Carroll, George MacDonald, and J. M. Barrie as writers of genius, and concludes:

> Is it an accident that all these writers, and those in the same group who are writing today are men? No. . . . Women can be excellent storytellers: their powers of invention and fancy are not inferior to that of men. But what they lack is the wholehearted abandonment to their inspiration: the power to enter the other world . . . without keeping some conscious hold on normality.[65]

Aside from the antifeminist bias of Lourie's conclusions, she seems to have overlooked a few authors. E. Nesbit and Selma Lagerlöf were both writing during the early years of children's fantasy. As for writers of Lourie's day, L. M. Boston, Rumer Godden, Carol Kendall, Mary Norton, and Philippa Pearce have produced unquestionable literary masterpieces. And today, Natalie Babbitt, Eleanor Cameron, Susan Cooper, Diana Wynne Jones, Ursula K. Le Guin, Anne McCaffrey, Robin McKinley, Margaret Mahy, Rosemary Sutcliff, and Patricia Wrightson are only a few of the masters of young people's fantasy who are women.

A Historical Overview of Children's and Young Adult Fantasy

> Most children's classics that have lasted from earlier times are fantasies, mainly because they are a literature least dependent upon the immediacy of time and surroundings.[66]

In *Thursday's Child: Trends and Patterns in Contemporary Children's Literature,* Sheila Egoff has done an impressive job of relating the historical development of children's literature to the evolution of Western society's attitude toward children. It seems so obvious now that Egoff has explained it, but her presentation is a unique one, and the following is an attempt to relate her theory to the development of European and American children's fantasy as a genre. In this edition of *Fantasy Literature for Children and Young Adults,* additional information has been added about the history of young adult fantasy.

Original fantasy stories for children and young adults are a fairly recent phenomenon. Invented tales of wonder and magic began appearing in English only around the middle of the nineteenth century, and fantasies written specifically for young adults did not really proliferate until after the middle of the twentieth century. *The Hope of the Katzekopfs,* written in 1844 by F. E. Paget, is considered to be the first English children's fantasy. It was preceded, of course, by a rich tradition of oral folklore, anonymous tales of magical creatures and occurrences, passed from one generation to the next. Before 1850, however, books written specifically for children tended to be didactic, moralistic tales, and the children themselves were regarded as miniature adults who were constantly admonished to be "good." There were no "teenagers" in the nineteenth century; young people in their teens were considered to be adults, and those who could read were given adult books.

Hans Christian Andersen was the first great writer of original fantasy for children. His tales, published in Denmark beginning in 1837, were translated into English in 1846 and are still among the most loved of all children's stories. Critic Margery Fisher describes Andersen's genius:

> There are plenty of writers since Andersen who have animated tin soldiers. . . . But to draw tears and smiles, quite spontaneous and genuine, on account of a lead soldier with one leg and a paper doll—that takes genius. Not cleverness or wit or ingenuity, but the power to compel truth out of yourself that has grown slowly out of childhood impressions. This is how writers of fairy tale work.[67]

The latter half of the nineteenth century has been called the first "golden age" of children's literature and it was during this period, the Victorian era, that Western children were finally deemed worthy of a literature of their own. Children were still seen as basically good, but different from adults. They were looked at as mischievous but perceptive, and they were finally given books with interesting characters and exciting plots.

Many of the Victorian fantasies are now considered classics. They include John Ruskin's *The King of the Golden River* (written in 1841, published in 1851), Mrs. Fairstar's *Memoirs of a London Doll* (1846 in England; 1852 in the United States), William Makepeace Thackeray's *The Rose and the Ring* (1855), Frances Browne's *Granny's Wonderful Chair* (1856 in England; 1900 in the United States), the Comtesse de Sègur's *The Enchanted Forest* (1856 in France; 1869 in the United States), Charles Kingsley's *The Water Babies* (1863), Lewis Carroll's *Alice's Adventures in Wonderland* (1865), Jean Ingelow's *Mopsa the Fairy* (1869), and George MacDonald's *At the Back of the North Wind* (1871, 1875) and *The Princess and the Goblin* (1872).

These books were followed by Mary L. Molesworth's *The Cuckoo Clock* (1877), Carlo Collodi's *The Adventures of Pinocchio* (written in Italy in 1880; published in the United States in 1892), Lucretia P. Hale's *The Peterkin Papers* (1880), Richard Jeffries's *Wood Magic* (1882), Louise de la Ramée's *The Nürnberg Stove* (1882 in France; 1901 in the United States), Frank R. Stockton's *The Bee-Man of Orn and Other Fanciful Tales* (1884), Howard Pyle's *Pepper and Salt* (1886) and *The Wonder Clock* (1887), Oscar Wilde's *The Selfish Giant* (1888), Andrew Lang's *Prince Prigio* (1889), Rudyard Kipling's *The Jungle Book* (1894), Laurence Housman's *A Doorway in Fairyland* (1894–1904 in England; 1905 in the United States), and Kenneth Grahame's *The Reluctant Dragon* (1898 in England; 1938 in the United States).

"An interesting fact," notes critic Naomi Lewis, "is that the fantasy genre was attracting (if briefly) most of the leading adult novelists. Ruskin, Thackeray, Dickens, Kingsley—MacDonald too—were all basically writers for adults when they turned to this new kind [of novel]; and though they chose themes of magic, they did not temper their manner or approach, so their books interest adults too."[68]

As a matter of fact, some of the "adult" fantasy works of this period are still read today, both by adults and young adults. This list might include Edward Bellamy's

Looking Backward: 2000–1887 (1888), Mark Twain's *A Connecticut Yankee in King Arthur's Court* (1889), Oscar Wilde's *The Picture of Dorian Gray* (1891), and William Morris's *The Well at the World's End* (1896). William Morris has been called the father of modern high fantasy, and his work influenced many others, including Lord Dunsany, J. R. R. Tolkien, and C. S. Lewis.

During the first half of the twentieth century, childhood was still considered an idyllic time, a period to be prolonged and kept separate from adulthood. This attitude was, of course, reflected in the books written for children. A decade-by-decade examination of the development of twentieth-century children's fantasy shows the surprising number of "old" books that are still read.

The early years of the century produced a number of memorable books, beginning with the first truly American children's fantasy, L. Frank Baum's *The Wizard of Oz* (1900). Those that followed include E. Nesbit's *The Five Children and It* (1902 in England; 1905 in the United States), *The Story of the Amulet* (1906 in England; 1907 in the United States), which was the first time travel fantasy was written for children, Howard Pyle's *The Story of King Arthur and His Knights* (1903), J. M. Barrie's *Peter and Wendy* (1904; retitled *Peter Pan* in 1911), Kenneth Grahame's *The Wind in the Willows* (1905 in England; 1908 in the United States), W. H. Hudson's *A Little Boy Lost* (1905 in England; 1918 in the United States), Frances Hodgson Burnett's *Racketty-Packetty House* (1906), Rudyard Kipling's *Puck of Pook's Hill* (1906), Selma Lagerlöf's *The Wonderful Adventures of Nils* (1907 in Sweden; 1908 in the United States), Friedrich de la Motte Fouqué's *Undine* (written in 1811; published in the United States in 1908), Walter de la Mare's *The Three Mulla-Mulgars* (1910 in England; 1919 in the United States), and E. F. Benson's *David Blaize and the Blue Door* (1918 in England; 1919 in the United States).

During and following World War I, there was a lull in the writing and/or publishing of children's and young adult fantasy. In contrast, the 1920s, a period of relative prosperity, produced a number of lighthearted fantasies, including talking toy and animal stories and tales of voyages to wondrous lands. Some of the better known books from this period are William Tarn's *Treasure of the Isle of Mist* (1919, 1920), Padraic Colum's *The Boy Apprenticed to an Enchanter* (1920), Hugh Lofting's *The Story of Doctor Dolittle* (1920), Carl Sandburg's *Rootabaga Stories* (1922), Stewart Edward White's *The Magic Forest* (1923), Margery Williams Bianco's *The Velveteen Rabbit* (1926), A. A. Milne's *Winnie-the-Pooh* (1926), Walter Brooks's Freddy books (1927–1958), John Masefield's *The Midnight Folk* (1927), Paul Fenimore Cooper's *Tal* (1929), Rachel Field's *Hitty* (1929), and Beatrix Potter's *The Fairy Caravan* (1929).

The years of the Great Depression produced two of the best loved English fantasies—P. L. Travers's *Mary Poppins* (1931) and J. R. R. Tolkien's *The Hobbit* (1937)—as well as Elizabeth Coatsworth's *The Cat Who Went to Heaven* (1930), Anne Parrish's *Floating Island* (1930), Eleanor Farjeon's *The Little Book Room* (1931 in England; 1956 in the United States), Ella Young's *The Unicorn with Silver Shoes* (1932), Kate Seredy's *The White Stag* (1937), Richard Atwater and Florence Atwater's *Mr. Popper's Penguins* (1938), Dr. Seuss's *The 500 Hats of Bartholomew Cubbins* (1938), Robert Lawson's *Ben and Me* (1939), and Alison Uttley's *A Traveller in Time* (1939).

During the 1920s and 1930s, teenagers were expected to read the classics, and school reading lists of this period often included Tennyson's Arthurian poem, "Idylls of the King," written in 1859. Westerns, mysteries, and adventure stories, rather than fantasies, seem to have been the recreational reading of young people at this time, although we should note that a number of the fantasies written for adults during the 1920s and 1930s are still read today by both adults and young adults.

These include E. R. Eddison's *The Worm Ouroboros* (1922 in England; 1926 in the United States), James Stephens's *Deirdre* (1923), Lord Dunsany's *The King of Elfland's Daughter* (1924), Thorne Smith's *Topper* (1926), Robert Nathan's *Portrait of Jenny* (1929), James Hilton's *Lost Horizon* (1933), Evangeline Walton's *The Virgin and the Swine* (1936, later retitled *The Island of the Mighty*), Stephen Vincent Benét's *The Devil and Daniel Webster* (1937), J. R. R. Tolkien's *The Hobbit* (1937), and T. H. White's *A Sword in the Stone* (1939).

Unlike the World War I period, a number of noteworthy children's fantasies were published during World War II. These include B. B.'s (D. J. Watkins-Pitchford) *The Little Grey Men* (1942 in England; 1949 in the United States), Enys Tregarthen's *The Doll Who Came Alive* (1942), Antoine de Saint-Exupéry's *The Little Prince* (1943), Julia L. Sauer's *Fog Magic* (1943), James Thurber's *Many Moons* (1943), Robert Lawson's *Rabbit Hill* (1944), Eric Linklater's *The Wind on the Moon* (1944), Mary Norton's *The Magic Bedknob* (1944 in England; 1957 in the United States), Astrid Lindgren's *Pippi Longstocking* (1945 in Sweden; 1950 in the United States), Carolyn Bailey's *Miss Hickory* (1946), Eleanor Farjeon's *The Glass Slipper* (1946 in England; 1956 in the United States), Elizabeth Goudge's *The Little White Horse* (1946), T. H. White's *Mistress Masham's Repose* (1946), William Pène Du Bois's *The Twenty-One Balloons* (1947), Rumer Godden's *The Doll's House* (1947), Ruth Stiles Gannett's *My Father's Dragon* (1948), Tove Jansson's *Finn Family Moomintroll* (1949 in Finland; 1958 in the United States), and Rumer Godden's *The Mousewife* (1951).

Following World War II, childhood came to be seen as preparation for adulthood. Adults were peripheral characters in the books of this era, and the children were depicted as resourceful and imaginative. The 1950s were again golden years for children's fantasy. Included among the many outstanding works were, according to critics,[69] three "perfect" fantasies: E. B. White's *Charlotte's Web* (1952), L. M. Boston's *The Children of Green Knowe* (1954 in England; 1967 in the United States), and Philippa Pearce's *Tom's Midnight Garden* (1958 in England; 1959 in the United States).

Many of the memorable children's fantasies from the 1950s and early 1960s were magic adventure tales: C. S. Lewis's Chronicles of Narnia (1951–1956), Edward Eager's *Half Magic* (1954), William Mayne's *A Grass Rope* (1957 in England; 1962 in the United States), Mary Chase's *Loretta Mason Potts* (1958), Elizabeth Marie Pope's *The Sherwood Ring* (1958), Agnes Smith's *An Edge of the Forest* (1959), and Norton Juster's *The Phantom Tollbooth* (1961).

A number of others involved miniature worlds, including Mary Norton's The Borrowers series (1952–1982), Carol Kendall's *The Gammage Cup* (1959), and Pauline Clarke's *The Return of the Twelves* (1962, 1963).

Still others involved humorous exaggeration or were lighthearted talking animal tales: Oliver Butterworth's *The Enormous Egg* (1956), Dodie Smith's *The Hundred and One Dalmatians* (1956, 1957), Eve Titus's Basil of Baker Street series (1958–1982), Margery Sharp's Miss Bianca books (1959–1978), Michael Bond's Paddington series (1960–1982), George Selden's *The Cricket in Times Square* (1960), Mary Stolz's *Belling the Tiger* (1961), Beverly Cleary's Ralph Mouse trilogy (1965–1982), and Maurice Sendak's *Higglety Pigglety Pop!* (1967).

One criticism could be leveled at many of the children's fantasies written during the 1950s: In spite of their fantastic adventures, the children in most of these stories never grew or changed. With the exception of a few books, such as Philippa Pearce's *Tom's Midnight Garden* (1958), L. M. Boston's *The Children of Green Knowe* (1959), and Mary Chase's *Loretta Mason Potts,* children with "problems" did not appear; the children were almost repetitiously pictured as happy and safe.

Most of the books popular with teenagers during the two decades following World War II were not fantasies, but were war stories, sports stories, car stories, and romances, beginning with Maureen Daly's *Seventeenth Summer* (1942). The immediate popularity of J. D. Salinger's realistic novel *The Catcher in the Rye* (1951) marked the beginning of a new body of literature written with the teenage reader in mind, although the term "young adult literature" did not come into use for more than 20 years.

In spite of the development of this "new" category of books aimed at teenagers, the fantasy novels written between 1945 and 1965 were still mainly "adult" works that only later gained popularity with young people. These works include George Orwell's *Animal Farm* (1945), Valentine Davies's *The Miracle on 34th Street* (1947), John Myers Myers's *Silverlock* (1949), Jack Vance's *Dying World* (1950), J. R. R. Tolkien's Lord of the Rings trilogy (1954–1956), Leonard Wibberley's *The Mouse That Roared* (1955), Mary Renault's *The King Must Die* (1958), T. H. White's *The Once and Future King* (1958), Peter Beagles's *A Fine and Private Place* (1960), Ray Bradbury's *Something Wicked This Way Comes* (1962), Marion Zimmer Bradley's first Darkover novel (*The Sword of Aldones,* 1962), and Andre Norton's *Witch World* (1963).

Contemporary Fantasy

It was not until the reissue of J. R. R. Tolkien's *The Hobbit* (1966) and Lord of the Rings trilogy (1967) that young adults began to find *fantasy* novels written specifically for them. Indeed, the term "young adult literature" first came into use in the early 1970s, along with the rise of problem novels aimed at young people, the first of which was S. E. Hinton's *The Outsiders* (1967). Many of the young adult fantasy novels written since the late 1960s utilize Arthurian or other "mythic" themes, as do some of the contemporary children's and adult fantasies.

The so-called crossover books have also become popular with young adults. Many readers who devoured children's and young adult fantasy novels have discovered the fast-growing genre of "adult" fantasy and have claimed these books for themselves. For a list of outstanding crossover titles as well as contemporary fantasy novels see Outstanding Contemporary Books and Series, which follows this Introduction.

Both children's and young adult books written since the mid-1960s have become much more open about what had previously been considered "adult" problems and emotions. In fantasy written today, magic is usually seen to have serious consequences, and those characters who have magic adventures are changed by them.

Conclusion

Natalie Babbitt has written that one of the special qualities of fantasy literature is that it not only lets us share the hero's hopes and triumphs but that it ends on a note of hope. She feels that fantasy "is not a sop for the terminally optimistic, but an affirmation of one of the things that makes us, as a species, unique: the always present hope that something will happen to change everything, once and for all, for the better."[70]

It is hoped that the authors of fantasy literature will continue to create stories that illuminate reality, delight us, refresh our hearts, provide us with hope for the future, and give us joy.

Notes

1. Natalie Babbitt, "The Purposes of Fantasy." In *Proceedings of the Ninth Annual Conference of the Children's Literature Association* (Ypsilanti, Mich.: Children's Literature Association, 1983), pp. 22, 29. Reprinted with permission. Reprinted in *Innocence & Experience,* ed. by Barbara Harrison and Gregory Maguire (New York: Lothrop, 1987), pp. 174–181.
2. Jane Yolen, "Tough Magic," *Top of the News* 35 (Winter, 1979): 186.
3. Sheila A. Egoff, *Thursday's Child: Trends and Patterns in Contemporary Children's Literature* (Chicago: ALA, 1981), p. 82.
4. Elizabeth Nesbit, *A Critical History of Children's Literature: A Survey of Children's Books in English,* rev. ed. Cornelia Meigs, Anne Thaxter Eaton, Elizabeth Nesbit, and Ruth Hill Viguers (New York: Macmillan, 1969), p. 347.
5. *The Oxford English Dictionary,* Vol. IV (Oxford, England: Oxford University Press, 1933), p. 67; and *1972 Supplement to The Oxford English Dictionary,* Vol. I, ed. by R. A. Birchfield (New York: Oxford University Press, 1972, reprinted 1986), p. 1031.
6. *The Random House Dictionary of the English Language* (New York: Random House, 1983), 698.
7. Everett F. Bleiler, *The Checklist of Fantastic Literature: A Bibliography of Fantasy, Weird and Science Fiction Published in the English Language* (Chicago: Shasta, 1948), p. 3; Perry Nodelman, "Defining Children's Literature," in *Children's Literature* 8 (New Haven, Conn.: Yale University Press, 1980), p. 187; Eric S. Rabkin, *The Fantastic in Literature* (Princeton, N.J.: Princeton University Press, 1976), p. 8; and Tsvetan Todorov, *The Fantastic: A Structural Approach to a Literary Genre* (Cleveland, Ohio: Case Western Reserve University Press, 1973), p. 25. "[Fantasy is] that hesitation experienced by a person . . . confronting an apparently supernatural event." *See also* Pierre Castex, *Le Conte Fantastique en France de Nodier à Maupassant* (Paris: Corti, 1951), quoted in Todorov, *The Fantastic,* p. 26. "[Fantasy is] the brutal intrusion of mystery [into real life.]"; H. P. Lovecraft, quoted in Todorov, *The Fantastic,* p. 34; Peter Penzoldt, *The Supernatural in Fiction* (Atlantic Highlands, N.J.: Humanities Press, 1965), quoted in Todorov, *The Fantastic,* p. 35. "A fantasy is a tale of fear and terror"; and Julius Kagarlitski, "Realism and Fantasy," in *Science Fiction: The Other Side of Realism—Essays in Modern Fantasy and Science Fiction,* ed. by Thomas D. Clareson. (Bowling Green, Ohio: Bowling Green University Popular Press, 1971), p. 29. "[Fantasy is a tale in which] disbelief arises side by side with belief."
8. Lin Carter, *Imaginary Worlds: The Art of Fantasy* (New York: Ballantine, 1973), p. 6. *See also* James E. Higgins, *Beyond Words: Mystical Fancy in Children's Literature* (New York: Columbia University Press, 1970), p. 5; Naomi Lewis, *Fantasy Books for Children,* rev. ed. (London: National Book League, 1977), p. 5; and Patrick Merla, " 'What Is Real?' Asked the Rabbit One Day; Realism vs. Fantasy in Children's and Adult Literature," in *Only Connect,* 2nd ed., ed. by Sheila Egoff, G. T. Stubbs, and L. F. Ashley (New York: Oxford University Press, 1980), p. 348. ". . . the essential element of any true work of fantasy is magic—a force that affects the lives and actions of all the creatures that inhabit the fantastic world. . . . Always it is a *supernatural* force whose use, *mis*use, or *dis*use irrevocably changes the lives of those it touches. . . . Real magic cannot be ex-

plained in material terms, nor manufactured with mechanical devices, nor achieved through ingested substances."

9. Louis Vax, *L'Art et la Littérature Fantastiques* (Paris: Presses Universitaires de France, 1960), quoted in Todorov, *The Fantastic*, p. 26. "The fantastic narrative generally describes men like ourselves, inhabiting the real world, suddenly confronted by the inexplicable." *See also* Roger Caillois, *Au Coeur de Fantastique* (Paris), quoted in Todorov, *The Fantastic*, p. 26. "The fantastic is always a break in the acknowledged order, an irruption of the inadmissible, within the changeless everyday legality."

10. Jane Mobley, ed., *Phantasmagoria: Tales of Fantasy and the Supernatural* (New York: Anchor Press, 1977), pp. 17, 23.

11. Brian Attebery, *The Fantasy Tradition in American Literature from Irving to Le Guin* (Bloomington: Indiana University Press, 1980), p. 2. "Any narrative which includes as a significant part of its make-up some violation of what the author clearly believes to be natural law—that is fantasy." *See also* W. R. Irwin, *The Game of the Impossible: A Rhetoric of Fantasy* (Champaign: University of Illinois Press, 1976), pp. 4, 9. "[The primary feature of fantasy is] an overt violation of what is generally accepted as possibility . . . a narrative is fantasy if it presents the persuasive establishment and development of an impossibility."; Leo P. Kelley, ed., *Fantasy: The Literature of the Marvelous* (New York: McGraw-Hill, 1974), p. v. "[Fantasy] tells us of events which could not occur in a universe whose major physical laws are known and necessarily obeyed"; and Marshall B. Tymn, Kenneth J. Zahorski, and Robert H. Boyer, *Fantasy Literature: A Core Collection and Reference Guide* (New York: Bowker, 1979), pp. 3, 4. "[Fantasies are] works in which events occur, or places or creatures exist that could not exist according to rational standards or scientific explanations. . . . Fantasy . . . has its own vision of reality."

12. Attebery, *Fantasy Tradition*, p. 3. "The most important thing [works of fantasy] share is a sense of wonder . . . invoke[d] . . . by making the impossible seem familiar and the familiar seem new and strange." See also C. N. Manlove, *Modern Fantasy: Five Studies* (New York: Cambridge University Press, 1975), p. 1. "A fantasy is 'A fiction evoking wonder and containing a substantial and irreducible element of the supernatural with which the mortal characters in the story or the readers become on at least partly familiar terms.' "

13. Ann Swinfen, *In Defense of Fantasy: A Study of the Genre in English and American Literature Since 1945* (Boston: Routledge, 1984), p. 234. Reprinted with permission of the publisher.

14. Egoff, *Thursday's Child*, p. 80. Reprinted with permission of the American Library Association, excerpt taken from "Thursday's Child: Trends and Patterns in Contemporary Children's Literature" by Sheila Egoff; copyright © 1981 by ALA.

15. Eleanor Cameron, *The Green and Burning Tree: On the Writing and Enjoyment of Children's Books* (Boston: Little, Brown, 1969), p. 16.

16. Jane Langton, "The Weak Place in the Cloth: A Study of Fantasy for Children," *Horn Book Magazine* 49 (October 1973): 433; Lloyd Alexander, "Wishful Thinking—Or Hopeful Dreaming?" *Horn Book Magazine* 44 (August 1968): 386; and Mollie Hunter, "One World," *Horn Book Magazine* 51 (December 1975): 557.

17. Ursula K. Le Guin, "From Elfland to Poughkeepsie," in *The Language of the Night: Essays on Fantasy and Science Fiction*, edited by Susan Wood. (New York: Putnam, 1979), pp. 84, 93. Reprinted with the permission of the editor's Estate, the Author, and their joint agent, Virginia Kidd.

18. Sheila Egoff, *The Republic of Childhood*, 2nd ed. (New York: Oxford University Press, 1975), p. 134.

19. Swinfen, *In Defense of Fantasy,* p. 231. Reprinted with permission of the publisher.
20. Alan Garner, "A Bit More Practice," [London] *Times Literary Supplement,* June 6, 1968, p. 577.
21. Jane Louise Curry, "On the Elvish Craft," *Signal* 2 (May 1970): 44.
22. Susan Cooper, "Escaping into Ourselves," in Betsy Hearne and Marilyn Kaye, *Celebrating Children's Books* (New York: Lothrop, 1981), pp. 22–23.
23. Paul Hazard, *Books, Children and Men,* 4th ed. (Boston: Horn Book, 1960), p. 157.
24. Cameron, *Green and Burning Tree,* pp. 15–16.
25. Natalie Babbitt, "Happy Endings? Of Course, and Also Joy," *New York Times Book Review,* November 8, 1970, p. 1.
26. Swinfen, *In Defense of Fantasy,* p. 2. Reprinted with permission of the publisher.
27. See, for example, Carter, *Imaginary Worlds,* p. 1; Louis Macneice, *Varieties of Parable* (New York: Cambridge University Press, 1965), p. 102. "When we reach the twentieth century, children's fantasy is represented, I suppose, typically by *Peter Pan,* a work which is not only frivolous but perverse"; and Isabelle Jan, *On Children's Literature* (New York: Schocken, 1974), pp. 67–68.
28. Donnarae MacCann, "Wells of Fancy, 1865–1965," *Wilson Library Bulletin* 40 (December 1965): 403.
29. Carter, *Imaginary Worlds,* p. 1.
30. Babbitt, "Happy Endings?" p. 50.
31. Egoff, *The Republic of Childhood,* p. 134. *See also* Cameron, *Green and Burning Tree,* pp. 87–88. "A writer, it seems to me, should feel himself no more under necessity to restrict the complexity of his plotting because of differences in child understanding . . . than he feels the necessity of restricting his vocabulary. What is important is not, I think, that a child shall have understood each turn of the author's thinking, but that his excitement be set simmering as vista after vista of mental and spiritual distances, hitherto unguessed at, open before him. [These implications and overtones of meaning] will haunt the child long after he has forgotten the plot. . . . [These stories] are satisfying to [an adult] in ways which the child is not yet aware of . . . but the child can experience a very deep sense of satisfaction without in the least knowing why."
32. Neil Philip, "Fantasy: Double Cream or Instant Whip?" *Signal* 35 (May 1981): 83.
33. Susan Cooper, "Newbery Award Acceptance Address," *Horn Book Magazine* 52 (August 1976): 362.
34. Le Guin, "Dreams Must Explain Themselves," in *Language of the Night,* p. 55. *See also* C. S. Lewis, "On Three Ways of Writing for Children," in *Of Other Worlds: Essays and Stories* (New York: Harcourt, 1967), p. 24. "I am almost inclined to set it up as a canon that a children's story which is enjoyed only by children is a bad children's story. The good ones last."
35. Curry, "On the Elvish Craft," pp. 42–43.
36. Ibid., pp. 43, 49. Other critics who divide fantasy into two basic categories are Frank Eyre, *British Children's Books in the Twentieth Century* (New York: Dutton, 1971), pp. 116–117. "[The first kind is] a story of ordinary life but with some extra quality added—wishes granted, time travel, talking animals, fairy creatures—the adventures happen in the real world. . . . [The second kind is] either about a different world altogether, or about our own world but in a completely different time in which everything is different"; Göte Klingberg, "The Fantastic and the Mythical as Reading for Modern Children and Young People," in *How Can Children's Literature Meet the Needs of Modern Children* (15th IBBY conference, 1976), p. 32. "I will call here a novel where some strange world is united with an everyday world . . . a fantastic tale, and a novel telling only of a mystical country wholly outside our ordinary world, a mythical tale"; Manlove, *Modern*

Fantasy, p. 11. "The two broad classes of fantasy are 'comic' or 'escapist' or 'fanciful' [in which] the point of the work . . . is the reader's pleasure in the invented characters or situations, [and] 'imaginative fantasy' [in which] the object is to enlist [the author's] experience and invention into giving a total version of reality transformed: that is to make their fantastic worlds as real as our own"; and Diana Waggoner, *The Hills of Faraway: A Guide to Fantasy* (New York: Atheneum, 1978). Waggoner uses the term "Magic in Operation" for tales set in our world and "Magic of Situation" for tales that take place in a magical world.

37. Egoff, *Thursday's Child,* p. 82; Ralph Lavender, "Other Worlds: Myth and Fantasy, 1970–1980," *Children's Literature in Education* 12, no. 3 (Autumn 1981): 141–142.
38. Egoff, *Thursday's Child,* p. 92.
39. Carter, *Imaginary Worlds,* p. 1; Elizabeth Cook, *The Ordinary and the Fabulous* (New York: Cambridge University Press, 1969), p. 5.
40. Cooper, "Escaping into Ourselves," pp. 15–16.
41. Lewis, "On Three Ways," pp. 29–30.
42. Curry, "On the Elvish Craft," p. 47.
43. J. R. R. Tolkien, *Tree and Leaf* (Boston: Houghton Mifflin, 1965), pp. 46–55.
44. Lloyd Alexander, "Substance and Fantasy," *Library Journal* 91 (December 15, 1966): 6158; and Lloyd Alexander, "The Truth about Fantasy," *Top of the News* 24 (January 1968): 174.
45. Kornei Chukovskii, *From Two to Five* (Berkeley: University of California Press, 1963), pp. 116–117, 124.
46. Alexander, "Wishful Thinking," p. 389.
47. Penelope Lively, "Children and Memory," *Horn Book Magazine* 49 (August 1973): 407.
48. Eleanor Cameron, "The Dearest Freshness Deep Down Things." Reprinted with the permission of Eleanor Cameron, *The Green and Burning Tree: On the Writing and Enjoyment of Children's Books* (Boston: Atlantic-Little, 1969), pp. 272–273; also in *Horn Book Magazine* 40 (October 1964): pp. 471–472.
49. Le Guin, "The Child and the Shadow," in *The Language of the Night,* pp. 68–69. *See also* Swinfen, *In Defense of Fantasy,* p. 229.
50. MacCann, "Wells of Fancy," p. 334.
51. Alan Garner, "Coming to Terms," *Children's Literature in Education* 2 (July 1970): 17; and Cooper, "Escaping into Ourselves," p. 16.
52. Isabelle Jan, *On Children's Literature* (New York: Schocken, 1974, published in France in 1969), pp. 44, 67, 75.
53. Bruno Bettleheim, *The Uses of Enchantment* (New York: Knopf, 1976), p. 144.
54. Mary J. Collier and Eugene L. Gaier, "Adult Reactions to Preferred Childhood Stories," *Child Development* 29 (March 1958): 97–103.
55. Egoff, *Thursday's Child,* p. 87; and Mobley, *Phantasmagoria,* p. 35.
56. Swinfen, *In Defense of Fantasy,* p. 229. Reprinted with permission of the publisher.
57. Helen Cresswell, "If It's Someone from Porlock, Don't Answer the Door," *Children's Literature in Education* 4 (March 1971): 37.
58. Roger W. Drury, "Realism Plus Fantasy Equals Magic," *Horn Book Magazine* 48 (April 1972): 119.
59. Lewis, "On Three Ways," p. 23.
60. Babbitt, "Happy Endings?," p. 50.
61. Cooper, "Escaping into Ourselves," p. 22.
62. Le Guin, "Myth and Archetype in Science Fiction," in *The Language of the Night,* pp. 78–79, edited by Susan Wood. Reprinted with permission of the editor's Estate, the Author, and their joint agent, Virginia Kidd. *See also* Attebery, *Fan-*

tasy Traditions, p. 15. "The materials of fantasy, the things that call forth feelings of wonder . . . are partly individual invention and partly community property."

63. Mollie Hunter, "One World," *Horn Book Magazine* 51 (December 1975): 562 (continued in 52 [January 1976]: 32–38).
64. Patricia Wrightson, "Stones into Pools," *Top of the News* 41 (Spring 1985): 286.
65. Helen Lourie, "Where Is Fancy Bred?" in Egoff, *Only Connect,* p. 110.
66. Egoff, *Thursday's Child,* p. 83.
67. Margery Fisher, *Intent upon Reading* (New York: Watts, 1962), p. 100.
68. Lewis, *Fantasy Books,* p. 5.
69. Frank Eyre, *British Children's Books in the Twentieth Century* (New York: Dutton, 1971), p. 128. *"Tom's Midnight Garden* and *The Children of Green Knowe* are the two perfect fantasies of our time." *See also* John Rowe Townsend, *Written for Children* (New York: Lothrop, 1967), pp. 127–128. *"Tom's Midnight Garden* . . . has not a flaw . . . it is as near to being perfect in its construction and its writing as any book I know. . . . If I were asked to name a single masterpiece of English children's literature since the last war . . . it would be this outstandingly beautiful and absorbing book"; and Eudora Welty, "Life in the Barn Was Very Good," *New York Times Book Review,* October 19, 1952, p. 49. "As a piece of work [*Charlotte's Web*] is just about perfect, and just about magical in the way it is done."
70. Babbitt, "The Purposes of Fantasy," p. 28.

OUTSTANDING CONTEMPORARY BOOKS AND SERIES

The following alphabetical lists of books and series published since 1960 are outstanding examples of fantasy literature for children and young adults. These lists are based on personal opinion as well as that expressed in professional review sources. For a list of the professional review sources used see Abbreviations of Books and Review Journals Cited. The first ten headings in this section correspond to Chapters 1 through 10. The final list, Crossover Books for Young Adults, includes those "adult" fantasy works that have become popular with young adults. Occasionally, a title will fit into two or more categories; if this is the case that title will appear on more than one list. To locate complete information on a specific book see the Title Index or the Author and Illustrator Index.

Allegorical Fantasy and Literary Fairy Tales

Outstanding examples of all types of children's and young adult fantasy have been written since the mid-1960s. Some fine examples from this category of allegorical fantasy and literary fairy tales include:

Brittain, Bill. *Dr. Dredd's Wagon of Wonders.* 1987
Fleischman, Paul. *Coming-and-Going Men.* 1985
Fleischman, Sid. *The Whipping Boy.* 1986
Garfield, Leon. *The Wedding Ghost.* 1985, 1987
Hoban, Russell. *The Mouse and His Child.* 1967
Lawson, John. *You Better Come Home with Me.* 1966
Le Vert, John. *The Flight of the Cassowary.* 1986
Moeri, Louise. *Star Mother's Youngest Child.* 1975
Price, Susan. *The Ghost Drum.* 1987
Wangerin, Walter. *The Book of the Dun Cow.* 1978

Animal Fantasy

Animal fantasy novels can be separated into two types: allegorical stories of animals attempting to escape human evils, which could be called beast tales; and the more lighthearted talking animal tales. Some of the best of the beast tales of the past two decades might include:

Adams, Richard. *Watership Down.* 1972, 1974
Bell, Clare. *Ratha's Creature.* 1983
Corbett, W. J. *The Song of Pentecost.* 1982, 1983
Hawdon, Robin. *A Rustle in the Grass.* 1984, 1985
Hoban, Russell. *The Mouse and His Child.* 1967
Jarrell, Randall. *The Animal Family.* 1965
Lively, Penelope. *The Voyage of QV66.* 1978, 1979
O'Brien, Robert C. *Mrs. Frisby and the Rats of NIMH.* 1971

In the talking animal category, E. B. White's classic *Charlotte's Web* (1952) has been followed by:

Cleary, Beverly. Ralph S. Mouse series. 1965–1982
Erickson, Russell E. Warton the Toad series. 1974–1986
Howe, James. Bunnicula series. 1979–1987
Jacques, Brian. *Redwall.* 1986, 1987
King-Smith, Dick. *Pigs Might Fly.* 1981, 1982
Selden, George. The Cricket in Times Square series. 1960–1987
Steig, William. *Abel's Island.* 1976

Fantasy Collections

During the so-called golden age of the fantasy short story genre—the latter half of the nineteenth and the early years of the twentieth centuries—classic stories were created by Hans Christian Andersen, Arthur Bowie Chrisman, Padraic Colum, Walter de la Mare, Eleanor Farjeon, Laurence Housman, Rudyard Kipling, E. Nesbit, Barbara Leonie Picard, Howard Pyle, Carl Sandburg, Frank R. Stockton, and Oscar Wilde.

Since the early 1970s there has been a renewed interest in the fantasy short story, leading to the publication of a number of excellent collections. These include:

Aiken, Joan. *Up the Chimney Down and Other Stories.* 1984, 1985
Asimov, Isaac, Waugh, Charles G., and Greenberg, Martin H. *Dragon Tales.* 1982
Babbitt, Natalie. *The Devil's Storybook.* 1974
Harris, Rosemary. *Sea Magic and Other Stories of Enchantment.* 1974
Housman, Laurence. *The Rat Catcher's Daughter.* 1974
Jones, Diana Wynne. *Warlock at the Wheel and Other Stories.* 1984, 1985
Kennedy, Richard. *Richard Kennedy: Collected Stories.* 1987
Le Guin, Ursula K. *The Wind's Twelve Quarters.* 1975
Lively, Penelope. *Uninvited Ghosts and Other Stories.* 1984, 1985
McKinley, Robin. *Imaginary Lands.* 1985
Pearce, Philippa. *Lion at School and Other Stories.* 1985, 1986
Singer, Isaac Bashevis. *Stories for Children.* 1984
Westall, Robert. *The Haunting of Chas McGill and Other Stories.* 1983
Williams, Jay. *The Practical Princess and Other Liberating Fairy Tales.* 1978
Yolen, Jane. *The Girl Who Cried Flowers and Other Tales.* 1974

Ghost Fantasy

The most memorable recent books in this category of ghost fantasy include:

Aiken, Joan. *The Shadow Guests.* 1980
Cameron, Eleanor. *The Court of the Stone Children.* 1973
Cassedy, Sylvia. *Behind the Attic Wall.* 1983
Cresswell, Helen. *A Game of Catch.* 1969, 1977
Garfield, Leon. *Mister Corbett's Ghost.* 1968
Hamilton, Virginia. *Sweet Whispers, Brother Rush.* 1982
Lively, Penelope. *The Ghost of Thomas Kempe.* 1973
Mahy, Margaret. *The Tricksters.* 1986, 1987
Westall, Robert. *The Watch House.* 1977, 1978

High Fantasy

The late 1960s and the 1970s were marked by the development of a relatively new type of children's and young adult novel—high fantasy, also called heroic fantasy or secondary world fantasy. The numerous books of high fantasy published during the last 25 years have been divided into three subcategories in this bibliography: (1) alternate world fantasy, stories set entirely in a secondary world; (2) myth fantasy, retellings of myth and stories of contemporary involvement in myth; and (3) travel to other worlds, stories in which a character from the "real" or primary world visits a secondary world.

ALTERNATE WORLDS OR HISTORIES. The outstanding alternate world fantasy novels written since Tolkien's *The Hobbit* (1937) include:

Alexander, Lloyd. Westmark trilogy. 1981–1984
Chetwin, Grace. Tales of Gom series. 1986–1988
Christopher, John. Winchester trilogy. 1970–1972
Dickinson, Peter. *The Blue Hawk.* 1976; Changes trilogy. 1968–1970
Downer, Ann. *The Spellkey.* 1987
Gloss, Molly. *Outside the Gates.* 1986
Halam, Ann. *The Daymaker.* 1987
Harris, Geraldine. Seven Citadels quartet. 1982–1984
Jones, Diana Wynne. *Cart and Cwidder.* 1975, 1977
King, Stephen. *The Eyes of the Dragon.* 1987
Le Guin, Ursula K. Earthsea trilogy. 1968–1972
Levin, Betty. *The Ice Bear.* 1986
McCaffrey, Anne. Harper Hall trilogy. 1976–1979
McKillip, Patricia. *The Forgotten Beasts of Eld.* 1974; *Moon-Flash.* 1984; Star-Bearer trilogy. 1976–1979
McKinley, Robin. *The Blue Sword.* 1982; *The Hero and the Crown.* 1984
Mark, Jan. *Aquarius.* 1982, 1984
Murphy, Shirley Rousseau. Nightpool trilogy. 1985–1988
Norton, Andre. *The Crystal Gryphon.* 1972
Pierce, Meredith Ann. *The Darkangel.* 1982
Pierce, Tamora. Song of the Lioness trilogy. 1983–1986

Wilder, Cherry. Rulers of Hylor trilogy. 1984–1986
Yolen, Jane. Pit Dragons trilogy. 1982–1987

MYTH FANTASY. T. H. White's *The Sword in the Stone* (1939) was the forerunner of
the retold-myth type of fantasy, represented more recently by:

Alexander, Lloyd. Chronicles of Prydain series. 1964–1968
Bradshaw, Gillian. *Hawk of May.* 1980
Briggs, K. M. *Kate Crackernuts.* 1979, 1980
Coolidge, Olivia. *The King of Men.* 1966
Gardner, John C. *Grendel.* 1971
Garfield, Leon, and Blishen, Edward. *The God Beneath the Sea.* 1970, 1971
Hamilton, Virginia. *The Magical Adventures of Pretty Pearl.* 1983
Harris, Rosemary. Reuben trilogy. 1968–1972
Ipcar, Dahlov. *The Queen of Spells.* 1973
Johnston, Norma. *Strangers Dark and Gold.* 1975
McKinley, Robin. *Beauty.* 1978
Seraillier, Ian. *The Challenge of the Green Knight.* 1967
Sutcliff, Rosemary. Sword and the Circle trilogy. 1979–1982

Outstanding stories of contemporary involvement with myth include:

Alcock, Vivien. *The Stonewalkers.* 1983
Babbitt, Natalie. *Tuck Everlasting.* 1975
Cooper, Susan. The Dark Is Rising sequence. 1966–1977
Curry, Jane Louise. *The Sleepers.* 1968
Dunlop, Eileen. *Clementina.* 1985, 1987
Farmer, Penelope. *A Castle of Bone.* 1972
Garner, Alan. *The Owl Service.* 1967, 1968; *The Weirdstone of Brisingamen.* 1960
Harris, Rosemary. *The Seal-Singing.* 1971
Hunter, Mollie. *A Stranger Came Ashore.* 1975
Lawrence, Louise. *Star Lord.* 1978
Lively, Penelope. *The Wild Hunt of the Ghost Hounds.* 1971, 1972
Mayne, William. *Earthfasts.* 1966, 1967
O'Shea, Pat. *The Hounds of the Morrigan.* 1985, 1986
Service, Pamela. *Winter of Magic's Return.* 1985
Wrightson, Patricia. Wirrun trilogy. 1977–1981

TRAVEL TO OTHER WORLDS. The best contemporary children's and young adult books
in the category of travel to other worlds include:

Alexander, Lloyd. *The First Two Lives of Lukas-Kasha.* 1978
Christopher, John. Fireball trilogy. 1981–1986
Cooper, Susan. *Seaward.* 1983
Duane, Diane. *So You Want to Be a Wizard.* 1983
Ende, Michael. *The Neverending Story.* 1983
Garner, Alan. *Elidor.* 1965, 1967
Le Guin, Ursula K. *The Beginning Place.* 1980
Pope, Elizabeth. *The Perilous Gard.* 1974
Wells, Rosemary. *Through the Hidden Door.* 1987
Westall, Robert. *The Devil on the Road.* 1979

Humorous Fantasy

Humorous fantasy continues to be popular, although more humorous stories seem to be written for children than for young adults. The well-loved stories by Dr. Seuss, Richard Atwater and Florence Atwater, William Pène du Bois, and Oliver Butterworth have been followed by:

Aiken, Joan. Dido Twite series. 1962–1986
Babbitt, Natalie. *The Devil's Storybook.* 1974
Cresswell, Helen. *The Piemakers.* 1967, 1980
Fleischman, Sid. Numerous tall tales. 1962–1978
King-Smith, Dick. *Harry's Mad.* 1986
Kotzwinkle, William. *Trouble in Bugland.* 1983
Le Vert, John. *The Flight of the Cassowary.* 1986
Nöstlinger, Christine. *Konrad.* 1977
Peck, Richard. Blossom Culp series. 1975–1986
Pinkwater, Daniel Manus. Numerous offbeat stories. 1976–1986
Raskin, Ellen. *Figgs and Phantoms.* 1974
Rodgers, Mary. Annabel Andrews trilogy. 1972–1983

Magic Adventure Fantasy

The magic adventure tradition of E. Nesbit, P. L. Travers, and C. S. Lewis has been continued in:

Brittain, Bill. *The Wish Giver.* 1983
Cassedy, Sylvia. *Behind the Attic Wall.* 1983
Cresswell, Helen. *The Secret World of Polly Flint.* 1982
Curry, Jane Louise. *Mindy's Mysterious Miniature.* 1970
Farmer, Penelope. *The Summer Birds.* 1962
Jones, Diana Wynne. *The Ogre Downstairs.* 1974
Konigsburg, E. L. *Up from Jericho Tel.* 1986
Langton, Jane. *The Fledgling.* 1980
Mahy, Margaret. *The Haunting.* 1982
Reid Banks, Lynne. *The Indian in the Cupboard.* 1980, 1981
Selden, George. *The Genie of Sutton Place.* 1973
Snyder, Zilpha Keatley. *Black and Blue Magic.* 1966
Townsend, John Rowe. *The Persuading Stick.* 1986, 1987
Van Allsburg, Chris. *Jumanji.* 1981

Time Travel Fantasy

The concept of time travel continues to fascinate readers of all ages, although its complexities can best be understood by young people from about age 10 up. Outstanding books that have followed in the footsteps of E. Nesbit's *The Story of the Amulet,* Alison Uttley's *A Traveller in Time,* and Philippa Pearce's *Tom's Midnight Garden* include:

Barber, Antonia. *The Ghosts.* 1969
Bond, Nancy. *A String in the Harp.* 1976
Cameron, Eleanor. *Beyond Silence.* 1980

Cresswell, Helen. *Moondial.* 1987; *Up the Pier.* 1971
Curry, Jane Louise. *Over the Sea's Edge.* 1971
Davies, Andrew. *Conrad's War.* 1978, 1980
Farmer, Penelope. *Charlotte Sometimes.* 1969
Garner, Alan. *The Red Shift.* 1973
Jones, Diana Wynne. *A Charmed Life.* 1977, 1978; *A Tale of Time City.* 1987
Levin, Betty. *The Keeping Room.* 1981
Mayne, William. *A Game of Dark.* 1971
Naylor, Phyllis Reynolds. York trilogy. 1980–1981
Park, Ruth. *Playing Beatie Bow.* 1982
Parker, Richard. *The Old Powder Line.* 1971
Paton Walsh, Jill. *A Chance Child.* 1978
Stolz, Mary. *Cat in the Mirror.* 1975
Westall, Robert. *The Devil on the Road.* 1978, 1980; *The Wind Eye.* 1976, 1977
Wiseman, David. *Jeremy Visick.* 1981

Toy Fantasy

Novels about toys or other inanimate objects that come to life are less common now than they were in the past, although such old favorites as Carlo Collodi's *The Adventures of Pinocchio,* E. T. A. Hoffmann's *The Nutcracker,* Margery Williams Bianco's *The Velveteen Rabbit,* and Rumer Godden's doll stories are still popular and frequently reprinted. The most memorable contemporary toy fantasies include:

Cassedy, Sylvia. *Behind the Attic Wall.* 1983
Gardam, Jane. *Through the Doll's House Door.* 1987
Kennedy, Richard. *Amy's Eyes.* 1985
O'Connell, Jean. *The Dollhouse Caper.* 1976
Reid Banks, Lynne. *The Indian in the Cupboard.* 1980, 1981
Sleator, William. *Among the Dolls.* 1975, 1985

Witchcraft and Sorcery Fantasy

The best of the contemporary witchcraft and sorcery novels for young people include:

Bedard, Michael. *A Darker Magic.* 1987
Brittain, Bill. *The Devil's Donkey.* 1981
Duane, Diane. *So You Want to Be a Wizard.* 1983
Furlong, Monica. *Wise Child.* 1987
Harris, Deborah Turner. *The Burning Stone.* 1987
Hunter, Mollie. *Thomas and the Warlock.* 1967, 1986
Jones, Diana Wynne. *Fire and Hemlock.* 1984; *Howl's Moving Castle.* 1986
McGowen, Tom. *The Magician's Apprentice.* 1987
Mahy, Margaret. *The Changeover.* 1984; *The Haunting.* 1982
Preussler, Otfried. *The Satanic Mill.* 1971, 1973

Crossover Books for Young Adults

Many readers who devoured children's and young adult fantasy novels have discovered the fast-growing genre of "adult" fantasy and have claimed these books for themselves. These crossover novels, many of which are part of a series, include:

Anderson, Poul. *The Merman's Children*. 1979
Anthony, Piers. Magic of Zanth series. 1977–1987
Asprin, Robert L. Myth Adventure series. 1978–1987
Beagle, Peter S. *The Last Unicorn*. 1968
Bradley, Marion Zimmer. Darkover series. 1962–1987
Butler, Octavia E. *Kindred*. 1979
Card, Orson Scott. *Seventh Son*. 1987
Cherryh, C. J. *Angel with the Sword*. 1985
Dickson, Gordon R. *The Dragon and the George*. 1976
Donaldson, Stephen R. Chronicles of Thomas Covenant, the Unbeliever. 1977–1983
Feist, Raymond E. *Silverthorn*. 1985
Finney, Jack. *Time and Again*. 1970
Goldstein, Lisa. *The Dream Years*. 1985
Hambley, Barbara. *Dragonsbane*. 1986
Kurtz, Katherine. Chronicles of Deryni series. 1970–1986
MacAvoy, R. A. *The Book of Kells*. 1985
McCaffrey, Anne. Dragonriders of Pern series. 1968–1986
Matheson, Richard. *Bid Time Return*. 1975
Shwartz, Susan. *Moonsinger's Friends*. 1985
Silverberg, Robert. *Lord Valentine's Castle*. 1980
Springer, Nancy. *Chains of Gold*. 1986
Stewart, Mary. Merlin quartet. 1970–1979
Warner, Sylvia Townsend. *Kingdoms of Elfin*. 1976
Wellman, Manly Wade. Silver John series. 1963–1984
Willard, Nancy. *Things Invisible to See*. 1985
Wolfe, Gene. Book of the New Sun series. 1980–1983
Zelazny, Roger. Amber series. 1970–1987

Part One
ANNOTATED BIBLIOGRAPHY

1
Allegorical Fantasy
and Literary Fairy Tales

The books in this chapter are tales with both simple and abstract levels of meaning. Literary fairy tales are short stories written by modern authors in the style of traditional folktales, often containing such elements as kings, princesses, dragons, and fairies. Modern allegorical fantasies, unlike traditional allegorical fables, often concern characters other than animals, and the full significance of the stories may not be obvious. Collections of literary fairy tales can be found in Chapter 3, Fantasy Collections. Retellings of legends and myths, which often have allegorical elements, can be found in Section 5B, Myth Fantasy.

C ABELL, Kathleen. *King Orville and the Bullfrogs*. Gr. 2–4.
   Three young princes are changed into frogs and banished after they outdo their father-in-law, King Orville, in a bagpipe contest. (BL 70:871; KR 42:239; LJ 99:1463)
   Illus. by Errol Le Cain, Little, 1974, 48 pp., o.p.

YA ADAMS, Hazard. *The Truth about Dragons: An Anti-Romance*. Gr. 10 up.
   Firedrake, an intellectual dragon living in California after an earthquake has severed the state from the rest of the United States, describes how Man ruined the Earth. (BL 67:685, 741; KR 39:15; LJ 96:653, 2938, 4160)
   Harcourt, 1971, 179 pp., o.p.

YA ADAMS, Richard (George). *Shardik*. Gr. 8 up. (Orig. British pub. 1974.)
   In Ortelga, a giant bear found by a young hunter is proclaimed Lord Shardik, the sacred messenger of God. (BL 71:892, 905; KR 43:251, 322; LJ 100:688)
   Simon, 1975, o.p.; Avon, 1976, pap., 525 pp.

C/YA ADAMS, Richard (George). *Watership Down*. Gr. 6 up. (Orig. British
[O]   pub. 1972.)
   Premonitions of destruction drive a small band of rabbits from their peace-

ful hillside warren into the wilderness. Carnegie Medal, 1972. (BL 70:852, 71:747, 72:1096, 1107, 80:351; CC:423; CCBB 27:121; Ch&Bks:248; HB 50:365, 405; JHC:342; LJ 99:1148, 1235; SHC:576; Suth 2:2)
Macmillan, 1974, 429 pp.; Avon, 1975, pap.

AIKEN, Joan (Delano). *A Harp of Fishbones and Other Stories.* See Chapter 3, Fantasy Collections.

C AIKEN, Joan (Delano). *The Moon's Revenge.* Gr. 2–5.
Young Sep angers the moon when he uses magic in learning to play the fiddle, but his musical ability eventually breaks the moon's curse on his town. (BL 84:929; HB 64:199; KR 55:1623; SLJ Feb 1988 p. 57)
Illus. by Alan Lee, Knopf, 1987, 32 pp.

AIKEN, Joan (Delano). *A Necklace of Raindrops and Other Stories.* See Chapter 3, Fantasy Collections.

AIKEN, Joan (Delano). *Past Eight O'Clock: Goodnight Stories.* See Chapter 3, Fantasy Collections.

AIKEN, Joan (Delano). *Smoke from Cromwell's Time and Other Stories.* See Chapter 3, Fantasy Collections.

C/YA AIKEN, Joan (Delano). *Street: A Play for Children.* Gr. 5–8.
[R]　In the town of Street, the theft of the toll bridge key by the village witch's eldest son caused deep hostilities between the inhabitants of the riverside and those of the forest side of Street's only thoroughfare. Only the love between the witch's younger son, Toomy, and Meg, a girl from the other side of the street, can heal the town's animosities and restore safety and justice. (BL 74:1247, 1251; HB 55:527; KR 46:696; SLJ May 1978 p. 62)
Illus. by Arvis Stewart, Viking, 1978, 128 pp., o.p.

ALDEN, Raymond Macdonald. *The Boy Who Found the King; a Tournament of Stories.* See Chapter 3, Fantasy Collections.

ALDEN, Raymond Macdonald. *Why the Chimes Rang and Other Stories.* See Chapter 3, Fantasy Collections.

ALEXANDER, Lloyd. *The Town Cats, and Other Tales.* See Section 2B, Talking Animal Fantasy.

ALLEN, Judy. *The Lord of the Dance.* See Section 5B, Myth Fantasy.

C/YA ALLEN, Judy. *The Spring on the Mountain.* Gr. 5–8.
An old woman sends Peter, Emma, and Michael in search of a magical, knowledge-giving spring that she, herself, once found. (BL 70:653; LJ 98:3142; TLS 1973 p. 1114)
Farrar, 1973, 153 pp., o.p.

YA AMADO, Jorge. *The Swallow and the Tom Cat: A Grown-Up Love Story.* Gr. 10 up (Written 1952.)
A fable by a major Brazilian novelist about star-crossed lovers, a swallow and a tom cat, whose families force them to marry others. (BL 79:90, 104; KR 50:943; LJ 107:1767)
Tr. by Barbara Shelby Merello, illus. by Carybé, Delacorte/Eleanor Friede, 1982, 96 pp., o.p.

ANDERSEN, Hans Christian. *Andersen's Fairy Tales.* See Chapter 3, Fantasy Collections.

C [R] ANDERSEN, Hans Christian. *The Emperor's New Clothes.* Gr. K–4.
(Written 1837, orig. U.S. pub. as a separate tale, 1848.)
Thieves pretending to create a magnificent new suit for the vain emperor
fool everyone in the kingdom except for one small boy. (BL 46:51, 70:336,
78:1155, 81:214, 82:341, 83:346; CC:426, 523; CCBB 2[Nov 1949]: 1, 13:25:
HB 25:523; KR 41:961; LJ 74:1533, 1612, 99:197; SLJ Apr 1982 p. 54, Dec
1984 p. 66, Jan 1987 p. 57; TLS 1973 pp. 384, 1121, Dec 1986 p. 1458)
Illus. by Virginia Lee Burton, Houghton, 1949, pap. 1979; tr. by H. W.
Dulcken, adapt. and illus. by Anne Rockwell, Harper, 1982, pap. 1987; retold
and illus. by Nadine Bernard Westcott, Atlantic, dist. by Little, 1984, hb and
pap.; adapt. and illus. by Janet Stevens, Holiday, 1985; retold by Anthea Bell,
illus. by Dorothée Duntze, North-South, dist. by Holt, 1986, 24 pp.

C [R] ANDERSEN, Hans Christian. *The Fir Tree.* Gr. K–4. (Orig. Danish pub.
1837, U.S. 1849.)
A little fir tree glories in being a Christmas tree, and then mourns the fate
that awaits him. (BL 67:375; CC:426; CCBB 24:53; Ch&Bks:263; HB 47:66;
KR 38:1142; LJ 96:3487; Suth: 13; TLS 1971 p. 1343)
Illus. by Nancy Ekholm Burkert, Harper, 1970, o.p.; Harper/Trophy,
1986, pap., 48 pp.

C [R] ANDERSEN, Hans Christian. *The Little Match Girl.* Gr. K–5. (Orig. Dan-
ish pub. 1846, U.S. 1870.)
A penniless young match-seller burns the last of her matches to keep warm
on Christmas Eve, and sees wondrous visions in the flames. (BL 84:387;
CC:426; CCBB 22:121; Ch&Bks:263; HB 63:716, 718; KR 36:1039, 55:1387;
LJ 93:3953; SLJ Oct 1987 p. 30; Suth:14; TLS 1987 p. 1284)
Illus. by Gustaf Tenggren, Grosset, 1944, o.p.; illus. by Blair Lent, Hough-
ton, 1968, o.p.; illus. by Rachel Isadora, Putnam, 1987, 30 pp.

C [R] ANDERSEN, Hans Christian. *The Little Mermaid.* Gr. K–5. (Written
1837, orig. Danish pub. 1846.)
A young mermaid in love with a human makes the tragic decision to give
up her undersea home and live as a mortal. (BL 32:80, 36:157, 202, 68:468,
81:585; Bookshelf 1935 p. 2; HB 16:43, 109, 48:142; KR 39:1124; LJ 97:771;
Mahony 3:200; SLJ Apr 1982 p. 65, Feb 1985 p. 70)
Tr. by M. R. James, illus. by Pamela Bianco, Holiday, 1935, o.p.; retold
and illus. by Dorothy P. Lathrop, Macmillan, 1939, o.p.; tr. by Eva Le
Gallienne, illus. by Edward Frascino, Harper, 1971, o.p.; tr. by M. R. James,
illus. by Josef Palaček, Faber, dist. by Merrimack, 1981; adapt. by Anthea
Bell, illus. by Chihiro Iwasaki, Picture Book, dist. by Alphabet, 1984, 33 pp.

C [R] ANDERSEN, Hans Christian. *The Nightingale.* Gr. K–5. (Written 1844,
orig. U.S. pub. 1896.)
A selfish emperor prefers a bejeweled mechanical bird to the faithful nightingale who loves him. (BL 31:385, 34:78, 59:113, 61:995, 78:705, 81:585,
82:564; CC:426, 433; CCBB 16:89, 18:157, 38:59, 39:41; Ch&Bks:263; HB
38:601; 41:389, 61:172, 62:78; KR 33:373; LJ 90:2393; Mahony 3:200; SLJ
Mar 1982 pp. 116, 126, Feb 1985 p. 61, Oct 1985 p. 166)
Tr. by Eva Le Gallienne, illus. by Nancy Ekholm Burkert, Harper, 1965,
Harper/Trophy, 1985; tr. by Erik Haugaard, illus. by Lemoine, Schocken,
1981, (entitled: *The Emperor's Nightingale*); tr. by Anthea Bell, illus. by
Lisbeth Zwerger, Picture Book, dist. by Alphabet, 1984; tr. and adapt. by
Alan Benjamin, illus. by Beni Montresor, Crown, 1985; adapt. by Anna
Bier, illus. by Demi, Harcourt, 1985, 30 pp.

C ANDERSEN, Hans Christian. *The Old House.* Gr. 2–5. (Orig. pub. in Denmark, orig. British pub. in this edition 1984.)

The tin soldier once given to a lonely old man by a neighbor boy reappears in a new house built for the now grown-up boy, on the site of the original house. (HB 68:364–365; SLJ Mar 1987 p. 139)

Tr. and adapt. by Anthea Bell, illus. by Jean Claverie, North-South, dist. by Holt, 1986, unp.

C ANDERSEN, Hans Christian. *The Red Shoes.* Gr. 1–4. (Orig. pub. in Denmark, this ed. orig. pub. in Austria.)

A young girl is punished for her vanity by a stern angel who decrees that she must never stop dancing in her new red shoes. (BL 79:1461; SLJ Sept 1983, p. 100)

Tr. by Anthea Bell, illus. by Chihiro Iwasaki, Neugebauer, dist. by Alphabet, 1983, 34 pp.; Oxford University Press, 1983, pap.

C [R] ANDERSEN, Hans Christian. *The Snow Queen.* Gr. 2–5. (Written 1845, orig. U.S. pub. 1849.)

Gerda faces many perils as she tries to save her friend, Kay, imprisoned in the Snow Queen's ice palace. (BL 39:37, 65:650, 69:531, 75:1627, 79:672, 684, 82:977, 84:470; Bookshelf 1921–1922 p. 8; CC:426, 463, 499; CCBB 22:21, 73, 36:121; Ch&Bks:263; HB 49:141; KR 36:820, 40:1307, 47:1205; LJ 67:884, 910, 93:3753, 3964, 98:999; SLJ Jan 1980 p. 64, Mar 1983 p. 154, Jan 1986 p. 53; Oct 1987 p. 109; Suth 3:16; TLS 1968 p. 586)

Tr. by R. P. Keigwin, illus. by June Corwin, Atheneum, 1968, o.p.; adapt. by Naomi Lewis, illus. by Errol Le Cain, Viking, 1979, o.p.; Penguin, 1982, pap.; adapt. by Amy Ehrlich, illus. by Susan Jeffers, Dial, 1982; tr. by Eva Le Gallienne, illus. by Arieh Zeldich, Harper, 1985; Macmillan, 1985; tr. and adapt. by Anthea Bell, illus. by Bernadette Watts, North-South, dist. by Holt, 1987, 24 pp.

C [R] ANDERSEN, Hans Christian. *The Steadfast Tin Soldier.* Gr. K–5. (Written 1838, orig. U.S. pub. 1846.)

A malevolent jack-in-the-box tries to separate two lovers, a tin soldier and a paper ballerina. (BL 50:18, 76:498, 78:595, 80:853; CC:426; CCBB 7:1; Ch&Bks:263; HB 29:347, 58:151; KR 21:532, 48:61; LJ 78:1544, 96:2373; SLJ Dec 1979 p. 71, Jan 1982 p. 58, Mar 1984 p. 137; Suth:216)

Tr. by M. R. James, illus. by Marcia Brown, Scribner, 1953, o.p.; illus. by Monika Laimgruber, Atheneum, 1971 (orig. pub. 1970), o.p.; illus. by Paul Galdone, Houghton/Clarion, 1979; illus. by Thomas Di Grazia, Prentice-Hall, 1981; illus. by Alain Vaës, Little, 1983; illus. by David Jorgensen, Knopf, 1986, 38 pp.

C [R] ANDERSEN, Hans Christian. *The Swineherd.* Gr. K–5. (Orig. Danish pub. 1841, U.S. 1924.)

Scorned by a self-centered princess, a prince decides to make a fool of her by wooing her disguised as a swineherd. (BL 55:27, 78:951, 83:1280; CC:427; CCBB 12:93; Ch&Bks:263; HB 34:38, 58:277; KR 26:605; LJ 55:27, 83:3004; SLJ Mar 1982 p. 127, June/July 1987 p. 75)

Tr. and illus. by Erik Blegvad, Harcourt, 1958, o.p.; tr. by Anthea Bell, illus. by Lisbeth Zwerger, Morrow, 1982; Picture Book, 1986, pap.; tr. by Naomi Lewis, illus. by Dorothée Duntze, North-South, dist. by Holt, 1987, 25 pp.

C [R] ANDERSEN, Hans Christian. *Thumbelina*. Gr. K–5. (Written 1835, orig. U.S. pub. Macmillan, 1928.)

A tiny, thumb-sized girl named Thumbelina is carried off by a frog, saved by a field mouse, and almost married to a mole before reaching the land of the flower people. (BL 58:228, 76:554, 77:112, 82:681; CC:427; CCBB 15:90, 33:145; Ch&Bks:263; HB 4[Aug 1928]:9, 38:41; KR 29:953, 48:209, 49:55; LJ 86:4357; SLJ Jan 1980 p. 53, Mar 1980 p. 116, Sept 1980 p. 55, Feb 1986 p.70)

Tr. by R. P. Keigwin, illus. by Adrienne Adams, Scribner, 1961, o.p.; adapt. by Amy Ehrlich, illus. by Susan Jeffers, Dial, 1979, pap., 1985; tr. by Richard Winston and Clara Winston, illus. by Lisbeth Zwerger, Morrow, 1980 (entitled: *Thumbeline*), o.p.; tr. by Anthea Bell, illus. by Lisbeth Zwerger, Picture Book, 1985, 29 pp.

C [R] ANDERSEN, Hans Christian. *The Ugly Duckling*. Gr. K–5. (Written 1842, orig. U.S. pub. 1850.)

Mistreated by the other ducks, the "ugly duckling" runs away to spend a terrible winter on his own, but when spring comes he has grown into a beautiful swan. (BL 62:270, 76:499, 82:681, 83:706, 1280; CC:427; CCBB 5:64, 19:141, 40:141; Ch&Bks:263; HB 41:627, 62:188; KR 33:899, 47:1206, 54:1719, 55:133; LJ 90:4602; SLJ Jan 1980 p. 54, Jan 1986 p. 53, Feb 1987 p. 63; Suth:216)

Tr. by R. P. Keigwin, illus. by Adrienne Adams, Scribner, 1965, o.p.; retold and illus. by Lorinda Bryan Cauley, Harcourt, 1979, o.p.; tr. by Anne Stewart, illus. by Monika Laimgruber, Greenwillow, 1985; adapt. by Joel Tuber and Clara Stites, illus. by Robert Van Nutt, Knopf, 1986; adapt. by Marianna Mayer, illus. by Thomas Locker, Macmillan, 1987, 38 pp.

C [R] ANDERSEN, Hans Christian. *The Wild Swans*. Gr. K–5. (Orig. pub. in Denmark, orig. U.S. pub. 1922.)

A young princess tries to break the spell that changed her eleven brothers into swans. *Swan's Wing* by Ursula Synge (see this chapter) is an extension of this story written for young adults. (BL 60:416, 78:646, 81:585; CC:427; CCBB 35:102; Ch&Bks:263; HB 39:601, 40:487; SLJ Jan 1982 p. 58, Dec 1984 p. 67)

Tr. by M. R. James, illus. by Marcia Brown, Scribner, 1963, o.p.; adapt. by Amy Ehrlich, illus. by Susan Jeffers, Dial, 1981, 1987, pap.; tr. by Naomi Lewis, illus. by Angela Barrett, Bedrick, dist. by Harper, 1984, 33 pp.

C ANDERSON, Mildred Napier. *A Gift for Merimond*. Gr. 4–6 (Orig. pub. in England.)

Prince Merimond's gift of having all his wishes granted causes him unexpected problems. (BL 49:273; CCBB 7:19; HB 29:119; KR 21:114; LJ 78:737)

Illus. by J. Paget-Fredericks, Oxford, 1953, 84 pp., o.p.

C ANDERSON, Mildred Napier. *Sandra and the Right Prince*. Gr. 3–5. (Orig. pub. in England.)

Princess Sandra rules out jousting and dragon-slaying as criteria in selecting her husband. (BL 47:369; CCBB 4:40; HB 27:179, 238; LJ 76:781)

Illus. by J. Paget-Fredericks, Oxford, 1951, 72 pp., o.p.

ANDREWS, Allen. *The Pig Plantagenet*. See Section 2A, Beast Tales.

ARKIN, Alan. *The Lemming Condition*. See Section 2A, Beast Tales.

C [R]   BABBITT, Natalie (Zane Moore). *Kneeknock Rise.* Gr. 3–5.
The people living closest to the hill called Kneeknock Rise are both proud and fearful of the noisy monster said to live there, until a boy named Egan discovers the real cause of the terrible noise. Newbery Medal Honor Book, 1971. (BL 67:99, 659; CC:429; CCBB 24:53; Ch&Bks:263; HB 46:295; KR 38:551; LJ 95:2306; Suth:24)
Illus. by the author, Farrar, 1970, 117 pp., 1984, pap.; Avon, 1981, pap.

C [R]   BABBITT, Natalie (Zane Moore). *The Search for Delicious.* Gr. 3–6.
While polling inhabitants on the exact definition of "delicious," Gaylen uncovers a plot by the queen's brother to take over the kingdom. (BL 66:53; CC:429; CCBB 23:21; Ch&Bks:263; HB 45:407; KR 37:373; LJ 95:3603; TLS 1975 p. 365)
Farrar, 1969, 167 pp.; Avon, 1980, pap.

BABBITT, Natalie (Zane Moore). *Tuck Everlasting.* See Section 5B, Myth Fantasy.

YA   BACH, Richard (David). *Jonathan Livingston Seagull.* Gr. 10 up.
Exiled from his flock for daring to fly for the joy of it, rather than following the dignified Gull family tradition, Jonathan discovers that his purpose in life is to help others find perfection. (BL 67:553; LJ 95:4187, 97:4093)
Macmillan, 1970, 93 pp.; Avon, 1973, pap.

BACON, Martha (Sherman). *Moth Manor: A Gothic Tale.* See Chapter 9, Toy Fantasy.

BAKER, Betty (Lou). *Dupper.* See Section 2A, Beast Tales.

C   BAKER, Betty (Lou). *Save Sirrushany! (Also Agotha, Princess Gwyn and All the Fearsome Beasts).* Gr. 4–6.
A dragon, a rare snail, and a girl named Agotha restore the fortunes of the Kingdom of Sirrushany. (CCBB 32:22; KR 46:496; SLJ May 1978 p. 62)
Illus. by Erick Ingraham, Macmillan, 1978, 134 pp., o.p.

C   BAKER, Betty (Lou). *Seven Spells to Farewell.* Gr. 4–6.
Orphaned Drucilla runs away from her uncle's inn with a talking raven and a performing pig and crosses the mountain to the town of Farewell to become a sorceress. (CCBB 35:162; SLJ Apr 1982, p. 65)
Macmillan, 1982, 123 pp.

C   BAKER, Margaret. *The Black Cats and the Tinker's Wife.* Gr. K–4.
The tinker's wife works magic with her good wishes. (BL 20:104; Bookshelf, 1923–1924 Suppl., p. 1; CCBB 5:42; LJ 77:71)
Illus. by Mary Baker, Dodd, 1939, 1951, 120 pp., o.p.

C   BAKER, Margaret. *Cat's-Cradles for His Majesty.* Gr. 2–4.
Pete, his mother, and Cinders the cat introduce the king to the game of cat's cradle. (BL 30:157, Bookshelf 1933 p. 6; HB 9:204; LJ 59:403)
Illus. by Mary Baker, Dodd, 1933, 115 pp., o.p.

C   BAKER, Margaret. *The Lost Merbaby.* Gr. 2–4.
The fisherman and his wife adopt a mischievous merbaby placed in the fisherman's basket by the mermaids. (BL 23:388; HB 3 [Aug 1927]:26–27; Mahony 2:130; Moore:345; TLS 1927 p. 873)
Illus. by Mary Baker, Duffield, 1927, o.p.; Dodd, 1941, 85 pp., o.p.

C BAKER, Margaret. *Noddy Goes A-Plowing.* Gr. 3–4.
A young man named Noddy wins a plowing match and the hand of the Princess. (BL 27:211; HB 6:319, 7:115; Mahony 3:104; TLS 1930 p. 982)
Illus. by Mary Baker, Duffield, 1930, 104 pp., o.p.

C BANCROFT, Alberta. *The Goblins of Haubeck.* Gr. 3–5.
A mischievous changeling makes trouble for the good goblins who help the housewives of Haubeck. (BL 22:167; HB 2[Nov 1925]:18; LJ 58:806; Mahony 2:272)
Illus. by Harold Sichel, McBride, 1925, 1933, 117 pp., o.p.

C BANKS, Richard. *The Mysterious Leaf.* Gr. 2–5.
A mysterious girl convinces three college professors to care for a tiny leaf which must never touch anything but the flesh of their hands. (BL 51:251; CCBB 8:74; HB 31:111; KR 22:633; LJ 79:2253)
Illus. by Irene Haas, Harcourt, 1954, 53 pp., o.p.

BARRETT, Nicholas. *Fledger.* See Section 2A, Beast Tales.

C BARRIE, Sir James M(atthew). *Peter Pan in Kensington Gardens.* Gr. 4–6. (Orig. British pub. as part of *The Little White Bird;* or, *Adventures in Kensington Gardens* 1902; pub. separately 1906.)
A very young Peter Pan comes to live among the fairies in Kensington Gardens. (BL 7:173)
Illus. by Arthur Rackham, Scribner, 1906, 1934, o.p.; Harmony Raine, 1980 (repr.), 123 pp.

BATO, Joseph. *The Sorcerer.* See Chapter 10, Witchcraft and Sorcery Fantasy.

C BAUM, L(yman) Frank. *The Surprising Adventures of the Magical Monarch of Mo and His People.* Gr. 3–6. (Orig. titles: *A New Wonderland,* Russell, 1900; *The Magical Monarch of Mo,* Bobbs-Merrill, 1901, 1947.)
Fourteen stories of princes, giants, wizards, and a dragon, set in the magical land of Mo where anything one wants can be picked from a tree. (LJ 72:1620; TLS 1969 p. 352)
Dover, 1968, pap.; Peter Smith (entitled *The Magical Monarch of Mo*), n.d.

BAXTER, Lorna. *The Eggchild.* See Chapter 10, Witchcraft and Sorcery Fantasy.

YA [R] BEAGLE, Peter S(oyer). *The Last Unicorn.* Gr. 10 up.
A magician and a very old but beautiful unicorn travel the world in search of others of her species. (BL 64:824; KR 36:19; LJ 93:2131; SHC:578; Tymn:50)
Viking, 1968, o.p.; Ballantine, 1976, 1988, pap., 218 pp.

C/YA BEHN, Harry. *The Faraway Lurs.* Gr. 5–8.
Heather, a girl from a peaceful forest tribe, falls in love with the son of the enemy chief who plans to cut down the sacred tree of the forest people, in this tragic love story set in prehistoric time. (BL 59:893, 896; HB 39:165; LJ 88:2140)
World, 1963, o.p.; Avon, 1968, pap., 127 pp., o.p.

C/YA [R] BENARY-ISBERT, Margot. *The Wicked Enchantment.* Gr. 5–7. (Orig. pub. in Germany.)
Anemone and her dog Winnie run away after an evil spell is cast over their

town. (BL 52:18; CCBB 9:18; Eakin:29; HB 31:374; 60:223; Kies:8; KR 23:538; LJ 80:2644)

Tr. by Richard and Clara Winston, illus. by Enrico Arno, Harcourt, 1955, o.p.; Ace, 1986, pap., 160 pp.

BENCHLEY, Nathaniel (Goddard). *Feldman Fieldmouse: A Fable.* See Section 2B, Talking Animal Fantasy.

C BIANCO, Margery Williams. *The Apple Tree.* Gr. 2–4.
An allegorical tale about spring and the renewal of life. (BL 22:425)
Illus. by Boris Artzybasheff, Doran, 1926, 47 pp., o.p.

C BIANCO, Margery Williams. *The House That Grew Smaller.* Gr. 2–4.
An uninhabited hillside house blows away and grows steadily smaller until it is just the right size for a special inhabitant. (BL 28:107; HB 7:317; Mahony 3:105)
Illus. by Rachel Field, Macmillan, 1931, 40 pp., o.p.

BIANCO, Margery Williams. *The Velveteen Rabbit; or, How Toys Became Real.* See Chapter 9, Toy Fantasy.

C BIANCO, Pamela. *The Starlit Journey, a Story.* Gr. 2–4.
A little princess begins her betrothal journey. (Bookshelf 1933 p. 6; LJ 58:898)
Illus. by the author, Macmillan, 1933, 46 pp., o.p.

C BIEGEL, Paul. *The King of the Copper Mountains.* Gr. 4–6. (Orig. Dutch pub. 1965.)
While awaiting the arrival of a doctor to save the king's life, several animals tell stories to distract the king. (CCBB 23:141; LJ 95:1632; Suth:38; TLS 1968 p. 1373)
Tr. by Gillian Hume and Paul Biegel, illus. by Babs Van Wely, Dent, dist. by Biblio, 1977 (repr. of 1968 ed.), 176 pp., o.p.

YA *Black Water: The Book of Fantastic Literature.* Ed. by Alberto Manguelo. Gr. 10 up. (Orig. Canadian pub. 1983.)
Seventy-two stories of fantasy and horror drawn primarily from England, the United States, and Latin America, whose authors include Henry James, D. H. Lawrence, and Tennessee Williams. (HB 60:634; LJ 109:824; VOYA 7:262)
Potter, dist. by Crown, 1984, pap., 967 pp.

C BODECKER, N(iels) M(ogens). *The Lost String Quartet.* Gr. 2–4.
The Daffodil String Quartet has a difficult time getting to their next concert: Sidney Periwinkle's cello is crushed by a trash compacter, Marcus Snowdrop's violin gets stuck in a tire, and frozen stringbeans stick to Jerome Crocus's violin. (CCBB 35:6; KR 49:796; SLJ Aug 1981 p. 63)
Illus. by the author, Atheneum, 1981, 28 pp., o.p.

C/YA BODGER, Joan (Mercer). *Clever-Lazy, the Girl Who Invented Herself.* Gr. 5–8.
Clever-Lazy and her husband flee the Emperor's Court to keep the gunpowder she invented from falling into the wrong hands. (BL 76:663; HB 56:53; SLJ Jan 1980 p. 77; VOYA 3 (June 1980):26)
Atheneum, 1979, 201 pp., o.p.

BOMANS, Godfried (Jan Arnold). *The Wily Witch and All the Other Fairy Tales and Fables.* See Chapter 3, Fantasy Collections.

BOURLIAGUET, Léonce. *The Giant Who Drank from His Shoe and Other Stories.* See Chapter 3, Fantasy Collections.

C BOWEN, William A(lvin). *The Enchanted Forest.* Gr. 3–5.
Six tales about the adventures of two young boys, Bojohn and Bildad, who meet elves, fairies, princesses, and princes. *Solario the Tailor* (1922) is the sequel. (BL 17:220; Bookshelf 1923–1924 p. 8)
Illus. by Maud Petersham and Miska Petersham, Macmillan, 1920, 1926, 197 pp., o.p.

C BOYLE, Kay. *The Youngest Camel.* Gr. 3–4. (Orig. pub. 1939.)
A lonely young camel wanders the world until he meets a caravan of white camels that circles the earth. (HB 15:295, 380, 35:387; LJ 64:870)
Illus. by Ronni Solbert, Harper, 1959, 96 pp., o.p.

BRADBURY, Ray (Douglas). *Something Wicked This Way Comes.* See Chapter 10, Witchcraft and Sorcery Fantasy.

YA BRADLEY, Marion Zimmer. *Night's Daughter.* Gr. 10 up.
A reinterpretation of Mozart's tale, "The Magic Flute," in which Prince Tamion and Princess Pamina face ordeals of earth, air, water, and fire as they try to unravel the conflict between the Queen of the Night and Sarastro, in order to rule their world in peace. (BL 81:1159, 1177; Kliatt 19(Spr 1985):24; VOYA 8:366)
Ballantine/Del Rey, 1985, pap., 249 pp.

C BRANCH, M(ary) L(ydia) (Bolles). *Guld the Cavern King.* Gr. 3–5.
(Orig. U.S. pub. 1917.)
Little Guld leads his people up into the light from the Koboldland caverns beneath the earth. (BL 15:189; Mahony 2:274)
Bookshop for Boys and Girls, 1918, 175 pp., o.p.

C BRENTANO, Clemens Maria. *Schoolmaster Whackwell's Wonderful Sons.*
Gr. 3–6. (Orig. pub. in Germany.)
The schoolmaster's five sons spend a year seeking their separate fortunes and then join forces to rescue a princess held captive by a giant. (BL 59:490; HB 39:58; LJ 87:4618)
Tr. by Doris Orgel, illus. by Maurice Sendak, Random, 1962. 88 pp. o.p.

C BRENTANO, Clemens Maria. *The Tale of Gockel, Hinkel and Gackeliah.*
Gr. 4–6. (Orig. German pub. 1838, U.S. Silver, 1914; entitled *Gockel, Hinkel and Gackeleia.*)
A magic ring brings good fortune to Gockel and his family, until his daughter is deceived into giving it to a stranger. (BL 58:444; HB 38:49; KR 29:504; LJ 86:2532)
Tr. by Doris Orgel, illus. by Maurice Sendak, Random, 1961, 143 pp. o.p.

BRIGGS, K(atharine) M(ary). *Kate Crackernuts.* See Section 5B, Myth Fantasy.

BRIGHT, Robert. *Richard Brown and the Dragon.* See Chapter 6, Humorous Fantasy.

C/YA BRITTAIN, Bill. *Dr. Dredd's Wagon of Wonders.* Gr. 4–7.
[R]   Orphaned Calvin Huckaway escapes from bondage to Dr. Dredd, a mysterious rain-maker, in time to save the townspeople of Coven Tree from trading away their souls. *The Wish Giver* (1983) and *The Devil's Donkey* (1981) are

also set in Coven Tree. (BL 83:1675; CCBB 40:182; HB 63:609; KR 55:922; SLJ Aug 1987 p. 78)
Illus. by Andrew Glass, Harper, 1987, 179 pp.

BRYHER, Winifred. *A Visa for Avalon.* See Section 5B, Myth Fantasy.

C [R] BUCHWALD, Emilie. *Gildaen: The Heroic Adventures of a Most Unusual Rabbit.* Gr. 4–6.
Gildaen Rabbit sets out on a quest to save the kingdom and to restore the memory of his friend, who changes from an owl to a prince to a peasant woman. (BL 69:1019; CCBB 26:167; KR 41:455; LJ 98:2191; Suth 2:63)
Illus. by Barbara Flynn, Harcourt, 1973, 189 pp., o.p.

C BULLA, Clyde Robert. *The Moon Singer.* Gr. 3–5.
Torr, a foundling who sings unearthly songs to the moon, is taken from his foster parents to be raised as a prince. (HB 45:671; KR 37:1111; LJ 95:2307)
Illus. by Trina Schart Hyman, Crowell, 1969, 48 pp., o.p.

C [R] BULLA, Clyde Robert. *My Friend the Monster.* Gr. 3–5.
Young Prince Hal rescues a monster named Humbert and the two become fast, but secret, friends. (BL 77:455; CCBB 34:107; HB 56:639; KR 49:6; SLJ Dec 1980 p. 58)
Illus. by Michele Chessare, Harper, 1980, 75 pp.

C [R] BULLA, Clyde Robert. *The Sword in the Tree.* Gr. 3–5.
Young Shan becomes a knight to avenge his father's loss of all rights to his uncle, Lord Weldon. (CC:440; HB 32:184; KR 21:1; LJ 81:764)
Illus. by Paul Galdone, Crowell, 1956, 113 pp.

C/YA BUNYAN, John. *The Pilgrim's Progress* (Orig. title: *The Pilgrim's Progress; from This World to That Which Is to Come,* 1881). Gr. 5 up.
A simplified retelling of Christian's allegorical journey from the City of Destruction to the Eternal City. (BL 36:76; HB 15:305, 16:17, 26, 126; KR 55:861; LJ 64:712; SHC:582)
Ed. by Mary Godolphin, illus. by Robert Lawson, Lippincott, 1939, 1976, o.p.; Dent, dist. by Biblio, 1954, 1979 (repr. of 1954 ed.); Dodd, 1979; adapt. by James Reeves, illus. by Joanna Troughton, Bedrick, dist. by Harper, 1987, 160 pp., pap.

BYFIELD, Barbara Ninde. *Andrew and the Alchemist.* See Chapter 10, Witchcraft and Sorcery Fantasy.

C CAMERON, Eleanor (Frances Butler). *The Beast with the Magical Horn.* Gr. 3–5.
Alison saves a unicorn and captures seven fabulous creatures for an evil queen. (BL 60:313; CCBB 17:75; HB 39:602; LJ 88:4471)
Illus. by Beth Krush and Joe Krush, Atlantic-Little, 1963, 73 pp., o.p.

C CAREW, Jan (Rynveld). *Children of the Sun.* Gr. 3–5.
The two sons of an earth woman and the sun set out to answer their father's query: "Would you like to be good men or great men?" (BL 76:1122; CCBB 33:187; KR 48:774; SLJ May 1980 p. 65)
Illus. by Leo Dillon and Diane Dillon, Little, 1980, 40 pp.

CAREY, Valerie Scho. *The Devil and Mother Crump.* See Chapter 6, Humorous Fantasy.

CARROLL, Lewis. *Alice's Adventures in Wonderland.* See Section 5C, Travel to Other Worlds.

C CARTER, Angela. *The Donkey Prince.* Gr. 1–4.
Even though he has been transformed into a donkey, Prince Bruno must find a magic apple to save the queen's life. (BL 67:662; CCBB 24:103; KR 38:1145; LJ 96:256)
Illus. by Eros Keith, Simon, 1970, 40 pp, o.p.

C [R] *A Cavalcade of Dragons.* Ed. by Roger Lancelyn Green. Gr. 4–7. (British title: *The Hamish Hamilton Book of Dragons,* 1970.)
Folktales, fantasy, and poetry about dragons, including "The Lady Dragonissa" by Andrew Lang, "The Fiery Dragon" by E. Nesbit, "The Hoard" by J. R. R. Tolkien, and "The Dragon Speaks" by C. S. Lewis. (BL 68:108; HB 47:283; Kies:93; KR 39:297; LJ 96:2130; TLS 1971 p. 388)
Illus. by Krystyna Turska, Walck, 1970, 256 pp., o.p.

C CAYLUS, Anne Claude Phillipe, Comte de. *Heart of Ice.* Gr. 2–3.
Kidnapped by a vengeful fairy at his christening, a tiny prince manages to scale the slopes of the Ice Mountain to win the hand of Princess Sabella. (BL 74:158; CCBB 31:76; KR 45:669; SLJ Oct 1977 p. 109)
Adapt. by Benjamin Appel, illus. by J. K. Lambert, Pantheon, 1977, 58 pp., o.p.

C/YA CERVANTES, Saavedra Miguel de. *The Adventures of Don Quixote de la*
[R] *Mancha.* Gr. 5 up. (Orig. Spanish pub. 1605, first English ed. 1612.)
Don Quixote and Sancho Panza, knight and page, ride off to defend the poor and rescue ladies in distress. (BL 46:47, 57:130; Bookshelf 1932 p.8; CCBB 11:51; HB 36:308; JHC:354; KR 28:621; LJ 85:3869; SHC:584; SLJ Jan 1981 p. 67; TLS Dec 4, 1951 p. xii, 1980 p. 1032)
Adapt. by Leighton Barret, illus. by Warren Chappell, Knopf, 1960, o.p.; illus. by Edward Ardizzone, Walck, 1960, o.p.; Dent, dist. by Biblio, 1983 (repr. of 1953 ed.); retold by James Reeves, illus. by Edward Ardizzone, Bedrick, 1985 (entitled: *Exploits of Don Quixote;* orig. British pub. in this ed. 1959), 219 pp., o.p.

YA CHERRYH, C. J. (pseud. of Carolyn Janice Cherry). *The Dreamstone.* Gr. 10 up. (Revised and expanded from the novella, "Ealdwood," 1981.)
Arafel, the last of the guardian spirits of Ealdwood, narrates this haunting tale of the last stand of faerie and magic against humanity and iron. The sequel is *The Tree of Swords and Jewels* (1983). (BL 79:1075, 1084; LJ 108:603; VOYA 6:148)
NAL/DAW 1983, 1987, pap., 192 pp.

C [R] COATSWORTH, Elizabeth (Jane). *The Cat Who Went to Heaven.* Gr. 4–6. (Orig. pub. 1930.)
When a poor Japanese artist paints his little white cat into a picture of the dying Buddha, he lets his pet into heaven. Newbery Medal winner, 1931. (BL 27:107, 55:191; Bookshelf 1932 p.8; CC:451; CCBB 12:60; Ch&Bks:244; HB 6:214, 7:119, 36:146, 62:344; LJ 56:279, 598; Moore:409, 431)
Illus. by Lynd Ward, Macmillan, 1967, 62 pp., hb and pap.

C [R] COATSWORTH, Elizabeth (Jane). *Cricket and the Emperor's Son.* Gr. 3–6. (Orig. pub. 1932.)
A little prince with insomnia is entertained each night by Cricket, an ap-

prentice with an endless number of stories to tell. (BL 29:118, 61:873; Bookshelf 1933 p. 6; CCBB 18:144; Ch&Bks:265; Eakin:77; HB 8:157, 41:275; KR 33:310; LJ 58:899, 90:2042)

Illus. by Juliette Palmer, Norton, 1965, 126 pp., o.p.

COATSWORTH, Elizabeth (Jane). *Marra's World*. See Section 5B, Myth Fantasy.

C [R]   COATSWORTH, Elizabeth (Jane). *The Princess and the Lion*. Gr. 4–6.

After the king surprises his court by naming Prince Michael heir to the throne, Princess Miriam journeys to the Prison of Princes to prevent Michael's escape. (BL 60:39; Eakin: 77; HB 39:281; LJ 88:2549)

Illus. by Evaline Ness, Pantheon, 1963, 77 pp. o.p.

C   COATSWORTH, Elizabeth (Jane). *Pure Magic* (pap. title: *The Werefox*). Gr. 4–5.

Johnny's new friend, Giles, has a secret: He can change into a fox, which proves dangerous when fox-hunting season begins. (BL 70:385; HB 49:464; KR 41:642; LJ 98:2649)

Illus. by Ingrid Fetz, Macmillan, 1973, 68 pp., o.p.

COLLINS, Meghan. *The Willow Maiden*. See Section 5B, Myth Fantasy.

COLLODI, Carlo. *The Adventures of Pinocchio*. See Chapter 9, Toy Fantasy.

COLUM, Padraic. *The Boy Apprenticed to an Enchanter*. See Chapter 10, Witchcraft and Sorcery Fantasy.

C   COLUM, Padraic. *The Children Who Followed the Piper*. Gr. 3–5.

John Ball, the miller's son, Golden Hood, the milk-woman's daughter, and Valentine, son of the Emperor, follow the Piper into adventure. (BL 19:91; Mahony 2:134)

Illus. by Dugald Stewart Walker, Macmillan, 1922, 1933, 1944, 152 pp., o.p.

C [R]   COLUM, Padraic. *The Girl Who Sat by the Ashes*. Gr. 3–5. (Orig. U.S. pub. 1919, 1939.)

An expanded version of the traditional "Cinderella" story. (BL 16:174; Bookshelf 1923–1924 p. 8; KR 36:336; LJ 45:980; Mahony 1:25, Mahony 2:134)

Illus. by Imero Gobbato, Macmillan, 1968, 117 pp., o.p.

C/YA   COLUM, Padraic. *The King of Ireland's Son*. Gr. 5–7. (Orig. pub. Holt 1916.)

The king's son falls in love with the daughter of Fedelma, the Enchanter. (BL 13:269, 18:95, 59:84; HB 39:75; Mahony 2:277)

Illus. by Willy Pogány, Macmillan, 1962, 275 pp., o.p.

COLUM, Padraic. *The Stone of Victory and Other Tales*. See Chapter 3, Fantasy Collections.

C   COOKE, Donald Edwin. *The Firebird*. Gr. 3–5.

A magical firebird helps the Red Prince pass through an enchanted land and defeat the evil Black Prince. This tale is taken from the same Russian source as Stravinski's "Firebird Suite." (BL 36:347; LJ 65:37)

Illus. by the author, Winston, 1939, 144 pp., o.p.

C COOMBS, Patricia. *Molly Mullett.* Gr. K–3.
Molly becomes a knight after she and her pet blackbird outwit an ogre. (CCBB 29:24; KR 43:69; SLJ Apr 1975 p. 43)
Illus. by the author, Lothrop, 1975, 32 pp., o.p.

C COOPER, Gale. *Unicorn Moon.* Gr. 4–5.
A princess must solve the riddle of true love before she can separate the young man imprisoned in her dreams from a real man she can love. (BL 81:786; CCBB 38:103; SLJ Dec 1984 p. 79)
Illus. by the author, Dutton, 1984, 32 pp., o.p.

C COOPER, Margaret. *The Ice Palace.* Gr. 3–5.
Princess Kasha is given a palace of ice, especially built to keep her cool. (CCBB 20:136; KR 34:574; LJ 91:4329)
Illus. by Harold Goodwin, Macmillan, 1966, 50 pp., o.p.

C COOPER, Paul Fenimore. *Dindle.* Gr. 3–5.
A rug-weaver named Dindle longs to rid the kingdom of the terrible white dragon whose tail turns living things to stone. (HB 40:174; LJ 89:951)
Illus. by Marion Cooper, Putnam, 1963, 64 pp., o.p.

COOPER (Grant), Susan (Mary). *The Selkie Girl.* See Section 5B, Myth Fantasy.

CORBETT, W(illiam) J(esse). *The Song of Pentecost.* See Section 2A, Beast Tales.

C CRANCH, Christopher P(earse). *The Last of the Huggermuggers, a Giant Story.* Gr. 4–6. (Orig. British pub. 1855, U.S. 1856.)
Shipwrecked on an island in the East Indies, a young sailor named Jacket is befriended by two kindly giants, or Huggermuggers. On a second visit described in the sequel, *Kobboltozo* (orig. British pub. 1856, U.S. 1857), Jacket finds that a race of dwarfs is trying to take over the island. (HB 20:172–175)
Illus. by J. Watson Davis, Burt, 1901, 170 pp., o.p.

C [R] CRESSWELL (Rowe), Helen. *The Night Watchmen.* Gr. 4–6. (Orig. British pub. 1969.)
Two tramps named Josh and Caleb tell Henry the secret of the Night Train. (BL 67:371; CCBB 24:121; HB 46:615; KR 38:1146; LJ 96:2128; Suth:94)
Illus. by Gareth Floyd, Macmillan, 1970, 122 pp., o.p.

CRESSWELL (Rowe), Helen. *Up the Pier.* See Chapter 8, Time Travel Fantasy.

C/YA [R] CRESSWELL (Rowe), Helen. *The Winter of the Birds.* Gr. 5–8. (Orig. British pub. 1975.)
Neighbors unite when old Mr. Rudge foretells the coming of "terrible steel birds" that kill live birds and bring evil to the town. (BL 72:1404; CC:457; CCBB 30:80; Ch&Bks:242; HB 52:404; KR 44:482; SLJ Sept 1976 p. 130; TLS 1975 p. 1457)
Macmillan, 1976, 243 pp. o.p.

C CROTHERS, Samuel McChord. *Miss Muffet's Christmas Party.* Gr. 4–6. (Written 1891, orig. U.S. pub. 1902.)
Miss Muffet and the spider invite all of her favorite literary characters to their Christmas party. (BL 25:401; LJ 53:810; Mahony 2:278)
Illus. by Olive M. Long, Houghton, 1929, 106 pp., o.p.

C CROWNFIELD, Gertrude. *Princess Whiteflame.* Gr. 4–6.
Prince Radiance breaks the spell that had turned Princess Whiteflame into a little tongue of flame. (BL 17:352; Mahony 1:39)
Illus. by Anne Merriman Peck, Dutton, 1920, 229 pp., o.p.

C/YA CUNNINGHAM, Julia (Woolfolk). *Come to the Edge.* Gr. 5–7.
Unable to trust adults after his father's betrayal and the loss of his friend, Gravel Winter continually runs away from foster homes. (BL 74:37; CCBB 31:11; HB 53:449; KR 45:4; SLJ May 1977 p. 60)
Pantheon, 1977, o.p.; Avon, 1985, pap.

C/YA CUNNINGHAM, Julia (Woolfolk). *Dorp Dead.* Gr. 5 up. (Orig. pub.
[R]   Pantheon 1965.)
Gilly is taken from an unhappy life in an orphanage to an even more miserable foster home, from which he escapes to avoid being kept in a cage. (CCBB 19:30; Ch&Bks:265; Eakin:87; JHC:362; LJ 90:2018)
Illus. by James Spanfeller, Knopf, 1987, hb and pap, 88 pp.

CUNNINGHAM, Julia (Woolfolk). *Maybe, a Mole.* See Section 2B, Talking Animal Fantasy.

C CUNNINGHAM, Julia (Woolfolk). *OAF.* Gr. 4–6.
Oaf, who has inherited three magic gifts, shares a dangerous adventure with a crow, a dog, a cat, and a rat. (BL 82:1016; CCBB 39:144; KR 54:544; SLJ Apr 1986 p. 86)
Illus. by Peter Sis, Knopf, 1986, 86 pp.

C/YA CUNNINGHAM, Julia (Woolfolk). *Tuppenny.* Gr. 5–8.
[R]   The appearance of a young girl named Tuppenny changes the lives of three families: one whose daughter ran away from home, one whose retarded daughter is institutionalized, and one whose daughter was murdered. (BL 75:371; CCBB 32:112; HB 55:639; KR 46:1309; SLJ Nov 1978 p. 72; Suth 2:111)
Dutton, 1978, o.p.; Avon, 1981, pap., 96 pp.

CUNNINGHAM, Julia (Woolfolk). *Viollet.* See Section 2B, Talking Animal Fantasy.

C/YA CUNNINGHAM, Julia (Woolfolk). *Wolf Roland.* Gr. 6–8.
A medieval peddler hunts down the huge yellow-eyed wolf that devoured his donkey friend, and the talking wolf agrees to take the donkey's place. (BL 79:1214; JHC:363; KR 51:522; SLJ May 1983 p. 80)
Pantheon, 1983, 108 pp.

CURLEY, Daniel. *Ann's Spring.* See Section 5B, Myth Fantasy.

CURLEY, Daniel. *Billy Beg and the Bull.* See Section 5B, Myth Fantasy.

C DAMJAN, Mischa (pseud.). *December's Travels.* Gr. 2–4. (Orig. German pub. 1986.)
The North Wind gives the boy, December, the magic gift of being able to visit March, June, and October. These visits give him a new appreciation of his winter home. (BL 83:127, 138; CCBB 40:103; SLJ Nov 1986 p. 74)
Illus. by Dušan Kállay, tr. by Anthea Bell, Dial, dist. by Dutton, 1986, 32 pp.

C DANK, Gloria Rand. *The Forest of App.* Gr. 4–6.
A young Rhymer, or storyteller, named Nob runs away and gets lost in an

enchanted forest, where he helps the creatures recover their lost magic. (CCBB 37:84; JHC:363; KR 51:202; SLJ Feb 1984 p. 67)
Greenwillow, 1983; Putnam, 1984, pap.

DANN, Colin (Michael). *The Animals of Farthing Wood.* See Section 2A, Beast Tales.

C DAY, David. *The Emperor's Panda.* Gr. 3–5. (Orig. Canadian pub. 1986.)
Wise and magical Lord Beishung, the Master Panda, helps young Kung, a poor flute player, gain wisdom, a princess, and an empire. (BL 83:1599; SLJ Aug 1987 p. 81)
Illus. by Eric Beddows, Dodd, 1987, 111 pp.

DE LA MARE, Walter (John). *The Three Royal Monkeys.* See Section 2B, Talking Animal Fantasy.

DE LINT, Charles. *Jack the Giant-Killer.* See Section 5B, Myth Fantasy.

DELL, Joan. *The Missing Boy.* See Section 5C, Travel to Other Worlds.

DE REGNIERS, Beatrice Schenk (Freedman). *The Boy, the Rat, and the Butterfly.* See Chapter 7, Magic Adventure Fantasy.

C [R] DE REGNIERS, Beatrice Schenk (Freedman). *Penny.* Gr. 1–4. (Orig. pub., illus. by Marvin Bileck, Viking, 1966, o.p.)
Penny is a tiny girl "no bigger than a penny" who is adopted and raised by an elderly couple, marries a young man just her size, and goes to live in the land of tiny people. (BL 83:1204; CCBB 20:107; HB 42:705; KR 34:1096, 55:135; LJ 91:6184)
Illus. by Betsy Lewin, Lothrop, 1987, 59 pp.

C DIAMOND, Donna (adapt.). *Swan Lake.* Gr. 3 up.
Prince Siegfried falls in love with the Swan Queen Odette but is fooled by a sorcerer into pledging his love to her lookalike, Odille. (BL 76:1289; KR 48:1082; SLJ May 1980 p. 66)
Illus. by the adaptor, Holiday, 1981, 32 pp.

C [R] DICKENS, Charles (John Huffam). *A Christmas Carol.* Gr. 4 up. (Orig. British pub. 1843.)
Mean old Ebenezer Scrooge is cured of his miserliness when he is visited by the ghosts of Christmases Past, Present, and Yet to Come. (BL 49:147, 58:194, 80:169, 406, 630, 633; Bookshelf 1928 p. 35; CC:460; CCBB 37:46; HB 59:731; JHC:365; KR 29:564; LJ 86:4046; SLJ Oct 1983 p. 179, Mar 1984 p. 172)
Illus. by Arthur Rackham, Lippincott, 1952, o.p.; illus. by John Groth, Macmillan, 1963, o.p.; illus. by Michael Foreman, Dial, 1983; illus. by Trina Schart Hyman, Holiday, 1983; illus. by Greg Hildebrandt, Simon, 1983, 122 pp.

C [R] DICKENS, Charles (John Huffam). *The Magic Fishbone.* Gr. 3–5. (Orig. British pub. 1868.)
Exhausted from caring for her nineteen brothers and sisters, Princess Alice is given a magic fishbone that will grant one wish. (Bookshelf 1923–1924 p. 8; CC:461; Eakin:99; HB 1[June 1925]:45; LJ 78:2226; Mahony 1:38; TLS 1971 p. 774)
Illus. by Louis Slobodkin, Vanguard, 1953, 36 pp.; Coach House, 1961, pap.

DICKINSON, Peter. *The Blue Hawk.* See Section 5A, Alternate Worlds or Histories.

C DICKINSON, Peter (pseud. of Malcolm De Brissac). *Giant Cold.* Gr. 4–6. (Orig. British pub. 1983.)
Giant Cold has awakened and turned tropical Apple Island to ice; when "you" try to stop the Giant, "you" are reduced to Lilliputian size. (CCBB 37:184; HB 60:50; SLJ Apr 1984 p. 122; TLS May 1984 p. 558)
Illus. by Alan E. Cober, Dutton, 1984, 69 pp.

C [R] DICKINSON, Peter (pseud. of Malcolm De Brissac). *The Iron Lion.* Gr. 2–4.
Princess Yasmin challenges Prince Mustapha to bring her the Iron Lion of Ferdustan, in order to win her hand in marriage. (CC:461; CCBB 25:120; HB 60:591; KR 40:135; LJ 97:1594; SLJ Nov 1984 p. 106; TLS 1973 p. 1431)
Illus. by Marc Brown, Little, 1972, o.p.; illus. by Pauline Baynes, Bedrick, 1984 (orig. British pub. in this ed. 1983), 32 pp.

C DOBBS, Rose. *Discontented Village.* Gr. 4–6.
A thick fog of gloom hangs over a pleasant town until a mysterious stranger teaches the villagers about contentment. (BL 43:173; HB 23:108; LJ 71:1466)
Illus. by Beatrice Tobias, Coward, 1946, 31 pp., o.p.

C [R] DOBBS, Rose. *No Room: An Old Story Retold.* Gr. 3–5.
An old man, who wishes to avoid sharing his house with his daughter's family, is given some unexpected advice. (BL 41:61; HB 20:375; KR 12:429; LJ 69:763, 865)
Illus. by Fritz Eichenberg, McKay, 1944, 44 pp., o.p.

DOLBIER, Maurice (Wyman). *A Lion in the Woods.* See Chapter 6, Humorous Fantasy.

C [R] DOLBIER, Maurice (Wyman). *Torten's Christmas Secret.* Gr. 2–4.
Torten, one of Santa's elves, decides to make his own gifts for the not-so-good children overlooked by Santa. (BL 48:51; CCBB 5:28; HB 27:401, 415; KR 19:388; LJ 76:1342)
Illus. by Robert Henneberger, Little, 1951, 61 pp., o.p.

DONOVAN, John. *Family: A Novel.* See Section 2A, Beast Tales.

C [R] DRUON, Maurice (Samuel Roger Charles). *Tistou of the Green Thumbs.* Gr. 4–6. (British title: *Tistou of the Green Fingers*; orig. French pub. 1957.)
Tistou makes flowers bloom, bringing beauty and happiness into the world and stopping a war. (BL 55:221; CCBB 12:130; HB 34:382, 61:84; KR 26:659; LJ 83:3006; TLS Nov 21, 1958 p. x)
Tr. by Humphrey Hare, illus. by Jacqueline Duhème, Scribner, 1958, 178 pp., o.p.

DU BOIS, William (Sherman) Pène. *Otto and the Magic Potatoes.* See Chapter 6, Humorous Fantasy.

C/YA DUNBAR, Aldis. *Once There Was a Prince.* Gr. 5–7. (Orig. pub. in England.)
Opposed to the oppression of his people, a young prince escapes in disguise to a neighboring land to learn how to rule fairly and wisely. (BL 25:216; HB 4:27)
Illus. by Maurice Day, Little, 1928, 302 pp., o.p.

DUNSANY, Lord. *The Charwoman's Shadow.* See Chapter 10, Witchcraft and Sorcery Fantasy.

YA DUNSANY, Lord (pseud. of Edward John Morton Drax Plunkett). *The King of Elfland's Daughter.* Gr. 10 up.
Prince Alveric of Erl crosses into Fairyland where, after many adventures, he wins the hand of Princess Lirazel; but their happiness is short-lived because the King of Elfland uses magic to bring his daughter back to him. (BL 21:111; TLS 1924 pp. 402, 466; Tymn:78)
Putnam, 1924, 301 pp., o.p.; Ballantine, 1969, o.p.

EDMONDS, Walter D. *Beaver Valley.* See Section 2A, Beast Tales.

C [R] ELIOT, Ethel (Augusta) Cook. *The Wind Boy.* Gr. 5–6. (Orig. pub. 1923.)
A winged boy from the Clear Land comes to play with two refugee children awaiting their father's return from war. (BL 20:105, 42:61; Bookshelf 1927 p. 7; HB 22:213; KR 13:370; LJ 70:980; Mahony 2:278)
Illus. by Robert Hallock, Viking, 1945, 244 pp., o.p.

C/YA *The Enchanter's Spell: Five Famous Tales.* Adapt. by Gennady Spirin. Gr.
[R] 3–7.
This collection of literary fairy tales contains Hans Christian Andersen's "The Emperor's New Clothes," Miguel de Cervantes' "The Beautiful Kitchen Maid," E. T. A. Hoffmann's "The Nutcracker," George MacDonald's "Little Daylight," and Alexander Pushkin's "Snow White." (BL 84:1608; CCBB 41:170; KR 56:128; SLJ Apr 1988 p. 100)
Illus. by the adaptor, Dial, 1988, 96 pp.

YA [R] ENDE, Michael. *Momo.* Gr. 10 up. (Orig. German pub. 1973; British title: *The Grey Gentlemen* 1975.)
A girl named Momo who lives in a ruined amphitheater is befriended by the poor people because she listens so carefully that everyone is able to think great thoughts. When her friends' lives are threatened by the "men in grey," who live off of others' spare time, only Momo can save them from the plague of deadly tedium. (BL 81:602; KR 52:1168; Kliatt 20[Spring 1986]:57; LJ Jan 1985 p. 100; VOYA 8:192)
Tr. by J. Maxwell Brownjohn, Doubleday, 1985; Penguin, 1986, pap., 240 pp.

C [R] ENRIGHT, Elizabeth (Wright). *Tatsinda.* Gr. 3–5.
In love with an outcast girl named Tatsinda, Prince Tackatan of Tatrajan determines to rescue her from the horrible giant who has kidnapped her. (BL 59:896; CCBB 16:159; Ch&Bks:266; Eakin:109; HB 39:382; LJ 88:2774; TLS 1964 p. 1081)
Illus. by Irene Haas, Harcourt, 1963, 80 pp., o.p.

C [R] ERSHOV, Petr Pavlovich. *The Little Hump-backed Horse: A Russian Tale.* Gr. 3–5. (Orig. U.S. pub. Harper, 1931, entitled *Humpy,* o.p.; Macmillan, 1942, entitled *Little Magic Horse,* o.p.; Putnam, 1942, entitled *The Little Hunchback Horse,* o.p.)
Ivan the Fool's magical horse helps him defeat his enemies, win a bride, and become tsar of Russia. (BL 28:354, 39:298, 77:513; CCBB 34:172; HB 19:34, 57:61; KR 48:1461; LJ 56:1058, 67:883, 68:38, 173; SLJ Dec 1980 p. 44)
Adapt. by Margaret Hodges from a poem by Petr Pavlovich Ershov, tr. by

Gina Kovarsky, illus. by Chris Conover, Farrar, 1980, 25 pp., o.p.; Farrar/ Sunburst, 1987, pap.

C/YA ESSEX, Rosamund (Sibyl). *Into the Forest.* Gr. 5–7. (Orig. British pub. 1963.)
Five children abandoned during the Great Destruction undertake a dangerous journey through the forest in search of a better world. (BL 62:716; KR 33:907; LJ 90:5512)
Coward-McCann, 1965, 156 pp. o.p.

EUSTIS, Helen. *Mr. Death and the Redheaded Woman.* See Chapter 6, Humorous Fantasy.

YA *Faery!* Ed. by Terri Windling. Gr. 10 up.
Twenty-three tales about the Kingdom of Faery, whose authors include Jane Yolen, Robin McKinley, Sherri Tepper, and Patricia McKillip. (BL 81:927, 945; Kies:100)
Ace, 1985, pap., 308 pp., o.p.

C FALKBERGET, Johan (Petter). *Broomstick and Snowflake.* Gr. 2–4. (Orig. pub. in Norway.)
Broomstick, the tanner's son, meets the North Mountain Giant's daughter, Snowflake. (BL 30:123; Bookshelf 1933 p. 5; HB 9:205; Mahony 3:172)
Illus. by Helen Sewell, Macmillan, 1933, 88 pp., o.p.

YA *The Fantastic Imagination: An Anthology of High Fantasy,* vol. I. Ed. by Robert H. Boyer and Kenneth J. Zahorski. Gr. 10 up.
Sixteen "high fantasy" short stories whose authors include George Mac-Donald, C. S. Lewis, J. R. R. Tolkien, Lloyd Alexander, Peter S. Beagle, Ursula K. Le Guin, Lord Dunsany, John Buchan, Frank R. Stockton, and Sylvia Townsend Warner. *The Fantastic Imagination,* vol. II (1978) is a companion volume. (BL 73:1338; Kliatt 11[Spring 1977]:9; Tymn:185)
Avon, 1977, pap., 325 pp., o.p.

FARBER, Norma. *Six Impossible Things before Breakfast.* See Chapter 3, Fantasy Collections.

C/YA FARJEON, Eleanor. *The Glass Slipper.* Gr. 5–7. (Orig. British pub.
[R] 1946.)
A humorous retelling of the Cinderella story. (BL 52:282, 83:350; CC 1987 Suppl., p. 56; HB 32:120, 63:84; KR 24:43; LJ 81:1309)
Illus. by Ernest Shepard, Viking, 1956, o.p.; Buccaneer, 1981 (repr.); Harmony, 1981, (repr.); Lippincott, dist. by Harper, 1986, 213 pp.

FARJEON, Eleanor. *The Little Bookroom: Eleanor Farjeon's Short Stories for Children Chosen by Herself.* See Chapter 3, Fantasy Collections.

C/YA FARJEON, Eleanor. *Martin Pippin in the Apple Orchard.* Gr. 5–7. (Orig. British pub. 1921, U.S., Stokes, 1922)
A minstrel named Martin Pippin frees an imprisoned farm girl by entertaining her six guards with his tales. The sequel is *Martin Pippin in the Daisy Field* (1937, 1963). (BL 19:53, 58:112; HB 37:557; KR 29:670; Mahony 2:279)
Illus. by Richard Kennedy, Lippincott, 1949, 1961, 305 pp., o.p.

C [R] FARJEON, Eleanor. *The Silver Curlew*. Gr. 3–6. (Orig. British pub. 1953.)
    A young queen must give up her child unless she can guess the Spindle-Imp's name. (BL 50:345; CCBB 8:29; HB 30:174; KR 22:114; LJ 79:1064)
    Illus. by Ernest Shepard, Viking, 1954, 162 pp., o.p.

FARMER (Mockridge), Penelope. *A Castle of Bone*. See Section 5B, Myth Fantasy.

FARMER, (Mockridge), Penelope. *The Summer Birds*. See Chapter 7, Magic Adventure Fantasy.

FAST, Howard (Melvin). *The General Zapped an Angel: New Stories of Fantasy and Science Fiction*. See Chapter 3, Fantasy Collections.

C/YA FENTON, Edward. *The Nine Questions*. Gr. 5–7.
[R]   Willy and Gabriella use a magical silver whistle and hunting cap to rescue the king, Willy's father. (BL 56:125; HB 36:129; KR 27:495; LJ 85:1302)
    Illus. by C. Walter Hodges, Doubleday, 1959, 235 pp., o.p.

C FENWICK, Elizabeth. *Cockleberry Castle*. Gr. 3–5.
    When the prince throws a banquet for the other palace children, they are afraid they are about to be punished. (KR 32:3; LJ 88:2550)
    Illus. by Fabio Rieti, Pantheon, 1963, 74 pp., o.p.

C [R] FLEISCHMAN, Paul (Taylor). *The Birthday Tree*. Gr. 3–4.
    An ex-sailor and his wife try to avoid losing a fourth son to the sea by moving inland and planting a Birthday Tree in honor of his birth. (BL 75:1535; CC:467; KR 47:573; SLJ Sept 1979 p. 110)
    Illus. by Marcia Sewall, Harper, 1979, 32 pp.

C/YA FLEISCHMAN, Paul (Taylor). *Coming-and-Going Men: Four Tales*. Gr. 6–9.
[O]   Four interconnected stories involving artisans and tradesmen passing through the town of New Caanan, Vermont, in 1800: a silhouette cutter who battles the devil, a poet who saves a man's soul, three artists whose works are destroyed, and a peddler who gives a woman back her life. (BL 81:1390, 1399; CC 1987 Suppl. p. 65; CCBB 39:7; HB 61:315; KR 53:J32; SLJ 31[Aug 1985]:75; VOYA 8:184)
    Illus. by Randy Gaul, Harper, 1985, 147 pp.

FLEISCHMAN, Paul (Taylor). *Finzel the Farsighted*. See Chapter 6, Humorous Fantasy.

FLEISCHMAN, Paul (Taylor). *The Half-a-Moon Inn*. See Chapter 10, Witchcraft and Sorcery Fantasy.

C/YA FLEISCHMAN, (Albert) Sid(ney). *The Whipping Boy*. Gr. 4–6.
[O]   Prince Brat decides to run away from home, taking his much-abused whipping boy, Jemmy, with him, but their roles are reversed when the boys are captured by the villains Cut-Water and Hold-Your-Nose-Billy. Newbery Award winner, 1986. (BL 82:1018, 83:1135; CC 1987 Suppl. p. 56; CCBB 39:126; HB 62:325; JHC 1987 Suppl. p. 65; KR 54:715; SLJ May 1986 p. 90)
    Illus. by Peter Sis, Greenwillow, 1986, 90 pp.

FLORA, James (Royer). *Wanda and the Bumbly Wizard*. See Chapter 10, Witchcraft and Sorcery Fantasy.

C FLORY, Jane Trescott. *The Lost and Found Princess.* Gr. 2–4.
Clues dropped by three robbers enable a cat, a dragon, and an old woman to rescue a captive princess. (BL 75:1156; KR 47:518; SLJ Apr 1979 p. 42)
Illus. by the author, Houghton, 1979, 48 pp., o.p.

C FOLLETT, Barbara Newhall. *The House without Windows and Eepersip's Life There.* Gr. 4–6
In this story written by a 9-year-old, a lonely little girl runs away to the woods, where she becomes a dryad. (BL 23:347; HB 3:41; Mahony 2:279; Moore:427)
Knopf, 1927, 166 pp., o.p.

YA FORD, Richard. *Quest for the Faradawn.* Gr. 10 up.
Abandoned in the woods by his parents, a human baby is taken in by badgers who raise him in fulfilment of a legend that foretold his becoming the savior of the world. (BL 78:1068, 1082; KR 50:374; LJ 107:1014; SLJ Sept 1982 p. 148; VOYA 5[Aug 1982]:39)
Illus. by Owain Bell, Delacorte/Eleanor Friede, 1982, o.p.; Dell, 1983, pap., 320 pp.

C FORST, S. *Pipkin.* Gr. 1–4.
Pipkin, the lost prince of the gnomes, is cared for by an old woman until he is able to find his way back into the Ladybug Kingdom. (HB 46:476; LJ 96:1007)
Illus. by Robin Jacques, Delacorte, 1970, 144 pp., o.p.

C FOSTER, Malcolm (Burton). *The Prince with a Hundred Dragons.* Gr. 2–4.
A gentle dragon agrees to help Prince Guy fool his father into thinking that Guy is a fearless dragon slayer. (CCBB 17:138; KR 31:656; LJ 88:4083)
Illus. by Barbara Remington, Doubleday, 1963, 60 pp., o.p.

FOX (Greenberg), Paula. *The Little Swineherd and Other Tales.* See Chapter 3, Fantasy Collections.

FRANKO, Ivan, and MELNYK, Bohdan. *Fox Mykyta.* See Section 2B, Talking Animal Fantasy.

C FREEMAN, Barbara C(onstance). *Broom-Adelaide.* Gr. 4–6. (Orig. British pub. 1963.)
No one at the castle suspects that the governess, Madame Crowberry, is actually a witch. (BL 62:219; HB 41:490; KR 33:626; LJ 90:3790; TLS 1963 p. 980)
Illus. by the author, Little, 1965, 124 pp., o.p.

GARDNER, John (Champlin) (Jr.). *Dragon, Dragon, and Other Timeless Tales.* See Chapter 3, Fantasy Collections.

YA GARDNER, John (Champlin) (Jr.). *In the Suicide Mountains.* Gr. 7 up.
A dwarf, a blacksmith's daughter, and a crown prince, all bent on suicide, meet in the mountains and find happiness together. (BL 74:22, 32; CCBB 31:126; HB 54:194; KR 45:868; LJ 102:1677; SLJ Dec 1977 p. 54)
Illus. by Joe Servello, Knopf, 1977, 159 pp.

YA [R] GARFIELD, Leon. *The Wedding Ghost.* Gr. 7 up. (Orig. British pub. 1985.)
Jack and Jill open a strange wedding gift: a mysterious map that leads Jack

through foggy London into a demonic forest where a dust-covered Sleeping Beauty lies in a golden mansion. (BL 83:1275; CCBB 40:144; HB 63:611; KR 55:637; SLJ June–July 1987 p. 106; TLS 1985 p. 350)
Illus. by Charles Keeping, Oxford/Salem, 1987, 64 pp.

GARNER, Alan. *Alan Garner's Fairytales of Gold.* See Chapter 3, Fantasy Collections.

GARNETT, David. *Two by Two: A Story of Survival.* See Section 5B, Myth Fantasy.

GATE, Ethel May. *The Fortunate Days.* See Chapter 3, Fantasy Collections.

GERRARD, Roy. *Sir Cedric.* See Chapter 6, Humorous Fantasy.

GERSTEIN, Mordicai. *The Seal Mother.* See Section 5B, Myth Fantasy.

C GIBSON, Katharine. *Cinders.* Gr. 3–5.
Overlooked when Cinderella's fairy-godmother turned the other servants back into animals, Cinders the coachman decides to go into service to the king. (BL 36:17; HB 15:296; LJ 64:712)
Illus. by Vera Bock, Longman, 1939, 133 pp., o.p.

C GIBSON, Katharine. *Jock's Castle.* Gr. 4–5.
The hunter rescued by Jock the miller turns out to be Crown Prince Henry. (BL 37:18; HB 16:343; LJ 65:714, 849)
Illus. by Vera Bock, Longman, 1940, 139 pp., o.p.

GILMAN, Dorothy. *The Maze in the Heart of the Castle.* See Section 5C, Travel to Other Worlds.

C [R] GODDEN (Dixon), (Margaret) Rumer. *The Dragon of Og.* Gr. 3–5.
The stubborn new lord of Og wants to get rid of the gentle local dragon, against the advice of his wife and chief minister. (BL 78:706; CC:474; CCBB 55:106; Ch&Bks:267; SLJ Nov 1981 p. 75; Suth 3:154)
Illus. by Pauline Baynes, Viking, 1981, 60 pp.

C [R] GODDEN (Dixon), (Margaret) Rumer. *The Mousewife.* Gr. 2–4.
A little mouse sets a caged dove free, in return for wondrous descriptions of the outside world. (BL 47:297, 79:777; CC:474; CCBB 4:50, 36:46; Eakin:143; HB 27:93, 102; KR 19:61; LJ 76:781; TLS 1951 p. 9)
Illus. by William Pène du Bois, Viking, 1951, o.p.; illus. by Heidi Holder, Viking, 1982, 31 pp.

YA GOLDMAN, William W. *The Princess Bride: S. Morgenstern's Classic Tale of True Love and High Adventure.* Gr. 8 up. (Orig. pub. Harcourt, 1973, o.p.)
In this parody of heroic fairy tales, Westley, the masked hero, tries to reclaim his beloved Buttercup from the evil Prince Humperdink of Florin, while Inigo Montoya, the great swordsman, continues his lifelong search for his father's murderer. (KR 41:704; LJ 98:2570; Tymn:91)
Ballantine, 1977, 1982, 1984, 1987, pap.

YA [R] GOLDSTEIN, Lisa. *The Red Magician.* Gr. 10 up.
Young Kicsi describes the battle between a wonder-working rabbi and a traveling magician who foretells the Holocaust, in this tale set in a small Hungar-

ian Jewish village. American Book Award winner, 1982. (BL 78:1004, 1014; Kies:31; VOYA 6:342)

Pocket/Timescape, 1982; pap., 1983, 156 pp.

GOODWIN, Harold Leland. *Magic Number.* See Section 2A, Beast Tales.

C/YA   GOUDGE, Elizabeth (de Beauchamp). *The Valley of Song.* Gr. 5–8
[R]   Tabitha lifts the spirits of her town's disheartened shipbuilders by leading them into the Valley of Song. (BL 49:92; CCBB 6:67; HB 28:395, 405; KR 20:552; LJ 77:1822; TLS 1951 p. 15)

Illus. by Richard Floethe, Coward, 1952, 281 pp., o.p.

C [O] GRAHAME, Kenneth. *The Reluctant Dragon.* Gr. 4–6. (Orig. British pub. 1898 in *Dream Days;* U.S. pub. 1938.)

St. George and his young friend find a dragon that is not at all like the one they had intended to slay. (BL 35:143, 80:680; CC:474; CCBB 7:29; Ch&Bks:267; Eakin:146; HB 15:29; LJ 64:118; SLJ Nov 1983 p. 77)

Illus. by Ernest Shepard, Holiday, 1953; illus. by Michael Hague, Holt, 1983, 42 pp.

GRAHAME, Kenneth. *The Wind in the Willows.* See Section 2B, Talking Animal Fantasy.

GRAY, Nicholas Stuart. *Mainly in Moonlight: Ten Stories of Sorcery and the Supernatural.* See Chapter 3, Fantasy Collections.

GRAY, Nicholas Stuart. *A Wind from Nowhere.* See Chapter 3, Fantasy Collections.

C   GREAVES, Margaret. *A Net to Catch the Wind.* Gr. 2–4.

A king uses his young daughter to trap a unicorn, causing both the girl and the unicorn to become ill. (BL 75:1438; KR 47:451; SLJ Sept 1979 p. 110)

Illus. by Stephen Gammell, Harper, 1979, 40 pp., o.p.

GREENE, Jacqueline Dembar. *The Leveller.* See Section 5B, Myth Fantasy.

GRIPARI, Pierre. *Tales of the Rue Broca.* See Chapter 3, Fantasy Collections.

C/YA   GRIPE, Maria (Kristina). *The Glassblower's Children.* Gr. 5–7. (Orig.
[R]   Swedish pub. 1964.)

Klaus and Klara, kidnapped and imprisoned by the Lord of All Wishes Town, lose all hope of rescue until a sorceress named Flutter Mildweather arrives to help them. (BL 70:170; CCBB 27:9; Ch&Bks:267; HB 62:756; KR 41:515, 1350; LJ 98:2194; Suth 2:192; TLS 1975 p. 365)

Tr. by Sheila LaFarge, illus. by Harald Gripe, Delacorte, 1973, 170 pp., o.p.

C/YA   GRIPE, Maria (Kristina). *In the Time of the Bells.* Gr. 5–9. (Orig. Swedish pub. 1965.)

Young Prince Arvid's disregard for his royal duties bodes ill for the kingdom, until the astrologers discover that his "whipping boy" is his brother and true heir to the throne. (BL 73:600, 606; CC:482; CCBB 30:76; HB 53:51; JHC:412; KR 44:982; SLJ Jan 1977 p. 92; TLS 1978 p. 767)

Tr. by Sheila La Farge, illus. by Harald Gripe, Delacorte, 1976, 208 pp., o.p.

C/YA GRIPE, Maria (Kristina). *The Land Beyond.* Gr. 5–8. (Orig. Swedish pub. 1967.)
    An explorer, a young king, and a princess travel to a world not found on any map. (HB 51:152; KR 42:949; LJ 99:3045; TLS 1975 p. 1457)
    Tr. by Sheila La Farge, illus. by Harald Gripe, Delacorte, 1974, 214 pp., o.p.

C [R] GUILLOT, René. *The Three Hundred Ninety-seventh White Elephant.* Gr. 3–6. (Orig. pub. in France. British title: *The Elephants of Sargabal.*)
    The young king is cured of his illness by Hong-Mo the Magnificent, a mysterious white elephant who becomes leader of the royal herd. Two British sequels are *Master of the Elephants* and *Great Land of the Elephant.* (BL 53:434; HB 33:221; KR 25:176; LJ 82:1102)
    Tr. by Gwen Marsh, illus. by Moyra Leatham, Phillips, 1957, 94 pp.

YA [R] GUY, Rosa (Cuthbert). *My Love, My Love, or the Peasant Girl.* Gr. 9 up.
    This touching story about the ill-fated love of a Caribbean peasant girl for a rich young man she rescued from a car crash, is based on Hans Christian Andersen's "The Little Mermaid." (BL 82:108, 124; KR 53:891; LJ Oct 15, 1985 p. 101; SHC:602; SLJ Jan 1986 p. 84; VOYA 9:30)
    Holt, 1985, 119 pp.

C [R] HACKETT, Walter Anthony. *The Swans of Ballycastle.* Gr. 3–5.
    Three children who were driven from home by their stepmother are changed into swans and find refuge on an island where time stands still. (BL 51:179; CCBB 8:51; HB 30:435; KR 22:479; LJ 79:2491)
    Illus. by Bettina, Ariel, 1954, 63 pp., o.p.

C [R] HALLOWELL, Priscilla. *The Long-Nosed Princess: A Fairy Tale.* Gr. 3–5.
    No one notices Princess Felicity's long nose until her self-centered fiancé brings it up. (BL 55:633; CCBB 12:168; HB 35:299; KR 27:88; LJ 84:2086)
    Illus. by Rita Fava, Viking, 1959, 61 pp., o.p.

HAMILTON, Virginia (Esther). *The Magical Adventures of Pretty Pearl.* See Section 5B, Myth Fantasy.

HANCOCK, Neil. *Dragon Winter.* See Section 2A, Beast Tales.

HANSEN, Ron. *The Shadowmaker.* See Chapter 7, Magic Adventure Fantasy.

C HAUFF, Wilhelm. *The Adventures of Little Mouk.* Gr. 3–4. (Orig. pub. in Germany.)
    Even Little Mouk's magic shoes and walking stick can't keep him out of the king's dungeon. (BL 71:866; CCBB 29:10; HB 51:257; KR 43:18; SLJ Apr 1975 p. 53)
    Tr. and adapt. by Elizabeth Shub, illus. by Monika Laimgruber, Macmillan, 1975, 36 pp., o.p.

HAUFF, Wilhelm. *The Caravan.* See Chapter 3, Fantasy Collections.

C [R] HAUFF, Wilhelm. *Dwarf Long-Nose.* Gr. 3–5. (Orig. pub. in Germany; orig. U.S. pub. 1881, 1916.)
    Transformed into an ugly dwarf by a wicked fairy, Long-Nose becomes a chef in the Duke's kitchen and searches for a special herb to break the spell. (BL 57:128; Eakin:151; HB 36:510; LJ 85; 3862)
    Tr. by Doris Orgel, illus. by Maurice Sendak; Random, 1960, 60 pp. o.p.

HAUFF, Wilhelm. *The Fairy Tales of Wilhelm Hauff.* See Chapter 3, Fantasy Collections.

C [R] HAUGAARD, Erik Christian. *Prince Boghole.* Gr. K–4.
King Desmond sends the three suitors for the hand of Princess Orla on a quest for the most magnificent of birds. (BL 83:1205; CCBB 40:146; KR 55:301; SLJ May 1987 p. 87)
Illus. by Julie Downing, Macmillan, 1987, 32 pp.

YA [R] HAWDON, Robin. *A Rustle in the Grass.* Gr. 10 up (Orig. British pub. 1984.)
A young soldier ant named Dreamer, struggling to work out his purpose in life, scouts the brutal red ant army and plays a key role in the war to defend his territory and his queen. (BL 81:1029, 1050; KR 53:150; LJ Apr 1, 1985 p. 158; SLJ Aug 1985 p. 86; VOYA 8:394, 10:23)
Dodd, 1985, 244 pp.

C HAWTHORNE, Julian. *Rumpty-Dudget's Tower: A Fairy Tale.* Gr. K–4.
(Orig. pub. in *St. Nicholas Magazine* 1879; orig. pub. in book form, illus. by George W. Hood, Stokes, 1924, o.p.)
An evil dwarf named Rumpty-Dudget kidnaps Prince Henry and locks him in a tower in order to turn the world into a desert, in this story written by Nathaniel Hawthorne's son. (BL 21:237, 84:862; Bookshelf 1924–1925 Suppl. p. 1; HB 1[Nov 1924]:7; KR 55:1515; LJ 50:803; Mahony 2:281)
Adapt. and illus. by Diane Goode, Knopf, 1987, 48 pp.

HAWTHORNE, Nathaniel. *The Snow Image.* See Chapter 3, Fantasy Collections.

C HAYWOOD, Carolyn. *A Valentine Fantasy.* Gr. 2–4.
Valentine's refusal to shoot the golden-hearted bluebird causes the king to imprison him, but the bird saves him. (BL 72:1113; KR 44:316; SLJ Apr 1976 p. 60)
Illus. by Glenys Ambrus and Victor Ambrus, Morrow, 1976, 32 pp.

YA HAZEL, Paul. *Yearwood* (Finnbranch trilogy, book 1). Gr. 10 up.
Finn, the bastard son of a Kell sorceress, sets out to find his birthright and discovers that his father was actually the High King. The sequels are *Undersea* (1982) and *Winter King* (1985). (HB 56:448; KR 48:150; SLJ Apr 1980 p. 124; VOYA 3[June 1980]:28, 3[Oct 1980]:32, 4[Aug 1981]:48)
Atlantic/Little, 1980, 276 pp., o.p.

HEARNE, Betsy. *South Star.* See Section 5A, Alternate Worlds or Histories.

C HEATH, W(illiam) L. *The Earthquake Men.* Gr. 4–6.
Sinn Fein, a troll-catching tinsmith, convinces Rafe and Ansel O'Grady that he can rid their farm of the troll living under the footbridge. (KR 49:213; SLJ Jan 1981, p. 61)
Beaufort, dist. by Scribner, 1980, 95 pp., o.p.

YA HELPRIN, Mark. *Winter's Tale.* Gr. 10 up.
Peter Lake escapes from a gang of murderous Manhattan thugs on the back of a flying milk-wagon horse, in this fast-moving Dickensian tale of romance, comedy, and adventure. (BL 79:1421; HB 60:229; KR 51:717; LJ 108:1502)
Harcourt, 1983; Pocket, 1984, pap., 704 pp.

HEWETT, Anita. *The Bull beneath the Walnut Tree and Other Stories.* See Chapter 3, Fantasy Collections.

C/YA HILGARTNER, Beth. *A Necklace of Fallen Stars,* Gr. 6–8.
Princess Kaela runs away rather than marry the man her father has chosen for her. (BL 76:558; KR 48:222; SLJ Oct 1979 p. 150)
Illus. by Michael R. Hague, Little, 1979, 209 pp., o.p.

C HOBAN, Russell C(onwell). *The Marzipan Pig.* Gr. 3–5.
After a marzipan pig falls behind the sofa, his sweetness and loving thoughts are absorbed by the mouse that eats him, and by the owl that eats the mouse, in this gentle and whimsical tale. (CCBB 40:210; KR 55:719; SLJ Sept 1987 p. 164; TLS Apr 3, 1987 p. 356)
Illus. by Quentin Blake, Farrar, 1987, 35 pp.

C/YA HOBAN, Russell C(onwell). *The Mouse and His Child.* Gr. 4 up.
[O] A broken windup mouse and his son set out to find happiness but are pursued by an evil rat intent on enslaving them. (BL 64:593; CC:483; CCBB 21:143; Ch&Bks:267; KR 35:1134; LJ 92:4612; Suth:185; TLS 1969 p. 357)
Illus. by Lillian Hoban, Harper, 1967; Avon, 1975, pap., 181 pp.

HOBAN, Russell C(onwell). *The Sea-Thing Child.* See Section 2B, Talking Animal Fantasy.

C HODGES, Elizabeth Jamison. *The Three Princes of Serendip.* Gr. 4–6.
The King of Serendip's sons search throughout India and Persia for a dragon-killing potion to save their kingdom. The sequel is *Serendipity Tales* (1966). (BL 60:1002; HB 40:281; KR 32:108; LJ 89:2219)
Illus. by Joan Berg, Atheneum, 1964, 158 pp., o.p.

HOFFMANN, E(rnst) T(heodor) A(madeus). *The Nutcracker.* See Chapter 9, Toy Fantasy.

C HOFFMANN, E(rnst) T(heodor) A(madeus). *The Strange Child.* Gr. 4–6.
(Orig. German pub. as part of a collection, 1857, orig. Austrian pub. in this edition, 1981.)
A mysterious child, the daughter of the queen of fairies, helps two human children get rid of their evil tutor. (BL 81:520; CC:433; CCBB 38:87; HB 61:177; SLJ Apr 1985 p. 88)
Tr. and adapt. by Anthea Bell, illus. by Lisbeth Zwerger, Picture Book Studio, dist. by Alphabet, 1984, 31 pp.

YA HOLDSTOCK, Robert. *The Emerald Forest.* Gr. 10 up.
Tommy Markham, a young boy lost in the Brazilian jungle, lives for ten years as the adopted son of the leader of a tribe of "the Invisible People," while his American father continues to search for him. (BL 82:28; Kies:37)
Zoetrope, 1985 (from the film script by Rospo Pallenberg), pap., 192 pp.

C/YA HOLLANDER, John. *The Quest of the Gole.* Gr. 6–8.
[R] Three princes search for the "Gole" to break the curse of darkness on their kingdom. (BL 63:418; HB 42:562; KR 34:982; LJ 91:4352)
Illus. by Reginald Pollack, Atheneum, 1966, 116 pp., o.p.

HOLMAN (Valen), Felice. *The Blackmail Machine.* See Chapter 6, Humorous Fantasy.

C [R] HOLT, Isabella. *The Adventures of Rinaldo.* Gr. 4–6.
Knight Rinaldo wins a bear, a stag, and a pig while searching for a wife and a castle. (BL 55:458; HB 35:131; KR 27:7; LJ 84:643)
Illus. by Erik Blegvad, Little, 1959, 142 pp., o.p.

C [R] HOOKS, William H(arris). *Moss Gown.* Gr. K–4.
Candace, disowned by her father and cast out by her older sisters, returns to their home as a scullery maid after she has been befriended by a witch. This rendition of a traditional southern tale contains elements of "King Lear" and "Cinderella." (BL 83:1206; CCBB 40:127; HB 63:599; KR 55:638; SLJ May 1987 p. 87, Dec 1987 p. 37)
Illus. by Donald Carrick, Clarion, 1987, 48 pp.

HORWITZ, Elinor Lander. *The Strange Story of the Frog Who Became a Prince.* See Chapter 10, Witchcraft and Sorcery Fantasy.

YA HORWOOD, William. *Duncton Wood.* Gr. 10 up.
The moles of Duncton Wood and all of southern England, are saved by a pair of star-crossed lovers and an epic battle between the forces of good and evil. (BL 76:1410; KR 48:152; LJ 105:1409; VOYA 4[Oct 1980]:32, 4[Aug 1981]:48)
McGraw-Hill, 1980, o.p.; Ballantine, 1981, pap., 736 pp.

C HOUSMAN, Laurence. *Cotton-Wooleena.* Gr. 2–4. (Orig. British pub. in this format, 1967.)
A newly crowned king discovers that a haughty fairy named Cotton-Wooleena has been ruling his country for the past 300 years. (BL 70:1056; KR 42:425; LJ 99:2270)
Illus. by Robert Binks, Doubleday, 1974, 58 pp., o.p.

HOUSMAN, Laurence. *The Rat-Catcher's Daughter: A Collection of Stories.* See Chapter 3, Fantasy Collections.

C HOWARD, Alice Woodbury. *Ching-Li and the Dragons.* Gr. 2–4.
Young King Ching Wong's magical jade flute sends him off to rescue a mighty dragon. (BL 28:265; HB 7:322; Mahony 3:205)
Illus. by Lynd Ward, Macmillan, 1931, 55 pp., o.p.

YA HUDSON, W(illiam) H(enry). *Green Mansions: A Romance of the Tropical Forest.* Gr. 10 up. (Orig. British pub. 1893, U.S. Putnam, 1904.)
The romance between a magical girl of the forest and an Amazon jungle adventurer ends tragically after he introduces her to the outside world and her paradise is destroyed. (BL 12:482, 22:428, 27:417, 41:304, 46:201; SHC:609)
Knopf, 1916, 1943, o.p.; illus. by Keith Henderson, World, 1931, o.p.; illus. by E. McKnight Kauffer, Random, 1944, o.p.; Airmont, 1966, © 1965, 191 pp., pap.; AMS (repr. of 1923 ed.).

C [R] HUDSON, W(illiam) H(enry). *A Little Boy Lost: A Tale for Children.* Gr. 4–6. (Orig. British pub. 1905; U.S. Knopf, 1918.)
A little boy following a mirage becomes lost in the wilds of South America, much to his delight. (BL 15:15, 35:70; Bookshelf 1932 p. 8; HB 14:147; LJ 63:817, 847, 76:660; Mahony 2:281)
Illus. by A. D. McCormick, Knopf, 1923, 1946, 1951, o.p.; illus. by Dorothy P. Lathrop, Knopf, 1920, 1939, o.p.; AMS (repr. of 1923 ed.), 222 pp.

HUGHES, Ted (Edward James). *How the Whale Became.* See Section 2B, Talking Animal Fantasy.

C HUGHES, Ted (Edward James). *The Iron Giant: A Story in Five Nights* (British title: *The Iron Man*). Gr. 3–6.
The people ask the Iron Giant for help against the hungry space-bat-angel-dragon who is terrorizing them. (BL 65:496; CCBB 41:208; KR 36:114; TLS 1968 p. 256)
Illus. by Robert Nadler, Harper, 1968, 1988, 58 pp.; Harper/Trophy, 1987, pap.

C [R] HUNTER, Mollie (pseud. of Maureen Mollie Hunter McVeigh McIlwraith). *The Kelpie's Pearls.* Gr. 4–6. (Orig. British pub. 1964, U.S. Funk, 1966.)
The pearl necklace that a water sprite gives to Morag MacLeod causes the old woman to be accused of witchcraft. (BL 63:451; CC:486; CCBB 20:109; Ch&Bks:268; HB 42:710; KR 34:688; LJ 91:5231; TLS 1964 p. 1081)
Harper, 1976, 112 pp., o.p.

C [R] HUNTER, Mollie (pseud. of Maureen Mollie Hunter McVeigh McIlwraith). *The Knight of the Golden Plain.* Gr. 1–4.
Daydreaming, a young boy is transformed into Sir Dauntless, Knight of the Golden Plain, who battles dragons, witches, and a nasty wizard to save the maiden Dorabella. The sequel is *The Three Day Enchantment* (1985). (BL 80:86; CC:486; CCBB 37:51; Ch&Bks:268; HB 60:54; KR 51:162; SLJ Sept 1983 p. 108)
Illus. by Marc Simont, Harper, 1983, 48 pp.; Harper/Trophy, 1986, pap.

C INGRAM, Tom (Thomas Henry). *Garranane* (British title: *The Hungry Cloud*, 1971.) Gr. 4–6.
Prince Kai and Princess Flor flee after discovering that the mysterious Miss Fenrir has trapped the King and Queen within her drawings. (BL 69:302; KR 40:623; LJ 98:261; TLS 1971 p. 767)
Illus. by Bill Geldart, Bradbury, 1972, 191 pp., o.p.

IPCAR, Dahlov (Zorach). *The Queen of Spells.* See Section 5B, Myth Fantasy.

IPCAR, Dahlov (Zorach). *The Warlock of Night.* See Chapter 10, Witchcraft and Sorcery Fantasy.

IRVING, Washington. *The Legend of Sleepy Hollow.* See Section 5B, Myth Fantasy.

IRVING, Washington. *Rip Van Winkle.* See Section 5B, Myth Fantasy.

ISH-KISHOR, Sulamith. *The Master of Miracle: A New Novel of the Golem.* See Section 5B, Myth Fantasy.

C/YA JACQUES, Brian. *Redwall.* Gr. 5–9. (Orig. British pub. 1986.)
[R] Young Matthias mouse helps defend Redwall Abbey against marauding rats bent on enslaving the peaceful mice who have taken refuge there. (BL 83:1519, 1522, 84:1248, 1441; CCBB 40:211; HB 64:71; KR 55:858; SLJ Aug 1987 p. 96, Dec 1987 p. 37)
Illus. by Gary Chalk, Philomel/Putnam, 1987, 351 pp.

C [R] JARRELL, Randall. *The Animal Family.* Gr. 4–6.
A lonely hunter and a mermaid fall in love and acquire a family consisting

of a bear cub, a lynx kitten, and a shipwrecked boy. Newbery Medal Honor Book, 1966. (BL 62:487; CC:489; CCBB 19:100; Ch&Bks:268; Eakin:171; HB 42:45, 61:714–716, 737; LJ 90:5516; TLS 1976 p. 392)
Illus. by Maurice Sendak, Pantheon, 1965, 1985, hb; 1987, pap.

C [R] JOHNSON, Elizabeth. *The Little Knight.* Gr. 3–5.
To avoid marrying a stranger, Princess Lenora dons armor and sets out to win the contest to determine the bravest knight in the land. (BL 54:28; HB 33:400; KR 25:412; LJ 82:2191)
Illus. by Ronni Solbert, Little, 1957, 56 pp. o.p.

C [R] JOHNSON, Elizabeth. *The Three-in-One Prince.* Gr. 3–4.
All three of King Frederick's sons enter the competition for Princess Alicia Anastasia Alfreda Anne's hand, but only Prince John, the middle son, can prove he is "three in one." (BL 57:498; HB 37:261; KR 29:102; LJ 86:1689)
Illus. by Ronni Solbert, Little, 1961, 58 pp. o.p.

YA [R] JONES, Adrienne. *The Hawks of Chelney.* Gr. 7–9.
In this haunting tale, a lonely boy named Siri is persecuted by superstitious village elders because of his friendship with the ospreys, "the Devil's servants." (BL 74:1108; CCBB 32:45; Ch&Bks:268; HB 54:283; JHC:384; KR 46:640; SLJ Apr 1978 p. 94; VOYA 1[Aug 1978]:35)
Illus. by Stephen Gammell, Harper, 1978, 245 pp.

JONES, Diana Wynne. *Cart and Cwidder.* See Section 5A, Alternate Worlds or Histories.

C JONES, Terry. *The Saga of Erik the Viking.* Gr. 4–6. (Orig. British pub. 1983.)
A band of Vikings has a series of fantastic adventures while searching for the land where the sun goes at night. (CCBB 37:149; SLJ Jan 1984 p. 78)
Illus. by Michael Foreman, Schocken, 1983; Penguin, 1986, pap., 144 pp.

C JUSTER, Norton. *Alberic the Wise and Other Journeys.* Gr. 4–6.
Three tales about a hero searching for wisdom, a boy who enters a painting, and two kings searching for happiness. (CCBB 19:150; HB 42:54; LJ 91:1064)
Illus. by Domenico Gnoli, Pantheon, 1965, 67 pp., o.p.

JUSTER, Norton. *The Phantom Tollbooth.* See Section 5C, Travel to Other Worlds.

KÄSTNER, Erich. *The Animal's Conference.* See Section 2A, Beast Tales.

C [R] KAYE, M(argaret) M(ary). *The Ordinary Princess.* Gr. 3–6. (Orig. British pub. 1981.)
Tired of suitors who consider her to be too ordinary to marry, Princess Amy runs away to find a prince who will like her just the way she is. (BL 81:641; CC:491; CCBB 38:8; HB 60:758; SLJ Mar 1985 p. 168)
Illus. by the author, Doubleday, 1984; Simon, 1986, pap.

C [R] KELLER, Beverly (Lou). *A Small, Elderly Dragon.* Gr. 4–6.
Terrorized by a feeble old dragon named Blystfylyl, the peasants of Minervia enlist the aid of the King, a princess, the Black Knight of Doum, and a sorceror whose sister turns the dragon into a parrot. (BL 80:1248; CCBB 37:188; HB 60:466; SLJ May 1984 p. 81; VOYA 7:147)
Illus. by Nola Langner Malone, Lothrop, 1984, 143 pp.

KENDALL, Carol (Seeger). *The Gammage Cup.* See Section 5A, Alternate Worlds or Histories.

C [R] KENNEDY, Richard (Jerome). *The Blue Stone.* Gr. 3–6.
The blue stone that fell from the sky brings magic into the peaceful lives of Bertie and Jack by turning people into animals, making poems come true, and changing a sparrow into a baby angel. (BL 73:323; CC:429; CCBB 30:127; KR 44:1094; SLJ Nov 1976 p. 60)
Illus. by Ronald Himler, Holiday, 1976, 93 pp.

YA KENNEDY, Richard (Jerome). *The Boxcar at the Center of the Universe.* Gr. 7–10.
An elderly bum who calls himself Ali meets a lost sixteen-year-old boy aboard a traveling boxcar and tells him the fabulous story of his search for the center of the universe. (BL 78:1307, 1314; CCBB 36:70; KR 50:496; SLJ Aug 1982 p. 126; VOYA 5[Aug 1982]:33)
Illus. by Jeff Kronen, Harper, 1982, 89 pp.

C [R] KENNEDY, Richard (Jerome). *Come Again in the Spring.* Gr. 4–6.
Old Hark is afraid to die and leave his birds to fend for themselves in midwinter, so he strikes a bargain with Death: If Hark can answer three questions, Death will wait until spring to take him. (BL 73:253; HB 53:154; KR 44:904; SLJ Feb 1977 p. 56)
Illus. by Marcia Sewall, Harper, 1976, 47 pp., o.p.

C/YA KENNEDY, Richard (Jerome). *The Dark Princess.* Gr. 5–7.
A princess's blinding beauty serves as a test for prospective suitors and prevents her from finding love, until the court fool risks blindness to declare his love. (HB 55:641; KR 46:1137; SLJ Dec 1978 p. 53)
Illus. by Donna Diamond, Holiday, 1978, 32 pp.

C [R] KENNEDY, Richard (Jerome). *Inside My Feet: The Story of a Giant.* Gr. 4–6.
A boy whose parents have been carried off by a giant frantically prepares for the giant's return. (BL 76:449; CCBB 33:155; Ch&Bks:268; KR 47:1210; SLJ Sept 1979 p. 141)
Illus. by Ronald Himler, Harper, 1979, 71 pp.

C KENNEDY, Richard (Jerome). *The Leprechaun's Story.* Gr. K–4.
A crafty leprechaun spins tale after tale to keep a man from winning his pot of gold. (HB 56:47; KR 47:1141; SLJ Dec 1979 p. 75)
Illus. by Marcia Sewall, Dutton, 1979, 40 pp.

C KENNEDY, Richard (Jerome). *The Lost Kingdom of Karnica.* Gr. 2–4.
In spite of the wise man's warning not to dig out a huge precious stone, the greedy king of Karnica orders his men to unearth it. (BL 76:44; CCBB 33:155; KR 47:998; SLJ Oct 1979 p. 142)
Illus. by Uri Shulevitz, Sierra Club, dist. by Scribner, 1979, 32 pp., o.p.

KENNEDY, Richard (Jerome). *The Mouse God.* See Section 2B, Talking Animal Fantasy.

KENNEDY, Richard (Jerome). *Richard Kennedy: Collected Stories.* See Chapter 3, Fantasy Collections.

C [R] KINGSLEY, Charles. *The Water Babies: A Fairy Tale for a Land Baby.* Gr. 4–6. (Orig. British pub. 1863, U.S. 1864.)
An apprentice chimney sweep named Tom runs away from his cruel master

and is taken in by fairies who change him into a tiny water baby. (BL 1:74, 5:63, 10:253, 12:204, 14:141, 53:538, 58:352; Bookshelf 1928 p. 10; Ch&Bks: 268; HB 1[June 1925]:32, 37:549; LJ 45:980; Mahony 2:282)

Illus. by Rosalie K. Fry, Dutton, 1905, 1957, o.p.; illus. by Jessie Willcox Smith, Dodd, 1910, 1937, o.p.; illus. by W. Heath Robinson, Houghton, 1915, 1923, o.p.; illus. by Maria L. Kirk, Lippincott, 1917, o.p.; adapt. by Kathleen Lines, illus. by Harold Jones, Watts, 1961, o.p.; illus. by Linley Sambourne, Garland, 1976 (repr. of 1864 ed.), o.p.; Peter Smith, 1979, o.p.; Dent, dist. by Biblio, 1982 (repr. of 1863 ed.), Penguin/Puffin, 1985, pap., 192 pp.

C [R]   KIPLING, (Joseph) Rudyard. *The Beginning of the Armadilloes*. Gr. 1–4 (Orig. British pub. in this edition 1982.)

In this tale from the *Just So Stories* (1897–1902) a hedgehog and a tortoise turn into armadillos while tricking a young jaguar out of his dinner. (BL 80:859, 82:262; CC:493; HB 60:357; SLJ Feb 1984 p. 60, Dec 1985 p. 75)

Illus. by Charles Keeping, Bedrick, dist. by Harper, 1983; illus. by Lorinda Bryan Cauley, Harcourt, 1985, 48 pp.

C [R]   KIPLING, (Joseph) Rudyard. *The Butterfly That Stamped*. Gr. 2–4. (Orig. British pub. in this edition 1982.)

This tale from Kipling's *Just So Stories* (1897–1902) explains the nature of butterflies. (BL 80:859; CC:493; SLJ Feb 1984 p. 60)

Illus. by Alan Baker, Bedrick, dist. by Harper, 1983, 31 pp.

C   KIPLING, (Joseph) Rudyard. *The Cat That Walked by Himself*. Gr. 2–4. (Orig. British pub. in this edition 1982.)

A tale from Kipling's *Just So Stories* (1897–1902), in which cats learn to be independent. (BL 80:859; CC:493; SLJ Feb 1984 p. 60)

Illus. by William Stobbs, Bedrick, dist. by Harper, 1983, 31 pp.

C [R]   KIPLING, (Joseph) Rudyard. *The Crab That Played with the Sea*. Gr. 2–4. (Orig. British pub. in this edition 1982.)

One of Kipling's *Just So Stories* (1897–1902), in which Eldest Magician creates huge ocean creatures that come into conflict with human beings. (BL 80:859; CC:493; HB 60:358; SLJ Feb 1984 p. 60)

Illus. by Michael Foreman, Bedrick, dist. by Harper, 1983, 31 pp.

C [R]   KIPLING, (Joseph) Rudyard. *The Elephant's Child*. Gr. K–4. (Orig. British pub. 1901.)

The familiar tale that explains how the elephant got his long trunk. (BL 80:87, 82:496; CC:494; CCBB 37:130; Ch&Bks:268; LJ 96:258; SLJ Oct 1983 p. 150, Feb 1986 p. 76)

Illus. by Leonard Weisgard, Walker, 1971; illus. by Lorinda Bryan Cauley, Harcourt, 1983; illus. by Louise Brierly, Bedrick, dist. by Harper, 1985, 31 pp.

C   KIPLING, (Joseph) Rudyard. *How the Camel Got His Hump*. Gr. K–4. (Orig. British pub. in this edition 1984.)

A lazy camel who refuses all work with a "Humph!" is given a hump on his back by the magical Djinn in charge of all deserts. (BL 82:496; CC 1987 Suppl. p. 60; SLJ Feb 1986 p. 76)

Illus. by Quentin Blake, Bedrick, dist. by Harper, 1985, 32 pp.

C [R]   KIPLING, (Joseph) Rudyard. *How the Leopard Got His Spots*. Gr. 1–4

The leopard and the Ethiopian change their skins to improve their hunting

abilities, in this tale from the *Just So Stories* (1897–1902). (BL 69:948; CC:494; KR 41:381; LJ 98:3139; TLS 1972 p. 1333)
Illus. by Leonard Weisgard, Walker, 1973; illus. by Caroline Ebborn, Bedrick, 1986, 32 pp.

C [R] KIPLING, (Joseph) Rudyard. *How the Rhinoceros Got His Skin.* Gr. 2–4.
A cake-thieving rhinoceros is punished by the Parsee who puts itchy cake crumbs inside the rhino's skin. (BL 70:1154, 83:1749; CC:494; CCBB 28:45; LJ 99:2250; Suth 2:257; TLS 1973 p. 1431)
Illus. by Leonard Weisgard, Walker, 1974; illus. by Jenny Thorne, Bedrick, dist. by Harper, 1987 (British pub. 1985), 31 pp.

C KIPLING, (Joseph) Rudyard. *How the Whale Got His Throat.* Gr. 2–4.
(Orig. British pub. in this edition 1983.)
A shipwrecked mariner swallowed by a whale convinces the creature to take him home. (BL 83:1749)
Illus. by Pauline Baynes, Bedrick, dist. by Harper, 1987, 32 pp.

KIPLING, (Joseph) Rudyard. *Just So Stories.* See Chapter 3, Fantasy Collections.

KORTUM, Jeanie. *Ghost Vision.* See Chapter 10, Witchcraft and Sorcery Fantasy.

C KOTZWINKLE, William. *Hearts of Wood: And Other Timeless Tales.* Gr. 4–6.
Five original fairy tales including stories about carousel animals that come to life, a man who becomes a butterfly, and a woodsman who becomes King of the fairies. Four of these tales were originally published as *The Oldest Man and Other Timeless Stories* (Pantheon, 1971). (CCBB 26:27, 40:129; KR 39:1013; LJ 97:1914; SLJ May 1987 p. 101)
Illus. by Joe Servello, Godine, 1986, 85 pp.

C KRENSKY, Stephen (Alan). *A Big Day for Scepters.* Gr. 4–6.
A boy named Corey teams up with Calandar, a magician, to oppose the villainous Prince Grogol in a race for possession of a powerful evil scepter. (BL 73:1576; KR 45:352; SLJ Apr 1977 p. 68)
Illus. by Bruce Degen, Atheneum, 1977, 112 pp., o.p.

C KRENSKY, Stephen (Alan). *The Perils of Putney.* Gr. 4–6.
A peace-loving giant, pressed into a search for a missing Fair Damsel and captured by a band of dwarfs, encounters a dragon, a witch, and a wizard. (BL 75:477; KR 46:1189; SLJ Oct 1978 p. 146)
Illus. by Jürg Obrist, Atheneum, 1978, 116 pp., o.p.

C [R] KRENSKY, Stephen (Alan). *A Troll in Passing.* Gr. 4–6.
Morgan, dissatisfied with troll life, saves his people from a band of giant trolls and sets off to see the world. (BL 76:1424; CCBB 33:175; KR 48:440; SLJ May 1980 p. 68; Suth 3:245)
Atheneum, 1980, 128 pp., o.p.

KROPP, Lloyd. *The Drift.* See Section 5C, Travel to Other Worlds.

KUMIN, Maxine (Winokur), and SEXTON, Anne. *The Wizard's Tears.* See Chapter 10, Witchcraft and Sorcery Fantasy.

C/YA KUSHNER, Donn. *Uncle Jacob's Ghost Story.* Gr. 6–10. (Orig. Canadian
    pub. 1980.)
    Uncle Jacob is reunited with the ghosts of his best friends, Simon and
    Esther, who died of typhus long ago, in this touching and sophisticated story.
    Canadian Library Association Best Book of the Year for Children, 1980. (BL
    82:1605, 1614; CCBB 39:170; KR 54:550; SLJ May 1986·p. 94)
    Holt, 1986, 132 pp.

C/YA KUSHNER, Donn. *The Violin-Maker's Gift.* Gr. 5–7. (Orig. Canadian
[R]   pub. 1981.)
    Gaspard the violin-maker rescues a beautiful bird and sets it free. As a
    reward, the bird tells him a secret that causes all of Gaspard's instruments to
    sing as though they had souls. Canadian Library Association Best Book of
    the Year for Children, 1981. (BL 78:1145; CCBB 35:191; SLJ Sept 1982 p.
    123; Suth 3:246)
    Illus. by Doug Panton, Farrar, 1982, 74 pp.

C [R] LAMORISSE, Albert (Emmanuel). *The Red Balloon.* Gr. 1–4. (Orig.
    French pub. 1956.)
    A young Parisian boy has trouble keeping his magical balloon safe from a
    gang of older boys. (BL 54:82; CC:495; KR 25:581; LJ 82:2187; TLS Nov 15,
    1957 p. xix)
    Illus. with photographs from the movie, Doubleday, 1957, 45 pp.; pap.
    1978

YA LA MOTTE FOUQUÉ, Friedrich Heinrich Karl baron de. *Sintram and
    His Companions: A Northern Romance.* Gr. 6 up. (Written, 1814; orig.
    U.S. pub. 1869.)
    A knight named Sintram struggles with the powers of evil. (BL 6:420;
    Mahony 1:31; Mahony 2:669)
    Lippincott, 1901, o.p.; illus. by Gordon Browne, Stokes, 1909, 1912, 279
    pp., o.p.

C/YA LA MOTTE FOUQUÉ, Friedrich Heinrich Karl baron de. *Undine.* Gr. 5
[R]   up. (Written in 1811, orig. U.S. pub. 1908.)
    Huldbrand, a knight married to the water nymph Undine, is threatened
    with death if he should ever betray her. (BL 5:195; Bookshelf 1923–1924 p.
    15; CCBB 25:5; KR 39:236; Mahony 2:283; TLS 1929 p. 180; Tymn:105)
    Tr. by Edmund Gosse, illus. by Arthur Rackham, R. West, 1978, o.p.;
    Hyperion, 1985 (repr. of 1912 ed.), 136 pp.

C LANCASTER, Osbert. *The Saracen's Head; or, the Reluctant Crusader.*
    Gr. 4–6. (Orig. British pub. 1948.)
    Cowardly Sir William de Littlehampton becomes a hero after he fights El
    Babooni. (BL 46:101; CCBB 3:7; HB 25:533; KR 17:302; LJ 74:1466; TLS
    1948 p. 712)
    Illus. by the author, Houghton, 1949, 67 pp., o.p.

C/YA LANG, Andrew. *My Own Fairy Book.* Gr. 5–7. (Orig. British pub. 1895,
    U.S. 1895.)
    This collection contains "Prince Prigio," "Prince Ricardo," and "The Gold
    of Fairnilee." (BL 24:75)
    Illus. by Gertrude A. Kay, McKay, 1927, 402 pp., o.p.

C [R] LANG, Andrew. *Prince Prigio and Prince Ricardo: The Chronicles of Pantouflia.* Gr. 4–6. (Orig. British pub. 1889, 1893.)

Prince Prigio and its sequel, *Prince Ricardo,* were originally published separately. *Prince Prigio,* the lighter of the two tales, is the story of an overly clever prince cursed by a fairy not invited to his christening. *Tales of a Fairy Court* (1906) is a related work. (BL 39:144; HB 18:423, 60:613; LJ 67:1069; SLJ Nov 1981 p. 94; TLS 1982 p. 795)

Illus. by Robert Lawson, Little, 1942, o.p.; illus. by Gordon Browne, Garland, 1976; illus. by Jeanne Titherington, Godine, 1981 (entitled *The Chronicles of Pantouflia: Prince Prigio and Prince Ricardo of Pantouflia*), 1984, 191 pp., pap.

C [R] LARSON, Jean (Russell). *The Silkspinners.* Gr. 3–5.

Li Po battles a sea monster and a sorcerer while searching for the lost silk spinners of China. (BL 64:448; CCBB 21:112; KR 35:1047; LJ 92:3852; Suth:239)

Illus. by Uri Shulevitz, Scribner, 1967, 93 pp., o.p.

LATHROP, Dorothy P(ulis). *The Colt from Moon Mountain.* See Chapter 7, Magic Adventure Fantasy.

C LATHROP, Dorothy P(ulis). *The Fairy Circus.* Gr. 2–4.

The fairies and the small woodland creatures stage a circus. Newbery Medal Honor Book, 1932. (BL 28:205; HB 7:315; Mahony 3:107)

Illus. by the author, Macmillan, 1931, 66 pp., o.p.

LAURENCE, Margaret (Wemyss). *Jason's Quest.* See Section 2B, Talking Animal Fantasy.

C/YA LAWRENCE, Ann (Margaret). *The Half Brothers.* Gr. 5–8.
[R]   All three of Duchess Ambra's cousins want to marry her, but only one is willing to let her be herself. (BL 70:341; CCBB 27:97; HB 50:51; LJ 99:891; Suth 2:274; TLS 1973 p. 685)

Walck, 1973, 172 pp., o.p.

C/YA LAWSON, John S(hults). *You Better Come Home with Me.* Gr. 5 up.
[R]   The lyrical tale of an orphaned boy searching for love, and the scarecrow who takes him home to stay. (BL 63:419; CCBB 20:92; HB 42:711; LJ 91:5232; Suth:241)

Illus. by Arnold Spilka, Crowell, 1966, 125 pp., o.p.

C LAWSON, Marie (Abrams). *Dragon John.* Gr. 2–4.

A small, unhappy dragon turns out to be an enchanted prince. (BL 40:64; HB 19:409; LJ 68:894)

Illus. by the author, Viking, 1943, 52 pp., o.p.

C LEE, Tanith. *Animal Castle.* Gr. 2–4.

Prince Rimtheed invites animals to live in his kingdom, but regrets his invitation when they take advantage of their hosts. (BL 69:948; KR 40: 1094; LJ 97:3797; TLS 1972 p. 808)

Illus. by Helen Craig, Farrar, 1972, 37 pp., o.p.

C LEE, Tanith. *The Dragon Hoard.* Gr. 4–6.

The witch Maligna's angry gift to Prince Jasleth—that he become a raven for one hour every day—comes in handy after he joins a quest for the Dragon Hoard treasure. (HB 48:49; KR 39:1120; TLS 1971 p. 1511)

Illus. by Graham Oakley, Farrar, 1971, o.p.; Ace, 1976, pap., 176 pp.

C [R] LEE, Tanith. *Princess Hynchatti and Some Other Surprises.* Gr. 4–6.
(Orig. British pub. 1972.)
A collection of twelve humorous fairy tales including one about a prince
who accidently falls in love with a witch, and another about a beautiful swan
who is transformed into an awkward, yellow-eyed princess. (BL 69:1021; HB
69:948; KR 41:457; LJ 98:2195; TLS 1972 p. 1332)
Illus. by Velma Ilsley, Farrar, 1973, 183 pp., o.p.

YA [R] LEE, Tanith. *Red as Blood; or Tales from the Sisters Grimmer.* Gr. 10 up.
A collection of well-known fairy tales such as "Snow White," "Cinderella,"
and "The Pied Piper of Hamelin," reworked with strange and original twists.
(BL 79:715, 719; LJ 108:147; Kies:46; VOYA 7:206)
NAL/DAW, 1983, 1986, pap., 208 pp.

LE GUIN, Ursula K(roebor). *A Wizard of Earthsea.* See Section 5A,
Alternate Worlds or Histories.

L'ENGLE, Madeleine. *Many Waters.* See Chapter 8, Time Travel
Fantasy.

C LESKOV, Nikolai. *The Steel Flea, a Story.* Gr. 3–5. (Orig. U.S. pub.
1943.)
The Czar challenges his friend Platov to create something even more inge-
nious than the dancing steel flea sent as a gift from England. (BL 40:167,
60:1004, CCBB 19:65; HB 40:178; LJ 69:73, 89:1452)
Adapt. by Babette Deutsch and Avrahm Yarmolinsky, illus. by Janina
Domanska, Harper, 1964 (rev. ed.), 56 pp., o.p.

YA [R] LE VERT, John. *The Flight of the Cassowary.* Gr. 8–12.
John's high school classmates label him as crazy after he tells them about
the intense moments during which he feels as though he has turned into an
animal. (BL 82:1136, 1142, 83:1592; CCBB 39:172; HB 62:332; JHC 1987
Suppl. p. 72; KR 54:869; SLJ May 1986 p. 105, Mar 1987 p. 120; TLS 1987 p.
1028; VOYA 9:80)
Atlantic, 1986, 288 pp.

YA LEVIN, Meyer. *The Spell of Time: A Tale of Love in Jerusalem.* Gr. 10 up.
Two male scientists working at an Israeli research institute fall in love with
a young French colleague, and make a mystical pact to exchange bodies while
retaining their own personalities, in order to test the young woman's ability to
find her true love. (BL 71:268, 285; HB 51:77; KR 42:829; LJ 99:2620)
Praeger, 1974, 127 pp., o.p.

C LEWIS, Beth (pseud. of Beth Lipkin). *The Blue Mountain.* Gr. 2–4.
Prince Desmond agrees to hold a mountain-climbing contest to choose his
bride, even though he is in love with Princess Noreen. (CCBB 10:52; HB
32:351; KR 24:519)
Illus. by Adrienne Adams, Knopf, 1956, 59 pp., o.p.

LEWIS, C(live) S(taples). *The Lion, the Witch, and the Wardrobe.* See
Section 5C, Travel to Other Worlds.

C LEY, Madeleine. *The Enchanted Eve.* Gr. 3 up. (Orig. French pub. 1935.)
On Saint Sylvain's Eve, Barbara, the crippled daughter of a Flemish
painter, is granted her wish for freedom—she is able to skate wherever she
wishes to go. (HB 23:263, 438; LJ 72:894)
Tr. by Willard Trask, illus. by Edy LeGrand, Howell, 1946, 48 pp., o.p.

LEZRA, Giggy (Grizzella Paull). *The Cat, the Horse, and the Miracle.* See Section 2B, Talking Animal Fantasy.

C [R] LIFTON, Betty Jean (Kirschner). *The Dwarf Pine Tree.* Gr. 3–5
To save the dying princess's life, a young pine tree agrees to undergo painful binding in order to become a dwarf-sized tree. (BL 60:262; Eakin:210; HB 39:499; LJ 88:116)
Illus. by Fuku Akino, Atheneum, 1963, 37 pp., o.p.

C/YA LINDGREN, Astrid. *The Brothers Lionheart.* Gr. 6–8. (Orig. Swedish pub. 1973.)
Two brothers, Jonathan and Karl, are reunited after death in a land called Nangiyala, where they fight a vicious tyrant and his dragon to liberate the other inhabitants. (HB 51:594; KR 43:777; SLJ Oct 1975 p. 100)
Tr. by Joan Tate; illus. by J. K. Lambert, Viking, 1975, o.p.; Penguin/Puffin, 1985, pap., 183 pp.

C/YA LISLE, Janet Taylor. *The Great Dimpole Oak.* Gr. 4–7.
The majestic old oak in the town of Dimpole has a mythic presence that draws both local inhabitants and the followers of a swami in India. (BL 84:150, 873; CCBB 41:121; HB 64:64; KR 55:1518; SLJ Dec 1987 p. 86)
Illus. by Richard Gammell, Watts/Orchard/Jackson, 1987, 135 pp.

LIVELY, Penelope (Margaret Low). *Astercote.* See Section 5B, Myth Fantasy.

C [R] LLOYD, (Mary) Norris. *The Desperate Dragons.* Gr. 2–4.
A young cowherd puts the knights of Rondo to shame by ridding the kingdom of the last twelve dragons on earth. (CCBB 13:151; HB 36:289; KR 28:88; LJ 85:2041)
Illus. by Joan Payne, Hastings, 1960, 64 pp., o.p.

C [R] LOVETT, Margaret (Rose). *The Great and Terrible Quest.* Gr. 4–6.
A runaway boy and a wounded knight join forces to search for the true heir to the throne. (BL 64:546; CCBB 21:30; HB 43:597; KR 35:879; LJ 92:4614; TLS 1967 p. 451)
Holt, 1967, 187 pp., o.p.

C [R] LOWREY, Janette Sebring. *The Lavender Cat.* Gr. 4–6
The little wild cat tamed by a lost boy named Jemmy eventually leads the boy home. (BL 41:127; HB 21:33; KR 12:431; LJ 69:1050)
Illus. by Rafaello Busoni, Harper, 1944, 180 pp., o.p.

C/YA LUENN, Nancy. *Arctic Unicorn.* Gr. 6–10.
Kala, a thirteen year old Eskimo girl, is torn between her attraction to a young hunter who could become her husband, and her visions of arctic unicorns that beckon her to accept her magical powers and become an angakok, or shaman. (CCBB 39:188; KR 54:869; SLJ Oct 1986 p. 179; VOYA 10:38)
Atheneum, 1986, 168 pp.

C LUENN, Nancy. *The Ugly Princess.* Gr. 3–5.
The veiled Princess Saralinde has difficulty choosing between handsome but vain Prince Phillip, and the kind but unattractive Dragonlord. (CCBB 35:90; HB 57:659; KR 50:201; SLJ Oct 1981 p. 144)
Illus. by David Wiesner, Little, 1981, 27 pp.

LUENN, Nancy. *Unicorn Crossing.* See Chapter 7, Magic Advanture Fantasy.

C LYNCH, Patricia (Nora). *Brogeen Follows the Magic Tune.* Gr. 4–6. (Orig. British pub. 1952.)
Brogeen the leprechaun is determined to retrieve the fairies' magic tune, stolen by a human fiddler. This story is preceded by *Brogeen and the Lost Castle* (British), *Brogeen and the Black Enchanter* (British), and *Brogeen and the Little Wind* (1963), and the sequels are *Brogeen and the Bronze Lizard* (1970), *Brogeen and the Red Fez* (British), and *Guests at the Beech Tree* (British). (BL 65:837; KR 36:1163; LJ 94:302)
Illus. by Ralph Pinto, Macmillan, 1968, 165 pp., o.p.

YA MACAULAY, David. *BAAA.* Gr. 6 up.
After humans disappear from the earth, sheep take up human clothing, possessions, and thoughts, become consumers, and eventually destroy themselves, rioting over inequities. (BL 82:53; CCBB 31:13; SLJ Oct 1985 p. 183)
Illus. by the author, Houghton, 1985, 61 pp.

C/YA MacDONALD, George. *At the Back of the North Wind.* Gr. 5–8. (Orig.
[R] British pub. 1871, U.S. 1875.)
A beautiful lady takes a boy named Diamond on fabulous journeys. The final journey is to the land at the back of the North Wind. (BL 6:146, 47:162; Bookshelf 1923–1924 p. 15; CC:503; CCBB 11:61; Ch&Bks:269; HB 1[Nov 1924]:7, 26:490, 34:122; LJ 26[no. 8]:67, 45:980, 50:803; Mahony 2:286; Tymn:132)
Illus. by George Hauman and Doris Hauman, Macmillan, 1964, o.p.; Garland, 1976 (repr. of 1871 ed.), o.p.; Schocken, 1978, pap.; Penguin, 1985, pap.; NAL, 1986, pap.

C MacDONALD, George. *The Fairy Fleet.* Gr. 2–4. (Orig. title: *The Carasoyn, Light Princess and Other Fairy Tales.)*
Young Colin rescues a changeling child from the fairy fleet. (BL 33:30; HB 12:289; LJ 61:733)
Illus. by Stuyvesant Van Veen, Holiday, 1936, 52 pp., o.p.

C/YA MacDONALD, George. *The Golden Key.* Gr. 4 up. (Orig. British pub.
[R] 1906.)
After Tangle discovers the key to the door at the end of the rainbow, he and his sister search for the mystical land beyond the door. (HB 43:464; KR 35:609; LJ 92:3187)
Illus. by Maurice Sendak, Farrar, 1976 rev. ed. 1985, 85 pp., hb and pap.

C [R] MacDONALD, George. *The Light Princess.* Gr. 3–6. (Orig. British title: *Dealing with Fairies,* 1867; orig. U.S. pub. 1926.)
Angry Aunt Makemnort's curse removes all of the princess's gravity, leaving her to laugh but never cry and to float but never walk on the ground. (BL 59:499, 66:623; Bookshelf 1926–1927 Suppl. p. 3; CC:504; CCBB 23:162; Ch&Bks:269; HB 2[Nov 1928]:45, 28:422, 38:605, 46:41; KR 37:1257, 56:365, LJ 87·427, 95:1640; Mahony 2:288; Suth:262)
Illus. by William Pène du Bois, Crowell, 1962, o.p.; illus. by Maurice Sendak, Farrar, 1977, 1985, rev. ed., 1984, pap.; adapt. by Robin McKinley, illus. by Katie Thamer Treherne, Harcourt, 1988, 48 pp.

YA MacDONALD, George. *Phantastes: A Faerie Romance for Men and Women.* Gr. 10 up. (Orig. British pub. 1858, U.S. 1871.)
On the morning of the hero's twenty-first birthday, his bedroom turns into a woodland glade and he sets out on a series of fantastic and dangerous adventures, in this somewhat dated Victorian allegory about growing up. (HB 3 [May 1927]: 17–22; TLS 1982 p. 1175)
McKay, 1911, o.p.; Dutton, 1916, 1923, 1940, 237 pp., o.p. (Pub. with *Lilith.* Eerdmans, 1964, o.p.); Eerdmans, 1964, 1981, pap.; Schocken, 1982, pap.; Biblio, 1983, pap.

C/YA MacDONALD, George. *The Princess and the Goblin.* Gr. 5–7. (Orig. Brit-
[O] ish pub. 1872.)
Curdie, a miner's son, overhears a plot by Goblins to flood the mines and take over the kingdom. The sequel is *The Princess and Curdie* (orig. pub. 1882; Macmillan, 1954, o.p.; Dell/Yearling, 1987, pap.). (BL 5:64, 83:354, 84:67; Bookshelf 1932 p. 8; CC:504, 1987 Suppl. p. 60; CCBB 4:45; Ch&Bks:269; HB 27:261, 63:84; LJ 26:67; Mahony 2:287; Moore:290; SLJ Oct 1987 p. 116; Tymn:133)
Illus. by Nora Unwin, Macmillan, 1951, o.p.; illus. by Arthur Hughes, Penguin, 1964, pap.; Zondervan, 1980; Dell/Yearling, 1985, pap.; illus. by Jessie Willcox Smith, Morrow, 1986; abr. by Oliver Hunkin, illus. by Alan Parry, Eerdmans, 1987, 93 pp.

C/YA MacDONALD, George. *The Wise Woman and Other Fantasy Stories.* Gr. 5–7. (Orig. British pub. 1875; retitled *The Lost Princess: A Double Story,* 1895.)
The paths of two little girls, a princess and a shepherd's daughter, converge at the home of the wise woman, who changes both their lives. (HB 42:306; SLJ Apr 1981 p. 129; TLS 1965 p. 1150)
Dutton, 1966 (entitled *The Lost Princess*), o.p.; Eerdmans, 1980, pap., 176 pp; illus. by D(enys) J(ames) Watkins-Pitchford, Zondervan, 1981, o.p.

C [R] McGINLEY, Phyllis (Louise). *The Plain Princess.* Gr. 2–4.
Dame Goodwit teaches a selfish young princess to be kind and helpful. (BL 42:133; Ch&Bks:269; HB 21:454, 447; KR 13:297; LJ 70:950, 1138)
Illus. by Helen Stone, Lippincott, 1945, 64 pp., o.p.

C [R] McGOWEN, Tom (Thomas E.). *Dragon Stew.* Gr. 1–3.
Gluttonous King Chubby holds a contest for the most unusual recipe, and dragon stew is the winner. (BL 65:1177; CCBB 23:114; HB 45:397; KR 37:171; LJ 94:1770)
Illus. by Trina Schart Hyman, Follett, 1969, 32 pp., o.p.

C McHARGUE, Georgess. *The Mermaid and the Whale.* Gr. K–3.
A mermaid asks Ichabod Paddock, the great whalemaster, to help her tame Long John, the whale she loves. (HB 50:46; KR 41:1157; LJ 99:883)
Illus. by Robert Andrew Parker, Holt, 1973, 34 pp., o.p.

McKILLIP, Patricia A(nne). *The Forgotten Beasts of Eld.* See Section 5A, Alternate Worlds or Histories.

McKINLEY, (Jennifer Carolyn) Robin. *Beauty: A Retelling of the Story of Beauty and the Beast.* See Chapter 5B, Myth Fantasy.

C/YA McKINLEY, (Jennifer Carolyn) Robin. *The Door in the Hedge.* Gr. 5–7.
[R] Two original tales, "The Hunting of the Hind" and "The Stolen Princess," and two familiar ones, "The Princess and the Frog" and "The Twelve Danc-

ing Princesses." (BL 77:810; CCBB 35:33; HB 57:433; JHC:434; Kies:51; KR 49:876; SLJ Aug 1981 p. 77)
Greenwillow, 1981; Berkley, 1987, pap., 224 pp.

MacLACHLAN, Patricia. *Tomorrow's Wizard.* See Chapter 10, Witchcraft and Sorcery Fantasy.

C MAETERLINCK, Maurice. *The Children's Blue Bird.* Gr. 3–5. (Orig. title: *The Blue Bird: A Fairy Play in Five Acts,* 1909; prose version, 1913.)
Two children search for the blue bird of happiness. (BL 5:174, 10:163; Bookshelf 1927 Suppl. p. 26; Mahony 1:34; Mahony 2:26; Mahony 3:37)
Adapt. by Georgette Leblanc (Maeterlinck), tr. by Alexander De Mattos, illus. by Herbert Paus, Dodd, 1962, o.p.; Philos, 1985 (entitled *The Blue Bird,* bound with *The Betrothal*), 304 pp., o.p.

MAGUIRE, Gregory. *The Dream Stealer.* See Chapter 10, Witchcraft and Sorcery Fantasy.

C MARIA, Consort of Ferdinand, King of Rumania. *The Story of Naughty Kildeen.* Gr. 2–4. (Orig. British pub. 1922.)
A spoiled young princess learns to control her temper and be more considerate of others. (BL 24:169; Bookshelf 1923–1924 Suppl. p. 2)
Illus. by Job, Harcourt, 1926, 95 pp., o.p.

C MAUGHAM, W. Somerset. *Princess September.* Gr. 3–5. (Orig. pub. as part of *The Gentleman in the Parlour,* 1930.)
A nightingale caged by Princess September nearly dies. (CCBB 22:31; HB 45:308; LJ 94:2104; TLS 1970 p. 420)
Illus. by Jacqueline Ayer, Harcourt, 1969, 33 pp., o.p.

MAYER, Marianna. *The Black Horse.* See Section 5B, Myth Fantasy.

C [R] MAYER, Marianna. *The Little Jewel Box.* Gr. K–3.
Isabel proves herself to be "brave, outspoken, and intelligent besides," as she performs the arduous tasks needed to win John for her husband. (BL 82:1086; CCBB 39:154; HB 62:443; KR 54:793; SLJ May 1986 p. 82)
Illus. by Margot Tomes, Dial, 1968, 32 pp.

C MAYER, Marianna. *The Unicorn and the Lake.* Gr. 1–4.
A powerful unicorn battles an evil serpent and restores a poisoned lake, bringing peace and good health to all of the other animals. (BL 79:779; SLJ Nov 1982 p. 70)
Illus. by Michael Hague, Dial, 1982, 1987, pap., 32 pp.

YA MAYHAR, Ardath. *The Saga of Grittel Sundotha.* Gr. 7–10.
Seven-foot-tall Grittel wanders the land of Garetha using her magical powers to rescue the helpless, as she searches for her true destiny. (BL 81:1051, 1060; SLJ 31[Aug 1985]:79)
Atheneum, 1985, 204 pp.

C [R] MAYNE, William (James Carter). *A Year and a Day.* Gr. 4–6.
Sara and Rebecca find a fairy changeling boy who brings happiness to their family, but only for a year and a day. (BL 72:1528; Ch&Bks:270; CCBB 29:178; HB 52:398, 60:223; KR 44:391; SLJ Apr 1976 p. 76; TLS 1976 p. 1241)
Dutton, 1976, 86 pp., o.p.

C/YA MEIGS, Cornelia (Lynde). *The Kingdom of the Winding Road.* Gr. 5–7.
Twelve tales in which the same wandering man with bright blue eyes plays on his silver pipe, summoning those he meets to adventure before he vanishes down the winding road. (BL 12:296; Bookshelf 1920–21 p. 15; HB 7:117)
Illus. by Frances White, Macmillan, 1915, 238 pp., o.p.

MENOTTI, Gian Carlo. *Amahl and the Night Visitors.* See Section 5B, Myth Fantasy.

C MENUHIN, Yehudi, and HOPE, Christopher. *The King, the Cat, and the Fiddle.* Gr. 1–4.
As an economy measure, the King fires his fiddlers, bringing on rebellion from his countrymen, who miss hearing music. (CCBB 37:33; KR 51:J153; SLJ Jan 1984 p. 79)
Illus. by Angela Barrett, Holt, 1983, 31 pp.

MERRILL, Jean (Fairbanks). *The Black Sheep.* See Section 2A, Beast Tales.

MERRILL, Jean (Fairbanks). *The Pushcart War.* See Chapter 6, Humorous Fantasy.

C [R] MERRILL, Jean (Fairbanks). *The Superlative Horse: A Tale of Ancient China.* Gr. 4–6.
After Hankan, the lowly stable boy, finds a wonderful horse for Duke Mu, he is made chief groom. (BL 58:287; Eakin:234; HB 38:48; LJ 87:334)
Illus. by Ronni Solbert, Addison-Wesley, 1961, 79 pp., o.p.

C MEYER, Zoe. *The Little Green Door.* Gr. 2–4.
Stories of how the Fairy of the Green Forest helped the robin get his spotted vest, the hermit thrush get his song, and the owl learn to fly at night. (BL 18:161; Bookshelf 1923–1924 p. 8)
Illus. by Clara E. Atwood, Little, 1921, 157 pp., o.p.

C/YA MILES, (Mary) Patricia. *The Gods in Winter.* Gr. 5–8.
[R] Strange things begin happening after Mrs. Korngold moves in as the Brambles' housekeeper. She changes cousin Crispin into a lizard, saves Lottie's life, and seems to be the cause of an extremely severe winter. (BL 75:51; CCBB 32:48; HB 55:518; KR 46:750; SLJ Oct 1978 p. 147; Suth 2:319; TLS 1978 p. 764)
Dutton, 1978, 140 pp., o.p.

C/YA MILNE, A(lan) A(lexander). *Once on a Time.* Gr. 5–7. (Orig. British and
[R] U.S. pub. 1917.)
After the kings go to war, the Kingdoms of Euralia and Barodia are ruled by women. (BL 19:87; Bookshelf 1928 p. 23; HB 2[Nov 1928]:45; KR 29:1086; LJ 87:842)
Illus. by Charles Robinson, Putnam, 1922, o.p.; illus. by Susan Perl, New York Graphic Society, 1962, 242 pp., o.p.

C MILNE, A(lan) A(lexander). *Prince Rabbit and the Princess Who Could Not Laugh.* Gr. 2–4.
Two humorous tales about an enchanted prince in rabbit-form, and a contest to make a princess laugh. (CCBB 20:61; LJ 92:329)
Illus. by Mary Shepard, Dutton, 1966, 72 pp., o.p.

C [O] MOERI, Louise. *Star Mother's Youngest Child.* Gr. 2 up.
A crochety old woman and Star Mother's Ugly Child spend Christmas

together, turning their otherwise lonely day into a warm and memorable one. (BL 72:304; CCBB 29:115; HB 51:582; KR 43:1180; SLJ Oct 1975 p. 81)
Illus. by Trina Schart Hyman, Houghton, 1975, 42 pp., 1980, pap.

C MOERI, Louise. *The Unicorn and the Plow.* Gr. 2–4.
A unicorn plows a starving farmer's field, turning it into a flourishing vegetable garden overnight. (BL 78:1527; CCBB 36:16; KR 50:419; SLJ Apr 1982 p. 60)
Illus. by Diane Goode, Dutton, 1982, 31 pp.

MOLESWORTH, Mary Louise (Stewart). *Fairy Stories.* See Chapter 3, Fantasy Collections.

MONTROSE, Anne. *The Winter Flower and Other Fairy Stories.* See Chapter 3, Fantasy Collections.

MOON, Sheila. *Knee-Deep in Thunder.* See Section 5C, Travel to Other Worlds.

MOORCOCK, Michael (John). *The Ice Schooner: A Tale.* See Section 5A, Alternate Worlds or Histories.

YA MOORCOCK, Michael. *The War Hound and the World's Pain: A Fable.*
Gr. 10 up. (Orig. U.S. pub. Timescape/Simon, 1981, o.p.)
Heartsick at the atrocities he has seen perpetrated in the name of God during the Thirty Years' War (1618–1648), Captain Von Beck is sent by Satan to find the "Cure for the World's Pain," in order to free his soul from the Devil's grip. The sequel is *The City in the Autumn Stars* (1987). (KR 49:1100; LJ 106:2052; SLJ Jan 1982 p. 92)
Ultramarine, 1981, 239 pp.; Pocket/Timescape, 1983, 1987, pap.

C [R] MOZART, Wolfgang Amadeus. *The Magic Flute.* Gr. 3–6.
Mozart's well-known opera retold in story form for children. (BL 59:615; HB 43:196; LJ 87:3896, 92:337)
Adapt. and illus. by John Updike and Warren Chappell, Knopf, 1962, o.p.; adapt. by Stephen Spender, illus. by Beni Montresor, Putnam, 1966, 40 pp., o.p.

C [R] MULOCK, Diana (pseud. of Dinah Craik). *The Little Lame Prince and His Travelling Cloak.* Gr. 4–6. (Orig. British pub. 1874.)
Prince Dolor, lame from an accident he had as a baby, uses magic to escape his greedy uncle and to gain his rightful throne. (BL 6:142, 45:145: Bookshelf 1932 p. 8; CCBB 2[Jan 1949]:2; HB 7:116; LJ 26 [no. 8]:67, 74:69; Mahony 2:278)
Grossett, 1948, o.p.; Garland, 1977 (repr. of 1874 ed., bound with *The Adventures of a Brownie*), o.p.

C [R] MURPHY, Shirley Rousseau. *Silver Woven in My Hair.* Gr. 4–6.
In an extended version of the Cinderella story, orphaned Thursey is abused by her stepmother and stepsisters until her friend, the goatherd, turns out to be a long-lost prince. (BL 73:1355; CCBB 31:51; HB 53:316; KR 45:224; SLJ Sept 1977 p. 134)
Illus. by Alan Tiegreen, Atheneum, 1977, 121 pp., o.p.

C [R] MURPHY, Shirley Rousseau. *Valentine for a Dragon.* Gr. K–4.
A shy demon's gifts to a lovey lady dragon keep going up in smoke, until he

comes up with the perfect gift and wins her heart. (BL 80:1550, 83:360; CCBB 37:171; SLJ Aug 1984 p. 63)
    Illus. by Kay Chorao, Atheneum, 1984, 48 pp., 1986, pap.

C MYERS, Walter Dean. *The Golden Serpent.* Gr. 3–5.
    A wise man finds the answer to the mystery of the golden serpent, but the king does not understand this answer. (BL 77:575; CCBB 34:157; HB 56: 636; SLJ Jan 1981 p. 53; TLS 1981 p. 343)
    Illus. by Alice Provensen and Martin Provensen, Viking, 1980, 40 pp.

YA [R] NATHAN, Robert (Gruntal). *Portrait of Jenny.* Gr. 10 up.
    Each time a struggling artist meets Jenny she has, mysteriously, grown older "in order to catch up with him," but tragedy intervenes after they fall in love. (BL 36:198; Kies:56; SHC:626; TLS 1940 p. 85)
    Knopf, 1929, 1940, 1949, 212 pp.

NESBIT (Bland), E(dith). *The Complete Book of Dragons.* See Chapter 3, Fantasy Collections.

C NESBIT (Bland), E(dith). *The Last of the Dragons.* Gr. 4–6. (Orig. British and U.S. pub. in *The Book of Dragons,* 1901; as a separate tale, 1925.)
    Faced with a Cornish princess and her suitor, England's last dragon reveals that he wants only to be loved. (CC:511; CCBB 34:115; SLJ Feb 1981 p. 69)
    Illus. by Peter Firmin, McGraw-Hill, 1980, 25 pp.

NESBIT (Bland), E(dith). *The Magic World.* See Chapter 7, Magic Adventure Fantasy.

C [R] NESS, Evaline (Michelow). *The Girl and the Goatherd, or This and That and Thus and So.* Gr. 1–4.
    A girl made beautiful after completing a witch's tasks can't understand why she is still unhappy. (BL 67:270; HB 47:159; KR 38:944; LJ 95:4038)
    Dutton, 1970, 32 pp., o.p.

NEWMAN, Robert (Howard). *Merlin's Mistake.* See Section 5B, Myth Fantasy.

NORTH, Joan. *The Cloud Forest.* See Chapter 7, Magic Adventure Fantasy.

C NYE, Robert. *The Mathematical Princess and Other Stories* Gr. 4–6. (British title: *Poor Pumpkin,* 1971.)
    Six stories, including the tale of a princess who puts all of her suitors to sleep with her lectures on Euclid. (HB 48:468; KR 40:673; LJ 98:646)
    Illus. by Paul Bruner, Hill, 1972, 125 pp.

C NYE, Robert. *Wishing Gold.* Gr. 3–5. (Orig. British pub. 1970.)
    Wishing Gold, the lost son of the King of Ireland, battles an evil queen and her three sons, and saves his father's life. (KR 39:52; LJ 96:1507; TLS 1970 p. 714)
    Illus. by Helen Craig, Hill, 1971, 109 pp., o.p.

OAKLEY, Graham. *Henry's Quest.* See Chapter 6, Humorous Fantasy.

O'BRIEN, Robert C. *Mrs. Frisby and the Rats of NIMH.* See Chapter 2A, Beast Tales.

YA   ORWELL, George (pseud. of Eric Hugh Blair). *Animal Farm*. Gr. 7 up.
[O]   (Orig. British pub. 1945, U.S. 1946, 1954.)
At Farmer Jones's farm, the pigs lead a revolt to drive out the humans and put themselves in charge of the new totalitarian state, in this classic satire of communism. (BL 43:18, 83:1592; JHC:403; KR 14:351; LJ 7:1048; SHC:627; TLS 1945 p. 401)
Illus. by Joy Batchelor and John Halas, Harcourt, 1982; Buccaneer, 1982 (repr. of 1945 ed.); NAL, 1974, 1983, pap., 128 pp.

OSBORNE, Maurice. *Ondine: The Story of a Bird Who Was Different.* See Section 2A, Beast Tales.

C   PAGET, (Reverend) F(rancis) E(dward) (used the pseud. William Churne of Staffordshire). *The Hope of the Katzekopfs; or, the Sorrow of Selfishness: A Fairy Tale.* Gr. 3–6. (Orig. British pub. 1844.)
Abracadabra, the uninvited fairy guest at the christening of the Fairy King and Queen's son, gives him the gift of "self-will," causing him to become selfish and mischievous. When the fairy is called back to take charge of him, she draws him out into a long elastic string, turns him into a ball, and bounces him all over the country. According to *The Oxford Companion to Children's Literature* (Oxford University Press, 1984) and Roger Lancelyn Green in *Tellers of Tales: British Authors of Children's Books from 1800–1964* (Watts, 1965), this book is generally regarded as the first English children's fantasy, and had a direct influence on Thackeray's *The Rose and the Ring* (1855) and Kipling's *Rewards and Fairies* (1910).
(Adapt. and retitled: *The Self-Willed Prince; or, The Hope of the Katzekopfs, a Fairy Tale Retold in Short Words*), illus. by J. L. Gilmour, Stokes, 1917, o.p.; Johnson, 1968 (repr. of 1844 ed.), 211 pp.

C   PALMER, Mary. *The Magic Knight*. Gr. 3–5.
Prince Gillian's page, Quist, helps him slay a dragon and tame a sea serpent. (CCBB 18:91; KR 32:955; LJ 90:382)
Illus. by Bill Sokol, Hale, 1964, 93 pp., o.p.

C [R]   PARKER, (James) Edgar (Jr.). *The Enchantress.* Gr. 3–5.
The enchantress-princess decides to help the young knight she loves to accomplish the three impossible tasks she set for prospective suitors. (BL 57:249; CCBB 14:99; HB 36:407; KR 28:816; LJ 85:3866)
Illus. by the author, Pantheon, 1960, 36 pp., o.p.

PARKER, (James) Edgar (Jr.). *The Flower of the Realm.* See Section 2B, Talking Animal Fantasy.

C [R]   PEARCE, (Ann) Philippa. *The Squirrel Wife.* Gr. 2–4. (Orig. British pub. 1971.)
Jealous of Jack's magic ring and fairy wife, Jack's brother has him imprisoned. (BL 68:822; CCBB 26:14; HB 48:265; KR 40:194, 1412; LJ 97:2479; Suth: 307)
Illus. by Derek Collard, Crowell, 1972, 61 pp., o.p.

PICARD, Barbara Leonie. *The Faun and the Woodcutter's Daughter.* See Chapter 3, Fantasy Collections.

PICARD, Barbara Leonie. *The Goldfinch Garden: Seven Tales.* See Chapter 3, Fantasy Collections.

PICARD, Barbara Leonie. *The Lady of the Linden Tree.* See Chapter 3, Fantasy Collections.

PICARD, Barbara Leonie. *The Mermaid and the Simpleton.* See Chapter 3, Fantasy Collections.

POLLAND, Madeleine A(ngela Cahill). *Deirdre.* See Section 5B, Myth Fantasy.

POPE, Elizabeth. *The Perilous Gard.* See Section 5C, Travel to Other Worlds.

C POSTGATE, Oliver, and FIRMIN, Peter. *King of the Nogs.* Gr. 2–4. (Orig. British pub. 1965.)
   Noggin battles the wicked Nogbad to gain a throne and a bride. The American sequels are *Noggin and the Whale* (1967), *The Ice Dragon* (1968), *Nogbad and the Elephants* (1967), and *Noggin and the Moon Mouse* (1967). The British sequels are *The Blackwash; The Flowers; The Game; The Icebergs; The Monster; Nogbad Comes Back; Noggin and the Dragon; Noggin and the Money; Noggin and the Storks; Noggin the King; Nogmania;* and *The Pie.* (KR 36:1220; LJ 94:1772; TLS 1965 p. 1149)
   Illus. by the authors, Holiday, 1968, 48 pp., o.p.

C/YA PRICE, Susan. *The Ghost Drum: A Cat's Tale.* Gr. 5–9. (Orig. British
[R]   pub. 1987.)
   A cat tells the story of the friendship between Chingis, a shaman who lives in a house on chicken legs, and Safa, the Czar's son, who has been imprisoned in a windowless room since birth. (BL 84:152; CCBB 41:36; KR 55:929; SLJ Sept 1987 p. 182, Dec 1987 p. 38; TLS 1987 p. 248; VOYA 10:245)
   Farrar, 1987, 167 pp.

C [R] *The Princesses: Sixteen Stories about Princesses.* Ed. by Sally Patrick Johnson. Gr. 4–6. (British title: *The Book of Princesses.*)
   One tale each by sixteen authors, including Hans Christian Andersen, Mary de Morgan, Somerset Maugham, Walter de la Mare, Eleanor Farjeon, Ruth Sawyer, and Rudyard Kipling. *The Harper Book of Princes* (1964) is a companion volume, containing stories by A. A. Milne, E. Nesbit, Frank R. Stockton, Laurence Housman, and Oscar Wilde. (BL 59:396; CCBB 16:96; Eakin:178; HB 38:603; LJ 87:187)
   Illus. by Beni Montresor, Harper, 1962, 318 pp.

C *Princesses and Peasant Boys: Tales of Enchantment.* Ed. by Phyllis Reid Fenner. Gr. 4–6.
   Included in this collection are stories by Hans Christian Andersen, Howard Pyle, and Margery Williams Bianco. (BL 41:126; KR 12:430; LJ 69:1049)
   Illus. by Henry C. Pitz, Knopf, 1944, 188 pp., o.p.

PUSHKIN, Alexander Sergeevich. *The Golden Cockerel and Other Stories.* See Chapter 3, Fantasy Collections.

C PUSHKIN, Alexander Sergeevich. *The Tale of Czar Saltan, or the Prince and the Swan Princess.* (British title: *The Tale of Tsar Saltan,* 1974.) Gr. 3–5.
   Abandoned in a foreign land, Czar Saltan's son is reunited with his family by an enchanted swan. (BL 72:167; SLJ Nov 1975 p. 82; TLS 1974 p. 1382)
   Tr. by Patricia Lowe, illus. by I. Bilbin, Crowell, 1975, 24 pp., o.p.

C [R]   PUSHKIN, Alexander Sergeevich. *The Tale of the Golden Cockerel*. Gr. 3–5. (Orig. U.S. pub. 1938.)
  The czar's magic cockerel warns him of enemy invasions, but cannot save him from the wiles of an enchantress. (BL 35:51, 72:167; CCBB 29:18; HB 14:298, 51:455; SLJ Oct 1975 p. 101; Suth 2:372)
  Tr. and retold by Patricia Tracy Lowe, illus. by I. Bilbin, Crowell, 1975, 24 pp., o.p.

PYLE, Howard. *The Garden behind the Moon: A Real Story of the Moon Angel*. See Section 5C, Travel to Other Worlds.

PYLE, Howard. *King Stork*. See Chapter 10, Witchcraft and Sorcery Fantasy.

PYLE, Howard. *The Wonder Clock; or, Four & Twenty Marvelous Tales*. See Chapter 3, Fantasy Collections.

C/YA   REEVES, James (pseud. of John Morris Reeves). *The Cold Flame*. Gr. 5–7.
  A soldier uses a witch's unquenchable blue flame to win himself a kingdom and a princess. (HB 45:419; LJ 94:1799; TLS 1967 p. 1142)
  Illus. by Charles Keeping, Meredith, 1967, 137 pp., o.p.

REEVES, James (pseud. of John Morris Reeves). *Maildun the Voyager*. See Section 5B, Myth Fantasy.

REEVES, James (pseud. of John Morris Reeves). *Sailor Rumbelow and Other Stories*. See Chapter 3, Fantasy Collections.

C   REID, Alastair. *Fairwater*. Gr. 3–5.
  A stone-cutter named Garth is barred from the Kingdom of Fairwater after he tries to rescue an enchanted princess. The sequel is *Allth* (1958). (CCBB 11:85; Eakin: 269; HB 33:222; KR 25:330; LJ 82:2192)
  Illus. by Walter Lorraine, Houghton, 1957, 47 pp., o.p.

C   REID BANKS, Lynne. *The Farthest-Away Mountain*. Gr. 4–6. (Orig. British pub. 1976.)
  Dakin and a prince-turned-frog set off for an unreachable mountain in order to break a witch's spell. (BL 74:809; CCBB 31:122; KR 46:2; SLJ Feb 1978 p. 54; TLS 1976 p. 1553)
  Illus. by Victor Ambrus, Doubleday, 1977, 140 pp., o.p.

C   RIORDAN, James. *The Three Magic Gifts*. Gr. K–4.
  Ivan the Rich manages to steal two of his poor brother's magic gifts, but the third time, Ivan the Poor outwits his brother and retrieves all of the gifts. (BL 77:967; CCBB 34:179; KR 99:210; SLJ Mar 1981 p. 136)
  Illus. by Errol Le Cain, Oxford, 1980, 29 pp., o.p.

ROBINSON, Joan (Mary) G(ale Thomas). *When Marnie Was There*. See Chapter 4, Ghost Fantasy.

ROCCA, Guido. *Gaetano the Pheasant: A Hunting Fable*. See Section 2A, Beast Tales.

C/YA   ROSS, Ramon Royal. *Prune*. Gr. 5–7.
  Two lonely animals, a magpie and a muskrat, befriend a talking prune who desperately wishes to return to his orchard. (BL 81:848, 84:1441; KR 52:98; SLJ Dec 1984 p. 94)
  Atheneum, 1984, 175 pp.

C [R] RUSKIN, John. *The King of the Golden River, or the Black Brothers: A Legend of Stiria.* Gr. 2–5. (Written 1841, orig. British pub. 1951, U.S. 1900.)

Little Gluck's cruel older brothers torment him until the King of the Golden River and the South-West Wind come to his aid. (BL 42:304; Bookshelf 1921–1922 p. 9; CCBB 13:120; Ch&Bks:271; HB 22:213, 28:422, 55:520; KR 46:1017; Mahony 2:296; SLJ Oct 1978 p. 138; Tymn:155)

Dover, 1974, pap.; illus. by Krystyna Turska, Greenwillow, 1978, 40 pp., o.p.; Putnam, 1988.

C/YA SAINT-EXUPÉRY, Antoine (Jean-Baptiste-Marie-Roger) de. *The Little*
[R] *Prince.* Gr. 5 up. (Orig. pub. in France.)

A pilot stranded in the Sahara meets a strange boy who tells him of his travels through the universe. (BL 39:354; CC:632; Ch&Bks:271; JHC:412; LJ 68:248; SHC:584)

Tr. by Katherine Woods, illus. by the author, Harcourt, 1943, 91 pp., 1982, pap.

C SANCHEZ-SILVA, José. *The Boy and the Whale.* Gr. 3–5. (Orig. Spanish pub. 1962.)

An imaginary whale helps a young boy deal with his grandmother's approaching death. (HB 40:376; KR 32:453; LJ 89:2662)

Tr. by Michael Heron, illus. by Margery Gill, McGraw-Hill, 1964, 80 pp., o.p.

SARGENT, Sarah. *Watermusic.* See Section 5B, Myth Fantasy.

C SAWYER, Ruth. *This Way to Christmas.* Gr. 3–5. (Orig. pub. 1916.)

A lonely boy and a fairy spend Christmas together listening to Christmas tales from around the world. (BL 13:185)

Illus. by Maginel Barney, Harper, 1952, rev. ed. 1967, 175 pp. o.p.

SCARBOROUGH, Elizabeth Ann. *The Harem of Aman Akbar; or The Djinn Decanted.* See Chapter 6, Humorous Fantasy.

C [R] SCHLEIN, Miriam. *The Raggle Taggle Fellow.* Gr. 2–4

Dick's father disapproves of his third and youngest son's ambition to become a minstrel. (BL 55:544; Eakin: 286; HB 35:286; KR 27:134; LJ 84:1690)

Illus. by Harvey Weiss, Abelard-Schuman, 1959, 62 pp., o.p.

C SCHMIDT, Werner (Felix). *The Forests of Adventure.* Gr. 3–6.

Eric's adventure-filled search for his missing guardian, Black Otto, includes archery battles with outlaws, escape from imprisonment, the rescue of a fair lady, and a king's coronation. (HB 39:174; LJ 88:2554)

Illus. by Artur Marokvia, Atlantic-Little, 1963, 161 pp., o.p.

C SCHRANK, Joseph. *The Plain Princess and the Lazy Prince.* Gr. 2–4.

In an attempt to marry off their unattractive daughter, the king and queen advertise for a dragon, but it is the princess who ends up rescuing the prince. (CCBB 12:74; KR 26:498; LJ 83:3012)

Illus. by Mircea Vasiliu, Day, 1958, 57 pp., o.p.

C SCHWARZ, Eugene M. *Two Brothers.* Gr. 1–4. (Orig. pub. in the Soviet Union.)

After he locks Little Brother out in the cold, Big Brother must save him from Great-grandfather Frost. (KR 41:559; LJ 98:2644)

Tr. by Elizabeth Hapgood, illus. by Gabriel Lisowski, Harper, 1973, 44 pp., o.p.

C [R] SÈGUR, Sophie (Rostopchine), Comtesse de. *The Enchanted Forest.* Gr. 2–4. (Orig. French pub. 1856, U.S. 1869 in *Fairy Tales for Little Folks.*) (Other editions: Penn, *Old French Fairy Tales,* 1920, o.p.; Macrae Smith, *Princess Rosette and Other Fairy Tales,* 1930, o.p.; British Book Service, *Blondine and Bear-Cub,* 1957, o.p.; Harlin Quist, *Forest of Lilacs,* 1969, illus. by Nicole Claveloux, o.p.)
A wicked queen banishes little Princess Blondine to the enchanted Forest of Lilacs where she is imprisoned by wicked fairies and rescued by good fairies and a young prince. (BL 17:127; Bookshelf 1932 p. 23; HB 51:54; KR 42:1251; LJ 83:649; SLJ Mar 1975 p. 86; TLS 1970 p. 419)
Adapt. by Beatrice Schenk de Regniers, illus. by Gustave Doré, Atheneum, 1974, 87 pp., o.p.

C SELFRIDGE, Oliver. *The Trouble with Dragons.* Gr. 4–6.
Although her older sisters' attempts at dragon slaying failed, Princess Celia succeeds and wins a prince's love in the bargain. (BL 74:1556; CCBB 31:184; SLJ Sept 1978 p. 148; Suth 2:402)
Illus. by Shirley Hughes, Addison-Wesley, 1978, 86 pp., o.p.

C SEREDY, Kate. *Lazy Tinka.* Gr. 3–4.
After Tinka is befriended by the forest animals, she learns to be more helpful at home. (BL 59:450; KR 62:683; LJ 88:98; TLS 1964 p. 605)
Illus. by the author, Viking, 1962, 56 pp., o.p.

C/YA SEREDY, Kate. *The White Stag.* Gr. 5–8.
[R] The white stag and the red eagle help guide Hunor, Magyar, Bendeguz, Attila, and their people to found the land of Hungary. Newbery Medal winner, 1938. (BL 34:197; CC:527; HB 13:366, 378; LJ 62:807, 63:34, 691)
Illus. by the author, Viking, 1937, 94 pp.; Penguin, 1979, pap.

C [R] SEUSS, Dr. (pseud. of Theodor Seuss Geisel). *The 500 Hats of Bartholomew Cubbins.* Gr. 1–4.
Even the king of Didd's most able wise men and sorcerers cannot take off all of Bartholomew's hats. The sequel is *Bartholomew and the Oobleck* (Random, 1949). (BL 35:102; Ch&Bks:253; HB 14:365, 377; LJ 63:818, 890)
Illus. by the author, Vanguard, 1938, 45 pp.

C SHAPIRO, Irwin. *Twice upon a Time.* Gr. 2–4.
Since the King of Gib-Gib has decreed that everything must be twice as much or twice as many, ought there be two kings? (CCBB 27:86; HB 50:40; KR 41:1032; LJ 98:3703)
Illus. by Adrienne Adams, Scribner, 1973, 35 pp., o.p.

C [R] SHARMA, Partap. *The Surangini Tales.* Gr. 4–6.
Beautiful Surangini refuses to reappear from within the carpet woven by her suitor, Kalu, until seventeen tales have been told. (BL 70:125; CCBB 26:176; HB 49:463; KR 41:386, 1351; LJ 98:2657; TLS 1974 p. 716)
Illus. by Demi Hitz, Harcourt, 1973, 125 pp., o.p.

C SHURA, Mary Francis (pseud. of Mary Francis Craig). *The Nearsighted Knight.* Gr. 4–6.
After learning that his sister must marry before he can leave home, Prince

Todd decides to help the Knight Before Glasses kill a dragon and win his sister's hand. (CCBB 17:130; HB 40:284; KR 32:61; LJ 89:1454)
Illus. by Adrienne Adams, Knopf, 1964, 111 pp., o.p.

YA [R] SIMAK, Clifford D(onald). *Enchanted Pilgrimage.* Gr. 10 up.
Mark and his traveling companions are set upon by witches, trolls, and other fearful creatures during their journey through the wildlands in search of "the old ones." (BL 71:863, 72:1038; KR 43:203; LJ 100:783; SLJ May 1975 p. 75; Tymn: 156)
Putnam, 1975, o.p.; Ballantine, 1983, pap., 256 pp.

C SINGER, Isaac Bashevis. *Alone in the Wild Forest.* Gr. 4–6.
Orphaned Joseph dreams of meeting and winning Princess Chassidah, but wicked Bal Makane plots against him. (CCBB 25:97; KR 39:1015; LJ 97:285)
Tr. by the author and Elizabeth Shub, illus. by Margot Zemach, Farrar, 1971, 79 pp.

C [R] SINGER, Isaac Bashevis. *The Fearsome Inn.* Gr. 4–6.
With his piece of magic chalk, Liebel, a young Cabala student, rescues three young girls held by a witch and a devil. Newbery Medal Honor Book, 1968. (BL 64:338; CCBB 21:67; Ch&Bks:271; HB 43:751, 61:595; KR 35:880; LJ 92:3190; Suth:367)
Tr. by the author and Elizabeth Shub, illus. by Nonny Hogrogian, Scribner, 1967, 45 pp., o.p.; Atheneum, 1984, pap.

C SINGER, Isaac Bashevis. *A Tale of Three Wishes.* Gr. 2–4.
Three children make wishes that cause unexpected problems on the night of Hoshanah Rabbah. (BL 72:1118; CCBB 30:18; KR 44:201; SLJ Apr 1976 p. 65)
Illus. by Irene Lieblich, Farrar, 1976, 30 pp.

SINGER, Isaac Bashevis. *Zlateh the Goat and Other Stories.* See Chapter 3, Fantasy Collections.

SLOBODKIN, Louis. *The Amiable Giant.* See Chapter 10, Witchcraft and Sorcery Fantasy.

C/YA SMITH, Agnes. *An Edge of the Forest.* Gr. 5–9. (Orig. pub. Viking
[R] 1959.)
An orphaned lamb who accidentally wanders into the forest is saved from death and adopted by a black leopardess. (BL 55:578; CCBB 13:21; Ch&Bks:272; Eakin:301; HB 35:10; KR 27:91; LJ 84:1700)
Illus. by Roberta Moynihan, Westwind, 1974, 202 pp.

SNYDER, Zilpha Keatley. *Below the Root.* See Section 5A, Alternate Worlds or Histories.

C [R] SNYDER, Zilpha Keatley. *The Changing Maze.* Gr. 2–4.
A shepherd boy lost in a maze created by an evil wizard searches for his stray pet lamb, ignoring the gold at the heart of the maze. (BL 82:269; CC:532; CCBB 39:57; HB 62:52; SLJ Dec 1985 p. 83)
Illus. by Charles Mikolaycak, Macmillan, 1985, 32 pp.

C SOYER, Abraham. *Adventures of Yemima.* Gr. 4–6. (Orig. pub. 1939.)
Six fables, including tales about a gift of flying money, greedy animals, and a brave little girl. (BL 75:1298; HB 55:305; KR 47:518; SLJ Apr 1979 p. 49)
Tr. by Rebecca Beagle and Rebecca Soyer, illus. by Raphael Soyer, Viking, 1979, 80 pp., o.p.

C/YA   STEARNS, Pamela (Fujimoto). *The Fool and the Dancing Bear.* Gr. 5–7.
Only a dancing bear can revive King Rolf's kingdom after its enchantment by a queen who is jealous of the king's love for her younger sister. (BL 75:1581; CCBB 33:57; HB 55:416; KR 47:742; SLJ Sept 1979 p. 148; Suth 3:408)
Illus. by Ann Strugnell, Atlantic-Little, 1979, 167 pp., o.p.

C   STEARNS, Pamela (Fujimoto). *The Mechanical Doll.* Gr. 4–6.
Jealous of the life-sized mechanical doll that has captured the king's fancy, Hulon, the court musician, breaks it and is banished from the court. (BL 75:1160; CCBB 32:184; KR 47:519; SLJ Nov 1979 p. 82)
Illus. by Trina Schart Hyman, Houghton, 1979, 45 pp., o.p.

STEELE, Mary Q(uintard Govan). *The Journey Outside.* See Section 5A, Alternate Worlds or Histories.

STEELE, Mary Q(uintard Govan). *The Owl's Kiss: Three Stories.* See Chapter 3. Fantasy Collections.

C/YA   STEELE, Mary Q(uintard Govan). *The True Men.* Gr. 5–7.
Driven from his home with the True Men because his skin has begun to glow in the dark, Ree is taken in by two weavers. (CCBB 30:82; HB 53:55; KR 44:1045; SLJ Jan 1977 p. 97)
Greenwillow/Morrow, 1976, 144 pp.

C   STEIN, Gertrude. *The World Is Round.* Gr. 1–4. (Orig. pub. 1939.)
A reissue of famed writer/philosopher Gertrude Stein's children's story about Rose, Willie, and Willie's pet lion. In this story the author experimented with rhythm and word patterns. (BL 36:180; HB 15:294; LJ 92:330; TLS 1939 p. 758)
Illus. by Clement Hurd, Young Scott, 1966, o.p.; Avon, 1972, pap., 96 pp.; Arion, 1986 (limited ed.).

C/YA   STEPHENS, James. *The Crock of Gold.* Gr. 6–9. (Orig. U.S. pub. Macmillan, 1912, 1960.)
Seumas and Brigid, children of two philosophers, meet extraordinary creatures in the woods, including leprechauns and the god Pan. (BL 10:245; TLS 1981 p. 348)
Illus. by Thomas MacKenzie, Telegraph Books, 1980 (repr. of 1912 ed.); Macmillan, 1986, pap., 240 pp.

STEVENS, Eden Vale. *Abba.* See Section 2B, Talking Animal Fantasy.

C/YA   STEVENSON, Robert Louis (Balfour). *The Touchstone.* Gr. 5–7.
Two rival princes searching for the "touchstone of truth" to exchange for the hand of a princess find very different solutions to their quest. (KR 44:844; SLJ Nov 1976 p. 63)
Illus. by Uri Shulevitz, Morrow, 1976, 47 pp., o.p.

C/YA   STEWART, Mary (Florence Elinor). *Ludo and the Star Horse.* Gr. 5–8. (Orig. British pub. 1974)
Ludo and his old horse fall into a hidden pit and journey through the twelve houses of the zodiac. (BL 71:967; KR 43:376; SLJ Sept 1975 p. 112; TLS 1974 p. 1380)
Illus. by Gino D'Achille, Morrow, 1975, 191 pp.

C [R] STOCKTON, Frank (Francis) R(ichard). *The Bee-Man of Orn.* Gr. 4–6. (Orig. pub. in *Fanciful Tales* 1884; as a separate tale, Holt, 1964.)
An old beekeeper, told by a sorcerer that he was transformed from another sort of being, decides to find out what he was originally. (BL 61:528; Ch&Bks:272; Eakin:312; HB 40:611, 63:491; LJ 89:4643; Mahony 1:27; TLS 1976 p. 376)
Illus. by Maurice Sendak, Harper, 1987, 48 pp.

C [R] STOCKTON, Frank (Francis) R(ichard). *The Griffin and the Minor Canon.* Gr. 3–5. (Orig. pub. in *Fanciful Tales,* 1884; as a separate tale, Holt, 1963.)
The last of the griffins threatens to stay in a terrified village because it so admires its likeness carved above the church door. (BL 59:900, 83:357; Eakin:313; HB 39:384, 63:84; LJ 88:2555)
Illus. by Maurice Sendak, Harper, 1986, 56 pp., 1987, pap.

STOCKTON, Frank (Francis) R(ichard). *The Queen's Museum and Other Fanciful Tales.* See Chapter 3, Fantasy Collections.

C [R] STOLZ, Mary (Slattery). *The Cuckoo Clock.* Gr. 4–6.
Ula, the old clockmaker, makes one final marvelous cuckoo clock before he dies, as part of a magical legacy for his assistant, a young foundling named Erich. (BL 83:652; CCBB 40:179; KR 55:376; SLJ Apr 1987 p. 105)
Illus. by Pamela Johnson, Godine, 1986, 84 pp.

C [R] STOLZ, Mary (Slattery). *The Leftover Elf.* Gr. 3–5
The survival of the last elf in the world depends on his finding someone who believes in him. (CCBB 5:69; HB 28:172; KR 20:188; LJ 77:653)
Illus. by Peggy Bacon, Harper, 1952, 57 pp., o.p.

C STOLZ, Mary (Slattery). *The Scarecrows and Their Child.* Gr. 3–5.
Two unemployed scarecrows, Handy and Blossom, marry and live peacefully with their cat child, Bohel, until they are kidnapped, whereupon Bohel sets out to find them. (BL 54:572; CCBB 41:77; KR 53:1467; SLJ Jan 1988 p. 76)
Illus. by Amy Schwartz, Harper, 1987, 67 pp.

C/YA STRANGER, Joyce (pseud. of Joyce Muriel Judson Wilson). *The Fox at Drummer's Darkness.* Gr. 6–9. (Orig. British pub. 1976.)
Poisoned by toxic chemicals in the water, a night watchman's ghost rises from his grave to warn the townspeople. (BL 73:1731; HB 53:534; KR 45:540; SLJ May 1977 p. 72)
Illus. by William Geldart, Farrar, 1977, 108 pp., o.p.

SUTCLIFF, Rosemary. *The Sword and the Circle: King Arthur and the Knights of the Round Table.* See Section 5B, Myth Fantasy.

YA SYNGE, (Phyllis) Ursula. *Swan's Wing.* Gr. 7 up.
In this extension of Hans Christian Andersen's story, "The Wild Swans," Lothar, the self-centered eleventh Prince who retained a swan's wing instead of one arm, Gerda, a goose-girl who loves him, and Matthew, a tormented sculptor in love with Gerda, travel the land in search of a cure for Lothar's affliction. (BL 81:436, 451; SLJ Mar 1985 p. 183; VOYA 8:366)
Bodley, dist. by Salem, 1984; Ace, 1985, pap., 160 pp.

TASSIN, Algernon de Vivier. *The Rainbow String.* See Chapter 3, *Fantasy Collections.*

C   TAZEWELL, Charles. *The Littlest Angel.* Gr. 3 up. (Orig. pub. 1946.)
The newest angel in Paradise is lonely among the well-behaved adult angels, until he is befriended by the Understanding Angel. (KR 14:592; LJ
71:1810)
Illus. by Sergio Leone, Childrens, 1966; Ideals, 1984, 1980, pap., 32 pp.

C [R]   TENNYSON, Noel. *The Lady's Chair and the Ottoman.* Gr. 1–4.
True love and loyalty win out in the end, after an ottoman becomes separated from the lady's chair he loves when their owner's home is sold. (BL
84:324; CCBB 41:79; KR 56:1326; SLJ Sept 1987 p. 183)
Illus. by the author, Lothrop, 1987, 32 pp.

C/YA   TERLOUW, Jan (Cornelis). *How to Become King.* Gr. 6–8. (Orig. British
pub. 1976.)
Seventeen-year-old Stark demands to know how he can become king, so
the Ministers of Katoren devise seven impossible tasks for him, including
silencing the Birds of Decibel, destroying the Dragon of Smog, and outwitting the Wizard of Equilibrium. (BL 74:1111; CCBB 31:135; SLJ Mar 1978 p.
134; Suth 2:445; VOYA 1 [Apr 1978]:65)
Hastings, 1977, 128 pp.

C/YA   THACKERAY, William Makepeace. *The Rose and the Ring; or the His-*
[R]   *tory of Prince Giglio and Prince Bulbo: A Fireside Pantomime for Great*
and Small Children. Gr. 5–8. (Orig. British pub. 1855.)
Princess Rosealba and Prince Giglio are restored to their rightful thrones
through the good offices of Fairy Blackstick. (BL 20:65; Bookshelf 1932 p.
23; HB 23:14, 35:480; Mahony 1:38)
Illus. by the author, John Gilbert, and Paul Hogarth, Pierpont Morgan,
1947, 212 pp., o.p.

C/YA   THEROUX, Paul. *A Christmas Card.* Gr. 5 up.
Lost in a blizzard on Christmas Eve, Marcel and his family are welcomed
into the house of a man called Pappy, whose magic helps them find their way
home. (BL 75:227; KR 46:1358; SLJ Oct 1978 p. 113)
Illus. by John Lawrence, Houghton, 1978, 96 pp.

C [R]   THURBER, James (Grover). *The Great Quillow.* Gr. 3–4.
Quillow the toymaker saves the town by outwitting an unruly giant named
Hunder. (BL 41:95; CC 539; Ch&Bks:23; HB 20:469, 482; KR 12:449; LJ
69:866, 1004)
Illus. by Doris Lee, Harcourt, 1944, o.p., 1975, 54 pp., pap.; Peter Smith,
hb.

C [R]   THURBER, James (Grover). *Many Moons.* Gr. K–4.
Only the court jester is wise enough to cure Princess Lenore's illness by
"giving" her the moon. (BL 40:20; CC:539; Ch&Bks:231; HB 19:318, 422,
20:21; LJ 68:672, 818)
Illus. by Louis Slobodkin, Harcourt, 1943, 46 pp., 1987, pap.

C/YA   THURBER, James (Grover). *The 13 Clocks.* Gr. 5 up.
[R]   To marry the princess, Prince Zorn must find a thousand jewels to start all
of the stilled clocks in the land. (BL 47:174; Ch&Bks: 272; Tymn:161)
Illus. by Marc Simont, Simon, 1950, 124 pp., o.p.

C/YA   THURBER, James (Grover). *The White Deer.* Gr. 5 up.
[R]   Since he once married a princess who appeared from the enchanted forest
in the guise of a white deer, King Clode and his three sons are tempted to

hunt in the forest when another white deer is sighted. (BL 42:57; HB 21:447; KR 13:43; Tymn:161)
    Illus. by the author and Don Freeman, Harcourt, 1945, o.p., 1968, pap., 115 pp.

C/YA THURBER, James (Grover). *The Wonderful O.* Gr. 5 up.
 [R]   Wicked Black and his pirate crew decide to destroy everything spelled with the letter "O." (BL 53:559; Ch&Bks:272; KR 25:308; LJ 82:1780)
    Illus. by Marc Simont, Simon, 1957, 72 pp., o.p.

  C TILLSTROM, Burr. *The Dragon Who Lived Downstairs.* Gr. 2–4.
    A friendly dragon releases the princess and her parents from an enchantment, and helps a nonroyal knight win the princess's hand. (CCBB 37:157; SLJ Aug 1984 p. 66)
    Illus. by David Small, Morrow, 1984, 44 pp.

C/YA TOLKIEN, J(ohn) R(onald) R(euel). *Farmer Giles of Ham.* Gr. 5–8.
 [R]   (Orig. pub. 1949.)
    Farmer Giles leads a simple life until the day he finds himself protecting his village from dragons. (CC:540; CCBB 4:23; Ch&Bks:272; HB 26:287; JHC:451; LJ 75:2084; Tymn:166)
    Illus. by Pauline Baynes, Houghton, 1978, 78 pp.

TOLKIEN, J(ohn) R(onald) R(euel). *Fellowship of the Ring.* See Section 5A, Alternate Worlds or Histories.

TOLKIEN, J(ohn) R(onald) R(euel). *The Hobbit; Or, There and Back Again.* See Section 5A, Alternate Worlds or Histories.

C/YA TOLKIEN, J(ohn) R(onald) R(euel). *Smith of Wootton Major.* Gr. 5–8.
    (Orig. pub. 1967.)
    After the blacksmith's son finds a magical star buried in a piece of cake, his life is completely changed. (CC:540; HB 44:63; KR 35:1164; LJ 92:4175; TLS 1967 p. 1153)
    Illus. by Pauline Baynes, Houghton, 1978, o.p.; Ballantine, 1984 (bound with *Farmer Giles of Ham*), pap., 160 pp.

  C TORREY, Marjorie (Chanslor Hood). *Artie and the Princess.* Gr. 2–4.
    Artie the lonely dragon child searches for a playmate and finds a princess. (BL 41:344; KR 13:181; LJ 70:343, 492)
    Illus. by the author, Howell, 1945, 107 pp., o.p.

  C TURKLE, Brinton (Cassaday). *The Fiddler of High Lonesome.* Gr. 3–6.
    When the magic of Lysander's fiddle-playing draws wild animals into a moonlight dance, his cruel cousins attempt to hunt the helpless creatures down. (BL 64:1189; CCBB: 21:166; HB 44:424; KR 36:338; LJ 93:2117)
    Illus. by the author, Viking, 1968, 47 pp., o.p.

  C URQUHART, Elizabeth. *Horace.* Gr. 3–5.
    A little girl named Miriam and a young dragon named Horace save the dragon's father from St. George. (BL 48:38; CCBB 5:25; HB 27:325; KR 19:387; LJ 76:1433)
    Illus. by Rosita Pastor, Dutton, 1951, 116 pp., o.p.

C [R] VAN ALLSBURG, Chris. *The Stranger.* Gr. K–4.
    It seems that autumn will never come, the year Farmer Bailey brings home

a leather-clad stranger who has lost his memory. (BL 83:276; CCBB 40:59; HB 62:741; KR 54:1452; SLJ Nov 1986 p. 84)

Illus. by the author, Houghton, 1986, 32 pp.

C [R] VAN ALLSBURG, Chris. *The Wreck of the Zephyr.* Gr. 2–5.

An old sailor tells a young boy about the wondrous night he learned to fly his sailboat through the skies. (BL 79:1273, 1279, 1284; CCBB 36:220; HB 59:295; KR 51:305; SLJ May 1983 pp. 33, 67)

Illus. by the author, Houghton, 1983, 28 pp.

Visions of Wonder: An Anthology of Christian Fantasy. Ed. by Robert H. Boyer and Kenneth J. Zahorski. See Chapter 3, Fantasy Collections.

C/YA VOEGELI, Max. *The Wonderful Lamp.* Gr. 5–7. (Orig. pub. in Germany 1952.)

In legendary Baghdad, Ali the beggar-boy searches for Aladdin's magic lamp and ends up aboard the ship of Sinbad the sailor. The sequel is *The Prince of Hindustan* (1961). (BL 51:455; CCBB 9:13; HB 31:260; KR 23:358)

Tr. by E. M. Prince, illus. by Felix Hoffmann, Oxford, 1955, 228 pp., o.p.

C WAECHTER, Friedrich, and EILERT, Bernd. *The Crown Snatchers.* Gr. 4–6. (Orig. German pub. 1972.)

Three children who help bring about the downfall of the Pig King are disappointed to find that the new king is also a tyrant. (BL 71:697; KR 43:377; SLJ Apr 1975 p. 60)

Tr. by Edite Kroll, illus. by the authors, Pantheon, 1975, 160 pp., o.p.

C WAHL, Jan (Boyer). *How the Children Stopped the Wars.* Gr. 4–6.

A shepherd boy envisions terrible wars, gathers children from all the surrounding villages, and marches them to the battlefield to stop the fighting. (CCBB 23:136; HB 46:164; KR 37:1260; LJ 95:782, 3610)

Illus. by Mitchell Miller, Farrar, 1969, o.p.; Avon, 1983, pap., 96 pp.

YA [R] WANGERIN, Walter, Jr. *The Book of the Dun Cow.* Gr. 8 up.

In this complex Christian allegory, Chaunticleer the rooster and Mundo Cani Dog save the world from the evils of the giant Wyrm and his "minion" Cockatrice. The sequel is *The Book of Sorrows* (1985). (BL 75:927; CCBB 32:92; KR 46:1255; SLJ Oct 1978 p. 160; Suth 2:469; TLS 1980 p. 368; VOYA 1(Feb 1979):43, 3(Oct 1980):49)

Harper, 1978, 241 pp.; Pocket, 1982, pap.

C WANGERIN, Walter, Jr. *Thistle.* Gr. 2–4.

Thistle, the youngest child, saves her family from being eaten by a giant potato, by daring to kiss an ugly witch. (CCBB 37:80; KR 51:J156; SLJ Nov 1983 p. 84)

Illus. by Marcia Sewall, Harper, 1983, 47 pp.

C/YA WARBURG, Sandol Stoddard (pseud. of Sandol Stoddard). *On the Way Home.* Gr. 6–9.

Alexi, his friend Bear, and Alexi's double, Twain, rescue a fair maiden, kill an ice-worm monster, and escape from the Monkey King. (BL 70:546; KR 41:1202, 1351; LJ 99:578)

Illus. by Daniel Stolpe, Houghton, 1973, 137 pp., o.p.

C WEIR, Rosemary (Green). *Albert the Dragon.* Gr. 4–6.

As a favor for a friend, Albert the vegetarian dragon pretends to let a knight defeat him in battle. The sequels are *Further Adventures of Albert the*

Dragon (1964) and *Albert the Dragon and the Centaur* (1968). *Albert and the Dragonettes* is a British sequel. (CCBB 15:68; KR 29:669)
Illus. by Quentin Blake, Abelard-Schuman, 1961, 107 pp., o.p.

C WERSBA, Barbara. *Let Me Fall before I Fly.* Gr. 3–5.
A young boy finds a two-inch-high circus giving daily performances in his garden. (CCBB 26:66; HB 47:616; KR 39:1124; LJ 97:1611)
Illus. by Mercer Mayer, Atheneum, 1971, o.p.; Creative, 1986, 48 pp.

C WERSBA, Barbara. *A Song for Clowns.* Gr. 4–6.
Humphrey the minstrel resents the fact that the king has abolished sheriffs, the color blue, love, hope, puddings, and minstrels. (CCBB 19:53; HB 41:629; KR 33:677; LJ 90:3797; TLS 1966 p. 1087)
Illus. by Mario Rivoli, Atheneum, 1965, 100 pp., o.p.

C WESTON, John (Harrison). *The Boy Who Sang the Birds.* Gr. 4–6.
Two boys try to stop a flock of strange birds from causing a catastrophic winter in their village. (BL 72:1272; KR 44:257; SLJ: Apr 1976 p. 79)
Illus. by Donna Diamond, Scribner, 1976, 106 pp., o.p.

C WETTERER, Margaret K. *The Giant's Apprentice.* Gr. 2–4.
When Liam McGowen, apprentice blacksmith, is kidnapped by a giant, only his uncle can save him. (BL 78:1261; HB 58:410; KR 50:492; SLJ May 1982 p. 67)
Illus. by Elise Primavera, Atheneum, 1982, 40 pp., o.p.

C WETTERER, Margaret K. *The Mermaid's Cape.* Gr. 2–4.
A mermaid, trapped into marriage and human form by a lonely fisherman, is freed when their beloved young son finds her magical cape. (BL 77:1302; HB 57:427; KR 49:506; SLJ May 1981 p. 60)
Illus. by Elise Primavera, Atheneum, 1981, 32 pp., o.p.

WHITE, E(lwyn) B(rooks). *Charlotte's Web.* See Section 2B, Talking Animal Fantasy.

WHITE, Eliza Orne. *The Enchanted Mountain.* See Section 5C, Travel to Other Worlds.

WHITE, T(erence) H(anbury). *The Sword in the Stone.* See Section 5B, Myth Fantasy.

C WIGGIN, Kate Douglas (Smith). *The Bird's Christmas Carol.* Gr. 3–5.
(Orig. pub. 1888.)
Carol Bird saves the Ruggles's Christmas. The sequel is *Polly Oliver's Problem* (1896). (BL 38:137; Bookshelf 1925–1926 p. 4; CC:545)
Illus. by Jessie Gillespie, Houghton, 1941, 84 pp., o.p.; Ballantine, 1987, pap.

C WILDE, Oscar (pseud. of Fingal O'Flahertie Wills). *The Birthday of the Infanta.* Gr. 3–5. (Orig. British pub. 1891, U.S. pub. 1906 in *A House of Pomegranates.* Orig. U.S. pub. 1905, as a separate tale.)
The princess of Spain is entertained on her birthday by an ugly dwarf. (BL 26:170; Mahony 3:486)
Illus. by Pamela Bianco, Macmillan, 1929, 57 pp., o.p.

C WILDE, Oscar (pseud. of Fingal O'Flahertie Wills). *The Birthday of the Infanta and Other Tales.* Gr. 4–6.

Five abridged fairy tales: "The Happy Prince," "The Selfish Giant," "The Nightingale and the Rose," "The Young King," and the title story. (BL 79:782; Ch&Bks:273; CCBB 36:139)

Illus. by Beni Montresor, Atheneum, 1982, 73 pp., o.p.

C [R] WILDE, Oscar (pseud. of Fingal O'Flahertie Wills). *The Happy Prince.* Gr. 3–6. (Orig. British pub. in *The Happy Prince and Other Stories,* 1888.)

A bejeweled statue of a prince, unhappy at the misery of the people around him, persuades a swallow to carry his riches to the needy. (BL 78:444; Bookshelf 1932 p. 24; HB 41:630; KR 45:1320; LJ 91:430; Mahony 1:37; SLJ Jan 1978 p. 92, Mar 1982 p. 153; TLS 1981 p. 343)

Illus. by Kaj Beckman, Methuen, 1977, o.p.; illus. by Jean Claverie, Oxford, 1981, 40 pp.; Penguin, 1985, pap.

C [R] WILDE, Oscar (pseud. of Fingal O'Flahertie Wills). *The Happy Prince and Other Stories.* Gr. 4–6. (Orig. British pub. 1888.)

A collection of magical tales about kings, queens, witches, mermaids, dwarfs, and sorcerers, including "The Happy Prince" and "The Selfish Giant." (CC:555; Ch&Bks:273; KR 36:826; TLS 1977 p. 352)

Illus. by Peggy Fortnum, Dent, dist. by Biblio, 1977 (repr. of 1968 ed.), 154 pp.

YA [R] WILDE, Oscar (pseud. of Fingal O'Flahertie Wills). *The Picture of Dorian Gray.* Gr. 10 up. (Orig. British pub. 1891, orig. U.S. pub. in an unauthorized ed. 1890.)

Granted eternal youth, Dorian Gray lives a wild, dissipated life while his portrait grows old and haggard. (BL 28:113; Kies:82; Kliatt 16 (Spring 1982):18; SHC:646; TLS 1974 p. 811)

Putnam 1909, 1916, o.p.; Modern Library, 1926, 1954, 1987; Dutton, 1930, o.p.; Dell/Laurel Leaf, 1956, pap.; NAL, 1962, pap.; Harper, 1965, o.p.; Oxford, 1974, 1981, pap.; Biblio, 1976, pap.; Penguin, 1986, pap.

C [R] WILDE, Oscar (pseud. of Fingal O'Flahertie Wills). *The Selfish Giant.* Gr. 1–4. (Orig. British pub. in *The Happy Prince and Other Stories,* 1888.)

A giant has a change of heart, allows children to play in his garden, and assures himself a place in heaven. (BL 75:551, 80:1631; CC:545; CCBB 8:56, 37:196; Ch&Bks:273; HB 60:463; KR 46:1242; LJ 93:2117; SLJ Jan 1979 p. 49, Jan 1980 p. 63, Sept 1984 p. 122, Apr 1987 p. 91; Suth 3:444; TLS 1967 p. 1137)

Illus. by Gertrude Reiner and Walter Reiner, Harvey, 1967, o.p.; illus. by Michael Foreman and Freire Wright, Methuen, 1978; illus. by Lisbeth Zwerger, Picture Book, 1984, o.p.; illus. by Dom Mansell, Prentice-Hall, 1986, 32 pp., pap.

C WILDE, Oscar (pseud. of Fingal O'Flahertie Wills). *The Star Child: A Fairy Tale.* Gr. 2–4. (Orig. British pub. 1891, U.S. 1906 in *A House of Pomegranates.*)

A selfish orphaned boy, searching for his mother, learns compassion and self-sacrifice before he learns his true identity. (BL 76:670; CCBB 33:123; SLJ Jan 1980 p. 63)

Adapt. by Jennifer Westwood, illus. by Fiona French, Four Winds, 1979, 30 pp., o.p.

C WILKINS, Mary E(leanor) (pseud. of Mary Eleanor Wilkins Freeman). *Princess Rosetta and the Popcorn Man.* Gr. 2–4. (Orig. pub. in *The Pot of Gold,* 1892, 1970.)

After the infant Princess of Romalia disappears during the annual bee festival, a wandering popcorn man finds her in a neighboring kingdom. (KR 39:94; LJ 97:1174)

Adapt. by Ellin Greene, illus. by Trina Schart Hyman, Lothrop, 1971, 40 pp., o.p.

C [R] WILKINS, Mary E(leanor) (pseud. of Mary Eleanor Wilkins Freeman). *The Pumpkin Giant.* Gr. 2–4. (Orig. pub. in *The Pot of Gold,* 1892, 1970).

A brave father kills the dreadful pumpkin-headed giant so that his plump son can marry the king's plump daughter, and they all feast on pumpkin pie. (BL 67:192; CCBB 24:68; HB 46:607; KR 38:870)

Retold by Ellin Greene, illus. by Trina Schart Hyman, Lothrop, 1970, 40 pp., o.p.

C WILLARD, Nancy. *The Marzipan Moon.* Gr. 4–5.

A hungry parish priest wishes for a marzipan moon to appear in his old crock every morning. When his wish is granted, an officious bishop steps in and tries to take charge of this miracle. (BL 77:1302; HB 57:418; KR 49:428; SLJ Aug 1981 p. 72)

Illus. by Marcia Sewall, Harcourt, 1981, hb and pap., 48 pp.

WILLARD, Nancy. *Sailing to Cythera, and Other Anatole Stories.* See Section 5C, Travel to Other Worlds.

YA [R] WILLARD, Nancy. *Things Invisible to See.* Gr. 10 up.

Struck on the head and paralyzed by a baseball hit by Ben, a young neighborhood baseball star, a girl named Ruth falls in love with him and saves his life. (BL 81:484, 82:753; Kies:82; Kliatt 20 [Spring 1986]:26; KR 52:1020; LJ 109:2301, Jan 1986 p. 50; SLJ May 1985 p. 115, Apr 1986 p. 31; VOYA 8:190)

Knopf, 1985, 263 pp.; Bantam, 1985, pap., o.p.

C/YA WILLETT, John (William Mills). *The Singer in the Stone.* Gr. 5–7.

Angelina is the only one who cares enough to help Rubythroat, the last of the Dreamers, bring back storytelling, song, and dance into the world of the Plain People. (BL 77:1342, 1348; CCBB 35:19; KR 49:636; SLJ Sept 1981 p. 132)

Houghton, 1981, 86 pp., o.p.

C WILLIAMS, Anne. *Secret of the Round Tower.* Gr. 4–6.

Melisande and Galpin must keep their discovery of a pure white unicorn secret from the king. (HB 45:47; KR 36:820; LJ 94:880)

Illus. by J. C. Kocsis, Random, 1968, 87 pp., o.p.

C WILLIAMS, Jay. *Petronella.* Gr. 2–4.

On her way to seek her fortune, Princess Petronella rescues an enchanted prince. This story has been republished in *The Practical Princess and Other Liberating Fairy Tales* (1978). (BL 70:176; KR 41:454; LJ 98:2646)

Illus. by Friso Henstra, Parents, 1973, 33 pp., o.p.

C WILLIAMS, Jay. *The Practical Princess.* Gr. 2–4.

The fairy gift of common sense helps a princess defeat a dragon and find her own prince. This story has been republished in *The Practical Princess and*

Other Liberating Fairy Tales (1978). (BL 65:1129; CCBB 23:68; KR 37:1774, 2073, and 4583)
Illus. by Friso Henstra, Parents, 1969, 40 pp., o.p.

C [R] WILLIAMS, Jay. *The Practical Princess and Other Liberating Fairy Tales.* Gr. 3–5.
Six lively tales originally published separately: "The Practical Princess," "Stupid Marco," "The Silver Whistle," "Forgetful Fred," "Petronella," and "Philbert the Fearful." (BL 75:937; CCBB 32:166; Ch&Bks:273; KR 47:7; SLJ Sept 1979 p. 124)
Illus. by Rick Schreiter, Parents, 1978, 99 pp., o.p.

C WILLIAMS, Kit. *Masquerade.* Gr. 4–6. (Orig. British pub. 1979.)
The moon, in love with the sun, gives him the gift of a jeweled hare. This book contains clues that touched off a three-year real-life treasure hunt in England. (BL 77:6; CCBB 34:103; SLJ Nov 1980 p. 80)
Illus. by the author, Schocken, 1980; Workman, 1983, pap., 48 pp.

YA WILLIAMS, Tad. *Tailchaser's Song.* Gr. 10 up.
The quest saga of a young ginger cat, Fritti Tailchaser, who is captured and enslaved by an evil cat-god while on a journey to find his lost mate. (BL 82:317, 332; KR 53:980; LJ Nov 15, 1985 p. 112; SLJ Nov 1985 p. 106)
NAL/DAW, 1985, 320 pp.

WILLIAMS, Ursula Moray. *Adventures of a Little Wooden Horse.* See Chapter 9, Toy Fantasy.

C/YA WILSON, Willie. *Up Mountain One Time.* Gr. 4–7.
A young shantytown-dwelling mongoose named Viggo decides to search for a better life in the bush country that his late mother longingly described to him. (BL 84:154, 1442; CCBB 41:40; KR 55:1076; SLJ Sept 1987 p. 184)
Illus. by Karen Bertrand, Orchard/Watts, 1987, 133 pp.

C/YA WOLITZER, Meg. *The Dream Book.* Gr. 5–7.
Eleven-year-olds Claudia Lemmon and Mindy (Danger) Roth attempt to share each other's dreams in order to find Claudia's missing father. (CCBB 40:59; JHC 1987 Suppl. p. 81; KR 54:1018; SLJ Nov 1986 p. 94; VOYA 9:224)
Greenwillow, 1986, 148 pp.

WRIGHTSON, (Alice) Patricia (Furlonger). *Moon Dark.* See Section 2A, Beast Tales.

YEP, Laurence (Michael). *Dragon of the Lost Sea.* See Section 5A, Alternate Worlds or Histories.

YOLEN (Stemple), Jane H(yatt). *The Acorn Quest.* See Section 2B, Talking Animal Fantasy.

C YOLEN (Stemple), Jane H(yatt). *The Bird of Time.* Gr. 2–4.
Pieter uses the magic of the Bird of Time to rescue a captive princess from a giant. (BL 68:509; CCBB 25:83; LJ 97:770)
Illus. by Mercer Mayer, Crowell, 1971, 32 pp., o.p.

C YOLEN (Stemple), Jane H(yatt). *The Boy Who Had Wings.* Gr. K–4.
Aetos uses his forbidden wings to rescue his father from a mountain blizzard. (BL 71:296; HB 50:687; LJ 99:3270)
Illus. by Helga Aichinger, Crowell, 1974, 25 pp., o.p.

YOLEN (Stemple), Jane H(yatt). *Dragonfield and Other Stories*. See Chapter 3, Fantasy Collections.

C [R] YOLEN (Stemple), Jane H(yatt). *The Girl Who Cried Flowers and Other Tales*. Gr. 4–6.
Five tales, including one about a girl who cries flowers instead of tears. (BL 71:48, 768; CCBB 28:88; Ch&Bks:273; KR 42:741; LJ 99:2744; SLJ Dec 1978 p. 33)
Illus. by David Palladini, Crowell, 1974; Harper, 1987, pap.

C [R] YOLEN (Stemple), Jane H(yatt). *The Girl Who Loved the Wind*. Gr. 1–4.
A wealthy merchant tries to protect his beautiful daughter from unhappiness by keeping her a prisoner in their palace, but a whispering wind makes the girl discontented with her life. (BL 69:575; CCBB 26:100; HB 48:585; KR 40:1353; LJ 98:998; TLS 1973 p. 1431)
Illus. by Ed Young, Crowell, 1972; Harper, 1987, pap., 31 pp.

YOLEN (Stemple), Jane H(yatt). *Greyling: A Picture Story from the Islands of Shetland*. See Section 5B, Myth Fantasy.

C YOLEN (Stemple), Jane H(yatt). *The Hundredth Dove and Other Tales*. Gr. 2–5.
Seven stories, including "The Lady and the Merman," "The White Seal Maid," and "The Wind Cap." (BL 74:817; CCBB 31:168; KR 45:1198; SLJ Jan 1978 p. 83)
Illus. by David Palladini, Harper, 1977, o.p.; Schocken, 1980, pap., 80 pp.

C/YA YOLEN (Stemple), Jane H(yatt). *The Magic Three of Solatia*. Gr. 5–7.
[R] A wisewoman named Sianna and her son, Lann, use three magic buttons to keep out of danger's way and to rescue an enchanted bird-girl from a wizard-king. (BL 71:574; CCBB 28:172; Ch&Bks:273; KR 42:1207; SLJ Jan 1975 p. 51; Suth 2:490; Tymn:180)
Illus. by Julia Noonan, Crowell, 1974, 172 pp.

YOLEN (Stemple), Jane H(yatt). *Merlin's Booke*. See Section 5B, Myth Fantasy.

C YOLEN (Stemple), Jane H(yatt). *The Moon Ribbon and Other Tales*. Gr. 3–5.
Six tales, including "The Moon Child," "Somewhen," "Rosechild," and "Honey-Stick Boy." (BL 73:328; KR 44:792; SLJ Feb 1977 p. 70)
Illus. by David Palladini, Crowell, 1976, 54 pp., o.p.

C [R] YOLEN (Stemple), Jane H(yatt). *The Seventh Mandarin*. Gr. 2–4.
The youngest mandarin must recover the lost kite containing the king's soul, or be put to death. (BL 67:343; CCBB 24:84; KR 38:1142; LJ 96:1112; Suth:432; TLS 1971 p. 388)
Illus. by Ed Young, Seabury, 1970, 36 pp., o.p.

YOLEN (Stemple), Jane H(yatt). *Sleeping Ugly*. See Chapter 6, Humorous Fantasy.

C/YA YOUNG, Ella. *The Unicorn with Silver Shoes*. Gr. 5–7.
[R] Ballor's Son and Flame of Joy escape to the Land of the Ever Young. (BL 29:80; Bookshelf 1933 p. 6; CCBB 11:104; HB 34:124; LJ 58:43; Mahony 3:213; TLS 1932 p. 893)
Illus. by Robert Lawson, McKay, 1932, 213 pp., o.p.

C   ZARING, Jane T(homas). *The Return of the Dragon*. Gr. 3–6.
Caradoc, the last Welsh dragon, decides to go home to Wales, in spite of the fact that the people do not want him to return. (HB 57:541; SLJ Feb 1982 p. 84)
Illus. by Polly Broman, Houghton, 1981, 146 pp.

C [R]   ZEMACH, Harve(y Fischtrom). *The Tricks of Master Dabble*. Gr. 1–3.
Playing upon the vanity of the castle inhabitants, Master Dabble tricks them into believing he is a painter and that his mirror is a masterpiece. (BL 62:164; HB 41:166; KR 33:3; LJ 90:1546)
Illus. by Margot Zemach, Holt, 1965, 32 pp., o.p.

C/YA   ZIMNIK, Reiner. *The Bear and the People*. Gr. 4–7. (Orig. German pub.
[R]   1956.)
Bearman and his talking bear, Brown One, entertain throughout the countryside, until jealous villagers attack them. (BL 68:670; KR 39:436; LJ 96:2367, 4160; TLS 1972 p. 1328)
Tr. by Nina Ignatowicz, illus. by the author, Harper, 1971, 78 pp., o.p.

ZINDEL, Paul. *Let Me Hear You Whisper: A Play*. See Section 2A, Beast Tales.

2
Animal Fantasy

There is sometimes only a fine line between realistic and fantastic portrayal of animals in literature. Thus, any tales in which the animal characters think or talk in a humanlike manner have been included in this list. The books in this chapter have been divided into two sections, Beast Tales and Talking Animal Fantasy. The latter tend to be lighter in tone, featuring dressed-up, anthropomorphic animals, and are often written for younger children. Beast Tales are more serious, often didactic stories of "realistic" animals trying to escape human evils, such as pollution or laboratory experimentation. This division is modeled on that used in Sheila Egoff's *Thursday's Child* (ALA, 1981).

A. BEAST TALES

ADAMS, Hazard. *The Truth About Dragons*. See Chapter 1, Allegorical Fantasy and Literary Fairy Tales.

YA [R] ADAMS, Richard (George). *The Plague Dogs*. Gr. 10 up.
After escaping from an animal research lab, two dogs run free in England's Lake District. They are befriended by a fox, but are hunted by humans as possible carriers of bubonic plague. (BL 74:975; Kliatt 13 [Spring 1979]:4; KR 46:54, 115; LJ 103:773; SLJ Sept 1978 p. 168)
Knopf, 1978, 390 pp., o.p.; Fawcett, 1983, pap.

ADAMS, Richard (George). *Shardik*. See Chapter 1, Allegorical Fantasy and Literary Fairy Tales.

ADAMS, Richard (George). *Watership Down*. See Chapter 1, Allegorical Fantasy and Literary Fairy Tales.

YA [R] ANDREWS, Allen. *The Pig Plantagenet*. Gr. 10 up. (Adapted from *Le Roman de Fulbert* by Michel Héloin.)
A domesticated thirteenth-century French pig becomes embroiled in a plot to save a family of wild boars from a massacre by the lord of the chateau. The

sequel is *Castle Crespin* (1984). (BL 77:286, 287; KR 48:1406; LJ 105:2513; TLS 1980 p. 1329; VOYA 4 [June 1981]:27)
Illus. by Michael Foreman, Viking, 1980, o.p.; Tor., 1984, pap., 200 pp.

C [R] ARKIN, Alan (Wolf). *The Lemming Condition.* Gr. 4–5.
Bubber's family and friends undertake their unquestioning journey toward the sea and death. In order to live, Bubber must fight not only the other lemmings, but his own instincts as well. The sequel is *The Clearing* (1986). (BL 72:1182; CC:428; HB 52:394; KR 44:389; SLJ Apr 1976 p. 68)
Illus. by Joan Sandin, Harper, 1976, 64 pp.

C/YA BAKER, Betty (Lou). *Dupper.* Gr. 5–7.
[R] Dupper is an outcast in the prairie dog world until his search for the Great Ants leads to a solution to the killer rattlesnake problem. (BL 73:140; CCBB 30:38; Ch&Bks:264; KR 44:684; SLJ Feb 1977 p. 60; Suth 2:24)
Illus. by Chuck Eckart, Greenwillow/Morrow, 1976, 147 pp.

YA BARRETT, Nicholas. *Fledger.* Gr. 10 up.
Goldie, a young puffin, leads his flock's fight against the deadly island rats who have destroyed their breeding grounds. (KR 53:647; LJ Oct 1, 1985 p. 110; SLJ Jan 1986 p. 83; VOYA 9:37)
Macmillan, 1985, 207 pp.

BEAGLE, Peter S(oyer). *A Fine and Private Place.* See Chapter 4, Ghost Fantasy.

YA [O] BELL, Clare. *Ratha's Creature.* Gr. 7–12.
Ratha, a yearling from a clan of intelligent cats living in an alternate prehistoric time, is exiled for learning to handle fire, and then caught up in a war between her clan and the Un-Named, a band of hunter cats. The sequel is *Clan Ground* (1984, 1987). (BL 79:956, 962; CCBB 36:202; JHC:347; SHC:579; SLJ Sept 1983 p. 130; VOYA 6:196)
Atheneum, 1983, 248 pp.; Dell/Laurel Leaf, 1987, pap.

YA [R] BELL, Clare. *Tomorrow's Sphinx.* Gr. 7–12.
Kichebo, a black and gold cheetah living in a post-ecological-disaster future time, is able to link minds with an ancient Egyptian cheetah who teaches her to accept a young human companion. (BL 83:344, 346, 83:776; CCBB 40:42; JHC 1987 Suppl. p. 59; KR 54:1372; SLJ Nov 1986 p. 96)
Atheneum, 1986, 312 pp.

C/YA BENCHLEY, Nathaniel (Goddard). *Kilroy and the Gull.* Gr. 5–7.
[R] Kilroy the killer whale and a seagull friend escape from an aquarium after frustrating attempts to communicate with humans, and search the sea for Kilroy's family. (BL 73:1086; CCBB 30:138; Ch&Bks:264; HB 53:309; KR 45:3; SLJ Oct 1977 p. 109; Suth 2:41)
Illus. by John Schoenherr, Harper, 1977, 118 pp., 1978, pap.

C [R] BODECKER, N(iels) M(ogens). *The Mushroom Center Disaster.* Gr. 2–4.
When the insect inhabitants of Mushroom Center find their peaceful community threatened by littering humans, William Beetle creates a "Garbage Emergency Plan" to recycle the debris. (BL 70:1054; CC:435; CCBB 28:24; KR 42:421; LJ 99:1464)
Illus. by Erik Blegvad, Atheneum, 1974, 48 pp., 1979, pap.

C CLIFFORD, Sandy. *The Roquefort Gang.* Gr. 2–4.
Nicole mouse joins forces with the Roquefort Gang to rescue hundreds of mice destined for laboratory experiments. (BL 77:1251; CCBB 34:189; KR 49:283; SLJ Apr 1981 p. 122)
Illus. by the author, Parnassus, dist. by Houghton, 1981, 79 pp.

YA CLINE, Linda. *The Miracle Season.* Gr. 10 up.
Crow discovers that mercury poisoning is the cause of his friends' mysterious deaths. (Kliatt 11 [Fall 1977]:4; KR 44:748; LJ 101:2084; SLJ Dec 1976 p. 74)
Berkley, 1976, 182 pp., o.p.

COATSWORTH, Elizabeth (Jane). *Pure Magic.* See Chapter 1, Allegorical Fantasy and Literary Fairy Tales.

C/YA CONLY, Jane Leslie. *Racso and the Rats of NIMH.* Gr. 5–8.
[R] Two young rodents, Timothy Frisby mouse and Racso rat, meet on their way to begin their education with the rats of NIMH, and quickly become involved in the rats' plan to destroy the dam that threatens their valley. This is the sequel to Robert C. O'Brien's *Mrs. Frisby and the Rats of NIHM* (1971) (see this section). Jane Conly is Robert C. O'Brien's daughter. (BL 82:1458, 83:794 84:1441; CC 1987 Suppl. p. 56; CCBB 39:182; HB 62:588; SLJ Apr 1986 p. 85; TLS 1986 p. 1042; VOYA 9:86, 10:23)
Illus. by Leonard Lubin, Harper, 1986, 278 pp.

YA COOK, Glen. *Doomstalker* (Darkwar trilogy, vol. 1). Gr. 10 up.
Marika, a young female member of an intelligent, caninelike race, survives the massacre of her tribe by nomads, only to be captured by the Silth Witches who want to use her psychic powers for their own battles with the nomads. The sequels are *Warlock* (1985) and *Ceremony* (1986). (BL 82:31, 52; VOYA 8:393)
Warner/Popular Library, 1985, pap., 272 pp.

C/YA CORBETT, W(illiam) J(esse). *The Song of Pentecost.* Gr. 5–9. (Orig. Brit-
[R] ish pub. 1982.)
A clan of harvest mice and their leader, Pentecost, leave their polluted home in search of utopia and truth. British Whitbread Award, 1982. The sequel is *Pentecost and the Chosen One* (1987). (BL 79:1463 84:1441; CC:456; CCBB 37:3; HB 59:450; JHC:360; SLJ Aug 1983 p. 63; TLS 1982 p. 1302)
Illus. by Martin Ursell, Dutton, 1983, 216 pp.; Dell, 1985, pap.

C [R] DANA, Barbara. *Zucchini.* Gr. 3–5.
Zucchini, a runaway ferret from the Bronx Zoo, is caught by the ASPCA. There, he meets Billy, a boy who loves him, and the ferret has to choose between escape and a real home. (BL 79:443; CC:458; CCBB 36:64; KR 50:1105; SLJ Oct 1982 p. 150)
Illus. by Eileen Christelow, Harper, 1982, o.p.; Bantam, 1984, pap. 160 pp.

YA DANN, Colin (Michael). *The Animals of Farthing Wood.* Gr. 7–10.
Led by Fox and Toad, the animal inhabitants of Farthing Wood unite and flee to a safer life in a nature preserve. (BL 77:110; LJ 105:2104)
Elsevier/Nelson, 1980, 255 pp., o.p.

C/YA DONOVAN, John. *Family: A Novel.* Gr. 6–9.
[R] Four apes escape from a scientific laboratory only to find that survival in the

wild is impossible for them. (BL 72:112, 80:95; CCBB 29:173; Ch&Bks:266; HB 52:404; KR 44:405; SLJ Sept 1976 p. 131; Suth 2:127)
Harper, 1976, 1986, 128 pp.

C EDMONDS, Walter D(umaux). *Beaver Valley*. Gr. 4–6
A young deermouse watches helplessly as the dams built by an ambitious beaver family destroy or displace the other wild creatures of the valley. (BL 67:797; HB 47:286; KR 39:432; LJ 96:2363)
Illus. by Leslie Morrill, Little, 1971, 70 pp., o.p.

FORD, Richard. *Quest for the Faradawn*. See Chapter 1, Allegorical Fantasy and Literary Fairy Tales.

YA [R] FREDDI, Cris. *Pork, and Other Stories*. Gr. 10 up.
A collection of connected animal tales set in a forest ruled by a magical stag. (BL 78:28, 36; KR 49:819; LJ 106:2048; SLJ Dec 1981 p. 88)
Knopf, dist. by Random, 1981, o.p.; Dutton, 1983, pap., 224 pp.

C GOODWIN, Harold Leland. *Magic Number*. Gr. 4–6.
In a bid for equal rights, the garden-dwelling animals declare war on the house pets at a veterinarian's home. (BL 66:206; CCBB 23:8; KR 37:559; LJ 95:3603)
Illus. by the author, Bradbury, 1969, 97 pp., o.p.

YA HANCOCK, Neil (Anderson). *Dragon Winter*. Gr. 8–12.
A mysterious voice unites a group of otters, beavers, squirrels, badgers, a muskrat, and a mole, all of whom have been driven from their homes. The voice convinces them to go on a magic quest to find a great silver bear. (Kliatt 12 [Spring 1978]:7; VOYA 7: 56)
Popular Library, 1978, 351 pp., o.p.; Warner, 1984, pap., o.p.

HAWDON, Robin. *A Rustle in the Grass*. See Chapter 1, Allegorical Fantasy and Literary Fairy Tales.

HOBAN, Russell C(onwell). *The Mouse and His Child*. See Chapter 1, Allegorical Fantasy and Literary Fairy Tales.

HORWOOD, William. *Duncton Wood*. See Chapter 1, Allegorical Fantasy and Literary Fairy Tales.

YA JEFFRIES, (John) Richard. *Wood Magic*. Gr. 7 up. (Orig. British pub. 1881.)
The animal inhabitants of an English meadow battle over dwelling rights, dominance, and survival, and are observed by a little boy named Bevis. The sequel is *Bevis: The Story of a Boy* (orig. British pub. 1882, U.S. Puffin, 1974). (BL 71:792; LJ 100:409; SLJ Apr 1975 p. 74)
Introduction by Richard Adams, Third, 1974, 271 pp., o.p.

JONES, Diana Wynne. *Dogsbody*. See Section 5C, Travel to Other Worlds.

C [R] KÄSTNER, Erich. *The Animal's Conference*. Gr. 4–6. (Orig. Swiss pub. 1949.)
The animals of the world unite and force the humans to make peace. (BL 49:380; CCBB 7:5; HB 29:271; KR 21:333)
Tr. by Zita de Schauensee, illus. by Walter Trier, McKay, 1953, 62 pp., o.p.

KENEALLY, Thomas (Michael). *Ned Kelly and the City of the Bees.* See Section 5C, Travel to Other Worlds.

LAMPMAN, Evelyn Sibley. *The City under the Back Steps.* See Section 5C, Travel to Other Worlds.

C/YA LANDSMAN, Sandy. *Castaways on Chimp Island.* Gr. 6–8.
Exiled to an island with other "unteachable" laboratory chimps, Danny and three friends hatch a plan for getting home. (BL 82:1614; CCBB 39:171; HB 62:597; JHC 1987 Suppl. p. 71; KR 54:869; SLJ Aug 1986 p. 94; VOYA 9:220)
Atheneum, 1986, 202 pp., o.p.; Archway, 1987, pap.

LAWSON, John S(hults). *You Better Come Home with Me.* See Chapter 1, Allegorical Fantasy and Literary Fairy Tales.

C LE GUIN, Ursula K(roeber). *Lesse Webster.* Gr. 1–4.
When Lesse Webster's palace is turned into a museum, her artistic spider webs are put on public display. (CCBB 34:14; KR 47:998; SLJ Nov 1979 p. 66)
Illus. by James Brunsman, Atheneum, 1979, 26 pp., o.p.

C/YA LIVELY, Penelope (Margaret Low). *The Voyage of Q V 66.* Gr. 6–8.
[R]   (Orig. British pub. 1978.)
In a future time when animals are the only survivors of a great flood, six creatures travel to London in hope of discovering Stanley's true identity. (BL 75:1627; CCBB 32:195; Ch&Bks:242; HB 55:415; KR 47:637; SLJ Dec 1979 p. 152; Suth 3:269)
Illus. by Harold Jones, Dutton, 1979, 172 pp., o.p.

MACAULAY, David. *BAAA.* See Chapter 1, Allegorical Fantasy and Literary Fairy Tales.

YA [R] *Magicats!* Ed. by Jack Dann and Gardner Dozois. Gr. 10 up.
Eighteen fantasy and science fiction tales involving cats, whose authors include Ursula K. Le Guin, Pamela Sargent, and Gene Wolfe. (BL 80:1599, 1609; Kliatt 18 [Fall 1984]:25; SLJ Sept 1984 p. 140; VOYA 7:267)
Berkley/Ace, 1984, pap., 270 pp., o.p.

C MERRILL, Jean (Fairbanks). *The Black Sheep.* Gr. 4–6.
A black sheep born into a community of white ones refuses to conform: Instead of knitting sweaters, he wears his own shaggy coat and spends his time gardening. (CCBB 23:131; LJ 95:1641, 1912, 3603; Suth:279)
Illus. by Ronni Solbert, Pantheon, 1969, 73 pp.

MOON, Sheila (Elizabeth). *Knee-Deep in Thunder.* See Section 5C, Travel to Other Worlds.

NEWMAN, Robert (Howard). *The Shattered Stone.* See Section 5A, Alternate Worlds or Histories.

NORTON, Andre. *Fur Magic.* See Chapter 7, Magic Adventure Fantasy.

C/YA O'BRIEN, Robert C. (pseud. of Robert Leslie Conly). *Mrs. Frisby and*
[O]   *the Rats of NIMH.* Gr. 4–7.
Mrs. Frisby, a field mouse with a problem, is befriended by a group of superintelligent laboratory rats and manages to save their lives. Newbery Medal Award winner, 1972. O'Brien's daughter, Jane Leslie Conly, has written a sequel entitled *Racso and the Rats of NIMH* (Harper, 1986) [see this

section]. (BL 67:955, 68:670, 80:96; CC:513; CCBB 25:29; Ch&Bks:248; HB 47:385; LJ 96:4159, 4186; Suth:298; TLS 1972 p. 1317)
Illus. by Zena Bernstein, Atheneum, 1971; Scholastic, 1982 (entitled *The Secret of NIMH*), pap.; Aladdin, 1975, pap., 240 pp.

ORWELL, George. *Animal Farm.* See Chapter 1, Allegorical Fantasy and Literary Fairy Tales.

C OSBORNE, Maurice. *Ondine: The Story of a Bird Who Was Different.* Gr. 4–6.
Ondine, a nonconformist sandpiper, is befriended by a seagull, an owl, and a hermit. (BL 56:690; Eakin:251; HB 36:290; LJ 85:2683)
Illus. by Evaline Ness, Houghton, 1960, 75 pp., o.p.

C/YA ROACH, Marilynne K(athleen). *Presto: Or, the Adventures of a Turnspit Dog.* Gr. 5–7.
Rescued by a traveling puppeteer, a dog named Presto finds adventure in the streets of eighteenth-century London. (BL 76:560; CCBB 33:117; HB 56:56; Suth 3:361)
Illus. by the author, Houghton, 1979, 148 pp., o.p.

C [R] ROCCA, Guido. *Gaetano the Pheasant: A Hunting Fable.* Gr. 3–5. (Orig. pub. 1961.)
Gaetano and his mate decide to escape from the threat of hunters' guns. (CCBB 20:115; HB 42:431; KR 34:418; LJ 91:3252; Suth:335)
Illus. by Giulio Cingoli and Giancarlo Carloni, Harper, 1966, 60 pp., o.p.

SMITH, Agnes. *An Edge of the Forest.* See Chapter 1, Allegorical Fantasy and Literary Fairy Tales.

C VAN DE WETERING, Janwillem. *Hugh Pine.* Gr. 2–4.
Hugh Porcupine decides to walk upright and wears a hat and coat in order to cross roads safely. The sequel is *Hugh Pine and the Good Place* (1986). (BL 77:122; CCBB 34:102; KR 48:1518; SLJ Mar 1981 p. 152)
Illus. by Lynn Munsinger, Houghton, 1980, 83 pp.

WAECHTER, Friedrich, and EILERT, Bernd. *The Crown Snatchers.* See Chapter 1, Allegorical Fantasy and Literary Fairy Tales.

WANGERIN, Walter, Jr. *The Book of the Dun Cow.* See Chapter 1, Allegorical Fantasy and Literary Fairy Tales.

C WEIR, Rosemary (Green). *Pyewacket.* Gr. 3–5.
Pyewacket leads the neighborhood cats in revolt against their owners. (KR 35:1210; LJ 93:297; TLS 1967 p. 1153)
Illus. by Charles Pickard, Abelard-Schuman, 1967, 123 pp., o.p.

WILLIAMS, Tad. *Tailchaser's Song.* See Chapter 1, Allegorical Fantasy and Literary Fairy Tales.

C/YA WRIGHTSON, (Alice) Patricia (Furlonger). *Moon Dark.* Gr. 5–8. (Orig.
[R] Australian pub. 1987.)
One dark night, a dog named Blue and the other animal inhabitants of a remote section of Australia, call on Keeting, an ancient moon spirit, to save their territory from encroaching human beings who have upset the natural balance. (CCBB 41:194; KR 56:462; SLJ Apr 1988 p. 106; VOYA 11:92)
Illus. by Noela Young, McElderry/Macmillan, 1988, 163 pp.

ZIMNIK, Reiner. *The Bear and the People.* See Chapter 1, Allegorical Fantasy and Literary Fairy Tales.

YA ZINDEL, Paul. *Let Me Hear You Whisper: A Play.* Gr. 7 up.
A short but moving play about a laboratory cleaning woman who discovers that the experimental subject, a dolphin, can talk, and tries to save him from being killed. (CCBB 27:188; KR 42:124; LJ 99:1234)
Illus. by Stephen Gammell, Harper, 1974, 44 pp., o.p.

B. TALKING ANIMAL FANTASY

AIKEN, Joan (Delano). *The Kingdom and the Cave.* See Section 5A, Alternate Worlds or Histories.

AIKEN, Joan (Delano). *A Necklace of Raindrops and Other Stories.* See Chapter 3, Fantasy Collections.

AINSWORTH (Gilbert), Ruth (Gallard). *The Bear Who Liked Hugging People and Other Stories.* See Chapter 3, Fantasy Collections.

C [R] ALEXANDER, Lloyd (Chudley). *The Cat Who Wished to Be a Man.* Gr. 4–6.
Lionel nags the wizard Stephanus to change him from a cat into a human. Stephanus grants his wish, only to find that he cannot reverse the process. (BL 70:168; CC:425; CCBB 27:21; Ch&Bks:263; HB 49:463; KR 41:639; LJ 98:2647; Suth 2:8).
Dutton, 1973, 107 pp., o.p.

C [R] ALEXANDER, Lloyd (Chudley). *The Town Cats, and Other Tales.* Gr. 4–6.
Eight fairy tales about wise and heroic cats. (BL 74:472; CC:550; CCBB 31:89; Ch&Bks:263; HB 54:42; KR 45:1096; SLJ Nov 1977 p. 52; Suth 2:9)
Illus. by Laszlo Kubinyi, Dutton, 1977, 144 pp.; Dell, 1981, pap.

C ALLAN, Ted. *Willie the Squowse.* Gr. 3–5. (Orig. British pub. 1977.)
Willie, the son of a mouse and a squirrel, gives a poor family the money their wealthy neighbors have stored in their walls. (CCBB 32:57; Ch&Bks:263; SLJ Nov 1978 p. 39; TLS 1977 p. 1414)
Illus. by Quentin Blake, Hastings, 1978, 57 pp.

AMADO, Jorge. *The Swallow and the Tom Cat: A Grown-Up Love Story.* See Chapter 1, Allegorical Fantasy and Literary Fairy Tales.

ANDERSEN, Hans Christian. *Thumbelina.* See Chapter 1, Allegorical Fantasy and Literary Fairy Tales.

ANDERSEN, Hans Christian. *The Ugly Duckling.* See Chapter 1, Allegorical Fantasy and Literary Fairy Tales.

C ANDERSON, Mary. *F*T*C* Superstar.* Gr. 4–6.
Freddie the cat dreams of becoming an actor, but when Emma, his pigeon friend, helps him attain his dream, stardom goes to his head. The sequel is *F*T*C* & Company* (1979). (BL 73:140; KR 44:320; SLJ Apr 1976 p. 68)
Illus. by Gail Owens, Atheneum, 1976, 156 pp., o.p.

C ANNETT (Pipitone Scott), Cora. *How the Witch Got Alf.* Gr. 3–5.
Alf, the old folks' donkey, feels unloved and decides to take drastic measures. He runs away and his adventures begin. (BL 71:864; CCBB 29:1; KR 43:70; SLJ Mar 1975 p. 84; Suth 2:16)
Illus. by Steven Kellogg, Watts, 1975, 47 pp., o.p.

C ANNETT (Pipitone Scott), Cora. *When the Porcupine Moved In.* Gr. 1–4.
Porcupine disrupts Rabbit's comfortable life by moving into Rabbit's house and bringing all of his relatives with him. (BL 68:626; CCBB 25:70; LJ 97:1593)
Illus. by Peter Parnall, Watts, 1971, 40 pp., o.p.

C ANNIXTER, Paul (pseud. of Howard Allison Sturtzel). *The Cat That Clumped.* Gr. 1–4.
Unhappy as a cat, Herbert decides to become a horse. (CCBB 19:157; KR 34:240; LJ 91:1694)
Illus. by Brinton Turkle, Holiday, 1966, 35 pp., o.p.

C ARUNDEL, Honor. *The Amazing Mr. Prothero* Gr. 3–5. (Orig. British pub. 1968.)
Scamp, a dog who prefers to be called Mr. Prothero, rescues Julia's baby brother from a runaway carriage. (BL 69:200; CCBB 26:101; KR 40:30; LJ 97:2928)
Illus. by Jane Paton, Nelson, 1972, 80 pp., o.p.

C ASCH, Frank. *Pearl's Promise.* Gr. 3–5.
Pearl mouse is horrified when her little brother, Tony, is given to the Pet Shop's new python, and she vows to rescue him. The sequel is *Pearl's Pirates* (1987). (BL 81:60; CCBB 37:160; HB 60:193; SLJ Apr 1984 p. 111)
Illus. by the author, Delacorte, dist. by Doubleday, 1984, 160 pp., o.p.; Dell, 1987, pap., 160 pp.

C [R] ATTWOOD, Frederic. *Vavache, the Cow Who Painted Pictures.* Gr. 3–5.
A young American boy visiting Normandy meets Vavache, a talking cow who paints with her tail. (BL 46:291; CCBB 3:39; HB 26:193; LJ 75:632, 1054)
Illus. by Roger Duvoisin, Aladdin, 1950, 77 pp., o.p.

C AVERILL, Esther. *Captains of the City Streets: A Story of the Cat Club.* Gr. 3–4.
Two tramp cats named Sinbad and the Duke move to New York City and become involved in a club run by the local cats. This is the sequel to *The Cat Club* (1944), *School for Cats* (1947), *Jenny's First Party* (1948), *Jenny's Moonlight Adventure* (1949), *How the Brothers Joined the Cat Club* (1953), and *The Hotel Cat* (1969), and is followed by *Jenny and the Cat Club* (1973). (BL 69:809; CCBB 26:149; HB 48:47; KR 40:1354; LJ 98:1678)
Illus. by the author, Harper, 1972, 147 pp., o.p.

C AYMÉ, Marcel (André). *The Wonderful Farm.* Gr. 4–6. (Orig. pub. in France.)
Marinette and Delphine don't know how to get around their parents' strict rules until the farm animals begin to talk to the girls and give them some unusual ideas. The sequel is *The Magic Pictures: More About the Wonderful Farm* (1954). (BL 48:161; CCBB 5:35; HB 27:406; LJ 76:2009)
Tr. by Norman Denny, illus. by Maurice Sendak, Harper, 1951, 182 pp., o.p.

BABCOCK, Betty. *The Expandable Pig.* See Chapter 7, Magic Adventure Fantasy.

BACH, Richard (David). *Jonathan Livingston Seagull.* See Chapter 1, Allegorical Fantasy and Literary Fairy Tales.

BACON, Peggy. *The Ghost of Opalina, or Nine Lives.* See Chapter 4, Ghost Fantasy.

BACON, Peggy. *The Lion-Hearted Kitten and Other Stories.* See Chapter 3, Fantasy Collections.

BACON, Peggy. *Mercy and the Mouse and Other Stories.* See Chapter 3, Fantasy Collections.

C BAILEY, Carolyn Sherwin. *Finnegan II: His Nine Lives.* Gr. 4–6.
Finnegan the cat proves to have more than nine lives. (BL 50:150; HB 29:455, 64:516; LJ 78:2225)
Illus. by Kate Seredy, Viking, 1953, 95 pp., o.p.

C BAKER, Betty (Lou). *Danby and George.* Gr. 3–4.
A wood rat and a deer mouse make a home for themselves at the zoo. (BL 77:1025; CCBB 35:4; KR 49:283; SLJ Jan 1982 p. 72)
Illus. by Adrienne Lobel, Greenwillow, 1981, 64 pp., o.p.

C [R] BAKER, Elizabeth Whitemore. *Sonny-Boy Sim.* Gr. 1–4.
The woodland animals decide to turn the tables on Sonny-Boy Sim and his hound dog. (BL 45:320; CCBB 2[May 1949]:1; HB 25:285; KR 17:177; LJ 74:666)
Illus. by Susanne Suba, Rand, 1948, 31 pp., o.p.

C BAKER, Margaret. *Three for an Acorn.* Gr. 1–4.
Mrs. Squirrel's shop sells dandelion lollipops, three for an acorn. (BL 32:45; Bookshelf 1935 p. 2; HB 11:289; LJ 60:857; Mahony 3:78)
Illus. by Mary Baker, Dodd, 1935, 96 pp., o.p.

C [R] BAKER, Margaret Joyce. *Homer the Tortoise* (British title: "*Nonsense!*" *Said the Tortoise,* 1949). Gr. 4–6.
Homer the educated tortoise comes to live with the Brown family. The sequels are *Homer Goes to Stratford* (1958) and *Homer Sees the Queen* (British). (BL 46:278; CCBB 3:33; KR 18:97; LJ 75:629, 986)
Illus. by Leo Bates, McGraw-Hill, 1950, 149 pp., o.p.

BAKER, Margaret Joyce. *Porterhouse Major.* See Chapter 7, Magic Adventure Fantasy.

BAKER, Olaf. *Bengey and the Beast.* See Chapter 7, Magic Adventure Fantasy.

C BECHDOLT, Jack (pseud. of John Ernest Bechdolt). *Bandmaster's Holiday.* Gr. 2–4.
Barko the circus sea lion decides to try living in the ocean. (HB 14:159; LJ 63:284, 690)
Illus. by Decie Merwin, Oxford, 1938, 71 pp., o.p.

BEEKS, Graydon. *Hosea Globe and the Fantastical Peg-Legged Chu.* See Chapter 6, Humorous Fantasy.

C BEHN, Harry. *Roderick*. Gr. 4–6.
A thoughtful, loving crow named Roderick unexpectedly becomes the leader of his flock. (HB 37:340; LJ 86:2353)
Illus. by Mel Silverman, Harcourt, 1961, 64 pp., o.p.

C [R] BENCHLEY, Nathaniel (Goddard). *Feldman Fieldmouse: A Fable*. Gr. 3–6.
Uncle Feldman's lessons in wild mouse survival are quite a change for Fendall, compared to his pampered life as a household pet. (BL 68:55; CC:433; CCBB 25:54; HB 47:285; KR 39:500; LJ 96:2128; Suth:33)
Illus. by Hilary Knight, Harper, 1971, 96 pp.

C BERESFORD, Elizabeth. *The Wombles*. Gr. 4–6. (Orig. pub. in England.)
Wombles are furry, subterranean creatures who survive by "collecting" things from human beings. The British sequels are *MacWomble's Pipe Band; The Invisible Womble; The Snow Womble; The Wandering Wombles; The Wombles at Work; The Wombles Book; The Wombles Go Round the World; The Wombles in Danger; The Wombles Make a Clean Sweep; The Wombles of Wimbledon;* and *The Wombles to the Rescue*. (KR 37:1147; LJ 95:1192; TLS 1968 p. 1376, 1973 p. 386)
Illus. by Margaret Gordon, Meredith, 1968, 183 pp., o.p.

BERGRENGREN, Ralph Wilhelm. *David the Dreamer: His Book of Dreams*. See Section 5C, Travel to Other Worlds.

BERTELLI, Luigi. *The Prince and His Ants*. See Chapter 7, Magic Adventure Fantasy.

C BEST, (Oswald) Herbert. *Desmond's First Case*. Gr. 3–5.
A dog detective named Desmond and his boy, Gus, solve the mystery of a missing banker. The sequels are *Desmond the Dog Detective: The Case of the Lone Stranger* (1962), *Desmond and the Peppermint Ghost, The Dog Detective's Third Case* (1965), and *Desmond and Dog Friday* (1968), all o.p. (KR 29:55; LJ 86:1980).
Illus. by Ezra Jack Keats, Viking, 1961, 96 pp., o.p.

C BESTERMAN, Catherine. *The Quaint and Curious Quest of Johnny Longfoot, the Shoe King's Son*. Gr. 4–6.
Johnny Longfoot and a group of animals search for buried treasure. Newbery Medal Honor Book, 1948. The sequel is *The Extraordinary Education of Johnny Longfoot in His Search for the Magic Hat* (1949). (BL 44:116; HB 23:435; 24:36; LJ 72:1618).
Bobbs-Merrill, 1947, 147 pp., o.p.

BETHANCOURT, T(homas) Ernesto. *The Dog Days of Arthur Cane*. See Chapter 7, Magic Adventure Fantasy.

C BIANCO, Margery (Winifred) Williams. *The Good Friends*. Gr. 4–6.
The animals on Farmer Hicks's farm must care for themselves after he goes into the hospital. (BL 31:67; Bookshelf 1934–1935 p. 5; HB 10:296; LJ 60:304; Mahony 3:200)
Illus. by Grace Paull, Viking, 1934, 142 pp., o.p.

BIANCO, Margery (Winifred) Williams. *Poor Cecco; the Wonderful Story of a Wonderful Wooden Dog Who Was the Jolliest Toy in the House Until He Went Out to Explore the World*. See Chapter 9, Toy Fantasy.

BIANCO, Margery (Winifred) Williams. *The Velveteen Rabbit; or, How Toys Became Real.* See Chapter 9, Toy Fantasy.

BIEGEL, Paul. *The King of the Copper Mountains.* See Chapter 1, Allegorical Fantasy and Literary Fairy Tales.

C BLACKWOOD, Algernon (Henry). *The Adventures of Dudley and Gilderoy* (Orig. British and U.S. title: *Dudley and Gilderoy: A Nonsense*, 1929). Gr. 1–4.
An aristocratic parrot and a ginger cat travel to London in search of adventure. (BL 26:159; HB 17:99; TLS 1929 p. 1030)
Adapt. by Marion Cothren, illus. by Feodor Rojankovsky, Dutton, 1941, 32 pp., o.p.

C BLADOW, Suzanne Wilson. *The Midnight Flight of Moose, Mops and Marvin.* Gr. 1–4.
Three mice from Mrs. Santa's kitchen stow away on Santa's sleigh. (BL 72:448; CCBB 29:91; KR 43:1118; SLJ Oct 1975 p. 78)
Illus. by Joseph Mathieu, McGraw-Hill, 1975, 40 pp., o.p.

C BLAISDELL, Mary Frances. *Bunny Rabbit's Diary.* Gr. 2–4. (Orig. pub. 1915.)
Eight tales about Bunny Rabbit and his friends, as recorded by Bunny Rabbit in his maple-leaf book. (KR 28:29; LJ 85:2025; Mahony 2:162)
Illus. by Anne Jauss, Little, 1960 (rev. ed.), 92 pp., o.p.

BLUNT, Wilfrid (Jasper Walter). *Omar; a Fantasy for Animal Lovers.* See Chapter 6, Humorous Fantasy.

C [O] BOND, (Thomas) Michael. *A Bear Called Paddington.* Gr. 3–5. (Orig. British pub. 1958.)
The Brown family decides to adopt a little Peruvian bear they find at Paddington railroad station, but life with Paddington isn't always easy. The sequels are *Paddington Helps Out* (1961), *More About Paddington* (1962), *Paddington at Large* (1963), *Paddington Marches On* (1965), *Paddington at Work* (1967), *Paddington Goes to Town* (1968), *Paddington Takes the Air* (1971), *Paddington Abroad* (1972), *Paddington's Garden* (Random, 1973), *Paddington at the Circus* (Random, 1974), *Paddington's Lucky Day* (1974), *Paddington Takes to TV* (1974), *Paddington on Top* (1975), *Paddington on Stage* (1977), *Paddington at the Seaside* (Random, 1978), *Paddington at the Tower* (Random, 1978), *Paddington Takes the Test* (1980), and *Paddington on Screen* (1982). *Paddington's Storybook* (1984) is a collection of stories from eight of the books. The British sequels are *The Adventures of Paddington; Fun and Games with Paddington; Paddington Bear; Paddington Does It Himself; Paddington Goes Shopping; Paddington Goes to the Sales; Paddington Hits Out; Paddington in the Kitchen;* and *Paddington's Birthday Party.* (BL 80:95; CC 435; CCBB 14:106; Ch&Bks:264; HB 37:53; KR 28:676; LJ 85:3856; Suth:42; TLS Nov 21, 1958 p. xiv)
Illus. by Peggy Fortnum, Houghton, 1960; Dell, 1968, pap., 128 pp.

C BOND, (Thomas) Michael. *Here Comes Thursday.* Gr. 3–5. (Orig. British pub. 1966.)
The "Help Yourself" sign posted by Thursday Mouse almost puts his family's store out of business. The sequels are *Thursday Rides Again* (1969) and

Thursday Ahoy! (1970). *Thursday in Paris* is a British sequel. (BL 64:541; CCBB 21:106; HB 43:748; KR 35:1204; LJ 93:1301; TLS 1966 p. 1087) Illus. by Daphne Rowles, Lothrop, 1967, 126 pp., o.p.

C [R] BOND, (Thomas) Michael. *Tales of Olga Da Polga*. Gr. 3–5. (Orig. British pub. 1972.)

Olga the guinea pig thinks very highly of herself, especially after she wins a pet show prize: Fattest Guinea Pig in the Show. The sequels are *Olga Meets Her Match* (Hastings, 1975), *Olga Carries On* (Hastings, 1977), *Olga Counts Her Blessings* (EMC, 1977, pap.), *Olga Makes a Friend* (EMC, 1977, pap.), *Olga Makes Her Mark* (EMC, 1977, pap.), *Olga Takes a Bite* (EMC, 1977, pap.), *Olga's New Home* (EMC, 1977, pap.), *Olga's Second Home* (EMC, 1977, pap.), *Olga's Special Day* (EMC, 1977, pap.), *Olga Makes a Wish* (EMC, 1977, pap.), and *The Complete Adventures of Olga Da Polga* (Delacorte, 1983). (BL 69:987, 70:826; CC:435; CCBB 27:38; Ch&Bks:264; HB 49:268; KR 41:60, 1349; LJ 98:1384; Suth 2:52)

Illus. by Hans Helweg, Macmillan, 1973, 113 pp., o.p.; Penguin, 1974, pap.; Dell, 1982, pap.

BONTEMPS, Arna, and CONROY, Jack. *The Fast Sooner Hound.* See Chapter 6, Humorous Fantasy.

C BOSHINSKI, Blanche. *Aha and the Jewel of Mystery*. Gr. 4–6.

Self-centered Aha the cat learns the value of friendship after he is rescued by an Egyptian slave who is searching for his true identity. (HB 45:168; LJ 94:868)

Illus. by Shirley Pulido, Parents, 1968, 155 pp., o.p.

BOYLE, Kay. *The Youngest Camel.* See Chapter 1, Allegorical Fantasy and Literary Fairy Tales.

C BRENNER, Barbara (Johnes). *Hemi: A Mule.* Gr. 4–6.

Hemionus, ex-farm mule and official mascot of West Point, runs away from army life to look for a farmhand who once befriended him. (BL 70:539; KR 41:1263; LJ 98:3142)

Illus. by J(effrey) Winslow Higginbottom, Harper, 1973, 120 pp., o.p., 1975, pap.

BRENTANO, Clemens Maria. *The Tale of Gockel, Hinkel and Gackeliah.* See Chapter 1, Allegorical Fantasy and Literary Fairy Tales.

C BRO, Margueritte (Harmon). *The Animal Friends of Peng-U*. Gr. 1–4.

Chickens, a fox, and a rabbit help farmer Peng-U find a wife. (BL 61:956; HB 41:274; KR 33:173)

Illus. by Seong Moy, Doubleday, 1965, 96 pp., o.p.

C [R] BROOKS, Walter Rollin. *Freddy Goes to Florida* (Orig. title: *To and Again*, 1927; British title: *Freddy's First Adventure*). Gr. 4–6.

Charles the Rooster suggests migration to avoid the cold, and Freddy the Pig goes along with the other farmyard animals. The other books in this series are *Freddy Goes to the North Pole* (1951; orig. title: *More To and Again*, 1930), *Freddy the Detective* (1932, 1987), *The Story of Freginald* (1936), *The Clockwork Twin* (1937), *Freddy the Politician* (1948, 1986, orig. title: *Wiggins for President*, 1939), *Freddy's Cousin Weedly* (1940), *Freddy and the Ignormus* (1941), *Freddy and the Perilous Adventure* (1942, 1986), *Freddy and the Bean Home News* (1943), *Freddy and Mr. Camphor* (1944), *Freddy and the*

Popinjay (1945), *Freddy the Pied Piper* (1946), *Freddy the Magician* (1947), *Freddy Goes Camping* (1948, 1986), *Freddy Plays Football* (1949), *Freddy Rides Again* (1951), *Freddy the Cowboy* (1951, 1987), *Freddy and Freginald* (1952), *Freddy the Pilot* (1952, 1986), *Collected Poems of Freddy the Pig* (1953), *Freddy and the Space Ship* (1953), *Freddy and the Men from Mars* (1954), *Freddy and the Baseball Team from Mars* (1955, 1987), *Freddy and the Dragon* (1955), *Freddy and Simon the Dictator* (1956), and *Freddy and the Flying Saucer Plans* (1958). (BL 24:30, 45:248; Bookshelf 1933 p. 8; CC:439; CCBB 2[Sept 1949]:1; Ch&Bks:264; HB 3[Aug 1927]:46, 3[Nov 1927]: 11, 7:116, 25:115; KR 17:58; LJ 74:559; Mahony 2:112; TLS 1927 p. 883)
Illus. by Kurt Wiese, Knopf, 1949, o.p.; 1987, pap., 208 pp.

C [R] BROWN, Palmer. *Hickory.* Gr. 3–5.
Hickory the field mouse's youth spent inside a grandfather clock does not prepare him for life in the fields, but a friendly grasshopper helps him overcome his loneliness. (CC:439; HB 55:513; KR 46:1137: SLJ Sept 1978 p. 104)
Illus. by the author, Harper, 1978, 42 pp., o.p.

C BUCHWALD, Emilie. *Floramel and Esteban.* Gr. 3–5.
Lonely Floramel, a Caribbean cow, gets all her news from her friend, Esteban, a cattle egret. After she learns to play music on conch shells, the President makes her a National Treasure. (BL 79:976; CC 1983 Suppl. p. 39; CCBB 36:3; SLJ Sept 1982 p. 104)
Illus. by Charles Robinson, Harcourt, 1982, 72 pp.

BUCHWALD, Emilie. *Gildaen: The Heroic Adventures of a Most Unusual Rabbit.* See Chapter 1, Allegorical Fantasy and Literary Fairy Tales.

C BURGESS, Thornton W(aldo). *Old Mother West Wind.* Gr. 2–4. (Orig. pub. 1910.)
Tales of Johnny Chuck, Reddy Fox, and the other animals living near the Green Meadows, the Smiling Pool, the Laughing Brook, and the Lone Little Path through the woods. Other books in the series are *Mother West Wind's Children* (1911; Little, 1962), *Mother West Wind's Animal Friends* (1912; Grosset, 1940), *Mother West Wind's Neighbors* (1913; Little, 1968), *The Adventures of Johnny Chuck* (1913; Grosset, 1952), *The Adventures of Reddy Fox* (1913; Grosset, 1950), *Mother West Wind's "Why" Stories* (1915; Grosset, 1941), *Mother West Wind's "How" Stories* (1916; Grosset, 1941), *The Adventures of Buster Bear* (1916; Grosset, 1941), *Mother West Wind's "When" Stories* (1917; Grosset, 1941), *Mother West Wind's "Where" Stories* (1918; Grosset, 1941), *The Adventures of Old Granny Fox* (Grosset, 1943), *The Adventures of Lightfoot the Deer* (Grosset, 1944), *The Adventures of Whitefoot the Woodmouse* (Grosset, 1944), *The Adventures of Chatterer the Red Squirrel* (Grosset, 1949), *The Adventures of Prickly Porky* (Grosset, 1949), *The Adventures of Sammy Jay* (Grosset, 1949), *The Adventures of Danny Meadowmouse* (Grosset, 1950), *The Adventures of Peter Cottontail* (Grosset, 1950), *The Adventures of Jerry Muskrat* (Grosset, 1951), *The Adventures of Unc' Billy Possum* (Grosset, 1951), *The Adventures of Grandfather Frog* (Grosset, 1952), *The Adventures of Old Man Coyote* (Grosset, 1952), *The Adventures of Poor Mrs. Quack* (Grosset, 1953), *The Adventures of Bob White* (Grosset, 1954), *The Adventures of Bobby Coon* (Grosset, 1954), *The Adventures of Jimmy Skunk* (Grosset, 1954), and *The Adventures of Ol' Mistah Buzzard* (Grosset, 1957). (BL 7:168; HB 36:526).

Illus. by Harrison Cady, Little, 1960, 140 pp., 1985, pap.; illus. by Harrison Cady and George Kerr, Grossett, 1976.

C/YA   BURMAN, Ben Lucien. *High Water at Catfish Bend*. Gr. 5–7.
The animals of Catfish Bend persuade the Army Corps of Engineers to build levees along the Mississippi River. The sequels are *Seven Stars for Catfish Bend* (1956, 1977), *The Owl Hoots Twice at Catfish Bend* (1961, 1977), *Blow a Wild Bugle for Catfish Bend* (1967, 1979), and *High Treason at Catfish Bend* (Vanguard, 1977). (BL 48:344; HB 28:174; KR 20:224; LJ 77:1018)
Illus. by Alice Caddy, Messner, 1952, 121 pp., o.p.; Avon, 1981, pap.

C   BUTTERS, Dorothy G(ilman). *Papa Dolphin's Table*. Gr. 4–6.
It was crowded enough in the Dolphin's apartment, without the enormous table Papa brought home. (BL 52:171; CCBB 9:82; Eakin:56; KR 23:597; LJ 80:2640)
Illus. by Kurt Werth, Knopf, 1955, 88 pp., o.p.

C   BUZZATI, Dino. *The Bears' Famous Invasion of Sicily*. Gr. 4–6.
King Leander's bear army conquers the island of Sicily. (BL 44:189; CCBB 1[Mar 1948]:2; HB 24:36; KR 15:625; LJ 72:1473)
Tr. by Frances Loeb, illus. by the author, Pantheon, 1947, 146 pp., o.p.

C   CAIRE, Helen. *Señor Castillo, Cock of the Island*. Gr. 3–4.
Castillo the old rooster boards a fishing boat to fulfill his dream of seeing the sea. (HB 24:195; LJ 73:604, 656)
Illus. by Christine Price, Rinehart, 1948, 76 pp., o.p.

C   CAMPBELL, Hope. *Peter's Angel: A Story about Monsters* (Pap. title: *The Monster's Room*, Scholastic, 1979, o.p.). Gr. 4–6.
After the monster posters in Peter's room come to life, his two mouse friends decide that an angel is needed to exorcise the creatures. (BL 72:1525; KR 44:467; SLJ Sept 1976 p. 112)
Illus. by Lilian Obligado, Four Winds, 1976, 151 pp., o.p.

CARLSON, Natalie Savage. *Alphonse, That Bearded One*. See Chapter 6, Humorous Fantasy.

C [R]   CARLSON, Natalie Savage. *Evangeline, Pigeon of Paris* (British title: *Pigeon of Paris*). Gr. 4–6.
Evangeline and her mate, Gabriel, become separated when the Parisian chief of police orders all pigeons trapped and deported. (BL 56:632; HB 36:215; KR 28:184; LJ 85:2475)
Illus. by Nicolas Mordvinoff, Harcourt, 1960, 72 pp., o.p.

C   CASSERLEY, Anne Thomasine. *Barney the Donkey*. Gr. 3–5.
Twelve humorous tales about a mischievous Irish donkey. (BL 34:304; HB 14:163; LJ 63:385)
Illus. by the author, Harper, 1938, 145 pp., o.p.

C   CASSERLEY, Anne Thomasine. *Roseen*. Gr. 2–4.
Twelve Irish tales about a little black pig named Roseen, a wild goat, Brock the badger, and Kerry the cow. The sequel is *Brian of the Mountain* (1931). (BL 26:165; HB 5:44–45, 49, 7:115; Mahony 3:105)
Illus. by the author, Harper, 1929, 152 pp., o.p.

CASSERLEY, Anne Thomasine. *The Whins on Knockattan.* See Chapter 3, Fantasy Collections.

C CAUFIELD, Don and CAUFIELD, Joan. *The Incredible Detectives.* Gr. 4–6.
   Reginald Bulldog, Madam Chang the Siamese cat, and Hennessy Crow solve their master's mysterious kidnapping. (CCBB 20:71; HB 42:708; KR 343:830; LJ 91:5771; Suth:67)
   Illus. by Kiyo Komoda, Harper, 1966, 75 pp., o.p.

CHASE, Mary. *Harvey, a Play.* See Chapter 6, Humorous Fantasy.

CHRISTIAN, Mary Blount. *Sebastian [Super-Sleuth] and the Crummy Yummies Caper.* See Chapter 6, Humorous Fantasy.

C CLARK, Ann Nolan. *Looking-for-Something: The Story of a Stray Burro of Ecuador.* Gr. 1–4.
   Grey Burro searches for someone to belong to. (BL 48:236; HB 28:96; KR 20:123; LJ 77:725)
   Illus. by Leo Politi, Viking, 1952, 53 pp., o.p.

C [O] CLEARY, Beverly (Bunn). *The Mouse and the Motorcycle.* Gr. 2–4.
   A boy named Keith shows a mouse named Ralph the joys of cycling on a toy motorcycle. The sequels are *Runaway Ralph* (1970) and *Ralph S. Mouse* (1982). (BL 62:270; CC:449; CCBB 19:60; Ch&Bks:265; Eakin:76; HB 41:628; KR 33:905; LJ 90:5510)
   Illus. by Louis Darling, Morrow, 1965, 158 pp.; Dell, 1980, pap.

C CLEARY, Beverly (Bunn). *Socks.* Gr. 3–5.
   The Brickers's new baby deprives a kitten named Socks of the family's undivided attention. (CC:449; CCBB 27:23; KR 41:599; LJ 98:2185)
   Illus. by Beatrice Darwin, Morrow, 1973, 156 pp.; Dell, 1980, pap.

C [R] COATSWORTH, Elizabeth (Jane). *The Cat and the Captain.* Gr. 2–4. (Orig. pub. 1927.)
   The captain's cat saves his master's house from burglary and earns a place in the housekeeper's heart. (BL 24:210; CCBB 28:40; HB 3[Nov 1927]:12, 28:421, 50:395; KR 42:364; LJ 53:484, 99:2242)
   Illus. by Bernice Loewenstein, Macmillan, 1974, 95 pp., o.p.

COATSWORTH, Elizabeth (Jane). *The Cat Who Went to Heaven.* See Chapter 1, Allegorical Fantasy and Literary Fairy Tales.

COATSWORTH, Elizabeth (Jane). *The Enchanted: An Incredible Tale.* See Section 5B, Myth Fantasy.

COBLENTZ, Catherine Cate. *The Blue Cat of Castle Town.* See Chapter 7, Magic Adventure Fantasy.

C COLOMA, Padre Luis. *Perez, the Mouse.* Gr. 1–4. (Orig. pub. in Spain, U.S. pub. 1915.)
   King Bube and Perez the Mouse travel throughout the kingdom. (BL 46:206; HB 26:99, 112; Mahoney 2:112)
   Adapt. by Lady Moreton, illus. by George Howard Vyse, Dodd, 1950, 63 pp., o.p.

C COLUM, Padraic. *The Boy Who Knew What the Birds Said.* Gr. 3–5.
   After an old crow teaches the Boy how to speak with the birds, each has a story to tell him. (BL 15:113; HB 1[June 1925]:30; Mahony 1:39)
   Illus. by Dugald Stewart Walker, Macmillan, 1918, 176 pp., o.p.

C   COLUM, Padraic. *Where the Winds Never Blew and the Cocks Never Crew.* Gr. 3–5.
Tibbie the cat and seven other animals live peacefully by the old woman's hearth until a beautiful swan's song lures each of them away. (BL 37:157; HB 16:429, 17:31)
Illus. by Richard Bennett, Macmillan, 1940, 96 pp., o.p.

C [R]   COLUM, Padraic. *The White Sparrow* (British title: *Sparrow Alone*). Gr. 3–5. (Orig. pub. 1933.)
Rescued from a street vendor, Jimmy the sparrow goes to work for a crocodile. (BL 29:344; Bookshelf 1933 p. 6; KR 40:1097; LJ 58:805, 98:259)
Illus. by Joseph Low, McGraw-Hill, 1972, 61 pp., o.p.

CONLY, Jane Leslie. *Racso and the Rats of NIMH.* See Section 2A, Beast Tales.

COOPER, Paul Fenimore. *Tal: His Marvelous Adventures with Noom-Zor-Noom.* See Section 5C, Travel to Other Worlds.

C   CREGAN, Maírín. *Old John.* Gr. 4–6. (Orig. pub. in Ireland.)
A fairy doctor disguised as a cat comes to live with the old shoemaker of Tir Aulin. (BL 32:330; HB 12:153; LJ 61:457,809)
Illus. by Helen Sewell, Macmillan, 1936, 184 pp., o.p.

C [R]   CROWLEY, Maude. *Azor and the Blue-Eyed Cow: A Christmas Story.* Gr. 1–4. (Orig. U.S. pub. Oxford, 1951.)
A young boy named Azor decides to prove the existence of Santa Claus. This is the sequel to *Azor* (1948) and *Azor and the Haddock* (1949); it is followed by *Tor and Azor* (1955). (BL 48:70; CCBB 5:13; HB 27:414; KR 19:530; LJ 76:2120)
Illus. by Helen Sewell, Gregg, 1980, 70 pp., o.p.

C [R]   CULLEN, Countee (Porter). *The Lost Zoo (A Rhyme for the Young, but Not Too Young) by Christopher Cat and Countee Cullen.* Gr. 3–6. (Orig. pub. Harper, 1940.)
Christopher Cat tells a tale in verse about some extraordinary beasts that Noah forgot to take on his ark. *My Lives and How I Lost Them, by Christopher Cat and Countee Cullen* (1942, 1964) is Christopher's second literary effort. (BL 37:292, 66:140; CCBB 23:157; HB 45:542, 62:78; LJ 94:4276)
Illus. By Joseph Low, Follett, 1969, 95 pp., o.p.

C [R]   CUNNINGHAM, Julia (Woolfolk). *Candle Tales.* Gr. 3–4.
Six animals tell a kind old man stories for his birthday. (BL 60:876; HB 40:376; KR 32:51; LJ 89:1448)
Illus. by Evaline Ness, Pantheon, 1964, 57 pp., o.p.

C [R]   CUNNINGHAM, Julia (Woolfolk). *Macaroon.* Gr. 3–5.
Macaroon, a raccoon who spends his winters in children's homes, decides one winter to choose the home of a selfish, surly child so that it won't be so hard to leave in the spring. (BL 59:288; HB 38:480; LJ 87:4266; TLS 1963 p. 980)
Illus. by Evaline Ness, Pantheon, 1962, 63 pp., o.p.; Dell, 1978, pap., o.p.

C   CUNNINGHAM, Julia (Woolfolk). *Maybe, a Mole.* Gr. 3–5.
Five episodes about a mole named Maybe who is rejected by his own kind because he is not blind, but is befriended by a fox, a mouse, and a turtle. (BL 71:506; CCBB 28:109; HB 51:51; KR 42:1303)

Illus. by Cyndy Szekeres, Pantheon, 1974, 81 pp., o.p.; Dell, 1975, pap., o.p.

CUNNINGHAM, Julia (Woolfolk). *OAF.* See Chapter 1, Allegorical Fantasy and Literary Fairy Tales.

C CUNNINGHAM, Julia (Woolfolk). *Viollet.* Gr. 4–6.
Oxford the dog, Warwicke the fox, and Viollet the thrush band together to save the life of Oxford's master. (CCBB 20:86; Ch&Bks:265; KR 34:1054; LJ 91:6190).
Illus. by Alan Cober, Pantheon, 1966, 82 pp., o.p.

C CUNNINGHAM, Julia (Woolfolk). *The Vision of Francois the Fox.* Gr. 1–4.
Francois is inspired by a vision to give up his greedy ways and become a saint. (HB 36:406; KR 28:617)
Illus. by Nicholas Angelo, Houghton, 1960, 35 pp., o.p.

CUNNINGHAM, Julia (Woolfolk). *Wolf Roland.* See Chapter 1, Allegorical Fantasy and Literary Fairy Tales.

C DAHL, Roald. *Fantastic Mr. Fox.* Gr. 3–5. (Orig. British and U.S. pub. 1970.)
Mr. Fox, his wife, and four children out-fox three of the meanest and stupidest farmers around. (BL 82:1538; CCBB 24:89; LJ 96:1106)
Illus. by Donald Chaffin, Knopf, 1986, 62 pp.; Bantam, 1978, pap.

DAHL, Roald. *James and the Giant Peach: A Children's Story.* See Chapter 7, Magic Adventure Fantasy.

C DALLAS-SMITH, Peter. *Trouble for Trumpets.* Gr. 2–4. (Orig. British pub. 1982.)
Pod, a little animal called a Trumpet, tells the story of the Trumpets' war against the hostile Grumpets. The sequel is *Trumpets in Grumpetland* (1985). (CCBB 38:104; Ch&Bks:265; SLJ Jan 1985 p. 73; Suth 3:112)
Illus. by Peter Cross, Random, 1984, 30 pp., o.p.

C DANA, Barbara. *Rutgers and the Watersnouts.* Gr. 3–5.
Rutgers the bulldog and his friends search for more of the prickly creatures he found on the beach. (BL 65:1075; KR 37:53; LJ 94:1324)
Illus. by Fred Brenner, Harper, 1969, o.p.; Avon, 1983, pap., 160 pp.

DAVIES, Andrew. *Marmalade and Rufus.* See Chapter 6, Humorous Fantasy.

C DAVIS, Mary Gould. *The Handsome Donkey.* Gr. 3–4.
Baldasarre the donkey becomes famous, in this story told through the eyes of a dachshund named Tedesco. (BL 30:51; HB 9:205; Mahony 3:242)
Illus. by Emma Brock, Harcourt, 1933, 67 pp., o.p.

C [R] DAVIS, Robert. *Padre Porko: The Gentlemanly Pig.* Gr. 4–6. (Orig. pub. 1939.)
Twelve tales about a pig who helps people and animals in distress. (BL 36:308; 45:17; CC:106; CCBB 1[Oct 1948]:2; HB 24:379; LJ 65:123, 74:134)
Illus. by Fritz Eichenberg, Holiday, 1948, 197 pp.

C DE LA MARE, Walter (John). *Mr. Bumps and His Monkey*. Gr. 4–6.
Jasper the English-speaking monkey is stolen from Mr. Bumps. (BL 39:73; HB 18:426; LJ 67:884, 955)
Illus. by Dorothy P. Lathrop, Holt, 1942, 69 pp., o.p.

C/YA DE LA MARE, Walter (John). *The Three Royal Monkeys*. (Orig. title:
[R] *The Three Mula Mulgars*). Gr. 5–7. (Orig. British pub. 1910, U.S. 1919.)
Three Mulgars, or monkeys, search for their father, the Prince, using a magic wonderstone. (BL 45:110; CCBB 2[Apr 1949]:3; HB 14:143; LJ 74:69; Mahony 2:278)
Illus. by Mildred Eldridge, Knopf, 1966, 277 pp., o.p.

DELANEY, M. C. *Henry's Special Delivery*. See Chapter 6, Humorous Fantasy.

DE LEEUW, Adele Louise. *Nobody's Doll*. See Chapter 9, Toy Fantasy.

DE REGNIERS, Beatrice Schenk (Freedman). *The Boy, the Rat, and the Butterfly*. See Chapter 7, Magic Adventure Fantasy.

DOLBIER, Maurice (Wyman). *A Lion in the Woods*. See Chapter 6, Humorous Fantasy.

C [R] DRURY, Roger W(olcott). *The Champion of Merrimack County*. Gr. 3–5.
O Crispin is the champion mouse bicyclist until a sliver of soap on the Berryfields' bathtub causes a bicycle wreck and a dislocated tail. (BL 73:1265; CC:462; CCBB 30:104; HB 53:50; KR 44:1092; SLJ Jan 1977 p. 91)
Illus. by Fritz Wegner, Little, 1976, 198 pp.

DU BOIS, William (Sherman) Pène. *Elisabeth the Cow Ghost*. See Chapter 4, Ghost Fantasy.

DU BOIS, William (Sherman) Pène. *The Forbidden Forest*. See Chapter 6, Humorous Fantasy.

DU BOIS, William (Sherman) Pène. *The Great Geppy*. See Chapter 6, Humorous Fantasy.

DU BOIS, William (Sherman) Pène. *Otto and the Magic Potatoes*. See Chapter 6, Humorous Fantasy.

DU BOIS, William (Sherman) Pène. *The Squirrel Hotel*. See Chapter 6, Humorous Fantasy.

C DUMAS, Gerald J. *Rabbits Rafferty*. Gr. 4–6.
Rabbits Rafferty stumbles into a fight with Mink Mumsey's tough gang who wants to tear down the other animals' homes. (CCBB 22:25; KR 36:510; LJ 93:2733; TLS 1970 p. 414)
Illus. by Wallace Tripp, Houghton, 1968, o.p.; Avon, 1981, pap., 209 pp.

DURRELL, Gerald. *The Talking Parcel*. See Section 5C, Travel to Other Worlds.

C [R] EAGER, Edward McMaken. *Mouse Manor*. Gr. 2–4.
Myrtilla, a poor but genteel country mouse, travels to London to see the Queen. (BL 49:19; CCBB 6:4; HB 28:399; KR 20:451; LJ 77:1310)
Illus. by Beryl Bailey-Jones, Ariel, 1952, 50 pp., o.p.

C EDMONDS, Walter D(umaux). *Time to Go House.* Gr. 4–6.
After her family's move to a vacant human house, Smalleata the field-mouse falls in love with Raffles the house-mouse. (BL 66:296; HB 45:535; KR 37:776; LJ 94:4284)
Illus. by Joan Victor, Little, 1969, 137 pp., o.p.

EDMONDSON, Madeline. *The Witch's Egg.* See Chapter 10, Witchcraft and Sorcery Fantasy.

C [O] ERICKSON, Russell E(verett). *A Toad for Tuesday.* Gr. 3–4.
Captured by an owl, Warton the toad becomes his housekeeper to avoid being eaten as birthday dinner. The sequels are *Warton and Morton* (1976), *Warton's Christmas Eve Adventure* (1977), *Warton and the King of the Skies* (1978), *Warton and the Traders* (1979), *Warton and the Castaways* (1982) and *Warton and the Contest* (1986). (BL 71:98; CC:464; CCBB 28:76; HB 51:48; KR 42:681; LJ 99:2244)
Illus. by Lawrence Di Fiori, Lothrop, 1974, 63 pp.

C ESTES, Eleanor. *Miranda the Great.* Gr. 3–5.
A Roman cat named Miranda, lost by her human family, gathers other strays and proclaims herself Queen of the Colosseum. (BL 63:948; CCBB 20:120; HB 43:201; KR 35:130; LJ 92:1315)
Illus. by Edward Ardizzone, Harcourt, 1967, 79 pp., o.p.

C EZO (pseud). *Avril.* Gr. 4–6. (Orig. pub. in France.)
When Avril runs away from her foster family, she is accompanied by a lamb, a cat, a bear, and a baby ghost. (KR 35:1046; LJ 92:4612)
Tr. by John Buchanan-Brown, illus. by Douglas Bissot, Abelard-Schuman, 1967, 94 pp., o.p.

EZO (pseud.) *My Son-In-Law, the Hippopotamus.* See Chapter 6, Humorous Fantasy.

FARALLA, Dana. *The Singing Cupboard.* See Chapter 7, Magic Adventure Fantasy.

FAST, Howard (Melvin). *The General Zapped an Angel: New Stories of Fantasy and Science Fiction.* See Chapter 3, Fantasy Collections.

C FEAGLES, Anita M(ac Rae). *Casey, the Utterly Impossible Horse.* Gr. 2–4.
Mike is not exactly pleased that Casey the talking horse has chosen him as a pet. (CCBB 14:78; LJ 85:4566)
Illus. by Dagmar Wilson, Addison-Wesley, 1960, 95 pp., o.p.

C [R] FIELD, Rachel (Lyman). *Little Dog Toby.* Gr. 3–5.
Toby performs in a Punch and Judy show during a Christmas party at Buckingham Palace. (BL 25:127, 49:147; Bookshelf 1929 p. 18; HB 4[Aug 1928]:9, 4[Nov 1928]:78, 7:115, 28:421; Mahony 2:118)
Illus. by the author, Macmillan, 1928, 1952, 116 pp., o.p.

C FLACK, Marjorie. *Walter the Lazy Mouse.* Gr. 2–4. (Orig. pub. 1937.)
Left behind during his family's move, Walter is befriended by Turtle and the three Frogs while he searches for his family. (CC:467; HB 13:284; LJ 62:782)
Illus. by Cyndy Szekeres, Doubleday, 1963, 95 pp., o.p.

FLORY, Jane (Trescott). *The Lost and Found Princess.* See Chapter 1, Allegorical Fantasy and Literary Fairy Tales.

C FOOTE, Timothy (Gilson). *The Great Ringtail Garbage Caper.* Gr. 4–6.
Oldest Raccoon and his gang heist a garbage truck to keep their friends in food. (BL 76:1363, 84:1441; HB 56:294; KR 48:583; SLJ May 1980 p. 66)
Illus. by Normand Chartier, Houghton, 1980, 66 pp.; Scholastic, 1982, pap.

FORBUS, Ina B(ell). *The Magic Pin.* See Chapter 7, Magic Adventure Fantasy.

FORST, S. *Pipkin.* See Chapter 1, Allegorical Fantasy and Literary Fairy Tales.

C [R] FORT, John. *June the Tiger.* Gr. 4–6.
Mrs. Pinckney's feisty dog, June, and her friend, Billy the Bull, declare war on a bear named Scratch who has ravaged Mrs. Pinckney's house. (BL 72:855, 84:1441; CCBB 29:143; HB 52:48; KR 43:1397; SLJ Mar 1976 p. 102)
Illus. by Bernice Loewenstein, Little, 1975, 59 pp., o.p.

C FOX, Denise P. *Through Tempest Trails.* Gr. 3–5.
Burr the raccoon, Minkley the mink, a peacock, and three shrews escape from outlaws and journey to Harbor Town, only to be captured by pirates. (BL 84:705, 1441; KR 55:1574; SLJ Dec 1987 p. 85)
Illus. by Judith Gwyn Brown, Atheneum, 1987, 116 pp.

C FOX (Greenburg), Paula. *Dear Prosper.* Gr. 3–5.
A dog named Chien writes his life story in a letter to the boy who was his first master. (KR 36:393; LJ 93:2733)
Illus. by Steve McLachlin, White, 1968, 67 pp., o.p.

FOX (Greenberg), Paula. *The Little Swineherd and Other Tales.* See Chapter 3, Fantasy Collections.

C FRANKO, Ivan, and MELNYK, Bohdan. *Fox Mykyta.* Gr. 4–5. (Orig. Ukrainian pub. 1890.)
The animals in Lion's court never manage to hurt wiley Fox Mykyta. (BL 75:933; HB 55:191)
Tr. by Bodhan Melnyk, illus. by William Kurelek, Tundra, dist. by Scribner, 1978, 148 pp., o.p.

FREEMAN, Barbara C(onstance). *Broom-Adelaide.* See Chapter 1, Allegorical Fantasy and Literary Fairy Tales.

C [R] FRESCHET, Bernice (Louise Speck). *Bernard of Scotland Yard.* Gr. 2–3.
Bernard the mouse helps his cousin Foster of Scotland Yard break up a gang of robber moles who are planning a heist of the crown jewels. This is the sequel to *Bernard Sees the World* (1976) and is followed by *Bernard and the Catnip Caper* (1981). (BL 75:750; CCBB 32:135; Ch&Bks:266; KR 47:3; SLJ Mar 1979 p. 121; Suth 2:156)
Illus. by Gina Freschet, Scribner, 1978, 48 pp., o.p.

C FRY, Rosalie K(ingsmill). *The Wind Call.* Gr. 2–4.
Mother Blackcap finds a lost baby of the Little People, names him Pierello, and raises him along with her three baby birds. (CCBB 10:50; HB 32:30; LJ 80:2916)
Illus. by the author, Dutton, 1955, 115 pp., o.p.

YA [R]   GALLICO, Paul (William). *The Abandoned* (British title: *Jennie*). Gr. 8 up.
Injured in an automobile accident, Peter imagines his transformation into a homeless cat. (BL 47:2, 39; HB 26:501; KR 18:394; LJ 75:2161)
Knopf, 1950, o.p.; International Polygonics, 1987, pap., 250 pp.

C/YA   GATES, Doris. *The Cat and Mrs. Cary.* Gr. 5–7.
Mrs. Cary is able to solve a mystery because she can understand cat language. (Eakin:135; HB 38:598; LJ 88:864)
Illus. by Peggy Bacon, Viking, 1962, 216 pp., o.p.

C   GAUNT, Michael (pseud. of [James] Dennis Robertshaw). *Brim's Boat.* Gr. 4–6. (Orig. British pub. 1964.)
A terrier named Brim finds an abandoned boat and decides to become a sailor. The sequels are *Brim Sails Out* (1966) and *Brim's Valley* (British). (BL 62:831; HB 42:305; KR 34:56; LJ 91:1063)
Illus. by Stuart Tresilian, Coward, 1966, 128 pp., o.p.

C/YA   GAUTIER, (Louise) Judith. *The Memoirs of a White Elephant.* Gr. 5–6. (Orig. pub. in France.)
A royal Indian elephant tells how he once saved his master's life and became the guardian of the baby princess of Golconda. (BL 13:269; Bookshelf 1921–1922 p. 13; Mahony 2:343)
Illus. by L. H. Smith and S. B. Kite, tr. by S. A. B. Harvey, Duffield, 1916, 233 pp., o.p.

C [R]   GODDEN (Dixon), (Margaret) Rumer. *Mouse House.* Gr. K–3.
Mary makes sure that her miniature house gets the right kind of tenants: a family of mice. (BL 54:28; CCBB 11:80; HB 33:483; KR 25:480; LJ 82:2693)
Illus. by Adrienne Adams, Viking, 1957, 63 pp., o.p.

GODDEN (Dixon), (Margaret) Rumer. *The Mousewife.* See Chapter 1, Allegorical Fantasy and Literary Fairy Tales.

C   GOODWIN, Murray. *Alonzo and the Army of Ants.* Gr. 4–6.
Alonzo the anteater must save his village from an invasion of army ants. (KR 34:419; LJ 91:3258)
Illus. by Kiyo Komoda, Harper, 1966, 104 pp., o.p.

C [R]   GRAHAME, Kenneth. *Bertie's Escapade.* Gr. 1–3. (Orig. U.S. pub. in this format, Lippincott, 1949.)
Bertie Pig and Peter and Benjie Rabbit's Christmas carolling efforts disturb Mr. Stone, who sets his dogs on them. This story was first published as part of *First Whispers of the Wind in the Willows* (1944 in England; 1945 in the U.S.). (BL 41:223; CCBB 2[Nov 1949]:4; HB 21:200, 25:413, 552; KR 13:31, 45:1094; LJ 70:264, 74:1533, 1681; TLS 1944 p. 369)
Illus. by Ernest Shepard, Harper, 1977, 28 pp., o.p.

C/YA [O]   GRAHAME, Kenneth. *The Wind in the Willows.* Gr. 4–8. (Orig. British pub. 1905, U.S. 1908.)
Ratty, Mole, and Toad battle the weasels and stoats that have taken over Toad Hall. A. A. Milne used this story as a basis for a play entitled *Toad of Toad Hall* (Scribner, 1929, 1957; Avon, 1982, pap.). Picture-book versions of four chapters from the novel have been published by Scribner—*The River Bank* (1977), *The Open Road* (1980), *Wayfarers All* (1981), and *Mole's Christmas, or, Home Sweet Home* (1983, 1986, pap.) Dixon Scott (see this section) has written a sequel for a slightly older audience entitled *A Fresh Wind in the*

Willows (orig. Brit. pub. 1983, Dell/Yearling, 1987, pap.). (BL 50:20, 77:1250, 80:85, 680; CC:475; CCBB 7:4, 34:111, 36:209; Ch&Bks:245; HB 1[June 1925]:34, 46, 7:118, 9:205, 30:83, 59:733, 60:357; Mahony 2:280; SLJ Nov 1980 p. 74, Sept 1983 p. 122; Suth 3:158, 159)

Illus. by Arthur Rackham, Heritage, 1940, o.p.; illus. by Ernest H. Shepard, Scribner/Macmillan, 1933, 1983, hb and pap.; illus. by Michael Hague, Ariel, 1982, o.p.; Bantam, 1982, pap; illus. by John Burningham, Viking, 1983, 239 pp.; Penguin/Puffin, 1984, pap.; illus. by Steven Smallman, Scholastic, 1988, pap.

GRAY, Nicholas Stuart. *Grimbold's Other World.* See Section 5C, Travel to Other Worlds.

GUILLOT, René. *Nicolette and the Mill.* See Chapter 7, Magic Adventure Fantasy.

GUILLOT, René. *The Three Hundred Ninety-seventh White Elephant.* See Chapter 1, Allegorical Fantasy and Literary Fairy Tales.

C/YA HAAS, Dorothy F. (Dee Francis). *The Bears Up Stairs.* Gr. 5–7.
Wendy befriends Otto and Ursula Ma'am, two bears hiding in her apartment building while they wait for transportation to the planet Brun. (BL 75:49; CCBB 32:44; KR 46:1248; SLJ Oct 1978 p. 144)
Greenwillow/Morrow, 1978, 192 pp., o.p.; Dell, 1981, pap., o.p.

C HAMILTON, Carol. *The Dawn Seekers.* Gr. 4–6.
Nocturnal young Quentin, a Kangaroo rat, joins forces with a bossy jerboa and a poetic centipede to venture out into the desert by day. (BL 83:1446, 84:1441; KR 55:56; SLJ Mar 1987 p. 160)
Illus. by Jeremy Guitar, Whitman, 1987, 160 pp.

C HASS, E. A. *Incognito Mosquito, Private Insective.* Gr. 3–5.
A mosquito detective describes five of his most serious cases, including the capture of the "bug napper" of baseball star Mickie Mantis. The sequels are *Incognito Mosquito Flies Again* (1985) and *Incognito Mosquito Takes to the Air* (1986). (CCBB 36:108; KR 50:1105; SLJ Dec 1982 p. 79)
Illus. by the author, Lothrop, 1982, 94 pp.; Random, 1985, pap.

C [R] HATCH, Richard Warren. *The Lobster Books* (Orig. title: *The Curious Lobster*, Harcourt, 1937; and *The Curious Lobster's Island*, Dodd, 1939). Gr. 4–6.
An old lobster meets a badger and a bear while exploring unknown territory up river. (BL 34:132; CCBB 4:50; HB 13:288, 15:383, 27:260; LJ 62:809, 881, 64:840, 904; TLS 1937 p. 948)
Illus. by Marion Freeman Wakeman, Houghton, 1951, 347 pp., o.p.

C HAYES, Geoffrey. *The Alligator and His Uncle Tooth: A Novel of the Sea.* Gr. 3–5.
Uncle Tooth's adventure-filled tales convince the old sea captain to sail again, with Corduroy as mate. (BL 73:1420; CCBB 31:33; HB 53:441; KR 45:350; SLJ Sept 1977 p. 109; TLS 1977 p. 1414)
Illus. by the author, Harper, 1977, 88 pp., o.p.

HEAL, (Berrien) Edith. *What Happened to Jenny.* See Chapter 7, Magic Adventure Fantasy.

HESS, Fjeril. *The Magic Switch.* See Chapter 7, Magic Adventure Fantasy.

HEWETT, Anita. *The Bull beneath the Walnut Tree and Other Stories.* See Chapter 3, Fantasy Collections.

HILLER, Catherine. *Abracatabby.* See Chapter 7, Magic Adventure Fantasy.

C HIMLER, Ronald (Norbert), and HIMLER, Ann. *Little Owl, Keeper of the Trees.* Gr. K–3.
Although Little Owl is afraid of high places, his favorite spot is the highest branch of the Old Sycamore Tree, where he dreams of being the mighty guardian of the forest. (BL 71:570; CCBB 28:148; KR 42:1103; SLJ Jan 1975 p. 39)
Illus. by Ronald Himler, Harper, 1974, 63 pp., o.p.

C HOBAN, Lillian. *It's Really Christmas.* Gr. K–3.
The family of a lame baby mouse named Gamey Joe nurses him back to health after a bad fall by creating Christmas in July. (BL 79:116; CCBB 36:27; KR 50:995; SLJ Oct 1982 p. 165)
Illus. by the author, Greenwillow, 1982, 39 pp.

C [R] HOBAN, Russell C(onwell). *Dinner at Alberta's.* Gr. 2–4.
Arthur Crocodile decides to learn table manners in preparation for dinner at Alberta Saurian's house. The sequel is *Arthur's New Power* (1978). (BL 72:302; CCBB 29:98; HB 52:46; KR 42:993; SLJ Dec 1975 pp. 31, 64; Suth 2:216)
Illus. by James Marshall, Crowell, 1975; Dell, 1980, pap., 48 pp.

C [R] HOBAN, Russell C(onwell). *The Sea-Thing Child.* Gr. 2–4.
Friendly shore creatures help a newborn sea-thing overcome its fear of flying. (CCBB 26:92; KR 40:1188, 1412; LJ 98:644; TLS 1972 p. 1323)
Illus. by Abrom Hoban, Harper, 1972, 35 pp., o.p.

HOFFMANN, E(rnest) T(heodor) A(madeus). *The Nutcracker.* See Chapter 9, Toy Fantasy.

C [R] HOFFMANN, Eleanor. *The Four Friends.* Gr. 3–5.
To avoid becoming Christmas dinner, a pig runs away in a rental car, along with a dog, a parrot, and a hen. (BL 43:173; HB 22:349; KR 14:422; LJ 71:1808)
Illus. by Kurt Wiese, Macmillan, 1946, 105 pp., o.p.

C HOLMAN (Valen), Felice. *The Cricket Winter.* Gr. 3–5.
A boy and a cricket communicate in Morse code to save a mouse family from a thieving rat. (BL 64:784; CCBB 21:111; LJ 92:3849; Suth:193)
Illus. by Ralph Pinto, Norton, 1967, 107 pp., o.p.

HORNE, Richard Henry. *The Good-Natured Bear: A Story for Children of All Ages.* See Chapter 6, Humorous Fantasy.

C [R] HORNE, Richard Henry. *King Penguin: A Legend of the South Sea Isles.* Gr. 3–5. (Orig. British pub. 1848, U.S. 1925.)
A remorseful sailor sets out to free the captive King of the Penguins. (BL 22:122; HB 2[Nov 1925]:19, 28:421; LJ 51:836; Mahony 2:148; Moore: 42)
Illus. by James Daugherty, Macmillan, 1952, 68 pp., o.p.

HORWITZ, Elinor Lander. *The Strange Story of the Frog Who Became a Prince.* See Chapter 10, Witchcraft and Sorcery Fantasy.

HOUGH, (Helen) Charlotte (Woodyatt). *Red Biddy and Other Stories.* See Chapter 3, Fantasy Collections.

C HOWARD, Joan (pseud. of Patricia Gordon). *The Taming of Giants.* Gr. 1–4.
A field mouse searching for a new home encounters a classroom full of "giants." (BL 47:16; CCBB 4:3; HB 26:375; KR 18:512)
Illus. by Garry MacKenzie, Viking, 1950, 57 pp., o.p.

C [R] HOWARD, Joan (pseud. of Patricia Gordon). *Uncle Sylvester.* Gr. 2–4.
In order to save their homes from destruction by erosion, Uncle Sylvester mole and his nephew, Digger, move the entire colony across the river to the Green Forest. (CCBB 3:35; HB 26:194; KR 18:176; LJ 75:629, 987)
Illus. by Garry MacKenzie, Oxford, 1950, 48 pp., o.p.

C [R] HOWE, Deborah and HOWE, James. *Bunnicula: A Rabbit Tale of Mystery.* Gr. 3–5.
Family pets Chester and Harold suspect that the bunny rabbit brought home from a Dracula movie is really a vampire. The sequels are *Howliday Inn* (1982), *The Celery Stalks at Midnight* (1983), and *Nighty-Nightmare* (1987). (BL 75:1439; CC:485; CCBB 32:192; Ch&Bks:268; KR 47:741; SLJ May 1979 p. 81; Suth 3:200)
Illus. by Alan Daniel, Atheneum, 1979; Avon, 1985, pap., 100 pp.

C HOWE, James. *Morgan's Zoo.* Gr. 3–5.
Morgan the zookeeper, two children, and all of the animals join forces to save their zoo from closing. (BL 81:448; SLJ Sept 1984 p. 119)
Illus. by Leslie Morrill, Atheneum, 1984; Avon/Camelot, 1986, pap, 192 pp.

C [R] HUGHES, Ted (Edward James). *How the Whale Became.* Gr. 2–5. (Orig. British pub. 1963.)
A collection of stories describing how the whale, the owl, the hare, the polar bear, and the hyena developed their individual personalities. (BL 61:482; HB 40:498; KR 32:650; LJ 89:4196)
Illus. by Rick Schreiter, Atheneum, 1964, 100 pp., o.p.

JACQUES, Brian. *Redwall.* See Chapter 1, Allegorical Fantasy and Literary Fairy Tales.

C JARRELL, Randall. *The Bat-Poet.* Gr. 3–5.
A young bat writes poetry about day-creatures to convince his nocturnal friends to stay awake during the day. (CC:489; Ch&Bks:268; LJ 89:2210)
Illus. by Maurice Sendak, Macmillan, 1964, 42 pp., 1977, pap.

JARRELL, Randall. *Fly by Night.* See Chapter 7, Magic Adventure Fantasy.

C JOHNSTON, Johanna. *Great Gravity the Cat.* Gr. 3–5.
Gravity's jealousy over the new baby in the house causes him to run away to seek his fortune. (CCBB 111:120; HB 34:195; KR 26:74; LJ 83:1602)
Illus. by Kurt Wiese, Knopf, 1958, 66 pp., o.p.

JONES, Diana Wynne. *Dogsbody.* See Section 5C, Travel to Other Worlds.

C KARAZIN, Nikolaí Nikoleavich. *Cranes Flying South.* Gr. 4–6. (Orig. pub. in the Soviet Union.)
A young Russian crane describes his summer of training with Longnose the Wise One, before his first flight south. (BL 27:506; HB 7:237, 238; Mahony 3:206)
Tr. by M. Pokrovsky, illus. by Vera Bock, Doubleday, 1931, 235 pp., o.p.

C KAUFMAN, Charles. *The Frog and the Beanpole.* Gr. 5–6.
Wesley, an invisible research laboratory frog, and a girl named Holly run away to join a traveling circus. (BL 76:1608; CCBB 33:174; KR 48:836; SLJ Aug 1980 p. 64)
Illus. by Troy Howell, Lothrop, 1980, 189 pp., o.p.

KELLER, Gottfried. *The Fat of the Cat and Other Stories.* See Chapter 3, Fantasy Collections.

C KELLEY, True Adelaide and LINDBLOM, Steven (Winther). *The Mouses' Terrible Christmas.* Gr. 2–3.
Santa gets into a sticky situation after he falls through a hole in the Mouse family's roof and lands on last year's recycled Christmas tree. The sequel is *The Mouses' Terrible Halloween* (1980). (BL 75:552; CCBB 32:64; KR 46:1187; SLJ Oct 1978 p. 114)
Illus. by True Adelaide Kelley, Lothrop, 1978, 63 pp., o.p.

C [R] KENNEDY, Richard (Jerome). *The Mouse God.* Gr. 2–5.
Too lazy to catch his own meals, a cat dresses up like a mouse god and convinces the mice to enter a special cage (mouse church) so he can catch them at his leisure. (BL 75:1440; HB 55:407; KR 47:385; SLJ May 1979 p. 52)
Illus. by Stephen Harvard, Atlantic-Little, 1979, 32 pp., o.p.

KENNEDY, X. J. (pseud. of Joseph Kennedy). *The Owlstone Crown.* See Section 5C, Travel to Other Worlds.

C KING, (David) Clive. *The Town That Went South.* Gr. 4–6.
A great storm sends the town of Ramsley drifting off across the ocean toward the South Pole. (HB 36:130; LJ 85:1305; TLS May 20, 1960 p. xv, 1969 p. 352)
Illus. by Maurice Bartlett, Macmillan, 1959, 117 pp., o.p.

C [R] KING-SMITH, Dick. *Babe: The Gallant Pig* (Orig. British title: *The Sheep-Pig,* 1983). Gr. 4–6.
Farmer Hogget's sheep dog, Fly, trains Babe the pig to become a champion sheepherder. (BL 81:1666, 82:1232; HB 61:449; SLJ Aug 1985 p. 66)
Illus. by Mary Rayner, Crown, 1985, 118 pp.

KING-SMITH, Dick. *Harry's Mad.* See Chapter 6, Humorous Fantasy.

C [R] KING-SMITH, Dick. *Magnus Powermouse.* Gr. 4–6. (Orig. British pub. 1982.)
Life with Magnus, the giant-sized mouse baby, proves to be somewhat difficult for his parents, in spite of his victory over a local cat and his father's liberation from a steel trap. (BL 80:1191; CC:493; CCBB 37:207; Ch&Bks:268; HB 60:329; KR 52:40; SLJ Aug 1984 p. 74; Suth 3:235)
Illus. by Mary Rayner, Harper, 1984, 120 pp.

C [R] KING-SMITH, Dick. *The Mouse Butcher.* Gr. 4–6. (Orig. British pub. 1981.)
A cat named Tom Plug is hired by a wealthy Persian cat family to be their

mouse butcher, but his life is endangered by a killer cat named Great Mog. (BL 78:1526; CCBB 36:71; Ch&Bks:268; HB 58:404; KR 50:605; SLJ Apr 1982 p. 71; Suth 3:236)
Illus. by Margot Apple, Viking, 1982, 132 pp.

C [R] KING-SMITH, Dick. *Pigs Might Fly* (Orig. British title: *Daggie Dogfoot,* 1980). Gr. 4–6.
Daggie, the dog-footed runt of the pig litter, learns to swim and rescues the other pigs during a flash flood. (BL 78:1368, 79:685, 978, 84:1441; CC:493; CCBB 36:29; Ch&Bks:268; HB 58:405; KR 50:419; SLJ Aug 1982 p. 99; Suth 3:236)
Illus. by Mary Rayner, Viking, 1982; Scholastic/Apple, 1984, pap., 168 pp.

KIPLING, (Joseph) Rudyard. *The Beginning of the Armadilloes.* See Chapter 1, Allegorical Fantasy and Literary Fairy Tales.

KIPLING, (Joseph) Rudyard. *The Elephant's Child.* See Chapter 1, Allegorical Fantasy and Literary Fairy Tales.

KIPLING, (Joseph) Rudyard. *How the Camel Got His Hump.* See Chapter 1, Allegorical Fantasy and Literary Fairy Tales.

KIPLING, (Joseph) Rudyard. *How the Leopard Got His Spots.* See Chapter 1, Allegorical Fantasy and Literary Fairy Tales.

KIPLING, (Joseph) Rudyard. *How the Rhinoceros Got His Skin.* See Chapter 1, Allegorical Fantasy and Literary Fairy Tales.

KIPLING, (Joseph) Rudyard. *The Jungle Book.* See Chapter 3, Fantasy Collections.

KIPLING, (Joseph) Rudyard. *Just So Stories.* See Chapter 3, Fantasy Collections.

C KIRBY, Mansfield. *The Secret of Thut-Mouse III; or Basil Beandesert's Revenge.* Gr. 3–5. (Orig. Dutch pub. 1983.)
A group of educated mice living in an art museum take revenge on the museum director for buying a cat, by producing fake Egyptian artifacts that look so real the director writes a book on his fabulous find. (BL 82:496; CCBB 39:70; SLJ Dec 1985 p. 90)
Illus. by Mance Post, Farrar, 1985, 60 pp.

KOTZWINKLE, William. *Trouble in Bugland: A Collection of Inspector Mantis Mysteries.* See Chapter 6, Humorous Fantasy.

C KRÜSS, James (Jacob Hinrich). *Eagle and Dove.* Gr. 3–5. (Orig. German pub. 1963.)
Trapped by an eagle, a dove distracts him by telling stories while she digs an escape hole. (BL 62:364; KR 33:624; LJ 90:3792)
Tr. by Edelgard von Heydekampf Brühl, illus. by Pat Kent, Atheneum, 1965, 69 pp., o.p.

KRÜSS, James. *The Happy Islands behind the Winds.* See Section 5C, Travel to Other Worlds.

LAGERLÖF, Selma (Ottiliana Lovisa). *The Wonderful Adventures of Nils.* See Chapter 7, Magic Adventure Fantasy.

C LANIER, Sterling E(dmund). *The War for the Lot: A Tale of Fantasy and Terror.* Gr. 4–6.
   Alec helps the woodland creatures living around his grandfather's farm to fight off the tyrannical rats. (BL 66:928; CCBB 24:61; HB 46:162; LJ 95:1945, 3603)
   Illus. by Robert Baumgartner, Follett, 1969, 256 pp., o.p.

   LATHROP, Dorothy P(ulis). *The Fairy Circus.* See Chapter 1, Allegorical Fantasy and Literary Fairy Tales.

   LATHROP, Dorothy P(ulis). *The Little White Goat.* See Chapter 7, Magic Adventure Fantasy.

C LATHROP, Dorothy P(ulis). *The Snail Who Ran.* Gr. 3–4.
   A moonbeam fairy gives one wish each to a mouse and a snail. (BL 31:177; Bookshelf 1935 p. 2; HB 10:357; LJ 59:854; Mahony 3:80)
   Illus. by the author, Stokes, 1934, 57 pp., o.p.

C LAUBER, Patricia (Grace). *Home at Last!: A Young Cat's Tale.* Gr. 2–4.
   Two kittens raised in a library set off to find a new home, fortified for their adventures by reading heroic books. (BL 77:406; HB 57:47; KR 49:7; SLJ Feb 1981 p. 58)
   Illus. by Mary Chalmers, Coward, 1980, 47 pp.

C/YA LAURENCE, Margaret (Wemyss). *Jason's Quest.* Gr. 5–7. (Orig. British pub. 1970.)
   Searching for a cure for his hometown's illness, Jason Mole travels to the city of Londinium and is captured by a gang of rats. (CCBB 24:29; LJ 96:3050; Suth:240; TLS 1970 p. 1458)
   Illus. by Staffen Torell, Knopf, 1970, 211 pp., o.p.

C/YA LAWSON, Robert. *Ben and Me: A New and Astonishing Life of Benjamin*
   [R] *Franklin as Written by His Good Mouse, Amos: Lately Discovered.* Gr. 4–7. (Orig. pub. 1939.)
   Amos Mouse discloses the fact that most of Ben Franklin's inventions were actually Amos's ideas, and describes their adventures together. (BL 36:117; CC:497; Ch&Bks:246; HB 15:388, 16:28; LJ 65:125)
   Illus. by the author, Little, 1951, 114 pp.; Dell, 1973, pap.; Little, 1988, hb and pap.

C/YA LAWSON, Robert. *Captain Kidd's Cat: Being the True and Dolorous*
   [R] *Chronicle of Wm. Kidd, Gentleman and Merchant of New York; Late Captain of the Adventure Galley; Of the Vicissitudes Attending His Unfortunate Cruise in Eastern Waters, Of His Unjust Trial and Execution, as Narrated by His Faithful Cat, McDermot, Who Ought to Know.* Gr. 4–7.
   McDermot doesn't think Captain Kidd deserves to be called a pirate. (BL 52:282; CCBB 9:115; Eakin:203; HB 32:121, 61:78; KR 24:3; LJ 81:767)
   Illus. by the author, Little, 1956, 151 pp., o.p.; pap., 1984, o.p.

C [R] LAWSON, Robert. *Edward, Hoppy and Joe.* Gr. 3–5.
   Father Rabbit struggles to educate his son Edward and friends Hoppy Toad and Joe Possum. (BL 48:303; HB 28:107; KR 20:224; LJ 77:907)
   Illus. by the author, Knopf, 1952, 122 pp., o.p.

C/YA LAWSON, Robert. *I Discover Columbus: A True Chronicle of the Great Admiral and His Finding of the New World, Narrated by the Venerable Parrot Aurelio, Who Shared in the Glorious Venture.* Gr. 4–7.
It is Aurelio, a Caribbean parrot stranded in Spain, who convinces Columbus to make his voyage to the New World. (BL 38:58; HB 17:366, 453; LJ 66:908)
Illus. by the author, Little, 1941, 110 pp., o.p.

C/YA LAWSON, Robert. *Mr. Revere and I: Being an Account of Certain Epi-*
[R] *sodes in the Career of Paul Revere, Esq., as Recently Revealed by His Horse, Scheherazade, Late Pride of His Royal Majesty's 14th Regiment of Foot.* Gr. 5–7.
Scheherazade, a former cavalry horse rescued by Sam Adams from the glue factory, tells of her subsequent life with Paul Revere's family. (BL 50:84; CC:497; CCBB 7:31; Ch&Bks:269; Eakin:204; HB 29:464; KR 21:357; LJ 78:1858)
Illus. by the author, Little, 1953, 152 pp.; Dell, 1973, pap.

C [R] LAWSON, Robert. *Mr. Twigg's Mistake* Gr. 4–6.
Super-vitamin-laced cereal transforms Mr. Twigg's pet mole. (BL 44:117; CCBB 2[Jan 1949]:4; KR 15:467; LJ 72:1543)
Illus. by the author, Little, 1947, 141 pp., o.p.; pap., 1985, o.p.

C [R] LAWSON, Robert. *Rabbit Hill.* Gr. 3–6.
Although they are happy that a new family is moving into the empty farmhouse, the animals on Rabbit Hill fear the newcomers may bring traps and guns. Newbery Medal winner, 1945. The sequels are *Robbut: A Tale of Tails* (1948) and *The Tough Winter* (1954). (BL 41:62; CC:497; Ch&Bks:246; HB 20:487; KR 12:403; LJ 69:866, 886)
Illus. by the author, Viking, 1944, 127 pp.; Penguin, 1977, pap.

LAZARUS, Keo Felker. *The Shark in the Window.* See Chapter 6, Humorous Fantasy.

LEE, Tanith. *Animal Castle.* See Chapter 1, Allegorical Fantasy and Literary Fairy Tales.

C LEONARD, Nellie Mabel. *The Graymouse Family.* Gr. 4–6. (Orig. pub. 1916; retitled: *The Mouse Book,* 1926.)
Mother Graymouse and her six children live in the walls of a human family's house. The sequel is *Grandfather Whiskers, M.D., a Graymouse Story* (1953; orig. title: *Grand-daddy Whiskers, M.D,* 1919). (CCBB 4:44; KR 18:330; LJ 75:2162)
Illus. by Barbara Cooney, Crowell, 1950, 209 pp., o.p.

LEWIS, C(live) S(taples). *The Lion, the Witch, and the Wardrobe.* See Section 5C, Travel to Other Worlds.

C LEZRA, Giggy (Grizzella Paull). *The Cat, the Horse, and the Miracle.* Gr. 4–6.
A lady in blue gives an unhappy cat and horse a golden thread that will lead them into their future. (CCBB 20:155; KR 35:198; LJ 92:1317; Suth:250)
Illus. by Zena Bernstein, Atheneum, 1967, 114 pp., o.p.

LIFTON, Betty Jean (Kirschner). *The Cock and the Ghost Cat.* See Chapter 4, Ghost Fantasy.

C LINDOP, Audrey E. *The Adventures of the Wuffle.* Gr. 4–6. (Orig. British pub. 1966.)
Wuffle's grandmother advises him to become important; so he and his friend, Norrie the tortoise, decide to become lawyers. (KR 36:150; LJ 93:2730; TLS 1966 p. 1087)
Illus. by William Stobbs, McGraw-Hill, 1968, 126 pp., o.p.

LINDSAY, Norman (Alfred William). *The Magic Pudding: Being the Adventures of Bunyip Bluegum and His Friends Bill Barnacle and Sam Sawnoff.* See Chapter 6, Humorous Fantasy.

LITTLE, Jane. *Sneaker Hill.* See Chapter 10, Witchcraft and Sorcery Fantasy.

C [R] LIVELY, Penelope. *A House Inside Out.* Gr. 3–6.
The Dixon family shares their home with thirty-nine animals and several thousand insects. Each chapter of this book is told through the eyes of one of the nonhuman inhabitants of 54 Pavilion Road. (BL 84:1265, 1441; CCBB 41:95; KR 55:1630; SLJ Feb 1988 p. 73; TLS 1987 p. 1176)
Illus. by David Parkins, Dutton, 1987, 127 pp.

LOFTING, Hugh. *The Story of Doctor Dolittle.* See Chapter 6, Humorous Fantasy.

C LOFTING, Hugh. *The Story of Mrs. Tubbs.* Gr. 2–4. (Orig. pub. 1923.)
A dog, a duck, and a pig care for old Mrs. Tubbs until she is strong enough to go home to her farm. (BL 20:63; Bookshelf 1927 p. 7; KR 36:393)
Illus. by the author, Lippincott, 1968, 91 pp., o.p.

The Lonely Little Pig and Other Animal Tales. Ed. by Wilhelmina Harper. See Chapter 3, Fantasy Collections.

LOWREY, Janette Sebring. *The Lavender Cat.* See Chapter 1, Allegorical Fantasy and Literary Fairy Tales.

C McCOY, Neely. *The Tale of the Good Cat Jupie.* Gr. 2–4.
A talking cat and a little girl set up housekeeping together. The sequels are *Jupie Follows His Tale* (1928) and *Jupie and the Wise Old Owl* (1931). (BL 23:276; HB 2[Nov 1926]:45; LJ 53:484)
Illus. by the author, Macmillan, 1926, 1932, 99 pp., o.p.

C [R] McGOWEN, Tom (Thomas E.). *Odyssey from River Bend.* Gr. 4–6.
Kip the badger leads a group of animals from River Bend into the Haunted Land to search for the secrets of the ancients. (BL 72:44; CCBB 29:82; KR 43:513; SLJ Sept 1975 p. 107; Suth 2:300)
Little, 1975, 166 pp., o.p.

C McINERNEY, Judith Whitelock. *Judge Benjamin: Superdog.* Gr. 4–6.
The O'Rileys' St. Bernard, Judge Benjamin, describes his busy life as family protector. The sequels are *Judge Benjamin: The Superdog Secret* (1983) *Judge Benjamin: The Superdog Rescue* (1984), *Judge Benjamin: The Superdog Surprise* (1985), *Judge Benjamin: The Superdog Gift* (1986), and *Judge Benjamin and the Purloined Sirloin* (1986). (BL 78:1315; CC:505; SLJ Aug 1982 p. 118)
Illus. by Leslie Morrill, Holiday, 1982, 142 pp.; Pocket, 1983, pap., o.p.

McINERNY, Ralph M. *Quick As a Dodo.* See Chapter 6, Humorous Fantasy.

C McPHAIL, (Michael) David. *Henry Bear's Park.* Gr. 2–4.
During the long wait for his balloonist father's return, Henry Bear devotes himself to beautifying their park. Stanley Raccoon's life story is told in the companion volume, *Stanley, Henry Bear's Friend* (1979). (BL 72:1408; KR 44:589; SLJ Sept 1976 p. 102)
Illus. by the author, Little, 1976, 47 pp.; Penguin, 1978, pap.

C MAJOR, Beverly. *Porcupine Stew.* Gr. 2–4.
Thomas gives up his favorite silver whistle for admission to the Perpetu-annual Porcupine Parade and Picnic, where he watches a quill-throwing contest and eats "porcupine stew." (BL 79:724, 1283; CCBB 36:93; KR 50:1057; SLJ Nov 1982 p. 70)
Illus. by Erick Ingraham, Morrow, 1982, 39 pp.

C MAMIN-SIBERIAK (pseud. of Dmitrii Narkisovich Mamin). *Verotchka's Tales.* Gr. 3–5. (Orig. pub. in the Soviet Union.)
A collection of Russian stories about animals, birds, and insects. (BL 19:129; Mahony 2:290)
Tr. by Ray Davidson, illus. by Boris Artzybasheff, Dutton, 1922, 190 pp., o.p.

C MARSHALL, James (Edward). *A Summer in the South.* Gr. 2–4.
Eleanor Owl, famous detective, solves the case of the ghostly figure frightening Marietta Chicken. (KR 45:1144; SLJ Dec 1977 p. 61)
Illus. by the author, Houghton, 1977, 97 pp.; Dell, 1980, pap., o.p.

C MARSHALL, James (Edward). *Taking Care of Carruthers.* Gr. 3–4.
Carruthers the bear, Eugene the turtle, and Emily the pig take a sightseeing trip downriver in a rowboat, traveling through skunk country to Stupendousberg where Carruthers stars in a production of "Goldilocks." This is the sequel to the picture book *What's the Matter with Carruthers?* (1972). (BL 78:598; KR 50:3; SLJ Jan 1981 p. 80)
Illus. by the author, Houghton, 1981, 128 pp.

MASEFIELD, John (Edward). *The Midnight Folk: A Novel.* See Chapter 7, Magic Adventure Fantasy.

C MASON, Miriam E(vangeline). *Hoppity.* Gr. 2–4. (Orig. pub. 1947.)
Hoppity the goat eats everything from crayons to ladies' hats, until the day he tastes the bee on a baby's nose. (BL 44:117; HB 23:34; KR 15:427)
Illus. by Cyndy Szekeres, Macmillan, 1962, 66 pp., o.p.

C MATTHIESSEN, Peter. *The Seal Pool.* Gr. 3–5.
While being transported to the Bronx Zoo, a Great Auk escapes and hides near the seal pool in Central Park. (CCBB 25:80; KR 40:724; LJ 98:645)
Illus. by William Pène Du Bois, Doubleday, 1972, 78 pp., o.p.

MAYNE, William (James Carter). *The Blue Boat.* See Chapter 7, Magic Adventure Fantasy.

MENUHIN, Yehudi, and HOPE, Christopher. *The King, the Cat, and the Fiddle.* See Chapter 1, Allegorical Fantasy and Literary Fairy Tales.

MILNE, A(lan) A(lexander). *Prince Rabbit and the Princess Who Could Not Laugh.* See Chapter 1, Allegorical Fantasy and Literary Fairy Tales.

MOLESWORTH, Mary Louisa (Stewart). *The Cuckoo Clock.* See Section 5C, Travel to Other Worlds.

MOLESWORTH, Mary Louisa (Stewart). *The Tapestry Room: A Child's Romance.* See Chapter 7, Magic Adventure Fantasy.

C [R] MOORE, Lilian. *I'll Meet You at the Cucumbers.* Gr. 2–5.
   Adam Mouse comes to the city to meet Amanda Mouse on her birthday, and during the course of a day of wondrous discovery, he realizes that he is a poet. (BL 84:1266, 1441; CCBB 41:142; KR 51:622; SLJ Apr 1988 p. 82)
   Illus. by Sharon Wooding, Atheneum, 1988, 64 pp.

C MOORE, Margaret Eileen. *Willie Without.* Gr. 1–4. (Orig. British pub. 1951.)
   Willy the poetic worm makes many new friends as he searches for a new hat. (CCBB 5:81; HB 28:108; KR 20:124; LJ 77:444)
   Illus. by Nora S. Unwin, Coward, 1952, 85 pp., o.p.

C MORGAN, Alison (Mary Raikes). *River Song.* Gr. 4–6.
   Timothy Wagtail adopts a young Flycatcher who has lost his family. (BL 72:457; HB 52:52; KR 43:1131; SLJ Sept 1975 p. 108)
   Illus. by John Schoenherr, Harper, 1975, 160 pp., o.p.

C/YA MURPHY, Shirley Rousseau. *Flight of the Fox.* Gr. 5–7.
   A kangaroo rat and a pet lemming ask a boy named Charlie to help them pilot a motorized model airplane. (BL 75:384; CCBB 32:142; KR 46:1358; SLJ Jan 1979 p. 56)
   Illus. by Donald Sibley, based on original designs by Richard Cuffari, Atheneum, 1978, 164 pp., o.p.

MURPHY, Shirley Rousseau. *Nightpool.* See Section 5A, Alternate Worlds or Histories.

MURPHY, Shirley Rousseau. *The Pig Who Could Conjure the Wind.* See Chapter 10, Witchcraft and Sorcery Fantasy.

C NEWELL, Averil. *Fly-By-Nights.* Gr. 2–4.
   A mouse family sets up housekeeping in a vacant house conveniently located between a toy shop and a bakery. (BL 44:253; CCBB 2[Jan 1949]:5; HB 24:190; KR 16:109; LJ 73:485)
   Illus. by Kathleen Hiken, Macmillan, 1948, 48 pp., o.p.

NEWMAN, Robert (Howard). *The Shattered Stone.* See Section 5A, Alternate Worlds or Histories.

C NICKLESS, Will. *Owlglass.* Gr. 4–6. (Orig. British pub. 1964.)
   Old Beak and Claws the owl is losing his vision, so the forest animals steal the villagers' eyeglasses for him. The British sequel is *Dotted Lines.* (BL 62:833; HB 42:307; LJ 91:2696)
   Illus. by the author, Day, 1966, 158 pp., o.p.

C NIXON, Joan Lowery. *Magnolia's Mixed-Up Magic.* Gr. 2–4.
   Magnolia Possum and her grandmother try out a few spells from an old magic book, but can't seem to undo them after Magnolia begins flying around

the house, and the mailman disappears. (BL 79:1403; CCBB 37:14; KR 51:618; SLJ Oct 1983 p. 152)
Illus. by Linda Bucholtz-Ross, Putnam, 1983, 43 pp., o.p.

C [R] OAKLEY, Graham. *The Church Mouse.* Gr. 2–4.
Despite his friendship with Sampson the cat, Arthur the church mouse was lonely. So he decided to fill the church with friendly mice. The sequels are *The Church Cat Abroad* (1973), *The Church Mice and the Moon* (1974), *The Church Mice Spread Their Wings* (1976), *The Church Mice Adrift* (1977), *The Church Mice at Bay* (1979), *The Church Mice at Christmas* (1980), *The Church Mice in Action* (1983), and *Diary of a Churchmouse* (1987). (CCBB 26:130; HB 49:132; LJ 98:1675; KR 40:1187; TLS 1972 p. 1327)
Illus. by the author, Atheneum, 1972, 33 pp., o.p.; 1980, pap., o.p.

C [R] ORMONDROYD, Edward. *Broderick.* Gr. 1–4. (Orig. pub. Parnassus, 1969.)
Broderick mouse stops chewing up library books long enough to read one about surfing, and is inspired to become a champion surfer. (BL 66:459; CCBB 23:104; HB 46:37; KR 37:1252; LJ 95:2303)
Illus. by John Larrecq, Houghton, 1975, hb, 1984, pap.

C OSBORNE, M(aurice) M. (Jr.). *Rudi and the Mayor of Naples.* Gr. 2–4.
It takes a very special cake to make Rudi the donkey get up and pull his cart again. (HB 35:33; LJ 84:641)
Illus. by Joseph Low, Houghton, 1958, 48 pp., o.p.

C OTTO, Margaret G(lover). *The Tiny Man.* Gr. 3–4.
Two sea gulls find a tiny man carved from the heart of an oak tree, and help him to find a home. (KR 23:647; LJ 81:240)
Illus. by Peter Burchard, Holt, 1955, 122 pp., o.p.

C PAINE, Albert Bigelow. *The Hollow Tree and Deep Woods Book.* Gr. 4–6. (Orig. pub. separately as *The Hollow Tree,* 1898 and *In the Deep Woods,* 1899.)
A Coon, a Possum, and a Big Black Crow live together in a hollow tree. The sequels are *Hollow Tree Nights and Days* (1916), *The Hollow Tree Snowed-In Book* (1910, 1937, 1938), *How Mr. Dog Got Even* (1915), *How Mr. Rabbit Lost His Tail* (1910, 1915), *Making Up with Mr. Dog* (1915), *Mr. Crow and the Whitewash* (1917), *Mr. Possum's Great Balloon Trip* (1915), *Mr. Rabbit's Big Dinner* (1901, 1915), *Mr. Rabbit's Wedding* (1917), *Mr. Turtle's Flying Adventure* (1917), and *When Jack Rabbit Was a Little Boy* (1910, 1915). (Bookshelf 1928 p. 9; HB 7:116; Mahony 2:113)
Illus. by J. M. Conde, Harper, 1898–1900, 1929, 1938, 272 pp., o.p.

C PALMER, Robin (Riggs). *Wise House.* Gr. 3–5.
A cat and a crow move a family of children and their house to a pirate's island. (KR 19:387; LJ 76:2124)
Illus. by Decie Merwin, Harper, 1951, 138 pp., o.p.

C PARKER, (James) Edgar (Jr.). *The Dream of the Dormouse.* Gr. 2–4.
Hibernating Dormouse is sure he must be dreaming when he is kidnapped by a pirate bulldog. (CCBB 17:144; HB 39:286; KR 3:53; LJ 88:2553)
Illus. by the author, Houghton, 1963, 48 pp., o.p.

C PARKER, (James) Edgar (Jr.). *The Duke of Sycamore.* Gr. 1–4.
When the Lion King announces an upcoming visit, a group of forest friends

search frantically for a castle to borrow. (BL 55:488; CCBB 12:154; HB 35:214; KR 27:264; LJ 84:1699)
Illus. by the author, Houghton, 1959, 38 pp., o.p.

C PARKER, (James) Edgar (Jr.). *The Flower of the Realm.* Gr. 3–5.
Sir Stephen Stag and Baron Roebuck duel for the love of a beautiful doe. (HB 42:564; KR 34:831; LJ 91:5236)
Illus. by the author, Houghton, 1966, 60 pp., o.p.

C PARKER, (James) Edgar (Jr.). *The Question of a Dragon.* Gr. 3–5.
A raccoon, a cat, and a frog are commanded to rid the forest of a dreadful dragon. (CCBB 19:16; HB 40:283; KR 32:232; LJ 89:2661)
Illus. by the author, Pantheon, 1964, 43 pp., o.p.

PARKER, (James) Edgar (Jr.). *Rogue's Gallery.* See Chapter 6, Humorous Fantasy.

PARRISH, Anne, and PARRISH, Dillwyn. *Knee-High to a Grasshopper.* See Chapter 7, Magic Adventure Fantasy.

C PAYNE, Joan Balfour. *Ambrose.* Gr. 2–4.
A spoiled dog named Ambrose searches for a family with children to adopt him. (CCBB 11:17; HB 32:445; KR 24:627)
Illus. by the author, Hastings, 1956, 48 pp., o.p.

C PAYNE, Joan Balfour. *The Piebald Princess.* Gr. 3–5.
A Siamese cat claiming to be a princess makes life difficult for witch Molly Pippin. (BL 50:327; CCBB 7:77; HB 30:95; KR 22:229; LJ 79:702, 865)
Illus. by the author, Farrar, 1954, 79 pp., o.p.

C PEET, Bill (William Bartlett). *Big Bad Bruce.* Gr. 2–4.
Bruce the bear bully is put in his place by a witch named Roxy, who shrinks him to chipmunk size. (BL 73:1172; CCBB 30:163; HB 53:302; KR 45:163)
Illus. by the author, Houghton, 1977, 38 pp., o.p., 1978, pap.

C [R] PEET, Bill (William Bartlett). *The Whingdingdilly.* Gr. 2–4.
Wishing to become a famous horse, Orvie's dog Scamp changes into a creature that is part elephant, camel, zebra, rhinoceros, and giraffe. (BL 66:1280; HB 46:291; KR 38:317; LJ 95:2309; TLS 1971 p. 1515)
Illus. by the author, Houghton, 1970, 60 pp., 1982, pap.

C [R] PINKWATER, D(aniel) Manus. *Blue Moose.* Gr. 1–4.
The maitre d' of Mr. Breton's gourmet restaurant in the wild is a talking blue moose. The sequels are *Return of the Moose* (1979) and *The Moospire* (1986). (BL 72:45; CC:519; CCBB 29:84; HB 52:46; KR 43:661; SLJ Sept 1975 p. 88; Suth 2:365)
Illus. by the author, Dodd, 1975, 47 pp., o.p.

PINKWATER, D(aniel) Manus. *The Hoboken Chicken Emergency.* See Chapter 6, Humorous Fantasy.

PINKWATER, D(aniel) Manus. *Jolly Roger: A Dog of Hoboken.* See Chapter 6, Humorous Fantasy.

PINKWATER, D(aniel) Manus. *Lizard Music.* See Chapter 6, Humorous Fantasy.

C PLENN, Doris. *The Green Song.* Gr. 4–6. (Orig. pub. 1954.)
Pepe, a green tree frog from Puerto Rico, comes to New York City. (HB 30:137; KR 22:152; LJ 79:1238)
Illus. by Paul Galdone, McKay, 1969, 126 pp., o.p.

C POLLACK, Penny. *Stall Buddies.* Gr. 3–5.
Scarlett the filly's friends, a rooster named Rufus and a goat named Merabel, boost her self-confidence in preparation for the big race. (BL 81:848; CCBB 38:115; SLJ Mar 1985 p. 170)
Illus. by Gail Owens, Putnam, 1984, 63 pp., o.p.

C [R] POTTER, (Helen) Beatrix (Heelis). *The Fairy Caravan.* Gr. 4–6. (Orig. British and U.S. pub. 1929.)
The animal caravan traveling through the English countryside includes Tuppeny the long-haired guinea pig, Pony Billy, Jenny Ferret, and Princess Xarifa the dormouse. (BL 47:278; CCBB 4:37; HB 5:9, 47–49, 28:163; LJ 76:660; Mahony 3:209; Moore: 120)
Warne, 1951, 1985; Penguin/Puffin, 1986, pap., 192 pp.

C POTTER, (Helen) Beatrix (Heelis). *The Tale of Little Pig Robinson.* Gr. K–4.
Sent to market by his Aunts Dorcas and Porcas, Little Pig Robinson becomes lost and ends up aboard a ship bound for Robinson Crusoe's island. (BL 27:266; TLS Nov 1930 p. 986)
Illus. by the author, Warne, 1930, 123 pp.

C POTTER, (Helen) Beatrix (Heelis). *The Tale of the Faithful Dove.* Gr. 2–4. (Orig. British and U.S. pub. 1955.)
A mother dove fleeing a falcon becomes trapped in a chimney, but a mouse family and a boy help her to escape. (CCBB 24:112; HB 46:604; KR 38:1141; LJ 96:1498; TLS 1971 p. 768)
Illus. by Marie Angel, Warne, 1970 (2nd ed.), 47 pp., o.p.

PRICE, Susan. *The Ghost Drum: A Cat's Tale.* See Chapter 1, Allegorical Fantasy and Literary Fairy Tales.

PUSHKIN, Alexander Sergeevich. *The Tale of Czar Saltan, or the Prince and the Swan Princess.* See Chapter 1, Allegorical Fantasy and Literary Fairy Tales.

QUACKENBUSH, Robert M(ead). *Express Train to Trouble: A Miss Mallard Mystery.* See Chapter 6, Humorous Fantasy.

C [R] RAYNER, Mary (Yoma, neé Grigson). *Mrs. Pig Gets Cross; and Other Stories.* Gr. K–3.
Seven short, humorous stories about Mrs. Pig and her untidy but clever piglets, who always manage to outwit fox and wolf. This is the sequel to three books for a slightly younger audience: *Mr. and Mrs. Pig's Evening Out* (Atheneum, 1976), *Garth Pig and the Ice-Cream Lady* (Atheneum, 1977) and *Mrs. Pig's Bulk Buy* (Atheneum, 1981). (BL 83:1209; CCBB 40:154; HB 58:338; KR 55:137; SLJ Mar 1987 p. 149)
Illus. by the author, Dutton, 1987, 64 pp.

C RAZZI, Jim (James), and RAZZI, Mary. *The Search for King Pup's Tomb.* Gr. 3–5.
Sherluck Bones, master canine detective, finds the lost treasure of King Pup's tomb, in this, his first full-length exploit. There are six short-mystery-

episode books in the related Sherluck Bones Mystery-Detective Book series published by Bantam. (BL 81:1337; SLJ May 1985 p. 110)
Illus. by Ted Enik, Bantam, 1985, 62 pp., pap.

REID BANKS, Lynne. *The Farthest-Away Mountain.* See Chapter 1, Allegorical Fantasy and Literary Fairy Tales.

C ROBINSON, Mabel L(ouise). *Back-Seat Driver.* Gr. 3–5.
A wirehair terrier who delights in giving his master backseat driving tips is given a car of his own. The sequels are *Skipper Riley* (1955) and *Riley Goes to Obedience School* (1956). (CCBB 3:18; KR 17:360; LJ 74:1918)
Illus. by Leonard Shortall, Random, 1949, 68 pp., o.p.

C ROBINSON, Marileta. *Mr. Goat's Bad Good Idea.* Gr. 2–4.
Three Navajo tales concerning Mr. Goat, Grandfather Sheep, and Jerry the prairie dog. (BL 75:1160; CCBB 33:17; KR 47:329; SLJ Apr 1979 p. 47)
Illus. by Arthur Getz, Crowell, 1979, 39 pp.

ROCCA, Guido. *Gaetano the Pheasant: A Hunting Fable.* See Section 2A, Beast Tales.

YA ROGERS, Mark E. *The Adventures of Samurai Cat.* Gr. 10 up.
A satirical fantasy starring Miaowara Tomokato, the Samurai Cat, who embarks on a quest for vengeance against the killers of his master. (BL 81:483; SLJ Feb 1985 p. 91)
Illus. by the author, Tor, dist. by St. Martin, 1984, pap.

ROSS, Ramon Royal. *Prune.* See Chapter 1, Allegorical Fantasy and Literary Fairy Tales.

C SAINTSBURY (Green), Dana. *The Squirrel That Remembered.* Gr. 2–4.
Grandma Nutcracker, an English squirrel living in New York's Central Park, tries to help a homesick English girl. (CCBB 5:54; HB 27:331; KR 19:388; LJ 76:1572)
Illus. by the author, Viking, 1951, 60 pp., o.p.

SANCHEZ-SILVA, José. *The Boy and the Whale.* See Chapter 1, Allegorical Fantasy and Literary Fairy Tales.

C SAYERS, Frances Clarke. *Mr. Tidy Paws.* Gr. 2–4.
A cat named Mr. Tidy Paws comes to the deserted village of Bear Blossom to help Christopher and his grandmother. (BL 32:78; Bookshelf 1935 p. 3; HB 11:197, 351; LJ 61:35; Mahony 3:209)
Illus. by Zhenya Gay, Viking, 1935, 64 pp., o.p.

C/YA SCOTT, Dixon. *A Fresh Wind in the Willows.* Gr. 5–7. (Orig. British pub. 1983.)
The inhabitants of Riverbank still find Toad's misbehavior to be trying, in this contemporary sequel to Kenneth Grahame's *The Wind in the Willows* (1908) (see this section), written for a slightly older audience. (Kliatt 21[Sept 1987]:29; SLJ Nov 1987 p. 107)
Illus. by Jonathon Coudrille, Dell/Yearling, 1987, pap., 111 pp.

C SEEMAN, Elizabeth (Brickel). *The Talking Dog and the Barking Man.* Gr. 3–5.
Candido the talking dog runs away from home and joins a traveling ventriloquist's show. (HB 36:291; LJ 85:2043)
Illus. by James Flora, Watts, 1960, 186 pp., o.p.

C SÈGUR, Sophie (Rostopchine) Comtesse de. *The Wise Little Donkey* (*Memoirs of a Donkey*). Gr. 3–5. (Orig. French pub. 1860, orig. U.S. pub. as *The Adventures of a Donkey*, 1880; as *The Story of a Donkey*, 1901, and *Memoirs of a Donkey*, Macmillan, 1924.)
Cadichon the learned donkey tells the story of his life. (BL 21:161, 28:313; Mahony 2:114)
Tr. by Louis Auguste Loiseaux, illus. by Emma Brock, Whitman, 1931, 191 pp., o.p.

C [R] SEIDLER, Tor. *A Rat's Tale*. Gr. 4–6.
An artistic young rat named Montague earns a fortune, brings honor to his family, and wins his girl friend's heart, all by selling his miniature shell paintings. (BL 83:788, 84:1441; CCBB 40:118; HB 63:212; KR 54:1511; SLJ Jan 1986 p. 79)
Illus. by Fred Marcellino, Farrar, 1986, 185 pp.

C [R] SELDEN, George (pseud. of George Selden Thompson). *The Cricket in Times Square*. Gr. 3–6.
Chester Cricket's beautiful music (as managed by Tucker Mouse) brings fame to Chester and fortune to the subway-station newspaper stand where they live. Newbery Medal Honor Book, 1961. The sequels are *Tucker's Countryside* (1969), *Harry Cat's Pet Puppy* (1974), *Chester Cricket's Pigeon Ride* (1981), *Chester Cricket's New Home* (1983), *Harry Kitten and Tucker Mouse* (1986), and *The Old Meadow* (1987). (BL 57:250, 80:96; CC:527; CCBB 14:86; Ch&Bks:247; Eakin:288; HB 36:407; LJ 85:4570; TLS 1982 p. 798)
Illus. by Garth Williams, Farrar, 1960, 151 pp.; Dell, 1970, pap.

C SELDEN, George (pseud. of George Selden Thompson). *Irma and Jerry*. Gr. 4–6.
Newly arrived in Greenwich Village, a proper cocker spaniel named Jerry meets a runaway cat named Irma, and the two manage to prevent a robbery and become actors in an off-Broadway play. (BL 79:780; HB 59:167; SLJ Nov 1982 p. 104)
Illus. by Leslie Morrill, Avon, 1982, pap., 207 pp.

C SELDEN, George (pseud. of George Selden Thompson). *Oscar Lobster's Fair Exchange* (orig. title: *The Garden under the Sea*, Viking, 1957). Gr. 3–5.
Oscar Lobster and his friends decide to retaliate for the humans' annual thievery of shells and rocks by making their own undersea garden using items stolen from the humans. (BL 53:508; CCBB 11:85; KR 25:37; LJ 82:1802, 91:3538)
Illus. by Peter Lippman, Harper, 1966, o.p.; Avon, 1974, pap., 174 pp.

C [R] SENDAK, Maurice (Bernard). *Higglety Pigglety Pop! Or, There Must Be More to Life*. Gr. 2–4.
Bored by life at home, a sheepdog named Jenny packs her bag and sets off to find happiness as the leading lady in the World Mother Goose Theater. (BL 64:451; CC:527; CCBB 21:66; Ch&Bks:241; HB 44:151, 161; KR 35:1209; LJ 92:4618; Suth:354)
Illus. by the author, Harper, 1967, 69 pp.

SEREDY, Kate. *Lazy Tinka*. See Chapter 1, Allegorical Fantasy and Literary Fairy Tales.

C [R] SHARP (Castle), Margery. *The Rescuers.* Gr. 3–6.

Miss Bianca and two other mice go on a dangerous mission to rescue a human poet from imprisonment in a deep dungeon. The sequels are *Miss Bianca* (1962), *The Turret* (1963), *Miss Bianca in the Salt Mines* (1966), *Miss Bianca in the Orient* (1970), *Miss Bianca in the Antarctic* (1971), *Miss Bianca and the Bridesmaid* (1972), *Bernard the Brave* (1977), and *Bernard into Battle* (1978). *Miss Bianca in the Arctic* is a British sequel. (BL 56:274; CC:528; CCBB 13:105; Ch&Bks:271; Eakin:295; HB 36:38; KR 27:617; LJ 84:3153; TLS Dec 4, 1959 p. xv)

Illus. by Garth Williams, Little, 1959, o.p.; Dell, 1974, pap., 160 pp.

C SHEEDY, Alexandra E. *She Was Nice to Mice: The Other Side of Elizabeth I's Character Never Before Revealed by Previous Historians.* Gr. 3–5.

Esther Long Whiskers Gray Hair Wallgate the 42nd, a mouse with a literary mind, finds the memoirs of one of her ancestors who lived at the court of Queen Elizabeth I, in this story written and illustrated by two young adolescents. (CCBB 29:86; KR 43:849; SLJ Oct 1975 p. 108)

Illus. by Jessica Levy, McGraw-Hill, 1975, 95 pp., o.p.

C/YA SHEEHAN, Carolyn, and SHEEHAN, Edmond. *Magnifi-Cat.* Gr. 6 up.

The arrival of a small grey cat with a saint's halo at the Pearly Gates jams Heaven's soul-processing computer. (BL 69:551, 570, 767; KR 40:887; LJ 97:2756)

Doubleday, 1972, 229 pp., o.p.

C SHULEVITZ, Uri. *The Strange and Exciting Adventures of Jeremiah Hush.* Gr. 3–6.

A middle-aged monkey named Jeremiah Hush leaves his quiet home to visit the Shake 'n' Roll Dancin' Hole, and to enter a chocolate-banana-pecan-cream pie eating contest. (BL 83:846; CCBB 40:135; KR 54:1795; SLJ Feb 1987 p. 84)

Illus. by the author, Farrar, 1986, 90 pp.

C [R] SHURA, Mary Francis (pseud. of Mary Francis Craig). *A Tale of Middle Length.* Gr. 3–6.

Dominic and Alec mouse discover that the strange object near the mouse colony is a mouse trap. (BL 63:268; CCBB 20:48; HB 42:566; KR 34:687; LJ 91:4343)

Illus. by Peter Parnall, Atheneum, 1966, 105 pp., o.p.

SILVERSTEIN, Shel. *Uncle Shelby's Story of Laficadio, the Lion Who Shot Back.* See Chapter 6, Humorous Fantasy.

C SIMONT, Marc. *Mimi.* Gr. 3–5.

A mouse named Mimi is secretly trained to run across the stage every time a famous concert singer needs to hit a high note. (HB 31:111; KR 22:726; LJ 80:193)

Illus. by the author, Harper, 1954, 56 pp., o.p.

C SINGER, Marilyn. *The Fido Frame-Up* (The Sam Spayed series). Gr. 4–6.

In this detective novel spoof, Samantha Spayed, dog detective, is the brains behind her master, Philip Barlowe's solutions to his dangerous cases. The sequels are *A Nose for Trouble* (1985) and *Where There's a Will, There's a Wag* (1986). (BL 80:576; HB 59:712; SLJ Dec 1983 p. 83)

Illus. by Andrew Glass, Warne, 1983, 90 pp.

C SISSON, Rosemary Anne. *The Adventures of Ambrose*. Gr. 2–4. (Orig. British pub. 1951.)
Ambrose and Simon mouse travel to London to meet the king and queen. (HB 28:406; KR 20:598; LJ 77:1662)
Illus. by Astrid Walford, Dutton, 1952, 118 pp., o.p.

SLEIGH, Barbara (de Riemer). *Carbonel: The King of the Cats*. See Chapter 7, Magic Adventure Fantasy.

C [R] SMITH, Dodie (Dorothy Gladys). *The Hundred and One Dalmatians*. Gr. 4–6. (Orig. British pub. 1956.)
Pongo and Missis Dalmatian rescue their fifteen puppies from Cruella DeVil, who dognapped them to make into fur coats. The sequel is *The Starlight Barking* (1967). (BL 53:588; HB 33:222; KR 25:75; LJ 82:1802)
Illus. by Janet Grahame-Johnstone and Anne Grahame-Johnstone, Viking, 1957, o.p.; Avon, 1976, pap., 208 pp.; Buccaneer, 1981.

C SMITH, Emma. *Emily: The Traveling Guinea Pig*. Gr. 3–5.
Emily Guinea Pig sets off to see the ocean, leaving behind her brother Arthur to look after her tidy little house. The sequel is *Emily's Voyage* (Harcourt, 1966). (HB 36:287; KR 28:232)
Illus. by Katherine Wigglesworth, Astor-Honor, 1960, 76 pp.

STEARNS, Pamela (Fujimoto). *Into the Painted Bear Lair*. See Section 5C, Travel to Other Worlds.

C [O] STEIG, William. *Abel's Island*. Gr. 3–6.
A storm sweeps Abel the mouse away from his new bride, Amanda, to a deserted island, where he develops a talent for sculpting. Newbery Medal Honor Book, 1977. (BL 73:181, 80:46; CC:535; CCBB 30:33; Ch&Bks:272; HB 52:500; KR 44:686; SLJ Oct 1976 p. 101; Suth 2:429; TLS 1977 p. 1248)
Illus. by the author, Farrar, 1976, 117 pp., 1985, pap.

C [R] STEIG, William. *Dominic*. Gr. 4–6.
An adventurous dog named Dominic finds an enchanted garden, is given a fortune by an old pig, and helps fight the Doomsday Gang. (BL 69:531; CC:535; CCBB 26:31; Ch&Bks:272; HB 48:470; KR 40:1414; LJ 97:2954; Suth 378; TLS 1973 p. 386)
Illus. by the author, Farrar, 1972, 145 pp., 1984, pap.

C [R] STEIG, William. *The Real Thief*. Gr. 2–5.
Angry over the theft of his jewels, the king accuses his loyal guard, Gawain the goose, in spite of Gawain's pleas of innocence. (BL 70:242, 827; CC:535; CCBB 27:102; HB 49:595; KR 41:756; LJ 98:3446; Suth 2:431)
Illus. by the author, Farrar, 1973, 58 pp., 1985, pap.

C STEVENS, Eden Vale. *Abba*. Gr. 3–6.
Abba, an orphaned elephant, searches for Einhorn, the Great White Buffalo, to help him rescue another elephant held captive by hunters. (BL 59:576; LJ 87:190)
Illus. by Anthony Stevens, Atheneum, 1962, 116 pp., o.p.

C STEVENSON, James. *Here Comes Herb's Hurricane!* Gr. 2–4.
Herb Rabbit develops a hurricane warning system that refuses to work

until a real hurricane comes along. (CCBB 27:150; KR 41:1310, 1351; LJ 98:3709)
Illus. by the author, Harper, 1973, 149 pp., o.p.

C STEVENSON, James. *Oliver, Clarence, and Violet.* Gr. 2–4.
Oliver Beaver's round-the-world boat trip is complicated by the numerous friends who decide to go with him, including a toad, a turkey, a turtle, and two bats. (BL 78:1370; KR 50:347; SLJ May 1952 p. 65)
Illus. by the author, Greenwillow, 1982, 96 pp., o.p.

C [R] STOLZ, Mary (Slattery). *Belling the Tiger.* Gr. 2–4.
Asa and Rambo mouse are selected to put a bell on Siri, the tigerlike housecat, bringing about an unexpected trip to the land of elephants and real tigers. Newbery Medal Honor Book, 1962. The sequels are *The Great Rebellion* (1961), *Siri the Conquistador* (1963), and *Maximilian's World* (1966). (BL 57:644; CCBB 14:149; Ch&Bks:272; Eakin:314; HB 37:339; KR 29:326; LJ 86:1989).
Illus. by Beni Montresor, Harper, 1961, 64 pp., o.p.

C [R] STOLZ, Mary (Slattery). *Cat Walk.* Gr. 3–6.
A six-toed black barn kitten runs away from the home where a little girl has dressed him up and named him Tootsie Wootsie, and searches for a home where he will be loved for himself. (BL 79:1223; CCBB 36:218; Ch&Bks:272; HB 59:306; KR 51:307; SLJ Aug 1983 p. 71; Suth 3:412)
Illus. by Erik Blegvad, Harper, 1983, 120 pp.; Harper/Trophy, 1985, pap.

C [R] STOLZ, Mary (Slattery). *Frédou.* Gr. 4–6.
Runaway Paul is taken in by a hotel-owning Parisian cat. (BL 59:84; CCBB 15:166; HB 38:370; KR 30:386; LJ 87:2625)
Illus. by Tomi Ungerer, Harper, 1962, 118 pp., o.p.

C STOLZ, Mary (Slattery). *Pigeon Flight.* Gr. 2–4.
Mr. and Mrs. Pigeon decide to leave New York City and move to New England. (CCBB 16:16; Eakin:317; HB 38:607; LJ 87:3206)
Illus. by Murray Tinkelman, Harper, 1962, 54 pp., o.p.

C [R] STOLZ, Mary (Slattery). *Quentin Corn.* Gr. 4–6.
Bored with life as a pig, Quentin Corn decides to live as a man; but while he is accepted by adults, the children are not all so accepting. (BL 82:270, 84:1441; CC 1987 Suppl. p. 63; CCBB 39:80; HB 61:737; SLJ Sept 1985 p. 140, Dec 1985 p. 34)
Illus. by Pamela Johnson, Godine, 1985, hb and pap., 122 pp.

C [R] STONG, Phil(ip Duffield). *Prince and the Porker.* Gr. 4–6.
A boy and a pig help a harness trotter named Prince to win blue ribbons. (BL 47:226; CCBB 3:71; HB 26:477; LJ 75:2083)
Illus. by Kurt Wiese, Dodd, 1950, 67 pp., o.p.

C SYMONDS, John. *Elfrida and the Pig.* Gr. 2–4. (Orig. British pub. 1959.)
Elfrida's secret friend, the pig next door, helps her find a doll of her very own. (CCBB 14:18; HB 36:292; LJ 85:2044; TLS Dec 4, 1959 p. xv)
Illus. by Edward Ardizzone, Watts, 1959, 48 pp., o.p.

TARN, Sir William Woodthorpe. *Treasure of the Isle of Mist: A Tale of the Isle of Skye.* See Chapter 7, Magic Adventure Fantasy.

C [R] TITUS, Eve. *Basil of Baker Street*. Gr. 3–5.
    Basil, an English mouse detective who idolizes Sherlock Holmes, solves one of Mousedom's most baffling and mysterious kidnapping cases. The sequels are *Basil and the Lost Colony* (1964), *Basil and the Pygmy Cats* (1971), *Basil in Mexico* (1975), and *Basil in the Wild West* (1982). (BL 54:593; CC:540; CCBB 11:124; Ch&Bks:272; HB 34:266; KR 26:335; LJ 83:1947)
    Illus. by Paul Galdone, McGraw-Hill, 1958, 128 pp.

C [R] TODD, Ruthven. *Space Cat*. Gr. 3–5.
    Flyball the cat not only makes an important scientific discovery on his way to the moon, but also saves the pilot's life. The sequels are *Space Cat Visits Venus* (1955), *Space Cat Meets Mars* (1957), and *Space Cat and the Kittens* (1959). (CCBB 6:28; Ch&Bks:272; HB 28:320; KR 20:657; LJ 77:1819)
    Illus. by Paul Galdone, Scribner, 1952, 69 pp., o.p.

C TOMLINSON, Jill. *Hilda the Hen Who Wouldn't Give Up*. Gr. 2–4.
    Hilda the hen is so enamored of her Aunt Emma's chicks that she decides to have a brood of her own, against Farmer Biddick's wishes. (BL 76:1612; KR 48:838; SLJ Aug 1980 p. 58)
    Illus. by Fernando Krahn, Harcourt, 1967, 1980, 96 pp., o.p.

C TREVOR, Elleston. *Deep Wood*. Gr. 4–6.
    Five friends, Badger, Otter, Owl, Squirrel, and Fox, live along the Wild River in Deep Wood. *Heather Hill* (1948) and *Badger's Wood* (1958, 1959) are the sequels. (BL 44:138; CCBB 1[Dec 1947]:7; HB 23:358; KR 45:394; LJ 73:126)
    Illus. by Stephen Voorhis, Longman, 1947, 282 pp., o.p.

   TURKLE, Brinton (Cassaday). *Mooncoin Castle; or Skulduggery Rewarded*. See Chapter 4, Ghost Fantasy.

C UNWIN, Nora S(picer). *Two Too Many*. Gr. 2–4.
    On Halloween night, two lost kittens are taken for a ride on a witch's broom. (Eakin:339; HB 38:473; LJ 87:4615; TLS 1965 p. 1141)
    Illus. by the author, McKay, 1962, 54 pp., o.p.

C [R] VAN LEEUWEN, Jean. *The Great Christmas Kidnapping Caper*. Gr. 3–5.
    The disappearance of Santa Claus mobilizes Marvin the Magnificent Mouse and his gang to the rescue. This is the sequel to *The Great Cheese Conspiracy* (Random, 1969) and is followed by *The Great Rescue Operation* (1982). (BL 72:169; CC:543; CCBB 29:54; KR 43:778; SLJ Oct 1975 p. 81; Suth 2:459)
    Illus. by Steven Kellogg, Dial, 1975, 133 pp.

C WABER, Bernard. *Dear Hildegarde*. Gr. 2–4.
    Hildegarde Owl is an advice columnist who tries to solve the problems of her fellow creatures. (CCBB 34:141; HB 57:54; KR 49:4; SLJ Feb 1981 p. 60)
    Illus. by the author, Houghton, 1980, 64 pp., o.p.

C WABER, Bernard. *Mice on My Mind*. Gr. 2–5.
    Suffering from an obsession with mice, a cat finally finds a cure for his malady. (CCBB 31:103; HB 53:526; KR 45:1045; SLJ Sept 1977 p. 117; Suth 2:464)
    Illus. by the author, Houghton, 1977, 48 pp., o.p.

C WAHL, Jan (Boyer). *Pleasant Fieldmouse*. Gr. 2–4.
    Pleasant Fieldmouse becomes a firefighter and courageously rescues Anx-

ious Squirrel's mother and Mrs. Worrywind Hedgehog. The sequels are *The Six Voyages of Pleasant Fieldmouse* (Delacorte, 1971), *Pleasant Fieldmouse's Halloween Party* (Putnam, 1974), *The Pleasant Fieldmouse Storybook* (Prentice-Hall, 1977), and *Pleasant Fieldmouse's Valentine Trick* (Dutton, 1977). (CCBB 18:94; HB 40:373; LJ 89:3477; TLS 1969 p. 1387)
Illus. by Maurice Sendak, Harper, 1964, 65 pp.

C WALLACE, Barbara Brooks. *Palmer Patch*. Gr. 4–6.
Thinking they are no longer wanted, the Patch family's pets run away from home. (BL 73:671; CCBB 30:116; SLJ Apr 1977 p. 72)
Illus. by Lawrence Di Fiori, Follett, 1976, 128 pp., o.p.

C WENNING, Elisabeth. *The Christmas Mouse* (British title: *The Christmas Churchmouse*). Gr. K–4.
Hungry little Kaspar Kleinmause helps Herr Gruber write the carol "Silent Night." (BL 56:225; HB 35:471; KR 27:756; LJ 84:3627)
Illus. by Barbara Remington, Holt, 1959, 44 pp., o.p.

WESTALL, Robert (Atkinson). *The Cats of Seroster*. See Section 5A, Alternate Worlds or Histories.

C [R] WHITE, Anne Hitchcock. *Junket*. Gr. 4–6.
It takes an entire summer for an airedale named Junket to teach his new owners about farm life. (BL 51:287; CCBB 9:31; Eakin:348; HB 31:114; KR 23:81; LJ 80:1259)
Illus. by Robert McCloskey, Viking, 1955, 183 pp., o.p.

C [R] WHITE, Anne Hitchcock. *The Story of Serapina*. Gr. 3–5.
Serapina the cat adopts the Salinus family, although they are not sure they want her. (BL 47:333; CCBB 4:47; Eakin:348; HB 27:180; LJ 76:970)
Illus. by Tony Palazzo, Viking, 1951, 128 pp., o.p.

C [O] WHITE, E(lwyn) B(rooks). *Charlotte's Web*. Gr. 3 up.
Wilbur the pig is destined for the annual fall slaughtering, but his resourceful friend, a spider named Charlotte, tries to save him. Newbery Medal Honor Book, 1953. (BL 49:2, 80:96; CC:545; CCBB 6:36; Ch&Bks:247; Eakin:348; HB 28:394, 407; KR 20:501; LJ 77:2185; TLS 1952 p. 7)
Illus. by Garth Williams, Harper, 1952, hb and pap., 184 pp.

C WHITE, E(lwyn) B(rooks). *Stuart Little*. Gr. 4–6.
Stuart Little is the second son of a normal American family—except that Stuart turns out to be a mouse instead of a boy. (CC:545; Ch&Bks:273; HB 21:455; KR 13:314)
Illus. by Garth Williams, Harper, 1945, hb and pap., 131 pp.

C [R] WHITE, E(lwyn) B(rooks). *The Trumpet of the Swan*. Gr. 4–6.
Lewis's father buys him a trumpet to overcome his speech defect and starts the young swan on a career as a nightclub entertainer. (BL 67:59, 661; CC:545; CCBB 24:35; Ch&Bks:273; HB 46:391; KR 38:455; LJ 95:2537, 4327; TLS 1970 p. 1458)
Illus. by Edward Frascino, Harper, 1970, hb and pap., 210 pp.

YA WHITELAW, Stella, GARDINER, Judith, and RONSON, Mark. *Grimalkin's Tales*. Gr. 10 up.
Twelve tales about cats, some of which are fantasy, including one about Leopold, a large cat who can fly. (KR 53:830; SLJ Jan 1986 p. 84)
St. Martin, 1985, 160 pp., o.p.

WIGGIN, Kate. *The Bird's Christmas Carol.* See Chapter 1, Allegorical Fantasy and Literary Fairy Tales.

WILDE, Oscar. *The Happy Prince.* See Chapter 1, Allegorical Fantasy and Literary Fairy Tales.

C WILLIAMS, Garth (Montgomery). *The Adventures of Benjamin Pink.* Gr. 2–4.
A rabbit named Benjamin Pink is shipwrecked while on a fishing trip. (HB 27:400; 28:27; KR 19:347; LJ 76:1710)
Illus. by the author, Harper, 1952, 152 pp., o.p.

C/YA WILLIAMS (John), Ursula Moray. *Bogwoppit.* Gr. 5–7. (Orig. British
[R] pub. 1978.)
Samantha's crusade to save the furry creatures who live in the drains of her aunt's mansion takes a new turn when her aunt is kidnapped by the Bogwoppits. (BL 75:54; CCBB 32:128; Ch&Bks:273; KR 46:879; SLJ Sept 1978 p. 152; Suth 2:481; TLS 1978 p. 765)
Nelson, 1978, 128 pp., o.p.

C [R] WILLIAMS (John), Ursula Moray. *The Nine Lives of Island MacKenzie* (Orig. U.S. title: *Island MacKenzie*). Gr. 4–6. (Orig. British pub. 1959.)
MacKenzie the cat and a cat-hating woman named Miss Pettifer survive shipwreck, sharks, and crocodiles to be cast up together on a desert island. (BL 57:157; CCBB 14:88; HB 36:503, 56:664; KR 28:498; LJ 85:3228; TLS Dec 4, 1959 p. xv)
Illus. by Edward Ardizzone, Morrow, 1960, o.p.; Chatto, dist. by Merrimack, 1980, 128 pp.

WILLIAMS (John), Ursula Moray. *Tiger Nanny.* See Chapter 6, Humorous Fantasy.

C WILSON, Gahan. *Harry the Fat Bear* (Orig. title: *Harry the Fat Bear Spy*). Gr. 4–6.
Harry would rather be a chef or a tap dancer than the bumbling spy he is, but he does manage to solve the case of the great Bearmania macaroons. The sequel is *Harry and the Sea Serpent* (1976). (KR 41:698; LJ 99:2281)
Illus. by the author, Scribner, 1973, o.p.; Dell, 1978, pap., 120 pp.

WILSON, Willie. *Up Mountain One Time.* See Chapter 1, Allegorical Fantasy and Literary Fairy Tales.

WOOD, James Playsted. *An Elephant in the Family.* See Chapter 6, Humorous Fantasy.

WRIGGINS, Sally. *The White Monkey King: A Chinese Fable.* See Section 5B, Myth Fantasy.

C WYNDHAM, Lee (pseud. of Jane Andrews Hyndman). *Mourka, the Mighty Cat.* Gr. 2–4.
Mourka the village cat pretends to be the mighty ruler of the forest. (HB 45:529; LJ 95:1192)
Illus. by Charles Mikolaycak, Parents, 1969, 41 pp., o.p.

C YEP, Laurence. *The Curse of the Squirrel.* Gr. 2–4.
Farmer Johnson's hunting dog, Howie, is cursed by Shag, the monster squirrel, into becoming a squirrel by night so that he can understand how it

feels to be "treed like a possum." (BL 84:325; CCBB 41:60, KR 55:1582; SLJ Dec 1987 p. 76)
Illus. by Dirk Zimmer, Random, 1987, hb and pap., 45 pp.

C [R] YOLEN (Stemple), Jane H(yatt). *The Acorn Quest*. Gr. 3–5.
King Earthor Owl of Woodland sends his wizard Squirrelin and his knights, a groundhog, a turtle, a rabbit, and a mouse, on a quest for the Golden Acorn, in this takeoff on an Arthurian legend. (BL 78:444; HB 58:48; KR 49:1346; SLJ Dec 1981 p. 59)
Illus. by Susanna Natti, Crowell, 1981, 57 pp.

C [R] YOLEN (Stemple), Jane H(yatt). *Hobo Toad and the Motorcycle Gang*. Gr. 3–5.
Hobo and his gang foil an attempted bank robbery and kidnapping. (BL 67:149; HB 46:391; KR 38:455; LJ 95:3056)
Illus. by Emily McCully, Collins + World, 1970, 62 pp., o.p.

C [R] YOLEN (Stemple), Jane H(yatt). *Piggins*. Gr. K–3.
Mr. and Mrs. Reynard's butler, Piggins, solves the mystery of Mrs. Reynard's stolen diamond lavaliere. The sequel is *Picnic with Piggins* (1988). (BL 83:1132; CCBB 40:160; HB 63:459; KR 55:304; SLJ Apr 1987 p. 91)
Illus. by Jane Dyer, Harcourt, 1987, 32 pp.

ZARING, Jane T(homas). *The Return of the Dragon*. See Chapter 1, Allegorical Fantasy and Literary Fairy Tales.

C/YA *Zoo 2000: Twelve Stories of Science Fiction and Fantasy Beasts*. Ed. by Jane H. Yolen. Gr. 6–9.
A collection of twelve science fiction and fantasy tales about animals of the future, including James Thurber's "Interview with a Lemming," and André Norton's "All Cats Are Grey." (BL 70:538, 546; CCBB 27:167; KR 41:1162; LJ 98:3715)
Seabury, 1973, 224 pp., o.p.

3
Fantasy Collections

Collections of fantastic tales in the form of short stories are listed in this chapter. These tales often resemble traditional folktales in style.

AHLBERG, Allan. *The Clothes Horse and Other Stories*. See Chapter 6, Humorous Fantasy.

C/YA AIKEN, Joan (Delano). *The Faithless Lollybird*. Gr. 5–8. (Orig. British [R] pub. 1977.)
These thirteen modern fairy tales include stories about a witch, a haunted tower, and a mermaid. (BL 74:1614; CCBB 31:153; HB 54:281; KR 46:594; SLJ Apr 1978 p. 90; Suth 2:6; TLS 1977 p. 863)
Illus. by Eros Keith, Doubleday, 1978, 255 pp., o.p.

YA [R] AIKEN, Joan (Delano). *The Far Forests: Tales of Romance, Fantasy and Suspense*. Gr. 8 up.
Fifteen sophisticated tales touched with humor, magic, and the macabre, including "As Gay as Cheese," "A Taxi to Solitude," "Furry Night," and "The Cold Flame." (CCBB 31:25; HB 53:536; JHC:431; KR 45:233, 363; LJ 102:827; Suth 2:6)
Viking, 1977, 154 pp., o.p.

C/YA AIKEN, Joan (Delano). *The Green Flash and Other Tales of Horror, Sus-* [R] *pense, and Fantasy*. Gr. 6–9. (Orig. British pubs. 1957, 1969.)
Fourteen tales, including "Marmalade Wine," "The Dead Language Master," and "The Windshield Weepers." (BL 68:428; HB 48:54; KR 39:1131; LJ 96:4200)
Holt, 1971, 163 pp., o.p.

C/YA AIKEN, Joan (Delano). *A Harp of Fishbones and Other Stories*. Gr. 5 up. (Orig. British pub. 1972.)
Thirteen fantasy tales, including "The Boy With a Wolf's Foot," "The Lost Five Minutes," and "The Prince of Darkness." (TLS 1972 p. 474; Tymn:39)
Puffin, 1975, pap., o.p.

C AIKEN, Joan (Delano). *The Last Slice of Rainbow: And Other Stories.*
  Gr. 3–6.
  Nine short fantasy stories, including one about a boy who wants to keep a
  rainbow. (BL 84:1338; CCBB 41:129; KR 56:613; SLJ May 1988 p. 94)
  Illus. by Alix Berenzy, Harper, 1988, 144 pp.

C AIKEN, Joan (Delano). *A Necklace of Raindrops and Other Stories.* Gr.
  3–5. (Orig. British pub. 1968.)
  Eight stories including "There's Some Sky in This Pie," "The Elves in the
  Shelves," and "The Patchwork Quilt." (CCBB 23:37; HB 45:530; KR 37:631;
  LJ 95:238)
  Illus. by Jan Pienkowski, Doubleday, 1969, 96 pp., o.p.

C/YA AIKEN, Joan (Delano). *Not What You Expected: A Collection of Short*
  [R] *Stories.* Gr. 6–9.
  Twenty-one tales, including "The Boy with a Wolf's Foot," "The Lost Five
  Minutes," and "The Third Wish." These stories were published in Great
  Britain in three collections: *A Small Pinch of Weather* (1971), *A Harp of
  Fishbones* (1971), and *All and More* (1971). (BL 71:377; CCBB 28:73;
  Ch&Bks:263; HB 51:151; KR 42:1258; SLJ Jan 1975 p. 42)
  Doubleday, 1974, 320 pp., o.p.

C AIKEN, Joan (Delano). *Past Eight O'Clock: Goodnight Stories.* Gr. 3–5.
  Eight magical tales about dreams, sleep, and the night. (CC 1988 Suppl. p.
  67; CCBB 40:201; SLJ Oct 1987 p. 124)
  Illus. by Jan Pienkowski, Viking, 1987, 128 pp.

C/YA AIKEN, Joan (Delano). *Smoke from Cromwell's Time and Other Stories.*
  [R] Gr. 4–7 (Orig. British pubs. 1959, 1966, 1969.)
  Fourteen tales, including "The King Who Stood All Night," "The Wolves
  and the Mermaids," and "The Parrot Pirate Princess." (BL 67:142; CCBB
  24:37; Ch&Bks:263; HB 46:476; KR 38:742; LJ 95:3044)
  Doubleday, 1970, 163 pp., o.p.

AIKEN, Joan (Delano). *A Touch of Chill: Tales for Sleepless Nights.* See
Chapter 4, Ghost Fantasy.

AIKEN, Joan (Delano). *Up the Chimney Down and Other Stories.* See
Chapter 6, Humorous Fantasy.

AIKEN, Joan (Delano). *A Whisper in the Night: Tales of Terror and
Suspense.* See Chapter 4, Ghost Fantasy.

C AINSWORTH (Gilbert), Ruth (Gallard). *The Bear Who Liked Hugging
  People and Other Stories.* Gr. K–4. (Orig. British pub. 1976.)
  Thirteen stories about witches, animals, and magic. (BL 74:1487; SLJ Oct
  1978 p. 141)
  Illus. by Antony Maitland, Crane Russak, 1978, 102 pp., o.p.

AINSWORTH (Gilbert), Ruth (Gallard). *The Phantom Carousel and
Other Ghostly Tales.* See Chapter 4, Ghost Fantasy.

C/YA *The Air of Mars; and Other Stories of Time and Space.* Ed. by Mirra
  [R] Ginsburg. Gr. 6–9. (Orig. Soviet Union pub. 1964–1972.)
  Nine Soviet Union fantasy and science fiction tales, including one about a
  woman whose husband turns into a garden. (BL 72:1592; HB 52:410; KR
  44:204; SLJ Apr 1976 p. 74)
  Tr. by the editor, Macmillan, 1976, 141 pp., o.p.

ALCOCK, Vivien (Dolores). *Ghostly Companions: A Feast of Chilling Tales.* See Chapter 4, Ghost Fantasy.

C ALDEN, Raymond Macdonald. *The Boy Who Found the King; a Tournament of Stories.* Gr. 3–5.

A young prince and princess hold a story tournament to choose an official storyteller, and the contestants tell the stories contained in this collection. (BL 19:127, 43:90; Mahony, 2:269).

Illus. by W. R. Lohse, Bobbs-Merrill, 1922, o.p. (Reissued in 1946, entitled: *Once There Was a King; a Tournament of Stories,* illus. by Evelyn Copelman, 176 pp., o.p.)

C ALDEN, Raymond Macdonald. *Why the Chimes Rang and Other Stories.* Gr. 3–6. (Orig. pub. 1908.)

Eleven tales of kings, knights, giants, and magic. (BL 42:170; LJ 80:188; Mahony 2:269).

Illus. by Rafaello Busoni, Bobbs-Merill, 1954, 146 pp., o.p.

YA ALDISS, Brian W(ilson). *Seasons in Flight.* Gr. 10 up.

Ten tales about the impact of modern cultures on ancient ones, including "The Other Side of the Lake," "The Gods in Flight," and "Incident in a Far Country." Some stories are related to Aldiss's Helliconia trilogy: *Helliconia Spring* (1982), *Helliconia Summer* (1983), and *Helliconia Winter* (1985). (BL 82:733, 750; KR 53:1293)

Atheneum, 1986, 157 pp., o.p.

Amazons! Ed. by Jessica Amanda Salmonson. See Section 5A, Alternate Worlds or Histories.

C/YA ANDERSEN, Hans Christian. *Fairy Tales.* Gr. 3 up. (Written in Denmark
[O] 1837–1845; orig. English tr. by Mary Howitt, entitled: *Wonderful Stories for Children* 1846.) Andersen was the first great writer of original fantasy for children, and his tales are still among the best loved of all children's stories. There have been numerous editions of Andersen's stories published in English, under various titles. These include the following, listed first in alphabetical order, then by publication date:

Andersen's Fairy Tales. Illus. by W. Heath Robinson, Houghton, 1931, 355 pp., o.p.

Andersen's Fairy Tales. Putnam, 1958, 352 pp., hb and pap.

Andersen's Fairy Tales. Sharon, 1981, 204 pp., pap.

Andersen's Fairy Tales. Wanderer, 1983, 300 pp.

[O] *Ardizzone's Hans Andersen: Fourteen Classic Tales.* Illus. by Edward Ardizzone, Atheneum, 1979, ©1978, 191 pp., o.p.

The Complete Fairy Tales and Stories. Doubleday, 1974, 1101 pp.

[O] *Dulac's The Snow Queen and Other Stories from Hans Andersen.* Illus. by Edmund Dulac, Doubleday, 1976, 143 pp.

Eighty Fairy Tales. Random, 1982, 394 pp.

Fairy Tales. Illus. by W. Heath Robinson, Holt, 1913, 288 pp., o.p.

Fairy Tales. Illus. by Kay Nielsen, Garden City, 1924, 1932, o.p.; Viking/
Metropolitan Museum of Art, 1981, 155 pp., o.p.

Fairy Tales. Illus. by Arthur Rackham, McKay, 1932, 287 pp., o.p.

Fairy Tales. Illus. by Fritz Kredel, Heritage, 1942, 297 pp., o.p.

Fairy Tales. Illus. by Vilhelm Pedersen, Scribner, 1950, 394 pp., o.p.

Fairy Tales from Hans Christian Andersen. (Orig. British pub. 1901). Illus.
by Thomas H. Robinson, Charles Robinson, and W. Heath Robinson,
Dutton, 1903, 1930, o.p.

Favorite Tales of Hans Andersen. Illus. by Robin Jacques, Faber, 1986,
pap., 168 pp.

[O] *Hans Andersen: His Classic Fairy Tales.* Illus. by Michael Foreman,
Doubleday, 1978, 196 pp.

Hans Andersen's Fairy Tales. Illus. by Maria L. Kirk and E. A. Lehmann,
Lippincott, 1911, 219 pp., o.p.

Hans Andersen's Fairy Tales. Illus. by W. Heath Robinson, Doran, 1924,
319 pp., o.p.

Hans Andersen's Fairy Tales. Illus. by Ernest H. Shepard, Walck, 1962, ©
1959, 327 pp., o.p.

Hans Andersen's Fairy Tales. Illus. by Shirley Hughes, Schocken, 1979,
pap.

Hans Andersen's Fairy Tales. Illus. by Sumiko, Schocken, 1980, 96 pp.,
o.p.

Hans Andersen's Fairy Tales. Illus. by Philip Gough, Penguin, 1981, pap.,
176 pp.

Hans Andersen's Fairy Tales: A Selection. Illus. by Lorenz Frolich and
Vilhelm Pedersen, Oxford, pap., 493 pp.

It's Perfectly True, and Other Stories. Illus. by Richard Bennett, Harcourt,
1938, 305 pp., o.p.

The Mermaid, and Other Fairy Tales. Illus. by Maxwell Armfield, Dutton,
1914, 1916, 127 pp., o.p.

[O] *Michael Hague's Favorite Hans Christian Andersen Fairy Tales.* Illus.
by Michael Hague, Holt, 1981, 176 pp.

[O] *Seven Tales.* Illus. by Maurice Sendak, Harper, 1959, 127 pp., o.p.

Stories from Hans Andersen. Illus. by Edmund Dulac, Hodder, 1911, 1922;
Doran, 1923, 1927, 1930, 250 pp., o.p.

The Stories of Hans Andersen. Illus. by Robin Lawrie, Silver, 1985, 80 pp.

Tales and Stories by Hans Christian Andersen. University of Washington
Press, 1980, 316 pp., hb and pap. (BL 20:109, 233, 28:110, 396, 34:303,
40:324, 47:241, 55:512, 58:797, 70:738, 73:1159, 74:1730, 75:1216, 78:241,
493; Bookshelf 1933 p. 5; CC:550, 551; CCBB 27:122, 35:101;
Ch&Bks:263; HB 1[Nov 1924]:6; 7:187–189, 9:152, 10:37, 13:25, 14:153,
20:46, 164, 27:93, 35:297, 50:269, 55:408, 58:539, KR 27:264, 30:111,

42:12, 46:879, 47:519, 49:1411; LJ 58:1050, 63:284, 69:72, 76:530, 84:1692, 87:2409, 99:568; Mahony 2:271; SLJ Feb 1977 p. 60, Nov 1978 p. 54, Apr 1979 p. 52, Dec 1981 p. 59; Suth 2:14; Suth 3:15, 16; TLS Dec 1, 1961 p. xii, 1974 p. 1377, 1981 p. 1360)

YA ANDERSON, Poul (William). *Fantasy.* Gr. 10 up.
A collection of Anderson's short fantasy fiction and essays, plus an introductory essay on Anderson's work by Sandra Miesel. (BL 78:425, 434; LJ 106:2409; SLJ Mar 1982 p. 162)
Tor/Pinnacle, 1981, pap., 334 pp., o.p.

YA *Another World; Adventures in Otherness: A Science Fiction Anthology.* Ed. by Gardner Dozois. Gr. 7–12.
Eleven tales of science fiction and fantasy written by Gene Wolfe, Ursula K. Le Guin, and Robert Silverberg, among others. (BL 73:1568; SLJ Oct 1977 p. 122)
Follett, 1977, 282 pp., o.p.

The April Witch and Other Strange Tales. Ed. by Barbara Ireson. See Chapter 4, Ghost Fantasy.

BABBITT, Natalie (Zane Moore). *The Devil's Storybook.* See Chapter 6, Humorous Fantasy.

C BACON, Peggy. *The Lion-Hearted Kitten and Other Stories.* Gr. 3–4.
A collection of short, humorous, folktalelike animal stories. (BL 24:124; Bookshelf 1929 p. 9; HB 3[Nov 1927]:19; LJ 53:484).
Illus. by the author, Macmillan, 1927, 102 pp., o.p.

C BACON, Peggy. *Mercy and the Mouse and Other Stories.* Gr. 2–4.
In the first of these animal stories, an ambitious young cellar cat becomes a household pet. (BL 25:289; HB 4[Aug 1928]:20, 4[Nov 1928]:76; Mahony 2:117; Moore:35)
Illus. by the author, Macmillan, 1928, 85 pp., o.p.

C BAILEY, Margery. *The Little Man with One Shoe.* Gr. 3–6.
Six magical fairy tales told by a fairy shoemaker. (BL 18:88; Bookshelf 1923–1924 p. 7; LJ 47:869; Mahony 2:271)
Illus. by Alice Bolan Preston, Little, 1921, 227 pp., o.p.

C BAILEY, Margery. *Seven Peas in the Pod.* Gr. 3–6.
Seven stories; one for each day of the week. (BL 16:137; Bookshelf 1923–1924 p. 7; LJ 45:980; Mahony 1:39; Mahony 2:272)
Illus. by Alice Bolan Preston, Little, 1919, 201 pp., o.p.

C BAILEY, Margery. *Whistle for Good Fortune, in Which It Is Shown How Six from Six Makes Six and One to Carry, with Other Riddles Here and There Along the Way.* Gr. 4–6.
Six original fairy tales told in folktale-style. (BL 36:308; LJ 65:260)
Illus. by Alice Bolan Preston, Little, 1940, 237 pp., o.p.

C BAKER, Margaret. *Fifteen Tales for Lively Children.* Gr. 2–4. (Orig. British pub. 1938. New British title: *The Goose Feather Gown,* 1982.)
This collection of humorous tales is a companion volume to *Tell Them Again Tales* (1934). (BL 35:292; LJ 64:380; TLS 1938 p. 789)
Illus. by Mary Baker, Dodd, 1939, 144 pp., o.p.

C BAKER, Margaret. *Pedlar's Ware*. Gr. 3–4.
Four fairy tales: "The Sad Princess," "The Leprechaun," "The Ghost and
the Shadow," and "The Princess and the Beggar Maid." (BL 21:386)
Illus. by Mary Baker, Duffield, 1925, 88 pp., o.p.

C BAKER, Margaret. *Tell Them Again Tales*. Gr. 2–4.
Eighteen tales about kings, animals, and princesses. *Fifteen Tales for
Lively Children* (1939) is a companion volume. (BL 31:67; Bookshelf 1934–
1935 p. 4; HB 10:296; LJ 60:403; Mahony 3:85)
Illus. by Mary Baker, Dodd, 1934, 143 pp., o.p.

C *A Baker's Dozen, Thirteen Stories to Tell and to Read Aloud*. Comp. by
Mary Gould Davis. Gr. 4–6.
A collection that includes stories by Laurence Housman, Carl Sandburg,
Mary E. Wilkins, Frank R. Stockton, and Gottfried Keller. (BL 27:108; HB
6:329; LJ 55:736; Mahony 3:158)
Illus. by Emma Brock, Harcourt, 1930, 207 pp., o.p.

BAUM, L(yman) Frank. *The Surprising Adventures of the Magical
Monarch of Mo and His People*. See Chapter 1, Allegorical Fantasy and
Literary Fairy Tales.

YA BEAGLE, Peter S(oyer). *The Fantasy Worlds of Peter S. Beagle*. Gr. 10
up.
This collection includes *A Fine and Private Place* and *The Last Unicorn*,
plus two short stories, "Lila the Werewolf" and "Come, Lady Death." (BL
75:598, 606; KR 46:977)
Viking, 1978, 430 pp., o.p.

BENNETT, John. *The Pigtail of Ah Lee Ben Loo, with Seventeen Other
Laughable Tales*. See Chapter 6, Humorous Fantasy.

C [R] BESTON, Henry B. (pseud. of Henry Beston Sheahan). *Henry Beston's
Fairy Tales*. Gr. 4–6.
Contains many of the stories from *The Firelight Fairy Book* (1919) and *The
Starlight Wonder Book* (1923) including "The Seller of Dreams," "The Lost
Half-Hour," and "The City Under the Sea." (BL 16:174, 20:62, 37:364,
49:76; Bookshelf 1932 p. 8; HB 28:311, 420; KR 20:546; LJ 77:1820; Mahony
1:39; Mahony 2:273; Moore:426)
Illus. by Fritz Kredel, Aladdin, 1952, 353 pp., o.p.

C BIANCO, Margery Williams. *A Street of Little Shops*. Gr. 3–5. (Orig.
pub. Doubleday, 1932.)
Seven tales about a street of shops in a small country town, including one
about a Cigar Store Indian who runs away. (Bookshelf 1932 p. 10; HB
21:191; LJ 58:899)
Illus. by Grace Paull, Gregg, 1981, 111 pp., o.p.

Black Water: The Book of Fantastic Literature. Ed. by Alberto Manguel.
See Chapter 1, Allegorical Fantasy and Literary Fairy Tales.

C [R] *The Blue Rose; a Collection of Stories for Girls*. Ed. by Eulalie Steinmetz
Ross. Gr. 4–6.
Stories by Hans Christian Andersen, Laurence Housman, Howard Pyle,
Walter de la Mare, Eleanor Farjeon, George MacDonald, and Ruth Sawyer.
(BL 63:186; HB 42:566; KR 34:106; LJ 91:4342; TLS 1966 p. 1092)
Illus. by Enrico Arno, Harcourt, 1966, 186 pp., o.p.

C [R] BOMANS, Godfried (Jan Arnold). *The Wily Witch and All the Other Fairy Tales and Fables.* Gr. 3–5. (An earlier Dutch ed. of selected tales pub. 1969; this ed. pub. 1975.)
Forty-five fairy tales, including "The Rich Blackberry Picker," "The Princess with Freckles," and "The Curse." Twenty-four of these tales were originally published in *The Wily Wizard and the Wicked Witch and Other Weird Stories* (Watts 1969). (BL 73:1726; CCBB 23:156, 31:6; Ch&Bks:264; LJ 95:777; SLJ Sept 1977 p. 121; Suth 2:51; TLS 1969 p. 3521)
Tr. by Patricia Crampton, illus. by Wouter Googendijk, Stemmer, 1977, 205 pp.

YA BORGES, Jorge Luis, with GUERRERO, Margarita. *The Book of Imaginary Beings.* Gr. 10 up. (Orig. Mexican pub. 1957.)
A treasury of carefully researched descriptions of one hundred and twenty legendary creatures from all over the world. (HB 46:186; LJ 94:4526; TLS 1971 p. 149)
Rev., enlarged, and tr. by Norman Thomas di Giovanni in collaboration with the author, Dutton, 1969, 256 pp., o.p.

YA BOUCHER, Anthony (pseud. of William Anthony Parker White). *The Compleat Werewolf; and Other Stories of Fantasy and Science Fiction.* Gr. 10 up.
Ten short stories and novellas about a werewolf, a demon, orgres, and a ghost. (BL 66:823, 837; KR 37:955; LJ 94:3665, 3839, 95:1913)
Simon, 1969, 256 pp., o.p.

C BOURLIAGUET, Léonce. *The Giant Who Drank from His Shoe and Other Stories.* Gr. 4–6. (Orig. pub. in France.)
Humorous tales about French villagers, giants, and animals. (KR 34:1979; LJ 91:3531; TLS 1965 p. 1140)
Tr. by John Buchanan Brown, illus. by Gerald Rose, Abelard-Schuman, 1966, 93 pp., o.p.

YA BRADBURY, Ray. *Dinosaur Tales.* Gr. 10 up.
A collection of Bradbury's stories and poems about dinosaurs, including "Tyrannosaurous Rex," "The Fog Horn," and "Besides a Dinosaur, Whatta Ya Wanna Be When You Grow Up?" (Kliatt 17[Fall 1983]:21; KR 51:339)
Illus. by Kenneth Smith, William Stout, Steranko, Moebius, Gahan Wilson, and David Wiesner, Bantam, 1983, pap., 144 pp., o.p.

YA [R] BRADBURY, Ray. *The Stories of Ray Bradbury.* Gr. 10 up.
One hundred of Bradbury's science fiction, fantasy, horror, and midwestern short stories. (BL 77:4, 7; KR 48:1120; LJ 105:1883; SHC:650; SLJ Dec 1980 p. 79; VOYA 4[June 1981]:36)
Knopf, dist. by Random, 1980, 884 pp.

C BRENTANO, Clemens Maria. *Fairy Tales from Brentano.* Gr. 4–6. (Orig. German pub. 1846–47, orig. U.S. pub. 1886.)
Seven original fairy tales selected from the works of this German storyteller. *More Fairy Tales from Brentano* (1888) is the companion volume. (BL 22:425)
Tr. by Kate Freiligrath Kroeker, illus. by F. Carruthers Gould, Stokes, 1925, 326 pp., o.p.

BRÖGER, Achim. *Bruno.* See Chapter 6, Humorous Fantasy.

BROWNE, Frances. *Granny's Wonderful Chair and Its Tale of Fairy Times.* See Chapter 7, Magic Adventure Fantasy.

BUCHAN, John. *The Watcher by the Threshold and Other Tales.* See Section 5B, Myth Fantasy.

BURGESS, Thornton W(aldo). *Old Mother West Wind.* See Section 2B, Talking Animal Fantasy.

C CANFIELD, Dorothy (pseud. of Dorothea Frances [Canfield] Fisher). *Made-to-Order Stories.* Gr. 4–6.
The author's ten-year-old son chose the elements used in these humorous stories. (BL 22:75; Bookshelf 1932 p. 12; HB 2[Nov 1925]:21, 14:208; LJ 51:836; Mahony 2:606)
Illus. by Dorothy P. Lathrop, Harcourt, 1925, 263 pp., o.p.

C CASSERLEY, Anne Thomasine. *Michael of Ireland.* Gr. 4–6. (Orig. British pub. 1926.)
The animals tell Michael stories about the fairy people. (BL 24:124; Bookshelf 1932 p. 8; HB 3[Nov 1927]:9–10; LJ 53:484, 1033; Mahony 2:132)
Illus. by the author, Harper, 1927, 139 pp., o.p.

C CASSERLEY, Anne Thomasine. *The Whins on Knockattan.* Gr. 2–4.
Pandeen and his grandmother share the whin-covered hillside of Knockattan with Little Black Lamb and Shaughran the red fox. (BL 25:215; Bookshelf 1929 p. 11; HB 4[Nov 1928]:30–32; Mahony 2:133; TLS 1929 p. 475)
Illus. by the author, Harper, 1928, 178 pp.

A Cavalcade of Dragons. Ed. by Roger Lancelyn Green. See Chapter 1, Allegorical Fantasy and Literary Fairy Tales.

C [R] *A Cavalcade of Goblins* (British title: *The Hamish Hamilton Book of Goblins*). Ed. by Alan Garner. Gr. 4–6.
A collection of myths, folktales, poems, and literary fairy tales about goblins and other fearsome creatures. (BL 66:129; CCBB 23:58; HB 45:531; LJ 94:4604; Suth:142)
Illus. by Krystyna Turska, Walck, 1969, 227 pp., o.p.

C [R] *A Cavalcade of Queens* (British title: *Hamish Hamilton Book of Queens,* 1965). Ed. by Eleanor Farjeon and William Mayne. Gr. 4–6.
A companion volume to *A Cavalcade of Kings* (1965), this collection includes stories by Andrew Lang, Nathaniel Hawthorne, and Rudyard Kipling. (BL 62:875; HB 42:193; LJ 91:1698; TLS 1965 p. 1136)
Illus. by Victor Ambrus, Walck, 1965, 243 pp., o.p.

CHANT, Joy. *The High Kings.* See Section 5B, Myth Fantasy.

C/YA CHESNUTT, Charles Waddell. *Conjure Tales.* Gr. 5–7.
[R] Seven tales of magic and witchcraft drawn from nineteenth-century U.S. black slave life. (CCBB 27:126; HB 50:48; KR 41:1035, 1152; LJ 98:3689, 3705; Suth 2:82)
Retold by Ray Shepard, illus. by John Ross and Clare Romano, Dutton, 1973, 99 pp., o.p.

C [R] CHRISMAN, Arthur Bowie. *Shen of the Sea: Chinese Stories for Children.* Gr. 5–8.
A collection of humorous Chinese fairy tales. Newbery Medal winner,

1926. *The Wind That Wouldn't Blow: Stories of the Merry Middle Kingdom for Children and Myself* (1927) is a companion volume. (BL 22:167; Bookshelf 1932 p. 8; CC:551; Ch&Bks:264; HB 2[Nov 1925]:20; LJ 51:836; Mahony 2:277; TLS 1969 p. 1193)

Illus. by Else Hasselriis, Dutton, 1926, 1968 (redesigned), 221 pp.

C/YA   CHRISMAN, Arthur Bowie. *The Wind That Wouldn't Blow: Stories of the Merry Middle Kingdom for Children and Myself.* Gr. 5–7.

A collection of stories that tell how things came to be as they are in China. This is a companion volume to *Shen of the Sea: Chinese Stories for Children* (1926, 1968). (BL 24:71; Bookshelf 1927 Suppl. p. 5; HB 3[Nov 1927]:47; Mahony 2:277)

Illus. by Else Hasselriis, Dutton, 1927, 355 pp., o.p.

Christmas Ghosts. Ed. by Kathryn Cramer and David G. Hartwell. See Chapter 4, Ghost Fantasy.

Christmas Ghosts: An Anthology. Ed. by Seon Manley and Gogo Lewis. See Chapter 4, Ghost Fantasy.

C   COATSWORTH, Elizabeth Jane. *The Snow Parlor and Other Bedtime Stories.* Gr. 3–4.

Five tales about talking animals, toys that come to life, a walking pine tree, and a boy who enters a mountain to find out where snow comes from. (CCBB 25:137; KR 39:1011; LJ 97:2476)

Illus. by Charles Robinson, Grosset, 1971, 64 pp., o.p.

C   COLUM, Padraic. *The Big Tree of Bunlahy: Stories of My Own Countryside.* Gr. 3–5.

A combination of Irish legends and original tales, including "Our Hen" and "The Three Companions." (BL 30:87; HB 10:33–36; LJ 59:482; Mahony 3:166)

Illus. by Jack B. Yeats, Macmillan, 1933, 166 pp., o.p.

COLUM, Padraic. *The Boy Who Knew What the Birds Said.* See Section 2B, Talking Animal Fantasy.

C   COLUM, Padraic. *The Fountain of Youth; Stories to Be Told.* Gr. 4–6.

Seventeen of Colum's tales chosen from several of his collections as being particularly good for storytelling. (BL 24:251; LJ 53:485)

Illus. by Jay Van Everen, Macmillan, 1927, 206 pp., o.p.

C   COLUM, Padraic. *The Peep-Show Man.* Gr. 1–3.

A peep-show man traveling the roads of Ireland tells a little boy three stories, one each for midsummer-day, Halloween, and Easter. (BL 21:71; Bookshelf 1924–1925 Suppl. p. 1; Mahony 3:85)

Illus. by Lois Lenski, Macmillan, 1924, 65 pp., o.p.

C [R]   COLUM, Padraic. *The Stone of Victory and Other Tales.* Gr. 4–6.

Irish tales drawn from Colum's previously published collections, including "The Twelve Silly Sisters," "The Wizard Earl," and "Kat Mary Ellen and the Fairies." (BL 63:794; HB 43:200; KR 34:980; LJ 91:5746; Suth:85)

Illus. by Judith Brown, McGraw-Hill, 1966, 121 pp., o.p.

CUNNINGHAM, Julia (Woolfolk). *Candle Tales.* See Section 2B, Talking Animal Fantasy.

C D'AULAIRE, Ingri Mortenson, and D'AULAIRE, Edgar Parin.
D'Aulaires' Trolls. Gr. 3–5.
In the mountains, forests, and waterways of Norway live bands of little creatures called trolls, gnomes, and hulder-people. (BL 69:404; HB 48:592; KR 40:1415; Suth:22)
Illus. by the authors, Doubleday, 1972, 62 pp., o.p.

C D'AULNOY, Marie Catherine Jumelle de Berneville, Comtesse. *The Children's Fairy Land*. Gr. 4–6.
Eight illustrated fairy tales. (BL 16:62; Bookshelf 1928 p. 10; LJ 45:980)
Illus. by Harriet Mead Olcott, Holt, 1919, 189 pp., o.p.

C [R] D'AULNOY, Marie Catherine Jumelle de Berneville, Comtesse. *The White Cat and Other Old French Fairy Tales*. Gr. 3–5. (Orig. pub. in France; orig. British title: *Fairy Tales by the Countess D'Aulnoy*, 1855; orig. U.S. title: *D'Aulnoy's Fairy Tales*, 1858; McKay, 1923. o.p.; orig. U.S. pub. with this title, 1928.)
A collection of old French folk tales, embroidered and adapted to take place in a palace, including "The Blue-Bird," "The Hind in the Wood," and "The Yellow Dwarf." (BL 20:303, 25:253; HB 4[Aug 1928]:11; LJ 53:811, 93:866; Mahony 2:195–197; Moore:290, 434.)
Adapt. by Rachel Field, illus. by Elizabeth MacKinstry, Macmillan, 1967, 150 pp., o.p.

DAVIS, Robert. *Padro Porko: The Gentlemanly Pig*. See Section 2B, Talking Animal Fantasy.

C/YA DE LA MARE, Walter (John). *Broomsticks and Other Tales*. Gr. 5–7.
[R] (Orig. British pub. 1925.)
Twelve stories including "The Lovely Myfanwy," "Alice's Godmother," and "Maria-Fly." (BL 22:252; HB 2[Nov 1925]:20, 18:180; LJ 67:892; TLS 1925 p. 797; Tymn:72)
Knopf, 1942, 334 pp., o.p.

C DE LA MARE, Walter (John). *The Dutch Cheese*. Gr. 3–5. (Orig. British pub. 1925.)
Two stories from *Broomsticks and Other Tales* (1925, 1942): "The Dutch Cheese" and "The Lovely Myfanwy." (BL 28:156; HB 7:223; Mahony 3:204)
Illus. by Dorothy P. Lathrop, Knopf, 1931, 75 pp., o.p.

C/YA DE LA MARE, Walter (John). *The Lord Fish*. Gr. 5–7.
Seven stories: "The Lord Fish," "A Penny a Day," "The Jacket," "Dick and the Beanstalk," "Hodmadod," "The Old Lion," and "Sambo and the Snow Mountains." (HB 10:232; Mahony 3:204)
Illus. by Rex Whistler, Faber, 1933, 289 pp., o.p.

C/YA DE LA MARE, Walter (John). *The Magic Jacket*. Gr. 5–7. (Orig. British
[R] pub. 1943.)
Ten tales of magic, including "The Magic Jacket," "The Riddle," and "Broomsticks." (BL 58:689; CCBB 16:93; Eakin:97; HB 38:276; KR 30:180; LJ 87:1316).
Illus. by Paul Kennedy, Knopf, 1962, 277 pp., o.p.

C/YA DE LA MARE, Walter (John). *A Penny a Day*. Gr. 4–7. (Orig. British
[R] pub. 1925.)
Six stories, including "The Three Sleeping Boys of Warwickshire," "Dick

and the Beanstalk," and "The Lord Fish." (BL 57:219; CCBB 14:78; Ch&Bks:265; Eakin:98; HB 36:503; LJ 85:4565)
Illus. by Paul Kennedy, Knopf, 1960, 209 pp., o.p.

C [R] DE LA MARE, Walter (John). *Tales Told Again* (Orig. title: *Told Again; Old Tales Told Again,* Knopf, 1927, 1943). Gr. 2–5.
This book contains all of the tales from *Broomsticks and Other Tales* (1942), *A Penny a Day* (1960), and *Animal Stories* (1940), including both traditional and modern fairy tales. (BL 24:324, 55:459; CCBB 12:130; HB 35:298; LJ 84:1694; TLS 1927 p. 873, Dec 4, 1959 p. xvi)
Scribner, 1940; Knopf, 1946; Faber, dist. by Merrimack, 1980, 208 pp., hb and pap.

C/YA DE MORGAN, Mary (Augusta). *The Complete Fairy Tales of Mary De Morgan.* Gr. 4–7.
Contains the stories from three of De Morgan's collections: *On a Pincushion* (orig. British pub. 1876, U.S. 1891), *The Necklace of Princess Fiorimonde* (orig. British pub. 1880, U.S. 1922), and *The Windfairies* (orig. British pub. 1900, U.S. 1901). A facsimile edition of *On a Pincushion* and *The Necklace of Princess Fiorimonde* was published by Garland, 1977, o.p. (LJ 88:4081)
Illus. by William De Morgan, Walter Crane, and Olive Cockerell, Watts, 1963, 412 pp., o.p.

C/YA DOLBIER, Maurice (Wyman). *The Half-Pint Jinni, and Other Stories.* Gr.
[R] 4–7.
Eight magical tales set in Baghdad. (BL 45:36; CCBB 1[Sept 1948]:2; KR 16:280; LJ 73:1097, 1457)
Illus. by Allan Thomas, Random, 1948, 242 pp., o.p.

DONALDSON, Stephen R. *Daughter of Regals and Other Tales.* See Section 5A, Alternate Worlds or Histories.

YA [R] *Dragon Tales.* Ed. by Isaac Asimov, Charles G. Waugh, and Martin Harry Greenberg. Gr. 7 up.
Twelve stories about dragons, including Anne McCaffrey's "Weyr Search" and Gordon Dickson's "The Dragon and the George." (BL 79:294, 304; JHC:433; SLJ Dec 1982 p. 86; VOYA 5[Dec 1982]:36)
Fawcett, 1982, pap., 318 pp., o.p.

Dragons and Dreams: A Collection of New Fantasy and Science Fiction Stories. Ed. by Jane Yolen, Martin H. Greenberg, and Charles G. Waugh. See Chapter 7, Magic Adventure Fantasy.

C/YA DUNBAR, Aldis. *The Sons O'Cormac, An' Tales of Other Men's Sons.* Gr. 5–7.
An old gardener tells children hero tales of Old Ireland. (BL 17:235, 26:77; Mahony 1:40)
Illus. by Myra Luxmoore, Longmans, 1904, o.p.; illus. by Ferdinand Huszti-Horvath, Dutton, 1920, 1929, 233 pp., o.p.

C EDGEWORTH, Maria. *Simple Susan and Other Tales.* Gr. 3–5. (Orig. U.S. pub. 1819.)
Eight of the author's best-known stories, including "The Cherry Orchard," "The Orange Man," and "The Purple Jar." (BL 26:169; HB 5:53)
Dutton, 1907, o.p.; illus. by Clara Burd, Macmillan, 1929, 216 pp., o.p.

Elsewhere, vol. I. Ed. by Terri Windling and Mark Alan Arnold. See Section 5A, Alternate Worlds or Histories.

YA *Elsewhere, Elsewhen, Elsehow.* Ed. by Miriam Allen De Ford. Gr. 10 up.
Eighteen fantasy, science fiction, and horror stories, including "The Old Woman" and "The Monster." (KR 39:465, 567; LJ 96:3641, 4205)
Walker, 1971, 180 pp., o.p.

C [R] *The Enchanted Book.* Ed. by Alice Dalgliesh. Gr. 3–5.
Twenty one stories of magical enchantment whose authors include Hans Christian Andersen and Marie D'Aulnoy. (BL 44:137; CCBB 1[Feb 1948]:2; HB 24:37; LJ 72:1436, 1690)
Illus. by Concetta Cacciola, Scribner, 1947, 246 pp., o.p.

The Enchanter's Spell: Five Famous Tales. Adapt. by Gennady Spirin. See Chapter 1, Allegorical Fantasy and Literary Fairy Tales.

C [R] ESTES, Eleanor. *The Sleeping Giant and Other Stories.* Gr. 2–5.
Three tales: "The Sleeping Giant," "The Lost Shadow," and "A Nice Room for Giraffes." (BL 45:123; CCBB 1[Nov 1948]4; HB 25:35; KR 16:571; LJ 73:1825)
Illus. by the author, Harcourt, 1948, 101 pp., o.p.

C EWING, Juliana (Horatia Gatty). *The Brownies and Other Stories* (orig. British title: *The Brownies and Other Tales,* 1870). Gr. 4–6. (Orig. U.S. pub. Macmillan, 1910.)
Seven tales, including "The Brownies," "Amelia and the Dwarfs," and "The Land of Lost Toys." (BL 7:85, 51:210; CCBB 9:44; Mahony 2:279)
Illus. by Ernest H. Shepard, Dent, dist. by Biblio, 1975 (repr. of 1954 ed.), 250 pp., o.p.

C *The Faber Book of Modern Fairy Tales.* Ed. by Sara Corrin and Stephen Corrin. Gr. 4–6. (Orig. British pub. 1981.)
Fifteen original tales by E. Nesbit, Laurence Housman, James Thurber, A. A. Milne, Philippa Pearce, and others. (CCBB 36:6; Ch&Bks:265; Suth 3:103; TLS 1981 p. 1356)
Illus. by Ann Strugnell, Faber, dist. by Merrimack, 1982, 312 pp.

Faery! Ed. by Terry Windling. See Chapter 1, Allegorical Fantasy and Literary Fairy Tales.

YA *Famous Tales of the Fantastic.* Ed. by Herbert Maurice Van Thal. Gr. 10 up.
Eleven American and British short stories whose authors include Ray Bradbury, Nathaniel Hawthorne, Washington Irving, and Robert Louis Stevenson. (BL 62:525; LJ 90:5303; TLS 1966 p. 29)
Illus. by Edward Pagram, Hill, 1965, 208 pp., o.p.

YA *Fantastic Creatures: An Anthology of Fantasy and Science Fiction.* Ed. by Isaac Asimov, Martin Greenberg, and Charles Waugh. Gr. 7–10.
A combination of eight fantasy and science fiction stories, including Anne McCaffrey's "The Smallest Dragonboy." (BL 78:434, 438; CCBB 35:142; SLJ Aug 1982 p. 123)
Watts, 1981, 155 pp., o.p.

The Fantastic Imagination: An Anthology of High Fantasy, vol. 1. Ed. by Robert H. Boyer and Kenneth J. Zahorski. See Chapter 1, Allegorical Fantasy and Literary Fairy Tales.

YA   *Fantasy Annual V.* Ed. by Terry Carr. Gr. 10 up.

A sampling of the best short fantasy of 1981, most of which are stories based in reality with a psychological rather than supernatural basis for the fantasy elements. Other books in the series are *The Year's Finest Fantasy, 1978* (Berkley 1978), *The Year's Finest Fantasy,* vol. 2 (1979), *Fantasy Annual III* (1981), and *Fantasy Annual IV* (1981). (BL 79:601; LJ 107:2192)

Timescape/Pocket, 1982, 240 pp.

YA   *Fantasy Hall of Fame.* Comp. by Robert Silverberg and Martin H. Greenberg. Gr. 10 up.

Twenty-three stories chosen as the best of modern fantasy by the 1982 and 1983 world fantasy conventions. The authors range from Edgar Allan Poe to Ursula K. Le Guin. (BL 80:397; JHC:433; LJ 108:1976)

Arbor House, 1983, 414 pp.

C   FARBER, Norma (Holzman). *Six Impossible Things before Breakfast.* Gr. 3–5.

Four poems and two short stories about magic, a unicorn, and a princess, each illustrated by a different artist. (CCBB 30:123; HB 53:307; SLJ Apr 1977 p. 66)

Illus. by Tomie dePaola, Trina Schart Hyman, Hilary Knight, Friso Henstra, Lydia Dabcovich, and Charles Mikolaycak, Addison-Wesley, 1977, 43 pp., o.p.

C [R]   FARJEON, Eleanor. *Italian Peepshow and Other Tales.* Gr. 3–5. (Orig. U.S. pub. 1926.)

Three children visiting Italy listen to a number of stories, including "Oranges and Lemons" and "Nella's Dancing Shoes." (BL 24:125, 57:274; Bookshelf 1928 p. 16; HB 3:18, 36:406; KR 28:904; LJ 85:4566; TLS Nov 25, 1960 p. vii)

Illus. by Edward Ardizzone, Walck, 1960, 96 pp., o.p.

C [R]   FARJEON, Eleanor. *Jim at the Corner* (Orig. title: *The Old Sailor's Yarn Box,* Stokes, 1934). Gr. 3–5.

Old Jim the sailor tells a young boy named Derry eight tales of the sea. This is a companion volume to *The Old Nurse's Stocking Basket* (1931, 1965). (BL 31:244, 55:192; Bookshelf 1935 p. 2; Eakin:113; HB 10:355; 34:473; LJ 60:403)

Illus. by Edward Ardizzone, Walck, 1958, 102 pp., o.p.

C/YA   FARJEON, Eleanor. *The Little Bookroom: Eleanor Farjeon's Short Sto-*
[R]   *ries for Children, Chosen by Herself.* Gr. 4–7. (Orig. British pub. 1931, U.S. Walck, 1956.)

Twenty-seven stories, including "The Giant and the Mite," "The Seventh Princess," and "The Glass Peacock." Carnegie Medal, 1955. (BL 52:415; CCBB 10:5; HB 32:179, 270, 61:77; LJ 81:1719)

Illus. by Edward Ardizzone, Oxford, 1979 (repr. of 1931 ed.), o.p.

FARJEON, Eleanor. *Martin Pippin in the Apple Orchard.* See Chapter 1, Allegorical Fantasy and Literary Fairy Tales.

C   FARJEON, Eleanor. *The Old Nurse's Stocking Basket.* Gr. 3–5. (Orig. British pub. 1931.)

The Old Nurse tells stories about caring for Hercules, the Princess of China, and the Spanish Infanta. A companion to *Jim at the Corner* (1958,

orig. title: *The Old Sailor's Yarn Box* 1934). (HB 42:193; LJ 91:2209; Mahony 3:86)
Illus. by Edward Ardizzone, Walck, 1965, 102 pp., o.p.

C [R] FARJEON, Eleanor. *One Foot in Fairyland: Sixteen Tales.* Gr. 4–6.
A collection of original fantasy tales and retellings of fairy tales. (BL 35:121; HB 14:381; LJ 63:978; TLS 1938 p. 789)
Illus. by Robert Lawson, Stokes, 1938, 261 pp., o.p.

C FARJEON, Eleanor. *The Tale of Tom Tiddler, with Rhymes of London Town.* Gr. 4–6. (Orig. British pub. 1929.)
While Tom Tiddler searches London for Jinny Jones, tales set in various parts of the city unfold. (BL 27:67)
Illus. by Norman Tealby, Stokes, 1930, 244 pp., o.p.

YA FAST, Howard (Melvin). *The General Zapped an Angel: New Stories of Fantasy and Science Fiction.* Gr. 10 up.
Nine short stories of allegorical fantasy and science fiction. (BL 66:955, 968; LJ 95:1047)
Morrow, 1970, 160 pp., o.p.

YA FAST, Howard (Melvin). *A Touch of Infinity: Thirteen New Stories of Fantasy and Science Fiction.* Gr. 10 up.
Thirteen satirical fantasy and science fiction tales, including one about a gnat-sized man on the back porch, and another about plucking breakfast rolls from the air. (BL 70:473, 484; KR 41:659; LJ 98,:2339, 2678)
Morrow, 1973, 182 pp., o.p.

FIELD, Rachel Lyman. *Eliza and the Elves.* See Section 5C, Travel to Other Worlds.

FINNEY, Jack. *About Time: Twelve Stories.* See Chapter 8, Time Travel Fantasy.

FLEISCHMAN, Paul (Taylor). *Graven Images: Three Stories.* See Chapter 4, Ghost Fantasy.

FLEISCHMAN, (Albert) Sid(ney). *Jim Bridger's Alarm Clock, and Other Tall Tales.* See Chapter 6, Humorous Fantasy.

FLORA, James. *Grandpa's Ghost Stories.* See Chapter 4, Ghost Fantasy.

C [R] FOX (Greenburg), Paula. *The Little Swineherd and Other Tales.* Gr. 3–6.
Five tales: four fables about a rooster, a pony, an alligator, and a raccoon and one story about an abandoned swineherd. (BL 75:292; CCBB 32:43; HB 55:516; KR 46:1071; SLJ Oct 1978 p. 144)
Illus. by Leonard Lubin, Dutton, 1978, o.p.; Dell, 1981, pap., 104 pp., o.p.

FRANKO, Ivan, and MELNYK, Bohdan. *Fox Mykyta.* See Section 2B, Talking Animal Fantasy.

FREDDI, Cris. *Pork, and Other Stories.* See Section 2A, Beast Tales.

Fun Phantoms: Tales of Ghostly Entertainment. Ed. by Seon Manley and Gogo Lewis. See Chapter 4, Ghost Fantasy.

C FYLEMAN, Rose. *Forty Good-Night Tales.* Gr. K–4. (Orig. British pub. 1923.)
Humorous tales and fairy stories to read aloud to young children at bed-

time. *Forty Good-Morning Tales* (Doubleday 1929, 1938) is a companion volume. (BL 21:200; HB 1[Oct 1924]:4; Mahony 2:57)
Illus. by Thelma Cudlipp Grosvenor, Doran, 1924, 131 pp., o.p.

C FYLEMAN, Rose. *Tea Time Tales*. Gr. 3–5.
Twenty humorous short stories to be read aloud. (BL 26:401; HB 6:210; LJ 55:995; Mahony 3:86)
Illus. by Erick Berry, Doubleday, 1930, 246 pp., o.p.

C/YA GARDNER, John (Champlin, Jr.). *Dragon, Dragon, and Other Timeless Tales*. Gr. 5–7.
Four fairy-tale spoofs about dragons, giants, and magic. (BL 72:684; CCBB 29:109; HB 52:154; KR 43:1129)
Illus. by Charles Shields, Knopf, 1975, 75 pp., o.p.

C GARNER, Alan. *Alan Garner's Fairytales of Gold*. Gr. 3–5. (Orig. pub. separately in England in 1979.)
Four original tales in the fairy-tale tradition: "The Golden Brothers," "The Girl of the Golden Gate," "The Three Golden Heads of the Well," and "The Princess and The Golden Mane." (BL 77:963; CCBB 34:132; KR 49:357; SLJ Mar 1981 p. 132)
Philomel, 1980, 200 pp., o.p.

C GATE, Ethel May. *The Broom Fairies and Other Stories*. Gr. 3–5.
Eight original fairy tales. (BL 14:172, 19:134; Mahony 2:280)
Illus. by Maud Petersham and Miska Petersham, Yale University Press, 1917, 110 pp., o.p.

C GATE, Ethel May. *The Fortunate Days*. Gr. 3–5.
Nine fairy tales about a tailor in Constantinople who follows his Persian cat through its nine lives. (BL 19:127; Bookshelf 1923–1924 p. 8; LJ 45:980; Mahony 2:280)
Illus. by Vianna Knowlton, Yale University Press, 1922, 127 pp., o.p.

C GATE, Ethel May. *Tales from the Enchanted Isles*. Gr. 3–5.
Seven fairy tales modeled on traditional folklore. (BL 23:235; HB 2[Nov 1925]:44; Mahony 2:280)
Illus. by Dorothy P. Lathrop, Yale University Press, 1927, 118 pp., o.p.

C GATE, Ethel May. *Tales from the Secret Kingdom*. Gr. 2–4.
Nine original fairy stories. (BL 16:138; LJ 45:980; Mahony 1:40)
Illus. by Katherine Buffum, Yale University Press, 1919, 93 pp., o.p.

Ghosts: An Anthology. Ed. by William Mayne. See Chapter 4, Ghost Fantasy.

The Ghost's Companion: A Haunting Anthology. Ed. by Peter Haining. See Chapter 4, Ghost Fantasy.

GODDEN (Dixon), (Margaret) Rumer. *Four Dolls*. See Chapter 9, Toy Fantasy.

GOROG, Judith. *No Swimming in Dark Pond: And Other Chilling Tales*. See Chapter 4, Ghost Fantasy.

GOROG, Judith. *A Taste for Quiet, and Other Disquieting Tales*. See Chapter 4, Ghost Fantasy.

GOULART, Ron(ald Joseph). *The Chameleon Corps and Other Shape Changers*. See Section 5A, Alternate Worlds or Histories.

C/YA GRAHAME, Kenneth. *The Golden Age*. Gr. 5–7. (Orig. British and U.S. pub. 1895.)
Five orphaned children take turns telling the stories in this book, and its companion volume, *Dream Days* (orig. pub. 1898; Garland, 1976; Beaufort, 1976). *Dream Days* includes the story "The Reluctant Dragon." (BL 25:176, 26:77; CCBB 18:129; HB 1[June 1925]:46, 7:324, 30:66)
Illus. by Maxfield Parrish, Garland, 1976 (repr. of 1900 ed.), o.p.; Avon, 1975, pap.; Beaufort, 1985 (repr. of 1898 ed.), 288 pp.

C [R] GRAY, Nicholas Stuart. *Mainly in Moonlight: Ten Stories of Sorcery and the Supernatural*. Gr. 4–6. (Orig. British pub. 1965.)
Tales of wizards, princes, and princesses, including "The Sorcerer's Apprentices," "The Reluctant Familiar," and "The Man Who Sold Magic." (HB 43:462; KR 35:207; LJ 92:2449; SLJ Feb 1980 p. 55; TLS 1965 p. 1130)
Illus. by Charles Keeping, Meredith, 1967, o.p.; Faber, dist. by Merrimack, 1979, pap., 181 pp., o.p.

C/YA GRAY, Nicholas Stuart. *A Wind from Nowhere*. Gr. 5–7.
Humorous fairy tales of dragons, princes, wizards, and demons. (HB 56:55; SLJ Dec 1979 p. 85)
Faber, dist. by Merrimack, 1979, 155 pp., o.p.

C GREEN, Kathleen. *Leprechaun Tales*. Gr. 3–5.
Irish-inspired tales of leprechauns, foolish human beings, pookas, and banshees. (BL 64:1042; HB 44:172; KR 36:340; LJ 93:1310)
Illus. by Victoria de Larrea, Lippincott, 1968, 127 pp., o.p.

C GREEN, Kathleen. *Philip and the Pooka and Other Irish Fairy Tales*. Gr. 4–6.
Ten tales about Irish fairy folk: the little people, pookas, Lochrimeh, and witches. (BL 62:831; CCBB 20:25; HB 42:305; LJ 91:2210)
Illus. by Victoria de Larrea, Lippincott, 1966, 93 pp., o.p.

GREEN, Roger Lancelyn. *A Cavalcade of Magicians*. See Chapter 10, Witchcraft and Sorcery Fantasy.

C/YA GRIPARI, Pierre. *Tales of the Rue Broca*. Gr. 5–7. (Selections from French pub. 1967.)
Six imaginative tales from France, including three about a good devil, a pair of shoes in love, and a hero with a ridiculous name. (CCBB 23:128; LJ 95:1942; KR 37:1112; Suth:159)
Tr. by Doriane Grutman, illus. by Emily McCully, Bobbs-Merrill, 1969, 111 pp., o.p.

HALDANE, J(ohn) B(urdon) (Sanderson). *My Friend Mr. Leakey*. See Chapter 10, Witchcraft and Sorcery Fantasy.

HALE, Lucretia P(eabody). *The Complete Peterkin Papers*. See Chapter 6, Humorous Fantasy.

C/YA [R] HARRIS, Rosemary (Jeanne). *Sea Magic and Other Stories of Enchantment* (British title: *The Lotus and the Grail: Legends from East to West*, 1974, includes eight additional stories). Gr. 6–8.
Ten tales of magic and superstition, including "The Graveyard Rose" and

"White Orchid, Red Mountain." (BL 70:819; CCBB 28:9; HB 50:145; KR 42:192; LJ 99:2290; Suth 2:203)
Macmillan, 1974, 178 pp., o.p.

C HARRISON, David Lee. *The Book of Giant Stories.* Gr. K–4.
Three tales about boys who use their wits either to escape or to befriend a giant. (KR 40:1021; LJ 98:253; TLS 1972 p. 1332)
Illus. by Philippe Fix, McGraw-Hill, 1972, 44 pp., o.p.

C/YA HAUFF, Wilhelm. *The Caravan.* Gr. 6 up. (Orig. pub. in Germany; orig.
[R]   U.S. pub. Appleton, 1850, entitled *The Caravan: A Collection of Popular Tales;* Stokes, 1912, entitled *Caravan Tales and Some Others.*)
Six suspenseful tales told by merchants traveling in a caravan across the desert. (BL 9:303, 61:656; HB 41:57; KR 32:1011; LJ 90:379)
Tr. by Alma Overholt, illus. by Burt Silverman, Crowell, 1964, 220 pp., o.p.

C/YA HAUFF, Wilhelm. *The Fairy Tales of Wilhelm Hauff.* Gr. 5–7. (Orig.
pub. in Germany; orig. U.S. pub. McKay, 1895; Dutton, 1910, entitled *Fairy Tales.*)
Magical adventure tales with an "Arabian Nights" flavor, including "Snout the Dwarf" and "The Inn in the Forest." (BL 66:1045; KR 37:1199; LJ 95:1638; Mahony 1:21; TLS 1969 p. 688)
Tr. by Anthea Bell, illus. by Ulrik Schramm, Abelard-Schuman, 1969, 223 pp., o.p.

The Haunted and the Haunters: Tales of Ghosts and Other Apparitions.
Ed. by Kathleen Lines. See Chapter 4, Ghost Fantasy.

Haunting Tales. Ed. by Barbara Ireson. See Chapter 4, Ghost Fantasy.

C HAWTHORNE, Nathaniel. *The Snow Image.* Gr. 4 up. (Orig. U.S. pub. 1851, 1899.)
A collection of allegorical and supernatural tales. (Bookshelf 1932 p. 23)
Illus. by Dorothy P. Lathrop, Macmillan, 1930, 1944, 69 pp., o.p.; Ohio State University Press, 1974 (entitled *Snow Image and Uncollected Tales*); Ayer, 1975 (entitled *The Snow Image and Other Twice-Told Tales*).

Hecate's Cauldron. Ed. by Susan M. Shwartz. See Chapter 10, Witchcraft and Sorcery Fantasy.

C [R] HEWETT, Anita. *The Bull beneath the Walnut Tree and Other Stories.*
Gr. K–4. (Orig. British pub. 1966.)
Eighteen short tales including "The Singing Witch" and "The Galloping Hedgehog." (BL 64:501; HB 43:588; KR 35:804; LJ 92:3178; TLS 1966 p. 1092)
Illus. by Imero Gobbato, McGraw-Hill, 1967, 155 pp., o.p.

C [R] HOUGH, (Helen) Charlotte (Woodyatt). *Red Biddy and Other Stories.*
Gr. 4–5. (Orig. British pub. 1966.)
Ten stories about princesses, dragons, giants, witches, and fairies. (CCBB 22:8; HB 43:463; KR 35:413; LJ 92:2450)
Illus. by the author, Coward, 1967, 127 pp., o.p.

C/YA HOUSMAN, Laurence. *A Doorway in Fairyland.* Gr. 4–7.
Twelve tales from *A Farm in Fairyland* (1894), *The House of Joy* (1895), *The Field of Clover* (1898), and *The Blue Moon* (1904) including "The Bound Princess" and "The Rat-Catcher's Daughter." (BL 20:24; Mahony 2:281)

Illus. by the author and Clemence Housman, Harcourt, 1905, 1922, 219 pp., o.p.

C/YA HOUSMAN, Laurence. *Moonshine and Clover*. Gr. 4–7. (Orig. British pub. 1922.)
Eighteen stories from *A Farm in Fairyland* (1894), *The House of Joy* (1895), *The Field of Clover* (1898), and *The Blue Moon* (1904), including "A Capful of Moonshine" and "The White Doe." (BL 20:24; Mahony 2:281)
Illus. by the author and Clemence Housman, Harcourt, 1923, 220 pp., o.p.

C/YA HOUSMAN, Laurence. *The Rat-Catcher's Daughter: A Collection of Sto-*
[R] *ries*. Gr. 4–7.
Twelve tales of princesses, magic, and little people, including "The White Doe" and "The Cloak of Friendship." (BL 70:874; HB 50:379; KR 42:244; LJ 99:1451, 1473)
Ed. by Ellin Greene, illus. by Julia Noonan, Atheneum, 1974, 169 pp., o.p.

HOWE, Deborah, and HOWE, James. *Teddy Bear's Scrapbook*. See Chapter 9, Toy Fantasy.

C [R] HUGHES, Richard (Arthur Warren). *The Wonder-Dog: The Collected Sto-ries of Richard Hughes* (Orig. titles: *The Spider's Palace and Other Sto-ries*, 1932 [British pub. 1931], and *Don't Blame Me!* 1940). Gr. 4–6.
Thirty illogical tales about a doll who owns a child, talking animals, and an evil motorbike. (Bookshelf 1932 p. 10; HB 37:53; KR 45:1197; LJ 65:849, 926; Mahony 3:206; SLJ Apr 1978 p. 84; TLS 1931 p. 957, 1940 p. 634, 1977 p. 1273)
Illus. by Antony Maitland, Greenwillow, 1977, 180 pp., o.p.

HUGHES, Ted (Edward James). *How the Whale Became*. See Section 2B, Talking Animal Fantasy.

C [R] HUNTER, Mollie. *A Furl of Fairy Wind: Four Stories*. Gr. 2–4.
Four Scottish tales involving the fairy world: "The Brownie," "The En-chanted Boy," "Hi Johnny," and "A Furl of Fairy Wind." (BL 74:613; CC:552; CCBB 31:142; Ch&Bks:268; HB 54:47; KR 45:1097; SLJ Sept 1977 p. 109; Suth 2:233)
Illus. by Stephen Gammell, Harper, 1977, 58 pp., o.p.

HUNTER, Norman (George Lorimer). *The Incredible Adventures of Professor Branestawm*. See Chapter 6, Humorous Fantasy.

Imaginary Lands. Ed. by Robin McKinley. See Section 5A, Alternate Worlds or Histories.

C *Imagine That! Fifteen Fantastic Tales*. Ed. by Sara Corrin and Stephen Corrin. Gr. 4–6.
Twelve folk tales, plus three original tales written by James Reeves, E. Nesbit, and William Hauff. (BL 83:648; KR 54:1648; SLJ Apr 1987 p. 93; TLS 1986 p. 1346)
Illus. by Jill Bennett, Faber, dist. by Harper, 1986, 175 pp.

YA *Into the Unknown: Eleven Tales of Imagination*. Ed. by Terry Carr. Gr. 7–9.
This collection of tales about unusual phenomena includes Ray Bradbury's

"McGillahee's Brat" and Robert Silverberg's "As Is." (BL 70:649, 654; KR 41:691; LJ 99:216)
Nelson, 1973, 192 pp., o.p.

YA *Isaac Asimov Presents the Best Fantasy of the 19th Century.* Ed. by Isaac Asimov, Charles G. Waugh, and Martin H. Greenberg. Gr. 10 up.
Fourteen tales whose authors include Charles Dickens, Washington Irving, Sir Arthur Conan Doyle, Oscar Wilde, and H. G. Wells. (LJ 107:2355; SHC:655)
Beaufort, 1982, 368 pp., o.p.

JONES, Diana Wynne. *Warlock at the Wheel and Other Stories.* See Chapter 10, Witchcraft and Sorcery Fantasy.

JONES, Louis C(lark). *Things That Go Bump in the Night.* See Chapter 4, Ghost Fantasy.

JONES, Terry. *Fairy Tales.* See Chapter 6, Humorous Fantasy.

JUSTER, Norton. *Alberic the Wise and Other Journeys.* See Chapter 1, Allegorical Fantasy and Literary Fairy Tales.

C [R] KELLER, Gottfried. *The Fat of the Cat and Other Stories.* Gr. 4–6.
Adaptations of Swiss legends and folktales about animals and witches. (BL 22:122; Bookshelf 1928 p. 10; HB 2(Nov 1925):20; LJ 51:836; Mahony 2:198; Moore:435)
Adapt. by Louis Untermeyer, illus. by Albert Sallak, Harcourt, 1925, 283 pp., o.p.

C/YA KENNEDY, Richard (Jerome). *Richard Kennedy: Collected Stories.* Gr. 4–9.
[R] Sixteen stories originally published separately, including "The Porcelain Man," "The Leprechaun's Story," and "The Dark Princess." (BL 84:625, 635; HB 64:359; KR 55:1629; SLJ Nov 1987 p. 105; VOYA 10:235)
Illus. by Marcia Sewall, Harper, 1987, 274 pp.

Kingdoms of Sorcery. Ed. by Lin Carter. See Section 5A, Alternate Worlds or Histories.

C/YA KIPLING, (Joseph) Rudyard. *All the Mowgli Stories.* Gr. 4–7.
Mowgli is a human boy raised by jungle animals. His stories were originally told in *The Jungle Books* (1893, 1895). (BL 32:333; HB 12:158; LJ 61:733)
Illus. by Kurt Wiese, Doubleday, 1936, 299 pp., o.p.

C/YA KIPLING, (Joseph) Rudyard. *The Jungle Book.* Gr. 4–7. (Orig. U.S.
[R] pub. Scribner, 1893.)
Tales of Mowgli, a boy adopted by wolves; Kotik the seal, Rikki-Tikki-Tavi, the mongoose; and other jungle animals. *The Second Jungle Book* (Scribner, 1895; Doubleday, 1923; Penguin/Puffin, 1987) is the sequel. (BL 47:162, 82:135; Bookshelf 1933 p. 9; CC:553; CCBB 5:15; HB 1[June 1925]:34; JHC:434; KR 32:1014; LJ 75:2085)
Illus. by John Lockwood Kipling, Doubleday, 1928, o.p.; illus. by Kurt Wiese, Doubleday, 1932, o.p.; illus. by Fritz Eichenberg, Grosset, 1950, hb and deluxe ed.; illus. by Robert Shore, Macmillan, 1964, o.p.; Doubleday, 1981, pap.; Schocken, 1984; adapt. by Robin McKinley, Random, 1985 (entitled *Tales from "The Jungle Book"*), 61 pp.; Bantam, 1986; Penguin/Puffin, 1987, pap.

C [R] KIPLING, (Joseph) Rudyard. *Just So Stories*. Gr. 3–5. (Orig. British pub. 1897–1902.)
Twelve animal tales, including "How the Camel Got His Hump," "How the Leopard Got His Spots," and "How the Rhinoceros Got His Skin." (BL 77:327, 79:778, 83:512, 84:709; Bookshelf 1928 p. 9; CC:553; CCBB 6:17, 26:93; Ch&Bks:245; Eakin:188; HB 1[June 1925]:45, 58:565; KR 40:940, 1413, 54:1450, 55:1159; LJ 98:1682; SLJ Nov 1987 p. 105)
Illus. by the author, Doubleday, 1902, o.p.; illus. by Feodor Rojankovsky, Doubleday, 1942, o.p.; illus. by Etienne Delessert, Doubleday, 1946 (anniversary ed.); NAL, 1974; illus. by Victor G. Ambrus, Rand, 1982, o.p.; Schocken, 1986; illus. by Meg Rutherford, Silver, 1986; illus. by Safaya Salter, Holt, 1987, 96 pp.; illus. by Michael Foreman, Viking/Kestrel, 1987, 127 pp.

KIPLING, (Joseph) Rudyard. *Phantoms and Fantasies: Twenty Tales.* See Chapter 4, Ghost Fantasy.

KOTZWINKLE, William. *Hearts of Wood: And Other Timeless Tales.* See Chapter 1, Allegorical Fantasy and Literary Fairy Tales.

KRÜSS, James. *Eagle and Dove.* See Section 2B, Talking Animal Tales.

LANG, Andrew. *My Own Fairy Book.* See Chapter 1, Allegorical Fantasy and Literary Fairy Tales.

LEACH, Maria. *The Thing at the Foot of the Bed and Other Scary Tales.* See Chapter 4, Ghost Fantasy.

C LEAMY, Edmund. *The Fairy Minstrel of Glenmalure, and Other Stories for Children.* Gr. 3–5. (Orig. pub. Warne, 1913.)
Three fanciful tales set in Ireland. (BL 27:216, 34:271; HB 14:106; Mahony 1:22)
Fitzgerald, 1913, o.p.; illus. by Vera Casseau, Roth, 1976, 92 pp.

C LEAMY, Edmund. *The Golden Spears and Other Fairy Tales.* Gr. 3–5. (Orig. pub. 1890, entitled *Irish Fairy Tales, a Collection of Seven Fairy Tales.*)
Seven tales set in Ireland, including "The Enchanted Cave," "The Fairy Tree of Dooros," and "Princess Finola and the Dwarf." (BL 8:278, 27:216, 35:33; HB 10:299; LJ 63:798; Mahony 3:206)
Fitzgerald, 1911, 1930, o.p.; illus. by Corinne Turner, Roth, 1976, 180 pp.

C LEBERMANN, Norbert. *New German Fairy Tales.* Gr. 3–6. (Orig. pub. in Germany.)
A combination of traditional and modern tales including one about an inventor-hero who conquers the goblins of electricity and steam. (HB 6:331; LJ 55:1023; Mahony 3:206)
Illus. by Margaret Freeman, Knopf, 1930, 247 pp., o.p.

YA LEE, Tanith. *Dreams of Dark and Light: The Great Short Fiction of Tanith Lee.* Gr. 10 up.
Twenty-three previously published tales written between 1977 and 1984, including "Because Our Skins Are Finer," "Tamastara," and "The Gorgon." (BL 82:1667; KR 54:978; VOYA 9:164, 10:22)
Arkham, 1986, 507 pp.

LEE, Tanith. *Princess Hynchatti and Some Other Surprises.* See Chapter 1, Allegorical Fantasy and Literary Fairy Tales.

LEE, Tanith. *Red as Blood; or Tales from the Sisters Grimmer*. See Chapter 1, Allegorical Fantasy and Literary Fairy Tales.

LEE, Tanith. *Tamastara; or the Indian Nights*. See Section 5B, Myth Fantasy.

YA [R] LE GUIN, Ursula K(roeber). *The Wind's Twelve Quarters: Short Stories*. Gr. 8 up.
Seventeen stories of fantasy and science fiction, including "Winter's King" and "The Day before the Revolution." (BL 72:615; KR 43:942; LJ 100:1950; SLJ Mar 1976 p. 120; TLS 1976 p. 950; Tymn:112)
Harper, 1975, 303 pp., o.p.; Bantam, 1976, pap., o.p.

Liavek. Ed. by Will Shetterly and Emma Bull. See Section 5A, Alternate Worlds or Histories.

LIVELY, Penelope. *Uninvited Ghosts and Other Stories*. See Chapter 6, Humorous Fantasy.

C *The Lonely Little Pig and Other Animal Tales*. Ed. by Wilhelmina Harper. Gr. 2–4.
Thirteen short humorous animal stories. (BL 35:160; HB 15:31)
Illus. by Vera Neville, McKay, 1938, 108 pp., o.p.

C [R] *The Lost Half-Hour: A Collection of Stories*. Ed. by Eulalie Steinmetz Ross. Gr. 4–6.
Stories by Rudyard Kipling, Ruth Sawyer, Howard Pyle, Barbara Freeman, Oscar Wilde, Kate Seredy, and others. (BL 60:210; HB 39:604; LJ 88:4088)
Illus. by Enrico Arno, Harcourt, 1963, 191 pp., o.p.

Lost Worlds, Unknown Horizons: Nine Stories of Science Fiction. Ed. by Robert Silverberg. See Section 5C, Travel to Other Worlds.

YA LYNN, Elizabeth A. *The Woman Who Loved the Moon, and Other Stories*. Gr. 10 up.
This collection of sixteen fantasy and horror short stories includes "Wizard's Domain" and "The Woman Who Loved the Moon," a World Fantasy Award, 1980, winning story. (BL 78:427, 435; Kliatt 16[Winter 1982]:22, VOYA 4[Dec 1981]:39)
Berkley, 1981, pap., 197 pp., o.p.

C/YA MacDONALD, George. *The Complete Fairy Tales of George MacDonald*
[R] (British title: *The Light Princess and Other Tales* 1901). Gr. 4–8.
Eight tales, including "The Light Princess," "The Giant's Heart," "The Golden Key," and "The Day Boy and the Night Girl." (BL 58:446, 74:1014; CC:553; CCBB 32:196; HB 38:177, 55:441)
Illus. by Arthur Hughes, Watts, 1961 (entitled: *The Light Princess and Other Tales, Being the Complete Fairy Stories of George MacDonald*), 288 pp., o.p.; illus. by Arthur Hughes, Schocken, 1979, hb and pap, 288 pp.

MacDONALD, George. *The Fairy Fleet*. See Chapter 1, Allegorical Fantasy and Literary Fairy Tales.

McKINLEY, (Jennifer Carolyn) Robin. *The Door in the Hedge*. See Chapter 1, Allegorical Fantasy and Literary Fairy Tales.

C MACOUREK, Miloš. *Curious Tales.* Gr. 3–5. (Orig. Czech pubs. 1966, 1971.)
Fourteen imaginative tales, including three about a turkey-eating plant, an alarm clock revolt, and an operatic kitchen sink. (BL 77:45; SLJ Sept 1981 p. 111)
Tr. by Marie Burg, illus. by Adolf Born, Oxford, 1980, 88 pp., o.p.

Magic in Ithkar. Ed. by Andre Norton and Robert Adams. See Section 5A, Alternate Worlds or Histories.

Magicats! Ed. by Jack Dann and Gardner Dozois. See Section 2A, Beast Tales.

MAMIN-SIBERIAK. *Verotchka's Tales.* See Chapter 2B, Talking Animal Fantasy.

MANLEY, Seon. *The Ghost in the Far Garden and Other Stories.* See Chapter 4, Ghost Fantasy.

Masters of Shades and Shadows: An Anthology of Great Ghost Stories. Ed. by Seon Manley and Gogo Lewis. See Chapter 4, Ghost Fantasy.

MAYNE, William (James Carter). *The Green Book of Hob Stories.* See Chapter 7, Magic Adventure Fantasy.

MEIGS, Cornelia (Lynde). *The Kingdom of the Winding Road.* See Chapter 1, Allegorical Fantasy and Literary Fairy Tales.

MENDOZA, George. *Gwot! Horribly Funny Hairticklers.* See Chapter 6, Humorous Fantasy.

MEYER, Zoe. *The Little Green Door.* See Chapter 1, Allegorical Fantasy and Literary Fairy Tales.

MILNE, A(lan) A(lexander). *Prince Rabbit and the Princess Who Could Not Laugh.* See Chapter 1, Allegorical Fantasy and Literary Fairy Tales.

C/YA *Modern Fairy Stories.* Ed. by Roger Lancelyn Green. Gr. 5–7. (Orig. British pub. 1955.)
Sixteen stories written by Lewis Carroll, Juliana Horatia Ewing, Andrew Lang, Mary Louise Molesworth, Oscar Wilde, E. Nesbit, John Ruskin, and others. (BL 52:369; HB 30:121)
Illus. by Ernest Shepard, Dutton, 1956, 270 pp., o.p.

C MOLESWORTH, Mary Louisa (Stewart). *Fairy Stories.* Gr. 4–6.
Eight tales of magic and enchantment including "The Reel Fairies" and "The Weather Maiden." (HB 34:478; KR 26:659; LJ 83:3002)
Ed. by Roger Lancelyn Green, Roy, 1958, 159 pp., o.p.

C MOLESWORTH, Mary Louisa (Stewart). *Stories by Mrs. Molesworth.* Gr. 4–6.
Nine tales, including "The Cuckoo Clock," "The Reel Fairies," "Six Poor Princesses," and "Blue Dwarfs." (BL 19:95; Mahony 2:291)
Comp. by Sidney Baldwin, illus. by Edna Cooke, Duffield, 1922, 353 pp., o.p.

C *Monsters, Ghoulies and Creepy Creatures: Fantastic Stories and Poems.* Gr. 4–6.
Stories by Natalie Babbitt, John Gardner, Natalie Savage Carlson, Tom

McGowen, and Lee Bennett Hopkins, about devils, dragons, monsters, and demons. (BL 74:1110; CCBB 31:178)
Comp. by Lee Bennett Hopkins, illus. by Vera Rosenberry, Whitman, 1977, 128 pp., o.p.

C MONTROSE, Anne. *The Winter Flower and Other Fairy Stories.* Gr. 4–6.
Thirteen stories about magic, kings, witches, and a dragon. (HB 40:611; KR 32:653; LJ 89:4642)
Illus. by Mircea Vasiliu, Viking, 1964, 143 pp., o.p.

YA [R] *Moonsinger's Friends: In Honor of Andre Norton.* Ed. by Susan Shwartz. Gr. 10 up.
Fourteen fantasy tales by such well-known authors as Marion Zimmer Bradley, C. J. Cherryh, Katherine Kurtz, Tanith Lee, Anne McCaffrey, Nancy Springer, and Jane Yolen. (BL 81:1637, 1657; KR 53:561; LJ Aug 1985 p. 121; SLJ Nov 1985 p. 106; VOYA 8:326)
Bluejay, dist. by St. Martin, 1985, hb and pap., 342 pp.

MÜNCHAUSEN, Karl. *The Adventures of Baron Münchausen.* See Chapter 6, Humorous Fantasy.

MUSSET, Paul Edmé de. *Mr. Wind and Madam Rain.* See Section 5B, Myth Fantasy.

C [R] NESBIT (Bland), E(dith). *The Complete Book of Dragons.* Gr. 4–6. (Written 1899, orig. U.S. pub. 1901, entitled *The Book of Dragons.*)
Nine tales about children confronting dragons, including "The Ice Dragon," "The Dragon Tamers," and "The Last of the Dragons." (BL 69:911; CCBB 26:142; HB 49:272; KR 41:6; LJ 26:167)
Illus. by Erik Blegvad, Macmillan, 1973, 198 pp., o.p.; Dell/Yearling, 1986, pap., o.p.

NYE, Robert. *The Mathematical Princess and Other Stories.* See Chapter 1, Allegorical Fantasy and Literary Fairy Tales.

YA *100 Great Fantasy Short Stories.* Ed. by Isaac Asimov, Terry Carr, and Martin H. Greenberg. Gr. 10 up.
The stories chosen for inclusion here were written by Roger Zelazny, Gene Wolfe, and Marion Zimmer Bradley, among others. (KR 52:114; LJ 109:600; SHC:657; TLS 1984 p. 1359; VOYA 7:207)
Doubleday, 1984, 311 pp.; Avon, pap.

The Other Side of the Clock: Stories Out of Time, Out of Place. Ed. by Philip Van Doren Stern. See Chapter 8, Time Travel Fantasy.

PAINE, Albert Bigelow. *The Hollow Tree and Deep Woods Book.* See Section 2B, Talking Animal Fantasy.

C PARRISH, Anne, and PARRISH, Dillwyn. *The Dream Coach.* Gr. 3–5.
Each night a dream coach travels across the sky, leaving dream stories along its way. (BL 21:158; HB 1(Nov 1924):12, 7:61–67)
Illus. by the authors, Macmillan, 1924, 143 pp., o.p.

PEARCE, (Ann) Philippa. *Lion at School: And Other Stories.* See Chapter 7, Magic Adventure Fantasy.

PEARCE, (Ann) Philippa. *The Shadow-Cage and Other Tales of the Supernatural.* See Chapter 4, Ghost Fantasy.

PEARCE, (Ann) Philippa. *Who's Afraid? And Other Strange Stories.* See Chapter 4, Ghost Fantasy.

YA *Phantasmagoria: Tales of Fantasy and the Supernatural.* Ed. by Jane Mobley. Gr. 10 up.
An anthology of English and American fantastic and supernatural tales whose authors include Lord Dunsany, George MacDonald, Ursula K. Le Guin, Andre Norton, and Peter Beagle. (BL 74:463, 470; Kliatt 12[Winter 1978]:14)
Anchor/Doubleday, 1977, pap., 439 pp., o.p.

C/YA *Phoenix Feathers: A Collection of Mythical Monsters.* Ed. by Barbara Silverberg. Gr. 6–10.
Tales of dragons, griffons, unicorns, and the phoenix. (BL 70:737; KR 41:820; LJ 98:3457)
Illus. with old prints, Dutton, 1973, 206 pp., o.p.

The Phoenix Tree: An Anthology of Myth Fantasy. Ed. by Robert H. Boyer and Kenneth J. Zahorski. See Chapter 5B, Myth Fantasy.

C/YA PICARD, Barbara Leonie. *The Faun and the Woodcutter's Daughter.* Gr.
[R] 4–7. (Orig. British pub. 1951.)
This collection of fourteen fairy tales begins with the story of a woodcutter's daughter who meets a faun in the woods and cannot live without him. (BL 61:436; CCBB 18:168; Ch&Bks:271; Eakin:261; HB 41:57; LJ 89:5010)
Illus. by Charles Stewart, Abelard-Schuman, 1964, 255 pp., o.p.

C/YA PICARD, Barbara Leonie. *The Goldfinch Garden: Seven Tales.* Gr. 4–7.
[R] (Orig. British pub. 1963.)
Seven original fairy tales about mortals who become involved with a witch, a water sprite, a fairy maiden, and other creatures. (BL 62:532; Ch&Bks:271; HB 42:55; KR 33:1042)
Illus. by Anne Linton, Criterion, 1965, 121 pp., o.p.

C/YA PICARD, Barbara Leonie. *The Lady of the Linden Tree.* Gr. 4–7. (Orig.
[R] British pub. 1954.)
Twelve tales of knights, princes, princesses, and enchantment, including "Findings Are Keepings," "The Castle in the Cornfield," and "The Piper with the Hoofs of a Goat." (BL 58:694; CCBB 16:14; Ch&Bks:271; Eakin:261; HB 38:276; KR 30:176; LJ 87:2027)
Illus. by Charles Stewart, Criterion, 1962, 214 pp., o.p.

C/YA PICARD, Barbara Leonie. *The Mermaid and the Simpleton.* Gr. 4–7.
[R] (Orig. British pub. 1949.)
Fifteen tales of princesses, witches, and magic, including "Heart of the Wind," "The Ivory Box," and "Three Wishes." (BL 47:225, 67:150; CCBB 4:15; Ch&Bks:271; HB 26:488; KR 18:642, 38:454; LJ 16:55, 95:2535, 4326)
Illus. by Philip Gough, Criterion, 1970, 253 pp., o.p.

C/YA PORTE, Barbara Ann. *Jesse's Ghost and Other Stories.* Gr. 4–6.
[R] A collection of thought-provoking stories told by a storyteller who "sits where three worlds meet, before and now and after." (BL 80:366; CC:554; CCBB 37:134; JHC:435; KR 51:J164; SLJ Nov 1983 p. 82)
Greenwillow, 1983, 105 pp.

PREUSSLER, Otfried. *The Wise Men of Schilda.* See Chapter 6, Humorous Fantasy.

The Princesses: Sixteen Stories about Princesses. Ed. by Sally Patrick Johnson. See Chapter 1, Allegorical Fantasy and Literary Fairy Tales.

Princesses and Peasant Boys: Tales of Enchantment. Ed. by Phyllis Reid Fenner. See Chapter 1, Allegorical Fantasy and Literary Fairy Tales.

C [R]   *The Provensen Book of Fairy Tales.* Ed. by Alice Provensen. Gr. 3–6.
Stories by Hans Christian Andersen, Henry Beston, Ruth Manning-Sanders, A. A. Milne, Barbara Picard, Howard Pyle, and Oscar Wilde. (CCBB 25:96; KR 39:1130; LJ 97:1916)
Illus. by Alice Provensen and Martin Provensen, Random, 1971, 140 pp., o.p.

C/YA   PUSHKIN, Alexander Sergeevich. *The Golden Cockerel and Other Stories.* Gr. 3–7. (Orig. pub. in Russia.)
Five poetic retellings of Russian folktales, including "The Tale of Tsar Saltan" and "The Tale of the Fisherman and the Little Golden Fish." (HB 46:384; LJ 95:3631; TLS 1970 p. 420)
Tr. by James Reeves, illus. by Ján Lebiš, Watts, 1969, 110 pp., o.p.

C/YA   PYLE, Howard. *Pepper and Salt; or, Seasoning for Young Folk.* Gr. 4–7.
[R]   (Orig. British pub. 1886.)
Eight tales, including "The Skillful Huntsman," "Clever Peter and the Two Bottles," and "The Apple of Contentment." (BL 20:384; Bookshelf 1932 p. 8; CC:95; Ch&Bks:271; HB 1[June 1925]:29; Mahony 1:37)
Illus. by the author, Harper, 1923, 109 pp., o.p.

PYLE, Howard. *Twilight Land.* See Section 5C, Travel to Other Worlds.

C/YA   PYLE, Howard. *The Wonder Clock; or, Four & Twenty Marvelous Tales,*
[R]   *Being One for Each Hour of the Day.* Gr. 5–7. (Orig. British pub. 1887.)
Twenty-four tales, including "One Good Turn Deserves Another," "The Princess Golden Hair and the Great Black Raven," and "King Stork." (Bookshelf 1932 p. 8; CC:95; Ch&Bks:271; HB 1[June 1925]:31, 19:48; Mahony 2:292)
Verses by Katharine Pyle, illus. by the author, Harper, 1943, o.p.; Peter Smith, 318 pp.

C   REEVES, James (pseud. of John Morris Reeves). *Sailor Rumbelow and Other Stories.* Gr. 4–6. (Orig. British pub. in two volumes: *Sailor Rumbelow and Britannia,* 1962 and *Pigeons and Princesses,* 1956.)
Two retellings of traditional tales, plus nine original stories, including "The Stonemason of Elphinstone." (BL 59:498; HB 38:605; LJ 87:3898)
Illus. by Edward Ardizzone, Dutton, 1962, 223 pp., o.p.

C/YA   *A Ring of Tales.* Ed. by Kathleen Lines. Gr. 4–7. (Orig. British pub.
[R]   1958.)
Tales by Alison Uttley, A. A. Milne, Hans Christian Andersen, Walter De la Mare, Eleanor Farjeon, and Selma Lagerlöf. (BL 55:488; HB 35:299; LJ 84:1698; TLS Nov 21, 1958 p. xvi)
Illus. by Harold Jones, Watts, 1959, 239 pp., o.p.

C/YA   RITCHIE, Alice. *The Treasure of Li-Po.* Gr. 4–7. (Orig. British pub.
[R]   1948.)
Six magical stories set in ancient China. (BL 46:17; CCBB 2(Sept 1949):4;
HB 25:416, 436; KR 17:393; LJ 74:1208, 1542)
Illus. by T. Ritchie, Harcourt, 1949, 154 pp., o.p.

C/YA   ROACH, Marilynne K(athleen). *Encounters with the Invisible World; Be-*
[R]   *ing Ten Tales of Ghosts, Witches, and the Devil Himself in New En-*
gland. Gr. 6–10.
Ten supernatural tales set in New England, about ghosts, piracy, witchcraft, and the devil. (BL 74:814; CC:554; HB 53:674; KR 45:991; SLJ Dec
1977 p. 55)
Illus. by the author, Crowell, 1977, 131 pp.

ROBINSON, Marileta. *Mr. Goat's Bad Good Idea.* See Section 2B,
Talking Animal Fantasy.

ROUNDS, Glen (Harold). *Mr. Yowder, The Peripatetic Sign Painter:
Three Tall Tales.* See Chapter 6, Humorous Fantasy.

SANDBURG, Carl. *Rootabaga Stories.* See Chapter 6, Humorous
Fantasy.

Shades of Dark: Stories. Ed. by Aidan Chambers. See Chapter 4, Ghost
Fantasy.

C/YA   SHANNON, Monica. *California Fairy Tales.* Gr. 5–7. (Orig. pub. Doubleday, 1926.)
Tales of the elves, fairies, and goblins living in California's orchards, gardens, and forests. *More Tales from California* (1960; orig. title: *Eyes for the
Dark,* 1928) is the companion volume. (BL 23:348; 54:310; HB 2[Nov
1926]:42, 344:124; Mahony 2:297; Moore:429)
Illus. by C. E. Millard, Stephen Daye, 1957, 298 pp., o.p.

C/YA   *Shape Shifters: Fantasy and Science Fiction Tales about Humans Who Can
Change Their Shapes.* Ed. by Jane H(yatt) Yolen (Stemple). Gr. 6–9.
Twelve tales about people who change into animals, monsters, and ma-
chines, including "The Boy Who Would Be a Wolf," "The Enchanted Vil-
lage," and "Judas Fish." (BL 74:1259; CCBB 32:40; JHC:436; KR 46:552;
SLJ Sept 1978 p. 167)
Seabury, 1978, 182 pp., o.p.

SHARMA, Partap. *The Surangini Tales.* See Chapter 1, Allegorical
Fantasy and Literary Fairy Tales.

The Silent Playmate: A Collection of Doll Stories. Ed. by Naomi Lewis.
See Chapter 9, Toy Fantasy.

SINGER, Isaac Bashevis. *The Fools of Chelm and Their History.* See
Chapter 6, Humorous Fantasy.

C/YA   SINGER, Isaac Bashevis. *Naftali the Storyteller and His Horse, Sus, and*
[R]   *Other Stories.* Gr. 4–7.
Eight tales, including stories about the foolish people of Chelm and an imp
called the lantuch. (BL 73:670; CC:555; CCBB 30:98; HB 53:162; KR
44:1139; SLJ Dec 1976 p. 56; Suth 2:415)
Tr. by Joseph Singer, Ruth Finkel, and the author, illus. by Margot
Zemach, Farrar, 1976, 129 pp.

C/YA SINGER, Isaac Bashevis. *Stories for Children.* Gr. 4–7.
[R]   A collection of most of Singer's children's stories, including those about the fools of Chelm, "Zlateh the Goat" and "Mazel and Shlimazel." (BL 81:592; CC:555; CCBB 38:73; HB 61:183; JHC:75; Suth 3:395; SLJ Dec 1984 p. 86)
Farrar, 1984, 337 pp., 1985, pap.

C/YA SINGER, Isaac Bashevis. *Zlateh the Goat and Other Stories.* Gr. 4–7.
[R]   Seven stories, including three tall tales about the foolish people of Chelm, two about the devil, and an allegorical tale about a young boy and his goat who are lost in a blizzard. Newbery Medal Honor Book, 1967. (BL 63:378; CC:96; CCBB 20:79; HB 42:712; KR 34:1045; LJ 91:6197; Suth:368)
Illus. by Maurice Sendak, Harper, 1966, 90 pp., 1984, pap.

C SLEIGH, Barbara (de Riemer). *Stirabout Stories, Brewed in Her Own Cauldron* (British title: *West of Widdershins,* 1971). Gr. 4–6.
Fourteen tales of magic, fairies, witches, and sea monsters. (CCBB 26:49; LJ 97:3808; TLS 1971 p. 1321)
Illus. by Victor Ambrus, Bobbs-Merrill, 1971, 143 pp., o.p.

Small Shadows Creep. Ed. by Andre Norton. See Chapter 4, Ghost Fantasy.

SOYER, Abraham. *Adventures of Yemima.* See Chapter 1, Allegorical Fantasy and Literary Fairy Tales.

C/YA *Spaceships and Spells: A Collection of New Fantasy and Science-Fiction Stories.* Ed. by Jane Yolen, Martin H. Greenberg, and Charles G. Waugh. Gr. 5–8.
Thirteen tales whose authors include Robert Lawson and Jane H. Yolen. (BL 84:868; CCBB 41:40; SLJ Dec 1987 p. 89; VOYA 10:292)
Harper, 1987, 182 pp.

C/YA STEELE, Mary Q(uintard Govan). *The Owl's Kiss: Three Stories.* Gr. 6–8.
In these three tales, a little girl fears owls will kill her for stealing her grandmother's fruit, an older girl longs to become a witch, and a man is falsely accused of theft. (BL 75:53; HB 55:522; KR 46:878; SLJ Dec 1978 p. 57)
Greenwillow/Morrow, 1978, 99 pp., o.p.

C/YA STOCKTON, Frank (Francis) R(ichard). *The Queen's Museum and Other Fanciful Tales.* Gr. 5–7. (Orig. pub. 1887.)
Ten stories, including "The Griffin and the Minor Canon," "The Bee-Man of Orn," and "Old Pipes and the Dryad." (BL 3:23; Bookshelf 1921–1922 p. 15; HB 1[June 1925]:45; Mahony 2:297)
Illus. by Frederick Richardson, Scribner, 1906, 219 pp., o.p.

C/YA STOCKTON, Frank (Francis) R(ichard). *The Reformed Pirate: Stories from The Floating Prince, Ting-a-Ling Tales and the Queen's Museum.* Gr. 5–7. (Orig. pub. 1881.)
Twelve imaginative tales about fairies, dragons, pirates, and kings. (BL 33:94; HB 13:36; LJ 62:126)
Illus. by Reginald Birch, Scribner, 1936, 342 pp., o.p.

C/YA STOCKTON, Frank (Francis) R(ichard). *The Storyteller's Pack, a Frank*
[R]   *R. Stockton Reader* (orig. title: *A Story-Teller's Pack* 1897). Gr. 5–7.
Seventeen stories, including "The Bee-Man of Orn," "The Griffin and the

Minor Canon," and "The Lady or the Tiger." (BL 65:1019; HB 45:60; LJ 94:891; Tymn:159)
Illus. by Bernarda Bryson, Scribner, 1968, 358 pp., o.p.

C/YA STOCKTON, Frank (Francis) R(ichard). *Ting-a-Ling Tales* (orig. title: *Ting-a-ling*, 1870). Gr. 4–7.
A collection of fanciful tales. (BL 52:110; CCBB 11:86; HB 31:445, 466)
Illus. by Richard Floethe, Scribner, 1955, 161 pp., o.p.

C *Stories for Nine-Year-Olds and Other Young Readers.* Ed. by Sara Corrin and Stephen Corrin. Gr. 4 up.
A combination of myths and modern fantasy by such authors as Helen Cresswell, Rudyard Kipling, Joan Aiken, Saki, and James Thurber, all appropriate for reading aloud. (BL 76:452; SLJ Apr 1980 p. 122; TLS 1979 p. 129)
Illus. by Shirley Hughes, Faber, dist. by Merrimack, 1979, 159 pp.

STORR, Catherine. *Cold Marble and Other Ghost Stories.* See Chapter 4, Ghost Fantasy.

Supernatural Stories: 13 Tales of the Unexpected. Ed. by Jean Russell. See Chapter 4, Ghost Fantasy.

Sword and Sorceress: An Anthology of Heroic Fantasy. Ed. by Marion Zimmer Bradley. See Section 5A, Alternate Worlds or Histories.

Tales out of Time. Ed. by Barbara Ireson. See Chapter 8, Time Travel Fantasy.

C TASSIN, Algernon de Vivier. *The Rainbow String.* Gr. 4–6.
Six humorous adventure tales about the romances of six princesses. (BL 18:291; Bookshelf 1923–1924 p. 8; Mahony 1:40)
Illus. by Anna Richards Brewster, Macmillan, 1921, 1929, 114 pp., o.p.

C [R] *Told Under the Magic Umbrella: Modern Fanciful Stories for Young Children.* Ed. by The Association for Childhood Education Literature Committee. Gr. 3–5.
Thirty-three fantasy stories written by Marjorie Williams Bianco, Carl Sandburg, Monica Shannon, Laurence Housman, Eleanor Farjeon, Ted Hughes, Anne Thomasine Casserley, Carol Ryrie Brink, and Betty Brock. (BL 35:312; HB 15:166; LJ 64:380)
Illus. by Elizabeth Orton Jones, Macmillan, 1939, 1955, 248 pp., o.p.

YA [R] *Tomorrow's Children: 18 Tales of Fantasy and Science Fiction.* Ed. by Isaac Asimov. Gr. 7–12.
Eighteen fantastic tales whose authors include Ray Bradbury and Clifford Simak. (BL 63:843; CCBB 20:69; HB 43:69; KR 34:993; LJ 91:6198)
Illus. by Emanuel Schoengut, Doubleday, 1966, 431 pp., o.p.

Trips in Time: Nine Stories of Science Fiction. Ed. by Robert Silverberg. See Chapter 8, Time Travel Fantasy.

YA *Unicorns!* Ed. by Jack Dann and Gardner Dozois. Gr. 10 up.
An anthology of humorous, mythic, and horror tales about unicorns written by Roger Zelazny, Ursula K. Le Guin, Gene Wolfe, Stephen R. Donaldson, and others. (BL 79:95, 106; Kies:92; VOYA 5[Oct 1982]:50)
Ace, 1982, pap., 310 pp.

YA   *Visions of Wonder: An Anthology of Christian Fantasy.* Ed. by Robert H.
Boyer and Kenneth J. Zahorski. Gr. 10 up.
A collection of fables, fairy tales, legends, allegories, and satires drawn
from Christian concepts, including material by George MacDonald. (BL
78:538, 546; Kliatt 16[Winter 1982]:20)
Avon, 1981, 1986, pap., 240 pp., o.p.

YA   *Wandering Stars: An Anthology of Jewish Fantasy and Science Fiction.* Ed.
by Jack Dann. Gr. 10 up.
Thirteen humorous science fiction and fantasy stories, whose authors include Robert Silverberg, Isaac Asimov, and Isaac Bashevis Singer. (BL
70:906, 932; KR 41:1287)
Harper, 1974, 239 pp., o.p.

WEAVER, Jack. *Mr. O'Hara.* See Chapter 6, Humorous Fantasy.

YA   WELLS, H(erbert) G(eorge). *The Door in the Wall and Other Stories.* Gr.
10 up. (Orig. British and U.S. pub. 1911; 1925, 1939.)
Eight short stories, including "The Door in the Wall," "A Moonlight Fable," and "The Country of the Blind." (BL 77:199, 206; Kliatt 15[Winter
1981]:19)
Photos by Alvin Langdon Coburn, Godine, 1980, 157 pp.

WESTALL, Robert (Atkinson). *The Haunting of Chas McGill and Other
Stories.* See Chapter 4, Ghost Fantasy.

YA [R]   WESTALL, Robert (Atkinson). *Rachel and the Angel and Other Stories.*
Gr. 8–12. (Orig. British pub. 1986.)
Seven fantasy and science fiction stories, including the title story, in which
a vicar's daughter tricks the angel of death into sparing the townspeople, in
spite of their faults. (BL 84:139, 154; CCBB 41:39; HB 64:74; KR 55:1399;
SLJ Dec 1987 p. 106; VOYA 10:239)
Greenwillow, 1987, 187 pp.

WHITELAW, Stella, GARDINER, Judith, and RONSON, Mark.
Grimalkin's Tales. See Section 2B, Talking Animal Fantasy.

WILDE, Oscar (pseud. of Fingal O'Flahertie Wills). *The Birthday of the
Infanta and Other Tales.* See Chapter 1, Allegorical Fantasy and Literary
Fairy Tales.

C/YA   WILDE, Oscar (pseud. of Fingal O'Flahertie Wills). *Fairy Tales.* Gr. 4–6.
(Orig. pub. in *The Happy Prince and Other Tales* (1888) and *The House
of Pomegranates* (1891, 1906).
Nine tales including "The Happy Prince" and "The Fisherman and His
Soul." (Bookshelf 1921–1922 p. 15; SLJ Oct 1980 p. 152)
Illus. by Charles Mozley, Watts, 1960, o.p.; Bodley Head, 1980, 189 pp.,
o.p.

WILDE, Oscar (pseud. of Fingal O'Flahertie Wills). *The Happy Prince
and Other Stories.* See Chapter 1, Allegorical Fantasy and Literary Fairy
Tales.

YA   WILHELM, Kate (Katie Gertrude). *The Downstairs Room, and Other
Speculative Fiction.* Gr. 10 up.
Fourteen fantastic, realistic, and science fiction short stories, including

"The Unbirthday Party," "Baby You Were Great," and "The Downstairs Room." (BL 65:440, 445; KR 36:719)
Doubleday, 1968, 215 pp., o.p.

C WILKINS, Mary Eleanor (pseud. of Mary Eleanor Wilkins Freeman). *The Pot of Gold, and Other Stories.* Gr. 3–6. (Orig. U.S. pub. Lothrop, 1892.)
Sixteen tales including "Princess Rosetta and the Pop-Corn-Man," "The Pumpkin Giant," and "The Silver Hen." (Mahony 1:27)
Books for Libraries, 1970, o.p.; Ayer, 1974 (repr. of 1892 ed.).

WILLARD, Nancy. *Sailing to Cythera, and Other Anatole Stories.* See Section 5C, Travel to Other Worlds.

C *William Mayne's Book of Giants* (English title: *The Hamish Hamilton Book of Giants,* 1968). Ed. by William Mayne. Gr. 4–6.
Nineteen tales whose authors include Oscar Wilde, Eleanor Farjeon, and Janet McNeill. (BL 65:1078; CCBB 22:179; HB 45:313; KR 37:181; LJ 94:2105; TLS 1968 p. 1373)
Illus. by Raymond Briggs, Dutton, 1969, 215 pp., o.p.

WILLIAMS, Jay. *The Practical Princess and Other Liberating Fairy Tales.* See Chapter 1, Allegorical Fantasy and Literary Fairy Tales.

Witches, Witches, Witches. Ed. by Helen Hoke. See Chapter 10, Witchcraft and Sorcery Fantasy.

With Cap and Bells: Humorous Stories to Tell and to Read Aloud. Ed. by Mary Gould Davis. See Chapter 6, Humorous Fantasy.

YA *Worlds Near and Far: Nine Stories of Science Fiction.* Ed. by Terry Carr. Gr. 7 up.
Nine science-fantasy tales, including Fritz Lieber's "Four Ghosts from Hamlet," Robert Silverberg's "Dybbuk of Mazel Tov IV," and Gene Wolfe's "Feather Tigers." (BL 71:34; KR 42:808; LJ 99:2744)
Nelson, 1974, 224 pp., o.p.

YA *The Year's Best Fantasy Stories, 6.* Ed. by Lin Carter. Gr. 10 up.
This annual anthology of fantasy contains tales by Roger Zelazny, Tanith Lee, and others. There have been thirteen annual volumes in this series, published between 1975 and 1987. Volumes 10–13, edited by Arthur W. Saha, are still in print. (BL 77:561; LJ 105:2437; VOYA 4[Apr 1981]:41; Tymn:191–193)
NAL/DAW, 1980, pap., 192 pp., o.p.

YA YOLEN (Stemple), Jane H(yatt). *Dragonfield and Other Stories.* Gr. 10 up.
Twenty stories and seven poems about dragons, angels, shapeshifters, mermen, selchies, princesses, and magic. (BL 81:1638, 1657; VOYA 8:397)
Berkley/Ace, 1985, 241 pp., pap., o.p.

C/YA YOLEN (Stemple), Jane H(yatt). *Dream Weaver.* Gr. 5–7.
Seven tales told by a blind old woman to passers-by. Two are somewhat lighter in tone, and the other five are more somber. (BL 75:1582; CCBB 33:84; KR 47:742)
Illus. by Michael R. Hague, Collins, 1979, 80 pp., o.p.

YOLEN (Stemple), Jane H(yatt). *The Girl Who Cried Flowers and Other Tales.* See Chapter 1, Allegorical Fantasy and Literary Fairy Tales.

YOLEN (Stemple), Jane H(yatt). *The Hundredth Dove and Other Tales.* See Chapter 1, Allegorical Fantasy and Literary Fairy Tales.

YOLEN (Stemple), Jane H(yatt). *The Moon Ribbon and Other Tales.* See Chapter 1, Allegorical Fantasy and Literary Fairy Tales.

YOLEN (Stemple), Jane H(yatt). *The Wizard Islands.* See Chapter 4, Ghost Fantasy.

Young Ghosts. Ed. by Isaac Asimov, Martin H. Greenberg, and Charles G. Waugh. See Chapter 4, Ghost Fantasy.

Young Witches and Warlocks. Ed. by Isaac Asimov, Martin H. Greenberg, and Charles G. Waugh. See Chapter 10, Witchcraft and Sorcery Fantasy.

YA ZELAZNY, Roger. *The Last Defender of Camelot.* Gr. 10 up.
Fourteen short stories and two novellas, including "He Who Shapes," "The Last Defender of Camelot," and "For Breath of Tarny." Some of the stories were originally published under the pseudonym Harrison Denmark. (BL 77:376, 377; LJ 105:2436; SLJ Mar 1981 p. 162; VOYA 4[June 1981]:55) Simon, dist. by Pocket/Timescape, 1980, pap., 308 pp.

Zoo 2000. Ed. by Jane H. Yolen. See Section 2B, Talking Animal Fantasy.

4
Ghost Fantasy

Tales about ghosts fascinate both children and adults. Ghost fantasies, however, should not be confused with tales of horror and the occult; many, although not all, of the tales listed here have an element of humor. Most are only mildly chilling. Novels about contemporary protagonists who become involved with ghosts from the past will also be found in this chapter. If the characters travel back into the past with these ghosts, however, the books will be found in Chapter 8, Time Travel Fantasy.

C/YA   ADLER, C(arole) S(chwerdtfeger). *Footsteps on the Stairs.* Gr. 5–7.
      Dodie, thirteen, and her stepsister, Anne, solve a mystery concerning the ghosts of two teenaged girls who haunt their summer house. (BL 78:1091; SLJ May 1982 p. 83; VOYA 5[Oct 1982]:39)
      Delacorte, 1982; Dell, 1984, pap, 160 pp.

C   ADLER, David A. *Jeffrey's Ghost and the Leftover Baseball Team.* Gr. 3–5.
      Jeffrey's baseball team isn't doing very well until Bradford, the baseball-playing ghost who lives in Jeffrey's house, joins the team, building up their skills and confidence. The sequels are: *Jeffrey's Ghost and the Fifth-Grade Dragon* (1985) and *Jeffrey's Ghost and the Ziffel Fair Mystery* (1987). (BL 80:1546; CCBB 38:39; SLJ Oct 1984 p. 153)
      Illus. by Jean Jenkins, Holt, 1984, 58 pp., o.p.

      AIKEN, Joan (Delano). *The Green Flash and Other Tales of Horror, Suspense, and Fantasy.* See Chapter 3, Fantasy Collections.

C/YA   AIKEN, Joan (Delano). *The Shadow Guests.* Gr. 6–8.
[R]   Cosmo learns of a family curse that may explain the mysterious disappearance of his mother and older brother. According to his cousin, Eunice, the eldest sons of the family are fated to die in battle, and their mothers to die of grief. (BL 77:41; CC:424; CCBB 34:85; Ch&Bks:263; HB 56:644; JHC:343; SLJ Oct 1980 p. 140; Suth 3:7; TLS 1980 p. 357; VOYA 3[Feb 1981]:27)
      Delacorte, 1980, 150 pp.; Dell/Yearling, 1986, pap.

YA [R]   AIKEN, Joan (Delano). *A Touch of Chill: Tales for Sleepless Nights.* Gr. 8 up. (Orig. British pub. 1979.)
Fifteen short stories combining realism, comedy, and fantasy, including "The Cat Flap and the Apple Pie" and "Listening." (BL 76:1416; CCBB 34:25; Kies:3; SHC:649; SLJ May 1980 p. 73; TLS 1979 p. 123)
Delacorte, 1980, 183 pp.

YA [R]   AIKEN, Joan (Delano). *A Whisper in the Night: Tales of Terror and Suspense.* Gr. 6–12. (Orig. British pub. 1982.)
Thirteen stunning stories of horror and fantasy, including "Snow Horse," "Miss Spitfire," and "Lob's Girl." (BL 81:582, 585; CCBB 38:59; Kies:3; KR 52:J102; SHC:649; SLJ Dec 1984 p. 87; VOYA 7:321, 8:46)
Delacorte, 1984, 203 pp., o.p.

C   AINSWORTH (Gilbert), Ruth (Gallard). *The Phantom Carousel and Other Ghostly Tales* (British title: *The Phantom Roundabout and Other Ghostly Tales,* 1977). Gr. 4–6.
Ten stories about children who meet ghosts. (BL 74:1489; KR 46:176; SLJ Feb 1978 p. 62; TLS 1977 p. 1414)
Illus. by Shirley Hughes, Follett, 1978, 176 pp., o.p.

C/YA   ALCOCK, Vivien (Dolores). *Ghostly Companions: A Feast of Chilling*
[R]   *Tales.* Gr. 6–10. (Orig. British pub. 1984.)
Ten ghostly tales with young protagonists, including "The Sea Bride," "Qwertyuiop," and "The Whisperer." (BL 83:1596; CCBB 40:161; HB 63:460; Kies:4; KR 55:789; SLJ Sept 1987 p. 194; VOYA 10:118)
Delacorte, 1987, 132 pp.

C/YA   ALCOCK, Vivien (Dolores). *The Haunting of Cassie Palmer.* Gr. 6–8.
[R]   (Orig. British pub. 1980.)
A ghost named Deverill, who is accidentally raised from the dead by Cassie, makes Cassie's life very difficult. (BL 78:1305, 1308; CCBB 35:161; Ch&Bks:263; HB 58:294, 62:616; KR 50:421; SLJ Apr 1982 p. 78; Suth 3:9)
Delacorte, 1982, 149 pp.; Dell/Yearling, 1985, pap.

C   ANASTASIO, Dina. *A Question of Time.* Gr. 4–6.
After her unwanted move from Manhattan to Minnesota, Syd discovers a connection between her new friend, Laura, some antique dolls, and an all-but-forgotten tragedy. (BL 75:287; CCBB 32:109; KR 46:1246; SLJ Dec 1978 p. 68)
Illus. by Dale Payson, Dutton, 1978, o.p.; Scholastic, 1983, pap., 96 pp.

YA   *The April Witch and Other Strange Tales* (Orig. British title: *Fantasy Tales,* 1977). Ed. by Barbara Ireson. Gr. 7–9.
Fourteen eerie stories by such well-known authors as Ray Bradbury, H. G. Wells, and Nicholas Stuart Gray. (BL 74:1676; KR 46:599; SLJ Sept 1978 p. 159)
Illus. by Richard Cuffari, Scribner, 1978, 238 pp., o.p.

C/YA   ARTHUR, Ruth M(abel). *The Autumn People.* Gr. 6–10.
[R]   Ghosts from the year 1901 reveal the truth about the death of Romilly's great-grandmother's suitor. (BL 69:1071; CCBB 27:21; HB 49:375; KR 41:122; LJ 98:1702; TLS 1973 p. 680)
Illus. by Margery Gill, Atheneum, 1973, 166 pp., o.p.

C/YA   ARTHUR, Ruth M(abel). *Miss Ghost.* Gr. 5–7.
The ghost that Elphie meets in the tower room of her boarding school

encourages her to make real friends. (BL 76:116; HB 55:53; KR 47:1262; SLJ Nov 1979 p. 73)

Atheneum, 1979, 119 pp., o.p.

C/YA ARTHUR, Ruth M(abel). *The Whistling Boy.* Gr. 6–9.
Deeply unhappy over her father's remarriage, Kristy falls in love with a young man haunted by visions of a suicidal ancestor. (BL 65:1173; HB 45:310; KR 37:244; LJ 94:1789; TLS 1969 p. 1199)
Illus. by Margery Gill, Atheneum, 1969, 200 pp., o.p.

BACON, Martha (Sherman). *Moth Manor: A Gothic Tale.* See Chapter 9, Toy Fantasy.

C/YA BACON, Peggy. *The Ghost of Opalina, or Nine Lives.* Gr. 4–7.
The talkative ghost of a Persian cat named Opalina haunts Philip, Ellen, and Jeb's new home. (BL 64:866; KR 35:648; LJ 92:4608)
Illus. by the author, Little, 1967, 243 pp., o.p.

BARBER, Antonia. *The Ghosts.* See Chapter 8, Time Travel Fantasy.

YA [R] BEAGLE, Peter S(oyer). *A Fine and Private Place, A Novel.* Gr. 10 up.
Michael Morgan and Laura Durand, two ghosts in the Yorkchester Cemetery, decide to force themselves to remember what it was like to be alive, in order to circumvent the oblivious forgetfulness of Death. (BL 56:601; Kies:7; KR 28:243; LJ 85:1822; Tymn:50)
Viking, 1960, o.p.; Ballantine, 1976, pap., 256 pp.

BEDARD, Michael. *A Darker Magic.* See Chapter 10, Witchcraft and Sorcery Fantasy.

C/YA BELLAIRS, John. *The House with a Clock in Its Walls.* Gr. 5–7.
[R] Lewis is impressed by his warlock uncle's magic abilities, but when he tries some magic himself, he unwittingly summons up a sinister ghost. The sequels are *The Figure in the Shadows* (1975) and *The Letter, the Witch and the Ring* (1977). (BL 70:227; CC:433; CCBB 27:37; Ch&Bks:264; Kies:7; KR 41:514; LJ 98:1701)
Illus. by Edward Gorey, Dial, 1973; Dell, 1974, pap., 192 pp.

C BENDICK, Jeanne. *The Goodknight Ghost.* Gr. 3–5.
Karen and Mike meet a ghostly knight and dragon when they are accidentally locked inside a museum overnight. (CCBB 10:62; HB 32:446; KR 24:432; LJ 82:584)
Illus. by the author, Watts, 1956, 51 pp., o.p.

BLAYLOCK, James P(aul). *Land of Dreams.* See Section 5C, Travel to Other Worlds.

C/YA BOSTON, L(ucy) M(aria Wood). *The Children of Green Knowe.* Gr. 4–7.
[O] (Orig. British pub. 1954.)
With the help of three of his ancestors, Tolly lifts the curse on his family's ancient home, Green Knowe. Tolly searches for lost family treasure in *The Treasure of Green Knowe* (British title: *The Chimneys of Green Knowe*) (1958, 1987), and battles a witch in *An Enemy at Green Knowe* (1964). *The Stones of Green Knowe* (Atheneum, 1976), *The River at Green Knowe* (1959), and *A Stranger at Green Knowe* (1961) are related stories, although the latter is not a fantasy. (BL 52:37, 80:95; CC:436; CCBB 9:33; Ch&Bks:239; Eakin:40; HB 31:375; KR 23:357; LJ 80:1965).

Illus. by Peter Boston, Harcourt, 1967, 157 pp., o.p., 1977, pap.; Peter Smith, 1988.

C   BRENNER, Anita. *The Timid Ghost: Or What Would You Do with a Sackful of Gold?* Gr. 3–5.
A man and his wife demand gold in exchange for answering a ghost's questions. (BL 62:954; HB 42:193; KR 34:179; LJ 91:2206)
Illus. by Jean Charlot, Addison-Wesley, 1966, 48 pp., o.p.

C [R]   BRITTAIN, Bill. *Who Knew There'd Be Ghosts?* Gr. 4–6.
Tommy Donahue and his friends find allies in two ghosts, Essie and Horace, as they try to save the vacant Parnell mansion from destruction and recover a mysterious treasure. (BL 81:1392, 83:585; CC 1987 Suppl. 54; HB 61:448; JHC:57; KR 53:31; SLJ May 1985 p. 108)
Illus. by Michele Chessare, Harper, 1985, 128 pp.

C [R]   BROCK, Betty. *The Shades.* Gr. 3–5.
In an old walled garden, Hollis meets the Shade family, ghosts of previous visitors to the garden. (BL 68:290; HB 48:47; KR 39:1069; LJ 96:4198; TLS 1973 p. 386)
Illus. by Victoria de Larrea, Harper, 1971, 128 pp., o.p.; Avon, 1983, pap.

C/YA   BROW, Thea J. *The Secret Cross of Lorraine.* Gr. 5–7.
Twyla is unable to return a medallion to the elusive old man who lost it, until she finds a secret passageway in the former Second World War-era bunker where her family lives. (BL 77:925, 81:1405; CCBB 34:208; HB 57:299; SLJ Apr 1981 p. 121)
Illus. by Allen Say, Houghton, 1981, 177 pp.

YA   BUNTING, (Anne) Eve(lyn Bolton). *The Ghosts of Departure Point.* Gr. 7–9.
Vicki and Ted, the ghosts of two teenaged auto accident victims, meet and fall in love while they attempt to prove to the town that a safer highway must be built. (BL 79:362, 365; CCBB 36:43; Kies:15; KR 50:1109; SLJ Apr 1983 p. 110)
Lippincott, dist. by Harper, 1982, 113 pp.; Scholastic, 1984, pap.

C   BYFIELD, Barbara Ninde. *The Haunted Spy.* Gr. K–4.
The spy discovers that his peaceful retirement home is haunted. The sequels are *The Haunted Churchbell* (1971), *The Haunted Ghost* (1973), and *The Haunted Tower* (1976). (CCBB 23:39; KR 37:923; LJ 94:3809; Suth:62)
Illus. by the author, Doubleday, 1969, 48 pp., o.p.

C/YA   CAMERON, Eleanor (Frances Butler). *The Court of the Stone Children.*
[O]   Gr. 5–8.
The ghost of a nineteenth-century French girl whose father was executed for treason, begs Nina Harmsworth to help prove her father's innocence. National Book Award, 1973. (BL 70:486, 826, 80:95; CC:444; CCBB 27:75; Ch&Bks:264; HB 50:151; Kies:15; KR 41:1159, 1349; LJ 98:3718; Suth 2:74)
Dutton, 1973, 191 pp.; Avon, 1982, pap.

C [R]   CARLSON, Natalie Savage. *The Ghost in the Lagoon.* Gr. 2–4.
Timmy Hawkins uses an old scarecrow to frighten off the pirate ghost guarding the treasure in the swamp. This is the sequel to *Spooky Night* (1982), a book for younger children. (BL 81:842; CC:445; CCBB 38:143; SLJ Feb 1985 p. 71)
Illus. by Andrew Glass, Lothrop, 1984, 40 pp.

C/YA CASSEDY, Sylvia. *Behind the Attic Wall.* Gr. 6–8.
[O] Twelve-year-old Maggie's life with her two unwelcoming great-aunts proves to be as lonely as her previous stays in foster homes and boarding schools, until voices draw her to a forgotten attic room where she finds a family of dolls who have lived there since a mysterious tragedy one hundred years before. (BL 80:566; CC:446; CCBB 37:45; HB 60:49; Kies:16; KR 51:J200; SLJ Oct 1983 p. 156; Suth 3:80; TLS May 1984 p. 506)
Crowell, 1983, 315 pp.; Avon/Camelot, 1985, pap.

CHASE, Mary (Coyle). *The Wicked Pigeon Ladies in the Garden.* See Chapter 8, Time Travel Fantasy.

YA *Christmas Ghosts.* Ed. by Kathryn Cramer and David G. Hartwell. Gr. 10 up.
Seventeen classic nineteenth- and twentieth-century ghost stories written by British and American authors. (BL 84:26, 52; VOYA 10:278)
Arbor House, 1987, 283 pp.

YA *Christmas Ghosts: An Anthology.* Ed. by Seon Manley and Gogo Lewis. Gr. 7 up.
Eleven short stories involving ghosts and Christmas, whose authors include Charles Dickens and Lord Dunsany. (BL 75:53; CCBB 32:68; SLJ Oct 1978 p. 113)
Doubleday, 1978, 227 pp., o.p.

C CHRISTOPHER, MATT. *Favor for a Ghost.* Gr. 4–6.
Lennie is haunted by the ghost of Billy Marble, a former school bully, who wants Lennie to dig up Billy's dog's grave and move it next to his own. (BL 80:966; 83:585; SLJ Feb 1984 p. 67)
Westminster, 1983, 107 pp.

C/YA CHURCH, Richard (Thomas). *The French Lieutenant: A Ghost Story.* Gr. 5–7. (Orig. British pub. 1971.)
Robert doesn't believe in the eighteenth-century ghost said to haunt the castle near his home, until he actually sees the ghost himself. (BL 69:44; KR 40:398; LJ 97:1927; TLS 1971 p. 766)
Day, 1972, 153 pp., o.p.

C/YA COBALT, Martin (pseud. of William Mayne). *Pool of Swallows* (British
[R] title: *Swallows,* 1972). Gr. 5–8.
A family of ghosts causes the ponds on Martin's farm to become an ocean that swallows up a herd of cattle and Martin's father as well. (BL 70:999; CCBB 28:26; Ch&Bks:265; LJ 99:2286; Suth 2:91)
Nelson, 1974, 139 pp., o.p.

C/YA COOKSON, Catherine (McMullen). *Mrs. Flannagan's Trumpet.* Gr. 6–8.
A ghostly figure and Eddy's stubborn Granny help rescue Eddy's younger sister from white slavers. (BL 76:1124; CCBB 34:5; KR 48:364; SLJ Oct 1980 p. 144)
Lothrop, 1980, 192 pp., o.p.

COOPER (Grant), Susan (Mary). *Jethro and the Jumbie.* See Chapter 7, Magic Adventure Fantasy.

C [R] CORBETT, Scott. *Captain Butcher's Body.* Gr. 4–6.
The ghost of the legendary pirate Captain Butcher is due to make its once-every-hundred-years appearance—and George and Leo don't want to

miss seeing it. (BL 73:1010, 75:305; CCBB 30:139; KR 44:973; SLJ Dec 1976 p. 68)
Little, 1976, 168 pp.

C/YA CORBETT, Scott. *The Discontented Ghost.* Gr. 5–7.
[R]   The ghost of Sir Simon de Canterville retells the Oscar Wilde tale *The Canterville Ghost* (1906, 1986) (see this chapter) and sets the record straight about his attempts to rid his home of its new American owners. (BL 75:859, 865, 928; CC:455; HB 55:190; KR 46:1307; SLJ Feb 1979 p. 62)
Dutton, 1978, 180 pp.

C [R] CRESSWELL (Rowe), Helen. *A Game of Catch.* Gr. 4–6. (Orig. British pub. 1969.)
Kate and Hugh's games of ice skating, tag, and catch near an old castle bring to life the children who played there long ago. (BL 73:895; CC:457; CCBB 30:173; Ch&Bks:242; HB 53:312; KR 45:4; SLJ Feb 1977 p. 62; Suth 2:109; TLS 1969 p. 1388)
Illus. by Ati Forberg, Macmillan, 1977, 48 pp., o.p.

CRESSWELL (Rowe), Helen. *Moondial.* See Chapter 8, Time Travel Fantasy.

C/YA CROSS, Gillian (Clare). *The Dark Behind the Curtain.* Gr. 6–9. (Orig. British pub. 1982.)
Only Colin and Ann realize that their rehearsals for the school play, "Sweeney Todd, the Demon Barber of Fleet Street," have called up miserable ghosts intent on reenacting the old legend. (HB 60:596; SLJ Aug 1984 p. 83; TLS 1982 p. 788; VOYA 7:263)
Illus. by David Parkins, Oxford, 1984, 159 pp., o.p.

C/YA CURRY, Jane Louise. *The Bassumtyte Treasure.* Gr. 5–7.
[R]   Clues to the lost family treasure lie in a cryptic riddle, two ancestral portraits, and an old medallion, but it is a sixteenth-century ghost named Lady Margaret who helps Tommy solve the family mystery. (BL 74:1347; CC:457; CCBB 32:6; HB 54:393; KR 46:243; SLJ May 1978 p. 84; TLS 1978 p. 1396)
Atheneum, 1978, 129 pp., o.p.

C/YA CURRY, Jane Louise. *Poor Tom's Ghost.* Gr. 6–9.
[R]   A hidden staircase is not the only secret held by the old house Roger's father inherits—ghostly sobbings and footsteps prove to be caused by Tom Garland, a seventeenth-century actor who involves Roger's family in danger. (BL 73:1413, 1419; CC:458; CCBB 31:12; HB 53:439; KR 45:426; SLJ May 1977 p. 67; TLS 1977 p. 864)
Atheneum, 1977, 178 pp., o.p.

DICKENS, Charles. *A Christmas Carol.* See Chapter 1, Allegorical Fantasy and Literary Fairy Tales.

C DU BOIS, William (Sherman) Pène. *Elisabeth the Cow Ghost* (Orig. title: *Elizabeth the Cow Ghost,* 1936). Gr. 3–5.
The ghost of Elisabeth the cow returns to haunt her former master. (HB 12:28, 40:120; KR:32:108; LJ 89:2208)
Illus. by the author, Viking, 1964, 41 pp., o.p.

C/YA DUNLOP, Eileen. *The House on the Hill.* Gr. 6–9. (Orig. British pub.
[R]   1987.)
Two cousins, Susan and Philip, uncover the cause of the mysterious light in

their Great Aunt Jane's old house. (BL 84:392, 1276; CCBB 41:63; KR 55:1461; SLJ Nov 1987 p. 115; TLS 1987 p. 529; VOYA 11:22)
Holiday, 1987, 147 pp.

C ERWIN, Betty K. *Who Is Victoria?* Gr. 4–6.
No one seems to know Victoria, the elusive girl in old-fashioned clothes who helps Margaret, Polly, and Emilie solve their problems. (BL 70:385; KR 41:1035; LJ 99:208)
Illus. by Kathleen Anderson, Little, 1973, 134 pp., o.p.

EZO. *Avril.* See Section 2B, Talking Animal Fantasy.

YA FINNEY, Jack. *Marion's Wall; A Novel.* Gr. 10 up.
Marion Marsh, the ghost of a promising young actress from the 1920s, returns to inhabit Jan Cheyney's body, after Jan and her husband uncover a message Marion left on the wall of their San Francisco apartment. (BL 70:221; KR 41:137; LJ 98:563)
Simon, 1973, 187 pp., o.p.

YA [R] FLEISCHMAN, Paul (Taylor). *Graven Images: Three Stories.* Gr. 7–9.
Two ghostly and one humorous short story entitled "The Binnacle Boy," "The Man of Influence," and "Saint Crispin's Follower." Newbery Medal Honor Book, 1983. (BL 79:368, 980; CC:552; CCBB 36:125; HB 58:656; KR 50:937; SLJ Sept 1982 p. 137; Suth 3:135)
Illus. by Andrew Glass, Harper, 1982, 85 pp, hb and pap., 96 pp.

C [R] FLEISCHMAN, (Albert) Sid(ney). *The Ghost in the Noonday Sun.* Gr. 4–6.
Pirates kidnap Oliver Finch in the hope that he will be able to see the ghost of Gentleman Jim, guardian of buried treasure. (BL 62:54; CC:462; CCBB 19:43; Ch&Bks:266; Eakin:121; HB 41:490; KR 33:245, 472; LJ 90:3790)
Illus. by Warren Chappell, Little, 1965, 173 pp., o.p.

C [R] FLORA, James (Royer). *Grandpa's Ghost Stories.* Gr. 2–4.
Grandpa has scary tales to tell: about a screaming skeleton, a ghost, a witch, and a werewolf. The sequel is *Grandpa's Witched-Up Christmas* (1982). (BL 75:216; HB 55:510; KR 46:1066; SLJ Oct 1978 p. 132, Apr 1982 p. 31)
Illus. by the author, Atheneum, 1978, 32 pp., 1980, pap., o.p.

C/YA FREEMAN, Barbara C(onstance). *A Haunting Air.* Gr. 5–7. (Orig. Brit-
[R] ish pub. 1976.)
Melissa and her neighbor search old letters and newspapers to discover why they keep hearing the ghostly singing of a Victorian child named Hanny. (BL 74:811; CCBB 31:141; HB 54:163; KR 45:1270; SLJ Feb 1978 p. 57; Suth 2:155)
Illus. by the author, Dutton, 1977, 158 pp., o.p.

YA FREEMAN, Barbara C(onstance). *A Pocket of Silence.* Gr. 7–9. (Orig. British pub. 1977.)
Zilia spins a tale of romance, kidnapping, and murder for Caroline, who discovers that Zilia has come from two hundred years in the past to help solve a mystery. (BL 75:804, 809; HB 55:192; KR 42:132; SLJ Apr 1979 p. 55; TLS 1977 p. 864)
Decorations by the author, Dutton, 1978, 171 pp., o.p.

C/YA   *Fun Phantoms: Tales of Ghostly Entertainment.* Ed. by Seon Manley and Gogo Lewis. Gr. 6–10.
Twelve humorous ghost stories by such authors as Frank Stockton, Philippa Pearce, Oscar Wilde, Saki, and James Thurber. (BL 75:860; KR 47:267; SLJ Mar 1979 p. 142).
Morrow/Lothrop, 1979, 192 pp., o.p.

YA   GARFIELD, Leon. *The Ghost Downstairs.* Gr. 7–9.
Dennis Fast eagerly gives up seven years of his life in exchange for a million pounds, but finds, to his dismay, that he is haunted by the ghost of himself as a child because he'd unwittingly given away the *first* seven years of his life. (CCBB 25:168; HB 48:599; KR 40:623; LJ 97:4056, 4087)
Illus. by Antony Maitland, Pantheon, 1972, 107 pp., o.p.

C/YA   GARFIELD, Leon. *Mister Corbett's Ghost.* Gr. 5–8.
[R]   The ghost of his former master, Mr. Corbett, returns to haunt Benjamin after his idle wish for the man's death is fulfilled. (BL 65:450, 84:1189; CCBB 22:92; HB 4:560; Kies:28; KR 36:824; LJ 73:8; Suth:141; TLS 1969 p. 350)
Pantheon, 1968, 87 pp., o.p.; Viking Kestrel, 1988.

C/YA   GARFIELD, Leon. *The Restless Ghost: Three Stories.* Gr. 5–7.
[R]   In the title story, a ghost returns to haunt his imitator. (CCBB 23:143; Ch&Bks:267; HB 46:45; KR 37:1122; LJ 94:4295; Suth:142)
Illus. by Saul Lambert, Pantheon, 1969, 132 pp., o.p.

GARFIELD, Leon. *The Wedding Ghost.* See Chapter 1, Allegorical Fantasy and Literary Fairy Tales.

C/YA   *Ghosts: An Anthology.* Ed. by William Mayne. Gr. 6–9.
Twenty-five stories and poems about ghosts and goblins, including works by Rudyard Kipling, Robert Louis Stevenson, and Walter de la Mare. (BL 68:430, 434; CCBB 25:12; HB 47:491; LJ 96:3478)
Nelson, 1971, 187 pp., o.p.

YA   *The Ghost's Companion: A Haunting Anthology.* Ed. by Peter Haining. Gr. 10 up.
Fifteen ghostly and supernatural tales whose authors include Ray Bradbury, M. R. James, and Rudyard Kipling. (BL 72:1090, 1103; KR 44:159; TLS 1976 p. 561)
Taplinger, 1976, 191 pp., o.p.

YA   GODDEN (Dixon), (Margaret) Rumer. *Take Three Tenses; A Fugue in Time* (orig. British title: *A Fugue in Time,* 1945). Gr. 10 up.
Ninety-nine years of Dane family history come to life for an American girl visiting her eighty-year-old great-uncle's London home. (BL 41:225; KR 13:38; TLS 1945 p. 245)
Little, 1945, 252 pp., o.p.; Avon, 1980, pap.

YA   GORDON, John. *The Ghost on the Hill.* Gr. 8 up. (Orig. British pub. 1976.)
The ghost of Tom Goodchild becomes entangled in the lives of three young villagers, Ralph, Jenny, and Joe. (CCBB 31:32; Kies:31; KR 45:290; SLJ May 1977 p. 78)
Viking, 1977, 171 pp., o.p.

C/YA GOROG, Judith. *No Swimming in Dark Pond: And Other Chilling Tales.* Gr. 6–10.
Thirteen shiver-producing tales, including "Flawless Beauty," "The Sufficient Prayer," and "No Swimming in Dark Pond." (BL 83:1590, 1601; CCBB 40:207; KR 55:227; SLJ Mar 1987 p. 158; VOYA 10:120)
Philomel, 1987, 112 pp.

C/YA GOROG, Judith. *A Taste for Quiet, and Other Disquieting Tales.* Gr. 6–10.
Twelve eerie tales, some in fairy-tale style and others in contemporary settings, including "Those Three Wishes," "A Story about Death," and "Critch." (BL 79:906; HB 59:170; KR 50:1295; SLJ Mar 1983 p. 192)
Illus. by Jeanne Titherington, Philomel, 1982, 128 pp.

C GRAY, Genevieve S(tuck). *Ghost Story.* Gr. 3–5.
A ghost family is kept busy haunting the vagrants who moved into their house. (BL 71:690; CCBB 28:177; KR 43:122; SLJ Apr 1975 p. 52; Suth 2:77)
Illus. by Greta Matus, Lothrop, 1975, 46 pp., o.p.

YA [R] HAMILTON, Virginia. *Sweet Whispers, Brother Rush.* Gr. 7–10.
Fifteen-year-old Tree (Teresa) has ghostly visions of the past that enable her to piece together the tragic history of her mother's family. Newbery Medal Honor Book, 1983. Boston Globe/Horn Book Award, 1984. (BL 78:1518, 1525; 79:685, 980, 80:352; CCBB 35:207; Ch&Bks:267; HB 58:505, 59:330; JHC:375; Kies:34; KR 50:801; SHC:602; SLJ Sept 1982 p. 138; Suth 3:172; VOYA 5 [Aug 1982]:31, [Feb 1983]:36)
Philomel, 1982; Avon, 1983, pap., 220 pp.

C/YA HARRIS, Christie (Lucy Irwin). *Secret in the Stlalakum Wild.* Gr. 4–7. (Orig. pub. in Canada.)
Spirits of the Northwest Coast Salish Indians send a little girl named Morann into the wilderness alone on a quest for treasure. (BL 68:908; CCBB 25:169; KR 40:478; LJ 97:1913)
Illus. by Douglas Tait, Atheneum, 1972, 186 pp.

HARRIS, Rosemary (Jeanne). *Sea Magic and Other Stories of Enchantment.* See Chapter 3, Fantasy Collections.

HARRIS, Rosemary (Jeanne). *The Seal-Singing.* See Chapter 5B, Myth Fantasy.

YA [R] *The Haunted and the Haunters: Tales of Ghosts and Other Apparitions.* Ed. by Kathleen Lines. Gr. 7–10.
Spine-tingling tales by Lucy Boston, Joan Aiken, and Walter de la Mare, among others. A companion volume to *The House of the Nightmare and Other Eerie Stories* (1968). (BL 72:358; HB 52:60; JHC:433; KR 43:1194; SLJ Dec 1975 p. 68)
Farrar, 1975, 275 pp.

C/YA *Haunting Tales.* Ed. by Barbara Ireson. Gr. 6–9. (Orig. British pub. 1973.)
Ghostly tales by E. Nesbit, Joan Aiken, Ray Bradbury, and Eleanor Farjeon. (BL 71:570; CC:548; HB 50:697; KR 42:1161)
Illus. by Freda Woolf, Dutton, 1974, 279 pp., o.p.

C HAYNES, Betsy. *The Ghost of the Gravestone Hearth.* Gr. 4–6.
Charlie spends the summer searching for buried treasure after an encoun-

ter with the ghosts of a drowned boy and his pirate enemies. (BL 74:41; CCBB 31:60; KR 45:351; SLJ May 1977 p. 77)

Nelson, 1977, 160 pp., o.p.

C/YA HEARNE, Betsy (Gould). *Eli's Ghost*. Gr 4–7.
[R] A young boy named Eli runs away from his mean father to search for his mother, almost drowns in a whirlpool, and releases a mischievous ghost. (BL 83:1205; CCBB 40:126; HB 63:612; KR 55:56; SLJ Apr 1987 p. 94)

Illus. by Ron Himler, Macmillan/McElderry, 1987, 104 pp.

HENDRICH, Paula (Griffith). *Who Says So?* See Chapter 7, Magic Adventure Fantasy.

C/YA HILDICK, E(dmund) W(allace). *The Ghost Squad Breaks Through*. Gr.
[R] 5–7.
Four ghosts and two live teenagers band together to solve crimes. The sequels are: *The Ghost Squad and the Halloween Conspiracy* (1985), *The Ghost Squad Flies Concorde* (1985), *The Ghost Squad and the Ghoul of Grünberg* (1986), and *The Ghost Squad and the Prowling Hermits* (1987). (BL 80:1398, 85:585; CC:483; JHC:379; SLJ 30 [May 1984]:101)

Dutton, 1984; Tor, dist. by St. Martin, 1986, pap., 144 pp.

HOWARD, Joan (pseud. of Patricia Gordon). *The Witch of Scrapfaggot Green*. See Chapter 10, Witchcraft and Sorcery Fantasy.

C HOYLAND, John. *The Ivy Garland*. Gr. 4–6. (Orig. British pub. 1982.)
Linda, Diane, and Jamie feel compelled to solve the mystery of the ghostly boy in old-fashioned clothes whom they meet in a mountain cave. (CCBB 36:211; SLJ Mar 1984 p. 160)

Illus. by Richard Vicary, Allison, dist. by Schocken, 1983, 96 pp.

C/YA IBBOTSON, Eva. *The Great Ghost Rescue*. Gr. 5–7.
So many of England's great mansions have become unhauntable that Humphrey the Horrible appeals to the prime minister for help. (HB 51:593; KR 43:605; SLJ May 1975 p. 70)

Illus. by Giulio Maestro, Walck, 1975, 135 pp., o.p.

IRVING, Washington. *The Legend of Sleepy Hollow*. See Section 5B, Myth Fantasy.

JAMES, M(ontague) R(hodes). *The Five Jars*. See Chapter 7, Magic Adventure Fantasy.

C/YA JONES, Louis C(lark). *Things That Go Bump in the Night*. Gr. 5–8.
Tales of ghosts, witches, and haunted houses. (BL 55:559; KR 27:205; LJ 84:1275)

Illus. by Erwin Austin, Hill, 1959, 208 pp., o.p.

C/YA KEMP, Gene. *Jason Bodger and the Priory Ghost*. Gr. 4–7. (Orig. British
[R] pub. 1985.)
A medieval ghost that only Jason can see convinces this tough boy to cooperate with his timid teachers. (BL 82:810; CCBB 39:169; SLJ Sept 1986 p. 136; TLS 1985 p. 1460)

Illus. by Elaine McGregor Turney, Faber, 1985, 140 pp.

YA KINSELLA, W(illiam) P(atrick). *Shoeless Joe*. Gr. 10 up.
Baseball fanatic Ray Kinsella joins forces with J. D. Salinger in resurrecting the long-deceased members of the Chicago Black Sox team, including

Shoeless Joe Jackson. (BL 78:941; KR 50:159; LJ 107:745; SLJ Aug 1982 p. 131, Dec 1982 p. 291)
Houghton, 1982, o.p.; Ballantine, 1983, pap., 265 pp.

C/YA KIPLING, (Joseph) Rudyard. *Phantoms and Fantasies: Twenty Tales.* Gr. 6–8.
Twenty ghostly stories set in India and England. (KR 33:533; LJ 90:3133)
Illus. by Burt Silverman, Doubleday, 1965, 302 pp., o.p.

C/YA KLAVENESS, Jan O'Donnell. *The Griffin Legacy.* Gr. 6–9.
[R]   Amy's resemblance to an eighteenth-century ancestor, Lucy Griffin, enables her to speak with apparitions of Lucy and of Seth Howes, a Loyalist shot to death by Lucy's father. With the help of friends, Amy solves the mystery of a lost family legacy, and brings peace to the souls of Lucy and Seth. (BL 80:297; CC:494; CCBB 37:110; HB 60:61; JHC:387; Kies:43; SLJ Dec 1983 p. 85; Suth 3:236; VOYA 7:32)
Macmillan, 1983, 184 pp.; Dell/Yearling, 1985, pap.

C/YA KNOWLES, Anne. *The Halcyon Island.* Gr. 5–7.
[R]   A ghostly boy named Giles teaches twelve-year-old Ken to overcome his fear of the water. (BL 77:1300; CCBB 34:213; HB 57:302; KR 49:571; SLJ Apr 1981 p. 128; Suth 3:240)
Harper, 1981, 120 pp.

KONIGSBURG, E(laine) L(obl). *Up from Jericho Tel.* See Chapter 7, Magic Adventure Fantasy.

KUSHNER, Donn. *Uncle Jacob's Ghost Story.* See Chapter 1, Allegorical Fantasy and Literary Fairy Tales.

C/YA LAMPMAN, Evelyn Sibley. *Captain Apple's Ghost.* Gr. 5–7.
The ghost of Captain Apple returns to save his former home. (HB 28:406; KR 20:405; LJ 77:1739, 78:70)
Illus. by Ninon MacKnight, Doubleday, 1952, 249 pp., o.p.

YA [R] LAWRENCE, Louise (pseud. of Elizabeth Rhoda Holden). *Sing and Scatter Daisies.* Gr. 8–10.
Seventeen-year-old Nicky Hennessy's jealousy of the love between his favorite aunt, Anna, and a ghost named John Hollis nearly blinds him to the fact that Anna is dying. This is the sequel to *The Wyndcliffe* (1975). (BL 73:1084, 1092; CCBB 30:162; HB 53:450; KR 45:358; SLJ Apr 1977 p. 77)
Harper, 1977, 256 pp.

LAWSON, John S(hults). *The Spring Rider.* See Chapter 8, Time Travel Fantasy.

YA LEACH, Christopher. *Rosalinda.* Gr. 7–9.
Rosalinda died in the 1700s at the age of seventeen, but anguish over a thwarted romance causes her to reach into the twentieth century to control the life of Anne, daughter of the curator of the Warrender estate. (BL 74:1552; CCBB 32:12; SLJ Sept 1978 p. 142; TLS 1978 p. 765)
Warne, 1978, 124 pp., o.p.

C/YA LEACH, Maria (pseud. of Alice Mary Doanne Leach). *The Thing at the Foot of the Bed and Other Scary Tales.* Gr. 5–7.
A collection of ghost and witch tales, including "The Thing at the Foot of

the Bed," "Wait til Martin Comes," and "The Golden Arm." (BL 55:543;
Eakin:204; KR 27:265; LJ 84:1697)
Illus. by Kurt Werth, Philomel, 1959, 1987; Dell, 1977, pap., 112 pp.

C/YA LEVIN, Betty. *A Binding Spell.* Gr. 6–8.
[R]   Only Wren and an extremely reclusive neighbor, Axel Pederson, can see
the ghostly horse that appears in the countryside near their homes. (BL
81:449; CC:498; CCBB 38:151; HB 60:759; SLJ Dec 1984 p. 101)
Dutton/Lodestar, 1984, 179 pp.

C [R] LIFTON, Betty Jean (Kirschner). *The Cock and the Ghost Cat.* Gr. 1–4.
Koko the rooster saves his master from the ghost of a huge cat. (BL 62:162;
CCBB 19:35; Eakin:210; HB 41:492; KR 33:672; LJ 90:4618)
Illus. by Fuku Akino, Atheneum, 1965, 32 pp., o.p.

YA LILLINGTON, Kenneth (James). *Full Moon.* Gr. 8–12. (Orig. pub. in
England.)
The unhappy ghosts of two sisters possess two teenaged girls who have
come to live in an old house and an antique shop inherited from their Great-
Aunt Clara. (BL 82:1455, 1462; KR 54:1022)
Faber, dist. by Harper, 1986, 136 pp.

YA LILLINGTON, Kenneth (James). *What Beckoning Ghost?* Gr. 7–10.
(Orig. British pub. 1983.)
The sobbing ghost of a young woman appears only to women who have
refused to marry men chosen by their parents. Sixteen-year-old Emma Nash
tries to understand the ghost's sadness, in this suspenseful tale. (BL 80:338,
360; CCBB 37:111; SLJ Dec 1983 p. 85)
Faber, 1983, 156 pp.

C LINDBERGH, Anne M(orrow). *The People in Pineapple Place.* Gr. 4–6.
Lonely after his move to a new home, August makes friends with a group
of invisible people from the past who take him on wonderful expeditions. The
sequel is *The Prisoner of Pineapple Place* (1988). (BL 79:116; CCBB 36:30;
HB 58:650; KR 50:1106; SLJ Oct 1982 p. 153; Suth 3:265)
Harcourt, 1982, 156 pp.

C/YA LIVELY, Penelope (Margaret Low). *The Driftway.* Gr. 5–7. (Orig. Brit-
[R]   ish pub. 1972.)
While running away from their father and his new wife, Paul and his sister
have visions of a Viking raid, a Civil War Battle, and an eighteenth-century
highway robbery along the "driftway." (BL 69:813; CCBB 26:172; HB
49:271; KR 41:188; LJ 98:2003; Suth 2:288; TLS 1972 p. 812)
Dutton, 1973, 140 pp., o.p.

C/YA LIVELY, Penelope (Margaret Low). *The Ghost of Thomas Kempe.* Gr.
[O]   4–6.
James Harrison becomes the unwilling apprentice of a seventeenth-century
sorcerer and ends up taking the blame for the mischief caused when Thomas
Kempe decides to start life anew in the twentieth century. Carnegie Medal,
1973. (BL 70:388, 80:96; CC:501; CCBB 27:81; Ch&Bks:242; HB 49:591;
Kies:48; KR 41:883; LJ 99:211; Suth 2:288; TLS 1973 p. 380)
Dutton, 1973; Berkley/Pacer, 1986, pap., 192 pp.

C/YA LIVELY, Penelope (Margaret Low). *The Revenge of Samuel Stokes.* Gr.
[R]   5–7.
Enraged at finding a housing development on the estate he landscaped

centuries before, the ghost of Samuel Stokes returns to haunt the residents. (BL 78:549, 550; CC:501; CCBB 35:175; HB 58:44; SLJ Oct 1981 p. 144; Suth 3:269; TLS 1982 p. 345)

Dutton, 1981, 122 pp.

C/YA LIVELY, Penelope (Margaret Low). *A Stitch in Time.* Gr. 4–7.
[R] Maria is convinced that the girl from the hundred-year-old photograph hanging in her summer house still lives in the house. (BL 73:610; CCBB 30:129; Ch&Bks:269; HB 53:52; KR 44:1169; SLJ Jan 1977 p. 94; Suth 2:289; TLS 1976 p. 885)

Dutton, 1976, 140 pp., o.p.

LIVELY, Penelope (Margaret Low). *Uninvited Ghosts and Other Stories.* See Chapter 6, Humorous Fantasy.

LIVELY, Penelope (Margaret Low). *The Wild Hunt of the Ghost Hounds.* See Section 5B, Myth Fantasy.

C/YA LUNN, Janet (Louise Swoboda). *Shadow in Hawthorn Bay.* Gr. 6–10.
[R] (Orig. pub. in Canada.)
Her cousin's ghost "calls" fifteen-year-old Mary Urquhart to make the difficult voyage from Scotland to Canada in 1815, only to find that he is summoning her into the lake where he committed suicide. Winner, Canadian Library Association Best Book of the Year for Children, 1988. (BL 83:1525; CCBB 40:192; HB 63:618, 641; KR 55:796; SLJ Sept 1987 p. 197; VOYA 10:122)

Scribner, 1987, 180 pp.

C/YA LUNN, Janet (Louise Swoboda). *Twin Spell* (Orig. Canadian title: *Double Spell,* 1968). Gr. 5–7.
An antique doll gives twins Jane and Elizabeth identical nightmares and intertwines their lives with a pair of twins from the past. (CCBB 23:101; HB 45:675; KR 37:1064; LJ 94:3821)

Illus. by Emily McCully, Harper, 1969, 158 pp., o.p.; Penguin/Puffin, 1986 (entitled *Double Spell*), pap.

C McGINNIS, Lila S(prague). *The Ghost Upstairs.* Gr. 3–6.
Albert Shook has trouble explaining his unusually good grades and tidy room, because they've been caused by Otis White, the ghost of a boy who died seventy-five years earlier. (BL 79:314, 83:586; SLJ Sept 1983 p. 124)

Illus. by Amy Rowen, Hastings, 1982, 119 pp.

McGOWEN, Tom (Thomas E.). *Sir Machinery.* See Chapter 10, Witchcraft and Sorcery Fantasy.

C/YA McGRAW, Eloise Jarvis. *A Really Weird Summer.* Gr. 6–8.
[R] While trying to cope with his parents' imminent divorce, Nels's secret friendship with Alan, a mysterious boy from the past, hurts his younger brother's feelings. (BL 73:1421; CCBB 31:62; HB 53:532; KR 45:427; SLJ Oct 1977 p. 126)

Atheneum, 1977, 218 pp., o.p.

C/YA MacKELLAR, William. *Alfie and Me and the Ghost of Peter Stuyvesant.* Gr. 5–7.
Peter Stuyvesant's ghost gives Billy and Alfie a map directing them to treasure buried beneath Times Square. (KR 42:877; LJ 99:3268)

Illus. by David Stone, Dodd, 1974, 150 pp., o.p.

C   MacKELLAR, William. *A Ghost around the House.* Gr. 4–6.
       While exploring Strowan Castle on Halloween night, Jasper meets a 250-year-old ghost. (KR 38:876; LJ 95:4352)
       Illus. by Marilyn Miller, McKay, 1970, 117 pp., o.p.

C [R]   MacKELLAR, William. *The Ghost in the Castle.* Gr. 4–6.
       A ghost tells Angus Campbell the truth about Bonnie Prince Charlie's secret mission to Dunnach. (BL 57:500; HB 36:396; KR 28:624; LJ 85:4568)
       Illus. by Richard Bennett, McKay, 1960, 86 pp., o.p.

       MacKELLAR, William. *The Witch of Glen Gowrie.* See Chapter 10, Witchcraft and Sorcery Fantasy.

C/YA   McKILLIP, Patricia A(nne). *The House on Parchment Street.* Gr. 5–7.
 [R]   Carol's cousins don't believe that she has seen ghosts from the seventeenth century in their cellar. (BL 69:1093; CC:505; CCBB 26:173; Kies:51; KR 41:115; LJ 98:1701)
       Illus. by Charles Robinson, Atheneum, 1973, 190 pp., o.p.

YA   MAHY, Margaret (May). *The Tricksters.* Gr. 9 up. (Orig. New Zealand
 [O]   pub. 1986.)
       Harry (Araidne) Hamilton accidentally calls up the spirit of Teddy Carnival, a former inhabitant of their vacation home, who appears in the form of triplet brothers claiming to be long-lost Carnival relations. (BL 83:1008, 84:1248; CCBB 40:131; HB 63:471; KR 55:60; SLJ Mar 1987 p. 172, Dec 1987 p. 38; VOYA 10:80)
       McElderry/Macmillan, 1987, 266 pp.; Scholastic, 1988, pap.

C/YA   MANLEY, Seon. *The Ghost in the Far Garden and Other Stories.* Gr. 6–9.
       Eleven original ghost stories based on legends, including "The Mistress of Montauk Point," "The Cats Here Speak Only Spanish," and "Evil One." (BL 74:1094, 1109; KR 45:1049; SLJ Jan 1978 p. 96)
       Illus. by Emanuel Schoengut, Lothrop/Morrow, 1977, 128 pp., o.p.

C [R]   MARTIN, Bill (William Ivan), and ARCHAMBAULT, John. *The Ghost-Eye Tree.* Gr. 2–3.
       A boy's older sister teases him about his fear of a ghostly tree, until she sees the ghost herself while out on an evening errand. (BL 83:586; CCBB 39:114; HB 62:51; SLJ Feb 1986 p. 76)
       Illus. by Ted Rand, Holt, 1985, 30 pp., o.p.

YA   *Masters of Shades and Shadows: An Anthology of Great Ghost Stories.* Ed. by Seon Manley and Gogo Lewis. Gr. 7 up.
       Sixteen ghost stories arranged chronologically, from Charles Dickens to Ray Bradbury. (BL 74:608; CCBB 31:164; KR 46:112; SLJ Dec 1977 p. 62)
       Doubleday, 1978, 216 pp., o.p.

C/YA   MAYNE, William (James Carter). *It.* Gr. 6–9. (Orig. British pub. 1977.)
 [R]   The ghost of a witch's familiar alerts Alice to other supernatural occurrences. (CCBB 32:84; Ch&Bks:270; HB 55:646; KR 46:1017; SLJ Dec 1978 p. 62; TLS 1978 p. 376; VOYA 1[Feb 1979]:40)
       Greenwillow, 1978, 189 pp., o.p.

       MIAN, Mary. *Take Three Witches.* See Chapter 10, Witchcraft and Sorcery Fantasy.

       MURPHY, Pat. *The Falling Woman: A Fantasy.* See Section 5B, Myth Fantasy.

MYERS, Walter Dean. *The Black Pearl and the Ghost; or, One Mystery after Another.* See Chapter 6, Humorous Fantasy.

YA [R] NATHAN, Robert (Gruntal). *Mia.* Gr. 10 up.
The ghost of a middle-aged woman's lost youth comes between her and a would-be lover, the retired novelist who tells this story. (BL 67:38; HB 46:502; KR 38:346; LJ 95:2181, 3080)
Knopf, 1970, 179 pp., o.p.

NAYLOR, Phyllis Reynolds. *Shadows on the Wall.* See Chapter 8, Time Travel Fantasy.

C NIXON, Joan Lowery. *Haunted Island.* Gr. 4–6.
While renovating an island inn, Chris Holt and his family discover that the island is haunted by the ghost of Amos Corley who died 175 years before. (BL 83:1132; Kliatt 21[Spr 1987]:24; SLJ May 1987 p. 102)
Scholastic/Apple, 1987, pap., 123 pp.

C/YA ORMONDROYD, Edward. *Castaways on Long Ago.* Gr. 5–7.
Richard, Linda, and Dudley explore the forbidden Long Ago Island and meet its ghostly inhabitant. (CCBB 27:99; HB 50:150; LJ 99:575; Suth 2:346)
Illus. by Ruth Robbins, Parnassus, 1973, 182 pp., o.p.; Bantam, 1983, pap.

PAYNE, Joan Balfour (Dicks). *The Leprechaun of Bayou Luce.* See Chapter 7, Magic Adventure Fantasy.

C/YA PEARCE, (Ann) Philippa. *The Shadow-Cage and Other Tales of the Super-*
[R] *natural.* Gr. 5–8.
Ten tales of ghostly encounters, including "The Shadow Cage," "The Dog Got Them," and "The Strange Illness of Mr. Arthur Cook." (BL 74:554; Kies:59; KR 45:934; SLJ Dec 1977 p. 50; TLS 1977 p. 864)
Illus. by Ted Lewin, Crowell, 1977, 144 pp., o.p.

C/YA PEARCE, (Ann) Philippa. *Who's Afraid? And Other Strange Stories.* Gr.
[R] 5–9.
Eleven strange tales of ghosts and the supernatural. (BL 83:1208; CCBB 40:152; HB 58:344; KR 55:375; SLJ May 1987 p. 116; VOYA 10:206)
Greenwillow, 1987, 152 pp.

C/YA PECK, Richard (Wayne). *The Ghost Belonged to Me: A Novel.* Gr. 5–9.
[O] Encounters with the ghost of a girl named Inez Dumaine convince Alexander Armsworth that he has second sight. In *Ghosts I Have Been* (1977; 1979), Alexander's friend, Blossom Culp's second sight involves her with a child who drowned on the Titanic, and earns her a visit to the Queen of England. In *The Dreadful Future of Blossom Culp* (Delacorte; dist. by Doubleday, 1983, 1987), Blossom makes an accidental trip from 1918 into the future world of the 1980's. In *Blossom Culp and the Sleep of Death* (Delacorte, 1986, 1987) the angry ghost of Egyptian Princess Sat-Hathor demands that Blossom and Alexander find the missing items plundered from her tomb and protect it from any future defilement. (BL 71:1129, 80:96; CC:517; CCBB 28:182; Ch&Bks:270; HB 51:471; JHC:406; Kies:59; KR 43:456; SLJ Sept 1975 p. 109, Dec 1976 p. 32; TLS 1977 p. 348)
Viking, 1975; Dell/Yearling, 1987, pap., 192 pp.

YA [R] PEYTON, K. M. (pseud. of Kathleen Wendy Peyton). *A Pattern of Roses.*
Gr. 7–9. (Orig. British pub. 1972.)
The old drawings Tim finds signed with his own initials enable him to see

the ghost of a young man whose death was never explained. (BL 70:124, 827; CCBB 27:49; Ch&Bks:270; HB 49:473, 60:361–364; JHC:407; KR 41:819; LJ 98:2661, 3691; Suth 2:361)
Illus. by the author, Crowell, 1973, 186 pp., o.p.

Phantasmagoria: Tales of Fantasy and the Supernatural. Ed. by Jane Mobley. See Chapter 3, Fantasy Collections.

POPE, Elizabeth. *The Sherwood Ring.* See Chapter 8, Time Travel Fantasy.

PORTE, Barbara Ann. *Jesse's Ghost and Other Stories.* See Chapter 3, Fantasy Collections.

POSTMA, Lidia. *The Witch's Garden.* See Chapter 7, Magic Adventure Fantasy.

C PREUSSLER, Otfried. *The Little Ghost.* Gr. 4–6. (Orig. pub. in Germany.)
A little ghost disregards the advice of his friend, Toowhoo the owl, and makes a daylight appearance at Town Hall. (KR 35:1271; LJ 92:4617; TLS 1967 p. 445)
Tr. by Anthea Bell, Abelard-Schuman, 1967, 126 pp., o.p.

RABINOWITZ, Ann. *Knight on Horseback.* See Chapter 8, Time Travel Fantasy.

ROACH, Marilynne K(athleen). *Encounters with the Invisible World; Being Ten Tales of Ghosts, Witches, and the Devil Himself in New England.* See Chapter 3, Fantasy Collections.

C/YA ROBINSON Joan (Mary) G(ale Thomas). *When Marnie Was There.* Gr. 5–7. (Orig. British pub. 1967.)
Anna, a lonely foster child, becomes friends with Marnie, an elusive girl from the house at the edge of the marsh. (CCBB 22:163; HB 45:56; KR 36:979; TLS 1967 p. 1141)
Coward, 1968, 256 pp., o.p.

C/YA RODOWSKY, Colby F. *The Gathering Room.* Gr. 4–7.
[R]   Angered by hints of an impending family move away from their cemetery gatehouse home, Mudge realizes that he will miss the friendship of the cemetery's ghostly inhabitants. (BL 78:394; CCBB 35:157; HB 57:537; KR 49:1297; SLJ Oct 1981 p. 146; Suth 3:363)
Farrar, 1981, hb and pap., 185 pp.

C ST. JOHN, Wylly Folk. *The Ghost Next Door.* Gr. 4–6.
Lindsey and Tammy discover that their neighbor, Sherry, can communicate with the ghost of her dead half-sister, Miranda. (BL 68:395; HB 48:147; Kies:65; KR 39:1014; LJ 96:4198)
Illus. by Trina Schart Hyman, Harper, 1971, 178 pp., o.p.

C SEFTON, Catherine (pseud. of Martin Waddell). *The Ghost and Bertie Boggin.* Gr. 3–5. (Orig. British pub. 1980.)
Bertie Boggin meets Ghost in his coal cellar, and is overjoyed to have made a friend at last. (BL 78:1261; SLJ Aug 1982 p. 105)
Illus. by Jill Bennett, Faber, dist. by Merrimack, 1982, 64 pp.

YA [R] SEVERN, David (pseud. of David Unwin). *The Girl in the Grove.* Gr. 7–
9.
Jonquil becomes jealous when her friend Paul spends more and more time
with a ghostly girl named Laura. (BL 71:93, 102; KR 42:1111; LJ 99:3277;
TLS 1974 p. 717)
Harper, 1974, 266 pp., o.p.

YA [R] *Shades of Dark: Stories.* Ed. by Aidan Chambers. Gr. 7 up. (Orig. British
pub. 1984.)
Eight ghost stories by British authors including Vivian Alcock, Helen
Cresswell, and Jan Mark. (BL 83:571, 581; CCBB 40:83; HB 63:215; JHC
1987 Suppl. p. 82; KR 54:1514)
Harper, 1986, 126 pp.

C [R] SHECTER, Ben. *The Whistling Whirligig.* Gr. 4–6. (Scholastic pap. title:
The Ghost and the Whistling Whirligig, o.p.)
While staying with his history teacher, Josh meets Matthew Hubbard, the
hundred-year-old ghost of a runaway slave, who has been hiding since the
Civil War. (BL 71:463; CCBB 28:138; HB 50:693; KR 42:1253; LJ 99:2721)
Harper, 1974, 143 pp.

C SHURA, Mary Francis (pseud. of Mary Francis Craig). *Happles and
Cinnamunger.* Gr. 3–5.
The Taggert children's new housekeeper, Ilsa, is haunted by a ghost, and it
is up to the children to free her from it. (BL 78:655; CCBB 35:116; HB
58:169; SLJ Jan 1982 p. 82)
Illus. by Bertram M. Tormey, Dodd, 1981, 157 pp.

C SHURA, Mary Francis (pseud. of Mary Francis Craig). *Simple Spigott.*
Gr. 3–5.
Simple Spigott is a small ghost searching for lost Irish treasure. (BL 56:609;
CCBB 13:169; Eakin:299; HB 36:291; LJ 85:2043)
Illus. by Jacqueline Tomes, Knopf, 1960, 90 pp., o.p.

C/YA SINGER, Marilyn. *Ghost Host.* Gr. 5–9.
High school football star Bart Hawkins enlists the help of a friendly ghost
and Arvie, a bright classmate, to deal with Stryker, a poltergeist inhabiting
Bart's home. (CCBB 40:218; KR 55:1076; SLJ Sept 1987 p. 182; VOYA
10:83)
Harper, 1987, 182 pp.

C/YA *Small Shadows Creep.* Ed. by Andre Norton. Gr. 6–10.
[R] Nine ghostly tales involving children or teenagers, including M. R. James's
"Lost Hearts" and Eleanor Farjeon's "Faithful Jenny Dove." (BL 71:687,
694; HB 51:279; KR 43:24; SLJ Apr 1975 p. 56)
Dutton, 1974, 195 pp., o.p.

YA SMITH, (James) Thorne. *Topper: An Improbable Adventure.* Gr. 7 up.
(Orig. pub. McBride, 1926, o.p.; Grossett, 1933, o.p.)
Ghosts George and Marian Kirby decide to shower good deeds on Topper,
their mild-mannered former banker. The sequel is *Topper Takes a Trip* (Dou-
bleday, 1932, 1962, o.p.; Amereon [repr. of 1974 ed.]; Ballantine, 1980).
(Kies:71)
Amereon, repr.; Ballantine, 1980, pap., 208 pp.

C/YA   SNYDER, Zilpha Keatley. *Eyes in the Fishbowl*. Gr. 6–9.
[R]   Dion thinks the strange girl he meets in the Alcott-Simpson Department
Store might be a ghost. (BL 64:1097; CCBB 21:181; HB 44:182; KR 36:124;
LJ 93:1804)
      Illus. by Alton Raible, Atheneum, 1968, 1970, 168 pp.; Aladdin, 1974,
pap.

C/YA   SNYDER, Zilpha Keatley. *The Truth about Stone Hollow*. Gr. 6–8.
      Jason, new in school, takes Amy to a strange valley where loops of time
come together, enabling them to see ghosts from the past. (BL 70:825; CCBB
27:164; HB 50:380; KR 42:245; LJ 99:576, 1451)
      Illus. by Alton Raible, Atheneum, 1974, 211 pp., o.p.; Dell, 1985, pap.

C/YA   SPEARING, Judith (Mary Harlow). *The Ghosts Who Went to School*. Gr.
      5–7.
      Bored with haunting the house, Wilbur and Mortimer Temple decide to go
to school. The sequel is *The Museum House Ghosts* (1969). (BL 62:920; HB
42:308; LJ 91:1710)
      Illus. by Marvin Glass, Atheneum, 1966, o.p.; Scholastic, 1986, pap., 186
pp.

C/YA   STAHL, Ben(jamin). *Blackbeard's Ghost*. Gr. 5–8.
      J.D. and Hank accidentally summon up the ghost of Blackbeard the pirate,
who discovers that the tavern he built three hundred years earlier is about to
be torn down. The sequel is *The Secret of Red Skull* (1971). (HB 41:393; KR
33:244; LJ 90:2897)
      Illus. by the author, Houghton, 1965, 184 pp., o.p.

C/YA   STORR, Catherine. *Cold Marble and Other Ghost Stories*. Gr. 6–10.
      (Orig. British pub. 1985.)
      Eleven poignant and humorous ghost stories, including "How to Be a
Ghost," "Pale Marble," and "Bill's Ghost." (BL 82:861, 871; SLJ Mar 1986
p. 179)
      Faber, dist. by Harper, 1985, 101 pp.

STRANGER, Joyce. *The Fox at Drummer's Darkness*. See Chapter 1,
Allegorical Fantasy and Literary Fairy Tales.

STRAUB, Peter (Francis). *Shadowland*. See Chapter 10, Witchcraft and
Sorcery Fantasy.

C/YA   SUDBERY, Rodie (Tutton). *The Silk and the Skin*. Gr. 6–8. (Orig. Brit-
[R]   ish. pub. 1976.)
      Guy Carmichael reluctantly joins the class bully's gang. They try to call up
the spirit of a long-dead wizard's bat and succeed by tricking Guy's slightly
retarded younger brother into doing the summoning. (BL 79:316; HB 58:523;
SLJ Nov 1982 p. 91; TLS 1976 p. 1554)
      Deutsch, dist. by Dutton, 1982, 144 pp.

C/YA   *Supernatural Stories: 13 Tales of the Unexpected*. Ed. by Jean Russell. Gr.
[R]   5–8
      Thirteen "pleasantly eerie" stories whose authors include Joan Aiken,
Joan Phipson, Patricia Miles, and Catherine Storr. Many of these stories
were previously published in England. (BL 84:55, 74; CCBB 41:75; HB
63:745; SLJ Sept 1987 p. 182; VOYA 10:283)
      Watts/Orchard, 1987, 156 pp.

SYKES, Pamela. *Mirror of Danger.* See Chapter 8, Time Travel Fantasy.

C/YA TAPP, Kathy Kennedy. *The Scorpio Ghosts and the Black Hole Gang.* Gr. 4–7.
Ryan, Josh, Carrie, and Brooke help a ghostly bus and its inhabitants break through the time barrier. (BL 83:1057; CCBB 40:136; KR 55:225; SLJ Apr 1987 p. 105)
Harper, 1987, 192 pp.

C/YA TOMALIN, Ruth. *Gone Away.* Gr. 5–7.
[R]   Francie becomes convinced that her secret friend is actually the ghost of a girl who lived in her house during the Middle Ages. (BL 76:452; CCBB 33:83; KR 47:933; SLJ Dec 1979 p. 89)
Faber, dist. by Merrimack, 1979, 158 pp., o.p.

  C TURKLE, Brinton (Cassaday). *Mooncoin Castle; or Skulduggery Rewarded.* Gr. 4–6.
A ghost, a witch, and a jackdaw join forces to save an Irish castle from demolition. (BL 67:149; KR 38:554; LJ 95:3054)
Viking, 1970, 141 pp., o.p.

C/YA WALLIN, Luke. *The Slavery Ghosts.* Gr. 5–7.
Jake and Livy pass through a time gate into a world where Mrs. Ruffin, the ghost of a former plantation slaveholder, holds captive the ghosts of her former slaves. (CCBB 37:20; Ch&Bks:272; SLJ Dec 1983 p. 70; Suth 3:439; VOYA 6:209)
Bradbury, 1983, 121 pp., o.p.

YA [R] WESTALL, Robert (Atkinson). *The Haunting of Chas McGill and Other Stories.* Gr. 7–12. (Orig. British pub. 1983.)
A collection of eerie stories including "The Haunting of Chas McGill," in which the hero of Westall's realistic novel, *The Machine Gunners* (1976), meets the ghost of a World War I army deserter just at the outbreak of World War II. (BL 80:490; CCBB 37:120; Ch&Bks:273; HB 60:66; JHC:437; KR 51:209; SLJ Jan 1984 p. 90; Suth 3:447; VOYA 7:98)
Greenwillow, 1983, 181 pp.

YA [R] WESTALL, Robert (Atkinson). *The Watch House.* Gr. 7–9. (Orig. British pub. 1977.)
Ghosts from the past haunt a museum of shipwreck salvage and ensnare Anne in their quest for vengeance. (BL 74:1356; CCBB 31:187; HB 54:405; Kies:81; KR 46:381; SLJ Apr 1978 p. 99, May 1978 p. 36; Suth 2:478; TLS 1977 p. 1408)
Greenwillow/Morrow, 1978, 218 pp., o.p.

C/YA WHITNEY, Phyllis A(yame). *The Island of Dark Woods.* Gr. 5–7. (Orig. pub. 1951.)
While visiting their Aunt Serena on Staten Island, Laurie and Celia Kane see the legendary phantom stagecoach, said to stop at the house next door where a young woman once died. (Kies:82; KR 35:1136; LJ 92:4271)
Westminster, 1967 (entitled *Mystery of the Strange Traveller*), o.p.; Signet/NAL, 1974, pap., 172 pp.

 YA WIBBERLEY, Leonard (Patrick O'Connor). *The Quest of Excalibur.* Gr. 10 up. (Orig. pub. Putnam, 1959.)
King Arthur's ghost appears in twentieth-century England to search for

Excalibur, and manages to save Princess Pamela from abdicating to marry an American. (BL 56:120, 246; HB 36:59; KR 27:612; LJ 84:3060.)
Borgo Press, 1979, hb and pap., 160 pp.

YA WILDE, Oscar (pseud. of Fingal O'Flahertie Wills). *The Canterville Ghost.* Gr. 7 up. (Orig. pub. 1906.)
After Virginia's American family buys a home in England, the resident ghost is outraged that they are not afraid of him. Scott Corbett's *The Discontented Ghost* (see this chapter) is a related work. (JHC 1987 Suppl. p. 81; SLJ Jan 1986 p. 85)
Illus. by Lisbeth Zwerger, Picture Book, dist. by Alphabet, 1986, unp.; Oxford, 1988.

C [R] WILLIAMS (John), Ursula Moray. *Castle Merlin.* Gr. 4–6.
While vacationing at Castle Merlin, Susie and Bryan meet two medieval ghosts. (BL 69:765; HB 48:471; KR 40:1029, 1414; LJ 98:265; TLS 1972 p. 474)
Nelson, 1972, 142 pp., o.p.

C WINDSOR, Patricia (Frances). *How a Weirdo and a Ghost Can Change Your Entire Life.* Gr. 4–6.
A Ouija board helps Martha and Teddy contact ghosts, who solve a number of neighborhood mysteries. (KR 54:1371; SLJ Nov 1986 p. 94)
Illus. by Jacqueline Rogers, Delacorte, 1986, 123 pp.

WISEMAN, David. *Jeremy Visick.* See Chapter 8, Time Travel Fantasy.

Worlds Near and Far: Nine Stories of Science Fiction. Ed. by Terry Carr. See Chapter 3, Fantasy Collections.

C WRIGHT, Betty Ren. *Christina's Ghost.* Gr. 4–6.
Christina's uncle refuses to believe that she has seen a ghost in a nearby haunted house, until he meets the ghost himself. (BL 82:815, 83:586; CCBB 39:120; Kies:84; SLJ Dec 1985 p. 96)
Holiday, 1985, 105 pp.; Scholastic, 1987, pap.

WRIGHTSON, (Alice) Patricia (Furlonger). *An Older Kind of Magic.* See Chapter 7, Magic Adventure Fantasy.

C/YA YOLEN (Stemple), Jane H(yatt). *The Wizard Islands.* Gr. 4–7.
A collection of legends about islands, some of which involve ghosts and pirate treasure. (CCBB 27:167; HB 50:162; KR 41:1368; LJ 99:1224)
Illus. by Robert Quackenbush, Crowell, 1973, 115 pp., o.p.

C/YA *Young Ghosts.* Ed. by Isaac Asimov, Martin H. Greenberg, and Charles G. Waugh. Gr. 6–9.
Twelve tales about the ghosts of children, written by Arthur Quiller-Couch, M. R. James, and Ray Bradbury, among others. (BL 82:862, 874; SLJ Dec 1985 p. 96)
Harper, 1985, 210 pp.

5

High Fantasy (Heroic or Secondary World Fantasy)

This chapter lists books that involve worlds other than our own. J. R. R. Tolkien suggested that these otherworlds be called "Secondary Worlds" and that the term "Primary World" be used for our own everyday world. It was his feeling that the only true fantasy stories are those involving a Secondary World. More recently, critics have used the terms "High Fantasy" and "Heroic Fantasy" for these works.

The books listed here are subdivided into three sections: Alternate Worlds or Histories (stories that take place entirely in a Secondary World), Myth Fantasy (retellings of myth or legend, as well as stories in which contemporary protagonists are drawn into the mythic struggle of good versus evil), and Travel to Other Worlds (tales involving travel between our world and another).

Although true science-fiction stories have not been included here, "science-fantasy" tales, in which science is used to explain the existence of the Secondary World and magic is used thereafter, are included in the Alternate Worlds or Histories section.

A. Alternate Worlds or Histories

YA ABBEY, Lynn (Marilyn Lorraine). *The Black Flame.* Gr. 10 up.
Exiled warrior-priestess Rifkind rides her horse Turin across the swamps of the Felmargue to find the Black Flame. At the Well of Knowledge she becomes involved in a magical battle of the gods. This is the sequel to *Daughter of the Bright Moon* (1979, 1985), which won Abbey the John W. Campbell Award for best new science fiction writer of 1979. (BL 77:29, 38; Kliatt 14[Fall 1980]:12; VOYA 3[Feb 1981]: 40)
Ace, 1980, 1985, pap., 376 pp.

ADAMS, Richard. *Shardik.* See Chapter 1, Allegorical Fantasy and Literary Fairy Tales.

C/YA AIKEN, Joan (Delano). *The Kingdom and the Cave.* Gr. 5–7. (Orig. Brit-
[R] ish pub. 1960.)
  Prince Michael's cat is kidnapped after Michael uncovers the invasion plans
  of the people Down Under. (BL 70:871; Ch&Bks:263; HB 50:146; KR
  42:108; LJ 99:2258)
  Illus. by Victor Ambrus, Doubleday, 1974, 160 pp., o.p.

C/YA AIKEN, Joan (Delano). *The Whispering Mountain.* Gr. 5–8. (Orig. Brit-
[R] ish pub. 1968.)
  Owen is falsely accused of stealing the legendary Golden Harp of Teirtu.
  (BL 66:563; CCBB 23:123; Ch&Bks:263; HB 46:39; KR 37:1146; LJ 94:4610;
  Suth:5)
  Illus. by Frank Bozzo, Doubleday, 1969, 240 pp., o.p.

AIKEN, Joan. *The Wolves of Willoughby Chase.* See Chapter 6,
Humorous Fanstasy.

C/YA ALEXANDER, Lloyd (Chudley). *The Book of Three* (The Chronicles of
[R] Prydain, book 1). Gr. 5–8.
  In this, the first volume of the Chronicles of Prydain, a young pig keeper
  named Taran and a warrior named Gwydion set out to battle the Horned
  King. In *The Black Cauldron* (Holt, 1965; Dell/Laurel Leaf, 1985, pap.),
  Taran and Prince Gwydion plan to destroy the Black Cauldron of the Lord of
  the Land of Death. *The Black Cauldron* was a Newbery Medal Honor Book,
  1966. In *The Castle of Llyr* (Holt, 1966; Dell, 1985, pap.) Taran and Prince
  Gwydion rescue the obstreperous Princess Eilonwy, who was kidnapped by
  the wicked Chief Steward. In *Taran Wanderer* (Holt, 1967; Dell, 1985, pap.)
  Taran has grown into a young man, journeying throughout Prydain in search
  of his true identity. In the final volume of the series, *The High King* (Holt,
  1968; Dell, 1985, pap.), Taran plays a leading role in the final struggle of the
  people of Prydain against the Lord of the Land of Death. *The High King* was
  the Newbery Medal winner, 1969. *Coll and His White Pig* (1965), *The Truthful Harp* (1967), and *The Foundling and Other Tales of Prydain* (1973) are
  also set in the land of Prydain. (BL 61:344, 346, 80:95; CC:425; CCBB
  18:157; Ch&Bks:233; Eakin:4; HB 40:496; KR 32:818; LJ 89:3465; TLS 1966
  p. 1089)
  Holt, 1964; Dell, 1985, pap., 192 pp.

C [R] ALEXANDER, Lloyd (Chudley). *Coll and His White Pig.* Gr. 2–4.
  The theft of his magical pig, Henwen, by Arawan, Lord of the Land of
  Death, drives Coll to attempt a dangerous rescue. (BL 62:407; CCBB 19:77;
  Eakin:4; HB 41:619; KR 33:115; LJ 90:5506)
  Illus. by Evaline Ness, Holt, 1965, 26 pp., o.p.

C [R] ALEXANDER, Lloyd (Chudley). *The Foundling and Other Tales of
  Prydain.* Gr. 4–6.
  Six tales of the land of Prydain before the birth of Taran, Assistant Pig
  Keeper, who is the main character of *The Book of Three* (1964) and its
  sequels. (BL 70:594, 826; CC:550; CCBB 27:122; HB 50:278; KR 41:1308; LJ
  98:3688, 3704; Suth 2:9)
  Illus. by Margot Zemach, Holt, 1973, 87 pp., o.p.; Dell, 1982, pap., o.p.

C [R] ALEXANDER, Lloyd (Chudley). *The Marvelous Misadventures of Sebastian: Grand Extravaganza, Including a Performance by the Entire Cast of
  the Gallimaufry Theatricus.* Gr. 4–6.
  Caught in a revolution, Sebastian saves a cat from a witch, rescues a

princess, and kills the regent by playing a magical violin. National Book Award, 1971. (BL 67:266, 659; CC:425; CCBB 24:85; Ch&Bks:233; HB 46:628; KR 38:949; LJ 95:4040, 4324; Suth:7)
Dutton, 1970, 204 pp.

C [R] ALEXANDER, Lloyd (Chudley). *The Truthful Harp.* Gr. 2–4.
Whenever King Fflewddar tells a lie, one of his harp strings breaks. (CCBB 21:89; HB 44:58; KR 35:1268; LJ 92:4608; Suth:7)
Illus. by Evaline Ness, Holt, 1967, 32 pp., o.p.

C/YA ALEXANDER, Lloyd (Chudley). *Westmark* (Westmark trilogy, book 1).
[O] Gr. 5–10.
Theo and Mickle, an orphaned boy and a runaway girl, turn the tables on the King's evil minister, Cabbarus, when he tries to use them in a plot to gain the throne for himself. In *The Kestrel* (Dutton, 1982; Dell, 1983, pap.), Theo becomes a blood-thirsty warrior known as the Kestrel, defending his love, Queen Mickle of Westmark. In *The Beggar Queen,* (Dutton, 1984; Dell/ Laurel Leaf, 1985, pap.), the government of Westmark is violently over-thrown by ex-prime minister Cabbarus, forcing Mickle and Theo to engineer a bloody resistance movement. (BL 77:1095, 80:351; CC:425; CCBB 34:185; Ch&Bks:233; HB 57:428; JHC:343; KR 49:934; SLJ May 1981 pp. 23, 62; Suth 3:10; VOYA 4[Oct 1981]:41)
Elsevier-Dutton, 1981; Dell, 1982, pap. 192 pp.

ALEXANDER, Lloyd. *The Wizard in the Tree.* See Chapter 10, Witchcraft and Sorcery Fantasy.

YA *Amazons!* Ed. by Jessica Amanda Salmonson. Gr. 10 up.
An anthology of stories on the theme of women warriors written by a number of fantasy writers including Andre Norton and C. J. Cherryh. Win-ner of the Sixth World Fantasy Award, Best Novel, 1980. A related work is *Amazons II* (1986). (BL 76: 932; LJ 104:2488; VOYA 3[Aug 1980]:51).
DAW, 1979, 1986, pap., 206 pp.

YA [R] ANDERSON, Poul (William). *The Merman's Children.* Gr. 10 up.
Two young merpeople of the dying faerie race who were driven from the coasts of Denmark by the rise of Christianity, fall in love and search together for a new home. (BL 76:216; Kliatt 15[Winter 1981]:11; KR 47:823; LJ 104:1592; SLJ Nov 1979 p. 96)
Berkley/Putnam, 1979, 258 pp., o.p.

YA ANDERSON, Poul (William). *A Midsummer Tempest.* Gr. 10 up.
In an alternate seventeenth-century England, faery King Oberon and Queen Titania help King Charles I in his final battle against Cromwell and the Puritans, by giving the Royalists a magical wand and book to awaken the sleeping powers of the land. This is the sequel to *Three Hearts and Three Lions* (1953, 1961, 1963, 1978, o.p.) and *Operation Chaos* (1971, o.p.). (BL 70:1080, 1098; KR 42:74; LJ 99:1733; Tymn:45)
Doubleday, 1974, o.p.; Del Rey, 1978, pap., o.p.; Tor, dist. by St. Martin, 1985, pap., 320 pp.

YA ANTHONY, Piers (pseud. of Piers A. D. Jacob). *Blue Adept.* Gr. 10 up.
Stile searches for an unknown enemy menacing him in both the magic world of Phaze and the science-fictional world of Proton. While in Phaze he is helped by a unicorn, kills a dragon, is given a magic flute, and gains the love

of Lady Blue. This is the sequel to *Split Infinity* (1980) and is followed by *Juxtaposition* (1981). (Kliatt 16[Fall 1982]:17; KR 49:390; LJ 106:1325)
Ballantine, 1981, pap., 336 pp.

YA ANTHONY, Piers (pseud. of Piers A. D. Jacob). *On a Pale Horse* (Incantations of Immortality series, book 1). Gr. 10 up.
When Zane's unsuccessful suicide attempt kills Death instead of himself, the young man finds that he must take over Death's job. The sequels are *Bearing the Hourglass* (1984), *With a Tangled Skein* (1985), *Wielding a Red Sword* (1986), and *Being a Green Mother* (1987). (BL 80:666, 676; KR 51:1020; VOYA 7:37)
Ballantine/Del Rey, 1983, 249 pp., 1984, 1988, pap.

YA [R] ANTHONY, Piers (pseud. of Piers A. D. Jacob). *A Spell for Chameleon* (The Magic of Xanth series, book 1). Gr. 10 up.
Exiled to Mundania from the magical land of Xanth for failing to demonstrate any magical talents, Bink and his friend Chameleon eventually discover that Bink's unique talent is that magic cannot harm him. *A Spell for Chameleon* won the British Fantasy Society Award, Best Novel of the Year, 1977. The sequels are *The Source of Magic* (1979), *Castle Roogna* (1979), *Centaur Aisle* (1981), *Ogre, Ogre* (1982), *Night Mare* (1982), *Dragon on a Pedestal* (1983), *Crewel Lye* (1984), *Golem in the Gears* (1986), and *Vale of the Vole* (1987). (Kliatt 12[Winter 1978]:12; LJ 102:2083; Tymn:43)
Ballantine/Del Rey, 1977, pap., 352 pp.; Ballantine, 1982 (entitled *The Magic of Xanth*, [3 vols.]), pap.

C/YA AVI. *Bright Shadow.* Gr. 5–8.
Morwenna becomes enmeshed in the conflict between an evil king and his subjects after a dying wizard leaves her the kingdom's last five magic wishes. (CCBB 39:102; SLJ Dec 1985 p. 86; VOYA 9:37)
Bradbury, 1985, 167 pp.

C/YA BABBITT, Lucy Cullyford. *The Oval Amulet.* Gr. 6–9.
Disguised as a boy, seventeen-year-old Paragrin escapes from a restrictive settlement with her only treasure, an oval amulet, determined to find the mysterious woman who once gave it to her. (BL 81:1249, 1250; CCBB 38:180; SLJ Sept 1985 p. 141; VOYA 8:191)
Harper, 1985, 244 pp.

BAXTER, Lorna. *The Eggchild.* See Chapter 10, Witchcraft and Sorcery Fantasy.

C [R] B. B. (pseud. of D(enys) J(ames) Watkins-Pitchford). *The Little Grey Men* (British title: *The Little Grey Men: A Story for the Young in Heart*, 1942). Gr. 4–6.
Three gnomes search the length of Folly Brook for their lost brother, Cloudberry. Carnegie Medal winner, 1942. The sequel is *Down the Bright Stream* (British pub. 1948). (BL 46:105; CCBB 2 [Nov 1949]:8; HB 25:533; KR 17:28; LJ 74:1541, 1919)
Illus. by the author, Scribner, 1949, 249 pp., o.p.

BELL, Clare. *Ratha's Creature.* See Section 2A, Beast Tales.

C BODECKER, N(iels) M(ogens). *Quimble Wood.* Gr. 2–4.
Four miniature people called Quimbles are forced to set up housekeeping in a forest. (BL 77:1296, KR 49:431; SLJ Sept 1981 p. 104)
Illus. by Branka Starr, Atheneum, 1981, 26 pp., o.p.

YA   *Borderland, No. 1.* Ed. by Terri Windling and Mark Arnold. Gr. 7–12.
Four short stories written by Steven R. Boyett, Bellamy Bach, Charles de Lint, and Ellen Kushner, all set in the magical world of Borderland, surrounded by other warring worlds. The sequel is *Bordertown* (1986). (BL 82:1184; Kliatt 20[Fall 1986]:30; VOYA 9:233, 10:21)
NAL/Signet, 1986, pap., 252 pp.

YA [R] BRADLEY, Marion Zimmer. *The Shattered Chain: A Darkover Novel.* Gr. 10 up.
Lady Rohana of Ardais and a female band of Free Amazons arrive in the Dry Towns of Darkover where all women are kept in chains, in order to free a royal captive and her slave-born daughter. The sequels are *Thendara House* (DAW, 1983, 1988) and *City of Sorcery* (DAW, 1984). *The Shattered Chain* has also been published in one volume with *Thendara House,* entitled *Oath of the Renunciates* (Doubleday, 1983). Bradley has written nineteen novels set in the alternate world of Darkover. *Darkover Landfall* (DAW, 1972) is the first in terms of internal chronology, but they need not be read in any specific order. The others in the series are: *The Sword of Aldones* (Ace, 1962), *The Planet Savers* (Ace, 1962), *The Bloody Sun* (Ace, 1964; DAW, 1969), *Star of Danger* (Ace, 1965), *Winds of Darkover* (Ace, 1970), *The World Wreakers* (Ace, 1971), *The Spell Sword* (DAW, 1974, 1988), *The Heritage of Hastur* (DAW, 1975, 1988), *The Forbidden Tower* (DAW, 1977, 1988), *Stormqueen* (DAW, 1978, 1989), *The Keeper's Price* (DAW, 1980), *Two to Conquer* (DAW, 1980), *Shaara's Exile* (DAW, 1981, 1988), *Sword of Chaos* (DAW, 1982), and *Hawkmistress!* (DAW, 1982, 1988). *The Keeper's Price and Other Stories* (1980), *The Other Side of the Mirror: And Other Darkover Stories* (NAL/DAW, 1987), and *Red Sun of Darkover* (1987) contain Darkover tales written by Bradley and by members of the Friends of Darkover. (BL 73:22; LJ 101:1227.)
DAW, 1976, pap., 287 pp.; Hall, 1979, o.p.

YA [R] BROOKS, Terry. *The Sword of Shannara.* Gr. 10 up. (Orig. pub. Random, 1977.)
A band of elves, dwarfs, and trolls, reluctantly led by orphaned Shea, set off to find the legendary Sword of Shannara and defeat the forces of evil. The sequels are *The Elfstones of Shannara* (1982) and *The Wishsong of Shannara* (1985). (BL 73:1147, 1155, 78:593; JHC:352; KR 45:108; LJ 102:946; SLJ Sept 1977 p. 152; Tymn:55; VOYA 2[Apr 1979]:49)
Illus. by the Brothers Hildebrandt, Ballantine, 1978, 1983, pap., 726 pp.

YA   CALDECOTT, Moyra. *The Tall Stones* (The Sacred Stones series). Gr. 10 up.
Karne and his sister Kyra are trained by Maal, the old priest of their Bronze-Age British village, in the powers and secrets held by the Circle of Stones, but their lives are threatened by an evil new priest. The sequels are *The Temple of the Sun* (1978) and *Shadow on the Stones* (1979). (BL 74:1174; KR 45:1057; LJ 103:383; SLJ May 1978 p. 89; TLS 1977 p. 864)
Hill/Farrar, 1977, 234 pp., o.p.

YA   CARD, Orson Scott. *Hart's Hope.* Gr. 10 up.
Black sorcery practiced by young Princess Asineth of Burland, who had been forced into an unloving marriage to her country's conquerer, brings centuries of despair to the kingdom and its rulers. (BL 79:1013; VOYA 6:212)
Berkley, 1983, pap., 272 pp., o.p.; TOR, 1988, pap.

YA [R] CARD, Orson Scott. *Seventh Son* (The Tales of Alvin Maker; book 1).
Gr. 10 up.
Something or someone is determined that young Alvin Miller, the seventh
son of a seventh son, will never grow up to use his powerful magic, in this
novel set on the frontier of an alternate early nineteenth-century America.
(BL 83:1314, 84:838, 855, 1246; KR 55:895; LJ June 15, 1987 p. 89; SLJ Dec
1987 p. 109; VOYA 10:243, 11:13)
Tor, 1987, 241 pp.

YA CARD, Orson Scott. *Songmaster.* Gr. 10 up.
Because nine-year-old Ansset's beautiful singing voice has captivated and
tamed the formerly tyrannical Emperor Mikal the Terrible, the emperor's
jealous advisors kidnap the boy and involve him in a plot to murder the
emperor. (KR 48:739; SLJ Oct 1980 p. 166; VOYA 3[Oct 1980]:31, 11:13)
Dial, 1980, o.p.; Tor, dist. by St. Martin, 1987, pap., 384 pp.

C/YA CARLYON, Richard. *The Dark Lord of Pengersick.* Gr. 5–9.
After young Mabby steals the sorcerer Pengersick's magic ring, her friend
Jago goes on a hazardous quest to learn the powers of enchantment so that he
can fight the evil enchanter and restore the land of Kernow to the people.
(BL 77:39, 42; SLJ Aug 1980 p. 61)
Farrar, 1980, 176 pp.

YA CARTER, Lin. *Mandricardo: New Adventures of Terra Magica* (Terra
Magica trilogy, book 3). Gr. 7–12.
A knight and his amazon companion encounter magic, monsters, and wiz-
ards in the lands of Terra Magica. The preceeding books in the trilogy are
Kesrick (1982) and *Dragonrouge* (1984). (Kliatt 21[Spring 1987]:20; VOYA
10:89, 11:13)
DAW, 1987, pap., 223 pp.

YA CHANT, Joy (pseud. of Eileen Joyce Rutter). *The Grey Mane of Morning*
(Khentor novels). Gr. 10 up.
In this story set in an earlier period of the history of Kendrinh than *Red
Moon and Black Mountain* (1976, see Section 5C, Travel to Other Worlds),
the nomadic Alnei tribe of Khentor and the Golden People of the Walled
Towns come into deadly conflict, and young Mor'anh emerges as an Alnei
hero. *When Voiha Wakes* (1983) is set in the same world. (BL 77:504; LJ
103:388; Tymn:62)
Unwin, 1977; illus. by Martin White, Bantam, 1980, pap., 332 pp., o.p.

YA [R] CHERRYH, C. J. (pseud. of Carolyn Janice Cherry). *Angel with the
Sword.* Gr. 10 up.
Seventeen-year-old Altair Jones rescues an unconscious man named Mon-
dragon from a canal, falls in love with him, and becomes determined to
protect him from his powerful enemies in the city of Merovingen. The sequels
are *Festival Moon* (Merovingen Nights, No. 1, 1987), *Fever Season* (Merovingen Nights, No. 2, 1987), and *Troubled Waters* (Merovingen Nights, No.
3, 1988). (BL 81:1596, 1599; LJ Sept 15, 1985 p. 96; SHC:584; SLJ Nov 1985
p. 105)
NAL/DAW, 1985, 293 pp. o.p.; DAW, 1986, pap.

YA [R] CHERRYH, C. J. (pseud. of Carolyn Janice Cherry). *Exile's Gate* (The
Quest of Morgaine, book 4). Gr. 10 up.
In this, the fourth volume of the Morgaine series, white-haired Morgaine
and her leigeman, Vanye, discover that Skarrin, the ruler of their world, is an

exiled member of the same ancient race to which Morgaine may belong. This is the sequel to *Gate of Ivrel* (1976), *The Well of Shiuan* (1978), and *The Fires of Azeroth* (1979). *Visible Light* (1986) contains one story set in Morgaine's world. (BL 84:417, 418; Kliatt 22[Apr 1988]:18; LJ Dec 1, 1987 p. 131; Tymn:65–66; VOYA 11:94)

DAW/NAL, 1988, 416 pp., pap.

C/YA CHETWIN, Grace. *Gom on Windy Mountain: From Tales of Gom* (Tales
[R]   of Gom series, vol. 1). Gr. 6–8.

The strange runestone left him by his mother, Harga, leads fatherless young Gom into mountain caves where he discovers the truth about his mother's disappearance on the day he was born. In the sequel *The Riddle and the Rune: From Tales of Gom in the Legends of Ulm* (1987) Gom travels across Ulm in search of Harga, making both friends and enemies while he struggles to solve a mysterious riddle. *The Crystal Stair* (1988) continues Gom's adventures. (BL 82:1308; HB 62:743; JHC 1987 Suppl. p. 61; SLJ May 1986 p. 89; VOYA 9:234)

Lothrop, 1986, 206 pp.

C/YA CHRISTOPHER, John (pseud. of Christopher Samuel Youd). *The Prince*
[O]   *in Waiting* (The Winchester trilogy, volume 1). Gr. 6–9.

After our world is destroyed by earthquakes, Luke is rescued by a seer who involves the youth in a struggle for power over the medieval civilization that has arisen. In *Beyond the Burning Lands* (1971, 1975, pap.) Luke must battle his half-brother, Peter, for the throne of Winchester. In the final volume of this trilogy, *The Sword of the Spirits* (1972, 1976, pap., Peter Smith, 1984), Luke's battle accomplishments have made him a hero, but he has become a lonely man, resigned to the fact that he will continually need to fight more battles. (BL 67:306; CCBB 24:154; Ch&Bks:265; HB 47:54; KR 38:1160; LJ 95:4051; Suth 2:72; TLS 1970 p. 1460)

Macmillan, 1970, o.p., 1974, pap., 182 pp.; Peter Smith, 1984.

YA CLAYTON, Jo. *A Bait of Dreams: A Five Summer Quest.* Gr. 10 up.

A jester, a dancer, and a young girl search out the source of the Ranga Eye jewels, deadly gems that drain the soul. (Kliatt 19[Spring 1985]:24; LJ Feb 15, 1985 p. 182; VOYA 8:192)

NAL/DAW, 1985, pap., 404 pp.

YA COLE, Adrian. *A Place among the Fallen.* Gr. 10 up.

A young girl has a vision that comes true when Korbillian, a man with great magical powers, arrives in Omara to save it from catastrophe. (BL 83:1655, 1672; VOYA 10:174)

Arbor House, 1987, 352 pp.

COOK, Glen. *Doomstalker.* See Section 2A, Beast Tales.

COOK, Hugh. *The Wizards and the Warriors.* See Chapter 10, Witchcraft and Sorcery Fantasy.

YA COWPER, Richard (pseud. of John Middleton-Murray). *The Road to*
    Corlay. Gr. 10 up.

The death of a boy named Thomas, whose magical piping charmed both beasts and men, brings about the formation of the cult of the White Bird, in this haunting story set in a post-technological thirtieth century. The sequel is *A Dream of Kinship* (1981). (BL 76:435, 438; Kliatt 14[Winter 1980]:16.

Pocket, 1979, 1986, pap., 239 pp.

C COX, Palmer. *The Brownies: Their Book*. Gr. 3–5. (Stories written 1883–1887; orig. pub. 1887.)

Twenty-four stories in verse about tiny creatures who go ice-skating, take a ballon ride, go to school, and put on a circus. The sequels are *Another Brownie Book* (1890, 1941, 1967), *The Brownies at Home* (1891, 1938), *The Brownies around the World* (1892, 1937), *The Brownies through the Union* (1894), *The Brownies Abroad* (1898, 1934), *The Brownies' Latest Adventure* (1900), *The Brownies in the Philippines* (1903, 1939), *The Brownies Many More Nights* (1912, 1939), and *The Brownies and Prince Florimel* (1918). (HB 41:406)

Illus. by the author, McGraw-Hill, 1967, o.p.; Dover, 1964 (repr. of 1887 edition), pap., 144 pp.

YA CURRY, Jane Louise. *The Wolves of Aam*. Gr. 7–9.

An orphan named Runner and his friends, Cat and Fith, journey north through the Land of Tiddi to the mountain citadel of Ozel, in search of Runner's lost stone of power. The sequel is *Shadow Dancers* (1983). (BL 77:1084, 1097; HB 57:196; SLJ Apr 1981 p. 124; VOYA 4[Oct 1981]:63)

Atheneum, 1981, 186 pp.

YA DALEY, Brian. *A Tapestry of Magics*. Gr. 10 up.

The heroic exploits of the reluctant young knight, Crassmor, include courting the Lady Willow, whose tapestry controls the future of this alternate world. (BL 79:1013, 1020; LJ 108:416)

Ballantine/Del Rey, 1983, pap., 304 pp., o.p.

De CAMP, L. Sprague, and De CAMP, Catherine Crook. *The Incorporated Knight*. See Chapter 6, Humorous Fantasy.

YA DELANY, Samuel R. *Tales of Nevèryön*. Gr. 10 up.

An adventure-filled tale of the life of Gorgik, a youth in the prehistoric empire of Nevèryön, who rises from mine slave to courtier to hero. The sequels are *Nevèryöna* (1983, o.p.), *Flight from Nevèryön* (1985, o.p.), and *The Bridge of Lost Desire* (1987). (BL 76:435; LJ 104:1593; VOYA 3[Apr 1980]:48)

Bantam, 1979, pap., 272 pp., o.p.

C/YA DE LARRABEITI, Michael. *The Borribles*. Gr. 6–9. (Orig. British pub. 1976.)

After eight Borribles (violent street urchins who look like children) successfully raid a group of enemy creatures called Rumbles, they return home to find betrayal and disillusionment. *The Borribles Go for Broke* is the British sequel. (BL 74:1420, 1429; CCBB 31:174; KR 46:182; SLJ May 1978 p. 76; Suth 2:120; TLS 1976 p. 1547)

Macmillan, 1978, o.p.; Ace, 1984, pap., 320 pp.

C/YA DERESKE, Jo. *Glom Gloom*. Gr. 5–7.

After Raymond's hated adversary, Gillus, is captured by the evil Weeuns, Raymond and his friends set out to free Gillus and to save their world. (BL 82:335; JHC 1986 Suppl. p. 61; SLJ Oct 1985 p. 171)

Atheneum, 1985, 195 pp., o.p.

YA DICKINSON, Peter (pseud. of Malcolm de Brissac). *The Blue Hawk*. Gr.
[O] 7–12.

In what could be ancient Egypt, a boy named Tron defies the high priests by saving a sacrificial hawk, hides in the dead king's coffin, and joins the new

king's fight to rule his own land. (BL 72:1584, 1595; HB 52:503; KR 44:490, 549; LJ 101:1142; SLJ Nov 1976 p. 74; TLS 1976 p. 375)
  Atlantic-Little, 1976, 229 pp.; Ballantine, 1982, pap., o.p.

C/YA DICKINSON, Peter (pseud. of Malcolm de Brissac). *The Devil's Children*
[R] (The Changes trilogy). Gr. 6–9.
  Nicky Gore becomes separated from her parents during the panic and confusion of The Changes and is taken in by Sikhs suspected of witchcraft. *The Weathermonger* (1968) and *Heartsease* (1969) are also set in England during The Changes. (BL 67:262, 267, 82:1604, 1611; CCBB 24:72; Ch&Bks:259; HB 46:616, 63:82; JHC 1987 Suppl. p. 63; LJ 95:4347; Suth:102; TLS 1970 p. 417; VOYA 9:236)
  Little, 1970, o.p.; Delacorte, dist. by Doubleday, 1986, 188 pp.; Dell, 1988, pap.

C/YA DICKINSON, Peter (pseud. of Malcolm de Brissac). *Heartsease* (The
[R] Changes trilogy). Gr. 6–9.
  Four young people and a foreign "witch" with mechanical know-how escape from an England immersed in The Changes and flee to Ireland. (Ch&Bks:259; HB 46:159; 63:82; JHC 1987 Suppl. p. 64; KR 37:1111; LJ 95:1638; TLS 1969 p. 687; VOYA 9:236)
  Illus. by Nathan Goldstein, Little, 1969, o.p.; Delacorte, dist. by Doubleday, 1986, 235 pp.; Dell, 1988, pap.

C/YA DICKINSON, Peter (pseud. of Malcolm de Brissac). *The Weathermonger*
[R] (The Changes trilogy). Gr. 6–9. (Orig. British pub. 1968.)
  Able to control the weather through magic, Geoffrey Tinker returns to an England that has reverted to the Middle Ages in hope of uncovering the cause of the enchantment. (BL 65:1075; CCBB 22:156; Ch&Bks:259; HB 63:82; JHC 1987 Suppl. p. 64; KR 37:501; LJ 94:2499; Suth:103; VOYA 9:236)
  Little, 1969, o.p.; Delacorte, dist. by Doubleday, 1986, 190 pp.

YA DONALDSON, Stephen R. *Daughter of Regals and Other Tales*. Gr. 10 up.
  Eight short stories of fantasy, adventure, and horror, including one left out (for space reasons) of *The Illearth War* (1977) (see section 5C, Travel to Other Worlds). (BL 80:1081, 1083; KR 52:173; LJ 109:825; VOYA 7:205)
  Ballantine/Del Rey, 1984, pap., 337 pp.

DOUGLAS, Carole Nelson. *Exiles of the Rynth*. See Chapter 10, Witchcraft and Sorcery Fantasy.

YA [R] DOWNER, Ann. *The Spellkey*. Gr. 7 up.
  Two young people journey unwillingly to far-off Ninthistile together: Caitlin, exiled on suspicion of witchcraft because she has one blue eye and one green, and Badger, an illegitimate stable boy. Their journey is full of strange adventures that are inexplicably involved with a spellkey that "unlocks all doors." (BL 84:384, 392; HB 63:742; KR 55:1068; SLJ Sept 1987 p. 194; VOYA 10:176)
  Atheneum, 1987, 208 pp.

Dragon Tales Ed. by Isaac Asimov, Charles G. Waugh, and Martin Harry Greenberg. See Chapter 3, Fantasy Collections.

DUANE, Diane. *So You Want to Be a Wizard*. See Chapter 10, Witchcraft and Sorcery Fantasy.

YA EASTON, M. Coleman. *The Fisherman's Curse.* Gr. 10 up.
Kyala, the only girl ever apprenticed to a Master of Glass, maker of protective glass talismans, returns home to battle three gigantic monsters. (BL 83:686; Kliatt 21[Spring 1987]:22)
Warner/Popular Library, 1987, pap., 236 pp.

YA EDDINGS, David. *Guardians of the West* (Mallorean, book 1). Gr. 10 up.
King Garion and his wife attempt to save their son from the evil sorcerer, Zandramas, in this first volume of a new series that is a sequel to his Belgariad series (see Chapter 10). The sequels are *King of the Murgos* (1988) and *Demon Lord of Karanda* (1988). (BL 83:947; KR 55:259; LJ Apr 15, 1987 p. 102)
Ballantine/Del Rey, 1987, 460 pp.

EDDINGS, David. *Queen of Sorcery.* See Chapter 10, Witchcraft and Sorcery Fantasy.

YA EDDISON, E(rik) R(ucker). *The Worm Ouroboros, a Romance.* Gr. 10 up. (Orig. British pub. 1922; U.S. Boni, 1926.)
In this classic fantasy tale, the King of Demonland embarks on a herioc quest to find and free his greatest warrior, who has been enchanted by the sorcerer King of Witchland. The books of the Zimiamvian trilogy are related: *The Menzian Gate* (British pub. 1958; Ballantine 1969), *A Fish Dinner in Memison* (Dutton 1941, 1942; Ballantine 1968), and *Mistress of Mistresses* (Dutton 1935; Ballantine 1967, 1978). (BL 23:38; TLS 1926 p. 676; Tymn:84)
Illus. by Keith Henderson, Dutton, 1952, o.p.; Ballantine, 1967, 1977, pap., 520 pp.

YA EISENSTEIN, Phyllis. *Sorcerer's Son.* Gr. 10 up.
A gentle sorceress's son named Cray searches for the father he has never met, only to discover that his father is, in fact, the demon Gildrum. (BL 75:1482, 1485, 78:594; VOYA 2[Dec 1979]:53)
Ballantine/Del Rey, 1979, pap., 387 pp.

C/YA ELDRIDGE, Roger. *The Shadow of the Gloom-World.* Gr. 6–9. (Orig. British pub. 1977.)
Exiled from their subterranean worlds, Fernfeather and Harebell search for a better world above the ground. (HB 54:401; SLJ May 1978 p. 76)
Dutton, 1978, 191 pp., o.p.

YA ELGIN, (Patricia Anne) Suzette Haden. *Twelve Fair Kingdoms* (The Ozark trilogy, book 1). Gr. 10 up.
A fourteen-year-old girl sets out to rally the Twelve Kingdoms in hopes of defeating a magician threatening her world. The sequels are *The Grand Jubilee* (1981, Berkley, 1982, pap.) and *And Then There'll Be Fireworks* (1981, Berkley, 1983, pap.). (BL 77:1433, 1444, 78:594; KR 49:390; LJ 106:1326)
Doubleday, 1981, 183 pp., o.p.

YA *Elsewhere, vol. I.* Ed. by Terri Windling and Mark Alan Arnold. Gr. 10 up.
An anthology of fantasy tales about other worlds, by such authors as Ursula K. Le Guin, Michael Moorcock, and Janny Wurts. The companion

volumes are *Elsewhere, vol. II* (1982) and *Elsewhere, vol. III* (1984). (BL 78:634; SLJ Apr 1982 p. 88; VOYA 4[Dec 1981]: 38)
Ace, 1981, pap., 366 pp., o.p.

C ENGH, M(ary) J(ane). *The House in the Snow*. Gr. 4–6.
Cloaks of invisibility help Benjamin lead a rebellion against a gang of robbers who enslave boys. (BL 84:476; CCBB 41:6; KR 55:990; SLJ Sept 1987 p. 179)
Illus. by Leslie Bowman, Orchard/Watts, 1987, 192 pp.

The Fantastic Imagination: An Anthology of High Fantasy. Ed. by Robert H. Boyer and Kenneth J. Zahorski. See Chapter 1, Allegorical Fantasy and Literary Fairy Tales.

YA [R] FEIST, Raymond E. *Silverthorn* (Riftwar trilogy, book 2). Gr. 10 up.
Prince Arutha and former bandit Jimmy the Hand set out on a perilous journey in search of the mythical silverthorn plant, needed to awaken the Prince's betrothed from an enchanted slumber. This book is preceded by *Magician* (1982, 1984) and the sequel is *A Darkness at Sethanon* (1986). *Daughter of the Empire* (1987; see this section), written by Feist and Janny Wurts, takes place in the same universe as this trilogy. (BL 81:1519; KR 53:450; LJ June 15, 1985 p. 74; VOYA 8:324)
Doubleday, 1985., 353 pp.

YA FEIST, Raymond E., and WURTS, Janny. *Daughter of the Empire*. Gr. 10 up.
Queen Mara of Acoma vows to avenge the deaths of her brother and father, even if it means killing her own husband. This book is set in the same universe as Feist's Riftwar trilogy (see previous entry, this section). (BL 83:1564; KR 55:755; LJ June 15, 1987 p. 88; VOYA 10:244, 287)
Doubleday, 1987, 394 pp.; Bantam, 1988, pap.

YA FINCH, Sheila. *Infinity's Web*. Gr. 10 up.
Anastasia Valerie Stein is confronted with four different possible lives, due to a leak between parallel universes: in one she is a witch in a Nazi-ruled England, and in the others she is an unhappy housewife, a teacher, and an aging hippie. (BL 82:317; LJ Aug 1985 p. 120; VOYA 8:365)
Bantam, 1985, pap., 230 pp., o.p.

C/YA FISHER, Paul R. *The Ash Staff*. Gr. 6–9.
An irrepressible boy named Mole becomes the leader of a group of orphans fighting the evil powers of the enchanter Ammar. The sequels are *The Hawks of Fellheath* (1980) and *The Princess and the Thorn* (1981). (BL 76:448; CCBB 33:151; KR 47:1067; SLJ Jan 1980 p. 68)
Atheneum, 1979, o.p.; Ace/Tempo, 1985, pap., 176 pp.

YA FISHER, Paul R. *Mont Cant Gold*. Gr. 7–10.
Rhian Mont Cant struggles to win the approval of each of the seven guardian fates to become High King of Rhewar. (BL 77:1191; SLJ Apr 1981 p. 126; VOYA 4[Oct 1981]:63)
Atheneum, 1981, o.p.; Ace, 1985, pap., 224 pp.

YA FRIESNER, Esther M. *Spells of Mortal Weaving* (The Twelve Kingdoms series, vol. 2). Gr. 10 up.
Prince Alban finds his curse of unrequited love fulfilled, when his quest for Lady Ursula takes him into the realm of the deadly Morgeld. This is the

sequel to *Mustapha and His Wise Dog* (1985). (BL 82:1360, 1388; LJ May 15, 1986 p. 81)
Avon, 1986, pap., 215 pp.

GARD, Joyce. *The Mermaid's Daughter.* See Chapter 10, Witchcraft and Sorcery Fantasy.

GILLILAND, Alexis A. *Wizenbeak.* See Chapter 10, Witchcraft and Sorcery Fantasy.

C/YA GLOSS, Molly. *Outside the Gates.* Gr. 6–9.
[R]   Exiled beyond the High Gates because of their magic abilities, Vren, a young boy, and a man called Rusche live peacefully until Rusche is kidnapped by the evil Spellbinder. (BL 83:270; CCBB 40:26; HB 68:209; JHC 1987 Suppl. p. 66; KR 54:1207; SLJ Mar 1987 p. 158; VOYA 10:38)
Atheneum, 1986, 120 pp.

GOLDMAN, William W. *The Princess Bride: S. Morgenstern's Classic Tale of True Love and High Adventure.* See Chapter 1, Allegorical Fantasy and Literary Fairy Tales.

YA GOULART, Ron(ald Joseph). *The Chameleon Corps and Other Shape Changers.* Gr. 10 up.
Five of these eleven humorous science fiction and fantasy tales concern Ben Jolson, a shape-changing lieutenant in the Chameleon Corps. These stories are preceded by *The Sword Swallower* (Doubleday, 1968). (BL 68:976, 998; KR 40:283, 341; LJ 97:1742, 3472)
Macmillan, 1972, 216 pp., o.p.

YA GOULART, Ron(ald Joseph). *The Prisoner of Blackwood Castle.* Gr. 8–12.
A humorous science fantasy set in 1897, featuring detective Harry Challange, a conjurer called the Great Lorenzo, and Princess Alicia of Orlandia, held prisoner by a vampire in Blackwood Castle. (Kliatt 18[Sept 1984]:28; VOYA 7:266)
Avon, 1984, pap., 174 pp.

C/YA GRIMSHAW, Nigel (Gilroy). *Bluntstone and the Wildkeepers.* Gr. 5–7.
(Orig. British pub. 1974.)
When the Wildkeepers are threatened by a builder named Bluntstone and his "yellow soil-eating monsters," the little people call on dark magic to save themselves. The sequel is *The Wildkeepers' Guest* (1978). (BL 75:1090; TLS 1974 p. 721)
Faber, dist. by Merrimack, 1978, 152 pp., o.p.

GRIPE, Maria. *In the Time of the Bells.* See Chapter 1, Allegorical Fantasy and Literary Fairy Tales.

YA [R] HALAM, Ann. *The Daymaker.* Gr. 7–10.
While studying magic at Covenant School, ten-year-old Zanne discovers a hidden cache of forgotten machines and searches for the legendary Daymaker, which can make machines run without magic. (BL 84:466, 478; CCBB 41:28; HB 64:70; KR 55:992; SLJ Oct 1987 p. 138; TLS 1987 p. 1205; VOYA 10:287)
Orchard/Watts, 1987, 173 pp.

HAMBLY, Barbara. *Dragonsbane.* See Chapter 10, Witchcraft and Sorcery Fantasy.

YA HAMBLY, Barbara. *The Ladies of Mandrigyn.* Gr. 10 up.
The women of Mandrigyn trick Sun Wolf, a mercenary captain, into rescuing their men from the wizard who has conquered their city. The sequel is *The Witches of Wenshar* (1987). (BL 80:1378; LJ 109:599)
Ballantine/Del Rey, 1984, 1987, pap., 320 pp.

HARDY, Lyndon. *Secret of the Sixth Magic.* See Chapter 10, Witchcraft and Sorcery Fantasy.

HARRIS, Deborah Turner. *The Burning Stone.* See Chapter 10, Witchcraft and Sorcery Fantasy.

YA [R] HARRIS, Geraldine (Rachel). *Prince of the Godborn* (The Seven Citadels quartet, book 1). Gr. 7–10. (Orig. British pub. 1982.)
Prince Kerish of Galkis is chosen to journey to the seven citadels of the sorcerers to find seven keys that will save his land from its enemies. *The Children of the Wind* (1983), *The Dead Kingdom* (1983), and *The Seventh Gate* (1984) complete the quartet. (BL 79:770, 777; CCBB 36:127; HB 59:312; JHC:376; KR 50:1335; SLJ Nov 1983 p. 93; Suth 3:175; VOYA 6:215)
Greenwillow, 1983, 186 pp.; Dell/Laurel Leaf, 1987, pap.

HARRIS, Rosemary. *The Moon in the Cloud.* See Section 5B, Myth Fantasy.

YA HARRISON, M(ichael) John. *The Pastel City.* Gr. 10 up.
Poet and swordsman Cromis vows to help Queen Methret of Virconium in her battle against the Northern Barbarians who have released powerful ancient golems. (BL 69:620, 644; KR 40:1164; LJ 97:3932)
Doubleday, 1972, 158 pp., o.p.

HAZEL, Paul. *Yearwood.* See Chapter 1, Allegorical Fantasy and Literary Fairy Tales.

C/YA HEARNE, Betsy (Gould). *South Star.* Gr. 4–7.
After her parents' murder, Megan, a girl giant, flees the Screamer and follows the South Star across a vast plain and plateau toward a colony of giants. The sequel is *Home* (1979). (BL 74:375; CCBB 31:78; HB 53:662; KR 45:990; SLJ Oct 1977 p. 112)
Illus. by Trina Schart Hyman, Atheneum, 1977, 84 pp., o.p.

YA HILL, Douglas (Arthur). *Blade of the Poisoner.* Gr. 6–10.
Three disciples of the good sorcerer Cyrl rescue 12-year-old Jarral from the malevolent Mephtik, who has cursed the boy with a deadly wound, and the four travel to find Cyrl and undo the curse. (BL 84:466, 480; KR 55:1240; SLJ Oct 1987 p. 139; VOYA 10:178)
McElderry/Macmillan, 1987, 192 pp.

HOBAN, Russell C. *The Mouse and His Child.* See Chapter 1, Allegorical Fantasy and Literary Fairy Tales.

YA HODGELL, P(atricia) C(hristine). *God Stalk.* Gr. 10 up.
In flight after her home is destroyed, Jame, one of the last of the magical race of Kencyrs, finds refuge and new friends in Taitastigon, where she becomes involved in political, religious, and magical intrigues. The sequel is *Dark of the Moon* (1985). (BL 79:189, 198; LJ 107:1772)
Macmillan, 1982, 293 pp., o.p.; Berkley, 1983, pap., o.p.

YA HOFFMAN, Lee. *Change Song*. Gr. 10 up.
   Young Dorey joins forces with a Nightman named Ryik, whose job it is to control the elements with magic, in an attempt to save the world from destruction by uncontrollable natural forces. (BL 68:931, 940; KR 40:15; LJ 97:217, 98:660)
   Doubleday, 1972, 203 pp., o.p.

YA [R] *Imaginary Lands*. Ed. by Robin McKinley. Gr. 7 up.
   Nine tales about imaginary worlds written by Peter Dickinson, P. C. Hodgell, Patricia McKillip, Robin McKinley, Joan D. Vigne, Robert Westall, and Jane Yolen. (BL 82:609, 621, 628; CCBB 39:152; HB 62:459; JHC 1987 Suppl. p. 82; KR 54:870; SLJ May 1986 p. 106; TLS 1987 p. 857; VOYA 9:162)
   Berkley/Ace, 1985, pap., o.p.; Greenwillow, 1986, 246 pp.

C [R] JANSSON, Tove (Marika). *Finn Family Moomintroll*. Gr. 4–6. (Orig. Finnish pub. 1949, orig. U.S. pub. Walck, 1951, entitled *The Happy Moomins;* retitled *Finn Family Moomintroll,* 1958.)
   Trouble comes to Moominvalley, home of the gnomelike Moomins, when Moomintroll, Sniff, and Snufkin bring home a hobgoblin's hat. The sequels are *Moominsummer Madness* (1961), *Moominland Midwinter* (1962), *Tales from Moominvalley* (1964), *The Exploits of Moominpappa* (1966), *Moominpappa at Sea* (1967), *A Comet in Moominland* (1968), *Moominvalley in November* (1971), and *Moomin, Mymble and Little My* (British). (CCBB 5:74; Ch&Bks:268; LJ 77:653)
   Tr. by Elizabeth Portch, illus. by the author, Walck, 1958, 1965, 170 pp., o.p.; Avon, 1975, 170 pp., pap.

C/YA JONES, Diana Wynne. *Cart and Cwidder*. Gr. 6–9. (Orig. British pub.
[R]   1975.)
   Moril inherits an ancient cwidder, a lutelike instrument, whose mystical powers save Moril and his family from the murderous Southern warriors. *Drowned Ammet* (1978) and *The Spellcoats* (1979) are also set in the land of Dalemark. (BL 73:1014; CCBB 30:161; HB 53:443; KR 45:224; SLJ May 1977 p. 70; TLS 1975 p. 764)
   Atheneum, 1977, 193 pp., o.p.

C/YA JONES, Diana Wynne. *Drowned Ammet*. Gr. 6–9.
[R]   Mitt's plot to revenge his father's death misfires, and he escapes by ship to the Holy Islands. *Cart and Cwidder* (1977) and *The Spellcoats* (1979) are also set in the land of Dalemark. (BL 74:1255; CCBB 31:161; HB 54:403; KR 46:177; SLJ Apr 1978 p. 85; TLS 1978 p. 377)
   Atheneum, 1978, 255 pp., o.p.

C/YA JONES, Diana Wynne. *The Homeward Bounders*. Gr. 6–9.
[R]   When Jamie accidentally stumbles on the headquarters of "Their" war games, "They" discard him to the worlds on the Bounds. There he joins other Homeward Bounders in a battle to banish "Them." (BL: 78:98, 108; CCBB 35:12; HB 57:542; JHC:385, KR 49:1164; SLJ Sept 1981 p. 137; TLS 1981 pp. 339, 1361)
   Greenwillow, 1981, 224 pp., o.p.; Berkley/Ace/Tempo, 1985, pap.

JONES, Diana Wynne. *The Magicians of Caprona*. See Chapter 10, Witchcraft and Sorcery Fantasy.

JONES, Diana Wynne. *The Power of Three*. See Section 5B, Myth Fantasy.

C/YA JONES, Diana Wynne. *The Spellcoats*. Gr. 6–10.
Tanaqui and her orphaned brother and sisters must flee their village because they look like the enemy Heathen. During their voyage, Tanaqui weaves their story into rugcoats, which prove to have magical powers. This story is set in the prehistory of Dalemark. (CCBB 33:111; HB 55:669; KR 47:1072; SLJ Nov 1979 p. 89; VOYA 2[Feb 1980]:30)
Atheneum, 1979, 249 pp., o.p.

YA JONES, McClure. *Cast Down the Stars*. Gr. 7–10.
Glory and her friend, Honor, must repair a gap in the ancient serpent line to keep out barbarian invaders. (BL 75:178; CCBB 32:100; HB 55:68; SLJ Dec 1978 p. 53)
Holt, 1978, 186 pp., o.p.

YA [R] KENDALL, Carol (Seeger). *The Firelings*. Gr. 7–9. (Orig. British pub. 1981.)
Marked by his fellow Firelings as a sacrifice to appease the Volcano, a boy named Tacky-obbie runs away and manages to fulfill an old prophecy. (BL 78:1161; CCBB 35:151; HB 58:299; SLJ May 1982 p. 70; TLS 1981 p. 1065; VOYA 5[Oct 1982]:49)
Atheneum, 1982, o.p.; Ace, 1986, pap., 256 pp.

C/YA KENDALL, Carol (Seeger). *The Gammage Cup* (British title: *The
[O] Minnipins*). Gr. 4–7.
Four nonconformists banished to the mountains by their fellow Minnipins risk their lives to save the country when it is invaded by the Mushroom People. Newbery Medal Honor Book, 1960. *A Whisper of Glocken* (1965) takes place in the same land at a later period of history. (BL 56:248; CC 1987 Suppl. p. 59; Ch&Bks:268; Eakin:187; HB 34:477; LJ 85:845; Tymn:99–100)
Illus. by Erik Blegvad, Harcourt, 1959, 221 pp., o.p., 1986, pap.

C/YA KENDALL, Carol (Seeger). *The Whisper of Glocken*. Gr. 5–7.
[R] Five Minnipins become heroes in the course of adventures forced on them when flooding drives them from their homes. This story is set in a later period of history than *The Gammage Cup* (1959). (BL 62:331; CCBB 19:84; Eakin:187; HB 42:54; KR 33:1042; LJ 90:5097)
Illus. by Imero Gobbato, Harcourt, 1965, 256 pp., o.p., 1986, pap.

YA KENNEALY (Morrison), Patricia. *The Copper Crown*. Gr. 10 up.
High Queen Aeron of Keltia proposes an alliance with Earth, precipitating a war with two hostile planetary systems, fought with magic as well as technology, in this blend of science fiction and fantasy. The sequel is *The Throne of Scone: A Novel of the Keltiad* (1986). (KR 52:936; LJ 109:2301; VOYA 8:364)
Bluejay, dist. by St. Martin, 1984, 329 pp.; NAL, 1986, pap.

KERR, Katharine. *Daggerspell*. See Chapter 10, Witchcraft and Sorcery Fantasy.

YA [R] KING, Stephen. *The Eyes of the Dragon*. Gr. 9 up.
After old King Roland mysteriously dies by poison, his eldest son, Peter, is imprisoned for the crime. Thomas, the younger son, assumes the throne, with the evil magician, Flagg, as his advisor. (BL 83:370, 84:856; JHC 1987 Suppl. p. 71; LJ Dec 1, 1986 p. 141; SLJ June–July 1987 p. 116; VOYA 10:121)
Illus. by David Palladini, Viking, 1987, 336 pp.

YA *Kingdoms of Sorcery.* Ed. by Lin Carter. Gr. 10 up.
Sixteen British and American tales of heroic fantasy, whose authors include J. R. R. Tolkien and Richard Adams. (BL 72:1393; KR 43:1308) Doubleday, 1976, 218 pp., o.p.

YA KURTZ, Katherine. *The Bishop's Heir* (The Histories of King Kelson, vol. 1). Gr. 10 up.
King Kelson of Gwynedd must deal with a resurgence of the ancient conflict between the human and Deryni races. The sequel is *The King's Justice* (1985). "The Chronicles of Deryni" are a related series. (KR 52:829; LJ 109:2162; SLJ Jan 1985 p. 92; VOYA 8:55, 364)
Ballantine/Del Rey, 1984, 1985, pap., 384 pp.

YA [R] KURTZ, Katherine. *The Deryni Archives* (The Chronicles of Deryni). Gr. 10 up.
Nine stories about the magical Deryni, including "Lords of Sorandor," an unpublished novella written in 1965, which served as the basis for *Deryni Rising* (1970). The series includes *Deryni Rising* (1970, 1976), *Deryni Checkmate* (1972, 1976), and *High Deryni* (1973, 1982). These books are related to two other series: "The Legends of Camber," which include: *Chamber of Culdi* (1976), *Saint Camber* (1978), and *Camber the Heretic* (1980), and "The Histories of King Kelson," which include: *The Bishop's Heir* (1984) (see this section) and *The King's Justice* (1985). (BL 82:1667, 1683; LJ Aug 1986 p. 174; SLJ Nov 1986 p. 116; Tymn:101–104; VOYA 9:238)
Ballantine/Del Rey, 1987, pap., 325 pp.

YA LAUMER, (John) Keith. *The Shape Changer: A Science Fiction Novel.* Gr. 10 up.
After examining a mysterious treasure, Lafayette O'Leary suddenly finds himself changing from shape to shape and traveling from world to world. (BL 68:753, 766; LJ 97:790)
Putnam, 1972, o.p.; Ace, 1984, pap., 240 pp.

YA LAWHEAD, Stephen R. *In the Hall of the Dragon King* (Dragon King trilogy, no. 1). Gr. 7 up.
Fifteen-year-old Quentin helps Queen Alinea rescue the imprisoned king, and save the land of Mensandor from the evil rule of the king's brother, Prince Jaspin, and Nimrood the Necromancer. The sequels are *The Warlords of Nin* (Good News, 1983) and *The Sword and the Flame* (1984). (KR 50:651; SLJ Nov 1982 p. 101)
Illus. by Jack Stockman, Crossway, 1982, pap., 351 pp.

YA LAWRENCE, Louise. *The Warriors of Taan.* Gr. 7–11. (Orig. British pub. 1986.)
Elana, destined to become the Reverend Mother of the Sisterhood of Taan, and Khian, heir to the throne, meet by chance and fall in love, after their world has been overrun by the Otherworlders. (BL 84:993, 1001; KR 56:56; SLJ Feb 1988 p. 84; VOYA 10:289)
Harper, 1988, 249 pp.

YA LEE, Tanith. *Anackire.* Gr. 10 up.
Young Prince Kesarh's ambitions for power over the land of Karmiss are complicated by his daughter, whose mother is an incarnation of the goddess Anackire, and by the appearance of a long-lost hero's son. This is the sequel

to *The Storm Lord* (1978, 1986) and is followed by *The White Serpent* (1988). (BL 80:469; VOYA 7:38)
DAW, 1983, pap., 414 pp., o.p.

YA LEE, Tanith. *Companions on the Road: Two Novellas.* Gr. 10 up. (Orig. British pub. separately as *Companions on the Road,* 1975, and *The Winter Players,* 1976.)
In "Companions on the Road," two soldiers and a "snatch purse" set off with the fabled cup of Avillis, but are pursued by three mysterious "undead": the evil Lord of Avillis, his son, and his daughter. In "The Winter Players," a wicked priest-lord uses a young man named Cyrdin and a seventeen-year-old priestess named Oaive as pawns in his attempt to gain power over a magical relic. (KR 45:1014; TLS 1976 p. 1242; Tymn:107, 108)
St. Martin, 1977, 256 pp., o.p.

YA LEE, Tanith. *Cyrion.* Gr. 10 up.
Seven short stories and a novella about a wanderer named Cyrion who uses logic to outwit sorcery. (BL 79:483; LJ 107:1772; VOYA 6:45)
DAW, 1982, pap., 304 pp. o.p.

YA [R] LEE, Tanith. *Dark Castle, White Horse.* Gr. 10 up. (Orig. British pub. separately, as *The Castle of Dark,* 1978, and *Prince on a White Horse,* 1982.)
In the first novella, "The Castle of Dark," a young harper must fight a fearsome creature to rescue a maiden; and in "Prince on a White Horse," a prince is puzzled by the angry maidens he has met and the useless battles he has fought. (Kliatt 20[Fall 1986]:26; LJ Apr 15, 1986 p. 98; TLS 1982 p. 797; VOYA 9:164)
DAW, dist. by NAL, 1986, pap., 302 pp.

YA LEE, Tanith. *East of Midnight.* Gr. 10 up. (Orig. British pub. 1977.)
Dekteon, a young slave, escapes through a Vortex Gate into a parallel world where he is tricked into exchanging lives with Zaister, the doomed Sun King-consort of the ruling Daughter of Night. (KR 46:334; TLS 1977 p. 1246; Tymn:109)
St. Martin, 1978, o.p.; Ace, 1985, pap., 176 pp.

YA LEE, Tanith. *Sung in Shadow.* Gr. 10 up.
This love story about Romulan and Iuletta is a retelling of "Romeo and Juliette," set in a magical alternate Renaissance Italy. (BL 79:1448; LJ 108:1019; VOYA 6:283)
DAW, 1983, pap., 349 pp., o.p.

C/YA LE GUIN, Ursula K(roeber). *A Wizard of Earthsea* (Earthsea trilogy, vol.
[O] 1). Gr. 6 up.
In this, the first volume of the Earthsea trilogy, young Ged, studying the art of wizardry, accidentally conjures up a terrifying creature that threatens the existence of the entire world of Earthsea. *A Wizard of Earthsea* won the National Book Award, 1969. In *The Tombs of Atuan* (Atheneum, 1971, 1985; Bantam, 1984 pap.) Ged, now a wizard, invades the forbidden undertomb and labyrinth of Atuan, forcing Tenar to choose between remaining as High Priestess to the Dark Ones or escaping from Atuan. *The Tombs of Atuan* was a Newbery Medal Honor Book, 1972. In the final volume, *The Farthest Shore* (Atheneum, 1972, 1985; Bantam, 1984, pap.), Ged, now Archmage of Roke, and Prince Arren of Enlad make an arduous journey into the Shadow Kindgom of the dead to confront an evil mage who has upset the

balance between life and death. *The Farthest Shore* won the National Book Award, 1973. (BL 65:546, 901, 80:95; CC:497; CCBB 22:144; Ch&Bks:234; HB 45:59; JHC:389; LJ 94:2073, 2104, 4582; TLS 1973 p. 379, 1977 p. 863; Tymn:110, 111)
　　Illus. by Ruth Robbins, Parnassus, 1968; Bantam, 1975, pap., 192 pp.

C/YA LEVIN, Betty (Lowenthal). *The Ice Bear.* Gr. 6–8.
[R]　After the evil Lord Uris orders the absent king's great white bear and her keeper killed, young Wat, a baker's assistant, helps the keeper's daughter, Kaila, escape with the last bear cub. (BL 83:580; CCBB 40:91; HB 63:56; JHC 1987 Suppl. p. 72; KR 54:1207; SLJ Oct 1986 p. 192; TLS 1987 p. 804; VOYA 9: 220)
　　Greenwillow, 1986, 179 pp.

YA　*Liavek.* Ed. by Will Shetterly and Emma Bull. Gr. 10 up.
　　Eleven tales set in the trading city of Liavek, at the mouth of the Cat River. Each story was written by a different author, including Gene Wolfe and Jane Yolen. *Liavek: The Players of Luck* (1986) and *Liavek: Wizard's Row* (1987) are companion works. (BL 81:1637, 1657; VOYA 8:325)
　　Berkley/Ace, 1985, pap., 288 pp., o.p.

　　LINDGREN, Astrid. *The Brothers Lionheart.* See Chapter 1, Allegorical Fantasy and Literary Fairy Tales.

C [R] LINDGREN, Astrid. *Ronia, the Robber's Daughter.* Gr. 4–6. (Orig. Swedish pub. 1981.)
　　Ronia and Birk, offspring of two rival robber chieftains, fall in love and run off together into the goblin and harpy-infested forest. (BL 79:1095; CC:499; Ch&Bks:269; HB 59:304; KR 51:459; SLJ Aug 1983 p. 67)
　　Viking, 1983, 176 pp.; Penguin, 1984, pap., o.p.

YA　LUKEMAN, Tim. *Witchwood.* Gr. 10 up.
　　In hopes of escaping from her life in the workhouse, orphaned Fiona attempts to revive the magic fading from the land of Therrilyn. (BL 80:944, 965; KR 51:1150; LJ 108:2346)
　　Pocket/Timescape, 1984, 192 pp., o.p.

YA　LYNN, Elizabeth A. *Watchtower* (The Chronicles of Tornor, book 1). Gr. 10 up.
　　Princess Sorren, disguised as a messenger, helps her brother, Errel, and his chief warrior, Ryke, to escape from imprisonment by the southern invaders who have captured their castle. They travel to Vanima, a utopian mountain community, where they learn the skills they need to defeat their enemies. The sequels are *The Dancers of Arun* (1979) and *The Northern Girl* (1980). (BL 75:1203, 1212; KR 46:1346; SLJ Apr 1979 p. 75)
　　Berkley, dist. by Putnam, 1979, 1986, pap., 240 pp.

YA [R] McCAFFREY, Anne (Inez). *Crystal Singer.* Gr. 10 up.
　　Killashandra Ree uses her musical talent to become one of the most successful crystal miners on the planet of Ballybran. The sequel is *Killashandra* (1985). (BL 78:1394; LJ 107:1487; SHC:619; SLJ Nov 1982 p. 106; VOYA 5[Feb 1983]:45)
　　Ballantine/Del Rey, 1982, 1986, pap., 320 pp.

YA [R] McCAFFREY, Anne (Inez). *Dragonflight* (The Dragonriders of Pern, vol. 1). Gr. 10 up. (Orig. British pub. 1968; U.S. Walker, 1969.)
　　In this first volume of McCaffrey's series set on the dragon-filled planet of

Pern, a young woman named Lessa joins the riders of the great winged dragons as they battle the deadly threads that periodically fall from the sky. The sequels are *Dragonquest* (orig. British pub 1971; Ballantine, 1979, 1981, pap.), *The White Dragon* (orig. British pub. 1978; Ballantine, 1979, 1980, pap.; Ultramarine, 1981), *Moreta: Dragon Lady of Pern* (Ballantine, 1983, 1984, pap.), *Nerilka's Story: A Pern Adventure* (Ballantine, 1986), and three books for younger readers: *Dragonsong* (1976), *Dragonsinger* (1977), and *Dragondrums* (1979). (JHC:393; SHC:619; TLS 1969 p. 1215).
Ballantine, 1981, 1975, pap., 303 pp.

C/YA McCAFFREY, Anne (Inez). *Dragonsong* (The Harper-Hall trilogy, vol.
[O]   1). Gr. 5–10.
Menolly, angered by her people's refusal to let a "mere woman" become a Harper, runs away to make her home with a family of fire dragons. In *Dragonsinger* (1977, 1978, pap.) Menolly struggles through her first year of Harper training and continues to care for her brood of fire lizards. In *Dragondrums* (1979, 1980, pap.) Piemer, a friend of Menolly, is trained as a drummer and sent on a mysterious journey by the Masterharper of Pern. (BL 72:1253, 1266, 80:353; CC:503; CCBB 29:177; Ch&Bks:269; HB 52:406; JHC:394; KR 44:391; SLJ Apr 1976 p. 91; Suth 2:294)
Atheneum, 1976, 204 pp.; Bantam, 1977, 1986, pap.

YA MACE, Elisabeth. *Out There* (British title: *Ransome Revisited*, 1975). Gr. 7–10.
An unnamed man undertakes a fearsome journey to escape his unhappy life and to find the legendary "Colony." *The Travelling Man* is the British sequel. (BL 74:807. CCBB 31:145; JHC 430; KR 46:111; SLJ Mar 1978 p. 138)
Greenwillow, 1978, 181 pp., o.p.

McGOWEN, Tom E. *The Magician's Apprentice.* See Chapter 10, Witchcraft and Sorcery Fantasy.

C/YA McKENZIE, Ellen Kindt. *Taash and the Jesters.* Gr. 5–7.
An orphan named Taash and two court jesters attempt to foil the Duke of Xon's plot to take over the kingdom. The sequel is *Kashka* (1987). (BL 65:451, 901; KR 36:1048)
Holt, 1968, 233 pp., o.p.

C/YA McKILLIP, Patricia A(nne). *The Forgotten Beasts of Eld.* Gr. 6–9.
[O]   Sybel, a sorceress, lovingly raises an abandoned baby named Tam, only to discover that his real father is the greatest enemy of the man she loves. First World Fantasy Award, Best Novel, 1975. (BL 71:173, 767; CCBB 28:82; Ch&Bks:269; KR 42:743; LJ 99:2748)
Atheneum, 1974; Berkley, 1984, pap., 224 pp.

YA McKILLIP, Patricia A(nne). *Moon-Flash.* Gr. 7–10.
[O]   Kyreol and her friend Terje set off in a boat to explore the world outside the boundaries of Riverworld, and in doing so, make some astonishing discoveries about the fate of Kyreol's mother and the true nature of their world. The sequel is *The Moon and the Face* (1985). (BL 81:636, 642; CC:505; CCBB 38:10; Ch&Bks:270; HB 60:763; JHC:394; SLJ Dec 1984 p. 92; Suth 3:287; VOYA 8:56)
Atheneum, 1984; Berkley, 1985, pap., 160 pp.

C/YA   McKILLIP, Patricia A(nne). *The Riddle-Master of Hed* (The Star-Bearer
[R]   trilogy, vol. 1). Gr. 6–9.
       Morgan, the peace-loving ruler of Hed, is driven to uncover the meaning of
       the three stars on his forehead. In *Heir of Sea and Fire* (1977, 1978, pap.),
       Raederle, Morgan's love, uses her magical powers to search for Morgan, who
       is inexplicably missing. In the final volume of this trilogy, *Harpist in the Wind*
       (1979, 1980, pap.), Morgan and Raederle battle numerous enemies during his
       struggle to become heir to the throne of the High One. (BL 73:468, 475;
       CC:506; CCBB 30:109; HB 52:625; JHC:394; Kliatt 12[Spring 1975]:13; KR
       44:1044; SLJ Oct 1976 p. 119; Tymn:136–138)
       Atheneum, 1976, 240 pp.; Ballantine, 1978, pap.

C   McKILLIP, Patricia A(nne). *The Throme of the Erril of Sherill.* Gr. 4–6.
    Before permitting his daughter to wed Cnite Caerles, King Magnus orders
    the young man to bring him the Throme, an ancient magical document.
    (CCBB 27:82; KR 41:686; LJ 98:2654; Tymn:135)
    Illus. by Julia Noonan, Atheneum, 1973, o.p.; Ace, 1987, pap., 160 pp.

C/YA   McKINLEY, Robin (Jennifer Carolyn). *The Blue Sword.* Gr. 6–12.
[O]   Harry Crewe is kidnapped by Corlath, King of the Damarians, and comes
       reluctantly to realize that they possess the same mysterious powers. Newbery
       Medal Honor Book, 1983. The prequel is *The Hero and the Crown* (1984).
       (BL 79:198, 247, 671, 980, 80:353; CC:506; CCBB 36:112; Ch&Bks:270;
       HB 58:660, 59:330; JHC:395; SLJ Jan 1983 p. 86; Suth 3:287; VOYA
       6:46)
       Greenwillow, 1982, 272 pp.; Berkley, 1982, pap., o.p.

C/YA   McKINLEY, Robin (Jennifer Carolyn). *The Hero and the Crown.* Gr. 6–
[O]   12.
       Princess Aerin of Damar becomes a legendary dragonslayer, fulfilling her
       destiny as savior of her kingdom, in this prequel to *The Blue Sword* (1982).
       The Hero and the Crown won the Newbery Medal, 1985. (BL 81:211, 250;
       CC:506; CCBB 38:30; Ch&Bks:270; HB 61:59; JHC:395; SLJ Oct 1984 p.
       169; Suth 3:287; TLS 1985 p. 958; VOYA 7:388)
       Greenwillow, 1984, 288 pp.; Berkley, 1985, pap.

YA [R]   *Magic in Ithkar.* Ed. by Andre Norton and Robert Adams. Gr. 10 up.
         Thirteen tales set in the magical kingdom of Ithkar, each written by a
         different author, including Andre Norton and C. J. Cherryh. *Magic in Ithkar
         2* (1985), *Magic in Ithkar 3* (1986), and *Magic in Ithkar 4* (1987) are compan-
         ion works. (BL 81:1436, 1448; JHC 1987 Suppl. p. 82; Kliatt 19[Fall 1985]:24;
         SLJ Aug 1985 p. 88; VOYA 8:268)
         Tor; dist. by St. Martin's 1985, pap., 317 pp.

YA [R]   MARK, Jan (pseud. of Janet Marjorie Brisland). *Aquarius.* Gr. 7–10.
         (Orig. British pub. 1982.)
         Because Viner's water-divining skills have made him an outcast in his rain-
         soaked land, he runs away in search of someone who can bring dryness and
         sunshine to his world. (CCBB 37:209; Ch&Bks:270; HB 60:598; SLJ Apr
         1985 p. 98; Suth 3:295; TLS 1982 p. 791)
         Atheneum, 1984, 223 pp.

YA [R]   MARK, Jan (pseud. of Janet Marjorie Brisland). *Divide and Rule.* Gr. 8
         up. (Orig. British pub. 1979.)
         Hanno spends a frightening year in the power of the temple priests, only to

learn that he will be sacrificed if he does not join them. (BL 76:1522; CCBB 33:196; HB 56:415; KR 48:516; SLJ Aug 1980 p. 77; TLS 1979 p. 122)
Crowell, 1980, 264 pp., o.p.

C/YA   MARTIN, Graham Dunstan. *Giftwish*. Gr. 5–8. (Orig. British pub. 1978.)
Ewan is tricked into going to the Castle Midnight to fight the wicked Necromancer, in order to fulfill an ancient prophecy. The sequel is *Catchfire* (1982), in which Ewan, newly crowned King of Feydom, and Catchfire, the witch girl, struggle to break the enchantment wrought by the wizard Hoodwill. (BL 77:1191, 1197; HB 57:197; SLJ Apr 1981 p. 129)
Houghton, 1981, 202 pp., o.p.

YA   MAYHAR, Ardath. *Lords of the Triple Moons*. Gr. 7–9.
Sixteen-year-old Johab, one of the last of the Old Lords of Rehar roth, uses his mental powers to escape from prison and to free his land fr(n the evil ones who murdered his family. (BL 79:1059, 1096; SLJ Sept 1983 p. 137; VOYA 6:148)
Atheneum, 1983; Ace, 1984, pap., 144 pp.

YA   MAYHAR, Ardath. *Makra Choria*. Gr. 7–9.
Choria uses her inherited powers to dethrone her older sister who gained the throne of Makraitis by having their father killed. (HB 58:347; KR 55:58; SLJ Apr 1987 p. 112; VOYA 10:92)
Atheneum, 1987, 193 pp.

YA   MAYHAR, Ardath. *Runes of the Lyre*. Gr. 7–12.
A science fantasy about Yinri, a runaway girl who discovers the secret gateway into the Kingdom of Hasyih, where she meets both her real and her foster fathers, becomes "The Queen Who Was to Come," and gathers her forces to battle the evil Hasyisi. (HB 58:520; SLJ Sept 1982 p. 141; VOYA 5[Feb 1983]:45)
Atheneum, 1982, o.p.; Ace, 1983, pap., 224 pp.

C/YA   MAYHAR, Ardath. *Soul-Singer of Tyrnos*. Gr. 6–9.
Trained as a Soul-Singer to keep goodness and justice in the souls of the people, Yeleeve is chosen to fight the evil that is corrupting the land of Tyrnos. *Runes of the Lyre* (1982) is a related work. (BL 78:98, 110; CCBB 35:91; JHC:396; SLJ Feb 1982 p. 90)
Atheneum, 1981, 195 pp., o.p.

YA   MIRRLEES, Hope. *Lud-in-the-Mist*. Gr. 10 up. (Orig. British pub. 1926.)
Master Chanticleer, the mayor of the seaport town of Mist, sets out to discover the identity of the smuggler bringing fairy fruits over the border from Fairyland into the sober land of Dorimare. (BL 23:384; TLS Jan 13, 1927 p. 26; Tymn:141)
Knopf, 1927, o.p.; Ballantine, 1970, 1977, 273 pp., o.p.

YA   MOORCOCK, Michael (John). *The Dragon in the Sword* (The Eternal Champion series, book 3). Gr. 10 up.
Erehose sets sail to search for his lost love, Ermizhad, and meets Count Von Bek, a refugee from the Third Reich. The series began with *The Eternal Champion* (Dell, 1970) and continues with *Phoenix in Obsidian* (Mayflower, 1970; Dell, 1973, entitled *The Silver Warriors*). (BL 83:34; KR 54:1072; LJ Sept 15, 1986 p. 102; VOYA 9:292, 11:12)
Ace, 1986, 1987, pap., 272 pp.

YA MOORCOCK, Michael (John). *The Ice Schooner: A Tale.* Gr. 10 up.
(Orig. British and U.S. pub. 1969.)
An ice-schooner captain, living at the end of a future ice age, makes an ill-fated pilgrimage to the sacred city of New York. (BL 73:1485, 1490; KR 45:509; LJ 102:1868)
Harper, 1977, o.p.; Berkley, 1969, 1987, pap., 208 pp.

YA MORRIS, William. *The Well at the World's End.* Gr. 10 up. (Orig. British
and U.S. pub. 1896.)
A boy named Ralph grows to manhood while undertaking an adventure-filled quest to find the well at the world's end. According to Tymn, Zahorski, and Boyer in *Fantasy Literature: A Core Collection and Reference Guide* (Bowker, 1979), Morris could be called the father of modern high fantasy, and this work is his most significant. His work influenced many others, including Lord Dunsany, J. R. R. Tolkien, and C. S. Lewis. (HB 3[May 1927]:20–22; Tymn:146)
Longman, 1903, 1913, 496 pp., o.p.; Ballantine, 1970, 1978, o.p.

YA [R] MURPHY, Shirley Rousseau. *Nightpool.* Gr. 7–10.
Young Prince Tebriel, badly injured by his father's murderer, is nursed by a colony of intelligent otters, until he is strong enough to seek out the legendary singing dragon and avenge his father's death. In *The Ivory Lyre* (1987) Tebriel and his telepathic dragon, Seastrider, join the resistance against the evil ones bent on taking over their world. *The Dragonbards* (1988) completes the trilogy. (BL 82:53, 67; CCBB 39:33; JHC 1986 Suppl. p. 69; SLJ Dec 1985 p. 104; VOYA 8:326)
Harper, 1985, 250 pp.; Harper/Starwanderer, 1987, pap.

YA MURPHY, Shirley Rousseau. *The Ring of Fire.* Gr. 7–9.
Zephy and Thorn search for a lost jade runestone that will protect them from the tyrants of Kubal. *The Wolf Bell* (1979) is set in a previous time, and the sequels are *The Castle of Hape* (1980), *Caves of Fire and Ice* (1980), and *The Joining of the Stone* (1981). (BL 74:368, 378; KR 45:791; SLJ Oct 1977 p. 116; VOYA 3 [June 1980]:46)
Atheneum, 1977, o.p.; Avon, 1979, pap., 226 pp.

C/YA NEWMAN, Robert (Howard). *The Shattered Stone.* Gr. 6–8.
In fulfillment of an ancient prophecy, two children without memories search for part of a stone inscription that will bring peace to their land. (BL 72:305; HB 51:465; KR 43:1186; SLJ Nov 1975 p. 81)
Illus. by John Gretzer, Atheneum, 1975, 231 pp., o.p.

NICHOLS, Ruth. *The Left-Handed Spirit.* See Chapter 10, Witchcraft and Sorcery Fantasy.

YA [R] NORTON, Andre (pseud. of Alice Mary Norton). *The Crystal Gryphon.*
Gr. 7–10.
Kerovan and his wife, Joisan, fight foreign invaders and the Dark Powers to regain the throne of Ulm. *The Jargoon Pard* (1974) is a companion volume, and *Gryphon in Glory* (1981) is the sequel. (BL 69:192, 204; Ch&Bks:270; JHC:401; KR 40:948; LJ 97:4080; SHC:626; TLS 1973 p. 1114; Tymn:152)
Atheneum, 1972, o.p.; Tor, dist. by St. Martin, 1985, pap., 256 pp.

YA [R] NORTON, Andre (pseud. of Alice Mary Norton). *The Jargoon Pard.* Gr.
7–9.
Kethan's magical powers save him from being used as a pawn in the power

struggle for the throne of the House of Car Do Prawn. This is a companion volume to *The Crystal Gryphon* (1972). (BL 71:46; Ch&Bks:270; HB 51:153; JHC:401; LJ 99:2748; TLS 1975 p. 1052)

Atheneum, 1974, 194 pp., o.p.; Fawcett, 1978, pap.

NORTON, Andre. *Quag Keep.* See Section 5B, Myth Fantasy.

ORR, A. *The World in Amber.* See Chapter 10, Witchcraft and Sorcery Fantasy.

PALMER, David R. *Threshold.* See Chapter 6, Humorous Fantasy.

YA PAXON, Diana L. *Lady of Light* (The First Book of Westria). Gr. 10 up.

King Jehan of Westria searches for a wife who will be able to use the jewels of the four natural elements to better the Kingdom. The sequels are *Lady of Darkness* (1983) and *Silverhair the Warrior* (1986). (Kliatt 17[Spring 1983]:16; LJ 107:2355)

Pocket/Timescape, 1982, pap., 261 pp., o.p.

YA PIERCE, Meredith Ann. *Birth of the Firebringer.* Gr. 7–10.

The son of the prince of unicorns discovers that he is Firebringer, destined to save his race from their enemies, the gryphons. (BL 82:861, 870; CCBB 39:94; KR 53:1090; SLJ Jan 1986 p. 70)

Four Winds, 1985, 234 pp.

C/YA PIERCE, Meredith Ann. *The Darkangel* (The Darkangel trilogy, vol. 1).
[R]   Gr. 6–10.

Even though she is falling in love with him, Aeriel must slay the beautiful but horrifying Darkangel vampire. In *A Gathering of Gargoyles* (1984, 1985, pap.) Aeriel makes a hazardous journey to gather five gargoyles in preparation for a final battle with the White Witch who enslaved her lover. (BL 78:1236, 1260, 80:353; CCBB 35:213; HB 58:416; JHC:408; KR 50:376; SLJ Mar 1982 p. 160; VOYA 5[June 1982]:40)

Atlantic, dist. by Little, 1982, 223 pp., o.p.; Tor, dist. by St. Martin, 1984, pap.

YA [R] PIERCE, Meredith Ann. *The Woman Who Loved Reindeer.* Gr. 7–12.

A young girl named Caribou and the magical reindeer she raised, lead her tribe on a dangerous journey to a new home. (BL 82:330, 340; CCBB 39:75; HB 62:208; KR 53:992; SLJ Dec 1985 p. 104; VOYA 9:41)

Atlantic, dist. by Little, 1985, 242 pp.

C/YA PIERCE, Tamora. *Alanna: The First Adventure* (Song of the Lioness,
[R]   book 1). Gr. 6–10.

Alanna and her twin brother, Alan, secretly change places as they are sent away from home for training: she is determined to ignore her magical powers and become a knight, while he wants to become a sorcerer, not a knight. In *In the Hand of the Goddess* (1984) Alanna has reached the level of squire to Prince Jonathan when she becomes suspicious that a sorcerer, Duke Roger, is plotting against the royal family. In *The Woman Who Rides Like a Man* (1986) Alanna, now a knight, proves her prowess as a warrior by aiding a tribe of desert raiders, who declare her their shaman. (BL 78:1236, 1260, 80:353; CCBB 35:213; HB 58:416; JHC:408; KR 50:376; SLJ Mar 1982 p. 160; VOYA 5[June 1982]:40)

Atheneum, 1983, 241 pp.

YA PRATT, (Murray) Fletcher. *The Well of the Unicorn.* Gr. 10 up.
Airar Alvarson leads the rebels of the Iron Ring in their battle against the Vulking invaders of Dalarna. (KR 15:628; LJ 72:1685; Tymn:154)
Sloane, 1948, 338 pp., o.p.; Ballantine, 1976, pap., o.p.

YA PREISS, Byron (Cary), and REAVES, J. Michael. *Dragonworld.* Gr. 10 up.
Falsely accused of being a spy for the murderous neighboring kingdom of Simballa, Amsel of Fandora travels to the land of the Dragons to discover who is killing both countries' children. (BL 76:544, 550, 78:594; SLJ Jan 1980 p. 82)
Bantam, 1979, 1983 (rev. ed.), pap., 560 pp.

YA RAY, Mary (Eva Pedder). *The Golden Bees.* Gr. 7–9. (Orig. British pub. 1984.)
Young Kenofer journeys across the oceans and mountains of Ancient Greece to retrieve a Princess's lost golden earring. This is the sequel to *Song of Thunder* (1978, o.p.). (CCBB 37:211; HB 60:477; JHC:410; SLJ Aug 1984 p. 86)
Faber, 1984, 152 pp., o.p.

C/YA REYNOLDS, Alfred. *Kiteman of Karanga.* Gr. 6–9.
Having used his Kitewing glider to escape from Karanga after being banished for cowardice, Karl discovers enemy forces plotting to invade his country. (BL 82:217; Kliatt 21[Winter]:18; SLJ Nov 1985 p. 90)
Knopf, 1985, 217 pp.

YA ROBERTS, Keith (John Kingston). *Pavane.* Gr. 10 up.
In an alternate Britain where Queen Elizabeth I was assassinated, the Armada triumphed, and the nonindustrial world is ruled by the Pope, a revolution of the oppressed is brewing. (KR 36:930; LJ 93:4580, 94:1347)
Doubleday, 1968, 288 pp., o.p.

YA SABERHAGEN, Fred. *Empire of the East.* Gr. 10 up.
After the wizard's troops murder the boy's parents and kidnap his sister, sixteen-year-old Rolf is recruited by a rebel band to battle Ominor, the wizard Emperor of the East. (Kliatt 14[Winter 1980]:18; SLJ Mar 1980 p. 147)
Ace/Grosset, 1979, 1983, pap., 558 pp., o.p.

YA SABERHAGEN, Fred. *The First Book of Lost Swords: Woundhealer's Story.* Gr. 10 up.
Prince Mark of Tasavalta seeks the magical sword, Woundhealer, to cure his blind and epileptic son. The sequels are *The Second Book of Lost Swords: Sightblinder's Story* (1987) and *The Third Book of Lost Swords: Stonecutter's Story* (1988). This is a companion series to Saberhagen's *Book of Swords* trilogy. (BL 82:1667, 1683; KR 54:1330; LJ Oct 15, 1986 p. 114; VOYA 9:293, 10:22)
Tor, dist. by St. Martin, 1986, 281 pp.

YA SALSITZ, R.A.V. *The Unicorn Dancer.* Gr. 10 up.
Princess Sharlin, her companion, Dar, and Turiana the golden dragon, search for the power to bring peace to the land of Rangard. (Kliatt 20[Fall 1986]:28; LJ Dec 1986 p. 142; VOYA 9:293, 10:24, 40)
Signet/NAL, 1986, pap., 256 pp., o.p.

YA   SCARBOROUGH, Elizabeth Ann. *Bronwyn's Bane* (The Aragonian series, vol. 3). Gr. 10 up.

Cursed at birth with an inability to tell the truth, amazonian Princess Bronwyn is sent away to her cousin Carol's for the duration of a war, whereupon the two young women attempt to lift Bronwyn's curse and end the war on their own. This book is preceded by *Song of Sorcery* (1982) and *The Unicorn Creed* (1983), and is followed by *The Christening Quest* (1985). (BL 80:847; LJ 108:2346; SLJ Apr 1984 p. 130)

Bantam, 1983, pap., 352 pp., o.p.

YA [R]   SILVERBERG, Robert. *The Gate of the Worlds.* Gr. 7–10.

If the Great Plague had killed three-quarters of the European population during the Middle Ages, perhaps North America today would be ruled by the Aztecs, South America by the Incas, and Europe by the Turks. It is in this version of the twentieth century that Dan Beauchamp sets sail from Turkish England to Aztec North America. (BL 64:250; CCBB 21:18; KR 35:609; LJ 92:3204; TLS 1978 p. 1396)

Holt, 1967, 244 pp., o.p.; Tor, dist. by St. Martin, 1984, pap., 256 pp.

YA [R]   SILVERBERG, Robert. *Lord Valentine's Castle.* Gr. 10 up.

Young Lord Valentine, ruler of Majipoor, wanders his land as an amnesiac juggler until he realizes that his mind and personality have been transferred to someone else's body, and that an imposter is ruling his kingdom. (BL 76:1110, 77:622, 1148, 78:594; JHC:416; Kliatt 15[Fall 1981]:23; KR 48:247; LJ 105:1008; SHC:634; SLJ Sept 1980 p. 93; TLS 1980 p. 1265; VOYA 3[Aug 1980]:53)

Harper, 1980, o.p.; Bantam, 1981, pap., 480 pp.

YA   SIMAK, Clifford D. *Where the Evil Dwells.* Gr. 10 up.

In an alternate Roman Middle Ages, a nobleman's son named Harcourt, the Abbot Guy, the maiden Yolanda, and the gruff thousand-year-old Knurly Man set off on a quest for the soul of a legendary saint. (BL 79:484, 490; KR 50:956; VOYA 5[Feb 1983]:46)

Ballantine/Del Rey, 1982, 256 pp.

C/YA   SMITH, Stephanie A. *Snow-Eyes.* Gr. 6–9.

Amarra, or Snow-Eyes, is taken from her family to become a "servitor" of the Lake Mother, where she learns occult skills from the other women servitors. *The Boy Who Was Thrown Away* (1987) is a companion volume. (CCBB 39:37; SLJ Oct 1985 p. 187; VOYA 9:42)

Atheneum, 1985, 184 pp.

C/YA   SNYDER, Zilpha Keatley. *Below the Root* (Green-Sky trilogy, vol. 1).
[R]   Gr. 5–8.

Raamo D'Ok's curiosity about the dreaded land beneath his treetop world of Green-Sky leads him to rescue a girl named Terra and uncover the secret of the world below. In *And All Between* (1976, 1985), Terra escapes from the underworld of Erd to Green-Sky, where she is rescued by Raamo and Neric, who plan to free all of the Erdlings. In *Until the Celebration* (1977, 1985), the Kindar and the Erdlings are finally about to be united, but plans for the celebration are disrupted by dissidents within each tribe, and by the disappearance of Pomma and Terra. (BL 71:764; CC:532; CCBB 28:186; Ch&Bks:272; KR 43:239; SLJ Sept 1975 p. 112; Suth 2:424)

Illus. by Alton Raible, Atheneum, 1975, o.p.; Tor, dist. by St. Martin, 1985, pap., 256 pp.

YA [R]   SPRINGER, Nancy. *Chains of Gold.* Gr. 10 up.
   The "year-King," destined to be sacrificed to bring fertility to the fields of Catena, falls in love with his "bride" and refuses to go through with the annual ritual. (BL 82:1667; KR 54:1074; LJ Aug 1986 p. 174; VOYA 9:241, 10:21)
   Arbor House, 1986, 230 pp.

YA   SPRINGER, Nancy. *Madbond* (The Sea King trilogy, book 1). Gr. 10 up.
   Two young men, Dannoc and Rad Korridun, become blood brothers and set out to find their parents, the Kings of the Seal Kindred and the Red Hart tribes, in order to fight the evil that has come to their land. The sequel is *Mindbond* (1987). (BL 84:31, 55; Kliatt 21[Sept 1987]:29; VOYA 10:180)
   Tor, dist. by St. Martin, 1987, pap., 214 pp.

YA   SPRINGER, Nancy. *The Sable Moon* (The Chronicles of Isle, book 3). Gr. 10 up.
   Crown Prince Trevyn completes a quest during which he is enslaved and freed, studies to become a sorcerer, visits the land of elves, and returns home to save his kingdom. This book is preceded by *The White Hart* (1979) and *The Silver Sun* (1980, 1983, revised from *The Book of Suns,* 1977). It is followed by *The Black Beast* (1982, 1986) and *The Golden Swan* (1983). The latter two books were published together as *The Book of Vale* (1985). (BL 77:1188; VOYA 4[Oct 1981]:64)
   Pocket, 1981, 1986, pap., 264 pp.

YA   SPRINGER, Nancy. *Wings of Flame.* Gr. 10 up.
   The orphan girl Seda saves Prince Kyrem of Devan after he is attacked by an evil wizard. (BL 81:1297, 1327; KR 53:117; LJ Mar 15, 1985 p. 75)
   Tor, dist. by St. Martin, 1985, 1986, pap., 256 pp.

C/YA   STEELE, Mary Q(uintard Govan). *The Journey Outside.* Gr. 5–8.
[R]   Dilar escapes the subterranean life of the Raft People and finds his way up to an unfamiliar sunlit world. Newbery Medal Honor Book, 1970. (BL 65:1276; CCBB 23:119; Ch&Bks:272, HB 45:309; KR 37:506; LJ 94:3227; TLS 1970 p. 1264)
   Illus. by Rocco Negri, Viking, 1969, 143 pp., o.p.; Penguin, 1979, pap.; Peter Smith.

STEELE, Mary Q. *The True Men.* See Chapter 1, Allegorical Fantasy and Literary Fairy Tales.

YA   STEUSSY, Marti. *Forest of the Night.* Gr. 10 up.
   A young woman named Hashti ventures alone into the wilds of New Lebanon seeking the highly intelligent feathered tigers said to roam this world. (BL 83:1564, 1591; LJ May 15, 1987 p. 101, VOYA 11:12)
   Ballantine/Del Rey, 1987, pap., 265 pp.

STEVENSON, Robert Louis. *The Touchstone.* See Chapter 1, Allegorical Fantasy and Literary Fairy Tales.

YA   SUCHARITKUL, Somtow. *Utopia Hunters: Chronicles of the High Inquest.* Gr. 10 up.
   Young Jenjen, a light-weaver who has been unwillingly appointed to the clan of Darkweavers, listens to an ancient Rememberer's tales of the Dispersal of Man, and overcomes her fear of Darkness. (LJ 109:2301; VOYA 8:140)
   Bantam, 1984, pap., 255 pp., o.p.

YA *Sword and Sorceress: An Anthology of Heroic Fantasy.* Ed. by Marion Zimmer Bradley. Gr. 10 up.

Fifteen tales of magical and warlike women, whose authors include Diana Paxon and Phyllis Ann Karr. *Sword and Sorceress II* (1985) and *Sword and Sorceress III* (1986) are companion volumes. (BL 80:1601, 1610; Kliatt 18[Fall 1984]:24; LJ 109:998)

DAW, 1984, pap., 255 pp.

YA TARR, Judith. *The Hall of the Mountain King* (Avaryan Rising, vol. 1). Gr. 10 up.

Prince Mirain's claim to the throne of Ianon is disputed by his treacherous mortal relatives, in this first volume of the Avaryan Rising series. The sequels are *The Lady of Han-Gilen* (1987) and *A Fall of Princes* (1988). (BL 83:192, 220; KR 54:1332; VOYA 9:293, 11:12)

Bluejay, dist. by St. Martin, 1986, 288 pp.; o.p.

YA [R] TARR, Judith. *The Isle of Glass* (The Hound and the Falcon trilogy, vol. 1). Gr. 10 up.

Brother Alfred, torn between his pursuits of healing and scholarship, and the secret knowledge of his elven blood, abandons his life at St. Ruan's Abbey after a seriously wounded ambassador of the elven King Gwydion places the fate of three fueding kingdoms in his hands. The sequels are *The Golden Horn* (1985) and *The Hounds of God* (1986). (BL 81:824, 838; Kies:75; Kliatt 20[Fall 1986]:30; KR 52:1172; LJ Feb 15, 1985 p. 182; VOYA 8:141, 194, 365)

Bluejay, dist. by St. Martin, 1985, 288 pp.; Tor, dist. by St. Martin, 1986, pap.

YA TEPPER, Sheri S. *Jinian Footseer* (Jinian trilogy). Gr. 10 up.

Young Jinian seeks out "sevens" of wizardly women to unleash her own magical powers in order to save the beings from the elder times. The sequels are *Dervish Daughter* (1986) and *Jinian Star-Eye* (1986). This trilogy is related to the Mavin Manyshaped trilogy (see below) and the True Game trilogy. (BL 82:380, 398; Kliatt 20[Winter 1986]:22; VOYA 8:366, 397)

Tor, dist. by St. Martin, 1985, pap., 284 pp.

YA TEPPER, Sheri S. *Northshore* (The Awakeners, vol. 1). Gr. 10 up.

A young girl escaping from the temples of Northshore after her mother's suicide becomes the object of pursuit by both humans and winged creatures. The sequel is *Southshore* (1987). (BL 83:530; KR 55:267; LJ Feb 15, 1987 p. 164; VOYA 10:93, 11:13)

Tor, dist. by St. Martin, 1987, 252 pp.

YA TEPPER, Sheri S. *The Song of Mavin Manyshaped* (Mavin Manyshaped trilogy). Gr. 10 up.

Mavin Manyshaped flees Danderbat Keep with her brother Mertin, and calls upon her shapeshifting talents to save a plague-stricken city. The sequels are *The Flight of Mavin Manyshaped* (1985) and *The Search of Mavin Manyshaped* (1985). There are two companion trilogies, the Jinian trilogy: *Jinian Footseer* (1985), *Dervish Daughter* (1986), and *Jinian Star-Eye* (1986); and the True Game trilogy: *Kings Blood Four* (1983), *Necromancer Nine* (1983), and *Wizard's Eleven* (1984). (BL 81:1297, 1327; VOYA 8:195)

Ace, 1985, pap., 183 pp.

YA   TOLKIEN, J(ohn) R(onald) R(euel). *The Fellowship of the Ring* (Lord of
[O]   the Rings trilogy, vol. 1). Gr. 8 up. (Orig. British and U.S. pub. 1954.)
        In this, the first volume of the trilogy set in Middle-Earth, as was *The
Hobbit* (1938; see this section), Frodo Baggins inherits a magic ring from his
uncle Bilbo and begins a journey to protect it from the evil powers who seek
it. In *The Two Towers* (orig. British pub. 1954; U.S. 1955; Houghton, 1967;
Ballantine, 1985, pap.), Frodo and Sam take the ring to the borders of the
Dark Kingdom while the members of the Company of the Ring battle the
wizard Saruman and his goblin army. In *The Return of the King* (orig. British
and U.S. pub. 1955; Houghton, 1967; Ballantine, 1985, pap.) Frodo and Sam
bring the Ring to Mount Doom where it is destroyed to help the forces of
good win their struggle against the Dark Lord. *The Adventures of Tom
Bombadil and Other Verses from 'The Red Book'* (1962, 1963) is a related
work. Tolkien's son, Christopher, has edited six collections of previously
unpublished legends about the history of Middle-Earth: *The Silmarillion*
(1979), *Unfinished Tales of Numenor and Middle-Earth* (1980, 1982), *The
Book of Lost Tales* (1983, 1984, 1986), *The Book of Lost Tales, Volume 2*
(1984), *The Lays of the Beleriad* (1985), and *The Shaping of Middle-Earth:
The Quenta, the Ambrakanta, and the Annals* (1986). (BL 51:204; HB 31:104,
43:491; JHC:421; KR 22:598; SHC:639; TLS 1954 p. 541; Tymn:153–166)
        Houghton, 1967 (rev. ed.), 423 pp.; Ballantine, 1985, pap.

C/YA TOLKIEN, J(ohn) R(onald) R(euel). *The Hobbit; Or, There and Back
[O]   Again.* Gr. 5 up. (Orig. pub. 1937.)
        A wizard tricks a peace-loving Hobbit named Bilbo Baggins into going on a
hazardous quest to recover stolen dwarf treasure from the dragon, Smaug.
The Lord of the Rings trilogy (see this section) continues the saga of Middle-
Earth. (BL 34:304, 80:52, 528; CC:540; CCBB 38:96; Ch&Bks:231; HB
14:92, 94, 174; JHC:421; LJ 63:385, 819; SHC:639; SLJ Dec 1984 p. 86; TLS
1937 p. 714; Tymn:162)
        Houghton, 1966 (rev. ed.); illus. by Michael Hague, Houghton, 1984 (col-
lector's ed.), 290 pp.

C/YA TURNBULL, Ann (Christine). *The Wolf King.* Gr. 5–7. (Orig. British
        pub. 1975.)
        Grayla and Coll search the wolf-infested forest for their father and brother,
aided by the Dark People and the magical Elder Folk. (BL 72:1339; KR
44:473; SLJ Sept 1976 p. 126; TLS 1975 p. 1450)
        Seabury, 1976, 141 pp., o.p.

YA [R] VANCE, Jack (pseud. of John Holbrook Vance). *Cugel's Saga* (Dying
        Earth Saga, book 3). Gr. 10 up.
        Cugel the Clever travels across half a world seeking vengeance against the
sorcerer Iucounu. This book is preceded by *The Dying Earth* (Lancer, 1950;
Pocket, 1982) and *The Eyes of the Overworld* (Ace, 1966, 1980). It is followed by *Rhialto the Marvellous* (1984). (BL 80:185; KR 51:979; LJ 108:2173;
VOYA 7:102)
        Pocket/Timescape, 1983, 1984, pap., 334 pp.

YA   VANCE, Jack (pseud. of John Holbrook Vance). *Suldrun's Garden*
        (Lyonesse, book 1). Gr. 10 up.
        Imprisoned by her father for refusing to help him gain control of the Elder
Isles, Princess Suldren manages to find a lover and escape. The sequel is *The
Green Pearl* (1986). (BL 79:1263, 1269; KR 51:213; VOYA 6:218)
        Berkley, 1983, pap., 436 pp., o.p.

YA VAN SCYOC, Sydney J(oyce) *Bluesong* (Darkchild trilogy, vol. 2). Gr. 10 up.
In this second volume of the science-fantasy trilogy that began with *Darkchild* (1982, 1985) and is followed by *Starsilk* (1984), Darkchild's son, Danior, and niece, Keva, search for her father among a tribe of desert dwellers. All three books have been published in one volume entitled *Daughters of the Sunstone* (SFBC, 1985, o.p.). (BL 79:1450, 1458; KR 51:272; VOYA 6:218)
Berkley, 1983, 1985, pap., 261 pp.

YA VAN SCYOC, Sydney J(oyce). *Drowntide*. Gr. 10 up.
Prince Keiris enters a world beneath the sea to search for his long-lost twin sister. (BL 83:1412, 1436; VOYA 10:181)
Berkley, 1987, pap., 220 pp.

WAECHTER, Friedrich, and EILERT, Bernd. *The Crown Snatchers*. See Chapter 1, Allegorical Fantasy and Literary Fairy Tales.

WANGERIN, Walter, Jr. *The Book of the Dun Cow*. See Chapter 1, Allegorical Fantasy and Literary Fairy Tales.

WARBURG, Sandol Stoddard. *On the Way Home*. See Chapter 1, Allegorical Fantasy and Literary Fairy Tales.

YA [R] WARNER, Sylvia Townsend. *Kingdoms of Elfin*. Gr. 10 up.
A collection of haunting, interconnected tales about the winged inhabitants of ancient Elfin Kingdoms beneath various European hillsides. (Kies:79; KR 44:1179, 1112; LJ 102:220; TLS 1977 p. 25; Tymn:172)
Viking, 1976, 222 pp, o.p.

WATT-EVANS, Lawrence. *With a Single Spell*. See Chapter 10, Witchcraft and Sorcery Fantasy.

YA [R] WESTALL, Robert (Atkinson). *The Cats of Seroster*. Gr. 7–12.
Gentle Cam becomes possessed by his magic dagger, which, with the help of some large, power-wielding cats, turns him into the Seroster, a legendary hero destined to lead his people against their enemies. (BL 81:362; CCBB 38:75; HB 61:188; KR 52:108; SLJ Jan 1985 p. 88; TLS 1984 p. 1375; VOYA 8:58)
Greenwillow, 1984, 349 pp.

YA [R] WILDER, Cherry (pseud. of Cherry Barbara Lockett Grimm). *A Princess of the Chameln* (The Rulers of Hylor trilogy, vol. 1). Gr. 8–12.
After Princess Aidris Am Firn's parents are assassinated, she flees to Athion where she becomes a cavalry soldier living under a false name until she can return to Chameln as Queen. In *Yorath the Wolf* (1984) young Yorath has been brought up in secret by the court magician because, as heir to the throne of Hylor, he is under a decree of death. In *The Summer's King* (1986), vain young King Sharn Am Zor is tricked by the sorcerer Rosmer into undergoing a deadly ordeal of trickery and magic. (BL 80:1111; HB 60:479; JHC:428; SLJ May 1984 p. 95; VOYA 7:269)
Atheneum, 1984, 272 pp.

WILLET, John. *The Singer in the Stone*. See Chapter 1, Allegorical Fantasy and Literary Fairy Tales.

YA [R] WILLIAMS, Jay. *The Time of the Kraken*. Gr. 7–10.
In this science-fantasy, two warring tribes unite in the face of the coming of

monstrous beasts called Kraken, while Thorgeir, his bride, and his blood brother set out for the legendary Temple of Arveid in search of help against the destructive beasts. (BL 74:609; CCBB 31:120; SLJ Sept 1977 p. 150; TLS 1978 p. 377)

Four Winds, 1977, 168 pp., o.p.

YA [R] WOLFE, Gene (Rodman). *The Shadow of the Torturer* (Book of the New Sun, vol. 1). Gr. 10 up.

In this first volume of a tetralogy that combines fantasy and science fiction, Severian, an exiled apprentice of the Torturer's Guild, travels across a future Earth immersed in winter due to its dying sun. As he travels toward his new appointment, his mysterious sword involves him in a duel with poisonous weapons, and he is given a strange jewel. The sequels are *The Claw of the Conciliator* (1981), *The Sword of Lictor* (1982), *The Citadel of the Autarch* (Ultramarine, 1983), and *The Urth of the New Sun* (1987). (BL 76:1594; KR 48:400; LJ 105:1192; SLJ Sept 1980 p. 93)

Simon, 1980, o.p.; Pocket, 1984, pap., 272 pp.

YA [R] WOLFE, Gene (Rodman). *Soldier of the Mist*. Gr. 10 up.

A head injury causes Latro, a young Greek soldier in 479 B.C., to lose his memory and wander the land, meeting gods, goddesses, and other supernatural beings. (BL 82:1475; KR 54:1324; LJ Nov 15, 1986 p. 112; VOYA 9:294, 10:23)

Tor, dist. by St. Martin, 1986, 335 pp.

YA WREDE, Patricia C. *The Seven Towers*. Gr. 10 up.

Jermain flees the Sevairn court and takes over command of the armies of the wizard King Carachel, in an attempt to preserve the Seven Kingdoms and destroy their monstrous enemy. (BL 80:1154, 1161; VOYA 7:148)

Ace, 1984, pap., 264 pp.

WURTS, Janny. *Stormwarden*. See Chapter 10, Witchcraft and Sorcery Fantasy.

C/YA YEP, Laurence M(ichael). *Dragon of the Lost Sea*. Gr. 5–8.
[R] Shimmer, banished princess of the Dragon Clan, joins forces with a thirteen-year-old boy named Thorn to win back the Lost Sea of the dragons from the enchantress Civit. In the sequel, *Dragon Steel* (1985), Shimmer and Thorn escape imprisonment in her undersea kingdom and fight numerous battles to restore the kingdom of the Inland Sea to the dragon clan. (BL 79:250, 978; CCBB 36:59; KR 50:1107; SLJ Nov 1982 p. 93; Suth 3:464; VOYA 5[Feb 1983]:47)

Harper, 1982, 224 pp.

YA [R] YOLEN (Stemple), Jane H(yatt) *Dragon's Blood*. (Pit Dragons trilogy, book 1). Gr. 7–10.

Jakkin steals and trains a young dragon to earn the money to buy his freedom. In *Heart's Blood* (1984), Jakkin oversees the hatching of his beloved Dragon's first clutch, is drawn into a terrorist plot, and is forced to flee with Akki, the daughter of his former master. In *A Sending of Dragons* (1987), Jakkin and Akki enter a subterranean labyrinth populated by a primitive race who practice sacrificial rituals. (BL 78:1236, 1262; CCBB 35:220; Ch&Bks:273; HB 58:418; JHC:429; SLJ Sept 1982 p. 146; Suth 3:466; VOYA 5[Oct 1982]:51)

Delacorte, 1982, 243 pp.; Dell, 1984, pap.

ZELAZNY, Roger. *Jack of Shadows.* See Chapter 10, Witchcraft and Sorcery Fantasy.

ZELAZNY, Roger. *Madwand.* See Chapter 10, Witchcraft and Sorcery Fantasy.

YA [R] ZELAZNY, Roger (Joseph Christopher). *Nine Princes in Amber* (The Amber series, book 1). Gr. 10 up.
Although he has lost all memory of his life in the land of Amber, Corwin slowly begins to recover his special powers and to fight for his princely birthright. The sequels are *The Guns of Avalon* (1972, 1974), *The Sign of the Unicorn* (1975, 1976), *The Hand of Oberon* (1976, 1977), *The Courts of Chaos* (1978, 1979), *Trumps of Doom* (1985), *Blood of Amber* (1986), and *Sign of Chaos* (1987). (BL 67:84, 142; KR 38:484; LJ 95:2513; Tymn:180–184)
Doubleday, 1970, o.p.; Avon, 1977, pap.; Gregg Press, 1979 (repr. of 1970 ed.), 188 pp., o.p.

ZIMNIK, Reiner. *The Bear and the People.* See Chapter 1, Allegorical Fantasy and Literary Fairy Tales.

B. Myth Fantasy

YA ABBEY, Lynn (Marilyn Lorraine). *Unicorn and Dragon.* Gr. 10 up.
The conflict between Alison, the last of the Druidic Saxon priestesses, and her foster-sister, Wildecent, a Norman sorceress, embodies the theme of an old culture reluctantly giving way before a new one, in this novel set in eleventh-century Saxon England. (Kliatt 21[Spring 1987]:19, LJ Feb 15, 1987 p. 165; SLJ June–July 1987 p. 115)
Avon, 1987, pap., 240 pp.

C/YA AIKEN, Joan (Delano). *Winterthing: A Play for Children.* Gr. 6–8.
Upon their arrival on mysterious Winter Island, four children and their peculiar old "aunt" take in a foundling baby. As the years go by, they realize that only the baby is aging. (BL 69:490; CCBB 26:85; HB 49:149; KR 40:1314; LJ 97:4075; TLS 1973 p. 681)
Illus. by Arvis Stewart, Holt, 1972, 79 pp., o.p.

C/YA ALCOCK, Vivien. *The Stonewalkers.* Gr. 5–8.
[R]   Lightning strikes the old metal bracelet Poppy has placed on the arm of a garden statue, and the statue comes to life, with frightening consequences. (BL 79:962; CCBB 36:181; HB 59:299; Kies:4; KR 51:120; SLJ May 1983 pp. 31, 68; Suth 3:9; VOYA 6:144)
Delacorte, 1983; Dell, 1985, pap., 192 pp.

ALEXANDER, Lloyd. *The Book of Three.* See Section 5A, Alternate Worlds or Histories.

C/YA ALLEN, Judy. *The Lord of the Dance.* Gr. 6–8. (Orig. British pub. 1976.)
In the rubble of a collapsed building, Mike meets the Sun King and the Earth Queen. (CCBB 31:25; HB 53:536; KR 45:580; SLJ Sept 1977 p. 139; TLS 1976 p. 1544)
Dutton, 1977, 124 pp., o.p.

C/YA BABBITT, Natalie (Zane Moore). *Tuck Everlasting.* Gr. 4–7.
[O]   After a sinister stranger uncovers the Tuck family secret—their discovery of the fountain of youth—it is left to a little girl named Winnie Foster to save

her friends from his evil plan. (BL 72:510, 80:95; CC:429; Ch&Bks:242; HB 52:47; KR 43:1181; SLJ Dec 1975 p. 50; Suth 2:22; Tymn:48)
Farrar, 1975, 139 pp., 1985, pap.; ABC-Clio, 1987 (repr. of 1975 ed.).

C [R]   BAKER, (Robert) Michael (Graham). *The Mountain and the Summer Stars: An Old Tale Newly Ended.* Gr. 4–6. (Orig. British pub. 1968.)
Owen Morgan, son of a Welsh farmer and a fairy, enters the land under Black Mountain to search for his mother. (BL 65:1122; CCBB 23:21; HB 45:303; KR 37:303; LJ 94:1178; TLS 1968 p. 1113)
Illus. by Erika Weihs, Harcourt, 1969, 124 pp., o.p.

YA   BEAGLE, Peter S(oyer). *The Folk of the Air.* Gr. 10 up.
Itinerant lutenist Joe Farrell, staying with old friends in California, becomes involved in acting out fantasy role-playing games, but things turn nasty when a young witch unleashes an evil, destructive power. (BL 83:370; KR 54:1738)
Ballantine/Del Rey, 1987, 336 pp.

YA [R]   BENÉT, Stephen Vicent. *The Devil and Daniel Webster.* Gr. 9 up.
Daniel Webster battles the devil for the soul of a poor New Hampshire farmer, in this version of the Faust legend. (BL 34:107; Kies:8; SHC:579; TLS 1938 p. 91)
Illus. by Harold Denison, Farrar, 1937, 61 pp., o.p.

YA [R]   BERGER, Thomas (Louis). *Arthur Rex: A Legendary Novel.* Gr. 10 up.
In this often humorous contemporary reworking of Thomas Malory's legend of Camelot, Arthur invents knightly conduct because of his guilt over Excalibur's invincibility, Guinevere is a liberated woman, and Launcelot is an anguished failure. (BL 75:275; Kies:11; KR 46:701; LJ 103:2260)
Delacorte, 1978; Dell, 1979, pap., 512 pp.

YA   BISSON, Terry. *Talking Man.* Gr. 10 up.
According to this contemporary extrapolation of the Book of Genesis, God was so pleased with his creation of our world, that he decided to stay here, marry a mortal woman, and have a daughter named Crystal. (BL 83:191, 217, 83:777; KR 54:1325; LJ Oct 15, 1986 p. 114; VOYA 9:290, 11:14)
Arbor House, 1986; Avon, 1987, pap., 192 pp.

BOND, Nancy. *A String in the Harp.* See Chapter 8, Time Travel Fantasy.

YA   BRADLEY, Marion Zimmer. *The Firebrand.* Gr. 10 up.
In this retelling of the legendary fall of Troy, King Priam's daughter, Kassandra, is cursed by the god Apollo, who decrees that her prophetic visions will be regarded as the ravings of a madwoman. (BL 84:90, 92; KR 55:1177; LJ Oct 15, 1987 p. 90)
Simon, 1987, 590 pp.

YA   BRADLEY, Marion Zimmer. *The Mists of Avalon.* Gr. 10 up.
Morgaine, Viviane, and Guinevere, King Arthur's sister, aunt, and wife, alternately tell the story of Arthur's rise to the throne, his betrayal, and his death. (BL 79:409, 410; Kies:12; KR 50:1200; LJ 107:2351)
Knopf, 1982; Ballantine/Del Rey, 1984, pap., 396 pp.

BRADLEY, Marion Zimmer. *Night's Daughter.* See Chapter 1, Allegorical Fantasy and Literary Fairy Tales.

YA [R]   BRADSHAW, Gillian (Marucha). *Hawk of May.* Gr. 10 up.
Young Gwalchmai, the son of evil Queen Morgawse, struggles for accep-

tance at King Arthur's court after Arthur rejects his offer of allegiance. The sequels are *Kingdom of Summer* (1981; NAL, 1982, pap.) and *In Winter's Shadow* (1982). (BL 76:1656, 1669, 77:1148; KR 48:378; LJ 105:1008; SLJ Aug 1980 p. 81)
Simon, 1980, 313 pp., o.p.

C/YA BRIGGS, K(atharine) M(ary). *Hobberdy Dick.* Gr. 6–8. (Orig. British
[R] pub. 1955.)
A hobgoblin named Hobberdy Dick uses his magic to help the children of the manor. (BL 73:1417; CC:438; CCBB 31:7; HB 53:311; KR 45:166; SLJ May 1977 p. 59)
Greenwillow, 1977, 239 pp., o.p.

C/YA BRIGGS, K(atharine) M(ary). *Kate Crackernuts.* Gr. 6–9. (Orig. British
[R] pub. 1979.)
Jealousy of her new stepdaughter, Katherine, drives Kate Maxwell's mother to bewitch the girl, and the two Kates run away together. A retelling of the folktale of the same name. (BL 76:1360; CC:438; HB 56:304; KR 48:369; SLJ May 1980 p. 73; VOYA 3[June 1980]:26)
Greenwillow, 1980, 223 pp.

YA BRINDEL, June Rachuy. *Ariadne.* Gr. 10 up.
Two narrators, Ariadne, the young high priestess of Crete, and Daedalus, the Greek refugee physician at the Cretan court, tell this exciting tale of Ariadne's love for Theseus of Athens and the end of matriarchal rule in the Western world. (KR 48:1094; LJ 105:2229; SLJ Jan 1981 p. 74)
St. Martin, 1980, o.p., 1981, pap., 246 pp.

YA BRUST, Steven K. (Zoltan). *Brokedown Palace.* Gr. 10 up.
A miraculous tree grows in Fenario, a land ruled by four brothers, in this tale adapted from Hungarian folklore. (BL 82:851; VOYA 9:86)
Ace, 1986, pap., 270 pp.

YA BRUST, Steven K. (Zoltan). *To Reign in Hell.* Gr. 10 up.
God and his angels battle Satan for control of the universe in this fantasy about the creation of the world. (Kies:14; VOYA 8:393)
SteelDragon, 1984; Ace, 1985, pap., 268 pp., o.p.

YA [R] BRYHER, Winifred (pseud. of Annie Winifred Ellerman). *A Visa for Avalon.* Gr. 8–10.
Six people whose world is engulfed in revolution escape to the legendary island of Avalon. (BL 61:980; CCBB 18:143; KR 33:198; LJ 90:1929)
Harcourt, 1965, 119 pp., o.p.

YA BUCHAN, John. *The Watcher by the Threshold and Other Tales.* Gr. 10 up. (Orig. British pub. 1902.)
Three of the five stories in this collection are fantasies: "The Far Islands," "The Watcher By The Threshold," and "The Outgoing of the Tide." "The Far Islands" is about a young man's tragic involvement with the Celtic legend of the Isle of the Apple-Trees. (BL 15:265; Tymn:56)
Doran, 1918, o.p.; Scholarly Press, 1971 (repr. of 1918 ed.), 312 pp.

YA BULL, Emma. *War for the Oaks.* Gr. 10 up.
Rock guitarist Eddi McCandry is drawn into a war between two Fairy Courts, in this fantasy set in contemporary Minneapolis. (BL 84:112, 132, 1246; VOYA 10:286)
Berkley/Ace, 1987, pap., 309 pp.

C/YA BURNFORD, Sheila (Philip [née Every] Cochrane). *Mr. Noah and the Second Flood.* Gr. 5 up. (Orig. Canadian pub., 1973.)
After Mr. Noah rebuilds the ark to escape a pollution-caused flood, he is shocked to discover how many animals have become extinct. (CCBB 27:59; KR 41:753; LJ 98:3474; TLS 1973 p. 386)
Illus. by Michael Foreman, Washington Square, 1974, pap., 64 pp., o.p.

CAMERON, Eleanor. *Time and Mr. Bass: A Mushroom Planet Book.*
See Chapter 8, Time Travel Fantasy.

YA CANNING, Victor. *The Crimson Chalice.* Gr. 10 up.
This retelling of the Arthurian epic concentrates on the Celtic chieftain Arturo's battles against the Saxon invaders of Roman Britain. (BL 74:1717, 1726; KR 46:649; LJ 103:1529)
Morrow, 1978, 540 pp., o.p.

YA CHANT, Joy (pseud. of Eileen Joyce Rutter). *The High Kings.* Gr. 10 up.
Retellings of tales about the Celtic heroes who ruled the British Isles before Arthur came to power. (Kies:17; Kliatt 20[Spring 1986]:19)
Bantam, 1983, 1985, pap., 244 pp. o.p..

CHANT, Joy. *Red Moon and Black Mountain: The End of the House of Kendreth.* See Section 5C, Travel to Other Worlds.

YA CHAPMAN, Vera. *The Green Knight* (The Three Damosels trilogy, book 2). Gr. 10 up. (Orig. British pub. 1975.)
This retelling of "Sir Gawain and the Green Knight" is told through the eyes of fifteen-year-old Vivian, niece of the sorceress Morgan Le Fay, and eighteen-year-old Gawain, whose knightly chastity is reluctantly tested by Vivian, at her aunt's insistence. The first book in this series, *The King's Damosel* (1976, 1978) describes the adventures of Lady Lynett, who is forced into an unwanted marriage, and then becomes King Arthur's damosel, or royal messenger to his Knights. In the final book, *King Arthur's Daughter* (1976, 1978), Lady Lynett comes to the aid of Ursulet, Arthur and Guinever's daughter and proclaimed heir to the throne, who is forced into hiding after Arthur's defeat and the breaking up of the Round Table. (Kies:17; Kliatt 12[Spr 1978]:5; Tymn:64)
Avon, 1978, pap., 173 pp., o.p.

YA CHRISTIAN, Catherine. *The Pendragon.* Gr. 10 up.
Bedivere, Arthur's boyhood friend and lifelong companion, narrates this story of Artus's life from age twelve through his initiation rites with Celidon the Merlin, his tragic love for Vivian (Ygern), his betrayal, and his death. (Kies:18; KR 46:1260; LJ 104:126)
Warner, 1978, 1984, pap., 607 pp., o.p.

C/YA CLARKE, Pauline (pseud. of Pauline [Clarke] Hunter Blair). *The Two Faces of Silenus.* Gr. 5–7.
Drusilla and Rufus's wish at an Italian fountain brings the ancient god, Silenus, to life. (CCBB 26:73; HB 48:594; KR 40:1244; TLS 1972 p. 1325)
Coward, 1972, 160 pp., o.p.

YA [R] COATSWORTH, Elizabeth (Jane). *The Enchanted: An Incredible Tale.*
Gr. 7–9. (Orig. U.S. pub. 1951.)
David Ross doesn't believe the Indian legends that the animals of the Enchanted Forest can assume human form, so he buys an abandoned farm on

the very edge of the forest. (BL 47:381; HB 27:316; KR 19:233, 36:343; LJ 76:1236, 93:2119)
Illus. by Mary Frank, Pantheon, 1968, 151 pp., o.p.

C [R] COATSWORTH, Elizabeth (Jane). *Marra's World*. Gr. 3–5.
Marra doesn't understand her grandmother's hatred or her father's disinterest until she discovers that her mother was a selkie, or seal-woman, who went back to live in the sea. (BL 72:448; CC:451; CCBB 29:107; Ch&Bks:265; HB 52:48; KR 43:1129; SLJ Apr 1976 p. 70; Suth 2:90)
Illus. by Krystyna Turska, Greenwillow/Morrow, 1975, 83 pp.

YA COATSWORTH, Elizabeth (Jane). *Silky: An Incredible Tale*. Gr. 7–10.
Silky, a young girl with strange powers, appears one day and helps Cephas Hewes control his temper and end his shiftless ways. (HB 29:229; LJ 78:1164; TLS 1953 p. 813)
Illus. by John Carroll, Pantheon, 1953, 144 pp., o.p.

YA COHEN, Barbara. *Roses*. Gr. 7–10.
Talented high school senior Isabel's relationships with a middle-aged florist and her would-be boyfriend, Rob, help her to overcome a fear of closeness with anyone but her father, in this modern version of "Beauty and the Beast." (BL 80:963; CCBB 37:163; Kies:18; SLJ Aug 1984 p. 82)
Lothrop, 1984, 224 pp.; Scholastic, 1985, pap.

YA [R] COHEN, Barbara. *Unicorns in the Rain*. Gr. 7–9.
Nikki falls in love with a young man whose family has been told by God to build an ark to save themselves and their animals (including two unicorns) from a disastrous flood. (BL 77:1148; CCBB 34:29; SLJ Sept 1980 p. 80; VOYA 3[Oct 1980]:31)
Atheneum, 1980, 164 pp., o.p.; Macmillan, 1988 (repr.), pap.

COLE, Joanna. *Bony-Legs*. See Chapter 10, Witchcraft and Sorcery Fantasy.

C COLLINS, Meghan. *The Willow Maiden*. Gr. 1–4.
A young man deeply in love with a Willow Maiden learns that he must let her go free every Spring and Summer or their love will die. (BL 82:625; SLJ Jan 1986 p. 55)
Illus. by Laszlo Gal, Dial, dist. by Dutton, 1985, 38 pp.

YA [R] COOLIDGE, Olivia E(nsor). *The King of Men*. Gr 7 up.
This retelling of Greek legends follows the life of King Agamemnon from his childhood to his marriage to Clytemnestra, alternating with scenes of the gods quarreling on Mount Olympus and affecting the fates of the mortals. (BL 63:37; CCBB 20:106; HB 42:438; KR 34:311; LJ 91:3264)
Illus. by Ellen Raskin, Houghton, 1966, 230 pp., o.p.

C/YA COONTZ, Otto. *Isle of the Shape-Shifters*. Gr. 5–8.
Theo's summer on Nantucket takes on frightening proportions when she discovers that the descendants of local Indian tribes plan to use her in their ancient shape-shifting rites to regain the island for themselves. (BL 80:856; CCBB 37:124; Kies:19; SLJ Mar 1984 p. 157)
Houghton, 1983, 209 pp.; Bantam, 1985, pap., o.p.

C/YA COOPER (Grant), Susan (Mary). *Over Sea, Under Stone* (The Dark Is
[O] Rising sequence, vol. 1). Gr. 5–8. (Orig. British pub. 1965.)
Simon, Jane, and Barney Drew set out to find King Arthur's grail, touching

off a struggle between good and evil forces, the Light and the Dark. In *The Dark Is Rising* (Atheneum, 1973; Macmillan/Collier, 1986, pap.), a boy named Will Stanton travels into the past in search of six magic signs needed by the forces of the Light to hold back the forces of Darkness. *The Dark Is Rising* was a Newbery Medal Honor Book, 1974. In *Greenwitch* (Atheneum, 1974; Macmillan/Collier, 1986, pap.), it falls to Jane, Simon, and Barney to retrieve from the sea creature, Greenwitch, a manuscript needed to interpret the inscription on King Arthur's grail. In *The Grey King* (Atheneum, 1975; Macmillan/Collier, 1986, pap.), Will and an albino boy named Bran Davies search for the golden harp needed to waken King Arthur's Knights for the final battle against the Dark. *The Grey King* won the Newbery Medal, 1976. In the final volume of this series, *Silver on the Tree* (Atheneum, 1977; Macmillan/Collier, 1986, pap.), all five children are summoned to a Welsh mountainside where Will and Bran search for the crystal sword, Eiras, while the Drews meet King Arthur and prepare for the ultimate battle against the forces of Darkness. (BL 63:118; CC:455; Ch&Bks:235; JHC:360; Kies:20; TLS 1965 p. 513; Tymn:67–71)

Illus. by Margery Gill, Harcourt, 1966, 252 pp.; Macmillan/Aladdin, 1987, pap. (boxed set).

C [R] COOPER (Grant), Susan (Mary). *The Selkie Girl*. Gr. K–4.

A young selkie, or seal-woman, is forced to live with her human husband, Donallan, for twenty years until her youngest son finds her seal-skin, freeing her to return to the sea. (BL 83:127; CC 1987 Suppl. p. 13; CCBB 40:46; HB 62:731; KR 54:1443; SLJ Nov 1986 p. 74)

Illus. by Warwick Hutton, Macmillan, 1986, 32 pp., o.p.

CROSS, Gillian. *The Dark Behind the Curtain*. See Chapter 4, Ghost Fantasy.

C CURLEY, Daniel. *Ann's Spring*. Gr. 4–6.

Spring reverts to winter when neighborhood boys lock Mother Nature's children in an old truck and prevent them from supervising the changing of the seasons. (CCBB 31:12; KR 45:46; SLJ Jan 1977 p. 90)

Illus. by Donna Diamond, Crowell, 1977, 48 pp., o.p.

C CURLEY, Daniel. *Billy Beg and the Bull*. Gr. 3–5.

Billy Beg flees his wicked stepmother and, with his friend the bull, sets out on an adventure-filled journey from Ireland to China. A retelling of tales from Irish folklore. (BL 74:1677; HB 54:289; KR 46:243; SLJ May 1978 p. 65)

Illus. by Frank Bozzo, Crowell, 1978, 127 pp., o.p.

C/YA CURRY, Jane Louise. *Beneath the Hill*. Gr. 5–8.
[R] When strip mining threatens the mountain home of the Fair Folk, Miggle, Dub, and Stevie help them return to their ancestral land. This is the sequel to *The Change Child* (1969). (BL 63:1146; CCBB 21:25; HB 43:461; LJ 92:2020; KR 35:61; TLS 1968 p. 1113)

Illus. by Imero Gobbato, Harcourt, 1967, 255 pp., o.p.

CURRY, Jane Louise. *The Daybreakers*. See Chapter 8, Time Travel Fantasy.

C/YA CURRY, Jane Louise. *The Sleepers*. Gr. 5–8.
[R] Four English young people meet Myrdain the Sorcerer who asks their help

in foiling a plot to murder King Arthur and his knights in their sleep. (BL 65:61; HB 44:427; KR 36:459; TLS 1969 p. 351)
Illus. by Gareth Floyd, Harcourt, 1968, 255 pp., o.p.

CURRY, Jane Louise. *The Watchers.* See Chapter 8, Time Travel Fantasy.

CUTT, W. Towrie. *Seven for the Sea.* See Chapter 8, Time Travel Fantasy.

YA DE LINT, Charles. *Jack the Giant-Killer.* Gr. 10 up. (Orig. pub. in Canada.)
A young Canadian named Jacky Rowan finds herself caught up in a Scottish fairy tale where she becomes Jack the Giant-Killer. (BL 84:752, 775; KR 55:1425; VOYA 11:38)
Berkley/Ace, 1987, 202 pp.

YA DE LINT, Charles. *Moonheart.* Gr. 10 up. (Orig. pub. in Canada.)
Sara Kendell is caught up in an ancient battle between good and evil after she finds four mysterious objects and meets Kieran Foy, apprentice to an ancient Welsh mage. (BL 81:558, 582; Kies:23; VOYA 7:335)
Berkley/Ace, 1984, pap., 496 pp., o.p.

C/YA DIXON, Marjorie (Mack). *The Forbidden Island.* Gr. 5–7. (Orig. pub. in
[R]   England.)
Libby makes a forbidden visit to the Irish island of Thunder, and finds it to be inhabited by an ancient race who live by violent, age-old laws. (HB 36:515; KR 28:760; LJ 86:4223; TLS May 20, 1960 p. iv)
Illus. by Richard Kennedy, Criterion, 1960, 201 pp., o.p.

C/YA DUNLOP, Eileen. *Clementina.* Gr. 6–10. (Orig. British pub. 1985.)
[R]   Spending a month visiting a friend at a Scottish estate, Daisy finds herself caught up in frightening events surrounding twentieth-century Clementina and her ties to a young woman who lived on the estate in 1746 and was involved in the death of a young man. (BL 83:1286, 1687; CCBB 40:186; HB 63:466; KR 55:635; SLJ May 1987 p. 109; VOYA 10:119)
Holiday, 1987, 156 pp.

YA ESTEY, Dale. *A Lost Tale.* Gr. 10 up.
Brigid falls in love with a wounded German soldier and enlists the aid of druids and a unicorn to protect him from the British authorities. (BL 76:1490, 1520, 77:621, 78:594; KR 48:305; LJ 105:1000; SLJ Dec 1980 p. 78)
St. Martin, 1980, 208 pp., o.p.; Berkley, 1984, pap., o.p.

C/YA FARMER (Mockridge), Penelope. *A Castle of Bone.* Gr. 5–8.
[R]   Hugh panics when his friend, Penn, enters a magic cupboard and is changed into a baby. (BL 69:572; CCBB 26:153; Ch&Bks:240; HB 49:52; KR 40:1201; LJ 98:652; TLS 1972 p. 802)
Atheneum, 1972, 151 pp., o.p.

YA FARMER (Mockridge), Penelope. *Year King.* Gr. 10 up.
Jealous of his twin brother's academic and social successes, Lan, 18, finds that he can enter his brother Lew's body and share his life, but these transformations make him feel even more inadequate and resentful of his twin.

(CCBB 31:125; Ch&Bks:266; HB 54:76; KR 45:1205; SLJ Jan 1978 p. 94; TLS 1977 p. 1246)

Atheneum, 1977, 232 pp., o.p.

YA FINNEY, Charles G(randison). *The Circus of Dr. Lao.* Gr. 10 up.

The mysterious Dr. Lao brings his magical menagerie of mythical beasts and legendary figures to a small Arizona town. (Kies:28; Kliatt 11[Winter 1977]:9)

Illus. by Boris Artzybasheff, Viking, 1935; Avon, 1980, pap.; Random, 1983, pap., 128 pp.

YA FLINT, Kenneth C. *The Dark Druid.* Gr. 10 up.

The Dark Druid is angered when legendary Irish hero Finn MacCumhal rescues a young woman from an evil enchantment. This is the sequel to *Challenge of the Clans* (1986) and *The Storm Shield* (1987). (LJ Aug 1987 p. 147; VOYA 10:287)

Bantam, 1987, pap., 326 pp.

YA FLINT, Kenneth C. *Riders of the Sidhe* (The Sidhe trilogy, vol. 1). Gr. 10 up.

Lugh of the Long Arm and his companions, Aine, the sea-god's sister, and Gilla the jester, battle the Formorian invaders of ancient Ireland, in this retelling of a Celtic legend. The sequels are *Champion of the Sidhe* (1984) and *Master of the Sidhe* (1984). (LJ 109:1253; VOYA 7:206)

Bantam, 1984, pap., 272 pp.

YA FRIEDMAN, Michael Jan. *The Seekers and the Sword.* Gr. 10 up.

In this retelling of Norse mythology, Vidar, one of the immortal but not invulnerable race of the Aesir, must find the lost Sword of Frey to restore peace to Alfheim. This is the sequel to *The Hammer and the Horn* (1985) and is followed by *The Glove of Maiden's Hair* (1987). (BL 82:733; LJ Dec 1985 p. 129)

Warner, 1985, pap., 263 pp.

C [R] FRY, Rosalie K(ingsmill). *The Secret of the Ron Mor Skerry* (British title: *Child of the Western Isles,* 1957). Gr. 4–6.

Fiona McConville searches the Western Isles for her little brother, Jamie, whose mysterious disappearance is connected to local legends about the selkies of Ron Mor Skerry. (BL 55:513; HB 35:214; KR 27:39; LJ 84:1696)

Illus. by the author, Dutton, 1959, 95 pp., o.p.

C/YA GARD, Joyce (pseud. of Joyce Reeves). *Talargain.* Gr. 6–8. (Orig. Brit-
[R] ish pub. 1964.)

A seventh-century orphan, fascinated by the seals near his Farne Island home, appears in modern England and describes his life and attempts to aid King Aldfrith in uniting the British tribes. (BL 61:1029; CCBB 19:8; Eakin:134; HB 41:175; KR 33:243; LJ 90:1558)

Holt, 1965, 251 pp., o.p.

C/YA GARDEN, Nancy. *Fours Crossing.* Gr. 6–8.

Melissa and her friend, Jed, are kidnapped by a hermit who has kept spring from coming to their New Hampshire town, Fours Crossing. *Watersmeet* (1983) and *The Door Between* (1987) are the sequels in this trilogy involving Celtic mythology. (BL 77:1252; CCBB 34:170; HB 57:431; SLJ May 1981 p. 72)

Farrar, 1981; Scholastic, pap., 240 pp.

YA [R] GARDNER, John C(hamplin, Jr.). *Grendel*. Gr. 10 up.
This version of the Anglo-Saxon legend of Beowulf is told from the point of view of Grendel, the marauding monster whom Beowulf sets out to destroy. (BL 68:353; Kies:28; KR 39:762; LJ 96:2670, 97:1180; TLS 1972 p. 793; Tymn:87)
Illus. by Emil Antonucci, Knopf, 1971, o.p.; Ballantine, 1972, 1975, pap., 140 pp.

YA [O] GARFIELD, Leon and BLISHEN, Edward. *The God beneath the Sea*.
Gr. 8 up. (Orig. British pub. 1970.)
This story poetically weaves together the legends of Greek mythology, including those about Prometheus, Pandora, and Persephone. This book was awarded the Carnegie Medal, 1970. (BL 68:144, 150; CCBB 25:56; HB 47:477; LJ 96:2137; TLS 1970 p. 1254)
Illus. by Zevi Blum, Pantheon, 1971, 212 pp., o.p.

YA [O] GARFIELD, Leon and BLISHEN, Edward. *The Golden Shadows: A Recreation of Greek Legends*. Gr. 7 up.
An old bard travels through ancient Greece collecting stories, which are woven into this powerful retelling of the myths surrounding the life of Heracles. (BL 70:592; CCBB 27:78; HB 50:45; KR 41:1370, LJ 99:1226; TLS 1973 p. 675)
Illus. by Charles Keeping, Pantheon, 1973, 159 pp., o.p.

GARNER, Alan. *Elidor*. See Section 5C, Travel to Other Worlds.

C/YA [O] GARNER, Alan. *The Owl Service*. Gr. 6–9. (Orig. British pub. 1967.)
A curse on the set of owl-decorated dishes found by Gwyn, Alison, and Roger turns the two boys against each other and threatens Alison's life. Carnegie Medal winner, 1967. (BL 65:310, 900; CC:471; Ch&Bks:267; HB 44:563; Kies:29; KR 36:1058; LJ 93:3980; Suth:143; TLS 1967 p. 1134, 1969 p. 1384; Tymn:89)
Walck, 1968, o.p.; Philomel, 1979, o.p.; Ballantine, 1981, pap., 192 pp.

C/YA [R] GARNER, Alan. *The Weirdstone of Brisingamen*. Gr. 5–8. (Orig. British pub. 1960.)
The stone on Susan's bracelet is the key to power over 140 knights who lie in an enchanted sleep within a nearby mountain. When this weirdstone is stolen, two dwarfs help Susan and her brother, Colin, make a torturous journey to recover and return it to its rightful owner. In the sequel, *The Moon of Gomrath* (orig. British pub. 1963; U.S. 1967, 1981) Susan's bracelet brings Morrigan the witch and her evil moon spirits into the twentieth century to battle the good dwarfs and elves. (BL 76:718; CC:471; CCBB 15:29; Ch&Bks:267; HB 46:45; Kies:29; KR 37:940; LJ 95:786; SLJ May 1980 p. 90; Tymn:87–88)
Walck, 1961, o.p.; Philomel, 1979, 224 pp., o.p.; Ballantine, 1981, pap.

YA GARNETT, David. *Two by Two: A Story of Survival*. Gr. 8 up. (Orig. British pub. 1963.)
Two girls disguise themselves as monkeys and stow away on Noah's ark in order to survive the flood. (BL 60:489; LJ 89:653; TLS 1963 p. 781)
Atheneum, 1964, 143 pp., o.p.

C [R] GERSTEIN, Mordicai (adapt.). *The Seal Mother*. Gr. K–4.
A fiddler playing to the seals on Midsummer's Eve tells a young boy the story of a seal who shed her skin to marry a human, bore a son, and eventu-

ally returned to her home in the sea. (BL 83:128; CCBB 40:48; HB 63:200; KR 54:1445; SLJ Nov 1986 p. 76)
Illus. by the adapt., Dial, 1986, 32 pp.

YA [R] GODWIN, Parke. *Beloved Exile.* Gr. 10 up.
King Arthur's widow, Queen Guenevere, narrates this story of her expulsion from Camelot after her husband's death, her enslavement, and her dream of returning to her homeland. This is the sequel to *Firelord* (Doubleday, 1980, o.p.). (BL 80:1273, 1274; KR 52:367; Kies:3; LJ 109:1253; SLJ Nov 1984 p. 145)
Bantam, 1984, pap., 422 pp.

C/YA GORDON, John (William). *The Giant under the Snow: A Story of Suspense.* Gr. 5–7. (Orig. British pub. 1968.)
An ancient brooch gives Jonquil, Bill, and Arthur the ability to fly in order to protect the Seal of Power from a huge Green Man. (BL 67:492; KR 38:1037; LJ 95:4374)
Illus. by Rocco Negri, Harper, 1970, 200 pp., o.p.

YA GORDON, John (William). *The House on the Brink: A Story of Suspense.* Gr. 8 up. (Orig. British pub. 1970.)
At "the house on the brink," Dick and Helen are drawn into a strange game involving divining for water and the lost treasure of King John. (HB 47:489; KR 39:683; LJ 96:4199; TLS 1970 p. 1251)
Harper, 1971, 217 pp., o.p.

YA [R] GREELEY, Andrew M(oran). *The Magic Cup: An Irish Legend.* Gr. 10 up.
King Cormac of Ireland falls in love with the slave girl, Brigid, while searching for the holy grail. (BL 76:540, 548; Kies:32; Kliatt 19[Spr 1985]:10; KR 47:1081; LJ 104:2118)
McGraw-Hill, 1979; Warner, 1985, 1987, pap., 304 pp.

C/YA GREENE, Jacqueline Dembar. *The Leveller.* Gr. 6–8.
Tom Cook is a young man who steals from the rich to help the poor, despite the fact that his mother signed his soul over to the devil to save him from death as a child. (BL 80:1549; CCBB 37:146; HB 60:474; SLJ Apr 1984 p. 114)
Walker, 1984, 117 pp.

YA GUARD, David. *Deirdre: A Celtic Legend.* Gr. 10 up.
A druidic prophecy that Deirdre's beauty would bring death and destruction to the land of Ulster, causes the King to imprison her, but she falls in love with a young knight and flees the country, bringing about war and their deaths. (BL 74:375; SLJ Nov 1977 p. 79)
Celestial Arts, 1981 (repr. 1977 ed.), 118 pp.

GUY, Rosa. *My Love, My Love, or, the Peasant Girl.* See Chapter 1, Allegorical Fantasy and Literary Fairy Tales.

YA HALDEMAN, Linda (Wilson). *Esbae: A Winter's Tale.* Gr. 10 up.
In order to pass his college finals, a lazy young man makes a bargain with the demon Asmodeas, which involves the sacrifice of a coed who has come under the protection of the exiled sprite, Esbae. (BL 78:537, 545, 594; Kliatt 16[Winter 1982]:21; VOYA 5[Apr 1982]:39)
Avon, 1981, 1984, pap., 224 pp.

YA HALDEMAN, Linda (Wilson). *The Lastborn of Elvinwood.* Gr. 10 up.
Ian James is captured by fairies in a local forest, reduced to fairy size, and becomes a reluctant participant in their plot to exchange a fairy for a female human child. (BL 75:860, 78:594; KR 46:962, 1077; TLS 1981 p. 1375)
Doubleday, 1978, 237 pp., o.p.; Avon, 1984, pap.

YA [R] HAMILTON, Virginia (Esther). *The Magical Adventures of Pretty Pearl.* Gr. 7–10.
Young Pretty Pearl is transformed from a god-child into a human as she helps relieve the suffering of the black slaves in the pre-Civil War South. (BL 79:1020, 1034; CC:479; CCBB 36:167; Ch&Bks:267; HB 59:312; KR 51:380; SLJ Apr 1983 p. 123, May 1983 p. 32; Suth 3:172; VOYA 6:215)
Harper, 1983, 311 pp., 1987, pap.

HAMLEY, Dennis. *Pageants of Despair.* See Chapter 8, Time Travel Fantasy.

C/YA HARRIS, Rosemary (Jeanne). *The Moon in the Cloud.* Gr. 6–8.
[O] In this, the first volume of a trilogy, Reuben agrees to go to Egypt in search of a pair of lions and a royal cat, in order to pay for his family's passage on Noah's Ark. *The Moon in the Cloud* was awarded the Carnegie Medal, 1968. In *The Shadow on the Sun* (1970) the young king of Egypt disguises himself to court the Chamberlain's daughter, Meri-Mekhmet. She is kidnapped, and he sends his friend Reuben to rescue her. In *The Bright and Morning Star* (1972), Reuben and Thamar arrive in Egypt to find a cure for their son's illness, and become enmeshed in a power struggle between the Prince and Princess's advisors. (BL 66:982; CCBB 23:159; Ch&Bks:267; HB 46:167, 64:236; KR 38:7; LJ 95:1911, 1953, 4325; Suth:169)
Macmillan, 1968, 182 pp., o.p.

YA [R] HARRIS, Rosemary (Jeanne). *The Seal-Singing.* Gr. 7–10.
Miranda's eerie resemblance to an infamous Scottish ancestor portends her own supernatural power over the seals. (BL 68:364; CCBB 25:57; Ch&Bks:267; HB 48:57; KR 39:954; LJ 96:4190; Suth:169; TLS 1971 p. 1318)
Macmillan, 1971, 245 pp., o.p.

C [R] HASTINGS, Selina. *Sir Gawain and the Green Knight.* Gr. 3 up.
A retelling of the Arthurian tale of young Gawain's testing by the Green Knight. *Sir Gawain and the Loathly Lady* (1985) is a companion volume. (BL 78:44; CC:119; HB 57:673; JHC:89; KR 49:1298; SLJ Oct 1981 p. 142; TLS 1981 p. 1360)
Illus. by Juan Wijngaard, Lothrop, 1981, 25 pp.

C/YA HIEATT, Constance B(artlett). *The Knight of the Cart.* Gr. 5–7.
[R] Sir Lancelot rescues Queen Guinevere from the evil Sir Malagant, in this Arthurian retelling from medieval sources. *Sir Gawain and the Green Knight* (1967), *The Knight of the Lion* (1968), *The Joy of the Court* (1971), *The Sword and the Grail* (1972), *The Castle of the Ladies* (1973), and *The Minstrel Knight* (1974) are companion volumes. (BL 66:516; CCBB 23:129; HB 45:671; KR 37:1067; LJ 95:242)
Illus. by John Gretzer, Crowell, 1969, 85 pp., o.p.

YA [R] HOLDSTOCK, Robert (P.) *Mythago Wood.* Gr. 10 up. (Orig. British pub. 1984.)
Upon his return from battle in World War II, Steven Huxley and his

brother Christian are inexorably drawn into a horrifying world within the forest near their home, a world where mythical creatures actually exist. (BL 82:468, 482; Kies:37; KR 53:1048; LJ Nov 15, 1985 p. 112; TLS 1985 p. 284; VOYA 9:40)

Arbor House, 1985; Berkley, 1986, pap., 288 pp.

C/YA   HUNTER, Mollie (pseud. of Maureen Mollie Hunter McVeigh
[R]   McIlwraith). *A Stranger Came Ashore.* Gr. 6–8.

No one but Robbie suspects that the handsome stranger who wishes to marry his sister may actually be the Great Selkie, a legendary seal-man who carries young girls off to the bottom of the sea. (BL 72:303, 80:95; CC:487; CCBB 29:79; Ch&Bks:268; HB 51:592; KR 43:1067; SLJ Dec 1975 p. 31; Suth 2:233; TLS 1975 p. 1053)

Harper, 1975, 192 pp., 1977, pap.

HUNTER, Mollie. *The Walking Stones: A Story of Suspense.* See Chapter 10, Witchcraft and Sorcery Fantasy.

INGRAM, Tom. *The Night Rider.* See Chapter 8, Time Travel Fantasy.

C/YA   IPCAR, Dahlov (Zorach). *The Queen of Spells.* Gr. 6–9.
[R]   In this retelling of the ballad of Tam Lin, Janet is able to enter the Green World to save her lover, Tom, but only on Halloween night. (BL 70:51; CCBB 27:45; KR 41:396; LJ 98:2665)

Viking, 1973, 128 pp., o.p.

C/YA   IRVING, Washington. *The Legend of Sleepy Hollow.* Gr. 4 up. (Orig.
[R]   U.S. pub. in *The Sketch-Book,* 1819; as a separate tale, 1849.)

Ichabod Crane, a superstitious schoolmaster courting a wealthy farmer's beautiful daughter, is frightened off by his rival Brom Bones, masquerading as the legendary headless horseman. (BL 25:174, 83:623, 641; Bookshelf 1929 p. 21; JHC:383; Kies:39; LJ 91:2210; Mahony 2:260)

Illus. by Arthur Rackham, McKay, 1928, o.p.; illus. by Leonard Everett Fisher, Watts, 1966, o.p.; Buccaneer, 1982 (repr. of 1849 ed.); retold by Robert D. San Souci, illus. by Daniel San Souci, Doubleday, 1986; illus. by Barry Moser, Harcourt, 1986 (entitled *Two Tales: Rip Van Winkle and The Legend of Sleepy Hollow*); adapt. by Diane Wolkstein, illus. by R. W. Alley, Morrow, 1987, 32 pp.

C/YA   IRVING, Washington. *Rip Van Winkle.* Gr. 4–7. (Orig. pub. in *The*
[R]   *Sketch-Book,* 1819; as a separate tale in 183?.)

After a drinking bout with some strange little men, Rip falls asleep for twenty years. (BL 18:65, 63:586, 81:589, 791, 84:64; CC:488; CCBB 38:150; JHC:385; Kies:39; LJ 47:869, 92:350; Mahony 2:260; SLJ Mar 1985 p. 154, Nov 1987 p. 92)

Illus. by Arthur Rackham, Doubleday, 1905, o.p.; illus. by Maria L. Kirk, Stokes, 1908, o.p.; illus. by Charles Robinson, Stokes, 1915, o.p.; illus. by N. C. Wyeth, McKay, 1921, o.p.; illus. by Arthur Rackham, Harper, 1967; Buccaneer, 1983 (repr.); retold by Catherine Storr, illus. by Peter Wingham, Raintree, 1984, hb and pap.; adapt. by Morrell Gipson, illus. by Daniel San Souci, Doubleday, 1984; illus. by Barry Moser, Harcourt, 1986 (entitled *Two Tales: Rip Van Winkle and The Legend of Sleepy Hollow*); illus. by N. C. Wyeth, Morrow, 1987, 110 pp.; Penguin, 1987, pap.

C/YA ISH-KISHOR, Sulamith. *The Master of Miracle: A New Novel of the*
[R] *Golem.* Gr. 5–8.
A huge clay being, created by the Rabbi of Prague to protect the Jews from
anti-Semitic attacks, goes on a rampage when its creators try to destroy it.
(BL 68:394, 669; HB 47:611; KR 39:1120; LJ 96:3902)
Illus. by Arnold Lobel, Harper, 1971, 108 pp., o.p.

C/YA JOHNSON, Dorothy M(arie). *Witch Princess.* Gr. 6–9.
The enchantress Medea creates the illusion of evil occurrences to escape
from Corinth with her sons and save her father's land from the Argonauts, in
this retelling of a Greek legend. (BL 64:681, 700; KR 35:1145; LJ 92:3850)
Illus. by Carolyn Cather, Houghton, 1967, 192 pp., o.p.

YA JOHNSTON, Norma. *Pride of Lions: The Story of the House of Atreus.*
Gr. 8–12.
A powerful retelling of the tragic story of Queen Clytemnestra and King
Agamemnon: the father who sacrifices his daughter, Iphigenia, to aid the
cause of the Trojan War, and the mother whose revenge on her husband
curses the lives of their other children, Electra and Orestes. (BL 76:110; HB
56:180; SLJ Nov 1979 p. 88)
Atheneum, 1979, 156 pp., o.p.

YA [R] JOHNSTON, Norma. *Strangers Dark and Gold.* Gr. 7–12.
A poetic retelling of the tragic Greek myth of Jason and Medea, the young
sailor questing for the golden fleece who wins the love of the virgin priestess
of Hecate, the princess of Colchis. (BL 71:1070, 1075; CCBB 29:12; KR
43:245; SLJ Apr 1975 p. 66)
Atheneum, 1975, 240 pp., o.p.

JONES, Diana Wynne. *Fire and Hemlock.* See Chapter 10, Witchcraft and
Sorcery Fantasy.

C/YA JONES, Diana Wynne. *The Power of Three.* Gr. 6–9. (Orig. British pub.
[R] 1976.)
An ancient curse is revived and entangles three psychic children, a race of
giants, and a group of shape-shifting Dorig in a struggle for water. (BL
74:298; KR 45:790; SLJ Nov 1977 p. 58; TLS 1976 p. 383)
Greenwillow, 1977, o.p.; Ace, 1984, pap., 208 pp.

YA KARR, Phyllis Ann. *The Idylls of the Queen.* Gr. 10 up.
After one of the knights of Arthur's Round Table dies of poisoning, Sir
Kay must conduct an investigation to clear Queen Guenevere of the suspicion
of murder. (BL 79:92, 105; VOYA 5[Dec 1982]:38)
Ace, 1982, pap., 352 pp., o.p.

YA KING, Bernard. *Starkadder.* Gr. 10 up.
The legendary Norse warrior Starkadder has been cursed with immortality
by the Fates and will be allowed to die only after committing three terrible
betrayals. The sequel is *Vargr-Moon* (1988). (KR 55:1355; LJ Oct 15, 1987 p.
95; VOYA 10:288)
St. Martin, 1987, 244 pp.

LA MOTTE FOUQUÉ, Friedrich Heinrich Karl baron de. *Undine.* See
Chapter 1, Allegorical Fantasy and Literary Fairy Tales.

YA LAUBENTHAL, Sanders Anne. *Excalibur.* Gr. 10 up.
Inspired by the legendary twelfth-century voyage of King Arthur's descen-

dant, Madoc, to the New World, this story describes the renewal of the battle between good and evil after the Holy Grail and Arthur's sword, Excalibur, are discovered in twentieth-century Mobile, Alabama. (Kies:45; Tymn:107)
Ballantine, 1973, pap., 236 pp., o.p.

YA LAWHEAD, Stephen R. *Taliesin* (Pendragon Cycle, book 1). Gr. 10 up.
A retelling of an Arthurian legend about the bard Taliesin and his love for Charis, the princess of Atlantis. (BL 84:31, 54; KR 55:965; LJ Aug 187 p. 146)
Good News/Crossways, 1987, pap., 452 pp.

YA [R] LAWRENCE, Louise (pseud. of Elizabeth Rhoda Holden). *The Earth Witch.* Gr. 7–12.
The belligerent old woman to whom young Owen is drawn becomes increasingly younger as Spring approaches. He falls in love with her and is devastated when she leaves him. (BL 77:1296; CCBB 35:33; HB 57:310: JHC:388; Kies:45; KR 49:745; SLJ May 1981 p. 74; VOYA 4[June 1981]:30)
Harper, 1981, o.p.; Ace, 1986, pap., 192 pp.

YA LAWRENCE, Louise (pseud. of Elizabeth Rhoda Holden). *Star Lord.*
[O] Gr. 8–10.
A young Star Lord crashes into the Welsh mountains and is hidden from the British Security by Rhys Williams and his family. (BL 75:369; CCBB 32:65; HB 55:525; KR 46:1310; SLJ Oct 1978 p. 156; Suth 2:274; VOYA 1[Dec 1978]:33)
Harper, 1978, 176 pp.

LAWSON, John S. *The Spring Rider.* See Chapter 8, Time Travel Fantasy.

LEE, Tanith. *Red as Blood; or Tales from the Sisters Grimmer.* See Chapter 1, Allegorical Fantasy and Literary Fairy Tales.

LEE, Tanith. *Sung in Shadow.* See Section 5A, Alternate Worlds or Histories.

YA [R] LEE, Tanith. *Tamastara; or the Indian Nights.* Gr. 10 up.
Seven supernatural tales set in India, drawn from the Hindu tradition, including "Foreign Skins," "Tamastara," and "Oh, Shining Star." (BL 80:1294, 1339; LJ 109:826; VOYA 7:206)
NAL/DAW, 1984, pap., 174 pp., o.p.

LE GUIN, Ursula K. *A Wizard of Earthsea.* See Section 5A, Alternate Worlds or Histories.

YA LEVIN, Betty (Lowenthal). *Landfall.* Gr. 7–10.
New Hampshire-born Liddy becomes convinced that she has spoken with a selkie, and uncovers a terrible crime against the seals during a visit to the Scottish island of Kelda. (CCBB 33:98; HB 55:669; KR 47:1005; SLJ Nov 1979 p. 89)
Atheneum, 1979, 216 pp., o.p.

LEVIN, Meyer. *The Spell of Time: A Tale of Love in Jerusalem.* See Chapter 1, Allegorical Fantasy and Literary Fairy Tales.

YA LILLINGTON, Kenneth. *Selkie.* Gr. 7–9. (Orig. British pub. 1985.)
Saved from drowning by a selkie or seal-woman, Cathy is determined to find her new friend's magical skin and return it, in spite of the villagers'

hatred and superstition. (BL 81:1179, 1196; SLJ May 1985 p. 111; TLS Feb 1985 p. 214; VOYA 8:325)
Faber, dist. by Harper, 1985, 145 pp.

C/YA LIVELY, Penelope (Margaret Low). *Astercote*. Gr. 6–8. (Orig. British pub. 1970.)
Mair and Peter Jenkins attempt to recover a missing medieval chalace said to have kept the Black Plague away from their town. (HB 47:172; Kies:48; TLS 1970 p. 421)
Dutton, 1971, 154 pp., o.p.

C/YA LIVELY, Penelope (Margaret Low). *The Whispering Knights*. Gr. 5–7.
[R] (Orig. British pub. 1971.)
William, Martha, and Susie inadvertently bring the sorceress Morgan le Fay to life. (BL 72:1467; CCBB 30:13; HB 52:499; KR 44:593; SLJ Sept 1976 p. 121; Suth 2:289; TLS 1971 p. 774)
Illus. by Gareth Floyd, Dutton, 1976, 160 pp.

C/YA LIVELY, Penelope (Margaret Low). *The Wild Hunt of the Ghost Hounds*
[R] (British title: *The Wild Hunt of Hagworthy*, 1971). Gr. 5–8.
Lucy uses magic to save her friend Kester from the ghostly horned riders who endanger his life when he takes part in an ancient stag-hunting dance. (BL 68:1004; CCBB 26:28; HB 48:376; Kies:48; KR 40:402; LJ 97:2964)
Dutton, 1972, o.p.; Ace, 1986, pap., 160 pp.

YA LLYWELYN, Morgan. *Bard: The Odyssey of the Irish*. Gr. 10 up.
Amergin, a visionary Celtic bard, inspires his Warrior clan, the Gaels, to cross the ocean from the Iberian peninsula to Ierne (Ireland), where they conquer the gentle inhabitants by force, in this retelling of fourth-century Irish history. (BL 81:3, 5; KR 52:706; LJ 109:1863; SLJ Sept 1985 p. 154)
Houghton, 1984, 463 pp.

LLYWELYN, Morgan. *The Horse Goddess*. See Chapter 10, Witchcraft and Sorcery Fantasy.

YA LLYWELYN, Morgan. *Lion of Ireland: The Legend of Brian Boru*. Gr. 10 up.
A spellbinding retelling of the rise of Brian Boru, warrior and King of tenth-century Ireland. (BL 76:757, 765; KR 47:1451; LJ 105:225.)
Houghton, 1979; Berkley, 1983, pap., 560 pp.

YA LOCKLEY, Ronald Mathias. *The Seal-Woman*. Gr. 8 up. (Orig. British pub. 1974.)
Convinced that she is a seal-princess, an Irish girl named Shian lives alone in the wild, awaiting the coming of her seal-prince. (BL 72:228, 1038; KR 43:869; SLJ Nov 1975 p. 96; TLS 1974 p. 1405)
Bradbury, 1975, 178 pp., o.p.; Avon, 1977, pap.

C/YA LOGAN, Carolyn F. *The Power of the Rellard*. Gr. 5–7. (Orig. Australian
[R] pub. 1986.)
While playing with an old toy theater, Lucy and her older brother and sister become enmeshed in an ancient struggle between good and evil, in the forms of a winged creature named Rowan, and four threatening strangers. (BL 83:1749, 84:1183; KR 56:281; SLJ Nov 1987 p. 105; VOYA 11:88)
Argus and Robertson, dist. by Salem House, 1987; Macmillan/McElderry, 1988, 278 pp.

YA [R] MacAVOY, R(oberta) A(nn). *Tea with the Black Dragon.* Gr. 10 up.
Searching for her missing daughter, Martha Macnamara seeks the help of Mayland Long, an oriental gentleman who claims to have the magical powers of a 1000-year-old Imperial Chinese black dragon. The sequel is *Twisting the Rope* (1986). (BL 79:1448, 1458; Kies:50; LJ 108:1018; VOYA 6:216)
Bantam, 1983, pap., 192 pp.

C/YA McKINLEY, (Jennifer Carolyn) Robin. *Beauty: A Retelling of the Story of*
[O] *Beauty and the Beast.* Gr. 5–9.
A beautiful girl marries a Beast and grows to love him in this novel-length version of the old French tale written by Madame le Prince de Beaumont. (BL 75:222; 80:96, 353; CC:506; CCBB 32:67; Ch&Bks:270; HB 55:201, 59:71; JHC:395; Kies:51; KR 46:1307; SLJ Nov 1978 p. 65; Suth 2:301; TLS 1983 p. 1312; VOYA 1[Feb 1979]:40)
Harper, 1978, 245 pp.; Pocket, 1982, 1985, pap.

YA [R] MALORY, Sir Thomas. *Le Morte D'Arthur.* Gr. 10 up. (Orig. British pub. 1485, orig. U.S. pub. Macmillan, 1879)
This medieval masterpiece, which combined the many legends about the reign of King Arthur and the quest for the Holy Grail, is the primary source used for contemporary retellings of the Arthurian legends.
There have been numerous adaptations of Malory's tales published over the years, with various titles. The following are arranged alphabetically by title:

Arthur Pendragon of Britain.
Ed. by John W. Donaldson, illus. by Andrew Wyeth, Putnam, 1943, o.p.

The Boy's King Arthur.
Illus. by N. C. Wyeth, Scribner, 1917, 1952, o.p.

King Arthur and His Knights.
Illus. by Mead Schaeffer and John R. Neill, Rand, 1924, 1936, o.p.; retold by Mary MacLeod, illus. by Howard Pyle, Parents, 1966, © 1964, o.p.; ed. by Eugene Vinaver, Oxford, 1975, pap.

The Romance of King Arthur and His Knights of the Round Table.
Ed. by Alfred W. Pollard, illus. by Arthur Rackham, Macmillan, 1917, 1927, o.p.

Stories of King Arthur.
Adapt. by U. Waldo Cutler, illus. by Elinore Blaisdell, Crowell, 1941, o.p.

Stories of King Arthur and His Knights.
Retold by Barbara Leonie Picard, illus. by Roy Morgan, Walck, 1955, o.p.

Tales of King Arthur.
Ed. and abridged by Michael Senior, Schocken, 1981, © 1980, o.p.

(BL 14:142, 39:460, 58:646, 78:694, 79:654; KR 30:82; LJ 66:798, 107:459, 108:208; SHC:148; TLS 1917 p. 613, 1967 p. 1126)
Macmillan, 1900, 1986, pap., 768 pp.; Dutton, 1908, 1941, o.p.; ed. by Ernest Rhys, Dent, dist. by Biblio, 1972 (2 vols.), hb and pap.; ed. by R. M. Lumiansky, Scribner, 1982.

C MAYER, Marianna. *The Black Horse.* Gr. 2–4.
In this retelling of a Celtic myth, Tim, a poor king's son, joins forces with a

magical black horse to rescue a princess, defeat an evil king, and break the enchantment holding the princess's brother. (BL 81:526; SLJ Jan 1985 p. 78) Illus. by Katie Thamer, Dial, 1984, hb, 1987, pap., 42 pp.

C/YA MAYNE, William (James Carter). *Earthfasts.* Gr. 6–8. (Orig. British pub.
[O] 1966.)
A curious cold-flamed candle, powerful enough to reverse time, endangers the lives of David and Keith when it brings King Arthur and his knights back to life. (BL 68:1050; CCBB 20:172; Ch&Bks:270; HB 43:343; KR 35:508; LJ 92:1750; Suth 274; TLS 1966 p. 1080; Tymn:139)
Dutton, 1967, 154 pp., o.p.

YA MEANY, Dee Morrison. *Iseult: Dreams That Are Done.* Gr. 10 up.
A retelling of the tragic love story of Tristan and Iseult. (BL 82:195, 216; Kies:53; VOYA 9:41)
Berkley/Ace, 1985, pap., 229 pp., o.p.

C [R] MENOTTI, Gian Carlo. *Amahl and the Night Visitors.* Gr. 1–5. (Orig. Italian pub. 1938.)
A narrative version of the Menotti opera about the crippled shepherd boy who leads the Three Kings to the Christ Child's manger and leaves his own special gift. (BL 49:112, 83:274, 1138; CC 1987 Suppl. p. 61; CCBB 6:40, 40:54; HB 28:310, 402, 61:762, 62:725–727; KR 20:550; LJ 77:1747, 2184; SLJ Oct 1986 p. 113)
Adapt. by Frances Frost, illus. by Roger Duvoisin, McGraw-Hill, 1952, 1962, o.p.; illus. by Michele Lemieux, Morrow, 1986, 64 pp.

YA MINOT, Stephen. *Surviving the Flood.* Gr. 10 up.
Noah's youngest son, Ham, decides to set the offical record straight, in this humorous report about what really happened aboard Noah's ark. (BL 78:178, 188; KR 49:895; LJ 106:2049)
Atheneum, 1981, o.p.; Second Chance, 1987 (repr. of 1981 ed.), 306 pp.

YA MORRIS, Kenneth. *The Book of the Three Dragons.* Gr. 10 up.
In this retelling of the fourth branch of the Welsh *Mabinogion,* the immortal hero, Manawyddan embarks on numerous adventures as he seeks to recover two treasures stolen from the gods: a magical breastplate and the divine harp of Alawn. This is the sequel to *The Fates of the Princes of Dyfed* (1913, 1914, 1978, 1980), which retells the first three branches of the *Mabinogion.* (BL 27:266; Tymn:143)
Longman, 1930, o.p.; ed. by R. Reginald and Douglas Melville, illus. by Ferdinand Huszti Horvath, Ayer, 1978 (repr. of 1930 ed.), 206 pp.

YA [R] MURPHY, Pat (pseud. of E[mmet] Jefferson Murphy). *The Falling Woman: A Fantasy.* Gr. 10 up.
Archeologist Elizabeth Butler, immersed in her work to escape an unhappy personal life, conjures up the ghost of a Mayan priestess who offers to change the world if Elizabeth will sacrifice the life of her own daughter. (BL 83:34, 52; KR 54:1319; LJ Oct 15, 1986 p. 114; VOYA 10:40)
Tor, dist. by St. Martin, 1986, 287 pp., 1987, pap.

C MUSSET, Paul Edmé de. *Mr. Wind and Madam Rain.* Gr. 3–5. (Orig. pub. in France; orig. U.S. pub. Harper, 1864.)
Magical adventures retold from the folklore of Brittany. (BL 1:23, 5:64; Mahony 1:23)

Putnam, 1905, o.p.; tr. by Emily Makepeace, illus. by Charles Bennett, Harper, 1908, 126 pp., o.p.

MYERS, John Myers. *Silverlock*. See Section 5C, Travel to Other Worlds.

YA NATHAN, Robert (Gruntal). *The Elixir*. Gr. 10 up.
An American historian and the mysterious girl he meets at Stonehenge travel back and forth through time, reliving the Arthurian legend of Merlin and Nimue. (BL 68:183; KR 39:608; LJ 96:2544, 3915, 4161)
Knopf, 1971, 177 pp., o.p.

C/YA NEWMAN, Robert (Howard). *Merlin's Mistake*. Gr. 5–8.
Tertius's knowledge of the future hampers Merlin's attempts to free himself from the bonds of Nimue. The sequel is *The Testing of Tertius* (1973, 1985). (BL 66:1162; HB 46:298, 60:223, 63:491; KR 38:174; LJ 95:2309; TLS 1971 p. 390)
Illus. by Richard Lebenson, Atheneum, 1970, 237 pp., o.p.; Peter Smith, 1985.

NEWMAN, Robert. *The Shattered Stone*. See Section 5A, Alternate Worlds or Histories.

YA [R] NEWMAN, Sharan. *Guinevere*. Gr. 10 up.
This is the story of Queen Guinevere's childhood love for a unicorn. The sequel is *Guinevere Evermore* (1985, 1986). (BL 77:796, 806; Kliatt 18[Fall 1984]:29; KR 48:1482; LJ 106:815; SLJ Apr 1981 p. 146)
St. Martin, 1981, hb, 1984, pap., 296 pp.

NORTON, Andre. *Here Abide Monsters*. See Section 5C, Travel to Other Worlds.

C/YA NORTON, Andre (pseud. of Alice Mary Norton.) *Huon of the Horn*. Gr. 6–9.
An exciting retelling of the legend of the Duke of Bordeaux from the Charlemagne saga. (KR 19:632; LJ 76:2126)
Illus. by Joe Krush, Harcourt, 1951, 208 pp., o.p.; Ballantine, 1987, pap.

YA [R] NORTON, Andre (pseud. of Alice Mary Norton). *Quag Keep*. Gr. 7–10.
With identical bracelets locked to their wrists, seven strangers journey to the lair of the powerful being who has enslaved them. (BL 74:1176; HB 54:285; JHC:400; SLJ Mar 1978 p. 139; VOYA 1[June 1978]:42, 2[Dec 1979]:58)
Atheneum, 1978, 224 pp., o.p.; DAW, 1987, pap.

NORTON, Andre. *Steel Magic*. See Section 5C, Travel to Other Worlds.

C/YA NYE, Robert. *Beowulf; a New Telling*. Gr. 5–8.
A modernized version of the Anglo-Saxon epic about the hero, Beowulf's conquest of the monsters Grendel, She, and the Firedrake. (BL 65:839; HB 45:49; Kies:58)
Illus. by Alan E. Cober, Hill, 1968, 116 pp., o.p.

C [R] OPPENHEIM, Shulamith (Levey). *The Selchie's Seed*. Gr. 4–6.
Marian never suspected that her ancestors were seal people until the night she is drawn to a white whale in the ocean near her island home. (BL 72:580; CCBB 29:129; KR 43:1287; SLJ Jan 1976 p. 49; Suth 2:345)
Illus. by Diane Goode, Bradbury, 1975, o.p.; Avon, 1977, 1983, pap., 83 pp.

YA ORLOCK, Carol (Ellen). *The Goddess Letters: The Demeter-Persephone Myth Retold.* Gr. 10 up.
    After her daughter's abduction by Hades, Demeter exchanges a series of letters with Persephone chronicling the decline of goddess worship on earth, in this unusual feminist retelling of Greek myth. (KR 55:415; SLJ Feb 1988 p. 95)
    St. Martin, 1987, 220 pp.

C/YA O'SHEA, Pat. *The Hounds of the Morrigan.* Gr. 6–9. (Orig. British pub.
[R]   1985.)
    The ancient book Pidge found brings the evil Queen Morrigan and her two witchlike assistants to his door, threatening the future of the world. (BL 82:1144; CCBB 39:215; HB 62:451; JHC 1984 Suppl. p. 76; KR 54:870; SLJ Mar 1986 p. 169, Feb 1987 p. 34, Apr 1987 p. 48; TLS Nov 1985 p. 1358; VOYA 10:22)
    Holiday, 1986, 469 pp.

    PEARCE, Philippa. *The Squirrel Wife.* See Chapter 1, Allegorical Fantasy and Literary Fairy Tales.

C/YA PHILIP, Neil. *The Tale of Sir Gawain.* Gr. 6–10.
[R]   Elderly and wounded, Sir Gawain tells his young squire old tales of the Round Table, tales of magic, love, adventure, and betrayal. (BL 84:774 787; CCBB 41:73; HB 64:78; TLS 1987 p. 1261)
    Illus. by Charles Keeping, Putnam/Philomel, 1987, 102 pp.

C/YA PHILLIPS, Ann. *The Oak King and the Ash Queen.* Gr. 6–8. (Orig. British pub. 1984.)
    Twelve-year-old English twins, Dan and Daisy, are reluctantly drawn into the battle between the Oak King and the Ash Queen, living trees who are fighting to preserve the balance of the forest. (BL 82:68; HB 61:458; SLJ Nov 1985 p. 100; VOYA 8:269)
    Oxford/Merrimack, 1985, 171 pp., o.p.

YA *The Phoenix Tree: An Anthology of Myth Fantasy.* Ed. by Robert H. Boyer and Kenneth J. Zahorski. Gr. 10 up.
    Sixteen short story retellings of myths, whose authors include Lord Dunsany, Richard Adams, Evangeline Walton, and Vera Chapman. (BL 77:309, 322; Kliatt 15[Winter 1981]:20)
    Avon, 1980, pap., 279 pp., o.p.

YA [R] POLLAND, Madeleine A(ngela Cahill). *Deirdre.* Gr. 7–9.
    Even though the old king keeps his daughter, Deirdre, imprisoned in a castle, he is unable to hide her from her tragic fate. (BL 63:1050; CCBB 21:16; HB 43:465; KR 35:424; TLS 1967 p. 1133)
    Illus. by Seon Morrison, Doubleday, 1967, 166 pp., o.p.

C/YA PRICE, Susan. *The Devil's Piper.* Gr. 6–9. (Orig. British pub. 1973.)
[R]   In this novel written by a sixteen-year-old, the parents of four children spirited off by a sly luchorpan ask the Devil for help. (BL 72:981; HB 52:292; KR 44:392; SLJ Apr 1976 p. 92; TLS 1973 p. 1429)
    Greenwillow/Morrow, 1976, 216 pp., o.p.

YA PURTILL, Richard. *Enchantment at Delphi.* Gr. 7–9.
    Visiting Greece to further her studies of Greek mythology, Alice Grant is transported into ancient times by a strange mist, and becomes involved in the struggle by the gods Apollo, Athena, and Dionysius to protect the Delphic

oracle from the Dark Powers. (CCBB 40:74; KR 54:1375; SLJ Nov 1986 p. 107)
Harcourt, 1986, 149 pp.

C/YA   PYLE, Howard. *The Story of King Arthur and His Knights.* Gr. 5–12.
[O]   (Orig. pub. 1903.)
This is the first of a classic four-volume retelling of the Arthurian legends. The three companion volumes are *The Story of the Champions of the Round Table* (1905, 1968, 1984), *The Story of Sir Launcelot and His Companions* (1907, 1985), and *The Story of the Grail and the Passing of Arthur* (1910, 1985). (BL 80:1392, 1401; CC:131; HB 60:359; Kliatt 20[Fall 1986]:28; JHC:90; SHC:148)
Dover, 1965, 312 pp., pap.; illus. by the author, Scribner, 1984 (repr. 1903 ed.), 312 pp.; Macmillan, 1984, 320 pp.; NAL, 1986, pap.

YA [R]   RAYNER, William. *Stag Boy.* Gr. 7–10. (Orig. British pub. 1972.)
Whenever Jim Hooper puts on an ancient stag-horn helmet, he enters the body of a huge black stag. (BL 69:902, 909; HB 49:387; KR 4:259; LJ 98:1692; TLS 1972 p. 1318; Tymn:155)
Harcourt, 1973, 160 pp., o.p.

C   REEVES, James (pseud. of John Morris Reeves). *Maildun the Voyager.* Gr. 4–6. (Orig. British pub. 1971.)
A retelling of an Irish legend about a young man who sails beyond the Western Isles to avenge his father's murder.
Illus. by Rocco Negri, Walck, 1972, 104 pp., o.p.

YA [R]   RENAULT, Mary (pseud. of Mary Challans). *The King Must Die.* Gr. 10 up.
Seventeen-year-old King Theseus joins a group of young people conscripted to become bull-dancers on the island of Crete. There he becomes renowned at the dangerous sport, and eventually manages to overthrow the Cretan Kingdom. The sequel is *The Bull from the Sea* (1962). (BL 54:574, 587; Kies:62; KR 26:341; LJ 83:2053; SHC:630; TLS 1958 p. 528)
Pantheon, 1958; Bantam, 1974, pap., 416 pp.

C [R]   ROBBINS, Ruth. *Taliesin and King Arthur.* Gr. 3–5.
When the young poet Taliesin tells the magical story of his birth at the Grand Contest of Poets, King Arthur proclaims him the greatest bard of all. (BL 67:452; CC:133; CCBB 24:98; HB 47:166; KR 38:1288; LJ 96:1119)
Illus. by the author, Parnassus, 1970, 31 pp., o.p.

YA   RUSH, Alison. *The Last of Danu's Children.* Gr. 7–10.
Matt and Kate enter the Otherworld, battle the forces of evil who have bewitched Kate's sister Anna, and call forth the Lord of Light to help save their world. (BL 79:364, 373; CCBB 36:96; Kies:64; Kliatt 18[Spr 1984]:22; SLJ Jan 1983 p. 87)
Houghton, 1982, 240 pp.; Tor, dist. by St. Martin, pap.

YA   SARGENT, Sarah. *Lure of the Dark.* Gr. 7–10.
Fourteen-year-old Ginny's empty home life with an alcoholic mother and an indifferent father leaves her vulnerable to the dark forces of Loki, the Norse god in wolf-form, who tempts her toward suicide. (BL 80:1551; CCBB 37:191; JHC:414; SLJ Aug 1984 p. 86; VOYA 7:332)
Four Winds, 1984, 118 pp.; Scholastic, 1985, pap.

C/YA SARGENT, Sarah. *Watermusic*. Gr. 6–9.
A haunting story in which Laura's flute-playing brings a huge white bat and a female ogre to life, and their battle symbolizes the struggle between love and intellect. (BL 82:1087; CCBB 39:195; SLJ May 1986 p. 109)
Clarion, dist. by Ticknor and Fields, 1986, 120 pp.

C SCHILLER, Barbara. *The Kitchen Knight*. Gr. 3–4.
King Arthur's nephew, Gareth, proves himself worthy of becoming a knight by laboring for a year as a palace kitchen boy. (HB 41:277; KR 33:374; LJ 90:3122)
Illus. by Nonny Hogrogian, Holt, 1965, 64 pp., o.p.

C/YA SERRAILLIER, Ian (Lucien). *The Challenge of the Green Knight*. Gr. 6–
[R]   9.
Gawain of Camelot is tested by a huge green knight who allows Gawain to behead him, then picks up his head and vows to return in twelve months to strike an exchange blow. (BL 64:275, 329; CCBB 21:84; HB 43:466; KR 35:653; LJ 92:3204; TLS 1966 p. 1078)
Illus. by Victor G. Ambrus, Walck, 1976, 56 pp., o.p.

C/YA SERVICE, Pamela F. *Winter of Magic's Return*. Gr. 5–8.
[R]   Welly and Heather befriend a young man who has lost his memory, and become embroiled in a struggle to awaken King Arthur and save Britain from evil. In *Tomorrow's Magic* (1987) a youthful Merlin and King Arthur appear from the past and join Heather and Welly in an attempt to use magic to unite Britain. (BL 82:269; CCBB 39:56; HB 61:742; Kliatt 21[Spring 1987]:25; SLJ Dec 1985 p. 94)
Atheneum, 1985, 192 pp.; Ballantine/Fawcett, 1986, pap.

YA SEYMOUR, Miranda (pseud. of Miranda Sinclair). *Medea*. Gr. 10 up.
Three narrators: Jason, Aegeus, and Medea, herself, tell this dramatic story of the king's daughter who agrees to become the priestess of Hecate, goddess of death, in exchange for promised political power, falls in love with Jason, and finally loses all chance for love or power. (KR 50:299; LJ 107:1013; SLJ Dec 1982 p. 88)
St. Martin, 1982, 248 pp., o.p.

YA [R] SILVERBERG, Robert. *Gilgamesh the King*. Gr. 10 up.
Young Gilgamesh grows to manhood, is crowned king, and must eventually face his own mortality, in this powerful retelling of the 5000-year-old Sumerian epic. (BL 81:3, 5; Kies:68; KR 52:874; LJ 109:1980; SHC:634)
Arbor House, 1984, 290 pp.

C/YA SINGER, Isaac Bashevis. *The Golem*. Gr. 5–7.
[R]   A clay giant named Joseph is brought to life to protect the endangered Jews of Prague. (BL 79:504, 980; CC:137; CCBB 36:97; HB 59:48, 331; JHC:91; KR 50:1237; SLJ Dec 1982 p. 68; Suth 3:394; TLS 1983 p. 776)
Illus. by Uri Shulevitz, Farrar, 1982, 96 pp.

C/YA SKURZYNSKI, Gloria (Joan). *What Happened in Hamelin*. Gr. 5–7.
[R]   A charismatic stranger with a silvery flute lures the rats and then the children out of the village of Hamelin, in this retelling of the legend, as seen through the eyes of Geist, an orphaned baker's apprentice. (BL 76:669; CCBB 33:119; HB 56:57; KR 47:1376; SLJ Jan 1980 p. 75)
Four Winds, 1979, 177 pp.

SNYDER, Zilpha Keatley. *The Truth about Stone Hollow.* See Chapter 4, Ghost Fantasy.

YA [R] STEINBECK, John (Ernst) (reteller). *The Acts of King Arthur and His Noble Knights from the Winchester Manuscripts of Thomas Malory and Other Sources.* Gr. 10 up.

Eight tales in a poetic translation of Thomas Malory's fifteenth-century manuscript, begun in 1958 and left incomplete at Steinbeck's death. (BL 73:294; HB 53:561; Kies:72; KR 44:1025; LJ 101:2178; SLJ Apr 1977 p. 84; TLS 1977 p. 536; VOYA 3[Dec 1980]:55)

Farrar, 1976, o.p.; Ballantine, 1980, 1985, pap., 464 pp.

YA [R] STEPHENS, James. *Deirdre.* Gr. 8 up. (Orig. British and U.S. pub. Macmillan, 1923.)

King Conachur raises Deirdre in exile to evade a fateful prophecy, but his jealousy of Deirdre's love for another man brings about the very tragedy he had sought to avoid. A retelling of an Irish legend. (BL 20:103; HB 46:395; KR 38:331; LJ 95:1957; TLS 1923 p. 618)

Illus. by Nonny Hogrogian, Macmillan, 1970, 202 pp., o.p.; Arden, 1977 (repr of 1924 ed.).

YA STEWART, Mary (Florence Elinor). *The Crystal Cave* (Merlin trilogy,
[O] vol. 1). Gr. 10 up.

In this first volume of Stewart's Arthurian trilogy, young Merlin has a difficult childhood at the court of the King of Wales. He is trained in magic by a learned wizard and eventually becomes involved in efforts to unite all of Britain. In *The Hollow Hills* (Morrow, 1973; Fawcett, 1984, pap.) Merlin brings up young Arthur and helps him search for the magical sword, Caliburn. *The Last Enchantment* (Morrow, 1979; Fawcett, 1984, pap.) deals with Arthur's reign and Merlin's death. *The Wicked Day* (orig. British pub. 1983; Morrow, 1984) is a related work in which Arthur's illegitimate son, Mordred, brings about the prophesied "wicked day," after he is left in charge of the kingdom while Arthur battles the Romans in Brittany. (BL 67:287, 305, 655; HB 46:503; JHC:419; Kies:73; KR 38:528; LJ 95:2830, 3082, 4328; SHC:636; Tymn:158)

Morrow, 1970, o.p.; Fawcett, 1984, pap., 521 pp.; also pub. in *Mary Stewart's Merlin Trilogy*, Morrow, 1980, 919 pp.

YA STORR, Catherine (Cole). *Thursday.* Gr. 7–10. (Orig. British pub. 1971.)

Bee Earnshaw believes that it was Thursday Townsend's involvement with the fairy folk, and not a nervous breakdown, that has made him so lonely and withdrawn. (BL 69:295, 303; HB 49:148; KR 40:730; LJ 97:3465)

Harper, 1972, 274 pp., o.p.

C/YA SUTCLIFF, Rosemary. *The Sword and the Circle: King Arthur and the*
[O] *Knights of the Round Table.* Gr. 6–10. (Orig. British pub. 1981.)

Thirteen Arthurian stories retold mainly from Sir Thomas Malory's *Le Morte d'Arthur*, involving King Arthur, Merlin, Sir Lancelot, and Morgan la Fay. Sutcliff's trilogy of Arthurian retellings continues with *The Light Beyond the Forest: The Quest for the Holy Grail* (orig. British pub. 1979; U.S. 1980) and *The Road to Camlann* (orig. British pub. 1981; U.S. 1982). *The Light Beyond the Forest* retells the adventures of Gawain, Bors, Percival, Lancelot, and Galahad as they search for the Holy Grail. In *The Road to Camlann*, Mordred, Arthur's illegitimate son, undermines the relationships between Arthur, Guenever, and Lancelot, to bring about the tragic end of the company

of the Round Table. (BL 78:644, 655; CCBB 35:96; Ch&Bks:217; HB 58:59; JHC:91; KR 50:141; SLJ Jan 1981 p. 90; Suth 3: 416; TLS 1981 p. 341)
Dutton, 1981, 261 pp.

YA [R] SUTCLIFF, Rosemary. *Sword at Sunset.* Gr. 10 up. (Orig. British pub. 1963.)
Artos the Bear leads his people in thrusting back the barbarian invaders of Britain, in this version of the Arthurian legend. (BL 59:814, 822; HB 39:634; LJ 88:2786, 2930; TLS 1963 p. 473)
Coward, 1963, 495 pp., o.p.

C/YA SUTCLIFF, Rosemary. *Tristan and Iseult.* Gr. 5–9.
[R] A poetic retelling of the legendary love story of Tristan and Iseult. (BL 68:431, 435, 670; CCBB 25:129; HB 47:620; KR 39:1015; TLS 1971 p. 764)
Dutton, 1971, 150 pp., o.p.

C/YA SYNGE, (Phyllis) Ursula. *Land of Heroes: A Retelling of the Kalevala*
[R] (British title: *Kalevala,* 1977). Gr. 6 up.
Three magician-heroes: Vainamoinen the singer, Ilmarinen the smith, and Lemminkainen the rogue, vie for the hand of the beautiful daughter of the sorceress, Mistress Louhi, in this retelling of Finnish folklore. (BL 74:1342, 1355; CCBB 32:55; HB 54:289; SLJ Sept 1978 p. 150; TLS 1977 p. 1410)
Atheneum, 1978, 222 pp., o.p.

SYNGE, Ursula. *Swan's Wing.* See Chapter 1, Allegorical Fantasy and Literary Fairy Tales.

C/YA SYNGE, (Phyllis) Ursula. *Weland, Smith of the Gods.* Gr. 5–8. (Orig. British pub. 1972.)
Crippled Weland and his brothers ignore their mother's warnings and leave home to find the Valkyries, in this retelling of Norse myth from the Icelandic poetic Edda. (BL 70:335, 343; LJ 99:577; TLS 1972 p. 1322)
Illus. by Charles Keeping, Phillips, 1973, 116 pp.

C/YA *Tales from the Mabinogion.* Gr. 5–9. (Orig. British pub. 1984.)
These medieval Welsh heroic fantasy tales form the basis of the works of many well-known authors of contemporary fantasy, including Alan Garner, Lloyd Alexander, and Susan Cooper. (BL 81:1123; CCBB 38:190)
Tr. by Thomas Gwyn and Kevin Crossley-Holland, illus. by Margaret Jones, Overlook, dist. by Viking, 1985, 88 pp.

YA TENNY, Dixie. *Call the Darkness Down.* Gr. 7–12.
American-born Morfa Owen's research into her Welsh heritage uncovers her family's ties to ancient Druidic powers, and almost costs her her life. (BL 80:1111, 1122; CCBB 37:175; KR 52[Mar 1, 1984]:J23; SLJ May 1984 p. 104; VOYA 7:198)
Atheneum, 1984, 185 pp., o.p.

C [R] TREGARTHEN, Enys (pseud. of Nellie Sloggett). *The White Ring.* Gr. 4–6.
In this retelling of a Cornish legend, the King and Queen of Fairyland take on the forms of an old man and a little girl until they are able to return to their own world. (BL 45:286; CCBB 2[June 1949]:6; HB 25:210; KR 17:150; LJ 74:557)
Ed. by Elizabeth Yates, illus. by Nora S. Unwin, Harcourt, 1949, 65 pp., o.p.

YA VALENCAK, Hannelore. *When Half-Gods Go.* Gr. 8–12. (Orig. Austrian pub. 1974.)
Tired of her lover Andreas's contemptuous treatment during an archaeological tour of Greece, Barbara strikes out on her own and is befriended by a young Greek named Alexander, who may be the god, Hermes, come to life. (BL 73:316, 327; CCBB 30:84; HB 52:630; KR 44:910; SLJ Oct 1976 p. 121)
Tr. by Patricia Crampton, Morrow, 1976, 192 pp.

VAN ALLSBURG, Chris. *The Stranger.* See Chapter 1, Allegorical Fantasy and Literary Fairy Tales.

Visions of Wonder: An Anthology of Christian Fantasy. Ed. by Robert H. Boyer and Kenneth J. Zahorski. See Chapter 3, Fantasy Collections.

C/YA WALKER, Kenneth Macfarlane, and BOUMPHREY, Geoffrey. *The Log of the Ark* (British title: *The Log of the Arc,* 1923; orig. U.S. title: *What Happened in the Arc?* Dutton, 1926). Gr. 5–7.
A humorous retelling of the story of Noah. (BL 23:139, 57:33; HB 36:217)
Pantheon, 1960, 214 pp., o.p.

YA WALTON, Evangeline (pseud. of Evangeline Ensley). *The Prince of Annwn* (The Mabinogion tetralogy, book 1). Gr. 10 up.
In this retelling of the first branch of the Welsh *Mabinogion,* Prince Pwyll of Dyfed (in Wales) battles Havgan, a ruler in the Kingdom of Death, and then travels into the Bright World in search of a bride, Rhiannon of the Birds. The sequels are *The Children of Llyr* (1971, 1978), *The Song of Rhiannon* (1972, 1978), and *The Virgin and the Swine* (Willett, 1936; repr. as *The Island of the Mighty,* 1970, 1979). (Kies:78; Tymn:169; VOYA 2[Apr 1979]:48)
Random, 1971, o.p.; Ballantine/Del Rey, 1974, 1978, pap., 178 pp., o.p.

WANGERIN, Walter, Jr. *The Book of the Dun Cow.* See Chapter 1, Allegorical Fantasy and Literary Fairy Tales.

YA WELLMAN, Manly Wade. *Cahena.* Gr. 10 up.
A retelling of the story of the Cahena, a legendary female warrior-priestess in eighth-century North Africa, who fought to her death against the Moslem conquest. (BL 83:625, 642; LJ Dec 1986 p. 141)
Doubleday, 1986, 182 pp.

YA [R] WELLMAN, Manly Wade. *The Old Gods Waken* (Silver John series, book 3). Gr. 10 up.
Only John, a wandering minstrel with a silver-stringed guitar, realizes the danger posed to his Appalachian home by the sinister revival of a druidic cult. This book is preceded by *Who Fears the Devil?* (1963) and *Worse Things Waiting* (1973). The sequels are *After Dark* (1980, 1984), *The Lost and the Lurking* (1981, 1984), *The Hanging Stones* (1982, 1984), *The Voice of the Mountain* (1984), and *The Valley So Low* (1987). (BL 76:758; Kies:79; KR 47:1292; LJ 104:2666)
Doubleday, 1979, o.p.; Berkley, 1984, pap., 186 pp., o.p.

WESTALL, Robert. *The Devil on the Road.* See Chapter 8, Time Travel Fantasy.

YA WHITE, T(erence) H(anbury). *The Once and Future King*. Gr. 10 up.
[O]   A revised omnibus edition of White's retelling of Arthurian legends. The first three sections of this book were originally published separately: *The Sword in the Stone* (1939), *The Witch in the Wood* (1939; here called "The Queen of Air and Darkness"), *The Illmade Knight* (1949), and the previously unpublished section, "The Candle in the Wind." *The Book of Merlyn*, written in 1941, was originally intended as the fifth and final book of the saga. It was first published by the University of Texas Press in 1977 and reissued by Berkley, 1978 (pap.). (BL 55:48; JHC:427; Kies:82; KR 26:429; LJ 83:2184; SHC:646; TLS 1958 p. 224; Tymn:174)
    Putnam, 1958, 677 pp.

C/YA WHITE, T(erence) H(anbury). *The Sword in the Stone*. Gr. 5–8. (Orig.
[R]   British pub. 1938.)
    Merlyn the sorcerer teaches young King Arthur about magic and history. This story and its sequel, *The Witch in the Wood* (1939), were revised to become the first two parts of *The Once and Future King* (1958). (BL 35:191; JHC:427; TLS 1938 p. 571)
    Illus. by the author, Putnam, 1939, 312 pp.

WIBBERLEY, Leonard Patrick O'Connor. *The Quest of Excalibur*. See Chapter 4, Ghost Fantasy.

YA [R] WIESEL, Elie(zer). *The Golem; the Story of a Legend*. Gr. 10 up.
    An old gravedigger in sixteenth-century Prague tells this story of Yossel, the huge clay figure created by Rabbi Yehuda Loew to protect the Jews from persecution. (BL 80:847, 853; LJ 109:510; SHC:150)
    Tr. by Anne Borchardt, illus. by Mark Podwal, Summit, 1983, 105 pp.

WILDE, Oscar. *The Picture of Dorian Gray*. See Chapter 1, Allegorical Fantasy and Literary Fairy Tales.

WILLIAMS, Thomas. *Tsuga's Children*. See Section 5C, Travel to Other Worlds.

YA WOOLLEY, Persia. *Child of the Northern Spring*. Gr. 10 up.
    This Arthurian legend is retold through the eyes of young Gwen, soon to become Queen Guinevere, in the first volume of a projected trilogy. (BL 83:1410, 1437, 84:1250; KR 55:422; LJ June 1, 1987 p. 131)
    Poseidon, 1987, 418 pp.

C [R] WRIGGINS, Sally. *The White Monkey King: A Chinese Fable*. Gr. 4–6.
    In ancient China, a monkey prankster with magical powers meets his match when he challenges the Buddha. (CCBB 31:104; HB 53:529; KR 45:487; SLJ Mar 1978 p. 135; Suth 2:487)
    Illus. by Ronni Solbert, Pantheon, 1977, 113 pp., o.p.

C/YA WRIGHTSON, (Alice) Patricia (Furlonger). *The Ice Is Coming* (Wirrun
[O]   trilogy, book 1). Gr. 6–9. (Orig. Australian pub. 1977.)
    Wirrun, a young Aborigine, discovers that the ancient ice people, or Ninya, are on the march, forming ice all over the land. He realizes that it is up to him to find the most ancient Nargun, or rock monster, to stop them. In *The Dark Bright Water* (1978; 1979) Wirrun uses magic to fight an enemy deep within the earth. In *Journey behind the Wind* (1981) the evil Wulgaru, master of a mysterious death-bringing thing, causes Wirrun's water-spirit wife to disappear, and Wirrun must confront Wulgaru to save the land. (BL 74:559;

CC:548; CCBB 31:104; Ch&Bks:219; HB 54:57; Kies:85; KR 45:996; SLJ Nov 1977 p. 65; Suth 2:487)
Atheneum, 1977, o.p.; Ballantine, 1986, pap., 222 pp.

WRIGHTSON, Patricia. *Moon Dark.* See Section 2A, Beast Tales.

C/YA WRIGHTSON, (Alice) Patricia (Furlonger). *The Nargun and the Stars.*
[R] Gr. 5–8. (Orig. Australian pub. 1973.)
The lives of Simon Brent and his elderly cousins are threatened by the Nargun, a rocklike monster from the past. (BL 70:1108, 71:768; 83:415; CC 1987 Suppl. p. 64; CCBB 28:72; Ch&Bks:232; HB 50:382, 63:84; KR 42:302; LJ 99:2300; Suth 2:488; TLS 1973 p. 1434; Tymn:179; VOYA 9:292)
Atheneum, 1974, 1986, 184 pp.; Penguin/Puffin, 1988, pap.

C [R] YOLEN (Stemple), Jane H(yatt). *Greyling: A Picture Story from the Islands of Shetland.* Gr. 2–4.
A selchie, or seal-boy, raised by a fisherman and his wife, reverts to his seal form to save his foster father's life. (CCBB 22:151; HB 45:44; LJ 94:2096; Suth:342; TLS 1969 p. 695)
Illus. by William Stobbs, Philomel, 1968, 29 pp., o.p.

YA YOLEN (Stemple), Jane H(yatt). *Merlin's Booke.* Gr. 7–12.
Ten stories and poems about the Arthurian wizard, Merlin, beginning with a ballad prophesying his birth and ending with an "Epitaph" in which an archaeological team proclaims the finding of Merlin's body to a group of skeptical journalists. (Kies:85; LJ Feb 1, 1987 p. 80; VOYA 9:242)
Illus. by Thomas Canty, SteelDragon, 1986, 176 pp.; Ace, 1986, pap., o.p.

YA YOUNG, Robert F. *The Vizier's Second Daughter.* Gr. 7–12.
Sent into the past to kidnap Scheherazade for duplication by a supplier of wax museum figures, Bill Billings grabs her younger sister, Dunyzad, by mistake, and meets up with Ali Baba when he tries to escape. (Kliatt 19[Spring 1985]:30; VOYA 8:196)
NAL/DAW, 1985, pap., 203 pp., o.p.

C. Travel to Other Worlds

C/YA ADAIR, Gilbert. *Alice Through the Needle's Eye: The Further Adventures*
[R] *of Lewis Carroll's "Alice."* Gr. 4–7. (Orig. British pub. 1984, entitled *Alice Through the Needle's Eye: A Third Adventure for Lewis Carroll's Alice.*)
In this contemporary sequel to Lewis Carroll's *Alice's Adventures in Wonderland* (see this section) and *Through the Looking Glass,* Alice slips through the eye of her needle and sets off on adventures with a Country Mouse, Jack and Jill, and the Red and White Queens. (BL 81:1188; KR 53:1; LJ Apr 15, 1985 p. 84; TLS Jan 4, 1985 p. 18)
Illus. by Jenny Thorne, Dutton, 1985, 184 pp.

AIKEN, Joan. *Winterthing: A Play for Children.* See Section 5B, Myth Fantasy.

C/YA ALEXANDER, Lloyd. *The First Two Lives of Lukas-Kasha.* Gr. 5–8.
[O] Lukas volunteers to participate in a magic act and unexpectedly ends up in the land of Abadan, where he is made king despite the objection of the

Grand Vizier. (BL 75:42; CC:425; CCBB 32:57; Ch&Bks:263; HB 55:513; JHC:343; KR 46:878; SLJ Oct 1978 p. 141; Suth 2:8)
Dutton, 1978; Dell, 1982, pap., 224 pp.

C/YA ALEXANDER, Lloyd. *The Illyrian Adventure* (Vesper Holly Adventure
[R]   series). Gr. 5–9.
In this adventure-filled romp set in the 1870s, young Vesper Holly travels to the kingdom of Illyria to continue her late father's research on Illyria's legendary magical warriors. In *The El Dorado Adventure* (1987) Vesper goes to the Central American country of El Dorado, where she is in constant danger from numerous villains as she attempts to save the homelands of the Chirica Indians. *The Drackenberg Adventure* (1988) continues Vesper's exploits. (BL 82:1134, 1137, 83:794, 1136; CC 1987 Suppl. p. 53; CCBB 39:142; HB 62:447; JHC 1987 Suppl. p. 58; Kliatt 21[Spring 1987]:19; KR 54:543; SLJ May 1986 p. 99; VOYA 9:232, 10:22)
Dutton, 1986, 132 pp.; Dell/Laurel Leaf, 1987, pap.

ALLEN, Judy. *The Lord of the Dance.* See Section 5B, Myth Fantasy.

ANDERSEN, Hans Christian. *The Snow Queen.* See Chapter 1, Allegorical Fantasy and Literary Fairy Tales.

BAKER, Michael. *The Mountain and the Summer Stars: An Old Tale Newly Ended.* See Chapter 5B, Myth Fantasy.

C [R] BARRIE, Sir J(ames) M(atthew). *Peter Pan.* Gr. 4–6. (Orig. pub. as a play, followed by a novel, both entitled *Peter and Wendy,* 1904; first pub. as *Peter Pan,* 1911.)
Peter Pan teaches three children to fly to Never Never Land, but a jealous fairy betrays them to Captain Hook's pirate band. *Peter Pan in Kensington Gardens* (abridged from *The Little White Bird,* 1892; orig. pub. in this format, 1902; Scribner, 1937, o.p.) is a related work that describes Peter's infant adventures with the birds and fairies of Kensington Gardens. (BL 8:171, 47:18, 77:807, 79:1140, 84:700, 858; Bookshelf 1923–1924 p. 15; CC:430; CCBB 3:66, 6:12, 11:66, 34:125, 36:162; Ch&Bks:237; HB 26:387, 56:661; Mahony 1:35; SLJ Dec 1980 p. 57, Aug 1983 p. 48; Suth 3:40; TLS 1981 p. 1363)
Illus. by Nora S. Unwin, Scribner, 1950, o.p.; Macmillan, 1972; illus. by Trina Schart Hyman, Scribner, 1980; Avon, 1982, pap.; ed. by Josette Frank, illus. by Diane Goode, Random, 1983; Bantam, 1985, pap.; Penguin/Puffin, 1986, pap.; illus. by Michael Hague, Holt, 1987; NAL, 1987, pap.; illus. by Jan Omerod, Viking/Kestrel, 1987, 204 pp.

C/YA BARTHOLOMEW, Barbara. *The Time Keeper* (The Timeways trilogy, book 1) (British title: *The Timekeeper,* 1986). Gr. 6–10.
Jeanette and her brother Neil are transported into a world with two moons where they are befriended by a boy named Jesse and his unicorn. The sequels are *Child of Tomorrow* (1985) and *When Dreamers Cease to Dream* (1985). (Kliatt 19[Fall 1985]:20; SLJ Dec 1985 p. 97; VOYA 8:323)
Signet, 1985, pap., 191 pp., o.p.

C BAUM, L(yman) Frank. *The Sea Fairies.* Gr. 4–6.
Zog the Terrible captures a little girl named Trott who is visiting the mermaids. The sequel is *Sky Island* (1912, 1970). (LJ 95:1936)

Illus. by John R. Neill, Reilly and Britton, 1911, 239 pp., o.p.; Contemporary Books, 1969, o.p.

C [R] BAUM, L(yman) Frank. *The Wizard of Oz* (Orig. title: *The Wonderful Wizard of Oz*, 1900). Gr. 3–6.
A cyclone blows Dorothy from Kansas to the Land of Oz. The price of her trip home is the death of the Wicked Witch of the West. There are forty-seven Oz sequels. Baum wrote the first thirteen: *The Land of Oz* (retitled *The Marvellous Land of Oz*) (1904), *Ozma of Oz* (1907; Peter Smith, 1985), *Dorothy and the Wizard in Oz* (1908; Peter Smith, 1984), *The Road to Oz* (1909), *The Emerald City of Oz* (1910), *The Patchwork Girl of Oz* (1913), *Tik-Tok of Oz* (1914), *The Scarecrow of Oz* (1915), *Rinki-tink of Oz* (1916), *The Lost Princess of Oz* (1917), *The Tin Woodman of Oz* (1918), *The Magic of Oz* (1919), and *Glinda of Oz* (1920). Baum also wrote *Little Wizard Stories of Oz* (1913; Schocken, 1985). The series was continued by Ruth Plumly Thompson, John Rea Neill, Jack Snow, Rachel R. Cosgrove, Eloise Jarvis McGraw, and Lauren McGraw Wagner. Thompson wrote *The Royal Book of Oz* (1921), *Kabumpo in Oz* (1922), *The Cowardly Lion of Oz* (1923), *Grampa in Oz* (1924), *The Lost King of Oz* (1925), *The Hungry Tiger of Oz* (1926), *The Gnome King of Oz* (1927), *The Giant Horse of Oz* (1928), *Jack Pumpkinhead of Oz* (1929), *The Yellow Knight of Oz* (1930), *Pirates in Oz* (1931), *The Purple Prince of Oz* (1932), *Ojo in Oz* (1933), *Speedy in Oz* (1934), *The Wishing Horse of Oz* (1935), *Captain Salt in Oz* (1936), *Handy Mandy in Oz* (1937), *The Silver Princess in Oz* (1938), and *Ozoplaning with the Wizard of Oz* (1939). Neill wrote *The Wonder City of Oz* (1940), *The Scalawagons of Oz* (1941), and *Lucky Bucky in Oz* (1942). Snow wrote *The Magical Mimics in Oz* (1946), *The Shaggy Man of Oz* (1949), and *Who's Who in Oz* (1954). Cosgrove wrote *The Hidden Valley of Oz* (1951), and McGraw and Wagner co-authored *Merry-Go-Round in Oz* (1963). Recent additions to the series include: *A Barnstormer in Oz* by Philip Jose Farmer (Berkley, 1982), *Ozma and the Wayward Wand* by Polly Berends (Random, 1985), *Dorothy and the Seven-Leaf Clover* by Dorothy Haas (Random, 1985), *Mister Tinker in Oz* by James Howe (Random, 1985), *Dorothy and the Magic Belt* by Susan Saunders (Random, 1985), and *Return to Oz* by Joan D. Vinge (Ballantine, 1985). (BL 79:673, 82:1661, 1682, 84:470; CC:431; CCBB 4:10, 36:21; Ch&Bks:264; HB 63:82; SLJ Oct 1982 p. 148; Suth 3:43; TLS 1982 p. 1308; Tymn:49)
Illus. by Evelyn Copelman, adapted from the illus. of W. W. Denslow, Putnam/Grosset, 1956, deluxe ed.; Dover, 1960, pap.; Dent, dist. by Biblio, 1975; Macmillan, pap.; illus. by W. W. Denslow, Peter Smith; Buccaneer, 1981 (repr. of 1900 ed.); illus. by Michael Hague, Holt, 1982; Penguin, 1983, pap.; adapt. by Deborah Hautzig, illus. by Joseph A. Smith, Random, 1984; illus. by L. Frank Ranger, Scholastic, 1984, pap.; Ballantine, 1985, pap.; illus. by Barry Moser, Univ. of California/Penroyal, 1986; illus. by W. W. Denslow, Morrow, 1987, 267 pp.

YA BEAR, Greg(orgy Dale). *The Infinity Concerto*, Gr. 10 up.
An old house is the gateway to another world entered by sixteen-year-old Michael Perrin, who meets the powerful Sidhe of Celtic legend. The sequel is *The Serpent Mage* (1986). (BL 81:557, 582; VOYA 8:54, 365)
Berkley, 1984, pap., 352 pp., o.p.; Ace, 1987, pap.

C BEATON-JONES, Cynon. *The Adventures of So Hi*. Gr. 4–6. (Orig. British pub. 1951.)
The wind carries a Chinese boy named So Hi and his kite across the sea,

where he meets a lovable dragon and embarks on a series of adventures. The sequel is *So Hi and the White Horse* (1952, 1957). (BL 53:228; CCBB 10:114; HB 32:445; LJ 82:224)
Illus. by John Ward, Vanguard, 1956, 178 pp., o.p.

C [R] BENSON, E(dward) F(rederic). *David Blaize and the Blue Door.* Gr. 4–6. (Orig. British pub. 1918.)
Six-year-old David locks the shining blue door to the real world behind him and escapes into a topsy-turvy nonsense world. *David Blaize* (1916) and *David Blaize of Kings* (1924; British title: *David of Kings*) are related stories but not fantasies. (BL 16:100; HB 3[May 1927]:17–23; LJ 45:980; Mahony 1:38; TLS 1918 p. 642)
Illus. by H. J. Ford, Doubleday, 1919, 217 pp., o.p.

C BERGENGREN, Ralph Wilhelm. *David the Dreamer: His Book of Dreams.* Gr. 2–4.
David and his dog, Fido, share many strange adventures in Dreamland. (BL 19:90; Bookshelf 1923–1924 p. 7; HB 3[May 1927]:18,21)
Illus. by Tom Freud, Atlantic, 1922, 67 pp., o.p.

C BERTON, Pierre. *The Secret World of Og.* Gr. 3–5. (Orig. Canadian pub. 1961.)
Five children are imprisoned in the subterranean world of Og, whose small green inhabitants learned to speak from comic books. (BL 58:688; HB 38:176; KR 30:181; LJ 87:2020)
Illus. by William Winter, Little, 1962, 146 pp., o.p.; Pocket, 1984, pap., o.p.

BIANCO, Pamela. *Little Houses Far Away.* See Chapter 9, Toy Fantasy.

YA BLAYLOCK, James P(aul). *Land of Dreams.* Gr. 10 up.
During Solstice, when visits to strange lands become possible, Skeezix and Jack find a boat-sized shoe on a California beach and travel to the "land of dreams." (KR 55:895; LJ Aug 1987 p. 146; VOYA 10:242)
Arbor House, 1987, 264 pp.

BOSTON, L. M. *The Castle of Yew.* See Chapter 7, Magic Adventure Fantasy.

C [R] BOSTON, L(ucy) M(aria Wood). *The Guardians of the House.* Gr. 4–6. (Orig. British pub. 1974.)
A collection of peculiar masks and carved heads in an old mansion lures Tom Morgan to a jungle temple, a submerged Roman villa, and an Indian cave. (CCBB 29:3; HB 51:265; KR 43:121; SLJ May 1975 p. 52; TLS 1974 p. 1373)
Illus. by Peter Boston, Atheneum, 1975, 52 pp., o.p.

BOSTON, L. M. *The Sea Egg.* See Chapter 7, Magic Adventure Fantasy.

C BOWEN, William A(lvin) *Merrimeg.* Gr. 3–5.
On her way to do some errands, a little girl named Merrimeg finds herself in strange places, meeting chimney imps, starlight fairies, appleseed elves, and gnomes. (BL 20:143; Bookshelf 1923–1924 Suppl. p. 1; Mahony 2:132)
Illus. by Emma Brock, Macmillan, 1923, 1938, 166 pp., o.p.

YA BOYER, Elizabeth H. *The Troll's Grindstone.* Gr. 10 up.
A man named Leif, kidnapped by elves to impersonate the enemy of the sorcerer Sorkvir, saves himself by stealing a magic sword. (BL 82:1587, 1604; VOYA 10:35)
Ballantine/Del Rey, 1986, pap., 342 pp., o.p.

YA BRADLEY, Marion Zimmer. *The House between the Worlds.* Gr. 10 up.
Cameron Fenton enters the faerie world while conducting an ESP experiment and stays to help battle an evil threat to the world. (BL 76:1409, 78:593; KR 48:397; LJ 105:1192)
Doubleday, 1980, o.p.; Ballantine, 1984, pap., 320 pp.

YA BRIN, David. *The Practice Effect.* Gr. 10 up.
Dennis Nuel, a young physicist, is transported to a magical alternate world where he discovers that he is a wizard. (BL 80:1377, 1391; LJ 109:600; VOYA 8:54)
Bantam, 1984, pap., 277 pp.

C [R] BROWN, Palmer. *The Silver Nutmeg: The Story of Anna Lavinia and Toby.* Gr. 4–6.
When Anna Lavinia discovers another world on the other side of a dew pond near her house, she decides to explore it. This is the sequel to *Beyond the Pawpaw Trees* (1954). (BL 52:367; CCBB 9:108; HB 32:187; Eakin:48; KR 24:244; LJ 81:1545)
Illus. by the author, Harper, 1956, 138 pp., o.p.; Avon, 1983, pap.

BRYHER, Winifred. *A Visa for Avalon.* See Section 5B, Myth Fantasy.

C CARLSEN, Ruth Christoffer. *Ride a Wild Horse.* Gr. 4–6.
Julie pretends to be suffering from memory loss while she searches for an escape hatch into her own world. (BL 67:338; KR 38:1145; LJ 96:264)
Illus. by Beth Krush and Joe Krush, Houghton, 1970, 164 pp., o.p.

YA CARPENTER, Christopher. *The Twilight Realm.* Gr. 7–12.
Five teenagers engaged in a fantasy role-playing game are suddenly pulled into the world of Xhandarre where they become warriors and enchanters fighting an evil sorcerer who is plotting to enter our world. (BL 82:1387, 1392; KR 54:549; SLJ Aug 1986 p. 99; VOYA 9:160)
Putnam, 1986; Berkley-Pacer, 1987, pap., 237 pp.

C/YA CARROLL, Lewis (pseud. of Charles Ludwidge Dodgson). *Alice's Adven-*
[O] *tures in Wonderland* (orig. title: *Alice's Adventures Underground,* written 1863; orig. pub. 1865). Gr. 5–8.
Alice has two adventures: First she follows a rabbit into a curious world where she meets the Mad Hatter and the Queen of Hearts. In *Through the Looking Glass and What Alice Found There* (written 1870; orig. U.S. pub. 1899; St. Martin, 1977; Knopf, 1986; Schocken, 1987), she steps through a mirror into a backward world. *Alice Through the Needle's Eye* is a contemporary sequel written by Gilbert Adair (Dutton, 1985; see this chapter). (BL 51:210, 63:189, 79:76, 80:678, 81:646, 1552, 82:682; Bookshelf 1932 p. 8; CC:446; CCBB 3:11, 5:21, 36, 9:66, 38:162; Ch&Bks:236, HB 1 [June 1925]:34; HB 5:48, 42:76, 326, 49:284, 56:80, 59:73, 59:732, 61:74, 62:344; LJ 91:5258; Mahony 2:276; SLJ Jan 1984 p. 73, Aug 1985 p. 62, Nov 1985 p. 82; TLS 1972 p. 1525, 1985 p. 18; Tymn:60)
Macmillan, 1962 (bound with *Through the Looking Glass*), pap.; illus. by Arthur Rackham, Watts, 1966, o.p.; Oxford, 1973, pap.; NAL, 1973; Dent,

dist. by Biblio, 1975 (bound with *Through the Looking Glass*) (repr. of 1929 ed.); illus. by Tove Jansson, Delacorte, 1977, o.p.; illus. by Mervyn Peake, Schocken, 1979 (bound with *Through the Looking Glass*), pap., o.p.; illus. by John Spiers, Messner, 1982 (bound with *Through the Looking Glass*), o.p.; illus. by Barry Moser, Univ. of California Press, 1982; ed. by Wendy Barrish, Wanderer, 1982; illus. by Michelle Wriggins, Ariel/Knopf, 1983, o.p.; Bantam, 1985, pap.; illus. by Justin Todd, Crown, 1985; illus. by Michael Hague, Holt, 1985; Penguin, 1985, pap.; illus. by John Tenniel, Scholastic, 1985, pap.; Holt, 1986 (entitled *Alice's Adventures Under Ground,* facsimile ed.), 112 pp.; Salem House, 1986.

C CARRYL, Charles Edward. *The Admiral's Caravan.* Gr. 4–6. (Orig. pub. in *St. Nicholas* magazine, 1891–1892.)
A little girl visits a land inhabited by the animals from Noah's ark. (Bookshelf 1928 p. 11; HB 3[May 1927]:21; Mahony 2:276)
Illus. by Reginald B. Birch, Houghton, 1909, 1920, 140 pp., o.p.

C CARRYL, Charles Edward. *Davy and the Goblin, or What Followed Reading "Alice's Adventures in Wonderland."* Gr. 3–5. (Reprint of 1885 ed.; orig. pub. in *St. Nicholas* magazine, 1884, 1885.)
After reading *Alice in Wonderland,* Davy sets off on a voyage with a goblin. (BL 25:173; Bookshelf 1932 p. 8; HB 3[May 1927]:18, 21, 7:115; Mahony 2:276)
Houghton, 1909, 1920, o.p.; illus. by E. B. Bensell and Herman I. Bacharach, University Microfilms, 1967, 160 pp., o.p.

C/YA CHANT, Joy (pseud. of Eileen Joyce Rutter). *Red Moon and Black Mountain: The End of the House of Kendreth* (Khentor novels). Gr. 6–10. (Orig. British pub. 1970.)
A prophecy calls three children into Kendrinh, the Starlit Land—Nick and Penelope to the Black Mountain lair of the sorcerer Fendarl, and Oliver to join a warrior band battling the Black Lord. *The Grey Mane of Morning* (1977, see Section 5A, Alternate Worlds or Histories) and *When Voiha Wakes* (1983) are set in the same world. (BL 72:1584, 1594; CCBB 30:22; KR 44:600; SLJ Sept 1976 p. 130; TLS 1970 p. 1449; Tymn:61)
Dutton, 1976, 227 pp., o.p.; Bantam, 1983, pap., o.p.

C [R] CHASE, Mary (Coyle). *Loretta Mason Potts.* Gr. 4–6.
Bewitched for seven years, Loretta refuses to live with her real family and draws her brother, Colin, into the enchantment with her. (BL 55:189; KR 26:711; LJ 84:248)
Illus. by Harold Berson, Lippincott, 1958, 221 pp., o.p.

C/YA CHETWIN, Grace. *Out of the Dark World.* Gr. 5–8.
Nightmares filled with cries for help convince Meg that she must enter the Dark World to rescue a young cousin whose spirit has been taken over by the forces of evil. (CCBB 39:105; JHC 1986 Suppl. p. 58; SLJ Jan 1986 p. 64)
Lothrop, 1985, 154 pp.

C/YA [R] CHRISTOPHER, John (pseud. of Christopher Samuel Youd). *Fireball.* Gr. 5–8.
Simon and his American cousin Brad are sent into the parallel world of twentieth-century Roman Britain, where they take part in a Christian revolution against the Romans, and escape on a ship bound for the New World. In *New Found Land* (1983), Brad, Simon, and their Roman friends, Bos and Curtius, make a dangerous journey across the North American conti-

nent, battling Algonquins and Vikings, and arrive at an Aztec settlement on the Pacific Coast. In *Dragon Dance* (1986), Simon and Brad are kidnapped by slavers and taken to China, where they learn the secret of the fireball which began their adventures. (BL 77:1083, 1097; CC:447; CCBB 35:7; HB 57:307; SLJ Apr 1981 p. 122; Suth 3:85; TLS 1981 p. 1069; VOYA 4[Dec 1981]:38)
Elsevier/Dutton, 1981, 148 pp.

C/YA   CLEMENTS, Bruce. *Two Against the Tide.* Gr. 5–7.
Tom and Sharon are kidnapped and taken to an island where the inhabitants have found the secret of everlasting youth. (BL 64:542; HB 43:587; KR 35:966, 1444; SLJ 93:289)
Farrar, 1967, 199 pp., o.p., 1987, pap.

C   COATSWORTH, Elizabeth (Jane). *Knock at the Door.* Gr. 3–5.
A half-fairy, half-mortal boy named Stephen helps his mortal father escape from imprisonment in Fairyland to the Outer World. (BL 28:155; HB 7:311; LJ 57:865; Mahony 3:202)
Illus. by F(rancis) D. Bedford, Macmillan, 1931, 73 pp., o.p.

COOMBS, Patricia. *The Lost Playground.* See Chapter 9, Toy Fantasy.

C [R]   COOPER, Paul Fenimore. *Tal: His Marvelous Adventures with Noom-Zor-Noom.* Gr. 4–6.
Tal's journey to the kingdom of Troom ends with the discovery that he is the king's long-lost son. (BL 26:285; HB 5:45, 49, 14:143, 34:124; Mahony 3:203; Moore 51:427; TLS 1930 p. 979)
Illus. by Ruth Reeves, Ungar, 1929, 305 pp., o.p.

C/YA   COOPER (Grant), Susan (Mary). *Seaward.* Gr. 6–9.
[R]   West and Cally become traveling companions after being wrenched into an unnamed world. Their treacherous journey takes them ever seaward, in search of parents they fear are dead. (BL 80:158, 168, 169; CC:455; CCBB 37:65; Ch&Bks:235; HB 60:59; JHC:360; KR 51:202; SLJ Oct 1983 p. 157; Suth 3:100; TLS 1983 p. 1317; VOYA 7:37)
Atheneum/Macmillan, 1983, 177 pp.; Macmillan/Aladdin, 1987, pap.

C   CORBETT, Scott. *The Mysterious Zetabet.* Gr. 1–3.
Zachary Zwicker finds Zyxland to be the perfect place for him: All the important places and things begin with Z. (CCBB 33:4; KR 47:576; SLJ Sept 1979 p. 107)
Illus. by John McIntosh, Atlantic-Little, 1979, 48 pp.

C/YA   CROSS, John Kier. *The Other Side of Green Hills* (British title: *The Owl and the Pussycat*, 1946). Gr. 5–7.
Five children exploring a world on the other side of their old house meet the Moon Folk and an evil sorcerer. (CCBB 1[Dec 1947]:2; HB 23:443; LJ 72:1473)
Illus. by Robin Jacques, Coward, 1947, 190 pp., o.p.

C   CROWNFIELD, Gertrude. *The Little Tailor of the Winding Way.* Gr. 3–5.
Jorin the tailor enters a land of happiness. (BL 14:230; Mahony 1:40)
Illus. by Willy Pogány, Macmillan, 1917, 132 pp., o.p.

DAHL, Roald. *James and the Giant Peach: A Children's Story.* See Chapter 7, Magic Adventure Fantasy.

YA DAVIDSON, Lionel. *Under Plum Lake.* Gr. 7 up.
A twelve-year-old boy exploring a smugglers' cave on the Cornwall coast enters the netherworld of Egon, an advanced civilization. (KR 48:1097; LJ 105:2236; TLS 1980 p. 1325; VOYA 4[June 1981]:54)
Knopf, 1980, 136 pp., o.p.

DE LINT, Charles. *Moonheart.* See Section 5B, Myth Fantasy.

YA DE LINT, Charles. *Yarrow: An Autumn Tale.* Gr. 10 up. (Orig. pub. in Canada.)
Canadian fantasy author Caitlin Midhir discovers that the only way to escape from the vampire who is feasting on her dreams is to enter an alternate world populated by gnomes and elves. (BL 83:625, 641; Kies:24; VOYA 9:291)
Ace, 1986, pap., 244 pp.

C DELL, Joan. *The Missing Boy.* Gr. 4–6.
A young cockney girl named Deborah puts on a pair of magical 3-D glasses and is transported into a five-dimensional world where she helps a young boy to see again. (HB 35:130; KR 26:819; LJ 84:249)
Illus. by Sheila Greenwald, Putnam, 1958, 192 pp., o.p.

DE REGNIERS, Beatrice Schenk. *Penny.* See Chapter 1, Allegorical Fantasy and Literary Fairy Tales.

YA [R] DICKSON, Gordon R(upert). *The Dragon and the George.* Gr. 10 up.
Eckert finds himself transplanted into the body of a dragon in an alternate world where his fiance is being held captive. Winner of the British Fantasy Award, Best Novel, 1976. This story is also contained in *Dragon Tales,* ed. by Isaac Asimov (Fawcett, 1982). (BL 73:994, 1001, 78:594; Kliatt 11[Spring 1977]: 10; Tymn:73; VOYA 1[Feb 1979]:54)
Ballantine, 1976, pap.

YA [R] DONALDSON, Stephen R(upert). *Lord Foul's Bane* (The Chronicles of Thomas Covenant, the Unbeliever, vol. 1). Gr. 10 up.
In this first volume of a complex and powerful fantasy trilogy, Thomas Covenant, a successful author shunned by family and friends because he has leprosy, is struck by a car and awakens in The Land, where he reluctantly agrees to help the Lords of Revelstone recover the Staff of Law, needed to thwart Lord Foul's destructive plans. The sequels are *The Illearth War* (1977, 1978) and *The Power that Preserves* (1977, 1979), which have been published in a three-volume boxed set entitled *The Chronicles of Thomas Covenant* (Ballantine, 1982). This trilogy is succeeded by a second trilogy called "The Second Chronicles of Thomas Covenant": *The Wounded Land* (1981), *The One Tree* (1983), and *White Gold Wielder* (1983). (BL 74:600, 606, 78:594; KR 45:865; LJ 102:2184; Tymn:74)
Holt, 1977, 369 pp., o.p.; Ballantine, 1978, pap.

YA DONALDSON, Stephen R(upert). *The Mirror of Her Dreams* (Mordant's Need series, book 1). Gr. 10 up.
Gerarden, a bumbling young sorcerer, is sent into our world to search for a champion to save the Kingdom of Mordant. He stumbles across Terisa Morgan, who makes the impulsive decision to return to Mordant with the sorcerer. *A Man Rides Through* (1987) is the second volume in the series. (BL 82:1633, 1636, 83:761; KR 54:1326; LJ Nov 15, 1986 p. 112)
Ballantine/Del Rey, 1986, 535 pp.

DOUGLAS, Carole Nelson. *Exiles of the Rynth*. See Chapter 10, Witchcraft and Sorcery Fantasy.

C/YA DRAGT, Tonke. *The Towers of February: A Diary by an Anonymous (for the Time Being) Author with Added Punctuation and Footnotes*. Gr. 5–9. (Orig. pub. in the Netherlands.)
In this science-fantasy, Tim convinces his scientist friend, Mr. Avla, to take him along on a travel experiment to a coexisting world. Once there, however, Tim realizes that he has lost his memory and his name. (BL 72:572, 577; CCBB 29:109; HB 52:163; KR 43:1192; SLJ Jan 1976 p. 45)
Tr. by Maryka Rudnik, Morrow, 1975, 251 pp., o.p.

DUANE, Diane. *So You Want to Be a Wizard*. See Chapter 10, Witchcraft and Sorcery Fantasy.

C DUGGAN, Maurice (Noel). *Falter Tom and the Water Boy*. Gr. 3–5. (Orig. British pub. 1958.)
A sea-boy invites an old sailor named Falter Tom to come and live in the realm of the sea kings. (CCBB 13:112; HB 36:128; LJ 84:3925; TLS 1975 p. 365)
Illus. by Kenneth Rowell, Phillips, 1959, 61 pp.

C DURRELL, Gerald (Malcolm). *The Talking Parcel*. Gr. 4–6. (Orig. British pub. 1974.)
A parrot, a spider, and a toad enlist the help of three children to save Mythologia after fire-breathing Cockatrices steal the books of magic. (BL 71:1127; HB 51:268; KR 43:453; SLJ May 1975 p. 54; TLS 1974 p. 1380)
Illus. by Pamela Johnson, Lippincott, 1975, 191 pp.

C [R] EAGER, Edward (McMaken). *Knight's Castle*. Gr. 4–6.
Roger, Ann, Jack, and Eliza find their way into a mixed-up medieval world where they become knights and battle giants. In the sequel *Time Garden* (1958, Peter Smith, 1985), they return to the past, and in *Half Magic* (1954) and *Magic by the Lake* (1957), their parents have magic adventures as children. (BL 52:281; HB 32:120; KR 23:859; LJ 81:766)
Illus. by N. M. Bodecker, Harcourt, 1956, 183 pp., 1985, pap.; Peter Smith, 1985.

C/YA ENDE, Michael. *The Neverending Story*. Gr. 5 up. (Orig. pub. in Ger-
[R] many.)
A boy named Bastian becomes so engrossed in reading a book about young Atreyu's quest to find a cure for the ailing Empress of Fantasiana, that he enters the book himself, saves Fantasiana, and sets off on his own adventures. (BL 80:488, 496; HB 60:228; KR 51:844; TLS 1983 p. 1317)
Tr. by Ralph Mannheim, illus. by Roswitha Quadflieg, Doubleday, 1983, 396 pp., o.p.; Penguin, 1984, pap.

FARMER, Penelope. *A Castle of Bone*. See Section 5B, Myth Fantasy.

C/YA FARMER (Mockridge), Penelope. *William and Mary: A Story*. Gr. 5–7.
[R] Mary and William find that a rare shell has the power to carry them into an aquarium, back to the fall of Atlantis, and to a world beneath the sea. (BL 71:168; CCBB 28:93; Ch&Bks:266; HB 50:690; KR 42:1160; LJ 99:3052; Suth 2:141; TLS 1974 p. 1380)
Atheneum, 1974, 160 pp., o.p.

C FARTHING, Alison. *The Mystical Beast.* Gr. 4–6. (Orig. British pub. 1976.)
   Sara and Henry enter the Other Side after meeting Lavinia, daughter of
the Hereditary Keeper of the Mystical Beast, and organize a hectic search for
the Beast, to avert a "terrible" occurrence. (CCBB 32:42; SLJ Oct 1978 p.
144; TLS 1976 p. 882)
   Illus. by Anne Mieke, Hastings, 1978, 123 pp., o.p.

FEYDY, Anne. *Osprey Island.* See Chapter 7, Magic Adventure Fantasy.

C FIELD, Rachel Lyman. *Eliza and the Elves.* Gr. 2–4.
   Tales and rhymes about elfin life and the possibility of stumbling into their
green land. (BL 23:136; HB 2[Nov 1925]:42; Mahony 2:279; Moore:130)
   Illus. by Elizabeth MacKinstry, Macmillan, 1926, 96 pp., o.p.

FIELD, Rachel Lyman. *The Magic Pawnshop; a New's Year Eve Fantasy.*
See Chapter 7, Magic Adventure Fantasy.

C FISCHER, Marjorie. *Red Feather.* Gr. 3–5. (Orig. pub. 1937.)
   When the Queen of Fairyland needs a new mortal child to be her maid, she
commands that a fairy child be exchanged for baby Rosemary, but the two
babies look identical and no one can tell them apart. (BL 34:112; CCBB 3:68;
LJ 75:1756, 2085)
   Illus. by Davine, Messner, 1950, 149 pp., o.p.

C/YA FLECKER, (Herman) James Elroy. *The King of Alsander.* Gr. 6–12.
   (Orig. British pub. 1914, U.S. pub. Putnam, 1914.)
   In this tale written by an English poet, Norman Price walks out of a
grocer's shop one day and steps into the legendary white city of Alsander.
(HB 3[May 1927]:18–22)
   Knopf, 1926, 286 pp., o.p.

C/YA FRANCE Anatole (pseud. of Jacques Anatole François Thibault). *Bee,
   the Princess of the Dwarfs* (orig. pub. in France; orig. U.S. title *Honey-
   Bee,* 1911, 1924). Gr. 5–7.
   After she is spirited away by nixies, Honey-Bee is crowned princess of the
dwarfs, but she longs for her home and her playmate, George. (BL 9:40;
Mahony 1:25)
   Tr. by Peter Wright, illus. by Charles Robinson, Dutton, 1912, 127 pp.,
o.p.

C [R] FRY, Rosalie K(ingsmill). *The Mountain Door.* Gr 4–6. (Orig. British
   pub. 1960.)
   Fenella returns to the fairies who once exchanged her for a human baby,
and meets Nell, the girl whose place she took. (BL 57:612; HB 37:269; KR
29:163; LJ 86:1983; TLS Nov 25, 1960 p. x)
   Illus. by the author, Dutton, 1961, 128 pp., o.p.

C GALL, Alice (Crew), and CREW, Fleming. *The Royal Mimkin.* Gr. 3–5.
   Binney and Mr. Tidd board a flying boat to another world. (BL 31:99;
Bookshelf 1934–1935 p. 5; HB 10:298; LJ 60:213; Mahony 3:205)
   Illus. by Camille Masline, Oxford, 1934, 128 pp., o.p.

GARFIELD, Leon. *The Wedding Ghost.* See Chapter 1, Allegorical
Fantasy and Literary Fairy Tales.

C/YA GARNER, Alan. *Elidor.* Gr. 6–8. (Orig. British pub. 1965, U.S. 1967.)
  [R]   Roland, Helen, Nicholas, and David unexpectedly stumble into the medi-

eval kingdom of Elidor, where they promise to protect four treasures from evil beings able to follow them back into twentieth-century England. (BL 63:1099; CC:471; HB 43:462; Kies:28; KR 35:269; LJ 92:2449; TLS 1965 p. 1131; Tymn:89)

Philomel, 1979, o.p.; Ballantine, 1981, pap., 160 pp.

C/YA   GEE, Maurice (Gough). *The Halfmen of O.* Gr. 5–8. (Orig. pub. in New Zealand, 1982.)

Susan and her cousin Nick are chosen to set things right in the Land of O, a country in turmoil ever since the invasion of the murderous Halfmen. (BL 79:1400; SLJ Sept 1983 p. 134; TLS 1982 p. 1302)

Oxford, dist. by Merrimack, 1983, 204 pp., o.p.

C   GEE, Maurice (Gough). *The World Around the Corner.* Gr. 3–6. (Orig. pub. in New Zealand, 1981.)

An old woman tells Caroline that she must keep her magical antique spectacles away from the evil Mr. Grimble. (CCBB 38:25; SLJ Oct 1981 p. 141, Apr 1985 p. 87)

Illus. by Gary Hebley, Oxford; dist. by Merrimack, 1984, 72 pp., o.p.

YA   GENTLE, Mary. *A Hawk in Silver.* Gr. 7–9.

A strange silver coin takes fifteen-year-olds Holly and Chris out of their tension-filled lives at an English school ruled by an abusive gang of girls, and draws them into a magical world where a unicorn helps them stop a bitter war between the hill-dwellers and the sea-people. (BL 81:1050, 1058; CCBB 38:125; SLJ May 1985 p. 100; VOYA 8:138)

Lothrop, 1985, 240 pp.; NAL 1986, pap., o.p.

C/YA   GILMAN (Butters), Dorothy. *The Maze in the Heart of the Castle.* Gr. 6–10.

The sudden deaths of his beloved parents compel sixteen-year-old Colin to undertake a perilous journey through a maze, deep within the castle atop Rheembeck Mountain. (BL 79:1138, 1143; CCBB 36:16; SLJ Dec 1983 p. 66; VOYA 6:214)

Doubleday, 1983, 230 pp.

YA [R]   GORDON, John (William). *The Edge of the World.* Gr. 7–9.

Tension and horror predominate as Tekker and Kit slip back and forth between the fens near their home and a bewitched land at the edge of the world, where they attempt to rescue a woman imprisoned by Ma Grist. (HB 59:581; KR 51:175; SLJ Jan 1984 p. 75; TLS 1983 p. 1047; VOYA 6:343)

Atheneum, 1983, 186 pp.

GOUDGE, Elizabeth. *The Valley of Song.* See Chapter 1, Allegorical Fantasy and Literary Fairy Tales.

C/YA   GOULD, Joan. *Otherborn.* Gr. 6–9.

Shipwrecked on a tropical island called the Land of Light, Mark and Allegra discover the inhabitants' secret: The young people are the tribal elders and the old people are the newborn children. (CCBB 34:53; HB 57:190; SLJ Sept 1980 p. 71; Suth 3:157)

Coward, 1980, 160 pp., o.p.

C/YA   GRAY, Nicholas Stuart. *Grimbold's Other World.* Gr. 5–7. (Orig. British pub. 1963; U.S. Meredith, 1968.)

A goatherd named Muffler gets himself into trouble when he returns to a

world of darkness shown him by Grimbold the cat. (BL 64:1185; KR 36:114; TLS 1963 p. 427)
Illus. by Charles Keeping, Faber, dist. by Merrimack, 1979, o.p.; Ace, 1986, pap., 192 pp.

C/YA GREAVES, Margaret. *The Dagger and the Bird: A Story of Suspense.* Gr.
[R]   4–7. (Orig. British pub. 1971.)
When Bridget and Luke discover that their brother, Simon, is actually a fairy changeling, they journey to the Kingdom of the Good People to find their real brother. (BL 71:618; HB 51:147; KR 43:374; SLJ May 1975 p. 70)
Illus. by Laszlo Kubinyi, Harper, 1975, 144 pp., o.p.

YA [R] GREGORIAN, Joyce Ballou. *The Broken Citadel.* Gr. 7–9.
A shaft of sunlight in an abandoned house takes Sibby into the lands of Tredana and Treclere, where she joins Prince Leron in his fight against Queen Simirimia. The sequels are *Castledown* (1977) and *The Great Wheel* (Tor, 1987). (BL 72:235; HB 52:154; KR 43:782; SLJ Nov 1975 p. 90; Tymn:92)
Illus. by the author, Atheneum, 1975, 373 pp.; Ace, 1982, pap., o.p.

GRIPE, Maria. *The Land Beyond.* See Chapter 1, Allegorical Fantasy and Literary Fairy Tales.

HACKETT, Walter Anthony. *The Swans of Ballycastle.* See Chapter 1, Allegorical Fantasy and Literary Fairy Tales.

YA HAMBLY, Barbara. *The Silent Tower.* Gr. 10 up.
Kidnapped and taken into an alternate world where magic works, Joanna, a young computer programmer, becomes embroiled in the intrigues of the Empire of Perryth. The sequels are *Search the Seven Hills* (1987) and *The Silcon Mage* (1988). (BL 83:550, 571; LJ Dec 1986 p. 142)
Ballantine/Del Rey, 1986, pap., 369 pp.

HENRY, Jan. *Tiger's Chance.* See Chapter 7, Magic Adventure Fantasy.

HILL, Elizabeth Starr. *Ever-After Island.* See Chapter 7, Magic Adventure Fantasy.

YA [R] HILTON, James. *Lost Horizon.* Gr. 8 up. (Orig. pub. 1922.)
Four survivors of a plane crash in Tibet find their way to the lamasery of Shangri-La, an oasis of eternal youth, but they long to return home. (BL 30:79; Kies:36; SHC:608; TLS 1933 p. 648)
Morrow, 1936 (repr. of 1922 ed.), 211 pp.; Pocket, 1984, pap.

HOFFMANN, E. T. A. *The Nutcracker.* See Chapter 9, Toy Fantasy.

C/YA HOWARD, Joan (pseud. of Patricia Gordon). *The Oldest Secret.* Gr. 6–8.
[R]   Clues in an ancient book lead Hugh to an island populated by legendary beings. (BL 50:84; CCBB 7:62; HB 29:362; KR 21:429)
Illus. by Garry MacKenzie, Viking, 1953, 128 pp., o.p.

HOWARD, Joan. *The Thirteenth Is Magic.* See Chapter 7, Magic Adventure Fantasy.

C HOWE, James. *Babes in Toyland.* Gr. 3–5.
In this story based on the libretto of Victor Herbert's 1903 operetta, Jane and Alan survive a shipwreck arranged by their greedy Uncle Barnaby, and escape to Toyland, where they meet Mother Goose characters and are

reunited with their true loves. (BL 83:352; KR 54:1370; SLJ Oct 1986 p. 112)

Illus. by Allen Atkinson, Harcourt, 1986, 96 pp.

C/YA HUNTER, Mollie. *The Haunted Mountain: A Story of Suspense.* Gr. 4–7.
[R]   A stubborn Highlander named MacAllister, enslaved by the fairy folk for refusing to pay a tithe, is rescued by his dog and his son. (BL 68:909; CC:486; CCBB 26:9; HB 48:269; Kies:39; KR 40:401; LJ 97:1928; Suth:203; TLS 1972 p. 1323)

Illus. by Laszlo Kubinyi, Harper, 1972, 1973, pap., 144 pp.

C [R] INGELOW, Jean. *Mopsa the Fairy.* Gr. 4–6. (Orig. U.S. pub. 1869.)
        A boy named Jack crawls into the hollow of an old thorn tree and finds himself in Fairyland. (BL 60:882; Bookshelf 1923–1924, p. 15; HB 3[Aug 1927]:48, 40:377; LJ 26 (no. 8):67; Mahony 2:281; Tymn:98)

Illus. by Dora Curtis and Diana Stanley, Dutton, 1964, 142 pp., o.p.; Garland, 1976 (repr.), o.p.

YA [R] IPCAR, Dahlov (Zorach). *A Dark Horn Blowing.* Gr. 7–10.
        Nora is unwillingly drawn into an unknown world to care for the infant son of a dying queen. (BL 74:1610; KR 46:510; SLJ Nov 1978 p. 82; VOYA 1[Dec 1978]:42, 3[Aug 1980]:55)

Viking, 1978, 228 pp., o.p.

IPCAR, Dahlov. *The Queen of Spells.* See Section 5B, Myth Fantasy.

C/YA JONES, Adrienne. *The Mural Master.* Gr. 5–7.
        Four children follow Til Pleeryn, the mural master, through one of his murals into the land of Pawthania, on a mission to free the captive king. (CCBB 28:44; HB 50:283; LJ 99:2271)

Illus. by David White, Houghton, 1974, 249 pp., o.p.

C/YA JONES, Diana Wynne. *Dogsbody.* Gr. 6–8. (Orig. British pub. 1976.)
[R]   Visiting Earth in search of a sacred object that fell from the sky, Sirius, the Dog Star, takes on a dog's form and befriends a lonely human girl. (BL 73:1414, 1421; CCBB 30:176; HB 53:319; KR 45:95; SLJ May 1977 p. 62; TLS 1976 p. 383; VOYA 2[Aug 1979]:57)

Greenwillow/Morrow, 1977, 242 pp., o.p.

C/YA JONES, Diana Wynne. *A Tale of Time City.* Gr. 6 up.
[R]   After Vivian Smith, age 11, is kidnapped by time travelers who mistake her for the "Time Lady," she plunges from London in 1939 to Time City, where she helps her kidnappers thwart the Time Lady's plans to alter history. (BL 84:569; CCBB 41:31; HB 64:71; KR 55:1158; SLJ Sept 1987 p. 196; TLS 1987 p. 1283; VOYA 10:288, 11:14)

Greenwillow, 1987, 288 pp.

JONES, Terry. *Nicobobinus.* See Chapter 6, Humorous Fantasy.

C/YA JUSTER, Norton. *The Phantom Tollbooth.* Gr. 5–7.
[R]   Finding a boy-sized car and tollbooth in his bedroom, Milo drives off to rescue the lost princesses, Rhyme and Reason, aided by the Spelling Bee and a watchdog named Tock. (CC:490; CCBB 15:112; Ch&Bks:268; LJ 87:332; TLS 1962 p. 892)

Illus. by Jules Feiffer, Random, 1961, hb and pap., 255 pp.

YA KAY, Guy Gavriel. *The Summer Tree.* (Fionavar Tapestry trilogy, book 1). Gr. 10 up.
        Five Canadian college students are summoned into the alternate world of

Fionavar, just as the evil Unraveller escapes its 1000 year imprisonment. These young people are destined to play legendary roles in the coming war against the Dark. The sequels are *The Wandering Fire* (1986) and *The Darkest Road* (1986). (BL 82:4; KR 53:984; LJ Oct 15, 1985 p. 104)

Arbor House, 1985, o.p.; Berkley, 1986, pap., 320 pp.

YA KAYE, Marvin. *The Incredible Umbrella*. Gr. 10 up.

A magic umbrella transports a young Pennsylvania college professor into a number of alternate literary worlds, including the London of Charles Dickens and Sir Arthur Conan Doyle, the Cornwall of Gilbert and Sullivan, and the worlds of the Arabian Nights, Frankenstein, and Flatland. The sequel is *The Amorous Umbrella* (1981). (BL 75:853, 860; LJ 104:213)

Doubleday, 1979, 218 pp., o.p.

C/YA KENEALLY, Thomas (Michael). *Ned Kelly and the City of the Bees*. Gr. 5–7.

Miniaturized by a kindly bee named Apis, Ned Kelly spends his summer recuperating from appendicitis, inside a bee hive. (HB 57:535; KR 49:1160; SLJ Nov 1981 p. 93)

Illus. by Stephen Ryan, Godine, 1981; Avon, 1985, pap., 122 pp.

C [R] KENNEDY, X. J. (pseud. of Joseph Kennedy). *The Owlstone Crown*. Gr. 4–6.

Twins Timothy and Verity Tibb enter the world of Owlstonia in search of their lost grandparents, and, with the help of talking animal friends, also manage to overthrow the villainous dictator. (BL 80:992; CC:429; KR 51:192; SLJ Jan 1984 p. 78)

Illus. by Michele Chessare, Atheneum, 1983, 210 pp.; Bantam/Skylark, 1985, pap.

C/YA KEY, Alexander (Hill). *The Forgotten Door*. Gr. 5–7.

Falling from another world into a remote mountain town, Jon's mind-reading ability generates fear and greed in the villagers who find him. (CCBB 18:151; HB 41:392; KR 33:117; LJ 90:972; TLS 1966 p. 449)

Westminster, 1965, 126 pp., o.p.; Scholastic, 1968, pap.

YA KING, Stephen, and STRAUB, Peter. *The Talisman*. Gr. 10 up.

As twelve-year-old Jack Sawyer travels cross-country from California, searching for a magic stone to save his mother's life, he visits the Territories, an alternate-past world where another woman's life is in danger. (BL 81:686, 708; KR 52:771; LJ 109:2080; SLJ Jan 1985 p. 92; VOYA 8:49)

Viking, 1984; Berkley, 1985, pap., 784 pp.

KINGSLEY, Charles. *The Water Babies: A Fairy Tale for a Land Baby*. See Chapter 1, Allegorical Fantasy and Literary Fairy Tales.

YA KROPP, Lloyd. *The Drift*. Gr. 10 up.

Becalmed in the Sargasso Sea, Peter Sutherland discovers an unknown ship-dwelling community called The Drift, whose inhabitants welcome him lovingly and urge him to stay. (BL 65:997, 1069; LJ 94:1162; TLS 1969 p. 910)

Doubleday, 1969, 240 pp., o.p.; Leisure, 1979, pap.

C KRÜSS, James (Jacob Hinrich). *The Happy Islands behind the Winds*. Gr. 3–6. (Orig. German pub. 1959.)

Captain Madirankowitsch and his crew discover an island paradise governed by talking animals. The sequel is *Return to the Happy Islands* (1967). (KR 34:1097; LJ 91:5750)

Tr. by Edelgard Brühl, illus. by Eberhart Binder-Strassfurt, Atheneum, 1966, 153 pp., o.p.

YA KUTTNER, Henry. *The Startling Worlds of Henry Kuttner.* Gr. 10 up.
Three novellas about people who travel to alternate worlds: "The Portal in the Picture," "Valley of the Flame" (orig. pub. Ace, 1964), and "The Dark World." (BL 83:550, 571; VOYA 10:130)
Warner/Popular Library, 1987, pap., 357 pp.

C LAMPMAN, Evelyn Sibley. *The City under the Back Steps.* Gr. 4–6.
After they insult the Queen ant, Craig and Jill dwindle to insect size and are put to work in the ant colony. (HB 36:510; KR 28:816; LJ 85:4567)
Illus. by Honoré Valintcourt, Doubleday, 1960, 210 pp., o.p.

LANGTON, Jane. *The Diamond in the Window.* See Chapter 7, Magic Adventure Fantasy.

LAWRENCE, Louise. *Star Lord.* See Section 5B, Myth Fantasy.

YA [R] LE GUIN, Ursula K(roeber). *The Beginning Place.* Gr. 8 up.
Irene resents Hugh's intrusion into the otherworld she has found, but the two unhappy young people are drawn together on their quest to destroy a terrible beast. (BL 76:756, 77:621, 1148; CCBB 34:14; Ch&Bks:269; HB 56:333; JHC:389; KR 47:1393, 1437; LJ 105:227; SHC:616; SLJ Apr 1980 p. 132; Suth 3:259; VOYA 3[Feb 1981]:38)
Harper, 1980, 183 pp.

C/YA LEWIS, C(live) S(taples). *The Lion, the Witch, and the Wardrobe* (The
[O] Chronicles of Narnia, book 1). Gr. 4–7. (Orig. British pub. 1951.)
The White Witch casts a spell over the land of Narnia, ensnaring Edmund, and drawing Susan, Peter, and Lucy into Narnia too, where they join the great lion Aslan's struggle to break the witch's enchantment. Lewis felt that the Narnia series ought to be read in the following order: first, *The Magician's Nephew* (1955; 1970; 1986, pap.), in which young Digory and Polly borrow his sorcerer-uncle's magic rings and are transported to Narnia, just as Aslan is singing it into existance. Many years later, four children exploring the now-elderly Digory's house, stumble through a magic wardrobe into Narnia, in *The Lion, the Witch, and the Wardrobe* (1951; 1983; 1986, pap.). In *The Horse and His Boy* (1954; 1986, pap.), two children and their talking horses flee into Narnia: Shasta to escape imprisonment and Aravis to avoid an unwanted marriage. In *Prince Caspian: The Return to Narnia* (1951; 1986, pap.) Lucy, Edmund, Susan, and Peter help Aslan save Prince Caspian from his murderous uncle and restore him to the throne of Narnia. In *The Voyage of the Dawn Treader* (1952; 1986, pap.), Edmund, Lucy, their cousin Eustace, and Prince Caspian sail to World's End aboard the Dawn Treader, in search of seven missing noblemen. In *The Silver Chair* (1953; 1986, pap.) Aslan sends Eustace and Jill on a quest to free King Caspian's missing son, Prince Rilian, from an enchantment, and bring him back to Narnia. In the final volume of this series, *The Last Battle* (1956; 1986, pap.), Aslan calls on all creatures who believe in and love Narnia, to return for the final battle against the forces of evil. *The Last Battle* won the Carnegie Medal, 1956. (BL 47:208, 80:96, 683; CC:498; CCBB 4:35; Ch&Bks:231; HB 27:54; JHC:391; KR 18:514; LJ 75:1756; SLJ Jan 1984 p. 79; Tymn:120–126)
Illus. by Pauline Baynes, Macmillan, 1951; illus. by Michael Hague, Macmillan, 1983, 183 pp.; Macmillan/Collier, 1986, pap.; boxed set of *The Chronicles of Narnia,* Macmillan/Collier, 1986, pap.

C LINDBERGH, Anne (Morrow Spencer). *Bailey's Window.* Gr. 4–6.
Anna, Carl, and their friend, Ingrid, are astonished to be able to step through a picture drawn by Anna's obnoxious cousin, Bailey, and have magical adventures visiting the past, a forest, and a carnival. (BL 80:1250; CCBB 37:208; SLJ May 1984 p. 82)
Illus. by Kinuko Craft, Harcourt, 1984, 115 pp.

C LINDGREN, Astrid. *Mio, My Son.* Gr. 4–6. (Orig. pub. in Sweden.)
After a genii carries Mio away from his unhappy foster home, he is adopted by the King of Faraway Land. (BL 53:304; KR 24:868; LJ 82:588)
Tr. by Marianne Turner, illus. by Ilon Wikland, Viking, 1956, 179 pp., o.p.

C/YA LINKLATER, Eric (Robert Russell). *The Pirates in the Deep Green Sea.*
[R]   Gr. 5–7.
Two boys travel beneath the sea to enlist the aid of Davy Jones in their battle with pirates. (BL 46:52; HB 25:411; KR 17:324; LJ 74:1105, 1542; TLS July 15, 1949 p. iii)
Illus. by William Reeves, Macmillan, 1949, 398 pp., o.p.

LITTLE, Jane. *Sneaker Hill.* See Chapter 10, Witchcraft and Sorcery Fantasy.

LOFTING, Hugh. *The Story of Doctor Dolittle.* See Chapter 6, Humorous Fantasy.

YA *Lost Worlds, Unknown Horizons: Nine Stories of Science Fiction.* Ed. by Robert Silverberg. Grade 10 up.
Nine stories of adventure in other-worlds, whose authors include Jack Finney, Edgar Allan Poe, H. G. Wells, and Robert Silverberg. (BL 75:745; KR 46:976, 1077; SLJ Apr 1979 p. 72; VOYA 2[June 1979]:48)
Nelson, 1978, 192 pp., o.p.

LOVEJOY, Jack. *The Rebel Witch.* See Chapter 10, Witchcraft and Sorcery Fantasy.

MacDONALD, George. *At the Back of the North Wind.* See Chapter 1, Allegorical Fantasy and Literary Fairy Tales.

MacDONALD, George. *The Golden Key.* See Chapter 1, Allegorical Fantasy and Literary Fairy Tales.

McGOWEN, Tom. *Odyssey from River Bend.* See Section 2B, Talking Animal Fantasy.

C McHARGUE, Georgess. *Elidor and the Golden Ball.* Gr. 3–4.
Elidor breaks the Faeries' trust when he steals a magic ball to prove to his mother that he really had lived with them. (BL 70:388; KR 41:1036; LJ 99:201)
Illus. by Emanuel Schoengut, Dodd, 1973, 61 pp., o.p.

C/YA McKENZIE, Ellen Kindt. *Drujienna's Harp.* Gr. 5–8.
A San Francisco curio shop is the entrance to the terror-ridden land of T'Pahl, where Tha and Duncan attempt to topple a tyrant from power. (BL 67:908; CCBB 25:12; HB 47:614; KR 39:434; LJ 96:1814)
Dutton, 1971, 305 pp., o.p.

C/YA McNEILL (Alexander), Janet. *Tom's Tower.* Gr. 5–7. (Orig. British pub. 1965.)
Tom is unexpectedly summoned into an unfamiliar world where he must

protect the king's treasure from two corrupt courtiers. (HB 43:464; KR 35:132; TLS 1965 p. 513)

Illus. by Mary Russon, Little, 1967, 182 pp., o.p.

C/YA MAGUIRE, Gregory. *The Daughter of the Moon.* Gr. 5–7.

Unhappy living with her stepmother in Chicago, Erikka is drawn into a watercolor painting of Canaan Lake, New York. (CCBB 33:219; HB 56:299; KR 48:585; SLJ May 1980 p. 69)

Farrar, 1980, 257 pp.

MASEFIELD, John. *The Midnight Folk: A Novel.* See Chapter 7, Magic Adventure Fantasy.

C/YA MAYNE, William. *All the King's Men.* Gr. 5 up. (Orig. British pub.
[R] 1982.)

Three unusual stories, including one fantasy: "Boy to Island," about two people captured by fairies in the west of Scotland. (CCBB 41:142; KR 56:203; SLJ Apr 1988 p. 103; TLS 1982 p. 788; VOYA 11:96)

Delacorte, 1988, 192 pp.

YA MERRITT, A(braham P.). *The Ship of Ishtar.* Gr. 10 up.

An ancient Babylonian stone sends John Kenton from New York City into an alternate world aboard the magical ship of Ishtar, where he falls in love with the princess Sharane and helps her to battle the Ruler of the Dead. (TLS 1926 p. 397; Tymn:140)

Illus. by Virgil Finlay, Borden, 1924, 1949, 309 pp., o.p.; Avon, 1926, 1951, 1966, pap.

C [R] MOLESWORTH, Mary Louisa (Stewart). *The Cuckoo Clock.* Gr. 4–6.

(Orig. British pub. 1877; U.S. Dutton, 1954.)

The cuckoo in Griselda's new home takes her through its clock into a magical land. The sequel is *A Christmas Child* (1880). (BL 18:95, 22:77, 27:216, 36:118, 51:48; Bookshelf 1932 p. 2; HB 1[June 1925]:32, 2[Nov 1925]:29; HB 3[May 1927]:17–22, 30:324, 344; 38:66; Mahony 2:291)

Illus. by Ernest Shepard, Dent, dist. by Biblio, 1974 (repr. of 1954 ed.); Garland, 1976 (bound with *The Tapestry Room*); illus. by Ernest Shepard, Peter Smith, 1980, 208 pp.; Dell/Yearling, 1987, pap.

YA MONACO, Richard. *Journey to the Flame.* Gr. 10 up.

British and German forces set out to discover the secrets of the lost city of Kôr, while World War I begins in Europe. This is a contemporary sequel to Sir H(enry) Rider Haggard's *She* (1886, 1911, 1961, 1976), *Ayesha, the Return of She* (1905, 1912), *She and Allan* (1920, 1931), and *Wisdom's Daughter* (1923). (Kies:55; LJ Nov 15, 1985, p. 112)

Bantam, 1985, pap., 203 pp., o.p.

C/YA MOON, Sheila (Elizabeth). *Knee-Deep in Thunder.* Gr. 6–9.
[R] A blue-green stone takes Maris to the Great Land, where she and her animal companions capture savage beasts that were terrifying the people. Maris returns to the Great Land in *Hunt Down the Prize* (1971). (BL 64:503; CCBB 21:98; HB 43:589; KR 35:968; LJ 92:3853; Suth:285)

Illus. by Peter Parnall, Atheneum, 1967, o.p.; Guild for Psychological Studies, 1986, pap., 307 pp.

YA MUNDY, Talbot. *OM, The Secret of Abhor Valley.* Gr. 10 up.

A young English adventurer in India during the 1920s sets out to find a piece of jade with supernatural powers and the hidden valley inhabited by a holy lama who can reveal the secrets of the universe. (BL 21:234; Kies:56; TLS 1925 p. 57)

Crown, 1924, o.p.; Point Loma, 1980, pap.; Amereon, repr. of 1924 ed.; Carroll, 1984, pap., 392 pp.

YA MYERS, John Myers. *Silverlock.* Gr. 10 up.

A young man shipwrecked in a land called the Commonwealth finds it to be populated by characters from classical literature, including Beowulf, Robin Hood, and Don Quixote. The sequel is *The Moon's Fire-Eating Daughter* (Donning, 1981). (BL 46:48; KR 17:310; LJ 74:1095)

Lippincott, 1949, o.p.; Ace, 1966, 1979, 1984, pap., 544 pp.

NASTICK, Sharon. *Mr. Radagast Makes an Unexpected Journey.* See Chapter 6, Humorous Fantasy.

NATHAN, Robert. *The Snowflake and the Starfish.* See Chapter 10, Witchcraft and Sorcery Fantasy.

C/YA NESBIT (Bland), E(dith). *The Magic City.* Gr. 5–7. (Orig. British pub. 1910; U.S. Coward, 1960.)

Awakening in the middle of the night, Philip finds himself in a city made of books, blocks, and toys. (BL 57:32; HB 36:309; LJ 85:3224)

Illus. by H. R. Millar, Gregg, 1981, 333 pp., o.p.

NESBIT, E. *Wet Magic.* See Chapter 7, Magic Adventure Fantasy.

C/YA NICHOLS, (Joanna) Ruth. *The Marrow of the World.* Gr. 5–7. (Orig. pub. in Canada.)

Summoned into another world by her dying half-sister, Linda is ordered to bring back the essence of life, in exchange for her freedom. (BL 69:717; KR 40:1191; LJ 98:262; Tymn:148)

Illus. by Trina Schart Hyman, Atheneum, 1972, 168 pp., o.p.

C/YA NICHOLS, (Joanna) Ruth. *A Walk out of the World.* Gr. 5–7. (Orig.
[R]   pub. in Canada.)

Judith and her brother, Tobit, follow a strange light into a world once ruled by their ancestors, where they mastermind a plot to overthrow the hated King Hagerrak. (BL 65:1178; CC:512; CCBB 22:180; HB 45:412; KR 37:304; LJ 94:2677)

Illus. by Trina Schart Hyman, Harcourt, 1969, o.p.; Ace, 1986, pap., 144 pp.

C/YA NORTH, Joan. *The Light Maze.* Gr. 6–9.
[R]   Kit Elting uses a circular medieval ornament called a Lightstone to enter the light maze and set Tom Nancarrow free. (BL 68:392; CCBB 26:12; HB 48:156; KR 39:1132; LJ 96:4192; Suth:297; TLS 1972 p. 1329)

Farrar, 1971, 185 pp., o.p.

YA NORTON, Andre (pseud. of Alice Mary Norton). *Here Abide Monsters.* Gr. 7–9.

Nick and Linda stumble into legendary Avalon where they become fugitives hunted by dangerous demons and mythical beasts. (BL 70:485; JHC:400; KR 41:760; LJ 98:3708)

Atheneum, 1974, o.p.; Tor, dist. by St. Martin, 1985, pap., 256 pp.

YA   NORTON, Andre (pseud. of Alice Mary Norton). *Knave of Dreams*. Gr. 7 up.
After crossing into a parallel world called Ulad, Ramsey Kimble becomes Kaskar, doomed son of the late emperor. (BL 72:294; KR 43:856; SLJ Nov 1975 p. 94; TLS 1976 p. 1242)
Viking, 1975, 252 pp., o.p.; Ace, 1980, pap.

YA   NORTON, Andre (pseud. of Alice Mary Norton). *Operation Time Search*. Gr. 7–10.
Ray Osborne is caught up in the conflict between the peoples of Atlantis and Mu after he steps from 1980s America through a time-space opening into an alternate world. (BL 64:442; HB 43:760; KR 35:747; LJ 92:3202)
Harcourt, 1967, o.p.; Fawcett, 1981, pap.; Ballantine, 1985, pap., 224 pp.

C/YA   NORTON, Andre (pseud. of Alice Mary Norton). *Steel Magic*. Gr. 5–7.
[R]   Eric, Sara, and Greg Lowry enter Avalon through a miniature castle, and search for Arthur's sword and Merlin's ring in order to save the land from evil. (CCBB 19:151; HB 41:629; LJ 90:5519; TLS 1967 p. 451; Tymn:152)
Illus. by Robin Jacques, World, 1965, 155 pp., o.p.

YA [R]   NORTON, Andre (pseud. of Alice Mary Norton). *Witch World* (Witch World series, vol. 1; Simon Tregarth sequence, Book 1). Gr. 8 up.
Simon Tregarth escapes from his post-World War II pursuers through a dimension portal into Estcarp, where the Witches use magic to battle their enemies. This book and the first five sequels listed below are called the Simon Tregarth sequence: *Web of the Witch World* (Ace, 1964; Gregg, 1977), *Three Against the Witch World* (Ace, 1965, pap.; Gregg, 1977), *Warlock of the Witch World* (Ace, 1967, pap.; Gregg, 1977), *Sorceress of the Witch World* (Ace, 1968, pap.; Gregg, 1977), and *Spell of the Witch World* (DAW, 1972, pap.; Gregg, 1977). The following are related books: *Year of the Unicorn* (Ace, 1965, pap.; Gregg, 1977), *The Crystal Gryphon* (Atheneum, 1972; Tor, 1985); *The Jargoon Pard* (Atheneum, 1974; Fawcett, 1978, pap.; Ballantine, 1986, pap.), *Trey of Swords* (Grosset, 1977; Ace, 1983, pap.), *Zarsthor's Bane* (Ace, 1978), *Horn Crown* (NAL/DAW, 1981, 1985, pap.), *Gryphon in Glory* (Atheneum, 1981; Ballantine, 1983, pap.), *'Ware Hawk* (Atheneum, 1983; Ballantine, 1984; pap.), *Gryphon's Eyrie* (Tor, 1984; 1985, pap.) by Andre Norton and A(nn) C(arol) Crispin, *Lore of the Witch World* (DAW, 1987), and *Gate of the Cat* (Ace, 1987). *Tales of the Witch World* (St. Martin, 1987) and *Tales of the Witch World, 2* (St. Martin, 1988) are anthologies of short stories by authors other than Norton. (JHC:401; SLJ 1977 p. 153; Tymn:149–152)
Ace, 1963, pap. o.p.; Gregg, 1977, 222 pp., o.p.

YA   NORTON, Andre (pseud. of Alice Mary Norton). *Wraiths of Time*. Gr. 7–12.
Radiation from a curious artifact thrusts Tallahassee Mitford into the Nubian kingdom of Meroë, where she takes on the memories and powers of Princess Ashake to battle evil forces from another world. (BL 73:138, 180; CCBB 30:96; Ch&Bks:270; KR 44:740; SLJ Oct 1976 p. 120; Suth 2:338)
Atheneum, 1976, 210 pp., o.p.; Fawcett, 1987, pap.

C   NORTON, Mary (Pearson). *Are All the Giants Dead?* Gr. 4–6.
James goes on a guided tour of fairy-tale land where he battles a giant to save Princess Dulcibel from an ill-fated marriage to a frog. (BL 72:627;

CCBB 29:129; HB 51:465; KR 43:1131; SLJ Sept 1975 p. 107; TLS 1975 p. 1053)
Illus. by Brian Froud, Harcourt, 1975, 123 pp., 1978, pap.

C/YA O'BRIEN, Robert C. (pseud. of Robert Leslie Conly). *The Silver Crown.* Gr. 5–8.
Ellen's bejeweled crown saves her from death by fire but endangers her life because of its potential for overthrowing the terrible Hieronymus Machine. (HB 44:174; LJ 93:1802; TLS 1973 p. 1115)
Illus. by Dale Payson, Atheneum, 1968, o.p., 1973, pap., 247 pp.

C/YA O'HANLON (Meek), Jacklyn. *The Door.* Gr. 5–8.
Rachel steps through "The Door" into a frightening world populated by the captives of Burt Pelf. (CCBB 32:49; KR 46:498; SLJ Apr 1978 p. 87)
Dial, 1978, 76 pp., o.p.

C PALMER, Mary. *The Dolmop of Dorkling.* Gr. 3–5.
On Dorkling Island, Stafford trains the watermelon-armed navy and is proclaimed king. (BL 64:335; CCBB 21:31; KR 35:652; LJ 92:2454)
Illus. by Fen Lasell, Houghton, 1967, 155 pp., o.p.

PATTEN, Brian. *Mr. Moon's Last Case.* See Chapter 7, Magic Adventure Fantasy.

PAYNE, Joan Balfour. *Magnificent Milo.* See Chapter 7, Magic Adventure Fantasy.

PINKWATER, D. Manus. *Lizard Music.* See Chapter 6, Humorous Fantasy.

C/YA POPE, Elizabeth. *The Perilous Gard.* Gr. 6–9.
[O] The centuries-old spell surrounding the castle of Perilous Gard envelops Kate Sutton when she is enslaved by the Fairy Folk. Newbery Medal Honor Book, 1975. (BL 70:1201; CC:520; HB 50:287; Kies:60; KR 42:433; LJ 99:1484)
Illus. by Richard Cuffari, Houghton, 1974, 280 pp.; Ace, 1984, pap., o.p.

C POSTMA, Lidia. *The Stolen Mirror.* Gr. 1–4. (Orig. pub. in the Netherlands.)
A magical bicycle takes Michael into a world of wizards, fairies, and a dragon. (BL 72:1468; CCBB 30:29; KR 44:532; SLJ Feb 1977 p. 58)
Illus. by the author, McGraw-Hill, 1976, 26 pp.

C PYLE, Howard. *The Garden behind the Moon: A Real Story of the Moon Angel.* Gr. 3–5. (Orig. U.S. pub. 1895.)
Davy follows the moonpath all the way to the moon. (Bookshelf 1921–1922 p. 15; Mahony 2:292)
Illus. by the author, Scribner, 1929, 192 pp., o.p.

C PYLE, Howard. *Twilight Land.* Gr. 5–6. (Orig. U.S. pub. 1894.)
The narrator visits Mother Goose's Inn, where he meets a number of well-known fairy tale characters, each of whom tells a tale. (Mahony 2:292; TLS 1968 p. 1120)
Illus. by the author, Harper, 1922, o.p.; Peter Smith, 1968 (repr. of 1894 ed.), 437 pp.

C REEVES, James (pseud. of John Morris Reeves). *The Strange Light*. Gr.
      4–6. (Orig. British pub. 1964.)
      Christina finds her way into a land whose occupants are characters in as yet
      unwritten books. (BL 63:491; CCBB 20:97; KR 34:689; LJ 91:5237; TLS
      1964 p. 602)
      Illus. by J. C. Kocsis, Rand, 1966, 152 pp., o.p.

C RHYS, Mimpsey. *Mr. Hermit Crab: A Tale for Children by a Child*. Gr.
      4–6.
      In this story written by a fourteen-year-old girl, ten-year-olds Lucia and
      Louisa enter a world of danger and enchantment. (BL 26:208; HB 5[Nov
      1929]:52–53; Mahony 3:413; Moore:30, 427)
      Illus. by Helen Sewell, Macmillan, 1929, 190 pp., o.p.

C RILEY, Louise. *Train for Tiger Lily*. Gr. 4–6. (Orig. Canadian pub.
      1954.)
      A magical train takes five children to Tiger Lily, where wishes are granted
      by a Master of Magic. Winner, Canadian Library Association Best Book of
      the Year for Children, 1956. The sequel is *A Spell at Scoggin's Crossing*
      (1960). (BL 51:117; KR 22:485; LJ 79:916, 80:192)
      Illus. by Christine Price, Viking, 1954, 186 pp., o.p.

YA ROSENBERG, Joel. *The Sleeping Dragon* (The Guardians of the Flame
      series, vol. 1). Gr. 10 up.
      Seven students engaged in a role-playing board game are transferred into
      their game world and must find their way home. The series continues with
      The Sword and the Chain (NAL, 1984) and *The Silver Crown* (1985). (Kliatt
      18[Winter 1984]:24; LJ 108:1976; VOYA 7:102)
      Signet/NAL, 1983, 1987, 256 pp.

C/YA RUBIN, Amy Kateman. *Children of the Seventh Prophecy*. Gr. 5–7.
      Alice and Bernard are recruited by Klig, a troll prince-child, to help outwit
      the evil Unking who is plotting to take control of both human and troll
      worlds. (BL 77:1449; CCBB 35:56; KR 49:801; SLJ Sept 1981 p. 129; VOYA
      4[Oct 1981]:44)
      Warne, 1981, 178 pp.

C/YA RUFFELL, Ann. *Pyramid Power*. Gr. 6–9.
      The mail-order pyramid with "magical powers" transports Martin into a
      dream world where he learns to cope with a potential stepfather he dislikes.
      (CCBB 35:36; SLJ Feb 1983 p. 82; TLS 1982 p. 345)
      Watts, 1981, 159 pp., o.p.

   RUSH, Alison. *The Last of Danu's Children*. See Section 5B, Myth
   Fantasy.

YA SABERHAGEN, Fred. *Pyramids*. Gr. 10 up.
      Tom Scheffler is transported to an alternate ancient Egypt whose gods are
      living beings. The sequel is *After the Fact* (1987). (BL 83:550, 571; VOYA
      10:93)
      Baen, dist. by Simon, 1987, pap., 311 pp.

   SAINT-EXUPÉRY, Antoine de. *The Little Prince*. See Chapter 1,
   Allegorical Fantasy and Literary Fairy Tales.

C/YA SCOTT, Evelyn. *Witch Perkins: A Story of the Kentucky Hills*. Gr. 6–8.
      A sinister witch in the shape of a white cat arrives at Ella's house and takes

her into a frightening dream world. (HB 5[Nov 1929]:30–33; Mahony 3:404; Moore:93)

Illus. by Vera Clare, Holt, 1929, 322 pp., o.p.

SIMAK, Clifford D. *Enchanted Pilgrimage.* See Chapter 1, Allegorical Fantasy and Literary Fairy Tales.

C/YA SINGER, Marilyn. *Horsemaster.* Gr. 6–9.

After dreaming of flight on a winged horse, Jessica is thrust into another world to become the protector of an ancient tapestry needed by the next Horsemaster to rule the war-torn land. (BL 81:1390, 1406; SLJ Sept 1985 p. 149; VOYA 8:194)

Atheneum, 1985, 179 pp.

SLEATOR, William. *Among the Dolls.* See Chapter 9, Toy Fantasy.

C/YA SMITH, L(isa) J. *Night of the Solstice.* Gr. 5–8.

Claudia, Alys, Charles, and Janie travel into the Wildworld to free the sorceress Morgana and battle an evil magician bent on enslaving our world. (CCBB 41:125; HB 64:212; KR 55:1397; SLJ Jan 1988 p. 76; VOYA 10:292)

Macmillan, 1987, 231 pp.

YA STASHEFF, Christopher. *Her Majesty's Wizard.* Gr. 10 up.

Reading a runic verse plunges Matt into an alternate world where he helps Princess Alisande to regain her throne. (BL 83:192, 220; LJ Oct 15, 1986 p. 114)

Ballantine/Del Rey, 1986, pap., 342 pp.

C STEARNS, Pamela (Fujimoto). *Into the Painted Bear Lair.* Gr. 4–6.

A visit to a toy store takes Gregory into a fairy-tale kingdom where a hungry bear and a knight help him rescue a princess from a dragon and awaken an enchanted prince. (BL 73:670; CCBB 30:133; HB 53:164; KR 44:1170; SLJ Dec 1976 p. 56)

Illus. by Ann Strugnell, Houghton, 1976, 153 pp., o.p.

C/YA STEPHENS, James. *In the Land of Youth.* Gr. 5–7. (Orig. pub. Macmillan, 1924.)

In the first of two tales retold from Irish folklore, Nera enters the Land of Faery on All Hallows' Eve, and in the second, Etain, the beautiful wife of Midir, is abducted and returned. (BL 21:199)

Century Bookbindery, 1980 (repr. of 1924 ed.), 304 pp.

STEWART, Mary. *Ludo and the Star Horse.* See Chapter 1, Allegorical Fantasy and Literary Fairy Tales.

STORR, Catherine. *Thursday.* See Section 5B, Myth Fantasy.

YA STRAUSS, Victoria. *Worldstone.* Gr. 7–12.

Alexina Taylor, orphaned and unhappy in her exile from New York City, discovers that she has psychic powers when a thief from another world links minds with her, enabling his escape into our world. (BL 82:398, 415; CCBB 39:159; SLJ Jan 1986 p. 75)

Macmillan, 1985, 324 pp.

C/YA SWAHN, Sven. *The Island through the Gate.* Gr. 6–8. (Orig. pub. in Sweden.)

Stranded on the isolated island of Oberair, Michael is prevented from

leaving by the superstitious islanders and their leader, Gourven the sorcerer. (BL 70:1059; HB 50:154; KR 42:187; LJ 99:2279)
Tr. by Patricia Crampton, Macmillan, 1974, 183 pp., o.p.

C/YA SWIFT, Jonathan. *Gulliver's Travels into Several Remote Nations of the*
[R]   *World.* Gr. 5 up. (Orig. British pub. 1726.)
In these editions adapted for young people, Gulliver is shipwrecked on an island of miniature people called Lilliput and then travels to Brobdingnag, Land of Giants. A contemporary sequel is *Castaways in Lilliput* by Henry Winterfeld (Harcourt, 1960; see this section). (BL 44:118, 45:145, 80:817; Bookshelf 1932 p. 23; CC:537; CCBB 2[May 1949]:6, 3:19; HB 1[Nov 1924]:8, 39:604; JHC 420; Mahony 2:297; SHC:638; SLJ Jan 1984 p. 82)
Illus. by Arthur Rackham, Dutton, 1957, o.p.; adapt. by Padraic Colum, illus. by Willy Pogany, Macmillan, 1962, o.p.; Penguin, 1967, pap.; ed. Ronald Storer, Oxford, 1972, pap.; Dent, dist. by Biblio, 1978 (repr. of 1952 ed.), 1984, pap.; illus. by David Small, Morrow, 1983, 94 pp.; NAL, pap.; illus. by Arthur Rackham, Outlet Book, n.d.

TARN, Sir William Woodthorpe. *Treasure of the Isle of Mist: A Tale of the Isle of Skye.* See Chapter 7, Magic Adventure Fantasy.

TOLKIEN, J. R. R. *Smith of Wootton Major.* See Chapter 1, Allegorical Fantasy and Literary Fairy Tales.

TOWNE, Mary. *Goldenrod.* See Chapter 7, Magic Adventure Fantasy.

TREGARTHEN, Enys. *The White Ring.* See Section 5B, Myth Fantasy.

C TROTT, Susan. *The Sea Serpent of Horse.* Gr. 4–6.
A young girl must choose between staying forever in an undersea world or returning to her unhappy life on land. (BL 70:546; KR 41:1045, 1358; LJ 99:577)
Illus. by Irene Burns, Little, 1973, 117 pp., o.p.

C TURNER, Nancy Byrd. *Zodiac Town: The Rhymes of Amos and Ann.* Gr. 3–5.
A rhyming story about a trip to Zodiac Town. (BL 18:93; LJ 47:869)
Illus. by Winifred Bromhall, Little, 1921, 131 pp., o.p.

C WALKER, Gwen. *The Golden Stile.* Gr. 4–6.
On the Golden Stile leading to the moon, Noel meets a little man who grants his wishes for adventure. (HB 34:479; KR 26:606; LJ 83:3304)
Illus. by C. Walter Hodges, Day, 1958, 188 pp., o.p.

C/YA WELLS, Rosemary. *Through the Hidden Door.* Gr. 6–9.
[R]   Barney Pennimen, target of the roughest boys in his private school, refuses to quit, because he and his friends have discovered a hidden cave housing the remains of a civilization of miniature people who lived hundreds of thousands of years ago. (BL 83:1296, 84:873, 1250; CCBB 40:220; HB 63:474; KR 55:728; SLJ Apr 1987 p. 114; VOYA 10:284)
Dial, dist. by Dutton, 1987, 256 pp.

C WERSBA, Barbara. *The Land of Forgotten Beasts.* Gr. 3–5.
Scientifically minded Andrew is magically transported to a land of mythical beasts who are doomed because people no longer believe in them. (HB 40:499; KR 32:651; LJ 89:3477; TLS 1965 p. 1130)
Illus. by Margot Tomes, Atheneum, 1964, 88 pp., o.p.

YA WHEELER, Thomas. *Loose Chippings*. Gr. 7–10.
Stranded after his car breaks down in the village of Loose Chippings, Bob Vickery finds the town to be full of secrets. (BL 66:50; KR 37:247; LJ 94:1802)
Phillips, 1969, 190 pp.

YA WHEELER, Thomas. *Lost Threshold: A Novel*. Gr. 8–10.
His father's disappearance brings James MacGregor into another world, where he leads an uprising against the tyrants in power and finds himself a wife. (BL 65:167; KR 36:467; LJ 93:3328)
Phillips, 1968, 189 pp.

C WHITE, Eliza Orne. *The Enchanted Mountain*. Gr. 3–5.
Four children are taken to an enchanted mountain where they learn to be polite and industrious. (BL 8:183; HB 3:17–22)
Illus. by E. Pollak Ottendorff, Houghton, 1911, 107 pp., o.p.

C/YA WICKENDEN, Dan. *The Amazing Vacation*. Gr. 5–7.
[R] Cousin Emmeline sends Ricky and Joanna through a magic window to search for her lost turquoise gem stone. (BL 53:230; HB 32:352; KR 24:475; LJ 82:230)
Illus. by Erik Blegvad, Harcourt, 1956, 216 pp., o.p.

C WILLARD, Nancy. *Sailing to Cythera, and Other Anatole Stories* (Anatole trilogy, book 1). Gr. 3–5.
Three stories about a boy named Anatole and his journeys to magical lands, including one tale in which he enters the wallpaper of his bedroom to meet the Blimlim. The sequels are *The Island of the Grass King: The Further Adventures of Anatole* (1979) and *Uncle Terrible: More Adventures of Anatole* (1982). (BL 71:573; CC:546; KR 43:19; LJ 99:2281)
Illus. by David McPhail, Harcourt, 1974, o.p., 1985, pap., 72 pp.

C/YA WILLIAMS, Jay. *The Hero from Otherwhere*. Gr. 5–7.
Jesse and Rich, sent to the principal's office for fighting, end up instead in the kingdom of Gwyliath, charged with finding a magic rope to shackle the fiendish wolf, Fenris. (BL 69:407; CCBB 26:99; KR 40:1193; LJ 98:1399)
Walck, 1972, 175 pp., o.p.

YA [R] WILLIAMS, Thomas (Alonzo). *Tsuga's Children*. Gr. 10 up.
Arn and Jen are two young children who find their way into a mythical valley beyond a waterfall, where they are taken in by Tsuga, leader of a peace-loving tribe. (BL 73:1327; KR 45:245; LJ 102:1046; SLJ Oct 1977 p. 130)
Random, 1977, 239 pp., o.p.

C/YA WINTERFELD, Henry. *Castaways in Lilliput*. Gr. 5–7. (Orig. German
[R] pub. 1958.)
Two hundred and fifty years after Gulliver's visit, the Lilliputians are again alarmed by the appearance of giants: three human children whose raft accidentally drifted to Lilliput. (BL 56:577; Eakin:355; HB 36:292; LJ 85:2484)
Tr. by Kyrill Schabert, illus. by William Hutchinson, Harcourt, 1960, 188 pp., o.p.

C [R] WINTHROP (Mahony), Elizabeth. *The Castle in the Attic*. Gr. 4–6.
Angry at his lifelong babysitter for planning to leave him, ten-year-old William uses a magic token to shrink her and himself small enough to enter

the world inside an elaborate toy castle. (BL 82:761; CC 1987 Suppl. p. 64; CCBB 39:40; HB 62:204; SLJ Feb 1986 p. 91; VOYA 9:37)

Illus. by Trina Schart Hyman, Holiday, 1985, 179 pp.; Bantam/Skylark, 1986, pap.

YOUNG, Robert F. *The Vizier's Second Daughter.* See Section 5B, Myth Fantasy.

6
Humorous Fantasy

Listed here are a variety of humorous and exaggerated tales, including those with fast-paced comic plots, tales of people with bizarre pets, tall tales, and amusing stories of inanimate objects that come to life.

ABELL, Kathleen. *King Orville and the Bullfrogs*. See Chapter 1, Allegorical Fantasy and Literary Fairy Tales.

ADLER, David A. *Jeffrey's Ghost and the Leftover Baseball Team*. See Chapter 4, Ghost Fantasy.

C AHLBERG, Allan. *The Clothes Horse and Other Stories*. Gr. 1–4. (Orig. British pub. 1987.)
Six short, humorous stories about people who take everyday expressions literally, including "The Jack Pot," in which a giant collects boys named Jack and keeps them in a pot. (KR 56:119; SLJ Apr 1988 p. 77)
Illus. by Janet Ahlberg, Viking, 1988, 32 pp.

C/YA AIKEN, Joan (Delano). *Arabel's Raven*. Gr. 4–7. (Orig. British pub. 1972, entitled *Tales of Arabel's Raven*.)
Life in the Jones's house just isn't the same after Mr. Jones brings home a raven named Mortimer who enjoys eating stairs and sleeping in the refrigerator. The sequels are *Arabel and Mortimer* (1981), *Mortimer's Cross* (1984), and *Mortimer Says Nothing* (1987). (CC:424; CCBB 28:1; Ch&Bks:263; HB 50:278; KR 42:478; LJ 99:2258)
Illus. by Quentin Blake, Doubleday, 1974, 118 pp., o.p.

C/YA AIKEN, Joan (Delano). *Armitage, Armitage, Fly Away Home*. Gr. 4–7.
[R] (Orig. British pub. 1965.)
Harriet and Mark's parents are proud of their unusual children's incredible adventures. (BL 65:183; CCBB 22:1; HB 44:558; KR 36:603; LJ 93:3296)
Illus. by Betty Fraser, Doubleday, 1968, 214 pp., o.p.

AIKEN, Joan. *The Faithless Lollybird*. See Chapter 3, Fantasy Collections.

C/YA　AIKEN, Joan (Delano). *Up the Chimney Down and Other Stories.* Gr. 5–
[R]　　8. (Orig. British pub. 1984.)
　　　Eleven eerie and humorous tales, including "The Missing Heir," "The
Midnight Rose," and "The Happiest Sheep in London." (BL 82:807; CC 1987
Suppl. p. 65; CCBB 39:121; HB 62:205; JHC 1986 Suppl. p. 74; KR 53:1139;
SLJ 32[Dec 1985]:85; TLS May 1984 p. 558; VOYA 8:323)
　　　Harper, 1985, 248 pp.

AIKEN, Joan. *The Whispering Mountain.* See Section 5A, Alternate
Worlds or Histories.

C/YA　AIKEN, Joan (Delano). *The Wolves of Willoughby Chase.* Gr. 5–7.
[R]　　In this, the first of five action-filled spoofs of Victorian melodrama set in
an England that never was, Bonnie and her cousin Sylvia run away from
their sinister governess, are chased by wolves, and end up in an orphanage.
With the help of a boy named Simon, they escape and thwart the plans of
the evil Miss Slighcarp. In *Black Hearts in Battersea* (1964; 1987, pap.; Peter
Smith, 1988), orphaned Simon and his friends, Dido and Justin, are kidnapped and shipwrecked before they uncover the true facts of their births.
In *Nightbirds on Nantucket* (1966; 1981, pap.; Peter Smith, 1988), Dido is
rescued from the sea, only to be put into the care of an evil woman who is
plotting against King James of England. In *The Cuckoo Tree* (1971), Dido
foils a plot to put St. Paul's Cathedral on rollers and push it into the Thames
to disrupt the royal coronation ceremony. In *The Stolen Lake* (1981), Dido
is sent on a dangerous diplomatic mission to New Cambria in Roman South
America, to help England's Queen Ginerva recover a stolen lake. And in
Dido and Pa (1986), Dido and Simon are reunited in an attempt to stop
Dido's wicked Pa from putting a Hanoverian pretender on England's throne.
(CC:424; Ch&Bks:263; Eakin:3; LJ 88:4076; TLS 1962 p. 901; VOYA 4 [Dec
1981]:58)
　　　Illus. by Pat Marriott, Doubleday, 1962, o.p.; Dell/Yearling, 1987, pap.,
176 pp.

ALEXANDER, Lloyd. *The Cat Who Wished to Be a Man.* See Section
2B, Talking Animal Fantasy.

ALEXANDER, Lloyd. *The Illyrian Adventure.* See Section 5C, Travel to
Other Worlds.

ANDERSON, Mary. *F*T*C Superstar.* See Section 2B, Talking Animal
Fantasy.

ANDERSON, Mildred Napier. *A Gift for Merimond.* See Chapter 1,
Allegorical Fantasy and Literary Fairy Tales.

ANDREWS, Allen. *The Pig Plantagenet.* See Section 2A, Beast Tales.

C　ANDREWS, Frank (Emerson). *The Upside-Down Town.* Gr. 3–5.
　　　Anne and Rickie visit a town where everything is done backward. (BL
54:449; CCBB 11:106; KR 26:34; LJ 83:1282)
　　　Illus. by Louis Slobodkin, Little, 1958, 60 pp., o.p.

ANGELL, Judie. *The Weird Disappearance of Jordan Hall.* See Chapter
7, Magic Adventure Fantasy.

ANNETT, Cora. *When the Porcupine Moved In.* See Section 2B, Talking
Animal Fantasy.

ANTHONY, Piers. *A Spell for Chameleon.* See Section 5A, Alternate Worlds or Histories.

ASPRIN, Robert L. *Hit or Myth.* See Chapter 10, Witchcraft and Sorcery Fantasy.

C [R] ATWATER, Richard (Tupper), and ATWATER, Florence (Hasseltine Carroll). *Mr. Popper's Penguins.* Gr. 3–5.
A paperhanger named Mr. Popper is given a penguin as a gift, but before he knows it, his problems multiply into twelve penguins. Newbery Medal Honor Book, 1939. (BL 35:86; CC:428; Ch&Bks:263; HB 14:370; LJ 63:818) Illus. by Robert Lawson, Little, 1938; Dell, 1986, pap., 144 pp.

C [R] AVI (pseud. of Avi Wortis). *Emily Upham's Revenge: Or, How Dead-wood Dick Saved the Banker's Niece: A Massachusetts Adventure.* Gr. 4–6.
Emily and her friend Seth need money to escape to Boston. Their plans to rob a bank go awry, but Emily triumphs in the end. (BL 74:1098; CC:110; CCBB 31:170; KR 46:304; SLJ Mar 1978 p. 24) Illus. by Paul Zelinsky, Pantheon, 1978, 172 pp.

C [O] BABBITT, Natalie (Zane Moore). *The Devil's Storybook.* Gr. 4–6.
Ten tales about Satan's battles with humans. *The Devil's Other Storybook* (1987) is a companion volume. (BL 71:37, 765; CC:551; CCBB 28:58; Ch&Bks:263; HB 50:134; KR 42:679; Suth 2:22; TLS 1976 p. 882) Illus. by the author, Farrar, 1974, 101 pp., 1985, pap.

C [R] BABBITT, Natalie (Zane Moore). *Goody Hall.* Gr. 4–6.
The mystery surrounding the death of young Willet Goody's father is solved after a seance visitation by Shakespeare and a nighttime visit to Mr. Goody's tomb. (BL 67:954; CC:429; CCBB 25:21; HB 47:380; KR 39:431; LJ 96:1780, 1820; Suth:23) Illus. by the author, Farrar, 1971; 1986, pap., 176 pp.

BABCOCK, Betty. *The Expandable Pig.* See Chapter 7, Magic Adventure Fantasy.

BAKER, Betty. *Save Sirrushany! (Also Agotha, Princess Gwyn and All the Fearsome Beasts).* See Chapter 1, Allegorical Fantasy and Literary Fairy Tales.

BAKER, Margaret. *Fifteen Tales for Lively Children.* See Chapter 3, Fantasy Collections.

BAKER, Margaret Joyce. *Porterhouse Major.* See Chapter 7, Magic Adventure Fantasy.

BEAGLE, Peter S. *A Fine and Private Place, A Novel.* See Chapter 4, Ghost Fantasy.

C BEEKS, Graydon. *Hosea Globe and the Fantastical Peg-Legged Chu.* Gr. 4–6.
Hosea and his talking dog are ordered to bring a scientist able to control cyclones and typhoons to their secret island home. (BL 71:813; KR 43:305; SLJ Oct 1975 p. 94) Illus. by Carol Nicklaus, Atheneum, 1974, 170 pp., o.p.

C BELL, Norman (Edward). *The Weightless Mother.* Gr. 4–6.
After Mrs. Flipping accidently swallows weightlessness pills, she floats out

of the house and off into the sky. (BL 64:384; HB 43:459; KR 35:339; LJ 92:2647)
Illus. by W. T. Mars, Follett, 1967, 144 pp., o.p.

C BENDICK, Jeanne. *The Blonk from beneath the Sea.* Gr. 3–5.
Peter and his uncle, Professor Pokeberry, discover a prehistoric sea creature (half-fish, half-seal), nickname it the Blonk, and put it on display at the oceanarium. (CCBB 11:90; HB 34:265; KR 26:133; LJ 83:1940)
Illus. by the author, Watts, 1958, 55 pp., o.p.

C BENNETT, John. *The Pigtail of Ah Lee Ben Loo, with Seventeen Other Laughable Tales.* Gr. 3–5.
This collection of humorous stories and poems was a Newbery Medal Honor Book, 1929. (BL 25:126; HB 4[Nov 1928]:82; Mahony 2:273; Moore:47, 430)
Illus. by the author, Longmans, 1928, 298 pp., o.p.

BERGER, Thomas. *Arthur Rex: A Legendary Novel.* See Section 5B, Myth Fantasy.

BEST, Herbert. *Desmond's First Case.* See Section 2B, Talking Animal Fantasy.

BETHANCOURT, T. Ernesto. *The Dog Days of Arthur Cane.* See Chapter 7, Magic Adventure Fantasy.

BLACKWOOD, Algernon. *The Adventures of Dudley and Gilderoy.* See Section 2B, Talking Animal Fantasy.

YA BLUNT, Wilfrid (Jasper Walter). *Omar; a Fantasy for Animal Lovers.* Gr. 10 up.
Omar, the rare talking bander-snatch, is given to Rose Bavistock for her fiftieth birthday. (BL 65:866, 875; KR 36:836; SLJ Dec 15, 1968 p. 4740)
Illus. by John Verney, Doubleday, 1968, 192 pp., o.p.

C BODECKER, N(iels) M(ogens). *Carrot Holes and Frisbee Trees.* Gr. 3–5.
The Plumtree family's love of gardening produces carrots big enough to "grow" postholes, bringing them unexpected business opportunities. (BL 80:404; HB 60:49; SLJ Jan 1984 p. 72)
Illus. by Nina Winters, Atheneum, 1983, 40 pp.

BODECKER, N. M. *The Lost String Quartet.* See Chapter 1, Allegorical Fantasy and Literary Fairy Tales.

BOND, Michael. *A Bear Called Paddington.* See Section 2B, Talking Animal Fantasy.

BOND, Michael. *Here Comes Thursday.* See Section 2B, Talking Animal Fantasy.

BOND, Michael. *Tales of Olga Da Polga.* See Section 2B, Talking Animal Fantasy.

C [R] BONTEMPS, Arna (Wendell), and CONROY, Jack. *The Fast Sooner Hound.* Gr. 1–4.
Sooner, the hound dog who would rather run than eat, can outrun any train to stay near his master, the Boomer railroad fireman. (BL 39:73; Ch&Bks 264; HB 18:417; LJ 67:882, 954)
Illus. by Virginia Lee Burton, Houghton, 1942, 28 pp.

BOUCHER, Anthony. *The Compleat Werewolf.* See Chapter 3, Fantasy Collections.

BOURLIAGUET, Léonce. *The Giant Who Drank from His Shoe and Other Stories.* See Chapter 3, Fantasy Collections.

C/YA BRELIS, Nancy (Burns). *The Mummy Market.* Gr. 5–7.
[R]   The Martin children visit the Mummy Market to select a new mother. (CCBB 20:38; HB 42:707; KR 34:757; LJ 91:5222; Suth:50)
   Illus. by Ben Shecter, Harper, 1966, 145 pp., o.p.

C [R] BRIGHT, Robert. *Richard Brown and the Dragon.* Gr. 2–4.
   Richard Brown uses a fire extinguisher to battle a dragon and win the hand of Princess Rosalie, in this story retold from an anecdote by Samuel Clemens. (BL 49:18; CCBB 6:13; HB 28:319; KR 20:498; LJ 77:1661)
   Illus. by the author, Doubleday, 1952, 81 pp., o.p.

C/YA BRINK, Carol Ryrie. *Andy Buckram's Tin Men.* Gr. 5–7.
[R]   A bolt of lightning brings Andy's tin-can robots to life in time to help him rescue two children from a flood. (BL 62:774; CCBB 19:143; Ch&Bks:264; KR 34:245; LJ 91:3255)
   Illus. by W. T. Mars, Viking, 1966, 192 pp., o.p.

C BRINK, Carol Ryrie. *Baby Island.* Gr. 3–5.
   Two little girls and two babies are shipwrecked on a desert island off the coast of Australia. (BL 34:196; HB 13:284; LJ 62:811, 881)
   Illus. by Helen Sewell, Macmillan, 1937, 1954, 172 pp., o.p., 1973, pap.

C BRITTAIN, Bill. *All the Money in the World.* Gr. 3–6.
   A group of friends who find all the money in the world deposited in their backyard are sought out by the army, kidnappers, and the President of the United States. (CC:439; CCBB 32:170; KR 47:328; SLJ Mar 1979 p. 135)
   Illus. by Charles Robinson, Harper, 1979, 1982, pap., 160 pp.

C BRÖGER, Achim. *Bruno.* Gr. 4–6. (Orig. German pub. 1973.)
   Amazing things keep happening to Bruno: A dinosaur comes for dinner, snowmen and statues talk to him, and he meets forty-two doubles of himself. The sequel is *Bruno Takes a Trip* (1978). (BL 72:622; KR 43:1128; SLJ Nov 1975 p. 71)
   Tr. by Hilda Van Stockum, illus. by Ronald Himler, Morrow, 1975, 160 pp.

C BRÖGER, Achim. *Little Harry.* Gr. 3–5. (Orig. German pub. 1979.)
   Seventeen tales from Little Harry's imagination, in which he meets a vacuum cleaner-witch, a human alarm clock, and learns to fly. (BL 75:1153; KR 47:451; SLJ May 1979 p. 50)
   Tr. by Elizabeth Crawford, illus. by Judy Morgan, Morrow, 1979, 189 pp., o.p.

YA BROOKS, Terry. *Magic Kingdom for Sale—Sold!* Gr. 10 up.
   The magic kingdom bought by Ben Holliday for a million dollars turns out to be possessed by a demon prince who has defeated all previous human rulers. The sequel is *The Black Unicorn* (1987). (BL 82:913, 83:1117; KR 54:254; LJ Apr 15, 1986 p. 97)
   Ballantine/Del Rey, 1986, 324 pp., 1987, pap.

BROOKS, Walter Rollin. *Freddy Goes to Florida.* See Section 2B, Talking Animal Fantasy.

C [R] BROWN, Jeff. *Flat Stanley*. Gr. 2–4.
    Stanley Lambchop, squashed flat as a pancake after a huge bulletin board
    falls on him, is lowered through sidewalk gratings, mailed to California, and
    disguised as a framed painting to capture art thieves. The sequel is *A Lamp
    for the Lambchops* (1983). (BL 60:875; HB 40:274; LJ 89:1850; TLS 1968 p.
    583)
    Illus. by Tomi Ungerer, Harper, 1964, 48 pp.

BUCHWALD, Emilie. *Floramel and Esteban*. See Section 2B, Talking
Animal Fantasy.

BURMAN, Ben Lucien. *High Water at Catfish Bend*. See Section 2B,
Talking Animal Fantasy.

C BURN, Doris. *The Tale of Lazy Lizard Canyon*. Gr. 2–4.
    The longstanding feud between the Hokums and the Burleys is settled by
    the marriage between Lafe Hokum and Mattie Mae Burley. (BL 73:1495; KR
    45:425; SLJ Sept 1977 p. 103)
    Illus. by the author, Putnam, 1977, 48 pp., o.p.

BUTTERS, Dorothy G. *Papa Dolphin's Table*. See Section 2B, Talking
Animal Fantasy.

C [R] BUTTERWORTH, Oliver. *The Enormous Egg*. Gr. 4–6.
    Nate Twitchell's new pet hatches from a leatherlike egg and turns out to be
    a baby Triceratops. In *The Narrow Passage* (1973) Nate and Nicol meet a
    prehistoric man. (BL 52:298; CCBB 9:91; Ch&Bks:264; Eakin:56; HB
    32:187; KR 24:45; LJ 81:1042)
    Illus. by Louis Darling, Little, 1956, 187 pp.; Dell, 1987, pap.

C [R] BUTTERWORTH, Oliver. *The Trouble with Jenny's Ear*. Gr. 4–6.
    After Jenny discovers that one of her ears is sensitive enough to hear other
    people's thoughts, her brothers concoct an ingenious money-making scheme.
    (BL 56:546; CCBB 13:143; Ch&Bks:264; Eakin:56; HB 36:215; KR 28:184;
    LJ 85:2034)
    Illus. by Julian de Miskey, Little, 1960, 275 pp., o.p.

BUZZATI, Dino. *The Bears' Famous Invasion of Sicily*. See Section 2B,
Talking Animal Fantasy.

BYFIELD, Barbara Ninde. *The Haunted Spy*. See Chapter 4, Ghost
Fantasy.

C/YA CALLEN, Larry (Lawrence Willard, Jr.). *Pinch*. Gr. 5–8.
  [R]   Pinch Grimball trains his pet pig, Homer, to be the best bird-hunting pig in
    Four Corners, Louisiana. (BL 72:1260, 73:1425; CCBB 30:5; HB 52:394; KR
    44:134; SLJ Apr 1976 p. 70, May 1976 p. 34)
    Illus. by Marvin Friedman, Little, 1976, 179 pp.

CANFIELD, Dorothy. *Made-to-Order Stories*. See Chapter 3, Fantasy
Collections.

C CAREY, Valerie Soho. *The Devil and Mother Crump*. Gr. 2–4.
    Old Mother Crump is so mean that she defeats both the Devil and Death.
    (BL 84:257; HB 64:50; KR 55:1316; SLJ Nov 1987 p. 87)
    Illus. by Arnold Lobel, Harper, 1987, 39 pp.

YA CARKEET, David. *I Been There Before*. Gr. 10 up.
    Halley's comet has brought Mark Twain back to life in 1985, and the

literary world begins to doubt that he was the true author of his famous works. (BL 82:307, 327; KR 53:801; SLJ Sept 1986 p. 152)

Harper, 1985; Penguin, 1987, pap., 320 pp.

C   CARLSEN, Ruth Christoffer. *Henrietta Goes West.* Gr. 4–6.

The Nelson family travels westward in their automobile, Henrietta. (CCBB 19:175; KR 34:475; LJ 91:3256)

Illus. by Wallace Tripp, Houghton, 1966, 185 pp., o.p.

CARLSEN, Ruth Christoffer. *Mr. Pudgins.* See Chapter 7, Magic Adventure Fantasy.

CARLSEN, Ruth Christoffer. *Sam Bottleby.* See Chapter 7, Magic Adventure Fantasy.

C [R] CARLSON, Natalie Savage. *Alphonse, That Bearded One.* Gr. 3–5.

Trained to take a clever woodsman's place as a soldier, Alphonse the bear causes chaos in the French-Canadian army. (BL 50:325; CCBB 7:70; Eakin:59; HB 30:174; KR 22:197; LJ 79:783)

Illus. by Nicolas Mordvinoff, Harcourt, 1954, 78 pp., o.p.

CARLSON, Natalie Savage. *Evangeline, Pigeon of Paris.* See Section 2B, Talking Animal Fantasy.

C   CARLSON, Natalie Savage. *Hortense, the Cow for a Queen.* Gr. 4–6.

A French cow named Hortense is kidnapped by pirates and shipwrecked on the coast of Africa. (BL 53:458; CCBB 11:92; HB 33:208, 298; KR 25:274; LJ 82:1684)

Illus. by Nicolas Mordvinoff, Harcourt, 1957, 95 pp., o.p.

CARTER, Lin. *Mandricardo.* See Section 5A, Alternate Worlds or Histories.

CASSERLEY, Anne Thomasine. *Barney the Donkey.* See Section 2B, Talking Animal Fantasy.

CATLING, Patrick Skene. *The Chocolate Touch.* See Chapter 7, Magic Adventure Fantasy.

CAUFIELD, Don, and CAUFIELD, Joan. *The Incredible Detectives.* See Section 2B, Talking Animal Fantasy.

C   CHARLES, Prince of Wales. *The Old Man of Lochnagar.* Gr. K–4. (Written, 1969.)

Six humorous episodes about a very old Scotsman's adventures, which include meeting a merman, being carried off by an eagle, and drinking a shrinking formula. (BL 77:807; CCBB 34:147; KR 49:209; SLJ Feb 1981 p. 55)

Illus. by Hugh Casson, Farrar, 1980, 46 pp., o.p.

YA CHASE, Mary (Coyle). *Harvey, a Play* (orig. title: *Harvey, a Comedy in Three Acts,* 1944, rev. version of the 1943 play entitled *The White Rabbit*). Gr. 6 up.

Elwood Down has an invisible rabbit friend named Harvey, in this humorous story adapted from the 1943 play, *The White Rabbit.* (BL 49:234; LJ 78:525)

Illus. by R. O. Blechman, Oxford, 1953, 89 pp., o.p.

CHASE, Mary. *Mrs. McThing: A Play.* See Chapter 10, Witchcraft and Sorcery Fantasy.

CHRISMAN, Arthur Bowie. *Shen of the Sea: Chinese Stories for Children.* See Chapter 3, Fantasy Collections.

C CHRISTIAN, Mary Blount. *Sebastian [Super-Sleuth] and the Crummy Yummies Caper.* Gr. 3–4.
Sebastian the dog detective uncovers a dognapping plot, saves Chummy the Wonder Dog, and captures the would-be thief, although his master manages to take all the credit. The sequels are *Sebastian [Super Sleuth] and the Hair of the Dog Mystery* (1982), *Sebastian [Super Sleuth] and the Bone to Pick Mystery* (1983), *Sebastian [Super Sleuth] and the Case of the Santa Claus Caper* (1984), *Sebastian [Super Sleuth] and the Secret of the Skewered Skier* (1984), *Sebastian [Super Sleuth] and the Clumsy Cowboy* (1985), *Sebastian [Super Sleuth] and the Purloined Sirloin* (1986), *Sebastian [Super Sleuth] and the Stars-in-His-Eyes Mystery* (1987) and *Sebastian [Super Sleuth] and the Egyptian Connection* (1988). (BL 79:1272; KR 51:375; SLJ May 1983 p. 91)
Illus. by Lisa McCue, Macmillan, 1983, 55 pp.

CLEARY, Beverly. *The Mouse and the Motorcycle.* See Section 2B, Talking Animal Fantasy.

COBALT, Martin. *Pool of Swallows.* See Chapter 4, Ghost Fantasy.

COONTZ, Otto. *Hornswoggle Magic.* See Chapter 7, Magic Adventure Fantasy.

COOPER, Susan. *Jethro and the Jumbie.* See Chapter 7, Magic Adventure Fantasy.

CORBETT, Scott. *The Discontented Ghost.* See Chapter 4, Ghost Fantasy.

C CORBETT, Scott. *Ever Ride a Dinosaur?* Gr. 4–6.
Bronson the talking brontosaurus visits his old friends at the Museum of Natural History. (CCBB 23:41; Ch&Bks: 265; HB 45:409; KR 37:558; LJ 94:2111; Suth:91)
Illus. by Mircea Vasiliu, Holt, 1969, 128 pp., o.p.

CORBETT, Scott. *The Great Custard Pie Panic.* See Chapter 10, Witchcraft and Sorcery Fantasy.

CORBETT, Scott. *The Lemonade Trick.* See Chapter 7, Magic Adventure Fantasy.

C [R] COREN, Alan. *Arthur the Kid.* Gr. 3–5. (Orig. British pub. 1976.)
Ten-year-old Arthur's career as leader of a gang of bank-robbing gunslingers takes an about-face when they save the bank from another gang. The sequels are *Buffalo Arthur* (1978), *The Lone Arthur* (1978), *Railroad Arthur* (1978), *Klondike Arthur* (1979), *Arthur's Last Stand* (1979), *Arthur and the Great Detective* (1980), *Arthur and the Purple Panic* (1984), *Arthur versus the Rest* (1985), and *Arthur and the Bellybutton Diamond* (British). (BL 74:1616; CC:456; CCBB 32:26; KR 46:594; SLJ Sept 1978 p. 133; Suth 2:103)
Illus. by John Astrop, Little, 1978; Bantam, 1984, pap., 80 pp.

COUNSEL, June. *A Dragon in Class 4.* See Chapter 7, Magic Adventure Fantasy.

CRESSWELL, Helen. *The Bongleweed.* See Chapter 7, Magic Adventure Fantasy.

C [R] CRESSWELL (Rowe), Helen. *The Piemakers.* Gr. 4–6. (Orig. U.S. pub. Lippincott, 1967.)
A family of bakers, competing with their cousins for the king's prize, concocts a meat pie big enough to serve 2,000 people. (BL 64:1041, 77:404; Ch&Bks:265; HB 56:662, 57:215; KR 36:261; LJ 93:2536; SLJ Sept 1980 p. 68; TLS 1967 p. 445)
Illus. by Judith Gwyn Brown, Macmillan, 1980, 117 pp., o.p.

C DAHL, Roald. *The BFG.* Gr. 4–6.
Kidnapped by the BFG (big friendly giant) and taken to Giant Country, orphaned Sophie and her vegetarian giant friend are horrified that the other giants eat "human beans," and ask the Queen of England to put a stop to it. (BL 79:608, 685; CCBB 36:86; HB 59:165; KR 50:1153; SLJ Dec 1982 p. 43; TLS 1982 p. 1303)
Illus. by Quentin Blake, Farrar, 1982, 221 pp.; Penguin/Puffin, 1985, pap., o.p.

DAHL, Roald. *Charlie and the Chocolate Factory.* See Chapter 7, Magic Adventure Fantasy.

DAHL, Roald. *Fantastic Mr. Fox.* See Section 2B, Talking Animal Fantasy.

DAHL, Roald. *The Magic Finger.* See Chapter 7, Magic Adventure Fantasy.

DAHL, Roald. *The Witches.* See Chapter 10, Witchcraft and Sorcery Fantasy.

DANA, Barbara. *Zucchini.* See Section 2A, Beast Tales.

DAVIES, Andrew. *Conrad's War.* See Chapter 8, Time Travel Fantasy.

C DAVIES, Andrew (Wynford). *Marmalade and Rufus.* Gr. 3–5. (Orig. British pub. 1979; 2nd ed. entitled *Marmalade Atkins' Dreadful Deeds.*)
Marmalade Atkins, the worst-behaved girl in the world, joins forces with an ornery talking donkey named Rufus to wreak havoc at the El Poco Nightclub, the Midnight Steeplechase, and a Christmas pageant. The British sequels are *Danger—Marmalade at Work, Marmalade Atkins Hits the Big Time, Marmalade Atkins in Space,* and *Educating Marmalade.* (BL 80:82; CCBB 37:46; HB 59:572; KR 51:659; SLJ Sept 1983 p. 121)
Illus. by Bert Dodson, Crown, 1983, 84 pp., o.p.

YA DAVIES, Valentine. *It Happens Every Spring.* Gr. 7 up.
A secret formula developed by a college professor enables him to pitch St. Louis to a World Series victory. (BL 45:359; KR 17:238; LJ 74:955, 1031)
Farrar, 1949, 224 pp., o.p.

C/YA DAVIES, Valentine. *The Miracle on 34th Street.* Gr. 4–7. (Orig. pub.
[R] 1947.)
Old Mr. Kringle tries to convince skeptics that he is Santa Claus, and gets a job as Macy's Christmas Santa to prove it. (BL 43:359, 81:190, 211, 245, 247; CCBB 38:43; JHC:364; KR 15:316; LJ 72:1033; SLJ Oct 1984 p. 175)
Harcourt, 1959; illus. by Tomie dePaola, Harcourt, 1984, 116 pp., 1987, pap.

YA De CAMP, L(yman) Sprague, and De CAMP, Catherine Crook. *The Incorporated Knight.* Gr. 10 up.
A bumbling knight named Sir Eudoric sets off on a series of adventures that eventually help to prove him worthy of his title. (BL 84:437, 466; LJ Oct 15, 1987 p. 95)
Phantasia Press, 1987, 256 pp.

C DELANEY, M. C. *Henry's Special Delivery.* Gr. 3–6.
Armed with a knapsack full of junk food, Henry sets out for the house of his secret love, Heather, determined to win her heart with the gift of a live, talking panda, ordered with two proof-of-purchase seals from his favorite cereal. (BL 80:1547; CCBB 37:202; SLJ Oct 1984 p. 156)
Illus. by Lisa McCue, Dutton, 1984, 138 pp.

C/YA De WEESE, (Thomas Eugene) Gene. *The Adventures of a Two Minute Werewolf.* Gr. 5–7.
One incredible day, fourteen-year-old Walt Cribbens discovers that he has turned into a werewolf. (BL 79:1274; SLJ May 1983 p. 91)
Illus. by Ronald Fritz, Doubleday, 1983; Putnam, 1984, pap., 128 pp.

DICKINSON, Peter. *The Iron Lion.* See Chapter 1, Allegorical Fantasy and Literary Fairy Tales.

DILLON, Barbara. *What's Happened to Harry?* See Chapter 10, Witchcraft and Sorcery Fantasy.

C [R] DOLBIER, Maurice (Wyman). *A Lion in the Woods.* Gr. 4–6.
A newspaper reporter makes up a story about 'lion at large in Forest Park. (BL 51:301; CCBB 8:77; HB 31:111; LJ 80:999)
Illus. by Robert Henneberger, Little, 1955, 115 pp., o.p.

DRURY, Roger W. *The Champion of Merrimack County.* See Section 2B, Talking Animal Fantasy.

C [R] DRURY, Roger W(olcott). *The Finches Fabulous Furnace.* Gr. 4–6.
The Finch family tries to keep the volcano in their basement a secret, yet safeguard their town. (BL 67:907; CCBB 25:4; HB 47:382; LJ 97:1169; Suth:108)
Illus. by Erik Blegvad, Little, 1971, 149 pp.

C [R] DU BOIS, William (Sherman) Pène. *The Alligator Case.* Gr. 3–5.
A case involving a circus alligator and three suspicious strangers is solved by a boy detective even before the crime is committed. *The Horse in the Camel Suit* (1967) is the sequel. (BL 62:330; CC:462; CCBB 19:31; Eakin:103; HB 41:497; KR 33:827; LJ 90:3788)
Illus. by the author, Harper, 1965, 63 pp., o.p.

C DU BOIS, William (Sherman) Pène. *Call Me Bandicoot.* Gr. 3–5.
A young con artist named Ermine Bandicoot is responsible for New York Harbor's tobacco-brown water color. (CCBB 24:105; KR 38:1095; LJ 95:4326, 4354; Suth:109)
Illus. by the author, Harper, 1970, 63 pp., o.p.

C DU BOIS, William (Sherman) Pène, *The Flying Locomotive.* Gr. 1–4.
A fairy godmother gives a special wish to a Swiss locomotive. (HB 17:356, 381; LJ 66:878)
Illus. by the author, Viking, 1941, 48 pp., o.p.

C [R] DU BOIS, William (Sherman) Pène. *The Forbidden Forest.* Gr. 3–5.
Lady Adelaide (a kangaroo), Buckingham the bulldog, and Spider Max the champion boxer are hailed as heroes for stopping World War I. (BL 75:215; CCBB 32:78; Ch&Bks:266; HB 55:515; KR 46:946; SLJ Sept 1978 p. 122; Suth 2:130; TLS 1978 p. 1397)
Illus. by the author, Harper, 1978, 56 pp., o.p.

C [R] DU BOIS, William (Sherman) Pène. *The Giant.* Gr. 4–6.
A gigantic eight-year-old boy named El Muchacho, whose toys are live wild animals and real trains and trucks, makes a visit to Paris. (BL 51:114; CCBB 8:98; Ch&Bks:266; Eakin:103; HB 30:434; KR 22:529; LJ 80:190; Suth:212)
Illus. by the author, Viking, 1954, 124 pp., o.p.; Dell/Yearling, 1987, pap.

C DU BOIS, William (Sherman) Pène. *The Great Geppy.* Gr. 4–6.
A red and white striped horse detective called The Great Geppy is hired to investigate problems at the Bolt Bros. Circus. (BL 36:368; HB 16:166, 175, 60:223; LJ 65:502, 847)
Illus. by the author, Viking, 1940, 1946, 92 pp., o.p.

C [R] DU BOIS, William (Sherman) Pène. *Otto and the Magic Potatoes.* Gr. 2–4.
In this sequel to *Otto at Sea* (1936, 1958, 1964), *Otto in Texas* (1959), and *Otto in Africa* (1961), Otto, a lovable giant-sized dog, is kidnapped by Baron Backgammon, who is trying to g ʾw gigantic potatoes and roses. (BL 66:1406; CCBB 24:57; Ch&Bks:266; KR 38:238; LJ 95:1940)
Illus. by the author, Viking, 1970, 48 pp., o.p.

C/YA DU BOIS, William (Sherman) Pène. *Peter Graves.* Gr. 5–7.
Peter uses a retired inventor's antigravity alloy to try such feats as tightrope walking upside down and the Indian rope trick. (BL 47:140; CCBB 4:19; HB 26:375; KR 18:518)
Illus. by the author, Viking, 1950, 168 pp., o.p.

C [R] DU BOIS, William (Sherman) Pène. *The Squirrel Hotel.* Gr. 3–6.
A retired toy dealer and bee-orchestra conductor describes his hotel for squirrels, equipped with all the modern conveniences. (BL 48:269; HB 28:106; KR 20:71; LJ 77:727)
Illus. by the author, Viking, 1952, o.p.; Gregg, 1980.

C DU BOIS, William (Sherman) Pène. *The Three Policemen, or Young Bottsford of Farbe Island.* Gr. 4–6.
The mystery of the stolen fishing nets on the fabulous island of Farbe is solved by three policemen, with the help of young Bottsford. (BL 57:190; HB 14:365, 375, 36:485; LJ 63:818, 978)
Illus. by the author, Viking, 1938, 1960, 95 pp., o.p.

C/YA DU BOIS, William (Sherman) Pène. *The Twenty-One Balloons.* Gr. 5–7.
[R] Professor William Waterman Sherman is tired of teaching arithmetic. He sails off in a balloon to see the world and lands on the volcanic island of Krakatoa. Newbery Medal winner, 1948. (BL 43:296; CC:462; Ch&Bks:237; HB 23:214; LJ 72:819)
Illus. by the author, Viking, 1947, o.p.; Penguin, 1986, pap., 184 pp.

DUTTON, Sandra. *The Magic of Myrna C. Waxweather.* See Chapter 7, Magic Adventure Fantasy.

C EDMONDS, Walter D(umaux). *Uncle Ben's Whale.* Gr. 3–5. (Orig. pub. 1931.)
A canal skipper named Uncle Ben harpoons a whale and sets up a museum inside it. (BL 52:60; KR 23:646; LJ 80:2641)
Illus. by William Gropper, Dodd, 1955, 90 pp., o.p.

EDMONDSON, Madeline. *Anna Witch.* See Chapter 10, Witchcraft and Sorcery Fantasy.

C EGNER, Thorbjørn. *The Singing Town.* Gr. 1–4. (Orig. Norwegian pub. 1955.)
A musical comedy about three robbers and a pet lion who frighten the villagers of Kardemomma. Awarded first prize by the Norwegian Ministry of Church and Education, 1955. (HB 35:387; LJ 84:3630; TLS Dec 4, 1959 p. iv)
Tr. by Evelyn Ramsden and Leila Berg, illus. by the author, Macmillan, 1959, 105 pp., o.p.

ERWIN, Betty K. *Aggie, Maggie, and Tish.* See Chapter 7, Magic Adventure Fantasy.

C/YA EUSTIS, Helen. *Mr. Death and the Redheaded Woman.* Gr. 5 up. (Orig. pub. in the *Saturday Evening Post,* 1950.)
Redheaded Maud Applegate sets out to convince Mr. Death to restore the life of her own true love, Billy-Be-Damn Bangtry. (BL 80:170; HB 60:50; SLJ Jan 1984 p. 84)
Illus. by Reinhard Michl, Green Tiger Press, 1983, pap., 32 pp.

C/YA EVARTS, Hal G. *Jay-Jay and the Peking Monster.* Gr. 6–9.
Aunt Hattie's experiments on ancient human bones bring a boy named Zurria to life, and involve Jay-Jay with the Marines, a Chinese attaché, and gangsters. (BL 74:1492; HB 54:401; KR 46:500; SLJ May 1978 p. 86)
Scribner, 1978, 185 pp., o.p.; Peter Smith, 1984.

C EZO (pseud.). *My Son-In-Law, the Hippopotamus.* Gr. 4–6. (Orig. pub. in France.)
Madame Hournarette's wild tales about her son-in-law, Baldomer the hippo, inspire two Parisian children to go to Africa in search of him. (HB 38:602; LJ 87:3201)
Tr. by Hugh Shelley, illus. by Quentin Blake, Abelard-Schuman, 1962, 160 pp., o.p.

FARJEON, Eleanor. *The Glass Slipper.* See Chapter 1, Allegorical Fantasy and Literary Fairy Tales.

C FARJEON, Eleanor. *Gypsy and Ginger.* Gr. 3–5. (Orig. pub. in England.)
Gypsy and Ginger are children who live in the weather house, emerging to visit London according to the weather. (BL 17:353).
Dutton, 1920, 164 pp., o.p.

FAST, Howard. *A Touch of Infinity: Thirteen New Stories of Fantasy and Science Fiction.* See Chapter 3, Fantasy Collections.

FEAGLES, Anita M. *Casey, the Utterly Impossible Horse.* See Section 2B, Talking Animal Fantasy.

FINNEY, Jack. *Marion's Wall; A Novel.* See Chapter 4, Ghost Fantasy.

FISHER, Leonard Everett. *Noonan: A Novel about Baseball, ESP, and Time Warps.* See Chapter 8, Time Travel Fantasy.

C [R] FLEISCHMAN, Paul (Taylor). *Finzel the Farsighted.* Gr. 2–4.
Although Finzel the fortune teller can barely see, his predictions enable him to outwit his greedy brother, Osip. (BL 80:407; CC:467; CCBB 37:86; Ch&Bks:266; KR 51:147; SLJ Dec 1983 p. 65; Suth 3:134)
Illus. by Marcia Sewall, Dutton, 1983, 46 pp.

FLEISCHMAN, Paul. *Graven Images: Three Stories.* See Chapter 4, Ghost Fantasy.

C [R] FLEISCHMAN, (Albert) Sid(ney). *By the Great Horn Spoon.* Gr. 4–6.
Jack Flagg runs away from home in Boston to make his fortune in the California gold fields, accompanied by Praiseworthy, his butler. (BL 60:207; CC:467; CCBB 17:110; Ch&Bks:266; HB 39:598; LJ 88:3348)
Illus. by Eric Von Schmidt, Little, 1963, 193 pp., 1987, pap.

C [R] FLEISCHMAN, (Albert) Sid(ney). *Chancy and the Grand Rascal.* Gr. 4–6.
Chancy, orphaned and searching for his long-lost sister, Indiana, meets a tall-tale-telling uncle and a sly villain named Colonel Plugg. (BL 63:119; CC:467; CCBB 20:41; Ch&Bks:266; HB 42:569; KR 34:625; LJ 91:5226; Suth:126; TLS 1967 p. 1145)
Illus. by Eric Von Schmidt, Little, 1966, 179 pp.

FLEISCHMAN, Sid. *The Ghost in the Noonday Sun.* See Chapter 4, Ghost Fantasy.

C [R] FLEISCHMAN, (Albert) Sid(ney). *The Ghost on Saturday Night.* Gr. 3–5.
Opie becomes a town hero when he exposes Dr. Pepper's traveling ghost-raising show as a front for bank robberies. (BL 70:1252; CC:468; CCBB 28:61; HB 50:379; KR 42:535; LJ 99:2267; Suth 2:148; TLS 1975 p. 770)
Illus. by Eric Von Schmidt, Little, 1974, 57 pp.

FLEISCHMAN, Sid. *The Hey Hey Man.* See Chapter 7, Magic Adventure Fantasy.

C [R] FLEISCHMAN, (Albert) Sid(ney). *Humbug Mountain.* Gr. 4–6.
Grandpa Flint's "property" in the boom town of Sunshine, Dakota, turns out to be no more than an abandoned riverboat in the ghost town of Sunshine, Nevada. But the family makes the best of it by setting off a gold rush. (BL 75:477, 80:95; CC:468; CCBB 32:113; HB 55:640; KR 46:1071; SLJ Sept 1978 p. 136; Suth 2:149)
Illus. by Eric Von Schmidt, Little, 1978, 149 pp., 1987, pap.

C [R] FLEISCHMAN, (Albert) Sid(ney). *Jim Bridger's Alarm Clock, and Other Tall Tales.* Gr. 2–4.
Three tall tales about an army scout and mountain man named Jim Bridger, including one in which he uses the echo of fireworks to outwit bank robbers. (BL 75:808; HB 55:191; KR 42:124; SLJ Apr 1979 p. 55)
Illus. by Eric Von Schmidt, Dutton, 1978, 56 pp., o.p.

C [R] FLEISCHMAN, (Albert) Sid(ney). *Jingo Django.* Gr. 4–6.
Orphaned Jingo Hawks and his benefactor, Mr. Peacock-Hemlock-Jones, travel from Boston to Mexico trying their hands at horse trading, river pilot-

ing, portrait painting, and treasure hunting. (BL 67:954, 68:669; CC:468; HB 47:383, 63:439; KR 39:432; LJ 96:2916; TLS 1971 p. 1509)

Illus. by Eric Von Schmidt, Little, 1971, 172 pp.

C [R] FLEISCHMAN, (Albert) Sid(ney). *McBroom Tells the Truth* (British title: *McBroom's Wonderful One Acre Farm*). Gr. 3–5.

Farmer McBroom's crops grow so fast that his eleven children can ride on the pumpkins and use the cornstalks for pogo sticks. The sequels, all published by Little, are *McBroom and the Big Wind* (1967; rev. ed. 1982), *McBroom's Ear* (1969), *McBroom's Ghost* (1971; rev. ed. 1981), *McBroom's Zoo* (1972; rev. ed. 1982), *McBroom the Rainmaker* (1973; rev. ed. 1982), *McBroom Tells a Lie* (1976; British title: *Here Comes McBroom!*), *McBroom and the Beanstalk* (1978), *McBroom and the Great Race* (1980), and *McBroom's Almanac* (1984). (BL 62:662; CC:468; CCBB 19:129; Ch&Bks:266; HB 42:193; KR 33:1187; LJ 91:424; Suth:127)

Illus. by Walter Lorraine, Grosset, 1966, o.p.; Little, 1981 (rev. ed.), hb and pap., 48 pp.

C [R] FLEISCHMAN, (Albert) Sid(ney). *Me and the Man on the Moon-Eyed Horse*. Gr. 3–5.

The circus train's visit to Furnace Flats is almost ruined by a desperado named Step-and-a-half Jackson, but young Clint saves the day. (BL 73:1652; HB 53:553; KR 45:46; SLJ May 1977 p. 61)

Illus. by Eric Von Schmidt, Atlantic-Little, 1977, 57 pp.

C [R] FLEISCHMAN, (Albert) Sid(ney). *Mister Mysterious and Company*. Gr. 4–6.

Mr. Mysterious and his magician family travel across the country in a covered wagon, entertaining people with wonderful feats of magic. (BL 58:728; CC:468; HB 38:279; LJ 87:1318)

Illus. by Eric Von Schmidt, Little, 1962, 151 pp.

C [R] FLEMING, Ian (Lancaster). *Chitty-Chitty Bang Bang: The Magical Car*. Gr. 4–6. (Orig. pub. Random, 1964.)

The Pott family's rattletrap auto can both fly and float, and it takes them across the English Channel to the underground hideout of England's worst gangster. (BL 61:435; CC:468; CCBB 18:73, 22:77; Ch&Bks:266; HB 41:167; LJ 89:4646)

Illus. by John Burningham, Aeonion Pr., 1976 (repr. of 1964 ed.), 111 pp.

FLORA, James. *Grandpa's Ghost Stories*. See Chapter 4, Ghost Fantasy.

FLORA, James. *Wanda and the Bumbly Wizard*. See Chapter 10, Witchcraft and Sorcery Fantasy.

FOOTE, Timothy. *The Great Ringtail Garbage Caper*. See Chapter 2B, Talking Animal Fantasy.

C FORESTER, C(ecil) S(cott). *Poo Poo and the Dragons*. Gr. 3–5.

Harold "Poo Poo" Brown brings home a dragon named Horatio. (HB 18:332; LJ 67:682; TLS 1942 p. 573)

Illus. by Robert Lawson, Little, 1942, 142 pp., o.p.

C [R] FOSTER, John T(homas). *Marco and the Tiger*. Gr. 4–6.

Marco concocts wild schemes to protect the aging Bengal tiger he met while delivering newspapers. (BL 64:273; HB 43:462; KR 35:57; LJ 92:2020)

Illus. by Lorence Bjorklund, Dodd, 1967, 128 pp., o.p.

FRESCHET, Bernice. *Bernard of Scotland Yard.* See Section 2B, Talking Animal Fantasy.

FROMAN, Elizabeth Hull. *Eba, the Absent-Minded Witch.* See Chapter 10, Witchcraft and Sorcery Fantasy.

Fun Phantoms: Tales of Ghostly Entertainment. Ed. by Seon Manley and Gogo Lewis. See Chapter 4, Ghost Fantasy.

C FYLEMAN, Rose. *The Strange Adventures of Captain Marwhopple.* Gr. 3–5. (Orig. British pub. 1931.)
   Uncle Billiwinks tells humorous stories of Captain Marwhopple's adventures. (LJ 57:864; TLS 1931 p. 957)
   Doubleday, 1932, 166 pp., o.p.

FYLEMAN, Rose. *Tea Time Tales.* See Chapter 3, Fantasy Collections.

C [R] GANNETT (Kahn), Ruth Stiles. *The Wonderful House-Boat-Train.* Gr. 2–4.
   A retired railroad engineer and his grandchildren move to a house in the country that looks like a train and floats like a boat. (BL 46:161; HB 26:37; KR 17:653; LJ 75:112)
   Illus. by Fritz Eichenberg, Random, 1949, 64 pp., o.p.

GARNETT, David. *Two by Two: A Story of Survival.* See Section 5B, Myth Fantasy.

C [R] GATHORNE-HARDY, Jonathan. *Operation Peeg* (British title: *Jane's Adventures on the Island of Peeg,* 1968). Gr. 4–6.
   After a rocket explosion sets the island of Peeg adrift in the Atlantic Ocean, two little girls and a housekeeper are caught up in a power struggle between two long-lost World War II soldiers and an evil billionaire. The sequels are *The Airship Ladyship Adventure* (1977) and *Jane's Adventures In and Out of the Book* (Overlook, 1981). (CCBB 28:77; HB 51:147; KR 42:1060, 43:6; LJ 99:2740; TLS 1968 p. 1377)
   Illus. by Glo Coalson, Lippincott, 1974, 192 pp.

C [R] GERRARD, Roy. *Sir Cedric.* Gr. 1–4.
   Balding Sir Cedric battles bullying Black Ned to free captive princess Fat Matilda, in this spoof of the age of chivalry. The sequel is *Sir Cedric Rides Again* (1986). (BL 81:246; CCBB 38:83; KR 52:J61; SLJ Jan 1985 p. 74; TLS 1984 p. 1139)
   Illus. by the author, Farrar, 1984, hb, 1986, pap., 32 pp.

GIBSON, Katharine. *Cinders.* See Chapter 1, Allegorical Fantasy and Literary Fairy Tales.

GILLILAND, Alexis A. *Wizenbeak.* See Chapter 10, Witchcraft and Sorcery Fantasy.

GOLDMAN, William W. *The Princess Bride: S. Morgenstern's Classic Tale of True Love and High Adventure.* See Chapter 1, Allegorical Fantasy and Literary Fairy Tales.

GORMLEY, Beatrice. *Fifth Grade Magic.* See Chapter 7, Magic Adventure Fantasy.

GORMLEY, Beatrice. *Paul's Volcano.* See Chapter 7, Magic Adventure Fantasy.

GOULART, Ron. *The Chameleon Corps and Other Shape Changers.* See Section 5A, Alternate Worlds or Histories.

GOULART, Ron. *The Prisoner of Blackwood Castle.* See Section 5A, Alternate Worlds or Histories.

GRAY, Nicholas Stuart. *The Apple Stone.* See Chapter 7, Magic Adventure Fantasy.

GRAY, Nicholas Stuart. *A Wind from Nowhere.* See Chapter 3, Fantasy Collections.

GREEN, Phyllis. *Eating Ice Cream with a Werewolf.* See Chapter 7, Magic Adventure Fantasy.

GREER, Gery, and RUDDICK, Bob. *Max and Me and the Time Machine.* See Chapter 8, Time Travel Fantasy.

GROSSER, Morton. *The Snake Horn.* See Chapter 8, Time Travel Fantasy.

C/YA HALE, Lucretia P(eabody). *The Complete Peterkin Papers* (British titles: [R] *The Peterkin Papers* and *The Last of the Peterkins*). Gr. 5–8. (Orig. pub. 1880.)
The Peterkin family's problems are solved by the common sense of the Lady from Philadelphia. (BL 57:190; Bookshelf 1932 p. 12; Ch&Bks:267; HB 1 [Nov 1924]:4–7, 1 [June 1925]:44; KR 28:905; LJ 50:803, 85:4567)
Illus. by the author, Houghton, 1960, 302 pp., o.p.

HASS, E. A. *Incognito Mosquito, Private Insective.* See Section 2B, Talking Animal Fantasy.

C HAUFF, Wilhelm. *A Monkey's Uncle.* Gr. 4–6. (Orig. pub. in Germany.)
A newcomer decides to introduce an orangutan as his nephew. (KR 37:1109; LJ 95:241)
Retold by Doris Orgel, illus. by Mitchell Miller, Farrar, 1969, 74 pp., o.p.

HAYES, Geoffrey. *The Alligator and His Uncle Tooth: A Novel of the Sea.* See Section 2B, Talking Animal Fantasy.

HAYNES, Betsy. *The Ghost of the Gravestone Hearth.* See Chapter 4, Ghost Fantasy.

C [R] HEIDE, Florence Parry. *The Shrinking of Treehorn.* Gr. 2–4.
No one believes that Treehorn is growing smaller and smaller every day. The sequels are *Treehorn's Treasure* (1981) and *Treehorn's Wish* (1984). (BL 68:564, 669; CC:481; CCBB 25:156; Ch&Bks:119; HB 48:45; KR 39:1118; LJ 97:763, 1884)
Illus. by Edward Gorey, Holiday, 1971, 60 pp.; Dell, 1983, pap. (entitled *The Adventures of Treehorn;* also includes *Treehorn's Treasure*).

HELPRIN, Mark. *Winter's Tale.* See Chapter 1, Allegorical Fantasy and Literary Fairy Tales.

HEWETT, Anita. *The Bull beneath the Walnut Tree and Other Stories.* See Chapter 3, Fantasy Collections.

C HILDICK, E(dmund) W(allace). *The Dragon That Lived under Manhattan.* Gr. 3–4.
Jimmy tries to convince the mayor of New York to allow a shy vegetarian dragon to live beneath the city. (BL 67:420; KR 38:1143; LJ 95:4337)
Illus. by Harold Berson, Crown, 1970, 62 pp., o.p.

HOBAN, Russell C. *Dinner at Alberta's.* See Section 2B, Talking Animal Fantasy.

C [R] HOBAN, Russell C(onwell). *How Tom Beat Captain Najork and His Hired Sportsmen.* Gr. 3–5.
Tom's Aunt Fidget Wonkham-Strong hires Captain Najork to teach Tom a lesson about foolish behavior, but even that doesn't stop him. The sequel is *A Near Thing for Captain Najork* (1976). (BL 71:766; CCBB 28:78; Ch&Bks: 268; HB 51:138; KR 42:1299, 43:2; LJ 99:2733; Suth 2:216; TLS 1974 p. 718)
Illus. by Quentin Blake, Atheneum, 1974, 32 pp., o.p.

C HOBAN, Russell C(onwell). *The Twenty-Elephant Restaurant.* Gr. K–4.
A wobbly table, strengthened enough for an elephant to dance on, inspires an old man to build a restaurant featuring twenty dancing elephants. (BL 74:1494; CCBB 32:10; KR 46:299; SLJ May 1978 p. 56)
Illus. by Emily McCully, Atheneum, 1978, 37 pp., o.p.

C HODGES, C(yril) Walter. *Sky High: The Story of a House That Flew* (British title: *The Flying House*). Gr. 3–5.
Uncle Ben's latest invention, super-inflating gas, causes Nicky and Linda's house to float off into the sky. (BL 44:189; HB 23:436; LJ 72:1543)
Illus. by the author, Coward, 1947, 112 pp., o.p.

HOFFMANN, Eleanor. *The Four Friends.* See Section 2B, Talking Animal Fantasy.

C [R] HOLMAN (Valen), Felice. *The Blackmail Machine.* Gr. 4–6.
A flying treehouse enables Murk and Arabella to "blackmail" the government into preserving wildlife and bringing peace to the world. (BL 64:995; CCBB 21:129; HB 44:173; KR 35:1472; LJ 93:870; TLS 1968 p. 1112)
Illus. by Victoria de Larrea, Macmillan, 1968, 182 pp., o.p.

C HOLMAN (Valen), Felice. *The Escape of the Giant Hogstalk.* Gr. 3–6.
A national emergency is declared after a gigantic plant at the Royal Botanic Gardens grows out of control. (CCBB 28:28; HB 50:283; KR 42:363; LJ 99:2270; Suth 2:223)
Illus. by Ben Shecter, Scribner, 1974, 96 pp., o.p.

C/YA HOLMAN (Valen), Felice. *The Future of Hooper Toote.* Gr. 5–7.
Hooper Toote can walk on air. (BL 69:529; CCBB 25:171; KR 40:259; LJ 97:2951; Suth:193)
Illus. by Gahan Wilson, Scribner, 1972, 138 pp., o.p.

HOLMAN, Felice. *The Witch on the Corner.* See Chapter 10, Witchcraft and Sorcery Fantasy.

C [R] HOOKS, William H(arris). *Mean Jake and the Devils.* Gr. 3–5.
Mean old Jake manages to outwit three generations of devils, in these three tales told to a boy by his grandmother. (BL 78:756; CCBB 35:172; HB 58:164; KR 50:202; SLJ Jan 1982 p. 77)
Illus. by Dirk Zimmer, Dial, 1981, 64 pp.

C HORNE, Richard Henry. *The Good-Natured Bear: A Story for Children of All Ages.* Gr. 4–6. (Orig. British pub. 1846; U.S. 1854.)

A good-natured uncle, disguised as a bear, tells the Littlepump children moralistic and humorous tales about his wandering life. (BL 24:168; HB 3[Nov 1927]:44; LJ 53:484, 1033; Mahony 2:147)

Illus. by Lisl Hummel, Macmillan, 1927, 159 pp., o.p.

HORWITZ, Elinor Lander. *The Strange Story of the Frog Who Became a Prince.* See Chapter 10, Witchcraft and Sorcery Fantasy.

HOWE, Deborah, and HOWE, James. *Bunnicula: A Rabbit Tale of Mystery.* See Section 2B, Talking Animal Fantasy.

HUGHES, Frieda. *Getting Rid of Aunt Edna.* See Chapter 10, Witchcraft and Sorcery Fantasy.

C [R] HUNTER, Mollie (pseud. of Maureen Mollie Hunter McVeigh McIlwraith). *The Smartest Man in Ireland* (British title: *Patrick Kentigen Keenan,* 1963). Gr. 4–6.

Patrick's boastful claim of being the smartest man in Ireland tempts the fairy folk to test him. (BL 62:487; HB 41:629; KR 33:821; TLS 1963 p. 427)

Illus. by Charles Keeping, Funk, 1965, 95 pp., o.p.

HUNTER, Mollie. *Thomas and the Warlock.* See Chapter 10, Witchcraft and Sorcery Fantasy.

C/YA HUNTER, Norman (George Lorimer). *The Incredible Adventures of Professor Branestawm.* Gr. 5–7. (Orig. British pub. 1933.)

Professor Branestawm's zany inventions include a clock that strikes thirteen and a time machine. The sequels are *The Best of Branestawm* (1981), *Professor Branestawm's Building Bust-Up* (1982), *Professor Branestawm's Mouse War* (1982), *The Peculiar Triumph of Professor Branestawm* (British), *Professor Branestawm up the Pole* (British), *Professor Branestawm's Great Revolution* (British), and *Professor Branestawm's Treasure Hunt* (British). (BL 76:558; SLJ Aug 1980 p. 64; TLS 1970 p. 1458)

Illus. by W. Heath Robinson, Bodley Head, dist. by Merrimack, 1979, 203 pp., o.p.

C [R] HUTCHINS, Pat (Goundry). *Follow That Bus!* Gr. 2–4.

After their teacher and schoolbus are hijacked by robbers, Miss Beaver's second-grade class rescues her and captures the bandits. The sequel is *The Mona Lisa Mystery* (1981). (BL 73:1498; CCBB 31:48; HB 53:442; KR 45:351; SLJ Apr 1977 p. 55; TLS 1977 p. 1412)

Illus. by Laurence Hutchins, Greenwillow/Morrow, 1977, 102 pp., o.p.

C [R] HUTCHINS, Pat (Goundry). *The House That Sailed Away.* Gr. 4–6.

A house that floats out to sea, a battle with pirates, a landing on a cannibal island, and the discovery of buried treasure are just some of the adventures in store for Morgan and his family. (BL 72:303; CCBB 29:64; HB 51:593; KR 43:777; SLJ Sept 1975 p. 84; TLS 1976 p. 882)

Illus. by Laurence Hutchins, Greenwillow/Morrow, 1975, 150 pp.

IBBOTSON, Eva. *The Great Ghost Rescue.* See Chapter 4, Ghost Fantasy.

YA IRVING, Washington. *Knickerbocker's History of New York* (Orig. title: *A History of New York, from the Beginning of the World to the End of the Dutch Dynasty . . . ,* 1812). Gr. 8 up.
   A shortened version of Irving's comic history of New York City. (BL 12:302, 25:174, 56:359, 450; HB 4[Aug 1928]:77; Moore:138, 431)
   Ed. by Anne Carroll Moore, illus. by James Daugherty, Doubleday, 1928, 1940, o.p.; Ungar, 1959, o.p., 1983, pap., 441 pp.

C/YA JANEWAY, Elizabeth (Hall). *Ivanov Seven.* Gr. 5–8.
   [R]   Stepan's curiosity and independence cause problems after he joins the Czar's army. (BL 64:502; HB 43:750; KR 35:1145; LJ 92:4261)
   Illus. by Eros Keith, Harper, 1967, 176 pp., o.p.

YA [R] JETER, K. W. *Infernal Devices: A Mad Victorian Fantasy.* Gr. 10 up.
   A witty, adventure-filled romp about the owner of a clock repair shop in Victorian London who becomes involved with a mechanical man, a pair of con men, a gentleman bent on blowing up the world, and the peculiar fishlike inhabitants of Wetwick. (BL 83:1253, 1275; KR 55:261; LJ Apr 15, 1987 p. 103; VOYA 10:130)
   St. Martin, 1987, 282 pp.; NAL, 1987, pap.

JONES, Diana Wynne. *Archer's Goon.* See Chapter 10, Witchcraft and Sorcery Fantasy.

JONES, Diana Wynne. *Howl's Moving Castle.* See Chapter 10, Witchcraft and Sorcery Fantasy.

JONES, Diana Wynne. *The Ogre Downstairs.* See Chapter 7, Magic Adventure Fantasy.

JONES, Diana Wynne. *A Tale of Time City.* See Section 5C, Travel to Other Worlds.

C JONES, Terry. *Fairy Tales.* Gr. 3–5. (Orig. British pub. 1981.)
   An oversized book containing thirty short, humorous tales for reading aloud. (CCBB 36:169; Ch&Bks:268; Suth 3:222; TLS 1981 p. 1360)
   Illus. by Michael Foreman, Schocken, 1983, 127 pp.

C/YA JONES, Terry. *Nicobobinus.* Gr. 5–7. (Orig. British pub. 1985.)
   Nicobobinus and his friend Rosie make a madcap journey to the Land of Dragons seeking a cure for Nicobobinus's enchanted golden foot. (BL 82:1613; SLJ Aug 1986 p. 94; TLS 1986 p. 174)
   Illus. by Michael Foreman, Bedrick, dist. by Harper, 1986, 175 pp.

C JONSSON, Runer. *Viki Viking* (British title: *Vike the Viking*). Gr. 4–6. (Orig. Swedish pub. 1963.)
   Chief Halvar's son, Viki, hates fighting but still manages to rescue his father's troops. (BL 64:1094; CCBB 21:129; HB 44:324; KR 35:1473; LJ 93:2114; TLS 1969 p. 689)
   Tr. by Birgit Rogers and Patricia Lowe, illus. by Ewert Karlsson, World, 1968, 143 pp., o.p.

JUSTER, Norton. *The Phantom Tollbooth.* See Section 5C, Travel to Other Worlds.

C [R] KÄSTNER, Erich. *The Little Man.* Gr. 4–6. (Orig. Swiss pub. 1963.)
   Two-inch-tall Maxie Pichelsteiner gains fame by becoming Professor Hokus Von Pokus's Invisible Right-Hand Man. The sequels are *The Little Man and*

the Big Thief (1970) and *The Little Man and the Little Miss* (British). (BL
63:728; CCBB 20:124; Ch&Bks:268; KR 34:1101; LJ 91:6192; Suth:220; TLS
1966 p. 1077)

Tr. by James Kirkup, illus. by Rick Schreiter, Knopf, 1966, o.p.; Avon,
1980, pap., 183 pp.

KAUFMAN, Charles. *The Frog and the Beanpole*. See Section 2B,
Talking Animal Fantasy.

KAYE, Marvin. *The Incredible Umbrella*. See Section 5C, Travel to Other
Worlds.

C/YA KEELE, Luqman, and PINKWATER, D(aniel) Manus. *Java Jack*. Gr. 4–
8.

Jack travels from Missouri to Indonesia in search of his missing parents. En
route, he is kidnapped, pilots an airplane, acquires a magic needle, fights a
gang of pirates, and voyages out of the universe. (HB 56:297; KR 48:584; SLJ
May 1980 p. 68)

Harper, 1980, 152 pp.

KEMP, Gene. *Jason Bodger and the Priory Ghost*. See Chapter 4, Ghost
Fantasy.

C KENNEDY, William, and KENNEDY, Brendan. *Charlie Malarkey and
the Belly-Button Machine*. Gr. 2–4.

Charlie Malarkey and Iggy Gowalowicz wake up to discover that their belly
buttons have been stolen by a salesman named Ben Bubie and his mysterious
machine. William Kennedy is a Pulitzer Prize-winning author, and Brendan
Kennedy is his son. (KR 54:1728; SLJ Dec 1986 p. 90)

Illus. by Glen Baxter, Atlantic, dist. by Little, 1986, 40 pp.

KING, Clive. *The Town That Went South*. See Chapter 2B, Talking
Animal Fantasy.

C [R] KING-SMITH, Dick. *Harry's Mad*. Gr. 3–6. (Orig. British pub. 1986.)

Just after Harry discovers that Madison, the parrot he inherited from a
great-uncle, can talk like a human, Mad is stolen by a burglar. (BL 83:1680,
84:1274; CCBB 40:171; HB 63:463; KR 55:221; SLJ May 1987 p. 101, Dec
1987 p. 37; TLS Nov 1986 p. 1347)

Illus. by Jill Bennet, Crown, 1987, 123 pp.

C KLEIN, Robin. *Thing*. Gr. 1–4. (Orig. British pub. 1982.)

Emily's pet rock hatches into a baby stegosaurus, who grows to the size of a
small rhinoceros and prevents a robbery in their landlady's apartment. (BL
79:1402; CCBB 37:52; SLJ Mar 1984 p. 146)

Illus. by Alison Lester, Oxford, dist. by Merrimack, 1983, 32 pp., o.p.

KONIGSBURG, E. L. *Up From Jericho Tel*. See Chapter 7, Magic
Adventure Fantasy.

YA KOTZWINKLE, William. *Trouble in Bugland: A Collection of Inspector
Mantis Mysteries*. Gr. 7 up.

Five short mystery tales starring Inspector Mantis and his grasshopper
sidekick, characters modeled after Sir Arthur Conan Doyle's Sherlock
Holmes and Dr. Watson. (BL 80:469, 490, 498; HB 60:196; KR 51:1022; SLJ
Feb 1984 p. 74)

Illus. by Joe Servello, Godine, 1983, hb, o.p., pap., 160 pp.

KRÜSS, James. *The Happy Islands behind the Winds.* See Section 5C, Travel to Other Worlds.

LAMPMAN, Evelyn Sibley. *Captain Apple's Ghost.* See Chapter 4, Ghost Fantasy.

C/YA LAMPMAN, Evelyn Sibley. *The Shy Stegosaurus of Cricket Creek.* Gr. 5–7.
Joey, Joan, and a shy dinosaur named George capture a thief. The sequel is *The Shy Stegosaurus of Indian Springs* (1962). (BL 52:150; HB 31:377; LJ 80:2386)
Illus. by Hubert Buel, Doubleday, 1955, 218 pp., o.p.

LAUMER, Keith. *The Shape Changer: A Science Fiction Novel.* See Section 5A, Alternate Worlds or Histories.

LAWSON, Robert. *Ben and Me: A New and Astonishing Life of Benjamin Franklin as Written by His Good Mouse, Amos: Lately Discovered.* See Section 2B, Talking Animal Fantasy.

LAWSON, Robert. *Captain Kidd's Cat: Being the True and Dolorous Chronicle of Wm. Kidd, Gentleman and Merchant of New York; Late Captain of the Adventure Galley; Of the Vicissitudes Attending His Unfortunate Cruise in Eastern Waters, Of His Unjust Trial and Execution, as Narrated by His Faithful Cat, McDermot, Who Ought to Know.* See Section 2B, Talking Animal Fantasy.

LAWSON, Robert. *The Fabulous Flight.* See Chapter 7, Magic Adventure Fantasy.

LAWSON, Robert. *I Discover Columbus: A True Chronicle of the Great Admiral and His Finding of the New World, Narrated by the Venerable Parrot Aurelio, Who Shared in the Glorious Venture.* See Section 2B, Talking Animal Fantasy.

C LAWSON, Robert. *McWhinney's Jaunt.* Gr. 3–5.
Professor McWhinney flies off to Hollywood on his z-gas powered bicycle. (BL 48:16; CCBB 5:6; KR 19:294; LJ 76:1341)
Illus. by the author, Little, 1951, 77 pp., o.p., 1985, pap.

LAWSON, Robert. *Mr. Revere and I: Being an Account of Certain Episodes in the Career of Paul Revere, Esq., as Recently Revealed by His Horse, Scheherazade, Late Pride of His Royal Majesty's 14th Regiment of Foot.* See Section 2B, Talking Animal Tales.

LAWSON, Robert. *Mr. Twigg's Mistake.* See Section 2B, Talking Animal Tales.

C [R] LAWSON, Robert. *Smeller Martin.* Gr. 4–6.
Davy Martin's extraordinary sense of smell helps the police solve a crime and makes him a celebrity at school. (BL 47:104; CCBB 4:5; HB 26:474; KR 18:470; LJ 75:2084)
Illus. by the author, Viking, 1950, 157 pp., o.p.

C LAZARUS, Keo Felker. *The Shark in the Window.* Gr. 4–6.
Shelly's new pet shark can swim through the air. (BL 69:357; CCBB 26:45; KR 40:940; LJ 97:3806; Suth:241)
Illus. by Laurel Schindelman, Morrow, 1972, 159 pp., o.p.

C/YA LEE, Robert C. *The Iron Arm of Michael Glenn*. Gr. 5–8.
After Mike's pitching arm is accidently exposed to Professor Von Heiner's experiment, he moves up from Little League baseball to pitching for the San Francisco Giants. The sequel is *The Day It Rained Forever* (1968). (KR 33:752; LJ 90:4636)
Illus. by Al Fiorentino, Little, 1965, 153 pp., o.p.

LEE, Tanith. *Princess Hynchatti and Some Other Surprises*. See Chapter 1, Allegorical Fantasy and Literary Fairy Tales.

C/YA LEESON, Robert (Arthur). *Genie on the Loose*. Gr. 6–8.
Keeping wily Abdul the genie in check proves to be more difficult than Alec Bowden bargained for. This is the sequel to the British book *The Third Class Genie*. (BL 81:524; SLJ Jan 1985 p. 87)
Hamish Hamilton, dist. by David and Charles, 1984, 127 pp.

C LE GRAND (pseud. of Le Grand Henderson). *How Baseball Began in Brooklyn*. Gr. 3–5.
It seems that baseball was accidently invented in New Amsterdam by ten Dutch colonial boys and a Native American. (BL 54:540; CCBB 11:97; Eakin:205; HB 34:108; LJ 83:1604)
Illus. by the author, Abingdon, 1958, 58 pp., o.p.

C LE GRAND (pseud. of Le Grand Henderson). *How Space Rockets Began*. Gr. 3–5.
Windwagon Smith invents a steam wagon that flies to the moon. (HB 36:289; KR 28:89; LJ 85:2040)
Illus. by the author, Abingdon, 1960, 64 pp., o.p.

C LE GRAND (pseud. of Le Grand Henderson). *Matilda*. Gr. 4–6.
A goat named Matilda becomes a student at Columbia University. (BL 53:52; Eakin:205; KR 24:353; LJ 81:2041)
Illus. by the author, Abingdon, 1956, 63 pp., o.p.

LE VERT, John. *The Flight of the Cassowary*. See Chapter 1, Allegorical Fantasy and Literary Fairy Tales.

C LEVITIN, Sonia (Wolff). *Jason and the Money Tree*. Gr. 4–6.
The ten-dollar bill Jason's grandfather gave him sprouts into a money tree, but leaves him with the problem of accounting for his sudden wealth. (BL 70:1057; CCBB 27:180; KR 42:300; LJ 99:2274)
Illus. by Pat Porter, Harcourt, 1974, 121 pp., o.p.

LEVOY, Myron. *The Magic Hat of Mortimer Wintergreen*. See Chapter 10, Witchcraft and Sorcery Fantasy.

C [R] LIFTON, Betty Jean (Kirschner). *The One-Legged Ghost*. Gr. 1–4.
The villagers decide that the strange bamboo object that fell from the sky must be a god. (BL 65:314; KR 36:1163; LJ 93:4396; Suth:251)
Illus. by Fuku Akino, Atheneum, 1968, 37 pp., o.p.

LILLINGTON, Kenneth. *An Ash-Blond Witch*. See Chapter 10, Witchcraft and Sorcery Fantasy.

C [R] LINDGREN, Astrid. *Pippi Longstocking*. Gr. 4–6. (Orig. Swedish pub. 1945.)
Life is never dull for Annika and Tommy after the strongest child in the world moves in next door with her pet monkey and horse. The sequels are

Pippi Goes on Board (1957; British title: *Pippi Goes Abroad*), *Pippi in the South Seas* (1959), and *Pippi on the Run* (1976). (BL 47:208; CC:499; CCBB 4:21; Ch&Bks:254; HB 26:376; KR 18:515; LJ 75:1754)
Tr. by Florence Lamborn, illus. by Louis Glanzman, Viking, 1950, 158 pp.; Penguin, 1977, pap.; Buccaneer, 1981 (repr. of 1950 ed.).

C LINDSAY, Norman (Alfred William). *The Magic Pudding: Being the Adventures of Bunyip Bluegum and His Friends Bill Barnacle and Sam Sawnoff.* Gr. 3–5. (Orig. Australian pub. 1918.)
A koala, a sailor, and a penguin find a magic pudding. (LJ 61:809, 62:38; TLS 1936 p. 974)
Illus. by the author, Farrar, 1936, 159 pp., o.p.

LINKLATER, Eric. *The Pirates in the Deep Green Sea.* See Section 5C, Travel to Other Worlds.

C LISLE, Janet Taylor. *The Dancing Cats of Applesap.* Gr. 4–6.
Ten-year-old Melba vows to save the drugstore home of Miss Toonie's fabulous dancing cats. (BL 80:1550; CCBB 37:208; SLJ Oct 1984 p. 159)
Illus. by Joelle Shefts, Bradbury, dist. by Macmillan, 1984, 169 pp.; Bantam/Sky Lark, 1985, pap.

LISLE, Janet Taylor. *The Great Dimpole Oak.* See Chapter 1, Allegorical Fantasy and Literary Fairy Tales.

C [R] LIVELY, Penelope (Margaret Low). *Uninvited Ghosts and Other Stories.* Gr. 4–6. (Orig. British pub. 1984.)
Eight hilarious tales about ghosts, a dragon, and a Martian who invade ordinary family life. (BL 81:1459; CC 1987 Suppl. p. 65; CCBB 38:189; HB 61:450; KR 53:34; SLJ 31[Aug 1985]:68; TLS 1984 p. 1381)
Illus. by John Lawrence, Dutton, 1985, 119 pp.

LOBE, Mira. *The Grandma in the Apple Tree.* See Chapter 7, Magic Adventure Fantasy.

LOCKE, Angela. *Mr. Mullett Owns a Cloud.* See Chapter 7, Magic Adventure Fantasy.

C [R] LOFTING, Hugh. *The Story of Doctor Dolittle.* Gr. 3–6.
When a great plague strikes the animals of Africa, Doctor Dolittle, the best animal doctor in the world, travels to Africa to save them. Lofting's depiction of black Africans has been criticized as racist; the Delacorte revised editions have changed or eliminated the prejudicial passages. The sequels are *The Voyages of Doctor Dolittle* (1922; Newbery Medal winner, 1923; rev. ed., 1988), *Doctor Dolittle's Post Office* (1923), *Doctor Dolittle's Circus* (1924), *Doctor Dolittle's Zoo* (1925), *Doctor Dolittle's Caravan* (1926), *Doctor Dolittle's Garden* (1927), *Doctor Dolittle in the Moon* (1928), *Gub-Gub's Book: An Encyclopedia of Food* (1932), *Doctor Dolittle's Return* (1933), *Doctor Dolittle and the Secret Lake* (1948), *Doctor Dolittle and the Green Canary* (1950), and *Doctor Dolittle's Puddleby Adventures* (1952). *Doctor Dolittle: A Treasury* (Dell, 1986, pap.) is a collection of tales. (BL 19:193, 84:1838; Bookshelf 1932 p. 8; Ch&Bks:269; HB 24:341; Mahony 2:284; Moore:426)
Illus. by the author, Lippincott, 1920, 172 pp., o.p.; Delacorte 1988 (rev. ed.), pap.

C   MacDONALD, Betty (Campbell Bard). *Mrs. Piggle-Wiggle.* Gr. 2–5.
(Orig. pub. 1947.)
Mrs. Piggle-Wiggle has magical cures for all children's ailments, including
the won't-pick-up-toys cure, the answer-backer cure, and the selfishness
cure. The sequels are *Mrs. Piggle-Wiggle's Farm* (1954), *Hello, Mrs. Piggle-Wiggle* (1957), and *Mrs. Piggle-Wiggle's Magic* (1957). (BL 43:260; HB
23:213; KR 15:127; LJ 72:590, 739)
Illus. by Hilary Knight, Lippincott, 1957 (rev. ed.), 118 pp.; Harper, 1957
(rev. ed.), pap.

C/YA McINERNY, Ralph M. *Quick As a Dodo.* Gr. 6 up.
Dormer, a literate dodo who hatches from a strange Easter egg, decides to
free a caged rabbit and escape from his owner's home. (BL 75:27, 39; LJ
103:973)
Illus. by Pam Butterworth, Juniper, 1977, o.p.; Vanguard, 1978, 116 pp.,
o.p.

MacKELLAR, William. *Alfie and Me and the Ghost of Peter Stuyvesant.*
See Chapter 4, Ghost Fantasy.

C [R] MAHY, Margaret (May). *The Great Piratical Rumbustification, and The
Librarian and the Robbers.* Gr. 3–6. (Orig. pub. in New Zealand, 1978.)
Two humorous stories about a pirate babysitter and a beautiful librarian
who rescues herself from kidnappers. (CCBB 40:92; KR 54:1584; SLJ Mar
1987 p. 163; TLS 1978 p. 1398)
Illus. by Quentin Blake, Godine, 1986, 62 pp.

C   MANES, Stephen. *Chicken Treck: The Third Strange Thing That Happened to Oscar Noodleman.* Gr. 4–6.
Oscar and his cousin, Dr. Prechtwinkle, attempt to win a prize offered by
the Bagful O' Chicken Company, using a Picklemobile that can travel in a
matter of seconds to any spot on Earth. This is the sequel to two humorous
science fiction tales: *That Game from Outer Space* (1983) and *The Oscar J.
Noodleman Television Network* (1984). (BL 83:1750; CCBB 41:13; KR
55:860; SLJ Aug 1987 p. 86)
Illus. by Ron Barrett, Dutton, 1987, 128 pp.

C   MANNING, Rosemary (Joy). *Dragon in Danger.* Gr. 4–6. (Orig. British
pub. 1959.)
The first dragon to appear in five hundred years, R. Dragon is offered a
starring role in the town's annual pageant. This is the sequel to *Green Smoke*
(1957), and is followed by *The Dragon's Quest* (1962) and *Dragon in Summer*
(British). (KR 28:775; LJ 85:4569; TLS May 29, 1959 p. xiii)
Illus. by Constance Marshall, Doubleday, 1960, 169 pp., o.p.

MARSHALL, James. *A Summer in the South.* See Section 2B, Talking
Animal Fantasy.

MARSHALL, James. *Taking Care of Carruthers.* See Chapter 2B, Talking
Animal Fantasy.

C   MENDOZA, George. *Gwot! Horribly Funny Hairticklers.* Gr. 3–5.
Three ghastly tales: a huge black snake that grows bigger each time its head
is chopped off, an old woman who eats a hairy toe, and the hunt for the
horrible Gumberoo. (KR 35:1048; LJ 92:4615)
Illus. by Steven Kellogg, Harper, 1967, 41 pp., o.p.

C/YA MERRILL, Jean (Fairbanks). *The Pushcart War.* Gr. 5–7.
[R]   Traffic congestion in New York City brings on a war between the truck drivers and the pushcart owners. (BL 61:219, 80:96; CC:508; Ch&Bks:254; Eakin:223; HB 40:378; LJ 89:2828)
    Illus. by Ronni Solbert, Harper, 1964; Dell, 1987, pap., 224 pp.; Peter Smith, 1988.

C [R] MERRILL, Jean (Fairbanks). *The Toothpaste Millionaire.* Gr. 4–5.
    Eleven-year-old Lucas starts his own toothpaste factory to compete with the higher-priced name-brand toothpastes. (BL 70:1254; CC:508; CCBB 28:49; HB 50:137; KR 42:480; Suth 2:316)
    Houghton, 1974, 90 pp.

MILNE, A. A. *Prince Rabbit and the Princess Who Could Not Laugh.* See Chapter 1, Allegorical Fantasy and Literary Fairy Tales.

MILNE, A. A. *Winnie-the-Pooh.* See Chapter 9, Toy Fantasy.

MINOT, Stephen. *Surviving the Flood.* See Section 5B, Myth Fantasy.

MOORE, Margaret Eileen. *Willie Without.* See Section 2B. Talking Animal Fantasy.

C MÜNCHAUSEN, Karl. *The Adventures of Baron Münchausen.* Gr. 3–6.
    (Orig. German pub. 1781–1783; U.S. pub. 1813.)
    These tales were originally printed anonymously in Germany, 1781–1783, and are sometimes attributed to Karl Friedrich Hieronymus, Baron Von Münchausen. They were translated into English and edited by Rudolf Erich Raspé in 1786, and first published in the U.S. (1813), entitled *Gulliver Redivivus; or the Curious and Entertaining Travels and Adventures by Sea and by Land of the Renowned Baron Munchausen; Including a Tour to the United States of America in the Year 1803; and the First Chapters of a Second Tour in 1816.* In *The Baron Rides Out* (Putnam/Philomel, 1985, 1986), the fabulous Baron Münchausen travels to a Ceylonese jungle where he meets a gigantic alligator, a huge lion, and an enormous giant called Peter the Great. Two companion volumes, both edited by Adrian Mitchell, are: *The Baron on the Island of Cheese* (1986), and *The Baron All at Sea* (1987). (BL 18:162, 25:87, 41:157; Bookshelf 1924–1925 p. 15, 1932 p. 23; HB 55:536; KR 12:483, 54:1451; LJ 69:1006, 86:575, 96:3470; SLJ Feb 1980 p. 60, May 1986 p. 82, Jan 1987 p. 76; TLS 1985 pp. 355, 1435)
    Illus. by W. Heath Robinson, Dutton, 1903 (entitled *The Surprising Travels and Adventures of Baron Münchausen*), o.p.; retold by John Martin (pseud. of Morgan Shepard), illus. by Gordon Ross, Houghton, 1921 (entitled *The Children's Münchausen*), o.p.; illus. by Gustave Doré, Pantheon, 1944, o.p.; retold by Erich Kästner, tr. by Richard Wilson and Clara Wilson, illus. by Walter Trier, Messner, 1951, 1957 (entitled *Baron Münchausen, His Wonderful Travels and Adventures*), o.p.; illus. by Fritz Kredel, Heritage, 1952 (entitled *The Singular Adventures of Baron Münchausen*), o.p.; ed. and illus. by Brian Robb, Deutsch, dist. by Elsevier-Dutton, 1979 (orig. British pub. 1947; entitled *12 Adventures of the Celebrated Baron Münchausen*), o.p.; ed. by Adrian Mitchell, illus. by Patrick Benson, Philomel/Putnam, 1986 (orig. British pub. 1985, entitled *The Baron Rides Out: A Baron Münchausen Tall Tale*), 28 pp.

C MYERS, Bernice. *Sidney Rella and the Glass Sneaker.* Gr. 2–4.
    In this Cinderella spoof, Sydney dreams of becoming a football hero, until

his fairy godmother magically takes over his household chores and provides a new uniform and a pair of glass sneakers. (BL 82:340; CCBB 39:155; SLJ Mar 1986 p. 150)
Illus. by the author, Macmillan, 1985, 32 pp.

C MYERS, Walter Dean. *The Black Pearl and the Ghost; or, One Mystery after Another.* Gr. 2–4.
Two humorous mystery stories, one involving a stolen pearl and the other a haunted manor house. (BL 76:1297; CCBB 33:180; HB 56:301; KR 48:514; SLJ May 1980 p. 85)
Illus. by Robert Quackenbush, Viking, 1980, 40 pp.

C [R] NASH, Mary (Hughes). *While Mrs. Coverlet Was Away.* Gr. 4–6.
After their father and their housekeeper are both called out of town, Molly, Malcolm, and Todd manage on their own. The sequels are *Mrs. Coverlet's Magicians* (1961) and *Mrs. Coverlet's Detectives* (1965). (BL 55:137; CCBB 12:52; Eakin:243; HB 34:386; KR 26:380; LJ 83:2502)
Illus. by Garrett Price, Little, 1958, 133 pp., o.p.

C/YA NASTICK, Sharon. *Mr. Radagast Makes an Unexpected Journey.* Gr. 4–7.
A seventh grade class is amazed to find that their experiment in immaterialism has made their teacher, Mr. Radagast, disappear. (BL 77:1346; KR 49:504; SLJ May 1981 p. 67)
Illus. by Judy Glasser, Crowell, 1981, 85 pp., o.p.

NESBIT, E. *The Last of the Dragons.* See Chapter 1, Allegorical Fantasy and Literary Fairy Tales.

NIXON, Joan Lowery. *Magnolia's Mixed-Up Magic.* See Section 2B, Talking Animal Fantasy.

C [O] NÖSTLINGER, Christine. *Konrad* (British title: *Conrad: The Hilarious Adventures of a Factory-made Child,* 1976). Gr. 4–6. (Orig. Austrian pub. 1975.)
Despite his unexpected arrival, a canned, mail-order child named Konrad is allowed to move in with Mrs. Bartolotti, but his perfect behavior disturbs his new mother and angers his classmates. (BL 74:482; CCBB 31:98; Ch&Bks:270; HB 53:665; SLJ Nov 1977 p. 60; Suth 2:339; TLS 1977 p. 348)
Tr. by Anthea Bell, illus. by Carol Nicklaus, Watts, 1977, o.p.; Avon, 1983, pap., 135 pp.

C/YA OAKLEY, Graham. *Henry's Quest.* Gr. 5 up.
[R] Sometime in a future post-technology England, the king sends shepherd Henry off on a quest for the magical substance "gasoline," in order to win the hand of Princess Isolde. (BL 83:893, 902; CCBB 40:133; KR 54:1374; SLJ Dec 1986 p. 107; TLS 1986 p. 1345)
Illus. by the author, Atheneum, 1986, 32 pp.

OLSON, Helen Kronberg. *The Strange Thing That Happened to Oliver Wendell Iscovitch.* See Chapter 7, Magic Adventure Fantasy.

ORMONDROYD, Edward. *Broderick.* See Section 2B, Talking Animal Fantasy.

ORMONDROYD, Edward. *David and the Phoenix.* See Chapter 7, Magic Adventure Fantasy.

PAGET, F. E. *The Hope of the Katzekopfs; or, the Sorrow of Selfishness: A Fairy Tale.* See Chapter 1, Allegorical Fantasy and Literary Fairy Tales.

YA [R] PALMER, David R. *Threshold.* Gr. 10 up.
Peter Cory is recruited as the savior of the universe by a beautiful witch who looks like Tinkerbell without wings, in this spoof of heroic fantasy. Two sequels are planned. (BL 82:468, 482; Kliatt 20[Spring 1986]:24; LJ Dec 1985 p. 130; VOYA 9:89)
Bantam, 1985, pap., 274 pp.

PALMER, Mary. *The Dolmop of Dorkling.* See Section 5C, Travel to Other Worlds.

PALMER, Robin. *Wise House.* See Section 2B, Talking Animal Fantasy.

PARKER, Edgar. *The Dream of the Dormouse.* See Section 2B, Talking Animal Fantasy.

PARKER, Edgar. *The Question of a Dragon.* See Section 2B, Talking Animal Fantasy.

C PARKER, (James) Edgar (Jr.). *Rogue's Gallery.* Gr. 4–6.
A crime story spoof starring master criminal Hoimie-the-stoat, Reynolds the policefox, and Matou, a tomcat gone straight. (CCBB 23:104; KR 37:1113)
Illus. by the author, Pantheon, 1969, 63 pp., o.p.

C PARKER, Nancy Winslow. *The Spotted Dog: The Strange Tale of a Witch's Revenge.* Gr. 2–4.
A witch turns the Cruikshank-Jones's baby, Eileen, into a dog, but the family doesn't seem to mind—they enjoy winning ribbons at dog shows. (BL 77:407; KR 48:1395; SLJ Dec 1980 p. 54)
Illus. by the author, Dodd, 1980, 46 pp.

C [R] PARRISH, Anne. *The Story of Appleby Capple.* Gr. 3–5.
A boy has alphabetical adventures while searching for a rare zebra moth. Newbery Medal Honor Book, 1951. (BL 47:225; CCBB 4:22; HB 26:457, 467, 27:20; KR 18:512; LJ 75:1745, 76:338)
Illus. by the author, Harper, 1950, 184 pp., o.p.

PASCAL, Francine. *Hangin' Out with Cici.* See Chapter 8, Time Travel Fantasy.

PECK, Richard. *The Ghost Belonged to Me: A Novel.* See Chapter 4, Ghost Fantasy.

PEET, Bill. *Big Bad Bruce.* See Section 2B, Talking Animal Fantasy.

PEET, Bill. *The Whingdingdilly.* See Section 2B, Talking Animal Fantasy.

C PETRIE, Stuart. *The Voyage of Barracks.* Gr. 4–6. (Orig. British pub. 1967.)
An English family ties their house to a hot-air balloon and soars off around the world. (BL 65:754; KR 36:643; LJ 93:3308; TLS 1967 p. 1133)
Illus. by the author, Meredith, 1968, 120 pp., o.p.

PINKWATER, D. Manus. *Blue Moose.* See Section 2B, Talking Animal Fantasy.

C [R] PINKWATER, D(aniel) Manus. *The Frankenbagel Monster.* Gr. 2–5.
Harold Frankenbagel creates Bagelnuculus in his quest to become the greatest bagel maker in history, but Harold must stop the monster bagel when it goes mad and heads off towards a lox warehouse. (BL 83:356; HB 62:742; KR 54:1584; SLJ Oct 1986 p. 165)
Dutton, 1986, 24 pp., o.p.

C [R] PINKWATER, D(aniel) Manus. *The Hoboken Chicken Emergency.* Gr. 3–5.
Arthur Bobowicz's adoption of a 266-pound chicken meets with opposition from his parents, the mayor, and the townspeople. (BL 73:1268; CC:520; CCBB 30:163; HB 53:316, 61:755; KR 45:166; SLJ Sept 1977 p. 134)
Illus. by the author, Prentice-Hall, 1977, 83 pp.; Scholastic, 1978, pap.; Prentice-Hall/Treehouse, 1984, pap.

C PINKWATER, D(aniel) Manus. *Jolly Roger: A Dog of Hoboken.* Gr. 3–5.
Jolly Roger (half husky, half chow chow) is befriended by The Kid, but soon becomes the leader of the Hoboken dock dogs. (BL 82:69; HB 61:559; KR 53:35; SLJ Sept 1985 p. 138)
Lothrop, 1985, 40 pp.

C/YA PINKWATER, D(aniel) Manus. *The Last Guru.* Gr. 5–7.
After twelve-year-old Harold Blatz invests his racetrack winnings in a hamburger chain and becomes a billionaire, the Blatz family tries to escape their newfound fame by moving to a castle in the Bavarian Alps and then to a village in India. (BL 75:548; CCBB 32:124; KR 46:1189; SLJ Nov 1978 p. 66)
Illus. by the author, Dodd, 1978, o.p.; Bantam, 1981, pap., 115 pp.

C [R] PINKWATER, D(aniel) Manus. *Lizard Music.* Gr. 4–6.
Victor can't understand why lizards and the Chicken Man turn up wherever he goes, until he is taken to an invisible, lizard-run island. (BL 73:41, 80:96; CC:520; CCBB 30:112; HB 53:161; KR 44:846; SLJ Oct 1976 p. 110)
Illus. by the author, Dodd, 1976, 157 pp.

C PINKWATER, D(aniel) Manus. *The Muffin Fiend.* Gr. 3–5.
Inspector Charles LeChat tracks down an extraterrestrial muffin thief who needs thousands of muffins to fuel his rocket for the trip home. (CCBB 39:156; HB 62:324, KR 54:475; SLJ Aug 1986 p. 97)
Illus. by the author, Lothrop, 1986, 48 pp.; Bantam/Skylark, 1987, pap.

C PINKWATER, D(aniel) Manus. *The Worms of Kukumlima.* Gr. 5–8.
Ronald Donald Almandotter, his grandfather, Seumas Finneganstein, and Sir Charles Pelicanstein go on a safari into wildest Kukumlima to capture a huge, intelligent worm. (BL 77:1034; CCBB 35:35; KR 49:571; SLJ May 1981 p. 68; VOYA 5[Apr 1982]:41)
Elsevier-Dutton, 1981, 152 pp.

C/YA PINKWATER, D(aniel) Manus. *Yobgorgle: Mystery Monster of Lake Ontario.* Gr. 5–7.
Only a corned beef sandwich will remove the curse on the captain of the "Flying Piggie" submarine. (BL 76:126; KR 47:1068; SLJ Nov 1979 p. 80)
Houghton, 1979, 138 pp., o.p.

C POMERANTZ, Charlotte. *Detective Poufy's First Case: Or the Missing Battery-Operated Pepper Grinder.* Gr. 3–5.
A lonely dragon named Dragobert turns out to be the robber who broke into Rosie Maloon's house and left all the electrical gadgets running. (BL 73:476; KR 44:796; SLJ Dec 1976 p. 65)
Illus. by Marty Norman, Addison-Wesley, 1976, 64 pp., o.p.

POMERANTZ, Charlotte. *The Downtown Fairy Godmother.* See Chapter 7, Magic Adventure Fantasy.

C POPHAM, Hugh. *The Fabulous Voyage of the Pegasus.* Gr. 4–6.
Lee-O! sets sail on the Pegasus in search of a Narwhal and the sea god, Poseidon. (HB 35:301; KR 27:176; LJ 84:1700)
Illus. by Graham Oakley, Phillips, 1959, 150 pp., o.p.

C [R] PORTER, David Lord. *Help! Let Me Out!* Gr. 2–5.
Hugo learns ventriloquism and throws his voice, only to have the voice take off for a life of its own. (BL 79:315; CCBB 36:75; KR 50:676; SLJ Sept 1982 p. 110)
Illus. by David Macaulay, Houghton, 1982, 32 pp.

POSTGATE, Oliver, and FIRMIN, Peter. *King of the Nogs.* See Chapter 1, Allegorical Fantasy and Literary Fairy Tales.

C/YA PREUSSLER, Otfried. *The Robber Hotzenplotz.* Gr. 5–7. (Orig. pub. in Germany.)
Kasperl and Seppel are trapped in the hideout of the notorious bandit, Hotzenplotz. The sequel is *Further Adventures of the Robber Hotzenplotz* (1971). *The Final Adventures of the Robber Hotzenplotz* is a British sequel. (KR 33:107; LJ 90:2409; TLS 1964 p. 1081)
Tr. by Anthea Bell, illus. by F. J. Tripp, Abelard-Schuman, 1965, 126 pp., o.p.

C PREUSSLER, Otfried. *The Wise Men of Schilda.* Gr. 4–6. (Orig. pub. in Germany.)
The foolish inhabitants of Schilda try to prove their cleverness to the rest of the world. (BL 60:44; CCBB 17:128; HB 39:286; LJ 88:2553)
Tr. by Anthea Bell, illus. by F. J. Tripp, Abelard-Schuman, 1963, 185 pp., o.p.

C QUACKENBUSH, Robert M(ead). *Express Train to Trouble: A Miss Mallard Mystery.* Gr. 2–4.
A humorous takeoff on Agatha Christie's *Murder on the Orient Express,* in which all of the characters are animals, including the detective, Miss Mallard. The sequels are *Dig to Disaster* (1982), *Stairway to Doom* (1983), *Gondola to Danger* (1983), *Rickshaw to Horror* (1984), *Taxi to Intrigue* (1984), *Stage Door to Terror* (1985), *Bicycle to Treachery* (1985), and *Dogsled to Dread* (1987). (BL 78:758; CC:520; SLJ Aug 1982 p. 104)
Illus. by the author, Prentice-Hall, 1981, 48 pp.

C/YA RASKIN, Ellen. *Figgs and Phantoms.* Gr. 5–7.
[R]   Mona Lisa Newton does not appreciate her kooky relatives—her tapdancing mother, twin brothers Romulus and Remus, contortionist Truman Figg, and cousin Fido Figg—until her beloved uncle dies. Newbery Medal Honor Book, 1975. (BL 71:46; CCBB 28:98; HB 50:138; KR 42:425; LJ 99:1451, 1475, 3247; Suth 2:374)
Illus. by the author, Dutton, 1974, 152 pp., o.p.; Avon, 1981, pap.

C/YA RASKIN, Ellen. *The Mysterious Disappearance of Leon (I Mean Noel)*.
[R]   Gr. 5–7.
      Married at five and seven years of age to solve their parents' business
problems, Caroline (Little Dumpling) and Leon (Noel) Carillon don't see
each other again for fourteen clue-, puzzle-, and secret code-filled
years. (BL 68:394, 670; CCBB 25:79; HB 48:51; KR 39:1122; LJ 96:4160;
Suth:323)
      Illus. by the author, Dutton, 1971, 149 pp., o.p.; Avon, 1980, pap.

C/YA RASKIN, Ellen. *The Tattooed Potato and Other Clues*. Gr. 5–7.
[R]   Dickory Dock's detective work leads her to the blackmailers of a brilliant
artist and the murderer of her parents. (BL 71:967; CC:520; CCBB 29:52;
HB 51:271; KR 43:457; SLJ Apr 1975 p. 69, Dec 1975 p. 32; Suth 2:374; TLS
1976 p. 1548)
      Dutton, 1975, 170 pp.; Avon, 1981, pap.

   RAYNER, Mary. *Mrs. Pig Gets Cross; and Other Stories*. See Section 2B,
   Talking Animal Fantasy.

   RAZZI, Jim, and RAZZI, Mary. *The Search for King Pup's Tomb*. See
   Section 2B, Talking Animal Fantasy.

  C REIT, Seymour. *Benvenuto*. Gr. 3–5.
      Paolo brings home a baby dragon from summer camp. (BL 70:878; KR
42:301; LJ 99:2276)
      Illus. by Will Winslow, Addison-Wesley, 1974, 126 pp., o.p.

C [R] RICHLER, Mordecai. *Jacob Two-Two Meets the Hooded Fang*. Gr. 3–5.
   (Orig. pub. in Canada.)
      Jacob is teased for his habit of saying everything twice, but he proves to be
courageous after his capture by the Slimers and their chief, the Hooded Fang.
Winner, Canadian Library Association Best Book of the Year for Children,
1976. The sequel is *Jacob Two-Two and the Dinosaur* (1987). (CCBB 28:184;
KR 43:568; SLJ Sept 1975 p. 90; TLS 1976 p. 376)
      Illus. by Fritz Wegner, Knopf, 1975, 87 pp., o.p.; Bantam, 1986, pap., o.p.

  C RINKOFF, Barbara (Jean). *Elbert, the Mind Reader*. Gr. 4–6.
      Elbert's new filling enables him to tune in on people's thoughts, a talent he
uses to impress the football coach so that he can join the team. (BL 64:594;
CCBB 21:65; KR 35:809; LJ 92:3855)
      Illus. by Paul Galdone, Lothrop, 1967, 112 pp., o.p.

  C RIOS, Tere (Teresa). *The Fifteenth Pelican*. Gr. 4–6.
      On the windy island of San Juan, Sister Bertrille's large white headpiece
enables her to fly like a pelican. (KR 33:782; LJ 90:4076)
      Illus. by Arthur King, Doubleday, 1965, 118 pp., o.p.

   ROBERTS, Willo Davis. *The Magic Book*. See Chapter 7, Magic
   Adventure Fantasy.

C/YA RODGERS (Guettel), Mary. *Freaky Friday*. Gr. 5–7.
[O]   One morning, Annabel Adams awakens to discover that she has turned
into her mother, and that her mother has taken over Annabel's own body. In
A Billion for Boris (1974, 1976), a television set that broadcasts tomorrow's
programs gives Annabel the urge to do good deeds, but inspires her friend
Boris to make a fortune at the racetrack. In *Summer Switch* (1982),
Annabel's brother, Ben, inadvertently trades bodies with his father, while

Ben is at summer camp and his father on a business trip in Hollywood. (BL 68:910, 80:96; CC:523; Ch&Bks:271; CCBB 26:15; HB 48:378; JHC:411; KR 40:267; LJ 97:1608)
Harper, 1972, 155 pp., 1976, pap.

ROGERS, Mark E. *The Adventures of Samurai Cat.* See Section 2B, Talking Animal Fantasy.

C [R] ROUNDS, Glen (Harold). *The Day the Circus Came to Lone Tree.* Gr. 3–4.
The townspeople of Lone Tree are treated to some unwelcome entertainment when a circus lion and his trainer stampede all of the town's livestock. The sequels are *Mr. Yowder and the Lion Roar Capsules* (1976), *Mr. Yowder and the Steamboat* (1977), *Mr. Yowder and the Giant Bull Snake* (1978), *Mr. Yowder and the Train Robbers* (1981), and *Mr. Yowder and the Windwagon* (1983). Three of the sequels have been published in a single volume entitled *Mr. Yowder, The Peripatetic Sign Painter* (1980; see below). (BL 70:545; CCBB 27:85; HB 52:393; KR 41:1155; LJ 99:203; Suth 2:387)
Illus. by the author, Holiday, 1973, 39 pp., o.p.

C [R] ROUNDS, Glen (Harold). *Mr. Yowder, The Peripatetic Sign Painter: Three Tall Tales.* Gr. 3–5.
Three tall tales about Mr. Yowder, now published in one volume, in which he sells canned lion roars, travels through Manhattan via steamboat, and hunts buffalo on a giant bull snake. (BL 76:1132; CC:524; KR 48:912; SLJ Sept 1980 p. 63)
Holiday, 1980, 126 pp.

SABERHAGEN, Fred. *Empire of the East.* See Section 5A, Alternate Worlds or Histories.

C/YA SANDBURG, Carl (August). *Rootabaga Stories.* Gr. 5–7. (Orig. pub. [R] 1922.)
A collection of forty-nine humorous tales written by the well-known poet. *Rootabaga Pigeons* (1923, 1974) and *Potato Face* (1930) are companion volumes. An omnibus volume was published in 1936. (BL 19:92; CC:554; Ch&Bks:271; HB 27:129; Moore:426)
Illus. by Maud Petersham and Miska Petersham, Harcourt, 1951, 218 pp., 1974, pap.

SCARBOROUGH, Elizabeth Ann. *Bronwyn's Bane.* See Section 5A, Alternate Worlds or Histories.

YA SCARBOROUGH, Elizabeth Ann. *The Drastic Dragon of Draco, Texas.* Gr. 10 up.
Even after she is captured by Indians and sold to the infamous Frank Drake, journalist Pelagia Harper never imagines she would meet a fire-breathing dragon in the Wild West. (Kies:66; LJ May 15, 1986 p. 81)
Bantam/Spectra, 1986, pap., 247 pp., o.p.

YA SCARBOROUGH, Elizabeth Ann. *The Harem of Aman Akbar; or The Djinn Decanted.* Gr. 10 up.
A nobleman turned into an ass while searching for a fourth wife, is forced to rely on his three other wives and his mother to rescue him. (BL 81:561, 583; LJ 109:1775)
Bantam, 1984, pap., 215 pp.

C SCULLARD, Sue. *Miss Fanshawe and the Great Dragon Adventure.* Gr. 2–4.

Renowned Victorian explorer, Miss Fansawe, captures a dragon in Patagonia, brings it back to London, and then chases down a thief who steals the dragon's egg. (BL 83:1526; KR 55:472)

St. Martin, 1987, 32 pp.

SEEMAN, Elizabeth. *The Talking Dog and the Barking Man.* See Section 2B, Talking Animal Fantasy.

SELDEN, George. *The Cricket in Times Square.* See Section 2B, Talking Animal Fantasy.

SELDEN, George. *The Genie of Sutton Place.* See Chapter 7, Magic Adventure Fantasy.

SELDEN, George. *Irma and Jerry.* See Section 2B, Talking Animal Fantasy.

SENDAK, Maurice. *Higglety Pigglety Pop! Or, There Must Be More to Life.* See Section 2B, Talking Animal Fantasy.

SEUSS, Dr. *The 500 Hats of Bartholomew Cubbins.* See Chapter 1, Allegorical Fantasy and Literary Fairy Tales.

Shape Shifters: Fantasy and Science Fiction Tales about Humans Who Can Change Their Shapes. Ed. by Jane H. Yolen. See Chapter 3, Fantasy Collections.

C SHARMAT, Marjorie Weinman. *The Trolls of Twelfth Street.* Gr. 1–3.

A troll family who arrives in Manhattan to spend a few hundred years above ground has problems dealing with human landlords, housewives, and children. (BL 76:838; CCBB 33:142; Ch&Bks:271; KR 48:214; SLJ May 1980 p. 84; Suth 3:387)

Illus. by Ben Shecter, Coward, 1979, 64 pp., o.p.

SHEEHAN, Carolyn, and SHEEHAN, Edmond. *Magnifi-Cat.* See Section 2B, Talking Animal Fantasy.

C SILVERSTEIN, Shel. *Uncle Shelby's Story of Laficadio, the Lion Who Shot Back.* Gr. 3–5.

Laficadio the lion teaches himself to shoot a hunting rifle and becomes a famous circus star. (CC:529; CCBB 17:85; LJ 88:4858)

Illus. by the author, Harper, 1963, 110 pp.

SIMAK, Clifford D. *The Goblin Reservation.* See Chapter 8, Time Travel Fantasy.

C [R] SIMONT, Marc. *The Contest at Paca.* Gr. 3–5.

The feuding soldiers and university students of Paca challenge each other to a stew-eating contest. (BL 55:634; HB 35:301; KR 27:300; LJ 84:2084; TLS Nov 25, 1960 p. iv)

Illus. by the author, Harper, 1959, 60 pp., o.p.

SIMONT, Marc. *Mimi.* See Section 2B, Talking Animal Fantasy.

C [R] SINGER, Isaac Bashevis. *The Fools of Chelm and Their History.* Gr. 4–6.

Angry that the whole world thinks them fools, the citizens of Chelm declare war, but attack the wrong town, and stage a revolution to depose the council of sages but replace them with thieves. (CC:529; CCBB 27:101; HB 49:593; KR 41:1037; LJ 99:213; TLS 1976 p. 376)

Tr. by the author and Elizabeth Shub, illus. by Uri Shulevitz, Farrar, 1973, 57 pp.

SINGER, Isaac Bashevis. *Naftali the Storyteller and His Horse, Sus, and Other Stories.* See Chapter 3, Fantasy Collections.

SINGER, Isaac Bashevis. *Stories for Children.* See Chapter 3, Fantasy Collections.

SINGER, Isaac Bashevis. *Zlateh the Goat and Other Stories.* See Chapter 3, Fantasy Collections.

SINGER, Marilyn. *The Fido Frame-Up.* See Section 2B, Talking Animal Fantasy.

C SLOTE, Alfred. *My Robot Buddy.* Gr. 2–4.

Jack is mistaken for his robot by a gang of robotnappers, but the robot rescues him from his captors. (BL 72:460; CCBB 29:102; KR 43:999; SLJ Oct 1975 p. 92)

Illus. by Joel Schick, Harper, 1975, 96 pp., 1986, pap.; Avon, 1984, pap.

SMITH, Thorne. *Topper: An Improbable Adventure.* See Chapter 4, Ghost Fantasy.

SNYDER, Zilpha Keatley. *Black and Blue Magic.* See Chapter 7, Magic Adventure Fantasy.

C SOMMER-BODENBURG, Angela. *My Friend the Vampire.* Gr. 3–5.

(Orig. German pub. 1982.)

Nine-year-old Tony makes friends with Rudolf, the young vampire he finds on his window sill, but worries about keeping his parents and his new friend's family apart. The sequels are *The Vampire Moves In* (1984) and *The Vampire Takes a Trip* (1985). (CCBB 38:56; HB 60:333; SLJ Aug 1984 p. 78)

Illus. by Amelie Glienke, Dial, 1984, 160 pp.; Simon, 1986, pap.

SPEARING, Judith. *The Ghosts Who Went to School.* See Chapter 4, Ghost Fantasy.

C SPURR, Elizabeth. *Mrs. Minetta's Car Pool.* Gr. 1–3.

Trips to school in Mrs. Minetta's car pool turn into fantastic adventures when the children fly off into the sky in her red convertible. (BL 81:1463; CCBB 38:195; SLJ Sept 1985 p. 126)

Illus. by Blanche Sims, Atheneum, 1985, 32 pp.

STAHL, Ben. *Blackbeard's Ghost.* See Chapter 4, Ghost Fantasy.

STASHEFF, Christopher. *Her Majesty's Wizard.* See Section 5C, Travel to Other Worlds.

C [R] STEELE, William O(wen). *Andy Jackson's Water Well.* Gr. 4–6.

Andy Jackson and Chief Ticklepitcher are traveling to East Tennessee to fetch a water well for drought-stricken Nashville, but Andy can't control his temper. (BL 55:426; Ch&Bks:272; Eakin:307; HB 35:214; KR 27:224; LJ 84:1700)

Illus. by Michael Ramos, Harcourt, 1959, 80 pp., o.p.

C STEELE, William O(wen). *Daniel Boone's Echo.* Gr. 3–5.

Daniel Boone helps Aaron Adamsale overcome his fear of the Sling-Tailed

Galootis and the One-Horned Sumpple. (BL 54:146; HB 33:490; KR 25:771; LJ 82:2976)
Illus. by Nicolas Mordvinoff, Harcourt, 1957, 79 pp., o.p.

C [R] STEELE, William O(wen). *Davy Crockett's Earthquake.* Gr. 3–5.
Davy Crockett meets up with a comet while out shooting bears in Tennessee. (BL 52:346; Eakin:308; HB 32:188; KR 24:242; LJ 81:2045)
Illus. by Nicolas Mordvinoff, Harcourt, 1956, 64 pp., o.p.

C [R] STEELE, William O(wen). *The No-Name Man of the Mountain.* Gr. 4–6.
A young man outwits his trick-playing older brothers. (BL 61:805; CCBB 18:110; Eakin:308; HB 41:58; KR 32:894; LJ 89:4642)
Illus. by Jack Davis, Harcourt, 1964, 79 pp., o.p.

STEVENSON, James. *Here Comes Herb's Hurricane!* See Section 2B, Talking Animal Fantasy.

STEVENSON, James. *Oliver, Clarence, and Violet.* See Section 2B, Talking Animal Fantasy.

YA STOCKTON, Frank (Francis) R(ichard). *The Casting Away of Mrs. Lecks and Mrs. Aleshine.* Gr. 7 up. (Orig. pub. 1886; bound with its sequel, *The Dusantes,* 1888.)
The humorous adventures of two New England widows. (BL 30:23; Bookshelf 1933 p. 9; HB 9:155; LJ 58:804; Mahony 3:484)
Illus. by George Richards, Appleton-Century, 1933, 290 pp., o.p.

STOLZ, Mary. *Quentin Corn.* See Section 2B, Talking Animal Fantasy.

C STORR, Catherine (Cole). *Clever Polly and the Stupid Wolf.* Gr. 3–5.
(Orig. British pub. 1955; U.S. 1970, entitled *The Adventures of Polly and the Wolf.*)
In spite of the wolf's attempts to disguise himself as a fox and as Father Christmas, he never manages to capture Polly. The British sequels are *Polly and the Wolf Again* and *Tales of Polly and the Hungry Wolf.* (LJ 95:3054; SLJ Jan 1980 p. 62)
Illus. by Marjorie-Ann Watts, Faber, dist. by Merrimack, 1979, 95 pp.

STRUGATSKII, Arkadii Natanovich, and STRUGATSKII, Boris Natanovich. *Monday Begins on Saturday.* See Chapter 10, Witchcraft and Sorcery Fantasy.

C [R] SWAYNE, Samuel, and SWAYNE, Zoa. *Great Grandfather in the Honey Tree.* Gr. 1–4.
With one round of ammunition and a net, Great-Grandfather captures a bear, a fish, twenty-four geese, a partridge, a deer, twelve turkeys, and a barrel of wild honey. (BL 46:86; CCBB 3:10; HB 25:411; KR 17:465; LJ 74:1531, 75:51)
Illus. by the authors, Viking, 1949, o.p.; Legacy House, 1982, pap., 54 pp.

THURBER, James. *The Wonderful O.* See Chapter 1, Allegorical Fantasy and Literary Fairy Tales.

TITUS, Eve. *Basil of Baker Street.* See Section 2B, Talking Animal Fantasy.

C TODD, Barbara Euphan (pseud. of Barbara Euphan [Todd] Bower). *Worzel Gummidge, the Scarecrow of Scatterbrook Farm* (British titles: *Worzel Gummidge,* 1936, and *Worzel Gummidge Again,* 1937). Gr. 3–6. Worzell Gummidge is a scarecrow who comes alive. The British sequels are *More about Worzel Gummidge* (1938), *Worzel Gummidge and Saucy Nancy* (1947), *Worzel Gummidge Takes a Holiday* (1949), *Earthy Mangold and Worzel Gummidge* (1949), *Worzel Gummidge and the Railway Scarecrows* (1955), *Worzel Gummidge at the Circus* (1956), and *Worzel Gummidge and the Treasure Ship* (1958). (KR 15:190; LJ 72:595)
Illus. by Ursula Koering, Putnam, 1947, 200 pp., o.p.

TODD, Ruthven. *Space Cat.* See Section 2B, Talking Animal Fantasy.

TOLLE, Jean Bashor. *The Great Pete Penney.* See Chapter 7, Magic Adventure Fantasy.

TRAVERS, P. L. *Mary Poppins.* See Chapter 7, Magic Adventure Fantasy.

VAN LEEUWEN, Jean. *The Great Christmas Kidnapping Caper.* See Section 2B, Talking Animal Fantasy.

C VAN STOCKUM, Hilda (Gerarda). *Kersti and Saint Nicholas.* Gr. 2–5.
Naughty Kersti convinces St. Nicholas to leave gifts for the bad children instead of the good ones. (BL 37:328; HB 16:435; LJ 65:849, 928)
Illus. by the author, Viking, 1940, 72 pp., o.p.

C VASILIU, Mircea. *Hark, the Little Angel.* Gr. 2–4.
A mischievous little angel spends a few days on earth disguised as a little boy. (CCBB 19:71; KR 33:979; LJ 90:4530)
Illus. by the author, Day, 1965, 48 pp., o.p.

C VAUGHAN, Agnes Carr. *Lucian Goes A-Voyaging.* Gr. 3–5.
Tall tales in a similar vein as the Baron Münchausen tales (see this chapter), adapted from the Greek of Lucian. (BL 27:68; HB 6:127–130, 146, 7:117; LJ 55:465; Mahony 3:213; TLS 1930 p. 717)
Illus. by Harrie Wood, Knopf, 1930, 139 pp., o.p.

WABER, Bernard. *Dear Hildegarde.* See Section 2B, Talking Animal Fantasy.

WABER, Bernard. *Mice on My Mind.* See Section 2B, Talking Animal Fantasy.

WAECHTER, Friedrich, and EILERT, Bernd. *The Crown Snatchers.* See Chapter 1, Allegorical Fantasy and Literary Fairy Tales.

WALKER, Kenneth Macfarlane, and BOUMPHREY, Geoffrey. *The Log of the Ark.* See Section 5B, Myth Fantasy.

WALLACE, Barbara Brooks. *Miss Switch to the Rescue.* See Chapter 10, Witchcraft and Sorcery Fantasy.

Wandering Stars: An Anthology of Jewish Fantasy and Science Fiction. Ed. by Jack Dann. See Chapter 3, Fantasy Collections.

WATT-EVANS, Lawrence. *With a Single Spell.* See Chapter 10, Witchcraft and Sorcery Fantasy.

WEALES, Gerald. *Miss Grimsbee is a Witch*. See Chapter 10, Witchcraft and Sorcery Fantasy.

C WEAVER, Jack. *Mr. O'Hara*. Gr. 4–6.
Mr. O'Hara entertains the customers in his general store with tall tales about his life in Ireland. (CCBB 7:34; HB 29:221; KR 21:115; LJ 78:705) Illus. by the author, Viking, 1953, 160 pp., o.p.

C [R] WERSBA, Barbara. *The Brave Balloon of Benjamin Buckley*. Gr. 2–4.
Benjamin and his cat stow away aboard a hot-air balloon. (BL 60:632; CCBB 17:102; HB 39:500; LJ 88:122) Illus. by Margot Jones, Atheneum, 1963, 66 pp., o.p.

WHITE, Anne Hitchcock. *Junket*. See Section 2B, Talking Animal Fantasy.

WHITE, Anne Hitchcock. *The Story of Serapina*. See Section 2B, Talking Animal Fantasy.

WHITE, E. B. *Stuart Little*. See Section 2B, Talking Animal Fantasy.

WHITE, E. B. *The Trumpet of the Swan*. See Section 2B, Talking Animal Fantasy.

C WIBBERLEY, Leonard (Patrick O'Connor). *McGillicuddy McGotham*. Gr. 4–6.
Timothy Patrick Fegus Kevin Sean Desmond McGillicuddy is the first leprechaun diplomat posted to America. (BL 52:312; KR 24:55; LJ 81:833) Illus. by Aldren A. Watson, Little, 1956, 111 pp., o.p.

YA [R] WIBBERLEY, Leonard (Patrick O'Connor). *The Mouse That Roared*. Gr. 7 up.
Attempting to revive its national economy, the tiny duchy of Grand Fenwick declares war on the United States, hoping for a quick defeat and large war reparations. But its twenty-three longbowmen not only win the war, they capture the top secret Q-Bomb! The sequels are *Beware of the Mouse* (1958), *The Mouse on the Moon* (1962), *The Mouse on Wall Street* (1969), and *The Mouse That Saved the West* (Morrow, 1981). (BL 51:190, 83:1593; JHC:428; KR 22:788; LJ 79:1506; SHC:646) Little, 1955, o.p.; Bantam, 1971, pap., 279 pp.

WIBBERLEY, Leonard. *The Quest of Excalibur*. See Chapter 4, Ghost Fantasy.

C WIEMER, Rudolf Otto. *The Good Robber, Willibald*. Gr. 2–4. (Orig. German pub. 1965.)
Willibald the robber steps out of Manni's storybook, ready for trouble. (CCBB 21:167; KR 36:181; TLS 1969 p. 699) Tr. by Barbara Kowall Gollob, illus. by Marie Marcks, Atheneum, 1968, 65 pp., o.p.

WILKINS, Mary E. *The Pumpkin Giant*. See Chapter 1, Allegorical Fantasy and Literary Fairy Tales.

WILLARD, Nancy. *The Marzipan Moon*. See Chapter 1, Allegorical Fantasy and Literary Fairy Tales.

WILLIAMS, Jay. *The Practical Princess and Other Liberating Fairy Tales*. See Chapter 1, Allegorical Fantasy and Literary Fairy Tales.

C [R] WILLIAMS (John), Ursula Moray. *The Cruise of the Happy-Go-Gay.* Gr. 3–5. (Orig. British pub. 1967.)
Aunt Hegarty and her five nieces sail off in search of burried treasure. (BL 64:1046; CCBB 22:87; HB 44:424; KR 35:1474; LJ 93:298; Suth:424)
Illus. by Gunvor Edwards, Meredith, 1968, 151 pp., o.p.

WILLIAMS, Ursula Moray. *The Nine Lives of Island Mackenzie.* See Section 2B, Talking Animal Fantasy.

C WILLIAMS (John), Ursula Moray. *Tiger Nanny* (British title: *Johnnie Tigerskin,* 1964). Gr. 4–6.
A tiger cub becomes the perfect nanny for the Harper children. (CCBB 28:140; HB 51:151; KR 42:805; SLJ Jan 1975 p. 42)
Illus. by Gunvor Edwards, Nelson, 1974, 128 pp., o.p.

WILSON, Gahan. *Harry the Fat Bear.* See Section 2B, Talking Animal Fantasy.

WINDSOR, Patricia. *How a Wierdo and a Ghost Can Change Your Entire Life.* See Chapter 4, Ghost Fantasy.

C *With Cap and Bells: Humorous Stories to Tell and to Read Aloud.* Ed. by Mary Gould Davis. Gr. 4–6.
Humorous tales by Carl Sandburg, Frank R. Stockton, Mary Eleanor Wilkins, and others. (BL 34:12; HB 13:286; LJ 62:782)
Illus. by Richard Bennett, Harcourt, 1937, 246 pp., o.p.

C WOOD, James Playsted. *An Elephant in the Family.* Gr. 2–4.
Three children and their parents adopt a talking elephant. The sequels are *The Elephant in the Barn* (Harper, 1961), *The Elephant on Ice* (Seabury, 1965), and *The Elephant Tells* (Reilly, 1968). (CCBB 11:32; HB 33:223; LJ 82:1803)
Illus. by Kurt Werth, Nelson, 1957, 64 pp., o.p.

C [R] WORK, Rhoda O. *Mr. Dawson Had a Farm.* Gr. 1–4.
A lazy farmer gets himself into humorous predicaments. The sequels are *Mr. Dawson Had an Elephant* (1959) and *Mr. Dawson Had a Lamb* (1963). (BL 47:386; CCBB 4:47; HB 27:247; LJ 76:880)
Illus. by Dorothy Maas, Bobbs-Merrill, 1951, 131 pp., o.p.

WRIGHTSON, Patricia. *An Older Kind of Magic.* See Chapter 7, Magic Adventure Fantasy.

YEP, Laurence. *The Curse of the Squirrel.* See Section 2B, Talking Animal Fantasy.

YOLEN, Jane H. *The Acorn Quest.* See Section 2B, Talking Animal Fantasy.

YOLEN, Jane H. *Hobo Toad and the Motorcycle Gang.* See Section 2B, Talking Animal Fantasy.

YOLEN, Jane H. *Piggins.* See Section 2B, Talking Animal Fantasy.

C [R] YOLEN (Stemple), Jane H(yatt). *Sleeping Ugly.* Gr. 2–4.
A beautiful but nasty princess named Miserella gets her comuppance when Prince Charming kisses awake homely but virtuous Plain Jane and forgets all

about sleeping Miserella. (BL 78:656; CC:550; CCBB 35:99; KR 49:1158; SLJ Dec 1981 p. 75; Suth 3:467)

Illus. by Diane Stanley, Coward, 1981, hb and pap., 64 pp.

YOUNG, Robert F. *The Vizier's Second Daughter.* See Section 5B, Myth Fantasy.

ZEMACH, Harve. *The Tricks of Master Dabble.* See Chapter 1, Allegorical Fantasy and Literary Fairy Tales.

7

Magic Adventure Fantasy

The majority of these books are about ordinary people who either gain magical powers or come in contact with magical objects, creatures, or events. A lighthearted tone usually prevails in this type of fantasy. Most tales involving extrasensory perception (ESP) or the occult have been excluded.

ADAIR, Gilbert. *Alice Through the Needle's Eye: The Further Adventures of Lewis Carroll's "Alice."* See Section 5C, Travel to Other Worlds.

AIKEN, Joan. *The Faithless Lollybird.* See Chapter 3, Fantasy Collections.

AIKEN, Joan. *Smoke from Cromwell's Time and Other Stories.* See Chapter 3, Fantasy Collections.

AIKEN, Joan. *Up the Chimney Down and Other Stories.* See Chapter 6, Humorous Fantasy.

ALCOCK, Vivien. *The Stonewalkers.* See Section 5B, Myth Fantasy.

ALLEN, Judy. *The Spring on the Mountain.* See Chapter 1, Allegorical Fantasy and Literary Fairy Tales.

C ANCKARSVÄRD, Karin (Inez Maria). *Bonifacius the Green.* Gr. 3–5. (Orig. Swedish pub. 1952.)
   Bonifacius the dragon helps children to gain self-confidence. (HB 38:314; KR 30:7; LJ 87:1314; TLS Dec 4, 1961 p. vii)
   Tr. by C. M. Anckarsvärd and K. H. Beales, illus. by Ingrid Rossell, Abelard-Schuman, 1961, 95 pp., o.p.

C [R] ANDERSON, Joy. *Juma and the Magic Jinn.* Gr. 2–4.
   Hoping to solve his problems at school, Juma calls up his family's magic jinn, who grants his wishes in unexpected ways. (BL 83:266; HB 62:729; KR 54:1123; SLJ Dec 1986 p. 78)
   Illus. by Charles Mikolaycak, Lothrop, 1986, 32 pp.

ANDREWS, Frank. *The Upside-Down Town.* See Chapter 6, Humorous Fantasy.

C/YA ANGELL, Judie. *The Weird Disappearance of Jordan Hall.* Gr. 5–8.
Hired as an assistant in his girlfriend's father's magic shop, Jordan Hall follows a black cat into the "disappearing box" and becomes invisible. (BL 84:52, 57; HB 64:61; SLJ Nov 1987 p. 102)
Watts, 1987, 121 pp.

BABBITT, Natalie. *Tuck Everlasting.* See Section 5B, Myth Fantasy.

C BABCOCK (Thompson), Betty (Elizabeth S.). *The Expandable Pig.* Gr. 3–5.
Pig suddenly expands like a balloon and takes Gary and his three dogs on a trip to England. (CCBB 2[Oct 1949]:1; HB 25:410, 436; KR 17:323; LJ 74:1541, 1760)
Illus. by the author, Scribner, 1949, 114 pp., o.p.

BACON, Martha. *The Third Road.* See Chapter 8, Time Travel Fantasy.

BACON, Peggy. *The Ghost of Opalina, or Nine Lives.* See Chapter 4, Ghost Fantasy.

C BACON, Peggy. *The Magic Touch.* Gr. 3–4.
Recipes from a witch's cookbook transform Ben, Esther, and Ted into animals. (BL 63:183; HB 44:556; KR 36:690; LJ 94:292)
Illus. by the author, Little, 1968, 112 pp., o.p.

C BAKER, Margaret. *Patsy and the Leprechauns.* Gr. 2–4. (Orig. British pub. 1932.)
Patsy decides that the quickest way to make money is to steal a leprechaun's gold. (BL 29:208; Bookshelf 1933 p. 6; LJ 58:710; Mahony 3:103; TLS 1932 p. 894)
Illus. by Mary Baker, Duffield, 1933, 109 pp., o.p.

C BAKER, Margaret. *Pollie Who Did as She Was Told.* Gr. 3–4.
Pollie accidentally washes out all of the magic potion-containing bottles when she tidies up the Wise Woman's house. (LJ 60:304; Mahony 3:104; TLS 1934 p. 838)
Illus. by Mary Baker, Dodd, 1934, 100 pp., o.p.

C BAKER, Margaret. *The Water Elf and the Miller's Child.* Gr. 2–4.
A mischievous young water elf plays tricks on the frogs, cranes, and fish living at the mill pond. (BL 25:126; HB 4[Nov 1928]:76; Mahony 2:131)
Illus. by Mary Baker, Duffield, 1928, 84 pp., o.p.

BAKER, Margaret Joyce. *Homer the Tortoise.* See Section 2B, Talking Animal Fantasy.

C BAKER, Margaret Joyce. *The Magic Sea Shell.* Gr. 3–5. (Orig. British pub. 1959.)
Three children find a magic sea shell and meet a wish-granting mermaid. (KR28:6, LJ 85:2033; TLS Dec 4, 1959 p. xxii)
Illus. by Susan Elson, Holt, 1960, 122 pp., o.p.

C BAKER, Margaret Joyce. *Porterhouse Major.* Gr. 4–6. (Orig. British pub. 1967.)
Rory uses her mother's magic books to create a gigantic cat named Porterhouse. (CCBB 21:105, 121; Suth:26; TLS 1967 p. 451)
Illus. by Shirley Hughes, Prentice-Hall, 1967, 116 pp., o.p.

C/YA BAKER, Olaf. *Bengey and the Beast.* Gr. 5–7.
Bengey uses magic to destroy the horrible Gunderbust. (BL 43:260; HB 23:212; LJ 72:466, 597)
Illus. by Victor J. Dowling, Dodd, 1947, 243 pp., o.p.

BARRIE, Sir J. M. *Peter Pan.* See Section 5C, Travel to Other Worlds.

BARZINI, Luigi. *The Little Match Man.* See Chapter 9, Toy Fantasy.

C [R] BAUER, Marion Dane. *Touch the Moon.* Gr. 4–6.
Jennifer's tiny china horse turns into Moonseeker, a talking palomino stallion, who teaches her how to ride, while she teaches him courage. (BL 84:144; CCBB 41:2; HB 63:608; KR 55:1388; SLJ Nov 1987 p. 102)
Illus. by Alix Berenzy, Clarion, 1987, 77 pp.

BEACHCROFT, Nina. *Well Met by Witchlight.* See Chapter 10, Witchcraft and Sorcery Fantasy.

C BEACHCROFT, Nina. *The Wishing People.* Gr. 4–6. (Orig. British pub. 1980.)
Released from a spell that imprisoned them inside a barometer, Tom and Mrs. Tom grant ten wishes to Martha and her friend, Jonathan. (BL 78:954; KR 50:553; SLJ Apr 1982 p. 65)
Dutton, 1982, 181 pp.

BEATON-JONES, Cynon. *The Adventures of So Hi.* See Section 5C, Travel to Other Worlds.

C BEAUMONT, Cyril W(illiam). *The Mysterious Toyshop: A Fairy Tale.* Gr. 4 up. (Orig. British pub. 1924.)
Only a few select customers are allowed to see the marvelous clockwork dolls, until the day a stranger forces his way into the magical toyshop that appeared almost overnight. (SLJ Mar 1986 p. 156)
Illus. by Wyndham Payne, Holt, 1985, 32 pp.

BEDARD, Michael. *A Darker Magic.* See Chapter 10, Witchcraft and Sorcery Fantasy.

C/YA BELL, Thelma Harrington. *Take It Easy.* Gr. 5–7.
Thirteen-year-old Margie rubs her brass elephant and an invisible genie comes forth. (KR 21:428; LJ 78:2042)
Illus. by Corydon Bell, Viking, 1953, 172 pp., o.p.

C BENCHLEY, Nathaniel (Goddard). *The Magic Sled* (British title: *The Magic Sledge*). Gr. 3–5.
No snow for his new sled? Fred finds that magic can make more snow than he ever dreamed of. (BL 68:1002; CCBB 25:134; KR 40:68; LJ 97:1593)
Illus. by Mel Furukawa, Harper, 1972, 44 pp.

BENDICK, Jeanne. *The Goodknight Ghost.* See Chapter 4, Ghost Fantasy.

BENSON, E. F. *David Blaize and the Blue Door.* See Section 5C, Travel to Other Worlds.

BERESFORD, Elisabeth. *Invisible Magic.* See Chapter 8, Time Travel Fantasy.

BERESFORD, Elisabeth. *Travelling Magic.* See Chapter 8, Time Travel Fantasy.

C BERGENGREN, Ralph Wilhelm. *Susan and the Butterbees.* Gr. 4–6.
Fairy Maud grants Susan's wish for forty-seven Butterbee uncles to appear whenever she needs entertainment or help. (HB 23:212; KR 15:163; LJ 72:643)
Illus. by Anne Vaughan, Longmans, 1947, 175 pp., o.p.

C/YA BETHANCOURT, T(homas) Ernesto (pseud. of Tom Paisley). *The Dog Days of Arthur Cane.* Gr. 6–9.
Arthur is changed into a stray mutt by a classmate he has ridiculed. (HB 53:157; KR 44:848; SLJ Jan 1977 p. 99; TLS 1978 p. 1082)
Holiday, 1976, 160 pp.

C BIANCO, Margery (Winifred) Williams. *The Hurdy-Gurdy Man.* Gr. 2–4. (Orig. U.S. pub. Oxford, 1933.)
The magical music of the hurdy-gurdy man changes the lives of the prim inhabitants of an overly tidy town. (BL 30:184; HB 9:204; LJ 58:897)
Illus. by Robert Lawson, Gregg, 1980, 56 pp.

C/YA BINNS, Archie (Fred). *The Radio Imp.* Gr. 4–7.
Jim Tompkins's second-hand Irish radio reports on the future as well as the past. The sequel is *Secret of the Sleeping River* (1952). (BL 46:266; CCBB 3:49; HB 26:193; KR 18:69; LJ 75:706)
Illus. by Rafaello Busoni, Winston, 1950, 216 pp., o.p.

C BONHAM, Frank. *The Friends of the Loony Lake Monster.* Gr. 4–6.
A baby dinosaur hatches from an orange egg and adopts Gussie as its mother. (BL 69:711; CCBB 26:71; KR 40:1097; LJ 97:3803)
Dutton, 1972, 135 pp., o.p.

C [R] BOSTON, L(ucy) M(aria Wood). *The Castle of Yew.* Gr. 3–5. (Orig. British pub. 1965.)
Two boys peer into a castle-shaped yew bush and find that they have shrunken to only a few inches in height and are inside the castle. (BL 62:327; CCBB 19:42; Ch&Bks:264; HB 42:192; KR 33:903; LJ 90:4609; TLS 1965 p. 513)
Illus. by Margery Gill, Harcourt, 1965, 58 pp., o.p.

BOSTON, L. M. *The Children of Green Knowe.* See Chapter 4, Ghost Fantasy.

C BOSTON, L(ucy) M(aria Wood). *The Fossil Snake.* Gr. 4–6. (Orig. British pub. 1975.)
The fossilized prehistoric snake that Rob hid under his radiator comes alive and begins to grow. (BL 72:1259; HB 52:287; KR 44:199; SLJ May 1976 p. 56; TLS 1975 p. 1060)
Illus. by Peter Boston, Atheneum, 1976, 53 pp., o.p.

BOSTON, L. M. *The Guardians of the House.* See Section 5C, Travel to Other Worlds.

C [R] BOSTON, L(ucy) M(aria Wood). *Nothing Said.* Gr. 3–5. (Orig. British pub. 1971.)
Libby meets a small, weeping dryad and promises to find her a new tree to replace the one felled by a storm. (BL 67:746; CCBB 25:2; Ch&Bks:264; HB 47:286; LJ 96:2128; TLS 1971 p. 1317)
Illus. by Peter Boston, Harcourt, 1971, 64 pp., o.p.

C/YA BOSTON, L(ucy) M(aria Wood). *The River at Green Knowe.* Gr. 5–7.
[R] While canoeing on the river near Green Knowe, Ping, Oskar, and Ida meet a hermit, a giant, and winged horses. Ping's adventures continue in *An Enemy at Green Knowe* (1964) and in a nonfantasy story, *A Stranger at Green Knowe* (1961). (CCBB 13:27; Ch&Bks:264; KR 27:701; LJ 84:3318; TLS Dec 4, 1959 p.xvii)
Illus. by Peter Boston, Harcourt, 1959, o.p., 1966, pap., 153 pp.; Peter Smith, 1959.

C [R] BOSTON, L(ucy) M(aria Wood). *The Sea Egg.* Gr. 4–5.
Toby and Joe find a green, egg-shaped stone that hatches into a sea boy. (BL 63:1045; CC:437; CCBB 21:1; HB 43:460; KR 35:498; LJ 92:2647; Suth:47; TLS 1967 p. 1133)
Illus. by Peter Boston, Harcourt, 1967, 94 pp.

BOWEN, William A. *Merrimeg.* See Section 5C, Travel to Other Worlds.

C/YA BOWEN, William A(lvin). *The Old Tobacco Shop: A True Account of*
[R] *What Befell a Little Boy in Search of Adventure.* Gr. 5–7.
Tales told by the old tobacco shop owner involve Freddie in thrilling pirate adventures. Newbery Medal Honor Book, 1922. (BL 18:159; Bookshelf 1923–1924 p. 8; LJ 47:869; Mahony 1:39; Moore:426)
Macmillan, 1921, 236 pp., o.p.

BRADBURY, Ray. *The Halloween Tree.* See Chapter 8, Time Travel Fantasy.

C [R] BRAND, (Mary) Christianna (Milne Lewis). *Nurse Matilda.* Gr. 2–5.
It takes only one stamp of Nurse Matilda's big black stick to straighten out the Browns' naughty children. The sequels are *Nurse Matilda Goes to Town* (1967) and *Nurse Matilda Goes to the Hospital* (British). (BL 61:436; HB 40:497; KR 32:732; LJ 89:3468; TLS 1964 p. 589)
Illus. by Edward Ardizzone, Dutton, 1964, o.p.; Gregg, 1980, 128 pp., o.p.

C/YA BRITTAIN, Bill. *The Wish Giver: Three Tales of Coven Tree.* Gr. 5–8.
[R] A stranger who appears out of nowhere offers to grant the wishes of four young people from Coven Tree. This book is related to *The Devil's Donkey* (1981) and *Dr. Dredd's Wagon of Wonders* (1987). (BL 79:1028; CC:439; CCBB 36:144; HB 59:300; KR 51:522; SLJ Apr 1983 p. 110, May 1983 p. 31)
Illus. by Andrew Glass, Harper, 1983, 1986, pap., 192 pp.

C BROCK, Betty. *No Flying in the House.* Gr. 3–5.
Annabel, a half-mortal, half-fairy child, is tempted by a wicked fairy to misuse her magic powers. (BL 66:1340; CCBB 24:38; KR 38:450; LJ 95:2531; Suth:52)
Illus. by Wallace Tripp, Harper, 1970, 139 pp., 1982, pap.; Avon, 1983, pap.

BROCK, Betty. *The Shades.* See Chapter 4, Ghost Fantasy.

C [R] BROWN, Palmer. *Beyond the Pawpaw Trees: The Story of Anna Lavinia.* Gr. 4–6.

Anna Lavinia has a number of strange adventures during a trip to her aunt's house, culminating in the discovery of her long-lost father. The sequel is *The Silver Nutmeg* (1956). (CCBB 8:66; HB 30:343; KR 22:385; LJ 79:2254)

Illus. by the author, Harper, 1954, 121 pp., o.p.; Avon, 1983, pap.

C [R] BROWNE, Frances. *Granny's Wonderful Chair and Its Tale of Fairy Times.* Gr. 4–6. (Orig. British pub. 1856; repr. 1887, retitled: *The Story of the Lost Fairy Book;* orig. U.S. pub. 1900, entitled: *The Wonderful Chair and the Tales It Told.*)

Snowflower's magical chair tells wondrous stories and helps her find the king's long-lost brother. (BL 59:859; Bookshelf 1928 p. 10; HB 1[June 1925]:30, 39:402; LJ 26:67, 50:803; Mahony 2:274)

Illus. by D(enys) J(ames) Watkins-Pitchford, Dutton, 1963, 150 pp., o.p.; Penguin, 1985, pap.

C BRUÈRE, Martha (Bensley). *Sparky-for-Short.* Gr. 3–4.

An electric spark released from the radio is really a radio photograph of a lost boy. (LJ 55:995; Mahony 3:132; Moore 131, 431)

Illus. by the author, Coward, 1930, 85 pp., o.p.

C/YA BUCHAN, John. *The Magic Walking Stick.* Gr. 5–7.

Bill's magic walking stick takes him to the South Pacific and to darkest Africa, where it helps him restore a prince to his throne. (Bookshelf 1933: 11; LJ 58:806; TLS 1932 pp. 840, 867)

Illus. by Arthur E. Becher, Houghton, 1932, 215 pp., o.p.

BULLETT, Gerald W. *The Happy Mariners.* See Chapter 8, Time Travel Fantasy.

C BURGESS, Thorton Waldo. *Tommy and the Wishing-Stone.* Gr. 4–6.

Tommy finds a Wishing-Stone in the meadow that can change him into any wild animal. The sequels are *Tommy's Change of Heart* (Little, 1921) and *Tommy's Wishes Come True* (Little, 1921). (BL 12:294; Mahony 1:24)

Illus. by Harrison Cady, Century, 1915, 290 pp., o.p.

C [R] BURNETT, Frances (Elizabeth) Hodgson. *Racketty-Packetty House.* Gr. 3–5. (Orig. British and U.S. pub. 1906.)

When Cynthia replaces her tumbledown doll house with an elegant new one, Queen Crosspatch of the fairies steps in to save the old discarded dolls. This is the sequel to *Queen Silverbell* (Century, 1906). (BL 2:249, 72:362; KR 43:1065; LJ 95:1192; Mahony 1:40; Mahony 2:127; SLJ Nov 1975 p. 42; TLS 1968 p. 589)

Illus. by Harold Berson, Scribner, 1961, o.p.; illus. by Holly Johnson, Lippincott, 1975, 60 pp.

BUTTERWORTH, Oliver. *The Enormous Egg.* See Chapter 6, Humorous Fantasy.

C/YA BYARS, Betsy (Cromer). *The Winged Colt of Casa Mia.* Gr. 5–7.

The colt Charles is given when he comes to live on his Uncle Coot's ranch is special—it has wings! (CCBB 27:107; HB 50:47; LJ 98:3448; Suth 2:71)

Illus. by Richard Cuffari, Viking, 1973, 128 pp., o.p.; Avon, 1975, pap.

C CALHOUN, Mary (pseud. of Mary Huiskamp Wilkins). *Magic in the Alley.* Gr. 4–6.
Cleery buys a box of magic items in an alley junk shop. (BL 67:55; HB 46:295; KR 38:242; LJ 95:1939)
Illus. by Wendy Watson, Atheneum, 1970, 167 pp., o.p.

C CALHOUN, Mary (pseud. of Mary Huiskamp Wilkins). *Ownself.* Gr. 4–6.
Laurabelle summons up a joyful fairy who convinces the girl to defy her stern father. (CCBB 29:59; HB 51:265; KR 43:371; SLJ Apr 1975 p. 50)
Harper, 1975, 160 pp., o.p.

C [R] CAMERON, Eleanor (Frances Butler). *The Terrible Churnadryne.* Gr. 4–6.
Few people believe the stories of a tremendous beast seen near Redwood Cove, so Tom and Jennifer decide to track it down themselves. (BL 56:247; Eakin:58; HB 35:481; KR 27:701; LJ 84:3629)
Illus. by Beth Krush and Joe Krush, Little, 1959, 125 pp.

C CARLSEN, Ruth Christoffer. *Mr. Pudgins.* Gr. 3–6.
When Mr. Pudgins babysits for John's family, the faucets run with soda pop and the bathtubs fly. (BL 47:240; CCBB 4:26; HB 27:1; LJ 76:415)
Illus. by Margaret Bradfield, Houghton, 1951, 163 pp., o.p.

C CARLSEN, Ruth Christoffer. *Sam Bottleby.* Gr. 4–6.
A fairy godfather cares for Trygve and Solveig after they are stranded at the airport. (KR 36:1282; LJ 94:1324)
Illus. by Wallace Tripp, Houghton, 1968, 151 pp., o.p.

CARROLL, Lewis. *Alice's Adventures in Wonderland.* See Section 5C, Travel to Other Worlds.

CASSEDY, Sylvia. *Behind the Attic Wall.* See Chapter 4, Ghost Fantasy.

C CATLING, Patrick Skene. *The Chocolate Touch.* Gr. 3–5. (Orig. pub. Morrow, 1952.)
John Midas transforms everyone, even his mother, into chocolate statues because of his insatiable craving for chocolate. The sequel is *John Midas in the Dreamtime* (1986). (BL 49:18, 75:1579; KR 20:369; SLJ Sep 1979 p. 131)
Illus. by Margot Apple, Morrow, 1979 (revision of 1952 ed.); Bantam, 1981, pap., 96 pp.

CHARLES, Prince of Wales. *The Old Man of Lochnagar.* See Chapter 6, Humorous Fantasy.

CHARNAS, Suzy McKee. *The Bronze King.* See Chapter 10, Witchcraft and Sorcery Fantasy.

CHASE, Mary. *Loretta Mason Potts.* See Section 5C, Travel to Other Worlds.

CHESNUTT, Charles Waddell. *Conjure Tales.* See Chapter 3, Fantasy Collections.

CHETWIN, Grace. *Out of the Dark World.* See Section 5C, Travel to Other Worlds.

CHEW, Ruth. *No Such Thing as a Witch.* See Chapter 10, Witchcraft and Sorcery Fantasy.

CLARKE, Pauline. *The Return of the Twelves.* See Chapter 9, Toy Fantasy.

CLARKE, Pauline. *The Two Faces of Silenus.* See Section 5B, Myth Fantasy.

COATSWORTH, Elizabeth. *Pure Magic.* See Chapter 1, Allegorical Fantasy and Literary Fairy Tales.

C COATSWORTH, Elizabeth (Jane). *Troll Weather.* Gr. 2–4.
Selma sees the trolls' golden castles on the mountainside above her Norwegian village. (BL 63:944; HB 43:198; KR 35:3; LJ 92:1309)
Illus. by Ursula Arndt, Macmillan, 1967, 41 pp., o.p.

C [R] COBLENTZ, Catherine Cate. *The Blue Cat of Castle Town.* Gr. 4–6.
A blue cat steps out of a rug and wanders through the town of Castleton. Newbery Medal Honor Book, 1950. (BL 46:15; CCBB 2[July 1949]:1; HB 25:412; LJ 74:1105)
Illus. by Janice Holland, McKay, 1949, o.p.; Countryman, 1986, pap., 128 pp.

COLE, Joanna. *Bony-Legs.* See Chapter 10, Witchcraft and Sorcery Fantasy.

COLE, Joanna. *Doctor Change.* See Chapter 10, Witchcraft and Sorcery Fantasy.

COLLODI, Carlo. *The Adventures of Pinocchio.* See Chapter 9, Toy Fantasy.

C COONTZ, Otto. *Hornswoggle Magic.* Gr. 3–5.
Jenny the shopping-bag lady has magical coins, or hornswoggles, which jam up the new vending machine and save Mr. Wiseman's newsstand from going out of business. (BL 78:705; SLJ Feb 1982 p. 73)
Illus. by the author, Little, 1981, 88 pp., o.p.

C [R] COOPER (Grant), Susan (Mary). *Jethro and the Jumbie.* Gr. 2–4.
Furious with his elder brother who has broken a promise to take him fishing, eight-year-old Jethro marches off into the bush and has a series of magical adventures. (BL 76:610; CCBB 33:91; Ch&Bks:265; HB 56:51; KR 48:120; SLJ Feb 1980 p. 44)
Illus. by Ashley Bryan, Atheneum, 1979, 28 pp.

COOPER, Susan. *Over Sea, Under Stone.* See Section 5B, Myth Fantasy.

CORBETT, Scott. *Ever Ride a Dinosaur?* See Chapter 6, Humorous Fantasy.

CORBETT, Scott. *The Great Custard Pie Panic.* See Chapter 10, Witchcraft and Sorcery Fantasy.

C [R] CORBETT, Scott. *The Lemonade Trick.* Gr. 4–6.
Kirby's new chemistry set can change a person's character, but the fun ends when it changes his friend, Bumps, into a bully. The sequels are *The Mailbox Trick* (1961), *The Disappearing Dog Trick* (1963), *The Limerick Trick* (1964), *The Turnabout Trick* (1967), *The Hairy Horror Trick* (1969), *The Hateful Plateful Trick* (1971), *The Home Run Trick* (1973), and *The Black*

Mask Trick (1976). (BL 56:633; CC:456; CCBB 13:128; HB 36:128; KR 28:90; LJ 85:2035)
Illus. by Paul Galdone, Little, 1960, o.p.; Scholastic, 1988, pap., 96 pp.

C COUNSEL, June. *A Dragon in Class 4.* Gr. 3–5. (Orig. British pub. 1984.)
An omniscient and vain young dragon named Scales adopts Sam as his boy and secretly manages to help him and his classmates with their school assignments. (CCBB 38:21; SLJ Dec 1984 p. 79)
Illus. by Jill Bennett, Faber, 1984, 102 pp.

C/YA CRESSWELL (Rowe), Helen. *The Beachcombers.* Gr. 5–8.
[R] On holiday at the coast, Ned is caught in a feud between the beachcombing Pickerings and the scavenging Dallakers, distant cousins searching for the lost family treasure. (BL 69:646; CCBB 26:74; HB 49:52)
Macmillan, 1972, 133 pp., o.p.

C/YA CRESSWELL (Rowe), Helen. *The Bongleweed.* Gr. 5–7.
[R] The magic seeds Becky plants change neatly manicured Pew Gardens into a jungle of bongleweed. (BL 70:540; CCBB 27:174; Ch&Bks:265; KR 41:1159; LJ 98:3143; Suth 2:109; TLS 1973 p. 1428)
Macmillan, 1973, 138 pp., o.p.

C/YA CRESSWELL (Rowe), Helen. *The Secret World of Polly Flint.* Gr. 5–7.
[R] (Orig. British pub. 1982.)
Banished to live with her Aunt Em during her father's recuperation from a mine accident, fanciful Polly Flint senses the magic surrounding an ancient maypole and becomes involved with the Time Gypsies, people who have "slipped the net of time" between Polly's world and the centuries-old village of Grimstone, which disappeared from that very site. (BL 80:1624; CC:457; CCBB 37:183; Ch&Bks:265; HB 60:465; KR 52 [May 1, 1984]:J38; SLJ Aug 1984 p. 70; Suth 3:107)
Illus. by Shirley Felts, Macmillan, 1984; Penguin, 1985, pap., 178 pp.

C CRESSWELL (Rowe), Helen. *The White Sea Horse.* Gr. 3–5.
Six donkeys mysteriously disappear after the mayor of Piskerton takes away the tiny white horse Molly's fisherman father drew up in his net. (KR 33:904; LJ 90:5511; TLS 1964 p. 605)
Illus. by Robin Jacques, Lippincott, 1964, 64 pp., o.p.

CROSS, John Kier. *The Other Side of Green Hills.* See Section 5C, Travel to Other Worlds.

CROTHERS, Samuel McChord. *Miss Muffet's Christmas Party.* See Chapter 1, Allegorical Fantasy and Literary Fairy Tales.

CURLEY, Daniel. *Ann's Spring.* See Section 5B, Myth Fantasy.

CURRY, Jane Louise. *Beneath the Hill.* See Section 5B, Myth Fantasy.

C [R] CURRY, Jane Louise. *Mindy's Mysterious Miniature* (Scholastic pap. title: *The Mysterious Shrinking House,* o.p.; British title: *The Housenapper*). Gr. 3–5.
Mindy and her neighbor, Mrs. Bright, are captured and shrunk to miniature size by Mr. Putt's miniaturizing machine. The "reducer" strikes again in *The Lost Farm* (1974), when Pete McCubbin and his family's entire farm are

miniaturized by the unscrupulous Professor Lilliput. (BL 67:340; HB 46:616; KR 38:1146; LJ 95:4374; Suth:96; TLS 1971 p. 774)

Illus. by Charles Robinson, Harcourt, 1970, 157 pp., o.p.

C [R] DAHL, Roald. *Charlie and the Chocolate Factory*. Gr. 3–6.

Charlie Bucket is one of five lucky children who win a tour of Wonka's wonderful chocolate factory. The sequel is *Charlie and the Great Glass Elevator* (1972). Dahl's depiction of Wonka's black helpers has provoked controversy. (CCBB 18:115; Ch&Bks:265; KR 32:1009; LJ 89:5004; TLS 1978 p. 1398)

Illus. by Joseph Schindelman, Knopf, 1964; Bantam, 1986, pap., 176 pp.

C DAHL, Roald. *James and the Giant Peach: A Children's Story*. Gr. 3–5.

A magic potion enables James to escape from his cruel aunts and travel across the ocean in a huge peach, with human-sized insects as traveling companions. Richard R. George has turned this story into a play entitled: *Roald Dahl's James and the Giant Peach: A Play* (Penguin, 1983, pap.). (CC:458; CCBB 15:57; Ch&Bks:265; KR 29:727; LJ 86:4036)

Illus. by Nancy Ekholm Burkert, Knopf, 1961, 118 pp.; Bantam, 1981, pap.

C [R] DAHL, Roald. *The Magic Finger*. Gr. 2–4.

Zak puts the Magic Finger on her teacher and her duck-hunting neighbors, changing the former into a cat and the latter into bird-sized people hunted by huge ducks. (BL 63:264; Ch&Bks:265; KR 34:830; LJ 91:5224)

Illus. by William Pène du Bois, Harper, 1966, 40 pp., 1983, pap.

DANK, Gloria Rand. *The Forest of App*. See Chapter 1, Allegorical Fantasy and Literary Fairy Tales.

DAVIES, Valentine. *The Miracle on 34th Street*. See Chapter 6, Humorous Fantasy.

DAWSON, Carley. *Mr. Wicker's Window*. See Chapter 8, Time Travel Fantasy.

C [R] DAWSON, Mitchell. *The Magic Firecrackers*. Gr. 4–6.

Uncle Dick brings the Carsons some six-hundred-year-old wish-granting Chinese firecrackers. (BL 46:144; CCBB 3:14; HB 26:36; KR 17:510)

Illus. by Kurt Wiese, Viking, 1949, 192 pp., o.p.

C DE LA MARE, Walter (John). *Crossings: A Fairy Play*. Gr. 4–6. (Orig. British pub. 1921.)

Four children spend their winter holiday at an old English country house inhabited by fairies. (BL 20:221; Mahony 2:383)

Illus. by Dorothy P. Lathrop, Knopf, 1923, 170 pp., o.p.

DE LA MARE, Walter. *The Magic Jacket*. See Chapter 3, Fantasy Collections.

C DE REGNIERS, Beatrice Schenk (Freedman). *The Boy, the Rat, and the Butterfly*. Gr. 2–4.

After he finds a jar of wish-granting bubble solution, Peter can stop worrying about his butterfly friend's short lifespan. (CCBB 25:104; HB 47:475; KR 39:805)

Illus. by Haig Shekerjian and Regina Shekerjian, Atheneum, 1971, 40 pp., o.p.

C DILLON, Barbara. *The Good-Guy Cake.* Gr. 2–4.
A "good-guy" cake baked in a magic oven turns Marvin into a suspiciously polite and helpful little boy. (BL 77:458; CCBB 34:91; KR 48:1163; SLJ Mar 1981 p. 130)
Illus. by Alan Tiegreen, Morrow, 1980, 64 pp.

DILLON, Barbara. *What's Happened to Harry?* See Chapter 10, Witchcraft and Sorcery Fantasy.

DIXON, Marjorie. *The Forbidden Island.* See Section 5B, Myth Fantasy.

DOLBIER, Maurice. *The Half-Pint Jinni, and Other Stories.* See Chapter 3, Fantasy Collections.

C [R] DOLBIER, Maurice (Wyman). *The Magic Shop.* Gr. 3–5.
Dick and Denise buy their father a magic wand as a birthday gift. (BL 43:19; HB 22:350, 456; KR 14:324; LJ 71:1054)
Illus. by Fritz Eichenberg, Random, 1946, 74 pp., o.p.

C/YA *Dragons & Dreams: A Collection of New Fantasy and Science Fiction Sto-*
[R]   *ries.* Ed. by Jane Yolen, Martin H. Greenberg, and Charles G. Waugh. Gr. 5–9.
Ten imaginative tales by Patricia McKillip, Jane Yolen, Diana Wynne Jones, Diane Duane, Patricia MacLachlan, Zilpha Keatley Snyder, and others. (BL 82:1219; CCBB 39:200; HB 62:459; JHC 1987 Suppl. p. 82: SLJ May 1986 p. 99; VOYA 9:87, 10:21)
Harper, 1986, 180 pp.

DRUON, Maurice. *Tistou of the Green Thumbs.* See Chapter 1, Allegorical Fantasy and Literary Fairy Tales.

YA DUNLOP, Eileen (Rhona). *The House on Mayferry Street* (Orig. British title: *A Flute in Mayferry Street,* 1976). Gr. 7–10.
Mysterious flute music and the search for hidden treasure bring excitement into the lives of Colin and his invalid sister, Marion. (BL 74:611; CCBB 31:91; HB 54:54; KR 45:990; SLJ Dec 1977 p. 62)
Illus. by Phillida Gili, Holt, 1977, 204 pp., o.p.

C DUTTON, Sandra. *The Magic of Myrna C. Waxweather.* Gr. 3–5.
Ten-year-old Bertha Zuchelli's fairy godmother appears with three magical items to help overcome her reputation as teacher's pet: a fan, a boa, and a black satin camisole. (BL 83:1745; CCBB 40:186; KR 55:372; SLJ Apr 1987 p. 93)
Illus. by Matthew Clark, Atheneum, 1987, 80 pp.

C [O] EAGER, Edward (McMaken). *Half Magic.* Gr. 3–6.
Jane, Mark, Katharine, and Martha find a coin that grants half of every wish they make. The sequel is *Magic by the Lake* (1957), and two related books, *Knight's Castle* (1956) and *Time Garden* (1958), describe the magical adventures of their children. (BL 50:363; CC:462; CCBB 7:86; Ch&Bks:266; HB 30:174; KR 22:232; LJ 79:784; TLS Nov 19, 1954 p. vii)
Illus. by N. M. Bodecker, Harcourt, 1954, 217 pp., 1985, pap.

EAGER, Edward. *Knight's Castle.* See Section 5C, Travel to Other Worlds.

C [R] EAGER, Edward (McMaken). *Magic or Not?* Gr. 4–6.
Did Laura, James, Lydia, and Kip's wishes come true because of magic, or

was it only coincidence? The sequel is *The Well-Wishers* (1960). (BL 55:424; CCBB 12:131; Ch&Bks:266; HB 35:213; KR 26:906; LJ 84:1332; TLS Dec 4, 1959 p. xiv)

Illus. by N. M. Bodecker, Harcourt, 1959, o.p., 1985, pap., 190 pp.; Peter Smith, 1984.

C [R]   EAGER, Edward (McMaken). *Seven Day Magic.* Gr. 4–6.
The main characters in Susan's library book turns out to be Susan, herself, and the friends who take part in seven magic adventures. (CC:462; CCBB 16:78; Ch&Bks:266; HB 38:602; LJ 88:863; TLS 1963 p. 427)
Illus. by N. M. Bodecker, Harcourt, 1962, 156 pp.; Peter Smith, 1984.

EDWARDS, Dorothy. *The Witches and the Grinnygog.* See Chapter 10, Witchcraft and Sorcery Fantasy.

C   ELIOT, Ethel Cook. *Buttercup Days.* Gr. 4–6.
Fairy Tim appears from Fairyland to spend the summer with the parsonage children. (BL 21:30; Bookshelf 1924–1925 Suppl. p. 1; Mahony 2:135; HB 1[Oct 1924]:4)
Illus. by Julia Daniels, Doubleday, 1924, 188 pp., o.p.

C   ELKIN, Benjamin. *Al and the Magic Lamp.* Gr. 2–4.
Every time Al tries to wish on Aladdin's magic lamp, something goes wrong. (BL 60:207; CCBB 16:125; HB 39:280; LJ 88:2550)
Illus. by William Wiesner, Harper, 1963, 31 pp., o.p.

ENDE, Michael. *The Neverending Story.* See Section 5C, Travel to Other Worlds.

C [R]   ENRIGHT, Elizabeth (Wright). *Zeee.* Gr. 2–4.
Pandora Smith gives a temperamental fairy a safe new home in her doll-house. (CCBB 18:127; Ch&Bks:266; HB 41:276; KR 33:309; LJ 90:2883)
Illus. by Irene Haas, Harcourt, 1965, 46 pp., o.p.

C   ERWIN, Betty K. *Aggie, Maggie, and Tish.* Gr. 3–5.
Three elderly sisters bring magic into the lives of the four Eliot children. The sequel is *Where's Aggie?* (1967). (BL 62:330; HB 41:628; KR 33:626; LJ 90:4615)
Illus. by Paul Kennedy, Little, 1965, 154 pp., o.p.

ESTES, Eleanor. *The Witch Family.* See Chapter 10, Witchcraft and Sorcery Fantasy.

C   EWING, Juliana (Horatia Gatty). *The Brownies.* Gr. 4–6. (Orig. British pub. 1865; U.S., 1901, in *The Brownies and Other Tales.*)
Lazy children become helpful brownies, in this story that gave rise to the Brownie Scout name. (BL 43:140; KR 14:523; LJ 72:83)
Illus. by Katherine Milhous, Scribner, 1946, 50 pp., o.p.; illus. by E. H. Shepard, Dutton, 1954, o.p.

C   FARALLA, Dana. *The Singing Cupboard.* Gr. 3–5. (Orig. British pub. 1962.)
A magical mouse takes Nils and Ulla on a journey from Denmark to England. (BL 60:630; HB 40:174; LJ 88:4852; TLS 1962 p. 900)
Illus. by Edward Ardizzone, Lippincott, 1963, 94 pp., o.p.

C [R]   FARALLA, Dana. *The Wonderful Flying-Go-Round.* Gr. 4–6.
Mr. and Mrs. Florabella drift across the town dump in a red balloon and

decide to create a playground complete with a Flying-Go-Round. (BL 62:528; CCBB 20:24; HB 42:52; KR 33:905; LJ 90:5076)
Illus. by Harold Berson, World, 1965, 94 pp., o.p.

FARBER, Norma. *Six Impossible Things before Breakfast.* See Chapter 3, Fantasy Collections.

C FARJEON, Eleanor. *Kaleidoscope.* Gr. 4–6. (Orig. British pub. 1928, U.S. 1929.)
A collection of short stories about a boy named Anthony who lives near a magical millpond where he searches for secrets. (LJ 88:4083)
Illus. by Edward Ardizzone, Walck, 1963, 152 pp., o.p.

C FARJEON, Eleanor. *Mr. Garden.* Gr. 3–5. (Orig. British pub. in this format 1965.)
A tiny man works wonders in Harry and Angela's garden. (CCBB 20:139; HB 42:429; LJ 91:4312; TLS 1966 p. 448)
Illus. by Jane Paton, Walck, 1966, 39 pp., o.p.

C/YA FARMER (Mockridge), Penelope. *The Magic Stone.* Gr. 5–7.
[R] Caroline and Alice's obsession with a magic stone blinds them to the growing rivalry between their younger brothers' gangs. (CCBB 18:53; HB 41:52; KR 32:898; LJ 89:4646; TLS 1965 p. 513)
Illus. by John Kaufmann, Harcourt, 1964, 223 pp., o.p.

C/YA FARMER (Mockridge), Penelope. *The Summer Birds.* Gr. 4–7.
[R] A strange boy spends the summer teaching Charlotte, Emma, and their friends to fly, but the magic ends when they learn his true identity. The sequels are *Charlotte Sometimes* (1969, see Chapter 8, Time Travel Fantasy) and *Emma in Winter* (1966). (BL 58:728; CCBB 15:124 Ch&Bks:240; HB 38:176; KR 30:58; LJ 87:2032; TLS 1985 p. 348)
Illus. by James Spanfeller, Harcourt, 1962, 155 pp., o.p.; Dell, 1987, pap.

FARMER, Penelope. *William and Mary: A Story.* See Section 5C, Travel to Other Worlds.

FARTHING, Alison. *The Mystical Beast.* See Section 5C, Travel to Other Worlds.

C/YA FAULKNER, William (Cuthbert). *The Wishing Tree.* Gr. 4 up. (Written 1927.)
A strange red-headed boy leads a birthday-girl and her friends on a magical hunt for the wishing tree, in this story by the Nobel Prize-winning author. (BL 63:1132; LJ 92:1176; TLS Nov 1967 p. 1133)
Illus. by Don Bolognese, Random, 1967 (© 1964), 81 pp.

C FEYDY, Anne (Lindbergh Sapieyevski). *Osprey Island.* Gr. 4–6.
Through magic, Lizzie, Charles, and Amy enter identical paintings of their houses and meet on an island called Carmar-Ogali-Retne. (CCBB 28:128; HB 51:146; KR 42:1201; LJ 98:3045)
Illus. by Maggie Smith, Houghton, 1974, 164 pp., o.p.

C FIELD, Rachel Lyman. *The Magic Pawnshop; a New Year's Eve Fantasy.* Gr. 3–5.
While tending Minerva MacLoon's shop on New Year's Eve, Prinda Bassett uses magic to spark a romance between Rose Martha and Christopher Marlowe Green. (BL 24:125; HB 3[Nov 1927]:47; LJ 53:484)
Illus. by Elizabeth MacKinstry, Dutton, 1927, 125 pp., o.p.

FINNEY, Charles G. *The Circus of Dr. Lao.* See Section 5B, Myth Fantasy.

C [R] FLEISCHMAN, (Albert) Sid(ney). *The Hey Hey Man.* Gr. 2–4.
A wood spirit called the Hey Hey Man magically punishes a thief who has stolen a farmer's gold. (BL 76:42; CC:468; HB 55:527; KR 47:1141; SLJ Sept. 1979 p. 135)
Illus. by Nadine Bernard Westcott, Atlantic, 1979, 32 pp.

C FORBUS, Ina B(ell). *The Magic Pin.* Gr. 4–6.
Neelie, the seventh grand-daughter of a seventh grand-daughter, inherits a broach enabling her to speak to animals. (CCBB 10:135; KR 24:435; LJ 81:2726)
Illus. by Corydon Bell, Viking, 1956, 138 pp., o.p.

FOSTER, Elizabeth. *Gigi: The Story of a Merry-Go-Round Horse.* See Chapter 9, Toy Fantasy.

FRANCHI, Anna. *The Little Lead Soldier.* See Chapter 9, Toy Fantasy.

C [R] FRAZIER, Neta Lohnes. *The Magic Ring.* Gr. 4–6.
Fairy child gives sensible Rebecca Osborn a magic ring and three wishes. (BL 56:247; HB 35:382; KR 27:402; LJ 84:3926)
Illus. by Kathleen Voute, Longmans, 1959, 149 pp., o.p.

C FRITZ, Jean (Guttery). *Magic to Burn.* Gr. 4–6.
On a ship bound for America, Stephen and Ann meet a stowaway boggart named Blaze. (BL 61:711; CCBB 18:74; LJ 89:3470)
Illus. by Beth Krush and Joe Krush, Coward, 1964, 255 pp., o.p.

C FROST, Frances. *Then Came Timothy.* Gr. 4–6.
Kathy and her grandparents have an eventful three-day visit from an Irish leprechaun. (BL 47:47; HB 26:375; KR 18:418; LJ 75:1834)
Illus. by Richard Bennett, Whittlesey, 1950, 155 pp., o.p.

FRY, Rosalie K. *The Mountain Door.* See Section 5C, Travel to Other Worlds.

C FRY, Rosalie K(ingsmill). *Mungo.* Gr. 3–5.
Richie's summer adventures with a sea monster take him to an uncharted isle inhabited by a shipwrecked sailor. (BL 68:1004; HB 48:370; KR 40:324)
Illus. by Velma Ilsley, Farrar, 1972, 123 pp., o.p.

C FYLEMAN, Rose (Amy). *A Princess Comes to Our Town.* Gr. 4–6.
Fairy princess Finestra grows tired of living in a fairy castle, and makes a sudden appearance in the town marketplace. (BL 25:127; Mahony 2:279)
Illus. by Erick Berry, Doubleday, 1928, 158 pp., o.p.

C [R] GAGE, Wilson (pseud. of Mary Q. Steele). *Miss Osborne-the-Mop.* Gr. 4–6.
Jody's magic abilities bring a dust mop to life, but she soon regrets her actions. (BL 59:747; CCBB 16:110; Eakin:133; HB 39:382; LJ 88:2143)
Illus. by Paul Galdone, Philomel, 1963, 156 pp., o.p.

GALL, Alice, and CREW, Fleming. *The Royal Mimkin.* See Section 5C, Travel to Other Worlds.

C/YA GALLICO, Paul (William). *The House That Wouldn't Go Away.* Gr. 5–7.
Visions of the Victorian mansion that once stood on the site of their apart-

ment building enable Miranda and her brothers to delve into the lives of their neighbors. (BL 76:1290; CCBB 32:189; HB 56:406; SLJ Aug 1980 p. 64) Delacorte, 1980, 234 pp., o.p.

C [R] GANNETT (Kahn), Ruth Stiles. *My Father's Dragon*. Gr. 3–5.
When a stray alley cat tells him about a captive baby dragon, Elmer Elevator decides to run away and rescue it. Newbery Medal Honor Book, 1949. The sequels are *Elmer and the Dragon* (1950, 1987) and *The Dragons of Blueland* (1951, 1987). (BL 44:320, 83:708; CC:470; CCBB 1[June 1948]:2; HB 26:266, 63:82; KR 16:194; LJ 73:604, 824)
Illus. by Ruth Chrisman Gannett, Random, 1948, 1986; Knopf, 1987, pap., 96 pp.

GARDEN, Nancy. *Fours Crossing*. See Section 5B, Myth Fantasy.

GEE, Maurice. *The World Around the Corner*. See Section 5C, Travel to Other Worlds.

GENTLE, Mary. *A Hawk in Silver*. See Section 5C, Travel to Other Worlds.

GORDON, John. *The Giant under the Snow: A Story of Suspense*. See Section 5B, Myth Fantasy.

C GORMLEY, Beatrice. *Fifth Grade Magic*. Gr. 4–6.
A delinquent apprentice-fairy godmother named Errora does a bungled job of granting fifth-grader Gretchen's wish to be the lead in the class play. (BL 79:564; HB 58:516; SLJ Oct 1982 p. 152)
Illus. by Emily Arnold McCully, Dutton, 1982; Avon, 1983, pap., 136 pp.

C GORMLEY, Beatrice. *Mail-Order Wings*. Gr. 4–6.
Andrea finds she can actually fly using her Wonda-Wings Kit, but she becomes frightened when the wings won't come off. The sequel is *The Ghastly Glasses* (1985). (BL 78:235; CCBB 35:107; SLJ Dec 1981 p. 63; Suth 3:157)
Illus. by Emily Arnold McCully, Elsevier-Dutton, 1981, 164 pp.; Avon, 1984, pap.

C/YA GORMLEY, Beatrice. *Paul's Volcano*. Gr. 4–7.
Paul and Adam's science project, a paper-mâché volcano, begins to grow during the night, and they fear that they've summoned up an ancient volcano god. (BL 83:1445; KR 55:552; SLJ Mar 1987 p. 158)
Illus. by Cat Bowen Smith, Houghton, 1987, 144 pp.

C/YA GOUDGE, Elizabeth (de Beauchamp). *Linnets and Valerians*. Gr. 5–7.
[R] After Mrs. Valerian takes in the runaway Linnet children, they decide to repay her kindness by searching for her long-lost son. On the way, they encounter a witch, giants, and magic cats. (BL 61:578; CCBB 18:74; Eakin:145; HB 40:615; TLS 1964 p. 1077)
Illus. by Ian Ribbons, Coward, 1946, o.p.; Gregg, 1981, 290 pp., o.p.; Avon, 1985, pap.

C/YA GOUDGE, Elizabeth (de Beauchamp). *The Little White Horse*. Gr. 5–8.
[R] Magical creatures help Maria Merryweather fight the evil Black Men of the forest. Carnegie Medal winner, 1946. (BL 43:349; HB 23:212; KR 15:167; LJ 72:738)
Illus. by C. Walter Hodges, Coward, 1946, o.p.; Gregg, 1980, 280 pp., o.p.; Avon, 1985, pap.

C/YA GOUDGE, Elizabeth (de Beauchamp). *Smoky-House.* Gr. 5–8.
Fairies help the Trequddick children save their father from betrayal as a smuggler. (BL 37:94; HB 16:343, 430; LJ 65:849, 878; TLS 1940 p. 634)
Illus. by Richard Floethe, Coward, 1940, o.p.; Buccaneer, 1983 (repr.), 391 pp.

C GRAY, Genevieve S(tuck). *The Seven Wishes of Joanna Peabody.* Gr. 3–5.
Joanna is granted seven wishes by Aunt Thelma, a Special Spirit who appears on Joanna's TV screen. (BL 69:493; CCBB 26:154; KR 40:939; LJ 97:3806)
Illus. by Elton Fax, Lothrop, 1972, 61 pp., o.p.

C/YA GRAY, Nicholas Stuart. *The Apple Stone.* Gr. 5–7. (Orig. British pub. 1965.)
A golden Apple Stone brings a stuffed bird, a model rocket, a leopard-skin rug, and a stone gargoyle to life. (BL 66:408; CCBB 23:128; KR 37:777; LJ 94:4582, 4606; TLS 1965 p. 1131)
Illus. by Charles Keeping, Hawthorn, 1969, 230 pp., o.p.

C GREEN, Phyllis. *Eating Ice Cream with a Werewolf.* Gr. 4–6.
When Brad and Nancy's wacky baby-sitter decides to try out her new hobby, witchcraft, the chicken that turns up in Nancy's bed is only one of many strange results. (BL 79:1465; CCBB 36:189; HB 59:302)
Illus. by Patti Stren, Harper, 1983, 121 pp.; Dell, 1985, pap.

GREEN, Roger Lancelyn. *A Cavalcade of Magicians.* See Chapter 10, Witchcraft and Sorcery Fantasy.

C GRIMBLE, Rosemary. *Jonothon and Large.* Gr. 2–4. (Orig. British pub. 1965.)
The sea-serpent that Jonothan raised returns to save him and his father from a hurricane at sea. (KR 38:340; LJ 92:2014; TLS 1965 p. 1131)
Illus. by the author, Bobbs-Merrill, 1966, 88 pp., o.p.

GROSSER, Morton. *The Snake Horn.* See Chapter 8, Time Travel Fantasy.

C GUILLOT, René. *Nicolette and the Mill.* Gr. 2–4. (Orig. pub. in France.)
An emerald fairy ring enables Nicolette to understand the language of animals. (KR 28:949; LJ 86:373; TLS May 20, 1960 p. vii)
Tr. by Gwen Marsh, illus. by Charles Mozley, Abelard-Schuman, 1960, 79 pp., o.p.

HAAS, Dorothy. *The Bears Up Stairs.* See Section 2B, Talking Animal Fantasy.

HACKETT, Walter Anthony. *The Swans of Ballycastle.* See Chapter 1, Allegorical Fantasy and Literary Fairy Tales.

HALAM, Ann. *The Daymaker.* See Section 5A, Alternate Worlds or Histories.

C HANLEY, Eve. *The Enchanted Toby Jug.* Gr. 3–5. (Orig. British pub. 1964.)
A Toby jug comes to life and tells stories to four children. (KR 33:6; LJ 90:960; TLS 1964 p. 602)
Illus. by Nora Unwin, Washburn, 1965, 134 pp., o.p.

C [R]   HANSEN, Ron. *The Shadowmaker*. Gr. 3–6.
Drizzle, the poorest child in town, manages to outwit the Shadowmaker, a mysterious man who sells shadows of people's secret dreams. (BL 83:1446; CCBB 40:125; HB 63:605; KR 55:719; SLJ Aug 1987 p. 83)
Illus. by Margot Tomes, Harper, 1987, 66 pp.

HARRIS, Rosemary. *Sea Magic and Other Stories of Enchantment*. See Chapter 3, Fantasy Collections.

HAUFF, Wilhelm. *The Adventures of Little Mouk*. See Chapter 1, Allegorical Fantasy and Literary Fairy Tales.

HAWTHORNE, Julian. *Rumpty-Dudget's Tower: A Fairy Tale*. See Chapter 1, Allegorical Fantasy and Literary Fairy Tales.

C   HEAL (Berrien), Edith. *What Happened to Jenny*. Gr. 3–5.
Neighborhood dogs take Jenny on a tour of the city although she is supposed to be in bed recovering from the measles. (HB 39:53, 76; KR 30:559)
Illus. by Abbi Giventer, Atheneum, 1962, 62 pp., o.p.

C   HENDRICH, Paula (Griffith). *Who Says So?* Gr. 4–6.
Lucinda conjures up an apparition and decides to use it as her science project at the county fair. (CCBB 26:56; KR 40:259; LJ 98:644)
Illus. by Trina Schart Hyman, Lothrop, 1972, 160 pp., o.p.

C [R]   HENRY, Jan. *Tiger's Chance*. Gr. 3–5.
A tiger rug with magic whiskers takes Jennifer and her cat, Midnight, to his jungle home. (BL 53:460; CCBB 10:130; Eakin:156; HB 33:222; KR 25:218; LJ 82:2190)
Illus. by Hilary Knight, Harcourt, 1957, 138 pp., o.p.

C   HESS, Fjeril. *The Magic Switch*. Gr. 2–4.
Marenka's magic birch switch enables her to talk to animals, trees, and flowers. (BL 26:166; HB 5:46, 49; Mahony 3:173)
Illus. by Neva Kanaga Brown, Macmillan, 1929, 74 pp., o.p.

C   HILL, Elizabeth Starr. *Ever-After Island*. Gr. 4–6.
Ryan and Sara search the Cavern of the Winds for the magic jewel needed to break the spell cast over their father. (BL 73:1497; CCBB 31:34; KR 45:575; SLJ Sept 1977 p. 130)
Dutton, 1977, 160 pp., o.p.

C   HILLER, Catherine. *Abracatabby*. Gr. 2–4.
Although Adam's black kitten, Abracatabby, can do magic and grant wishes, the cat doesn't want anyone else to know his secret. (BL 77:1350; KR 49:799; SLJ Nov 1981 p. 77)
Illus. by Victoria de Larrea, Coward, 1981, 62 pp., o.p.

HOFFMANN, E. T. A. *The Nutcracker*. See Chapter 9, Toy Fantasy.

C   HOFFMANN, Eleanor. *Mischief in Fez*. Gr. 4–6.
Mousa's new stepmother brings evil Djinns to disrupt the household, but a desert fox flies the boy over the mountains to find a magical solution to his problems. (BL 39:373; HB 19:170; LJ 68:433, 825)
Illus. by Fritz Eichenberg, Holiday, 1943, 109 pp., o.p.

C   HOPP, Zinken. *The Magic Chalk*. Gr. 3–5. (Orig. Norwegian pub. 1948.)
John uses a witch's magic chalk to draw a boy who comes to life. (KR 27:492; LJ 85:844; TLS Nov 25, 1960 p. x)

Tr. by Suzanne Bergensdahl, illus. by Malvin Neset, McKay, 1959, 127 pp., o.p.

HOUGH, Charlotte. *Red Biddy and Other Stories*. See Chapter 3, Fantasy Collections.

HOUSMAN, Laurence. *The Rat-Catcher's Daughter: A Collection of Stories*. See Chapter 3, Fantasy Collections.

C HOWARD, Alice (Woodbury). *Sokar and the Crocodile: A Fairy Story of Egypt*. Gr. 3–5.
A young Egyptian boy named Sokar finds himself inside a fairy story and goes on a quest in search of the magic lotus bud. (BL 25:170; HB 4[Nov 1928]:79, 4[Aug 1928]:19, 7:115; Mahony 2:424)
Illus. by Coleman Kubinyi, Macmillan, 1928, 1948, 58 pp., o.p.

HOWARD, Joan. *The Oldest Secret*. See Section 5C, Travel to Other Worlds.

C [R] HOWARD, Joan (pseud. of Patricia Gordon). *The Thirteenth Is Magic*. Gr. 4–6.
A black cat takes Ronnie and Gillian up to the magical thirteenth floor of their apartment building. The sequel is *The Summer Is Magic* (1952). (BL 47:224; CCBB 4:20; HB 27:31; KR 18:725; LJ 76:338)
Illus. by Adrienne Adams, Lothrop, 1950, 170 pp., o.p.

HOYLAND, John. *The Ivy Garland*. See Chapter 4, Ghost Fantasy.

C HUNT, Marigold. *Hester and the Gnomes*. Gr. 2–5.
Hester discovers that a group of gnomes have set up housekeeping in a hollow tree on her father's farm. (HB 31:376; KR 23:417; LJ 80:2645)
Illus. by Jean Charlot, Whittlesey, 1955, 124 pp., o.p.

C HUNTER, Mollie (pseud. of Maureen Mollie Hunter McVeigh McIlwraith). *The Ferlie*. Gr. 4–6.
Hob the herd boy enters into a battle of wits with a ferlie over some stolen cattle. (BL 65:498; CCBB 22:95; HB 45:55)
Illus. by Joseph Cellini, Funk, 1968, 128 pp., o.p.

C/YA HUNTER, Mollie (pseud. of Maureen Mollie Hunter McVeigh
[R] McIlwraith). *The Wicked One*. Gr. 5–8.
Scottsman Colin Grant moves his family to America to avoid the devilish tricks of the Grollican, only to find that the demon has followed them. (BL 73:1339, 1352; CC:487; CCBB 30:160; HB 53:442; KR 45:426; SLJ May 1977 pp. 36, 62; Suth 2:234)
Harper, 1977, 128 pp., 1980, pap.

C HURLBUTT, Isabelle B. *Little Heiskell*. Gr. 3–4.
Little Heiskell, a soldier-shaped weather-vane, descends from the market-house roof to bring Christmas cheer to the children of Hagerstown. (BL 25:127; Bookshelf 1929 p. 12; HB 4[Nov 1928]:80); Mahony 2:716)
Illus. by Alida Conover, Dutton, 1928, 59 pp., o.p.

INGELOW, Jean. *Mopsa the Fairy*. See Section 5C, Travel to Other Worlds.

IRVING, Washington. *Rip Van Winkle*. See Section 5B, Myth Fantasy.

YA JAMES, M(ontague) R(hodes). *The Five Jars.* Gr. 7 up.
The magical contents of five jars discovered by an Englishman reveal the fairy world all around him. (BL 19:224; HB 3[May 1927]:22)
Longman, 1922, 172 pp., o.p.; Ayer, 1976 (repr. of 1922 ed.), o.p.

JANE, Pamela. *Noelle of the Nutcracker.* See Chapter 9, Toy Fantasy.

C [R] JARRELL, Randall. *Fly by Night.* Gr. 3–4.
A young boy floats out into the night, sees into dreams, listens to animals talking, and visits an owl's nest to hear a bedtime poem-story. (BL 73:474; CCBB 30:92; HB 53:52, 62:616; KR 44:1137; SLJ Nov 1976 p. 59; Suth 2:241)
Illus. by Maurice Sendak, Farrar, 1976, 31 pp., 1986, pap., o.p.

C JOHNSON, Elizabeth. *Break a Magic Circle.* Gr. 3–5.
An invisible boy asks Tilly to help break the magical spell over him. (BL 68:109; CCBB 25:27; HB 47:482; KR 39:676)
Illus. by Trina Schart Hyman, Little, 1971, 70 pp., o.p.

C JOHNSON, Elizabeth. *No Magic, Thank You.* Gr. 3–4.
Gordon and Debbie's belief in magic helps them win a contest against the Unlucks, bringing more good luck into the world. (CCBB 18:119; HB 40:499; KR 32:550)
Illus. by Garrett Price, Little, 1964, 55 pp., o.p.

C [R] JOHNSON, Elizabeth. *Stuck with Luck.* Grade 3–5.
Tom wishes for a dog but gets a powerless leprechaun instead. (BL 64:198; HB 43:589; KR 35:740; LJ 92:3187)
Illus. by Trina Schart Hyman, Little, 1967, 88 pp., o.p.

JONES, Adrienne. *The Mural Master.* See Section 5C, Travel to Other Worlds.

C/YA JONES, Diana Wynne. *The Ogre Downstairs.* Gr. 6–8. (Orig. British pub.
[O] 1974.)
Amazing things happen when Johnny and Malcolm use the chemistry sets given to them by "The Ogre," their new stepfather. (BL 71:1075; CCBB 28:179; CH&Bks:268; HB 51:464; KR 43:453; SLJ Sept 1975 p. 105; Suth 2:246)
Dutton, 1975, 191 pp., o.p.

JONES, Diana Wynne. *Warlock at the Wheel and Other Stories.* See Chapter 10, Witchcraft and Sorcery Fantasy.

C JONES, Elizabeth Orton. *Twig.* Gr. 3–5.
A little girl named Twig finds a fairy living in a tomato can. (BL 39:256; HB 19:102; LJ 67:884, 68:173)
Illus. by the author, Macmillan, 1942, 152 pp., o.p.

KAYE, Marvin. *The Incredible Umbrella.* See Section 5C, Travel to Other Worlds.

KEELE, Luqman, and PINKWATER, D(aniel) Manus. *Java Jack.* See Chapter 6, Humorous Fantasy.

KEMP, Gene. *Mr. Magus Is Waiting for You.* See Chapter 10, Witchcraft and Sorcery Fantasy.

KENNEDY, Richard. *Amy's Eyes.* See Chapter 9, Toy Fantasy.

C KENNEDY, Richard (Jerome). *Crazy in Love.* Gr. 3–5.
Kindness to an old woman gains Diana a husband who worries that Diana is a "crazy wife" because she talks to a donkey. (BL 77:625; HB 57:51; KR 49:7; SLJ Jan 1981 p. 62)
Illus. by Marcia Sewall, Elsevier-Dutton/Unicorn, 1980, 57 pp., o.p.

KENNEDY, William, and KENNEDY, Brendan. *Charlie Malarkey and the Belly-Button Machine.* See Chapter 6, Humorous Fantasy.

KING-SMITH, Dick. *Harry's Mad.* See Chapter 6, Humorous Fantasy.

C [R] KING-SMITH, Dick. *The Queen's Nose.* Gr. 3–6.
A mysterious coin grants Harmony Parker seven wishes. (BL 82:262; CCBB 38:209; HB 61:555; SLJ Aug 1985 p. 66)
Illus. by Jill Bennett, Harper, 1985, 111 pp.

C/YA KOFF, Richard M(yram). *Christopher.* Gr. 5–8.
The mysterious "Headmaster" shows Christopher how to use his supernatural powers to read minds, change his size, and make himself invisible. (CCBB 35:110; SLJ Feb 1982 p. 78; VOYA 4[Feb 1982]:34)
Illus. by Barbara Reinertson, Dawne-Leigh/Celestial Arts, 1981; Bantam, 1985, pap., 160 pp.

C/YA KONIGSBURG, E(laine) L(obl). *Up from Jericho Tel.* Gr. 5–9.
[R] Jeanmarie and Malcolm are summoned into ghostly Tallulah's underground boudoir, where they are made invisible in order to recover Tallulah's missing Regina Stone necklace. (BL 82:1304, 1312, 1313, 83:794, 1136; CC 1987 Suppl. p. 60; CCBB 39:131; HB 62:327; JHC 1987 Suppl. p. 71; KR 54:209; SLJ May 1986 p. 93, Apr 1987 p. 48; VOYA 9:219)
Atheneum, 1986, 178 pp.; Dell, 1987, pap.

KOOIKER, Leonie. *The Magic Stone.* See Chapter 10, Witchcraft and Sorcery Fantasy.

C [R] KORSCHUNOW, Irina. *Adam Draws Himself a Dragon.* Gr. 1–4. (Orig. German pub. 1978; British pub. 1982, entitled *Johnny's Dragon.*)
Adam's imaginary dragon friend gives him the confidence to do better at school, to make friends, and to lose some excess weight. (BL 82:1312; CCBB 40:11; HB 62:587; KR 54:638; SLJ Sept 1986 p. 123)
Tr. by James Skofield, illus. by Mary Rahn, Harper, 1986, 57 pp.

C KRENSKY, Stephen (Alan). *The Dragon Circle.* Gr. 4–6.
The Wynd children are kidnapped by five dragons who plan to use the children's magic powers to search for treasure. The sequels are *The Witching Hour* (1981) and *A Ghostly Business* (1984). (BL 74:477; CCBB 31:97; KR 45:728; SLJ Oct 1977 p. 115)
Illus. by A. Delaney, Atheneum, 1977, 116 pp., o.p.

C/YA LAGERLÖF, Selma (Ottilliana Lovisa). *The Wonderful Adventures of*
[R] *Nils.* Gr. 5–7. (Orig. Swedish pub. 1906–1907; U.S. 1908.)
An elf turns a boy named Nils into a Thumbling, smaller than the animals he once mistreated. *The Further Adventures of Nils* (1907) is included in this edition. (BL 4:22, 22:171, 44:118; Bookshelf 1932 p. 8; CCBB 1[Feb 1948]:4; HB 1[June 1925]:30, 7:118, 23:451; LJ 72:1544; Mahony 2:283)
Doubleday, 1925, o.p.; tr. by Velma Swanston Howard, illus. by H. Baumhauer, Pantheon, 1947, 539 pp., o.p.

LAMORISSE, Albert. *The Red Balloon.* See Chapter 1, Allegorical Fantasy and Literary Fairy Tales.

LAMPMAN, Evelyn Sibley. *The Shy Stegosaurus of Cricket Creek.* See Chapter 6, Humorous Fantasy.

C LANCASTER, Clay. *Periwinkle Steamboat.* Gr. 2–4.
   Nothing ever happens on Pennypacker Square until the night a flying-ferry-boat takes Timmy and his friends to the other side of the world. (HB 37:261; LJ 86:1984)
   Illus. by the author, Viking, 1961, 54 pp., o.p.

C/YA LANGTON, Jane (Gillson). *The Diamond in the Window.* Gr. 5–7.
[R]   The mysterious disappearance of two children and an Indian prince intrigues Eleanor and Eddie, who decide to find the key to the mystery: the Star of India Diamond. In *The Swing in the Summerhouse* (1967) Eleanor and Eddie go on magic adventures by swinging out through each of the summerhouse's six sides. In *The Astonishing Stereoscope* (1971), an optical toy sends Eleanor into the past. *The Fledgling* (1980) (see below) is a related work. (CCBB 16:30; Ch&Bks:269; HB 38:481; LJ 87:3895; Tymn:106)
   Illus. by Erik Blegvad, Harper, 1962, o.p., 1973, pap., 256 pp.

C/YA LANGTON, Jane (Gillson). *The Fledgling.* Gr. 5–7.
[O]   Georgie's parents fear for her safety after an old Canada goose teaches the little girl to fly. Newbery Medal Honor Book, 1981. *The Fragile Flag* (1984) is a non-fantasy sequel. Georgie's cousins, Eleanor and Eddie, have their own magic adventures in *The Diamond in the Window* (1962), *The Swing in the Summerhouse* (1967), and *The Astonishing Stereoscope* (1971). (BL 76:1365, 80:95; CC:496; CCBB 33:218; Ch&Bks:269; HB 56:408; KR 48:513; SLJ Sept 1980 p. 73)
   Harper, 1980, 1981, pap., 192 pp.

C LATHROP, Dorothy P(ulis). *The Colt from Moon Mountain.* Gr. 3–5.
   (Orig. pub. 1941.)
   Cynthy befriends an elusive snow-white colt who runs wild on Moon Mountain. (BL 38:162; HB 17:460; LJ 66:879, 67:42)
   Illus. by the author, Macmillan, 1956, 62 pp., o.p.

C LATHROP, Dorothy P(ulis). *The Dog in the Tapestry Garden.* Gr. 2–4.
   The dog in the tapestry on Maria's wall comes to life. (CCBB 16:83; HB 38:481; LJ 87:3203)
   Illus. by the author, Macmillan, 1962, 40 pp., o.p.

C LATHROP, Dorothy P(ulis). *The Little White Goat.* Gr. 2–4.
   On May Day Eve, a magical goat leads Debby and Pats into the forest, where they play with the forest creatures. (BL 30:185; HB 9:206; LJ 59:321; Mahony 3:80)
   Illus. by the author, Macmillan, 1933, 58 pp., o.p.

C LATHROP, Dorothy P(ulis). *The Lost Merry-Go-Round.* Gr. 3–5.
   Each child has a magic adventure while riding merry-go-round animals through Flittermouse Wood at night. (BL 31:177; Bookshelf 1934–1935 p. 6; HB 10:360; Mahony 3:107)
   Illus. by the author, Macmillan, 1934, 104 pp., o.p.

C LAURIN, Anne (pseud. of Anne McLaurin). *Perfect Crane*. Gr. 1–4.
   Gami the magician has always lived apart, until the perfect crane he brings
   to life causes his neighbors to become friendly. (BL 77:1105; KR 49:568; SLJ
   Apr 1981 p. 114)
   Illus. by Charles Mikolaycak, Harper, 1981, 31 pp.

C LAWRENCE, Ann (Margaret). *Tom Ass: Or the Second Gift*. Gr. 4–6.
   (Orig. British pub. 1972.)
   Two elfin gifts bring fortune and adventure to Tom and his wife, Jennifer.
   (BL 70:173; CCBB 27:46; HB 49:378; KR 41:600)
   Illus. by Mila Lazarevich, Walck, 1973, 132 pp., o.p.

C [R] LAWSON, Robert. *The Fabulous Flight*. Gr. 4–6.
   Seven-year-old Peter Peabody Pepperell III shrinks to four inches in height
   and flies off on a seagull's back. (BL 46:37; CCBB 2[Nov 1949]:5; HB 25:410,
   61:77; KR 17:394; LJ 74:1542, 1682)
   Illus. by the author, Little, 1949, 152 pp., o.p., 1984, pap.

LEWIS, C. S. *The Lion, the Witch, and the Wardrobe*. See Section 5C,
Travel to Other Worlds.

LEWIS, Hilda. *The Ship That Flew*. See Chapter 8, Time Travel Fantasy.

LINDBERGH, Anne. *Bailey's Window*. See Section 5C, Travel to Other
Worlds.

LINDBERGH, Anne. *The Hunky-Dory Dairy*. See Chapter 8, Time
Travel Fantasy.

LINDBERGH, Anne. *The Shadow on the Dial*. See Chapter 8, Time
Travel Fantasy.

C LINDE, Gunnel (Geijerstam). *The White Stone*. Gr. 4–6. (Orig. Swedish
   pub. 1964.)
   Fia and Hampus are transformed into fearless Fideli and Prince Perilous.
   This book won the Nils Holgersson Award for best Swedish children's book
   of 1964. (BL 63:734; CCBB 20:156; HB 42:717; KR 34:1053; LJ 91:5232)
   Tr. by Richard Winston and Clara Winston, illus. by Imero Gobbato,
   Harcourt, 1966, 185 pp., o.p.

C LINDGREN, Astrid. *Karlsson-on-the-Roof*. Gr. 3–5. (Orig. Swedish pub.
   1955; British pub. 1958.)
   No one believes Eric's story that a small, mischievous flying man is living
   on his roof. *Karlson Flies Again, Erik and Karlson on the Roof,* and *The
   World's Best Karlson* are the British sequels. (CCBB 26:28; KR 39:1156; LJ
   97:1168; TLS 1975 p. 373)
   Tr. by Marianne Turner, illus. by Jan Pyk, Viking, 1971, 128 pp., o.p.

LINDGREN, Astrid. *Mio, My Son*. See Section 5C, Travel to Other
Worlds.

C/YA LINKLATER, Eric (Robert Russell). *The Wind on the Moon*. Gr. 5–7.
 [R]   A magical wind from the moon turns two girls into kangaroos and helps
   them rescue their father. Carnegie Medal winner, 1944. (BL 41:140; HB
   21:112; KR 12:458; TLS 1944 p. 574)
   Illus. by Nicolas Bentley, Macmillan, 1944, 323 pp., o.p.

C [R] LOBE, Mira. *The Grandma in the Apple Tree.* Gr. 2–4. (Orig. Austrian pub. 1965.)
Andi's imaginary grandma takes him on tiger hunts and voyages to pirate-infested seas. (BL 67:703; CCBB 24:126; HB 47:163; LJ 96:1109)
Tr. by Doris Orgel, illus. by Judith Gwyn Brown, McGraw-Hill, 1970, 95 pp., o.p.

C LOCKE, Angela. *Mr. Mullett Owns a Cloud.* Gr. 3–5. (Orig. British pub. 1982.)
A shepherd named Mr. Mullett is given a small cloud named Napoleon as a gift, but the cloud proves to be quite vain and impulsive. (HB 60:196; SLJ Feb 1984 p. 75)
Illus. by Ian Newsham, Chatto, dist. by Merrimack, 1983, 128 pp., o.p.

C/YA LOFTING, Hugh. *The Twilight of Magic.* Gr. 5–7. (Orig. pub. Stokes, 1930.)
Anne and Giles learn about magic from Agnes the wise woman, who many people believe to be a witch. (BL 27:367; KR 35:60; LJ 56:278)
Illus. by Lois Lenski, Harper, 1967 (repr. of 1930 ed.), 303 pp.

LOGAN, Carolyn F. *The Power of the Rellard.* See Section 5B, Myth Fantasy.

LORING, Selden M. *Mighty Magic: An Almost-True Story of Pirates and Indians.* See Chapter 8, Time Travel Fantasy.

LOVEJOY, Jack. *The Rebel Witch.* See Chapter 10, Witchcraft and Sorcery Fantasy.

C LUENN, Nancy. *Unicorn Crossing.* Gr. 3–5.
Jenny longs to see a unicorn while staying at Unicorn Crossing, but only her family's elderly hostess, Mrs. Donovan, takes her wish seriously. (BL 84:67; CCBB 41:12; KR 55:1395; SLJ Oct 1987 p. 126)
Illus. by Peter E. Hanson, Atheneum, 1987, 64 pp.

C LYNCH, Patricia (Nora). *The Turf-Cutter's Donkey: An Irish Story of Mystery and Adventure.* Gr. 4–6. (Orig. British pub. 1934.)
Eileen, Seamus, and Long Ears the Donkey meet a leprechaun and travel through ancient Ireland. The sequels are *The Turf-Cutter's Donkey Goes Visiting* (1936) and *The Turf-Cutter's Donkey Kicks Up His Heels* (1939). (BL 32:22; Bookshelf 1935 p. 3; HB 11:295; LJ 61:115; Mahony 3:207)
Illus. by Jack B. Yeats. Dutton, 1935, 245 pp., o.p.

C MacALPINE, Margaret H(esketh Murray). *The Black Gull of Corie Lachan.* Gr. 4–6. (Orig. British pub. 1964.)
When Morag and Rory search for their missing father, rumored to have been abducted by the wee folk, they are followed by a strange black gull. (CCBB 19:102; KR 33:627; LJ 91:427; TLS 1964 p. 602)
Illus. by James Armstrong, Prentice-Hall, 1965, 105 pp., o.p.

MacDONALD, Betty. *Mrs. Piggle-Wiggle.* See Chapter 6, Humorous Fantasy.

C/YA MacDONALD, Greville. *Billy Barnicoat: A Fairy Romance for Young and Old.* Gr. 5–8. (Orig. British pub. 1922.)
In this story, written by George MacDonald's son, a boy cast up by the sea onto the Cornish coast searches for his inheritance while battling smugglers,

storms, and a witch. The sequel is *Count Billy* (1928). (BL 20:146; Bookshelf 1932 p. 8; Mahony 2:290; Moore:426)
Illus. by Francis D. Bedford, Dutton, 1923, 230 pp., o.p.

C McGRAW, Eloise Jarvis. *Joel and the Great Merlini.* Gr. 3–5.
The Great Merlini teaches Joel how to perform real magic. (CCBB 33:156; SLJ Feb 1980 p. 58)
Illus. by Jim Arnosky, Pantheon, 1979, 59 pp.

C/YA McHARGUE, Georgess. *Stoneflight.* Gr. 5–7.
[R] When Jane's home life becomes unbearable, she discovers the joys of night flight on the back of a stone griffin come to life. (BL 71:762; CCBB 29:50; HB 51:268; KR 43:239; SLJ Mar 1975 p. 98)
Illus. by Arvis Stewart, Viking, 1975, 222 pp., o.p.; Avon, 1982, pap.

C MacKELLAR, William. *The Smallest Monster in the World.* Gr. 3–5.
A kelpie introduces Wullie Watson to Maggie the sea monster. (BL 66:621; HB 46:36; KR 37:1064; LJ 95:1628)
Illus. by Ursula Koering, McKay, 1969, 113 pp., o.p.

MacLEOD, Charlotte. *The Curse of the Giant Hogweed.* See Chapter 8, Time Travel Fantasy.

C McNEILL (Alexander), Janet. *A Monster Too Many.* Gr. 3–5.
Sam and Joe circumvent their sea monster's incarceration in a zoo by returning it to the sea. (BL 68:1004; KR 40:136; LJ 97:2232)
Illus. by Ingrid Fetz, Little, 1972, 60 pp., o.p.

McNEILL, Janet. *Tom's Tower.* See Section 5C, Travel to Other Worlds.

MAETERLINCK, Maurice. *The Children's Blue Bird.* See Chapter 1, Allegorical Fantasy and Literary Fairy Tales.

Magicats! Ed. by Jack Dann and Gardner Dozois. See Section 2A, Beast Tales.

MAGUIRE, Gregory. *The Daughter of the Moon.* See Section 5C, Travel to Other Worlds.

MAGUIRE, Gregory. *Lightning Time.* See Chapter 8, Time Travel Fantasy.

MAHY, Margaret. *The Haunting.* See Chapter 10, Witchcraft and Sorcery Fantasy.

MANES, Stephen. *Chicken Treck: The Third Strange Thing That Happened to Oscar Noodleman.* See Chapter 6, Humorous Fantasy.

C MARIA, Consort of Ferdinand, King of Rumania. *The Magic Doll of Rumania; a Wonder Story in Which East and West Do Meet; Written for American Children.* Gr. 4–6.
An American girl named Nancy travels throughout Rumania with her magic doll. (Bookshelf 1925–1926 Suppl. p. 1; Mahony 3:54)
Illus. by Maud Petersham and Miska Petersham, Stokes, 1929, 319 pp., o.p.

C/YA MASEFIELD, John (Edward). *The Midnight Folk: A Novel.* Gr. 5–7.
[R] (Orig. British pub. 1927.)
Five animals help Kay solve the mystery of his great-grandfather's stolen treasure. In *The Box of Delights: Or, When the Wolves Were Running* (1935,

1984), Kay battles evil forces to save the magical Box of Delights. (BL 24:264, 287, 28:396, 401; Bookshelf 1932 p. 24; LJ 53:856; Moore: 332, 427; TLS 1927 p. 906)

Illus. by Rowland Hilder, Macmillan, 1932, o.p.; Dell, 1985, pap., 176 pp.

C/YA MASON, Arthur. *The Wee Men of Ballywooden.* Gr. 4–7. (Orig. U.S.
[R] pub. Doubleday, 1930.)

Times were hard for Danny Fay and the others until the Wee Men returned to their Irish village. The sequel is *From the Horn of the Moon* (1931). (BL 27:167; CCBB 6:34; HB 6:331, 7:121, 29:62; LJ 56:452, 77:1747; Mahony 3:207; Moore:435)

Illus. by Robert Lawson, Viking, 1952, 214 pp., o.p.

C [R] MAXWELL, William (Keepers). *The Heavenly Tenants.* Gr. 3–5.

The constellations descend from the sky to care for the Marvells' farm. (BL 43:90, 277; HB 22:455; KR 14:455; LJ 71:1412, 1720)

Illus. by Ilonka Karasz, Harper, 1946, 56 pp., o.p.

C [R] MAYNE, William (James Carter). *The Blue Boat.* Gr. 4–6. (Orig. British pub. 1957.)

Christopher and Hugh meet a goblin and a giant while exploring a magical lake. (BL 56:609; CCBB 14:178; KR 28:49; LJ 85:2479)

Illus. by Geraldine Spence, Dutton, 1960, 173 pp., o.p.

C [R] MAYNE, William (James Carter). *The Glass Ball.* Gr. 3–5. (Orig. pub. in England.)

Max and Niko follow a rolling glass ball. (BL 58:796; Eakin:228; HB 38:374; LJ 87:2026)

Illus. by Janet Duchesne, Dutton, 1962, 63 pp., o.p.

C [R] MAYNE, William (James Carter). *A Grass Rope.* Gr. 4–6. (Orig. British pub. 1957.)

Four children weave a special rope to capture a unicorn. Carnegie Medal, 1957. (Eakin:224; HB 38:600; LJ 87:4622)

Illus. by Lynton Lamb, Dutton, 1962, 166 pp., o.p.

C [R] MAYNE, William (James Carter). *The Green Book of Hob Stories.* Gr. 2–3. (Orig. British pub. 1984.)

Five tales about an invisible two-foot-tall man who magically smooths out household problems. Hob's adventures continue in: *The Blue Book of Hob Stories* (1984), *The Yellow Book of Hob Stories* (1984), and *The Red Book of Hob Stories* (1984). (BL 80:1550; CCBB 38:32; HB 60:468; SLJ Oct 1984 p. 160; Suth 3:298; TLS Mar 3, 1984 p. 338)

Illus. by Patrick Benson, Putnam/Philomel, 1984, 25 pp.

C MEIGS, Cornelia (Lynde). *The Wonderful Locomotive.* Gr. 3–5.

A little boy named Peter takes old engine number 44 for its last exciting cross-country run. (BL 25:171; Bookshelf 1932 p. 8; HB 4[Aug 1928]:13, 32–33, 4[Nov 1928]:76, 7:115, 20:347–349; Mahony 2:141)

Illus. by Berta Hader and Elmer Hader, Macmillan, 1928, 104 pp., o.p.

MILES, Patricia. *The Gods in Winter.* See Chapter 1, Allegorical Fantasy and Literary Fairy Tales.

MOERI, Louise. *Star Mother's Youngest Child.* See Chapter 1, Allegorical Fantasy and Literary Fairy Tales.

MOLESWORTH, Mary Louisa. *The Cuckoo Clock.* See Section 5C, Travel to Other Worlds.

C MOLESWORTH, Mary Louisa (Stewart). *The Tapestry Room: A Child's Romance.* Gr. 4–6. (Orig. British and U.S. pubs., 1879.)
A family of French children living in an old chateau have wonderful dreams and adventures. (HB 38:66; Mahony 2:291)
Illus. by Walter Crane, Random, 1961, 217 pp., o.p.; Garland, 1976 (bound with *The Cuckoo Clock* 1877, 1954), o.p.

C MONATH, Elizabeth. *Topper and the Giant.* Gr. 3–5.
Mat and his dog, Topper, are given a magic charm by a giant whom they rescued from an avalanche. (HB 36:216; KR 28:144; LJ 85:2029)
Illus. by the author, Viking, 1960, 60 pp., o.p.

C/YA MOON, Grace Purdie, and MOON, Carl. *Lost Indian Magic: A Mystery Story of the Red Man as He Lived Before the White Men Came.* Gr. 5–7.
A brave young Indian boy must recover his tribe's magic jewel, a turquoise elephant stolen long ago. (BL 15:1512; Mahony 2:538)
Illus. by Carl Moon, Stokes, 1918, 301 pp., o.p.; Gordon, 1977.

C MOORE, Annie Carroll. *Nicholas: a Manhattan Christmas Story.* Gr. 4–6.
An eight-inch-tall Dutch boy arrives in New York City on Christmas Eve, determined to see everything of interest, past and present. The sequel is *Nicholas and the Golden Goose* (1932). (BL 21:158; Bookshelf 1927 p. 10; HB 1[Nov 1924]:13; LJ 50:803; Mahony 2:717)
Illus. by Jay Van Everen, Putnam, 1924, 331 pp., o.p.

C MORGAN, Helen (Gertrude Louise Axford). *Satchkin Patchkin.* Gr. 2–4. (Orig. British pub. 1966.)
Satchkin Patchkin is a small green man who lives in an apple tree. *Mother Farthing's Luck* is the British sequel. (CCBB 24:63; LJ 95:4340; TLS 1966 p. 1092)
Illus. by Shirley Hughes, M. Smith, 1970, 64 pp., o.p.

C MULOCK, Diana (pseud. of Dinah Craik). *The Adventures of a Brownie as Told to My Child.* Gr. 3–5. (Orig. British pub. 1872.)
Six tales in which only children can see the brownie work his mischief. (BL 15:153, 20:224; HB 28:422; LJ 50:803; Mahony 1:36)
Illus. by Mary Seaman, Macmillan, 1952, 122 pp., o.p.; Garland, 1977 (bound with *The Little Lame Prince,* 1874, 1948), o.p.

MYERS, Bernice. *Sidney Rella and the Glass Sneaker.* See Chapter 6, Humorous Fantasy.

NASTICK, Sharon. *Mr. Radagast Makes an Unexpected Journey.* See Chapter 6, Humorous Fantasy.

NESBIT, E. *The Complete Book of Dragons.* See Chapter 3, Fantasy Collections.

C [R] NESBIT (Bland), E(dith). *The Deliverers of Their Country.* Gr. 3–5.
(Orig. British pub. in *Strand Magazine,* 1899; U.S. pub. in *The Book of Dragons,* 1901, 1973; this ed. orig. pub. in Austria, 1985.)
Harry and Effie awaken a marble statue of St. George to ask his advice on

fighting the plague of dragons infesting England. (BL 82:759; CCBB 39:93; HB 62:195; SLJ Apr 1986 p. 91; TLS July 1986 p. 789)
Illus. by Lisbeth Zwerger, Picture Book, 1985, 24 pp.

C/YA NESBIT (Bland), E(dith). *The Enchanted Castle.* Gr. 5–7. (Orig. British
[R]   pub. 1907.)
A magical ring transports Gerald, Jimmy, and Cathy to a garden of stone monsters surrounding a castle. (BL 30:24, 60; Bookshelf 1933 p. 9; HB 8:153, 214; KR 32:293; LJ 58:1052; Mahony 3:208)
Illus. by H. R. Millar, Coward, 1933, o.p.; illus. by Cecil Leslie, Dutton, 1964, o.p.; Dent, dist. by Biblio, 1968 (repr. of 1964 ed.), 231 pp., o.p.; Penguin/Puffin, 1986, pap.

C/YA NESBIT (Bland), E(dith). *Five Children and It.* Gr. 5–7. (Orig. British
[R]   pub. 1902; U.S. Looking Glass, dist. by Dodd, 1905.)
Anthea, Jane, Robert, Cyril, and the Baby uncover a Psammead or Sand Fairy, who reluctantly agrees to grant their wishes. In *The Phoenix and the Carpet* (1904, 1949, 1960, 1987) a magic carpet carrying a phoenix egg takes the children on magical journeys to Persia. In *The Story of the Amulet* (orig. British pub. 1906; U.S. 1907, 1949, 1960, 1987), which was the first time travel fantasy ever written for children, the Sand Fairy helps the children travel to ancient Egypt, Babylon, and Rome. All three books were published in one volume entitled *The Five Children; Containing the Five Children and It; The Phoenix and the Carpet; The Story of the Amulet* (Coward, 1930). (BL 27:215; HB 6:332, 25:297, 579; LJ 74:618; Mahony 2:291)
Illus. by J. S. Goodall, Looking Glass, dist. by Random, 1948,1959, o.p.; illus. by H. R. Millar, Coward, 1949, 1963, o.p.; illus. by J. S. Goodall, Buccaneer, 1981, 253 pp.; Dell/Yearling, 1986, pap.

NESBIT, E. *The House of Arden.* See Chapter 8, Time Travel Fantasy.

NESBIT, E. *The Magic City.* See Chapter 5C, Travel to Other Worlds.

C/YA NESBIT (Bland), E(dith). *The Magic World.* Gr. 5–7. (Orig. British pub.
[R]   1912.)
Twelve fantasy tales including "The Cat-hood of Maurice," "Accidental Magic," and "The Magician's Heart." (BL 57:32; HB 36:309; LJ 85:3224; TLS 1981 p. 348)
Illus. by H. R. Millar and Spencer Pryse, Coward, 1960, o.p.; British Book Center, 1974 (repr. of 1912 ed.), 280 pp., o.p.

C/YA NESBIT (Bland), E(dith). *Wet Magic.* Gr. 5–7. (Orig. British pub. 1910.)
Four children rescue a mermaid and are taken on an undersea adventure. (BL 57:32; HB 13:378, 36:309; LJ 62:881, 63:691)
Illus. by H. R. Millar, Coward, 1960, 244 pp., o.p.

C/YA NESBIT (Bland), E(dith). *The Wonderful Garden; or the Three C's.* Gr. 5–7. (Orig. British pub. 1911.)
Carolyn, Charlotte, and Charles find an old book of magic and a magical garden. (BL 32:80, 57:32; Bookshelf 1935 p. 2; HB 11:296, 36:309, 61:196; LJ 60:830, 85:3224; Mahony 3:209)
Illus. by H. R. Millar, Coward, 1960, o.p.; British Book Center, 1974 (repr. of 1911 ed.), 293 pp., o.p.

C/YA NIMMO, Jenny. *The Snow Spider.* Gr. 4–7. (Orig. British pub. 1986.)
[R]   On his tenth birthday, Gwyn's grandmother gives him five magic gifts to

help solve the mystery of his sister's disappearance in the Welsh mountains. (BL 83:1751; CCBB 40:216; HB 63:613; KR 55:861; SLJ Aug 1987 p. 87) Dutton, 1987, 128 pp.

C NIXON, Joan Lowery. *The Gift.* Gr. 4–6.
   Brian's Irish grandfather enchants him with tales of pookas, fairies, and leprechauns, and he resolves to bring a real leprechaun home with him. (BL 79:1036; CCBB 36:214; KR 51:524; SLJ May 1983 p. 74)
   Illus. by Andrew Glass, Macmillan, 1983, 96 pp.

NIXON, Joan Lowery. *Magnolia's Mixed-Up Magic.* See Section 2B, Talking Animal Fantasy.

C/YA NORTH, Joan. *The Cloud Forest.* Gr. 5–8. (Orig. British pub. 1965.)
   [R]   The Annerlie Ring causes Andrew to have disturbing dreams of the Cloud Forest. (BL 63:326; CCBB 20:96; HB 42:564; Suth:297; TLS 1965 p. 1133) Farrar, 1966, 180 pp., o.p.

C/YA NORTON, Andre (pseud. of Alice Mary Norton). *Fur Magic.* Gr. 5–7.
   Corey is afraid of everything on his foster uncle's ranch until the Changer, part-coyote and part-man, turns him into a beaver named Yellow Shell. (HB 45:172; KR 36:1164; LJ 94:877; TLS 1969 p. 689)
   Illus. by John Kaufmann, World, 1968, 174 pp., o.p.

NORTON, Andre. *Lavender Green Magic.* See Chapter 8, Time Travel Fantasy.

C/YA NORTON, Andre (pseud. of Alice Mary Norton), and MILLER, Phyllis. *Seven Spells to Sunday.* Gr. 5–7.
   Gifts and spells found in a purple and silver mailbox bring hope into the lives of two foster children named Monnie and Bim. (BL 75:1219; JHC:401; KR 47:741; SLJ Mar 1979 p. 143)
   Atheneum, 1979, 144 pp., o.p.

C [O] NORTON, Mary (Pearson). *Bedknob and Broomstick.* Gr. 4–6. (Orig.
   pub. separately in England as *The Magic Bedknob or; How to Become a Witch in Ten Easy Lessons,* 1944, and *Bonfires and Broomsticks,* 1947.)
   In this two-part story, a witch gives Paul, Carey, and Charles a magical bedknob, enabling their bed to fly through time. (BL 54:177; CC:512; CCBB 11:98; Ch&Bks:270; HB 33:489; KR 25:638; LJ 69:355, 82:3248; TLS Nov 15, 1957 p. iii)
   Illus. by Erik Blegvad, Harcourt, 1957, 189 pp., 1975, pap.

C/YA NORTON, Mary (Pearson). *The Borrowers.* Gr. 4–7. (Orig. British pub.
   [O]   1952.)
   Pod, Homily, and Arrietty Clock, a family of tiny people who live by "borrowing" from humans, must flee for their lives after Arrietty makes friends with a human boy. Carnegie Medal, 1952. In *The Borrowers Afield* (1955), the Clocks live precariously outdoors in an old boot, until they are rescued from the winter snows by Arietty's friend, the game-keeper's son. In *The Borrowers Afloat* (1959), a young Borrower named Spiller guides the family on an exciting trip through the drains to the river, where they settle in a tea kettle, only to be washed away by a flood. In *The Borrowers Aloft* (1961), the Clocks' safe, happy life in a miniature railway village is interrupted when they are kidnapped by greedy Mr. and Mrs. Platter. In *Poor Stainless* (1971), Homily tells Arrietty about Stainless, a young Borrower who spent a glorious week in a candy store, while his worried family

searched for him. In *The Borrowers Avenged* (1982, Peter Smith, 1988), the Clocks move into a rectory and rid themselves forever of the money-hungry Platters and their plot to put the Borrowers on display. (BL 50:4, 40, 80:96; CC:513; CCBB 7:25; Ch&Bks:238; Eakin:249; HB 29:456; KR 21:483; LJ 78:1699)

    Illus. by Beth Krush and Joe Krush, Harcourt, 1953, 1986, pap., 192 pp.

C O'FAOLÁIN, Eileen. *The Little Black Hen; An Irish Fairy Story.* Gr. 4–6. (Orig. pub. in Ireland.)

    Garret and Julie lift a spell laid on a changeling hen by Cliona, the fairy queen. Garret has other magic adventures in *King of the Cats* (Morrow, 1942), *Miss Pennyfeather and the Pooka* (Random, 1946), and *Miss Pennyfeather in the Springtime* (published in Ireland, 1946). (BL 37:20; HB 16:339, 342; LJ 65:715, 848; TLS 1940 p. 633)

    Illus. by Aldren Watson, Random, 1940, 135 pp., o.p.

C [R] OLSON, Helen Kronberg. *The Strange Thing That Happened to Oliver Wendell Iscovitch.* Gr. 1–4.

    Oliver Wendell's fat cheeks enable him to hold his breath and float through the air. (BL 79:1221; CCBB 37:14; SLJ Sept 1938 p. 110; Suth 3:328)

    Illus. by Betsy Lewin, Dodd, 1983, 62 pp.

OPPENHEIM, Shulamith. *The Selchie's Seed.* See Section 5B, Myth Fantasy.

C [R] ORMONDROYD, Edward. *David and the Phoenix.* Gr. 4–6.

    David meets the Phoenix on a mountain ledge and helps him outwit a scientist bent on capturing the mythical creature. (BL 54:113; CCBB 11:38; HB 33:401; KR 25:583; LJ 82:3249)

    Illus. by Joan Raysor, Follett, 1957, 173 pp., o.p.

ORMONDROYD, Edward. *Time at the Top.* See Chapter 8, Time Travel Fantasy.

C OUIDA (pseud. of [Marie] Louise de la Ramée). *The Nürnberg Stove.* Gr. 4–6. (Orig. British pub. 1882, in *Stories for Children;* U.S. pub. in *The Nürnberg Stove and Other Stories,* 1901, 1928.)

    A boy named August hides inside his family's porcelain stove and goes on a journey when the stove is sold. (BL 12:392, 21:160, 25:253, 49:209; HB 4[Aug 1928]:9, 28:421; Mahony 2:296)

    Illus. by Maria Kirk, Lippincott, 1905, 1916, o.p.; illus. by Frank Boyd, Macmillan, 1928, 1952, 122 pp., o.p.

C PALMER, Mary. *The Teaspoon Tree.* Gr. 3–5.

    A girl named Andulasia searches for the magical Teaspoon Tree. (CCBB 16:115; HB 39:174; LJ 88:1769)

    Illus. by Carlota Dodge, Houghton, 1963, 114 pp., o.p.

C PARKER, Richard. *M for Mischief.* Gr. 3–5. (Orig. British pub. 1965.)

    Andrew and Milly find an old-fashioned stove with a magical dial that cooks foods which cause invisibility and change people into animals. (HB 42:307; KR 34:57; LJ 91:2697; TLS 1965 p. 513)

    Illus. by Charles Geer, Hawthorn, 1966, 90 pp., o.p.

PARKER, Richard. *The Old Powder Line.* See Chapter 8, Time Travel Fantasy.

C PARKER, Richard. *Spell Seven*. Gr. 3–5.
Carolyn gives her brother, Norman, a magic wand. (HB 47:385; LJ 96:2920; TLS 1971 p. 774)
Illus. by Trevor Ridley, Nelson, 1971, 127 pp., o.p.

C PARRISH, Anne, and PARRISH, Dillwyn. *Knee-High to a Grasshopper*. Gr. 4–6.
Little Man "ungrows" to the size of a meadow mouse. (BL 20:107; Bookshelf 1923–1924 Suppl. p. 2; HB 7:61–67; LJ 50:803; Mahony 2:291)
Illus. by the authors, Macmillan, 1923, 209 pp., o.p.

C/YA PATTEN, Brian. *Mr. Moon's Last Case*. Gr. 5–8. (Orig. British pub. 1975.)
A leprechaun called Nameon, who accidentally entered the human world, is pursued by a detective named Mr. Moon and aided by the members of the Secret Society for the Protection of Leprechauns as he desperately tries to get home. (BL 73:410; CCBB 30:111; HB 52:626; KR 44:974; SLJ Feb 1977 p. 67)
Illus. by Mary Moore, Scribner, 1976, 158 pp., o.p.

C [R] PAYNE, Joan Balfour (Dicks). *The Leprechaun of Bayou Luce*. Gr. 3–5.
Josh helps a leprechaun win back gold stolen by pirate ghosts. (BL 54:208; CCBB 11:39; HB 33:489; KR 25:689; LJ 83:240)
Illus. by the author, Hastings, 1957, 60 pp., o.p.

C PAYNE, Joan Balfour (Dicks). *Magnificent Milo*. Gr. 3–5.
A young centaur named Milo accidentally falls from his mountain home into the world of men, where he joins a traveling circus and tries to find his way home again. (BL 55:137; HB 34:478; KR 26:605; LJ 84:253)
Illus. by the author, Hastings, 1958, 64 pp., o.p.

C [R] PEARCE, (Ann) Philippa. *A Dog So Small*. Gr. 4–6. (Orig. British pub. 1962.)
Ben's powerful imaginary chihuahua comes to life whenever Ben closes his eyes, and almost leads him to disaster. (BL 59:946; CCBB 16:131; HB 39:284, 60:499; LJ 88:2149; TLS 1962 p. 397)
Illus. by Antony Maitland, Lippincott, 1963, 142 pp., o.p.

C [R] PEARCE, (Ann) Philippa. *Lion at School: And Other Stories*. Gr. 3–5. (Orig. British pub. 1985.)
Nine tales, including "The Lion at School," "The Executioner," and "The Crooked Little Finger." (BL 82:1616; CCBB 39:177; KR 54:716; SLJ Sept 1986 p. 138)
Illus. by Caroline Sharpe, Greenwillow, 1986, 122 pp.

C [R] PEARCE, (Ann) Philippa. *Mrs. Cockle's Cat*. Gr. 2–4. (Orig. British pub. 1961.)
The wind sweeps a balloon-seller named Mrs. Cockle off in search of her lost cat. (BL 58:694; CCBB 15:130; HB 38:172; LJ 87:2026; TLS Dec 1, 1961 p. xiv)
Illus. by Antony Maitland, Lippincott, 1962, 32 pp., o.p.

PEARCE, Philippa. *Tom's Midnight Garden*. See Chapter 8, Time Travel Fantasy.

PEASE, Howard. *The Gypsy Caravan*. See Chapter 8, Time Travel Fantasy.

PHILLIPS, Ann. *The Oak King and the Ash Queen.* See Chapter 5B, Myth Fantasy.

C PINKWATER, D(aniel) Manus. *Magic Camera.* Gr. 2–3.
Charles's antique camera can make real things disappear and imaginary things become real. (BL 70:878; KR 42:53)
Illus. by the author, Dodd, 1974, 35 pp., o.p.

PINKWATER, D. Manus. *Wingman.* See Chapter 8, Time Travel Fantasy.

C POLESE, Carolyn. *Something about a Mermaid.* Gr. 2–4.
The mermaid Janie finds at the beach does not adjust well to life in an apartment. (BL 75:867; KR 47:66; SLJ Mar 1979 p. 129)
Illus. by Gail Owens, Dutton, 1978, 27 pp., o.p.

C POMERANTZ, Charlotte. *The Downtown Fairy Godmother.* Gr. 3–5.
Olivia's fairy godmother turns out to be an amateur who needs a lot of practice to perfect her wish-granting abilities. (CCBB 32:70; Ch&Bks:271; KR 46:1190; SLJ Nov 1978 p. 67)
Illus. by Susanna Natti, Addison-Wesley, 1978, 45 pp., o.p.

PORTE, Barbara Ann. *Jesse's Ghost and Other Stories.* See Chapter 3, Fantasy Collections.

POSTMA, Lidia. *The Stolen Mirror.* See Section 5C, Travel to Other Worlds.

C POSTMA, Lidia. *The Witch's Garden.* Gr. 1–3. (Orig. pub. in the Netherlands.)
Seven children exploring the garden of a tumbledown house meet some elves and see circus ghosts dancing in a magic tree. (CCBB 33:54; SLJ 26[Sept 1979]:119; Suth 3:352)
Illus. by the author, McGraw-Hill, 1979, 23 pp., o.p.

C POTTER, Miriam (S.) Clark. *Sally Gabble and the Fairies.* Gr. 3–5.
Old Sally Gabble makes friends with the fairies after she catches a particularly troublesome one in a trap. (BL 26:237; HB 5:49; Mahony 3:109)
Illus. by Helen Sewell, Macmillan, 1929, 87 pp., o.p.

C PROYSEN, Alf. *Little Old Mrs. Pepperpot and Other Stories.* Gr. 3–5.
(Orig. Swedish pub. 1957; British pub. 1959.)
Twelve stories, mostly about a woman who can shrink to the size of a pepper shaker. The sequels are *Mrs. Pepperpot Again* (1961), *Mrs. Pepperpot to the Rescue* (Pantheon, 1964), *Mrs. Pepperpot in the Magic Wood* (Pantheon, 1968), and *Mrs. Pepperpot's Outing* (Pantheon, 1971). Three British sequels are *Mrs. Pepperpot's Busy Day, Mrs. Pepperpot's Christmas,* and *Mrs. Pepperpot's Year.* (HB 36:216; KR 28:235; LJ 85:2042; TLS May 29, 1959 p. xiii)
Tr. by Marianne Helwig, illus. by Bjorn Berg, Astor-Honor, 1960, 95 pp.

PYLE, Howard. *King Stork.* See Chapter 10, Witchcraft and Sorcery Fantasy.

C PYLE, Katherine. *The Counterpane Fairy.* Gr. 3–5. (Orig. pub. 1898.)
While Teddy is sick in bed, he is entertained by the stories of the Counterpane Fairy. (BL 25:174; Mahony 1:40; Mahony 2:136)
Illus. by the author, Dutton, 1928, 191 pp., o.p.

C [R] RAWLINGS (Baskin), Marjorie Kinnan. *The Secret River.* Gr. 2–4.
Calpurnia stumbles upon a beautiful river, but when she tries to find it again, it has disappeared. (CCBB 9:12; BL 51:436; HB 31:254, 258; KR 23:327; LJ 80:1508)
Illus. by Leonard Weisgard, Scribner, 1955, 56 pp., o.p; Sams/Macmillan (repr. of 1955 ed.).

C/YA REID BANKS, Lynne. *The Indian in the Cupboard.* Gr. 4–7. (Orig. Brit-
[O] ish pub. 1980.)
An old wall cupboard turns Patrick and Omri's toy cowboy and Indian into miniature people named Boone and Little Bear, who immediately begin to fight. In *The Return of the Indian* (1986), Omri and Patrick reinstitute the magic after Little Bear is gravely wounded in the French and Indian Wars. (CCBB 35:22; HB 57:662; SLJ Dec 1981 p. 59; TLS 1980 p. 1326)
Illus. by Brock Cole, Doubleday, 1981, 181 pp.; Avon, 1982, pap.

REIT, Seymour. *Benvenuto.* See Chapter 6, Humorous Fantasy.

RHYS, Mimpsey. *Mr. Hermit Crab: A Tale for Children by a Child.* See Section 5C, Travel to Other Worlds.

RILEY, Louise. *Train for Tiger Lily* See Section 5C, Travel to Other Worlds.

C ROBERTS, Willo Davis. *The Magic Book.* Gr. 4–6.
Alex is hopeful that a book called *Magic Spells and Potions for the Beginner,* will help disarm Norm, the neighborhood bully. (BL 82:1400; CCBB 39:195; KR 54:866; SLJ May 1986 p. 97)
Atheneum, 1986, 146 pp.

C/YA ROCKWELL, Thomas. *Tin Cans.* Gr. 5–7.
The police begin searching for David and Jane after a magical soup can makes them wealthy. (BL 72:240; KR 43:714; SLJ Oct 1975 p. 101)
Illus. by Saul Lambert, Bradbury, 1975, 70 pp., o.p.

RODGERS, Mary. *Freaky Friday.* See Chapter 6, Humorous Fantasy.

RUFFELL, Ann. *Pyramid Power.* See Section 5C, Travel to Other Worlds.

C [R] SARGENT, Sarah. *Weird Henry Berg.* Gr. 4–6.
Millie Levenson wants to help a Welsh dragon recover its lost baby, but Henry Berg does not want to give up his pet "lizard." (BL 77:48; CC:526; CCBB 34:20; Ch&Bks:271: HB 56:642; KR 48:1164; SLJ Sept 1980 p. 78; Suth 3:375)
Crown, 1980, 113 pp., o.p.

SAUER, Julia L. *Fog Magic.* See Chapter 8, Time Travel Fantasy.

C SAWYER, Ruth. *The Enchanted Schoolhouse.* Gr. 4–6.
A leprechaun's magic helps Lobster Cove build a new school. (BL 53:182; HB 32:450; KR 24:70)
Illus. by Hugh Troy, Viking, 1956, 128 pp., o.p.

C [R] SAWYER, Ruth. *The Year of the Christmas Dragon.* Gr. 3–5.
A little boy and an ancient Chinese dragon enliven a Mexican Christmas fiesta. (BL 57:249; Eakin:283; HB 36:504; KR 28:556; LJ 85:4570)
Illus. by Hugh Troy, Viking, 1960, 88 pp., o.p.

C SEFTON, Catherine (pseud. of Martin Waddell). *The Emma Dilemma.*
Gr. 3–5. (Orig. British pub. 1982.)
A bump on the head brings a mischievous transparent twin into Emma's
life. (BL 79:1098; CCBB 37:37; SLJ May 1983 p. 77)
Illus. by Jill Bennett, Faber, dist. by Harper, 1983, 96 pp.

C/YA SELDEN, George (pseud. of George Selden Thompson). *The Genie of*
[R] *Sutton Place.* Gr. 5–7.
Nothing is quite the same after Abdulla, the genie, is released from 1,000
years of captivity in an Arabian carpet. (BL 69:861; CC:527; CCBB 26:176;
HB 49:382; KR 41:116; LJ 98:1398, 1656)
Farrar, 1973, hb and pap., 175 pp.

C [R] SENDAK, Maurice (Bernard). *Kenny's Window.* Gr. 1–4. (Orig. pub.
1956.)
Kenny must find the answers to seven difficult questions asked by a four-
legged rooster. (BL 52:393; CCBB 10:13; HB 32:108; KR 24:242; LJ
81:1546)
Illus. by the author, Harper, 1964, 54 pp.

SEREDY, Kate. *Lazy Tinka.* See Chapter 1, Allegorical Fantasy and
Literary Fairy Tales.

Shape Shifters. Ed. by Jane H. Yolen. See Chapter 3, Fantasy Collections.

C SHOWELL, Ellen Harvey. *Cecelia and the Blue Mountain Boy.* Gr. 4–6.
Long ago, the townspeople of Chester began holding an annual music
festival to cheer up a girl named Cecelia who had been enchanted by a fiddler
on Blue Mountain. (BL 79:1468; CCBB 36:178; SLJ Aug 1983 p. 70)
Illus. by Margot Tomes, Lothrop, 1983, 76 pp., o.p.

C [R] SHURA, Mary Francis (pseud. of Mary Francis Craig). *A Shoe Full of*
Shamrock. Gr. 3–5.
Davie O'Sullivan's secret wish comes true after he returns a pouch of fairy
gold to a leprechaun. (BL 62:222; CCBB 19:68; Eakin:299; HB 41:500; KR
33:677; LJ 90:4622)
Illus. by N. M. Bodecker, Atheneum, 1965, 64 pp., o.p.

SHURA, Mary Francis. *Happles and Cinnamunger.* See Chapter 4, Ghost
Fantasy.

SINGER, Isaac Bashevis. *A Tale of Three Wishes.* See Chapter 1,
Allegorical Fantasy and Literary Fairy Tales.

C SLATER, Jim. *Grasshopper and the Unwise Owl.* Gr. 3–5. (Orig. British
pub. 1979.)
Magic candy makes Graham Hooper small enough to undermine Mr.
Groll's plot to cheat Graham's widowed mother out of her home. (BL 77:812;
CCBB 34:161; SLJ Mar 1981 p. 152)
Illus. by Babette Cole, Holt, 1980, 88 pp.

C/YA SLEIGH, Barbara (de Riemer). *Carbonel: The King of the Cats* (British
[R] title: *Carbonel,* 1955). Gr. 4–7.
Rosemary tries to break the spell on the witch's cat that came with her new
broom. The sequels are *The Kingdom of Carbonel* (1960) and *Carbonel and*
Calidor (British). (BL 54:30; CCBB 11:40; Eakin:300; HB 33:408; LJ
82:2702; TLS 1978 p. 765)
Illus. by V. H. Drummond, Bobbs-Merrill, 1956, 253 pp., o.p.

SMITH, L. J. *Night of the Solstice*. See Section 5C, Travel to Other Worlds.

C/YA SNYDER, Zilpha Keatley. *Black and Blue Magic*. Gr. 5–7.
[R]   Mr. Mazzeek's magic lotion causes Harry Houdini Marco to sprout wings. (BL 62:878; CCBB 20:48; HB 42:308; KR 34:108; LJ 91:2214; Suth:371) Illus. by Gene Holtan, Atheneum, 1966, 186 pp., o.p.

C/YA SNYDER, Zilpha Keatley. *A Season of Ponies*. Gr. 5–7.
Her father's amulet enables Pamela to make friends with a beautiful pastel pony and escape from the pig woman in the swamp. (CCBB 18:20; HB 40:284; KR 32:108; LJ 89:1862) Illus. by Alton Raible, Atheneum, 1964, 133 pp., o.p., 1973, pap.

SOMMER-BODENBURG, Angela. *My Friend the Vampire*. See Chapter 6, Humorous Fantasy.

SPURR, Elizabeth. *Mrs. Minetta's Car Pool*. See Chapter 6, Humorous Fantasy.

C STANLEY (Zuromskis), Diane. *The Good-Luck Pencil*. Gr. 2–4.
Mary Ann's magic pencil brings to life an outrageous composition describing her family: it turns her mother into a famous ballerina, her father into an astronaut, and her house into a mansion. (BL 82:1317; SLJ Aug 1986 p. 88) Illus. by Bruce Degen, Macmillan/Four Winds, 1986, 32 pp.

C STEELE, Mary Q(uintard). *Wish, Come True*. Gr. 4–6.
The magic ring that Meg finds while she and her brother are staying at Great-Aunt Louise's enables them to miniaturize themselves, breathe under water, and search for treasure. (BL 76:47, 1545; KR 48:128; SLJ Sept 1979 p. 148) Illus. by Muriel Batherman, Greenwillow, 1979, 160 pp.

C STERMAN, Betsy, and STERMAN, Samuel. *Too Much Magic*. Gr. 3–6.
Bill and his younger brother, Jeff, find a magic wish-granting cube, but discover that the consequences are difficult to handle. (BL 83:1130; KR 54:1796; SLJ Feb 1987 p. 86) Illus. by Judy Glasser, Lippincott, 1987, 160 pp.

STOLZ, Mary. *The Cuckoo Clock*. See Chapter 1, Allegorical Fantasy and Literary Fairy Tales.

C/YA STORR, Catherine (Cole). *The Magic Drawing Pencil* (British title: *Marianne Dreams*, 1958). Gr. 5–7.
Everything that Marianne draws comes to life in her dreams, including a boy named Mark. (LJ 86:378; TLS 1958 p. 355) Illus. by Marjorie-Ann Watts, Barnes, 1960, 191 pp., o.p.

STORR, Catherine. *Thursday*. See Section 5B, Myth Fantasy.

STOVER, Marjorie Filley. *When the Dolls Woke*. See Chapter 9, Toy Fantasy.

SYKES, Pamela. *Mirror of Danger*. See Chapter 8, Time Travel Fantasy.

C TAPP, Kathy Kennedy. *Moth-Kin Magic*. Gr. 3–5.
Six tiny people, or Moth-Kins, who were captured by "giants" and imprisoned in a classroom terrarium, carry out a daring escape. The sequel is *Flight*

of the Moth-Kin (1987). (BL 80:685; CC:538; CCBB 37:98; KR 51:166; SLJ Mar 1984 p. 166)
   Illus. by Michele Chessare, Atheneum, 1983, 122 pp.

C/YA   TARN, Sir William Woodthorpe. *Treasure of the Isle of Mist: A Tale of*
[R]   *the Isle of Skye.* Gr. 4–7. (Orig. British pub. 1919; U.S. 1920.)
   Fiona's search for lost treasure becomes a frantic hunt for a friend held captive in an elfin cave on the Isle of Mist. (BL 17:119, 31:38; HB 10:236, 14:143; LJ 47:814; Mahony 2:298; TLS 1919 p. 740)
   Illus. by Robert Lawson, Putnam, 1934, 192 pp., o.p.

   THEROUX, Paul. *A Christmas Card.* See Chapter 1, Allegorical Fantasy and Literary Fairy Tales.

C   TOLLE, Jean Bashor. *The Great Pete Penney.* Gr. 3–5.
   A leprechaun gives Pete (short for Priscilla) Penney a magic ring, enabling her to throw a curve ball well enough to be called up from Little League to major league baseball. (BL 76:358; CCBB 33:121; KR 47:1002; SLJ Dec 1979 p. 100)
   Atheneum, 1979, 90 pp., o.p.

C/YA   TOWNE, Mary (pseud. of Mary Spelman). *Goldenrod.* Gr. 5–7.
   Goldenrod, the babysitter, can magically transport the Madder children anywhere they choose to go. (CCBB 31:149; KR 45:852; SLJ Nov 1977 p. 64)
   Atheneum, 1977, 180 pp., o.p.

C [R]   TOWNSEND, John Rowe. *The Persuading Stick.* Gr. 4–6. (Orig. British
   pub. 1986.)
   Quiet Sarah, the youngest sister of an angry and depressed older brother, finds a small magical stick that forces people to do whatever she wishes. (BL 84:486; CCBB 41:38; HB 64:205; KR 55:1398; SLJ Sept 1987 p. 184; TLS 1986 p. 1344)
   Lothrop, 1987, 96 pp.

C   TOWNSEND, Ralph M. *A Journey to the Garden Gate.* Gr. 2–4.
   Prudence-Anne is reduced to insect size after she goes through the small end of a telescope. (BL 16:208; Mahony 2:298)
   Illus. by Milo Winter, Houghton, 1919, 127 pp., o.p.

C [R]   TRAVERS, P(amela) L(yndon). *Mary Poppins.* (Orig. British and U.S.
   pub. 1934.)
   Mary Poppins blows in on an East Wind and becomes the Banks children's nanny, bringing hilarious and magical adventures. These adventures continue in *Mary Poppins Comes Back* (1935, 1963), *Mary Poppins Opens the Door* (1943), *Mary Poppins in the Park* (1952; Peter Smith, 1988), *Mary Poppins from A to Z* (1962), and *Mary Poppins in Cherry Tree Lane* (1982). (BL 31:178, 78:709; Bookshelf 1935 p. 3; CC:541; Ch&Bks:253; Mahony 3:212; SLJ Feb 1982 p. 82; TLS 1934 p. 637)
   Illus. by Mary Shepard, Harcourt, 1962, 1981 (rev. ed), 206 pp., o.p., 1985, pap., o.p.; Buccaneer, 1981 (reprint).

   TWOHILL, Maggie. *Jeeter, Mason and the Magic Headset.* See Chapter 9, Toy Fantasy.

C   VAMBA (pseud. of Luigi Bertelli). *The Prince and His Ants.* Gr. 4–6.
   (Orig. pub. in Italy.)
   A little Italian boy learns all about the lives of ants, bees, and wasps after

he is transformed into an ant. (BL 7:81; Bookshelf 1921–1922 p. 9, 1935 p. 3; LJ 61:116; Mahony 2:107)

Tr. by S. F. Woodruff, Holt, 1911, o.p.; tr. by Nicola di Pietro, illus. by the author, Crowell, 1935 (entitled *Emperor of the Ants*), 239 pp., o.p.

C [R] VAN ALLSBURG, Chris. *Ben's Dream*. Gr. 2–4.
Ben and his friend, Margaret, find they have had the same dream: sailing across a flooded world in their half-submerged houses. (BL 78:1371; CCBB 35:217; HB 58:396; KR 50:487; SLJ May 1982 p. 66; Suth 3:429)
Illus. by the author, Houghton, 1982, 31 pp.

C [R] VAN ALLSBURG, Chris. *The Garden of Abdul Gasazi*. Gr. 1–5.
Alan chases Miss Hester's dog, Fritz, into a magician's garden where he finds Fritz changed into a duck. (BL 76:510; CC:623; CCBB 33:121; HB 56:49; SLJ Jan 1980 pp. 40, 62; Suth 3:429; TLS 1981 p. 1067)
Illus. by the author, Houghton, 1979, 31 pp.

C [O] VAN ALLSBURG, Chris. *Jumanji*. Gr. 1–5.
A frightening jungle world is unleashed as Peter and Judy play the magical board game they brought home from the park. Caldecott Medal Winner, 1982. (BL 77:1258; CC:542; CCBB 35:18; HB 57:416; KR 49:737; SLJ May 1981 pp. 24, 60; Suth 3:430)
Illus. by the author, Houghton, 1981, 28 pp.

VAN ALLSBURG, Chris. *The Wreck of the Zephyr*. See Chapter 1, Allegorical Fantasy and Literary Fairy Tales.

VAN STOCKUM, Hilda. *Kersti and Saint Nicholas*. See Chapter 6, Humorous Fantasy.

WALKER, Gwen. *The Golden Stile*. See Section 5C, Travel to Other Worlds.

C [R] WALLACE, Barbara Brooks. *The Barrel in the Basement*. Gr. 3–5.
After their protector, an elderly man named Noah, disappears, three elves living in his house face danger in the form of an inquisitive nine-year-old boy. (BL 81:1260; CCBB 38:177; HB 61:561; KR 53:14; SLJ Sept 1985 p. 140)
Illus. by Sharon Wooding, Atheneum, 1985, 127 pp.

C WALLACE, Barbara Brooks. *The Interesting Thing That Happened at Perfect Acres, Inc.* Gr. 4–6.
Perfecta and Puck set out to discover the secret of the only old, "imperfect" house in the Perfect Acres housing development. (BL 84:1269; CCBB 41:172; KR 56:287; SLJ Apr 1988 p. 105)
Illus. by Blanche Sims, Atheneum, 1988, 144 pp.

C/YA WARD, Patricia A(nn). *The Secret Pencil* (British title: *The Silver Pencil*, 1959). Gr. 5–7.
Spending the summer with her uncle on the coast of Wales, Anna finds a magical silver pencil. (HB 36:217; KR 28:90; LJ 85:2045)
Illus. by Nicole Hornby, Random, 1960, 277 pp., o.p.

C WEBB, Clifford (Cyril). *The North Pole Before Lunch*. Gr. 2–4. (Orig. U.S. pub. 1936.)
Michael and Jennifer make a fast trip to the North Pole. (HB 2:349, 27:261; LJ 61:808)
Illus. by the author, Warne, 1951, 63 pp., o.p.

C WHITE, Stewart Edward. *The Magic Forest: A Modern Fairy Story.* Gr. 4–6. (Orig. pub. Macmillan, 1923.)
   Jimmy Ferris steps off a Canadian Pacific Railroad car into an enchanted forest where he lives with an Ojibway Indian tribe. (BL 20:303, 49:209; Bookshelf 1932 p. 12; HB 1[June 1925]:32, 28:422)
   Lightyear, 1976, 146 pp.

C/YA WHITE, T(erence) H(anbury). *Mistress Masham's Repose.* Gr. 5–7.
[O]   Maria discovers a group of Lilliputians living on her rundown estate and resolves to save them from her greedy governess, who is plotting to sell them to a circus. (BL 43:36; HB 57:565; KR 14:529; LJ 71:2107; Tymn:173)
   Illus. by Fritz Eichenberg, Putnam, 1946, 255 pp., o.p.; Gregg, 1980, 255 pp., o.p.; Berkley, 1984, pap.

WHITEHEAD, Victoria. *The Chimney Witches.* See Chapter 10, Witchcraft and Sorcery Fantasy.

WICKENDEN, Dan. *The Amazing Vacation.* See Secton 5C, Travel to Other Worlds.

C [R] WILLARD, Nancy. *The Mountains of Quilt.* Gr. 1–4.
   After the narrator's grandmother accidentally sews the magic carpet belonging to the Magician of the Mountains of Cleveland into her crazy quilt, the carpet flies her up into the clouds to have lunch with four Magicians. (BL 84:325; CCBB 41:105; HB 63:732; KR 55:1399; SLJ Oct 1987 p. 119)
   Illus. by Tomie dePaola, Harcourt, 1987, 32 pp.

WILLIAMS, Jay. *The Hero from Otherwhere.* See Section 5C, Travel to Other Worlds.

C [R] WILLIAMS, Jay. *The Magic Grandfather.* Gr. 4–6.
   Sam and his cousin, Sarah, experiment with magic to bring back their missing grandfather. (BL 75:1631; CC:546; HB 55:418; SLJ Sept 1979 p. 151)
   Illus. by Gail Owens, Macmillan, 1979, 149 pp.

WILLIAMS, Ursula Moray. *Castle Merlin.* See Chapter 4, Ghost Fantasy.

C [R] WILLIAMS (John), Ursula Moray. *The Moonball.* Gr. 3–5. (Orig. British pub. 1958.)
   The children who find a strange, furry, round creature decide to protect it from scientific investigations. (BL 63:1194; CCBB 21:19; Ch&Bks:273; HB 43:344; KR 35:201; LJ 92:2024; Suth:425)
   Illus. by Jane Paton, Hawthorn, 1967, 138 pp., o.p.

WINDSOR, Patricia. *How a Weirdo and a Ghost Can Change Your Entire Life.* See Chapter 4, Ghost Fantasy.

WINTHROP, Elizabeth. *The Castle in the Attic.* See Section 5C, Travel to Other Worlds.

C/YA WISEMAN, David. *Blodwen and the Guardians.* Gr. 5–7.
   Blodwen, ten, and Tiddy, her six-year-old brother, join forces with the fairy "Guardians" of the ancient Grove, to save their home from a road-construction project. (BL 80:504; HB 60:58; SLJ Jan 1982 p. 82; VOYA 7:102)
   Houghton, 1983, 163 pp.

C/YA WRIGHTSON, (Alice) Patricia (Furlonger). *A Little Fear.* Gr. 6 up.
[R] (Orig. Australian pub. 1983.)
Mrs. Tucker escapes from a nursing home to set up an independent life in a rural cottage, but her peace is disturbed by a mischievous Njimbin, or forest gnome, who wants the cottage for himself. (BL 80:404, 422; CC:548; Ch&Bks:273; CCBB 37:60; HB 60:66; JHC:429; KR 51:210; SLJ Nov 1983 p. 98; Suth 3:462; VOYA 7:36)
Atheneum, 1983, 111 pp.; Penguin/Puffin, 1987, pap.

C/YA WRIGHTSON, (Alice) Patricia (Furlonger). *An Older Kind of Magic* (Australian title: *An Older Form of Magic*). Gr. 4–7.
On the night a comet streaks through the sky, aboriginal spirits appear and Rupert, Selina, and Benny save the Botanical Gardens by using ancient spells. (BL 69:247; CCBB 26:35; Ch&Bks:232; HB 48:472; KR 40:1100; LJ 97:3458; TLS 1972 p. 1325)
Illus. by Noela Young, Harcourt, 1972, 186 pp., o.p.

C [R] WUORIO, Eva-Lis. *Tal and the Magic Barruget.* Gr. 3–5.
Tal conjures up a bottle-imp, or barruget, to help with the housework. (BL 62:414; HB 41:630; KR 33:981; LJ 91:430)
Illus. by Bettina, World, 1965, 76 pp., o.p.

C YOLEN (Stemple), Jane H(yatt). *The Mermaid's Three Wisdoms.* Gr. 4–6.
Jess comes to terms with her deafness with the help of Melusina, an exiled mermaid who is unable to speak. (BL 74:1738; KR 46:638; SLJ Nov 1978 p. 71)
Illus. by Laura Rader, Collins + World, 1978, o.p.; Philomel, 1981, 112 pp.

YOLEN, Jane H. *The Wizard of Washington Square.* See Chapter 10, Witchcraft and Sorcery Fantasy.

C YORK, Carol Beach. *Miss Know-It-All; A Butterfield Square Story.* Gr. 3–4.
Miss Know-It-All's box of magic chocolates and her marvelous memory create quite a stir in the orphanage at number 18 Butterfield Square. The sequels are *The Christmas Dolls* (1967) and *Miss Know-It-All Returns* (1972). (CCBB 20:52; LJ 91:4345)
Illus. by Victoria de Larrea, Watts, 1966, 87 pp., o.p.

C ZOLOTOW, Charlotte S(hapiro). *The Man With Purple Eyes.* Gr. 2–4.
The odd-looking seed Anna is given grows into a beautiful purple plant that helps her invalid father recover from his illness. (CCBB 15:152; HB 37:340; LJ 86:2361)
Illus. by Joe Lasker, Abelard-Shuman, 1961, 60 pp., o.p.

8

Time Travel Fantasy

Tales about people who step into another time can be the most memorable of all types of fantasy. This chapter includes books about travel from our time to the past and future, and stories in which travelers from the past or future visit the twentieth century. A few stories deal with two time periods that somehow touch, permitting glimpses into the past or future without any actual traveling. In fantasy, the means of time travel must be magical, not scientific. Tales of travelers to other worlds, rather than other times, are found in Section 5C, Travel to Other Worlds. Stories about people who meet ghosts from the past have been placed in Chapter 4, Ghost Fantasy, if the ghosts, not the human protagonists, travel through time.

C/YA   ADKINS, Jan. *A Storm without Rain.* Gr. 6–9.
      After sailing to an island off the coast of Cape Cod, fifteen-year-old Jack is caught in a storm and finds himself in the year 1904, where he is befriended by young John Swain, his own grandfather. (BL 79:1089; HB 59:448; KR 51:662; SLJ Oct 1983 p. 155; VOYA 6:212)
      Little, 1983, 179 pp.

      AIKEN, Joan. *The Shadow Guests.* See Chapter 4, Ghost Fantasy.

C/YA   ALLAN, Mabel E(sther). *Romansgrove.* Gr. 5–7.
      Wandering through the ruins of the old manor house called Romansgrove, Clare and Richard find themselves in the year 1902, attempting to save Emily Roman and her family from death by fire. (BL 72:295; CCBB 29:89; HB 52:54; KR 43:776; SLJ Oct 1975 p. 93)
      Illus. by Gail Owens, Atheneum, 1975, 192 pp., o.p.

C/YA   ALLAN, Mabel E(sther). *Time to Go Back.* Gr. 5–8.
      Sarah reads her late Aunt Larke's poetry and finds herself living in the year 1942, where her friend, Larke, has a tragic wartime love affair. (CCBB 26:70; KR 40:1105; LJ 98:257)
      Abelard-Schuman, 1972, 134 pp., o.p.

      ALLEN, Judy. *The Spring on the Mountain.* See Chapter 1, Allegorical Fantasy and Literary Fairy Tales.

C/YA   ANDERSON, Margaret Jean. *In the Circle of Time.* Gr. 5–8.
A strange fog swirling around an ancient Scottish stone circle sweeps Jennifer and Robert into the year 2179, where they attempt to help a peace-loving tribe escape enslavement by the mechanized Barbaric Ones. This is the sequel to *In the Keep of Time* (Random, 1977) and is followed by *The Mists of Time* (Knopf, 1984). (BL 75:1533; CCBB 32:185; KR 47:635; SLJ Apr 1979 p. 52)
Knopf, 1979, 181 pp., o.p.

C/YA   ANDERSON, Margaret Jean. *To Nowhere and Back.* Gr. 5–7.
On a path near her home, Elizabeth travels 100 years into the past and becomes a girl named Ann. (BL 71:961; CCBB 28:157; HB 51:379; KR 43:181; SLJ Mar 1975 p. 91)
Knopf, 1975, 141 pp., o.p.

C/YA   ANDREWS, J(ames) S(ydney). *The Green Hill of Nendrum* (British title: *The Bell of Nendrum,* 1969). Gr. 6–8.
Nial Ross is caught in a storm while sailing and transported 1,000 years back through time to the island monastery of Nendrum. (BL 67:266; HB 46:613; TLS 1969 p. 690)
Hawthorn, 1970, 214 pp., o.p.

ARTHUR, Ruth M. *The Autumn People.* See Chapter 4, Ghost Fantasy.

C/YA   ARTHUR, Ruth M(abel). *On the Wasteland.* Gr. 5–7.
When Betony travels into the past, she is transformed from a friendless orphan into Estrith, a Viking chief's daughter engaged to a Saxon prince. (BL 72:163; HB 51:459; KR 43:710; SLJ Oct 1975 p. 94; TLS 1975 p. 1455)
Illus. by Margery Gill, Atheneum, 1975, 159 pp., o.p.

C/YA   ARTHUR, Ruth M(abel). *Requiem for a Princess.* Gr. 6–9.
[R]   Willow Forrester's upsetting discovery that she is adopted brings on nightmares, in which she becomes a sixteenth-century Spanish girl fated to die by drowning. (BL 63:1098; CC:428; CCBB 21:138; HB 43:211; KR 35:61; LJ 92:1744; TLS 1967 p. 1141)
Illus. by Margery Gill, Atheneum, 1967, 182 pp., o.p.

C/YA   BACON, Martha (Sherman). *The Third Road.* Gr. 5–8.
A twentieth-century girl named Fox becomes stranded in seventeenth-century Spain. (KR 39:943; LJ 96:4182)
Illus. by Robin Jacques, Little, 1971, 188 pp., o.p.

C/YA   BARBER, Antonia (pseud. of Barbara Anthony). *The Ghosts.* Gr. 5–7.
[O]   Lucy and Jamie move to an old country house where they meet two ghostly children, and make a frightening journey into the past to save the ghosts from a fiery death. (BL 66:563; CCBB 23:92; HB 45:532; Kies:6; KR 37:854; LJ 95:777; TLS 1969 p. 689)
Farrar, 1969, 189 pp., o.p.; Archway, 1982, pap.

YA   BELLAMY, Edward. *Looking Backward: 2000–1887.* Gr. 10 up. (Orig. U.S. pub. 1888.)
Wealthy nineteenth-century Bostonian Julian West awakens in the year 2000, in a Massachusetts that has become a cooperative utopia, where he falls in love with his fiancé's great-granddaughter. The sequel is *Equality* (1897, 1924). (BL 25:403, 39:141, 42:59; SHC:579)
Houghton, 1915, 1941, hb, 1966, pap.; Harvard University Press, 1967;

Amereon (repr. of 1888 ed.); Amsco, 1979, pap.; Hendricks, 1979, pap., 272 pp.; NAL/Signet, pap.; Random, 1982, pap.; Penguin, 1982, pap.

C BERESFORD, Elizabeth. *Invisible Magic*. Gr. 4–6. (Orig. British pub. 1975.)
   Princess Elfrida-of-the-Castle decides she likes life in the twentieth century better than in her own time, and welcomes the chance to trade places with Mr. Patrick. (BL 74:1185; CCBB 32:23; TLS 1975 p. 763)
   Illus. by Reg Gray, Hart-Davis/Granada, 1977, 158 pp., o.p.

C BERESFORD, Elizabeth. *Travelling Magic*. Gr. 4–6. (Orig. British pub. 1965.)
   Kate and Marcus meet a magician from Ancient Britian who has come to the twentieth century as part of his studies. (BL 74:1185; TLS 1965 p. 1130)
   Illus. by Judith Valpy, Granada, 1977, 163 pp., o.p.

YA BETHANCOURT, T(homas) Ernesto (pseud. of Tom Paisley). *Tune in Yesterday*. Gr. 8–10.
    A love for jazz propels two friends into the past to 1942, but racial prejudice and Nazi plots make life more complicated than they had anticipated. In *The Tomorrow Connection* (1984), Richie and Matty escape their problems by traveling to 1912 and then 1906, but Matty is forced to endure more racial prejudice while they search for a tomorrow gate to take them home. (BL 74:1420, 80:351; HB 54:400; KR 46:311; SLJ May 1978 p. 73)
    Holiday, 1978, 156 pp., o.p.

C/YA BOND, Nancy (Barbara). *A String in the Harp*. Gr. 6–8.
[R]   Unhappy over his mother's recent death and the family's move to Wales, Peter Morgan is drawn into the sixth-century period of Taliesin by the tuning key of an ancient harp. Newbery Medal Honor Book, 1977. (BL 72:1108, 80:95; CC:436; CCBB 29:171; Ch&Bks:264; HB 52:287; JHC:349; KR 44:255; SLJ Apr 1976 p. 84; Suth 2:52; Tymn:54)
        Atheneum, 1976, 370 pp.; Penguin/Puffin, 1987, pap.

YA BOSSE, Malcolm J(oseph). *Cave beyond Time*. Gr. 7–9.
    Bitten by a rattlesnake while on an Arizona archaeological dig, Ben travels back in time for a series of encounters with two Native American tribes. His experiences in the past help him adjust to the recent loss of his parents. (BL 77:400, 402; CCBB 34:66; HB 57:57; SLJ Nov 1980 p. 83; VOYA 3[Dec 1980]:37)
    Harper, 1980, 187 pp.

BOSTON, L. M. *The Children of Green Knowe*. See Chapter 4, Ghost Fantasy.

C [R] BOSTON, L(ucy) M(aria Wood). *The Stones of Green Knowe*. Gr. 4–6.
       In the year 1120, a boy named Roger discovers two magical stones at the building site of Green Knowe manor house, and is sent into the future to meet Toby, Linnet, Susan, and Tolly, the protagonists in *The Children of Green Knowe* (1954, 1967; see Chapter 4, Ghost Fantasy). (BL 73:141; Ch&Bks:264; HB 52:623; KR 44:845; SLJ Jan 1977 p. 87; Suth 2:53; TLS 1976 p. 881)
       Illus. by Peter Boston, Atheneum, 1976, 118 pp., o.p.

C/YA BRADBURY, Ray (Douglas). *The Halloween Tree*. Gr. 5–8.
[R]   Eight Halloween-costumed boys search through ancient Egypt, druidic Britain, medieval Europe, and some Mexican catacombs for a friend who

vanished from a haunted house. (BL 69:404; JHC:350; KR 40:801; Kies:12; LJ 97:4086)

Illus. by Joseph Mugnaini, Knopf, 1972, 145 pp., o.p.; Bantam, 1982, pap.

C/YA BRANDEL, Marc (pseud. of Marcus Beresford). *The Mine of Lost Days.*
[R] Gr. 4–7.

Deep inside an abandoned Irish copper mine, Henry discovers four people who have lived without aging for over one hundred years, but who would die if they emerged into the modern world. (BL 71:241; KR 42:876; LJ 99:2738)

Illus. by John Verling, Harper, 1974, 185 pp., o.p.

C/YA BUCHAN, John. *Lake of Gold.* Gr. 5–7. (Orig. Canadian pub. 1941; British title: *The Long Traverse,* 1941.)

Bored by his history lessons, a young boy on a camping trip is given the chance to take part in Canadian history. (HB 17:367, 476; LJ 66:737)

Illus. by S. Levenson, Houghton, 1941, 190 pp., o.p.

C BULLETT, Gerald W(illiam). *The Happy Mariners* (Orig. British title: *The Spanish Mariners,* 1928). Gr. 4–6.

The four Robinson children accidentally break a bottle containing a model of an Elizabethan ship, propelling them on an adventure-filled journey involving pirates, buried treasure, and cannibals. (HB 12:355; TLS 1930 p. 805)

Illus. by C. Walter Hodges, Dodge, 1936, 247 pp., o.p.

YA BURFORD, Lolah. *The Vision of Stephen: An Elegy.* Gr. 7 up.

Fleeing a sentence of execution, Prince Stephen escapes from the seventh-century Anglo-Saxon period into Victorian England. (BL 69:26, 292, 299; KR 40:344; LJ 97:2640, 3473)

Illus. by Bill Greer, Macmillan, 1972, 192 pp., o.p.

YA [R] BUTLER, Octavia E. *Kindred.* Gr. 10 up.

Dana, a young black writer living in Los Angeles in 1976, undergoes a series of unexpected and dangerous trips into the year 1819 to rescue Rufus, the young son of a Maryland slaveholder. (KR 47:587; LJ 104:1585; VOYA 2[Feb 1980]:28, 4[Aug 1981]:47)

Doubleday, 1979, 264 pp., o.p.; Pocket Books, 1981, pap.

C/YA CAMERON, Eleanor (Frances Butler). *Beyond Silence.* Gr. 6–10.
[R] Andy is plagued by nightmares and unsettling visits to the past when he and his father visit their ancestral home in Scotland, following his brother's death. (BL 77:205, 207; CC:444; CCBB 34:88; HB 56:646, 62:616; KR 49:78; SLJ Jan 1981 p. 67; VOYA 4[Dec 1981]:28)

Dutton, 1980, 197 pp.; Dell/Laurel Leaf, 1985, pap.

CAMERON, Eleanor. *The Court of the Stone Children.* See Chapter 4, Ghost Fantasy.

C [R] CAMERON, Eleanor (Frances Butler). *Time and Mr. Bass: A Mushroom Planet Book.* Gr. 4–6.

Forces of evil reach through Mycetian history to ensnare Tyco Bass and his friends, Chuck and David, after they visit ancient Wales to translate an old scroll. *The Wonderful Flight to the Mushroom Planet* (1954), *Stowaway to the Mushroom Planet* (1956), *Mr. Bass's Planetoid* (1958), and *A Mystery for Mr. Bass* (1960) are science-fiction stories that precede this book in the Mushroom Planet series. (BL 63:988; HB 43:460; KR 35:56; LJ 92:1314)

Illus. by Fred Meise, Little, 1967, 247 pp.

CARKEET, David. *I Been There Before*. See Chapter 6, Humorous Fantasy.

C [R] CHASE, Mary (Coyle). *The Wicked Pigeon Ladies in the Garden.* Gr. 4–6.

Maureen Swanson, trespassing at the Old Messerman Place, finds a strange bracelet and meets seven evil ghosts who try to trap her in the past. (BL 65:493, 82:682; CCBB 22:90; HB 45:52, 63:491; KR 36:1162; LJ 94:293; Suth:69)

Illus. by Don Bolognese, Knopf, 1968, 115 pp., o.p.; Peter Smith, 1985.

CHURCH, Richard. *The French Lieutenant: A Ghost Story*. See Chapter 4, Ghost Fantasy.

COOPER, Susan. *Over Sea, Under Stone* (see discussion of *The Dark Is Rising* and *Silver on the Tree*). See Section 5B, Myth Fantasy.

CRESSWELL, Helen. *A Game of Catch*. See Chapter 4, Ghost Fantasy.

C/YA   CRESSWELL (Rowe), Helen. *Moondial*. Gr. 5–8.
[R]   Minty Kane feels compelled to travel back through time to rescue the ghosts of two abused children she meets while spending the summer near an old English manor house. (BL 84:317, 873; CCBB 41:86; HB 66:68; KR 55:1238; SLJ Nov 1987 p. 104; TLS 1987 p. 1285; VOYA 10:243)
Macmillan, 1987, 192 pp.

CRESSWELL, Helen. *The Secret World of Polly Flint*. See Chapter 7, Adventure Fantasy.

C [R] CRESSWELL (Rowe), Helen. *Up the Pier*. Gr. 4–6.
Lonely Carrie meets the invisible Pontifex family, who were unwillingly transported from 1921 to 1971 and need Carrie's help to break the spell that holds them in the wrong time. (BL 68:1002; CCBB 26:40; Ch&Bks:265; HB 48:368; KR 40:477; LJ 97:4070; Suth:94; TLS 1971 p. 1516)
Illus. by Gareth Floyd, Macmillan, 1971, 144 pp., o.p.

CURRY, Jane Louise. *The Bassumtyte Treasure*. See Chapter 4, Ghost Fantasy.

C/YA   CURRY, Jane Louise. *The Daybreakers*. Gr. 5–7.
Researching the history of Apple Lock, Callie, Liss, and Harry are drawn back through time to Abáloc, a primitive village whose people need the children's help to defeat their enemies. The sequel is *The Birdstones* (1977). Both stories are related to *Over the Sea's Edge* (1971) (see this chapter). (BL 66:1406; HB 46:296; KR 38:452; LJ 95:3626; TLS 1970 p. 1251)
Illus. by Charles Robinson, Harcourt, 1970, 191 pp., o.p.

C/YA   CURRY, Jane Louise. *Over the Sea's Edge*. Gr. 5–7.
[R]   An ancient medallion causes Dave Reese to exchange places with a twelfth-century Welsh boy named Dewi. He accompanies the exiled Prince Maduac to the legendary island of Antillia where they are drawn into a struggle between the fairy people of Abáloc and a Native-American civilization. *The Daybreakers* (1970, see above) and *The Birdstones* (1977) are related stories. (BL 68:333; HB 47:610; KR 39:1079; LJ 96:3474; TLS 1971 p. 1510)
Illus. by Charles Robinson, Harcourt, 1971, 182 pp., o.p.

C CURRY, Jane Louise. *Parsley, Sage, Rosemary and Time.* Gr. 3–6.
An herb from her aunt's garden sends Rosemary into Pilgrim times, where she helps a woman accused of witchcraft. The sequel is *The Magical Cupboard* (1976). (KR 43:306; SLJ Apr 1975 p. 51)
Illus. by Charles Robinson, Atheneum, 1975, 108 pp., o.p.

CURRY, Jane Louise. *Poor Tom's Ghost.* See Chapter 4, Ghost Fantasy.

CURRY, Jane Louise. *The Sleepers.* See Section 5B, Myth Fantasy.

C/YA CURRY, Jane Louise. *The Watchers.* Gr. 6–8.
[R] Ray Silver joins the family battle against a coal company threatening their land, and when a stone splinter sends him sixteen hundred years into the past, he becomes involved in a tragedy surrounding his ancestors. (BL 72:451; CCBB 29:108; KR 43:988; SLJ Nov 1975 p. 73; Suth 2:112; TLS 1976 p. 392)
Illus. by Trina Schart Hyman, Atheneum, 1975, 235 pp., o.p.

C/YA CUTT, W(illiam) Towrie. *Seven for the Sea.* Gr. 6–8. (Orig. British pub. 1972.)
Two cousins travel 100 years into the past to investigate rumors of Selkie ancestors. This is the sequel to *Message from Arkmae* (pub. in England). (BL 71:507; HB 50:690; LJ 99:3276)
Follett, 1974, 96 pp., o.p.

C/YA DAVIES, Andrew (Wynford). *Conrad's War.* Gr. 5–8. (Orig. British pub.
[O] 1978.)
The tank and the model plane Conrad built allow his "leak" through time to World War II, where he becomes a pilot imprisoned in a German POW camp. Guardian Award winner, 1978. (BL 76:883; CC:459; CCBB 33:130; HB 56:171; JHC:364; KR 48:364; SLJ Apr 1980 p. 107; Suth 3:113)
Crown, 1980, 120 pp., o.p.; Dell, 1986, pap.

C/YA DAWSON, Carley. *Mr. Wicker's Window.* Gr. 5–7.
Chris travels from an antique shop into the Revolutionary War period, where he is sent on a dangerous mission to China. The sequels are *The Sign of the Seven Seas* (1954) and *Dragon's Run* (1955). (BL 49:160; CCBB 6:31; HB 29:53; LJ 78:68)
Illus. by Lynd Ward, Houghton, 1952, 272 pp., o.p.

C/YA DOTY, Jean Slaughter. *Can I Get There by Candlelight?* Gr. 5–7.
Gail's horse, Candlelight, takes her through a long-unused gate to Babylon, a nineteenth-century estate, where she befriends a girl named Hilary. (BL 76:980; HB 56:405; JHC:366; KR 48:364; SLJ Mar 1980 p. 130)
Illus. by Ted Lewin, Macmillan, 1980, 111 pp.

C/YA DUNLOP, Eileen (Rhona). *Elizabeth, Elizabeth* (British title: *Rob-*
[R] *insheugh,* 1975). Gr. 6–9.
On a lonely visit to her aunt at the Melville manor house, Elizabeth escapes through an old looking glass into the eighteenth century, but she soon fears for her life. (BL 73:1349; CCBB 30:174; Ch&Bks:266; HB 53:314; Kies:26; SLJ May 1977 p. 67; Suth 2:131; TLS 1975 p. 733)
Illus. by Peter Farmer, Holt, 1977, 185 pp., o.p.

C/YA DUNLOP, Eileen (Rhona). *The Maze Stone.* Gr. 6–10. (Orig. British pub. 1982.)
After Fanny's suspicions about their new drama teacher are aroused by the unusual pendant he wears, she must take quick action to save her sister from

a terrifying fate. (BL 80:337, 356; CCBB 37:85; KR 51[Sept 1, 1983]:J173; SLJ Dec 1983 p. 84; TLS 1982 p. 1302; VOYA 7:29)
Coward, 1983, 159 pp.

C/YA EAGAR, Frances. *Time Tangle.* Gr. 5–7.
Beth spends a lonely Christmas at boarding school until she meets a boy from the sixteenth century who involves her in a plot to save a hidden cleric. (CCBB 31:45; KR 45:539; SLJ Oct 1977 p. 88)
Nelson, 1977, 172 pp., o.p.

YA EISENBERG, Lawrence B(enjamin). *The Villa of the Ferromonte.* Gr. 10 up.
While visiting his elderly Aunts Elizabeth and Amy in their run-down Manhattan apartment, Norman Dickens realizes that both he and they can travel into the past. (BL 71:22, 34; KR 42:443; LJ 99:1847)
Simon, 1974, 191 pp., o.p.

EVARTS, Hal G. *Jay-Jay and the Peking Monster.* See Chapter 6, Humorous Fantasy.

FARMER, Penelope. *A Castle of Bone.* See Section 5B, Myth Fantasy.

C/YA FARMER (Mockridge), Penelope. *Charlotte Sometimes.* Gr. 5–7.
[O] Charlotte Makepeace discovers that she has a double named Claire who slept in the same boarding school bed in the year 1918, and that she and Claire can exchange places in time. This is the sequel to *The Summer Birds* (1962, see Chapter 7, Magic Adventure Fantasy) and *Emma in Winter* (1966, see below). (BL 66:457; CCBB 23:158; Ch&Bks:240; HB 45:675, 60:223; KR 37:1121; LJ 94:4604; Suth:120; TLS 1969 p. 1190, 1985 p. 348)
Illus. by Chris Conor, Harcourt, 1969, 192 pp., o.p.; Dell/Yearling, 1987, pap.

C/YA FARMER (Mockridge), Penelope. *Emma in Winter.* Gr. 5–7.
[R] Lonely Emma and Bobby find themselves sharing a dream in which they travel so far back through time that they are in danger of not being able to return to the real world. (BL 63:488: Ch&Bks:266; LJ 91:5747; TLS 1966 p. 1071)
Illus. by James J. Spanfeller, Harcourt, 1966, 160 pp., o.p.; Dell/Yearling, 1987, pap.

YA FINNEY, Jack (pseud. of Walter Branden Finney). *About Time: Twelve Stories.* Gr. 10 up. (Orig. pub. separately, 1950–1969.)
Twelve witty and romantic stories about time and time travel, including "Second Change," "Of Missing Persons," and "I'm Scared." (BL 83:34, 52, 83:777; Kliatt 21[Winter 1987]:16; KR 54:1078)
Simon, 1986, pap., 219 pp.

YA [R] FINNEY, Jack (pseud. of Walter Branden Finney). *Time and Again.* Gr. 10 up.
Simon Morley agrees to move into the Dakota apartment building in Manhattan, where he will travel back to the year 1882 as part of a U.S. government project, but he balks at altering historical events after he falls in love with Julia, a nineteenth-century girl. (BL 67:36, 95, 654; HB 46:502; KR 38:272, 473; LJ 95:3304, 3649)
Simon, 1970, 399 pp., o.p., 1978, 1986, pap.

C/YA   FISHER, Leonard Everett. *Noonan: A Novel about Baseball, ESP, and Time Warps.* Gr. 6–9.
    In 1896, young hopeful Johnny Noonan, a baseball pitcher, is hit by a foul ball and sent one hundred years into the future, where his psychokinetic ability to control a baseball leads to stardom. (BL 74:1733; CCBB 32:60; KR 46:749; SLJ May 1978 p. 87)
    Doubleday, 1978, o.p.; Avon, 1981, pap., 125 pp.

C/YA   FREEMAN, Barbara C(onstance). *The Other Face.* Gr. 5–8. (Orig. British pub. 1975.)
    A miniature china cottage transports Betony 150 years into the past where she becomes involved in an ancestor's romance. (BL 73:832; KR 44:1169; SLJ Jan 1977 p. 91; TLS 1975 p. 733)
    Illus. by the author, Dutton, 1976, 151 pp., o.p.

FREEMAN, Barbara C. *A Pocket of Silence.* See Chapter 4, Ghost Fantasy.

GARD, Joyce. *Talargain.* See Section 5B, Myth Fantasy.

YA [R]   GARNER, Alan. *The Red Shift.* Gr. 8 up.
    The lives of three British teenagers from different time periods—the Roman occupation, the Civil War, and contemporary Britain—are linked by an ancient stone ax. (BL 70:801; CCBB 27:142; HB 49:580; Kies:29; KR 41:989; TLS 1973 p. 1112; Tymn:90)
    Macmillan, 1973, o.p.; Ballantine, 1981, pap., 197 pp.

GARNER, Alan. *The Weirdstone of Brisingamen* (see discussion of *The Moon of Gomrath*). See Section 5B, Myth Fantasy.

YA   GERROLD, David. *The Man Who Folded Himself.* Gr. 10 up.
    Danny Eakins's timebelt shows him numerous versions of himself, occupying many different time lines. (BL 69:835; KR 40:1445; LJ 98:436; TLS 1974 p. 163)
    Random, 1973, 148 pp., o.p.; Amereon, 1976 (repr. of 1973 ed.)

YA [R]   GOLDSTEIN, Lisa. *The Dream Years.* Gr. 10 up.
    A young Parisian surrealist painter living during the 1920s is transported in his dreams to the future of 1968, where he falls in love with a student named Solange and becomes involved in the student protests. (BL 81:1637; Kies:30; Kliatt 20[Fall 1986]:24; KR 53:678; LJ Aug 1985 p. 120; SLJ Dec 1985 p. 110)
    Bantam, 1985, 181 pp.; Bantam/Spectra, 1986, pap.

C/YA   GREAVES, Margaret. *Cat's Magic.* Gr. 5–7. (Orig. British pub. 1980.)
    An Egyptian cat goddess rewards Louise for rescuing a drowning kitten by enabling her to travel through time to visit ancient Egypt and Victorian England. (BL 77:1028; CCBB 35:9; KR 49:633; SLJ Apr 1981 p. 127; TLS 1980 p. 360; VOYA 3[June 1981]:38)
    Harper, 1981, 183 pp.

C/YA   GREER, Gerry, and RUDDICK, Bob. *Max and Me and the Time Ma-*
[R]   *chine.* Gr. 4–7.
    Max's doubts about his friend Steve's time machine are dispelled after they find themselves in medieval England: Steve inside the body of a famous knight, and Max inside his horse. The sequel is *Max and Me and the Wild*

West (1988). (BL 79:1465; CCBB 37:28; HB 59:443; KR 51:660; SLJ May 1983 pp. 32, 71; VOYA 6:214)
Harcourt, 1983, 114 pp.

C/YA GROSSER, Morton. *The Snake Horn.* Gr. 5–7.
When Danny blows his antique horn, a seventeenth-century music-master appears and teaches the boy's father music that makes him famous. (BL 70:50; CCBB 26:171; KR 41:114; LJ 98:1387; Suth 2:193)
Illus. by David Stone, Atheneum, 1973, 131 pp., o.p.

HAMILTON, Virginia. *Sweet Whispers, Brother Rush.* See Chapter 4, Ghost Fantasy.

C/YA HAMLEY, Dennis. *Pageants of Despair.* Gr. 6–8.
Giles helps the Pageant Master of a medieval English town fight off the devil's influence on the annual miracle plays. (BL 71:618; KR 42:1065; SLJ Jan 1975 p. 54; TLS 1974 p. 717)
Phillips, 1974, 175 pp.

C/YA HANLON, Emily. *Circle Home.* Gr. 5–7.
A Stone Age girl named Mai finds herself in the twentieth century, trapped inside the body of a nine-year-old girl who is recovering from a near-fatal automobile accident. (BL 78:706; CCBB 35:130; KR 50:208; SLJ May 1982 p. 70; VOYA 5[Apr 1982]:39)
Bradbury, dist. by Dutton, 1981, 237 pp.

HAYNES, Betsy. *The Ghost of the Gravestone Hearth.* See Chapter 4, Ghost Fantasy.

C/YA HOUGHTON, Eric. *Steps Out of Time.* Gr. 5–8.
[R] New in town and lonely, Jonathan is able to step through the dense fog into another time, where he lives in the same house but seems to have a sister who calls him Peter. (BL 77:405; CCBB 34:12; SLJ Sept 1980 p. 72; Suth 2:119; VOYA 3[Feb 1981]:38)
Lothrop, 1980, 128 pp.

C/YA HURMENCE, Belinda. *A Girl Called Boy.* Gr. 6–8.
[R] Blanch Overtha Yoncey learns about the hardships of slavery firsthand when she goes back through time to become one of her ancestors, a slave girl named Overtha, in North Carolina during the 1850s. (BL 78:1445; CCBB 36:12; KR 50:490; HB 58:404; SLJ May 1982 p. 63)
Clarion/Houghton, 1982, 168 pp.

C/YA INGRAM, Tom (Thomas Henry). *The Night Rider.* Gr. 5–8.
A cursed golden bracelet lures Laura to pre-Roman Britain where she becomes a girl called Merta, desperate to find the matching necklace and destroy it before the curse kills her. (BL 71:1128; CCBB 29:47; KR 43:521; SLJ Sept 1975 p. 105)
Bradbury, 1975, 176 pp., o.p.

C/YA JONES, Diana Wynne. *A Charmed Life.* Gr. 5–8. (Orig. British pub.
[R] 1977.)
After Cat and Gwen Chant are adopted by the mysterious Chrestomanci, Gwen uses witchcraft to change places with a twentieth-century girl, leaving Cat to fend for himself. The prequel is *The Lives of Christopher Chant* (1988). *The Magicians of Caprona* (1980) and *Witch Week* (1982) are related works, and there are short stories about Chrestomanci in *Warlock at the*

Wheel (1985) and *Dragons and Dreams* (Ed. by Jane Yolen, Harper, 1986). (BL 74:1009; CCBB 31:113; HB 54:396; KR 46:177; SLJ Apr 1978 p. 94; Suth 2:45; TLS 1977 p. 348)
    Greenwillow/Morrow, 1978, 217 pp.

JONES, Diana Wynne. *A Tale of Time City.* See Section 5C, Travel to Other Worlds.

YA [R] KENNEMORE, Tim. *Changing Times.* Gr. 7–10. (Orig. British pub. 1984.)
    After a junk-shop-purchased 24-hour alarm clock propels Victoria back into her own past, at ages fourteen, eight, and fifteen months, she begins to understand the roots of her parents' miserable marriage. (BL 81:436, 449; CCBB 38:110; HB 61:58; SLJ Sept 1984 p. 129; Suth 3:229; TLS Nov 1984 p. 1383)
    Faber, 1984, 149 pp.

C/YA KEY, Alexander (Hill). *The Sword of Aradel.* Gr. 5–7.
    Brian and Merra escape from medieval England into twentieth-century Manhattan, searching for the magic sword of Aradel. (BL 73:1728; CCBB 31:35; SLJ Sept 1977 p. 146)
    Westminster, 1977, 144 pp. o.p.

C/YA KIPLING, (Joseph) Rudyard. *Puck of Pook's Hill.* Gr. 5–8.
[R]   Puck, the last of the English fairies, takes Don and Una into the past to meet well-known figures from England's history. The sequel is *Rewards and Fairies* (1910). (BL 2:216; HB 61:84; LJ 32:260; TLS 1906 p. 536)
    Illus. by Arthur Rackham, Doubleday, 1906, 275 pp., o.p.; Penguin/Puffin, 1987, pap.

C/YA KITTLEMAN, Laurence R. *Canyons beyond the Sky.* Gr. 6–8.
    While visiting his archaeologist father on a dig, Evan Ferguson falls off a cliff and awakens 5000 years in the past, where he is befriended by a Native-American boy and his people. (BL 82:810; CCBB 39:111; SLJ Nov 1985 p. 86)
    Atheneum, 1985, 212 pp.

YA LAMPLUGH, Lois. *Falcon's Tor.* Gr. 7–10.
    Aiden Westleigh awakens after a riding accident to find that it is 1915 and he has become Arthur Morchand, son of a wealthy British family experiencing the difficulties of wartime life. (BL 81:130; CCBB 38:9; SLJ Dec 1984 p. 91; TLS 1984 p. 335)
    Andre Deutsch, 1984, 121 pp., o.p.

LAMPMAN, Evelyn. *Captain Apple's Ghost.* See Chapter 4, Ghost Fantasy.

LANGTON, Jane. *The Diamond in the Window* (see discussion of *The Astonishing Stereoscope*). See Chapter 7, Magic Adventure Fantasy.

YA [R] LASKI, Marghanita. *The Victorian Chaise Lounge.* Gr. 10 up. (Orig. pub. Houghton, 1953, 1954.)
    Twentieth-century Melanie Langdon falls asleep on her antique Victorian chaise longue and awakens in 1864, inside the body of Milly Baines, the consumptive young mother of an illegitimate child. (BL 50:420; Kies:45; Kliatt 18[Fall 1984]:14; KR 22:249; TLS 1953 p. 705)
    Academy Chicago, 1984, pap., 119 pp.

YA LASKY (Knight), Kathryn. *Home Free.* Gr. 7–10.
An endangered eagle takes Sam, fifteen, and an autistic girl back in time to meet Gus (the old man who first inspired them to help the eagles) as a young man. (BL 82:751, 758; CCBB 39:112; KR 53:1198; SLJ Mar 1986 p. 176; VOYA 9:145)
Macmillan/Four Winds, 1985, 245 pp.

LAWRENCE, Louise. *Sing and Scatter Daisies.* See Chapter 4, Ghost Fantasy.

C/YA LAWSON, John S(hults). *The Spring Rider.* Gr. 5–8.
[R]   Jacob and his sister, Gray, meet the ghost of a Union soldier whose bugle call brings a Civil War battle to life once again. (BL 65:254; HB 44:564; KR 36:699; Suth:240)
Crowell, 1968, 147 pp., o.p.

C/YA LEE, Robert C. *Timequake.* Gr. 6–8.
Caught in a "timequake" while on a canoe trip, Randy and his cousin Morgan are thrown forward in time to the year 2027. They discover a United States run by state police, where rationed food, computer designated death, and cannibals are all part of daily life. (BL 79:907; CCBB 36:128; SLJ Feb 1983 p. 79; VOYA 6:148)
Westminster, 1982, 151 pp.

C/YA L'ENGLE, Madeleine. *Many Waters.* Gr. 6–10.
Twins Sandy and Dennys Murry are stranded in Biblical times, where they become involved in a struggle surrounding Noah and his ark. This is the sequel to *A Wrinkle in Time* (1962), *A Wind in the Door* (1973), and *A Swiftly Tilting Planet* (1978), three "science-fantasies" that tend more toward science-fiction than fantasy. *A Wrinkle in Time* was the Newbery Medal winner, 1962. (BL 82:1633, 1636, 84:1248; CCBB 40:54; KR 54:1374; JHC 1987 Suppl. p. 72; SLJ Nov 1986 p. 104; VOYA 9:238)
Farrar, 1986, 310 pp., 1987, pap.

YA [R] LEVIN, Betty (Lowenthal). *The Keeping Room.* Gr. 7 up.
Hal is drawn into the past when he reads the journal of a girl named Hannah who disappeared during the nineteenth century. (BL 77:620; CCBB 34:155; HB 57:190; KR 49:507; SLJ May 1981 p. 86)
Greenwillow, 1981, 247 pp., o.p.

C/YA LEVIN, Betty (Lowenthal). *The Sword of Culann.* Gr. 6–9.
Claudia and Evan are transported from coastal Maine to Iron Age Ireland where they become involved in terrifying mythic battles. The sequels are *A Griffon's Nest* (1975) and *The Forespoken* (1976). (KR 41:1212; LJ 98:3156)
Macmillan, 1973, 288 pp., o.p.

C LEVY, Elizabeth. *Running Out of Magic with Houdini.* Gr. 4–6.
Three young joggers are swept back in time by a mysterious fog to 1912, where they help save Harry Houdini's life. This is the sequel to *Running Out of Time* (1980), in which the fog takes them back to Ancient Rome. (BL 78:390; SLJ Dec 1981 p. 86)
Illus. by Blanche Sims and Jenny Rutherford, Knopf, dist. by Random, 1981, hb and pap., 121 pp.

C/YA LEWIS, Hilda (Winifred). *The Ship That Flew.* Gr. 5–7. (Orig. British pub. 1939.)
A dwarf-made toy Viking ship takes four modern children to Ancient

Egypt, Norman Britain, and Sherwood Forest. (BL 54:509; CCBB 11:121; HB 34:109; KR 26:77; LJ 83:1286)

Illus. by Nora Lavrin, Phillips, 1958, 246 pp.

C [R] LINDBERGH, Anne (Morrow). *The Hunky-Dory Dairy.* Gr. 4–6.

Zannah's old-fashioned horse and buggy dairy wagon enables her to enter a small town "removed" by witchcraft from the nineteenth to the twentieth century, where she befriends a girl named Utopia Graybeal. (BL 82:1143; CCBB 40:12; KR 54:865; SLJ Aug 1986 p. 95)

Illus. by Julie Brinkloe, Harcourt, 1986, 147 pp.; Avon/Camelot, 1987, pap.

LINDBERGH, Anne. *The People in Pineapple Place.* See Chapter 4, Ghost Fantasy.

C/YA LINDBERGH, Anne (Morrow). *The Shadow on the Dial.* Gr. 5–7.

Marcus and Dawn find a coupon that promises to deliver their heart's desire. They use it to travel back and forth in time trying to fulfill their uncle's dream of becoming a flautist. (BL 83:1680; CCBB 40:191; HB 63:463; KR 55:927; SLJ June–July 1987 p. 97; VOYA 10:90)

Harper, 1987, 160 pp.

C LITTLE, Jane. *The Philosopher's Stone.* Gr. 4–6.

A sorcerer named Nyvrem needs a rock from Stephen's collection to convert copper into gold, but he accidentally transports Stephen from Indiana to the twelfth-century Castle Mordemagne. (BL 68:367; KR 39:1121; LJ 96:2918)

Illus. by Robin Hall, Atheneum, 1971, 123 pp., o.p.

LIVELY, Penelope. *The Driftway.* See Chapter 4, Ghost Fantasy.

LIVELY, Penelope. *The Ghost of Thomas Kempe.* See Chapter 4, Ghost Fantasy.

C/YA LIVELY, Penelope (Margaret Low). *The House in Norham Gardens.* Gr.
[R]   6–9.

A New Guinean ceremonial shield brought home by Clare Mayfield's great-grandfather has the power to transport Clare from present-day England to the primitive jungles of New Guinea. (BL 71:767; CCBB 28:96; Ch&Bks:242; HB 51:55; Kies:48; KR 42:1161; LJ 99:3273; Suth 2:289; TLS 1974 p. 717)

Dutton, 1974, 154 pp.

LIVELY, Penelope. *A Stitch in Time.* See Chapter 4, Ghost Fantasy.

LIVELY, Penelope. *The Whispering Knights.* See Chpater 5B, Myth Fantasy.

C LORING, Selden M(elville). *Mighty Magic: An Almost-True Story of Pi-rates and Indians.* Gr. 3–5. (Orig. pub. 1937.)

Granny Matten gives Jack Hollis a magic Indian drum. (HB 13:151; KR 32:738; LJ 62:564).

Illus. by Brinton Turkle, Holiday, 1964, 126 pp., o.p.

Lost Worlds, Unknown Horizons. Ed. by Robert Silverberg. See Section 5C, Travel to Other Worlds.

C/YA LUNN, Janet. *The Root Cellar.* Gr. 5–7. (Orig. Canadian pub. 1981.)
[R]   Orphaned Rose escapes from her adoptive relatives by hiding in an old root cellar. There, she travels back in time to 1860 and helps a young woman

search for her missing lover, a soldier in the American Civil War. Winner, Canadian Library Association Best Book of the Year for Children, 1982. (BL 79:1402; CC:503; HB 59:575; KR 51:661; SLJ Sept 1983 p. 124)
Scribner, 1983, 229 pp.; Penguin/Puffin, 1984, pap.

LUNN, Janet. *Twin Spell.* See Chapter 4, Ghost Fantasy.

YA [R] MacAVOY, R(oberta) A(nn). *The Book of Kells.* Gr. 10 up.
A professor of Irish history and an unemployed Canadian artist are pulled back through time by the spirals of a Celtic cross to tenth-century Ireland, where the survivors of a Viking raid are yearning for vengeance. (BL 82:195; Kies:49; LJ Aug 1985 p. 120; VOYA 8:364, 394)
Bantam, 1985, pap., 352 pp.

C/YA MacDONALD, Reby Edmond. *The Ghosts of Austwick Manor.* Gr. 5–7.
[R]   Hilary and Heather MacDonald travel into the past through an exact model of their old family homestead in England and uncover a family curse that threatens their brother's life. (BL 78:961; CC:504; HB 58:406; SLJ May 1982 p. 85; VOYA 5[Aug 1982]:34)
Atheneum, 1982, 144 pp., o.p.

C/YA MACE, Elisabeth. *The Ghost Diviners.* Gr. 5–7. (Orig. British pub. 1977.)
Martin's sister, Jackie, travels back in time to the turn of the century, where she witnesses a murder on the future site of their house. (BL 74:299; KR 46:3; SLJ Sept 1977 p. 132; TLS 1977 p. 864)
Nelson, 1977, 160 pp., o.p.

C/YA MACE, Elisabeth. *The Rushton Inheritance.* Gr. 5–7. (Orig. British pub. 1978.)
Two generations of Rushtons search for treasure after Steve visits the nineteenth century. (BL 75:1093; CCBB 32:179; HB 55:195; KR 42:126; SLJ Dec 1978 p. 54; TLS 1978 p. 1083)
Nelson, 1978, 173 pp., o.p.

McGRAW, Eloise Jarvis. *A Really Weird Summer.* See Chapter 4, Ghost Fantasy.

MacKELLAR, William. *Alfie and Me and the Ghost of Peter Stuyvesant.* See Chapter 4, Ghost Fantasy.

MacKELLAR, William. *The Ghost in the Castle.* See Chapter 4, Ghost Fantasy.

McKILLIP, Patricia A. *The House on Parchment Street.* See Chapter 4, Ghost Fantasy.

YA MacLEOD, Charlotte (Matilda Hughes). *The Curse of the Giant Hogweed.* Gr. 10 up.
Three Massachusetts horticultural professors suddenly find themselves in medieval Wales battling a plant that is taking over the countryside. (BL 81:823, 838; Kies:51; KR 52:1170)
Doubleday, 1985, hb, o.p., 1986, pap.; Avon, 1986, pap., 176 pp.

C/YA MAGUIRE, Gregory. *Lightning Time.* Gr. 6–8.
Daniel is distressed to learn of construction plans for the mountain where his grandmother lives and where magic occurs whenever lightning strikes.

The sequel is *Lights on the Lake* (1981). (BL 74:1680; HB 55:517; KR 46:750; SLJ Sept 1978 p. 143)
Farrar, 1978, 256 pp.

YA   MARZOLLO, Jean. *Halfway Down Paddy Lane.* Gr. 7–10.
Kate awakens to discover that she has gone back in time to 1850 and become Kate O'Hara, daughter of Irish immigrants who work exhausting twelve-hour days in the New England cotton mills. (BL 77:1198; Kies:53; KR 49:1165; SLJ 27[May 1981]:76; VOYA 4[Dec 1981]:33)
Dial, 1981, 178 pp.; Scholastic, 1984, pap.

YA [R]   MATHESON, Richard (Burton). *Bid Time Return.* Gr. 10 up.
Knowing that he is about to die, Richard Collier manages to pull himself back through time from 1971 to 1896 to search for a beautiful girl he once saw in an old photograph. Winner of the Second World Fantasy Award, Best Novel, 1975. (BL 71:1008; KR 42:1320; LJ 100:410; SLJ May 1975 p. 36, Dec 1975 p. 32)
Viking, 1975, o.p.; Buccaneer, 1986, 280 pp.

MAYNE, William. *Earthfasts.* See Section 5B, Myth Fantasy.

C/YA   MAYNE, William (James Carter). *A Game of Dark.* Gr. 6–9.
[R]   Feeling increasingly helpless and guilty over his father's critical illness, Donald finds himself traveling into the past to a land menaced by a huge man-eating worm, or dragon, that only he can destroy. (BL 68:629; CCBB 25:61; Ch&Bks:270; HB 48:58; KR 39:1022; LJ 97:2490; Suth:274; TLS 1971 p. 1319)
Dutton, 1971, 143 pp., o.p.

C/YA   MAYNE, William (James Carter). *The Hill Road* (British title: *Over the Hills and Far Away*). Gr. 5–7.
Sara, Dolly, and Andrew ride their ponies back through time to post-Roman Britain, where Sara is mistaken for an accused witch. (CCBB 22:161; HB 45:171; KR 37:55; LJ 94:1783)
Dutton, 1968, 144 pp., o.p.

C/YA   MAZER, Norma Fox. *Saturday, the Twelfth of October.* Gr. 6–9.
[R]   Furious at her family, Zan Ford wishes so intensely to be elsewhere that she crosses the "river of time" into the Stone Age and is adopted by a tribe of cave dwellers. (BL 72:44; CCBB 29:67; KR 43:1195; SLJ Nov 1975 p. 93; Suth 2:312)
Delacorte, 1975, 247 pp., o.p.; Dell, 1976, pap.

C/YA   MELLING, O. R. *The Singing Stone.* Gr. 6–9. (Orig. Canadian pub. 1986.)
Eighteen-year-old Kay Warrick, abandoned at birth, visits Ireland in hopes of discovering her true identity. There, she is swept back through time to ancient Ireland where she meets an amnesiac young woman named Ahorne and learns that their destinies are intertwined. (BL 84:135, 150, 576; CCBB 41:71; SLJ Sept 1987 p. 198)
Viking, 1987, 206 pp.

C/YA   MILLER (Mandelkorn), Eugenia. *The Sign of the Salamander.* Gr. 5–7. (Orig. British pub. 1982.)
After he plunges through a French castle floor, twentieth-century Henry

Carter suddenly finds himself inside the body of a sixteenth-century would-be apprentice to Leonardo Da Vinci. (HB 43:464; KR 35:600; LJ 92:2022)
Holt, 1967, 233 pp., o.p.

C MOORE, Katherine (Davis). *The Little Stolen Sweep.* Gr. 4–6.
Staying with relatives in his father's boyhood village, Daniel makes a series of journeys into the past. There he befriends a child chimney sweep named Jim, and offers to change places in order to help the boy escape his cruel master. (CCBB 36:131; SLJ Mar 1983 p. 181; TLS 1982 p. 345)
Illus. by Pat Marriott, Allison, dist. by Schocken, 1982, 121 pp., o.p.

C/YA MOSKIN, Marietta D(unston). *Dream Lake.* Gr. 5–8.
Spending an unhappy summer with her great aunt, Hilary is drawn to a lake she has seen in nightmares, where she is transformed into Margaret Mooney, an eighteenth-century serving girl. (BL 77:1024, 1032, 81:1408; CCBB 35:51; KR 49:635; SLJ Mar 1981 p. 149)
Atheneum, 1981, 156 pp., o.p.

NATHAN, Robert. *The Elixer.* See Section 5B, Myth Fantasy.

C/YA NAYLOR, Phyllis Reynolds. *Shadows on the Wall* (The York trilogy,
[R] book one). Gr. 6–10.
Visiting England with his parents, Dan Roberts makes two disturbing discoveries: that he may have a hereditary illness, Huntington's disease, and that he can see ghostly soldiers from Roman times. In *Faces in the Water* (1981), Dan and his family have returned home to Pennsylvania, where he continues to worry about his father's illness, and is unexpectedly sent back through time to fourteenth-century Britain. In *Footprints at the Window* (1981), Dan returns to fourteenth-century Britain, where he tries to help the gypsy girl Orlenda elude the Black Death. (BL 77:118; CCBB 34:115; HB 56:649; KR 48:1465; SLJ Jan 1981 p. 71; VOYA 4[Apr 1981]:35)
Atheneum, 1980, 165 pp., o.p.

C/YA NESBIT (Bland), E(dith). *The House of Arden.* Gr. 5–7. (Orig. British pub. 1908.)
In the ruins of Arden Castle lives a magical creature called Mouldiwarp with the power to send Edred and Elfrida into the past in search of lost Arden treasure. The sequel is *Harding's Luck* (1910, 1960). (BL 57:32; HB 36:309; LJ 85:3224)
Illus. by H. R. Millar, Coward, 1960, o.p.; illus. by Clarke Hutton, Dutton, 1968, 244 pp., o.p.; Penguin/Puffin, 1986, pap.

C/YA NESBIT (Bland), E(dith). *The Story of the Amulet.* Gr. 5–7. (Orig. British pub. 1906, U.S. 1907.)
In this, the first time-travel fantasy written with children as protagonists, Cyril, Robert, Anthea, and Jane make journeys to ancient Egypt, Babylon, and Rome with the help of their old friend, the Sand Fairy. This is the sequel to *Five Children and It* (1902, see Chapter 7, Magic Adventure Fantasy) and *The Phoenix and the Carpet* (1904). (BL 3:206, 27:215, 46:146; CCBB 3:21)
Illus. by J. S. Goodall, Coward, 1949, o.p.; illus. by J. S. Goodall, Looking Glass Lib, dist. by Random, 1960, o.p.; illus. by H. R. Millar, Penguin/Puffin, 1965, pap., 281 pp., o.p.; Dell/Yearling, 1987, pap.

YA   NICHOLS, (Joanna) Ruth. *Song of the Pearl.* Gr. 7–10. (Orig. Canadian
         pub. 1976.)
         Margaret Redmond, a withdrawn and troubled young woman, dies in 1900
     at the age of seventeen, only to regain consciousness and health on a silent
     island where she learns about her three previous lives: as the wife of an
     Elizabethan explorer, as an Indian slave girl, and as a young Sumerian
     prince. (CCBB 30:110; HB 53:59; KR 44:740; SLJ Oct 1976 p. 120; VOYA
     2[Oct 1979]:63)
         Macmillan, 1976, 158 pp., o.p.

     NICHOLS, Ruth. *A Walk out of the World.* See Section 5C, Travel to
     Other Worlds.

C/YA   NORTON, Andre (pseud. of Alice Mary Norton). *Dragon Magic.* Gr.
         5–7.
         Each of four boys who complete a dragon puzzle are sent into a different
     era of the past. (BL 68:1004; CCBB 25:160; HB 48:373; KR 40:485; LJ
     97:2244)
         Illus. by Robin Jacques, Crowell, 1972, 213 pp., o.p.

C/YA   NORTON, Andre (pseud. of Alice Mary Norton). *Lavender Green Magic.*
[R]   Gr. 5–7.
         A maze at their grandparents' home causes Holly Wade and her brother
     and sister to travel into the past and meet two witches, one good and one evil.
     (BL 71:101; Ch&Bks:270; HB 50:137; LJ 99:2275)
         Illus. by Judith Brown, Crowell, 1974, o.p; Ace, 1982, pap., 256 pp.

C/YA   NORTON, Andre (pseud. of Alice Mary Norton). *Octagon Magic.* Gr.
         5–7.
         Lorrie enters a doll-sized replica of Octagon House and goes back in time
     to the Civil War period where she takes part in the Underground Railroad
     rescue of escaped slaves. (KR 35:610; LJ 92:2656; TLS 1968 p. 584)
         Illus. by Mac Conner, World, 1967, 189 pp., o.p.

C/YA   NORTON, Andre (pseud. of Alice Mary Norton). *Red Hart Magic.* Gr.
         5–7.
         Mutual dreams of an old English inn draw Charles and Nan, step- brother
     and sister, together, as they travel through history and learn to deal with
     problems in their own lives. (BL 73:610; CCBB 30:110; HB 53:160; KR
     44:974; SLJ Nov 1976 p. 61)
         Illus. by Donna Diamond, Crowell, 1976, 179 pp.

     NORTON, Mary. *Bedknob and Broomstick.* See Chapter 7, Magic
     Adventure Fantasy.

C [R]   ORMONDROYD, Edward. *Time at the Top.* Gr. 4–6.
         Susan Shaw takes the elevator to the top floor of her apartment building and
     steps out into the world of 1881, where she helps two children search for lost
     treasure. The sequel, *All in Good Time* (1975), describes what happens after
     Susan's father follows her into the past. (BL 60:262; CC:514; Ch&Bks:270;
     Eakin:251; HB 39:603; LJ 88:4478; TLS 1976 p. 392)
         Illus. by Peggie Bach, Parnassus, 1963, 176 pp., o.p.; Bantam, 1986, pap.

YA   *The Other Side of the Clock: Stories Out of Time, Out of Place.* Ed. by
         Philip Van Doren Stern. Gr. 10 up.
         Twelve stories speculating on the nature of time, whose authors include

H. G. Wells and Jack Finney. (BL 66:1139, 1157; CCBB 23:152; KR 37:1089; LJ 95:1661)
Van Nostrand Reinhold, 1969, 192 pp., o.p.

C/YA PARDOE, M. *Curtain of Mist* (British title: *Argyle's Mist,* 1956). Gr. 6–8.
Three twentieth-century children step through a "curtain of mist" into Celtic Britain. The British sequels are *Argyle's Causeway* and *Argyle's Oracle.* (CCBB 11:73; HB 34:38; KR 25:485; LJ 83:652)
Illus. by Leslie Atkinson, Funk, 1957, 246 pp., o.p.

C/YA PARK, (Rosina) Ruth (Lucia). *Playing Beatie Bow.* Gr. 5–8. (Orig. Aus-
[O]   tralian pub. 1980.)
Angry at her parents' upcoming remarriage and move to Norway, Abigail follows a waiflike girl named Beatie Bow one hundred years into the past. Best Australian Children's Book, 1981; Boston Globe Horn Book Award, 1982. (BL 78:1307, 1315, 79:685, 980; CC:515; CCBB 35:156; Ch&Bks:270; HB 58:487, 59:331; JHC:404; SLJ May 1982 p. 64; Suth 3:336; TLS 1981 p. 1354; VOYA 5[Aug 1982]:35)
Atheneum, 1982, 196 pp.; Penguin/Puffin, 1984, pap.

C/YA PARKER, Richard. *The Old Powder Line.* Gr. 5–8.
[R]   Brian Kane embarks on a dangerous journey when he boards an antiquated steam train to rescue his friend, Mr. Mincing, trapped somewhere in the past. (BL 68:676; CCBB 25:78; KR 39:677; Suth:306; TLS 1971 p. 744)
Nelson, 1971, 143 pp., o.p.

C/YA PARKER, Richard. *A Time to Choose: A Story of Suspense.* Gr. 6–9.
[R]   (Orig. British pub. 1973.)
Stephen and Mary are given the choice of staying in a peaceful, unpolluted future world or returning to their unhappy twentieth-century lives. (CCBB 27:183; HB 50:385; KR 42:309; LJ 99:1488; TLS 1973 p. 1434)
Harper, 1974, 151 pp., o.p.

YA [R] PASCAL, Francine. *Hangin' Out with Cici.* Gr. 7–9.
After Victoria's disruptive behavior gets her expelled from school, a bump on the head transports her to 1944 where she makes friends with a strangely familiar girl. (BL 73:1355; HB 53:541; JHC 404; Kies:59; KR 45:99; SLJ Sept 1977 p. 134)
Viking, 1977, 152 pp.; Dell, 1986, pap.

C/YA PATON WALSH, Jill (Gillian Bliss). *A Chance Child.* Gr. 6–9.
[R]   Abused by his twentieth-century mother, Creep enters an even crueler time, that of the nineteenth century before child labor laws, where he and two runaways must work to survive. (BL 75:1215, 1222; CC:516; CCBB 32:147; HB 55:64; Kies:78; KR 46:1359; SLJ Jan 1979 p. 63)
Farrar, 1978, 186 pp., o.p.; Avon, 1980, pap., 186 pp.

C/YA PEARCE, (Ann) Philippa. *Tom's Midnight Garden.* Gr. 5–8. (Orig. Brit-
[O]   ish pub. 1958; U.S. Lippincott, 1959.)
When the grandfather clock strikes thirteen, Tom Long is able to enter an old-fashioned garden to meet Hatty, a mysterious girl who seems to have grown older each time he visits her. Carnegie Medal, 1958. (BL 56:126; CC:517; CCBB 13:18; Ch&Bks:239; Eakin:254; HB 35:478; KR 27:492; LJ 84:3930; TLS Nov 21, 1958 p. x)
Illus. by Susan Einzig, Harper, 1984, 229 pp.; Dell, 1986, pap.

C/YA   PEASE, (Clarence) Howard. *The Gypsy Caravan; Being the Merry Tale of the Travels of Betty and Joe With the Gypsies—Their Amazing Adventures with Robin Hood—with Richard-the-Lion-Hearted—with Roland—and Sundry Other Great and Famous Persons.* Gr. 5–7.
Two children join a gypsy caravan and embark on a series of adventures with heroes from their history books. (HB 6:331; LJ 56:179; Mahony 3:209)
Illus. by Harrie Wood, Doubleday, 1930, 1946, 254 pp., o.p.

PECK, Richard. *The Ghost Belonged to Me* (see discussion of *Ghosts I Have Been*). See Chapter 4, Ghost Fantasy.

PEYTON, K. M. *A Pattern of Roses.* See Chapter 4, Ghost Fantasy.

C/YA   PHIPSON, Joan (pseud. of Margaret Fitzhardinge). *The Way Home.* Gr. 5–7.
Prue, Peter, and Richard are thrown over a cliff during a car accident and swept downstream into a world of enormous monsters and volcanic eruptions. (HB 50:52; KR 41:760; LJ 98:2656; TLS 1973 p. 1114)
Atheneum, 1973, 184 pp., o.p.

C   PINKWATER, D(aniel) Manus. *Wingman.* Gr. 4–6.
Wingman flies truant Daniel Chen off of the George Washington Bridge and into ancient China. (KR 43:375; SLJ Sept 1975 p. 109)
Illus. by the author, Dodd, 1975, 63 pp., o.p.

C/YA   POPE, Elizabeth. *The Sherwood Ring.* Gr. 6 up.
The American Revolutionary period comes alive for Peggy when she meets the ghost of her ancestor, Barbara Grahame, and sympathizes with Barbara's forbidden love affair with a British soldier. (BL 54:567; CCBB 11:22; Eakin:265; HB 34:112, 613, 35:399; KR 26:38; LJ 83:2073)
Illus. by Evaline Ness, Houghton, 1958, 266 pp., o.p.; Berkley/Ace, 1985, pap.

PURTILL, Richard. *Enchantment at Delphi.* See Section 5B, Myth Fantasy.

C/YA   RABINOWITZ, Ann. *Knight on Horseback.* Gr. 6–8.
While on a tour of England, Eddy Newby meets the ghost of Richard III, who mistakes the thirteen-year-old American boy for his son, Edward. (BL 84:572; CCBB 41:73; SLJ Oct 1987 p. 142; VOYA 10:245)
Macmillan, 1987, 187 pp.

REID BANKS, Lynne. *The Indian in the Cupboard.* See Chapter 7, Magic Adventure Fantasy.

ROBINSON, Joan G. *When Marnie Was There.* See Chapter 4, Ghost Fantasy.

C/YA   RODOWSKY, Colby. *Keeping Time.* Gr. 6–9.
Drew Wakeman is drawn back into the past to Elizabethan London, where he is befriended by an apprentice minstrel, Symon Ives, who helps the youth learn to communicate with his taciturn father. (BL 80:419; CCBB 37:116; HB 60:203; SLJ Jan 1984 p. 85)
Farrar, 1983, 137 pp.

SABERHAGEN, Fred. *Pyramids.* See Section 5C, Travel to Other Worlds.

C ST. GEORGE, Judith. *The Mysterious Girl in the Garden.* Gr. 3–5.
Led back through time into 1805 by a small white dog, Terrie meets Princess Charlotte Augusta. Both girls miss their mothers' companionship and a friendship develops, culminating in a plan to exchange places in time. (BL 78:599; 81:1408; KR 50:7; SLJ Dec 1981 p. 68)
Illus. by Margot Tomes, Putnam, 1981, 64 pp., o.p.

C [R] SAUER, Julia L(ina). *Fog Magic.* Gr. 4–6.
While in search of a friend her own age, Greta Addington wanders through the Nova Scotia fog and enters Blue Cove, a village from one hundred years in the past. Newbery Medal Honor Book, 1944. (BL 40:83; HB 19:405, 422, 56:548–551; LJ 68:822, 963; TLS 1977 p. 1409)
Viking, 1943, o.p.; Penguin/Puffin, 1986, pap., 128 pp.; Peter Smith, 1988.

SELDEN, George. *The Genie of Sutton Place.* See Chapter 7, Magic Adventure Fantasy.

C/YA SERVICE, Pamela F. *The Reluctant God.* Gr. 6–9.
Ameni escapes from his princely responsibilities in ancient Egypt by traveling to twentieth-century London, where he is befriended by Lorna, an archaeologist's daughter. (BL 84:1131, 1186; CCBB 41:167; SLJ June/July 1988 p. 106; VOYA 11:97)
Atheneum, 1988, 206 pp.

C/YA SEVERN, David (pseud. of David Unwin). *Dream Gold.* Gr. 6–8. (Orig. British pub. 1949.)
Peter and Guy have frightening experiences involving pirates and their "dream gold," while vacationing in Cornwall. (HB 29:53; KR 20:412; LJ 77:2079)
Illus. by Isami Kashiwagi, Viking, 1952, 192 pp., o.p.

SEVERN, David. *The Girl in the Grove.* See Chapter 4, Ghost Fantasy.

SHECTER, Ben. *The Whistling Whirligig.* See Chapter 4, Ghost Fantasy.

C/YA SHERBURNE, Zoa (Morin). *Why Have the Birds Stopped Singing?* Gr. 5–7.
An epileptic seizure at an ancestor's birthplace sends Katie into the nineteenth century where she becomes Kathryn, a girl imprisoned by her uncle. (BL 70:1202; LJ 99:1488)
Morrow, 1974, 189 pp., o.p.

YA SIEGEL, Robert (Harold). *Alpha Centauri.* Gr. 7–9.
Rebecca finds herself in pre-Druid Britain, where she must complete a dangerous quest to save the half-horse, half-human centaurs who have befriended her. (BL 77:40, 48; LJ 105:1665)
Illus by Kurt Mitchell, Good News, 1980, o.p., 1981, pap., 256 pp.

YA SIMAK, Clifford D(onald). *The Goblin Reservation.* Gr. 10 up.
Time travel permits goblins, trolls, Shakespeare, a Neanderthal man, and a ghost to live together on The Reservation. (BL 65:484, 492; KR 36:722; LJ 94:1164, 2074; SLJ Dec 15, 1968 p. 4740)
Putnam, 1968, 192 pp., o.p.

C/YA SLEIGH, Barbara (de Riemer). *Jessamy.* Gr. 5–7.
[R] Jessamy travels to the period of World War I to solve a mystery surround-

ing a rare, missing book. (BL 63:1195; CCBB 21:33; HB 43:343; KR 35:416; LJ 92:2024; TLS 1967 p. 451)
Bobbs-Merrill, 1967, 246 pp., o.p.

SNYDER, Zilpha Keatley. *The Truth about Stone Hollow.* See Chapter 4, Ghost Fantasy.

C/YA STEWART, Mary (Florence Elinor). *A Walk in Wolf Wood.* Gr. 5–8.
[R]   John and Margaret help Mardian, a man forced to become a ferocious wolf each night, to defeat the enchanter who has taken Mardian's place as the king's adviser. (BL 77:40, 49; CCBB 34:42; Ch&Bks:272; Kies:73; KR 48:1300; SLJ Sept 1980 p. 78; TLS 1980 p. 806)
Illus. by Emanuel Schoengut, Morrow, 1980, 1984, 160 pp.; Fawcett, 1984, pap.

C/YA STOLZ, Mary (Slattery). *Cat in the Mirror.* Gr. 5–7.
[R]   Difficulties in coping with a disinterested mother and unfriendly classmates lead to two lives for Erin Gandy, one in the twentieth century and the other in ancient Egypt. (BL 72:628; CC:546; CCBB 29:70; Ch&Bks:272; HB 51:597; JHC:419; KR 45:999; SLJ Oct 1975 p. 103; Suth 2:434)
Harper, 1975, 199 pp., o.p.

C/YA SYKES, Pamela. *Mirror of Danger* (British title: *Come Back, Lucy,*
[R]   1973). Gr. 5–7.
Orphaned Lucy comes to live with distant cousins and is befriended by Alice, the ghost of a Victorian girl, who tries to trap Lucy permanently in the past. The sequel is *Lucy Beware!* (1984). (BL 70:1007; Kies:75; LJ 99:2742; TLS 1973 p. 1117)
Nelson, 1974, o.p.; Archway, 1983, pap., 175 pp.

C/YA SYMONS, (Dorothy) Geraldine. *Crocuses Were Over, Hitler Was Dead* (British title: *Now and Then,* 1977). Gr. 5–7.
Jassy travels back in time to the period of World War II, where she helps a British solider accomplish a secret mission behind German lines. (BL 75:550; CCBB 32:145; KR 46:1308; SLJ Oct 1978 p. 151; TLS 1977 p. 864)
Harper, 1978, 158 pp., o.p.

YA   *Tales out of Time.* Ed. by Barbara Ireson. Gr. 7 up.
Fourteen fantasy and science-fiction time-travel tales written by John Rowe Townsend, Ray Bradbury, H. G. Wells, and others. (BL 77:1342; CCBB 35:11; SLJ Sept 1981 p. 136)
Philomel/Putnam, 1981, 247 pp., o.p.

C/YA TANNEN, Mary. *The Wizard Children of Finn.* Gr. 5–7.
Magic brings Fiona and Bran into ancient Ireland where they help Finn McCool claim his kingdom. The sequel is *The Lost Legend of Finn* (1982). (BL 77:1157; Kies:75; KR 49:505; SLJ Sept 1981 p. 131)
Illus. by John Burgoyne, Knopf, dist. by Random, 1981, o.p.; Avon, 1983, pap., 216 pp.

TAPP, Kathy Kennedy. *The Scorpio Ghosts and the Black Hole Gang.* See Chapter 4, Ghost Fantasy.

C/YA TOWNSEND, John Rowe. *The Visitors* (British title: *The Xanadu Manu-*
[R]   *script,* 1977). Gr. 6–10.
Katherine Wyatt and her parents are sent from the world of 2149 A.D. back into the twentieth century, but they need John Dunham's help to survive and

stay out of trouble. (BL 74:34, 45; CC:541; CCBB 31:87; HB 53:671; JHC 422; KR 45:856; SLJ Nov 1977 p. 75; Suth 2:454)
Lippincott, 1977, 221 pp.

YA *Trips in Time: Nine Stories of Science Fiction.* Ed. by Robert Silverberg. Gr. 9 up.
Nine time-travel tales by Poul Anderson, Roger Zelazny, Robert Silverberg, and others. (BL 74:369; KR 45:884, 941)
Nelson, 1977, 192 pp., o.p.

YA [R] TWAIN, Mark (pseud. of Samuel Clemens). *A Connecticut Yankee in King Arthur's Court* (British title: *A Connecticut Yankee in the Court of King Arthur*). Gr. 8 up. (Orig. pub. Harper, 1889, 1925.)
An accidental blow on the head sends Hank Morgan 1300 years back through time to King Arthur's court, where he uses his knowledge of history and modern technology to replace Merlin as Court Magician. (BL 22:170; HB 2[Nov 1925]:30, 60:359; JHC:423; SHC:640)
Penguin, 1972, pap.; Regents, 1982; Buccaneer, 1982 (repr.); University of California Press, 1983, 479 pp.; Bantam, 1985, pap.

C/YA UTTLEY, Alison (pseud. of Alice Jane [Taylor] Uttley). *A Traveller in*
[R]   *Time.* Gr. 6–8. (Orig. British pub. 1939.)
While visiting her family's ancient country home, Penelope Cameron is drawn back through time to Elizabethan England, where she becomes involved in an ill-fated plot to save Mary, Queen of Scots. (BL 61:581; HB 40:612, 58:721; Kies:77; LJ 65:923, 89:4653; SLJ Oct 1981 p. 154; TLS 1939 p. 667)
Illus. by Phyllis Bray, Viking, 1940, 1964, o.p.; Faber, dist. by Merrimack, 1981, 331 pp.

C/YA VOIGT, Cynthia. *Building Blocks.* Gr. 4–7.
[R]   A fortress made of children's blocks takes Brann Connell back into the time of his father's boyhood, where he comes to better understand the man he had thought of as a loser. (BL 80:1350; CC:543; CCBB 37:157; Ch&Bks:272; HB 60:470; JHC:425; KR 52:24; SLJ May 1984 p. 85; Suth 3:435)
Atheneum, 1984; Ballantine/Fawcett Juniper, 1985, pap., 128 pp.

WALLIN, Luke. *The Slavery Ghosts.* See Chapter 4, Ghost Fantasy.

YA WELCH, Ronald (pseud. of Ronald Oliver Felton). *The Gauntlet.* Gr. 7–9. (Orig. British pub. 1951.)
A medieval gauntlet sends Peter Staunton into the fourteenth century where he lives in his ancestors' castle and takes part in their battles. (BL 49:53; HB 29:53; KR 20:456; LJ 77:1522)
Illus. by T. R. Freeman, Oxford, 1952, 248 pp., o.p.

C/YA WELDRICK, Valerie. *Time Sweep.* Gr. 5–7. (Orig. Australian pub. 1976.)
Laurie's bed is the means by which he travels from twentieth-century Sydney, Australia, to 1862 London, where he and his new friend, Frank, avert a robbery. (CCBB 32:127; HB 55:196; KR 47:7; SLJ Jan 1978 p. 58; Suth 2:474)
Illus. by Ron Brooks, Lothrop, 1978, 157 pp., o.p.

YA [R] WESTALL, Robert (Atkinson). *The Devil on the Road.* Gr. 8 up. (Orig. British pub. 1978.)
John Webster becomes convinced of the innocence of Johanna, a

seventeenth-century girl accused of witchcraft, and manages to bring her into the twentieth century. (BL 75:1532, 76:1199; CCBB 32:204; Ch&Bks:272; HB 55:541; JHC:426; KR 47:860; Kies:80; SLJ May 1979 pp. 36, 76)
Greenwillow, 1979, 256 pp.

WESTALL, Robert. *The Haunting of Chas McGill and Other Stories*. See Chapter 4, Ghost Fantasy.

WESTALL, Robert. *The Watch House*. See Chapter 4, Ghost Fantasy.

C/YA WESTALL, Robert (Atkinson). *The Wind Eye*. Gr. 6–9. (Orig. British
[O]   pub. 1976.)
A boat that once belonged to a medieval monk carries Mike, Beth, and Sally across time into the seventh century, where St. Cuthbert changes both their lives and those of their parents. (BL 74:370, 381; CC:540; CCBB 31:103; Ch&Bks:273; HB 54:56; JHC:427; KR 45:1104; SLJ Nov 1977 p. 77; Suth 2:248; TLS 1976 p. 1547)
Greenwillow/Morrow, 1977, 213 pp., o.p.

C/YA WIBBERLEY, Leonard (Patrick O'Connor). *The Crime of Martin Co-*
[R]   *verly*. Gr. 6–8.
Nick Ormsby is drawn into the eighteenth century for shipboard adventures with his ancestor, pirate Martin Coverly. (BL 76:1538; HB 56:418; KR 48:986; SLJ May 1980 p. 80; VOYA 3[June 1981]:34)
Farrar, 1980, 167 pp.; Scholastic, 1983, pap.

WILLIAMS, Ursula Moray. *Castle Merlin*. See Chapter 4, Ghost Fantasy.

YA WILLIS, Connie. *Lincoln's Dreams*. Gr. 10 up.
Historical researcher Jeff Johnston attempts to help a young woman named Annie who is haunted by the Civil War-ravaged dreams of Robert E. Lee. (BL 83:1098, 1117; KR 55:519; LJ Apr 15, 1987 p. 102; VOYA 10:182)
Spectra/Bantam, 1987, hb, 1988, pap., 224 pp.

C/YA WISEMAN, David. *Adam's Common*. Gr. 5–7.
Peggy uses her ability to glimpse townspeople from the past to solve a mystery and protect the town common from a proposed transformation into a shopping mall. (BL 81:592; CC:547; CCBB 38:97; KR 52:98; SLJ Nov 1984 p. 129)
Houghton, 1984, 175 pp.

C/YA WISEMAN, David. *Jeremy Visick* (British title: *The Fate of Jeremy*
[O]   *Visick*, 1981). Gr. 5–8.
Having learned about a twelve-year-old boy named Jeremy who died in the Cornish mines in 1852, Matthew begins visiting Jeremy's time in an attempt to save his life. (BL 77:1397, 80:96; CC:547; CCBB 35:20; HB 57:193; KR 49:741; SLJ Apr 1981 p. 134, May 1981 p. 25; Suth 3:456)
Houghton, 1981, 170 pp.

C/YA WISEMAN, David. *Thimbles*. Gr. 5–7.
Two old thimbles propel Cathy into the year 1819, where she becomes, alternately, two girls involved in a dangerous demonstration by thousands of workers pleading for the right to vote. (BL 78:965, 980; CCBB 35:219; KR 50:556; SLJ Mar 1982 p. 153; TLS 1983 p. 1318)
Houghton, 1982, 134 pp.

9
Toy Fantasy

Tales of toys that talk or exhibit other magical abilities are listed in this chapter. Most are about dolls, but there are a few about carousel horses, stuffed animals, toy soldiers, and windup toys.

C ALBRECHT, Lillie Vanderveer. *Deborah Remembers*. Gr. 4–6.
  Deborah describes to the other museum dolls the events she witnessed during the American Revolution. (BL 56:246; HB 38:381; KR 27:548)
  Illus. by Rita Newton, Hastings, 1959, 111 pp., o.p.

ANASTASIO, Dina. *A Question of Time*. See Chapter 4, Ghost Fantasy.

ANDERSEN, Hans Christian. *The Steadfast Tin Soldier*. See Chapter 1, Allegorical Fantasy and Literary Fairy Tales.

C AVERILL, Esther. *The Adventures of Jack Ninepins*. Gr. 3–4.
  Jack Ninepins, Charlotte's favorite toy, is determined to follow her across the ocean to France. (HB 20:471, 480; KR 12:399; LJ 69:863, 1104)
  Harper, 1944, 63 pp., o.p.

C/YA BACON, Martha (Sherman). *Moth Manor: A Gothic Tale*. Gr. 5–7.
  A ghostly moth sparks Monica's interest in the mystery surrounding her great-aunt's dollhouse. (BL 75:42; CCBB 32:93; Ch&Bks:264; KR 46:1188; SLJ Sept 1978 p. 130)
  Illus. by Gail Burroughs, Atlantic-Little, 1978, 160 pp., o.p.

C [R] BAILEY, Carolyn Sherwin. *Miss Hickory*. Gr. 3–5.
  Miss Hickory, a doll with a hickory-nut head, is forgotten by her family and has a winter full of adventure. Newbery Medal, 1947. (BL 43:74; CC:430; Ch&Bks:264; HB 22:465; KR 14:387; LJ 71:1412, 1544)
  Illus. by Ruth Chrisman Gannett, Viking, 1946, 123 pp.; Penguin, 1977, pap.

C BAKER, Margaret. *Victoria Josephine* (British title: *The Roaming Doll*, 1936). Gr. 2–4.
  Freed after seventy years in a box, Victoria Josephine is determined to travel. (HB 12:350; LJ 62:217)
  Illus. by Mary Baker, Dodd, 1936, 95 pp., o.p.

C BAKER, Margaret Joyce. *The Shoe Shop Bears.* Gr. 3–5. (Orig. British pub. 1963.)
Three Teddy bears leave the shoe shop in search of a truly loving home. The sequels are *Hannibal and the Bears* (1966), *Bears Back in Business* (1967), and *Hi Jinks Joins the Bears* (1969). (CCBB 19:41; LJ 90:3785; TLS 1964 p. 605)
Illus. by C. Walter Hodges, Ariel, 1965, 96 pp., o.p.

C BARRINGER, Marie. *Martin the Goose Boy.* Gr. 3–5.
Only Gustel knew that his wooden goose-boy doll, Martin, could talk. (BL 29:77; Bookshelf 1932 p. 6; LJ 58:711; Mahony 3:53)
Illus. by Maud Petersham and Miska Petersham, Doubleday, 1932, 1936, 188 pp., o.p.

C BARZINI, Luigi (Giorgio, Jr.). *The Little Match Man.* Gr. 4–6. (Orig. Italian pub. 1909.)
A little man made out of matches comes to life. (BL 14:202; Bookshelf 1923–1924 p. 8)
Illus. by Hattie Longstreet, Penn, 1917, 1923, 164 pp., o.p.

BEAUMONT, Cyril W. *The Mysterious Toyshop: A Fairy Tale.* See Chapter 7, Magic Adventure Fantasy.

C BEMELMANS, Ludwig. *The Happy Place.* Gr. 2–4.
Unsold by Easter, Winthrop the toy rabbit is turned loose in Central Park, where the zoo animals befriend him. (KR 20:499; LJ 77:1661)
Illus. by the author, Little, 1952 (c. 1951), 58 pp., o.p.

C BIANCO, Margery (Winifred) Williams. *The Adventures of Andy.* Gr. 4–6.
A doll named Andromeda sets off on an adventurous journey after her owner grows up and gets married. (HB 3[Nov 1927]:47; Mahony 2:122; Moore:124)
Illus. by Leon Underwood, Doran, 1927, 227 pp., o.p.

C [R] BIANCO, Margery (Winifred) Williams. *The Little Wooden Doll.* Gr. 2–4.
A lonely doll found in the attic is transformed into a princess doll. (BL 22:121; Bookshelf 1928 p. 9; HB 2[Nov 1925]:18; LJ 51:836; Moore:426)
Illus. by Pamela Bianco, Macmillan, 1925, 65 pp., o.p.

C [R] BIANCO, Margery (Winifred) Williams. *Poor Cecco: The Wonderful Story of a Wonderful Wooden Dog Who Was the Jolliest Toy in the House Until He Went Out to Explore the World.* Gr. 3–5. (Orig. U.S. and British pubs. 1925.)
Cecco the wooden dog and his friends, Jensina the doll and Bulka the toy rabbit, leave their home in the toy cupboard to search for adventure. (BL 22:121; Bookshelf 1926–1927 p. 5; HB 2[Nov 1925]:13, 19, 20; Mahony 2:122; Moore:426; TLS 1925 p. 809)
Illus. by Arthur Rackham, Doubleday, 1945, 175 pp., o.p.

C [O] BIANCO, Margery (Winifred) Williams. *The Velveteen Rabbit; or, How Toys Became Real.* Gr. K–4. (Orig. British pub. 1926.)
A well-loved toy is transformed into a real rabbit after it is worn out and discarded. The sequel is *The Skin Horse* (orig. British pub. 1927, 1978). (BL 77:137, 79:1337, 1443, 82:632, 84:401; Bookshelf 1923–1924 p. 7; CC:546;

CCBB 37:2, 39:59; Ch&Bks:264; KR 51:374; Moore:426; SLJ Dec 1981 p. 58, Aug 1983 p. 60; Jan 1986 p. 62)
Illus. by William Nicholson, Doubleday, 1958; illus. by Michael Hague, Holt, 1983; illus. by Allen Atkinson, Knopf, 1983, o.p.; Avon, 1987, pap.; illus. by Ilsa Plume, Harcourt, 1987, 31 pp.

C BIANCO, Pamela. *Little Houses Far Away.* Gr. 1–4.
Paula explores the teddy-bear and doll world she saw from a train window. (BL 48:174; CCBB 5:26; HB 27:324; KR 19:614; LJ 76:2009)
Illus. by the author, Oxford, 1951, 87 pp., o.p.

C BIANCO, Pamela. *Toy Rose.* Gr. 3–5.
A talking doll named Toy Rose comes between Joy and Jessica, twins who are also best friends. (CCBB 11:77; HB 33:398; KR 25:479; LJ 82:3241)
Illus. by the author, Lippincott, 1957, 91 pp., o.p.

C BLOCH, Marie Halun. *The Dollhouse Story.* Gr. 3–5.
Three dollhouse dolls come to life to get rid of a cat who frightened away their friend, Mouse. (BL 58:488; HB 38:176; LJ 87:329)
Illus. by Walter Erhard, Walck, 1961, 63 pp., o.p.

BRINK, Carol Ryrie. *Andy Buckram's Tin Men.* See Chapter 6, Humorous Fantasy.

C BROWN, Abbie Farwell. *The Lonesomest Doll.* Gr. 3–5. (Orig. U.S. pub. 1901.)
The porter's daughter teaches a princess how to play with her lonesome doll. (BL 25:173; Bookshelf 1923–1924 p. 12; HB 4[Nov 1928]:76; Mahony 1:40; Mahony 2:127)
Illus. by Arthur Rackham, Houghton, 1928, 80 pp., o.p.

C BUCK, David. *The Small Adventures of Dog.* Gr. 3–5. (Orig. British pub. 1968.)
A discarded leather pig called "Dog" finds he can talk with other toys and real animals. (CCBB 24:5; LJ 95:778; TLS 1968 p. 1376)
Illus. by the author, Watts, 1969, 76 pp., o.p.

BURNETT, Frances Hodgson. *Racketty-Packetty House.* See Chapter 7, Magic Adventure Fantasy.

C BYARS, Betsy (Cromer). *Clementine.* Gr. 3–4.
Clementine, a dragon made from an old green sock, grows dissatisfied with her toy-shelf home and insists on moving to a cave in the country. (KR 30:280; LJ 87:3199)
Illus. by Charles Wilton, Houghton, 1962, 72 pp., o.p.

CASSEDY, Sylvia. *Behind the Attic Wall.* See Chapter 4, Ghost Fantasy.

C CLARKE, Pauline (pseud. of Pauline [Clarke] Hunter Blair). *Five Dolls in a House.* Gr. 3–5. (Orig. British pub. 1961.)
After she shrinks to doll-size, Elizabeth sees what life is like for her own five dolls. The sequels are *Five Dolls in the Snow* (1967), *Five Dolls and Their Friends* (British), *Five Dolls and the Duke* (British), and *Five Dolls and the Monkey* (British). (CCBB 19:145; HB 41:627; LJ 91:1696; TLS 1961 p. 451)
Illus. by Aliki (Brandenberg), Prentice-Hall, 1965, 143 pp., o.p.

C/YA CLARKE, Pauline (pseud. of Pauline [Clarke] Hunter Blair). *The Return*
[R]   *of the Twelves* (British title: *The Twelve and the Genii*, 1962). Gr. 4–7.
      Max Morley discovers that his twelve toy soldiers are alive, and he helps
      them reach their ancestral home. Carnegie Medal, 1962. (BL 60:701;
      Ch&Bks:265; Eakin:74; HB 39:602, 60:223; LJ 89:390; TLS 1962 p. 901)
      Illus. by Bernarda Bryson, Coward, 1963, o.p.; Gregg, 1981, 251 pp., o.p.;
      Dell, 1986, pap.

C [R] COATSWORTH, Elizabeth (Jane). *All-of-a-Sudden Susan*. Gr. 3–5.
      Susan finds that her doll, Emelida, can speak, after they are accidentally
      left behind when her family abandons their house during a flood. (BL 71:506;
      CCBB 28:128; KR 42:1303; SLJ Mar 1975 p. 86)
      Illus. by Richard Cuffari, Macmillan, 1974, 74 pp., o.p.

C/YA COLLODI, Carlo (pseud. of Carlo Lorenzini). *The Adventures of*
[R]   *Pinocchio*. Gr. 4–8. (Written 1880; pub. serially beginning in 1881; orig.
      Italian pub. in book form, 1882, U.S. pub. 1892.)
      A wooden puppet named Pinocchio longs to become a real boy. Five
      sequels were written by authors other than Collodi and published in the U.S.:
      Pinocchio in Africa (Ginn, 1911) by Eugenio Cherubini, *Pinocchio under the
      Sea* (Macmillan, 1913) by Gemma Mongiardini Rembadi, *The Heart of
      Pinocchio* (Harper, 1919) by Paolo Lorenzini, *Pinocchio in America* (Double-
      day, 1928) by Angelo Patri, and *Puppet Parade* (Longmans, 1932) by Carol-
      [yn M.] Della Chiesa). (BL 12:299, 21:238, 60:307, 79:674; 80:856; Bookshelf
      1928 p. 9; CC:453, 508; CCBB 2[Jan 1949]:4, 4:45, 11:67, 37:105, 144;
      Ch&Bks:250; HB 2[Nov 1925]:29, 27:260, 59:70, 60:357, 61:588; KR 37:719;
      LJ 95:258, June 15, 1985 p. 71; Mahony 2:286; SLJ Feb 1984 p. 56, Feb 1986
      p. 72, Mar 1987 p. 156; Suth 3:97)
      Tr. by Carol Della Chiesa, illus. by Atillo Mussino, Macmillan, 1969, 1978,
      o.p.; illus. by Richard Floethe, Philomel, 1982, pap., o.p.; adapt. by Neil
      Morris, illus. by Frank Baber, Macmillan, 1982; illus. by Fritz Kredel, Put-
      nam, 1982, hb and pap.; tr. by M. L. Rosenthal, illus. by Troy Howell,
      Lothrop, 1983; adapt. by Stephanie Spinner, illus. by Diane Goode, Ran-
      dom, 1983; tr. by James T. Teahan, illus. by Alexa Jaffurs, Schocken, 1985;
      tr. and illus. by Francis Wainwright, Holt, 1986, 96 pp.

C   COOMBS, Patricia. *The Lost Playground*. Gr. 1–4.
      Accidentally left in the park, Mostly, June's home-made stuffed animal,
      floats off to the Lost Playground where all lost toys go. (CCBB 17:153; HB
      39:380)
      Illus. by the author, Lothrop, 1963, 46 pp., o.p.

C   DE LEEUW, Adele Louise. *Nobody's Doll*. Gr. 2–5.
      Susan Araminta is rescued from the trash by Mr. McHugh, a Scottie who
      helps her find a new owner. (BL 42:319; HB 22:268; LJ 71:827)
      Illus. by Anne Vaughan, Little, 1946, 85 pp., o.p.

C   DIAZ, Abby (Morton). *Polly Cologne*. Gr. 3–5. (Orig. pub. 1881.)
      A rag doll named Polly Cologne goes for a ride in a dog's mouth and gets
      lost. (BL 27:215; HB 6:332, 7:116; Mahony 1:14)
      Illus. by Morgan J. Sweeney, Lothrop, 1930, 215 pp., o.p.

C   DILLON, Barbara. *The Teddy Bear Tree*. Gr. 3–5.
      Bertine buries a worn-out teddy bear's glass eye, and a tree full of teddy
      bears grows there. (BL 79:244; KR 50:734; SLJ Oct 1982 p. 150)
      Illus. by David Rose, Morrow, 1982, 79 pp.

C DILLON, Barbara. *Who Needs a Bear?* Gr. 2–4.
Three old toys leave the safety of their attic home, searching for new owners who really care about them. (BL 78:104; CCBB 35:84; KR 49:1159; SLJ Nov 1981 p. 90)
Illus. by Diane de Groat, Morrow, 1981, 63 pp.

C DU BOIS, William (Sherman) Pène. *Gentleman Bear.* Gr. 4–6.
Bayard the gentleman teddy bear accompanies his owner, Sir Billy Browne-Browne, from age four through adulthood. (BL 82:1080; CCBB 39:145; SLJ Apr 1986 p. 86)
Illus. by the author, Farrar, 1985, 78 pp.

ESTES, Eleanor. *The Witch Family.* See Chapter 10, Witchcraft and Sorcery Fantasy.

C [R] FAIRSTAR, Mrs. (pseud. of Richard Henry Horne). *Memoirs of a London Doll, Written by Herself.* Gr. 4–6. (Orig. British pub. 1846, U.S. 1852.)
Maria Poppet describes her harrowing experiences as she is passed from owner to owner. This story has been reprinted in *The Silent Playmate* (Macmillan, 1979, 1981), ed. by Naomi Lewis (see this chapter). (BL 65:257; Bookshelf 1928 p. 16; CCBB 22:79; Ch&Bks:266; HB 44:560; KR 36:642; TLS 1967 p. 1143)
Illus. by Margaret Gillies and Richard Smith, Macmillan, 1968, 143 pp., o.p.

C FANCIULLI, Guiseppe. *The Little Blue Man.* Gr. 4–6. (Orig. pub. in Italy.)
The story of the adventures of a small blue puppet-man. (BL 23:234; HB 2[Nov 1926]:42; Mahony 2:123)
Tr. by May M. Sweet, illus. by Herman I. Bacharach, Houghton, 1926, 198 pp., o.p.

C [R] FIELD, Rachel (Lyman). *Hitty, Her First Hundred Years.* Gr. 4–6. (Orig. pub. 1929.)
The adventures of a carved-wood doll named Hitty include being shipwrecked while traveling from Maine to the South Seas. Newbery Medal, 1930. (BL 26:125; Bookshelf 1932 p. 12; CC:465; Ch&Bks:266; HB 5:53, 6:22; LJ 54:986, 55:603, 996; Moore:235, 427)
Illus. by Dorothy P. Lathrop, Macmillan, 1937, 207 pp.

C FOSTER, Elizabeth. *Gigi: The Story of a Merry-Go-Round Horse.* Gr. 4–6.
A merry-go-round horse has many adventures while traveling from Vienna to Paris, London, and America. The sequel is *Gigi in America: Further Adventures of a Merry-Go-Round Horse* (1946, 1983). (BL 40:116; HB 19:319; LJ 68:820, 1008)
Illus. by Ilse Bischoff, Houghton, 1943, o.p.; North Atlantic Books, 1983, 118 pp.

C FRANCHI, Anna. *The Little Lead Soldier.* Gr. 3–5.
Tamburino, a French lead soldier, tells two Italian children the story of his life and adventures. (BL 16:316; Bookshelf 1923–1924 p. 8)
Illus. by Hattie Longstreet Price, Penn, 1919, 186 pp., o.p.

C [R] FYLEMAN, Rose (Amy). *The Dolls' House.* Gr. 2–4. (Orig. British pub. 1930.)
The doll house family has a number of adventures while their owner is gone. (BL 28:66; HB 7:220; LJ 56:958; TLS 1930 p. 986)
Illus. by Erick Berry, Doubleday, 1931, 99 pp., o.p.

C/YA   GARDAM, Jane. *Through the Dolls' House Door.* Gr. 4–8. (Orig. British
[R]   pub. 1987.)
       Forgotten for many years after their playmates have moved away, the
       "creatures" living in an antique doll house (a Dutch doll, a rag doll, a soldier,
       a little girl doll, and a china cat) despair that they will never be found and
       played with again. (BL 84:318; CCBB 41:48; KR 55:1155; SLJ Oct 1987 p.
       125; TLS 1987 p. 751; VOYA 11:39)
       Greenwillow, 1987, 121 pp.

C [R] GODDEN (Dixon), (Margaret) Rumer. *Candy Floss.* Gr. 2–4.
       A spoiled little girl named Clementina decides to steal Jack's doll, Candy
       Floss. This story has been reprinted in *Four Dolls* (Greenwillow, 1984; see
       this chapter). (BL 56:633; CCBB 13:147; Ch&Bks:267; Eakin:141; HB
       36:212; KR 28:144; LJ 85:247; TLS Nov 25, 1960 p. iv)
       Illus. by Adrienne Adams, Viking, 1959, 63 pp., o.p.

C [R] GODDEN (Dixon), (Margaret) Rumer. *The Dolls' House.* Gr. 3–5.
       Life in a Victorian dollhouse changes drastically when a haughty new doll ar-
       rives. (BL 45:53, 59:292; CC:474; CCBB 2[Jan 1949]:3, 13:147; Ch&Bks:252;
       Eakin:141; HB 24:347, 457, 39:75; KR 16:363; LJ 73:1097; TLS 1947 p. 636)
       Illus. by Tasha Tudor, Viking, 1947, 1962, 136 pp., o.p.; Penguin, 1976,
       pap.

C [R] GODDEN (Dixon), (Margaret) Rumer. *The Fairy Doll.* Gr. 2–4.
       The fairy doll atop the Christmas tree helps Elizabeth to gain self-
       confidence. This story has been reprinted in *Four Dolls* (Greenwillow, 1984;
       see this chapter). (BL 53:51; Ch&Bks:267; HB 34:453; KR 24:431; LJ
       81:2720; TLS Nov 23, 1956 p. xv)
       Illus. by Adrienne Adams, Viking, 1956, 67 pp., o.p.

C [R] GODDEN (Dixon), (Margaret) Rumer. *Four Dolls* (Orig. titles: *Impunity
       Jane,* Viking, 1954; *The Fairy Doll,* Viking, 1956; *The Story of Holly
       and Ivy,* Viking, 1958; *Candy Floss,* Viking, 1960). Gr. 3–5. (Orig. Brit-
       ish pub. in this edition 1983.)
       Four timeless tales about spirited little dolls and their resourceful owners.
       (BL 81:306; CC:552; HB 60:615; SLJ Nov 1984 p. 124)
       Illus. by Pauline Baynes, Greenwillow, 1984; Dell/Yearling, 1986, pap.,
       206 pp.

C [R] GODDEN (Dixon), (Margaret) Rumer. *Home Is the Sailor.* Gr. 3–5.
       A Welsh doll named Curley sets sail for France to search for his older
       brother, Thomas. (Ch&Bks:267; Eakin:141; HB 41:56; LJ 90:960; TLS 1964
       p. 1081)
       Illus. by Jean Primrose, Viking, 1964, 128 pp., o.p.

C [R] GODDEN (Dixon), (Margaret) Rumer. *Impunity Jane: The Story of a
       Pocket Doll.* Gr. 2–4.
       Impunity Jane grows bored sitting on a dollhouse cushion all day, and longs
       to take a ride in someone's pocket. This story has been reprinted in *Four Dolls*
       (Greenwillow, 1984; see this chapter). (BL 51:47; CCBB 9:23; Ch&Bks:252;
       Eakin:142; HB 30:330; KR 22:383; LJ 79:1913, 2018)
       Illus. by Adrienne Adams, Viking, 1954, 47 pp., o.p.

C [R] GODDEN (Dixon), (Margaret) Rumer. *Miss Happiness and Miss Flower.*
       Gr. 3–5.
       Nona and her cousins build a Japanese-style house for her two Japanese

dolls. The sequel is *Little Plum* (1962). (BL 57:580; CCBB 14:143; Ch&Bks:252; Eakin:142; HB 37:269; KR 29:328; LJ 86:1983; TLS May 19, 1961 p. iv)

Illus. by Jean Primrose, Viking, 1961, o.p.; Penguin/Puffin, 1987, pap., 88 pp.

C GODDEN (Dixon), (Margaret) Rumer. *The Story of Holly and Ivy.* Gr. 2–4.

The Christmas wishes of an orphaned girl named Ivy, a doll named Holly, and a lonely woman named Mrs. Jones, are all granted. This story can also be found in *Four Dolls* (Greenwillow, 1984; see this chapter). (BL 55:53, 82:261, 417; CCBB 12:47, 39:27; Ch&Bks:267; Eakin:143; HB 34:461; KR 26:453; LJ 83:3572; SLJ Oct 1985 p. 190; TLS Nov 21, 1958 p. xv)

Illus. by Adrienne Adams, Viking, 1957, o.p.; illus. by Barbara Cooney, Viking/Kestrel, 1985, 31 pp.; Penguin/Puffin, 1987, pap.

C GREENWALD, Sheila (pseud. of Sheila Green) *The Secret Museum.* Gr. 3–5.

Jennifer comes upon some antique dolls who agree to take part in plays to earn money to help Jennifer's parents. (BL 70:1104; CCBB 27:177; KR 42:424; LJ 99:1473)

Illus. by the author, Lippincott, 1974, 127 pp., o.p.

HOBAN, Russell C. *The Mouse and His Child.* See Chapter 1, Allegorical Fantasy and Literary Fairy Tales.

C/YA HOFFMANN, E(rnst) T(heodor) A(madeus). *The Nutcracker.* Gr. 2 up.
[O] (Orig. German pub. 1819; U.S. pub. 1853, entitled: *Nutcracker and Mouse-King.*)

In a little girl's Christmas Eve dream, her toy nutcracker comes to life and takes her to a magical world. (BL 35:139, 55:78, 56:225, 72:791, 76:452, 78:304, 80:417, 81:146; CC:432, 483, 526; CCBB 32:153, 37:30, 38:67; HB 6:329, 34:460, 35:487, 61:53; KR 26:606, 27:597, 49:1292, 52:75; LJ 55:924; 83:2496, 84:2731; SLJ Oct 1979 p. 118, Oct 1981 p. 155, Feb 1984 p. 73, Nov 1984 p. 125, Oct 1987 p. 31; Suth 3:194, 195; TLS 1985 p. 75)

Whitman, 1930, o.p.; adapt. and illus. by Warren Chappell, Knopf, 1958; adapt. by Janet Schulman, illus. by Kay Chorao, Dutton, 1979, o.p.; illus. by Rachel Isadora, Macmillan, 1981; tr. and adapt. by Anthea Bell, illus. by Lisbeth Zwerger, Picture Book Studio, 1983, 1987 (entitled *The Nutcracker and the Mouse-King*), 33 pp.; tr. by Ralph Manheim, illus. by Maurice Sendak, Crown, 1984, 102 pp.

C HOWE, Deborah, and HOWE, James. *Teddy Bear's Scrapbook.* Gr. 2–4.

Teddy tells his owner seven adventure-filled tales. His exploits include visiting the abominable snowman and becoming a cowboy, a circus performer, and a movie star. (BL 76:1424; CCBB 34:13; KR 48:911; SLJ Sept 1980 p. 60)

Illus. by David S. Rose, Atheneum, 1980; Avon, 1981, pap.; Macmillan, 1987, pap., 80 pp.

C JANE, Pamela. *Noelle of the Nutcracker.* Gr. 3–5.

A ballerina doll who dreams of a dancing career is desperately desired by second-graders Ilyana Ingram and her arch-rival, wealthy Mary Jane Igoe. (BL 83:132; CCBB 40:28; KR 54:1125; SLJ Oct 1986 p. 112)

Illus. by Jan Brett, Houghton, 1986, 60 pp.

C JOHNSON, Crockett (pseud. of David Leisk). *Ellen's Lion: Twelve Stories*. Gr. 2–4.
Ellen and her talking toy lion go on twelve adventures together. (HB 35:379; KR 27:370; LJ 84:3625)
Illus. by the author, Harper, 1959, o.p.; Godine, 1984, pap., 64 pp.

C [R] JONES, Elizabeth Orton. *Big Susan*. Gr. 2–4. (Orig. pub. 1947.)
Big Susan helps the Doll family come to life on Christmas Eve. (BL 44:138, CCBB 1[Dec 1947]:3; HB 24:39; KR 15:547; LJ 72;1692)
Illus. by the author, Macmillan, 1967, 82 pp., o.p.

C/YA KENNEDY, Richard (Jerome). *Amy's Eyes*. Gr. 5–7.
[R] Orphaned Amy's love for her sailor doll, Captain, causes him to grow into a real sailor who runs away from the Home for Girls, vowing to return for Amy once he has made his fortune. (BL 81:1254, 82:1234; CC 1987 Suppl. p. 59; CCBB 38:150; HB 61:554; KR 53:42; SLJ May 1985 p. 90; VOYA 8:193)
Illus. by Richard Egielski, Harper, 1985, 437 pp.

C KING, Beulah. *Ruffs and Pompons*. Gr. 4–6.
Finney Foo, the clown-doll, leaves the toy shop to see the world. (HB 1[Oct 1924]:4, 8, 1[June 1925]:32; Mahony 2:282)
Illus. by Maurice Day, Little, 1924, 256 pp., o.p.

C KNIGHT, Marjorie. *Alexander's Christmas Eve*. Gr. 2–4.
Three Christmas toys escape from Santa's pack and set out to see the world and find their own home. The sequels are *Alexander's Birthday* (1940), and *Alexander's Vacation* (1943). (HB 14:413; LJ 63:798)
Illus. by Howard Simon, Dutton, 1938, 93 pp., o.p.

C KROEBER, Theodora (Kracow). *Carrousel*. Gr. 2–4.
When Pegason the winged horse falls into a giant city, his friends Gryphon and Pyggon must rescue him. (CCBB 31:97; HB 53:664; KR 45:1198; SLJ Nov 1977 p. 49)
Illus. by Douglas Tait, Atheneum, 1977, 91 pp., o.p.

LAMORISSE, Albert (Emmanuel). *The Red Balloon*. See Chapter 1, Allegorical Fantasy and Literary Fairy Tales.

C [R] LATHROP, Dorothy P(ulis). *An Angel in the Woods*. Gr. 2–4. (Orig. pub. 1947.)
A toy Christmas angel brings the Christmas spirit to the forest animals. (BL 44:156; HB 24:37; KR 15:578; LJ 72:1784)
Illus. by the author, Macmillan, 1955, 42 pp., o.p.

LATHROP, Dorothy P. *The Lost Merry-Go-Round*. See Chapter 7, Magic Adventure Fantasy.

MARIA, Consort of Ferdinand, King of Rumania. *The Magic Doll of Rumania*. See Chapter 7, Magic Adventure Fantasy.

C [O] MILNE, A(lan) A(lexander). *Winnie-the-Pooh*. Gr. 2–4. (Orig. pub. 1926.)
The adventures of Christopher Robin and his friends, Winnie-the-Pooh, Tigger, Eeyore, Piglet, Rabbit, Owl, Kanga, and Baby Roo; including Pooh's tangles with honeybees, and Piglet's encounter with a Heffalump. The sequels are *The House at Pooh Corner* (1961; orig. pub. 1928) and *The Hums of Pooh* (1930). Collections of tales about Pooh include *The World of Pooh*

(1957), *The Pooh Story Book* (1965), and *The Christopher Robin Story Book* (1966). (BL 23:137; Bookshelf 1928 p. 9; CC:509; Ch&Bks:250; HB 2[Nov 1925]:42, 34:122; KR 39:1213; LJ 52:1017; Moore:427; TLS 1926 p. 861, 1971 p. 1614)
Illus. by Ernest Shepard, Dutton, 1954; Dell, 1970, pap., 176 pp.

NESBIT, E. *The Magic City.* See Section 5C, Travel to Other Worlds.

C [R] O'CONNELL, Jean S. *The Dollhouse Caper.* Gr. 4–6.
Although the Dollhouse family is unable to warn the Humans about an upcoming robbery, they manage to scare the burglars off by themselves. (BL 72:1049; CCBB 29:149; Ch&Bks:270; HB 52:291; KR 44:70; SLJ Apr 1976 p. 63; Suth 2:341)
Illus. by Erik Blegvad, Crowell, 1976, 87 pp.; Scholastic, 1977, pap.

C [R] PARRISH, Anne. *Floating Island.* Gr. 3–5.
The adventures of a family of dolls who are shipwrecked on a deserted island. Newbery Medal Honor Book, 1931. (BL 27:214; Bookshelf 1932 p. 12; HB 6:331, 7:60, 116; Moore: 280, 427; TLS 1930 p. 1043)
Illus. by the author, Harper, 1930, 265 pp., o.p.

C PETERSHAM, Maud (Fuller), and PETERSHAM, Miska. *Get A-Way and Háry János.* Gr. 2–4.
In a far-off land where old toys become new, a worn-out toy horse and a one-armed wooden soldier doll go on an adventure. (BL 30:90; Mahony 3:59)
Illus. by the authors, Viking, 1933, 64 pp., o.p.

C PHILLIPS, Ethel Calvert. *Little Rag Doll.* Gr. 3–5.
Mrs. Thimbletop, the doll fairy, befriends a neglected rag doll named Dilly and they go to live with a cat named Grandma Reddy, inside a child's play-house. (BL 27:214; HB 6:322; LJ 55:955, 56:279; Mahony 3:56)
Illus. by Lois Lenski, Houghton, 1930, 174 pp., o.p.

C PHILLIPS, Ethel Calvert. *The Popover Family.* Gr. 2–4.
Ellen meets the Popover doll family who live in her Aunt Amelia's old red dollhouse. (BL 24:73; HB 3[Nov 1927]:43; LJ 53:1033; Mahony 2:128)
Illus. by E. F. Butler, Houghton, 1927, 132 pp., o.p.

C PHILLIPS, Ethel Calvert. *Pretty Polly Perkins.* Gr. 3–5.
Grandmother King settles the disagreement among three little girls who each claim an old-fashioned rag doll as their own. (BL 22:123; HB 2[Nov 1925]:17; Mahony 2:128)
Illus. by E. F. Butler, Houghton, 1924, 122 pp., o.p.

REID BANKS, Lynne. *The Indian in the Cupboard.* See Chapter 7, Magic Adventure Fantasy.

SCOTT, Evelyn. *Witch Perkins: A Story of the Kentucky Hills.* See Section 5C, Travel to Other Worlds.

C SHECTER, Ben. *The Stocking Child.* Gr. 2–4.
Sam and his friend, Epaphroditus, search far and wide for a missing button eye, and wind up at Sam's own house. (BL 73:669; CCBB 30:114; KR 44:1038; SLJ Jan 1977 p. 85)
Illus. by the author, Harper, 1976, 32 pp. o.p.

C SIEBE, Josephine. *Kasperle's Adventures.* Gr. 3–5. (Orig. German pub. 1928.)
Kasperle, a mischievous wooden doll, comes to life after Master Friedolm finishes carving him. (BL 26:126; Bookshelf 1930–1931 p. 9; HB 5:46–47, 49, 7:117; Mahony 3:56)
Tr. by Florence Geiser, illus. by Frank Dobias, Macmillan, 1929, 1939, 199 pp., o.p.

C *The Silent Playmate: A Collection of Doll Stories.* Ed. by Naomi Lewis. Gr. 4–6. (Orig. British pub. 1979.)
Doll stories from various sources, including Mrs. Fairstar's *Memoirs of a London Doll* (1846, 1852; see this chapter). (BL 78:589; CCBB 35:89; HB 58:44; SLJ Feb 1982 p. 78)
Illus. by Harold Jones, Macmillan, 1981, 223 pp., o.p.

C [R] SLEATOR, William (Warner III). *Among the Dolls.* Gr. 3–5.
Vicky learns a painful lesson when she shrinks to doll size and must suffer the ill-temper of the dolls she had mistreated. (BL 72:628; CC:259; CCBB 29:118; HB 52:53; KR 43:1186; SLJ Dec 1975 p. 55)
Illus. by Trina Schart Hyman, Dutton, 1975, 1985, 70 pp.

C SLOBODKIN, Louis. *The Adventures of Arab.* Gr. 3–5. (Orig. pub. 1946.)
Arab is not happy as a merry-go-round horse, so he changes places with a coach horse. (BL 43:148; HB 22:349; KR 14:386; LJ 72:167)
Illus. by the author, Vanguard, 1967, 123 pp.

STEARNS, Pamela. *The Mechanical Doll.* See Chapter 1, Allegorical Fantasy and Literary Fairy Tales.

C STOVER, Marjorie Filley. *When the Dolls Woke.* Gr. 3–6.
Great-Great-Aunt Abigail's dollhouse holds a treasure, if only the doll family can remember where it is hidden in time to help Abigail, now a destitute old woman. (BL 82:814; SLJ Jan 1986 p. 71)
Illus. by Karen Loccisano, Whitman, 1985, 136 pp.

C [R] SYMONDS, John. *Away to the Moon.* Gr. 2–4.
Two dollhouse dolls named Hetty and Betty set off to visit the moon. (BL 53:101; HB 32:349; KR 24:571; LJ 81:2723)
Illus. by Pamela Bianco, Lippincott, 1956, 64 pp., o.p.

C [R] TREGARTHEN, Enys (pseud. of Nellie Sloggett). *The Doll Who Came Alive.* Gr. 3–5. (Orig. U.S. pub. 1942.)
A little girl's great love for her wooden doll brings it to life. (BL 69:911; CC:541; CCBB 4:51, 26:33; HB 48:596; KR 40:860; LJ 67:884, 98:1009; TLS 1973 p. 387)
Ed. by Elizabeth Yates, illus. by Nora S. Unwin, Day, 1972 (repr. of 1942 ed.), 75 pp., o.p.

C TWOHILL, Maggie. *Jeeter, Mason and the Magic Headset.* Gr. 3–5.
Ten-year-old Jeeter's Cabbage Patch doll, Morgan, suddenly begins talking to Jeeter through her radio headphones. (CCBB 39:18; SLJ Sept 1985 p. 140)
Bradbury, 1985, 103 pp.; Dell, 1986, pap.

C WILLIAMS (John), Ursula Moray. *Adventures of a Little Wooden Horse.* Gr. 4–6. (Orig. British pub. 1938.)
A "real" wooden horse, searching for his former master, has misadven-

tures at a race track, at a circus, in a coal mine, and a cave, before being reunited with Uncle Peder. (LJ 65:37)

Illus. by Joyce Brisley, Lippincott, 1939, o.p.; illus. by Peggy Fortnum, Penguin, 1959, 170 pp., pap., o.p.

C [R] WILLIAMS (John), Ursula Moray. *The Toymaker's Daughter.* Gr. 4–6. (Orig. British pub. 1968.)

A doll-girl named Marta escapes from Malkin, the evil toymaker, and crosses the mountains, hoping to become a real girl. The sequels are *The Three Toymakers* (1970, 1971) and *Malkin's Mountain* (Nelson, 1971, 1972). (CCBB 23:68; HB 45:538; KR 37:507; LJ 94:3209; TLS 1968 p. 1377)

Illus. by Shirley Hughes, Meredith, 1969, 134 pp., o.p.

YOUNG, Miriam. *The Witch Mobile.* See Chapter 10, Witchcraft and Sorcery Fantasy.

10

Witchcraft and Sorcery Fantasy

These are tales of magic as practiced by witches and wizards, enchanters and enchantresses, sorcerers and magicians. Most have a lighthearted quality, distinguishing them from the more serious and at times terrifying tales of the occult, or horror fiction, which have not been included in this bibliography.

AIKEN, Joan. *The Faithless Lollybird*. See Chapter 3, Fantasy Collections.

AIKEN, Joan. *The Kingdom and the Cave*. See Section 5A, Alternate Worlds or Histories.

AIKEN, Joan. *Smoke from Cromwell's Time and Other Stories*. See Chapter 3, Fantasy Collections.

AINSWORTH, Ruth. *The Bear Who Liked Hugging People and Other Stories*. See Chapter 3, Fantasy Collections.

ALCOCK, Vivian. *The Haunting of Cassie Palmer*. See Chapter 4, Ghost Fantasy.

ALEXANDER, Lloyd. *The Cat Who Wished to Be a Man*. See Section 2B, Talking Animal Fantasy.

ALEXANDER, Lloyd. *The Marvelous Misadventures of Sebastian*. See Section 5A, Alternate Worlds or Histories.

C [R] ALEXANDER, Lloyd (Chudley). *The Wizard in the Tree*. Gr. 4–6.
A firm belief in magic helps Mallory, an overworked, orphaned servant girl, to release a crotchety old wizard from imprisonment in an oak tree. (BL 71:813; CC:425; CCBB 28:173; Ch&Bks:263; HB 51:377; KR 43:451; SLJ May 1975 pp. 34, 45; Suth 2:9)
Illus. by Laszlo Kubinyi, Dutton, 1975, 160 pp.; Dell, 1981, pap.

ANDERSEN, Hans Christian. *The Snow Queen*. See Chapter 1, Allegorical Fantasy and Literary Fairy Tales.

ANTHONY, Piers. *A Spell for Chameleon.* See Section 5A, Alternate Worlds or Histories.

YA ASPRIN, Robert L(ynn). *Hit or Myth* (Myth Adventure series, book 4). Gr. 10 up.
In this, the fourth book of Asprin's pun-filled Myth Adventure series, Skeeve, a bumbling apprentice wizard, is left without the aid of his demon-mentor Aahz to fight off numerous magical enemies. The other books in the series are: *Another Fine Myth* (1978), *Myth Conceptions* (1980), *Myth Directions* (1982, 1986), *Myth-ing Persons* (1984), *Little Myth Marker* (1985, 1987), *M.Y.T.H. Inc. Link* (1986), and *Myth-Nomers and Im-Perfections* (1987). (BL 80:715; LJ 108:2174)
Ed. by Kay Reynolds, Donning, 1983, hb and pap., 172 pp.; Ace, 1986, pap.

AVI. *Bright Shadow.* See Section 5A, Alternate Worlds or Histories.

BACON, Peggy. *The Magic Touch.* See Chapter 7, Magic Adventure Fantasy.

YA BATO, Joseph. *The Sorcerer.* Gr. 7–10.
Cro-Magnon Ao'h's sorcery brings him power, but eventually causes his downfall. (BL 73:890, 893; HB 53:165; KR 44:1174; SLJ Nov 1976 p. 65)
Ed. by Katherine Donnelly, illus. by the author, McKay, 1976, 171 pp., o.p.

BAUM, L. Frank. *The Sea Fairies.* See Section 5C, Travel to Other Worlds.

BAUM, L. Frank. *The Wizard of Oz.* See Section 5C, Travel to Other Worlds.

C BAXTER, Caroline. *The Stolen Telesm.* Gr. 4–6 (Orig. British pub. 1975.)
David and Lucy escape on a winged colt from the evil magic of Marada the sorceress. (KR 44:794; SLJ Oct 1976 p. 104; TLS 1975 p. 1457)
Lippincott, 1976, 192 pp., o.p.

C/YA BAXTER, Lorna. *The Eggchild.* Gr. 5–7. (Orig. British pub. 1978.)
Two children with magic powers try to rescue a baby who can transform itself into a glowing egg, from Doppel the Enchanter. (BL 76:663; CCBB 33:126; KR 47:1325; SLJ Jan 1980 p. 65; TLS 1978 p. 1089)
Dutton, 1979, 157 pp., o.p.

C BEACHCROFT, Nina. *Well Met by Witchlight.* Gr. 4–6. (Orig. British pub. 1972.)
Three children help a good witch fight the evil power of Mrs. Black. (BL 70:595; KR 41:1199; LJ 99:205)
Atheneum, 1973, 137 pp., o.p.

BEAGLE, Peter S. *The Folk of the Air.* See Section 5B, Myth Fantasy.

C/YA BEDARD, Michael. *A Darker Magic.* Gr. 6–9.
[R] Emily and her elderly teacher, Miss Potts, attempt to thwart the evil plans of Professor Mephisto, whose magic show was responsible for the death of one of Miss Potts's friends, back in 1936. (BL 84:59; CCBB 41:2; KR 55:1235; SLJ Sept 1987 p. 177; VOYA 10:242)
Atheneum, 1987, 208 pp.

BEHN, Harry. *The Faraway Lurs*. See Chapter 1, Allegorical Fantasy and Literary Fairy Tales.

YA BELLAIRS, John. *The Face in the Frost*. Gr. 8 up.
Two bumbling wizards search for the powerful being causing eerie dreams, terrifiying gray shadows, and frost faces on the windows of their land. (BL 65:1209; KR 36:1395; LJ 94:776; Tymn:51)
Illus. by Marilyn Fitschen, Macmillan, 1969, o.p.; Ace, 1986, pap., 112 pp.

BELLAIRS, John. *The House with a Clock in Its Walls*. See Chapter 4, Ghost Fantasy.

BENARY-ISBERT, Margot. *The Wicked Enchantment*. See Chapter 1, Allegorical Fantasy and Literary Fairy Tales.

C [R] BENNETT, Anna Elizabeth. *Little Witch*. Gr. 3–5.
Even though she can perform all kinds of exciting and unusual feats, Miniken does not want to be a witch. She wants to go to school like a real little girl. (CC:434; CCBB 7:51; HB 29:356; LJ 78:1855)
Illus. by Helen Stone, Lippincott, 1953, 127 pp., 1981, pap.

BERESFORD, Elizabeth. *Travelling Magic*. See Chapter 8, Time Travel Fantasy.

BOMANS, Godfried. *The Wily Witch and All the Other Fairy Tales and Fables*. See Chapter 3, Fantasy Collections.

BOSTON, L. M. *An Enemy at Green Knowe* (see discussion under *The Children of Green Knowe*). See Chapter 4, Ghost Fantasy.

BOYER, Elizabeth H. *The Troll's Grindstone*. See Section 5C, Travel to Other Worlds.

YA [R] BRADBURY, Ray (Douglas). *Something Wicked This Way Comes*. Gr. 8 up.
Two boys attending a carnival freak show become the targets of an evil magician who imprisons them in the Wax Museum. (BL 59:163; Kies:12; SHC:580; TLS 1963 p. 189)
Simon, 1962, 317 pp., o.p.; Bantam, pap.; Knopf, 1983.

BRADLEY, Marion Zimmer. *The Mists of Avalon*. See Section 5B, Myth Fantasy.

YA BRADLEY, Marion Zimmer, and McINTYRE, Vonda. *Lythande*. Gr. 10 up.
Six tales about the journeys of the magician Lythande. (BL 82:1667; VOYA 9:290)
NAL/DAW, 1986, pap., 240 pp.

BRIGGS, K. M. *Hobberdy Dick*. See Section 5B, Myth Fantasy.

BRIN, David. *The Practice Effect*. See Section 5C, Travel to Other Worlds.

C [R] BRITTAIN, Bill (William). *The Devil's Donkey*. Gr. 3–6.
Turned into a donkey by Old Magda for stealing wood from the witches' tree, Dan'l must confront the devil himself to be freed of the curse. *The Wish Giver: Three Tales of Coven Tree* (1983) and *Dr. Dredd's Wagon of Wonders* (1987, see Chapter 1, Allegorical Fantasy and Literary Fairy Tales) are re-

lated works. (BL 77:1097; CC:439; HB 57:420; KR 49:503; SLJ Mar 1981 p. 141, May 1981 p. 23)
Illus. by Andrew Glass, Harper, 1981, 120 pp., 1982, pap.

YA BROWN, Mary. *The Unlikely Ones*. Gr. 10 up.
Seven human and animal companions, all under a witch's curse, set out to break their enchantment. (BL 83:191, 217; KR 54:1223; LJ Oct 15, 1986 p. 114)
McGraw-Hill, 1986, 425 pp.; Baen, 1987, pap.

BUCHWALD, Emilie. *Gildaen: The Heroic Adventures of a Most Unusual Rabbit*. See Chapter 1, Allegorical Fantasy and Literary Fairy Tales.

C [R] BYFIELD, Barbara Ninde. *Andrew and the Alchemist*. Gr. 4–6.
Andrew's "easy" job as apprentice to an alchemist goes wrong after he is accused of misusing his power to steal the king's treasure. (BL 73:128; CCBB 30:172; HB 53:312; KR 44:1264; SLJ Jan 1977 p. 88; Suth 2:71)
Illus. by Deanne Hollinger, Doubleday, 1976, 129 pp., o.p.

CALHOUN, Mary. *Magic in the Alley*. See Chapter 7, Magic Adventure Fantasy.

CARD, Orson Scott. *Hart's Hope*. See Section 5A, Alternate Worlds or Histories.

CARD, Orson Scott. *Seventh Son*. See Section 5A, Alternate Worlds or Histories.

CARLYON, Richard. *The Dark Lord of Pengersick*. See Section 5A, Alternate Worlds or Histories.

CARPENTER, Christopher. *The Twilight Realm*. See Section 5C, Travel to Other Worlds.

CAYLUS, Anne Claude Philippe, Comte de. *Heart of Ice*. See Chapter 1, Allegorical Fantasy and Literary Fairy Tales.

CHANT, Joy. *Red Moon and Black Mountain: The End of the House of Kendreth*. See Section 5C, Travel to Other Worlds.

CHAPMAN, Vera. *The Green Knight*. See Section 5B, Myth Fantasy.

C/YA CHARNAS, Suzy McKee. *The Bronze King*. Gr. 5–8.
An elderly man with magical powers needs Tina and Joel's help to defeat a monster hiding in the depths of Manhattan's subway system. The sequel is *The Silver Glove* (Bantam, 1988). (CCBB 39:82; KR 53:1087; SLJ Nov 1985 p. 94)
Houghton, 1985; Bantam, 1987, pap., 208 pp.

C/YA CHASE, Mary (Coyle). *Mrs. McThing: A Play*. Gr. 5 up.
[R] A witch punishes a wealthy woman who objected to her son's friendship with the witch's daughter. (BL 49:101, 111; CCBB 6:37; HB 28:310, 418; LJ 77:1814)
Illus. by Madeleine Gekiere and Helen Sewell, Oxford, 1952, 141 pp., o.p.

CHESNUTT, Charles W. *Conjure Tales*. See Chapter 3, Fantasy Collections.

CHETWIN, Grace. *Gom on Windy Mountain*. See Section 5A, Alternate Worlds or Histories.

C CHEW, Ruth (Silver). *No Such Thing as a Witch*. Gr. 2–4. (Orig. pub. Scholastic, 1972, pap.)
Fudge made by Nora and Tad's neighbor, Maggie, turns people into animals. (CCBB 33:168; SLJ May 1980 p. 52)
Illus. by the author, Hastings, 1980, 112 pp.; Scholastic, 1986, pap.

C COLE, Joanna. *Bony-Legs*. Gr. 1–4.
Sasha uses a magical mirror and comb to escape from Bony-Legs, the witch with the iron teeth, in this adaptation of a Russian Baba Yaga tale. (CCBB 37:123; HB 60:47; SLJ Dec 1983 p. 79)
Illus. by Dirk Zimmer, Four Winds, 1983, 44 pp.

C [R] COLE, Joanna. *Doctor Change*. Gr. K–4.
Young Tom learns the tricks of magical transformation in order to escape from his mysterious employer, Doctor Change. (BL 83:127; CCBB 40:46; HB 62:730; KR 54:934; SLJ Oct 86 p. 158)
Illus. by Donald Carrick, Morrow, 1986, 32 pp.

C [R] COLUM, Padraic. *The Boy Apprenticed to an Enchanter*. Gr. 4–6. (Orig. pub. 1920.)
Merlin the magician and a girl called Bird of Gold help Eean escape from a wicked enchanter. (BL 63:493; HB 42:708; LJ 92:333; Mahony 1:39; Tymn: 67)
Illus. by Edward Leight, Macmillan, 1966, 150 pp., o.p.

COLUM, Padraic. *The Stone of Victory and Other Tales*. See Chapter 3, Fantasy Collections.

COOK, Glen. *Doomstalker*. See Section 2A, Beast Tales.

YA COOK, Hugh. *The Wizards and the Warriors* (Chronicles of an Age of Darkness, no. 1). Gr. 10 up. (Orig. pub. in New Zealand, 1986.)
Miphon and the other members of the Confederation of Wizards form an uneasy alliance with their ancient enemies, the Warriors of Rovac, to battle a renegade sorcerer threatening to end the world. The sequel is *The Wordsmiths and the Warguild* (1988). (BL 83:1252, 1273; LJ Apr 15, 1987 p. 102)
Smyth, dist. by Dufour, 1987, 351 pp.

C [R] COOMBS, Patricia. *Dorrie and the Blue Witch*. Gr. 2–4.
Shrinking powder enables young Dorrie witch to capture the bad blue witch and win first prize for witch-catching. Other titles in this series are *Dorrie's Magic* (1962), *Dorrie's Play* (1965), *Dorrie and the Weather-Box* (1966), *Dorrie and the Witch Doctor* 1967), *Dorrie and the Wizard's Spell* (1968), *Dorrie and the Haunted House* (1970), *Dorrie and the Birthday Eggs* (1971), *Dorrie and the Goblin* (1972), *Dorrie and the Fortune Teller* (1973), *Dorrie and the Amazing Magic Elixir* (1974), *Dorrie and the Witch's Imp* (1975), *Dorrie and the Halloween Plot* (1976), *Dorrie and the Dreamyard Monsters* (1977), *Dorrie and the Screebit Ghost* (1979), *Dorrie and the Witchville Fair* (1980), and *Dorrie and the Witches' Camp* (1983). (BL 61:217; CCBB 18:51; HB 40:488; KR 32:595; LJ 89:3458)
Illus. by the author, Lothrop, 1964, o.p.; Dell, 1980, pap., 48 pp.

C CORBETT, Scott. *The Great Custard Pie Panic*. Gr. 2–4.
Nick thwarts Dr. Merlin's diabolical plot to use Nick's dog's brain to create the smartest dog in the world. This is the sequel to *Dr. Merlin's Magic Shop*

(1973) and is followed by *The Foolish Dinosaur Fiasco* (1978). (BL 70:1252; CCBB 28:26; KR 42:580)

Illus. by Joseph Mathieu, Little, 1974, 47 pp., o.p.

CURLEY, Daniel. *Billy Beg and the Bull.* See Section 5B, Myth Fantasy.

CURRY, Jane Louise. *The Sleepers.* See Section 5B, Myth Fantasy.

C [R] DAHL, Roald. *The Witches.* Gr. 4–6.

A boy and his grandmother thwart the plans of England's witches to turn all children into mice. (BL 80:567; CC:458; CCBB 37:105; HB 60:194; KR 51:190; SLJ Jan 1984 p. 74)

Illus. by Quentin Blake, Farrar, 1983, 202 pp.; Penguin/Puffin, 1985, pap.

DAWSON, Carley. *Mr. Wicker's Window.* See Chapter 8, Time Travel Fantasy.

DIAMOND, Donna, adapt. *Swan Lake.* See Chapter 1, Allegorical Fantasy and Literary Fairy Tales.

DICKINSON, Peter. *The Weathermonger.* See Section 5A, Alternate Worlds or Histories.

C DILLON, Barbara. *What's Happened to Harry?* Gr. 3–5.

A mischievous witch captures Harry on Halloween, changes him into a poodle, and takes over his real body. (BL 78:1255; CCBB 36:7; HB 58:399; SLJ Aug 1982, p. 114)

Illus. by Chris Conover, Morrow, 1982, 125 pp.

YA DOUGLAS, Carole Nelson. *Exiles of the Rynth.* Gr. 10 up.

Propelled through a magic gate into the Rynth, Irissa, the last of the Torloc sorceresses, is captured by the wizard Sofistron, and her lover, Kendric, joins a band of outlaws. This is the sequel to *Six of Swords* (1982) and is followed by *Keepers of Edanvant* (Tor, 1987). The latter book also begins a new trilogy about Irissa and Kendric, called Sword and Circlet. Book 2 of this trilogy is *Heir of Rengarth* (1988). (BL 80:1586, 1608; LJ 109:1253)

Ballantine/Del Rey, 1984, pap., 343 pp.

YA DUANE, Diane (Elizabeth). *The Door into Fire* (The Epic Tales of the Five series, book 1). Gr. 10 up.

Herewiss Hearn's son, a young sorcerer, has difficulty controlling the extra portion of Fire within him, until the Goddess helps him to better understand himself. *The Door into Shadow* (Bluejay, 1984) is the first of a number of projected sequels. (BL 75:1482; VOYA 2[Oct 1979]:58)

Dell, 1979, o.p.; Tor, dist. by Warner & St. Martin, 1985, 304 pp., pap.

C/YA DUANE, Diane (Elizabeth). *So You Want to Be a Wizard.* Gr. 5–8.
[R] Two novice wizards, Nita and Kit, journey into a frightening alternate Manhattan full of evil machines and terrified people, where they attempt to fight the powers of darkness who are destroying the world. The sequel is *Deep Wizardry* (1985). *Dragons and Dreams* (Harper, 1986, see Chapter 7, Magic Adventure Fantasy) contains a related story. (CCBB 37:106; HB 59:716; JHC:366; Kliatt 18[Fall 1984]:26; SLJ Jan 1984 p. 74; VOYA 6:342)

Delacorte, 1983, 226 pp.; Dell, pap., 1986

YA DUNSANY, Lord (pseud. of Edward John Morton Drax Plunkett). *The Charwoman's Shadow.* Gr. 10 up.

Having sold his shadow to the Magician in exchange for the magical secrets

needed to create a dowry and a love potion for his sister, Ramon attempts to use his new-found knowledge to regain his shadow and that of the Magician's kindly charwoman. (BL 23:38; TLS 1926 p. 262; Tymn:79)
Putnam, 1926, 294 pp., o.p.

YA EDDINGS, David. *Queen of Sorcery* (The Belgariad Saga, book 2). Gr. 10 up.
A Sorcerer, his daughter, and a young wizard struggle to keep the Orb of Aldur from being used to revive an evil god. This book is preceded by *Pawn of Prophecy* (1982, 1984), and followed by *Magician's Gambit* (1983, 1984), *Castle of Wizardry* (1984), and *Enchanter's End Game* (1984). This series is related to the Mallorean series, which begins with *Guardians of the West* (1987). (BL 79:714; Kliatt 17[Winter 1983]:17; SLJ Jan 1983 p. 90)
Ballantine/Del Rey, 1982, 1985, pap., 327 pp.

C EDMONDSON, Madeline. *Anna Witch*. Gr. 2–4.
Angry at her mother's disappointment in her daughter's lack of magical prowess, Anna surprises herself by turning her mother into a frog. (BL 79:608; CCBB 36:24; SLJ Dec 1982 p. 64)
Illus. by William Pène Du Bois, Doubleday, 1982, 88 pp., o.p.

C EDMONDSON, Madeline. *The Witch's Egg*. Gr. 2–4.
A crabby witch named Agatha who is living in an abandoned eagle's nest becomes the foster mother of a baby bird. (BL 70:939; KR 42:182; LJ 99:1465)
Illus. by Kay Chorao, Seabury, 1974, o.p.; Dell, 1976, pap.

C/YA EDWARDS, Dorothy (Brown). *The Witches and the Grinnygog*. Gr. 5–7. (Orig. British pub. 1981.)
Seven children who uncover the history of the last three witches to live in their village, bring the old magic to life in time for the Midsummer's Eve festival. (BL 79:1400; CCBB 37:47; KR 51:4; SLJ Sept 1983 p. 132)
Faber, dist. by Harper, 1983, 176 pp.

EISENSTEIN, Phyllis. *Sorcerer's Son*. See Section 5A, Alternate Worlds or Histories.

ELGIN, Suzette Haden. *Twelve Fair Kingdoms*. See Section 5A, Alternate Worlds or Histories.

C [R] EMBRY, Margaret (Jacob). *The Blue-Nosed Witch*. Gr. 2–4.
On her way to the witches' Halloween flight meeting, a young witch named Blanche joins a group of trick-or-treating children. (BL 53:154; CC:463; CCBB 11:23; HB 32:366, 63:495; KR 24:514; LJ 81:2720)
Illus. by Carl Rose, Holiday, 1956, 45 pp.; Bantam, 1986, pap.

ERWIN, Betty K. *Aggie, Maggie and Tish*. See Chapter 7, Magic Adventure Fantasy.

C [R] ESTES, Eleanor. *The Witch Family*. Gr. 3–5.
Two girls drawing witches are amazed when their drawings come to life. Amy has another magic adventure in *The Curious Adventures of Jimmy McGee* (1987). (BL 57:329; CC:464; CCBB 14:57; Ch&Bks:266; HB 36:395; KR 28:817; LJ 85:4558; TLS 1962 p. 393)
Illus. by Edward Ardizzone, Harcourt, 1960, 186 pp., 1975, pap.

FARTHING, Alison. *The Mystical Beast.* See Section 5C, Travel to Other Worlds.

FEIST, Raymond E. *Silverthorn.* See Section 5A, Alternate Worlds or Histories.

C [R] FLEISCHMAN, Paul (Taylor). *The Half-a-Moon Inn.* Gr. 4–6.
Sinister Miss Grackle, thieving innkeeper and dream reader, holds a mute boy named Aaron prisoner after he wanders away from home in search of his mother. (BL 76:1531; CC:467; HB 56:294; KR 48:513; SLJ Oct 1980 p. 145)
Illus. by Kathy Jacobi, Harper, 1980, 88 pp.

FLORA, James. *Grandpa's Ghost Stories.* See Chapter 4, Ghost Fantasy.

C FLORA, James (Royer). *Wanda and the Bumbly Wizard.* Gr. 2–4.
An inept wizard and an orphaned girl named Wanda tame a giant and save the queen's castle. (BL 76:1056; KR 48:511; SLJ Mar 1980 p. 120)
Illus. by the author, Atheneum, 1980, 32 pp., o.p.

FREEMAN, Barbara C. *Broom-Adelaide.* See Chapter 1, Allegorical Fantasy and Literary Fairy Tales.

C FROMAN, Elizabeth Hult. *Eba, the Absent-Minded Witch.* Gr. 3–5.
Eba the witch is so absent-minded that she has forgotten how to fly. (CCBB 20:24; HB 41:491; KR 33:824; LJ 90:5514; TLS 1968 p. 256)
Illus. by Dorothy Maas, World, 1965, 64 pp., o.p.

C/YA FURLONG, Monica (Navis). *Wise Child.* Gr. 6–8. (Orig. British pub.
[R] 1987.)
Wise Child, a headstrong young orphan, is taken in by Juniper, a mysterious healer, who teaches the girl the arts of witchcraft. (BL 84:632, 1276; CCBB 41:116; HB 64:206; KR 55:1461; SLJ Sept 1987 p. 195; TLS 1987 p. 964)
Knopf, 1987, 228 pp.

YA [R] GARD, Joyce (pseud. of Joyce Reeves). *The Mermaid's Daughter.* Gr. 7–9.
Astria, High Priestess of a mystical cult of woman worshippers, travels from the Scilly Islands to Britain to defeat a Roman plot to destroy her cult. (BL 66:564; CCBB 23:176; HB 46:166; LJ 95:1202; Suth:139; TLS 1969 p. 690)
Holt, 1969, 319 pp., o.p.

GARNER, Alan. *The Weirdstone of Brisingamen.* See Section 5B, Myth Fantasy.

YA GILLILAND, Alexis A(rnaldus). *Wizenbeak.* Gr. 10 up.
Wizard Wizenbeak, sent into the outlands to establish a new settlement, is asked by the Witch-Queen Shaia to protect her two children from their royal half-brother, and to help them take control of the throne of Cymdulock. The sequel is *The Shadow Shaia* (1987). (BL 82:1361, 1388; KR 54:587; VOYA 9:237)
Bluejay, 1986, 288 pp.

GILMAN, Dorothy. *The Maze in the Heart of the Castle.* See Section 5C, Travel to Other Worlds.

GLOSS, Molly. *Outside the Gates.* See Section 5A, Alternate Worlds or Histories.

GOLDSTEIN, Lisa. *The Red Magician.* See Chapter 1, Allegorical Fantasy and Literary Fairy Tales.

GORDON, John. *The Edge of the World.* See Section 5C, Travel to Other Worlds.

GORDON, John. *The Giant under the Snow.* See Section 5B, Myth Fantasy.

GOUDGE, Elizabeth. *Linnets and Valerians.* See Chapter 7, Magic Adventure Fantasy.

GRAY, Nicholas Stuart. *Mainly in Moonlight: Ten Stories of Sorcery and the Supernatural.* See Chapter 3, Fantasy Collections.

GREEN, Kathleen. *Philip and the Pooka and Other Irish Fairy Tales.* See Chapter 3, Fantasy Collections.

GREEN, Phyllis, *Eating Ice Cream with a Werewolf.* See Chapter 7, Magic Adventure Fantasy.

C/YA GREEN, Roger Lancelyn. *A Cavalcade of Magicians* (British title: *A*
[R]   *Book of Magicians,* 1973). Gr. 5–7.
       Legends, folktales, and original tales about magic and magicians, including "The Sorcerer's Apprentice" and the story of Merlin. (BL 70:291; HB 49:461; KR 41:645; LJ 98:2664; TLS 1973 p. 1115)
       Illus. by Victor Ambrus, Walck, 1973, 274 pp., o.p.

GRIPE, Maria. *The Glassblower's Children.* See Chapter 1, Allegorical Fantasy and Literary Fairytales.

C/YA HAHN, Mary Downing. *The Time of the Witch.* Gr. 5–7.
[R]   Laura convinces an old woman with witch powers to cast a spell that will reunite her parents, but the spell goes wrong and makes Laura's younger brother very ill. (BL 79:311; HB 59:44; JHC:374; SLJ Nov 1982 p. 84)
       Clarion, dist. by Ticknor and Fields, 1982, 162 pp.

C   HALDANE, J(ohn) B(urdon) S(anderson). *My Friend Mr. Leakey.* Gr. 3–5. (Orig. British pub. 1937.)
       A collection of eerie tales, many of which concern a magician named Mr. Leakey. (HB 14:382)
       Illus. by L. H. Rosoman, Harper, 1938, 179 pp., o.p.

HALDEMAN, Linda. *The Lastborn of Elvinwood.* See Section 5B, Myth Fantasy.

YA   HAMBLY, Barbara. *Dragonsbane.* Gr. 10 up.
[O]   Mage Jenny Waynest unites her powers with those of the Black Dragon that her lover, John Aversin, has pledged to destroy, in order to defeat an evil sorceress threatening the kingdom. (BL 82:851, 860, 83:777, 1118; LJ Feb 15, 1986 p. 196, SLJ Sept 1986 p. 152; VOYA 9:162, 10:21)
       Ballantine, 1986, pap., 341 pp.

HAMBLY, Barbara. *The Ladies of Mandrigyn.* See Section 5A, Alternate Worlds or Histories.

HAMBLY, Barbara. *The Silent Tower.* See Section 5C, Travel to Other Worlds.

HANSEN, Ron. *The Shadowmaker.* See Chapter 7, Magic Adventure Fantasy.

YA HARDY, Lyndon. *Secret of the Sixth Magic.* Gr. 10 up.
A bumbling apprentice magician, attempting to master the five magics that govern his world, stumbles upon a demonic sixth magic controlled by the evil Melazar. This is the sequel to *Master of the Five Magics* (1980). (BL 81:25, 58; LJ 109:1776; SLJ Jan 1985 p. 92)
Ballantine/Del Rey, 1984, pap., 384 pp.

YA [R] HARRIS, Deborah Turner. *The Burning Stone* (Mages of Garillon, book 1). Gr. 10 up.
Young Carodoc Penlluathe seeks revenge against Borthen Berigeld, the man responsible for expelling the young mage from his order. The sequel is *The Gauntlet of Malace* (1988). (BL 83:1097, 1116; Kliatt 21[Spring 1987]:22; SLJ Sept 1987 p. 204; VOYA 10:90; 11:12)
Tor, dist. by St. Martin, 1987, pap., 307 pp.

YA *Hecate's Cauldron.* Ed. by Susan M. Shwartz. Gr. 10 up.
An anthology of fantasy stories based on European, African, and Japanese tales of witchcraft, written by Katherine Kurtz, C. J. Cherryh, Tanith Lee, and Andre Norton, among others. (BL 78:1299, 1307; Kliatt 16[Spring 1982]:29; VOYA 5[Aug 1982]:39)
NAL/DAW, 1982, pap., 256 pp., o.p.

HEWETT, Anita. *The Bull beneath the Walnut Tree and Other Stories.* See Chapter 3, Fantasy Collections.

HILL, Douglas. *Blade of the Poisoner.* See Section 5A, Alternate Worlds or Histories.

HILL, Elizabeth Starr. *Ever-After Island.* See Chapter 7, Magic Adventure Fantasy.

HOFFMANN, Eleanor. *Mischief in Fez.* See Chapter 7, Magic Adventure Fantasy.

C [R] HOLMAN (Valen), Felice. *The Witch on the Corner.* Gr. 3–5.
Miss Pinchon tries to fly on a broomstick, but realizes that her magic is meant for gardening. (CCBB 20:108; KR 34:1101; LJ 92:335; TLS 1967 p. 1133)
Illus. by Arnold Lobel, Norton, 1966, 88 pp., o.p.

HOOKS, William H. *Moss Gown.* See Chapter 1, Allegorical Fantasy and Literary Fairy Tales.

HOPP, Zinken. *The Magic Chalk.* See Chapter 7, Magic Adventure Fantasy.

C HORWITZ, Elinor Lander. *The Strange Story of the Frog Who Became a Prince.* Gr. 1–4.
A witch changes a happy frog into a prince and can neither understand his dissatisfaction, nor remember how to change him back. (HB 47:282; KR 39:428; LJ 96:2906)
Illus. by John Heinly, Delacorte, 1971, 45 pp., o.p.

HOUGH, Charlotte. *Red Biddy and Other Stories.* See Chapter 3, Fantasy Collections.

YA HOUSTON, James A(rchibald). *Spirit Wrestler.* Gr. 10 up.
Shoonah, an orphaned Eskimo boy, longs to become a hunter and lead a normal life, rather than follow in his adoptive mother's footsteps and become the tribal shaman. (BL 76:700, 713; Kies:38; KR 47:1342, 1382; LJ 10:120) Harcourt, 1980; Avon, 1981, pap., 288 pp.

C [R] HOWARD, Joan (pseud. of Patricia Gordon). *The Witch of Scrapfaggot Green.* Gr. 3–5.
A witch's ghost brings trouble to a small English village. (BL 44:228; CCBB 1[May 1948]:2; HB 24:191; KR 16:49; LJ 73:609, 657) Illus. by William Pène Du Bois, Viking, 1948, 78 pp., o.p.

C HUGHES, Frieda. *Getting Rid of Aunt Edna.* Gr. 3–5. (Orig. British title: *Getting Rid of Edna,* 1985.)
Miranda helps her Aunt Agatha, a witch, put a stop to the inept spells cast by her other aunt, Edna. (BL 82:1612; CCBB 39:211; KR 54:715; SLJ Oct 1986 p. 177; TLS Aug 1, 1986 p. 850) Illus. by Ed Levine, Harper, 1986, 74 pp.

HUNTER, Mollie. *The Ferlie.* See Chapter 7, Magic Adventure Fantasy.

HUNTER, Mollie. *The Kelpie's Pearls.* See Chapter 1, Allegorical Fantasy and Literary Fairy Tales.

HUNTER, Mollie. *A Stranger Came Ashore.* See Section 5B, Myth Fantasy.

C [R] HUNTER, Mollie (pseud. of Maureen Mollie Hunter McVeigh McIlwraith). *Thomas and the Warlock.* Gr. 4–6.
Thomas, the village blacksmith, manages to rescue his wife from an angry warlock and drive all of the witches out of the Scottish lowlands. (BL 64:450; CCBB 21:60; HB 43:749, 61:84, 63:492; KR 35:808; LJ 92:3850; Suth:204; TLS 1967 p. 451) Illus. by Joseph Cellini, Funk, 1967, o.p.; Peter Smith, 1986, 128 pp.

C [R] HUNTER, Mollie (pseud. of Maureen Mollie Hunter McVeigh McIlwraith). *The Walking Stones: A Story of Suspense* (British title: *The Bodach,* 1970). Gr. 4–6.
An elderly Bodach, or sorcerer, lets Donald Campbell take over his magical powers in order to save his stone circle from the waters of a new hydroelectric plant. (BL 67:228; CCBB 24:157; Ch&Bks:268; HB 47:51; KR 38:800; LJ 95:4375; Suth:204; TLS 1970 p. 1251) Illus. by Trina Schart Hyman, Harper, 1970, 143 pp., o.p.

IPCAR, Dahlov (Zorach). *The Queen of Spells.* See Section 5B, Myth Fantasy.

C/YA IPCAR, Dahlov (Zorach). *The Warlock of Night.* Gr. 5–7.
A young apprentice to the dreaded Warlock of the Land of Night tries to use magic to save his country. (KR 37:1195; LJ 95:789, 1911) Viking, 1969, 159 pp., o.p.

JOHNSON, Dorothy M. *Witch Princess.* See Section 5B, Myth Fantasy.

C/YA JONES, Diana Wynne. *Archer's Goon.* Gr. 6–9.
[O] Howard Sykes and his sister, Awful, are determined to discover how their

father's writings have kept the mysterious and powerful Archer from leaving their town to rule the world. (BL 80:1060; CCBB 37:167; Ch&Bks:268; HB 60:202; JHC:385; SLJ Mar 1984 p. 160; Suth 3:220; TLS 1984 p. 1198; VOYA 7:101)
Greenwillow, 1984, 241 pp.; Berkley, 1987, pap.

JONES, Diana Wynne. *A Charmed Life.* See Chapter 8, Time Travel Fantasy.

YA JONES, Diana Wynne. *Fire and Hemlock.* Gr. 7–12.
[O]   When Polly's vague memories of the year that she was ten and first met Thomas Lynn become clearer, she is horrified to realize that someone has erased Tom's existence from both her memory and that of the world at large, and that his life is in her hands. (BL 81:300, 307; CCBB 38:68; HB 61:58; JHC 1986 Suppl. p. 66; Kies:85; SLJ Oct 1984 p. 167; Suth 3:221; VOYA 7:266, 8:365)
Greenwillow, 1984; Berkley, 1986, pap., 228 pp.

YA JONES, Diana Wynne. *Howl's Moving Castle.* Gr. 7–12.
[O]   After a witch turns Sophie into an old woman, she moves into Wizard Howl's moving castle and attempts to tame him, even as she is falling in love with him. (BL 82:1455, 1461, 83:777, 1118, 1138, 1274, 1592; CC 1987 Suppl. p. 59; CCBB 39:187; HB 62:331; JHC 1987 Suppl. p. 70; KR 54:868; SLJ Aug 1986 p. 101, Apr 1987 p. 48; TLS 1986 p. 1410)
Greenwillow, 1986, 212 pp.

C/YA JONES, Diana Wynne. *The Magicians of Caprona.* Gr. 5–7.
[R]   When an evil enchantress tries to destroy Caprona by dividing its two families of magicians, two young children and the wizard, Chrestomanci, join forces to defeat her. This book is related to *A Charmed Life* (1978), *Witch Week* (1982) and *The Lives of Christopher Chant* (1988), which is a prequel to this story. Two collections contain short stories about Chrestomanci: *Dragons and Dreams* ed. by Jane Yolen (Harper, 1986) and *Warlock at the Wheel* by Diana Wynne Jones (Greenwillow, 1985). (BL 76:1676; CC:490; CCBB 33:216; Ch&Bks:268; HB 56:407; KR 48:1163; SLJ Oct 1980 p. 147; Suth 3:221; TLS 1980 p. 360)
Greenwillow, 1980, 223 pp., o.p.; Ace, pap.

JONES, Diana Wynne. *A Tale of Time City.* See Section 5C, Travel to Other Worlds.

C/YA JONES, Diana Wynne. *Warlock at the Wheel and Other Stories.* Gr. 6–8.
[R]   (Orig. British pub. 1984.)
Eight stories of fantasy and magic, warlocks and wizards, including one about Chrestomanci (see *The Magicians of Caprona*, this chapter). (BL 81:1196; CCBB 38:129; HB 61:453; JHC 1986 Suppl. p. 74; SLJ Apr, 1985 p. 97; TLS 1984 p. 1198; VOYA 8:139)
Greenwillow, 1985, 156 pp.

C/YA JONES, Diana Wynne. *Witch Week.* Gr. 5–7.
[R]   Magical chaos fills Class 6B when a group of witch orphans begins playing magic tricks. This book is related to *A Charmed Life* (1978) and *The Magicians of Caprona* (1980). (BL 79:246; CC:490; CCBB 36:49; Ch&Bks:268; HB 59:44; KR 50:938; SLJ Nov 1982 p. 86; Suth 3:221; TLS 1982 p. 797; VOYA 6:38)
Greenwillow, 1982, 213 pp.

C/YA   JONES, Diana Wynne. *Witch's Business* (British title: *Wilkin's Tooth,*
1973). Gr. 5–7.
Jess and Frank's "revenge business" runs into competition from a nasty
local witch. (KR 42:186; LJ 99:1220; TLS 1973 p. 387)
Dutton, 1974, 168 pp., o.p.

KAY, Guy Gavriel. *The Summer Tree.* See Section 5C, Travel to Other
Worlds.

KELLER, Beverly. *A Small, Elderly Dragon.* See Chapter 1, Allegorical
Fantasy and Literary Fairy Tales.

KELLER, Gottfried. *The Fat of the Cat and Other Stories.* See Chapter 3,
Fantasy Collections.

C/YA   KEMP, Gene. *Mr. Magus Is Waiting for You.* Gr. 4–7.
Four young people's lives are endangered after they enter an ancient house
surrounded by a strangely beautiful garden. (SLJ Sept 1987 p. 180; TLS May
1987 p. 529)
Illus. by Alan Baker, Faber, 1987, hb and pap., 91 pp.

YA [R]   KERR, Katharine. *Daggerspell.* Gr. 10 up.
Nevyn, an ancient sorcerer, who has become immortal in order to right the
wrong he once did to a certain woman, must follow her through several
incarnations. The sequel is *Darkspell* (1987). (BL 82:1667, 1683; KR 54:1071;
LJ Aug 1986 p. 174; VOYA 9:237, 10:21)
Doubleday, 1986, 414 pp.

C [R]   KIMMEL, Margaret Mary. *Magic in the Mist.* Gr. 2–4.
Although he is studying to be a wizard, young Thomas's spells cannot even
warm his own hut until his pet toad, Jeremy, leads him to a tiny dragon. (BL
71:867; CC:493; CCBB 29:28; HB 51:139; KR 43:119; SLJ Apr 1975 p. 46)
Illus. by Trina Schart Hyman, Atheneum, 1975, 31 pp.

C [R]   KOOIKER, Leonie (pseud. of Johanna Maria Kooyker-Romijn). *The
Magic Stone.* Gr. 4–6. (Orig. Dutch pub. 1974.)
Frank's grandmother's magic stone enables his friend, Chris, to control
other people's behavior, but when the witch's association wants the stone
back, she is determined that he keep it. In *Legacy of Magic* (orig. Dutch pub.
1979; U.S. 1981) Chris, now a witch's apprentice, thinks that his friend Alec's
book of magic may help them find buried treasure. (BL 74:1494; CCBB
32:65; Ch&Bks:269; HB 54:396; KR 46:595; SLJ May 1978 p. 68; Suth 2:263)
Tr. by Richard Winston and Clara Winston, illus. by Carl Hollander, Morrow, 1978, 224 pp., o.p.

C/YA   KORTUM, Jeanie. *Ghost Vision.* Gr. 5–8.
A young Greenland Eskimo named Panipaq's visions teach him that he is
becoming an *angakok,* or wise one, with special powers allowing him to see
into other worlds. (BL 80:814; CCBB 37:110; SLJ Jan 1984 p. 78)
Illus. by Dugald Stermer, Sierra Club, dist. by Pantheon, 1983, 143 pp.

KRENSKY, Stephen. *A Big Day for Scepters.* See Chapter 1, Allegorical
Fantasy and Literary Fairy Tales.

KRENSKY, Stephen. *The Dragon Circle.* See Chapter 7, Magic
Adventure Fantasy.

KRENSKY, Stephen. *The Perils of Putney.* See Chapter 1, Allegorical Fantasy and Literary Fairy Tales.

C [R] KUMIN, Maxine (Winokur), and SEXTON, Anne (Harvey). *The Wizard's Tears.* Gr. 1–3.
The new young wizard of Drocknock goes too far with his magical powers and is rescued by the former wizard and a dalmation. (CCBB 29:99; HB 51:587; KR 43:911; SLJ Nov 1975 p. 64, Dec 1975 p. 31; Suth 2:266)
Illus. by Evaline Ness, McGraw-Hill, 1975, 48 pp., o.p.

YA KURTZ, Katherine. *Lammas Night.* Gr. 10 up.
On Lammas night in 1940, a coven of witches gathers to use the "old religion" to keep Hitler from invading England. (BL 80:846, 853; Kies:44)
Ballantine/Del Rey, 1983, pap., 438 pp., o.p.

LARSON, Jean. *The Silkspinners.* See Chapter 1, Allegorical Fantasy and Literary Fairy Tales.

C LAUGHLIN, Florence (Young). *The Little Leftover Witch.* Gr. 2–4.
When Felina witch's broomstick breaks in midair, she falls out of the sky and is stranded on earth for an entire year. (BL 57:362; CCBB 14:82; HB 36:396; KR 28:496; LJ 85:4226; TLS 1967 p. 1153)
Illus. by Sheila Greenwald, Macmillan, 1960, 1971, 107 pp., 1973, pap.

LAWRENCE, Louise. *The Earth Witch.* See Section 5B, Myth Fantasy.

LEACH, Maria. *The Thing at the Foot of the Bed and Other Scary Tales.* See Chapter 4, Ghost Fantasy.

C/YA LEE, Josephine. *Joy Is Not Herself.* Gr. 5–7. (Orig. British pub. 1962.)
Melisanda Montgomery discovers that she is part witch. (HB 39:174; LJ 88:1768; TLS 1962 p. 393)
Illus. by Pat Marriott, Harcourt, 1963, 154 pp., o.p.

LEE, Tanith. *Cyrion.* See Section 5A, Alternate Worlds or Histories.

LEE, Tanith. *The Dragon Hoard.* See Chapter 1, Allegorical Fantasy and Literary Fairy Tales.

LEE, Tanith. *Princess Hynchatti and Some Other Surprises.* See Chapter 1, Allegorical Fantasy and Literary Fairy Tales.

LE GUIN, Ursula K. *A Wizard of Earthsea.* See Section 5A, Alternate Worlds or Histories.

C/YA LEVOY, Myron. *The Magic Hat of Mortimer Wintergreen.* Gr. 4–7.
Orphaned Joshua and Amy Bains are rescued from the clutches of evil Aunt Vootch by the magic hat of Wizard Mortimer Q. Wintergreen. (BL 84:1001; CCBB 41:121; KR 55:1734; SLJ Mar 1988 p. 197)
Illus. by Andrew Glass, Harper, 1988, 224 pp.

LEWIS, C. S. *The Lion, the Witch, and the Wardrobe.* See Section 5C, Travel to Other Worlds.

YA LILLINGTON, Kenneth. *An Ash-Blond Witch.* Gr. 7 up.
A young woman from the twenty-second century "beyond the mountains," arrives in the old-fashioned village of Urstwhile and becomes the rival of the local witch. (BL 83:776, 1274, 1592; KR 55:60)
Faber, dist. by Harper, 1987, 138 pp.

LITTLE, Jane. *The Philosopher's Stone.* See Chapter 8, Time Travel Fantasy.

C LITTLE, Jane. *Sneaker Hill.* Gr. 3–5.
After Matthew's mother, a witch-in-training, forgets to take her owl with her, Matthew and Susan follow her into a magic land. (CCBB 21:29; LJ 92:1738)
Illus. by Nancy Grossman, Atheneum, 1967, 176 pp., o.p.

C LITTLE, Jane. *Spook.* Gr. 3–5.
Grimalda the witch is allergic to cats and tries to make do with a small dog named Spook, but a boy named Jamie wants Spook too. (CCBB 19:35; HB 41:492; LJ 90:3812)
Illus. by Suzanne Larsen, Atheneum, 1965, 110 pp., o.p.

LIVELY, Penelope. *The Ghost of Thomas Kempe.* See Chapter 4, Ghost Fantasy.

LIVELY, Penelope. *The Whispering Knights.* See Section 5B, Myth Fantasy.

YA [R] LLYWELYN, Morgan. *The Horse Goddess.* Gr. 10 up.
Destined from birth to become the Shaman of her father's Celtic tribe, Epona runs away with Kazhak, leader of a nomadic band of horsemen from Asia Minor. (BL 78:1483, 1485; Kies:49; KR 50:818; LJ 107:1170; SLJ Dec 1982 p. 87)
Houghton, 1982; Pocket, 1983, pap., 464 pp.

LOFTING, Hugh. *The Twilight of Magic.* See Chapter 7, Magic Adventure Fantasy.

C LOVEJOY, Jack. *The Rebel Witch.* Gr. 4–6.
A magic wand enables Suzie, an apprentice witch, to enter the witch world of Veneficon to search for her teacher, Madame Mengo. (BL 75:50; KR 46:1248; SLJ Dec 1978 p. 54)
Illus. by Judith Brown, Lothrop/Morrow, 1978, 201 pp., o.p.

LUENN, Nancy. *Arctic Unicorn.* See Chapter 1, Allegorical Fantasy and Literary Fairy Tales.

YA [R] MacAVOY, R(oberta) A(nn). *Damiano.* Gr. 10 up.
Damiano, a fourteenth-century Italian wizard, is forced by marauders to flee with his wise dog, Macchiata. His determination for vengeance leads him on an adventurous quest. The sequels are *Damiano's Lute* (1984) and *Raphael* (1984). (BL 80:1099, 1110; Kies:50; SLJ Nov 1984 p. 146; VOYA 7:101)
Bantam, 1984, pap., 243 pp.

YA MacAVOY, R(oberta) A(nn). *The Grey Horse.* Gr. 10 up.
The Irish village of Carraroe is thrown into turmoil upon the arrival of Ruairi MacEibhir, a faerie in search of the woman he loves. (BL 83:1655, 1672; LJ Apr 15, 1987 p. 103; VOYA 10:179)
Bantam/Spectra, 1987, pap., 247 pp.

MacDONALD, Greville. *Billy Barnicoat: A Fairy Romance for Young and Old.* See Chapter 7, Magic Adventure Fantasy.

C/YA McGOWEN, Tom (Thomas E.). *The Magician's Apprentice.* Gr. 5–7.
[R] A wily street urchin named Tigg is befriended by the magician Armindor,

who takes him to the Wild Lands in search of magical artifacts from an earlier civilization. (BL 83:580, 84:873; CCBB 40:113; KR 54:1649; SLJ Jan 1987 p. 76)
Lodestar/Dutton, 1987, 119 pp.

C [R] McGOWEN, Tom (Thomas E.). *Sir Machinery.* Gr. 3–6.
Merlin the wizard joins forces with a physicist to battle an ancient race of demons bent on taking over the world. (BL 68:367; HB 48:49; KR 39:1071; LJ 96:4191)
Illus. by Trina Schart Hyman, Follett, 1971, 155 pp., o.p.

C/YA MacKELLAR, William. *The Witch of Glen Gowrie.* Gr. 5–7.
Old Meg's ghost keeps everyone but young Gavin Fraser from finding her treasure. (BL 74:1109; CCBB 32:34; SLJ May 1978 p. 85)
Illus. by Ted Lewin, Dodd, 1978, 134 pp., o.p.

McKENZIE, Ellen Kindt. *Taash and the Jesters.* See Section 5A, Alternate Worlds or Histories.

McKILLIP, Patricia A. *The Forgotten Beasts of Eld.* See Section 5A, Alternate Worlds or Histories.

McKILLIP, Patricia A. *The Riddle-Master of Hed.* See Section 5A, Alternate Worlds or Histories.

C MacLACHLAN, Patricia. *Tomorrow's Wizard.* Gr. 3–5.
Tomorrow's Wizard and his apprentice, Murdoch, travel the kingdom solving problems and fulfilling the wishes of the inhabitants. (CC:553; HB 58:290; SLJ Apr 1982 p. 72)
Illus. by Kathy Jacobi, Harper, 1982, 80 pp., o.p.

C [R] McLEOD, Emilie Warren. *Clancy's Witch.* Gr. 2–4.
Clancy's next-door neighbor is a witch. (BL 55:543; Eakin:224; HB 35:131; KR 26:905; LJ 84:1686)
Illus. by Lisl Weil, Little, 1959, 38 pp., o.p.

McNEILL, Janet. *Tom's Tower.* See Section 5C, Travel to Other Worlds.

C [R] MAGUIRE, Gregory. *The Dream Stealer.* Gr. 3–5.
Pasha and Lisette set out to consult the fearsome hag Baba Yaga about their encounter with a Firebird and rumors of a marauding demon wolf called the Blood Prince. (BL 80:299; CC:128; HB 59:576; KR 51:164; SLJ Feb 1984 p. 75)
Harper, 1983, 118 pp.

C/YA MAHY, Margaret (May). *The Changeover: A Supernatural Romance.* Gr.
[O]   6–10. (Orig. pub. in New Zealand.)
Laura Chant must undergo a changeover to become a witch, in order to save the life of her brother Jacko, who has been bewitched by a demon. Carnegie Medal winner, 1985. (BL 81:122, 132; CC:507; CCBB 38:11; Ch&Bks:270; HB 60:764; JHC 1986 Suppl. p. 68; Kies:52; KR 52:81; SLJ Sept 1984 p. 132; Suth 3:292; TLS 1984 p. 794; VOYA 8:50, 364)
Atheneum, 1984; Scholastic/Point, 1985, pap., 256 pp.

C/YA MAHY, Margaret (May). *The Haunting.* Gr. 5–8. (Orig. pub. in New
[O]   Zealand.)
Eight-year-old Barney's frightening messages from a long-lost uncle bring to light a secret family curse. Carnegie Medal winner, 1982. (BL 79:117;

CC:507; CCBB 36:31; Ch&Bks:270; HB 59:46; KR 50:1155; SLJ Aug 1982 p. 119; Suth 3:293; TLS 1982 p. 1001)
Atheneum, 1982; Scholastic, 1984, pap., 144 pp.

MARTIN, Graham Dunstan. *Giftwish.* See Section 5A, Alternate Worlds or Histories.

MASEFIELD, John. *The Midnight Folk: A Novel.* See Chapter 7, Magic Adventure Fantasy.

MAYNE, William. *The Hill Road.* See Chapter 8, Time Travel Fantasy.

C/YA   MIAN, Mary (Lawrence Shipman). *Take Three Witches.* Gr. 6–8.
Three sixth-graders, three witches, and a ghost join forces to prevent their town from spraying bird-killing insecticide. The sequel is *The Net to Catch War* (1975). (HB 47:485; LJ 96:2133)
Illus. by Eric Von Schmidt, Houghton, 1971, 279 pp., o.p.

MONTROSE, Anne. *The Winter Flower and Other Fairy Stories.* See Chapter 3, Fantasy Collections.

MOZART, Wolfgang Amadeus. *The Magic Flute.* See Chapter 1, Allegorical Fantasy and Literary Fairy Tales.

C   MURPHY, Shirley Rousseau. *The Pig Who Could Conjure the Wind.* Gr. 2–4.
Miss Folly, a flying witch pig, rescues the wind demon's victims. (BL 74:1436; HB 54:278; KR 46:239; SLJ Apr 1978 p. 73).
Illus. by Mark Lefkowitz, Atheneum, 1978, 58 pp., o.p.

C   NATHAN, Robert (Gruntal). *The Snowflake and the Starfish.* Gr. 3–4.
A lonely sea-witch takes Vicky and Thomas into the sea with her. (HB 35:478; LJ 84:3930)
Illus. by Leonard Weisgard, Knopf, 1959, 68 pp., o.p.

NESS, Evaline. *The Girl and the Goatherd, or This and That and Thus and So.* See Chapter 1, Allegorical Fantasy and Literary Fairy Tales.

NEWMAN, Robert. *Merlin's Mistake.* See Section 5B, Myth Fantasy.

NEWMAN, Robert. *The Shattered Stone.* See Section 5A, Alternate Worlds or Histories.

YA   NICHOLS, (Joanna) Ruth. *The Left-Handed Spirit.* Gr. 8–10.
Kidnapped by the Chinese ambassador to the Roman Empire, Mariana is expected to use her healing powers to save the life of the ambassador's twin brother. (BL 75:469; CCBB 32:85; KR 46:1254; SLJ Oct 1978 p. 158; VOYA 1[Dec 1978]:43)
Atheneum, 1978, 260 pp., o.p.

NICHOLS, Ruth. *The Marrow of the World.* See Section 5C, Travel to Other Worlds.

NORTON, Andre. *Lavender Green Magic.* See Chapter 8, Time Travel Fantasy.

NORTON, Andre. *Witch World.* See Section 5C, Travel to Other Worlds.

NORTON, Mary. *Bedknob and Broomstick.* See Chapter 7, Magic Adventure Fantasy.

O'HANLON, Jacklyn. *The Door.* See Chapter 5C, Travel to Other Worlds.

YA ORR, A. *The World in Amber.* Gr. 10 up.
Court sorcerer Judah Hila transports complacent King Ambrose and his minstrel son Isme to magical locations, and transforms Queen Maldive into a palace cat, all in an attempt to improve their ability to rule the land of Phar-Tracil. The sequel is *In the Ice King's Palace* (1986). (KR 53:679; VOYA 10:105)
Bluejay, dist. by St. Martin, 1985, 214 pp.; Tor, 1987, pap.

O'SHEA, Pat. *The Hounds of the Morrigan.* See Section 5B, Myth Fantasy.

PALMER, David R. *Threshold.* See Chapter 6, Humourous Fantasy.

PARKER, Edgar. *The Enchantress.* See Chapter 1, Allegorical Fantasy and Literary Fairy Tales.

PARKER, Nancy Winslow. *The Spotted Dog: The Strange Tale of a Witch's Revenge.* See Chapter 6, Humorous Fantasy.

PAYNE, Joan B. *The Piebald Princess.* See Section 2B, Talking Animal Fantasy.

PEET, Bill. *Big Bad Bruce.* See Section 2B, Talking Animal Fantasy.

PEET, Bill. *The Whingdingdilly.* See Section 2B, Talking Animal Fantasy.

PICARD, Barbara Leonie. *The Goldfinch Garden: Seven Tales.* See Chapter 3, Fantasy Collections.

PICARD, Barbara Leonie. *The Mermaid and the Simpleton.* See Chapter 3, Fantasy Collections.

PIERCE, Meredith Ann. *The Darkangel.* See Section 5A, Alternate Worlds or Histories.

PIERCE, Tamora. *Alanna: The First Adventure.* See Section 5A, Alternate Worlds or Histories.

C PLACE, Marian T(empleton). *The Resident Witch.* Gr. 3–5.
Living with her aunt while her mother is away, Witcheena is working hard at becoming a Junior Witch when she makes the mistake of befriending some earthlings. (CCBB 24:65; KR 38:244; LJ 95:2309)
Illus. by Marilyn Miller, Washburn, 1970, 119 pp., o.p.; Avon, 1985, pap.

C PLACE, Marian T(empleton). *The Witch Who Saved Halloween.* Gr. 4–6.
When pollution threatens both witches and humans, Witchard comes up with a plan to save them. (BL 75:306; CCBB 25:1281; KR 39:1072; LJ 97:284)
Illus. by Marilyn Miller, Washburn, 1971, 150 pp., o.p.; Avon, 1985, pap.

POSTMA, Lidia. *The Witch's Garden.* See Chapter 7, Magic Adventure Fantasy.

YA PRANTERA, Amanda. *The Cabalist.* Gr. 10 up. (Orig. British pub. 1985.)
Joseph Kestler, a modern-day Cabalist with a terminal illness, searches for

someone to inherit his magical powers. (BL 82:1663, 1683; KR 54:966; LJ Aug 1986 p. 172; TLS 1985 p. 1266)
Atheneum, 1986, 192 pp.

C [R] PREUSSLER, Otfried. *The Little Witch.* Gr. 3–5. (Orig. pub. in Germany.)
Little Witch plots revenge on the older witches who took away her magic broomstick on Walpurgis Night. (BL 58:450; CCBB 15:84; KR 29:843; LJ 86:4040; TLS May 19, 1961 p. iv)
Tr. by Anthea Bell, illus. by Winnie Gayler, Abelard-Schuman, 1961, 127 pp., o.p.

PREUSSLER, Otfried. *The Robber Hotzenplotz.* See Chapter 6, Humorous Fantasy.

C/YA PREUSSLER, Otfried. *The Satanic Mill.* Gr. 6–9. (Orig. German pub.
[O]   1971; U.S. Macmillan, 1973.)
Krabat thinks he has been apprenticed to a miller, but discovers that the mill is actually a school of black magic run by an evil magician. (BL 69:1073, 70:827, 82:677, 686; CCBB 26:143; Ch&Bks:271; HB 49:147; 61:84, 63:492; KR 41:61, 1351; LJ 98:1398, 1655; Suth 2:369; TLS 1972 p. 1489)
Tr. by Anthea Bell, Peter Smith, 1985, 250 pp.

PRICE, Susan. *The Ghost Drum.* See Chapter 1, Allegorical Fantasy and Literary Fairy Tales.

PUSHKIN, Alexander Sergeevich. *The Golden Cockerel and Other Stories.* See Chapter 3, Fantasy Collections.

C [R] PYLE, Howard. *King Stork.* Gr. 2–4. (Orig. pub. in *The Wonder Clock,* 1887.)
A beautiful but wicked witch is tamed and won by a poor drummer and King Stork's magic. (BL 70:174; CC:131; HB 49:373; KR 41:455; LJ 98:2643)
Illus. by Trina Schart Hyman, Little, 1973, 48 pp., o.p., 1985, pap.

REEVES, James. *The Cold Flame.* See Chapter 1, Allegorical Fantasy and Literary Fairy Tales.

REID, Alastair. *Fairwater.* See Chapter 1, Allegorical Fantasy and Literary Fairy Tales.

REID BANKS, Lynne. *The Farthest-Away Mountain.* See Chapter 1, Allegorical Fantasy and Literary Fairy Tales.

ROACH, Marilynne K. *Encounters with the Invisible World.* See Chapter 3, Fantasy Collections.

YA ROHAN, Michael Scott. *The Anvil of Ice* (Winter of the World trilogy, vol. 1). Gr. 10 up.
A young magesmith defies his master and attempts to use his growing magical powers to battle the evil Ice Age threatening to destroy the world. (KR 54:1330; LJ Oct 15, 1986 p. 112; SLJ Feb 1987 p. 99)
Morrow, 1986, 344 pp.

RUSH, Alison. *The Last of Danu's Children.* See Section 5B, Myth Fantasy.

SABERHAGEN, Fred. *Empire of the East.* See Section 5A, Alternate Worlds or Histories.

SALSITZ, R.A.V. *The Unicorn Dancer.* See Section 5A, Alternate Worlds or Histories.

C SENDAK, Jack. *The Second Witch.* Gr. 3–5.
   Andrew tries to save Vivian, an unpopular witch, from the wrath of the villagers of Platzenhausen, in this story written by Maurice Sendak's brother. (KR 33:751; LJ 90:4620)
   Illus. by Uri Shulevitz, Harper, 1965, 94 pp.

SERVICE, Pamela F. *Winter of Magic's Return.* See Section 5B, Myth Fantasy.

SINGER, Isaac Bashevis. *Alone in the Wild Forest.* See Chapter 1, Allegorical Fantasy and Literary Fairy Tales.

SINGER, Isaac Bashevis. *The Fearsome Inn.* See Chapter 1, Allegorical Fantasy and Literary Fairy Tales.

SLEIGH, Barbara. *Carbonel: The King of the Cats.* See Chapter 7, Magic Adventure Fantasy.

SLEIGH, Barbara. *Stirabout Stories, Brewed in Her Own Cauldron.* See Chapter 3, Fantasy Collections.

C SLOBODKIN, Louis. *The Amiable Giant.* Gr. 1–4.
   A little girl uncovers a wizard's plot to terrify the villagers with lies about a friendly local giant. (BL 52:173; KR 23:784)
   Illus. by the author, Vanguard, 1955, 36 pp.

SMITH, L. J. *Night of the Solstice.* See Section 5C, Travel to Other Worlds.

SMITH, Stephanie A. *Snow-Eyes.* See Section 5A, Alternate Worlds or Histories.

SNYDER, Zilpha Keatley. *The Changing Maze.* See Chapter 1, Allegorical Fantasy and Literary Fairy Tales.

SNYDER, Zilpha Keatley. *A Season of Ponies.* See Chapter 7, Magic Adventure Fantasy.

STASHEFF, Christopher. *Her Majesty's Wizard.* See Section 5C, Travel to Other Worlds.

STEARNS, Pamela. *The Fool and the Dancing Bear.* See Chapter 1, Allegorical Fantasy and Literary Fairy Tales.

STEELE, Mary Q. *The Owl's Kiss: Three Stories.* See Chapter 3, Fantasy Collections.

STEELE, Mary Q. *Wish, Come True.* See Chapter 7, Magic Adventure Fantasy.

STEWART, Mary. *The Crystal Cave.* See Section 5B, Myth Fantasy.

C STEWART, Mary (Florence Elinor). *The Little Broomstick.* Gr. 3–5.
   (Orig. British pub. 1971.)
   Mary goes to witch school to learn enough magic to rescue her black cat. (BL 68:822; CCBB 25:146; HB 48:271; KR 40:5; LJ 97:1610; Suth:382)
   Illus. by Shirley Hughes, Morrow, 1972, 192 pp., o.p.

STEWART, Mary. *A Walk in Wolf Wood.* See Chapter 8, Time Travel Fantasy.

STOCKTON, Frank R. *The Bee-Man of Orn.* See Chapter 1, Allegorical Fantasy and Literary Fairy Tales.

YA STRAUB, Peter (Francis). *Shadowland.* Gr. 10 up.
Tom and Del, two high school students drawn together by an interest in magic, visit Shadowland, home of renowned magician, Coleman Collins, who wants Tom to be his successor in the practice of black magic. (Kies:74; KR 48:1187; LJ 105:2235; SLJ Feb 1981 p. 82; TLS 1981 p. 430)
Coward, 1980, o.p.; Berkley, 1981, 1985, pap., 480 pp.

YA STRUGATSKII, Arkadii Natanovich, and STRUGATSKII, Boris Natanovich. *Monday Begins on Saturday.* Gr. 10 up.
A computer scientist studying witchcraft and magic in a secret laboratory produces a time-traveling sofa, an unspendable coin, a talking cat, and a house on hen's legs, in this satire of Russian scientific research. (BL 74:899, 905; Kliatt 12[Winter 1978]:11)
Tr. by Leonid Renen, DAW, 1977, pap., 220 pp., o.p.

SWAHN, Sven. *The Island through the Gate.* See Section 5C, Travel to Other Worlds.

SYNGE, Ursula. *Land of Heroes: A Retelling of the Kalevala.* See Section 5B, Myth Fantasy.

TENNY, Dixie. *Call the Darkness Down.* See Section 5B, Myth Fantasy.

TEPPER, Sheri S. *Jinian Footseer.* See Section 5A, Alternate Worlds or Histories.

TEPPER, Sheri S. *The Song of Mavin Manyshaped.* See Section 5A, Alternate Worlds or Histories.

TERLOUW, Jan. *How to Become King.* See Chapter 1, Allegorical Fantasy and Literary Fairy Tales.

TOLKIEN, J. R. R. *The Hobbit; or There and Back Again.* See Section 5A, Alternate Worlds or Histories.

TURKLE, Brinton. *Mooncoin Castle; or Skulduggery Rewarded.* See Chapter 4, Ghost Fantasy.

C [R] TURNBULL, Ann (Christine). *The Frightened Forest.* Gr. 4–6. (Orig. British pub. 1974.)
Responsible for releasing a witch from an abandoned tunnel, Gillian and her cousins make a midnight attempt to recapture the malevolent creature. (BL 71:1018; HB 51:385; KR 43:460; SLJ May 1975 p. 59; TLS 1974 p. 714)
Illus. by Gillian Gaze, Seabury, 1975, 125 pp., o.p.

UNWIN, Nora S. *Two Too Many.* See Section 2B, Talking Animal Fantasy.

VAN ALLSBURG, Chris. *The Garden of Abdul Gasazi.* See Chapter 7, Magic Adventure Fantasy.

VANCE, Jack. *Cugel's Saga.* See Section 5A, Alternate Worlds or Histories.

YA [R] VINGE, Joan D(ennison). *Ladyhawke*. Gr. 10 up.
Orphaned Phillipe escapes death in the Bishop's prison and goes into the service of the mysterious Navarre, whose beautiful lover, Isabeau, has been transformed into a hawk by the evil Bishop. (Kies:77; Kliatt 19[Fall 1985]:27; TLS 1985 p. 345; VOYA 8:195)
NAL, 1985, pap., 252 pp., o.p.

C WALLACE, Barbara Brooks. *Miss Switch to the Rescue*. Gr. 3–6.
Miss Switch saves the day after a witch turns Rupert, Amelia, and their entire fifth grade class into toads. This is the sequel to *The Trouble With Miss Switch* (1981). (BL 78:760; SLJ Mar 1982 p. 152)
Illus. by Kathleen Garry McCord, Abingdon, 1981, 158 pp.; Archway, 1982, pap.

WANGERIN, Walter, Jr. *Thistle*. See Chapter 1, Allegorical Fantasy and Literary Fairy Tales.

YA WARNER, Sylvia Townsend. *Lolly Willowes: or, the Loving Huntsman*. Gr. 10 up. (Orig. pub. Viking, 1926, 1928.)
Laura Willowes leads an uneventful, spinsterly life until the age of forty-seven, when she decides to take up witchcraft, and makes a pact with the devil. (BL 22:332, 25:83; Kies:79; TLS 1926 p. 78, 1978 p. 273)
Academy Chicago, 1978, 1979, hb and pap., 252 pp.; Charles River Books, pap.

YA WATT-EVANS, Lawrence (pseud. of Richard Watt Evans). *With a Single Spell*. Gr. 10 up.
An inexperienced wizard's apprentice joins a dragon hunt and comes across a magical tapestry linked to another world. This book is set in the same world as *Misenchanted Sword* (1985). (BL 83:983, 1009; LJ Mar 15, 1987 p. 93)
Del Rey, 1987, pap., 263 pp.

C WEALES, Gerald (Clifford). *Miss Grimsbee Is a Witch*. Gr. 3–5.
Jimmy is the only one who believes that Miss Grimsbee is a real witch. The sequel is *Miss Grimsbee Takes a Vacation* (1965). (BL 53:435; CCBB 10:138; HB 33:140; KR 25:74; LJ 82:884)
Illus. by Lita Scheel, Little, 1957, 123 pp., o.p.

WHITE, T. H. *The Once and Future King*. See Section 5B, Myth Fantasy.

C WHITEHEAD, Victoria. *The Chimney Witches*. Gr. 4–6. (Orig. British pub. 1986.)
On Halloween Eve, Lucy finally meets the witches she suspected of living in her chimney: Weird Hannah and her bumbling son, Rufus. (BL 84:154; CCBB 41:59; SLJ Nov 1987 p. 107)
Illus. by Linda North, Watts/Orchard, 1987, 117 pp.

WICKENDEN, Dan. *The Amazing Vacation*. See Section 5C, Travel to Other Worlds.

WILDE, Oscar. *The Happy Prince*. See Chapter 1, Allegorical Fantasy and Literary Fairy Tales.

WILLARD, Nancy. *The Mountains of Quilt*. See Chapter 7, Magic Adventure Fantasy.

WILLIAMS, Anne. *Secret of the Round Tower.* See Chapter 1, Allegorical Fantasy and Literary Fairy Tales.

WILLIAMS, Jay. *The Magic Grandfather.* See Chapter 7, Magic Adventure Fantasy.

WILLIAMS, Jay. *Petronella.* See Chapter 1, Allegorical Fantasy and Literary Fairy Tales.

WILLIAMS, Ursula Moray. *The Toymaker's Daughter.* See Chapter 9, Toy Fantasy.

C/YA *Witches, Witches, Witches.* Ed. by Helen Hoke. Gr. 5–8. (Orig. British pub. 1958.)
Twenty-five tales about folktale and fantasy witches, whose authors include Oscar Wilde and Andrew Lang. (BL 55:190; KR 26:663; LJ 83:3572)
Illus. by W. R. Lohse, Watts, 1966, 230 pp., o.p.

WREDE, Patricia C. *The Seven Towers.* See Section 5A, Alternate Worlds or Histories.

WRIGGINS, Sally. *The White Monkey King: A Chinese Fable.* See Section 5B, Myth Fantasy.

WRIGHTSON, Patricia. *An Older Kind of Magic.* See Chapter 7, Magic Adventure Fantasy.

YA WURTS, Janny. *Stormwarden.* Gr. 10 up.
A brother and sister named Emien and Taen, and a young scholar named Jaric are caught up in a battle between opposing sorceresses. (BL 81:484, 520; VOYA 8:141)
Berkley/Ace, 1984, pap., 325 pp.

YOLEN, Jane H. *The Magic Three of Solatia.* See Chapter 1, Allegorical Fantasy and Literary Fairy Tales.

YOLEN, Jane H. *Merlin's Booke.* See Section 5B, Myth Fantasy.

C YOLEN (Stemple), Jane H(yatt). *The Wizard of Washington Square.* Gr. 4–6.
A tiny wizard is distressed to discover how many children have forgotten that he exists. (CCBB 23:170; KR 37:1150; LJ 95:783)
Illus. by Ray Cruz, Collins + World, 1969, 126 pp., o.p.

C YOUNG, Miriam. *The Witch Mobile.* Gr. 2–4.
Nanette, the smallest witch in the toy shop, does not want to work revengeful spells like her older sisters. (KR 37:995; LJ 95:1192)
Illus. by Victoria Chess, Lothrop, 1969, 48 pp., o.p.

C/YA *Young Witches and Warlocks.* Ed. by Isaac Asimov, Martin H. Greenberg, and Charles G. Waugh. Gr. 6–9.
Ten stories about adolescents with unusual abilities, including "Teregram," "The Entrance Exam," and two by Ray Bradbury and Elizabeth Coatsworth. (BL 83:1673, 1683; CCBB 40:202; KR 55:921; SLJ Jan 1988 p. 83; VOYA 10:93)
Harper, 1987, 207 pp.

YA ZELAZNY, Roger (Joseph Christopher). *Jack of Shadows.* Gr. 10 up.
Jack, a shadow magician from the dark side of the world who was unjustly

punished for thievery, is determined to have vengeance. (BL 68:320; LJ 97:217; Tymn:184)

Walker, 1971, 207 pp., o.p.; NAL, 1985, pap.

YA ZELAZNY, Roger (Joseph Christopher). *Madwand.* Gr. 10 up.

Pol Detson must use his newly learned magician's skills to battle a sorcerer bent on ruling the world. This is the sequel to *Changeling* (Ace, 1980). (BL 78:850; VOYA 5:41)

Phantasia Press, dist. by Fantasy and Science Fiction Book, 1981, o.p.; illus. by Judy King Rieniets, Ace, 1981, pap., 281 pp., o.p.

Part Two
RESEARCH GUIDE

11
Reference and Bibliography

The works listed here include bibliographies of fantasy (such as Naomi Lewis's *Fantasy Books for Children*), indexes to fantasy criticism (such as Tymn's *The Year's Scholarship in Fantastic Literature*), biographical directories (such as *Something about the Author*), and atlases and dictionaries of the faerie world (such as J. B. Post's *An Atlas of Fantasy*). Multivolume reference works and those works commonly known by title (such as *Children's Catalog*) have been listed by title, rather than by editor.

The Preface contains a list of the major sources of the information in Chapters 11 through 14.

American Writers for Children before 1900 (*Dictionary of Literary Biography*, vol. 42). Edited by Glenn E. Estes. Detroit: Gale, 1985.
American Writers for Children, 1900–1960 (*Dictionary of Literary Biography*, vol. 22). Edited by John Cech. Detroit: Gale, 1983.
American Writers for Children since 1960: Fiction (*Dictionary of Literary Biography*, vol. 52). Edited by Glenn E. Estes. Detroit: Gale, 1986.
Anderson, Hugh, ed. *The Singing Roads: A Guide to Australian Children's Authors and Illustrators*. Sydney: Wentworth Press, 1965.
Ashley, Mike. *Who's Who in Horror and Fantasy Literature*. London: Elm Tree Books, 1977.
Bell, John. "Time Voyageurs: An Annotated Checklist of Juvenile Books Involving Fantastic Journeys in Canadian History." *Canadian Children's Literature* 38 (1985): 26–28.
"Best Science Fiction/Fantasy [1985–1986]." *VOYA* 10 (Apr. 1987): 21–24. (bibliography)
"Best Science Fiction/Fantasy [1987]." *VOYA* 11 (Apr. 1988): 11–14. (bibliography)
Bingham, Jane, ed. *Writers for Children: Critical Surveys of Major Authors since the Seventeenth Century*. New York: Scribner, 1988.
Bleiler, Everett Franklin. *The Checklist of Fantastic Literature: A Bibliography of Fantasy, Weird and Science Fiction Published in the English Language*. Chicago: Shasta, 1948. 2nd ed. Mercer Island, WA: Fax, 1972.
Briggs, Katharine M. *An Encyclopedia of Fairies: Hobgoblins, Brownies, Bogies, and Other Supernatural Creatures*. New York: Pantheon, 1976.
Briney, Robert E., and Wood, Edward. *Science Fiction Bibliographies: An Annotated*

Bibliography of Bibliographic Works on Science Fiction and Fantasy Fiction. Chicago: Advent, 1972.

Children's Authors and Illustrators: An Index to Biographical Dictionaries. 4th ed. Edited by Joyce Nakamura. Detroit: Gale, 1986.

Children's Catalog. 15th ed. Edited by Richard H. Isaacson, Ferne E. Hillegas, and Juliette Yaakov. New York: Wilson, 1986 (Suppl., 1987).

Children's Literature Review: Excerpts from Reviews, Criticism and Commentary on Books for Children and Young People. 14 vols. Edited by Carolyn Riley. Detroit: Gale, 1976–.

Clareson, Thomas D. *Science Fiction Criticism: An Annotated Checklist.* Kent, OH: Kent State Univ. Press, 1972.

Contemporary Authors. 122 vols. Edited by Hal May and Susan M. Trosky. Detroit: Gale, 1962–.

Contemporary Literary Criticism. 47 vols. Edited by Daniel J. Marowski and Roger Matuz. Detroit: Gale, 1973–.

Cooper, Ilene. "Popular Reading—After *The Borrowers.*" *Booklist* 81 (Nov. 15, 1984): 452–453. (bibliography)

Currey, L. W. *Science Fiction and Fantasy Authors: A Bibliography of First Printings of Their Fiction and Selected Non-Fiction.* Boston: G. K. Hall, 1979.

Davidson, Don Adrian. "Sword and Sorcery Fiction: An Annotated Book List." *English Journal* 61 (1972): 43–51.

Dictionary of Literary Biography. 52 vols. Detroit: Gale, 1981–. Each volume has its own editor and subject matter; vols. 22, 42, and 52 are devoted to children's literature.

Dooley, Patricia. "Finding Fantasy." *School Library Journal* 27 (Dec. 1980): 32–33. (bibliography)

Doyle, Brian. *The Who's Who of Children's Literature.* New York: Schocken, 1968.

Eaglen, Audrey B. "Alternatives: A Bibliography of Books and Periodicals on Science Fiction and Fantasy." *Top of the News* 39 (Fall 1982): 96–103.

Eakin, Mary, ed. *Good Books for Children, 1950–1965.* 3rd ed. Chicago: Univ. of Chicago Press, 1966.

Elleman, Barbara. "Popular Reading: Animal Fantasy." *Booklist* 76 (Feb. 15, 1980): 839–841. (bibliography)

———. "Popular Reading—Animal Fantasy: Update." *Booklist* 84 (Apr. 15, 1988): 1441–1442. (bibliography)

———. "Popular Reading—Ghosts, Witches, and Such: Update." *Booklist* 83 (Dec. 1, 1986): 585–586. (bibliography)

———. "Popular Reading: Time Fantasy." *Booklist* 74 (June 1, 1978): 1558–1560. (bibliography)

———. "Popular Reading—Time Fantasy Update." *Booklist* 81 (June 1, 1985): 1407–1408. (bibliography)

The Encyclopedia of Science Fiction and Fantasy through 1986: A Bibliographic Survey of the Fields of Science Fiction, Fantasy and Weird Fiction through 1968. 2 vols. Edited by Donald Henry Tuck. Chicago: Advent, 1974–1978. Previous edition entitled *A Handbook of Science Fiction and Fantasy.* Hobart, Tasmania, Australia, 1959.

Estes, Sally. "Fantastic Reading: Selected Fantasy for Young Adults." *Booklist* 78 (Jan. 1, 1982): 593–594.

———. "Science Fiction/Fantasy in Series." Speech given at the Young Adult Books Open Forum at the ALA Conference, July 1985. *Booklist* 82 (Nov. 1, 1985): 393–396. (bibliography)

"Fiction for Children 1970–1980: Myth and Fantasy." *Children's Literature in Education* 12 (Autumn 1981): 119–139.

Fifth Book of Junior Authors and Illustrators. Edited by Sally Holmes Holtze. New York: Wilson, 1983.

Fourth Book of Junior Authors and Illustrators. Edited by Doris de Montreville and Elizabeth D. Crawford. New York: Wilson, 1978.

Gallo, Donald R. *Books for You: A Booklist for Senior High Students.* Urbana, IL: National Council of Teachers of English, 1985. "Fantasy," pp. 121–132.

Gillispie, John. *The Elementary School Paperback Collection.* Chicago: American Library Association, 1985. "Fantasy." pp. 126–139.

———. *The Junior High School Paperback Collection.* Chicago: American Library Association, 1985. "Fantasy," pp. 30–37; "Science Fiction," pp. 95–107.

———. *The Senior High School Paperback Collection.* Chicago: American Library Association, 1986. "Fantasy and Science Fiction," pp. 55–94.

Gillespie, John T., and Gilbert, Christine B., eds. *Best Books for Children.* 3rd ed. New York: Bowker, 1985. "Fantasy," pp. 134–149. (bibliography)

Greene, David L. "Children's Literature Periodicals on Individual Authors, Dime Novels, Fantasy." *Phaedrus* 3, no. 1 (Spring 1976): 22–25.

Hall, Halbert W. *Science Fiction Book Review Index, 1921–1973.* Detroit: Gale, 1975.

Hannabus, Stuart; Litherland, Barry; and Morland, Stephanie, comps. "Fiction for Children, 1970–1980. 1. Myth and Fantasy." *Children's Literature in Education* 12 (Autumn 1981): 119–139. (bibliography)

Helbig, Alethea K., and Perkins, Agnes R. *Dictionary of American Children's Fiction, 1859–1959: Books of Recognized Merit.* Westport, CT: Greenwood Press, 1985.

———. *Dictionary of American Children's Fiction, 1960–1984.* Westport, CT: Greenwood Press, 1986.

Hendrickson, Linnea. *Children's Literature: A Guide to the Criticism.* Boston: G. K. Hall, 1987. "Fantasy," pp. 402–411.

Hoffman, Miriam, and Samuels, Eva. *Authors and Illustrators of Children's Books: Writings of Their Lives and Works.* New York: Bowker, 1972, pp. 56–61, 70–107, 165–171, 186–192, 256–267, 280–301, 340–342, 364–393, 407–411. Essays on Carlson, Cleary, Coatsworth, Hamilton, Lawson, Lewis, Lindgren, M. Norton, Seuss, Sendak, Seredy, and E. B. White.

Hopkins, Lee Bennett. "Fantasy Flights Circa 1976." *Teacher* 93 (Apr. 1976): 34+. (bibliography)

Hutchinson, Tom. *British Science Fiction and Fantasy.* London: National Book League and the British Council, 1975. "Children's Books," pp. 39–45. (bibliography)

The Junior Book of Authors. 2nd rev. ed. Edited by Stanley J. Kunitz and Howard Haycraft. New York: Wilson, 1951.

Junior High School Library Catalog. 5th ed. Edited by Richard H. Isaacson. New York: Wilson, 1985 (Suppl. 1986).

Kies, Cosette N. *Supernatural Fiction for Teens: 500 Good Paperbacks to Read for Wonderment, Fear, and Fun.* Littleton, CO: Libraries Unlimited, 1987. (bibliography)

Lacy, Norris J. *The Arthurian Encyclopedia.* New York: Garland, 1986.

Lehan, Terri, and Murray, Peggy. "Fantasy: A Reader's List." *VOYA* 5, no. 4 (Oct. 1982): 28–34.

Leif, Irving P. *Children's Literature: A Historical and Contemporary Bibliography.* Troy, NY: Whitson, 1977.

Lewis, Naomi. *Fantasy Books for Children.* rev. ed. London: National Book League, 1975, 1977. (bibliography)

Lurker, Manfred, ed. *Dictionary of Gods and Goddesses, Devils and Demons.* New York: Routledge; dist. by Methuen, 1987.

McGeehon, C. "I Have Read Everything by Tolkien." *Unabashed Librarian* 50 (1980): 25. (bibliography)

McGhan, Barry, ed. *Science Fiction and Fantasy Pseudonyms*. rev. ed. Dearborn, MI: Misfit Press, 1979.

Mahony, Bertha E. *Books for Boys and Girls: A Suggestive Purchase List*. Boston: Women's Educational and Industrial Union, Bookshop for Boys and Girls, 1916. "Modern Fairy Tales," pp. 23–27. (2nd ed. 1917, pp. 15, 23–27; 3rd ed. 1919, pp. 14, 23–26; 4th rev. ed. 1922, pp. 35–40)

Mahony, Bertha E., and Whitney, Elinor. *Five Years of Children's Books 1930–1935: A Supplement to Realms of Gold*. Garden City, NY: Doubleday, 1936. "Creations of Fancy—Modern Fairy Tales," pp. 195–214.

———. *Realms of Gold in Children's Books* (5th ed. of *Books for Boys and Girls—A Suggestive Purchase List*, previously published by the Bookshop for Boys and Girls, Women's Educational and Industrial Union, Boston). Garden City, NY: Doubleday, 1929. "Creations of Fancy—Modern Fairy Tales," pp. 263–298.

Manguel, Alberto, and Guagalupi, Gianni. *The Dictionary of Imaginary Places*. New York: Macmillan, 1980.

Masterworks of Children's Literature: 1550–1900. 9 vols. Edited by Jonathan Cott. New York: Stonehill/Chelsea House, 1983–1986. Vol. VI: *The Victorian Era, 1837–1900*. Edited by Robert Lee Wolf. Includes Thackeray, Browne, Ruskin, Kingsley. Vol. VIII: *The Twentieth Century*. Edited by William T. Moynihan and Mary E. Shaner. Includes a chapter on contemporary fantasy.

Means, H. J. "Books for Young Adults: Science Fiction, Fantasy, and the Occult." *English Journal* 62 (Oct. 1973): 1059–1060. (bibliographic essay)

Miller, C. "Science Fiction, Fantasy, and Horror: The Year in Review." *A.B. Bookman's Weekly* 80 (Oct. 26, 1987): 1576–1578. (bibliography)

More Junior Authors. Edited by Muriel Fuller. New York: Wilson, 1963.

Muller, Al, and Sullivan, C. W., III. "Science Fiction and Fantasy Series Books." *English Journal* 69 (Oct. 1980): 71–74. (bibliography)

Nelms, Beth, and Nelms, Ben. "The Farfaring Imagination: Recent Fantasy and Science Fiction." *English Journal* 74 (Apr. 1985): 83–86. (bibliography)

Olcott, F. J. "Fairy Tales for Children: Bibliography No. 13." *New York Special Library Report*, 1898.

The Oxford Companion to Children's Literature. Edited by Humphrey Carpenter and Mari Prichard. New York: Oxford Univ. Press, 1984. "Fantasy," pp. 181–182.

Parish, M. "Children's Fantasy for Young Adults." *English Journal* 66 (Oct. 1977): 92–93. (bibliography)

Pflieger, Pat, and Hill, Helen M. *A Reference Guide to Modern Fantasy for Children*. Westport, CT: Greenwood Press, 1984.

Phillips, R. A. "Discovering New Worlds." *Curriculum Review* 19 (Sept. 1980): 336–337. (bibliographic essay)

Post, J. B. *An Atlas of Fantasy*. rev. ed. New York: Ballantine, 1979. Expanded edition of articles published in *Special Library Association Geography and Map Division Bulletin* 75 (Mar. 1969): 11–13, and 101 (Sept. 1975): 12–14.

Raburn, Josephine. "Ghost Stories." *School Library Journal* 31 (Nov. 1984): 25–27. (bibliography)

———. "Shuddering Shades! A Ghostly Book List." *Top of the News* 41 (Spring 1985): 275–281.

Rahn, Suzanne. *Children's Literature: An Annotated Bibliography of the History and Criticism*. New York: Garland, 1981. "Fantasy," pp. 83–92.

Reginald, Robert, ed. *Science Fiction and Fantasy Literature: A Checklist from 1700–1974* (bound with *Contemporary Science Fiction Authors*. II). 2 vols. Detroit: Gale, 1979.

Richards, George M. *The Fairy Dictionary*. New York: Macmillan, 1932.

Roginski, Jim, ed. *Newbery and Caldecott Medalists and Honor Book Winners: Bibliog-

raphies and Resource Material through 1977. Littleton, CO: Libraries Unlimited, 1982.

Rovin, Jeff. *The Fantasy Almanac.* New York: Dutton, 1979.

Schlobin, Roger C. *The Literature of Fantasy: An Annotated Bibliography of Modern Fantasy Fiction.* New York; Garland, 1979.

Schlobin, Roger C., and Tymn, Marshall B. "The Year's Scholarship in Science Fiction and Fantasy: 1974." *Extrapolation* 18 (Dec. 1976): 73–96.

————. "The Year's Scholarship in Science Fiction and Fantasy, 1975." *Extrapolation* 19 (May 1978): 156–199.

————. "The Year's Scholarship in Science Fiction and Fantasy, 1976." *Extrapolation* 20 (Spring 1979): 60–99.

————. "The Year's Scholarship in Science Fiction and Fantasy, 1977." *Extrapolation* 20 (Fall 1979): 238–287.

————. "The Year's Scholarship in Science Fiction and Fantasy, 1978." *Extrapolation* 21 (Spring 1980): 45–89.

————. "The Year's Scholarship in Science Fiction and Fantasy, 1979." *Extrapolation* 22 (Spring 1981): 25–91.

"Science Fiction and Fantasy for Young Adults." *VOYA* 8 (Feb. 1986): 363–367. (bibliography)

Science Fiction and Fantasy Literature: 1975–1984 Supplement. 2 vols. Edited by Robert Reginald. Detroit: Gale, 1987.

Science Fiction and Fantasy Reference Index: 1973–1985: An International Author and Subject Index to History and Criticism. 2 vols. Edited by H. W. Hall. Detroit: Gale, 1987. Updates and will be followed by the annual *Science Fiction and Fantasy Research Index* published by Borgo Press. More emphasis on Science Fiction than Fantasy. Includes children's writers who have also written for adults.

Science Fiction and Fantasy Series and Sequels: A Bibliography. Vol. 1: *Books.* Edited by Tim Cottrill, Martin H. Greenberg, and Charles G. Waugh. New York: Garland, 1986.

Science Fiction Writers: Critical Studies of the Major Authors from the Early Nineteenth Century to the Present Day. Edited by E. F. Bleiler. New York: Scribner, 1982.

Searles, Baird; Meacham, Beth; and Franklin, Michael. *A Reader's Guide to Fantasy.* New York: Avon, 1982. pap. Includes both children's and adult books. (bibliography)

Seattle (Washington) Public Library. "After *Mary Poppins:* Book List." *Top of the News* 23 (Nov. 1966): 31–34.

Shapiro, Lillian. *Fiction for Youth: A Guide to Recommended Books.* 2nd ed. New York: Neal-Schuman, 1985.

Sleigh, Bernard. *An Ancient Mappe of Fairyland, with a Guide to the Map of Fairyland; Newly Discovered and Set Forth.* rev. ed. New York: Dutton, 1920, 1925. Originally published in England, 1920.

Something about the Author: Autobiography Series. 4 vols. Edited by Adele Sarkissian. Detroit: Gale, 1985–.

Something about the Author: Facts and Pictures about Authors and Illustrators of Books for Young People. 51 vols. Edited by Anne Commire. Detroit: Gale, 1971–.

South, Malcolm. *Mythical and Fabulous Creatures: A Source Book and Research Guide.* Westport, CT: Greenwood Press, 1987.

Stott, John C. *Children's Literature from A to Z: A Guide for Parents and Teachers.* New York: McGraw-Hill, 1984. "Fantasy," pp. 104–108.

Supernatural Fiction Writers: Fantasy and Horror. 2 vols. Edited by E. F. Bleiler. New York: Scribner, 1985.

Survey of Modern Fantasy Literature. 5 vols. Edited by Frank N. Magill. Englewood Cliffs, NJ: Salem Press, 1983.

Sutherland, Zena, ed. *The Best in Children's Books, 1966–1972.* Chicago: Univ. of Chicago Press, 1973.

——. *The Best in Children's Books, 1973–1978.* Chicago: Univ. of Chicago Press, 1980.

——. *The Best in Children's Books: The University of Chicago Guide to Children's Literature, 1979–1984.* Chicago: Univ. of Chicago Press, 1986.

Third Book of Junior Authors. Edited by Doris de Montreville and Donna Hill. New York: Wilson, 1972.

Twentieth-Century Children's Writers. Edited by D. L. Kirkpatrick. New York: St. Martin's Press, 1978.

Twentieth Century Literary Criticism. 15 vols. Edited by Dennis Poupard and James E. Persorn, Jr. Detroit: Gale, 1978–.

Twentieth Century Science Fiction Writers. 2nd ed. Edited by Curtis C. Smith. Chicago: St. James Press, 1986. Original publication, St. Martin's Press, 1981. "Major Fantasy Writers," pp. 863–870.

Tymn, Marshall B. *American Fantasy and Science Fiction: Toward a Bibliography of Works Published in the United States, 1948–1973.* San Bernardino, CA: Borgo Press, 1980.

——. "An Annotated Bibliography of Critical Studies and Reference Works on Fantasy." *CEA Critic* 40 (Jan. 1978): 43–47. Expanded version: *Recent Critical Studies on Fantasy Literature: An Annotated Checklist, Exchange Bibliography #1522.* Chicago: Council of Planning Librarians, 1978.

——. "Bibliography of Fantastic Scholarship: History and Culture, Themes and Motifs, Author Studies, Children's Literature." In *The Scope of Fantastic—Culture, Biography, Themes, Children's Literature: Selected Essays from the First International Conference on the Fantastic in Literature and Film.* Edited by Robert A. Collins and Howard D. Pearce. Westport, CT: Greenwood Press, 1985, pp. 267–270.

——. "Fantasy Literature: A Survey." *Analytical and Enumerative Bibliography* 5 (1981): 25–34.

——. "Guide to Science Fiction and Fantasy Scholarship: 1980–1982." In *Science Fiction Dialogues.* Edited by Gary K. Wolfe. Chicago: Academy Chicago, 1982, pp. 215–227.

——. "Modern Critical Studies and Reference Works on Fantasy." In *The Aesthetics of Fantasy Literature and Art.* Edited by Roger C. Schlobin. South Bend, IN: Univ. of Notre Dame Press, 1982, pp. 262–270.

——. "Science Fiction and Fantasy in the School Curriculum: Part I: A Checklist of Articles, 1967–1975." *English Language Arts Bulletin* 21 (Fall/Winter 1981): 24–27.

——. "Science Fiction and Fantasy Scholarship, 1982: The Year in Review." *Fantasy Review* 64 (1984): 52–54.

——. "The Year's Scholarship in Fantastic Literature: 1986." *Extrapolation* 28 (Fall 1987): 201–254.

——. *The Year's Scholarship in Science Fiction, Fantasy, and Horror Literature, 1980.* Kent, OH: Kent State Univ. Press, 1983.

——. *The Year's Scholarship in Science Fiction, Fantasy, and Horror Literature, 1981.* Kent, OH: Kent State Univ. Press, 1984.

——. *The Year's Scholarship in Science Fiction, Fantasy, and Horror Literature, 1982.* Kent, OH: Kent State Univ. Press, 1985.

——. "The Year's Scholarship in Science Fiction, Fantasy, and Horror Literature, 1983." *Extrapolation* 26 (Summer 1985): 85–142.

——. "The Year's Scholarship in Science Fiction, Fantasy, and Horror Literature: 1984." *Extrapolation* 26 (Winter 1985): 316–377.

——. "The Year's Scholarship in Science Fiction, Fantasy, and Horror Literature: 1985." *Extrapolation* 27 (Summer 1986): 123–173.

Tymn, Marshall B., and Schlobin, Roger C. "Checklist of American Critical Works on Science Fiction: 1972–1973." *Extrapolation* 17 (Dec. 1975): 78–96.

————, eds. *The Year's Scholarship in Science Fiction and Fantasy, 1972–1975*. Kent, OH: Kent State Univ. Press, 1979. Followed by *The Year's Scholarship in Science Fiction and Fantasy: 1976 to 1979*. Kent, OH: Kent State Univ. Press, 1983. Compilations of annual checklists published between 1974 and 1981 in *Extrapolation: A Science-Fiction Newsletter*.

Tymn, Marshall B.; Schlobin, Roger C.; and Currey, L. W. *A Research Guide to Science Fiction Studies: An Annotated Checklist of Primary and Secondary Materials on Fantasy and Science Fiction*. New York: Garland, 1977.

Tymn, Marshall B.; Zahorski, Kenneth J.; and Boyer, Robert H. *Fantasy Literature: A Core Collection and Reference Guide*. New York: Bowker, 1979. Mainly lists adult books, except for a "core collection" of children's books. (bibliography)

Waggoner, Diana. *The Hills of Faraway: A Guide to Fantasy*. New York: Atheneum, 1978. Lists both adult and children's books. (bibliography)

Ward, Martha E., and Marquardt, Dorothy A. *Authors of Books for Young People*. 2nd ed. Metuchen, NJ: Scarecrow Press, 1971.

Werner, Nancy. *Flights of Fancy. Resources in Education*. ED 025-401. Washington, DC: U.S. Office of Education, 1968. (bibliography)

Wolf, Gary K. *Critical Terms for Science Fiction and Fantasy: A Glossary and Guide to Scholarship*. Westport, CT: Greenwood Press, 1986.

Writers for Young Adults: Biographies Master Index. 2nd ed. Edited by Adele Sarkissian. Detroit: Gale, 1984.

Yesterday's Authors of Books for Children: Facts and Pictures about Authors and Illustrators of Books for Young People, from Early Times to 1960. 2 vols. Edited by Anne Commire. Detroit: Gale, 1977–1978.

12
History and Criticism

This chapter lists general studies of children's and young adult fantasy, such as Brian Attebery's "Fantasy for American Children" and James E. Higgins's *Beyond Words: Mystical Fancy in Children's Literature*. Works about children's and young adult literature that discuss fantasy, like Sheila Egoff's *Thursday's Child* and Cornelia Meigs's *A Critical History of Children's Literature*, are found here as well, with citations to the particular chapters or pages devoted to fantasy.

Also listed are collections of interviews and critical studies by and/or about children's and young adult fantasists, such as Edward Blishen's *The Thorny Paradise* and Sheila Egoff's *Only Connect*. Books on fantastic illustration have been included here, as well.

A list of the major sources of the information found in this chapter is located in the Preface.

Articles and studies on the educational or psychological uses of fantasy, like Bruno Bettelheim's *The Uses of Enchantment* and Marshall Tymn's *Teacher's Guide to Fantasy Literature,* as well as audiovisual materials on fantasy literature, are located in Chapter 13, Teaching Resources.

For information about individual fantasists, see Chapter 14, Author Studies.

Abbey, K. "Science Fiction and Fantasy: A Collection Proposal." *Wilson Library Bulletin* 55 (Apr. 1981): 584–588.

Adams, Bess Porter. *About Books and Children: Historical Survey of Children's Literature.* New York: Holt, 1953, pp. 456–460, 473–477, 495–497, 534–535.

Adams, J. "Linkages: Science Fiction and Science Fantasy." *School Library Journal* (May 1980): 23–28, and (Nov. 1980): 3.

Alberghene, Janice Marie. "From Alcott to *Abel's Island:* The Image of the Artist in American Children's Literature." Ph.D. dissertation, Brown University, 1980.

Alderson, Brian, ed. *Children's Books in England: Five Centuries of Social Life.* Orig. pub. 1932, ed. by F. J. Harvey Darton. 3rd ed. New York: Cambridge Univ. Press, 1982, pp. 252–266, 281–285, 308–315. Discusses Kinsley, Carroll, Potter, Kipling, and Barrie.

Alexander, Lloyd. "Fantasy as Images: A Literary View." *Language Arts* 55 (1978): 440–446.

———. "Substance and Fantasy." *Library Journal* 91 (Dec. 15, 1966): 6157–6159.

————. "The Truth about Fantasy." *Top of the News* 24 (Jan. 1968): 168–174.

————. "Wishful Thinking—Or Hopeful Dreaming?" *Horn Book* 44 (Aug. 1968): 383–390.

Alpers, Hans Joachim. "Loincloth, Double Ax, and Magic: 'Heroic Fantasy' and Related Genres." *Science–Fiction Studies* 5 (1978): 19–32.

Anderson, William, and Groff, Patrick. *A New Look at Children's Literature.* Belmont, CA: Wadsworth, 1972. "Fantasy," pp. 66–93, 254–266.

Antczak, Janice. *Science Fiction: The Mythos of a New Romance.* New York: Neal–Schuman, 1985. "Science Fantasy," pp. 184–189.

Anthony, Piers. "In Defense of Fantasy." *Isaac Asimov's Science Fiction Magazine,* Dec. 1983, pp. 71–87.

Aquino, John. *Fantasy in Literature.* Washington, DC: National Education Association, 1977, "Fantasy Literature," pp. 13–19, 23–26; 28–29, 40–47.

"Are Fairy Tales Outgrown?" *Literary Digest* 63 (1919): 32.

Armstrong, Judith. "Ghost Stories: Exploiting the Convention." *Children's Literature in Education* 11 (Autumn 1980): 117–123.

Arrowsmith, Nancy, and Moorse, George. *A Field Guide to the Little People.* New York: Hill, 1977.

Asche, Geoffrey. *The Discovery of King Arthur.* Garden City, NY: Anchor Press/ Doubleday, 1985.

————. *King Arthur: In Fact and Legend.* New York: Nelson, 1971.

Asker, David Barry Desmond. "The Modern Bestiary: Animal Fiction from Hardy to Orwell." Ph.D. dissertation, University of British Columbia, 1978.

Astbury, E. A. "Other and Deeper Worlds." *Junior Bookshelf* 39 (Oct. 1975): 301–305.

Attebery, Brian L. "America and the Materials of Fantasy." Ph.D. dissertation, Brown University, 1979.

————. *The Fantasy Tradition in American Literature: From Irving to Le Guin.* Bloomington: Indiana Univ. Press, 1980. "Fantasy for American Children," pp. 59–108, 134–153.

————. "Women's Coming of Age in Fantasy." *Extrapolation* 28 (Spring 1987): 10–22.

Auerbach, N. "Falling Alice, Fallen Women, and Victorian Dream Children." *English Language Notes* 20 (Dec. 1982): 46–64.

Avery, Gillian. "American Distaste for Fairy Tales." *Horn Book* 62 (July–Aug. 1986): 486–489.

————. "The Quest for Fairyland." *Quarterly Journal of the Library of Congress* 38 (Fall 1981): 220–227.

Babbitt, Natalie. "The Purposes of Fantasy." In *Proceedings of the Ninth Annual Conference of the Children's Literature Association.* University of Florida, March 1982. Ypsilanti, MI: Children's Literature Association, 1983, pp. 22–29.

Bailey, W. L. "Fairy Tales as Character-Builders." *Libraries* 31 (1926): 44–46.

Bainton, George, ed. *The Art of Authorship: Literary Reminiscences, Methods of Work, and Advice to Young Beginners, Personally Contributed by Leading Authors of the Day.* London: James Clarke, 1890.

Baker, F. T. "Old and Modern Fairy Tales." *Teachers College Record* 9 (Jan. 1908): 9–23.

Barnes, Myra Edwards. "Linguistics and Languages in Science Fiction–Fantasy." Ph.D. dissertation, East Texas State University, 1971. Reprinted. New York: Arno Press, 1975.

Barth, Melissa Ellen. "Problems in Generic Classification: Toward a Definition of Fantasy Fiction." Ph.D. dissertation, Purdue University, 1981.

Bator, Robert. *Signposts to Criticism of Children's Literature.* Chicago: American Library Association, 1983. "Fantasy," pp. 240–264.

Beard, Patten. "Why Punish the Fairy Tale?" *Libraries* 34 (1929): 457–459.

Becker, May Lamberton. *First Adventures in Reading: Introducing Children to Books*. New York: Stokes, 1936. "The Fairy-Tale Age," pp. 43–66; "Animals in Books," pp. 67–87.

Berman, Ruth. "A Note on the Mythopoeic Holdings in the Kerlan Collection." *Mythlore* 6 (Fall 1979): 32, 42. Survey of the holdings of the Children's Literature Collection of the University of Minnesota of works by Bellairs, Lewis, MacDonald, Coatsworth, Ipcar, Nichols, Pope, and Yolen.

———. "Victorian Dragons: The Reluctant Brood." *Children's Literature in Education* 15 (Winter 1984): 220–233.

Billman, Carol. "Reading and Mapping: Directions in Children's Fantasy." In *Proceedings of the Ninth Annual Conference of the Children's Literature Association*. University of Florida, March 1982. Ypsilanti, MI: Children's Literature Association, 1983, pp. 40–46.

Bisenieks, Dainis. "Children, Magic and Choices." *Mythlore* 6 (Winter 1979): 13–16. Discussion of Le Guin, Alexander, Garner, Cooper, and Lewis.

Blackham, H. J. *The Fable as Literature*. Dover, NH: Athlone Press, 1985.

Blishen, Edward, ed. *The Thorny Paradise: Writers on Writing for Children*. Boston: Horn Book, 1975, pp. 25–52, 58–61, 65–76, 81–92, 103–116, 123–145, 163–173. Originally published in Great Britain in 1975. Articles written by Storr, Gordon, Aiken, Walsh, Hoban, Garfield, Le Guin, Farmer, Cresswell, Peyton, Hunter, Pearce, and Adams.

Blount, Margaret. *Animal Land: The Creatures of Children's Fiction*. New York: Morrow, 1975. "Animal Fantasy," pp. 95–244, 258–324.

Borges, Jorge Luis, with Guerreo, Margarita. *The Book of Imaginary Beings*. New York: Dutton, 1969. Revised and enlarged from original Mexican publication in 1957.

Boyer, Robert H., and Zahorski, Kenneth J., eds. *Fantasists on Fantasy: A Collection of Critical Reflections by Eighteen Masters of the Art*. New York: Avon/Discus, 1984.

Bradley, Marion Zimmer. "Fantasy and the Contemporary Occult Novel: Social and Intellectual Approaches." *Fantasy Review* 80 (1985): 10–12.

———. "Fantasy and the Contemporary Occult Novel: Social and Intellectual Approaches II." *Fantasy Review* 81 (1985): 31–32.

Branham, Robert J. "Fantasy and Ineffability: Fiction at the Limits of Language." *Extrapolation* 24 (Spring 1983): 66–79.

Briggs, Katherine Mary. *The Fairies in Tradition and Literature*. London: Routledge & Kegan Paul, 1967.

———. *The Vanishing People: Faery Lore and Legends*. Illus. by Mary I. French. New York: Pantheon; dist. by Random, 1978.

Britton, J. "The Role of Fantasy." *English in Education* 5, no. 3 (Winter 1971): 39–44.

Brooks–Rose, Christine. *A Rhetoric of the Unreal: Studies in Narrative and Structure, Especially of the Fantastic*. New York: Cambridge Univ. Press, 1983.

Buechner, Frederick. "If Not God, Old Scratch." *New York Times Book Review*, sect. 7, pt. II, May 6, 1973, pp. 3, 14–16.

Burns, Linda Lattin. "High Fantasy: A Definition." Ph.D. dissertation, University of Missouri-Columbia, 1979.

Burns, Marjorie Jean. "Victorian Fantasists from Ruskin to Lang: A Study in Ambivalence." Ph.D. dissertation, University of California at Berkeley, 1978.

Butler, Francelia, and Rotert, Richard, eds. *Reflections on Literature for Children: Selected from the Annual "Children's Literature."* Hamden, CT: Shoe String Press, 1984. Essays on Baum, Milne, Potter, Singer, Travers, E. B. White, Collodi, Mac-Donald, Ruskin, Barrie, Nesbit, Grahame, Lewis, and Sendak.

———, eds. *Triumphs of the Spirit in Children's Literature*. Hamden, CT: Shoe String Press, 1986. Anderson, pp. 122–126; Sendak, pp. 142–149; Collodi, pp. 171–179.

Butts, Dennis, ed. *Good Writers for Young Readers*. St. Albans, England: Hart-Davis, 1977, pp. 12–49, 57–66, 79–128. Articles about Aiken, Boston, Garfield, Garner, Hoban, Mayne, M. Norton, Pearce, Peyton, Adams, and Le Guin.

Cadogan, Mary, and Craig, Patricia. *You're a Brick, Angela! A New Look at Girls' Fiction from 1839 to 1975*. London: Gollancz, 1976.

Cameron, Eleanor. "The Dearest Freshness Deep Down Things." *Horn Book* 40 (Oct. 1964): 459–472.

――――. "The Eternal Moment." *Children's Literature Association Quarterly* 9 (Winter 1984/1985): 157–164.

――――. "Fantasy." In *The Green and Burning Tree*. 2nd ed. Boston: Atlantic/Little, Brown, 1985, pp. 3–134, 258–274.

――――. "The Inmost Secret." *Horn Book* 59 (Feb. 1983): 17–24.

――――. "Into Something Rich and Strange: Of Dreams, Art, and the Unconscious." *Quarterly Journal of the Library of Congress* 5 (1978): 92–107. Reprinted in *The Openhearted Audience*. Washington, DC: Library of Congress, 1980, pp. 152–176.

Campbell, P. "Young Adult Perplex: Adult Fantasy Illustration." *Wilson Library Bulletin* 54 (Feb. 1980): 392–393.

Canadian Children's Literature: A Journal of Criticism and Review. "A Double Issue on Fantasy," nos. 15 and 16 (1980).

Carpenter, Humphrey. *Secret Gardens: A Study of the Golden Age of Children's Literature*. Boston: Houghton Mifflin, 1985. Discusses Kingsley, Carroll, MacDonald, Grahame, Nesbit, Potter, Barrie, Milne, Jeffries.

Cart, Michael. "A Light in the Darkness: Humor Returns to Children's Fantasy." *School Library Journal* 33 (April 1987): 48–49.

Carter, Lin. *Imaginary Worlds: The Art of Fantasy*. New York: Ballantine, 1973.

Chambers, Aidan. *Booktalk: Occasional Writing on Literature and Children*. New York: Harper and Row, 1986. Original British publication, Bodley Head, 1985.

――――. "Letter from England: Magical Thinking." *Horn Book* 58 (Feb. 1982): 94–105.

Chambers, Nancy, ed. *The Signal Approach to Children's Books*. Metuchen, NJ: Scarecrow Press, 1980.

Children and Books. 7th ed. Edited by Zena Sutherland and May Hill Arbuthnot. Glenview, IL: Scott, Foresman, 1985. "Modern Fantasy," pp. 226–272.

Children's Literature: The Great Excluded, vol. 1. Edited by Francelia Butler. Annual of the Modern Language Association Seminar on Children's Literature and the Children's Literature Association. Storrs, CT: Journal of the Modern Language Association, 1972, pp. 42–45, 54–57, 62–73, 98–103, 152–172. Articles on Bunyan, Carroll, Ruskin, Baum, and Milne.

Children's Literature (The Great Excluded), 2. Storrs, CT: Journal of the Modern Language Association, 1973, pp. 11–17, 50–66, 77–86, 110–122, 221–223. Articles on Milne, Tolkien, E. B. White, Collodi, Baum, and Potter.

Children's Literature (The Great Excluded), 3. Storrs, CT: Journal of the Modern Language Association, 1974, pp. 12–35, 66–75, 103–106, 140–164, 173–176. Articles on Lewis, Collodi, Wilde, Nesbit, and Baum.

Children's Literature (The Great Excluded), 4. Philadelphia: Temple Univ. Press, 1975, pp. 15–22, 80–104. Articles on Travers, Grahame, and Kipling.

Children's Literature (The Great Excluded), 5. Philadelphia: Temple Univ. Press, 1976, pp. 74–91, 148–156. Articles on Baum and Ouida.

Children's Literature, 6. Philadelphia: Temple Univ. Press, 1977, pp. 77–92, 165–181. Articles on d'Aulnoy and Barrie.

Children's Literature, 7. Storrs, CT: Parousia Press, 1978, pp. 78–92, 115–128, 242–247. Articles on Carroll and Grahame.

Children's Literature, 8. New Haven, CT: Yale Univ. Press, 1980, pp. 53–140, 184–190. Articles on Boston, Ruskin, Hoban, Collodi.

Children's Literature, 9. New Haven, CT: Yale Univ. Press, 1981, pp. 19–27. Article on Barrie.

Children's Literature, 10. New Haven, CT: Yale Univ. Press, 1982, pp. 37–55, 113–140, 153–158. Articles on Barrie, Le Guin, Steig, and Baum.

Children's Literature, 11. New Haven, CT: Yale Univ. Press, 1983, pp. 32–48, 64–75, 125–134, 145–155, 201–210. Articles on Carroll, Collodi, Jarrell, and Boston.

Children's Literature, 12. New Haven, CT: Yale Univ. Press, 1984. Sendak, pp. 3–24; Cameron, pp. 122–146; Lewis, pp. 105–121.

Children's Literature, 13. New Haven, CT: Yale Univ. Press, 1985. Ruskin, pp. 3–30; E. B. White, pp. 109–127; Raskin, pp. 128–138.

Children's Literature, 15. New Haven, CT: Yale Univ. Press, 1987. pp. 106–119.

Chubb, Percival. "The Value and Place of Fairy Stories in the Education of Children." *National Education Association Journal* (1905): 871–879.

Chukovskii, Kornei. *From Two to Five.* Translated and edited by Miriam Morton. Berkeley: Univ. of California Press, 1963. Originally published in Russia, 1925. "The Battle for the Fairy Tale," pp. 114–139.

Cianciolo, Patricia Jean. "A Look at Modern Fantasy Currently Available to Young Readers." Syracuse, NY: ERIC Educational Document Reproduction Service, 1977.

Clancy, Joseph P. *Pendragon: Arthur and His Britain.* New York: Praeger, 1971.

Clark, Rosalind Elizabeth. "Goddess, Fairy Mistress, and Sovereignty: Women of the Irish Supernatural." Ph.D. dissertation, University of Massachusetts, 1985.

Cline, Ruth K. J. *A Guide to Literature for Young Adults: Background, Selection, and Use.* Glenview, IL: Scott, Foresman, 1983.

Cohen, John Arthur. "An Examination of Four Key Motifs Found in High Fantasy for Children." Ph.D. dissertation, Ohio State University, 1975.

Collings, Michael R., ed. *Reflections on the Fantastic: Selected Essays from the Fourth International Conference on the Fantastic in the Arts.* Westport, CT: Greenwood Press, 1986.

Collins, Robert A., and Pearce, Howard D., eds. *The Scope of the Fantastic—Culture, Biography, Themes, Children's Literature: Selected Essays from the First International Conference on the Fantastic in Literature and Film.* Westport, CT: Greenwood Press, 1985. "Fantasy and Children's Literature," pp. 221–270.

———. *The Scope of the Fantastic—Theory, Technique, Major Authors: Selected Essays from the First International Conference on the Fantastic in Literature and Film.* Westport, CT: Greenwood Press, 1985.

Cook, Elizabeth. *The Ordinary and the Fabulous.* New York: Cambridge Univ. Press, 1969.

Cooper, Susan. "Escaping into Ourselves." In Betsy Hearne and Marilyn Kaye. *Celebrating Children's Books.* New York: Lothrop, 1981, pp. 14–23.

Cott, Jonathan. *Pipers at the Gates of Dawn: The Wisdom of Children's Literature.* New York: Random, 1983. Interviews with Sendak, Lindgren, Seuss, Steig, and Travers.

———, ed. *Beyond the Looking Glass: Extraordinary Works of Fantasy and Fairy Tales.* New York: Stonehill, 1973. Anthology of ten Victorian children's tales by Ruskin, de Morgan, MacDonald, and others.

Cox, Harvey. *The Feast of Fools: A Theological Essay on Festivity and Fantasy.* Cambridge, MA: Harvard Univ. Press, 1969, pp. 59–97.

Crago, Hugh. "Terra Incognita, Cognita." In Margaret Trask. *Fantasy, Science Fiction, Science Materials.* Kensington, NSW, Australia: Univ. of New South Wales, School of Librarianship, 1972, pp. 41–68.

Crago, Hugh, and Crago, Maureen. "A World beneath the Waves: The Imagery of the

Underwater Otherworld in Children's Fiction 1840–1971." *Signal* 11 (May 1973): 74–87; continued in 12 (Sept. 1973): 123–134.

Crouch, Marcus S. "Experiments in Time." *Junior Bookshelf* 20 (Jan. 1956): 5–11. Discusses Kipling, Nesbit, H. Lewis, Uttley, others.

―――. "Guest Essay, New Faces, New Directions in Britain." *Children's Literature Review,* vol. 11. Edited by Gerard J. Senick. Detroit: Gale, 1986, pp. 11–18.

―――. *The Nesbit Tradition: Children's Novels 1945–1972.* Totowa, NJ: Rowman & Littlefield, 1972. "Laughter," pp. 101–111; "Magic Casements," pp. 112–141.

―――. *Treasure Seekers and Borrowers: Children's Books in Britain, 1900–1960.* London: The Library Association, 1961, amended ed. 1970, pp. 15–21, 36, 43–49, 61–67, 91–92, 101–103, 115–118.

Crouch, Marcus, and Ellis, Alec, eds. *Chosen for Children: An Account of the Books Which Have Been Awarded the Library Association Carnegie Medal, 1936–1975.* 3rd ed. London: The Library Association, 1977, pp. 30–49, 66–69, 78–99, 117–123, 141–149, 164–172. B. B., Linklater, Goudge, de la Mare, M. Norton, Farjeon, C. S. Lewis, Mayne, Pearce, Clarke, Garner, R. Harris, Adams, and Lively.

Cullinan, Bernice E. *Literature and the Child.* New York: Harcourt Brace Jovanovich, 1981. "Fantasy and Science Fiction," pp. 209–245.

Cunningham, Michael Henry. "The Triumph of Fantasy: Childhood and Children's Literature in Victorian England." Ph.D. dissertation, New School for Social Research, 1978.

Curry, Jane Louise. "On the Elvish Craft." *Signal* 2 (May 1970): 42–49. Reprinted in Aidan Chambers. *Signal Approach to Children's Books.* Metuchen, NJ: Scarecrow Press, 1971, pp. 83–93.

Dalgliesh, Alice. *First Experiences with Literature.* New York: Scribner, 1932, pp. 87–99, 148–152.

Dalphin, Marcia. "I Give You the End of a Golden String." *Horn Book* 14 (Apr. 1938): 143–149.

Dankert, B. "Phantastiche Kinder—Und Jugend—Literatur und Märchen [Fantastic Children's and Youth Books and Fairy Tales]." *Buch und Bibliothek* 34 (June 1982): 496–498+.

Darton, F. J. Harvey. "Battles Long Ago: War against Fairyland." *Cornhill Magazine* (London) 68 (March 1930): 330–337.

de Camp, L. Sprague. *Blond Barbarians and Noble Savages.* Baltimore: T-K Graphics, 1975.

―――. *Lost Continents: The Atlantis Theme in History, Science, and Literature.* New York: Gnome Press, 1954.

de Camp, L. Sprague, and Ley, Willy. *Lands Beyond.* New York: Rinehart, 1952.

DeLuca, Geraldine, and Natov, Roni. "The State of the Field in Children's Fantasy: An Interview with George Woods." *The Lion and the Unicorn* 1, no. 2 (Fall 1977): 4–16.

Dickinson, Peter. "Fantasy: The Need for Realism." *Children's Literature in Education* 17 (Spring 1986): 39–51. Paper given at the Fourth *Bookquest* Conference, Brighton Polytechnic, Spring 1984.

―――. *The Flight of Dragons.* Illus. by Wayne Anderson. New York: Harper and Row, 1979.

Digg, Sandra Elizabeth. "The Identification and Analysis of Contemporary and Universal Themes in Selected Books of Children's Literary Fantasy, Published between 1965 and 1970." Ph.D. dissertation, University of Chicago, 1971.

Di Lauro, Stephen. "100 Years of Fantasy Illustrations." *TZM* (June 1981): 36–41.

Disney, Walt. "Children Love Fantasy." *Instructor* 64 (Jan. 1955): 42.

Donaldson, Stephen R. *Epic Fantasy in the Modern World: A Few Observations.* Kent, OH: Kent State Univ. Libraries, 1986.

Donelson, Kenneth L., and Nilsen, Alleen Pace. *Literature for Today's Young Adults.* Glenview, IL: Scott, Foresman, 1980. "Fantasy," pp. 265–272.

Dooley, Patricia, ed. *The First Steps: Articles and Columns from the "Children's Literature Association Newsletter/Quarterly,"* vols. I–VI. West Lafayette, IN: Children's Literature Association Publications, 1984.

Drury, Roger W. "Realism Plus Fantasy Equals Magic." *Horn Book* 78 (Apr. 1972): 113–119. Reprinted in Heins. *Crosscurrents of Criticism.* Boston: Horn Book, 1977, pp. 178–184.

Eaton, Anne. "Extensions of Reality." *Horn Book* 3 (May 1927): 17–22.

Eaton, Anne Thaxter. *Reading with Children.* New York: Viking Press, 1940, pp. 13–23, 78–106, 310–330.

———. *Treasure for the Taking: A Book List for Boys and Girls.* rev. ed. New York: Viking Press, 1957. Original publication 1946. "Talking Beasts and Other Fanciful Creatures," pp. 28–33; "Modern Wonder Stories," pp. 72–86.

Ebert, G. "Zwischen Phantasie und Personlichkeit—neue Tendenzen Sozialisatischer Kinderliteratur [Between Fantasy and Reality: New Trends in Socialist Children's Literature]." *Bibliothekar* 35 (March 1981): 133–137.

Edwards, Malcolm, and Holdstock, Robert. *Realms of Fantasy.* Garden City, NY: Doubleday, 1983. Tolkien, pp. 11–22; Hilton, pp. 27–31; Le Guin, pp. 87–97.

Egoff, Sheila A. "Beyond the Garden Wall: Some Observations on Current Trends in Children's Literature." May Hill Arbuthnot Lecture. *Top of the News* 35 (Spring 1979): 257–271.

———. *The Republic of Childhood: A Critical Guide to Canadian Children's Literature in English.* New York: Oxford Univ. Press, 1967, 1975. "Books of Fantasy," pp. 131–149, 157–159.

———. *Thursday's Child: Trends and Patterns in Contemporary Children's Literature.* Chicago: American Library Association, 1981. "The New Fantasy," pp. 80–129.

Egoff, Sheila; Stubbs, G. T.; and Ashley, L. F., eds. *Only Connect: Readings on Children's Literature.* 2nd ed. New York: Oxford Univ. Press, 1980, pp. 106–120, 133–175, 183–220, 233–243, 337–355. Articles written by Tolkien, Travers, and Lewis; others about Baum, Lewis, Andersen, and Carroll.

Elgin, Don D. *The Comedy of the Fantastic: Ecological Perspectives on the Fantasy Novel.* Westport, CT: Greenwood Press, 1985.

Elleman, Barbara. "*A Game of Catch.*" Speech given at the 1985 Children's Books Open Forum at the ALA Annual Conference, July 1985. *Booklist* 82 (Nov. 15, 1985): 494–496. (time travel)

Ellis, Alec. "Little Folk and Young People." *Junior Bookshelf* 30, no. 2 (Apr. 1966): 97–102. Discusses Andersen, Carroll, Clarke, M. Norton, Swift, Tolkien, and T. H. White.

Emerson, Caroline D. "The Contemporaneous in Fairy Lore." *Horn Book* 3 (Nov. 1927): 38–41.

Epstein, Connie C. "Young Adult Books." *Horn Book* 63 (Nov.–Dec. 1987): 774–777. Contemporary fantasy and science fiction.

Esmonde, Margaret. "Death and Deathlessness in Children's Fantasy." *Fantasiae* 7 (Apr. 1979): 8–11.

Evans, Gwyneth. " 'Nothing Odd *Ever* Happens Here': Landscape in Canadian Fantasy." *Canadian Children's Literature* 15–16 (1980): 15–30.

Evans, W. D. Emrys. "The Welsh Mabinogion: Tellings and Retellings." *Children's Literature in Education* 28, no. 9 (Spring 1978): 17–33. Discusses Alexander and Garner.

Eyre, Frank. *British Children's Books in the 20th Century.* New York: Dutton, 1971. "Fantasy," pp. 115–147.

―――. "Twentieth Century British Fantasy Writers." In Margaret Trask. *Fantasy Science Fiction, Science Materials.* Kensington, NSW, Australia: Univ. of New South Wales, School of Librarianship, 1972, pp. 177–204.

Farmer, Penelope. " 'Jorinda and Jorindel' and Other Stories." *Children's Literature in Education* 7 (Mar. 1972): 23–37. Reprinted in Fox. *Writers, Critics and Children.* New York: Agathon, 1976, pp. 55–72.

Farrell, Eleanor M. " 'And Clove the Wind from Unseen Shores': The Sea Voyage Motif in Imaginative Literature." *Mythlore* 45 (1986): 43–47, 60.

Field, Elinor Whitney, comp. *Horn Book Reflections on Children's Books and Reading, 1949–1966.* Boston: Horn Book, 1969, pp. 6–13, 49–53, 203–249, 260–275, 286–290. Articles written by Coatsworth, Pearce, Eager, and Alexander; others about MacDonald, Nesbit, Lofting, C. S. Lewis, P. F. Cooper, Lynch, de la Mare, Grahame, and Carroll.

Finch-Reyner, S. "The Unseen Shore: Thoughts on the Popularity of Fantasy." *Journal of Popular Culture* 18 (Spring 1985): 127–134.

Fisher, Margery. *Intent upon Reading: A Critical Appraisal of Modern Fiction for Children.* New York: Watts, 1962. "Fantasy," pp. 36–169.

Ford, Boris, ed. *Young Writers, Young Readers: An Anthology of Children's Writing and Reading.* London: Hutchinson, 1960.

Fox, Geoff P., et al., eds. *Writers, Critics and Children: Articles from "Children's Literature in Education."* New York: Agathon Press, 1976, pp. 15–26, 55–124, 211–223. Articles written by Aiken, Farmer, Dickinson, Hughes, and Hoban; others about E. B. White, C. S. Lewis, and Le Guin.

Frank, Josette. *Your Child's Reading Today.* rev. ed. Garden City, NY: Doubleday, 1969, pp. 81–86, 97–98, 243–246, 265–268, 272–273. Original title: *What Books for Children?* 1937.

Fryatt, Norma R. *A Horn Book Sampler: On Children's Books and Reading (1924–1948).* Boston: Horn Book, 1959, pp. 4–7, 50–54, 133–139, 146–149.

Gagnon, Laurence. "Philosophy and Fantasy." In *Children's Literature: The Great Excluded,* vol. 1. Storrs, CT: Journal of the Modern Language Association, 1972, pp. 98–103.

Gardner, Emelyn E., and Ramsey, Eloise. *A Handbook of Children's Literature: Methods and Materials.* Darby, PA: Arden Library, 1981. Original publisher Scott, Foresman, 1927. "Modern Fairy Tales," pp. 82–83, 209–213.

Garthwaith, Marion. "The Acid Test." *Horn Book* 39 (Aug. 1963): 408–411. Discusses witchcraft and sorcery fantasy.

Geer, Caroline. "Land of Faerie: The Disappearing Myth." *Mythlore* 5 (Autumn 1978): 3–5.

Georgiou, Constantine. *Children and Their Literature.* Englewood Cliffs, NJ: Prentice-Hall, 1969. "Fantasy in Children's Literature," pp. 240–301.

Giblin, James Cross. "Forum: Does It Have to Be Fantasy to Be Imaginative?" *Children's Literature in Education* 30, no. 9 (Autumn 1978): 151–155. Reply from Göte Klingberg. *Children's Literature in Education* 10 (Spring 1979): 49–51.

Gillespie, Margaret C., and Conner, John W. *Creative Growth through Literature for Children and Adolescents.* Columbus, OH: Merrill, 1975. "Fantasy," pp. 11–14.

Glassman, Peter. "Juvenile Fantasy—An Overview." *A.B. Bookman's Weekly* 76 (Oct. 28, 1985): 3108–3113. (bibliographic essay)

Glazer, Joan I., and Williams, Gurney. *Introduction to Children's Literature.* New York: McGraw-Hill, 1979. "Modern Fantasy," pp. 256–301.

Golden, Joanne Marie. "A Scheme for Analyzing Responses to Literature Applied to the Responses of Fifth and Eighth Graders to Realistic and Fantastic Short Stories." Ph.D. dissertation, Ohio State University, 1978.

Goldthwaite, John. "The Black Rabbit: Part One." *Signal* 47 (May 1985): 86–111; "The Black Rabbit: Part Two." *Signal* 48 (Sept. 1985): 148–167. Reprinted in Goldthwaite. *The Natural History of Make-Believe: A Study of Imaginative Children's Literature from Perrault to Sendak.* London: Oxford Univ. Press, 1987.

Goodrich, Norma Lorre. *King Arthur.* New York: Watts, 1986.

———. *Merlin.* New York: Watts, 1987.

Goodrich, Peter Hampton. "Merlin: The Figure of the Wizard in English Fiction." Ph.D. dissertation, University of Michigan, 1983.

Graham, Eleanor. "Nonsense in Children's Literature." *Junior Bookshelf* 9 (July 1945): 61–68.

Gray, Irene. "The Shadow Line between Reality and Fantasy: The Development of Fantasy in Australian Children's Literature." M. Ed. dissertation, University of Tasmania, 1985.

Green, Roger Lancelyn. *Tellers of Tales: British Authors of Children's Books from 1800–1964.* New York: Watts, 1965, pp. 23–39, 49–73, 97–115, 202–224, 238–257, 269–279.

Greene, Ellin. "Literary Uses of Traditional Themes: From 'Cinderella' to *The Girl Who Sat by the Ashes* and *The Glass Slipper.*" *Children's Literature Association Quarterly* 11 (Fall 1986): 128–132.

Hallowell, Lillian. *A Book of Children's Literature.* New York: Farrar, 1938. "Modern Fairy Tales," pp. 177–282.

Hambleton, A. "Canadian Fantasy." *British Columbia Library Quarterly* 26 (Oct. 1962): 11–13.

Hannabus, Stuart; Litherland, Barry; and Morland, Stephanie, comps. "Fiction for Children, 1970–1980. 1. Myth and Fantasy." *Children's Literature in Education* 12, no. 3 (Autumn 1981): 119–139.

Harmes, Jean McLain. "Children's Responses to Fantasy in Relation to Their Stages of Intellectual Development." Ph.D. dissertation, Ohio State University, 1972.

Hartmann, Waltraut. "Identification and Projection in Folk Fairy Tales and in Fantastic Stories for Children." *Bookbird* 7, no. 2 (1969): 8–17.

Hathaway, Nancy. *The Unicorn.* New York: Viking Press, 1980; Outlet Book Co., 1984.

Haviland, Virginia. *Children and Literature: Views and Reviews.* Glenview, IL: Scott, Foresman, 1973, pp. 50–63, 71–77, 140–159, 220–249. Articles written by de la Mare, E. B. White, Aiken, Babbitt, Buchan, C. S. Lewis, Alexander, and Travers.

———. "Fairy Tales and Creativity." In *How Can Children's Literature Meet the Needs of Modern Children?* 15th IBBY Conference, 1976, pp. 56–61.

Hazard, Paul. *Books, Children, and Men.* 4th ed. Boston: Horn Book, 1960, pp. 92–105, 111–118, 135–141, 157–165. Originally published in France, 1932.

Hedges, Ned Samuel. "The Fable and the Fabulous: The Use of Traditional Forms in Children's Literature." Ph.D. dissertation, University of Nebraska, 1968.

Heins, Paul. "Mythic Journeys." In *Innocence & Experience.* Edited by Barbara Harrison and Gregory Maguire. New York: Lothrop, 1987, pp. 129–137.

———, ed. *Crosscurrents of Criticism: Horn Book Essays 1968–1977.* Boston: Horn Book, 1977, pp. 3–6, 98–125, 169–204, 226–233, 277–282, 311–314, 333–348. Articles written by Lindgren, Cameron, Dahl, Le Guin, Alexander, Drury, Langton, Fleischman, and Lively; others about Andersen, Adams, Le Guin, and Lively.

Helson, Ravenna. "The Creative Spectrum of Authors of Fantasy." *Journal of Personality* 45 (June 1977): 310–326. An examination of 98 books for 8-to-12-year olds written between 1930 and 1972.

———. "Experiences of Authors in Writing Fantasy: Two Relationships Between

Creative Process and Product." *Altered States of Consciousness* 3, no. 3 (1977–1978): 235–248.

———. "Fantasy and Self-Discovery." *Horn Book* 46 (Apr. 1970): 121–134. Reprinted in M. L. White. *Children's Literature*. Columbus, OH: Merrill, 1976, pp. 117–125.

———. "From Magical Woman to Wizard: Comparisons of Literary Fantasy in the Nineteenth and Twentieth Centuries." In *Proceedings of the XVIIth International Congress of Applied Psychology*. Brussels: Editest, 1972, pp. 1515–1519.

———. "Heroic and Tender Modes in Women Authors of Fantasy." *Journal of Personality* 41 (Dec. 1973): 493–512. Twenty-eight women authors of children's fantasy written since 1930.

———. "The Heroic, the Comic, and the Tender: Patterns of Literary Fantasy and Their Authors." *Journal of Personality* 41 (June 1973): 163–184. Twenty-seven male authors of children's fantasy written since 1930.

———. "The Imaginative Process in Children's Literature: A Quantitative Appraisal." *Poetics* 7 (1978): 135–153.

———. "Sex-Specific Patterns in Creative Literary Fantasy." *Journal of Personality* 38, no. 3 (Sept. 1970): 344–363.

———. "Through the Pages of Children's Books." *Psychology Today,* 7, no. 6 (Nov. 1973): 107–117.

Helson, Ravenna, and Proysen, Alf. "The Psychological Origins of Fantasy for Children in Mid-Victorian England." In *Children's Literature,* vol. 3. Storrs, CT: Journal of the Modern Language Association, 1974, pp. 66–75.

Hendrix, Miriam Jenson. "Flight to Fantasy." *Christianity Today,* Sept. 13, 1974, pp. 29–32.

Hennelly, Mark M., Jr. "Alice's Big Sister: Fantasy and the Adolescent Dream." *Journal of Popular Culture* 16 (Summer 1982): 72–87.

Hibbert, Christopher. *The Search for King Arthur.* New York: Harper and Row, 1969.

Hieatt, Constance B. "Analyzing Enchantment: Fantasy after Bettelheim." *Canadian Children's Literature* 15–16 (1980): 6–14.

Higgins, James E. *Beyond Words: Mystical Fantasy in Children's Literature.* New York: Teachers College Press, Columbia Univ., 1970.

———. "Five Authors of Mystical Fantasy for Children: A Critical Study." Ed.D. dissertation, Columbia University, 1965. Discusses Hudson, C. S. Lewis, Saint-Exupéry, MacDonald, and Tolkien.

Hoffield, Laura. "Where Magic Begins." *The Lion and the Unicorn* 3 (Spring 1979): 4–13.

Holdstock, Robert, and Edwards, Malcolm. *Lost Realms.* Englewood Cliffs, NJ: Salem Press, 1985. Illustrated landscapes of fantasy fiction.

Hollinger, V. "Deconstructing the Time Machine." *Science Fiction Studies* 14 (July 1987): 201–221. Discusses time travel in literature.

Honig, Edith Lazaros. "A Quiet Rebellion: The Portrait of the Female in Victorian Children's Fantasy." Ph.D. dissertation, Fordham University, 1986.

Hopkins, Lee Bennett. *Books Are by People: Interviews with 104 Authors and Illustrators of Books for Young Children.* New York: Citation Press, 1969, pp. 107–120, 125–127, 226–229, 250–258, 289–291, 299–302. Interviews with Ipcar, Lathrop, Raskin, Sendak, Seuss, Turkle, and Warburg.

———. *More Books by More People: Interviews with Sixty-five Authors of Books for Children.* New York: Citation Press, 1974, pp. 10–17, 24–28, 35–40, 68–77, 88–99, 105–114, 138–140, 147–152, 199–207, 303–307, 312–322, 343–350, 355–362, 375–380. Interviews with Alexander, Babbitt, M. Bond, Byars, Carlson, Cleary, Coatsworth, Cunningham, Dahl, Edmonds, Estes, Hamilton, Selden, Singer, Snyder, Stolz, Travers, and E. B. White.

Hughes, Felicity A. "Children's Literature: Theory and Practice, Part 2." *English Literary History* 45 (1978): 552–561. Reprinted in Robert Bator. *Signposts to Criticism of Children's Literature.* Chicago: American Library Association, 1983, pp. 242–248.

Hume, Kathryn. *Fantasy and Mimesis: Responses to Reality in Western Literature.* New York: Methuen, 1984.

Hunt, Caroline. "Form as Fantasy—Fantasy as Form." *Children's Literature Association Quarterly* 12 (Spring 1987): 7–11.

Hunt, Peter. "Landscapes and Journeys, Metaphors and Maps: The Distinctive Feature of English Fantasy." *Children's Literature Association Quarterly* 12 (Spring 1987): 11–15.

Hunter, Mollie. "One World." *Horn Book* 51 (Dec. 1975): 557–563; continued in 52 (Jan. 1976): 32–38.

Hürlimann, Bettina. "Fantasy and Reality." In *Three Centuries of Children's Books in Europe.* Cleveland: World, 1968, pp. 76–92.

Huygen, Wil. *Gnomes.* New York: Abrams, 1977. Illus. by Rien Poortvliet. New York: Bantam, 1979. pap. A companion volume is *Faeries* by Brian Froud and Alan Lee. New York: Abrams, 1978.

Inglis, Fred. *The Promise of Happiness: Value and Meaning in Children's Fiction.* New York: Cambridge Univ. Press, 1981.

Innocence & Experience: Essays & Conversations on Children's Literature. Edited by Barbara Harrison and Gregory Maguire. New York: Lothrop, 1987. "Mythic Patterns," pp. 87–164; "Fantasy: The Perilous Realm," pp. 165–210.

Issayeva, A. "The Contemporary Children's Tale: Images and Intent." *Bookbird* 22 (1984): 18–32.

Jackson, Rosemary. *Fantasy: The Literature of Subversion.* London: Methuen, 1981. "Victorian Fantasies," pp. 141–156.

Jan, Isabelle. *On Children's Literature.* Edited by Catherine Storr. New York: Schocken, 1974, pp. 42–89. Originally published in France, 1969.

Jarvis, Sharon, ed. *Inside Outer Space: Science Fiction Professionals Look at Their Craft.* New York: Ungar, 1985.

Jenkins, Sue. " 'I Will Take the Ring': Responsibility and Maturity in Modern Fantasy Fiction for Young People." In Peter Hunt. *Further Approaches to Research in Children's Literature.* Cardiff: Univ. of Wales, 1982.

Johnson, Diana L. *Fantastic Illustration and Design in Britain, 1850–1930.* Providence: Museum of Art, Rhode Island School of Design, 1979.

Johnson, Edna; Sickels, Evelyn R.; and Sayers, Frances Clark. *Anthology of Children's Literature.* Originally published 1959, 4th ed. Boston: Houghton Mifflin, 1970. "Fantasy," pp. 607–750.

Jones, Cornelia, and Way, Olivia R. *British Children's Authors: Interviews at Home.* Chicago: American Library Association, 1976, pp. 3–10, 31–40, 49–100, 127–154. Interviews with Aiken, Arthur, M. Bond, Boston, Clarke, Farmer, Gard, Garner, Peyton, Picard, and Sutcliff.

Jordan, Alice M. "Animals in Fairyland." *Horn Book* 17 (Nov.–Dec. 1941): 439–444. Reprinted in Norma Fryatt. *A Horn Book Sampler.* Boston: Horn Book, 1959, pp. 146–149.

Keightley, Thomas. *The World Guide to Gnomes, Fairies, Elves and Other Little People.* New York: Avenel, 1978. Originally published in 1880 as *The Fairy Mythology.*

Kiefer, B. Z. "Wales as a Setting for Children's Fantasy." *Children's Literature in Education* 13 (Summer 1982): 95–102.

Kincaid, Paul. "The Realms of Fantasy." *Vector* 117 (1983): 10–14.

Kingman, Lee, ed. *Newbery and Caldecott Medal Books: 1966–1975, with Acceptance*

Papers, Biographies and Related Material Chiefly from the Horn Book Magazine. Boston: Horn Book, 1975. Alexander, O'Brien, pp. 45–55, 79–92.

————. *Newbery and Caldecott Medal Books, 1976–1985.* Boston: Horn Book, 1986. Cooper, McKinley, and Van Allsburg.

Kinney, Thomas L. "Arthurian Romances." In *Supernatural Fiction Writers*, vol. 1. Edited by E. F. Bleiler. New York: Scribner, 1985, pp. 11–18.

Klingberg, Göte. "The Fantastic and the Mythical as Reading for Modern Children and Young People." In *How Can Children's Literature Meet the Needs of Modern Children?* 15th IBBY Conference, 1976, pp. 32–35.

————. *The Fantastic Tale for Children: A Genre Study from the Viewpoints of Literary and Educational Research.* LIGRU Monograph no. 2. Gothenburg, Sweden: Gothenburg School of Education, 1970.

————. "The Fantastic Tale for Children: Its Literary and Educational Problems." *Bookbird* 5, no. 3 (1967): 13–20.

Knoblauch, C. J. "Recent Trends in Fantasy in Children's Literature." Research paper. Kent, OH: Kent State Univ. Press, 1975.

Knoepflmacher, U. C. "The Balancing of Child and Adult: An Approach to Victorian Fantasies for Children." *19th Century Fiction* 37 (Mar. 1983): 497–530.

Kobil, Daniel T. "The Elusive Appeal of the Fantastic." *Mythlore* 4 (June 1977): 17–19.

Kurth, R. J. "Realism in Children's Books of Fantasy." *California Librarian* 39 (July 1978): 39–40.

Kuznets, Lois R. "Games of Dark: Psychofantasy in Children's Literature." *The Lion and the Unicorn* 1 (1977): 17–24.

Lacy, Norris J., ed. *The Arthurian Encyclopedia.* New York: Garland, 1986.

Landow, G. P. "And the World Became Strange: Realms of Literary Fantasy." *Georgia Review* 33 (Spring 1979): 7–42. Reprinted in Diana Johnson. *Fantastic Illustration and Design in Britain 1850–1930.* Providence: Rhode Island School of Design, 1979, pp. 28–43; and in Roger Schlobin. *The Aesthetics of Fantasy Literature and Art.* Notre Dame, IN: University of Notre Dame Press, 1982, pp. 105–142.

Landsberg, Michele. *Michele Landsberg's Guide to Children's Books.* New York: Penguin, 1985. "Fantasy," pp. 120–140; "Travelling in Time," pp. 141–154.

Lanes, Selma. *Down the Rabbit Hole: Adventures and Misadventures in the Realm of Children's Literature.* New York: Atheneum, 1976. "America as Fairy Tale," pp. 91–111.

Langton, Jane. "The Weak Place in the Cloth: A Study of Fantasy for Children." *Horn Book* 49 (Oct. 1973): 433–441; continued in 49 (Dec. 1973): 570–578. Reprinted in Paul Heins, ed. *Crosscurrents of Criticism.* Boston: Horn Book, 1977, pp. 185–196.

"A Large Youthful Appetite for Magic and Fantasy." *London Times Literary Supplement*, Sept. 9, 1960, pp. xxi–xxii.

Larkin, David. *The Fantastic Kingdom: A Collection of Illustrations from the Golden Days of Storytelling.* New York: Ballantine, 1974.

Laurence, M. J. P. "Animals and Dressed Animals." *Junior Bookshelf* 21 (Dec. 1957): 289–294.

————. "Fantasy and Fashion." *Junior Bookshelf* 18 (Oct. 1954): 169–174.

Lavender, Ralph. "Other Worlds: Myth and Fantasy, 1970–1980." *Children's Literature in Education* 12, no. 3 (Autumn 1981): 140–150.

Le Guin, Ursula K. "In Defense of Fantasy." *Horn Book* 49 (June 1973): 239. Reprinted in Paul Heins. *Crosscurrents of Criticism.* Boston: Horn Book, 1977, p. 169.

————. *The Language of the Night: Essays on Fantasy and Science Fiction.* New York: Putnam, 1979.

L'Engle, Madeleine. "What Is Real?" *Language Arts* 55 (1977): 447–451.

Lenz, Millicent. "Fantasy and Survival." *Catholic Library World* 48 (Sept. 1976): 56–61.

Lenz, Millicent, and Mahood, Ramona M., comps. *Young Adult Literature: Background and Criticism.* Chicago: American Library Association, 1980, pp. 415–445.

Lewis, Naomi. "The Road to Fantasy." In *Children's Literature,* vol. 11. New Haven, CT: Yale Univ. Press, 1983, pp. 201–210.

Lindskoog, John, and Lindskoog, Kay. *How to Grow a Young Reader.* Elgin, IL: Cook, 1978. "Flights of Fancy: Fantastic Tales Today," pp. 62–88.

Lochhead, Marion. *Renaissance of Wonder: The Fantasy Words of J. R. R. Tolkien, C. S. Lewis, George MacDonald, E. Nesbit and Others.* New York: Harper & Row, 1980. Originally published in England in 1977 as *The Renaissance of Wonder in Children's Literature.* Major chapters on MacDonald, Nesbit, Kipling, Masefield, de la Mare, Stephens, Lynch, C. S. Lewis, and Tolkien.

Loder Reed, Elizabeth. "Personal Identity Concepts in the Context of Children's Fantasy Literature." Ph.D. dissertation, Boston University, 1979.

Lourie, Helen. "Where Is Fancy Bred?" *New Society,* Dec. 6, 1962. Reprinted in Sheila A. Egoff. *Only Connect.* New York: Oxford Univ. Press, 1980, pp. 106–110.

Lowentrout, Peter. "The Rags of Lordship: Science Fiction, Fantasy, and the Reenchantment of the World." *Mythlore* 41 (1985): 47–51, 57.

Lukens, Rebecca J. *A Critical Handbook of Children's Literature.* 3rd ed. Glenview, IL: Scott, Foresman, 1986. "Fantasy," pp. 18–19, 95–97, 106–107, 140–141, 161, 167–168.

Lupak, Alan C. "Modern Arthurian Novelists on the Arthurian Legend." *Studies in Medievalism* 2 (Fall 1983): 79–88.

Lüthi, Max. *Once upon a Time: On the Nature of Fairy Tales.* New York: Ungar, 1970.

MacCann, Donnarae. "Wells of Fancy, 1865–1965." *Wilson Library Bulletin* 40 (Dec. 1965): 334–343. Reprinted in Sheila A. Egoff. *Only Connect.* New York: Oxford Univ. Press, 1980, pp. 133–149.

MacDonald, Ruth. "The Tale Retold: Feminist Fairy Tales." *Children's Literature Association Quarterly* 7 (Summer 1982): 18–20.

McDonough, Irma, ed. *Profiles.* rev. ed. Ottawa: Canadian Library Association, 1975.

———. *Profiles 2: Authors and Illustrators, Children's Literature in Canada.* Ottawa: Canadian Library Association, 1982.

McGillis, Roderick. "Fantasy as Adventure: 19th Century Children's Fiction." *Children's Literature Association Quarterly* 8 (Fall 1983): 18–22.

Macneice, Louis. *Varieties of Parable.* New York: Cambridge Univ. Press, 1965, pp. 82–102.

MacVeagh, Charles Peter, and Shands, Frances. "Fairy Stories: Fantasy, Fact, or . . . Forecast?" *Language Arts* 59 (1982): 328–335.

McVitty, Walter. *Innocence and Experience: Essays on Contemporary Australian Children's Writers.* Melbourne, Australia: Nelson, 1981.

Mahon, R. L. "The Epic Tradition in Science Fiction and Fantasy." *Teaching in a Two-Year College* 14 (Fall 1987): 47–51.

Manlove, C. N. "Comic Fantasy." *Extrapolation* 28 (Spring 1987): 37–44.

———. "The Elusiveness of Fantasy." *Fantasy Review* 90 (1986): 13–14+.

———. *The Impulse of Fantasy Literature.* Kent, OH: Kent State Univ. Press, 1983, pp. 7–14, 31–114. Major chapters on Thackeray, Le Guin, Nesbit, MacDonald, and T. H. White.

———. *Modern Fantasy: Five Studies.* New York: Cambridge Univ. Press, 1975. "On the Nature of Fantasy," pp. 1–12. Reprinted in Roger Schlobin. *The Aesthetics of Fantasy Literature and Art.* Notre Dame, IN: Univ. of Notre Dame Press, 1982, pp. 16–35. Discusses Kingsley, MacDonald, C. S. Lewis, and Tolkien.

Manuel, Diane. "The Realm of the Imagination: Enduring Fantasy." *Christian Science Monitor* (Nov. 6, 1987): B1–2.

May, Jill P., ed. *Children and Their Literature: A Readings Book.* West Lafayette, IN:

Children's Literature Association Publications, 1983. Includes articles on Mac-Donald and Aiken.

Meek, Margaret. "Speaking of Shifters." In *Changing English: Essays for Harold Rosen.* London: Heinemann, 1984. Reprinted in *Signal* 45 (Sept., 1984): 152–167.

Meek, Margaret; Warlow, Aidan; and Barton, Griselda. *The Cool Web: The Pattern of Children's Reading.* New York: Atheneum, 1978, pp. 76–79, 103–105, 120–128, 157–158, 166–187, 196–200, 216–221, 265–271, 284–293, 314–330. Articles by C. S. Lewis, Storr, Aiken, Pearce, Garner, and Boston.

Meigs, Cornelia; Eaton, Anne Thaxter; Nesbitt, Elizabeth; and Viguers, Ruth Hill. *A Critical History of Children's Literature: A Survey of Children's Books in English* (originally published 1953), rev. ed. New York: Macmillan, 1969, pp. 165–174, 182–183, 186–202, 278–284, 310–348, 446–483, 512–513.

Merla, Patrick. " 'What Is Real?' Asked the Rabbit One Day: Realism vs. Fantasy in Children's and Adult Literature." *Saturday Review,* Nov. 4, 1972, pp. 43–50. Reprinted in Sheila A. Egoff. *Only Connect.* New York: Oxford Univ. Press, 1980, pp. 337–355.

Millar, John Hepburn. "On Some Books for Boys and Girls." In *A Peculiar Gift: Nineteenth Century Writings on Books for Children.* Edited by Lance Salway. Harmondsworth, England: Penguin, 1976, pp. 154–161. Reprinted from *Blackwood's Magazine* 159 (Mar. 1896): 389–395.

Miller, Bertha Mahony, and Field, Elinor Whitney, eds. *Newbery Medal Books: 1922–1955.* Boston: Horn Book, 1957. Lofting, pp. 17–27; Chrisman, pp. 39–43; Field, pp. 74–88; Coatsworth, pp. 89–98; Seredy, pp. 157–165; Lawson, pp. 255–267; Bailey, pp. 288–299; Du Bois, pp. 300–317.

Miller, Patricia. "The Importance of Being Earnest: The Fairy Tale in 19th Century England." *Children's Literature Association Quarterly* 7 (Summer 1982): 11–14.

Milne, Rosemary. "Fantasy in Literature for Early Childhood." In Moira Robinson, ed. *Readings in Children's Literature: Proceedings of the National Seminar on Children's Literature.* Frankston, Australia: Frankston State College, 1975.

Milnes, P. C. "Analysis of British and American Fantasy in Children's Literature." Research paper. Long Island University, 1969.

Milosh, Joseph E., Jr. "Reason and Mysticism in Fantasy and Science Fiction." In *Young Adult Literature: Background and Criticism.* Edited by Millicent Lenz and Ramona M. Mahood. Chicago: American Library Association, 1980, pp. 433–439.

Mobley, Jane. "Magic Is Alive: A Study of Contemporary Fantasy Fiction." Ph.D. dissertation, University of Kansas, 1974.

———. "Toward a Definition of Fantasy Fiction." *Extrapolation* 15 (May 1974): 117–128. Reprinted in Robert Bator. *Signposts to Criticism of Children's Literature.* Chicago: American Library Association, 1983, pp. 249–260.

———, ed. *Phantasmagoria: Tales of Fantasy and the Supernatural.* New York: Anchor Press, 1977. "Preface," pp. 13–18; "The Wondrous Fair: Magical Fantasy," pp. 21–35.

Molson, Francis. "Children's Fantasy and Science Fiction." In Marshall B. Tymn, ed. *The Science Fiction Reference Book.* Mercer Island, WA: Starmont, 1981, pp. 19–32.

———. "Ethical Fantasy for Children." In Roger Schlobin. *The Aesthetics of Fantasy Literature and Art.* Notre Dame, IN: Univ. of Notre Dame Press, 1982, pp. 82–104.

Montgomery, Marion. "Prophetic Poet and the Loss of Middle Earth." *Georgia Review* 33 (Spring 1979): 63–88.

Moorcook, Michael. "The Heroes in Heroic Fantasy." *Dragonfields* 3 (1980): 50–61.

Moore, Anne Carroll. *The Three Owls: A Book about Children's Books, Their Authors, Artists and Critics.* New York: Macmillan, 1925. Followed by *The Three Owls: Second Book. Contemporary Critics of Children's Books.* New York: Coward-

McCann, 1928; and *The Three Owls, Third Book.* New York: Coward-McCann, 1931.

Moore, Annie E. *Literature Old and New for Children: Materials for a College Course.* Boston: Houghton Mifflin, 1934. "The Modern Fanciful Tale," pp. 352–387.

Morris, John S. "Fantasy in a Mythless Age." In *Children's Literature,* vol. 2. Storrs, CT: Journal of the Modern Language Association, 1973, pp. 77–86.

Moss, Anita West. "Children and Fairy Tales: A Study in Nineteenth Century British Fantasy." Ph.D. dissertation, Indiana University, 1979.

————. "Crime and Punishment—Or Development—In Fairy Tales and Fantasy." *Mythlore* 8 (Spring 1981): 26–28, 42.

————. "Varieties of Literary Fairy Tale." *Children's Literature Association Quarterly* 7 (Summer 1982): 15–17.

Moss, Elaine. *Part of the Pattern: A Personal Journey through the World of Children's Books, 1960–1985.* New York: Greenwillow Press, 1986.

Mountjoy, Harry W. "The Comic Fantasy in English Fiction of the Victorian Period." Ph.D. dissertation, University of Pennsylvania, 1934.

Muir, Percival Horace. *English Children's Books, 1600–1900.* Original U.S. publication, Praeger, 1954. North Pomfret, VT: David and Charles, 1979, pp. 105–107, 136–143, 153–160.

Mulderig, Gerald P. "Alice and Wonderland: Subversive Elements in the World of Victorian Children's Fiction." *Journal of Popular Culture* 11 (1978): 320–329.

Muta, Orie. "The Development of Fantasy in Australian Children's Literature." Master's dissertation, University of Sydney (Australia), 1983.

Natov, Roni, and DeLuca, Geraldine. "Current Trends in Children's Books: Fantasy and Realism." *U.S.A. Today* 109 (July 1980): 42–47.

Newman, Anne Royall. "Images of the Bear in Children's Literature." *Children's Literature in Education* 18 (Fall 1987): 131–138. Milne, Bond, Kipling, and Stearns.

Nodelman, Perry. "Defining Children's Literature." In *Children's Literature,* vol. 8. New Haven, CT: Yale Univ. Press, 1980, pp. 184–190.

————. "Interpretation and the Apparent Sameness of Children's Novels." *Studies in Literary Imagination* 18 (Fall 1985): 5–20. (time travel)

————. "Some Presumptuous Generalizations about Fantasy." *Children's Literature Association Quarterly* 4 (Summer 1979): 5–6, 18. Reprinted in *Festschrift: A Ten Year Retrospective.* Edited by Perry Nodelman and Jill P. May. West Lafayette, IN: Children's Literature Association Publications, 1983, pp. 26–27; and in *The First Steps.* Edited by Patricia Dooley. West Lafayette, IN: Children's Literature Association Publications, 1984, pp. 15–16.

————, ed. *Touchstones: Reflections on the Best in Children's Literature,* vol. 1. West Lafayette, IN: Children's Literature Association Publications, 1985.

Nodelman, Perry, and May, Jill P. *Festschrift: A Ten Year Retrospective.* West Lafayette, IN: Children's Literature Association Publications, 1983. "Fantasy," pp. 26–35.

Norton, Donna E. *Through the Eyes of a Child: An Introduction to Children's Literature.* 2nd ed. Columbus, OH: Merrill, 1983, 1987. "Modern Fantasy," pp. 264–325.

Norton, Eloise D., ed. *Folk Literature of the British Isles: Readings for Librarians, Teachers and Those Who Work with Children and Young Adults.* Metuchen, NJ: Scarecrow Press, 1978.

Olcott, Frances Jenkins. *The Children's Reading.* rev. ed. Boston: Houghton Mifflin, 1927. "Fables, Myths and Fairy Tales," p. 90.

The Openhearted Audience: Ten Authors Talk about Writing for Children. Washington, DC: Library of Congress, 1980. Joan Aiken, pp. 46–67; Eleanor Cameron, pp. 152–175; Ursula Le Guin, pp. 100–113; and P. L. Travers, pp. 2–23.

Osborne, E. "Fairy Tales and Fantasy." *Library Association Record* 45 (Dec. 1943): 211–212.

Owen, Helen Hammet. "In Defense of Fairy Tales." *Horn Book* 7 (Aug. 1931): 131–139.

Parish, Helen Rand. "Children's Books in Latin America: Part II. Fantasy and Other Modern Trends." *Horn Book* 24 (July–Aug. 1948): 257–262.

Pawling, Christopher, ed. *Popular Fiction and Societal Changes.* New York: St. Martin's Press, 1984.

Paxon, Diana. "The Tolkien Tradition." *Mythlore* 39 (1984): 23–27, 37. Includes Adams, Alexander, Brooks, Le Guin, Lewis.

Peel, Doris. "Books That Enchant." *Horn Book* 25 (May 1949): 242–247. Grahame and St. Exupéry.

Peppin, Brigid. *Fantasy: Book Illustration 1860–1920.* London: Thames and Hudson, 1977.

———. *Fantasy: The Golden Age of Fantastic Illustration.* Original British publication, 1975. New York: New American Library, 1976.

Peterson, Linda Kauffman, and Solt, Marilyn Leathers. "The Newbery Medal and Honor Books, 1922–1981: Fantasy." *Children's Literature Association Quarterly* 6 (Fall 1981): 23.

Petrich, Shirley. "A Note on Contemporary Soviet Fantasies." In *Children's Literature,* vol. 2. Storrs, CT: Journal of the Modern Language Association, 1973, pp. 221–223.

Philip, Neil. "Fantasy: Double Cream or Instant Whip?" *Signal* 35 (May 1981): 82–90.

Plank, Robert. "The Golem and the Robot." *Literature and Psychology* 13–15 (1963–1965): 12–27.

Platt, Charles. *Dream Makers: Science Fiction and Fantasy Writers at Work.* New York: Ungar, 1987. Interviews.

———. "In Defense of the Real World." *Isaac Asimov's Science Fiction Magazine,* Nov. 1983, pp. 53–66.

Poskanzer, Susan Cornell. "A Case for Fantasy." *Elementary English* 52 (Apr. 1975): 472–475.

Post, J. B. "Cartographic Fantasy." *Bulletin of the Geography and Map Division, Special Libraries Association* 101 (1975): 12–14.

Prickett, Stephen. "Religious Fantasy in the Nineteenth Century." In Frank N. Magill. *Survey of Modern Fantasy Literature,* vol. 5. Englewood Cliffs, NJ: Salem Press, 1983, pp. 2369–2382.

———. *Victorian Fantasy.* Bloomington: Indiana Univ. Press, 1979. Discusses Carroll, Kingsley, MacDonald, Kipling, and Nesbit.

Quayle, Eric. *The Collector's Book of Children's Books.* New York: Potter; dist. by Crown, 1971. "Fairy, Folk Tales and Fantasy," pp. 36–46.

———. *Early Children's Books: A Collector's Guide.* New York: Barnes and Noble, 1983, pp. 74–88, 176–181.

Rabkin, Eric S. "The Appeal of the Fantastic: Old Worlds for New." In *The Scope of the Fantastic—Theory, Technique, Major Authors.* Edited by Robert A. Collins and Howard D. Pearce. Westport, CT: Greenwood Press, 1985.

———. *The Fantastic in Literature.* Princeton: Princeton Univ. Press, 1975.

———. *Fantastic Worlds: Myths, Tales, and Stories.* New York: Oxford Univ. Press, 1979. Anthology plus critical essay.

Radu, Kenneth. "Canadian Fantasy." *Canadian Children's Literature* 1, no. 2 (Summer 1975): 73–79.

Rausch, Helen Martha. "The Debate over Fairy Tales." Ph.D. dissertation, Columbia University Teachers College, 1977.

Rawlinson, Eleanor. *Introduction to Literature for Children.* rev. ed. New York: Norton, 1937. "Fanciful Tales," pp. 337–340.

Ray, Sheila G. *Children's Fiction: A Handbook for Librarians.* rev. ed. London: Brockhampton, 1972. "Fantasy," pp. 23–33.

Rees, David. *The Marble in the Water: Essays on Contemporary Writers of Fiction for Children and Young Adults.* Boston: Horn Book, 1980, pp. 1–13, 36–89, 185–198. Articles on Farmer, Pearce, Garner, E. B. White, Le Guin, and Lively.

———. *Painted Desert, Green Shade: Essays on Contemporary Writers of Fiction for Children and Young Adults.* Boston: Horn Book, 1984. Includes Boston, Dickinson, Hamilton, Hoban, T. Hughes, Mark, Langton, Townsend, and Westall.

"Reflections on Fantasy and Science Fiction." *Top of the News* 39 (Fall 1982): 39–96. Issue on fantasy.

Richardson, Carmen C. "The Reality of Fantasy." *Language Arts* 53 (1976): 549–551, 563.

Robinson, Evelyn R., ed. *Readings about Children's Literature.* New York: McKay, 1966, pp. 302–312.

Robinson, Moira, ed. *Readings in Children's Literature: Proceedings of the National Seminar on Children's Literature.* Frankston, Australia: Frankston State College, 1975.

Rochelle, Larry. "Quest: The Search for Meaning through Fantasy." *English Journal* 66 (October 1977): 54–55.

Roginski, Jim. *Behind the Covers: Interviews with Authors and Illustrators of Books for Children and Young Adults.* Littleton, CO: Libraries Unlimited, 1985.

Rottensteiner, Franz. "European Theories of Fantasy." In Frank N. Magill. *Survey of Modern Fantasy Literature,* vol. 5. Englewood Cliffs, NJ: Salem Press, 1983, pp. 2235–2246.

———. *The Fantasy Book: An Illustrated History from Dracula to Tolkien.* New York: Macmillan, 1978, pp. 96–98, 108–115.

Rupert, Pamela Rae. "An Analysis of the Need Fulfillment Imagery in Fantasy Literature for Children." Ph.D. dissertation, University of Akron, 1979.

Rustin, Margaret. "Deep Structures of Fantasy in Modern British Children's Books." *The Lion and the Unicorn* 10 (1986): 60–82.

Rustin, Michael, and Rustin, Margaret. *Narratives of Love and Loss: Studies in Modern Children's Fiction.* London: Verso, 1987. Fox, Godden, Hoban, Lewis, Nesbit, M. Norton, Fred Banks, Pearce, E. B. White.

Ryan, John S. *Australian Fantasy and Folklore.* Armidale, NSW, Australia: Univ. of New England, 1981.

Safford, Barbara Ripp. "High Fantasy: An Archetypal Analysis of Children's Literature." D.L.S. dissertation, Columbia University, 1983.

Sale, Roger. "The Audience in Children's Literature." In George Slusser, Eric Rabkin, and Robert Scholes. *Bridges to Fantasy.* Carbondale: Southern Illinois Univ. Press, 1982, pp. 78–89.

———. *Fairy Tales and After: From Snow White to E. B. White.* Cambridge, MA: Harvard Univ. Press, 1978. Discusses Carroll, Grahame, Kipling, Baum, Brooks, and E. B. White.

Salway, Lance, ed. *A Peculiar Gift: Nineteenth Century Writings on Books for Children.* Harmondsworth, Middlesex: Kestrel, 1976. "Fairy Tale Never Dies," pp. 111–167, 173–194. Articles by Dickens, Ruskin, Lang, Molesworth, MacDonald, and Horne.

Sargent, Abby L. "Books for Children: Fairy Tales. *Library Journal* 26, no. 8 (1901): 66–69. Discusses Browne, Ingelow, Craik, MacDonald, and Nesbit.

Saxby, H. M., and Cotton, Marjorie. *A History of Australian Children's Literature, 1941–1970.* Sydney: Wentworth Books, 1971. "Fantasy," pp. 139–154.

Sayers, Frances Clarke. "Walt Disney Accused. An Interview with Frances Clarke Sayers." *Horn Book* 41 (Dec. 1965): 602–611.

Scherf, Walter. "Magic Tales as an Invitation to a Child's Necessary Scaling Off." In

How Can Children's Literature Meet the Needs of Modern Children? 15th IBBY Conference, 1976, pp. 36–41.

Schlobin, Roger C. "Fantasy Versus Horror." In Frank N. Magill. *Survey of Modern Fantasy Literature,* vol. 5. Englewood Cliffs, NJ: Salem Press, 1983, pp. 2259–2266.

———. "In the Looking Glasses: The Popular and Cultural Fantasy Response." In *The Scope of the Fantastic—Culture, Biography, Themes, Children's Literature.* Edited by Robert A. Collins and Howard D. Pearce. Westport, CT: Greenwood Press, 1985.

———, ed. *The Aesthetics of Fantasy Literature and Art.* Notre Dame, IN: University of Notre Dame Press, 1982.

Schmidt, Nancy J. *Children's Fiction about Africa in English.* New York: Conch Magazine, 1981.

Schorr, Karl. "The Rewards of Reading Fantasy." *Mythlore* 41 (1985): 9–15.

Schwarcz, H. Joseph. "Machine Animism in Modern Children's Literature." In Sara Fenwick. *A Critical Approach to Children's Literature.* Chicago: Univ. of Chicago Press, 1967, pp. 78–95. Originally published in *The Library Quarterly,* Jan. 1967.

Searles, Baird; Meacham, Beth; and Franklin, Michael. *A Reader's Guide to Fantasy.* New York: Avon, 1982.

Sebesta, Sam Leaton, and Iverson, William J. *Literature for Thursday's Child.* Palo Alto, CA: Science Research Associates, 1975. "Fanciful Fiction," pp. 177–242.

Shaner, Mary E. "Twentieth Century Fantasy." In *Masterworks of Children's Literature,* vol. VIII. New York: Stonehill/Chelsea House, 1986, pp. 119–158.

Shannon, George. "All Times in One." *Children's Literature Association Quarterly* 10 (Winter 1986): 178–181. Discusses time travel.

Shapiro, Lillian L. *Fiction for Youth: A Guide to Recommended Books.* 2nd ed. New York: Neal–Schuman, 1985.

Shippey, Tom. "The Golden Bough and the Incorporation of Magic in Science Fiction." *Foundation* 11/12 (1977): 119–134.

Shochet, Lois. "Fantasy and English Children." *Top of the News* 24 (April 1968): 311–320.

Singh, Michael J. "Law and Emotion in Fantasy." *Orana* 18 (May 1982): 49–54.

Slusser, George; Rabkin, Eric; and Scholes, Robert, eds. *Bridges to Fantasy.* Carbondale: Southern Illinois Univ. Press, 1982. Children's literature, pp. 78–89; Twain, pp. 130–141.

Smaridge, Norah. *Famous Modern Storytellers for Young People.* New York: Dodd, 1969. Brink, Coatsworth, Enright, Farjeon, Godden, Lindgren, Lofting, Milne, M. Norton, Travers, and E. B. White.

Smith, Curtis C., ed. *Twentieth Century Science–Fiction Writers.* 2nd ed. Chicago: St. James Press, 1986.

Smith, James Steel. *A Critical Approach to Children's Literature.* New York: McGraw-Hill, 1967. "Sensibility," pp. 171–202.

Smith, Karen Patricia. "The English Psychological Fantasy Novel: A Bequest of Time." *School Library Journal* 31 (May 1985): 44–45.

———. "The Keys to the Kingdom: From Didacticism to Dynamism in British Children's Fantasy, 1780–1979." Ed.D., Columbia University, 1982.

Smith, Lillian. *The Unreluctant Years: A Critical Approach to Children's Literature.* Chicago: American Library Association, 1953. "Fantasy," pp. 149–162.

Stableford, Brian. "The Mythology of Faerie." In Frank N. Magill. *Survey of Modern Fantasy Literature,* vol. 5. Englewood Cliffs, NJ: Salem Press, 1983, pp. 2283–2298.

Stewig, John Warren. *Children and Literature.* Skokie, IL: Rand McNally, 1980, pp. 396–449, 452–461.

Stohler, Sara L. "The Mythic World of Childhood." *Children's Literature Association Quarterly* 12 (Spring 1987): 28–32.

Stott, Jon C. "Midsummer Night's Dream: Fantasy and Self-Realization in Children's Fiction." *The Lion and the Unicorn* 1 (1977): 25–39.

Sullivan, Charles Williams, III. "The Influence of Celtic Myth and Legend on Modern Imaginative Fiction." Ph.D. dissertation, University of Oregon, 1976.

———. "Traditional Ballads and Modern Children's Fantasy: Some Comments on Structure and Intent." *Children's Literature Association Quarterly* (Fall 1986): 145–147.

———. "Traditional Welsh Materials in Modern Fantasy, 3rd Bibliography." *Extrapolation* 28 (Spring 1987): 87–97.

———. "Women of Power: Mythic and Cultural Sources." *Fantasy Review* 91 (1986): 7–8, 42.

———, ed. "Special Section: Fantasy." *Children's Literature Association Quarterly* 12 (Spring 1987): 6–32.

Summerfield, Geoffrey. *Fantasy and Reason: Children's Literature in the 18th Century.* Athens: Univ. of Georgia Press, 1985.

Survey of Modern Fantasy Literature. 5 vols. Edited by Frank N. Magill. Englewood Cliffs, NJ: Salem Press, 1983. 500 essay-reviews.

Svenson, Å. "Opening Windows onto Unreality, Some Elements of Fantasy in Scandinavian Children's Literature." *International Review of Children's Literature and Librarianship* 2 (Spring 1987): 1–9. (bibliographic essay)

Swinfen, Ann. *In Defense of Fantasy: A Study of the Genre in English and American Literature since 1945.* Boston: Routledge, 1984. Animal fantasy, pp. 12–43; time fantasy, pp. 44–74; secondary worlds, pp. 75–99; allegory, pp. 100–122; magical powers, pp. 123–146.

———. "The Sub-Creative Art: An Examination of Some Aspects of the Use of Fantasy, Principally in English Children's Literature, 1945–1975." Ph.D. dissertation, University of Dundee (Scotland), 1979.

Taylor, Robert. " 'Wishful Thinking' or 'Hopeful Dreaming'?" *Horn Book* 59 (Aug. 1983): 398–399.

Taylor, Una Ashworth. "Fairy Tales as Literature." *Signal* 21 (Sept. 1976): 123–138; continued in 22 (Jan. 1977): 48–56.

Terry, June S. "To Seek and to Find: Quest Literature for Children." *School Librarian* 18 (Dec. 1970): 399–404. Reprinted in M. L. White. *Children's Literature.* Columbus, OH: Merrill, 1976, pp. 138–143. Discusses Garner, de la Mare, Andersen, Tolkien, MacDonald, and C. S. Lewis.

Thompson, Hillary. "Doorways to Fantasy." *Canadian Children's Literature* 21 (1981): 8–16.

Thompson, Raymond H. "Arthurian Legend and Modern Fantasy." In Frank N. Magill. *Survey of Modern Fantasy Literature,* vol. 5. Englewood Cliffs, NJ: Salem Press, 1983, pp. 2299–2315.

———. "Commentary: King Arthur in Modern Fantasy." *Fantasy Review* 86 (Dec. 1985): 12–13.

———. "The Enchanter Awakes: Merlin in Modern Fantasy." In *Death and the Serpent: Immortality in Science Fiction and Fantasy.* Edited by Carl B. Yoke and Donald M. Hassler. Westport, CT: Greenwood Press, 1985, pp. 49–56.

———. "Modern Fantasy and Medieval Romance. A Comparative Study." In Roger Schlobin. *The Aesthetics of Fantasy Literature and Art.* Notre Dame, IN: University of Notre Dame Press, 1982, pp. 211–225.

———. *The Return from Avalon: A Study of the Arthurian Legend in Modern Fiction.* Westport, CT: Greenwood Press, 1985.

Thwaite, Mary F. *From Primer to Pleasure in Reading*. Boston: Horn Book, 1963. "Fairy Lore and Fantasy," pp. 106–125.

Timmerman, John H. *Other Worlds: The Fantasy Genre*. Bowling Green, OH: Bowling Green Univ., 1983.

Toijer–Nilsson, Ying. *Fantasins Underland. Myt Och Ide I Den Fantastika Berättelsen* [*The Wonderland of Fantasy. Myth and Ideology in Fantasy Literature*]. Stockholm: Efs-Förlaget, 1981.

Tolkien, J. R. R. "On Fairy-Stories." In *Tree and Leaf*. Boston: Houghton Mifflin, 1965, pp. 3–84.

Tolstoy, Nikolai. *The Quest for Merlin*. Boston: Little, Brown, 1985.

Townsend, John Rowe. "Guest Essay: Heights of Fantasy." *Children's Literature Review*, vol. 5. Detroit: Gale, 1983, pp. 7–12.

———. *A Sense of Story: Essays on Contemporary Writers for Children*. Philadelphia: Lippincott, 1971, pp. 9–27, 39–47, 57–67, 97–119, 130–153, 163–181, 204–214. Essays on Aiken, Boston, Christopher, Cresswell, Estes, Garfield, Garner, Mayne, M. Norton, Pearce, Peyton, and Wrightson.

———. *A Sounding of Storytellers: New and Revised Essays on Contemporary Writers for Children*. Philadelphia: Lippincott, 1979, pp. 41–55, 66–110, 125–178, 194–206. Essays on Dickinson, Garfield, Garner, Hamilton, Lively, Mayne, Walsh, Peyton, and Wrightson.

———. *Written for Children: An Outline of English-Language Children's Literature*. 2nd. rev. ed. Philadelphia: Lippincott, 1983, pp. 90–110, 120, 124–130, 163–177, 235–259, 330–344.

Trask, Margaret. "Fantasy and the Young Child—A Personal View." In Margaret Trask. *Fantasy, Science Fiction, Science Materials*. Kensington, NSW, Australia: Univ. of New South Wales School of Librarianship, 1972, pp. 117–138.

Trease, Geoffrey. *Tales Out of School*. 2nd ed. London: Heinemann; dist. by Dufour, 1964. "Fancy Free," pp. 40–52.

Valli, Luigi. "Shakespeare and Fantasy: Modern Theories and Interpretations of the Genre." Ph.D. dissertation, Bowling Green University, 1981.

Varlejs, Jana, ed. *Young Adult Literature in the Seventies: A Selection of Readings*. Metuchen, NJ: Scarecrow Press, 1978.

Veglahn, Nancy. "Images of Evil: Male and Female Monsters in Heroic Fantasy." In *Children's Literature*, vol. 15. New Haven, CT: Yale Univ. Press, 1987, pp. 106–119.

Viguers, Ruth Hill. "Out of the Abundance." *Horn Book* 34 (Oct. 1958): 341. Reprinted in Elinor Field. *Horn Book Reflections*. Boston: Horn Book, 1969, pp. 248–249.

Wagenknecht, Edward. "The Little Prince Rides the White Deer: Fantasy and Symbolism in Recent Literature." *College English* 7, no. 8 (May 1946): 431–437.

Watt, Lois Belfield. "Fantasy," *Selection* 2, no. 1 (Autumn 1982): 9–10.

Webber, Rosemary. "Folklore and Fantasy—Mix or Match." Syracuse, NY: ERIC Educational Document Reproduction Service, 1978.

Weinberg, R. "Collecting Fantasy and Science Fiction." *A B. Bookman's Weekly* 76 (Oct. 28, 1985): 3101–3107.

West, Mark Irwin. "Imagination Defended: Nineteenth Century Critics of Fanciful Children's Literature." In *Proceedings of the Eighth Annual Conference of the Children's Literature Association*. University of Minnesota, March 1981. Ypsilanti, MI: Children's Literature Association, 1982, pp. 126–131.

Whetton, Betty B. "In This Year of the Dragon: An Invitation to a Retrospective of Fantasy Literature, or a New Look at an Age-Old Genre Many Thought to Have Been Replaced by Realistic Fiction." *Arizona English Bulletin* 18 (Apr. 1976): 110–115.

Whitaker, Muriel. "Swords at Sunset and Bag-Puddings: Arthur in Modern Fiction." *Children's Literature in Education* 27, no. 8 (Winter 1977): 143–153. Discusses Mayne and T. H. White.

White, Dorothy M. *About Books for Children.* New York: Oxford Univ. Press, 1949. Originally published in New Zealand by Whitcombe and Tombs, 1946. "Modern Fairy Tales," pp. 51–67.

White, Mary Lou. *Children's Literature: Criticism and Response.* Columbus, OH: Merrill, 1976, pp. 56–68, 75–77, 112–130, 138–143, 191–201. Articles on Garner, Collodi, Travers, Alexander, and C. S. Lewis.

Wilson, Andrew J. "If It's Wednesday This Must Be Narnia: Exploring the Links between Phantasy and Reality." *Dark Horizons* 24 (1981): 19–23.

Wilson, Anne. "Magical Thought in Story." *Signal* 36 (Sept. 1981): 138–151.

Wintle, Justin, and Fisher, Emma. *The Pied Pipers: Interviews with the Influential Creators of Children's Literature.* London: Paddington Press, 1974, pp. 20–24, 101–170, 192–248, 263–294. Interviews with Sendak, Dahl, Seuss, E. B. White, Adams, Gray, Aiken, Garfield, Alexander, Garner, Townsend, Peyton, Boston, and Godden.

Witucke, Virginia. "The Treatment of Fantasy and Science Fiction in Juvenile and Young Adult Literature Texts." *Top of the News* 39 (Fall 1982): 77–91.

Wolfe, Gary Kent. "Contemporary Theories of Fantasy." In Frank N. Magill. *Survey of Modern Fantasy Literature,* vol. 5. Englewood Cliffs, NJ: Salem Press, 1983, pp. 2220–2234.

———. *Critical Terms for Science Fiction and Fantasy: A Glossary and Guide to Scholarship.* Westport, CT: Greenwood Press, 1986.

———. "Fairy Tales, Märchen, and Modern Fantasy." In Frank N. Magill. *Survey of Modern Fantasy Literature,* vol. 5. Englewood Cliffs, NJ: Salem Press, 1983, pp. 2267–2282.

———. "The Symbolic Fantasy in England." Ph.D. dissertation, University of Chicago, 1972.

Wortley, John, ed. "Faerie, Fantasy and Pseudo-Mediavalia in 20th Century Literature." Special issue of *Mosaic* 10, no. 2 (Winter 1977): 1–195.

Wrightson, Patricia. "The Nature of Fantasy." In Moira Robinson, ed. *Readings in Children's Literature.* Frankston, Australia: Frankston State College, 1975.

Writers for Children: Critical Studies of Major Authors since the Seventeenth Century. Edited by Jane M. Bingham. New York: Scribner, 1988.

Yates, Jessica. "In Defense of Fantasy." *Use of English* 32 (Summer 1981): 70–73. Response to Andrew Stibbs. "For Realism in Children's Fiction." *Use of English* 32 (Fall 1980): 18–24.

Yep, Laurence. "Fantasy and Reality." *Horn Book* 54 (Apr. 1978): 137–143.

Yoke, Carl B., and Hassler, Donald M., eds. *Death and the Serpent: Immortality in Science Fiction and Fantasy.* Westport, CT: Greenwood Press, 1985.

Yolen, Jane. "Here There Be Dragons." *Top of the News* 39 (Fall 1982): 54–56.

———. "The Literary Underwater World." *Language Arts* 57 (1980): 403–412. Stories of merfolk and selchies.

———. *Touch Magic: Fantasy, Faerie and Folklore in the Literature of Childhood.* New York: Philomel, 1981.

———. "The Voice of Fantasy." *Advocate* 3 (Fall 1983): 50–56.

———. "The Wood between the Worlds." *Mythlore* 41 (1985): 5–7. Fifteenth mythopoetic conference guest of honor speech on fantasy.

Zahorski, Kenneth J., and Boyer, Robert H. "The Secondary Worlds of High Fantasy." In Roger C. Schlobin. *The Aesthetics of Fantasy Literature and Art.* Notre Dame, IN: Univ. of Notre Dame Press, 1982, pp. 56–81.

Zanger, Jules. "Goblins, Warlocks, and Weasels: Classic Fantasy and the Industrial Revolution." *Children's Literature in Education* 8 (Winter 1977): 154–162.

Zipes, Jack. "The Age of Commodified Fanaticism: Reflections of Children's Literature and the Fantastic." *Children's Literature Association Quarterly* 9 (Winter 1984–85): 187–190.

———. *Breaking the Magic Spell: Radical Theories of Folk and Fairy Tales.* Austin: Univ. of Texas Press, 1979; reprinted New York: Methuen, 1984.

———. *Don't Bet on the Prince: Contemporary Feminist Fairy Tales in North America and England.* New York: Methuen, 1986. Sixteen tales, including four by Tanith Lee, Jay Williams, Angela Carter, and Jane Yolen, plus four essays of feminist literary criticism.

———. "The Potential of Liberating Fairy Tales for Children." *New Literary History* 13 (1982): 309–325.

———. "Towards a Social History of the Literary Fairy Tale for Children." *Children's Literature Association Quarterly* 7 (Summer 1982): 23–25.

———, ed. *Victorian Fairy Tales: The Revolt of the Fairies and Elves.* New York: Methuen, 1987. Anthology of fairy tales written between 1830 and 1902, including tales by Dickens, Wilde, and Carroll.

13
Teaching Resources

This chapter lists articles and studies on the educational and psychological uses of fantasy literature, as well as audiovisual materials on fantasy literature in general. Audiovisual materials on individual fantasists are also listed in Chapter 14, Author Studies.

A list of the major sources of the information in this chapter is located in the Preface.

Abramson, R. F. "Classroom Uses for the Books of William Steig." *Reading Teacher* 32 (Dec. 1978): 307–311.

Alberghene, Janice M. "The Writing in *Charlotte's Web*." *Children's Literature in Education* 16 (Spring 1985): 32–44.

Allen, A. T. "On Keeping the Sense of Wonder: Fantasy for Children." *The Record* 69 (Feb. 1968): 513–516.

Aquino, John. *Fantasy in Literature*. Washington, DC: National Education Association, 1977, pp. 13–19, 23–26, 28–29, 40–47.

Bailey, W. L. "Fairy Tales as Character-Builders." *Libraries* 31 (1926): 44–46.

Bettelheim, Bruno. *The Uses of Enchantment*. New York: Knopf, 1976, pp. 143–147.

Bingham, Jane M., and Scholt, Grayce. "Enchantment Revisited: Or, Why Teach Fantasy?" *The CEA Critic* 39 (Jan. 1978): 11–15. Reprinted in Robert Bator. *Signposts to Criticism of Children's Literature*. Chicago: American Library Association, 1983, pp. 261–264.

Bodem, Marguerite M. "The Role of Fantasy in Children's Reading." *Elementary English* 52 (Apr. 1975): 470–471, 538.

Bortolussi, Marisa. "Fantasy, Realism and the Dynamics of Reception: The Case of the Child Reader." *Canadian Children's Literature* 41 (1986): 32–43.

Boyer, Robert H., and Zahorski, Kenneth J. "Science Fiction and Fantasy Literature: Clarification through Juxtaposition." *Wisconsin English Journal* 18 (1976): 2–8.

Chubb, Percival. "The Value and Place of Fairy Stories in the Education of Children." *N.E.A. Journal* (1905): 871–879.

Chukovskii, Kornei. *From Two to Five*. Translated and edited by Miriam Morton. Berkeley: Univ. of California Press, 1963. Originally published in Russia in 1925. "The Battle for the Fairy Tale," pp. 114–139.

Clark, Beverly Lyon. "Crossword Puzzle: *The Hobbit.*" *Children's Literature Association Quarterly* 9 (Summer 1984): 76, 95.

Cooper, Ilene. "Popular Reading—After *The Borrowers.*" *Booklist* 81 (Nov. 15, 1984): 452–453. (bibliography)

Crossley, Robert. "Education and Fantasy." *College English* 37 (1975): 281–293.

———. "Teaching the Course in Fantasy: An Elvish Counsel." *Extrapolation* 22 (Fall 1981): 242–251.

Davidson, D. A. "Sword and Sorcery Fiction: An Annotated Booklist." *English Journal* 61 (Jan. 1972): 43–51.

Derby, J. "Anthropomorphism in Children's Literature; Or, Mom, My Doll's Talking Again." *Elementary English* 47 (Fall 1970): 190–192.

Donelson, Kenneth L., and Nilsen, Alleen Pace. *Literature for Today's Young Adults.* Glenview, IL: Scott, Foresman, 1980. "Fantasy," pp. 265–272.

Elleman, Barbara. "Popular Reading—Animal Fantasy Update." *Booklist* 84 (Apr. 15, 1988): 1441–1442. (bibliography)

———. "Popular Reading—Time Fantasy Update." *Booklist* 81 (Jan. 1, 1985): 1407–1408. (bibliography)

Fantasy and Reality. North Hollywood, CA: Center for Cassette Studies, 1972. (audiocassette)

"Fantasy and Science Fiction; by Children." *Elementary English* 52 (May 1975): 620–630.

Fantasy Literature. Peoria, IL: Thomas S. Klise, 1981. (filmstrip and audiocassette)

George Orwell. Peoria, IL: Thomas S. Klise, 1985. (filmstrip and audiocassette)

Getting Hooked on Fantasy. White Plains, NY: Guidance Associates, 1976. (filmstrip and audiocassette) Contains Juster's *The Phantom Tollbooth;* Lewis's *The Lion, The Witch, and The Wardrobe;* Boston's *The Treasure of Green Knowe;* Lindgren's *Pippi Longstocking;* White's *Charlotte's Web;* Selden's *The Genie of Sutton Place;* Eager's *Half Magic;* Butterworth's *The Enormous Egg;* Norton's *The Borrowers;* Babbitt's *The Search for Delicious;* and Alexander's *The Book of Three.*

Getting Hooked on Science Fiction. White Plains, NY: Guidance Associates, 1976. (filmstrip and audio-cassette) Includes O'Brien's *Mrs. Frisby and the Rats of NIMH.*

Gillespie, John Thomas. *The Elementary School Paperback Collection.* Chicago: American Library Association, 1985. "Fantasy," pp. 126–139.

———. *The Junior High School Paperback Collection.* Chicago: American Library Association, 1985. "Fantasy," pp. 30–37.

———. *The Senior High School Paperback Collection.* Chicago: American Library Association, 1986. "Fantasy and Science Fiction," pp. 55–94.

Gillespie, Margaret C., and Conner, John W. *Creative Growth through Literature for Children and Adolescents.* Columbus, OH: Merrill, 1975. "Fantasy," pp. 11–14.

Golden, Joanne Marie. "A Scheme for Analyzing Response to Literature Applied to the Responses of 5th and 8th Graders to Realistic and Fantastic Short Stories." Ph.D. dissertation, Ohio State University, 1978.

Goodwin, P. "Elements of Utopias in Young Adult Literature." *English Journal* 74 (Oct. 1985): 66–69.

Green, Roland J. "Modern Science Fiction and Fantasy: A Frame of Reference." *Illinois Schools Journal* 57 (Fall 1977): 45–53.

Greene, Ellin. "A Peculiar Understanding: Recreating the Literary Fairy Tale." *Horn Book* 59 (June 1983): 270–278.

Guthrie, John T. "Research Views: Fantasy as Purpose." *Reading Teacher* 32 (1978): 106–108.

Harms, Jean McLain. "Children's Responses to Fantasy in Literature." *Language Arts* 52 (Oct. 1975): 942–946.

————. "Children's Responses to Fantasy in Relation to Their Stages of Intellectual Development." Ph.D. dissertation, Ohio State University, 1972.

Harrell, P. "Hooray for Fantasy!" *Elementary English* 39 (Nov. 1962): 710–712.

Hartmann, Waltraut. "Identification and Projection in Folk Fairy Tales and in Fantastic Stories for Children." *Bookbird* 7, no. 2 (1969): 8–17.

Haviland, Virginia. "Fairy Tales and Creativity." In *How Can Children's Literature Meet the Needs of Modern Children?* 15th IBBY Conference, 1976, pp. 56–61.

Helson, Ravenna. "Fantasy and Self-Discovery." *Horn Book* 46 (Apr. 1970): 121–34. Reprinted in M. L. White. *Children's Literature*. Columbus, OH: Merrill, 1976, pp. 117–125.

"The Hobbit": Reading Motivation Unit. Wilton, CT: Current Affairs, 1977. (filmstrip and audiocassette)

Hopkins, Lee Bennett. "Fantasy Flights Circa 1976." *Teacher* 93 (Apr. 1976): 34+. (bibliography)

An Hour with Katherine Kurtz: An Introduction to the Author and Her Work. Garden Grove, NY: Hourglass Productions, 1979. (audiocassette)

An Hour with Marion Zimmer Bradley: A Personal Note. Garden Grove, NY: Hourglass Productions, 1979. (audiocassette)

Huck, Charlotte S. "Modern Fantasy." *Elementary English* 41 (May 1964): 473–474, 515.

Huck, Charlotte S.; Hepler, Susan; and Hickman, Janet. *Children's Literature in the Elementary School*. 4th ed. New York: Holt, 1987. "Modern Fantasy," pp. 335–377.

Hughes, M. "Confessions of a Science Fiction Reader: Notes upon Values Taught to Adolescents by Fantasy and Science Fiction." In *Reaching Young People through Media*. Littleton, CO: Libraries Unlimited, 1983, pp. 69–80.

Hunter, C. Bruce. "Generating Magic in the English Classroom." *Curriculum Review* 21 (Feb. 1982): 41–43.

Jacobs, James S. "The Focus of Fantasy." *Arizona English Bulletin* 18 (Apr. 1976): 199–202.

Klingberg, Göte. *The Fantastic Tale for Children: A Genre Study from the Viewpoints of Literary and Educational Research*. LIGRU Monograph, no. 2. Gothenburg, Sweden: Gothenburg School of Education, 1970.

————. "The Fantastic Tale for Children: Its Literary and Educational Problems." *Bookbird* 5, no. 3 (1967): 13–20.

Koss, H. G. "Relevancy and Children's Literature." *Elementary English* 49 (Nov. 1972): 991–992.

Latshaw, Jessica Louise. "An In-Depth Examination of Four Pre-Adolescents' Responses to Fantasy Literature." Ph.D. dissertation, University of Saskatchewan, 1986.

L'Engle, Madeleine. "What Is Real?" *Language Arts* 55 (1977): 447–451.

Lewis, Claudia. "Fairy Tales and Fantasy in the Classroom." *Childhood Education* 49 (Nov. 1972): 64–67.

Liddell, Sharon. "Recommended: Anne McCaffrey." *English Journal* 73 (Nov. 1984): 89.

Loder Reed, Elizabeth. "Personal Identity Concepts in the Context of Children's Fantasy Literature." Ph.D. dissertation, Boston University, 1979.

McGeehon, C. "I Have Read Everything by Tolkien." *Unabashed Librarian* 50 (1984): 25. (bibliography)

Mahon, R. L. "The Epic Tradition in Science Fiction and Fantasy." *Teaching English in the Two-Year College* 14 (Feb. 1987): 47–51.

May, Jill. "The American Literary Fairy Tale and Its Classroom Uses." *Journal of Reading* 22 (Nov. 1978): 148–152.

Means, H. J. "Books for Young Adults: Science Fiction, Fantasy, and the Occult." *English Journal* 62 (Oct. 1973): 1059–1060. (bibliography)

Meek, Margaret; Warlow, Aidan; and Barton, Griselda. *The Cool Web; The Pattern of Children's Reading.* New York: Atheneum, 1978.

Meraklis, Michael. "Fairy Tales and Their Pedagogical Content." In *How Can Children's Literature Meet the Needs of Modern Children?* 15th IBBY Conference, 1976, pp. 53–55.

Miller, A. I. "My Eighth Graders Like Fantasy." *Journal of Education* 124 (Sept. 1941): 199–201.

Montgomery, J. W. "*The Chronicles of Narnia* and the Adolescent Reader." *Religious Education* 54 (Sept. 1959): 418–428.

Muller, A., and Sullivan, C. W. "Science Fiction and Fantasy Series Books." *English Journal* 69 (Oct. 1980): 71–74. (bibliography)

Mura, J. "Pern Puzzle." *VOYA* 9 (June 1986): 69; Erratum *VOYA* 9 (Aug.–Oct. 1986): 133. (Anne McCaffrey)

Nelms, Beth, and Nelms, Ben. "The Farfaring Imagination: Recent Fantasy and Science Fiction." *English Journal* 74 (Apr. 1985): 83–86. (bibliography)

O'Donnell, H. "Once upon a Time in the Classroom. ERIC/RCS Report." *Language Arts* 55 (Apr. 1978): 534–537.

Olson, Miken Rae. "Exposure to Fantasy Literature, Related Activities, and Creativity in Kindergarten." Ph.D. dissertation, Arizona State University, 1977.

Owen, Linda. "Dragons in the Classroom." *English Journal* 73 (Nov. 1984): 76–77.

Parish, Margaret. "Children's Fantasies for Young Adults." *English Journal* 66 (Nov. 1977): 92–93. (bibliography)

Petersen, Vera D. "Dragons in General." *Elementary English* 39 (Jan. 1962): 3–6.

Phillips, R. A. "Discovering New Worlds." *Curriculum Review* 19 (Sept. 1980): 336–337. (bibliography)

Poskanzer, Susan Cornell. "A Case for Fantasy." *Elementary English* 52 (Apr. 1975): 472–475.

———. "Thoughts on C. S. Lewis and *The Chronicles of Narnia.*" *Language Arts* 53 (1976): 523–526.

Rausch, Helen Martha. "The Debate over Fairy Tales." Ph.D. dissertation, Columbia University Teachers College, 1977.

Ray Bradbury as Philosopher. North Hollywood, CA: Center for Cassette Studies, 1974. (audiocassette)

Read, Arthea J. S. *Reaching Adolescents: The Young Adult Book and the School.* New York: Holt, 1985. "Fantasy and Science Fiction," pp. 86–95, 108–111.

Richardson, Carmen C. "The Reality of Fantasy." *Language Arts* 53 (1976): 549–551, 563.

Robert Silverberg. North Hollywood, CA: Center for Cassette Studies, 1974. (audiocassette)

Roberts, Thomas J. "Before You Dump Those 'Junk' Books." *Media & Methods* 15 (May–June 1979): 27–28, 46.

Rochelle, Larry. "Quest: The Search for Meaning through Fantasy." *English Journal* 66 (Oct. 1977): 54–55.

Rollin, L. W. "Exploring Earthsea: A Sixth Grade Literature Project." *Children's Literature in Education* 16 (Winter 1985): 195–202. (Ursula K. Le Guin)

Salisi, Rosemary A. "Fanciful Literature and Reading Comprehension." Ann Arbor, MI: ERIC Educational Document Reproduction Service, 1978.

Sams, Edwin Boyer. "Studies in Experiencing Fantasy." *Teaching English in the Two-Year College* 5 (1979): 235–237.

Scherf, Walter. "Magic Tales as an Invitation to a Child's Necessary Scaling Off." In

How Can Children's Literature Meet the Needs of Modern Children? 15th IBBY Conference, 1976, pp. 36–41.

Science Fiction and Fantasy. Pleasantville, NY: Educational Audio-Visual, 1975. (filmstrip and audiocassette)

"Science Fiction and Fantasy: Symposium." *Media and Methods* 16 (Nov. 1979): 18–20+.

Science Fiction and Time Fiction. Tarrytown, NY: Prentice-Hall Media, 1977. (filmstrip and audiocassette)

Sellers, F. E. "Fantasy." *New Jersey School Librarian* 14 (Spring 1960): 2–5.

Sloane, B. L. "The Real World of the Imagination." *English Journal* 67 (Feb. 1978): 74–75.

Stein, R. M. "Changing Styles in Dragons: From Fáfnir to Smaug." *Elementary English* 45 (Feb. 1968): 179–183+.

Studier, Catherine Elizabeth. "A Comparison of the Responses of Fifth Grade Students to Modern Fantasy and Realistic Fiction." Ed.D. dissertation, University of Georgia, 1978.

Sullivan, F. "Boggarts and Such: Books of Fantasy for Children." *P.T.A. Magazine* 62 (Mar. 1968): 34–35.

Toothaker, Roy E. "What's Your Fantasy I.Q?" *Language Arts* 54 (1976): 11–24.

Tunnell, Michael D. "Books in the Classroom." *Horn Book* 63 (July–Aug. 1987): 509–511. Discusses Natalie Babbitt's *Tuck Everlasting.*

Tymn, Marshall B. "A Guide to Audio-Visual Resources in Science Fiction and Fantasy." *Media and Methods* 16 (Nov. 1979): 40–42, 56–57.

———. "Guide to Resource Materials for Science Fiction and Fantasy Teachers." *English Journal* 68 (Jan. 1979): 68–74.

———. "Resource Materials for Science Fiction and Fantasy Teachers." *Arizona English Bulletin* 19 (1977): 54–58.

———. "Science Fiction and Fantasy in the School Curriculum: Part I: A Checklist of Articles, 1967–1975." *English Language Arts Bulletin* 21 (Fall/Winter 1981): 24–27.

———. *A Teacher's Guide to Fantastic Literature.* Mercer Island, WA: Starmont, 1986.

Tyre, Richard H. "You Can't Teach Tolkien." *Media and Methods* 15 (Nov. 1978): 18–20, 54.

The Unexpected: Stories of Humor and Fantasy. Pleasantville, NY: Educational Audio Visual, 1979. (filmstrip and audiocassette)

Ursula Le Guin: Woman of Science Fiction. North Hollywood, CA: Center for Cassette Studies, 1973. (audiocassette)

Watanabe, S. "Study of Children's Literature, Syllabus II: Fantasy." *Library and Information Science* 7 (1969): 67–78.

Winfield, Evelyn T. "Fantasy Stories: A Passport to Lands of Enchantment." *PTA Today* 10 (Feb. 1985): 12.

Zipes, Jack. "The Liberating Potential of the Fantastic Projection in Fairy Tales for Children." In *The Scope of the Fantastic—Culture, Biography, Themes, Children's Literature.* Edited by Robert A. Collins and Howard D. Pearce. Westport, CT: Greenwood Press, 1985 pp. 257–266.

———. "The Use and Abuse of Folk and Fairy Tales with Children." In Jill P. May. *Children and Their Literature.* West Lafayette, IN: Children's Literature Association Publications, 1983, pp. 14–33.

Zuck, J. E. "Religion and Fantasy." *Religious Education* 70 (Nov. 1975): 586–604.

14
Author Studies

The works in this chapter are arranged alphabetically by fantasist. The works include books, articles, dissertations, and biographical information by and about a particular fantasist, as well as interviews with them, bibliographies of their work, the published texts of their speeches, and audiovisual materials about them. A list of the major sources of the information found in this chapter is located in the Preface.

Additional information regarding individual fantasists can be found in the following Gale Research publications: *Children's Literature Review, Contemporary Authors, Contemporary Authors Autobiography Series, Contemporary Literary Criticism, Dictionary of Literary Biography, Something about the Author, Something about the Author: Autobiography Series, Twentieth Century Literary Criticism,* and *Yesterday's Authors of Books for Children.*

Adams, Richard (George)

Adams, Richard. "Musings on *Watership Down.*" *Books for Your Children* (London) 8 (Aug. 1973).

———. "Some Ingredients of *Watership Down.*" *Children's Book Review* 4 (Autumn 1974): 92–95. Reprinted in Edward Blishen. *The Thorny Paradise.* Boston: Horn Book, 1975, pp. 163–173.

Anderson, Celia. "Troy, Carthage, and *Watership Down.*" *Children's Literature Association Quarterly* 8 (Spring 1983): 12–13.

Chambers, Aidan. "Letter from England: Great Leaping Lapins!" *Horn Book* 49 (June 1973): 253–255.

Chapman, Edgar L. "The Shaman as Hero and Spiritual Leader: Richard Adams' Mythmaking in *Watership Down* and *Shardik.*" *Mythlore* 5, 18 (1978).

Fritz, Jean. "An Evening with Richard Adams." *Children's Literature in Eduation* 9, no. 29 (Summer 1975): 67–72.

Gentle, Mary. "Godmakers and Worldshapers: Fantasy and Metaphysics." *Vector* 106 (1982): 8–14.

Green, Timothy. "Richard Adams' Long Journey from *Watership Down.*" *Smithsonian* 10, no. 4 (July 1979): 76–83.

Hammond, Graham. "Trouble with Rabbits." *Children's Literature in Education* 12 (Sept. 1973): 48–63.

Heins, Paul. *"Watership Down,* a Review." *Horn Book* 50 (Aug. 1974): 365.
Hunt, Peter. "Landscapes and Journeys, Metaphors and Maps: The Distinctive Feature of English Fantasy." *Children's Literature Association Quarterly* 12 (Spring 1987): 11–15.
Inglis, Fred. *The Promise of Happiness: Value and Meaning in Children's Fiction.* New York: Cambridge Univ. Press, 1981, pp. 201–210.
———. "Spellbinding and Anthropology: The Work of Richard Adams and Ursula Le Guin." In Dennis Butts. *Good Writers for Young Readers.* St. Albans, England: Hart-Davis, 1977, pp. 114–128.
Jordan, Tom. "Breaking Away from the Warren." In Douglas Street. *Children's Novels and the Movies.* New York: Ungar, 1985, pp. 227–235.
Morgan, Chris. "Shardik." In Frank N. Magill. *Survey of Modern Fantasy Literature,* vol. 3. Englewood Cliffs, NJ: Salem Press, 1983, pp. 1387–1391.
Nelson, Marie. "Non–Human Speech in the Fantasy of C. S. Lewis, J. R. R. Tolkien and Richard Adams." *Mythlore* 5, 17 (1978): 37–39.
The Oxford Companion to Children's Literature. Edited by Humphrey Carpenter and Mari Prichard. New York: Oxford Univ. Press, 1984, pp. 3, 563.
Pawling, Christopher. *"Watership Down:* Rolling Back the 1960's." In *Popular Fiction and Social Change.* New York: St. Martin's Press, 1984.
Paxon, Diana. "The Tolkien Tradition." *Mythlore* 39 (1984): 23, 27, 37.
Petzold, Dieter. "Fantasy Out of Myth and Fable: Animal Stories in Rudyard Kipling and Richard Adams." *Children's Literature Association Quarterly* 12 (Spring 1987): 15–19.
Pflieger, Pat, and Hill, Helen M. *A Reference Guide to Modern Fantasy for Children.* Westport, CT: Greenwood Press, 1984, pp. xv, 4–6, 582–583.
Reed, Julia R. *"The Plague Dogs."* In *Survey of Modern Fantasy Literature,* vol. 3. Edited by Frank N. Magill. Englewood Cliffs, NJ: Salem Press, 1983, pp. 1268–1270.
Searles, Baird; Meacham, Beth; and Franklin, Michael. *A Reader's Guide to Fantasy.* New York: Avon, 1982, pp. 19–20.
Shippey, T. A. *"Watership Down."* In Frank N. Magill. *Survey of Modern Fantasy Literature,* vol. 5. Englewood Cliffs, NJ: Salem Press, 1983, pp. 2079–2083.
Stone, James S. "The Rabbitness of *Watership Down." English Quarterly* 13 (Spring 1980): 37–46.
Stott, Jon C. *Children's Literature from A to Z.* New York: McGraw-Hill, 1984, p. 3.
Swinfen, Ann. *In Defense of Fantasy.* London: Routledge, 1984, pp. 37–42, 218–229. *Watership Down.*
Thomas, Jane Resh. "Old Worlds and New: Anti-Feminism in *Watership Down." Horn Book* 50 (Aug. 1974): 405–408. Reprinted in Paul Heins. *Crosscurrents of Criticism.* Boston: Horn Book, 1977, pp. 311–314.
Twentieth Century Children's Writers. 2nd ed. Edited by D. L. Kirkpatrick. New York: St. Martin's Press, 1983, pp. 13–14.
Vine, Phillip. "Richard Adams." *Words* 2 (1985): 20–29.
———. "Richard Adams: A Personal View." *Words* 2 (1985): 14–18.
"Watership Down." In M. Crouch and A. Ellis. *Chosen for Children.* 3rd ed. London: The Library Association, 1977, pp. 164–167.
Wintle, Justin, and Fisher, Emma. "Richard Adams." In *The Pied Pipers,* New York: Paddington Press, 1974, pp. 32–46.

Adkins, Jan

Fifth Book of Junior Authors and Illustrators. Edited by Sally Holmes Holtze. New York: Wilson, 1983, pp. 2–4.

Aiken, Joan (Delano)

Aers, Lesley. "Joan Aiken's Historical Fantasies." In Dennis Butts. *Good Writers for Young Readers*. St. Albans, England: Hart-Davis, 1977, pp. 12–24. Originally published in *Use of English* 22 (Summer 1971): 336–344, entitled "Writers for Children—Joan Aiken."

Aiken, Joan. "Between Family and Fantasy: An Author's Perspectives on Children's Books." *Quarterly Journal of the Library of Congress* 29 (Oct. 1972): 308–326. Reprinted in *The Openhearted Audience*. Washington, DC: Library of Congress, 1980, pp. 46–67.

———. " 'Bred an Bawn in a Briar-Patch'—Dialect and Language in Children's Books." *Children's Literature in Education* 9 (Nov. 1972): 7–23.

———. "A Free Gift." In Edward Blishen. *The Thorny Paradise*. Boston: Horn Book, 1975, pp. 36–52.

———. "Hope Is the Spur." *Signal* 45 (Sept. 1984): 146–151.

———. "International Children's Book Day Message." *Horn Book* 50 (Apr. 1974): 229.

———. "Interpreting the Past." *Children's Literature in Education* 16 (Summer 1985): 67–83.

———. "A Letter to a Boy in Leicester." *London Times Saturday Review* 14 (Apr. 1973): 7. Reprinted in *Horn Book* 49 (Oct. 1973): 450–452.

———. "On Imagination." *Horn Book* 60 (Nov.–Dec. 1984): 735–741. Reprinted in *Innocence & Experience*. Edited by Barbara Harrison and Gregory Maguire. New York: Lothrop, 1987, pp. 45–58.

———. "Purely for Love." *Books* (London, National Book League) 2 (Winter 1970). Reprinted in Margaret Meek. *The Cool Web*. New York: Atheneum, 1978, pp. 166–181; and in Virginia Haviland. *Children and Literature*. Glenview, IL: Scott, Foresman, 1973, pp. 141–154.

———. "A Thread of Mystery." *Children's Literature in Education* 2 (July 1970): 30–47. Reprinted in Geoff Fox. *Writers, Critics and Children*. New York: Agathon Press, 1976, pp. 15–26, entitled "Writing for Enjoyment."

———. "Using History to Create Fiction." In *Prelude, Series 6; Mini-Seminars on Using Books Creatively*. New York: Children's Book Council, 1982. Cassette–taped lecture plus bibliography.

———. *The Way to Write for Children*. New York: St. Martin's Press, 1983.

Apseloff, Marilyn. "Joan Aiken: Literary Dramatist." *Children's Literature Association Quarterly* 9 (Fall 1984): 116–118.

Cadogan, Mary, and Craig, Patricia. *You're a Brick, Angela! A New Look at Girls' Fiction from 1839 to 1975*. London: Gollancz, 1976, pp. 357–360.

Crouch, Marcus. *The Nesbit Tradition: The Children's Novel in England 1945–1970*. London: Benn, 1972, pp. 38–39.

Ellis, A. "Writers for Children: Joan Aiken." *School Librarian* 18 (June 1970): 147–151.

Jones, Cornelia, and Way, Olivia R. "Joan Aiken." In *British Children's Authors*. Chicago: American Library Association, 1976, pp. 3–10.

McGillis, Rod. " 'A Fair Amount of Chaos.' The World of Joan Aiken." *World of Children's Books* 6 (1981): 3–9.

The Oxford Companion to Children's Literature. Edited by Humphrey Carpenter and Mari Prichard. New York: Oxford Univ. Press, 1984, pp. 10, 577.

Searles, Baird; Meacham, Beth; and Franklin, Michael. *A Reader's Guide to Fantasy*. New York: Avon, 1982, pp. 20–21.

Stott, Jon C. *Children's Literature from A to Z*. New York: McGraw-Hill, 1984, p. 5.

Third Book of Junior Authors. Edited by Doris De Montreville and Donna Hill. New York: Wilson, 1972, pp. 4–5.
Townsend, John Rowe. "Joan Aiken." In *A Sense of Story*. Philadelphia: Lippincott, 1971, pp. 9–16.
————. "Joan Aiken." *Signal 5* (May 1971): 72–77.
Twentieth Century Children's Writers. 2nd ed. Edited by D. L. Kirkpatrick. New York: St. Martin's Press, 1983, pp. 16–18.
Usrey, Malcolm. "America's Gift to British Children: The Tall Tales of Joan Aiken." In *Proceedings of the Sixth Annual Conference of the Children's Literature Association,* University of Toronto, March 1979. Ypsilanti, MI: Children's Literature Association, 1981, pp. 196–203. Reprinted in Jill P. May. *Children and Their Literature.* West Lafayette, IN: Children's Literature Association Publications, 1983, pp. 58–64.
Wintle, Justin, and Fisher, Emma. "Joan Aiken." In *The Pied Pipers.* New York: Paddington Press, 1974, pp. 161–170.

Ainsworth (Gilbert), Ruth (Gallard)

Doyle, Brian. *The Who's Who of Children's Literature.* New York: Schocken, 1968, pp. 3–4.
Twentieth Century Children's Writers. 2nd ed. Edited by D. L. Kirkpatrick. New York: St. Martin's Press, 1983, pp. 18–20.

Alcock, Vivien (Dolores)

Helbig, Alethea K., and Perkins, Agnes Regan. *Dictionary of American Children's Fiction, 1960–1984.* Westport, CT: Greenwood Press, 1986, pp. 7–8.
Twentieth Century Children's Writers. 2nd ed. Edited by D. L. Kirkpatrick. New York: St. Martin's Press, 1983, p. 20.

Alexander, Lloyd (Chudley)

Alexander, Lloyd. "The Alchemical Experience." *Library News Bulletin* 37 (Jan. 1970): 28–29.
————. "The American Book Award Acceptance." *Horn Book* 58 (Oct. 1982): 571–583.
————. "Books Remembered." *The Calendar* (now *CBC* [Children's Book Council] *Features*) 38 (Mar.–Oct. 1981).
————. "Fantasy and the Human Condition. In *Prelude, Series 2; Mini-Seminars on Using Books Creatively.* New York: Children's Book Council, 1977. Cassette-taped lecture plus bibliography.
————. "Fantasy as Images: A Literary View." *Language Arts* 55 (Apr. 1978): 440–446.
————. "The Flat-Heeled Muse." *Horn Book* 41 (Apr. 1965): 141–146. Reprinted in Elinor Field. *Horn Book Reflections.* Boston: Horn Book, 1969, pp. 242–247; and in Virginia Haviland. *Children and Literature.* Glenview, IL: Scott, Foresman, 1973, pp. 241–245.
————. "Foreword." In Marshall B. Tymn, Kenneth J. Zahorski, and Robert H. Boyer. *Fantasy Literature: A Core Collection and Reference Guide.* New York: Bowker, 1979, pp. vii–x.
————. "Foreword." In John Gillespie and Diana Lembo. *Introducing Books: A Guide for the Middle Grades.* New York: Bowker, 1970, pp. xi–xiv.
————. "Future Conditional." *Children's Literature Association Quarterly* 10 (Winter 1986): 164–166.

————. "High Fantasy and Heroic Romance." *Horn Book* 47 (Dec. 1971): 577–584. Reprinted in Paul Heins. *Crosscurrents of Criticism*. Boston: Horn Book, 1977, pp. 170–177.

————. "How Does the Author View His Relationship to His Audience?" *Elementary English* 45 (Nov. 1968): 932–933.

————. "Identification and Identities." *Wilson Library Bulletin* 45 (Oct. 1970): 144–148.

————. "Literature, Creativity, and Imagination." *Childhood Education* 47 (Mar. 1971): 307–310. Reprinted in Patricia Maloney Markun. *Association for Childhood Education International*. Wheaton, MD: Association for Childhood Education International, 1973, pp. 3–6.

————. "Meet the Newbery Author—A Series." New York: Random/Miller-Brody, 1974. (filmstrip and audiocassette)

————. "Newbery Award Acceptance." *Horn Book* 45 (Aug. 1969): 378–381.

————. "No Laughter in Heaven." *Horn Book* 46 (Feb. 1970): 11–19.

————. "Notes on the Westmark Trilogy." *Advocate* 4 (Fall 1984): 1–6.

————. "On Responsibility and Authority." *Horn Book* 50 (Aug. 1974): 363–364. Reprinted in *Michigan Librarian* 41 (Summer 1974): 14–15; and in *Nebraska Library Association Quarterly* 5 (Fall 1974): 17–19.

————. "Outlooks and Insights." In Helen W. Painter. *Reaching Children and Young People through Literature*. Newark, DE: International Reading Association, 1971, pp. 19–29.

————. "A Recorded Message to Loughborough '83." In *Loughborough '83: Proceedings*. Welsh National Centre for Children's Literature, 1984, pp. 77–78.

————. "A Second Look: *Five Children and It*." *Horn Book* 61 (May–June 1985): 354–355.

————. "Seeing with the Third Eye." *English Journal* 63 (May 1974): 35–40.

————. "Substance and Fantasy." *School Library Journal* 13 (Dec. 1966): 19–21; *Library Journal*, Dec. 15, 1966, pp. 6157–6159.

————. "Travel Notes." In *Innocence & Experience*. Edited by Barbara Harrison and Gregory Maguire. New York: Lothrop, 1987, pp. 59–65.

————. "The Truth about Fantasy." *Texas Library Journal* 43 (Fall 1967): 101–102. Reprinted in *Top of the News* 24 (Jan. 1968): 168–174.

————. "Where the Novel Went." *Saturday Review*, Mar. 22, 1969, p. 62.

————. "Wishful Thinking—Or Hopeful Dreaming?" *Horn Book* 44 (Aug. 1968): 383–390. Reprinted in *Bookbird* 7 (1969): 3–9; and in Boyer and Zahorski. *Fantasists on Fantasy*. New York: Avon, 1984, pp. 137–150.

Anon. "NBA Winner Stresses Seriousness of Fantasy." *Library Journal*, Apr. 15, 1971, pp. 1412–1413.

Bisenieks, Dainis. "Children, Magic and Choices." *Mythlore* 6 (Winter 1979): 13–16.

————. "Tales from the 'Perilous Realm': Good News for the Modern Child." *Christian Century*, June 5, 1974, pp. 617–620.

Carr, Marion G. "Classic Hero in a New Mythology." *Horn Book* 47 (Oct. 1971): 508–513. Reprinted in White. *Children's Literature*. Columbus, OH: Merrill, 1976, pp. 112–116.

Colbath, Mary Lou. "Worlds as They Should Be: Middle-Earth, Narnia and Prydain." *Elementary English* 48 (Dec. 1971): 937–945.

Deitz, Thomas F. "The Foundling and Other Tales of Prydain." In Frank N. Magill. *Survey of Modern Fantasy Literature*, vol. 2. Englewood Cliffs, NJ: Salem Press, 1983, pp. 571–574.

Durell, Ann. "Lloyd Alexander: Newbery Winner." *Library Journal*, May 15, 1969, pp. 2066–2068.

————. "Who's Lloyd Alexander?" *Horn Book* 45 (Aug. 1969): 382–384.

Evans, W. D. Emrys. "The Welsh Mabinogion: Tellings and Retellings." *Children's Literature in Education* 28, no. 9 (Spring 1978): 17–33.

Glass, Rona. "*A Wrinkle in Time* and *The High King:* Two Couples, Two Perspectives." *Children's Literature Association Quarterly* 6 (Fall 1981): 15–18. Reprinted in Patricia Dooley. *The First Steps.* West Lafayette, IN: Children's Literature Association Publications, 1984, pp. 119–121.

Greenlaw, M. Jean. "Profile: Lloyd Alexander." *Language Arts* 61 (Apr. 1984): 406–413.

Heins, Paul. "*The Marvelous Misadventures of Sebastian*, a Review." *Horn Book* 46 (Dec. 1970): 628.

Helbig, Alethea K., and Perkins, Agnes Regan. *Dictionary of American Children's Fiction, 1960–1984.* Westport, CT: Greenwood Press, 1986, pp. 8, 56–57, 67–68, 98, 101, 213–214, 286–287, 354–355, 404, 644, 709–710.

"The High King." In Lee Kingman. *Newbery and Caldecott Medal Books: 1966–1975.* Boston: Horn Book, 1975, pp. 45–55.

Hopkins, Lee Bennett. "Lloyd Alexander." In *More Books by More People.* New York: Citation Press, 1974, pp. 10–17.

Ingram, Laura. "Lloyd Alexander." In *American Writers for Children since 1960: Fiction. Dictionary of Literary Biography,* vol. 52. Detroit: Gale, 1986, pp. 3–21.

Jacobs, James Swenson. "Lloyd Alexander: A Critical Biography." Ed.D. dissertation, University of Georgia, 1978.

————. "A Personal Look at Lloyd Alexander." *Advocate* 4 (Fall 1984): 8–18.

Kuznets, Lois R. " 'High Fantasy' in America: Alexander, Le Guin and Cooper." An unpublished paper delivered at the Conference on Fantasy and Social Values in German and American Children's Literature, Humanities Institute of Brooklyn College, March 1984.

Lane, Elizabeth. "Lloyd Alexander's *Chronicles of Prydain* and the Welsh Tradition." *Orcrist* 7 (1973): 25–29.

Livingston, Myra C. *Tribute to Lloyd Alexander.* Philadelphia: Drexel Institute, 1976.

McGovern, John Thomas. "Lloyd Alexander—Bard of Prydain: A Study of the Prydain Cycle." Ph.D. dissertation, Temple University, 1980.

May, Jill P. "Lloyd Alexander's Truthful Harp." *Children's Literature Association Quarterly* 10 (Spring 1985): 37–38.

Miklovic, J. "Biography–Bibliography of Lloyd Alexander, with an Analysis of Some of His Fantasy Works." Research paper. Kent, OH: Kent State University, 1973.

Molson, Francis J. "The Chronicles of Prydain." In Frank N. Magill. *Survey of Modern Fantasy Literature,* vol. 1. Englewood Cliffs, NJ: Salem Press, 1983, pp. 256–261.

Omdal, Marsha de Prez. "For Wayfarers Still Journeying: *Taran Wanderer.*" *Language Arts* 55 (Apr. 1978): 501–502.

The Oxford Companion to Children's Literature. Edited by Humphrey Carpenter and Mari Prichard. New York: Oxford Univ. Press, 1984, pp. 14, 428.

Painter, Helen W. "Lloyd Alexander: The Man and His Books for Children." In Helen W. Painter. *Reaching Children and Young People through Literature.* Newark, DE: International Reading Association, 1971, pp. 30–36.

Patterson, Nancy-Lou. "Homo Monstrous: Lloyd Alexander's Gurgi and Other Shadow Figures of Fantastic Literature." *Mythlore* 3, 11 (1976): 24–28.

Paxon, Diana. "The Tolkien Tradition." *Mythlore* 39 (1984): 23–27, 37.

"The Perilous Realms: A Colloquy." In *Innocence & Experience.* Edited by Barbara Harrison and Gregory Maguire. New York: Lothrop, 1987, pp. 195–210.

Pflieger, Pat, and Hill, Helen M. *A Reference Guide to Modern Fantasy for Children.*

Westport, CT: Greenwood Press, 1984, pp. xiii–xvi, 8–11, 61–62, 71–73, 97–99, 100–101, 186–187, 240–243, 350–351, 522–524, 533–535, 609–611.

Roginski, Jim, ed. *Newbery and Caldecott Medalists and Honor Book Winners.* Littleton, CO: Libraries Unlimited, 1982, pp. 29–30.

Rossman, Douglas A., and Rossman, Charles E., eds. *Pages from 'The Book of Three': A Prydain Glossary.* Baltimore: T-K Graphics, 1975.

Searles, Baird; Meacham, Beth; and Franklin, Michael. *A Reader's Guide to Fantasy.* New York: Avon, 1982, pp. 21–22.

"*SLJ* Meets Lloyd Alexander." *Library Journal,* Apr. 15, 1971, pp. 1421–1423. *School Library Journal* 18 (Apr. 1971): 23–25.

Stott, Jon C. *Children's Literature from A to Z.* New York: McGraw-Hill, 1984, p. 9.

———. "Lloyd Alexander's *Chronicles of Prydain:* The Nature of Beginnings." In *Touchstones.* Edited by Perry Nodelman. West Lafayette, IN: Children's Literature Association Publications, 1985, pp. 21–29.

Stuart, Dee, ed. "An Exclusive Interview with Lloyd Alexander." *Writer's Digest* 53 (Apr. 1973): 32–35, 58–59.

Sullivan, Charles Williams, III. "The Influence of Celtic Myth and Legend on Modern Imaginative Fiction." Ph.D. dissertation, University of Oregon, 1976.

———. "Traditional Welsh Materials in Modern Fantasy." *Extrapolation* 28 (Spring 1987): 87–97.

Swinfen, Ann. *In Defense of Fantasy.* London: Routledge, 1984. Prydain series, pp. 77–78, 80, 83–85, 88, 94–95, 101–103.

Third Book of Junior Authors. Edited by Doris De Montreville and Donna Hill. New York: Wilson, 1972, pp. 6–7.

Townsend, John Rowe. "Guest Essay: Heights of Fantasy." In *Children's Literature Review,* vol. 5. Detroit: Gale, 1983, pp. 8–9.

Trautman, Patricia Ann. "Welsh Mythology and Arthurian Legend in the Novels of Lloyd Alexander and Susan Cooper: Parallels of Motif, Character, and Other Elements." Ph.D. dissertation, Vanderbilt University, 1984.

Tunnell, Michael O. "An Analytical Companion to Prydain." Ph.D. dissertation, Brigham Young University, 1986.

Tunnell, Michael O., and Jacobs, James S. "Alexander's Chronicles of Prydain: 20 Years Later." *School Library Journal* 34 (Apr. 1988): 27–31.

Twentieth Century Children's Writers. 2nd ed. Edited by D. L. Kirkpatrick. New York: St. Martin's Press, 1983, pp. 20–22.

Waggoner, Diana. "Lloyd Alexander." In *Supernatural Fiction Writers,* vol. 2. Edited by E. F. Bleiler. New York: Scribner, 1985, pp. 965–972.

West, Richard C. "The Tolkienians." *Orcrist* 2 (1967): 4–15.

Whetton, Betty B. "Who Will Read Prydain?" *Arizona English Bulletin* 14 (Apr. 1972): 51–53.

Wintle, Justin, and Fisher, Emma. "Lloyd Alexander." In *The Pied Pipers.* New York: Paddington Press, 1974, pp. 208–220.

Zahorski, Kenneth J., and Boyer, Robert H. *Lloyd Alexander, Evangeline Walton Ensley, Kenneth Morris: A Primary and Secondary Bibliography.* Boston: G. K. Hall, 1981, pp. 1–110.

Ziefer, Barbara Z. "Wales as a Setting for Children's Fantasy." *Children's Literature in Education* 13 (Summer 1982): 95–102.

Allan, Mabel E(sther)

Twentieth Century Children's Writers. 2nd ed. Edited by D. L. Kirkpatrick. New York: St. Martin's Press, 1983, pp. 22–24.

Andersen, Hans Christian

American–Scandinavian Review 18, no. 4 (Apr. 1930). Hans Christian Andersen Anniversary issue.

Andersen, Hans Christian. *The Fairy Tale of My Life: An Autobiography*. Translated by Horace E. Scudder. London: Hurd & Houghton, 1871; reprinted London: Paddington Press, 1975.

Anderson, Celia Catlett. "Andersen's Heroes and Heroines: Relinquishing the Reward." In *Triumphs of the Spirit in Children's Literature*. Edited by Francelia Butler and Richard Rotert. Hamden, CT: Shoe String Press, 1986, pp. 122–126.

Auden, W. H. "Grimm and Andersen." In W. H. Auden. *Forewords and Afterwords*. New York: Random, 1973, pp. 198–208.

Bianco, Margery. "Four Tales from Andersen." *Horn Book* 12 (Mar.–Apr. 1936): 89–90.

———. *"It's Perfectly True*—A New Andersen." *Horn Book* 14 (May 1938): 153–155.

———. "The Mackinstry Andersen." *Horn Book* 10 (Jan. 1934): 37.

———. "The Real Andersen." *Horn Book* 7 (Aug. 1931): 187–189

Bianco, Margery Williams. "The Stories of Hans Andersen." *Horn Book* 3 (May 1927): 29–34. Reprinted in Anne Carroll Moore and Bertha Mahony Miller. *Writing and Criticism*. Boston: Horn Book, 1951, pp. 58–62.

———. "The Story of a Storyteller." *Horn Book* 19 (May 1934): 186–189.

Böök, Fredrik. *Hans Christian Andersen: A Biography*. Translated by George C. Schoolfield. Norman: Univ. of Oklahoma Press, 1962.

Bredsdorff, Elias. "A Critic's Guide to the Literature on Hans Christian Andersen." *Scandinavica* 6, no. 2 (Nov. 1967): 108–125.

———. "Hans Christian Andersen: A Bibliographic Guide to His Works." *Scandinavica* 6, no. 1 (May 1967): 26–42.

———. *Hans Christian Andersen: The Story of His Life and Work, 1805–1875*. New York: Scribner, 1975.

Catalog of the Jean Hersholt Collection of Hans Christian Andersen. Washington, DC: Library of Congress, 1954.

Cimino, Maria. "Children Illustrate Andersen's Tales." *Horn Book* 30 (Oct. 1954): 318–324.

Clausen, Julius. "Hans Christian Andersen Abroad and at Home." *American–Scandinavian Review* 18 (Apr. 1930): 228–234.

Dahl, Svend, and Topsöe–Jensen, H. G., eds. *A Book on the Danish Writer Hans Christian Andersen, His Life and Work, Published on the 150th Anniversary of His Birth*. Translated by W. Glyn Jones. Copenhagen: Det Berlingske Bogtry Kkeri, 1955.

Dal, Erik. "Hans Christian Andersen's Tales and America." *Scandinavian Studies* 40, no. 1 (Feb. 1968): 1–25.

———. "Research on Hans Christian Andersen: Trends, Results, and Desiderata." *Orbis Litterarum* 17 (1962): 166–183.

Dooley, Patricia. "Porcelain, Pigtails, Pagodas: Images of China in 19th and 20th Century Illustrated Editions of 'The Nightingale.' " In *Proceedings of the Sixth Annual Conference of the Children's Literature Association*. University of Toronto, March 1979. Ypsilanti, MI: Children's Literature Association, 1981, pp. 94–105.

Doyle, Brian. *The Who's Who of Children's Literature*. New York: Schocken, 1968, pp. 7–8.

Ellwood, Gracia Fay. "Matters of Grave Import." *Mythlore* 8, 28 (1981).

Fell, Christine E. "Symbolic and Satiric Aspects of Hans Andersen's Fairy-Tales." *Leeds Studies in English*. n.s. 1 (1967): 83–91.

Freeman, Ann. "A Comparative Study of Hans Christian Andersen and Charles Dickens: The Relationship between Spiritual and Material Value Systems as Defined by Their Treatment of the Child." Ph.D. dissertation, University of California, Berkeley, 1979.

Fullam, Victoria Ann. "Mermaid." Ph.D. dissertation, University of Minnesota, 1984. An original opera adapted from "The Little Mermaid."

Godden, Rumer. *Hans Christian Andersen: A Great Life in Brief.* New York: Knopf, 1955.

Grabowski, Simon. "The Refrigerated Heart: A Comparative Study of Novalis' 'Marchen von Hyacinth und Rosenblute' and Hans Christian Andersen's 'Sneedronninger' ['The Snow Queen']." *Scandinavica* 10, no. 1 (May 1971): 43–58.

Griffith, John. "Personal Fantasy in Andersen's Fairy Tales." *Kansas Quarterly* 16 (Summer 1984): 81–88.

Grønbech, Bo. *Hans Christian Andersen.* Boston: Twayne, 1980.

Haugaard, Erik Christian. "Hans Christian Andersen." In *Writers for Children: Critical Studies of Major Authors since the Seventeenth Century.* Edited by Jane M. Bingham. New York: Scribner, 1988, pp. 7–14.

———. "Hans Christian Andersen: A Twentieth Century View." *Scandinavian Review* 63 (Dec. 1975): 4–12.

———. "The Poet Who Lives." *Horn Book* 51 (Oct. 1975): 443–448.

———. *Portrait of a Poet: Hans Christian Andersen and His Fairy Tales.* Washington, DC: Library of Congress, 1973. Reprinted in *The Openhearted Audience.* Washington, DC: Library of Congress, 1980, pp. 68–81.

———. "Random Thoughts by a Translator of Andersen." *Horn Book* 48 (Dec. 1972): 557–562. Reprinted in Paul Heins. *Crosscurrents of Criticism.* Boston: Horn Book, 1977, pp. 277–282.

———. "The Simple Truth." *Signal* 11 (May 1973): 69–73.

———. "A Translator's Opinions." *Quarterly Journal of the Library of Congress* 30 (Apr. 30, 1973): 89–94.

Hazard, Paul. "Hans Christian Andersen." *Junior Bookshelf* 4 (Dec. 1939): 65–77.

———. "Prince of Story–Tellers." *Horn Book* 19 (May–June 1943): 141–147. Reprinted in Paul Hazard. *Books, Children, and Men.* Boston: Horn Book, 1960, pp. 92–105.

Hearn, Michael Patrick. "Afterword." In Kate Greenway. *Original Drawings for 'The Snow Queen' by Hans Christian Andersen.* New York: Schocken, 1981, pp. 53–58.

Heins, Paul. "*Hans Christian Andersen: The Complete Fairy Tales and Stories,* a Review." *Horn Book* 50 (June 1974): 269.

Hersholt, Jean. "Hans Andersen Fairy Tales Published First in America." *The Colophon* 1, no. 4 (Feb. 1940): 5–12.

———. "Hans Christian Andersen's First Book." *The New Colophon* 3 (1950): 44–48.

Hürlimann, Bettina. "Hans Christian Andersen." In *Three Centuries of Children's Books in Europe.* Edited by Brian W. Alderson. Cleveland: World, 1968, pp. 42–52.

Jan, Isabelle. "Hans Christian Andersen or Reality." In *On Children's Literature.* New York: Schocken, 1974, pp. 45–55.

The Junior Book of Authors. 2nd rev. ed. Edited by Stanley J. Kunitz and Howard Haycraft. New York: Wilson, 1951, pp. 5–6.

Kromann-Kelly, I. "Hans Christian Andersen's Tales: Alive and Well in Denmark?" *Top of the News* 36 (Summer 1980): 381–383.

Lavender, R. "Hans Christian Andersen and Erik Christian Haugaard." *School Librarian* 23 (June 1975): 113–119.

Lederer, Wolfgang. *The Kiss of the Snow Queen: Hans Christian Andersen and Man's Redemption by Woman.* Berkeley: Univ. of California Press, 1986.

Lowry, Betty. "An Andersen Anniversary." *Horn Book* 62 (May–June 1986): 378–379.

Meynell, Esther. *Story of Hans Andersen.* New York: H. Schuman, 1950.
Mishler, William. "Hans Christian Andersen's 'Tin Soldier' in a Freudian Perspective." *Scandinavian Studies* 50, no. 4 (Autumn 1975): 389–395.
Molesworth, Mary. "Hans Christian Andersen." In Lance Salway. *A Peculiar Gift.* Harmondsworth, Middlesex: Kestrel, 1976, pp. 137–145.
Möller, Kai Friis. "The Poet and the Fair Sex." *American–Scandinavian Review* 18 (Apr. 1930): 220–227.
The Oxford Companion to Children's Literature. Edited by Humphrey Carpenter and Mari Prichard. New York: Oxford Univ. Press, 1984, pp. 20–23, 166, 317, 378, 427, 489, 495, 509–510, 528, 549, 571.
Potter, R. A. "The World of Hans Christian Andersen." *A.B. Bookman's Weekly* 80 (Dec. 7, 1987): 2237–2242.
Robb, Nesca A. "Hans Andersen." In *Four in Exile.* Stroudsburg, PA: Hutchinson Ross, 1945, pp. 120–158.
Rubeck, Mary Ann. "Annotations Documenting and Interpreting the Reflections of Hans Christian Andersen's Life in His Fairy Tales." Ph.D. dissertation, State University of New York at Buffalo, 1981.
Rubow, Paul V. "Hans Andersen and His Fairy Tales." *Life and Letters* (London) 53 (May 1947): 92–98.
———. "Idea and Form in Hans Christian Andersen's Fairy Tales." In *A Book on the Danish Writer Hans Christian Andersen: His Life and Work.* Edited by Svend Dahl and H. G. Topse-Jensen. Copenhagen: Det Berlingske Bogtrykkeri, 1955, pp. 97–135.
Sale, Roger. *Fairy Tales and After.* Cambridge, MA: Harvard Univ. Press, 1978, pp. 63–73.
Scudder, Horace E. "Andersen's Short Stories." *Atlantic Monthly* 36 (Nov. 1875): 598–602.
———. "Hans Christian Andersen." *Atlantic Monthly* 36 (Nov. 1875): 203–234. Reprinted in Horace E. Scudder. *Childhood in Literature and Art.* Boston: Houghton Mifflin, 1894; reprinted, Folcroft, 1978, pp. 201–216; and in Virginia Haviland. *Children and Literature.* Glenview, IL: Scott, Foresman, 1973, pp. 50–56.
Searles, Baird; Meacham, Beth; and Franklin, Michael. *A Reader's Guide to Fantasy.* New York: Avon, 1982, p. 22.
Sicherman, Ruth. "Time to Tell an Andersen Tale." *Top of the News* 30 (Jan. 1974): 161–168.
Spink, Reginald. *Hans Christian Andersen and His World.* New York: Putnam, 1972.
Stirling, Monica. *The Wild Swan: The Life and Times of Hans Christian Andersen.* New York: Harcourt Brace Jovanovich, 1965.
Stott, Jon C. *Children's Literature from A to Z.* New York: McGraw-Hill, 1984, p. 12.
Sutherland, Zena. "Hans Christian Andersen." In *Children and Books.* 7th ed. Edited by Zena Sutherland and May Hill Arbuthnot. Glenview, IL: Scott, Foresman, 1985, pp. 228–230.
Toksvig, Signe. "Good News for Lovers of Andersen." *Horn Book* 12 (Mar.–Apr. 1936): 87–88.
———. *The Life of Hans Christian Andersen.* New York: Harcourt Brace Jovanovich, 1934.
Topsöe-Jensen, Helge, and Rubow, Paul V. "Hans Christian Andersen the Writer." *American-Scandinavian Review* 18 (Apr. 1930): 205–212.
Trapp, F. " 'The Emperor's Nightingale': Some Aspects of Mimesis." *Critical Inquiry* 4 (Aug. 1977): 85–103.
Tucker, Alan. "Andersen Complete." *Signal* 16 (Jan. 1975): 12–17.
Williams, Alan Moray. "Hans Christian Andersen." *Time and Tide* (Feb. 1963): 9–13.

Reprinted in Sheila A. Egoff. *Only Connect.* 2nd ed. New York: Oxford Univ. Press, 1980, pp. 233–237.
Yolen, Jane. "The Literary Underwater World." *Language Arts* 57 (1980): 403–412.

Anderson, Margaret J(ean)

Fifth Book of Junior Authors and Illustrators. Edited by Sally Holmes Holtze. New York: Wilson, 1983, pp. 7–9.

Anderson, Poul (William)

Anderson, Poul. "Concerning Future Histories." *Bulletin of the Science Fiction Writers of America* 14 (1979): 7–14.
———. *Fantasy.* New York: Pinnacle, 1981.
———. "Star-Flights and Fantasies: Sagas Still to Come." In *The Craft of Science Fiction.* Edited by Reginald Bretnor. New York: Harper and Row, 1976.
Brenner, Malcolm. "Interview: Poul Anderson." *Future Life* 109 (1981): 26–28.
Clark, Judith A. *"A Midsummer Tempest."* In *Survey of Modern Fantasy Literature,* vol. 2. Edited by Frank N. Magill. Englewood Cliffs, NJ: Salem Press, 1983, pp. 1025–1028.
Dean, John. "A Curious Note in the Wind: The New Literary Genre of Heroic Fantasy." *New Mexico Humanities Review* 2 (Summer 1979): 34–41.
De Camp, L. Sprague, ed. *The Blade of Conan.* New York: Ace, 1979.
Dietz, Thomas F. *"The Merman's Children."* In *Survey of Modern Fantasy Literature,* vol. 2. Edited by Frank N. Magill. Englewood Cliffs, NJ: Salem Press, 1983, pp. 1021–1024.
Elliot, Jeffrey M. *Science Fiction Voices #2.* San Bernardino, CA: Borgo Press, 1979.
Elliott, Elton T. "An Interview with Poul Anderson." *Science Fiction Review* 7 (May 1978): 32–37.
McGuire, Patrick L. *"Operation Chaos."* In *Survey of Modern Fantasy Literature,* vol. 3. Edited by Frank N. Magill. Englewood Cliffs, NJ: Salem Press, 1983, pp. 1160–1163.
Miesel, Sandra. *Against Time's Arrow: The High Crusade of Poul Anderson.* San Bernardino, CA: Borgo Press, 1978.
Morgan, Chris. "The Short Fiction of Anderson." In *Survey of Modern Fantasy Literature,* vol. 3. Edited by Frank N. Magill. Englewood Cliffs, NJ: Salem Press, 1983, pp. 1417–1419.
———. *"Three Hearts and Three Lions."* In *Survey of Modern Fantasy Literature,* vol. 2. Edited by Frank N. Magill. Englewood Cliffs, NJ: Salem Press, 1983, pp. 1913–1917.
Pierce, Hazel Beasley. *A Literary Symbiosis: Science Fiction/Fantasy Mystery.* Westport, CT: Greenwood Press, 1983.
Platt, Charles. *Dream Makers II: The Uncommon Men and Women Who Write Science Fiction.* New York: Berkley, 1983, pp. 151–158.
Shippey, Tom. "The Golden Bough and the Incorporation of Magic in Science Fiction." *Foundation* 11/12 (1977): 119–134.
Tweet, Roald D. "Poul Anderson." In *Supernatural Fiction Writers,* vol. 2. Edited by E. F. Bleiler. New York: Scribner, 1985, pp. 973–980.
Twentieth-Century Science Fiction Writers. 2nd ed. Edited by Curtis C. Smith. Chicago: St. James Press, 1986, pp. 11–14.
Walker, Paul. *Speaking of Science Fiction.* Oradell, NJ: Luna, 1978, pp. 107–120. Interview.

Andrews, J(ames) S(idney)

Taylor, Anne. "Traveling in Time—Towards a Project." *Children's Literature in Education* 13 (1974): 68–79.

Annett (Pipitone Scott), Cora

Helbig, Alethea K., and Perkins, Agnes Regan. *Dictionary of American Children's Fiction, 1960–1984.* Westport, CT: Greenwood Press, 1986, pp. 19, 300–301.

Anthony, Piers (pseud. of Piers A[nthony] D[illingham] Jacob)

Anthony, Piers. "In Defense of Fantasy." *Isaac Asimov's Science Fiction Magazine,* Dec. 1983, pp. 71–87.

Biggers, Cliff. "An Interview with Piers Anthony." *Science Fiction Review* 6 (Nov. 1977): 56–62.

Clark, Judith A. "The Xanth Novels." In *Survey of Modern Fantasy Literature,* vol. 5. Edited by Frank N. Magill. Englewood Cliffs, NJ: Salem Press, 1983, pp. 2185–2191.

Collings, Michael R. *Reader's Guide to Piers Anthony.* Mercer Island, WA: Starmont, 1983.

———. "Words and Worlds: The Creation of a Fantasy Universe in Zelazny, Lee and Anthony." In *The Scope of the Fantastic—Theory, Technique, Major Authors.* Edited by Robert A. Collins and Howard D. Pearce. Westport, CT: Greenwood Press, 1985, pp. 173–182.

Collins, Robert A. "Piers Anthony: A Twenty-Year Trek to the Top." *Fantasy Newsletter* 59 (1983): 12–16.

Lane, Daryl; Vernon, William; and Carlson, David. *The Sound of Wonder: Interviews from "The Science Fiction Radio Show,"* vol 2. Phoenix, AZ: Oryx Press, 1985, pp. 1–28.

Platt, Charles. *Dream Makers.* New York: Ungar, 1987, pp. 221–230. Interview.

———. "Profile: Piers Anthony." *Science Fiction Review* 49 (1983): 35–38.

Scarborough, John. "Piers Anthony." In *Supernatural Fiction Writers,* vol. 2. Edited by E. F. Bleiler. New York: Scribner, 1985, pp. 981–986.

Searles, Baird; Meacham, Beth; and Franklin, Michael. *A Reader's Guide to Fantasy.* New York: Avon, 1982, pp. 24–25.

Smith, Scott S. "Interview with Piers Anthony." *Thrust* 25 (1986): 9–13.

Twentieth–Century Science Fiction Writers. 2nd ed. Edited by Curtis C. Smith. Chicago: St. James Press, 1986, pp. 14–18.

Arthur, Ruth M(abel)

Crouch, Marcus. *The Nesbit Tradition.* London: Benn, 1972, pp. 205–206, 218.

———. "The Painful Art of Growing Up: The Novels of Ruth M. Arthur." *Junior Bookshelf* 42 (Oct. 1978): 239–244.

Fifth Book of Junior Authors and Illustrators. Edited by Sally Holmes Holtze. New York: Wilson, 1983, pp. 13–14.

Jones, Cornelia, and Way, Olivia R. "Ruth M. Arthur." In *British Children's Authors.* Chicago: American Library Association, 1976, pp. 31–40.

Twentieth Century Children's Writers. 2nd ed. Edited by D. L. Kirkpatrick. New York: St. Martin's Press, 1983, pp. 39–40.

Arundel (McCrindle), Honor (Morfydd)

Boyd, Celia. "Growing Pains: A Survey of Honor Arundel's Novels." *Signal* 4 (Jan. 1973): 38–51.
Fourth Book of Junior Authors and Illustrators. Edited by Doris De Montreville and Elizabeth D. Crawford. New York: Wilson, 1978, pp. 16–17.
Russell, J. "Honor Arundel." *Junior Bookshelf* 37 (Dec. 1973): 367–369.
Twentieth Century Children's Writers. 2nd ed. Edited by D. L. Kirkpatrick. New York: St. Martin's Press, 1983, pp. 40–41.

Asch, Frank

Fourth Book of Junior Authors and Illustrators. Edited by Doris De Montreville and Elizabeth D. Crawford. New York: Wilson, 1978, pp. 17–18.

Asprin, Robert L(ynn)

Searles, Baird; Meacham, Beth; and Franklin, Michael. *A Reader's Guide to Fantasy.* New York: Avon, 1982, pp. 25–26.
Twentieth-Century Science Fiction Writers. 2nd ed. Edited by Curtis C. Smith. Chicago: St. James Press, 1986, pp. 27–28.

Atwater, Richard (Tupper), and Atwater, Florence (Hasseltine Carroll)

Helbig, Alethea K., and Perkins, Agnes Regan. *Dictionary of American Children's Fiction, 1859–1959.* Westport, CT: Greenwood Press, 1985, pp. 28, 360–361.
Jameyson, Karen. "A Second Look: *Mr. Popper's Penguins.*" *Horn Book* 64 (Mar.–Apr. 1988): 186–187.
More Junior Authors. Edited by Muriel Fuller. New York: Wilson, 1963, pp. 3–4.
The Oxford Companion to Children's Literature. Edited by Humphrey Carpenter and Mari Prichard. New York: Oxford Univ. Press, 1984, p. 366.
Roginski, Jim, ed. *Newbery and Caldecott Medalists and Honor Book Winners.* Littleton, CO: Libraries Unlimited, 1982, p. 36.
Twentieth Century Children's Writers. 2nd ed. Edited by D. L. Kirkpatrick. New York: St. Martin's Press, 1983, pp. 43–44.

Averill, Esther

The Junior Book of Authors. 2nd rev. ed. Edited by Stanley J. Kunitz and Howard Haycraft. New York: Wilson, 1951, pp. 13–14.

Avi (pseud. of Avi Wortis)

Avi. "All That Glitters." *Horn Book* 63 (Sept.–Oct. 1987): 569–576.
———. "Some Thoughts on the Young Adult World." *VOYA* 7 (Oct. 1984): 183–184.
Fifth Book of Junior Authors and Illustrators. Edited by Sally Holmes Holtze. New York: Wilson, 1983, pp. 15–16.
Helbig, Alethea K., and Perkins, Agnes Regan. *Dictionary of American Children's Fiction, 1960–1984.* Westport, CT: Greenwood Press, 1986, pp. 31–32, 191.
Roginski, Jim. *Behind the Covers: Interviews with Authors and Illustrators of Books for Children and Young Adults.* Littleton, CO: Libraries Unlimited, 1985, pp. 33–41.

Aymé, Marcel (André)

Brand, Patricia Petrus. "The Modern French Fairy Tale: Aspects of 'Le Merveilleux' in Aymé, Supervielle, Saint-Exupéry and Sabatier." Ph.D. dissertation, University of Colorado at Boulder, 1983.

Loy, J. R. "The Reality of Marcel Aymé's World." *French Review* 28 (Dec. 1954): 115–127.

Voorhees, R. J. "Marcel Aymé: Neglected Novelist." *Midwest Quarterly* 25 (Autumn 1983): 74–89.

Babbitt, Natalie (Zane Moore)

Babbitt, Natalie. "Between Innocence and Maturity." *Horn Book* 48 (Dec. 1972): 33–37. Reprinted in Varlejs. *Young Adult Literature in the Seventies*. Metuchen, NJ: Scarecrow Press, 1978.

———. "Easy Does It." *Top of the News* 43 (Summer 1987): 376–382.

———. "The Fantastic Voyage." *The Five Owls* (July–Aug 1987).

———. "Fantasy and the Classic Hero." In *Innocence & Experience*. Edited by Barbara Harrison and Gregory Maguire. New York: Lothrop, 1987, pp. 148–155. Reprinted in *School Library Journal* 34 (Oct. 1987): 25–29.

———. "The Great American Novel for Children—And Why Not." *Horn Book* 50 (Apr. 1974): 176–185.

———. "Happy Endings? Of Course, and Also Joy." *New York Times Book Review*, pt. II, Nov. 8, 1970, pp. 1, 50. Reprinted in Virginia Haviland. *Children and Literature*. Glenview, IL: Scott, Foresman, 1973, pp. 155–159.

———. "How Can We Write Children's Books If We Don't Know Anything about Children?" *Publishers Weekly* 200 (July 19, 1971): 64–66.

———. "The Purposes of Fantasy." In *Proceedings of the Ninth Annual Conference of the Children's Literature Association*. University of Florida, March 1982. Ypsilanti, MI: Children's Literature Association, 1983, pp. 22–29. Reprinted in *Innocence & Experience*. Edited by Barbara Harrison and Gregory Maguire. New York: Lothrop, 1987, pp. 174–181.

———. "Saying What You Think." *Quarterly Journal of the Library of Congress* 39 (Spring 1982): 80–89.

———. "What Makes a Book Worth Reading?" *Language Arts* 52 (Oct. 1975): 924–927ff.

———. "Who Is the Child?" *Horn Book* 62 (Mar.–Apr. 1986): 161–166.

De Luca, Geraldine. "Extensions of Nature: The Fantasies of Natalie Babbitt." *The Lion and the Unicorn* 1, no. 2 (Fall 1977): 47–70.

Fourth Book of Junior Authors and Illustrators. Edited by Doris De Montreville and Elizabeth D. Crawford. New York: Wilson, 1978, pp. 22–23.

Hartvigsen, M. Kip, and Hartvigsen, Christen Brog. " 'Rough and Soft, Both at Once': Winnie Foster's Initiation in *Tuck Everlasting*." *Children's Literature in Education* 18 (Fall 1987): 176–183.

Helbig, Alethea K., and Perkins, Agnes Regan. *Dictionary of American Children's Fiction, 1960–1984*. Westport, CT: Greenwood Press, 1986, pp. 35, 248, 364, 579–580, 680–681.

Hirsch, Corinne. "Toward Maturity: Natalie Babbitt's Initiatory Journeys." In *Proceedings of the Seventh Annual Conference of the Children's Literature Association*. Baylor University, March 1980. Ypsilanti, MI: Children's Literature Association, 1982, pp. 107–113.

Hopkins, Lee Bennett. "Natalie Babbitt." In *More Books by More People*. New York: Citation Press, 1974, pp. 24–28.

Lanes, Selma G. "A Second Look: *The Devil's Storybook.*" *Horn Book* 64 (May–June 1988): 329–331.

———. "A Talk with Natalie Babbitt." *New York Times Book Review,* Nov. 14, 1982, pp. 44, 54.

Lynch, Catherine M. "Winnie Foster and Peter Pan: Facing the Dilemma of Growth." In *Proceedings of the Ninth Annual Conference of the Children's Literature Association.* University of Florida, March 1982. Ypsilanti, MI: Children's Literature Association, 1983, pp. 107–111.

Mercier, J. "Natalie Babbitt, Admired Author–Illustrator for Children." *Publishers Weekly* 208 (July 28, 1975): 66–67.

Moss, Anita. "Crime and Punishment—Or Development—In Fairy Tales and Fantasy." *Mythlore* 8 (Spring 1981): 26–28, 42.

———. "Natalie Babbitt." In *American Writers for Children since 1960: Fiction. Dictionary of Literary Biography,* vol. 52. Detroit: Gale, 1986, pp. 22–29.

———. "Pastoral and Heroic Patterns: Their Uses in Children's Fantasy." In *The Scope of the Fantastic—Culture, Biography, Themes, Children's Literature.* Edited by Robert A. Collins and Howard D. Pearce. Westport, CT: Greenwood Press, 1985, pp. 231–238.

———. "A Second Look: *The Search for Delicious.*" *Horn Book* 60 (Nov.–Dec. 1984): 779–783.

The Oxford Companion to Children's Literature. Edited by Humphrey Carpenter and Mari Prichard. New York: Oxford Univ. Press, 1984, p. 40.

"The Perilous Realms: A Colloquy." In *Innocence & Experience.* Edited by Barbara Harrison and Gregory Maguire. New York: Lothrop, 1987, pp. 195–210.

Pflieger, Pat, and Hill, Helen M. *A Reference Guide to Modern Fantasy for Children.* Westport, CT: Greenwood Press, 1984, pp. xii, 33–35, 485–486, 555–556.

Ragsdale, W. "Presentation of the Recognition of Merit to Natalie Babbitt." *Claremont Reading Conference Yearbook* 43 (1979): 199–203.

Roginski, Jim, ed. *Newbery and Caldecott Medalists and Honor Book Winners.* Littleton, CO: Libraries Unlimited, 1982, p. 36.

Stott, Jon C. *Children's Literature from A to Z.* New York: McGraw-Hill, 1984, p. 22.

Tunnell, Michael D. "Books in the Classroom." *Horn Book* 63 (July–Aug. 1987): 509–511. *Tuck Everlasting.*

Twentieth Century Children's Writers. 2nd ed. Edited by D. L. Kirkpatrick. New York: St. Martin's Press, 1983, p. 49.

Bach, Richard (David)

Watson, Christine. "*Jonathan Livingston Seagull.*" In *Survey of Modern Fantasy Literature,* vol. 2. Edited by Frank N. Magill. Englewood Cliffs, NJ: Salem Press, 1983, pp. 808–810.

Bacon, Martha (Sherman)

Helbig, Alethea K., and Perkins, Agnes Regan. *Dictionary of American Children's Fiction, 1960–1984.* Westport, CT: Greenwood Press, 1986, pp. 35–36.

Twentieth Century Children's Writers. 2nd ed. Edited by D. L. Kirkpatrick. New York: St. Martin's Press, 1983, pp. 49–50.

Bailey, Carolyn Sherwin

Bailey, Carolyn Sherwin. "*Miss Hickory:* Her Geneology. The Newbery Acceptance Paper." *Horn Book* 23 (July–Aug. 1947): 239–242.

Davis, Dorothy R. *Carolyn Sherwin Bailey, 1876–1961: Profile and Bibliography.* Bloomington, IN: Eastern Press, 1967.

————. *Carolyn Sherwin Bailey Historical Collection of Children's Books: A Catalog.* New Haven: Southern Connecticut State College, 1966.

Helbig, Alethea K., and Perkins, Agnes Regan. *Dictionary of American Children's Fiction, 1859–1959.* Westport, CT: Greenwood Press, 1985, pp. 33, 34, 348.

The Junior Book of Authors. 2nd rev. ed. Edited by Stanley J. Kunitz and Howard Haycraft. New York: Wilson, 1951, pp. 14–15.

Lindquist, Jennie. "Books and an Apple Orchard." *Horn Book* 23 (July–Aug. 1947): 243–249.

"*Miss Hickory.*" In Bertha Miller and Elinor Field. *Newbery Medal Books: 1922–1955.* Boston: Horn Book, 1957, pp. 288–299.

Pflieger, Pat, and Hill, Helen M. *A Reference Guide to Modern Fantasy for Children.* Westport, CT: Greenwood Press, 1984, pp. xii–xvi, 37–40, 369–370.

Roginski, Jim, ed. *Newbery and Caldecott Medalists and Honor Book Winners.* Littleton, CO: Libraries Unlimited, 1982, pp. 37–39.

Twentieth Century Children's Writers. 2nd ed. Edited by D. L. Kirkpatrick. New York: St. Martin's Press, 1983, pp. 52–53.

Baker, Betty (Lou)

Helbig, Alethea K., and Perkins, Agnes Regan. *Dictionary of American Children's Fiction, 1960–1984.* Westport, CT: Greenwood Press, 1986, p. 36.

Third Book of Junior Authors. Edited by Doris De Montreville and Donna Hill. New York: Wilson, 1972, pp. 24–25.

Twentieth Century Children's Writers. 2nd ed. Edited by D. L. Kirkpatrick. New York: St. Martin's Press, 1983, pp. 53–54.

Baker, Margaret

The Junior Book of Authors. 2nd rev. ed. Edited by Stanley J. Kunitz and Howard Haycraft. New York: Wilson, 1951, pp. 15–17.

Baker, Margaret J(oyce)

Baker, Margaret J. "Beginning of *The Shoe Shop Bears.*" *Junior Bookshelf* 34 (Dec. 1970): 337–340.

More Junior Authors. Edited by Muriel Fuller. New York: Wilson, 1963, pp. 6–7.

Twentieth Century Children's Writers. 2nd ed. Edited by D. L. Kirkpatrick. New York: St. Martin's Press, 1983, pp. 54–56.

Baker, Olaf

The Junior Book of Authors. 2nd rev. ed. Edited by Stanley J. Kunitz and Howard Haycraft. New York: Wilson, 1951, p. 17.

Barrie, Sir J(ames) M(atthew)

Alderson, Brian, ed. *Children's Books in England.* 3rd ed. New York: Cambridge Univ. Press, 1982, pp. 309–312.

Asquith, Lady Cynthia. *Portrait of Barrie.* New York: Dutton, 1955.

Barrie, J(ames) M. "Captain Hook at Eton." *M'Connachie and J. M. B. The Works of J. M. Barrie—Peter Pan Edition,* vol. 35. New York: Scribner, 1940, pp. 108–121.

Birkin, Andrew. *J. M. Barrie and the Lost Boys: The Love Story That Gave Birth to Peter Pan*. New York: Potter, 1979.

Blackburn, William. "*Peter Pan* and the Contemporary Adolescent Novel." In *Proceedings of the Ninth Annual Conference of the Children's Literature Association*. University of Florida, March 1982. Ypsilanti, MI: Children's Literature Association, 1983, pp. 47–53.

———. "The Quest for Values in Contemporary Adolescent Fiction." Ann Arbor, MI: ERIC Educational Document Reprint Service, 1982.

Blake, Kathleen. "The Sea-Dream: *Peter Pan* and *Treasure Island*." In *Children's Literature*, vol. 6. Philadelphia: Temple Univ. Press, 1977, pp. 165–181. Reprinted in *Reflections on Literature for Children*. Hamden, CT: Shoe String Press, 1984, pp. 215–228.

Burson, Linda. "Fantasy Components of Sir James Matthew Barrie: A Study through Selected Plays." Ph.D. dissertation, University of Georgia, 1983.

Carpenter, Humphrey. "J. M. Barrie and *Peter Pan*: 'That Terrible Masterpiece.' " In *Secret Gardens: A Study of the Golden Age of Children's Literature*. Boston: Houghton Mifflin, 1985, pp. 170–187.

Chalmers, Patrick R. *The Barrie Inspiration*. London: Davies, 1938.

Clayton, Walter. "An Interrupted Pan Resumes His Piping." *Forum* 41 (Jan. 1909): 83–85.

Doyle, Brian. *The Who's Who of Children's Literature*. New York: Schocken, 1968, pp. 20–22.

Dunbar, Janet. *J. M. Barrie: The Man behind the Image*. Boston: Houghton Mifflin, 1970.

Egan, Michael. "The Neverland of Id: Barrie, *Peter Pan*, and Freud." In *Children's Literature*, vol. 10. New Haven, CT: Yale Univ. Press, 1982, pp. 37–55.

Garland, Herbert. *A Bibliography of the Writings of Sir James Matthew Barrie Bart., OM*. London: Bookman's Journal, 1928.

Green, Martin. "The Charm of *Peter Pan*." In *Children's Literature*, vol. 9. New Haven, CT: Yale Univ. Press, 1981, pp. 19–27.

Green, Roger Lancelyn. "Barrie and *Peter Pan*." *Junior Bookshelf* 24 (Oct. 1960): 197–204.

———. *Fifty Years of Peter Pan*. London: Davies, 1954.

———. *J. M. Barrie*. New York: Walck, 1961. Reprinted in Edward Blishen, Margaret Meek, and Roger Lancelyn Green. *Hugh Lofting/Geoffrey Trease/J. M. Barrie*. London: Bodley Head, 1968.

Griffin, John. "Making Wishes Innocent: *Peter Pan*." *The Lion and the Unicorn* 3, no. 1 (Sept. 1979): 28–37.

Haill, Catherine. *Dear Peter Pan*. Winchester, MA: Faber, 1984.

Hodges, J. M. "J. M. Barrie." In *Writers for Children: Critical Studies of Major Authors since the Seventeenth Century*. Edited by Jane M. Bingham. New York: Scribner, 1988, pp. 29–36.

Hunter, Lynette. "J. M. Barrie: The Rejection of Fantasy." *Scottish Literary Journal* 5 (1978): 39–52.

———. "J. M. Barrie's Islands of Fantasy." *Modern Drama* 23 (1980): 65–74.

Karpe, Marietta. "The Origins of Peter Pan." *Psychoanalytic Review* 43, no. 1 (Jan. 1956): 104–110.

Lurie, Alison. "The Boy Who Couldn't Grow Up." *New York Review of Books* 6 (Feb. 1975): 11–15.

Lynch, Catherine M. "Winnie Foster and Peter Pan: Facing the Dilemma of Growth." In *Proceedings of the Ninth Annual Conference of the Children's Literature Association*. University of Florida, March 1982. Ypsilanti, MI: Children's Literature Association, 1983, pp. 107–111.

McGowan, Maureen Ann. "An Analysis of the Fantasy Plays of James M. Barrie Utilizing Vladimir Propp's Structural Model of the Fairy Tale." Ph.D. dissertation, New York University, 1984.

Mackail, Denis. *Barrie: The Story of J. M. B.* New York: Scribner, 1941.

Marsh, Corinna. "Eleven Little Girls and *Peter Pan.*" *Horn Book* 31 (June 1955): 199–206.

Master, Helen. "Peter's Kensington." *Horn Book* 10 (Sept. 1934): 316–321.

Meisel, Frederick L. "The Myth of Peter Pan." *Psychoanalytic Study of the Child* 32 (1977): 545–563.

The Oxford Companion to Children's Literature. Edited by Humphrey Carpenter and Mari Prichard. New York: Oxford Univ. Press, 1984, pp. 45–48, 320–321, 403–407.

Pflieger, Pat, and Hill, Helen M. *A Reference Guide to Modern Fantasy for Children.* Westport, CT: Greenwood Press, 1984, pp. xii–xiii, 42–46, 432–436.

Philip, Neil. "Letters." *Signal* 38 (May 1982): 129–132. A response to Tucker, below.

Roy, James A. *James Matthew Barrie: An Appreciation.* New York: Scribner, 1938.

Russell, Patricia Read. "Parallel Romantic Fantasies: Barrie's *Peter Pan* and Spielberg's *E. T.: The Extraterrestrial.*" *Children's Literature Association Quarterly* 8 (Winter 1983): 28–30.

Skinner, John. "James M. Barrie, or the Boy Who Wouldn't Grow Up." *American Imago* 14 (Summer 1947): 111–141.

Smith, Louisa A. "*Peter Pan.*" In Frank N. Magill. *Survey of Modern Fantasy Literature,* vol. 3. Englewood Cliffs, NJ: Salem Press, 1983, pp. 1230–1233.

Stableford, Brian M. "J. M. Barrie." In *Supernatural Fiction Writers,* vol. 1. Edited by E. F. Bleiler. New York: Scribner, 1985, pp. 405–410.

Stevenson, Lionel. "A Source for Barrie's *Peter Pan.*" *Philological Quarterly* 8, no. 2 (Apr. 1929): 210–214.

Stott, Jon C. *Children's Literature from A to Z.* New York: McGraw-Hill, 1984, p. 23.

Tucker, Nicholas. "Fly Away, Peter?" *Signal* 37 (Jan. 1982): 43–49.

Twentieth Century Children's Writers. 2nd ed. Edited by D. L. Kirkpatrick. New York: St. Martin's Press, 1983, pp. 61–64.

Bauer, Marion Dane

Helbig, Alethea K., and Perkins, Agnes Regan. *Dictionary of American Children's Fiction, 1960–1984.* Westport, CT: Greenwood Press, 1986, p. 40.

Baum, L(yman) Frank

Abraham, Paul M., and Kenter, Stuart. "Tik-Tok and the Laws of Robotics." *Science–Fiction Studies* 5 (Mar. 1978): 67–80.

The American Book Collector. Special issue on Baum 13, no. 4 (Dec. 1962).

Attebery, Brian. "The Oz Books." In Frank N. Magill. *Survey of Modern Fantasy Literature,* vol. 3. Englewood Cliffs, NJ: Salem Press, 1983, pp. 1196–1208.

Baughman, Roland. "L. Frank Baum and the 'Oz Books.'" *Columbia Library Columns* 4 (May 1955): 15–35.

Baum, Frank Joslyn, and McFall, Russell P. *To Please a Child: A Biography of L. Frank Baum.* Chicago: Reilly and Lee, 1961.

Baum, Harry Neal. "How My Father Wrote the Oz Books." *American Book Collector* 13 (Dec. 1962): 17.

Baum, Joan, and Baughman, Roland. *L. Frank Baum: The Wonderful Wizard of Oz. An Exhibition of His Published Writings, in Commemoration of the Centenary of His Birth, May 15, 1856.* New York: Columbia University Libraries, 1956.

Baum, L. Frank. "Modern Fairy Tales." *The Advance,* Aug. 19, 1909.

————. *The Wizard of Oz.* Edited by Michael Patrick Hearn. New York: Schocken, 1983. Complete text plus 20 critical essays.

The Baum Bugle: A Journal of Oz. Kinderhook, IL: International Wizard of Oz Club, 1957– .

Beckwith, Osmond. "The Oddness of Oz." In *Children's Literature,* vol. 5. Philadelphia: Temple Univ. Press, 1976, pp. 74–91.

Bewley, Marius. "The Land of Oz: America's Great Good Place." *New York Review of Books,* Dec. 3, 1964. Reprinted in Marius Bewley. *Masks and Mirrors: Essays in Criticism.* New York: Atheneum, 1970, pp. 255–267.

Billman, Carol. " 'I've Seen the Movie': Oz Revisited." In Douglas Street. *Children's Novels and the Movies.* New York: Ungar, 1983, pp. 92–100.

Brotman, Jordan. "A Late Wanderer in Oz." *Chicago Review* 18, no. 2 (1965): 63–73. Reprinted in Sheila A. Egoff. *Only Connect.* New York: Oxford Univ. Press, 1980, pp. 156–169.

Callahan, Jean. "I Have the Feeling We're Not in Kansas Any More." *American Film* 10 (May 1985): 24.

Cath, Stanley H., and Cath, Claire. "On the Other Side of Oz: Psychoanalytic Aspects of Fairy Tales." *Psychoanalytic Study of the Child* 33 (1978): 621–639.

Collins, Robert G. "*Star Wars:* The Pastiche of Myth and the Yearning for a Past Future." *Journal of Popular Culture* 11 (Summer 1977): 1–10.

De Luca, Geraldine, and Natov, Roni. "Researching Oz: An Interview with Michael Patrick Hearn." *The Lion and the Unicorn* 11 (Oct. 1987): 51–62.

Dempsey, David. "The Wizardry of L. Frank Baum." In William Targ. *Bibliophile in the Nursery.* Chicago: World, 1957, pp. 387–391.

Downing, David C. "Waiting for Godoz: A Post-Nasal Deconstruction of the Wizard of Oz." *Christianity and Literature* 33 (Winter 1984): 28–30.

Doyle, Brian. *The Who's Who of Children's Literature.* New York: Schocken, 1968, pp. 22–26.

Elms, Alan C. "Oz in Science Fiction Film." *The Baum Bugle* 27 (Winter 1983): 2–7.

Erisman, Fred. "L. Frank Baum and the Progressive Dilemma." *American Quarterly* 20 (Fall 1968): 616–623.

Eyles, Allen. *The World of Oz.* Tucson, AZ: HP Books, 1985.

Fisher, Eugene J. "Gopher Prairie and the Emerald City: A Comparison of Themes and Techniques of Sinclair Lewis and L. Frank Baum." *The Baum Bugle* 26 (Winter 1982): 14–16.

Ford, Alla T., and Martin, Dick. *The Musical Fantasies of L. Frank Baum.* Torrance, CA: Wizard Press, 1958.

Gardner, Martin. "A Child's Garden of Bewilderment: *Alice's Adventures in Wonderland* and *The Wonderful Wizard of Oz* Compared." *Saturday Review,* July 17, 1965, pp. 18–19, and Aug. 14, 1965, p. 26. Reprinted in Sheila A. Egoff. *Only Connect.* New York: Oxford Univ. Press, 1980, pp. 150–155.

————. "John Dough and the Cherub." *Children's Literature,* vol. 2. Storrs, CT: Journal of the Modern Language Association, 1973, pp. 110–118.

————. "Librarians in Oz." *Saturday Review,* Apr. 11, 1959, pp. 18–19.

————. "Why Librarians Dislike Oz." *Library Journal* 88 (Feb. 1963): 834–836; *School Library Journal* 10 (Feb. 1963): 22–24. Reprinted from *American Book Collector* 13 (Dec. 1962): 14–16.

Gardner, Martin, and Nye, Russell B. *The Wizard of Oz and Who He Was.* East Lansing: Michigan State Univ. Press, 1957.

Glassman, P. "The Wonderful World of Oz." *A.B. Bookman's Weekly* 72 (Nov. 14, 1983): 3329–3334. (bibliographic essay)

————. "The World of Oz Lives On." *A.B. Bookman's Weekly* 76 (Aug. 19–26, 1985): 1198–1203.

Greene, David L. "The Concept of Oz." In *Children's Literature,* vol. 3. Storrs, CT: Journal of the Modern Language Association, 1974, pp. 173–176.

———. "L. Frank Baum: Science Fiction and Fantasy." *Children's Literature Association Quarterly* 5 (Winter 1981): 13–16. Reprinted in Patricia Dooley. *The First Steps.* West Lafayette, IN: Children's Literature Association Publications, 1984, pp. 60–61.

Greene, David L., and Martin, Dick. *The Oz Scrapbook.* New York: Random, 1977.

Greene, Douglas G. "Bibliographical Baumania." *The Baum Bugle* 29 (Autumn 1985): 20–21.

Hamilton, Margaret. "There's No Place Like Oz." In *Children's Literature,* vol. 10. New Haven, CT: Yale Univ. Press, 1982, pp. 153–158.

Hanff, Peter E., and Greene, Douglas G. *Bibliographia Oziana: A Concise Bibliographical Checklist of the Oz Books by L. Frank Baum and His Successors.* Demorest, GA: International Wizard of Oz Club, 1976.

Harmetz, Aljean. *The Making of 'The Wizard of Oz.'* New York: Knopf, 1977; reprinted New York: Limelight, 1984, #1060.

Hearn, Michael Patrick. "Discovering Oz (The Great and Terrible) at the Library of Congress." *Quarterly Journal of the Library of Congress* 39 (Spring 1982): 70–79.

———. "L. Frank Baum." In *American Writers for Children, 1900–1960. Dictionary of Literary Biography,* vol. 22. Detroit: Gale, 1983, pp. 13–36.

———. "L. Frank Baum." In *Writers for Children: Critical Studies of Major Authors since the Seventeenth Century.* Edited by Jane M. Bingham. New York: Scribner, 1988, pp. 37–48.

———. "L. Frank Baum and the Modernized Fairy Tale." *Children's Literature in Education* 33 (Summer 1979): 57–67.

———. "The Wizard of Oz." Unpublished paper. Presented at the meeting of the Modern Language Association, 1974.

———, ed. *The Annotated Wizard of Oz.* New York: Potter, 1973.

———, ed. *The Wizard of Oz: The Critical Heritage.* New York: Schocken, 1983.

Helbig, Alethea K., and Perkins, Agnes Regan. *Dictionary of American Children's Fiction, 1859–1959.* Westport, CT: Greenwood Press, 1985, pp. 37, 576–577.

Indick, Ben P. "L. Frank Baum: The Wonderful Wizard of Oz." *Anduril* 7 (1979): 7–14.

Jackson, Shirley. "The Lost Kingdom of Oz." *The Reporter,* Dec. 10, 1959, pp. 42–43.

Jones, Alan. "*Return to Oz.*" *Cinefantastique* 15 (July 1985): 27–31.

Jones, Vernon H. "The Oz Parade." *New Orleans Review* 3 (1973): 375–378.

Keller, Karl. "L. Frank Baum: The Wizard of Coronado." *Seacoast* 2 (Feb. 1981): 52–55.

Kopp, Sheldon. "The Wizard of Oz behind the Couch." *Psychology Today* 3, no. 10 (Mar. 1970): 70.

Littlefield, Henry M. "The Wizard of Oz: Parable on Populism." *American Quarterly* 16 (Spring 1964): 47–58.

Luehrs, R. B. "Nineteenth-Century Profile: L. Frank Baum and the Land of Oz: A Children's Author as Social Critic." *Nineteenth Century* 6, no. 3 (Aug. 1980): 55–57.

MacFall, Russell P. "L. Frank Baum—Shadow and Substance." *American Book Collector* 13 (Dec. 1962): 9, 11.

Mannix, Daniel P. "The Father of *The Wizard of Oz.*" *American Heritage* 16 (Dec. 1964): 36–47, 108–109.

Martin, Dick. "The First Edition of *The Wonderful Wizard.*" *American Book Collector* 13 (Dec. 1962): 26–27.

Moore, Raylyn. *Wonderful Wizard, Marvelous Land.* Bowling Green, OH: Bowling Green University Press, 1974.

Nye, Russell B. "The Wizardess of Oz—And Who She Is." In *Children's Literature,* vol. 2. Storrs, CT: Journal of the Modern Language Association, 1973, pp. 119–122.

The Oxford Companion to Children's Literature. Edited by Humphrey Carpenter and Mari Prichard. New York: Oxford Univ. Press, 1984, pp. 50–51, 578–579.

Pattrick, Robert B. *Unexplored Territory in Oz: An Excursion through Hitherto Uncharted Regions.* Demorest, GA: International Wizard of Oz Club, 1975.

Prentice, Ann E. "Have You Been to See the Wizard: Oz Revisited." *Top of the News* 27 (Nov. 1970): 32–44.

Sackett, S. J. "The Utopia of Oz." *Georgia Review* 14 (Fall 1960): 275–291.

Sale, Roger. "Baum's Magic Powder of Life." *Children's Literature,* vol. 8. New Haven: Yale University Press, 1980, pp. 157–163.

———. "Child Reading and Man Reading: Oz, Babar and Pooh." In *Children's Literature,* vol. 1. Storrs, CT: Journal of the Modern Language Association, 1972, pp. 162–172. Reprinted in *Reflections on Literature for Children.* Hamden, CT: Shoe String Press, 1984, pp. 19–31.

———. *Fairy Tales and After: From Snow White to E. B. White.* Cambridge, MA: Harvard Univ. Press, 1978, pp. 223–244.

———. "L. Frank Baum and Oz." *Hudson Review* 25 (Winter 1972–1973): 571–592.

Schuman, Samuel. "Out of the Fryeing Pan and Into the Pyre: Comedy, Myth and *The Wizard of Oz.*" *Journal of Popular Culture* 7 (Fall 1973): 302–304. Reprinted as "Comic Mythos and Children's Literature—Or, Out of the Fryeing Pan and Into the Pyre." In *It's a Funny Thing, Humor.* Edited by Antony J. Chapman and Hugh C. Foot. Elmsford, NY: Pergamon Press, 1977, pp. 119–121.

Searles, Baird; Meacham, Beth; and Franklin, Michael. *A Reader's Guide to Fantasy.* New York: Avon, 1982, pp. 26–27.

Smyers, R. P. "A Librarian Looks at Oz." *Library Occurrent* (Indiana State University) 21 (Dec. 1964): 190–192.

Snow, Jack. *Who's Who in Oz.* Chicago: Reilly and Lee, 1954.

Stott, Jon C. *Children's Literature from A to Z.* New York: McGraw-Hill, 1984, p. 25.

Street, Douglas. "The Wonderful Wiz That Was: The Curious Transformation of *The Wizard of Oz.*" *Kansas Quarterly* 16 (Summer 1984): 91–98.

Third Book of Junior Authors. Edited by Doris De Montreville and Donna Hill. New York: Wilson, 1972, pp. 28–29.

Thurber, James. "The Wizard of Chitenago." *New Republic* (Dec. 12, 1934): 141–142. Reprinted in Boyer and Zahorski. *Fantasists on Fantasy.* New York: Avon, 1984, pp. 59–66.

Twentieth Century Children's Writers. 2nd ed. Edited by D. L. Kirkpatrick. New York: St. Martin's Press, 1983, pp. 65–66.

Vidal, Gore. "On Rereading the Oz Books." *New York Review of Books,* Oct. 13, 1977, pp. 38–42.

———. "The Wizard of *The Wizard.*" *New York Review of Books,* Sept. 29, 1977, pp. 10–15.

Vogel, Carl S. "The Amazonia of Oz." *The Baum Bugle* 26 (Autumn 1982): 4–8.

Wagenknecht, Edward. *Utopia America.* Seattle: Univ. of Washington Press, 1929; rev. ed. entitled "The Yellow Brick Road." In *As Far as Yesterday: Memories and Reflections.* Stillwater: Univ. of Oklahoma Press, 1968, pp. 63–79.

———. " 'Utopia America' A Generation Afterwards." *American Book Collector* 13 (Dec. 1962): 12–13.

B. B. (pseud. of D[enys] J[ames] Watkins–Pitchford)

Doyle, Brian. *The Who's Who of Children's Literature.* New York: Schocken, 1968, pp. 284–285.

Fisher, Marjorie T. "B. B. As a Writer for Young People." *Bookbird* 5, no. 3 (1967): 21–27.
"The Little Grey Men." In M. Crouch and A. Ellis. *Chosen for Children.* 3rd ed. London: The Library Association, 1977, pp. 30–34.
The Oxford Companion to Children's Literature. Edited by Humphrey Carpenter and Mari Prichard. New York: Oxford Univ. Press, 1984, p. 52.
Ryan, J. S. " 'B. B.'—Delineator of England's Natural Glories." *Orana* 19 (Feb. 1983): 11–24.
Third Book of Junior Authors. Edited by Doris De Montreville and Donna Hill. New York: Wilson, 1972, pp. 32–33.
Twentieth Century Children's Writers. 2nd ed. Edited by D. L. Kirkpatrick. New York: St. Martin's Press, 1983, pp. 804–805.

Beachcroft, Nina

Twentieth Century Children's Writers. 2nd ed. Edited by D. L. Kirkpatrick. New York: St. Martin's Press, 1983, pp. 69–70.

Beagle, Peter S(oyer)

Foust, R. E. "Fabulous Paradigm: Fantasy, Meta-Fantasy, and Peter S. Beagle's *The Last Unicorn.*" *Extrapolation* 21 (1980): 5–20.
Hark, I. R. "The Fantasy Worlds of Peter Beagle." In *Survey of Modern Fantasy Literature,* vol. 2. Edited by Frank N. Magill. Englewood Cliffs, NJ: Salem Press, 1983, pp. 526–534.
Manlove, C. N. *The Impulse of Fantasy Literature.* Kent, OH: Kent State Univ. Press, 1983, pp. 148–154.
" 'A Myth, a Memory, a Will–O' the–Wish': Peter Beagle's Funny Fantasy." In *Reflections on the Fantastic.* Edited by Michael R. Collings. Westport, CT: Greenwood Press, 1986.
Norford, Don Parry. "Reality and Illusion in Peter Beagle's *The Last Unicorn.*" *Critique: Studies in Modern Fiction* 19 (1987): 93–104.
Olsen, Alexandra Hennessey. "The Anti-Consolatio: Boethius and *The Last Unicorn.*" *Mosaic* 13 (Spring/Summer 1980): 133–144.
Samuelson, David N. "Peter S. Beagle." In *Supernatural Fiction Writers,* vol. 2. Edited by E. F. Bleiler. New York: Scribner, 1985, pp. 987–992.
Schlobin, Roger C. "The Fool and the Fantastic." *Fantasy Newsletter* 43 (1981): 6–9, 29.
Searles, Baird; Meacham, Beth; and Franklin, Michael. *A Reader's Guide to Fantasy.* New York: Avon, 1982, pp. 28–29.
Stevens, David. "Incongruity in a World of Illusion: Patterns of Humor in Peter Beagle's *The Last Unicorn.*" *Extrapolation* 20 (1979): 230–237.
Tobin, Jean. "Introduction." By Peter S. Beagle. *The Last Unicorn.* Boston: Gregg, 1978, pp. v–xxiv.
Van Becker, David. "Time, Space, and Consciousness in the Fantasy of Peter S. Beagle." *San José Studies* 1 (1975): 52–61.

Bear, Greg(ory Dale)

Bear, Greg. "Beneath the Dream: Tomorrow through the Past." *Bulletin of the Science Fiction Writers of America* 14 (1979): 38–40.
Klein, Jay Kay. "Greg Bear." *Analog* (June 1983): 37.

Twentieth-Century Science Fiction Writers. 2nd ed. Edited by Curtis C. Smith. Chicago: St. James Press, 1986, pp. 42–43.

Beaumont, Madame le Prince de

Barchilon, J. "A Note on the Original Text of 'Beauty and the Beast.' " *Modern Language Review* 56 (Jan. 1961): 81–82.

Mintz, Thomas. "The Meaning of Rose in 'Beauty and the Beast.' " *Psychoanalytic Review* 56 (1969–1970): 615–620.

Zipes, Jack. "The Dark Side of 'Beauty and the Beast': The Origins of the Literary Fairy Tale for Children." In *Proceedings of the Eighth Annual Conference of the Children's Literature Association.* University of Minnesota, March 1981. Ypsilanti, MI: Children's Literature Association, 1982, pp. 119–125.

Behn, Harry

Behn, Harry. "A Definition Implied." *Horn Book* 43 (Oct. 1967): 561–564.

———. "The Golden Age." *Horn Book* 36 (Apr. 1960): 109–115.

———. "Poetry, Fantasy, and Reality." *Elementary English* 43 (Apr. 1965): 355–361.

———. "Poetry for Children." *Horn Book* 42 (Apr. 1966): 163–175.

Helbig, Alethea K., and Perkins, Agnes Regan. *Dictionary of American Children's Fiction, 1960–1984.* Westport, CT: Greenwood Press, 1986, pp. 46, 204.

More Junior Authors. Edited by Muriel Fuller. New York: Wilson, 1963, pp. 12–13.

Richardson, Carmen C. "Harry Behn: Wizard of Childhood." *Elementary English* 51 (Oct. 1974): 975–976, 1002.

Roop, Peter. "Profile: Harry Behn." *Language Arts* 62 (Jan. 1985): 92–94.

Twentieth Century Children's Writers. 2nd ed. Edited by D. L. Kirkpatrick. New York: St. Martin's Press, 1983, pp. 72–73.

Viguers, Ruth H. "*The Faraway Lurs,* a Review." *Horn Book* 39 (Apr. 1963): 164.

Bell, Thelma Harrington

Helbig, Alethea K., and Perkins, Agnes Regan. *Dictionary of American Children's Fiction, 1960–1984.* Westport, CT: Greenwood Press, 1986, pp. 46, 543–544.

Third Book of Junior Authors. Edited by Doris De Montreville and Donna Hill. New York: Wilson, 1972, pp. 35–36.

Bellairs, John

Burgess, Mary A. "*The Face in the Frost.*" In Frank N. Magill. *Survey of Modern Fantasy Literature,* vol. 1. Englewood Cliffs, NJ: Salem Press, 1983, pp. 508–510.

Fifth Book of Junior Authors and Illustrators. Edited by Sally Holmes Holtz. New York: Wilson, 1983, pp. 26–27.

Schmidt, Gary D. "See How They Grow: Character Development in Children's Series Books." *Children's Literature in Education* 18 (1987): 34–44.

Searles, Baird; Meacham, Beth; and Franklin, Michael. *A Reader's Guide to Fantasy.* New York: Avon, 1982, p. 30.

Bellamy, Edward

Gies, Joseph. "Looking Forward to Utopia." *Vocational Education* 57 (Jan.–Feb. 1982): 30–31.

Jehmlich, Reimer. "Cog-Work: The Organization of Labor in Edward Bellamy's *Look-*

ing Backward and in Later Utopian Fiction." In *Clockwork Worlds.* Edited by
Richard D. Erlich and Thomas P. Dunn. Westport, CT: Greenwood Press, 1983.
Kerr, Howard; Crowley, John W.; and Crowley, Charles W., eds. *The Haunted Dusk:
American Supernatural Fiction, 1820–1920.* Athens: Univ. of Georgia Press, 1983.
Pfaelzer, Jean. "A State of One's Own: Feminism as Ideology in American Utopias
1880–1915." *Extrapolation* 24 (Winter 1983): 311–328.
Thomas, W. K. "The Underside of Utopias." *College English* 38 (1976): 356–372.
Twentieth-Century Science Fiction Writers. 2nd ed. Edited by Curtis C. Smith. Chi-
cago: St. James Press, 1986, pp. 44–45.
Williams, Raymond. "Utopia and Science Fiction." *Science Fiction Studies* 5 (1978):
203–214.
Winters, Donald E. "The Utopianism of Survival: Bellamy's *Looking Backward* and
Twain's *A Connecticut Yankee.*" *American Studies* 21 (1980): 23–28.

Bemelmans, Ludwig

More Junior Authors. Edited by Muriel Fuller. New York: Wilson, 1963, pp. 14–15.

Benary–Isbert, Margot

Benary-Isbert, Margot. "An Author's Reflections." *Library Journal* 82 (May 15,
1957): 1329–1334.
———. "Editorial: The Light in the Darkness." *Horn Book* 34 (Dec. 1958): 443.
———. "The Need of Understanding in Our Shrinking World." *Horn Book* 31 (June
1955): 167–176.
———. "On Words, Singleness of Mind, and the Genius Loci." *Horn Book* 40 (Apr.
1964): 202–208.
More Junior Authors. Edited by Muriel Fuller. New York: Wilson, 1963, p. 15.

Benchley, Nathaniel (Goddard)

Fourth Book of Junior Authors and Illustrators. Edited by Doris De Montreville and
Elizabeth D. Crawford. New York: Wilson, 1978, pp. 36–37.
Helbig, Alethea K., and Perkins, Agnes Regan. *Dictionary of American Children's
Fiction, 1960–1984.* Westport, CT: Greenwood Press, 1986, pp. 47–48.
Twentieth Century Children's Writers. 2nd ed. Edited by D. L. Kirkpatrick. New York:
St. Martin's Press, 1983, pp. 77–79.

Bendick, Jeanne

More Junior Authors. Edited by Muriel Fuller. New York: Wilson, 1963, p. 16.

Benét, Stephen Vincent

Bromley, Robin. "Stephen Vincent Benét." In *Supernatural Fiction Writers: Fantasy
and Horror,* vol. 2. Edited by E. F. Bleiler. New York: Scribner, 1985, pp. 797–804.

Bennett, John

Bennett, John. "The Love of Grotesquerie." *Horn Book* 4 (Aug. 1928): 67–70.
Bennett, M. "Youth in Pleasant Places." *Horn Book* 36 (June 1960): 245–247.
Coyle, William, ed. *Ohio Authors and Their Books.* Cleveland: World, 1962.
Gunterman, Bertha. "The Astrologer's Tower." *Horn Book* 4 (Aug. 1928): 63–66.

The Junior Book of Authors. 2nd rev. ed. Edited by Stanley J. Kunitz and Howard Haycraft. New York: Wilson, 1951, pp. 27–28.

Roginski, Jim, ed. *Newbery and Caldecott Medalists and Honor Book Winners.* Littleton, CO: Libraries Unlimited, 1982, pp. 44–45.

Smith, Janie M. "Author for Children in the South." *Horn Book* 18 (Mar. 1942): 83–87.

———. "John Bennett of Chillicothe." *Horn Book* 19 (Jan. 1943): 427–433.

Benson, E(dward) F(rederic)

Morgan, Chris. "E. F. Benson." In *Supernatural Fiction Writers,* vol. 1. Edited by E. F. Bleiler. New York: Scribner, 1985, pp. 491–496.

The Oxford Companion to Children's Literature. Edited by Humphrey Carpenter and Mari Prichard. New York: Oxford Univ. Press, 1984, p. 142.

Searles, A. L. "The Short Fiction of Benson." In *Survey of Modern Fantasy Literature,* vol. 3. Edited by Frank N. Magill. Englewood Cliffs, NJ: Salem Press, 1983, pp. 1433–1435.

Beresford, Elisabeth

Twentieth Century Children's Writers. 2nd ed. Edited by D. L. Kirkpatrick. New York: St. Martin's Press, 1983, pp. 80–81.

Berger, Thomas (Louis)

Chapman, Edgar L. "*Arthur Rex.*" In *Survey of Modern Fantasy Literature,* vol. 1. Edited by Frank N. Magill. Englewood Cliffs, NJ: Salem Press, 1983, pp. 57–60.

Thompson, Raymond H. "Humor and Irony in Modern Arthurian Fantasy: Thomas Berger's *Arthur Rex.*" *Kansas Quarterly* 16 (Summer 1984): 45–49.

Berton, Pierre

Hambleton, A. "Canadian Fantasy." *British Columbia Library Quarterly* 26 (Oct. 1962): 11–13.

Sigman, Joseph. "Pierre Berton and the Romantic Tradition." *Canadian Children's Literature* 7 (1977): 21–27.

Stott, Jon C. "An Interview with Pierre Berton." *Canadian Children's Literature* 23/24 (1981): 4–19.

Best, (Oswald) Herbert

The Junior Book of Authors. 2nd rev. ed. Edited by Stanley J. Kunitz and Howard Haycraft. New York: Wilson, 1951, pp. 32–33.

Twentieth Century Children's Writers. 2nd ed. Edited by D. L. Kirkpatrick. New York: St. Martin's Press, 1983, pp. 83–84.

Besterman, Catherine

Helbig, Alethea K., and Perkins, Agnes Regan. *Dictionary of American Children's Fiction, 1859–1959.* Westport, CT: Greenwood Press, 1985, pp. 46, 417.

Beston, Henry B.

The Junior Book of Authors. 2nd rev. ed. Edited by Stanley J. Kunitz and Howard Haycraft. New York: Wilson, 1951, pp. 33–34.

Bethancourt, T. Ernesto (pseud. of Tom Paisley)

Fifth Book of Junior Authors and Illustrators. Edited by Sally Holmes Holtze. New York: Wilson, 1983, pp. 31–32.

Bianco, Margery (Winifred) Williams
[Prior to 1925, she wrote as Margery Williams.]

Bechtel, Louise Seaman. "A Tribute to Margery Bianco." *Elementary English Review* 12 (June 1935): 147–149, 165.

Bianco, Margery Williams. "Easter Rabbits—And Others." *Horn Book* 27 (Mar.–Apr. 1951): 131–134.

———. "Our Youngest Critics." In Anne Carroll Moore and Bertha Mahony Miller. *Writing and Criticism.* Boston: Horn Book, 1951, pp. 47–57.

———. "Writing Books for Boys and Girls." *Elementary English Review* 14 (May 1937): 161–164.

Doyle, Brian. *The Who's Who of Children's Literature.* New York: Schocken, 1968, pp. 28–29.

Helbig, Alethea K., and Perkins, Agnes Regan. *Dictionary of American Children's Fiction, 1859–1959.* Westport, CT: Greenwood Press, 1985, p. 47.

The Junior Book of Authors. 2nd rev. ed. Edited by Stanley J. Kunitz and Howard Haycraft. New York: Wilson, 1951, pp. 34–36.

Moore, Anne Carroll. "Margery Williams Bianco, 1881–1944." *Horn Book* 21 (May–June 1945): 157–164.

Moore, Anne Carroll, and Miller, Bertha Mahony, eds. *Writing and Criticism: A Book for Margery Bianco.* Boston: Horn Book, 1951.

The Oxford Companion to Children's Literature. Edited by Humphrey Carpenter and Mari Prichard. New York: Oxford Univ. Press, 1984, pp. 59–60.

Roginski, Jim, ed. *Newbery and Caldecott Medalists and Honor Book Winners.* Littleton, CO: Libraries Unlimited, 1982, pp. 48–50.

Ryan, J. S. "The Young Child as Sub–Creator: A Theology of Toys." *Orana* 18 (Nov. 1982): 117–119.

Seaman, Louise. "About the Biancos." *Horn Book* 2 (Mar. 1926): 17–25.

Stott, Jon C. *Children's Literature from A to Z.* New York: McGraw–Hill, 1984, p. 34.

Twentieth Century Children's Writers. 2nd ed. Edited by D. L. Kirkpatrick. New York: St. Martin's Press, 1983, pp. 85–86.

Whalen–Levitt, Peggy. "Margery Williams Bianco." In *Writers for Children: Critical Studies of Major Authors since the Seventeenth Century.* Edited by Jane M. Bingham. New York: Scribner, 1988, pp. 63–68.

Bianco, Pamela

Helbig, Alethea K., and Perkins, Agnes Regan. *Dictionary of American Children's Fiction, 1859–1959.* Westport, CT: Greenwood Press, 1985, pp. 47, 301–302.

Seaman, Louise. "About the Biancos." *Horn Book* 2 (Mar. 1926): 17–25.

Biegel, Paul

Biegel, Paul. "Tell Me a Story." *Horn Book* 58 (Feb. 1982): 87–93.

Binns, Archie (Fred)

Helbig, Alethea K., and Perkins, Agnes Regan. *Dictionary of American Children's Fiction, 1859–1959*. Westport, CT: Greenwood Press, 1985, p. 51.

Blackwood, Algernon (Henry)

Columbo, John Robert. *Blackwood's Books: A Bibliography Devoted to Algernon Blackwood*. Toronto: Hounslow, 1981.

Hudson, Derek. "A Study of Algernon Blackwood." In *Essays and Studies for 1961*. Edited by Derek Hudson. London: Murray, 1961, pp. 102–114.

Letson, Russell Francis. "The Approaches to Mystery: The Fantasies of Arthur Machen and Algernon Blackwood." Ph.D. dissertation, Southern Illinois University, 1975.

Punter, David. "Algernon Blackwood." In *Supernatural Fiction Writers: Fantasy and Horror*, vol. 1. Edited by E. F. Bleiler. New York: Scribner, 1985, pp. 463–469.

Searles, Baird; Meacham, Beth; and Franklin, Michael. *A Reader's Guide to Fantasy*. New York: Avon, 1982, pp. 31–32.

Stevenson, Lionel. "Purveyors of Myth and Magic." In *Yesterday and After: The History of the English Novel*. Totowa, NJ: Barnes and Noble, 1967, pp. 111–154.

Bloch, Marie Halun

Fourth Book of Junior Authors and Illustrators. Edited by Doris De Montreville and Elizabeth D. Crawford. New York: Wilson, 1978, pp. 44–46.

Helbig, Alethea K., and Perkins, Agnes Regan. *Dictionary of American Children's Fiction, 1960–1984*. Westport, CT: Greenwood Press, 1986, p. 59.

Bodecker, N(iels) M(ogens)

Twentieth Century Children's Writers. 2nd ed. Edited by D. L. Kirkpatrick. New York: St. Martin's Press, 1983, pp. 103–104.

Bond, (Thomas) Michael

Blount, Margaret. "Animals Are Equal: A Bear in a London Family." In *Animal Land*. New York: Morrow, 1975, pp. 307–322.

Bond, Michael. "Jumping In at the Deep End: On Writing for Children." *Horn Book* 56 (June 1980): 335–339.

Doyle, Brian. *The Who's Who of Children's Literature*. New York: Schocken, 1968, pp. 32–33.

Hopkins, Lee Bennett. "Michael Bond." In *More Books by More People*. New York: Citation Press, 1974, pp. 35–40.

Jones, Cornelia, and Way, Olivia R. "Michael Bond." In *British Children's Authors*. Chicago: American Library Association, 1976, pp. 49–54.

The Oxford Companion to Children's Literature. Edited by Humphrey Carpenter and Mari Prichard. New York: Oxford Univ. Press, 1984, pp. 70, 393.

Stott, Jon C. *Children's Literature from A to Z*. New York: McGraw-Hill, 1984, p. 44.

Third Book of Junior Authors. Edited by Doris De Montreville and Donna Hill. New York: Wilson, 1972, pp. 40–41.
Twentieth Century Children's Writers. 2nd ed. Edited by D. L. Kirkpatrick. New York: St. Martin's Press, 1983, pp. 104–105.

Bond, Nancy (Barbara)

Bond, Nancy. "Conflict in Children's Literature." *Horn Book* 60 (June 1984): 297–306.
———. "Landscape of Fiction." In *Loughborough '83: Proceedings*. Welsh National Centre for Children's Literature, 1984, pp. 91–99.
———. "On Not Teaching Creative Writing." In *Innocence & Experience*. Edited by Barbara Harrison and Gregory Maguire. New York: Lothrop, 1987, pp. 445–446.
———. "A Writer's Freedom." *Catholic Library World* 56 (Nov. 1984): 169–171.
Fifth Book of Junior Authors and Illustrators. Edited by Sally Holmes Holtze. New York: Wilson, 1983, pp. 38–40.
Helbig, Alethea K., and Perkins, Agnes Regan. *Dictionary of American Children's Fiction, 1960–1984*. Westport, CT: Greenwood Press, 1986, pp. 65, 630–631.
Sullivan, C. W., III. "Nancy Bond and Welsh Traditions." *Children's Literature Association Quarterly* 11 (Spring 1986): 33–37.
———. *"A String in the Harp."* In Frank N. Magill. *Survey of Modern Fantasy Literature,* vol. 4. Englewood Cliffs, NJ: Salem Press, 1983, pp. 1851–1853.
———. "Traditional Welsh Materials in Modern Fantasy." *Extrapolation* 28 (Spring 1987): 87–97.
Twentieth Century Children's Writers. 2nd ed. Edited by D. L. Kirkpatrick. New York: St. Martin's Press, 1983, pp. 106–107.

Bonham, Frank

Third Book of Junior Authors. Edited by Doris De Montreville and Donna Hill. New York: Wilson, 1972, pp. 42–43.

Bontemps, Arna (Wendell)

Bontemps, Arna. "The *Lonesome Boy* Theme." *Horn Book* 42 (Dec. 1966): 672–680.
———. "Sad-Faced Author." *Horn Book* 15 (Jan.–Feb. 1939): 7–12.
The Junior Book of Authors. 2nd rev. ed. Edited by Stanley J. Kunitz and Howard Haycraft. New York: Wilson, 1951, pp. 39–40.
Ryder, Ione Morrison. "Arna Bontemps." *Horn Book* 15 (Jan.–Feb. 1939): 13–20.

Borges, Jorge Luis

Balderston, Daniel. *The Literary Universe of Jorge Luis Borges: An Index to References and Allusions to Persons, Titles, and Places in His Writings*. Westport, CT: Greenwood Press, 1986.
Barnstone, Willis, ed. *Borges at Eighty: Conversations*. Bloomington: Indiana Univ. Press, 1982.
Bell-Villada, Gene H. *Borges and His Fiction: A Guide to His Mind and Art*. Chapel Hill: Univ. of North Carolina Press, 1981.
Foster, David William. *Jorge Luis Borges: An Annotated Primary and Secondary Bibliography*. New York: Garland, 1984.
Fulton, Patricia Teague. "Borges, Hawthorne, and Poe: A Study of Significant Parallels in Their Theories and Methods of Short Story Writing." Ph.D. dissertation, Auburn University, 1979.

Gordon, Ambrose, Jr. "A Quiet Betrayal: Some Mirror Work in Borges." *Texas Studies in Literature and Language* 17 (1975): 207–218.

Hager, Stanton. "Places of the Looking Glass: Borges's Deconstruction of Metaphysics." In *The Scope of the Fantastic.* Edited by Robert A. Collins and Howard D. Pearce. Westport, CT: Greenwood Press, 1985, pp. 231–238.

Menton, S. "Jorge Luis Borges, Magic Realist." *Hispanic Review* 50 (Autumn 1982): 411–426.

Philmus, Robert M. "Wells and Borges and the Labyrinths of Time." *Science Fiction Studies* 1, pt. 4 (1974): 237–248.

Twentieth–Century Science Fiction Writers. 2nd ed. Edited by Curtis C. Smith. Chicago: St. James Press, 1986, pp. 838–839.

Bosse, Malcolm J(oseph)

Fifth Book of Junior Authors and Illustrators. Edited by Sally Holmes Holtze. New York: Wilson, 1983, pp. 40–42.

Boston, L(ucy) M(aria Wood)

Blatt, G. T. "Profile: Lucy M. Boston." *Language Arts* 60 (Fall 1983): 220–225.

Boston, Lucy M. "Christmas at Green Knowe." *Horn Book* 31 (Dec. 1955): 473.

———. *Memory in a House.* New York: Macmillan, 1974.

———. "A Message from Green Knowe." *Horn Book* 39 (June 1963): 259–264. Originally published as "The Place That Is Green Knowe." *Junior Bookshelf* 26 (Dec. 1962): 295–301. Reprinted in Meek. *The Cool Web.* New York: Atheneum, 1978, pp. 216–221.

———. *Perverse and Foolish: A Memoir of Childhood and Youth.* New York: Atheneum, 1979.

Campbell, Alastair K. D. "Children's Writers: Lucy Boston." *School Librarian* 26 (Sept. 1978): 212–217.

Chambers, Aidan. *Booktalk: Occasional Writing on Literature and Children.* New York: Harper and Row, 1986, pp. 19, 49–58. Original British publication, 1985.

———. "Why *The Children of Green Knowe.*" *Signal* 23 (May 1977): 64–68. Reprinted in Chambers. *Signal Approach to Children's Books.* Metuchen, NJ: Scarecrow Press, 1980, pp. 267–275.

Crouch, Marcus S. "Lucy Boston at 80." *Junior Bookshelf* 36 (Dec. 1972): 355–357.

———. "A Visit to Green Knowe." *Junior Bookshelf* 26 (Dec. 1962): 302–305.

Doyle, Brian. *The Who's Who of Children's Literature.* New York: Schocken, 1968, pp. 33–34.

Hatch, Jane. "Lucy M. Boston." *Wilson Library Bulletin* 37 (Oct. 1962): 188.

Hollindale, Peter. "The Novels of L. M. Boston." In Butts. *Good Writers for Young Readers.* St. Albans, England: Hart-Davis, 1977, pp. 25–33.

Jones, Cornelia, and Way, Olivia R. "L. M. Boston." In *British Children's Authors.* Chicago: American Library Association, 1976, pp. 55–64.

Lively, Penelope. "The World of Green Knowe." *Books for Your Children* 5, no. 2 (Winter 1969–1970).

Livo, Norma J. "Lucy Boston at 80." *Junior Bookshelf* 36 (Dec. 1972): 355–357.

Meek, Margaret. "A Private House." *Times Literary Supplement,* June 15, 1973, p. 676. Reprinted in Margaret Meek. *The Cool Web.* New York: Atheneum, 1978, pp. 325–330.

The Oxford Companion to Children's Literature. Edited by Humphrey Carpenter and Mari Prichard. New York: Oxford Univ. Press, 1984, pp. 76–77, 473.

Pflieger, Pat, and Hill, Helen M. *A Reference Guide to Modern Fantasy for Children.*

Westport, CT: Greenwood Press, 1984, pp. 79–82, 108–112, 175–176, 476–477, 504–505.

Rees, David. "Green Thought in Green Shade—L. M. Boston." In *Painted Desert, Green Shade.* Boston: Horn Book, 1984, pp. 1–16.

Robbins, Sidney. "A Nip of Otherness, Like Life: The Life of Lucy Boston." *Children's Literature in Education* 6 (Nov. 1971): 6–16.

Rose, Jasper. *Lucy Boston.* New York: Walck, 1966.

Rosenthal, Lynne. "The Development of Consciousness in Lucy Boston's *The Children of Green Knowe.*" In *Children's Literature,* vol. 8. New Haven, CT: Yale Univ. Press, 1980, pp. 53–67.

Stott, Jon C. *Children's Literature from A to Z.* New York: McGraw–Hill, 1984, p. 46.

———. "From Here to Eternity: Aspects of Pastoral in the Green Knowe Series." In *Children's Literature,* vol. 11. New Haven, CT: Yale Univ. Press, 1983, pp. 145–155.

Swinfen, Ann. *In Defense of Fantasy.* London: Routledge, 1984, pp. 49, 55–56.

Third Book of Junior Authors. Edited by Doris De Montreville and Donna Hill. New York: Wilson, 1972, pp. 44–45.

Townsend, John Rowe. "L. M. Boston." In *A Sense of Story.* Philadelphia: Lippincott, 1971, pp. 17–27.

Travers, P. L. "World Beyond World." *Book Week* (May 7, 1967): 4–5. Reprinted in Haviland. *Children and Literature.* Glenview, IL: Scott, Foresman, 1973, pp. 246–249.

Twentieth Century Children's Writers. 2nd ed. Edited by D. L. Kirkpatrick. New York: St. Martin's Press, 1983, pp. 110–111.

Wintle, Justin, and Fisher, Emma. "L. M. Boston." In *The Pied Pipers.* New York: Paddington Press, 1974, pp. 277–284.

Boucher, Anthony (pseud. of W[illiam] A[nthony] P[arker] White)

Boucher, Anthony. "The Publishing of Science Fiction." In *Modern Science Fiction: Its Meaning and Its Future.* 2nd ed. Edited by Reginald Bretnor. Chicago: Advent, 1979.

Fredericks, Casey. *The Future of Eternity: Mythologies of Science Fiction and Fantasy.* Bloomington: Indiana Univ. Press, 1982.

Pierce, Hazel Beasley. *A Literary Symbiosis: Science Fiction/Fantasy Mystery.* Westport, CT: Greenwood Press, 1983.

Twentieth–Century Science Fiction Writers. 2nd ed. Edited by Curtis C. Smith. Chicago: St. James Press, 1986, pp. 65–67.

Bourliaguet, Leonce

Fourth Book of Junior Authors and Illustrators. Edited by Doris De Montreville and Elizabeth D. Crawford. New York: Wilson, 1978, pp. 51–52.

Bowen, William (Alvin)

Helbig, Alethea K., and Perkins, Agnes Regan. *Dictionary of American Children's Fiction, 1859–1959.* Westport, CT: Greenwood Press, 1985, pp. 61, 379–380.

Bradbury, Ray (Douglas)

Albright, Donn. "Ray Bradbury Index: Part I." *Xenophile* 13 (May 1975).

———. "Ray Bradbury Index: Part II." *Xenophile* 26 (Sept. 1976): 4–10.

———. "Ray Bradbury Index: Part III." *Xenophile* 36 (1977): 2–7.

Ash, Lee. "WLB Biography—Ray Bradbury." *Wilson Library Bulletin* 39 (Nov. 1964): 268, 280.

Atkins, T. R. "Illustrated Man: Interview." *Sight & Sound* 43 (Spring 1974): 96–100.

Bradbury, Ray. "How, Instead of Being Educated in College, I Was Graduated from Libraries, or, Thoughts from a Chap Who Landed on the Moon in 1932." *Wilson Library Bulletin* 45 (May 1971): 842–851.

———. "Rationale for Bookburners: A Further Word from Ray Bradbury." *ALA Bulletin* 55 (May 1961): 403–404.

———. "Science Fiction as Modern Romance." *Intellect* 104 (1976): 490. Summary of speech.

———. "The Secret Mind." In David Wingrove, ed. *The Science Fiction Source Book.* New York: Van Nostrand Reinhold, 1984, pp. 72–74.

Dimeo, Richard Steven. "The Mind and Fantasies of Ray Bradbury." Ph.D. dissertation, University of Utah, 1970.

Elliot, Jeffrey M. "The Bradbury Chronicles." *Future* 5 (1978): 22–26. Interview.

———. "An Interview with Ray Bradbury." *Science Fiction Review* 6 (Nov. 1977): 48–50. Reprinted from *San Francisco Review of Books,* June 1977.

———. *Science Fiction Voices #2.* San Bernardino, CA: Borgo Press, 1979.

Fantasy and Reality. North Hollywood, CA: Center for Cassette Studies, 1972. (audiocassette)

Foster, Mark Anthony. "Write the Other Way: The Correlation of Style and Theme in Selected Prose Fiction of Ray Bradbury." Ph.D. dissertation, Florida State University, 1973.

Grabowski, William J. "Whales, Libraries, and Dreams: Ray Bradbury." *Fantasy Review* 93 (1986): 11, 16.

Jacobs, Robert. "*The Writer's Digest* Interview: Bradbury." *Writer's Digest* (Feb. 1976): 18–25.

Johnson, Wayne L. *Ray Bradbury.* New York: Ungar, 1980.

Kilworth, Garry. "The Profession of Science Fiction 31: Confessions of a Bradbury Eater." *Foundation* 29 (1983): 5–10.

Linkfield, Thomas P. "The Fiction of Ray Bradbury: Universal Themes in Midwestern Settings." *Midwestern Miscellany* 8 (1980): 44–101.

McNelly, Willis E. "Bradbury Revisited." *CEA Critic* 31 (Mar. 1969): 4, 6.

———. "Ray Bradbury." In *Science Fiction Writers.* Edited by E. F. Bleiler. New York: Scribner, 1982, pp. 171–178.

———. "Ray Bradbury." In *Supernatural Fiction Writers,* vol. 2. Edited by E. F. Bleiler. New York: Scribner, 1985, pp. 917–924.

———. "Ray Bradbury—Past, Present and Future." In *Voices for the Future: Essays on Major Science Fiction Writers,* vol. 1. Edited by Thomas D. Clareson. Bowling Green, OH: Bowling Green Univ. Popular Press, 1976.

McReynolds, Douglas J. "The Short Fiction of Bradbury." In *Survey of Modern Fantasy Literature,* vol. 3. Edited by Frank N. Magill. Englewood Cliffs, NJ: Salem Press, 1983, pp. 1471–1481.

Mogen, David. *Ray Bradbury.* Boston: Twayne, 1986.

Moskowitz, Sam. *Seekers of Tomorrow; Masters of Modern Science Fiction.* New York: Ballantine, 1967, pp. 352–375.

Nolan, William F. *The Ray Bradbury Companion: A Life and Career History, Photolog, and Comprehensive Checklist of Writings with Facsimiles from Ray Bradbury's Unpublished and Uncollected Work in All Media.* Detroit: Gale, 1975. Originally published in *Xenophile,* May 1975.

Orlander, Joseph D., and Greenberg, Martin Harry, eds. *Ray Bradbury.* New York: Taplinger, 1979.

Plank, R. "Expedition to the Planet of Paranoia." *Extrapolation* 22 (Summer 1981): 171–185.

Platt, Charles. "Ray Bradbury." In *Dream Makers: The Uncommon People Who Write Science Fiction.* New York: Berkley, 1980; rev. ed. New York: Ungar, 1987, pp. 161–172. Interview.

Ray Bradbury as Philosopher. North Hollywood, CA: Center for Cassette Studies, 1974. (audiocassette)

Reilly, Robert. "The Artistry of Ray Bradbury." *Extrapolation* 13 (Dec. 1971): 64–74.

Searles, Baird; Meacham, Beth; and Franklin, Michael. *A Reader's Guide to Fantasy.* New York: Avon, 1982, pp. 36–37.

Slusser, George Edgar. *The Bradbury Chronicles.* San Bernardino, CA: Borgo Press, 1977.

Stupple, A. James. "The Past, the Future and Ray Bradbury." In *Voices for the Future: Essays on Major Science Fiction Writers,* vol. 1. Edited by Thomas D. Clareson. Bowling Green, OH: Bowling Green Univ. Popular Press, 1976.

Sullivan, Anita T. "Ray Bradbury and Fantasy." *English Journal* 61 (1972): 1309–1314.

Touponce, William F. *Ray Bradbury and the Poetics of Reverie: Fantasy, Science Fiction and the Reader.* Ann Arbor, MI: University of Michigan Research Press, 1984.

Twentieth-Century Science Fiction Writers. 2nd ed. Edited by Curtis C. Smith. Chicago: St. James Press, 1986, pp. 72–75.

Wolfe, Gary K. "*Something Wicked This Way Comes.*" In Frank N. Magill. *Survey of Modern Fantasy Literature,* vol. 4. Englewood Cliffs, NJ: Salem Press, 1983, pp. 1769–1773.

Bradley, Marion Zimmer

Arbur, Rosemarie. "*Darkover.*" In *Survey of Modern Fantasy Literature,* vol. 1. Edited by Frank N. Magill. Englewood Cliffs, NJ: Salem Press, 1983, pp. 488–492.

———. *Leigh Brackett, Marion Zimmer Bradley, Anne McCaffrey: A Primary and Secondary Bibliography.* Boston: G. K. Hall, 1982.

———. *Reader's Guide to Marion Zimmer Bradley.* Mercer Island, WA: Starmont, 1985.

Bradley, Marion Zimmer. "An Evolution of Consciousness: Twenty-five Years of Writing about Women in Science Fiction." *Science Fiction Review* 6 (Aug. 1977): 34–45.

———. "Experiment Perilous: The Art and Science of Anguish in Science Fiction." In *Experiment Perilous: Three Essays on Science Fiction.* Edited by Andrew Porter. New York: Algol Press, 1976.

———. "Fandom: It's Value to the Professional." In *Inside Outer Space.* Edited by Sharon Jarvis. New York: Ungar, 1985.

———. "Fantasy and the Contemporary Occult Novel: Social and Intellectual Approaches." *Fantasy Review* 80 (1985): 10–12. Part II. *Fantasy Review* 81 (1985): 31–32.

———. "Introduction." *The Bloody Sun and "To Keep the Oath."* Boston: Gregg, 1979.

———. "Introduction." *The Forbidden Tower.* Boston: Gregg, 1979.

———. "Introduction." *The Shattered Chain.* Boston: Gregg, 1979.

———. "Introduction." *The Spell Sword.* Boston: Gregg, 1979.

———. "Introduction." *Star of Danger.* Boston: Gregg, 1979.

————. "Introduction." *Stormqueen!* Boston: Gregg, 1979.

————. "Introduction." *The Winds of Darkover*. Boston: Gregg, 1979.

————. "Introduction." *The World Wreakers*. Boston: Gregg, 1979.

————. "The Maverick View." *Bulletin of the Science Fiction Writers of America* 14 (1979): 17–21.

————. *Men, Halflings and Hero Worship*. Baltimore: T-K Graphics, 1973. Discusses Tolkien.

————. "My Trip through Science Fiction." *Algol* 15 (Winter 1978): 10–20.

————. "Two Worlds of Fantasy." *Haunted: Studies in Gothic Fiction* 1 (June 1968): 82–85.

————. "Why Did My Story Get Rejected?" In *The Writer's Handbook*. Edited by Sylvia K. Burack. Boston: The Writer, 1985.

Breen, Walter. *The Darkover Concordance: A Reader's Guide*. Berkeley, CA: Pennyfarthing Press, 1979.

————. *The Gemini Problem: A Study in Darkover*. New York: Berkley, 1973; reprinted Baltimore: T-K Graphics, 1976.

Day, Phyllis J. "Earthmother/Witchmother: Feminism and Ecology Renewed." *Extrapolation* 23 (1982): 12–21.

De Camp, L. Sprague, ed. *The Blade of Conan*. New York: Ace, 1979. pap.

Godwin, Parke. "The Road to Camelot: A Conversation with Marion Zimmer Bradley." *Science Fiction and Fantasy Review* 66 (1984): 6–9.

Hanna, Judith. "Though He Was No Arthur." *Vector* 123 (1984): 20–21.

Heldreth, L. M. "The Darkover Novels." In *Survey of Modern Fantasy Literature*, vol. 1. Edited by Frank N. Magill. Englewood Cliffs, NJ: Salem Press, 1983, pp. 341–346.

Herbert, Rosemarie. "The Authors' Visions." *Publishers Weekly*, May 23, 1986, pp. 42–45.

An Hour with Marion Zimmer Bradley: A Personal Note. Garden Grove, NY: Hourglass Productions, 1979. (audiocassette)

Kimpel, R. *"The Mists of Avalon/Die Nebel Von Avalon:* Marion Zimmer Bradley's German Best Seller." *Journal of American Culture* 9 (Fall 1986): 25–28.

Lacy, N. J. *The Arthurian Encyclopedia*. New York: Garland, 1986, pp. 59–60.

Leith, Linda. "Marion Zimmer Bradley and Darkover." *Science–Fiction Studies* 7 (1980): 28–35.

Lupoff, Richard A. "Introduction." In Marion Zimmer Bradley. *The Sword of Aldones*. Boston: Gregg, 1977.

"Marion Zimmer Bradley." In Daryl Lane, William Vernon, and David Carlson. *The Sound of Wonder: Interviews from "The Science Fiction Radio Show,"* vol. 2. Phoenix, AZ: Oryx Press, 1985, pp. 111–132.

Roberts, Thomas J. "Before You Dump Those 'Junk' Books." *Media and Methods* 15 (May–June 1979): 27–28, 46.

Russ, Joanna. "Recent Feminist Utopias." In *Future Females*. Edited by Marleen S. Barr. Bowling Green, OH: Bowling Green Univ. Press, 1984, pp. 71–87.

Shwartz, Susan M. "Marion Zimmer Bradley's Ethic of Freedom." In *The Feminine Eye: Science Fiction and the Women Who Write It*. Edited by Tom Staicar. New York: Ungar, 1982, pp. 73–88.

————. "Other Worlds: By the Light of the Bloody Sun." *Fantasy Newsletter* 32 (1981): 12–15.

Sturgeon, Theodore. "Introduction." In Marion Zimmer Bradley. *Darkover Landfall*. Boston: Gregg, 1978.

Twentieth–Century Science Fiction Writers. 2nd ed. Edited by Curtis C. Smith. Chicago: St. James Press, 1986, pp. 75–77.

Wise, S. *The Darkover Dilemma: Problems of the Darkover Series.* Baltimore: T-K Graphics, 1976.

Wood, Susan. "Introduction." In Marion Zimmer Bradley. *The Heritage of Hastur.* Boston: Gregg, 1977.

Brand, Christianna (pseud. of Mary [Christianna Milne] Lewis)

The Oxford Companion to Children's Literature. Edited by Humphrey Carpenter and Mari Prichard. New York: Oxford Univ. Press, 1984, p. 80.

Twentieth Century Children's Writers. 2nd ed. Edited by D. L. Kirkpatrick. New York: St. Martin's Press, 1983, pp. 112–113.

Brenner, Barbara (Johnes)

Fourth Book of Junior Authors and Illustrators. Edited by Doris De Montreville and Elizabeth D. Crawford. New York: Wilson, 1978, pp. 55–56.

Briggs, K(atherine) M(ary)

Briggs, K. M. "Fairies in Children's Books." Lecture given at Mississippi University for Women, 1977. In *Folk Literature of the British Isles.* Metuchen, NJ: Scarecrow Press, 1978, pp. 11–21.

Fifth Book of Junior Authors and Illustrators. Edited by Sally Holmes Holtze. New York: Wilson, 1983, pp. 49–50.

Hodges, Margaret. "Katherine M. Briggs: A Memoir." *Children's Literature in Education* 43, no. 4 (Winter 1981): 209–213.

Moss, Elaine. "K. M. Briggs, Novelist." *Signal* 30 (Sept. 1979): 133–139.

The Oxford Companion to Children's Literature. Edited by Humphrey Carpenter and Mari Prichard. New York: Oxford Univ. Press, 1984, pp. 82–83.

Philip, Neil. "The Goodwill of Our Hearts: K. M. Briggs as Novelist." *Folklore* 92 (1981): 155–159.

Searles, Baird; Meacham, Beth; and Franklin, Michael. *A Reader's Guide to Fantasy.* New York: Avon, 1982, pp. 37–38.

Twentieth Century Children's Writers. 2nd ed. Edited by D. L. Kirkpatrick. New York: St. Martin's Press, 1983, pp. 118–119.

Bright, Robert

More Junior Authors. Edited by Muriel Fuller. New York: Wilson, 1963, pp. 28–29.

Twentieth Century Children's Writers. 2nd ed. Edited by D. L. Kirkpatrick. New York: St. Martin's Press, 1983, pp. 120–121.

Brin, David

Klein, Jay Kay. "David Brin." *Analog* (Nov. 1983): 119.

Brink, Carol Ryrie

Brink, Carol Ryrie. "*Caddy Woodlawn:* Newbery Medal Winner 1936: Her History." *Horn Book* 12 (July–Aug. 1936): 248–250.

———. "Keep the Bough Green." *Horn Book* 43 (Aug. 1967): 447–452.

Hadlow, Ruth M. "*Caddie Woodlawn.*" *Elementary English* 37 (Apr. 1960): 221–226, 237.

Helbig, Alethea K. "Carol Ryrie Brink." In *Writers for Children: Critical Studies of Major Authors since the Seventeenth Century.* Edited by Jane M. Bingham. New York: Scribner, 1988, pp. 85–90.

Helbig, Alethea K., and Perkins, Agnes Regan. *Dictionary of American Children's Fiction, 1859–1959.* Westport, CT: Greenwood Press, 1985, pp. 69–70.

Hopkins, Lee Bennet. *More Books by More People: Interviews with Sixty-five Authors of Books for Children.* New York: Citation Press, 1974, pp. 53–59.

The Junior Book of Authors. 2nd rev. ed. Edited by Stanley J. Kunitz and Howard Haycraft. New York: Wilson, 1951, pp. 45–46.

Orland, Norine. "Carol Ryrie Brink and *Caddie Woodlawn.*" *Elementary English* 45 (Apr. 1968): 425–428, 451.

The Oxford Companion to Children's Literature. Edited by Humphrey Carpenter and Mari Prichard. New York: Oxford Univ. Press, 1984, pp. 83–84.

Reed, M. E. "Carol Ryrie Brink: Legacy of an Idaho Childhood." *Idaho Librarian* 34 (Oct. 1982): 142–147.

Roginski, Jim, ed. *Newbery and Caldecott Medalists and Honor Book Winners.* Littleton, CO: Libraries Unlimited, 1982, pp. 54–55.

Smaridge, Norah. *Famous Modern Storytellers for Young People.* New York: Dodd, 1969, pp. 52–56.

Twentieth Century Children's Writers. 2nd ed. Edited by D. L. Kirkpatrick. New York: St. Martin's Press, 1983, pp. 121–122.

Brittain, Bill (William)

Fifth Book of Junior Authors and Illustrators. Edited by Sally Holmes Holtze. New York: Wilson, 1983, pp. 50–51.

Helbig, Alethea K., and Perkins, Agnes Regan. *Dictionary of American Children's Fiction, 1960–1984.* Westport, CT: Greenwood Press, 1986, pp. 75, 730–731.

Bro, Marguerite (Harmon)

More Junior Authors. Edited by Muriel Fuller. New York: Wilson, 1963, pp. 30–31.

Brooks, Terry

Paxon, Diana. "The Tolkien Tradition." *Mythlore* 39 (1984): 23–27, 37.

Searles, Baird; Meacham, Beth; and Franklin, Michael. *A Reader's Guide to Fantasy.* New York: Avon, 1982, p. 38.

Watson, Christine. "*The Sword of Shannara.*" In *Survey of Modern Fantasy Literature,* vol. 4. Edited by Frank N. Magill. Englewood Cliffs, NJ: Salem Press, 1983, pp. 1866–1868.

Brooks, Walter R(ollin)

Cart, Michael. "Fanfare for *Freddy:* A Classic Neglected No Longer." *School Library Journal* 32 (Feb. 1986): 25–27.

———. "Freddy, St. Peter, and Me." *Children's Literature in Education* 14 (Autumn 1983): 142–148.

The Junior Book of Authors. 2nd rev. ed. Edited by Stanley J. Kunitz and Howard Haycraft. New York: Wilson, 1951, pp. 51–52.

Kurth, Ruth Justine. "Realism in Children's Books of Fantasy." *California Librarian* 39 (July 1978): 39–40.

Sale, Roger. *Fairy Tales and After: From Snow White to E. B. White.* Cambridge, MA: Harvard Univ. Press, 1978, pp. 245–258.
Speth, Lee. "The Pig in the Widow's Shawl." *Mythlore* 6, 22 (Fall 1979): 7–8.
Twentieth Century Children's Writers. 2nd ed. Edited by D. L. Kirkpatrick. New York: St. Martin's Press, 1983, p. 125.

Brown, Abbie Farwell

"Abbie Farwell Brown." *Horn Book* 3 (May 1927): 15–16.

Brown, Palmer

Bader, Barbara. *American Picturebooks.* New York: Macmillan, 1976, pp. 492–494.
Fifth Book of Junior Authors and Illustrators. Edited by Sally Holmes Holtze. New York: Wilson, 1983, pp. 55–56.
Twentieth Century Children's Writers. 2nd ed. Edited by D. L. Kirkpatrick. New York: St. Martin's Press, 1983, pp. 127–128.

Browne, Frances

Doyle, Brian. *The Who's Who of Children's Literature.* New York: Schocken, 1968, pp. 39–40.
"Frances Browne: *Granny's Wonderful Chair.*" In *Masterworks of Children's Literature,* vol. VI. New York: Stonehill/Chelsea House, 1984, pp. 137–162.
The Oxford Companion to Children's Literature. Edited by Humphrey Carpenter and Mari Prichard. New York: Oxford Univ. Press, 1984, p. 219.

Buchan, John

Blackburn, William. "John Buchan's *Lake of Gold:* A Canadian Imitation of Kipling." *Canadian Children's Literature* 14 (1979): 5–13.
Buchan, John. "The Novel and the Fairy Tale." In *Children and Literature: Views and Reviews.* Edited by Virginia Haviland. New York: Lothrop, 1973, pp. 220–229.
Morgan, Chris. "The Short Fiction of John Buchan." In *Survey of Modern Fantasy Literature,* vol. 3. Edited by Frank N. Magill. Englewood Cliffs, NJ: Salem Press, 1983, pp. 1482–1484.
The Oxford Companion to Children's Literature. Edited by Humphrey Carpenter and Mari Prichard. New York: Oxford Univ. Press, 1984, p. 87.

Bulla, Clyde Robert

Bulla, Clyde Robert. *A Grain of Wheat: A Writer Begins.* Boston: Godine, 1985.
Griese, Arnold A. "Clyde Robert Bulla: Master Story Weaver." *Elementary English* 48 (Nov. 1971): 766–778. Reprinted in *Authors and Illustrators of Children's Books.* Edited by Miriam Hoffman and Eva Samuels. New York: Bowker, 1972, pp. 28–40.
Helbig, Alethea K., and Perkins, Agnes Regan. *Dictionary of American Children's Fiction, 1859–1959.* Westport, CT: Greenwood Press, 1985, pp. 73, 504.
———. *Dictionary of American Children's Fiction, 1960–1984.* Westport, CT: Greenwood Press, 1986, pp. 78–79.
More Junior Authors. Edited by Muriel Fuller. New York: Wilson, 1963, p. 34.
Twentieth Century Children's Writers. 2nd ed. Edited by D. L. Kirkpatrick. New York: St. Martin's Press, 1983, pp. 134–135.

Bunting, (Anne) Eve(lyn Bolton)

Fifth Book of Junior Authors and Illustrators. Edited by Sally Holmes Holtze. New York: Wilson, 1983, pp. 60–61.

Twentieth Century Children's Writers. 2nd ed. Edited by D. L. Kirkpatrick. New York: St. Martin's Press, 1983, pp. 136–137.

Bunyan, John

Bator, Robert. "John Bunyan." In *Writers for Children: Critical Studies of Major Authors since the Seventeenth Century.* Edited by Jane M. Bingham. New York: Scribner, 1988, pp. 97–102.

Batson, E. Beatrice. *John Bunyan, Allegory and Imagination.* Totowa, NJ: Barnes and Noble, 1984.

MacDonald, Ruth K. "The Case for *The Pilgrim's Progress.*" *Children's Literature Association Quarterly* 10 (Spring 1985): 29–30.

White, Alison. "*Pilgrim's Progress* as Fairy Tale." In *Children's Literature,* vol. 1. Storrs, CT: Journal of the Modern Language Association, 1972, pp. 42–45.

Burgess, Thornton Waldo

Agosta, Lucien L. "Thornton W. Burgess." In Cech. *American Writers for Children, 1900–1960. Dictionary of Literary Biography,* vol. 22. Detroit: Gale, 1983, pp. 71–87.

Bixler, Phyllis, and Agosta, Lucien L. "Formula Fiction and Children's Literature: Thornton Waldo Burgess and Frances Hodgson Burnett." *Children's Literature in Education* 15 (Summer 1984): 63–72.

Burgess, Thornton W. *Now I Remember: Autobiography of an Amateur Naturalist.* Boston: Little, Brown, 1960.

Doyle, Brian. *The Who's Who of Children's Literature.* New York: Schocken, 1968, pp. 42–43.

Fox, Dorothea Magdalene. "A 90–Year Romance with Nature." *Audubon Magazine* 66, no. 5 (Sept.–Oct. 1964): 312–313.

Goldthwaite, John. "The Black Rabbit: Part One." *Signal* 47 (May 1985): 86–111; "The Black Rabbit: Part Two." *Signal* 48 (Sept. 1985): 148–167. Reprinted in Goldthwaite. *The Natural History of Make–Believe.* New York: Oxford Univ. Press, 1987.

The Junior Book of Authors. 2nd rev. ed. Edited by Stanley J. Kunitz and Howard Haycraft. New York: Wilson, 1951, pp. 60–61.

Lovell, Russell A., Jr. *The Cape Cod Story of Thornton W. Burgess.* Thornton W. Burgess Centennial Committee 1874–1974, in conjunction with William S. Sullwold Publishing (Taunton, MA), 1974.

O'Neil, Paul. "Fifty Years in the Green Meadow." *Life,* Nov. 14, 1960, p. 112.

The Oxford Companion to Children's Literature. Edited by Humphrey Carpenter and Mari Prichard. New York: Oxford Univ. Press, 1984, p. 386.

Stott, Jon C. *Children's Literature from A to Z.* New York: McGraw-Hill, 1984, p. 57.

Twentieth Century Children's Writers. 2nd ed. Edited by D. L. Kirkpatrick. New York: St. Martin's Press, 1983, pp. 138–140.

Burman, Ben Lucien

Helbig, Alethea K., and Perkins, Agnes Regan. *Dictionary of American Children's Fiction, 1859–1959.* Westport, CT: Greenwood Press, 1985, pp. 74, 462–463.

Twentieth Century Children's Writers. 2nd ed. Edited by D. L. Kirkpatrick. New York: St. Martin's Press, 1983, pp. 140–141.

Burnett, Frances (Elizabeth) Hodgson

Baker, Margaret J. "Mrs. Burnett of Maytham Hall." *Junior Bookshelf* 13 (Oct. 1949): 126–136.

Bixler, Phyllis. "The Oral-Formulaic Training of a Popular Fiction Writer: Frances Hodgson Burnett." *Journal of Popular Culture* 15 (Spring 1982): 44–52.

Bixler, Phyllis, and Agosta, Lucien. "Formula Fiction and Children's Literature: Thornton Waldo Burgess and Frances Hodgson Burnett." *Children's Literature in Education* 15 (Summer 1984): 63–72.

Burnett, Constance Buel. "Frances Hodgson Burnett: Episodes in Her Life." *Horn Book* 41 (Feb. 1965): 86–94.

Burnett, Frances Hodgson. *The One I Knew Best of All: A Memory of the Mind of a Child.* New York: Scribner, 1893.

Burnett, Vivian. *The Romantick Lady (Frances Hodgson Burnett): The Life Story of an Imagination.* New York: Scribner, 1927.

Doyle, Brian. *The Who's Who of Children's Literature.* New York: Schocken, 1968, pp. 43–45.

Laski, Marghanita. *Mrs. Ewing, Mrs. Molesworth, and Mrs. Hodgson Burnett.* New York: Oxford Univ. Press, 1951.

Molson, Francis J. "Frances Hodgson Burnett (1848–1924)." *American Literary Realism 1870–1910* 8, no. 1 (Winter 1975): 35–41.

Stott, Jon C. *Children's Literature from A to Z.* New York: McGraw-Hill, 1984, p. 58.

Thwaite, Ann. *Waiting for the Party: The Life of Frances Hodgson Burnett 1849–1924.* New York: Scribner, 1974.

Twentieth Century Children's Writers. 2nd ed. Edited by D. L. Kirkpatrick. New York: St. Martin's Press, 1983, pp. 141–143.

Burnford, Sheila (Philip [née Every] Cochrane)

Fourth Book of Junior Authors and Illustrators. Edited by Doris De Montreville and Elizabeth D. Crawford. New York: Wilson, 1978, pp. 63–65.

Stott, Jon C. *Children's Literature from A to Z.* New York: McGraw-Hill, 1984, p. 60.

Twentieth Century Children's Writers. 2nd ed. Edited by D. L. Kirkpatrick. New York: St. Martin's Press, 1983, pp. 143–144.

Butler, Octavia E(stelle)

Barr, Marleen S., et al. *Reader's Guide to Suzy McKee Charnas, Octavia Butler and Joan Vinge.* Mercer Island, WA: Starmont, 1985.

Elliot, Jeffrey. "Interview with Octavia Butler." *Thrust* 12 (Summer 1979): 19–22.

Foster, Frances Smith. "Octavia Butler's Black Female Future Fiction." *Extrapolation* 23 (1982): 37–49.

Friend, Beverly. "Time Travel as a Feminist Didactic in Works by Phyllis Eisenstein, Marlys Millhiser and Octavia Butler." *Extrapolation* 23 (1982): 50–55.

Govan, Sandra Y. "Connections, Links, and Extended Networks: Patterns in Octavia Butler's Science Fiction." *Black American Literature Forum* 18 (1984): 82–87.

Salvaggio, Ruth. "Octavia Butler and the Black Science Fiction Heroine." *Black American Literature Forum* 18 (1984): 78–81.

Twentieth-Century Science Fiction Writers. 2nd ed. Edited by Curtis C. Smith. Chicago: St. James Press, 1986, pp. 109–110.

Weinkauf, Mary S. "So Much for the Gentle Sex." *Extrapolation* 20 (1985): 231–239.
Weixlmann, Joe. "An Octavia E. Butler Bibliography." *Black American Literature Forum* 18 (1984): 88–89.

Butterworth, Oliver

Fourth Book of Junior Authors and Illustrators. Edited by Doris De Montreville and Elizabeth D. Crawford. New York: Wilson, 1978, pp. 65–66.
Helbig, Alethea K., and Perkins, Agnes Regan. *Dictionary of American Children's Fiction, 1859–1959.* Westport, CT: Greenwood Press, 1985, pp. 75, 149.
———. *Dictionary of American Children's Fiction, 1960–1984.* Westport, CT: Greenwood Press, 1986, pp. 83, 677–678.
Twentieth Century Children's Writers. 2nd ed. Edited by D. L. Kirkpatrick. New York: St. Martin's Press, 1983, pp. 147–148.

Byars, Betsy (Cromer)

Byars, Betsy. "Authoress Betsy Byars Tells It Like It Is." *West Virginia Libraries* (Fall 1971).
———. "Beginnings, 'Human Things' and the Magical Moments." *Proceedings of the Eighth Annual Conference of the Children's Literature Association.* Ypsilanti, MI: Children's Literature Association, 1982, pp. 4–8.
———. "Newbery Award Acceptance." *Horn Book* 47 (Aug. 1971): 354–358.
———. "Spinning Straw into Gold." *School Libraries* 34 (Mar. 1986): 6–13. Shortened transcript of talk given at 1985 SLA Course, Christ Church College.
———. "Writing for Children." *Signal* 37 (Jan. 1982): 3–10.
Byars, Edward F. "Betsy Byars." *Horn Book* 47 (Oct. 1971): 459–462.
Chambers, Aidan. "Letter from England: Arrows—All Pointing Upward." *Horn Book* 54 (Dec. 1978): 680–684.
Hansen, I. V. "A Decade of Betsy Byars' Boys." *Children's Literature in Education* 15 (Spring 1984): 3–11.
Helbig, Alethea K., and Perkins, Agnes Regan. *Dictionary of American Children's Fiction, 1960–1984.* Westport, CT: Greenwood Press, 1986, pp. 83–84.
Hopkins, Lee Bennett. *More Books by More People: Interviews with Sixty–five Authors of Books for Children.* New York: Citation Press, 1974, pp. 68–72.
Kingman, Lee, ed. *Newbery and Caldecott Medal Books: 1966–1975.* Boston: Horn Book, 1975, pp. 66–75.
Kuznets, Lois T. "Betsy Byars' Slice of 'American Pie.' " *Children's Literature Association Quarterly* 5 (1981): 31–33.
The Oxford Companion to Children's Literature. Edited by Humphrey Carpenter and Mari Prichard. New York: Oxford Univ. Press, 1984, p. 91.
Rees, David. "Little Bit of Ivory—Betsy Byars." In *Painted Desert, Green Shade.* Boston: Horn Book, 1984, pp. 33–46.
Robertson, Ina. "Profile: Betsy Byars—Writer for Today's Child." *Language Arts* 57 (Mar. 1980): 328–334.
Roginski, Jim, ed. *Newbery and Caldecott Medalists and Honor Book Winners.* Littleton, CO: Libraries Unlimited, 1982, pp. 59–60.
Segel, Elizabeth. "Betsy Byars." In *American Writers for Children since 1960: Fiction. Dictionary of Literary Biography,* vol. 52. Detroit: Gale, 1986, pp. 52–65.
———. "Betsy Byars: An Interview." *Children's Literature in Education* 13 (Winter 1984): 171–179.
Stott, Jon C. *Children's Literature from A to Z.* New York: McGraw-Hill, 1984, p. 66.

Third Book of Junior Authors. Edited by Doris De Montreville and Donna Hill. New York: Wilson, 1972, p. 55.
Twentieth Century Children's Writers. 2nd ed. Edited by D. L. Kirkpatrick. New York: St. Martin's Press, 1983, pp. 148–149.
Watson, Ken. "The Art of Betsy Byars." *Orana* 16 (Feb. 1980): 3–5.

Caldecott, Moyra

Searles, Baird; Meacham, Beth; and Franklin, Michael. *A Reader's Guide to Fantasy.* New York: Avon, 1982, pp. 40–41.

Calhoun, Mary (pseud. of Mary Huiskamp Wilkins)

Barnett, D. "Mary Calhoun Visits Green River Schools." *Wyoming Library Roundup* 39 (Winter 1984): 66–67.
Batman, G. "Interview with Mary Calhoun." *Colorado Libraries* 9 (Dec. 1983): 36–39.
Calhoun, Mary. "Tracking Down Elves in Folklore." *Horn Book* 45 (June 1969): 278–281.
Third Book of Junior Authors. Edited by Doris De Montreville and Donna Hill. New York: Wilson, 1972, pp. 56–57.

Callen, Larry (Lawrence Willard, Jr.)

Fifth Book of Junior Authors and Illustrators. Edited by Sally Holmes Holtze. New York: Wilson, 1983, pp. 63–64.

Cameron, Eleanor (Frances Butler)

Cameron, Eleanor. "Art and Morality." In *Proceedings of the Seventh Annual Conference of the Children's Literature Association.* Baylor University, March 1980. Ypsilanti, MI: Children's Literature Association, 1982, pp. 30–44. Reprinted in *Festschrift: A Ten Year Retrospective.* Edited by Perry Nodelman and Jill P. May. West Lafayette, IN: Children's Literature Association Publications, 1983, pp. 28–35.
———. "Books Remembered." *CBC (Children's Book Council) Features* 41 (Jan.–Aug. 1987).
———. "The Dearest Freshness Deep Down Things." *Horn Book* 40 (Oct. 1964): 459–472.
———. "The Eternal Moment." *Children's Literature Association Quarterly* 9 (Winter 1984–1985): 157–163.
———. "Fantasy, Science Fiction and the *Mushroom Planet* Books." *Children's Literature Association Quarterly* 5 (Winter 1981): 1, 5–9. Reprinted in *Signposts to Criticism of Children's Literature.* Edited by Robert Bator. Chicago: American Library Association, 1983, pp. 294–300; and in *The First Steps.* Edited by Patricia Dooley. West Lafayette, IN: Children's Literature Association Publications, 1984, pp. 55–57.
———. *The Green and Burning Tree: On the Writing and Enjoyment of Children's Books.* Boston: Little, Brown, 1969. "Fantasy," pp. 3–134.
———. "The Inmost Secret." *Horn Book* 59 (Feb. 1983): 17–23.
———. "Into Something Rich and Strange: Of Dreams, Art and the Unconscious." *Quarterly Journal of the Library of Congress* 35 (Apr. 1978): 92–107. Reprinted in *The Openhearted Audience.* Washington, DC: Library of Congress, 1980, pp. 152–176.
———. "McLuhan, Youth, and Literature." *Horn Book* 48 (Oct. 1972): 433–440,

(Dec. 1972): 572–579, and 49 (Feb. 1973): 79–85. Reprinted in Paul Heins. *Crosscurrents of Criticism*. Boston: Horn Book, 1977, pp. 98–120.

———. "Of Style and the Stylist." *Horn Book* 40 (Feb. 1964): 25–32.

———. "One Woman as Writer and Feminist." *Children's Literature Association Quarterly* 7 (Winter 1982–1983): 3-6ff.

———. "A Question of Taste: A Reply to Anne Merrick." *Children's Literature in Education* 21 (Summer 1976): 59–63.

———. "A Reply to Perry Nodelman's 'Beyond Explanation.' " In *Children's Literature*, vol. 12. New Haven, CT: Yale Univ. Press, 1984, pp. 134–146.

———. "An Unforgettable Glimpse." *Wilson Library Bulletin* 37 (Oct. 1962): 147–153. Revised for *The Green and Burning Tree*. Boston: Little, Brown, 1969, pp. 3–47.

———. "Why *Not* for Children?" *Horn Book* 42 (Feb. 1966): 21–33.

———. "With Wrinkled Brow and Cool Fresh Eye. Part I." *Horn Book* 61 (May–June 1985): 280–288; "Part II." *Horn Book* 61 (July–Aug. 1985): 426–431.

———. "A Writer's Journey." In *Innocence & Experience*. Edited by Barbara Harrison and Gregory Maguire. New York: Lothrop, 1987, pp. 30–44.

Helbig, Alethea K., and Perkins, Agnes Regan. *Dictionary of American Children's Fiction, 1859–1959*. Westport, CT: Greenwood Press, 1985, p. 84.

———. *Dictionary of American Children's Fiction, 1960–1984*. Westport, CT: Greenwood Press, 1986, pp. 90–91, 133, 661–662.

Nodelman, Perry. "Beyond Explanation, and Beyond Inexplicability, in Eleanor Cameron's *Beyond Silence*." Abstract. In *Proceedings of the Ninth Annual Conference of the Children's Literature Association*. University of Florida, March 1982. Ypsilanti, MI: Children's Literature Association, 1983, pp. 128–129. Reprinted in *Children's Literature*, vol. 12. New Haven, CT: Yale Univ. Press, 1984, pp. 122–133.

———. "The Depths of All She Is: Eleanor Cameron." *Children's Literature Association Quarterly* 4 (Winter 1980): 6–8.

Pflieger, Pat, and Hill, Helen M. *A Reference Guide to Modern Fantasy for Children*. Westport, CT: Greenwood Press, 1984, pp. 93–95, 127–129.

Stott, Jon C. *Children's Literature from A to Z*. New York: McGraw-Hill, 1984, p. 71.

Sulerud, Grace, and Garness, Sue. "Eleanor Cameron." In *American Writers for Children since 1960: Fiction. Dictionary of Literary Biography*, vol. 52. Detroit: Gale, 1986, pp. 66–74.

Third Book of Junior Authors. Edited by Doris De Montreville and Donna Hill. New York: Wilson, 1972, pp. 57–58.

Twentieth Century Children's Writers. 2nd ed. Edited by D. L. Kirkpatrick. New York: St. Martin's Press, 1983, pp. 149–150.

Card, Orson Scott

Card, Orson Scott. "On Sycamore Hill: A Personal View." *Science Fiction Review* 55 (1985): 6–11.

———. "The Well-Ground Axe: On Themes." *Bulletin of the Science Fiction Writers of America* 73 (1980): 10–12.

———. "The Well-Ground Axe: Using Criticism." *Bulletin of the Science Fiction Writers of America* 73 (1980): 43–45.

Moser, Cliff. "An Interview with Orson Scott Card." *Science Fiction Review* 8 (Aug. 1979): 32–35.

Carlson, Natalie Savage

Carlson, Julie McAlpine. "Family Unity in Natalie Savage Carlson's Books for Children." *Elementary English* 45 (Feb. 1968): 214–217. Reprinted in Miriam Hoffman and Eva Samuels. *Authors and Illustrators of Children's Books.* New York: Bowker, 1972, pp. 56–61.

Helbig, Alethea K., and Perkins, Agnes Regan. *Dictionary of American Children's Fiction, 1960–1984.* Westport, CT: Greenwood Press, 1986, pp. 94–95.

Hopkins, Lee Bennett. "Natalie Savage Carlson." In *More Books by More People.* New York: Citation Press, 1974, pp. 73–77.

McAlpine, Julie Carlson. "Fact and Fiction in Natalie Savage Carlson's Autobiographical Stories." *Children's Literature,* vol. 5. Philadelphia: Temple University Press, 1976, pp. 157–161.

More Junior Authors. Edited by Muriel Fuller. New York: Wilson, 1963, pp. 34–35.

Roginski, Jim, ed. *Newbery and Caldecott Medalists and Honor Book Winners.* Littleton, CO: Libraries Unlimited, 1982, pp. 60–61.

Twentieth Century Children's Writers. 2nd ed. Edited by D. L. Kirkpatrick. New York: St. Martin's Press, 1983, pp. 150–151.

Carroll, Lewis (pseud. of Charles Lutwidge Dodgson)

Adams, Gillian. "Student Responses to *Alice's Adventures in Wonderland* and *At the Back of the North Wind.*" *Children's Literature Association Quarterly* 10 (Spring 1985): 6–9.

Adelman, Richard Parker. "Comedy in Lewis Carroll's *Alice's Adventures in Wonderland* and *Through the Looking Glass.*" Ph.D. dissertation, Temple University, 1979.

Alderson, Brian, ed. *Children's Books in England.* 3rd ed. New York: Cambridge Univ. Press, 1982, pp. 255–261.

Alexander, Peter. *Logic and the Humor of Lewis Carroll.* London: Chorley and Pickersgill, 1951. Originally published in the *Proceedings of the Leeds Philosophy and Literature Society* 6 (May 1951): 551–566.

Arnoldi, Richard. "Parallels between *Our Mutual Friend* and the *Alice* Books." In *Children's Literature,* vol. 1. Storrs, CT: Journal of the Modern Language Association, 1972, pp. 54–57.

Auden, W. H. "Lewis Carroll." In W. H. Auden. *Forewords and Afterwords.* New York: Random, 1973, pp. 283–293.

Auerbach, Nina. "Alice and Wonderland: A Curious Child." *Victorian Studies* 17 (Sept. 1973): 31–47.

———. "Falling *Alice,* Fallen Women, and Victorian Dream Children." *English Language Notes* 20 (Dec. 1982): 46–64.

Ayres, Harry Morgan. *Carroll's Alice.* New York: Columbia Univ. Press, 1936.

Bacon, Deborah. "The Meaning of Non–Sense: A Psychoanalytic Approach to Lewis Carroll." Ph.D. dissertation, Columbia University, 1950.

Baker, Margaret J. "Jo Meets the Reverend C. L. Dodgson." *Junior Bookshelf* 8 (July 1944): 45–54.

Baldwin, Honor. "*Alice* and Louise Stimson." *Horn Book* 24 (May 1948): 181–188.

Bartley, William Warren, III. "Lewis Carroll's Lost Book on Logic." *Scientific American* 227 (July 1972): 38–46.

———, ed. *Lewis Carroll's Symbolic Logic.* New York: Potter, 1977.

Bassett, Lisa. *Very Truly Yours, Charles L. Dodgson, Alias Lewis Carroll.* New York: Lothrop, 1987.

Baum, Alwin L. "Carroll's *Alice:* The Semiotics of Paradox." *American Imago* 34 (1977): 86–108.

Bedinger, Margery. "Guide Books for *Alice* in the Wonderland of Life." *Horn Book* 8 (Feb. 1932): 33–40.

Berman, Ruth. "White Knight and Leech Gatherer: The Poet as Boor." *Mythlore* 9 (Autumn 1982): 29–31.

Birns, Margaret Boe. "Solving the Mad Hatter's Riddle." *Massachusetts Review* 25 (1984): 457–468.

Blackburn, William. " 'A New Kind of Rule': The Subversive Narrator in *Alice's Adventures in Wonderland* and 'The Pied Piper of Hamelin.' " *Children's Literature in Education* 17 (Fall 1986): 181–190.

Blake, Kathleen. *Play, Games, and Sport: The Literary Works of Lewis Carroll.* Ithaca, NY: Cornell Univ. Press, 1974.

———. "The Play Theme in the Imaginative Writing of Lewis Carroll." Ph.D. dissertation, University of California, San Diego, 1971.

Bohem, Hilda. "Alice's Adventures with Altemus (and Vice Versa)." *Papers of the Bibliographic Society of America* 73 (1979): 423–442.

Bond, W. H. "The Publication of *Alice's Adventures in Wonderland.*" *Harvard Library Bulletin* 10 (Autumn 1956): 306–324.

Bowman, Isa. *Lewis Carroll As I Knew Him.* London: Dent, 1899; Dover, 1972. Originally published as *The Story of Lewis Carroll.*

Briggs, Elizabeth D. "Lewis Carroll, Friend of Children. 1832–1932." *Elementary English Review* 9 (Jan. 1932): 5–7, 11.

Bushnell, John Palmer. "Powerless to Be Born: Victorian Struggles in Romantic Landscapes of Adolescence." Ph.D. dissertation, Rutgers University, 1983.

Carpenter, Humphrey. "*Alice* and the Mockery of God." In *Secret Gardens: A Study of the Golden Age of Children's Literature.* Boston: Houghton Mifflin, 1985, pp. 44–69.

Carroll, Lewis. "Alice on the Stage." In *The Lewis Carroll Picture Book.* Edited by Stuart Dodgson Collingwood. London: Unwin, 1899, pp. 163–170.

Cixous, Helene. "Introduction to Lewis Carroll's *Through the Looking Glass* and *The Hunting of the Snark.*" *New Literary History* 13 (1982): 231–251.

Clark, Anne. *Lewis Carroll: A Biography.* London: Dent, 1979.

———. *The Real Alice: Lewis Carroll's Dream Child.* New York: Stein and Day, 1982.

Clark, Beverly Lyon. "Carroll's Well–Versed Narrative: *Through the Looking Glass.*" *English Language Notes* 20 (Dec. 1982): 65–76.

———. "Lewis Carroll's *Alice* Books: The Wonder of Wonderland." In *Touchstones.* Edited by Perry Nodelman. West Lafayette, IN: Children's Literature Association Publications, 1985, pp. 44–52.

———. "The Mirror Worlds of Carroll, Nabokov, and Pynchon: Fantasy in the 1860's and 1960's." Ph.D. dissertation, Brown University, 1979.

———. *Reflections of Fantasy: The Mirror Worlds of Carroll, Nabokov and Pynchon.* New York: Lang, 1986.

———. "What Went Wrong with Alice?" *Children's Literature Association Quarterly* 11 (Spring 1986): 29–33.

Cohen, Morton N. "Another Wonderland: Lewis Carroll's *The Nursery 'Alice.'* " *The Lion and the Unicorn* 7/8 (1983–1984): 120–126.

———. "Lewis Carroll and the House of Macmillan." *Browning Institute for Studies in Victorian Literature and Cultural History* 7 (1979): 31–70.

———. "Lewis Carroll's *Memoria Technica.*" *Library Chronicle of the University of Texas* 11 (1979): 77–88.

———, ed. *The Selected Letters of Lewis Carroll.* New York: Pantheon, 1982.

Collingwood, Stuart Dodgson. *The Life and Letters of Lewis Carroll.* New York: Century, 1898; reprinted Detroit: Gale, 1967.

———, ed. *The Lewis Carroll Picture Book.* London: Unwin, 1899.

Cornwell, Charles Landrum. "From Self to the Shire: Studies in Victorian Fantasy." Ph.D. dissertation, University of Virginia, 1972.

Cripps, Elizabeth A. "*Alice* and the Reviewers." In *Children's Literature,* vol. 11. New Haven, CT: Yale Univ. Press, pp. 32–48.

Cunningham, Michael Henry. "The Triumph of Fantasy: Childhood and Children's Literature in Victorian England." Ph.D. dissertation, New School for Social Research, 1978.

D'Ambrosio, Michael A. *"Alice* for Adolescents." *English Journal* 59 (Nov. 1970): 1074–1075, 1085.

Davies, Ivor. "Looking–Glass Chess." *Anglo–Welsh Review* 19 (Autumn 1970): 189–191.

De la Mare, Walter. *Lewis Carroll.* London: Faber, 1932.

———. "Lewis Carroll—A Biography." *Fortnightly Review,* Sept. 1, 1930, pp. 319–331. Reprinted in Virginia Haviland. *Children and Literature.* Glenview, IL: Scott, Foresman, 1973, pp. 57–63.

De la Roche, Wayne William. "Privacy and Community in the Writings of Lewis Carroll." Ph.D. dissertation, Columbia University, 1975.

Dohm, J. H. *"Alice* in America." *Junior Bookshelf* 29 (Oct. 1965): 261–267.

Doyle, Brian. *The Who's Who of Children's Literature.* New York: Schocken, 1968, pp. 46–50.

Dreyer, Lawrence M. "The Mathematic References to the Adoption of the Gregorian Calendar in Lewis Carroll's *Alice's Adventures in Wonderland." American Notes and Queries* 19 (1980): 41–44.

Ede, L. "The Nonsense Literature of Edward Lear and Lewis Carroll." Ph.D. dissertation, Ohio State University, 1975.

Edes, Mary Elizabeth. "Alice Liddell of Wonderland." *Publishers Weekly,* July 2, 1962, pp. 112–115. Reprinted in *Readings about Children's Literature.* Edited by Evelyn R. Robinson. New York: McKay, 1966, pp. 304–312.

Empson, William. *"Alice in Wonderland:* The Child as Swain." In *Some Versions of Pastoral.* London: Chatto, 1935, pp. 251–294.

Evans, Luther H. "The Return of *Alice's Adventures under Ground." Columbia Library Columns* 15 (Nov. 1965): 29–35.

Fisher, John, ed. *The Magic of Lewis Carroll.* New York: Simon & Schuster, 1973.

Flesher, Jacqueline. "The Language of Nonsense in *Alice." Yale French Studies* 43 (1969): 128–144.

Furniss, Harry. "Recollections of Lewis Carroll." Edited by Lance Salway. *Signal* 19 (Jan. 1976): 45–50. Originally published in *Strand Magazine* 35 (Jan. 1908): 48–52.

Gabriele, Mark. *"Alice in Wonderland:* Problems of Identity—Aggressive Content and Form Control." *American Imago* 39 (Winter 1982): 369–389.

Gardner, Martin. "An Anniversary for *Alice.* A Child's Garden of Bewilderment [*Alice's Adventures in Wonderland* and *The Wonderful Wizard of Oz* Compared]." *Saturday Review,* July 17, 1965, pp. 18–19, and Aug. 14, 1965, p. 26. Reprinted in Sheila A. Egoff. *Only Connect.* New York: Oxford Univ. Press, 1980, pp. 150–155.

———. "The Games and Puzzles of Lewis Carroll." *Scientific American* 202 (Mar. 1960): 172–174ff.

———, ed. *The Annotated Alice.* New York: Potter, 1960.

Gattegno, Jean. *Lewis Carroll: Fragments of a Looking–Glass.* New York: Crowell, 1976.

Glastonbury, M. "In and Out of Wonderland." *Times Educational Supplement* 3192 (Aug. 6, 1976): 16.

Goodacre, Selwyn H. "1865 *Alice:* A New Appraisal and a Revised Census." *English Language Notes* 20 (Dec. 1982): 77–96.

Gordon, Jan B., and Guiliano, Edward. "From Victorian Textbook to Ready–Made: Lewis Carroll and the Black Art." *English Language Notes* 20 (Dec. 1982): 1–25.

Graham, Eleanor. "Nonsense in Children's Literature." *Junior Bookshelf* 9 (July 1945): 61–68.

Gray, Donald J., ed. *Lewis Carroll's "Alice in Wonderland."* New York: Norton, 1971.

Green, David L. "Children's Literature Periodicals on Individual Authors, Dime Novels, Fantasy." *Phaedrus* 3 (1976): 22–24.

Green, Roger Lancelyn. "Bibliographer in Wonderland." *Private Libraries* 4 (Oct. 1962): 62–65.

———. *Lewis Carroll*. London: Bodley Head, 1960; New York: Walck, 1962. Reprinted in Green, Bell, and Nesbitt. *Lewis Carroll, E. Nesbit and Howard Pyle*. London: Bodley Head, 1968.

———. "The Lewis Carroll Handbook." New York: Oxford Univ. Press, 1962. Revision of original edition by Sidney Herbert Williams and Falconer Madan.

———. "More Aspects of *Alice*." *Jabberwocky* 13 (Winter 1972): 9–14.

———. "Picnic in Wonderland." *Junior Books* 26 (July 1962): 110–114.

———, ed. *The Diaries of Lewis Carroll*. 2 vols. New York: Oxford Univ. Press, 1954.

Greenacre, Phyllis. *Swift and Carroll: A Psychoanalytic Study of Two Lives*. New York: International Universities Press, 1955.

Grotjahn, Martin. "About the Symbolization of *Alice's Adventures in Wonderland*." *American Imago* 4 (Dec. 1947): 32–41.

Guiliano, Edward. "Lewis Carroll: A Sesquicentennial Guide to Research." *Dickens Studies Annual* 10 (1982): 263–310.

———. *"Lewis Carroll: An Annotated International Bibliography, 1960–1977*. Charlottesville: Univ. Press of Virginia, 1981.

———. "Lewis Carroll in a Changing World: An Interview with Morton N. Cohen." *English Language Notes* 20 (Dec. 1982): 97–108.

———. "150th Anniversary: Lewis Carroll: His Genius Was 'Frabjous.' " *A.B. Bookman's Weekly*, Jan. 18, 1982, pp. 355–356ff.

———. "Popular and Critical Responses to Lewis Carroll: A Comparative Survey of Publishers since 1960." Ph.D. dissertation, State University of New York at Stony Brook, 1978.

———, ed. *Lewis Carroll, a Celebration*. New York: Potter; dist. by Crown, 1981.

———, ed. *Lewis Carroll Observed: A Collection of Unpublished Photographs, Drawings, Poetry, and New Essays*. New York: Potter, 1976.

Hancher, Michael. "The Placement of Tenniel's *Alice* Illustrations." *Harvard Library Bulletin* 30 (July 1982): 237–252.

———. *The Tenniel Illustrations to the 'Alice' Books*. Columbus: Ohio State Univ. Press, 1985.

Hazard, Paul. *Books, Children and Men*, 4th ed. Boston: Horn Book, 1960, pp. 135–140.

Hearn, Michael Patrick. "*Alice*'s Other Parent: John Tenniel as Lewis Carroll's Illustrator." *American Book Collector* 3 (May–June 1984): 11–20.

Heath, Peter. "Carroll through the Pillar–Box." *Virginia Quarterly Review* 56 (1980): 552–558.

Hedberg, Johannes. "Dodgson, Charles Lutwidge = Lewis Carroll." *Artes* 6 (1983): 98–108.

Helson, Ravenna, and Proysen, Alf. "The Psychological Origins of Fantasy for Children in Mid-Victorian England." *Children's Literature,* vol. 3. Storrs, CT: Journal of the Modern Language Association, 1974, pp. 66–75.

Hentoff, N. "Looking Backward and Ahead with *Alice*." *Wilson Library Journal* 45 (Oct. 1970): 169–171.

Herson, Flodden W. "The 1866 Appleton *Alice*." *The Colophon* 1 (Winter 1936): 422–427.

Holešovsky, František. "Contribution to the Lewis Carroll Jubilee by Illustrators of the BIB." *Bookbird* 1 (1984): 52–55.

Holmes, Roger W. "The Philosopher's *Alice in Wonderland*." *Antioch Review* 19 (Summer 1959): 133–149.

Hubbell, George Shelton. "Triple *Alice.*" *Sewanee Review* 48, no. 2 (Apr.–June 1940): 174–196.

Hudson, Derek. *Lewis Carroll: An Illustrated Biography.* London: Constable, 1954; New York: Potter, 1977.

"In Honor of the Lewis Carroll Centenary." *Horn Book* 8 (Feb. 1932): 41–43.

Inglis, Fred. *The Promise of Happiness.* New York: Cambridge Univ. Press, 1981, pp. 103–109.

Jabberwocky: The Journal of the Lewis Carroll Society. Lewis Carroll Society (British), 1969– .

Jackson, Rosemary. *Fantasy: The Literature of Subversion.* New York: Methuen, 1980.

Johnson, Paula. "*Alice* among the Analysts." *Hartford Studies in Literature* 4 (1972): 114–122.

Jorgens, Jack. "*Alice,* Our Contemporary." In *Children's Literature,* vol. 1. Storrs, CT: Journal of the Modern Language Association, 1972, pp. 152–161.

Kelly, Richard. *Lewis Carroll.* Boston: G. K. Hall, 1977.

Kibel, Alvin C. "Logic and Satire in *Alice in Wonderland.*" *American Scholar* 43, no. 4 (Autumn 1974): 605–629.

Kincaid, James R. "*Alice's* Invasion of Wonderland." *Publications of the Modern Language Association* 33 (Jan. 1973): 92–99.

The Knight Letter. Lewis Carroll Society of North America, 1974– .

Knoepflmacher, U. C. "Avenging Alice: Christina Rossetti and Lewis Carroll." *Nineteenth–Century Literature* 41 (Dec. 1986): 299–328.

Kolbe, Martha Emily. "Three Oxford Dons as Creators of Other Worlds for Children: Lewis Carroll, C. S. Lewis, and J. R. R. Tolkien." Ph.D. dissertation, University of Virginia, 1981.

Leach, Elsie. "*Alice in Wonderland* in Perspective." *Victorian Newsletter* 25 (Spring 1964): 9–11.

Lebovitz, Richard. "Alice as Eros." *Jabberwocky* 10 (Winter 1981): 72–87.

Lee, Hermione. "Mr. Dodgson and the Little Girls." *New Statesman* (Nov. 2, 1979): 684–685.

Lennon, Florence Becker. *The Life of Lewis Carroll.* rev. ed. New York: Collier, 1962. Original title: *Victoria through the Looking-Glass: The Life of Lewis Carroll.* New York: Simon & Schuster, 1945.

Levin, Harry. "Wonderland Revisited." *Kenyon Review* 27 (Autumn 1965): 591–616.

Little, Edmund. *The Fantasists: Studies in J. R. R. Tolkien, Lewis Carroll, Mervyn Peake, Nikolay Gogol and Kenneth Grahame.* Amersham, England: Avebury, 1984.

Little, Judith. "Liberated *Alice:* Dodgson's Female Hero as Domestic Rebel." *Women's Studies* 3 (1976): 195–205.

McGillis, Roderick F. "Fantasy as Adventure: Nineteenth Century Children's Fiction." *Children's Literature Association Quarterly* 8 (Fall 1983): 18–22.

———. "Novelty and Roman Cement: Two Versions of *Alice.*" In Douglas Street. *Children's Novels and the Movies.* New York: Ungar, 1983, pp. 15–27.

———. " 'What *Is* the Fun?' Said Alice." *Children's Literature in Education* 17 (Spring 1986): 25–36.

Matthews, Charles. "Satire in the *Alice* Books." *Criticism* 12 (Spring 1970): 105–119.

Meacham, Margaret McKeen Ramsey. "*Alice in Wonderland,* a Chamber Opera in One Act." Original composition. D.M.A. dissertation, University of Maryland, 1982.

Molson, Francis J. "*Alice's Adventures in Wonderland* and *Through the Looking Glass.*" In *Survey of Modern Fantasy Literature,* vol. 1. Edited by Frank N. Magill. Englewood Cliffs, NJ: Salem Press, 1983, pp. 7–16.

Morton, Lionel. "Memory in the *Alice* Books." *Nineteenth–Century Fiction* 33 (Dec. 1978): 285–308.

Morton, Richard. "*Alice's Adventures in Wonderland* and *Through the Looking–Glass.*" *Elementary English* 37 (Dec. 1960): 509–513.

Moss, Anita. "Lewis Carroll." In *Writers for Children: Critical Studies of Major Authors since the Seventeenth Century.* Edited by Jane M. Bingham. New York: Scribner, 1988, pp. 117–128.

Mulderig, G. "*Alice* and *Wonderland:* Subversive Elements in the World of Victorian Children's Fiction." *Journal of Popular Culture* 11 (Fall 1977): 320–329.

Myer, Michael Grosvenor. "Some Omissions from Martin Gardner's *The Annotated Alice.*" *Notes and Queries* 30 (Aug. 1983): 302–303.

Natov, Roni. "The Persistence of *Alice.*" *The Lion and the Unicorn* 3, no. 1 (Spring 1979): 38–61.

O'Brien, Hugh B. "Alice's Journey in *Through the Looking–Glass.*" *Notes and Queries* 14 (Oct. 1967): 380–382.

Ovenden, Graham. *The Illustrators of "Alice in Wonderland" and "Through the Looking Glass."* New York: St. Martin's Press, 1972; rev. ed. 1980.

———. *Lewis Carroll.* London: Macdonald, 1984.

The Oxford Companion to Children's Literature. Edited by Humphrey Carpenter and Mari Prichard. New York: Oxford Univ. Press, 1984, pp. 15–19, 97–102, 382, 512, 527.

Page, Jane Izzard. "Enduring *Alice.*" Ph.D. dissertation, University of Washington, 1970.

Peterson, Calvin R. "Time and Stress: *Alice in Wonderland.*" *Journal of the History of Ideas* 46 (1985): 427–433.

Pfeiffer, John R. "Lewis Carroll." In *Supernatural Fiction Writers: Fantasy and Horror,* vol. 1. Edited by E. F. Bleiler. New York: Scribner, 1985, pp. 247–254.

Phillips, Robert, ed. *Aspects of "Alice": Lewis Carroll's Dreamchild as Seen through the Critics' Looking-Glasses, 1865–1971.* New York: Vanguard, 1970.

Platzner, R. L. "Child's Play: Games and Fantasy in Carroll, Stevensen, and Grahame." In *Proceedings of the Fifth Annual Conference of the Children's Literature Association.* Harvard University, March 1978. Ypsilanti, MI: Children's Literature Association, 1979, pp. 78–86.

Potter, Greta Lagro. "Millions in Wonderland." *Horn Book* 41 (Dec. 1965): 593–597.

Preston, Michael J. *Concordance to Lewis Carroll's "Alice's Adventures in Wonderland" and "Through the Looking Glass."* New York: Garland, 1986.

———. *A Concordance to the Verse of Lewis Carroll.* New York: Garland, 1985.

Prickett, Stephen. "Religious Fantasy in the Nineteenth Century." In Frank N. Magill. *Survey of Modern Fantasy Literature,* vol. 5. Englewood Cliffs, NJ: Salem Press, 1983, pp. 2369–2382.

———. *Victorian Fantasy.* Bloomington: Indiana Univ. Press, 1979.

Pritchett, V. S. "Lewis Carroll." *The New Yorker* 56 (Mar. 3, 1980): 123–128.

Pudney, John. *Lewis Carroll and His World.* New York: Scribner, 1976.

Pycior, Helena M. "At the Intersection of Mathematics and Humor: Lewis Carroll's *Alice* and Symbolical Algebra." *Victorian Studies* 28 (1984): 149–170.

Rackin, Donald. "Alice's Journey to the End of Night." *PMLA* 81 (1966): 313–326. Reprinted in Robert Phillips, ed. *Aspects of Alice.* New York: Vanguard, 1970.

———. "Corrective Laughter: Carroll's Alice and Popular Children's Literature of the 19th Century." *Journal of Popular Culture* 1 (1967): 343–355.

———. "The Critical Interpretation of *Alice in Wonderland:* A Survey and Suggested Reading." Ph.D. dissertation, University of Illinois, 1964.

452 *Author Studies*

————. "Love and Death in Carroll's *Alices*." *English Language Notes* 20 (Dec. 1982): 26–45.

————. "What You Always Wanted to Know about Alice but Were Afraid to Ask." *Victorian Newsletter* 44 (Feb. 1973): 1–5.

Rapaport, Herman. "The Disarticulated Image: Gazing in Wonderland." *Encomia* 6 (Fall 1982): 57–77.

Reardon, Margaret. "A Present for Alice." *Horn Book* 38 (June 1962): 243–247. Reprinted in Elinor Field. *Horn Book Reflections*. Boston: Horn Book, 1969, pp. 286–290.

Reed, Langford. "The Life of Lewis Carroll." London: Foyle, 1932.

Reichertz, Ronald. "Carroll's *Alice in Wonderland*." *Explicator* 43 (Winter 1985): 21–22.

Richardson, J. "Dodgson in Wonderland." *History Today* 25 (Feb. 1975): 110–117.

Rottensteiner, Franz. *The Fantasy Book: An Illustrated History from Dracula to Tolkien*. New York: Macmillan, 1978, pp. 108–111.

Sale, Roger. *Fairy Tales and After: From Snow White to E. B. White*. Cambridge, MA: Harvard Univ. Press, 1978, pp. 101–126.

Sams, Edwin Boyer. "Studies in Experiencing Fantasy." *Teaching English in a Two-Year College* 5 (1979): 235–237.

Sapire, D. "*Alice in Wonderland:* A Work of Intellect." *English Studies in Africa* 15 (Mar. 1972): 53–62.

Schaefer, David, and Schaefer, Maxine. "The Movie Adventures of Lewis Carroll's *Alice*." *American Classic Screen* 5 (Sept.–Oct. 1981): 9–12.

Searles, Baird; Meacham, Beth; and Franklin, Michael. *A Reader's Guide to Fantasy*. New York: Avon, 1982, p. 42.

Sewell, Elizabeth. *The Field of Nonsense*. London: Chatto, 1952.

Sibley, Brian. "Through a Darkling Glass: An Appreciation of Mervyn Peake's Illustrations to *Alice*." *The Mervyn Peake Review* 6 (1978): 25–29 and 7 (1978): 26–29.

Skinner, John. "Lewis Carroll's *Adventures in Wonderland*." *American Imago* 4 (Dec. 1947): 3–31.

Spacks, Patricia Meyer. "Logic and Language in *Through the Looking-Glass*." *ETC* 18, no. 1 (Apr. 1961): 91–100.

Steveson, Lynn Bradley. "Lewis Carroll's *Through the Looking Glass* as a Kaleidoscope of English History: A Critical Approach to Scripting Interpreters Theatre." Ph.D. dissertation, Southern Illinois University at Carbondale, 1983.

Stott, Jon C. *Children's Literature from A to Z*. New York: McGraw-Hill, 1984, p. 73.

Stowell, Phyllis. "We're All Mad Here." *Children's Literature Association Quarterly* 8 (Summer 1983): 5–8.

Suchan, James. "Alice's Journey from Alien to Artist." In *Children's Literature*, vol. 7. Storrs, CT: Parousia Press, 1978, pp. 78–92.

Sutherland, Robert D. "Language and Lewis Carroll." Ph.D. dissertation, University of Iowa, 1964.

————. *Language and Lewis Carroll*. The Hague and Paris: Mouton, 1970.

Taylor, Alexander L. *The White Knight: A Study of C. L. Dodgson*. London: Oliver, 1952.

Thurber, James. "Tempest in a Looking Glass." *Forum* (Apr. 1937): 236–238. Reprinted in Boyer and Zahorski. *Fantasists on Fantasy*. New York: Avon, 1985, pp. 67–74.

Twentieth Century Children's Writers. 2nd ed. Edited by D. L. Kirkpatrick. New York: St. Martin's Press, 1983, p. 863.

Warren, A. "Carroll and His *Alice* Books." *Sewanee Review* 88 (Summer 1980): 331–353.

Weaver, Warren. "*Alice's Adventures in Wonderland:* Its Origin and Its Author." *Princeton University Library Chronicle* 13 (Autumn 1951): 1–17.
———. "In Pursuit of Lewis Carroll." *Library Chronicle of the University of Texas* 2 (Nov. 1970): 38–45.
White, Alison. "*Alice* after a Hundred Years." *Michigan Quarterly Review* 4 (Fall 1965): 261–264.
Williams, Sidney Herbert. *A Bibliography of the Writings of Lewis Carroll.* London: Bookman's Journal, 1924.

Carryl, Charles E(dward)

Sargent, Constance Carryl. "The Carryls—Father and Son." *Horn Book* 8 (May 1932): 105–113.
Street, Douglas. "Charles E. Carryl." In *American Writers for Children before 1900. Dictionary of Literary Biography,* vol. 42. Detroit: Gale, 1985, pp. 122–126.

Carter, Angela

Twentieth–Century Science Fiction Writers. 2nd ed. Edited by Curtis C. Smith. Chicago: St. James Press, 1986, pp. 122–123.

Carter, Lin

Twentieth–Century Science Fiction Writers. 2nd ed. Edited by Curtis C. Smith. Chicago: St. James Press, 1986, pp. 124–125.

Cassedy, Sylvia

Cassedy, Sylvia. *In Your Own Words: A Beginner's Guide to Writing.* Garden City, NY: Doubleday, 1979.

Casserley, Anne Thomasine

Casserley, Anne. "The Home of *Michael of Ireland.*" *Horn Book* 3 (Nov. 1927): 28–29.
The Junior Book of Authors. 2nd rev. ed. Edited by Stanley J. Kunitz and Howard Haycraft. New York: Wilson, 1951, pp. 67–68.

Chant, Joy (pseud. of Eileen Joyce Rutter)

"Attracting the Reader." *Times Literary Supplement* 42 (Sept. 19, 1980): 1028.
Berman, Ruth. "Discussion Reports." *Mythlore* 7, 24 (1980).
Chant, Joy. *Fantasy and Allegory in Literature for Young Readers.* Student Project no. 2. Aberystwyth, Wales: University College of Wales, 1971.
———. "A Letter from Joy Chant." *Mythlore* 3, 9 (1976).
———. "Niggle and Numenor." *Children's Literature in Education* 19 (Winter 1975): 161–171.
Elgin, Don D. *The Comedy of the Fantastic: Ecological Perspectives on the Fantasy Novel.* Westport, CT: Greenwood Press, 1985.
Hanna, Judith. "Though He Was No Arthur." *Vector* 123 (1984): 20–21.
Searles, Baird; Meacham, Beth; and Franklin, Michael. *A Reader's Guide to Fantasy.* New York: Avon, 1982, pp. 44–45.

Sullivan, C. W., III. "The Khendiol Novels." In *Survey of Modern Fantasy Literature,* vol. 2. Edited by Frank N. Magill. Englewood Cliffs, NJ: Salem Press, 1983, pp. 839–843.

Swinfen, Ann. *In Defense of Fantasy.* London: Routledge, 1984, pp. 97–98, 106–107.

Chapman, Vera

Miller, M. Y. "The Three Damosels Trilogy." In *Survey of Modern Fantasy Literature,* vol. 4. Edited by Frank N. Magill. Englewood Cliffs, NJ: Salem Press, 1983, pp. 1908–1912.

Charnas, Suzy McKee

Barr, Marleen S., et al. *Reader's Guide to Suzy McKee Charnas, Octavia Butler, and Joan Vinge.* Mercer Island, WA: Starmont, 1985.

Bartokowski, Frances. "Toward a Feminist Eros: Readings in Feminist Utopian Fiction." Ph.D. dissertation, University of Iowa, 1982.

Bogstad, Janice. "Interview: Suzy McKee Charnas." *Janus* 5 (Spring 1979): 20–23.

Charnas, Suzy McKee. "A Woman Appeared." In *Future Females.* Edited by Marleen S. Barr. Bowling Green, OH: Bowling Green Univ. Press, 1981, pp. 103–108.

Charnas, Suzy McKee, and Winter, Douglas. "Mostly I Want to Break Your Heart." *Fantasy Review* 7 (Sept. 1984): 5–6, 41.

Day, Phyllis J. "Earthmother/Witchmother: Feminism and Ecology Renewed." *Extrapolation* 23 (1982): 12–21.

Howard, Susan E. "*Unicorn Tapestry:* A Modern Romance." *Extrapolation* 27 (1986): 39–48.

Miller, Margaret. "The Ideal Woman in Two Feminist Science Fiction Utopias." *Science Fiction Studies* 10 (July 1983): 191–198.

Russ, Joanna. "Recent Female Utopias." In *Future Females.* Edited by Marleen S. Barr. Bowling Green, OH: Bowling Green Univ. Press, 1981, pp. 71–87.

Twentieth–Century Science Fiction Writers. 2nd ed. Edited by Curtis C. Smith. Chicago: St. James Press, 1986, pp. 132–133.

Wilgus, Neal. "*Algol* Interview: Suzy McKee Charnas." *Algol* 16 (Winter 1979): 21–25.

Cherryh, C. J. (pseud. of Carolyn Janice Cherry)

Brizzi, Mary T. "C. J. Cherryh and Tomorrow's New Sex Roles." In *The Feminine Eye.* Edited by Tom Staicar. New York: Ungar, 1982, pp. 32–47.

Burnick, Gale. "An Interview with C. J. Cherryh." *Science Fiction Review* 7 (Nov.–Dec. 1978): 14–18.

Cherryh, C. J. "Female Characters in Science Fiction and Fantasy." *Bulletin of the Science Fiction Writers of America* 77 (1982): 22–29.

―――. "Goodbye Star Wars. Hello Alley-Oop." In *Inside Outer Space.* Edited by Sharon Jarvis. New York: Ungar, 1985.

―――. "Linguistic Sexism in Science Fiction and Fantasy: A Modest Proposal." *Bulletin of the Science Fiction Writers of America* 73 (1980): 7–9, 26.

―――. "The Use of Archaeology in Worldbuilding." *Bulletin of the Science Fiction Writers of America* 13 (1978): 5–10.

Lane, Daryl; Vernon, William; and Carlson, David. "C. J. Cherryh." In *The Sound of Wonder: Interviews from "The Science Fiction Radio Show,"* vol. 1. Phoenix, AZ: Oryx Press, 1985, pp. 22–51.

McGuire, Patrick. "Water into Wine: The Novels of C. J. Cherryh." *Starship* 16 (Spring 1979): 47–49.
Twentieth-Century Science Fiction Writers. 2nd ed. Edited by Curtis C. Smith. Chicago: St. James Press, 1986, pp. 133–135.
Vance, Michael. "C. J. Cherryh: The Quiet Berserker." *Science Fiction and Fantasy Review* 65 (1984): 9–10, 22.
Williams, Lynn F. "Women and Power in C. J. Cherryh's Novels." *Extrapolation* 27 (1986): 85–92.

Chrisman, Arthur Bowie

Chrisman, Arthur Bowie. "The Father of Children's Books." *Horn Book* 3 (Aug. 1927): 14–17. (John Newbery)
Jordan, Mrs. Arthur M. "Arthur Chrisman—Newbery Medalist." *Elementary English Review* 3 (Oct. 1926): 251, 267.
The Junior Book of Authors. 2nd rev. ed. Edited by Stanley J. Kunitz and Howard Haycraft. New York: Wilson, 1951, pp. 69–70.
Roginski, Jim, ed. *Newbery and Caldecott Medalists and Honor Book Winners.* Littleton, CO: Libraries Unlimited, 1982, p. 65.
"Shen of the Sea." In Bertha Mahony Miller and Elinor Field. *Newbery Medal Books: 1922–1955.* Boston: Horn Book, 1957, pp. 39–43.
Twentieth Century Children's Writers. 2nd ed. Edited by D. L. Kirkpatrick. New York: St. Martin's Press, 1983, pp. 169–170.

Christopher, John (pseud. of Christopher Samuel Youd)

Antczak, Janice. *Science Fiction: The Mythos of a New Romance.* New York: Neal–Schuman, 1985, pp. 46–48, 144.
Crago, Hugh, and Crago, Maureen. "John Christopher: An Assessment with Reservations." *Children's Book Review* 1 (June 1971): 77–79.
Crouch, Marcus. *The Nesbit Tradition.* Totowa, NJ: Rowman and Littlefield, 1972, pp. 50–52.
Fourth Book of Junior Authors and Illustrators. Edited by Doris De Montreville and Elizabeth D. Crawford. New York: Wilson, 1978, pp. 78–79.
Fraser, John. "The Worlds of John Christopher." *Space Voyager* 9 (1984): 52–54.
Gough, John. "An Interview with John Christopher." *Children's Literature in Education* 15 (Summer 1984): 93–102.
The Oxford Companion to Children's Literature. Edited by Humphrey Carpenter and Mari Prichard. New York: Oxford Univ. Press, 1984, p. 117.
Ragsdale, W. "Presentation of the Recognition of Merit to John Christopher for the *White Mountains Trilogy.*" *Claremont Reading Conference Yearbook* 41 (1977): 76–79.
Swinfen, Ann. *In Defense of Fantasy.* London: Routledge, 1984, pp. 202–218, 227–229.
Townsend, John Rowe. "John Christopher." In *A Sense of Story.* Philadelphia: Lippincott, 1971, pp. 39–47.
Twentieth Century Children's Writers. 2nd ed. Edited by D. L. Kirkpatrick. New York: St. Martin's Press, 1983, pp. 170–171.
Twentieth-Century Science Fiction Writers. 2nd ed. Edited by Curtis C. Smith. Chicago: St. James Press, 1986, pp. 137–139.
Wehmeyer, Lillian B. "The Future of Religion in Junior Novels." *Catholic Library World* 54 (Apr. 1983): 366–369.
Williams, Jay. "John Christopher: Allegorical Historian." *Signal* 4 (Jan. 1971): 18–23.

Christopher, Matt(hew F.)

Fifth Book of Junior Authors and Illustrators. Edited by Sally Holmes Holtze. New York: Wilson, 1983, pp. 68–69.

Church, Richard (Thomas)

Church, Richard. *The Golden Sovereign.* London: Heinemann, 1957.
———. *Over the Bridge.* London: Heinemann, 1955.
———. *The Voyage Home.* London: Heinemann, 1964.
Doyle, Brian. *The Who's Who of Children's Literature.* New York: Shocken, 1968, p. 51.
Hannabuss, Stuart. "The Motive in the Actuality: Richard Church as Writer for Children." *Children's Literature Review* 2 (June 1972): 69–70.
More Junior Authors. Edited by Muriel Fuller. New York: Wilson, 1963, p. 47.
Twentieth Century Children's Writers. 2nd ed. Edited by D. L. Kirkpatrick. New York: St. Martin's Press, 1983, pp. 171–172.

Churne of Staffordshire, William *see* Paget, F. E.

Clapp, Patricia

Fifth Book of Junior Authors and Illustrators. Edited by Sally Holmes Holtze. New York: Wilson, 1983, pp. 69–71.
Twentieth Century Children's Writers. 2nd ed. Edited by D. L. Kirkpatrick. New York: St. Martin's Press, 1983, pp. 175–176.

Clare, Helen *see* Clarke, Pauline

Clark, Ann Nolan

Bishop, Claire Huchet. "Ann Nolan Clark." *Catholic Library World* 34 (Feb. 1963): 280–286, 333.
Clark, Ann Nolan. *Journey to the People.* New York: Viking Press, 1969.
———. "Newbery Award Acceptance." *Horn Book* 29 (Aug. 1953): 249–257.
Gilbert, Ophelia. "Ann Nolan Clark." In *American Writers for Children since 1960: Fiction. Dictionary of Literary Biography,* vol. 52. Detroit: Gale, 1986, pp. 75–83.
Griese, Arnold A. "Ann Nolan Clark—Building Bridges of Cultural Understanding." *Elementary English* 49 (May 1972): 648–658.
The Junior Book of Authors. 2nd rev. ed. Edited by Stanley J. Kunitz and Howard Haycraft. New York: Wilson, 1951, p. 71.
Massee, May. "Ann Nolan Clark." *Horn Book* 29 (Aug. 1953): 258–262.
Miller, Bertha Mahony, and Field, Elinor Whitney. *Newbery Medal Books: 1922–1955.* Boston: Horn Book, 1957, pp. 388–404.
Twentieth Century Children's Writers. 2nd ed. Edited by D. L. Kirkpatrick. New York: St. Martin's Press, 1983, pp. 176–178.
Wenzel, Evelyn. "Ann Nolan Clark: 1953 Newbery Award Winner." *Elementary English* 30 (Oct. 1953): 327–332. Reprinted in *Authors and Illustrators of Children's Books.* Edited by Miriam Hoffman and Eva Samuels. New York: Bowker, 1972, pp. 62–69.

Clarke, Pauline (pseud. of Pauline [Clarke] Hunter Blair) (a.k.a. Helen Clare)

Clarke, Pauline. "Chief Genii Branwell, the Inspiration behind *The Twelve and the Genii.*" *Junior Bookshelf* 27 (July 1963): 119–123.

Doyle, Brian. *The Who's Who of Children's Literature.* New York: Schocken, 1968, pp. 51–52.

Jones, Cornelia, and Way, Olivia R. "Pauline Clarke." In *British Children's Authors.* Chicago: American Library Association, 1976, pp. 65–76.

Pflieger, Pat, and Hill, Helen M. *A Reference Guide to Modern Fantasy for Children.* Westport, CT: Greenwood Press, 1984, pp. xiv, 115–116, 558–559.

Swinfen, Ann. *In Defense of Fantasy.* London: Routledge, 1984, pp. 127–128.

Third Book of Junior Authors. Edited by Doris De Montreville and Donna Hill. New York: Wilson, 1972, p. 67.

"*The Twelve and the Genii.*" In M. Crouch and A. Ellis. *Chosen for Children.* 3rd ed. London: The Library Association, 1977, pp. 117–123.

Twentieth Century Children's Writers. 2nd ed. Edited by D. L. Kirkpatrick. New York: St. Martin's Press, 1983, pp. 181–182.

Cleary, Beverly (Atlee Bunn)

Bauer, Caroline Feller. "Laura Ingalls Wilder Award Presentation." *Horn Book* 51 (Aug. 1975): 359–360.

Burns, Paul C., and Hines, Ruth. "Beverly Cleary: Wonderful World of Humor." *Elementary English* 44 (Nov. 1967): 743–747, 752.

Cleary, Beverly. "Books Remembered." *The Calendar* (now *CBC Features*) 38 (July 1982–Feb. 1983).

———. *A Girl from Yamhill: A Memoir.* New York: Morrow, 1988.

———. "The Laughter of Children." *Horn Book* 58 (Oct. 1981): 555–564.

———. "Laura Ingalls Wilder Award Acceptance." *Horn Book* 51 (Aug. 1975): 361–364.

———. "Low Man in the Reading Circle: Or, A Blackbird Takes Wing." *Horn Book* 45 (June 1969): 287–293.

———. "Newbery Medal Acceptance." *Horn Book* 60 (Aug. 1984): 429–438.

Helbig, Alethea K., and Perkins, Agnes Regan. *Dictionary of American Children's Fiction, 1859–1959.* Westport, CT: Greenwood Press, 1985, pp. 105–106.

———. *Dictionary of American Children's Fiction, 1960–1984.* Westport, CT: Greenwood Press, 1986, pp. 117, 435–436, 564–565.

Hopkins, Lee Bennett. "Beverly Cleary." In *More Books by More People.* New York: Citation Press, 1974, pp. 88–94.

More Junior Authors. Edited by Muriel Fuller. New York: Wilson, 1963, pp. 49–50.

Novinger, Margaret. "Beverly Cleary: A Favorite Author of Children." *Southeastern Librarian* 18 (Fall 1968): 194–202. Reprinted in Miriam Hoffman and Eva Samuels. *Authors and Illustrators of Children's Books.* New York: Bowker, 1972, pp. 70–83.

Rees, David. "Middle of the Way: Rodie Sudbery and Beverly Cleary." In *Marble in the Water.* Boston: Horn Book, 1980, pp. 90–103.

Reuther, David. "Beverly Cleary." *Horn Book* 60 (Aug. 1984): 439–443.

Roggenbuck, Mary June. "Profile: Beverly Cleary—The Children's Force at Work." *Language Arts* 56 (Jan. 1979): 55–60.

Roozen, N. "Presentation of the Recognition of Merit Award to Beverly Cleary." *Claremont College Reading Conference Yearbook* (1983): 86–90.

Trout, Anita. "Beverly Cleary." In *American Writers for Children since 1960: Fiction. Dictionary of Literary Biography,* vol. 52. Detroit: Gale, 1986, pp. 84–90.

Twentieth Century Children's Writers. 2nd ed. Edited by D. L. Kirkpatrick. New York: St. Martin's Press, 1983, pp. 182–184.

Clements, Bruce

Fifth Book of Junior Authors and Illustrators. Edited by Sally Holmes Holtze. New York: Wilson, 1983, pp. 71–72.
Twentieth Century Children's Writers. 2nd ed. Edited by D. L. Kirkpatrick. New York: St. Martin's Press, 1983, pp. 185–186.

Coatsworth, Elizabeth (Jane)

Abbott, Barbara. "To Timbuctoo and Back: Elizabeth Coatsworth's Books for Children." *Horn Book* 6 (Nov. 1930): 283–289.
Bechtel, Louise Seaman. "Elizabeth Coatsworth: Poet and Writer." *Horn Book* 12 (Jan. 1936): 27–31.
"The Cat Who Went to Heaven." In Bertha Miller and Elinor Field. *Newbery Medal Books: 1922–1955.* Boston: Horn Book, 1957, pp. 89–98.
Coatsworth, Elizabeth. *Personal Geography: Almost an Autobiography.* Brattleboro, VT: Stephen Green Press, 1976.
———. "Upon Writing for Children." *Horn Book* 24 (Sept. 1948): 389–395. Reprinted in Elinor Field. *Horn Book Reflections.* Boston: Horn Book, 1969, pp. 6–13.
Doyle, Brian. *The Who's Who of Children's Literature.* New York: Schocken, 1968, pp. 53–54.
Helbig, Alethea K., and Perkins, Agnes Regan. *Dictionary of American Children's Fiction, 1859–1959.* Westport, CT: Greenwood Press, 1985, pp. 89–90, 106–107.
———. *Dictionary of American Children's Fiction, 1960–1984.* Westport, CT: Greenwood Press, 1986, pp. 121–122.
Hopkins, Lee Bennett. "Elizabeth Coatsworth." In *More Books by More People.* New York: Citation Press, 1974, pp. 95–99.
Jacobs, L. "Elizabeth Coatsworth." *Instructor* 72 (Nov. 1962): 100ff.
The Junior Book of Authors. 2nd rev. ed. Edited by Stanley J. Kunitz and Howard Haycraft. New York: Wilson, 1951, pp. 71–73.
Kuhn, Doris Young. "Elizabeth Coatsworth: Perceptive Impressionist." *Elementary English* 46 (Dec. 1969): 991–1007. Reprinted in Miriam Hoffman and Eva Samuels. *Authors and Illustrators of Children's Books.* New York: Bowker, 1972, pp. 84–107.
Lukens, Rebecca. "Elizabeth Coatsworth." In *American Writers for Children, 1900–1960. Dictionary of Literary Biography,* vol. 22. Detroit: Gale, 1983, pp. 94–101.
Meigs, Cornelia. "Alice-All-by-Herself." *Horn Book* 14 (Mar. 1938): 77–80.
The Oxford Companion to Children's Literature. Edited by Humphrey Carpenter and Mari Prichard. New York: Oxford Univ. Press, 1984, p. 122.
Rice, Mabel F. "The Poetic Prose of Elizabeth Coatsworth." *Elementary English* 31 (Jan. 1954): 3–10.
Roginski, Jim, ed. *Newbery and Caldecott Medalists and Honor Book Winners.* Littleton, CO: Libraries Unlimited, 1982, pp. 67–70.
Schmidt, Nancy. *Children's Fiction about Africa in English.* New York: Conch Magazine, 1981, pp. 178–179.
Smaridge, Norah. *Famous Modern Storytellers for Young People.* New York: Dodd, 1969, pp. 57–62.
Twentieth Century Children's Writers. 2nd ed. Edited by D. L. Kirkpatrick. New York: St. Martin's Press, 1983, pp. 190–192.
Yolen, Jane. "The Literary Underwater World." *Language Arts* 57 (1980): 403–412.

Cobalt, Martin *see* Mayne, William

Coblentz, Catherine Cate

Coblentz, Catherine Cate. "Through a Diamond Pane." *Horn Book* 19 (Sept. 1943): 309–313.

———. "Wading into Yesterday." *Horn Book* 20 (July 1944): 293–298.

Helbig, Alethea K., and Perkins, Agnes Regan. *Dictionary of American Children's Fiction, 1859–1959.* Westport, CT: Greenwood Press, 1985, pp. 57, 107.

The Junior Book of Authors. 2nd rev. ed. Edited by Stanley J. Kunitz and Howard Haycraft. New York: Wilson, 1951, pp. 73–74.

Quimby, Harriet B. "A Second Look: *The Blue Cat of Castle Town.*" *Horn Book* 61 (July–Aug. 1985): 481–491.

Roginski, Jim, ed. *Newbery and Caldecott Medalists and Honor Book Winners.* Littleton, CO: Libraries Unlimited, 1982, p. 70.

Cohen, Barbara

Fifth Book of Junior Authors and Illustrators. Edited by Sally Holmes Holtze. New York: Wilson, 1983, pp. 75–76.

Karp, Hazel B., and Veal, Sibley. "Point of View." *Advocate* 1 (Winter 1982): 122–125.

Cole, Joanna

Fifth Book of Junior Authors and Illustrators. Edited by Sally Holmes Holtze. New York: Wilson, 1983, pp. 77–78.

Collodi, Carlo (pseud. of Carlo Lorenzini)

Bacon, Martha. "Puppet's Progress: *Pinocchio.*" *Atlantic Monthly* 225 (Apr. 1970): 88–90, 92. Reprinted in Virginia Haviland. *Children and Literature.* Glenview, IL: Scott, Foresman, 1973, pp. 71–77.

Cambon, Glauco. "*Pinocchio* and the Problem of Children's Literature." In *Children's Literature,* vol. 2. Storrs, CT: Journal of the Modern Language Association, 1973, pp. 50–60.

Cech, John. "The Triumphant Transformations of *Pinocchio.*" In *Triumphs of the Spirit in Children's Literature.* Edited by Francelia Butler and Richard Rotert. Hamden, CT: Shoe String Press, 1986, pp. 171–179.

Doyle, Brian. *The Who's Who of Children's Literature.* New York: Schocken, 1968, pp. 56–57.

Gannon, Susan R. "A Note on Collodi and Lucian." In *Children's Literature,* vol. 8. New Haven, CT: Yale Univ. Press, 1980, pp. 98–102.

———. "*Pinocchio:* The First Hundred Years." *Children's Literature Association Quarterly* 6 (Winter 1981–1982): 1, 5–8. Reprinted in *The First Steps.* Edited by Patricia Dooley. West Lafayette, IN: Children's Literature Association Publications, 1984, pp. 131–133.

Hawkes, Louise Restieaux. *Before and after "Pinocchio": A Study of Italian Children's Books.* Paris: Puppet Press, 1933.

Hazard, Paul. *Books, Children and Men,* 4th ed. Boston: Horn Book, 1960, pp. 111–119. Excerpted in *Horn Book* 19 (Mar.–Apr. 1943): 119–126.

Heins, Paul. "A Second Look: *The Adventures of Pinocchio.*" *Horn Book* 58 (Apr. 1982): 200–204.

Heisig, James. "*Pinocchio:* Archetype of the Motherless Child." In *Children's Literature*, vol. 3. Storrs, CT: Journal of the Modern Language Association, 1974, pp. 23–35. Reprinted in *Reflections on Literature for Children.* Edited by Francelia Butler. Hamden, CT: Shoe String Press, 1984, pp. 155–170.

The Junior Book of Authors. 2nd rev. ed. Edited by Stanley J. Kunitz and Howard Haycraft. New York: Wilson, 1951, pp. 74–76.

Mayne, W. G. "*Pinocchio* Turns Fascist." *Living Age* 359, no. 4493 (Feb. 1941): 569–571. Reprinted in Mary Lou White. *Children's Literature.* Columbus, OH: Merrill, 1976, pp. 56–58.

Melegari, V. "*Pinocchio, Cuore,* and Other Italian Books." *Junior Bookshelf* 19 (Mar. 1955): 71–77.

Morrissey, Thomas J. "Alive and Well but Not Unscathed: A Reply to Susan R. Gannon's '*Pinocchio* at 100.' " *Children's Literature Association Quarterly* 7 (Summer 1982): 37–38.

Morrissey, Thomas J., and Wunderlich, Richard. "Death and Rebirth in Pinocchio." In *Children's Literature,* vol. 11. New Haven, CT: Yale Univ. Press, 1983, pp. 64–75.

The Oxford Companion to Children's Literature. Edited by Humphrey Carpenter and Mari Prichard. New York: Oxford Univ. Press, 1984, pp. 123, 413–414.

Petrini, E. "Collodi and His Times." *Bookbird* 13, no. 1 (1975): 24–26.

Poesio, Carla. "*Pinocchio's* Centenary Celebrations." *Horn Book* 58 (Apr. 1982): 235–239; *Bookbird* 21 (1983): 29–30.

Redmont, Dennis. "*Pinocchio* Lives at 100." *The Gainsville Sun* (Nov. 28, 1980).

Schroeder, Ida. "Homage to Pinocchio." *Horn Book* 35, no. 5 (Oct. 1959): 368–373. Reprinted in Robinson. *Readings about Children's Literature.* New York: McKay, 1966, pp. 302–303.

Segal, Elizabeth. "Beastly Boys: A Century of Mischief." *Children's Literature in Education* 18 (1987): 3–12.

Stott, Jon C. *Children's Literature from A to Z.* New York: McGraw-Hill, 1984, p. 80.

Street, Douglas. "*Pinocchio*—From Picaro to Pipsqueak." In Douglas Street. *Children's Novels and the Movies.* New York: Ungar, 1983, pp. 47–57.

Teahan, James T. "Carlo Collodi." In *Writers for Children: Critical Studies of Major Authors since the Seventeenth Century.* Edited by Jane M. Bingham. New Yꞓ ꓥ: Scribner, 1988, pp. 129–138.

Wunderlich, Richard, and Morrissey, Thomas J. "Carlo Collodi's *The Adventures of Pinocchio:* A Classic Book of Choices." In *Touchstones.* Edited by Perry Nodelman. West Lafayette, IN: Children's Literature Association Publications, 1985, pp. 53–63.

———. "The Desecration of *Pinocchio* in the United States." In *Proceedings of the Eighth Annual Conference of the Children's Literature Association.* University of Minnesota, March 1981. Ypsilanti, MI: Children's Literature Association, 1982, pp. 106–118. Reprinted in *Horn Book* 58 (Apr. 1982): 205–211.

———. "*Pinocchio* before 1920: The Popular and Pedagogical Traditions." *Italian Quarterly* 23 (Spring 1982): 61–72.

Colum, Padraic

Bechtel, Louise Seaman. "Padraic Colum: A Great Storyteller of Today." *Catholic Library World* 32 (Dec. 1960): 159–160.

Bowen, Zackary R. "*Padraic Colum: A Biographical–Critical Introduction.* Carbondale: Southern Illinois Univ. Press, 1970.

Colum, Padraic. "Imagination and the Literature of Children." *Illinois Libraries* 7 (1925): 50–52.

———. "Patterns for the Imagination: Acceptance of the 1961 Regina Medal Award." *Horn Book* 36 (Feb. 1962): 82–86.

———. "Storyteller's Story: The Power of Imagination." *New York Public Library Bulletin* 70 (Oct. 1966): 528–532.

———. "Storytelling in Ireland." *Horn Book* 10 (May 1934): 190–194.

———. "Storytelling New and Old." In *The Fountain of Youth.* New York: Mac-Millan, 1927, 1968. Reprinted in *Horn Book* 59 (June 1983): 358–377.

Dolbier, Maurice. "Padraic Colum." *N.Y. Herald Tribune Book Review* (June 9, 1957).

Greene, Ellin. "Literary Uses of Traditional Themes: From 'Cinderella' to *The Girl Who Sat by the Ashes* and *The Glass Slipper.*" *Children's Literature Association Quarterly* 11 (Fall 1986): 128–132.

Helbig, Alethea K., and Perkins, Agnes Regan. *Dictionary of American Children's Fiction, 1859–1959.* Westport, CT: Greenwood Press, 1985, pp. 108–109, 559–560.

The Junior Book of Authors. 2nd rev. ed. Edited by Stanley J. Kunitz and Howard Haycraft. New York: Wilson, 1951, pp. 76–77.

Mahony, Bertha E. "Tir-Nan-Oge and Tir Tairngire." *Horn Book* 10 (Jan. 1934): 31–36.

Myers, Andrew. " 'In the Wild Earth a Grecian Vace!' For Padraic Colum (1881–1972)." *Columbia Library Columns* 22 (Feb. 1973): 11–21.

Nichols, L. "A Talk with Padraic Colum." *New York Times Book Review* 15 (June 23, 1957): 1.

The Oxford Companion to Children's Literature. Edited by Humphrey Carpenter and Mari Prichard. New York: Oxford Univ. Press, 1984, p. 125.

Roginski, Jim, ed. *Newbery and Caldecott Medalists and Honor Book Winners.* Littleton, CO: Libraries Unlimited, 1982, pp. 71–73.

Seaman, Louise H. "Stories Out of the Youth of the World—As Recreated by Padraic Colum." *Horn Book* 1 (Mar. 1925): 16–20.

Twentieth Century Children's Writers. 2nd ed. Edited by D. L. Kirkpatrick. New York: St. Martin's Press, 1983, pp. 194–196.

Warren, Dorothea C. "Padraic Colum." In *Writers for Children: Critical Studies of Major Authors since the Seventeenth Century.* Edited by Jane M. Bingham. New York: Scribner, 1988, pp. 139–146.

Coolidge, Olivia E(nsor)

Helbig, Alethea K., and Perkins, Agnes Regan. *Dictionary of American Children's Fiction, 1960–1984.* Westport, CT: Greenwood Press, 1986, pp. 129–130.

More Junior Authors. Edited by Muriel Fuller. New York: Wilson, 1963, pp. 52–53.

Cooper, Paul F(enimore)

Dalphin, Marcia. "I Give You the End of a Golden String." *Horn Book* 14 (May 1938): 143–149. Reprinted in Norma Fryatt. *A Horn Book Sampler.* Boston: Horn Book, 1959, pp. 133–139.

Jones, Louis C. "Paul Fenimore Cooper and *Tal.*" *Horn Book* 26 (Jan.–Feb. 1950): 30–32. Reprinted in Elinor Field. *Horn Book Reflections.* Boston: Horn Book, 1969, pp. 238–241.

Cooper (Grant), Susan (Mary)

Bisenieks, Dainis. "Children, Magic and Choices." *Mythlore* 6 (Winter 1979): 13–16.

Carlson, Dudley Brown. "A Second Look: *Over Sea, Under Stone.*" *Horn Book* 52 (Oct. 1976): 522–523.

Cooper, Susan. "Address Delivered at the Children's Round Table Breakfast: Is There Really Such a Species Called Children's Books?" *Texas Library Journal* 52 (May 1976): 52–54.

———. "A Dream of Revels." *Horn Book* 55 (Dec. 1979): 633–640.

———. "Escaping into Ourselves." In Betsy Hearne and Marilyn Kaye. *Celebrating Children's Books: Essays on Children's Literature in Honor of Zena Sutherland.* New York: Lothrop, 1981, pp. 14–23. Reprinted in Boyer and Zahorski. *Fantasists on Fantasy.* New York: Avon, 1984, pp. 277–287.

———. "In Defense of the Artist." In *Proceedings of the Fifth Annual Conference of the Children's Literature Association.* Harvard University, March 1978. Ypsilanti, MI: Children's Literature Association, 1979, pp. 20–28. Reprinted in Robert Bator. *Signposts to Criticism of Children's Literature.* Chicago: American Library Association, 1983, pp. 98–108.

———. "A Love Letter to the *Horn Book.*" *Horn Book* 50 (Oct. 1974): 182–183.

———. "My Links with Wales." In *Loughborough '83: Proceedings.* Welsh National Centre for Children's Literature, 1984, pp. 79–81.

———. "Nahum Tarune's Book." *Horn Book* 56 (Oct. 1980): 497–507. Reprinted in *Innocence & Experience.* Edited by Barbara Harrison and Gregory Maguire. New York: Lothrop, 1987, pp. 76–86.

———. "Newbery Award Acceptance Address." *Horn Book* 52 (Aug. 1967): 361–366; *Top of the News* 33 (Fall 1976): 39–43.

———. "Susan Cooper—A Famous Author from Wales Who Writes about Wales." *Bookbird* 17, no. 4 (1979): 19–21.

Esmonde, Margaret. Articles on Susan Cooper's *Dark Is Rising* sequence. *Fantasiae* (Nov. 1974): 6–7, (Jan. 1975): 7–9, (Feb. 1975): 5–6, (Feb. 1976): 7–8.

Fourth Book of Junior Authors and Illustrators. Edited by Doris De Montreville and Elizabeth D. Crawford. New York: Wilson, 1978, pp. 98–99.

Gilderdale, B. "Susan Cooper, *The Dark Is Rising,* and the Legends." *Children's Literature Association Yearbook* (Auckland, New Zealand), vol. 7 (1978), pp. 11–23.

"*The Grey King.*" In *Newbery and Caldecott Medal Books 1976–1985.* Edited by Lee Kingman. Boston: Horn Book, 1986, pp. 3–17.

Heins, Ethel L. "*The Dark Is Rising,* a Review." *Horn Book* 49 (June 1973): 286.

Helbig, Alethea K., and Perkins, Agnes Regan. *Dictionary of American Children's Fiction, 1960–1984.* Westport, CT: Greenwood Press, 1986, pp. 130, 144–145, 257–258, 496–497.

Hipolito, Jane. "*The Dark Is Rising* Series." In Frank N. Magill. *Survey of Modern Fantasy Literature,* vol. 1. Englewood Cliffs, NJ: Salem Press, 1983, pp. 331–335.

Kuznets, Lois R. " 'High Fantasy' in America: Alexander, Le Guin and Cooper." An unpublished paper delivered at the Conference on Fantasy and Social Values in German and American Children's Literature, Humanities Institute of Brooklyn College, March 1984.

———. "Susan Cooper: A Reply." *Children's Literature Association Newsletter* 3 (Spring–Summer 1978): 14–16. Reprinted in Robert Bator. *Signposts to Criticism of Children's Literature.* Chicago: American Library Association, 1983, pp. 109–113.

Levin, Betty. "Journey through Mountain and Mist: *The Grey King.*" *Horn Book* 52 (Aug. 1976): 443–445.

McElderry, Margaret K. "Susan Cooper." *Horn Book* 52 (Aug. 1976): 367–372.

The Oxford Companion to Children's Literature. Edited by Humphrey Carpenter and Mari Prichard. New York: Oxford Univ. Press, 1984, pp. 130, 141–142.

Pearson, Maisie K. "High Magic and the Presence of Good and Evil in the Novels of Susan Cooper." Paper presented at the 1982 Popular Culture/American Culture Association Meeting, Louisville, KY, April 1982.

"The Perilous Realms: A Colloquy." In *Innocence & Experience.* Edited by Barbara Harrison and Gregory Maguire. New York: Lothrop, 1987, pp. 195–210.

Pflieger, Pat, and Hill, Helen M. *A Reference Guide to Modern Fantasy for Children.* Westport, CT: Greenwood Press, 1984, pp. xii–xiv, 122–125, 138–140, 216–218, 414–415, 492–494.

Philip, Neil. "Fantasy: Double Cream or Instant Whip?" *Signal* 35 (May 1981): 82–90.

Plante, Raymond L. "Object and Character in *The Dark Is Rising.*" *Children's Literature Association Quarterly* 11 (Spring 1986): 37–41.

Rees, David. "Children's Writers: Susan Cooper." *School Librarian* 32 (Summer 1984): 197–205.

Roginski, Jim, ed. *Newbery and Caldecott Medalists and Honor Book Winners.* Littleton, CO: Libraries Unlimited, 1982, p. 76.

Schmidt, Gary D. "See How They Grow: Character Development in Children's Series Books." *Children's Literature in Education* 18 (1987): 34–44.

Searles, Baird; Meacham, Beth; and Franklin, Michael. *A Reader's Guide to Fantasy.* New York: Avon, 1982, pp. 47–48.

Spraggs, Gillian. "A Lawless World: The Fantasy Novels of Susan Cooper." *Use of English* 33 (Spring 1982): 23–31.

Stott, Jon C. "The Nature of Fantasy: A Conversation with Ruth Nichols, Susan Cooper, and Maurice Sendak." *World of Children's Books* 3, no. 2 (Fall 1978): 32–43.

Sullivan, C. W., III. "Traditional Welsh Materials in Modern Fantasy." *Extrapolation* 28 (Spring 1987): 87–97.

Swinfen, Ann. *In Defense of Fantasy: A Study of the Genre in English and American Literature since 1945.* Boston: Routledge, 1984, pp. 141–146.

Thompson, Hillary. "Doorways to Fantasy." *Canadian Children's Literature* 21 (1981): 8–16.

Thwaite, Ann. "Gooseflesh and Nameless Longings." *Times Literary Supplement* March 29, 1985, p. 348.

Townsend, John Rowe. "Guest Essay: Heights of Fantasy." *Children's Literature Review,* vol. 5. Detroit: Gale, 1983, pp. 9–10.

Trautmann, Patricia Ann. "Welsh Mythology and Arthurian Legend in the Novels of Lloyd Alexander and Susan Cooper: Parallels of Motif, Character and Other Elements." Ph.D. dissertation, Vanderbilt University, 1984.

Twentieth Century Children's Writers. 2nd ed. Edited by D. L. Kirkpatrick. New York: St. Martin's Press, 1983, pp. 198–200.

Ziefer, Barbara Z. "Wales as a Setting for Children's Fantasy." *Children's Literature in Education* 13 (Summer 1982): 95–102.

Corbett, Scott

Fourth Book of Junior Authors and Illustrators. Edited by Doris De Montreville and Elizabeth D. Crawford. New York: Wilson, 1978, pp. 99–100.

Helbig, Alethea K., and Perkins, Agnes Regan. *Dictionary of American Children's Fiction, 1960–1984.* Westport, CT: Greenwood Press, 1986, pp. 130–131.

Twentieth Century Children's Writers. 2nd ed. Edited by D. L. Kirkpatrick. New York: St. Martin's Press, 1983, pp. 200–201.

Cosgrove (Payes), Rachel R.

Hanff, Peter E., and Greene, Douglas G. *Bibliographia Oziana.* Demorest, GA: International Wizard of Oz Club, 1976.

Cowper, Richard (pseud. of John Middleton–Murray, Jr.)

Cowper, Richard. "Apropos: The White Bird of Kinship." *Vector* 110 (1982): 6–13.
———. "Is There a Story in It Somewhere?" In *The Science Fiction Sourcebook.* New York: Van Nostrand Reinhold, 1984, pp. 74–75.
———. "The Profession of Science Fiction: X: Backwards Across the Frontier." *Foundation* 9 (1975): 4–21.
Elliot, Jeffrey. "Interview: Richard Cowper." *Fantasy Newsletter* 36 (1981): 17–24, 30.
Twentieth–Century Science Fiction Writers. 2nd ed. Edited by Curtis C. Smith. Chicago: St. James Press, 1986, pp. 162–163.

Cox, Palmer

Cummins, R. W. *Humorous but Wholesome: A History of Palmer Cox and the Brownies.* Watkins Glen, NY: Century, 1973.
The Oxford Companion to Children's Literature. Edited by Humphrey Carpenter and Mari Prichard. New York: Oxford Univ. Press, 1984, p. 132.
Spivak, Charlotte. "Palmer Cox." In *American Writers for Children before 1900. Dictionary of Literary Biography,* vol. 42. Detroit: Gale, 1985, pp. 133–138.
Twentieth Century Children's Writers. 2nd ed. Edited by D. L. Kirkpatrick. New York: St. Martin's Press, 1983, pp. 864–865.

Cranch, Christopher P(earse)

The Oxford Companion to Children's Literature. Edited by Humphrey Carpenter and Mari Prichard. New York: Oxford Univ. Press, 1984, p. 133.

Cregan, Mairin

Patee, Doris. "Mairin Cregan and *Old John.*" *Horn Book* 12 (May 1936): 165–166.

Cresswell (Rowe), Helen

Cresswell, Helen. "Ancient and Modern and Incorrigibly Plural." In Edward Blishen. *The Thorny Paradise.* Boston: Horn Book, 1975, pp. 108–116.
———. "If It's Someone from Porlock, Don't Answer the Door." *Children's Literature in Education* 4 (Mar. 1971): 32–39.
Crouch, Marcus S. "Helen Cresswell, Craftsman." *Junior Bookshelf* 34 (June 1970): 135–139.
Elleman, Barbara. "*A Game of Catch.*" *Booklist* 82 (Nov. 15, 1985): 494–496. Speech given at the 1985 Children's Books Open Forum, 1985 ALA Conference.
Fourth Book of Junior Authors and Illustrators. Edited by Doris De Montreville and Elizabeth D. Crawford. New York: Wilson, 1978, pp. 105–106.
Greaves, Margaret. "Warm Sun, Cold Wind: The Novels of Helen Cresswell." *Children's Literature in Education* 5 (July 1971): 51–59.
Maguire, Gregory. "A Second Look: *The Piemakers.*" *Horn Book* 57 (Apr. 1981): 215–217.
Merrick, Anne. "*The Nightwatchmen* and *Charlie and the Chocolate Factory* as Books to Be Read to Children." *Children's Literature in Education* 16 (Spring 1975): 21–30.

The Oxford Companion to Children's Literature. Edited by Humphrey Carpenter and Mari Prichard. New York: Oxford Univ. Press, 1984, p. 134.

Swinfen, Ann. *In Defense of Fantasy: A Study of the Genre in English and American Literature since 1945.* Boston: Routledge, 1984, pp. 72–74.

Townsend, John Rowe. "Helen Cresswell." In *A Sense of Story.* Philadelphia: Lippincott, 1971, pp. 57–67.

Twentieth Century Children's Writers. 2nd ed. Edited by D. L. Kirkpatrick. New York: St. Martin's Press, 1983, pp. 204–207.

Cross, Gillian (Clare)

Twentieth Century Children's Writers. 2nd ed. Edited by D. L. Kirkpatrick. New York: St. Martin's Press, 1983, p. 210.

Cross, John Keir

Cross, John Keir. *Aspect of Life: An Autobiography of Youth.* London: Selwyn and Blount, 1937.

Doyle, Brian. *The Who's Who of Children's Literature.* New York: Schocken, 1968, pp. 66–67.

Twentieth–Century Science Fiction Writers. 2nd ed. Edited by Curtis C. Smith. Chicago: St. James Press, 1986, pp. 166–167.

Crownfield, Getrude

The Junior Book of Authors. 2nd rev. ed. Edited by Stanley J. Kunitz and Howard Haycraft. New York: Wilson, 1951, p. 83.

Cullen, Countee (Porter)

Fourth Book of Junior Authors and Illustrators. Edited by Doris De Montreville and Elizabeth D. Crawford. New York: Wilson, 1978, pp. 110–112.

Shucard, Alan R. *Countee Cullen.* Boston: Twayne, 1984.

Cunningham, Julia (Woolfolk)

Cunningham, Julia. "The Creative Spirit and Children's Literature: A Symposium." Paper presented at the University of California, Berkeley, July 1977. *Wilson Library Bulletin* 53 (Oct. 1978): 155–160.

———. "Dear Characters." *Horn Book* 43 (Apr. 1967): 233–234.

———. "From Another Edge of the Forest." *Horn Book* 42 (June 1966): 291.

Helbig, Alethea K., and Perkins, Agnes Regan. *Dictionary of American Children's Fiction, 1960–1984.* Westport, CT: Greenwood Press, 1986, pp. 82–83, 126, 136, 165, 217–218, 673–674.

Hopkins, Lee Bennett. "Julia Cunningham." In *More Books by More People.* New York: Citation Press, 1974, pp. 105–109.

Keyser, Elizabeth Lennox. "A Contemporary Gothic for Girls: Julia Cunningham's *Tuppenny.*" *Children's Literature in Education* 17 (Summer 1986): 88–100.

Third Book of Junior Authors. Edited by Doris De Montreville and Donna Hill. New York: Wilson, 1972, pp. 70–71.

Twentieth Century Children's Writers. 2nd ed. Edited by D. L. Kirkpatrick. New York: St. Martin's Press, 1983, pp. 213–215.

Curry, Jane L(ouise)

Curry, Jane Louise. "On the Elvish Craft." *Signal* 2 (May 1970): 42–49. Reprinted in Nancy Chambers. *Signal Approach to Children's Books*. Metuchen, NJ: Scarecrow Press, 1981, pp. 83–93.

Fourth Book of Junior Authors and Illustrators. Edited by Doris De Montreville and Elizabeth D. Crawford. New York: Wilson, 1978, pp. 112–113.

Helbig, Alethea K., and Perkins, Agnes Regan. *Dictionary of American Children's Fiction, 1960–1984*. Westport, CT: Greenwood Press, 1986, pp. 38–39, 137, 521–522.

Pflieger, Pat, and Hill, Helen M. *A Reference Guide to Modern Fantasy for Children*. Westport, CT: Greenwood Press, 1984, pp. xiii–xvi, 47–49, 53–54, 58–60, 105–106, 132–134, 143–145, 323–325, 341–342, 366–367, 415–418, 424–425, 446–448, 495–497, 576–578, 613–614.

Twentieth Century Children's Writers. 2nd ed. Edited by D. L. Kirkpatrick. New York: St. Martin's Press, 1983, pp. 215–216.

Cutt, W(illiam) Towrie

Aldritt, Judith Morse. "Profile: W. Towrie Cutt." *In Review* 14 (Apr. 1980): 12–15.

McDonough, Irma, ed. "William Towrie Cutt." In *Profiles 2: Authors and Illustrators, Children's Literature in Canada*. Ottowa: Canadian Library Association, 1982.

Twentieth Century Children's Writers. 2nd ed. Edited by D. L. Kirkpatrick. New York: St. Martin's Press, 1983, p. 216.

Dahl, Roald

Bouchard, Lois Kalb. "A New Look at Old Favorites: *Charlie and the Chocolate Factory*." *Interracial Books for Children, Bulletin* 3 (1970): 3, 8. Reprinted in MacCann. *The Black American in Books for Children*. Metuchen, NJ: Scarecrow Press, 1972, pp. 112–115.

Cameron, Eleanor. "McLuhan, Youth, and Literature." *Horn Book* 48 (Oct. 1972): 433–440. Reprinted in Paul Heins. *Crosscurrents of Criticism*. Boston: Horn Book, 1977, pp. 98–125.

———. "A Question of Taste." *Children's Literature in Education* 21 (Summer 1976): 59–63.

———. "A Reply to Roald Dahl." *Horn Book* 49 (Apr. 1973): 127–128. Reprinted in Paul Heins. *Crosscurrents of Criticism*. Boston: Horn Book, 1977, pp. 123–125.

Campbell, A. K. D. "Children's Writers: Roald Dahl." *School Librarian* 29 (June 1981): 108–114.

Chesterfield-Evans, Jan. "Roald Dahl: A Discussion and Comparison of His Stories for Children and Adults." *Orana* 19 (Nov. 1983): 165–168.

Corner, Calla. "The Weird Writing World of Roald Dahl." *Writers Digest* 60 (Aug. 1980): 40–42, 47.

Dahl, Roald. *Boy: Tales of Childhood*. New York: Farrar, 1984. Autobiography.

———. "*Charlie and the Chocolate Factory:* A Reply." *Horn Book* 49 (Feb. 1973): 77–78. Reprinted in Paul Heins. *Crosscurrents of Criticism*. Boston: Horn Book, 1977, pp. 121–122.

———. *Going Solo*. New York: Farrar, 1986. Autobiography.

Hopkins, Lee Bennett. "Roald Dahl." In *More Books by More People*. New York: Citation Press, 1974, pp. 110–114.

Merrick, Anne. "*The Nightwatchmen* and *Charlie and the Chocolate Factory* as Books to Be Read to Children." *Children's Literature in Education* 16 (Spring 1975): 21–30.

Moss, Anita. "*Charlie and the Chocolate Factory* and *James and the Giant Peach.*" In *Part of the Pattern*. New York: Greenwillow, 1986, p. 28.

———. "Crime and Punishment—Or Development—In Fairy Tales and Fantasy." *Mythlore* 8 (Spring 1981): 26–28, 42.

The Oxford Companion to Children's Literature. Edited by Humphrey Carpenter and Mari Prichard. New York: Oxford Univ. Press, 1984, pp. 108, 139.

Seiter, Richard D. "The Bittersweet Journey from *Charlie* to 'Willy Wonka.'" In *Douglas Street. Children's Novels and the Movies*. New York: Ungar, 1983, pp. 191–196.

Stott, Jon C. *Children's Literature from A to Z*. New York: McGraw-Hill, 1984, p. 86.

Third Book of Junior Authors. Edited by Doris De Montreville and Donna Hill. New York: Wilson, 1972, pp. 73–74.

Twentieth Century Children's Writers. 2nd ed. Edited by D. L. Kirkpatrick. New York: St. Martin's Press, 1983, pp. 216–218.

West, Mark I. "Regression and Fragmentation of the Self in *James and the Giant Peach.*" *Children's Literature in Education* 16 (Winter 1985): 219–226.

Wintle, Justin, and Fisher, Emma. "Roald Dahl." In *The Pied Pipers*. New York: Paddington Press, 1974, pp. 101–112.

Dalgliesh, Alice

Helbig, Alethea K., and Perkins, Agnes Regan. *Dictionary of American Children's Fiction, 1859–1959*. Westport, CT: Greenwood Press, 1985, p. 119.

D'Aulaire, Edgar Parin, and D'Aulaire, Ingri (Mortenson)

Bader, Barbara. "Ingri and Edgar Parin D'Aulaire." In *American Picturebooks: From Noah's Ark to the Beast Within*. New York: Macmillan, 1976, pp. 42–46.

Children's Literature Review Board. "Review." In MacCann. *Cultural Conformity in Books for Children*. Metuchen, NJ: Scarecrow Press, 1977, pp. 144–145.

Crago, Hugh. "Ingri and Edgar D'Aulaire." In *American Writers for Children, 1900–1960. Dictionary of Literary Biography*, vol. 22. Detroit: Gale, 1983, pp. 102–109.

D'Aulaire, Ingri, and D'Aulaire, Edgar Parin. "Working Together on Books for Children." *Horn Book* 16 (July 1940): 247–256.

Farquhar, M. C. "The Magic Rug of Ingri and Edgar Parin D'Aulaire." *Elementary English* 30 (Apr. 1953): 197–201.

Mahony, Bertha E., and Mitchell, Marguerite M. "Ingri and Edgar Parin D'Aulaire." *Horn Book* 16 (July 1940): 257–264.

Stott, Jon C. *Children's Literature from A to Z*. New York: McGraw-Hill, 1984, p. 89.

Twentieth Century Children's Writers. 2nd ed. Edited by D. L. Kirkpatrick. New York: St. Martin's Press, 1983, pp. 225–226.

D'Aulnoy, Countess Marie Catherine de Berneville

Degraff, Amy Vanderlyn. "The Tower and the Well: A Study of Form and Meaning in Mme. d'Aulnoy's Fairy Tales." Ph.D dissertation, University of Virginia, 1979.

Doyle, Brian. *The Who's Who of Children's Literature*. New York: Schocken, 1968, p. 69.

Filstrup, Jane Merrill. "Individuation in 'La Chatte Blanche.'" *Children's Literature*, vol. 6. Philadelphia: Temple University Press, 1977, pp. 77–92.

Hearn, Michael Patrick. "Preface." In Marie Catherine, Comtesse d'Aulnoy. *The Tales of the Fairies in Three Parts, Compleat . . .* New York: Garland, 1977.

Mitchell, Jane. "Thematic Analysis of Mme. Comtesse d'Aulnoy's *Contes de Fées.*" Ph.D. dissertation, University of North Carolina at Chapel Hill, 1973.

The Oxford Companion to Children's Literature. Edited by Humphrey Carpenter and Mari Prichard. New York: Oxford Univ. Press, 1984, pp. 35–36, 67, 568–569, 583.

Palmer, Melvin Delmar. "Madame d'Aulnoy in England." Ph.D. dissertation, University of Maryland, 1969.

Palmer, Nancy, and Palmer, Melvin D. "English Editions of French Contes de Fées Attributed to Mme. d'Aulnoy." *Studies in Bibliography* 27 (1974): 227–232.

———. "The French 'Conte de Fée' in England." *Studies in Short Fiction* 11, no. 1 (Winter 1974): 35–44.

Sale, Roger. *Fairy Tales and After.* Cambridge, MA: Harvard Univ. Press, 1978, pp. 54–58.

Williams, Elizabeth Detering. "The Fairy Tales of Madame d'Aulnoy." Ph.D. dissertation, Rice University, 1982.

Davies, Andrew (Wynford)

Fifth Book of Junior Authors and Illustrators. Edited by Sally Holmes Holtze. New York: Wilson, 1983, pp. 94–95.

Twentieth Century Children's Writers. 2nd ed. Edited by D. L. Kirkpatrick. New York: St. Martin's Press, 1983, pp. 226–227.

Davis, Robert

Helbig, Alethea K. and Perkins, Agnes Regan. *Dictionary of American Children's Fiction, 1859–1959.* Westport, CT: Greenwood Press, 1985, pp. 125–126.

The Junior Book of Authors. 2nd rev. ed. Edited by Stanley J. Kunitz and Howard Haycraft. New York: Wilson, 1951, pp. 95–96.

De Camp, L(yon) Sprague

De Camp, L. Sprague. *Blond Barbarians and Noble Savages.* Baltimore: T-K Graphics, 1975.

———. "Ghost Trouble." *Fantasy Newsletter* 26 (1980): 12–13.

———. "Imaginative Fiction and Creative Fiction." In *Modern Science Fiction.* 2nd ed. Edited by Reginald Bretnor. Chicago: Advent, 1979.

———. *Literary Swordsmen and Sorcerers: The Makers of Heroic Fantasy.* Sauk City, WI: Arkham House, 1976.

———, ed. *The Blade of Conan.* New York: Ace, 1979. Essays on sword-and-sorcery fantasy.

Fredericks, Casey. *The Future of Eternity: Mythologies of Science Fiction and Fantasy.* Bloomington: Indiana Univ. Press, 1982.

Laughlin, Charlotte, and Levack, Daniel J. H. *De Camp: An L. Sprague De Camp Bibliography.* Columbia, PA: Underwood-Miller, 1983.

Moskowitz, Sam. *Seekers of Tomorrow; Masters of Modern Science Fiction.* New York: Ballantine, 1967, pp. 151–166.

Schlobin, Roger C. "The Fool and the Fantastic." *Fantasy Newsletter* 43 (1981): 6–9, 29.

Schuyler, William M., Jr. "Recent Developments in Spell Construction." In *The Aesthetics of Fantasy Literature and Art.* Edited by Roger C. Schlobin. Notre Dame, IN: Univ. of Notre Dame Press, 1982, pp. 237–248.

Schweitzer, Darrell. *Science Fiction Voices #1.* San Bernardino, CA: Borgo Press, 1979.

————, ed. *Science Fiction Voices.* Baltimore: T-K Graphics, 1976.

Schweitzer, Darrell, and Geis, Richard E. "An Interview with: L. Sprague De Camp." *Science Fiction Review* 4 (1975): 11–14.

Stableford, Brian M. "L. Sprague De Camp and Fletcher Pratt." In *Supernatural Fiction Writers,* vol. 2. Edited by E. F. Bleiler. New York: Scribner, 1985, pp. 925–932.

Twentieth-Century Science Fiction Writers. 2nd ed. Edited by Curtis C. Smith. Chicago: St. James Press, 1986, pp. 178–181.

De La Mare, Walter (John)

Auden, W. H. "Walter de la Mare." In W. H. Auden. *Forewords and Afterwords.* New York: Random, 1973, pp. 384–394.

Bianco, Margery. "De la Mare." *Horn Book* 18 (May–June 1942): 141–147. Reprinted in Anne Carroll Moore and Bertha Mahony Miller. *Writing and Criticism.* Boston: Horn Book, 1951, pp. 67–77.

Bianco, Pamela. "Editorial: Walter de la Mare." *Horn Book* 29 (June 1953): 173.

————. "Walter de la Mare." *Horn Book* 33 (June 1957): 242–247. Reprinted in Elinor Field. *Horn Book Reflections.* Boston: Horn Book, 1969, pp. 265–270.

Buchan, S. "Walter de la Mare for Children." *Spectator* (London), August 24, 1918, pp. 200–201.

Chapman, Vera. "Forerunner to Tolkien? Walter de la Mare's *The Three Royal Monkeys.*" *Mythlore* 8 (Summer 1981): 32–33.

Clark, Keith. "A Child of Mature Years: Walter de la Mare, 1873–1956." *Junior Bookshelf* 37 (Apr. 1973): 89–93.

Clark, Leonard. *Walter de la Mare.* New York: Walck, 1960. Reprinted in Hugh Shelley, Rosemary Sutcliff, and Leonard Clark. *Arthur Ransome, Rudyard Kipling and Walter de la Mare.* London: Bodley Head, n.d.

Clute, John. "The Short Fiction of Walter de la Mare." In Frank N. Magill. *Survey of Modern Fantasy Literature,* vol. 3. Englewood Cliffs, NJ: Salem Press, 1983, pp. 1492–1495.

————. "Walter de la Mare." In *Supernatural Fiction Writers: Fantasy and Horror,* vol. 1. Edited by E. F. Bleiler. New York: Scribner, 1985, pp. 497–504.

"Collected Stories for Children." In M. Crouch and A. Ellis. *Chosen for Children.* 3rd ed. London: The Library Association, 1977, pp. 45–49.

Cooper, Susan. "Naham Tarune's Book." *Horn Book* 56 (Oct. 1980): 497–507.

Crouch, Marcus S. "Farewell to Walter de la Mare." *Junior Bookshelf* 20 (Oct. 1956): 187–191.

————. "Walter de la Mare and His Illustrators." *Junior Bookshelf* 17 (Mar. 1953): 51–60.

Dalphin, Marcia. "I Give You the End of a Golden String." *Horn Book* 14 (May 1938): 143–149. Reprinted in Norma Fryatt. *A Horn Book Sampler.* Boston: Horn Book, 1959, pp. 133–139.

Degan, James Nerhood. "The Short Fiction of Walter de la Mare." Ph.D. dissertation, University of Iowa, 1982.

De la Mare, Walter. "A Sort of Interview." *London Mercury* 35 (Dec. 1936): 165–171.

Doyle, Brian. *The Who's Who of Children's Literature.* New York: Schocken, 1968, pp. 73–74.

Farjeon, Eleanor. "Walter de la Mare." *Horn Book* 33 (June 1957): 197–205.

Gardner, Jane E. "Walter de la Mare's Stories for Children: An Analysis of Variant Texts." *Private Libraries* 3rd series 1, no. 3 (Autumn 1978): 101–118.

Graham, Eleanor. "The Riddle of Walter de la Mare: An Appreciation of His Work for Children." *Junior Bookshelf* 12 (July 1948): 59–65.

Greene, Ellin. "Walter de la Mare." In *Writers for Children: Critical Studies of Major Authors since the Seventeenth Century*. Edited by Jane M. Bingham. New York: Scribner, 1988, pp. 173–180.

Gulliver, Lucile. "Walter de la Mare: A Godfather Fairy." *Horn Book* 2 (Nov. 1925): 36–42.

Hopkins, Kenneth. *Walter de la Mare*. rev. ed. London: Longman, 1957.

Horn Book Magazine. Walter de la Mare special issues 18 (May–June 1942): 139–157, 33 (Oct. 1957): 195–247.

The Junior Book of Authors. 2nd rev. ed. Edited by Stanley J. Kunitz and Howard Haycraft. New York: Wilson, 1951, pp. 97–98.

Lathrop, Dorothy P. "Illustrating de la Mare." *Horn Book* 18 (May–June 1942): 188–196.

Lochhead, Marion. *Renaissance of Wonder*. New York: Harper and Row, 1980, pp. 70–76.

McCrosson, Doris Ross. *Walter de la Mare*. Boston: Twayne, 1966.

Megroz, Rodolphe Louis. *Walter de la Mare: A Biographical and Critical Study*. New York: Doran, 1924.

Miller, Bertha E. Mahony, ed. "The Books of Walter de la Mare." *Horn Book* 33 (June 1957): 235–241.

Murphy, Michael William. "The British Tale in the Early 20th Century: Walter de la Mare, A. E. Coppard, and T. F. Powys." Ph.D. dissertation, University of Wisconsin, 1971.

The Oxford Companion to Children's Literature. Edited by Humphrey Carpenter and Mari Prichard. New York: Oxford Univ. Press, 1984, pp. 145, 526.

Pflieger, Pat, and Hill, Helen M. *A Reference Guide to Modern Fantasy for Children*. Westport, CT: Greenwood Press, 1984, pp. 146–147, 529–531.

Read, Herbert. "Walter de la Mare." *Horn Book* 33 (June 1957): 209–210.

Reid, Forrest. *Walter de la Mare: A Critical Study*. London: Faber, 1929.

Stott, Jon C. *Children's Literature from A to Z*. New York: McGraw-Hill, 1984, p. 90.

Twentieth Century Children's Writers. 2nd ed. Edited by D. L. Kirkpatrick. New York: St. Martin's Press, 1983, pp. 235–237.

Walsh, William. "De la Mare's Small World." In Ford. *Young Writers, Young Readers*. London: Hutchinson, 1960, pp. 107–114.

Zanger, Jules. "*The Three Mulla Mulgars*." In *Survey of Modern Fantasy Literature*, vol. 4. Edited by Frank N. Magill. Englewood Cliffs, NJ: Salem Press, 1983, pp. 1926–1929.

Delany, Samuel R(ay), Jr.

Barbour, Douglas. "Cultural Invention and Metaphor in the Novels of Samuel R. Delany." *Foundation* 7/8 (1975): 105–121.

———. "Patterns of Meaning in the Science Fiction Novels of Ursula K. Le Guin, Joanna Russ and Samuel R. Delany, 1962–1972." Ph.D. dissertation, Queen's University (Ontario, Canada), 1976.

———. "Samuel R. Delany, Jr." In *Science Fiction Writers*. Edited by E. F. Bleiler. New York: Scribner, 1982, pp. 329–336.

———. *Worlds Out of Words: The Science Fiction Novels of Samuel R. Delany*. Frome, Somerset, U.K.: Bran's Head, 1978.

Brasswell, Laurel. "The Visionary Voyage in Science Fiction and Medieval Allegory." *Mosaic* 14 (Winter 1981): 125–142.

Bravard, Robert S., and Peplow, Michael W. "Through a Glass Darkly: Bibliographing Samuel R. Delany." *Black American Literature Forum* 18 (1984): 69–75.

Canary, Robert H. "Science Fiction as Fictive History." *Extrapolation* 16 (1974): 81–95.

Delany, Samuel R. "Generic Protocols: Science Fiction and Mundane." In *The Technological Imagination: Theories and Fictions*. Edited by Teresa De Laurentis, Andreas Huyssen, and Kathleen Woodward. Madison, WI: Coda Press, 1980, pp. 175–193.

———. "The Profession of Science Fiction: VIII: Shadows—Part 1." *Foundation* 6 (1974): 31–60. "Shadows—Part 2." *Foundation* 7/8 (1975): 122–154.

———. "Reflections on Historical Models of Modern English Language Science Fiction." *Science Fiction Studies* 7 (1980): 135–149.

———. *Starboard Wine: More Notes on the Language of Science Fiction*. Pleasantville, NY: Dragon Press, 1984.

Fox, Robert Elliot. "The Mirrors of Caliban: A Study of the Fiction of LeRoi Jones, Ishmael Reed and Samuel R. Delany." Ph.D. dissertation, State University of New York at Buffalo, 1976.

Govan, Sandra Y. "The Insistent Presence of Blackfolk in the Novels of Samuel R. Delany." *Black American Literature Forum* 18 (1984): 43–48.

Hausdorff, Don. "Introduction." In Samuel R. Delany. *The Jewels of Aptor*. Boston: Gregg, 1976.

Littlefield, Ralph Emerson. "Character and Language in Eight Novels by Ursula K. Le Guin and Samuel R. Delany." Ph.D. dissertation, Florida State University, 1984.

McEvoy, Seth. *Samuel R. Delany*. New York: Ungar, 1984.

Peplow, Michael W. "Meet Samuel Delany: Black Science Fiction Writer." *The Crisis* 86 (Apr. 1979): 115–121.

Peplow, Michael W., and Bravard, Robert S. *Samuel R. Delany: A Primary and Secondary Bibliography, 1962–1979*. Boston: G. K. Hall, 1980.

———. "Samuel R. Delany: A Selective Primary and Secondary Bibliography, 1979–1983." *Black American Literature Forum* 18 (1984): 75–77.

Platt, Charles. *Dream Makers: The Uncommon People Who Write Science Fiction*. New York: Berkley, 1980, pp. 69–76. Interview.

Rabkin, Eric S. "Metalinguistics and Science Fiction." *Critical Inquiry* 6 (1979): 79–97.

Samuelson, David N. "Tales of Nevèrÿon." In *Survey of Modern Fantasy Literature*, vol. 4. Edited by Frank N. Magill. Englewood Cliffs, NJ: Salem Press, 1983, pp. 1875–1879.

Schuyler, William M., Jr. "Heroes and History." In *The Intersection of Science Fiction and Philosophy*. Edited by Robert E. Myers. Westport, CT: Greenwood Press, 1983, pp. 197–210.

Schweitzer, Darrell. "*Algol* Interview: Samuel R. Delany." *Algol* 13 (1976): 16–20.

Searles, Baird; Meacham, Beth; and Franklin, Michael. *A Reader's Guide to Fantasy*. New York: Avon, 1982, pp. 53–54.

Slusser, George Edgar. *The Delany Intersection: Samuel R. Delany Considered as a Writer of Semi-Precious Words*. San Bernardino, CA: Borgo Press, 1977.

Somay, Bulent. "Towards an Open-Ended Utopia." *Science Fiction Studies* 11 (1984): 25–38.

Spencer, Kathleen L. "Deconstructing *Tales of Nevèrÿon:* Delany, Derrida, and 'The Modular Calculus, Parts I–IV.' " *Essays in Arts and Sciences* 14 (May 1985): 59–89.

Sullivan, Charles W., III. "*The Jewels of Aptor*." In *Survey of Modern Fantasy Literature*, vol. 2. Edited by Frank N. Magill. Englewood Cliffs, NJ: Salem Press, 1983, pp. 798–800.

Twentieth-Century Science Fiction Writers. 2nd ed. Edited by Curtis C. Smith. Chicago: St. James Press, 1986, pp. 184–186.

Weedman, Jane Branham. "Art and the Artist's Role in Delany's Works." In *Voices for the Future,* vol. 3. Edited by Thomas D. Clareson and Thomas L. Wymer. Bowling Green, OH: Bowling Green Univ. Press, 1984, pp. 151–187.
———. *Reader's Guide to Samuel R. Delany.* Mercer Island, WA: Starmont, 1982.
———. "Samuel R. Delany: Present-Day Cultures in Future Literary Worlds." Ph.D. dissertation, State University of New York at Buffalo, 1979.

De Larrabeiti, Michael

Zipes, Jack. "The Adventure of Fantasy as Struggle for Survival." *Children's Literature,* vol. 7. Storrs, CT: Parousia Press, 1978, pp. 242–247.

De Leeuw, Adele Louise

The Junior Book of Authors. 2nd rev. ed. Edited by Stanley J. Kunitz and Howard Haycraft. New York: Wilson, 1951, pp. 98–100.

Denslow, W(illiam) W(allace)

Fourth Book of Junior Authors and Illustrators. Edited by Doris De Montreville and Elizabeth D. Crawford. New York: Wilson, 1978, pp. 113–115.
Hanff, Peter E., and Greene, Douglas G. *Bibliographia Oziana.* Demorest, GA: International Wizard of Oz Club, 1976.

De Regniers, Beatrice Schenk (Freedman)

More Junior Authors. Edited by Muriel Fuller. New York: Wilson, 1963, p. 65.
Twentieth Century Children's Writers. 2nd ed. Edited by D. L. Kirkpatrick. New York: St. Martin's Press, 1983, pp. 239–241.

De Weese, (Thomas Eu)Gene

Twentieth–Century Science Fiction Writers. 2nd ed. Edited by Curtis C. Smith. Chicago: St. James Press, 1986, pp. 193–194.

Dickens, Charles (John Huffam)

Adrian, Arthur A. *Dickens and the Parent–Child Relationship.* Athens: Ohio Univ. Press, 1984.
Dickens, Charles. "Frauds on the Fairies." *Household Words* 8 (Oct. 5, 1853): 97–100. Reprinted in *Masterworks of Children's Literature,* vol. VI. New York: Stonehill/ Chelsea House, 1984, pp. 55–62; and in Lance Salway. *A Peculiar Gift.* Harmondsworth, Middlesex: Kestrel, 1967, pp. 111–118.
Doyle, Brian. *The Who's Who of Children's Literature.* New York: Schocken, 1968, pp. 75–76.
Fraden, Rena. "The Sentimental Tradition in Dickens and Hawthorne." Ph.D. dissertation, Yale University, 1983.
Freeman, Ann. "A Comparative Study of Hans Christian Andersen and Charles Dickens: The Relationship between Spiritual and Material Value Systems as Defined by Their Treatment of the Child." Ph.D. dissertation, University of California, Berkeley, 1979.
Glancy, Ruth R. *Dickens's Christmas Books, Children's Stories, and Other Short Fiction: An Annotated Bibliography.* New York: Garland, 1985.

Hearn, Michael Patrick. "Charles Dickens." In *Writers for Children: Critical Studies of Major Authors since the Seventeenth Century.* Edited by Jane M. Bingham. New York: Scribner, 1988, pp. 181–192.

Hodges, Margaret. "Dickens for Children." *Horn Book* 58 (Dec. 1982): 626–635.

Jackson, Rosemary. *Fantasy: The Literature of Subversion.* New York: Methuen, 1980, pp. 5, 10, 15, 47, 108, 123–124, 126–127, 133, 153, 172, 180.

Miller, Patricia. "The Importance of Being Earnest: The Fairy Tale in 19th-Century England." *Children's Literature Association Quarterly* 7 (Summer 1982): 11–14.

Stableford, Brian. "Charles Dickens." In *Supernatural Fiction Writers: Fantasy and Horror,* vol. 1. Edited by E. F. Bleiler. New York: Scribner, 1985, pp. 213–218.

———. "Christmas Stories." In *Survey of Modern Fantasy Literature,* vol. 1. Edited by Frank N. Magill. Englewood Cliffs, NJ: Salem Press, 1983, pp. 242–247.

Stone, Harry. "Dark Corners of the Mind: Dickens' Childhood Reading." *Horn Book* 39 (June 1963): 306–321.

Tremper, Ellen. "Commitment and Escape: The Fairy Tales of Thackeray, Dickens, and Wilde." *The Lion and the Unicorn* 2 (Spring 1978): 38–47.

Dickinson, Peter (pseud. of Malcolm de Brissac)

Antczak, Janice. *Science Fiction: The Mythos of a New Romance.* New York: Neal–Schuman, 1985, pp. 53, 162, 186.

Crouch, Marcus. *The Nesbit Tradition.* Totowa, NJ: Rowman and Littlefield, 1972, pp. 50–52.

Dickinson, Mike. "The Blue Hawk." In *Survey of Modern Fantasy Literature,* vol. 1. Edited by Frank N. Magill. Englewood Cliffs, NJ: Salem Press, 1983, pp. 132–136.

Dickinson, Peter. "The Burden of the Past." In *Innocence & Experience.* Edited by Barbara Harrison and Gregory Maguire. New York: Lothrop, 1987, pp. 91–101.

———. "The Day of the Tennis Rabbit." *Quarterly Journal of the Library of Congress* 38 (Fall 1981): 203–220.

———. "Fantasy: The Need for Realism." *Children's Literature in Education* 17 (Spring 1986): 39–51. Paper given at the Fourth *Bookquest* Conference, Brighton Polytechnic, Spring 1984.

Fourth Book of Junior Authors and Illustrators. Edited by Doris De Montreville and Elizabeth D. Crawford. New York: Wilson, 1978, pp. 117–118.

Grimshaw, Nigel. "Peter Dickinson's Children's Stories." *School Librarian* 22 (Sept. 1974): 219–223.

Hutchison, Joanna. "Peter Dickinson Considered, In and Out of the Classroom." *Children's Literature in Education* 17 (Summer 1975): 88–98.

The Oxford Companion to Children's Literature. Edited by Humphrey Carpenter and Mari Prichard. New York: Oxford Univ. Press, 1984, pp. 148–149.

Rees, David. "Plums and Roughage—Peter Dickinson." In *Painted Desert, Green Shade.* Boston: Horn Book, 1984, pp. 153–167.

Searles, Baird; Meacham, Beth; and Franklin, Michael. *A Reader's Guide to Fantasy.* New York: Avon, 1982, pp. 55–56.

Townsend, John Rowe. "Peter Dickinson." In *A Sounding of Storytellers.* Philadelphia: Lippincott, 1979, pp. 41–54.

Twentieth Century Children's Writers. 2nd ed. Edited by D. L. Kirkpatrick. New York: St. Martin's Press, 1983, pp. 243–245.

Twentieth–Century Science Fiction Writers. 2nd ed. Edited by Curtis C. Smith. Chicago: St. James Press, 1986, pp. 197–199.

Williams, Jay. "Very Iffy Books: An Interview with Peter Dickinson." *Signal* 13 (Jan. 1974): 21–29.

Dickson, Gordon R(upert)

Clute, John. "Gordon Dickson." In *Science Fiction Writers*. Edited by E. F. Bleiler. New York: Scribner, 1982, pp. 345–350.

Dickson, Gordon R. "Plausibility in Science Fiction." In *Science Fiction Today and Tomorrow*. Edited by Reginald Bretnor. New York: Harper and Row, 1974, pp. 295–308.

Lane, Daryl; Vernon, William; and Carlson, David. *The Sound of Wonder: Interviews from "The Science Fiction Radio Show,"* vol. 2. Phoenix, AZ: Oryx Press, 1985, pp. 159–173.

McMurry, Clifford. "An Interview with Gordon R. Dickson." *Science Fiction Review* 7 (July 1978): 6–12.

Miesel, Sandra. "*Algol* Interview: Gordon R. Dickson." *Algol* 15 (Spring 1978): 33–38.

———. "The Plume and the Sword; Gordon Dickson: A Biographical Sketch of the Man and His Work." *Destinies* 2 (1980): 116–131.

Schweitzer, Darrell, ed. *Science Fiction Voices*. Baltimore: T–K Graphics, 1976. Interview.

Searles, Baird; Meacham, Beth; and Franklin, Michael. *A Reader's Guide to Fantasy*. New York: Avon, 1982, pp. 56–57.

Thompson, Raymond H. *Gordon R. Dickson: A Primary and Secondary Bibliography*. Boston: G. K. Hall, 1983.

———. "Gordon R. Dickson: Science Fiction for Young Canadians." *Canadian Children's Literature* 15/16 (Summer 1980): 38–46.

Twentieth–Century Science Fiction Writers. 2nd ed. Edited by Curtis C. Smith. Chicago: St. James Press, 1986, pp. 199–201.

Watson, Christine. "*The Dragon and the George*." In *Survey of Modern Fantasy Literature*, vol. 1. Edited by Frank N. Magill. Englewood Cliffs, NJ: Salem Press, 1983, pp. 418–422.

Dolbier, Maurice (Wyman)

Helbig, Alethea K., and Perkins, Agnes Regan. *Dictionary of American Children's Fiction, 1859–1959*. Westport, CT: Greenwood Press, 1985, pp. 132–133, 323.

More Junior Authors. Edited by Muriel Fuller. New York: Wilson, 1963, p. 69.

Donaldson, Stephen R.

Bacon, Jonathan. "Interview with Stephen R. Donaldson." *Fantasy Crossroads* 15 (1979): 11–16.

Barkley, Christine. "Donaldson as Heir to Tolkien." *Mythlore* 38 (1984): 50–57.

Clute, John. "*The Chronicles of Thomas Covenant the Unbeliever* and *The Second Chronicles of Thomas Covenant*." In *Survey of Modern Fantasy Literature*, vol. 1 Edited by Frank N. Magill. Englewood Cliffs, NJ: Salem Press, 1983, pp. 266–274.

Donaldson, Stephen R. *Epic Fantasy in the Modern World: A Few Observations*. Kent, OH: Kent State Univ. Libraries, 1986.

Fonstad, Karen Wynn. *The Atlas of the Land*. New York: Del Rey, 1985.

Gentle, Mary. "Godmakers and Worldshapers: Fantasy and Metaphysics." *Vector* 106 (1982): 8–14.

Godfrey, R. J. "Peake and Donaldson: A Comparative Study of Their Fantasies." *The Mervyn Peake Review* 11 (1980): 26–34.

"An Interview with Stephen Donaldson." *Extro Science Fiction* (Feb.–Mar. 1982): 7–9.

Lane, Daryl; Vernon, William; and Carlson, David. *The Sound of Wonder: Interviews from "The Science Fiction Radio Show,"* vol. 1. Phoenix, AZ: Oryx Press, 1985 pp. 1–21.

Myers, Walter E. "Stephen R. Donaldson." In *Supernatural Fiction Writers: Fantasy and Horror,* vol. 2. Edited by E. F. Bleiler. New York: Scribner, 1985, pp. 1009–1014.

Paulsen, Steven. "An Interview with Stephen Donaldson." *Dark Horizons* 27 (1984): 3–8.

Paxon, Diana. "The Tolkien Tradition." *Mythlore* 39 (1984): 23–27, 37.

Rich, Calvin, and Ingersol, Earl. "A Conversation with Stephen R. Donaldson." *Mythlore* 46 (1986): 23–26.

Slethaug, Gordon E. "No Exit: The Hero as Victim in Donaldson." *Mythlore* 40 (1984): 22–27.

Timmerman, John H. *Other Worlds: The Fantasy Genre.* Bowling Green, OH: Bowling Green Univ. Press, 1983, pp. 103–115.

Vance, Michael. "Interview: Stephen Donaldson." *Fantasy Review* 85 (1985): 8–10, 14.

Wilgus, Neal. "An Interview with Stephen R. Donaldson." *Science Fiction Review* 8 (Mar.–Apr. 1979): 26–29.

Wilson, Andrew J. "Melding for Beginners: Language and Names in *The Illearth War.*" *Dark Horizons* 24 (1981): 9–13.

Donovan, John

Fifth Book of Junior Authors and Illustrators. Edited by Sally Holmes Holtze. New York: Wilson, 1983, pp. 103–104.

Goldman, Suzy. "John Donovan: Sexuality, Stereotypes and Self." *The Lion and the Unicorn* 2 (Fall 1978): 27–36.

Helbig, Alethea K., and Perkins, Agnes Regan. *Dictionary of American Children's Fiction, 1960–1984.* Westport, CT: Greenwood Press, 1986, pp. 163–164.

Twentieth Century Children's Writers. 2nd ed. Edited by D. L. Kirkpatrick. New York: St. Martin's Press, 1983, p. 248.

Drury, Roger W(olcott)

Drury, Roger W. "Realism Plus Fantasy Equals Magic." *Horn Book* 48 (Apr. 1972): 113–119. Reprinted in Heins. *Crosscurrents of Criticism.* Boston: Horn Book, 1977, pp. 178–184.

Helbig, Alethea K., and Perkins, Agnes Regan. *Dictionary of American Children's Fiction, 1960–1984.* Westport, CT: Greenwood Press, 1986, pp. 107–108, 171.

Duane, Diane (Elizabeth)

Duane, Diane. "Watching the Sparks Fly Upward: Six Months after *The Door into Fire.*" *Empire* 4 (Sept. 1979): 10–12.

Elliot, Jeffrey. "Interview with Diane Duane." *Starship* 40 (1980): 17–24.

Reimer, James D. "Masculinity and Feminist Fantasy Authors." *Science Fiction and Fantasy Review* 66 (1984): 19–21.

Twentieth–Century Science Fiction Writers. 2nd ed. Edited by Curtis C. Smith. Chicago: St. James Press, 1986, pp. 210–211.

Du Bois, William (Sherman) Pène

Bader, Barbara. *American Picturebooks.* New York: Macmillan, 1976, pp. 175–186.

Burkert, Nancy Ekholm. "A Second Look: *Lion.*" *Horn Book* 56 (Dec. 1980): 671–676.

Doyle, Brian. *The Who's Who of Children's Literature.* New York: Schocken, 1968, pp. 81–82.

Du Bois, William Pène. "Animal History Will Bear This Out." In *Contents of the Basket and Other Papers on Children's Books and Reading.* New York: New York Public Library, 1960, pp. 35–39.

———. "Newbery Acceptance Paper—1947." *Horn Book* 24 (July 1948): 235–244.

Du Bois, Yvonne. "William Pène Du Bois, Boy and Artist." *Horn Book* 24 (July 1948): 245–249.

Helbig, Alethea K., and Perkins, Agnes Regan. *Dictionary of American Children's Fiction, 1859–1959.* Westport, CT: Greenwood Press, 1985, pp. 139–140, 165–166, 180–181, 539.

———. *Dictionary of American Children's Fiction, 1960–1984.* Westport, CT: Greenwood Press, 1986, p. 172.

The Junior Book of Authors. 2nd rev. ed. Edited by Stanley J. Kunitz and Howard Haycraft. New York: Wilson, 1951, pp. 102–104.

Miller, Bertha Mahony, and Field, Elinor Whitney, eds. *Newbery Medal Books: 1922–1955.* Boston: Horn Book, 1957, pp. 300–317.

The Oxford Companion to Children's Literature. Edited by Humphrey Carpenter and Mari Prichard. New York: Oxford Univ. Press, 1984, pp. 158, 547.

Roginski, Jim, ed. *Newbery and Caldecott Medalists and Honor Book Winners.* Littleton, CO: Libraries Unlimited, 1982, pp. 91–92.

Stott, Jon C. *Children's Literature from A to Z.* New York: McGraw-Hill, 1984, p. 95.

Twentieth Century Children's Writers. 2nd ed. Edited by D. L. Kirkpatrick. New York: St. Martin's Press, 1983, pp. 250–251.

Duggan, Maurice (Noel)

Twentieth Century Children's Writers. 2nd ed. Edited by D. L. Kirkpatrick. New York: St. Martin's Press, 1983, p. 251.

Dunsany, Lord (pseud. of Edward John Morton Drax Plunkett)

Branham, Robert J. "Fantasy and Inaffability: Fiction at the Limits of Language." *Extrapolation* 24 (1983): 66–79.

Cantrell, Brent. "British Fairy Tradition in *The King of Elfland's Daughter.*" *The Romantist* 4–5 (1980–1981): 51–53.

Clute, John. "*The King of Elfland's Daughter.*" In *Survey of Modern Fantasy Literature,* vol. 2. Edited by Frank N. Magill. Englewood Cliffs, NJ: Salem Press, 1983, pp. 848–851.

De Camp, L. Sprague. *Literary Swordsmen and Sorcerers: The Makers of Heroic Fantasy.* Sauk City, WI: Arkham House, 1976.

De Casseres, Benjamin. "Lord Dunsany." *Studies in Weird Fiction* 1 (Summer 1986): 33–34.

Eckley, Grace. "The Short Fiction of Dunsany." In *Survey of Modern Fantasy Literature,* vol. 3. Edited by Frank N. Magill. Englewood Cliffs, NJ: Salem Press, 1983, pp. 1507–1510.

Gardner, Martin. "Lord Dunsany." In *Supernatural Fiction Writers,* vol. 1. Edited by E. F. Bleiler. New York: Scribner, 1985, pp. 471–478.

Mahoney, Patrick. "Lord Dunsany's Centennial: A Memoir." *Érie* 14 (1979): 126–130.

Manlove, C. N. *The Impulse of Fantasy Literature*. Kent, OH: Kent State Univ. Press, 1983.

Ringel, Faye Joyce. "Patterns of the Hero and the Quest: Epic, Romance, Fantasy." Ph.D. dissertation, Brown University, 1979.

Schweitzer, Darrell. "Lord Dunsany: Grand Master of Wonder." *The Eildon Tree* 1, no. 1 (1974): 4–7.

———. "The Novels of Lord Dunsany." *Mythlore* 25 (1980): 39–42. "Part 2." *Mythlore* 26 (1981): 39–41.

Shippey, T. A. *"The Charwoman's Shadow."* In *Survey of Modern Fantasy Literature*, vol. 1. Edited by Frank N. Magill. Englewood Cliffs, NJ: Salem Press, 1983, pp. 232–235.

Twentieth–Century Science Fiction Writers. 2nd ed. Edited by Curtis C. Smith. Chicago: St. James Press, 1986, p. 863.

Eager, Edward (McMaken)

Doyle, Brian. *The Who's Who of Children's Literature*. New York: Schocken, 1968, pp. 83–84.

Eager, Edward. "Daily Magic." *Horn Book* 34 (Oct. 1958): 349–358.

———. "A Father's Minority Report." *Horn Book* 24 (March 1948): 104–109.

Helbig, Alethea K., and Perkins, Agnes Regan. *Dictionary of American Children's Fiction, 1859–1959*. Westport, CT: Greenwood Press, 1985, pp. 141, 200, 276–277, 322–323.

———. *Dictionary of American Children's Fiction, 1960–1984*. Westport, CT: Greenwood Press, 1986, pp. 179, 588.

More Junior Authors. Edited by Muriel Fuller. New York: Wilson, 1963, pp. 71–72.

Searles, Baird; Meacham, Beth; and Franklin, Michael. *A Reader's Guide to Fantasy*. New York: Avon, 1982, pp. 59–60.

Spivack, Charlotte. "Edward Eager." In Cech. *American Writers for Children, 1900–1960. Dictionary of Literary Biography*, vol. 22. Detroit: Gale, 1983, pp. 135–139.

Twentieth Century Children's Writers. 2nd ed. Edited by D. L. Kirkpatrick. New York: St. Martin's Press, 1983, pp. 257–258.

Eddison, E(rik) R(ucker)

Attebery, Brian. "E. R. Eddison." In *Supernatural Fiction Writers: Fantasy and Horror*, vol. 2. Edited by E. F. Bleiler. New York: Scribner, 1985, pp. 529–534.

———. "The Zimiamvian Trilogy." In *Survey of Modern Fantasy Literature*, vol. 5. Edited by Frank N. Magill. Englewood Cliffs, NJ: Salem Press, 1983, pp. 2206–2213.

De Camp, L. Sprague. *Literary Swordsmen and Sorcerers: The Makers of Heroic Fantasy*. Sauk City, WI: Arkham House, 1976.

———, ed. *The Blade of Conan*. New York: Ace, 1979.

Fredericks, Casey. *The Future of Eternity: Mythologies of Science Fiction and Fantasy*. Bloomington: Indiana Univ. Press, 1982.

Lewis, C. S. *On Stories and Other Essays on Literature*. Edited by Walter Hooper. New York: Harcourt Brace Jovanovich, 1982.

Paul, Terri. *"The Worm Ouroboros:* Time Travel, Imagination and Entropy." *Extrapolation* 24 (1983): 272–279.

Pesch, Helmut W. "The Sign of the Worm: Images of Death and Immortality in the Fiction of E. R. Eddison." In *Death and the Serpent*. Edited by Carl B. Yoke and Donald M. Hassler. Westport, CT: Greenwood Press, 1985, pp. 91–102.

Schuyler, William M., Jr. "Recent Developments in Spell Construction." In *The Aes-*

thetics of Fantasy Literature and Art. Edited by Roger C. Schlobin. South Bend, IN: Univ. of Notre Dame Press, 1982, pp. 237–248.

Stableford, Brian. *"The Worm Ouroboros."* In *Survey of Modern Fantasy Literature,* vol. 5. Edited by Frank N. Magill. Englewood Cliffs, NJ: Salem Press, 1983, pp. 2180–2184.

Twentieth-Century Science Fiction Writers. 2nd ed. Edited by Curtis C. Smith. Chicago: St. James Press, 1986, p. 863.

Wilson, Andrew J. "If It's Wednesday This Must Be Narnia: Exploring the Links between Phantasy and Reality." *Dark Horizons* 24 (1981): 19–23.

Wilson, Sharon. "The Doctrine of Organic Unity: E. R. Eddison and the Romance Tradition." *Extrapolation* 25 (1984): 12–19.

Edmonds, Walter D(umaux)

Carmer, C. "Walter Edmonds of Black River Valley." *Publishers Weekly* 141 (June 27, 1942): 2346–2348.

Helbig, Alethea K., and Perkins, Agnes Regan. *Dictionary of American Children's Fiction, 1859–1959.* Westport, CT: Greenwood Press, 1985, p. 144.

———. *Dictionary of American Children's Fiction, 1960–1984.* Westport, CT: Greenwood Press, 1986, p. 185.

Hopkins, Lee Bennett. "Walter D. Edmonds." In *More Books by More People.* New York: Citation Press, 1974, pp. 138–140.

Miller, Bertha Mahony, and Field, Elinor Whitney, eds. *Newbery Medal Books, 1922–1955.* Boston: Horn Book, 1957, pp. 208–224.

More Junior Authors. Edited by Muriel Fuller. New York: Wilson, 1963, p. 73.

Roginski, Jim, ed. *Newbery and Caldecott Medalists and Honor Book Winners.* Littleton, CO: Libraries Unlimited, 1982, pp. 98–99.

Twentieth Century Children's Writers. 2nd ed. Edited by D. L. Kirkpatrick. New York: St. Martin's Press, 1983, pp. 258–260.

Wyld, Lionel D. *Walter D. Edmonds, Storyteller.* Syracuse, NY: Syracuse Univ. Press, 1982.

Edwards, Dorothy (Brown)

Twentieth Century Children's Writers. 2nd ed. Edited by D. L. Kirkpatrick. New York: St. Martin's Press, 1983, pp. 260–261.

Eisenstein, Phyllis

Eisenstein, Phyllis. "The Profession of Science Fiction, 28: Science Fiction and Me." *Foundation* 25 (1982): 31–35.

Friend, Beverly. "Time Travel as a Feminist Didactic in Works by Phyllis Eisenstein, Marlys Millhiser, and Octavia Butler." *Extrapolation* 23 (1982): 50–55.

Sanders, Jo. *"Sorcerer's Son."* In *Survey of Modern Fantasy Literature,* vol. 4. Edited by Frank N. Magill. Englewood Cliffs, NJ: Salem Press, 1983, pp. 1780–1783.

Searles, Baird; Meacham, Beth; and Franklin, Michael. *A Reader's Guide to Fantasy.* New York: Avon, 1982, pp. 61–62.

Twentieth–Century Science Fiction Writers. 2nd ed. Edited by Curtis C. Smith. Chicago: St. James Press, 1986, pp. 218–219.

Elgin, (Patricia Anne) Suzette Haden

Attebery, Brian. "Women's Coming of Age in Fantasy." *Extrapolation* 28 (Spring 1987): 10–22.

Bray, Mary Kay. "The Naming of Things: Men and Women, Language and Reality in Suzette Haden Elgin's *Native Tongue.*" *Extrapolation* 27 (1986): 49–61.

Chapman, Edgar L. "Sex, Satire, and Feminism in the Science Fiction of Suzette Haden Elgin." In *The Feminine Eye.* Edited by Tom Staicar. New York: Ungar, 1982.

Jakiel, S. James, and Levinthal, Rosandra E. "The Laws of Time Travel." *Extrapolation* 21 (1980): 130–138.

"Suzette Haden Elgin Creates 'Women's Language.' " *Science Fiction Chronicle* 6 (Aug. 1985): 4.

Twentieth–Century Science Fiction Writers. 2nd ed. Edited by Curtis C. Smith. Chicago: St. James Press, 1986, pp. 223–225.

Elkin, Benjamin

Fourth Book of Junior Authors and Illustrators. Edited by Doris De Montreville and Elizabeth D. Crawford. New York: Wilson, 1978, pp. 120–122.

Ende, Michael

Filmer, Kath. "Beware the Nothing: An Allegorical Reading of Ende's *The Neverending Story.*" *Mythlore* 46 (1986): 34–36.

Fleischer, Leonore. "Talk of the Trade: Off to Fantastica." *Publishers Weekly* 244 (Oct. 7, 1983): 95.

Luserke, Uwe. "*The Neverending Story.*" *Space Voyager* 14 (1985): 56–59.

Neumeyer, Peter F. "An Exhortation: Michael Ende, Father Goose, and the Confusion of Categories." *Journal of Aesthetic Education* 21 (Fall 1987): 45–51.

Enright, Elizabeth (Wright)

Cameron, Eleanor. "The Art of Elizabeth Enright." *Horn Book* 45 (Dec. 1969): 641–651; continued in 46 (Feb. 1970): 26–30.

Enright, Elizabeth. "Acceptance Speech, Newbery Medal." *Horn Book* 15 (July 1939): 231–236.

———. *Doublefields: Memories and Stories.* New York: Harcourt Brace Jovanovich, 1966.

———. "Realism in Children's Literature." *Horn Book* 43 (Apr. 1967): 165–170.

Gendron, Charisse. "Elizabeth Enright." In Cech. *American Writers for Children, 1900–1960. Dictionary of Literary Biography,* vol. 22. Detroit: Gale, 1983, pp. 140–145.

Helbig, Alethea K., and Perkins, Agnes Regan. *Dictionary of American Children's Fiction, 1859–1959.* Westport, CT: Greenwood Press, 1985, p. 150.

———. *Dictionary of American Children's Fiction, 1960–1984.* Westport, CT: Greenwood Press, 1986, pp. 196–197, 647–648.

The Junior Book of Authors. 2nd rev. ed. Edited by Stanley J. Kunitz and Howard Haycraft. New York: Wilson, 1951, p. 113.

Miller, Bertha Mahony, and Field, Elinor Whitney, eds. *Newbery Medal Books: 1922–1955.* Boston: Horn Book, 1957, pp. 166–175.

The Oxford Companion to Children's Literature. Edited by Humphrey Carpenter and Mari Prichard. New York: Oxford Univ. Press, 1984, p. 168.

Roginski, Jim, ed. *Newbery and Caldecott Medalists and Honor Book Winners*. Littleton, CO: Libraries Unlimited, 1982, pp. 103–104.

Smaridge, Norah. *Famous Modern Storytellers for Young People*. New York: Dodd, 1969, pp. 38–43.

Smedman, M. Sarah. "Elizabeth Enright." In *Writers for Children: Critical Studies of Major Authors since the Seventeenth Century*. Edited by Jane M. Bingham. New York: Scribner, 1988, pp. 215–220.

Twentieth Century Children's Writers. 2nd ed. Edited by D. L. Kirkpatrick. New York: St. Martin's Press, 1983, pp. 264–265.

Ensley, Evangeline *see* Walton, Evangeline

Ershov, Petr Pavlovich

The Oxford Companion to Children's Literature. Edited by Humphrey Carpenter and Mari Prichard. New York: Oxford Univ. Press, 1984, pp. 315–316.

Estes, Eleanor

Altsteter, Mabel F. "Eleanor Estes and Her Books." *Elementary English* 29 (May 1952): 245–251.

Donnelly, E. "The 'Way' of Eleanor Estes." *Ontario Library Review* 40 (May 1956): 93–94.

Estes, Eleanor. "Gathering Honey." *Horn Book* 36 (Dec. 1960): 487–494.

———. "Newbery Award Acceptance." *Horn Book* 28 (Aug. 1952): 261–270.

———. "What Makes a Good Book?" *Writer* 48 (Nov. 1935).

———. "Writing for Children." *Writer* 66 (Apr. 1953): 109–111.

Helbig, Alethea K., and Perkins, Agnes Regan. *Dictionary of American Children's Fiction, 1859–1959*. Westport, CT: Greenwood Press, 1985, pp. 150–151.

———. *Dictionary of American Children's Fiction, 1960–1984*. Westport, CT: Greenwood Press, 1986, pp. 199, 735.

Hopkins, Lee Bennett. "Eleanor Estes." In *More Books by More People*. New York: Citation Press, 1974, pp. 147–152.

The Junior Book of Authors. 2nd rev. ed. Edited by Stanley J. Kunitz and Howard Haycraft. New York: Wilson, 1951, pp. 114–115.

Miller, Bertha Mahony, and Field, Elinor Whitney, eds. *Newbery Medal Books: 1922–1955*. Boston: Horn Book, 1957, pp. 372–387.

Rice, Mabel R. "Eleanor Estes: A Study in Versatility." *Elementary English* 45 (May 1968): 553–557.

Roginski, Jim, ed. *Newbery and Caldecott Medalists and Honor Book Winners*. Littleton, CO: Libraries Unlimited, 1982, pp. 104–105.

Sayers, Frances Clarke. "The Books of Eleanor Estes." *Horn Book* 28 (Aug. 1952): 257–260. Reprinted in Sayers. *Summoned by Books*. New York: Viking Press, 1965, pp. 116–121.

Stott, Jon C. *Children's Literature from A to Z*. New York: McGraw-Hill, 1984, p. 100.

Townsend, John Rowe. *A Sense of Story: Essays on Contemporary Writers for Children*. Philadelphia: Lippincott, 1971, pp. 79–88.

Twentieth Century Children's Writers. 2nd ed. Edited by D. L. Kirkpatrick. New York: St. Martin's Press, 1983, pp. 265–266.

Wolf, Virginia L. "Eleanor Estes." In Cech. *American Writers for Children, 1900–1960. Dictionary of Literary Biography*, vol. 22. Detroit: Gale, 1983, pp. 146–156.

Ewing, Juliana (Horatia Gatty)

Avery, Gillian. "Juliana Horatia Ewing." In *Writers for Children: Critical Studies of Major Authors since the Seventeenth Century.* Edited by Jane M. Bingham. New York: Scribner, 1988, pp. 221–226.

———. *Mrs. Ewing.* New York: Walck, 1964. Originally published London: Bodley Head, 1961.

Binding, P. M. "Mrs. Ewing: A Critical Appreciation of Her Work." B. Litt. thesis, Oxford University, 1969.

Downie, Mary Alice. "Mrs. Ewing in Canada." *Horn Book* 43 (Dec. 1967): 721–725.

Doyle, Brian. *The Who's Who of Children's Literature.* New York: Schocken, 1968, pp. 90–91.

Kent, Muriel. "Juliana Horatia Ewing (1841–1885)." *Junior Bookshelf* 5 (Dec. 1941): 123–128.

Kilby, H. T. "Yorkshire Genius: Juliana Horatia Ewing; A Note on Her Popular Children's Books and Their Illustrators." *Apollo* 41 (Apr. 1945): 102–103.

Laski, Marghanita. *Mrs. Ewing, Mrs. Molesworth, and Mrs. Hodgson Burnett.* New York: Oxford Univ. Press, 1951.

Maxwell, Christabel. *Mrs. Gatty and Mrs. Ewing.* London: Constable, 1949.

The Oxford Companion to Children's Literature. Edited by Humphrey Carpenter and Mari Prichard. New York: Oxford Univ. Press, 1984, pp. 86, 171–172, 323.

Twentieth Century Children's Writers. 2nd ed. Edited by D. L. Kirkpatrick. New York: St. Martin's Press, 1983, p. 867.

Whitney, Elinor. "Country Tales of Juliana Horatia Ewing." *Horn Book* 2 (Mar. 1926): 12–16.

Yates, Elizabeth. "Juliana Horatia Ewing." *Junior Bookshelf* 2 (July 1938): 183–186.

Fairstar, Mrs. *see* Horne, Richard Henry

Farber, Norma (Holzman)

Bagnall, Norma. "Profile: Norma Farber." *Language Arts* 58 (Apr. 1981): 481–486.

Harrison, Barbara. "Norma H. Farber 1909–1984." *Horn Book* 60 (June 1984): 404.

Helbig, Alethea K. "Bravura and Skill Yield Kernels of Truth: Norma Farber's Poetry for the Young." *Children's Literature Association Quarterly* 9 (Summer 1984): 79–80.

Twentieth Century Children's Writers. 2nd ed. Edited by D. L. Kirkpatrick. New York: St. Martin's Press, 1983, pp. 268–269.

Farjeon, Eleanor

Andrews, Sheryl R. "A Second Look: *The Glass Slipper.*" *Horn Book* 53 (Apr. 1977): 193–194.

Blakelock, Denys. *Eleanor: Portrait of a Farjeon.* London: Gollancz, 1966.

———. "In Search of Elsie Piddock: An Echo of Eleanor Farjeon." *Horn Book* 44 (Feb. 1968): 17–23; and *Junior Bookshelf* 32, no. 1 (Feb. 1968): 17–23.

Cameron, Eleanor. "A Fine Old Gentleman." In *The Green and Burning Tree.* Boston: Little, Brown, 1962, pp. 317–334.

Colwell, Eileen H. *Eleanor Farjeon.* New York: Walck, 1961.

———. "Eleanor Farjeon: A Centenary View." *Horn Book* 57 (July 1981): 280–287.

———. "Our Friend, Eleanor Farjeon." *Junior Bookshelf* 28 (Aug. 1965): 205–208.

Crouch, Marcus S. "Eleanor Farjeon." *Junior Bookshelf* 20 (July 1956): 110–114.

Doyle, Brian. *The Who's Who of Children's Literature.* New York: Schocken, 1968, pp. 93–95.

Farjeon, Annabel. *Morning Has Broken: A Biography of Eleanor Farjeon.* New York: Watts, 1986.

Farjeon, Eleanor. "A Comedy in Wax, or Lucy and Their Majesties." *Horn Book* 41 (Aug. 1965): 358–363.

———. "A London Letter from Eleanor Farjeon." *Horn Book* 19 (Mar. 1941): 90–92.

———. *Magic Casements.* London: Allen & Unwin, 1941.

———. *A Nursery in the Nineties.* rev. ed. New York: Oxford Univ. Press, 1960. Original U.S. title: *Portrait of a Family,* 1934.

———. "A Pepperpot Question." *Horn Book* 18 (May 1942): 149–151.

———. "Regina Award Acceptance." *Horn Book* 35 (Apr. 1959): 105–108.

Fish, Helen Dean. "The Spring–Green Lady: Eleanor Farjeon." *Horn Book* 6 (Feb. 1930): 10–16.

Fisher, Margery. "Eleanor Farjeon: In Memorium." *Bookbird* 4 (1965): 3–10.

Graham, Eleanor. "Eleanor Farjeon—A Study and an Appreciation." *Junior Bookshelf* 5 (July 1941): 81–86.

Greene, Ellin. "Eleanor Farjeon." In *Writers for Children: Critical Studies of Major Authors since the Seventeenth Century.* Edited by Jane M. Bingham. New York: Scribner, 1988, pp. 227–234.

———. "Eleanor Farjeon: The Shaping of a Literary Imagination." Ed.D. dissertation, Rutgers University, 1979. Reprinted in *Proceedings of the Ninth Annual Conference of the Children's Literature Association.* University of Florida, March 1983. Ypsilanti, MI: Children's Literature Association, 1983, pp. 61–70.

———. "Literary Uses of Traditional Themes: From 'Cinderella' to *The Girl Who Sat by the Ashes* and *The Glass Slipper.*" *Children's Literature Association Quarterly* 11 (Fall 1986): 128–132.

The Junior Book of Authors. 2nd rev. ed. Edited by Stanley J. Kunitz and Howard Haycraft. New York: Wilson, 1951, pp. 117–119.

Junior Bookshelf. Eleanor Farjeon special issue 29 (Aug. 1965): 195–208.

Lewis, Naomi, comp. *The Eleanor Farjeon Book: A Tribute to Her Life and Work, 1881–1965.* London: Hamish Hamilton, 1966.

"*The Little Bookroom.*" In M. Crouch and A. Ellis. *Chosen for Children.* 3rd ed. London: The Library Association, 1977, pp. 78–82.

Miller, Bertha Mahony. "Editorial: Honour to Eleanor Farjeon." *Horn Book* 32 (Oct. 1956): 333.

———. "Little Brother and Sister." *Horn Book* 12 (May 1936): 167–174.

Morgan, M. E. "Eleanor Farjeon: An Evaluation." *Junior Bookshelf* 18 (Oct. 1954): 175–179.

The Oxford Companion to Children's Literature. Edited by Humphrey Carpenter and Mari Prichard. New York: Oxford Univ. Press, 1984, pp. 182–183.

Sayers, Frances Clarke. "Eleanor Farjeon's Room with a View." *Horn Book* 32 (Oct. 1956): 335–345. Reprinted in *Horn Book* 57 (June 1981): 337–346; and in Frances Clarke Sayers. *Summoned by Books.* New York: Viking Press, 1965, pp. 122–132.

Smaridge, Norah. *Famous Modern Storytellers for Young People.* New York: Dodd, 1969, pp. 21–25.

Twentieth Century Children's Writers. 2nd ed. Edited by D. L. Kirkpatrick. New York: St. Martin's Press, 1983, pp. 269–273.

Viguers, Ruth Hill, ed. "Eleanor Farjeon." *Horn Book* 41 (Aug. 1965): 419–420.

Farmer (Mockridge), Penelope (Jane)

Cameron, Eleanor. "Afterword." In Penelope Farmer. *Charlotte Sometimes.* New York: Dell/Yearling, 1987.

Crago, Hugh. "Penelope Farmer's Novels." *Signal* 17 (May 1975): 81–90.

Esmonde, Margaret P. "Narrative Methods in Penelope Farmer's *A Castle of Bone.*" *Children's Literature in Education* 14 (Autumn 1983): 171–179.

Farmer, Penelope. "Discovering the Pattern." In Edward Blishen. *The Thorny Paradise.* Boston: Horn Book, 1975, pp. 103–107.

———. " 'Jorinda and Jorindel' and Other Stories." *Children's Literature in Education* 7 (Mar. 1972): 23–34. Reprinted in Geoff Fox. *Writers, Critics, and Children.* New York: Agathon Press, 1976, pp. 55–72.

———. "On the Effects of Collecting Myth for Children and Others." *Children's Literature in Education* 27, no. 4 (Winter 1977): 176–185.

———. "Patterns on a Wall." *Horn Book* 50 (Oct. 1974): 169–176.

Fourth Book of Junior Authors and Illustrators. Edited by Doris De Montreville and Elizabeth D. Crawford. New York: Wilson, 1978, pp. 124–126.

Hewitt, Marion R. "Emergent Authors: Penelope Farmer." *Junior Bookshelf* 27 (Jan. 1963): 20–22.

Jones, Cornelia, and Way, Olivia R. "Penelope Farmer." In *British Children's Authors.* Chicago: American Library Association, 1976, pp. 77–84.

McElderry, Margaret K. "Penelope Farmer: The Development of an Author." *Elementary English* 51 (Sept. 1974): 799–805.

Meek, Margaret. "Inwardly Adolescent." *Times Literary Supplement* March 29, 1985, p. 348.

Rees, David. "The Marble in the Water: The Real World in Penelope Farmer's Novels." *Horn Book* 52 (Oct. 1976): 471–478. Reprinted in David Rees. *The Marble in the Water.* Boston: Horn Book, 1980, pp. 1–13.

Salway, Lance, and Chambers, Nancy. "Book Post." *Signal* 25 (Jan. 1978): 49–55; "Book Post Returns." *Signal* 26 (May 1978): 92–98.

Swinfen, Ann. *In Defense of Fantasy.* London: Routledge, 1984. *Charlotte Sometimes,* pp. 53, 56–58; *Castle of Bone,* pp. 67–71; *The Magic Stone, The Summer Birds, William and Mary,* pp. 138–141.

Twentieth Century Children's Writers. 2nd ed. Edited by D. L. Kirkpatrick. New York: St. Martin's Press, 1983, pp. 273–274.

Fast, Howard (Melvin)

Burgess, E. E. "This Man, Howard Fast." *Top of the News* 21 (Jan. 1965): 138–141.

Twentieth–Century Science Fiction Writers. 2nd ed. Edited by Curtis C. Smith. Chicago: St. James Press, 1986, pp. 244–246.

Faulkner, William (Cuthbert)

Brown, Calvin S. "Faulkner's Rowan Oak Tales." *Mississippi Quarterly* 34 (Summer 1981): 367–374.

Ditsky, John. "William Faulkner's *The Wishing Tree:* Maturity's First Draft." *The Lion and the Unicorn* 2 (Spring 1978): 56–64.

Gidley, Mick. "William Faulkner and Children." *Signal* 3 (Sept. 1970): 91–102.

Feagles, Anita M(acRae)

Fourth Book of Junior Authors and Illustrators. Edited by Doris De Montreville and Elizabeth D. Crawford. New York: Wilson, 1978, pp. 128–129.

Fenton, Edward

Third Book of Junior Authors. Edited by Doris De Montreville and Donna Hill. New York: Wilson, 1972, pp. 82–83.
Twentieth Century Children's Writers. 2nd ed. Edited by D. L. Kirkpatrick. New York: St. Martin's Press, 1983, pp. 277–278.

Field, Rachel (Lyman)

Bechtel, Louise Seaman. "Rachel's Gifts." *Horn Book* 18 (July–Aug. 1942): 230–236.
Benét, Laura. "Rachel Field—A Memory." *Horn Book* 18 (July–Aug. 1942): 227–229.
Bianco, Margery Williams. *"Hitty, Her First Hundred Years."* In Anne Moore and Bertha Miller. *Writing and Criticism.* Boston: Horn Book, 1951, pp. 63–66.
Field, Rachel Lyman. "How *Hitty* Happened." *Horn Book* 6 (Feb. 1930): 22–26.
———. "A Hunt Breakfast—Authors' Symposium." *Horn Book* 2 (Nov. 1926): 35–36.
Griffin, Deuel N. "Rachel Field." In Cech. *American Writers for Children, 1900–1960. Dictionary of Literary Biography,* vol. 22. Detroit: Gale, 1983, pp. 170–175.
Hale, F. "Concerning *Hitty: Her First Hundred Years.*" *Grade Teacher* 48 (Nov. 1930):189.
Helbig, Alethea K. "Rachel Lyman Field." In *Writers for Children; Critical Studies of Major Authors since the Seventeenth Century.* Edited by Jane M. Bingham. New York: Scribner, 1988, pp. 235–240.
Helbig, Alethea K., and Perkins, Agnes Regan. *Dictionary of American Children's Fiction, 1859–1959.* Westport, CT: Greenwood Press, 1985, pp. 160, 220–221.
Horn Book Magazine. A Memorial *Horn Book* for Rachel Field. *Horn Book* 18 (July–Aug. 1942).
The Junior Book of Authors. 2nd rev. ed. Edited by Stanley J. Kunitz and Howard Haycraft. New York: Wilson, 1951, pp. 123–126.
Lane, Margaret. "Rachel Field and Her Contribution to Children's Literature." In Siri Andrews. *The Hewins Lectures. 1947–1962.* Boston: Horn Book, 1963, pp. 343–375.
Lathrop, Dorothy P. "A Test of Hitty's Pegs and Patience." *Horn Book* 6 (Feb. 1930): 27–30.
Mahony, Bertha E. "Of Rachel Field and Letters." *Horn Book* 18 (July–Aug. 1942): 237–250.
Miller, Bertha Mahony, and Field, Elinor Whitney, eds. *Newbery Medal Books: 1922–1955.* Boston: Horn Book, 1957, pp. 74–88.
Quinnam, Barbara. "Rachel Field Collection of Old Children's Books in The District of Columbia Public Library: A Catalogue." Thesis, George Washington University, 1961.
Roginski, Jim, ed. *Newbery and Caldecott Medalists and Honor Book Winners.* Littleton, CO: Libraries Unlimited, 1982, pp. 107–109.
Titzell, Josiah. "Rachel Field, 1894–1942." *Horn Book* 18 (July–Aug. 1942): 216–225.
———. "Rachel Field: Portrait of a Troubadour." *Horn Book* 3 (Nov. 1927): 22–27.
Twentieth Century Children's Writers. 2nd ed. Edited by D. L. Kirkpatrick. New York: St. Martin's Press, 1983, pp. 280–282.
Usrey, Malcolm. "The Child Persona in *Taxis and Toadstools.*" *Children's Literature Association Quarterly* 7 (Summer 1982): 39–49.

Finney, Charles G(randison)

Schlobin, Roger C. "The Fool and the Fantastic." *Fantasy Newsletter* 43 (1981): 6–9, 29.

Smith, Curtis C. "Charles Finney." In *Supernatural Fiction Writers: Fantasy and Horror,* vol. 2, Edited by E. F. Bleiler. New York: Scribner, 1985, pp. 821–826.
Wolfe, Gary K. *"The Circus of Dr. Lao."* In *Survey of Modern Fantasy Literature,* vol. 1. Edited by Frank N. Magill. Englewood Cliffs, NJ: Salem Press, 1983, pp. 282–286.

Finney, Jack (pseud. of Walter Braden Finney)

Landon, Brooks. "Time and Again." In *Survey of Modern Fantasy Literature,* vol. 4. Edited by Frank N. Magill. Englewood Cliffs, NJ: Salem Press, 1983, pp. 1938–1942.
Searles, Baird; Meacham, Beth; and Franklin, Michael. *A Reader's Guide to Fantasy.* New York: Avon, 1982, pp. 63–64.
Twentieth-Century Science Fiction Writers. 2nd ed. Edited by Curtis C. Smith. Chicago: St. James Press, 1986, p. 253.

Fisher, Dorothy (Frances) Canfield

Maguire, Gregory. "A Second Look: *Understood Betsy.*" *Horn Book* 50 (Oct. 1979): 558–560.
Twentieth Century Children's Writers. 2nd ed. Edited by D. L. Kirkpatrick. New York: St. Martin's Press, 1983, pp. 288–290.
Washington, Ida H. *Dorothy Canfield Fisher: A Biography.* Shelburne, VT: New England Press, 1982.

Fisher, Leonard Everett

Fisher, Leonard Everett. "The Artist at Work: Creating Non Fiction." *Horn Book* 64 (May–June 1988): 315–323.
Third Book of Junior Authors. Edited by Doris De Montreville and Donna Hill. New York: Wilson, 1972, pp. 84–85.

Flack, Marjorie

Bader, Barbara. *American Picturebooks.* New York: Macmillan, 1976, pp. 61–64.
Twentieth Century Children's Writers. 2nd ed. Edited by D. L. Kirkpatrick. New York: St. Martin's Press, 1983, pp. 293–294.

Flecker, (Herman) James Elroy

Eaton, Anne. "Extensions of Reality." *Horn Book* 3 (May 1927): 17–22.
Speth, Lee. "Cavalier Treatment: James Elroy Flecker's *King of Alsander.*" *Mythlore* 5, 19 (1978), and 6 (Winter 1979): 17.

Fleischman, Paul (Taylor)

Fifth Book of Junior Authors and Illustrators. Edited by Sally Holmes Holtze. New York: Wilson, 1983, pp. 114–116.
Fleischman, Paul. "Sid Fleischman." *Horn Book* 63 (July–Aug. 1987): 429–432.
———. "Sound and Sense." *Horn Book* 62 (Sept.–Oct. 1986): 551–555.

Fleischman, (Albert) Sid(ney)

Dane, C. "Presentation of the Eighth Recognition of Merit to Sid Fleischman for *By the Great Horned Spoon.*" *Claremont Reading Conference Yearbook* 36 (1972): 94–96.

Fleischman, Paul. "Sid Fleischman." *Horn Book* 63 (July–Aug. 1987): 429–432.
Fleischman, Sid. "Boston Globe–Horn Book Acceptance." *Horn Book* 56 (Feb. 1980): 94–96.
———. "Laughter and Children's Literature." *Horn Book* 52 (Oct. 1976): 465–470. Reprinted in Paul Heins. *Crosscurrents of Criticism.* Boston: Horn Book, 1977, pp. 199–204; and in *The Claremont Reading Conference Yearbook* 40 (1976): 88–92.
———. "Newbery Medal Acceptance." *Horn Book* 63 (July–Aug. 1987): 423–428.
———. "1987 Newbery Acceptance Speech." *Top of the News* 48 (Summer 1987): 385–390.
Helbig, Alethea K., and Perkins, Agnes Regan. *Dictionary of American Children's Fiction, 1960–1984.* Westport, CT: Greenwood Press, 1986, pp. 84–85, 108–109, 216, 237–238, 302, 410, 439–440.
Johnson, Emily R. "Profile: Sid Fleischman." *Language Arts* 59 (Oct. 1982): 754–759, 772.
The Oxford Companion to Children's Literature. Edited by Humphrey Carpenter and Mari Prichard. New York: Oxford Univ. Press, 1984, p. 188.
Third Book of Junior Authors. Edited by Doris De Montreville and Donna Hill. New York: Wilson, 1972, pp. 86–87.
Twentieth Century Children's Writers. 2nd ed. Edited by D. L. Kirkpatrick. New York: St. Martin's Press, 1983, pp. 294–295.

Fleming, Ian (Lancaster)

Fifth Book of Junior Authors and Illustrators. Edited by Sally Holmes Holtze. New York: Wilson, 1983, pp. 116–117.
West, Mark. "Fleming's Flying Flivver Flops on Film." In Douglas Street. *Children's Novels and the Movies.* New York: Ungar, 1983, pp. 197–204.

Flora, James (Royer)

Third Book of Junior Authors. Edited by Doris De Montreville and Donna Hill. New York: Wilson, 1972, pp. 87–89.
Twentieth Century Children's Writers. 2nd ed. Edited by D. L. Kirkpatrick. New York: St. Martin's Press, 1983, pp. 295–296.

Follett, Barbara Newhall

Follett, Barbara Newhall. "In Defense of Butterflies." *Horn Book* 9 (Feb. 1933): 24–28.
Follett, Wilson. "Notes on a Junior Author: With a Glance at Precocity." *Horn Book* 4 (May 1928): 6–13.

Fox (Greenberg), Paula

Bach, Alice. "Cracking Open the Geode: The Fiction of Paula Fox." *Horn Book* 53 (Oct. 1977): 514–521.
Baker, Augusta. "Paula Fox." *Horn Book* 50 (Aug. 1974): 351–353.
Council on Interracial Books for Children. "*The Slave Dancer:* Critiques of This Year's Newbery Award Winner." *Interracial Books for Children* 5 (1974): 4–6, 8.
Fourth Book of Junior Authors and Illustrators. Edited by Doris De Montreville and Elizabeth D. Crawford. New York: Wilson, 1978, pp. 135–136.
Fox, Paula. "Hans Christian Andersen Medal Acceptance." *Horn Book* 55 (Apr. 1979): 222–223.
———. "Newbery Award Acceptance." *Horn Book* 50 (Aug. 1974): 345–350.

———. "Other Places [Children and the Complexity of Life]." *Horn Book* 63 (Jan./ Feb. 1987): 21–27.

Heins, Paul. "Editorial: Paula Fox: Hans Christian Andersen Medal Winner." *Horn Book* 54 (Oct. 1978): 486–487.

Helbig, Alethea K., and Perkins, Agnes Regan. *Dictionary of American Children's Fiction, 1960–1984*. Westport, CT: Greenwood Press, 1986, pp. 222–223.

Inglis, Fred. *The Promise of Happiness*. New York: Cambridge Univ. Press, 1981, pp. 281–283.

Kingman, Lee, ed. *Newbery and Caldecott Medal Books: 1966–1975*. Boston: Horn Book, 1975, pp. 113–125.

McDonnell, Christine. "A Second Look: *The Stone-Faced Boy*." *Horn Book* 60 (Apr. 1984): 219–222.

Moss, Anita. "Paula Fox." In *American Writers for Children since 1960: Fiction. Dictionary of Literary Biography*, vol. 52. Detroit: Gale, 1986, pp. 143–155.

The Oxford Companion to Children's Literature. Edited by Humphrey Carpenter and Mari Prichard. New York: Oxford Univ. Press, 1984, pp. 189–190.

Parker, Patricia Anne Falstad. "Responses of Adolescents and Librarians to Selected Contemporary Fiction." Ph.D. dissertation, University of Minnesota, 1974.

Rees, David. "'The Colour of Saying': Paula Fox." In *Marble in the Water*. Boston: Horn Book, 1980, pp. 114–127.

Rustin, Michael. "Finding Oneself among Strangers: Three Stories by Paula Fox." In *Narratives of Love and Loss*. London: Verso, 1987, pp. 215–247.

Townsend, John Rowe. "Paula Fox." In *A Sounding of Storytellers*. New York: Lippincott, 1979, pp. 55–65.

———. *A Sense of Story: Essays on Contemporary Writers for Children*. Philadelphia: Lippincott, 1971, pp. 89–96.

Twentieth Century Children's Writers. 2nd ed. Edited by D. L. Kirkpatrick. New York: St. Martin's Press, 1983, pp. 298–300.

France, Anatole (pseud. of Jacques Anatole Francois Thibault)

Stableford, Brian M. "Anatole France." In *Supernatural Fiction Writers: Fantasy and Horror*, vol. 1. New York: Scribner, 1985, pp. 67–73.

Freeman, Barbara C(onstance)

Twentieth Century Children's Writers. 2nd ed. Edited by D. L. Kirkpatrick. New York: St. Martin's Press, 1983, pp. 300–302.

Freschet, Berniece (Louise Speck)

Fourth Book of Junior Authors and Illustrators. Edited by Doris De Montreville and Elizabeth D. Crawford. New York: Wilson, 1978, pp. 130–139.

Fritz, Jean (Guttery)

Ammon, Richard. "Profile: Jean Fritz." *Language Arts* 60 (Mar. 1983): 365–369.

Busbin, O. Mell. "Jean Fritz." In *American Writers for Children since 1960: Fiction. Dictionary of Literary Biography*, vol. 52. Detroit: Gale, 1986, pp. 156–167.

Fritz, Jean. "Making It Real." *Children's Literature in Education* 22 (Autumn 1976): 125–127.

———. "On Writing Historical Fiction." *Horn Book* 43 (Oct. 1967): 565–570.

———. "There Once Was." 1986 Laura Ingalls Wilder Award Acceptance Speech.

Top of the News 42 (Summer 1986): 401–404; *Horn Book* 62 (July–Aug. 1986): 432–435.

———. "Turning History Inside Out." *Horn Book* 61 (Jan. 1985): 29–34.

Heins, Ethel L. "Presentation of the 1986 Laura Ingalls Wilder Medal." *Horn Book* 62 (July/Aug. 1986): 430–431.

Helbig, Alethea K., and Perkins, Agnes Regan. *Dictionary of American Children's Fiction, 1960–1984; Recent Books of Recognized Merit.* Westport, CT: Greenwood Press, 1986, pp. 226–227.

Hopkins, Lee Bennett. *More Books by More People.* New York: Citation Press, 1974, pp. 172–177.

Roginski, Jim. *Behind the Covers: Interview with Authors and Illustrators of Books for Children and Young Adults.* Littleton, CO: Libraries Unlimited, 1985, pp. 73–84.

Third Book of Junior Authors. Edited by Doris De Montreville and Donna Hill. New York: Wilson, 1972, pp. 94–95.

Fry, Rosalie K(ingsmill)

Third Book of Junior Authors. Edited by Doris De Montreville and Donna Hill. New York: Wilson, 1972, pp. 95–97.

Twentieth Century Children's Writers. 2nd ed. Edited by D. L. Kirkpatrick. New York: St. Martin's Press, 1983, pp. 304–305.

Fyleman, Rose (Amy)

Adams, Lady Agnes. "Rose Fyleman." *Bookman* 77 (Oct. 1929): 27–28.

———. "Rose Fyleman, the Fairies' Laureate." *Elementary English Review* 6 (Mar. 1929): 61–63.

Doyle, Brian. *The Who's Who of Children's Literature.* New York: Schocken, 1968, pp. 104–105.

Fyleman, Rose. "How I Came to Write for Children." *Horn Book* 5 (Aug. 1929): 22–23.

———. "Writing Poetry for Children." *Horn Book* 16 (Jan.–Feb. 1940): 58–66.

———. "Writing Verse for Children." *Horn Book* 13 (May 1937): 144–146.

The Junior Book of Authors. 2nd ed. rev. Edited by Stanley J. Kunitz and Howard Haycraft. New York: Wilson, 1951, pp. 133–134.

The Oxford Companion to Children's Literature. Edited by Humphrey Carpenter and Mari Prichard. New York: Oxford Univ. Press, 1984, p. 193.

Shippen, Elizabeth P. "Rose Fyleman." *Elementary English* 35 (Oct. 1958): 358–365.

Twentieth Century Children's Writers. 2nd ed. Edited by D. L. Kirkpatrick. New York: St. Martin's Press, 1983, pp. 306–309.

Whitney, Elinor. "A Pilgrim Fairy." *Horn Book* 5 (Aug. 1929): 18–21.

Gage, Wilson *see* Steele, Mary Q.

Gall, Alice Crew, and Crew, Fleming H.

The Junior Book of Authors. 2nd ed. rev. Edited by Stanley J. Kunitz and Howard Haycraft. New York: Wilson, 1951, pp. 136–137.

Gallico, Paul (William)

Searles, Baird; Meacham, Beth; and Franklin, Michael. *A Reader's Guide to Fantasy.* New York: Avon, 1982, pp. 65–66.

Gannett (Kahn), Ruth Stiles

Fourth Book of Junior Authors and Illustrators. Edited by Doris De Montreville and Elizabeth D. Crawford. New York: Wilson, 1978, pp. 143–144.

Helbig, Alethea K., and Perkins, Agnes Regan. *Dictionary of American Children's Fiction, 1859–1959.* Westport, CT: Greenwood Press, 1985, pp. 174–175, 365.

Roginski, Jim, ed. *Newbery and Caldecott Medalists and Honor Book Winners.* Littleton, CO: Libraries Unlimited, 1982, p. 123.

Twentieth Century Children's Writers. 2nd ed. Edited by D. L. Kirkpatrick. New York: St. Martin's Press, 1983, pp. 309–310.

Gard, Joyce (pseud. of Joyce Reeves)

Jones, Cornelia, and Way, Olivia R. "Joyce Gard." In *British Children's Authors.* Chicago: American Library Association, 1976, pp. 85–93.

Twentieth Century Children's Writers. 2nd ed. Edited by D. L. Kirkpatrick. New York: St. Martin's Press, 1983, pp. 310–311.

Gardam, Jane

Gardam, Jane. "Mrs. Hookaneye and I." In Edward Blishen. *The Thorny Paradise.* Boston: Horn Book, 1975, pp. 77–80.

———. "On Writing for Children: Some Wasps in the Marmalade, Part I." *Horn Book* 54 (Oct. 1978): 489–496. "Part II." *Horn Book* 54 (Dec. 1978): 672–679.

Garden, Nancy

Chelton, Mary K. "Interview with Nancy Garden." *VOYA* 5 (Feb. 1983): 15–16.

Fifth Book of Junior Authors and Illustrators. Edited by Sally Holmes Holtze. New York: Wilson, 1983, pp. 126–127.

Gardner, John (Champlin, Jr.)

De Luca, Geraldine, and Natov, Roni. "Modern Moralities for Children: John Gardner's Children's Books." In *John Gardner: Critical Perspectives.* Edited by Robert A. Morace and Kathryn Van Spanckeren. Carbondale: Southern Illinois Univ. Press, 1982, pp. 89–96.

Evans, W. D. Emrys. "The Welsh Mabinogion: Tellings and Retellings." *Children's Literature in Education* 28, no. 9 (Spring 1978): 17–33.

Fifth Book of Junior Authors and Illustrators. Edited by Sally Holmes Holtze. New York: Wilson, 1983, pp. 127–129.

Foust, R. E. "Monstrous Image: Theory of Fantasy Antagonists." *Genre* 13 (1981): 441–453.

Howell, John M. *John Gardner: A Bibliographic Profile.* Carbondale: Southern Illinois Univ. Press, 1980.

Merrill, Robert. "John Gardner's *Grendel* and the Interpretation of Modern Fables." *American Literature* 56 (1984): 162–180.

Morace, Robert A. *John Gardner: An Annotated Secondary Bibliography.* New York: Garland, 1984.

Morace, Robert A., and Morace, Kathryn, eds. *John Gardner.* Carbondale: Southern Illinois Univ. Press, 1982.

Morris, G. L. *World of Order and Light: The Fiction of John Gardner.* Athens: Univ. of Georgia Press, 1984.

Myers, Walter E. *"Grendel."* In *Survey of Modern Fantasy Literature,* vol. 2. Edited by Frank N. Magill. Englewood Cliffs, NJ: Salem Press, 1983, pp. 675–679.

Natov, Roni, and De Luca, Geraldine. "An Interview with John Gardner." *The Lion and the Unicorn* 2 (Spring 1979): 114–136.

Tuso, Joseph F. *"Grendel:* Chapter I: John Gardner's Perverse Prologue." *College Literature* 12 (1985): 184–186.

Garfield, Leon

Camp, Richard. "Garfield's Golden Net." *Signal* 5 (May 1971): 47–55.

Crouch, Marcus. *The Nesbit Tradition.* London: Benn, 1972, pp. 34–38.

Doyle, Brian. *The Who's Who of Children's Literature.* New York: Schocken, 1968, pp. 105–106.

Fourth Book of Junior Authors and Illustrators. Edited by Doris De Montreville and Elizabeth D. Crawford. New York: Wilson, 1978, pp. 144–145.

Garfield, Leon. "And So It Grows." *Horn Book* 44 (Dec. 1968): 668–672. Reprinted from *Children's Book News* (Mar.–Apr. 1968).

———. "Bookmaker and Punter." In Edward Blishen. *The Thorny Paradise.* Boston: Horn Book, 1975, pp. 81–86.

———. "An Evening with Leon Garfield." In *One Ocean Touching.* Edited by Sheila A. Egoff. Metuchen, NJ: Scarecrow Press, 1979, pp. 110–120.

———. "Writing for Childhood." *Children's Literature in Education* 2 (July 1970): 56–63.

Garfield, Leon; Blishen, Edward; and Keeping, Charles. "Greek Myths and the Twentieth Century Reader." *Children's Literature in Education* 3 (Nov. 1970): 48–65.

Holland, Phillip. "Shades of the Prison House: The Fiction of Leon Garfield." *Children's Literature in Education* 9 (Winter 1978): 159–172.

Jones, Rhodri. "Writers for Children—Leon Garfield." *The Use of English* 23 (Summer 1972): 293–299. Reprinted in Dennis Butts. *Good Writers for Young Readers.* St. Albans, England: Hart-Davis, 1977, pp. 34–44.

Natov, Roni. " 'Not the Blackest of Villains . . . Not the Brightest of Saints.' Humanism in Leon Garfield's Adventure Novels." *Lion and Unicorn* 2 (Fall 1978): 44–71.

The Oxford Companion to Children's Literature. Edited by Humphrey Carpenter and Mari Prichard. New York: Oxford Univ. Press, 1984, pp. 196–198.

Stott, Jon C. *Children's Literature from A to Z.* New York: McGraw-Hill, 1984, p. 120.

Sucher, Mary Wadsworth. "Recommended: Leon Garfield." *English Journal* 72 (Sept. 1983): 71–72.

Swinfen, Ann. *In Defense of Fantasy.* London: Routledge, 1984. Discussion of *The Ghost Downstairs,* pp. 55, 116–117, 159–168, 187–189.

Townsend, John Rowe. "Leon Garfield." In *A Sense of Story.* Philadelphia: Lippincott, 1971, pp. 97–107.

———. "Leon Garfield." In *A Sounding of Storytellers.* Philadelphia: Lippincott, 1979, pp. 66–80.

Twentieth Century Children's Writers. 2nd ed. Edited by D. L. Kirkpatrick. New York: St. Martin's Press, 1983, pp. 312–314.

Wintle, Justin, and Fisher, Emma. "Leon Garfield." In *The Pied Pipers.* New York: Paddington Press, 1974, pp. 192–207.

Garner, Alan

Aers, Lesley. "Alan Garner: An Opinion." *Use of English* 22 (Winter 1978): 141–147, 153.

Alderson, Valerie. "*Red Shift*—Some Aspects Considered." *Children's Book Review* 4 (Summer 1974): 49.

Attebery, Brian. "Alan Garner." In *Supernatural Fiction Writers: Fantasy and Horror,* vol. 2. Edited by E. F. Bleiler. New York: Scribner, 1985, pp. 1023–1030.

Bartle, F. R. "Alan Garner." *Children's Libraries Newsletter* 8 (May 1972): 38–47.

Benton, Michael. "Detective Imagination." *Children's Literature in Education* 13 (1974): 5–12.

Berman, Ruth. "Who's Lleu?" *Mythlore* 4, 16 (June 1977): 20–21.

Bisenieks, Dainis. "Children, Magic and Choices." *Mythlore* 6 (Winter 1979): 13–16.

Blishen, Edward. "Ambiguous Triptych." *Times Educational Supplement* (Oct. 12, 1973): 22.

"Books of International Interest: Forum of Children's Books." *Bookbird* 6 (1968): 27–30.

Brewer, Rosemary. "Alan Garner: A Perspective." *Orana* 14 (Nov. 1978): 127–133.

Cadogan, Mary, and Craig, Patricia. *You're a Brick Angela!* London: Gollancz, 1976, pp. 367–371.

Cameron, Eleanor. "*The Owl Service: A Study.*" *Wilson Library Bulletin* 44 (Dec. 1969): 425–433. Reprinted in Mary Lou White. *Children's Literature: Criticism and Response.* Columbus, OH: Merrill, 1976, pp. 191–201.

Chambers, Aidan. *Booktalk: Occasional Writing on Literature and Children.* New York: Harper and Row, 1986, pp. 70, 83, 87.

———. "An Interview with Alan Garner." *Signal* 27 (Sept. 1978): 119–137. Reprinted in Aidan Chambers. *Signal Approach to Children's Books.* Metuchen, NJ: Scarecrow Press, 1981, pp. 276–328.

———. "Letter from England: A Matter of Balance." *Horn Book* 53 (Aug. 1977): 479–482.

———. "Letter from England: Literary Crossword Puzzle . . . or Literary Masterpiece?" *Horn Book* 49 (Oct. 1973): 494–497. Discussion of *Red Shift.*

Clute, John. "*Elidor.*" In *Survey of Modern Fantasy Literature,* vol. 1. Edited by Frank N. Magill. Englewood Cliffs, NJ: Salem Press, 1983, pp. 472–474.

Doyle, Brian. *The Who's Who of Children's Literature.* New York: Schocken, 1968, pp. 106–107.

Farrell, Jacqueline M. "Recommended: Alan Garner." *English Journal* 70 (Sept. 1981): 65–66.

Garner, Alan. "Achilles in Altjira." *Children's Literature Association Quarterly* 8 (Fall 1983): 5–10. Reprinted In *Innocence & Experience.* Edited by Barbara Harrison and Gregory Maguire. New York: Lothrop, 1987, pp. 116–128.

———. "A Bit More Practice." *Times Literary Supplement,* June 6, 1968, pp. 577–578. Reprinted in Meek. *The Cool Web.* New York: Atheneum, 1978, pp. 196–200.

———. "Coming to Terms." *Children's Literature in Education* 2 (July 1970): 15–29.

———. "The Death of Myth." *Children's Literature in Education* 3 (1970): 69–71.

———. "The Edge of the Ceiling." *Horn Book* 60 (Sept./Oct. 1984): 559–565. Reprinted from *Loughborough 1983: Proceedings.* Welsh National Centre for Children's Literature, 1984, pp. 72–76.

———. "Inner Time." In Peter Nicholl. *Science Fiction at Large.* New York: Harper and Row, 1976, pp. 119–138.

———. "Real Mandrakes in Real Gardens." *New Statesman,* Nov. 1, 1968, pp. 591–592.

Gillies, Carolyn. "Possession and Structure in the Novels of Alan Garner." *Children's Literature in Education* 18 (Fall 1975): 107–117.

Gough, John. "Alan Garner, the Critic and Self-Critic." *Orana* 20 (Aug. 1984): 110–118.

Heins, Paul. "Off the Beaten Path." *Horn Book* 49 (Dec. 1973): 580–581. Reprinted in Paul Heins. *Crosscurrents of Criticism*. Boston: Horn Book, 1977, p. 319. *Discussion of The Jersey Shore*.

Hellings, Carol. "Alan Garner: His Use of Mythology and Dimension in Time." *Orana* 15 (May 1979): 66–73.

Herbert, Kathleen. "*The Owl Service* and the Fourth Branch of the Maginogion." *Labrys* 7 (Nov. 1981): 115–122.

Hunt, Peter. "Landscapes and Journeys, Metaphors and Maps: The Distinctive Feature of English Fantasy." *Children's Literature Association Quarterly* 12 (Spring 1987): 11–15.

Inglis, Fred. *The Promise of Happiness*. New York: Cambridge Univ. Press, 1981, pp. 242–245.

Jones, Cornelia, and Way, Olivia R. "Alan Garner." In *British Children's Authors*. Chicago: American Library Association, 1976, pp. 94–100.

Kohler, Margaret. "Author Study: Alan Garner." *Orana* 16 (May 1980): 39–48.

McMahon, Patricia. "A Second Look—*Elidor*." *Horn Book* 56 (June 1980): 328–331.

Mould, G. H. "*Weirdstone of Brisingamen:* A Four-Way Experience with the Novel by Alan Garner." *School Librarian* 15 (July 1967): 146–150.

"*The Owl Service*." In M. Crouch and A. Ellis. *Chosen for Children*. 3rd ed. London: The Library Association, 1977, pp. 141–145.

The Oxford Companion to Children's Literature. Edited by Humphrey Carpenter and Mari Prichard. New York: Oxford Univ. Press, 1984, pp. 164–165, 198–200, 392, 444–445, 498, 564.

Pearce, Philippa. "*The Owl Service*." *Children's Book News* (1967). Reprinted in Margaret Meek. *The Cool Web*. New York: Atheneum, 1978, pp. 291–293.

Pflieger, Pat, and Hill, Helen M. *A Reference Guide to Modern Fantasy for Children*. Westport, CT: Greenwood Press, 1984, pp. xiv, 169–171, 199–201, 377–379, 418–420, 585–587.

Philip, Neil. *A Fine Anger: A Critical Introduction to the Work of Alan Garner*. New York: Collins/Philomel, 1981.

Rees, David. "Alan Garner: Some Doubts." *Horn Book* 55 (July 1979): 282–289. Reprinted as "Hanging in Their True Shapes." In David Rees. *The Marble in the Water*. Boston: Horn Book, 1980, pp. 56–67.

Searles, Baird; Meacham, Beth; and Franklin, Michael. *A Reader's Guide to Fantasy*. New York: Avon, 1982, pp. 66–67.

Stableford, Vivien. "*The Owl Service*." In *Survey of Modern Fantasy Literature,* vol. 3. Edited by Frank N. Magill. Englewood Cliffs, NJ: Salem Press, 1983, pp. 1188–1190.

———. "*The Weirdstone of Brisingamen* and *The Moon of Gomrath*." In *Survey of Modern Fantasy Literature,* vol. 5. Edited by Frank N. Magill. Englewood Cliffs, NJ: Salem Press, 1983, pp. 2087–2089.

Stott, Jon C. *Children's Literature from A to Z*. New York: McGraw-Hill, 1984, p. 121.

Sullivan, C. W., III. "Traditional Welsh Materials in Modern Fantasy." *Extrapolation* 28 (Spring 1987): 87–97.

Swinfen, Ann. *In Defense of Fantasy*. London: Routledge, 1984. Discussion of *The Owl Service*, pp. 101, 107–109.

Third Book of Junior Authors. Edited by Doris De Montreville and Donna Hill. New York: Wilson, 1972, pp. 99–100.

Thompson, Hillary. "Doorways to Fantasy." *Canadian Children's Literature* 21 (1981): 8–16.

Townsend, John Rowe. "Alan Garner." In *A Sense of Story*. Philadelphia: Lippincott, 1971, pp. 108–119.

———. "Alan Garner." In *A Sounding of Storytellers*. Philadelphia: Lippincott, 1979, pp. 81–96.

Twentieth Century Children's Writers. 2nd ed. Edited by D. L. Kirkpatrick. New York: St. Martin's Press, 1983, pp. 314–315.

Walsh, Robin. "Alan Garner: A Study." *Orana* 13 (May 1977): 31–39.

Watkins, Tony. "Alan Garner." *The Use of English* 21, no. 2 (Winter 1969): 114–117. Reprinted in Dennis Butts. *Good Writers for Young Readers.* St. Albans, England: Hart-Davis, 1977, pp. 45–49.

———. "Alan Garner's *Elidor.*" *Children's Literature in Education* 7 (Mar. 1972): 56–63.

Watson, Victor. "In Defense of Jan: Love and Betrayal in *The Owl Service* and *Red Shift.*" *Signal* 41 (May 1983): 77–87.

West, Richard C. "The Tolkinians." *Orcrist* 2 (1967): 4–15.

Whitaker, Muriel A. " 'The Hollow Hills': A Celtic Motif in Modern Fantasy." *Mosaic* 13 (Spring/Summer 1980): 165–178.

Wintle, Justin, and Fisher, Emma. "Alan Garner." In *The Pied Pipers.* New York: Paddington Press, 1974, pp. 221–235.

Ziefer, Barbara Z. "Wales as a Setting for Children's Fantasy." *Children's Literature in Education* 13 (Summer 1982): 95–102.

Garnett, David

Clute, John. "David Garnett." In *Supernatural Fiction Writers: Fantasy and Horror,* vol. 2. Edited by E. F. Bleiler. New York: Scribner, 1985, pp. 535–539.

Gates, Doris

Gates, Doris. "Along the Road to Kansas." *Horn Book* 31 (Oct. 1955): 382–390.

Helbig, Alethea K., and Perkins, Agnes Regan. *Dictionary of American Children's Fiction, 1960–1984.* Westport, CT: Greenwood Press, 1986, pp. 99, 231.

The Junior Book of Authors. 2nd ed. rev. Edited by Stanley J. Kunitz and Howard Haycraft. New York: Wilson, 1951, pp. 137–138.

Rollins, Charlemae. "The Work of Doris Gates." *Elementary English* 31 (Dec. 1954): 459–465. Reprinted in *Authors and Illustrators of Children's Books.* Edited by Miriam Hoffman and Eva Samuels. New York: Bowker, 1972, pp. 157–164.

Twentieth Century Children's Writers. 2nd ed. Edited by D. L. Kirkpatrick. New York: St. Martin's Press, 1983, pp. 316–317.

Gee, Maurice (Gough)

Twentieth Century Children's Writers. 2nd ed. Edited by D. L. Kirkpatrick. New York: St. Martin's Press, 1983, pp. 317–318.

Gentle, Mary

Barrett, D. V. "Mary Gentle Interviewed." *Vector* 116 (Sept. 1983): 7–12.

Twentieth-Century Science Fiction Writers. 2nd ed. Edited by Curtis C. Smith. Chicago: St. James Press, 1986, p. 276.

Gibson, Katharine (Wicks)

Helbig, Alethea K., and Perkins, Agnes Regan. *Dictionary of American Children's Fiction, 1859–1959.* Westport, CT: Greenwood Press, 1985, pp. 102–103, 181.

The Junior Book of Authors. 2nd ed. rev. Edited by Stanley J. Kunitz and Howard Haycraft. New York: Wilson, 1951, pp. 140–141.

Gilliland, Alexis A(rnaldus)

Lowell, Priscilla. "Interview: Alexis Gilliland." *Thrust* 22 (Spring/Summer 1985): 23–24, 32.

Twentieth-Century Science Fiction Writers. 2nd ed. Edited by Curtis C. Smith. Chicago: St. James Press, 1986, p. 282.

Godden (Dixon), (Margaret) Rumer

De Temple, J. "The Magic of Rumer Godden." *Canadian Library* 18 (July 1961): 23.

Doyle, Brian. *The Who's Who of Children's Literature.* New York: Schocken, 1968, pp. 112–113.

Godden, Rumer. "A Little Tale That Anyone Could Write." *Horn Book* 63 (May–June 1987): 301–307.

———. "Shining Popocatapetl: Poetry for Children." *Horn Book* 64 (May–June 1988): 305–314.

———. *A Time to Dance, No Time to Weep.* New York: Morrow, 1987. Autobiography.

———. "The Writer Must Become as a Child." *Writer* 68 (June 1955): 229.

Godden, Rumer, and Godden, Jon. *Two under the Indian Sun.* New York: Knopf, 1966. Autobiography.

Hines, Ruth, and Burns, Paul C. "Rumer Godden." *Elementary English* 44 (Feb. 1967): 101–104.

More Junior Authors. Edited by Muriel Fuller. New York: Wilson, 1963, pp. 101–102.

Moss, Elaine. "Rumer Godden: Prince of Storytellers." *Signal* 17 (May 1975): 55–60. Reprinted in *Part of the Pattern.* New York: Greenwillow, 1986, pp. 75–80.

The Oxford Companion to Children's Literature. Edited by Humphrey Carpenter and Mari Prichard. New York: Oxford Univ. Press, 1984, pp. 209–210.

Rustin, Michael. "The Life of Dolls: Rumer Godden's Understanding of Children's Imaginative Play." In *Narratives of Love and Loss.* London: Verso, 1987, pp. 84–103.

Simpson, Hassell A. *Rumer Godden.* Boston: Twayne, 1973.

Smaridge, Norah. *Famous Modern Storytellers for Young People.* New York: Dodd, 1969, pp. 68–72.

Stott, Jon C. *Children's Literature from A to Z.* New York: McGraw-Hill, 1984, p. 125.

Twentieth Century Children's Writers. 2nd ed. Edited by D. L. Kirkpatrick. New York: St. Martin's Press, 1983, pp. 322–323.

Willard, Nancy. "Afterword." In Rumer Godden. *Four Dolls.* New York: Dell, 1987.

Wintle, Justin, and Fisher, Emma. "Rumer Godden." In *The Pied Pipers.* New York: Paddington Press, 1974, pp. 285–294.

Godwin, Parke

Godwin, Parke. "There Goes Deuteronomy." In *Inside Outer Space.* Edited by Sharon Jarvis. New York: Ungar, 1985.

Goldman, William (W.)

Walter, E. M. "*The Princess Bride.*" In *Survey of Modern Fantasy Literature,* vol. 3. Edited by Frank N. Magill. Englewood Cliffs, NJ: Salem Press, 1983, pp. 1286–1290.

Goldstein, Lisa

"Lisa Goldstein Wins American Book Award." *Locus* 16 (June 1983): 1.

Gordon, John (William)

Blishen, Edward. "The Bare Pebble: The Novels of John Gordon." *Signal* 3 (May 1972): 62–73.

———. "The Slow Art of John Gordon." *Signal* 40 (Jan. 1983): 12–17.

Gordon, John. "On Firm Ground." In Edward Blishen. *The Thorny Paradise*. Boston: Horn Book, 1975, pp. 34–35.

Twentieth Century Children's Writers. 2nd ed. Edited by D. L. Kirkpatrick. New York: St. Martin's Press, 1983, pp. 323–324.

Gordon, Patricia *see* Howard, Joan

Goudge, Elizabeth (De Beauchamp)

Colwell, Eileen H. "Elizabeth Goudge." *Junior Bookshelf* 11 (July 1947): 58–61.

Doyle, Brian. *The Who's Who of Children's Literature*. New York: Schocken, 1968, pp. 115–117.

Goudge, Elizabeth. *The Joy of the Snow*. New York: Coward-McCann, 1974.

———. "Today and Tomorrow." *Junior Bookshelf* 11 (July 1947): 53–57.

———. "West Country Magic." *Horn Book* 23 (Mar. 1947): 100–103.

Gough, John. "Rediscovering *The Little White Horse*." *Signal* 48 (Sept. 1985): 168–175.

"*The Little White Horse*." In M. Crouch and A. Ellis. *Chosen for Children*. 3rd ed. London: The Library Association, 1977, pp. 40–44.

Searles, Baird; Meacham, Beth; and Franklin, Michael. *A Reader's Guide to Fantasy*. New York: Avon, 1982, pp. 68–69.

Third Book of Junior Authors. Edited by Doris De Montreville and Donna Hill. New York: Wilson, 1972, pp. 105–107.

Twentieth Century Children's Writers. 2nd ed. Edited by D. L. Kirkpatrick. New York: St. Martin's Press, 1983, pp. 324–325.

Goulart, Ron(ald Joseph)

Goulart, Ron. "Historical Hysteria or Humor in Science Fiction." In *Inside Outer Space*. Edited by Sharon Jarvis. New York: Ungar, 1985.

Pierce, Hazel Beasley. *A Literary Symbiosis: Science Fiction/Fantasy Mystery*. Westport, CT: Greenwood Press, 1983.

Shapiro, David. "Introduction." In Ron Goulart. *After Things Fell Apart*. Boston: Gregg, 1977.

Twentieth-Century Science Fiction Writers. 2nd ed. Edited by Curtis C. Smith. Chicago: St. James Press, 1986, pp. 294–296.

Grahame, Kenneth

Battiscombe, Georgina. "Exile from the Golden City." *Times Literary Supplement*, Mar. 13, 1959, p. 144. Reprinted in Margaret Meek. *The Cool Web*. New York: Atheneum, 1978, pp. 284–290.

Berman, R. "Victorian Dragons: The Reluctant Brood." *Children's Literature in Education* 15 (Winter 1984): 220–233.

Braybrooke, Neville. "Kenneth Grahame—1859–1932: A Centenary Study." *Elementary English* 36 (Jan. 1959): 11–15.

———. "A Note on Kenneth Grahame." *Horn Book* 46 (Oct. 1970): 504–507.

Carpenter, Humphrey. "Kenneth Grahame and the Search for Arcadia." In *Secret*

Gardens: A Study of the Golden Age of Children's Literature. Boston: Houghton Mifflin, 1985, pp. 115–125.

———. *"The Wind in the Willows."* In *Secret Gardens: A Study of the Golden Age of Children's Literature.* Boston: Houghton Mifflin, 1985, pp. 151–169.

Chalmers, Patrick R. *Kenneth Grahame: Life, Letters and Unpublished Work.* London: Methuen, 1933.

Cornwell, Charles Landrum. "From Self to the Shire: Studies in Victorian Fantasy." Ph.D. dissertation, University of Virginia, 1972.

Cripps, Elizabeth A. "Kenneth Grahame: Children's Author?" *Children's Literature in Education* 40, no. 12 (Spring 1981): 15–23.

Doyle, Brian. *The Who's Who of Children's Literature.* New York: Schocken, 1968, pp. 118–121.

Fadiman, Clifton. "Professionals and Confessionals: Dr. Seuss and Kenneth Grahame." In Egoff. *Only Connect.* 2nd ed. New York: Oxford Univ. Press, 1980, pp. 277–283.

Fletcher, D. "The Book That Cannot Be Illustrated: *The Wind in the Willows."* *Horn Book* 44 (Feb. 1968): 87–90.

Forsyth, A. *"The Wind in the Willows*—50 Years Later." *Junior Bookshelf* 22 (Mar. 1958): 57–62.

Gagnon, Laurence. "Philosophy and Fantasy." *Children's Literature* 1 (1972): 98–103.

Goldthwaite, John. "The Black Rabbit: Part One." *Signal* 47 (May 1985): 86–111. "Part Two." *Signal* 48 (Sept. 1985): 148–167. Reprinted in Goldthwaite. *The Natural History of Make-Believe.* New York: Oxford Univ. Press, 1987.

Graham, Eleanor. *Kenneth Grahame.* New York: Walck, 1963.

Grahame, Kenneth. *First Whisper of "The Wind in the Willows."* Edited by Elspeth Grahame. Philadelphia: Lippincott, 1945.

———. "Introduction." In *A Hundred Fables of Aesop.* New York: Dodd, 1924, pp. i–xv. Originally published 1898.

Green, Peter. *Beyond the Wild Wood: The World of Kenneth Grahame, Author of 'The Wind in the Willows.'* New York: Facts on File, 1983. An abridged version of Green's 1959 biography.

———. *Kenneth Grahame: A Biography.* Chicago: World, 1959.

———. "The Rentier's Rural Dream." Introduction to *The Wind in the Willows.* New York: Oxford Univ. Press, 1983. Reprinted in the *Times Literary Supplement,* Nov. 26, 1982, pp. 1299–1301.

Green, Roger Lancelyn. "The Magic of Kenneth Grahame." *Junior Bookshelf* 23 (Mar. 1959): 47–58.

Hedges, Ned Samuel. "The Fable and the Fabulous: The Use of Traditional Forms in Children's Literature." Ph.D. dissertation, University of Nebraska, 1968.

Hodges, M. "Happy Birthday, *The Wind in the Willows."* *Top of the News* 14 (Mar. 1958): 7–10.

Hunt, Peter. "Landscapes and Journeys, Metaphors and Maps: The Distinctive Feature of English Fantasy." *Children's Literature Association Quarterly* 12 (Spring 1987): 11–15.

Inglis, Fred. *The Promise of Happiness.* New York: Cambridge Univ. Press, 1981, pp. 117–123.

Kuznets, Lois R. "Kenneth Grahame." In *Writers for Children; Critical Studies of Major Authors since the Seventeenth Century.* Edited by Jane M. Bingham. New York: Scribner, 1988, pp. 247–254.

———. "Toad Hall Revisited." *Children's Literature,* vol. 7. Storrs, CT: Parousia Press, 1978, pp. 115–128.

Lippman, Charles. "All the Comforts of Home." *Antioch Review* 41 (1983): 409–420.

Little, Edmund. *The Fantasts: Studies in J. R. R. Tolkien, Lewis Carroll, Mervyn*

Peake, Nikolay Gogol, and Kenneth Grahame. Amersham, England: Avebury, 1984.

Lowe, Elizabeth Cochran. "Kenneth Grahame and the Beast Tale." Ph.D. dissertation, New York University, 1976.

Luenn, Nancy. "A Visit to Toad Hall and Pooh Forest." *Horn Book* 62 (July–Aug. 1986): 507–508.

McGillis, Roderick. "Utopian Hopes: Criticism Beyond Itself." *Children's Literature Association Quarterly* 9 (Winter 1984–1985): 184–186.

Macy, George. "Arthur Rackham and *The Wind in the Willows.*" *Horn Book* 16 (May–June 1940): 153–158. Reprinted in Norma Fryatt. *A Horn Book Sampler.* Boston: Horn Book, 1959, pp. 50–54.

Moore, Anne Carroll. "Kenneth Grahame, 1859–1932." *Horn Book* 10 (Mar. 1934): 73–81.

The Oxford Companion to Children's Literature. Edited by Humphrey Carpenter and Mari Prichard. New York: Oxford Univ. Press, 1984, pp. 216–219, 573–575.

Pflieger, Pat, and Hill, Helen M. *A Reference Guide to Modern Fantasy for Children.* Westport, CT: Greenwood Press, 1984, pp. xv, 210–213, 606–607.

Philip, Neil. "Kenneth Grahame's *The Wind in the Willows:* A Companionable Vitality." In *Touchstones.* Edited by Perry Nodelman. West Lafayette, IN: Children's Literature Association Publications, 1985, pp. 96–105.

Platzner, R. L. "Child's Play: Games and Fantasy in Carroll, Stevenson, and Grahame." In *Proceedings of the Fifth Annual Conference of the Children's Literature Association.* Harvard University, March 1978. Ypsilanti, MI: Children's Literature Association, 1979, pp. 78–86.

Poss, Geraldine D. "An Epic in Arcadia: The Pastoral World of *The Wind in the Willows.*" In *Children's Literature,* vol. 4. Philadelphia: Temple Univ. Press, 1975, pp. 80–90. Reprinted in *Reflections on Literature for Children.* Edited by Francelia Butler and Richard Rotert. Hamden, CT: Shoe String Press, 1984, pp. 237–246.

Price, J. "*The Wind in the Willows:* Kenneth Grahame's Creation of a Wild Wood." *A. B. Bookman's Weekly* 81 (Jan. 25, 1988): 265–266 ff.

Ray, Laura Krugman. "Kenneth Grahame and the Literature of Childhood." *English Literature in Transition* 20 (1977): 3–12.

Ryan, J. S. "The Wild Wood—Place of Dander, Place of Protest." *Orana* 19 (Aug. 1983): 133–140.

Sale, Roger. *Fairy Tales and After: From Snow White to E. B. White.* Cambridge, MA: Harvard Univ. Press, 1978, pp. 165–194.

Sayers, Frances Clarke. "Editorial: *The Wind in the Willows.*" *Horn Book* 35 (June 1959): 189.

Searles, Baird; Meacham, Beth; and Franklin, Michael. *A Reader's Guide to Fantasy.* New York: Avon, 1982, p. 69.

Shepard, Ernest H. "Illustrating *The Wind in the Willows.*" *Horn Book* 30 (Apr. 1954): 83–86. Reprinted in Elinor Field. *Horn Book Reflections.* Boston: Horn Book, 1969, pp. 273–275.

Slobodkin, Louis. "Artist's Choice: *Bertie's Escapade.*" *Horn Book* 26 (July 1950): 293–295.

Smith, Kathryn A. "Kenneth Grahame and the Singing Willows." *Elementary English* 45 (Dec. 1968): 1024–1035.

Smith, Louisa A. "*The Wind in the Willows.*" In *Survey of Modern Fantasy Literature,* vol. 5. Edited by Frank N. Magill. Englewood Cliffs, NJ: Salem Press, 1983, pp. 2132–2135.

Steig, Michael. "At the Back of *The Wind in the Willows:* An Experiment in Biographical and Autobiographical Interpretation." *Victorian Studies* 24 (Spring 1981): 303–323.

Sterck, Kenneth. "Rereading *The Wind in the Willows." Children's Literature in Education* 12 (Sept. 1973): 20–28.

Stott, Jon C. *Children's Literature from A to Z.* New York: McGraw-Hill, 1984, p. 126.

Stridsberg, A. B. "On Illustrating Kenneth Grahame." *Yale University Library Gazette* 24 (July 1949): 28–35.

Taylor, S. Keith. "Universal Themes in Kenneth Grahame's *The Wind in the Willows."* Ph.D. dissertation, Temple University, 1967.

Tucker, Nicholas. "The Children's Falstaff." In Nicholas Tucker. *Suitable for Children? Controversies in Children's Literature.* Berkeley: Univ. of California Press, 1976, pp. 160–164. Originally published in *Times Literary Supplement,* June 26, 1969.

Twentieth Century Children's Writers. 2nd ed. Edited by D. L. Kirkpatrick. New York: St. Martin's Press, 1983, pp. 329–331.

Waddey, Lucy E. "Home in Children's Fiction: Three Patterns." *Children's Literature Association Quarterly* 8 (Spring 1983): 13–15.

Watkins, Tony. " 'Making a Break for the Real England': The River-Bankers Revisited." *Children's Literature Association Quarterly* 9 (Spring 1984): 34–35.

Williams, Jay. "Reflections on *The Wind in the Willows." Signal* 21 (Sept. 1976): 103–107.

Zanger, Jules. "Goblins, Morlocks, and Weasels: Classic Fantasy and the Industrial Revolution." *Children's Literature in Education* 27, no. 4 (1977): 154–162.

Gray, Nicholas Stuart

Crouch, Marcus. "Revels Ended." *Junior Bookshelf* 45 (June 1981): 101–103.

Twentieth Century Children's Writers. 2nd ed. Edited by D. L. Kirkpatrick. New York: St. Martin's Press, 1983, pp. 331–333.

Wintle, Justin, and Fisher, Emma. "Nicholas Stuart Gray." In *The Pied Pipers.* New York: Paddington Press, 1974, pp. 147–160.

Greaves, Margaret

Twentieth Century Children's Writers. 2nd ed. Edited by D. L. Kirkpatrick. New York: St. Martin's Press, 1983, pp. 333–334.

Greenwald, Sheila (pseud. of Sheila Ellen Green)

Fifth Book of Junior Authors and Illustrators. Edited by Sally Holmes Holtze. New York: Wilson, 1983, pp. 139–140.

Gripe, Maria (Kristina)

Gripe, Maria. "A Word and a Shadow." *Bookbird* 12 (1974): 4–10.

Heins, Paul. *"The Glassblower's Children,* a Review." *Horn Book* 49 (Aug. 1973): 365.

Mannheimer, Carin. "Maria Gripe." *Bookbird* 11 (1973): 24–34.

Stanton, Lorraine. "Shadows and Motifs: A Review and Analysis of the Works of Maria Gripe." *Catholic Library World* 51 (May 1980): 447–449.

Third Book of Junior Authors. Edited by Doris De Montreville and Donna Hill. New York: Wilson, 1972, pp. 113–114.

Guillot, René

Crouch, Marcus. *The Nesbit Tradition*. London: Benn, 1972, pp. 39–40.
Doyle, Brian. *The Who's Who of Children's Literature*. New York: Schocken, 1968, pp. 126–127.
Marsh, Gwen. "René Guillot." *Horn Book* 41 (Apr. 1965): 192–194.
More Junior Authors. Edited by Muriel Fuller. New York: Wilson, 1963, pp. 104–105.
Schmidt, Nancy J. *Children's Books about Africa in English*. New York: Conch Magazine, 1981, pp. 114–118.

Guy, Rosa (Cuthbert)

Fifth Book of Junior Authors and Illustrators. Edited by Sally Holmes Holtze. New York: Wilson, 1983, pp. 140–141.
Twentieth Century Children's Writers. 2nd ed. Edited by D. L. Kirkpatrick. New York: St. Martin's Press, 1983, pp. 334–335.

Haldane, J(ohn) B(urdon) S(anderson)

The Oxford Companion to Children's Literature. Edited by Humphrey Carpenter and Mari Prichard. New York: Oxford Univ. Press, 1984, p. 368.
Twentieth Century Children's Writers. 2nd ed. Edited by D. L. Kirkpatrick. New York: St. Martin's Press, 1983, pp. 348–350.
Twentieth-Century Science Fiction Writers. 2nd ed. Edited by Curtis C. Smith. Chicago: St. James Press, 1986, pp. 310–312.

Haldeman, Linda (Wilson)

Searles, Baird; Meacham, Beth; and Franklin, Michael. *A Reader's Guide to Fantasy*. New York: Avon, 1982, p. 72.

Hale, Lucretia Peabody

Doyle, Brian. *The Who's Who of Children's Literature*. New York: Schocken, 1968, p. 132.
Gay, Carol. "Lucretia Peabody Hale." In *American Writers for Children before 1900. Dictionary of Literary Biography*, vol. 42. Detroit: Gale, 1985, pp. 207–216.
Heins, Paul. "Lucretia P. Hale." In *Writers for Children; Critical Studies of Major Authors since the Seventeenth Century*. Edited by Jane M. Bingham. New York: Scribner, 1988, pp. 265–268.
Helbig, Alethea K., and Perkins, Agnes Regan. *Dictionary of American Children's Fiction, 1859–1959*. Westport, CT: Greenwood Press, 1985, pp. 200, 403–404.
The Oxford Companion to Children's Literature. Edited by Humphrey Carpenter and Mari Prichard. New York: Oxford Univ. Press, 1984, pp. 235, 404.
Twentieth Century Children's Writers. 2nd ed. Edited by D. L. Kirkpatrick. New York: St. Martin's Press, 1983, p. 870.
Wankmiller, Madelyn C. "Lucretia P. Hale and *The Peterkin Papers*." *Horn Book* 34 (Apr. 1958): 95–103, 137–147. Reprinted in Siri Andrews. *The Hewins Lectures. 1947–1962*. Boston: Horn Book, 1963, pp. 235–249.
White, Eliza Orne. "Lucretia P. Hale: The Author of *The Peterkin Papers*." *Horn Book* 16 (Sept.–Oct. 1940): 317–322.

————. "Some New England Authors and Their Stories." *Horn Book* 1 (June 1925): 11–21.

Whitney, Elinor. "The Peterkins Visit the Bookshop." *Horn Book* 2 (Nov. 1924): 4–6. Reprinted in *Horn Book* 53 (Apr. 1977): 215–216.

Hambly, Barbara

"Barbara Hambly: Saved by the Ax." *Locus* 305 (1986): 27ff.

Hamilton (Adoff), Virginia (Esther)

Apseloff, Marilyn F. "A Conversation with Virginia Hamilton." *Children's Literature in Education* 14 (Winter 1983): 204–213.

————. "Creative Geography in the Ohio Novels of Virginia Hamilton." *Children's Literature Association Quarterly* 8 (Spring 1983): 17–20.

————. "Virginia Hamilton." In *American Writers for Children since 1960: Fiction. Dictionary of Literary Biography*, vol. 52. Detroit: Gale, 1986, pp. 207–212.

Dressel, Janice Hartwick. "The Legacy of Ralph Ellison in Virginia Hamilton's *Justice Trilogy*." *English Journal* 73 (Nov. 1984): 42–48.

Fourth Book of Junior Authors and Illustrators. Edited by Doris De Montreville and Elizabeth D. Crawford. New York: Wilson, 1978, pp. 162–164.

Hamilton, Virginia. "Ah, Sweet Rememory!" Based on a paper given at the Simmons College Center for the Study of Children's Literature, March 14, 1981. *Horn Book* 57 (Dec. 1981): 633–651. Reprinted in *Innocence & Experience*. Edited by Barbara Harrison and George Maguire. New York: Lothrop, 1987, pp. 6–12.

————. "Boston Globe—Horn Book Award Acceptance." *Horn Book* 60 (Feb. 1984): 24–28.

————. "Changing Woman, Working." In Betsy Hearne. *Celebrating Children's Books*. New York: Lothrop, 1981, pp. 54–61.

————. "Coretta Scott King Award Acceptance." *Horn Book* 62 (Nov./Dec. 1986): 683–687.

————. "High John's Risen Again." *Horn Book* 51 (Apr. 1975): 113–121.

————. "Illusion and Reality." In Haviland. *The Openhearted Audience*. Washington, DC: Library of Congress, 1980, pp. 115–131.

————. "The Known, the Remembered, and the Imagined: Celebrating Afro-American Folktales." *Children's Literature in Education* 18 (Summer 1987): 67–76.

————. "The Mind of a Novel: The Heart of the Book." *Children's Literature Association Quarterly* 8 (Fall 1983): 10–14.

————. "Newbery Award Acceptance." *Horn Book* 51 (Aug. 1975): 337–343.

————. "On Being a Black Writer in America." *The Lion and the Unicorn* 10 (1986): 15–17.

————. "Portrait of the Author as a Working Writer." *Elementary English* 48 (Apr. 1971): 237–240 ff. Reprinted in Miriam Hoffman and Eva Samuels. *Authors and Illustrators of Children's Books*. New York: Bowker, 1972, pp. 186–192.

————. "Writing the Source: In Other Words." *Horn Book* 54 (Dec. 1978): 609–619.

Heins, Ethel L. "*Sweet Whispers, Brother Rush*." *Horn Book* 58 (Oct. 1982): 505–506. Review.

Heins, Paul. "Virginia Hamilton." *Horn Book* 51 (Aug. 1975): 344–348.

Helbig, Alethea K., and Perkins, Agnes Regan. *Dictionary of American Children's Fiction, 1960–1984; Recent Books of Recognized Merit*. New York: Greenwood Press, 1986, pp. 269, 639–640.

Hopkins, Lee Bennett. "Virginia Hamilton." *Horn Book* 48 (Dec. 1972): 563–569.

Reprinted in *More Books by More People.* New York: Citation Press, 1974, pp. 199–207.

Kingman, Lee, ed. *Newbery and Caldecott Medal Books: 1966–1975.* Boston: Horn Book, 1975, pp. 126–140.

Langton, Jane. "Virginia Hamilton the Great." *Horn Book* 50 (Dec. 1971): 671–673.

Mikkelsen, Nina. "But Is It a Children's Book? A Second Look at Virginia Hamilton's *The Magical Adventures of Pretty Pearl.*" *Children's Literature Association Quarterly* 11 (Fall 1986); 134–142.

The Oxford Companion to Children's Literature. Edited by Humphrey Carpenter and Mari Prichard. New York: Oxford Univ. Press, 1984, p. 237.

"Profile of an Author: Virginia Hamilton." *Top of the News* 25 (June 1969): 376–380.

Rees, David. "Ride through a Painted Desert—Virginia Hamilton." In *Painted Desert, Green Shade.* Boston: Horn Book, 1984, pp. 168–184.

Roginski, Jim, ed. *Newbery and Caldecott Medalists and Honor Book Winners.* Littleton, CO: Libraries Unlimited, 1982, p. 136.

Rush, Theresa Gunnell; Myers, Carol Fairbanks; and Arata, Esther Spring, comps. *Black American Writers, Past and Present,* vol. 1. Metuchen, NJ: Scarecrow Press, 1975, pp. 351–352.

Stott, Jon C. *Children's Literature from A to Z.* New York: McGraw-Hill, 1984, p. 135.

Townsend, John Rowe. "Virginia Hamilton." In *A Sounding of Storytellers.* Philadelphia: Lippincott, 1974, pp. 97–110.

Twentieth Century Children's Writers. 2nd ed. Edited by D. L. Kirkpatrick. New York: St. Martin's Press, 1983, pp. 353–354.

Wilson, Geraldine. "Review." *Interracial Books for Children* 1–2 (1983): 32. Review of *Sweet Whispers, Brother Rush.*

Hancock, Neil (Anderson)

Paxon, Diana. "The Tolkien Tradition." *Mythlore* 39 (1984): 23–27, 37.

Harris, Christie (Lucy Irwin)

Ellison, Shirley, and Mishra, Mary. "Award-Winning Canadian Author Christie Harris." *Bookbird* 19, no. 4 (1981): 19–22.

Fourth Book of Junior Authors and Illustrators. Edited by Doris De Montreville and Elizabeth D. Crawford. New York: Wilson, 1978, pp. 165–167.

Harris, Christie. "Christie Harris on Fantasy." *In Review* 15 (Oct. 1981): 5–8.

———. "In Tune with Tomorrow." *Canadian Children's Literature* 10 (Autumn 1978): 26–30.

———. "My Heroine Helped Me." *Horn Book* 41 (Aug. 1964): 361–363.

———. "Never Underestimate an Indian Village." *Horn Book* 39 (Apr. 1963): 156–161.

———. "The Shift from Feasthouse to Book." *Canadian Children's Literature* 31/32 (1983): 9–11.

McDonough, Irma, ed. "Christie Harris." In *Profiles.* rev. ed. Ottowa: Canadian Library Association, 1975.

Radu, Kenneth. "Canadian Fantasy." *Canadian Children's Literature* 1 (Summer 1975): 75–79.

Stott, Jon C. *Children's Literature from A to Z.* New York: McGraw-Hill, 1984, p. 138.

Twentieth Century Children's Writers. 2nd ed. Edited by D. L. Kirkpatrick. New York: St. Martin's Press, 1983, pp. 358–359.

Wood, Susan. "Stories and Stlalakums: Christie Harris and the Supernatural World." *Canadian Children's Literature* 15 and 16 (1980): 47–56.

Harris, Rosemary (Jeanne)

Fourth Book of Junior Authors and Illustrators. Edited by Doris De Montreville and Elizabeth D. Crawford. New York: Wilson, 1978, pp. 167–168.

Harris, Rosemary. "The Moon in the Cloud." *Junior Bookshelf* 33 (Aug. 1969): 223–226.

"The Moon in the Cloud." In M. Crouch and A. Ellis. *Chosen for Children.* 3rd ed. London: The Library Association, 1977, pp. 146–149.

The Oxford Companion to Children's Literature. Edited by Humphrey Carpenter and Mari Prichard. New York: Oxford Univ. Press, 1984, p. 242.

Schmidt, Nancy J. *Children's Fiction about Africa in English.* New York: Conch Magazine, 1981, pp. 157–158.

Twentieth Century Children's Writers. 2nd ed. Edited by D. L. Kirkpatrick. New York: St. Martin's Press, 1983, pp. 360–361.

Yolen, Jane. "The Literary Underwater World." *Language Arts* 57 (1980): 403–412.

Harrison, M(ichael) John

Darlington, Andy. "M. John Harrison: The Condition of Falling." *Vector* 122 (1984): 3–5.

Fowler, Christopher. "The Last Rebel: An Interview with M. John Harrison." *Foundation* 23 (1981): 5–30.

Twentieth-Century Science Fiction Writers. 2nd ed. Edited by Curtis C. Smith. Chicago: St. James Press, 1986, pp. 322–323.

Hatch, Richard Warren

Doyle, Brian. *The Who's Who of Children's Literature.* New York: Schocken, 1968, p. 138.

Hatch, Richard W. "Too Good to Be Forgotten." *Horn Book* 19 (July 1943): 251–252.

Hauff, Wilhelm

Cobbs, Alfred L. "Wilhelm Hauff." In *Supernatural Fiction Writers: Fantasy and Horror,* vol. 1. Edited by E. F. Bleiler. New York: Scribner, 1985, pp. 107–110.

Doyle, Brian. *The Who's Who of Children's Literature.* New York: Schocken, 1968, pp. 138–139.

The Oxford Companion to Children's Literature. Edited by Humphrey Carpenter and Mari Prichard. New York: Oxford Univ. Press, 1984, p. 242.

Haugaard, Erik Christian

Haugaard, Erik Christian. "A Writer Comments." *Horn Book* 43 (Aug. 1967): 444–446.

Kuznets, Lois R. "Other People's Children: Erik Haugaard's 'Untold Tales.' " *Children's Literature in Education* 11 (Summer 1980): 62–68. Reprinted from *Proceedings of the Sixth Annual Conference of the Children's Literature Association,* 1979. Ypsilanti, MI: Children's Literature Association, 1981, pp. 128–135.

Lavender, Ralph. "Hans Christian Andersen and Erik Christian Haugaard." *School Librarian* 23 (June 1975): 113–119.
Nist, Joan. *"Places of Freedom:* Erik Christian Haugaard's Historical Fiction." *Advocate* 2 (Winter 1985): 114–120.
Root, Shelton L., and Greenlaw, M. Jean. "Profile: An Interview with Erik Christian Haugaard." *Language Arts* 56 (May 1979): 549–561.
Third Book of Junior Authors. Edited by Doris De Montreville and Donna Hill. New York: Wilson, 1972, pp. 120–121.
Twentieth Century Children's Writers. 2nd ed. Edited by D. L. Kirkpatrick. New York: St. Martin's Press, 1983, pp. 361–362.

Hawthorne, Nathaniel

Becker, Allienne Rimer. "The Fantastic in the Fiction of Hoffmann and Hawthorne." Ph.D. dissertation, Pennsylvania State University, 1984.
Billman, Carol. "Nathaniel Hawthorne: 'Revolutionizer' of Children's Literature." *Studies in American Fiction* 10 (1982): 107–114.
Bonney, Agnes Mavis. "Artistic Uses of Supernaturalism in the Fiction of Brown, Irving and Hawthorne." Ph.D. dissertation, Washington University, 1978.
Doyle, Brian. *The Who's Who of Children's Literature.* New York: Schocken, 1968, pp. 139–140.
Fraden, Rena. "The Sentimental Tradition in Dickens and Hawthorne." Ph.D. dissertation, Yale University, 1983.
Fulton, Patricia Teague. "Borges, Hawthorne and Poe: A Study of Significant Parallels in Their Theories and Methods of Short Story Writing." Ph.D. dissertation, Auburn University, 1979.
Jordan, Alice M. "The Dawn of Imagination in American Books for Children." *Horn Book* 20 (May 1944): 168–175.
Kerr, Howard; Crowley, John W.; and Crowley, Charles W., eds. *The Haunted Dusk: American Supernatural Fiction, 1820–1920.* Athens: Univ. of Georgia Press, 1983, pp. 67–98.
Lee, A. Robert, ed. *Nathaniel Hawthorne, New Critical Essays.* Totowa, NJ: Barnes and Noble, 1982.
Martin, Terence. *Nathaniel Hawthorne.* rev. ed. Boston: Twayne, 1983.
Neilson, Keith. "The Short Fiction of Nathaniel Hawthorne." In *Survey of Modern Fantasy Literature,* vol. 3. Edited by Frank N. Magill. Englewood Cliffs, NJ: Salem Press, 1983, pp. 1536–1543.
The Oxford Companion to Children's Literature. Edited by Humphrey Carpenter and Mari Prichard. New York: Oxford Univ. Press, 1984, pp. 243, 516, 577–578.
Rupprecht, Erich S. "Nathaniel Hawthorne." In *Supernatural Fiction Writers: Fantasy and Horror,* vol. 2. Edited by E. F. Bleiler. New York: Scribner, 1985, pp. 707–716.
Stott, Jon C. "Nathaniel Hawthorne." In *Writers for Children; Critical Studies of Major Authors since the Seventeenth Century.* Edited by Jane M. Bingham. New York: Scribner, 1988, pp. 277–282.

Haywood, Carolyn

Burns, Paul C., and Hines, Ruth. "Carolyn Haywood." In *Authors and Illustrators of Children's Books.* Edited by Miriam Hoffman and Eva Samuels. New York: Bowker, 1972, pp. 193–196. Reprinted from *Elementary English* 47 (Feb. 1970): 172–175.
The Junior Book of Authors. 2nd ed. rev. Edited by Stanley J. Kunitz and Howard Haycraft. New York: Wilson, 1951, pp. 155–156.

Shaken, Grace. "Our Debt to Carolyn Haywood." *Elementary English* 32 (Jan. 1955): 3–8.
Twentieth Century Children's Writers. 2nd ed. Edited by D. L. Kirkpatrick. New York: St. Martin's Press, 1983, pp. 363–364.

Hazel, Paul

Searles, Baird; Meacham, Beth; and Franklin, Michael. *A Reader's Guide to Fantasy.* New York: Avon, 1982, p. 73.

Heide, Florence Parry

Chambers, Aidan. *Booktalk: Occasional Writing on Literature and Children.* New York: Harper and Row, 1986, pp. 33, 62, 76, 80, 120.
Fourth Book of Junior Authors and Illustrators. Edited by Doris De Montreville and Elizabeth D. Crawford. New York: Wilson, 1978, pp. 172–173.
Twentieth Century Children's Writers. 2nd ed. Edited by D. L. Kirkpatrick. New York: St. Martin's Press, 1983, pp. 364–366.

Helprin, Mark

Twentieth-Century Science Fiction Writers. 2nd ed. Edited by Curtis C. Smith. Chicago: St. James Press, 1986, pp. 328–329.

Hess, Fjeril

The Junior Book of Authors. 2nd ed. rev. Edited by Stanley J. Kunitz and Howard Haycraft. New York: Wilson, 1951, pp. 157–159.
Seaman, Louise. "From California to the Volga with Fjeril Hess." *Horn Book* 10 (Nov. 1934): 385–389.

Hewett, Anita

Twentieth Century Children's Writers. 2nd ed. Edited by D. L. Kirkpatrick. New York: St. Martin's Press, 1983, pp. 371–372.

Hildick, E(dmund) W(allace)

Doyle, Brian. *The Who's Who of Children's Literature.* New York: Schocken, 1968, pp. 143–144.
Fourth Book of Junior Authors and Illustrators. Edited by Doris De Montreville and Elizabeth D. Crawford. New York: Wilson, 1978, pp. 174–176.
Twentieth Century Children's Writers. 2nd ed. Edited by D. L. Kirkpatrick. New York: St. Martin's Press, 1983, pp. 374–376.

Hilton, James

Crawford, John W. "The Utopian Dream Alive and Well." *Cuyahoga Review* 2 (Spring–Summer 1984): 27–33.
Edwards, Malcolm, and Holdstock, Robert. "Lost Worlds." In *Realms of Fantasy.* Garden City, NY: Doubleday, 1983, pp. 27–31.
Stableford, Brian. "*Lost Horizon.*" In *Survey of Modern Fantasy Literature,* vol. 2. Edited by Frank N. Magill. Englewood Cliffs, NJ: Salem Press, 1983, pp. 920–923.

Hoban, Russell C(onwell)

Allison, Alida. "Russell Hoban." In *American Writers for Children since 1960: Fiction. Dictionary of Literary Biography,* vol. 52. Detroit: Gale, 1986, pp. 192–201.

Archer, John. "Interview with Russell Hoban." *Hard Times* (University College, Cardiff, Wales) 2 (Dec. 1974).

Blount, Margaret. *Animal Land: The Creatures of Children's Fiction.* New York: Morrow, 1975, pp. 186–188.

Bowers, Joan A. "From Badgers to Turtles: The Fantasy World of Russell Hoban." In *Proceedings of the Sixth Annual Conference of the Children's Literature Association.* University of Toronto, March 1979. Ypsilanti, MI: Children's Literature Association, 1981, pp. 86–93. Reprinted in *Children's Literature,* vol. 8. New Haven, CT: Yale Univ. Press, 1980, pp. 80–97.

Branscomb, J. "The Quest for Wholeness in the Fiction of Russell Hoban." *Critique* 28 (Fall 1986): 29–38.

Bunbury, Rhonda M. " 'Always a Dance Going On in the Stone': An Interview with Russell Hoban." *Children's Literature in Education* 17 (Fall 1986): 139–149.

Hamilton, Alex. "Interview with Russell Hoban." *The Guardian,* Mar. 24, 1975.

Helbig, Alethea K., and Perkins, Agnes Regan. *Dictionary of American Children's Fiction, 1960–1984.* Westport, CT: Greenwood Press, 1986, pp. 291, 434–435.

Hoban, Russell. "One Pays Attention." *Puffin Post* (London) 10, no. 2 (1976): 14.

———. "Thoughts on a Shirtless Cyclist, Robin Hood, Johann Sebastian Bach and One or Two Other Things." *Children's Literature in Education* 4 (Mar. 1971): 5–23. Reprinted in Geoff Fox. *Writers, Critics and Children.* New York: Agathon Press, 1976, pp. 95–103.

———. "Thoughts on Being and Writing." In Edward Blishen. *The Thorny Paradise.* Boston: Horn Book, 1975, pp. 65–76.

———. "Time Slip, Uphill Lean, Laminar Flow, Place-to-Place Talking and Hearing the Silence." *Children's Literature in Education* 9 (Nov. 1972): 33–47.

Inglis, Fred. *The Promise of Happiness.* New York: Cambridge Univ. Press, 1981, pp. 303–304.

Kincaid, Paul. "The Mouse, the Lion and *Ridley Walker:* Russell Hoban Interviewed." *Vector* 124/125 (1985): 5–9.

Lenz, Millicent. "Russell Hoban's *The Mouse and His Child* and the Search to Be Self-Winding." In *Proceedings of the Fifth Annual Conference of the Children's Literature Association.* Harvard University, March 1978. Ypsilanti, MI: Children's Literature Association, 1979, pp. 64–69.

Lynn, Joanne. "Threadbare Utopia: Hoban's Modern Pastoral." *Children's Literature Association Quarterly* 11 (Spring 1986): 19–24.

MacKillop, Ian D. "Russell Hoban: Returning to the Sunlight." In Dennis Butts. *Good Writers for Young Readers.* St. Albans, England: Hart-Davis, 1977, pp. 57–66.

McMahon-Hill, Gillian. "A Narrow Pavement Says 'Walk Alone': The Books of Russell Hoban." *Children's Literature in Education* 20 (Spring 1976): 41–55.

Morrissey, Thomas J. "Armageddon from Huxley to Hoban." *Extrapolation* 25 (Fall 1984): 197–213.

The Oxford Companion to Children's Literature. Edited by Humphrey Carpenter and Mari Prichard. New York: Oxford Univ. Press, 1984, pp. 254–255, 365.

Rees, David. "Beyond the Last Visible Dog—Russell Hoban." In *Painted Desert, Green Shade.* Boston: Horn Book, 1984, pp. 138–152.

Rustin, Michael. "Making Out in America: *The Mouse and His Child.*" In *Narratives of Love and Loss.* London: Verso, 1987, pp. 181–195.

Singh, Michael J. "Law and Emotion in Fantasy." *Orana* 18 (May 1982): 49–54.

Swinfen, Ann. *In Defense of Fantasy.* London: Routledge, 1984. A discussion of *The Mouse and His Child*, pp. 21, 31–34, 105, 193–202, 228–229.

Third Book of Junior Authors. Edited by Doris De Montreville and Donna Hill. New York: Wilson, 1972, pp. 129–130.

Toomey, Philippa. "Interview with Russell Hoban." *The* [London] *Times,* Nov. 15, 1974.

Townsend, John Rowe. "A Second Look—*The Mouse and His Child.*" *Horn Book* 51 (Oct. 1975): 449–451. Reprinted in Paul Heins. *Crosscurrents of Criticism.* Boston: Horn Book, 1977, pp. 330–332.

Twentieth Century Children's Writers. 2nd ed. Edited by D. L. Kirkpatrick. New York: St. Martin's Press, 1983, pp. 377–379.

Twentieth-Century Science Fiction Writers. 2nd ed. Edited by Curtis C. Smith. Chicago: St. James Press, 1986, pp. 338–339.

Hodges, C(yril) Walter

Crouch, Marcus S. "Illustrated by C. Walter Hodges." *Junior Bookshelf* 15 (July 1951): 79–84.

Hodges, C. Walter. "Adventures with a Problem." *Horn Book* 16 (Sept.–Oct. 1940): 331–333.

———. "On Writing about King Alfred." *Horn Book* 43 (Apr. 1967): 179–182; *Junior Bookshelf* 31 (June 1967): 159–163. Reprinted in *Folk Literature of the British Isles.* Edited by Eloise S. Norton. Metuchen, NJ: Scarecrow Press, 1978, pp. 67–70.

Long, Sidney. "A Second Look: *The Namesake.*" *Horn Book* 53 (Aug. 1977): 477–482.

Third Book of Junior Authors. Edited by Doris De Montreville and Donna Hill. New York: Wilson, 1972, pp. 130–132.

Twentieth Century Children's Writers. 2nd ed. Edited by D. L. Kirkpatrick. New York: St. Martin's Press, 1983, pp. 379–381.

Hodges, Elizabeth Jamison

Hodges, Elizabeth Jamison. "The Magic of Serendipity." *Horn Book* 43 (June 1967): 370–374. "Part II." *Horn Book* 45 (Aug. 1969): 436–439.

Hoffmann, Eleanor

Helbig, Alethea K., and Perkins, Agnes Regan. *Dictionary of American Children's Fiction, 1859–1959.* Westport, CT: Greenwood Press, 1985, p. 221.

The Oxford Companion to Children's Literature. Edited by Humphrey Carpenter and Mari Prichard. New York: Oxford Univ. Press, 1984, pp. 256, 384.

Hoffmann, E(rnst) T(heodor) A(madeus)

Becker, Allienne Rimer. "The Fantastic in the Fiction of Hoffmann and Hawthorne." Ph.D. dissertation, Pennsylvania State University, 1984.

Doyle, Brian. *The Who's Who of Children's Literature.* New York: Schocken, 1968, p. 144.

Duroche, Leonard L. "E. T. A. Hoffmann." In *Writers for Children; Critical Studies of Major Authors since the Seventeenth Century.* Edited by Jane M. Bingham. New York: Scribner, 1988, pp. 283–288.

Goff, Penrith. "E. T. A. Hoffmann." In *Supernatural Fiction Writers: Fantasy and Horror,* vol. 1. Edited by E. F. Bleiler. New York: Scribner, 1985, pp. 111–120.

Jackson, Rosemary. *Fantasy: The Literature of Subversion.* New York: Methuen, 1980, pp. 14, 37, 43–44, 50, 55, 66–67, 104, 107, 123, 172, 176.

Searles, Baird; Meacham, Beth; and Franklin, Michael. *A Reader's Guide to Fantasy.* New York: Avon, 1982, pp. 75–76.

Wolfe, Gary K. "The Short Fiction of E. T. A. Hoffmann." In *Survey of Modern Fantasy Literature,* vol. 4. Edited by Frank N. Magill. Englewood Cliffs, NJ: Salem Press, 1983, pp. 1547–1553.

Holdstock, Robert (P.)

Kincaid, Paul. "The Novels of Robert Holdstock." *Arena* 9 (Aug. 1979): 27–32.

Rippington, Geoff. "Robert Holdstock Interviewed." *Arena* 9 (Aug. 1979): 18–26.

Twentieth-Century Science Fiction Writers. 2nd ed. Edited by Curtis C. Smith. Chicago: St. James Press, 1986, pp. 346–347.

Holman (Valen), Felice

Fourth Book of Junior Authors and Illustrators. Edited by Doris De Montreville and Elizabeth D. Crawford. New York: Wilson, 1978, pp. 182–183.

Helbig, Alethea K., and Perkins, Agnes Regan. *Dictionary of American Children's Fiction, 1960–1984.* Westport, CT: Greenwood Press, 1986, p. 293.

Holman, Felice. "*Slake's Limbo:* In Which a Book Switches Authors." *Horn Book* 52 (Oct. 1976): 479–485.

Holt, Isabella

Helbig, Alethea, and Perkins, Agnes Regan. *Dictionary of American Children's Fiction, 1859–1959.* Westport, CT: Greenwood Press, 1985, pp. 7–9, 223.

Hopkins, Lee Bennett

Fifth Book of Junior Authors and Illustrators. Edited by Sally Holmes Holtze. New York: Wilson, 1983, pp. 155–157.

Horne, Richard Henry

Blainey, Ann. *The Farthing Poet: A Biography of Richard Hengist Horne, 1802–1884, a Lesser Literary Lion.* London: Longmans, 1968.

Fisher, Margery. "Introduction and Notes" to *Memoirs of a London Doll Written by Herself,* by Mrs. Fairstar. Reproduction of 1846 edition. New York: Macmillan, 1967.

Horne, Richard Henry. "A Witch in the Nursery." *Household Words,* Sept. 20, 1851, pp. 601–609. Reprinted in Lance Salway. *A Peculiar Gift.* Harmondsworth, Middlesex: Kestrel, 1976, pp. 173–194.

The Oxford Companion to Children's Literature. Edited by Humphrey Carpenter and Mari Prichard. New York: Oxford Univ. Press, 1984, pp. 261, 348.

Pearl, Cyril. *Always Morning: The Life of Richard Henry "Orion" Horne.* Melbourne, Australia: F. W. Cheshire, 1960.

Horwood, William

Morgan, Chris. "*Duncton Wood.*" In *Survey of Modern Fantasy Literature,* vol. 1. Edited by Frank N. Magill. Englewood Cliffs, NJ: Salem Press, 1983, pp. 436–444.

Hough, (Helen) Charlotte (Woodyatt)

Twentieth Century Children's Writers. 2nd ed. Edited by D. L. Kirkpatrick. New York: St. Martin's Press, 1983, pp. 387–388.

Housman, Laurence

The Oxford Companion to Children's Literature. Edited by Humphrey Carpenter and Mari Prichard. New York: Oxford Univ. Press, 1984, p. 262.

Houston, James A(rchibald)

Fourth Book of Junior Authors and Illustrators. Edited by Doris De Montreville and Elizabeth D. Crawford. New York: Wilson, 1978, pp. 183–185.

Howard, Joan (pseud. of Patricia Gordon)

Helbig, Alethea K., and Perkins, Alice Regan. *Dictionary of American Children's Fiction, 1859–1959.* Westport, CT: Greenwood Press, 1985, p. 189.

Howe, James

Brainard, D. "James Howe." *Publishers Weekly* 225 (Feb. 24, 1984): 144–145. Interview.

Howe, James. "Writing for the Hidden Child." *Horn Book* 61 (Mar.–Apr. 1985): 156–161.

Raymond, A. "James Howe: Corn, Ham, and Punster Cheese." *Teaching K–8* 17 (Feb. 1987): 32–34.

Hudson, W(illiam) H(enry)

Dalphin, Marcia. "I Give You the End of a Golden String." *Horn Book* 14 (May 1938): 143–149. Reprinted in Norma Fryatt. *A Horn Book Sampler.* Boston: Horn Book, 1959, pp. 133–139.

Higgins, James Edward. "Five Authors of Mystical Fancy for Children: A Critical Study." Ed.D. dissertation, Columbia University, 1965.

Ronner, Amy D. *W. H. Hudson: The Man, the Novelist, the Naturalist.* New York: AMS Press, 1986.

Stableford, Brian. *"Green Mansions."* In *Survey of Modern Fantasy Literature,* vol. 2. Edited by Frank N. Magill. Englewood Cliffs, NJ: Salem Press, 1983, pp. 670–674.

Tomalin, Ruth. *W. H. Hudson: A Biography.* London: Faber, 1982.

Hughes, Richard (Arthur Warren)

Doyle, Brian. *The Who's Who of Children's Literature.* New York: Schocken, 1968, pp. 149–150.

Parker, Geoffrey. "Richard Hughes' *The Spider Palace and Other Stories.*" *Children's Literature in Education* 20 (Spring 1976): 32–40.

———. "*The Wonder-Dog:* The Collected Children's Stories of Richard Hughes." *Children's Literature in Education* 27, no. 4 (1977): 163–175.

Stevenson, Lionel. "Purveyors of Myth and Magic." In *Yesterday and After: The History of the English Novel.* Totowa, NJ: Barnes and Noble, 1967, pp. 111–154.

Twentieth Century Children's Writers. 2nd ed. Edited by D. L. Kirkpatrick. New York: St. Martin's Press, 1983, pp. 392–393.

Hughes, Ted (Edward James)

Adams, John. "Dark Rainbow: Reflections of Ted Hughes." *Signal* 5 (May 1971): 65–71. Reprinted in Chambers. *The Signal Approach to Children's Literature.* Metuchen, NJ: Scarecrow Press, 1980, pp. 101–108.

Bradman, T. "Giant Singer: The Children's Books of Ted Hughes." *Junior Bookshelf* 44 (Aug. 1980): 163–165.

Hughes, Ted. "Myth and Education." *Children's Literature in Education* 1 (Mar. 1970): 55–70. Reprinted in Geoff Fox. *Writers, Critics and Children.* New York: Agathon Press, 1976, pp. 77–94.

Inglis, Fred. *The Promise of Happiness.* New York: Cambridge Univ. Press, 1981, pp. 248–250.

The Oxford Companion to Children's Literature. Edited by Humphrey Carpenter and Mari Prichard. New York: Oxford Univ. Press, 1984, p. 264.

Paul, Lissa. "Inside the Lurking-Glass with Ted Hughes." *Signal* 49 (Jan. 1986): 52–63.

Rees, David. "Hospitals Where We Heal—Ted Hughes." In *Painted Desert, Green Shade.* Boston: Horn Book, 1984, pp. 47–61. Reprinted from *San Jose Studies* (July 1983).

Twentieth Century Children's Writers. 2nd ed. Edited by D. L. Kirkpatrick. New York: St. Martin's Press, 1983, pp. 395–397.

Hunter, Mollie (pseud. of Maureen Mollie Hunter McVeigh McIlwraith)

Cook, S. "Children's Writers: Mollie Hunter." *School Librarian* 26 (June 1978): 108–111.

Dooley, Patricia. "Profile: Mollie Hunter." *Children's Literature Association Quarterly* 3 (Autumn 1978): 3–6.

Hickman, J. "Profile: The Person behind the Book: Mollie Hunter." *Language Arts* 56 (Mar. 1979): 302–306.

Hollindale, Peter. "World Enough and Time: The Work of Mollie Hunter." *Children's Literature in Education* 26, no. 3 (1977): 109–119.

Hunter, Mollie. "Folklore—One Writer's View." In *Folk Literature of the British Isles.* Edited by Eloise S. Norton. Metuchen, NJ: Scarecrow Press, 1978, pp. 124–133.

———. "If You Can Read." *Horn Book* 54 (June 1978): 257–262.

———. "The Last Lord of Redhouse Castle." In *Children's Books International 1; Proceedings and Book Catalog.* Boston: Boston Public Library, 1976, pp. 26–32. Reprinted in Edward Blishen. *The Thorny Paradise.* Boston: Horn Book, 1975, pp. 128–139.

———. "A Need for Heroes." In *Proceedings of the Sixth Annual Conference of the Children's Literature Association.* University of Toronto, March 1979. Ypsilanti, MI: Children's Literature Association, 1981, pp. 52–66. Reprinted in *Horn Book* 59 (Apr. 1983): 146–154.

———. "One World." *Horn Book* 51 (Dec. 1975): 557–563, and 52 (Jan. 1976): 32–38. Reprinted in Mollie Hunter. *Talent Is Not Enough.* New York: Harper and Row, 1976, pp. 57–77; and in Boyer and Zahorski. *Fantasists on Fantasy.* New York: Avon, 1984, pp. 211–230.

———. "Talent Is Not Enough." In *The Arbuthnot Lectures, 1970–1979*. Chicago: American Library Association, 1980, pp. 105–119.

———. *Talent Is Not Enough: Mollie Hunter on Writing for Children*. New York: Harper and Row, 1976. "One World," pp. 57–77; "The Other World," pp. 78–102.

———. "The Third Eye." In *Innocence & Experience*. Edited by Barbara Harrison and Gregory Maguire. New York: Lothrop, 1987, pp. 243–249.

Kaye, Marilyn J. "Mollie Hunter: An Interview." *Top of the News* 41 (Winter 1985): 141–146.

Rowe, M. "Mollie Hunter." Auckland, New Zealand: *Children's Literature Association Yearbook* 6 (1974): 33–38.

Ryan, J. S. "The Spirit of Old Scotland: Tone in the Fiction of Mollie Hunter." *Orana* 20 (May 1984): 93–101; continued in (Aug. 1984): 138–145.

Third Book of Junior Authors. Edited by Doris De Montreville and Donna Hill. New York: Wilson, 1972, pp. 140–141.

Twentieth Century Children's Writers. 2nd ed. Edited by D. L. Kirkpatrick. New York: St. Martin's Press, 1983, pp. 400–401.

Yolen, Jane. "The Literary Underwater World." *Language Arts* 57 (1980): 403–412.

Hunter, Norman (George Lorimer)

Doyle, Brian. *The Who's Who of Children's Literature*. New York: Schocken, 1968, pp. 151–152.

The Oxford Companion to Children's Literature. Edited by Humphrey Carpenter and Mari Prichard. New York: Oxford Univ. Press, 1984, pp. 266, 427.

Twentieth Century Children's Writers. 2nd ed. Edited by D. L. Kirkpatrick. New York: St. Martin's Press, 1983, pp. 401–402.

Hutchins, Pat (Goundry)

Fourth Book of Junior Authors and Illustrators. Edited by Doris De Montreville and Elizabeth D. Crawford. New York: Wilson, 1978, pp. 189–191.

Moss, Elaine. "Pat Hutchins: A Natural." *Signal* 10 (Jan. 1973): 32–36.

Thompson, Hillary. "An Interview with Pat Hutchins." *Children's Literature Association Quarterly* 10 (Summer 1985): 57–59.

Twentieth Century Children's Writers. 2nd ed. Edited by D. L. Kirkpatrick. New York: St. Martin's Press, 1983, pp. 402–403.

Hyndman, Jane Andrews Lee *see* Wyndham, Lee

Ingelow, Jean

Attebery, Brian. "Women's Coming of Age in Fantasy." *Extrapolation* 28 (Spring 1987): 10–22.

Black, Helen C. "Jean Ingelow." In *Notable Women Authors of the Day: Biographical Sketches*. Glasgow: David Bryce, 1893.

Doyle, Brian. *The Who's Who of Children's Literature*. New York: Schocken, 1968, pp. 152–153.

Lewis, Naomi. "A Lost Pre-Raphaelite." *Times Literary Supplement*, Dec. 8, 1972, pp. 1487–1488.

McGillis, Roderick. "Fantasy as Adventure: Nineteenth Century Children's Fiction." *Children's Literature Association Quarterly* 8 (Fall 1983): 18–22.

The Oxford Companion to Children's Literature. Edited by Humphrey Carpenter and Mari Prichard. New York: Oxford Univ. Press, 1984, pp. 271, 357.

Peters, Maureen. *Jean Ingelow: Victorian Poetess.* Ipswich: Boydell Press, 1972.

Pflieger, Pat, and Hill, Helen M., eds. *A Reference Guide to Modern Fantasy for Children.* Westport, CT: Greenwood Press, 1984, pp. xiii–xvi, 259–261, 380–383.

Some Recollections of Jean Ingelow and Her Early Friends. 1901. Reprinted by Kennikat Press, Port Washington, NY, 1972.

Twentieth Century Children's Writers. 2nd ed. Edited by D. L. Kirkpatrick. New York: St. Martin's Press, 1983, pp. 873–874.

Ipcar, Dahlov (Zorach)

Hopkins, Lee Bennett. "Dahlov Ipcar." In *Books Are by People.* New York: Citation Press, 1969, pp. 107–120.

Ipcar, Dahlov. "The Artist at Work: Combining Dinobase and Wash on Paper." *Horn Book* 42 (Feb. 1966): 83–86.

———. "Making Pictures on the Farm." *Horn Book* 37 (Oct. 1961): 460–464.

Searles, Baird; Meacham, Beth; and Franklin, Michael. *A Reader's Guide to Fantasy.* New York: Avon, 1982, pp. 78–79.

Sullivan, C. W., III. "Traditional Ballads and Modern Children's Fantasy: Some Comments on Structure and Intent." *Children's Literature Association Quarterly* 11 (Fall 1986): 145–147.

Third Book of Junior Authors. Edited by Doris De Montreville and Donna Hill. New York: Wilson, 1972, pp. 145–146.

Irving, Washington

Aderman, R. M. "Mary Shelley and Washington Irving Once More." *Keats-Shelley Journal* 31 (1982): 24–28.

Bashore, J. Robert, Jr. "Washington Irving." In *Writers for Children; Critical Studies of Major Authors since the Seventeenth Century.* Edited by Jane M. Bingham, New York: Scribner, 1988, pp. 303–308.

Bonney, Agnes Mavis. "Artistic Uses of Supernaturalism in the Fiction of Brown, Irving, and Hawthorne." Ph.D. dissertation, Washington University, 1978.

Brooks-Rose, Christine. *A Rhetoric of the Unreal: Studies in Narration and Structure, Especially of the Fantastic.* New York: Cambridge Univ. Press, 1983, pp. 106–112.

Doyle, Brian. *The Who's Who of Children's Literature.* New York: Schocken, 1968, pp. 153–155.

Fisher, Franklin, IV. "Washington Irving." In *Supernatural Fiction Writers: Fantasy and Horror,* vol. 2. Edited by E. F. Bleiler. New York: Scribner, 1985, pp. 685–692.

Franklin, Bruce H. *Future Perfect: American Science Fiction of the 19th Century.* rev. ed. New York: Oxford Univ. Press, 1978.

Helbig, Alethea K., and Perkins, Agnes Regan. *Dictionary of American Children's Fiction, 1859–1959.* Westport, CT: Greenwood Press, 1985, pp. 237, 287–288, 433–434.

Masiello, Lea. "Speaking of Ghosts: Style in Washington Irving's Tales of the Supernatural." Ph.D. dissertation, University of Cincinnati, 1983.

Morsberger, Robert E. "The Short Fiction of Washington Irving." In *Survey of Modern Fantasy Literature,* vol. 4. Edited by Frank N. Magill. Englewood Cliffs, NJ: Salem Press, 1983, pp. 1554–1562.

The Oxford Companion to Children's Literature. Edited by Humphrey Carpenter and Mari Prichard. New York: Oxford Univ. Press, 1984, pp. 272, 308, 452.

Thompson, G. R. "Washington Irving and the American Ghost Story." In Howard Kerr. *The Haunted Dusk: American Supernatural Fiction, 1820–1920.* Athens: Univ. of Georgia Press, 1983, pp. 11–36.

Ish-Kishor, Sulamith

Fifth Book of Junior Authors and Illustrators. Edited by Sally Holmes Holtze. New York: Wilson, 1983, pp. 160–161.

Helbig, Alethea K., and Perkins, Agnes Regan. *Dictionary of American Children's Fiction, 1960–1984.* Westport, CT: Greenwood Press, 1986, p. 313.

Kingston, Carolyn T. *The Tragic Mode in Children's Literature.* New York: Teacher's College Press, 1974, pp. 46–48.

Roginski, Jim, ed. *Newbery and Caldecott Medalists and Honor Book Winners.* Littleton, CO: Libraries Unlimited, 1982, pp. 145–146.

Twentieth Century Children's Writers. 2nd ed. Edited by D. L. Kirkpatrick. New York: St. Martin's Press, 1983, pp. 403–404.

Jacob, Piers A(nthony) D(illingham) *see* Anthony, Piers

James, M(ontague) R(hodes)

Ashley, Mike. "M. R. James." *TZM* (Dec. 1981): 55–59.

Donaldson, Norman. "M. R. James." In *Supernatural Fiction Writers: Fantasy and Horror,* vol. 1. Edited by E. F. Bleiler. New York: Scribner, 1985, pp. 429–436.

Kidd, A. F. "M. R. James: An English Humorist." *Ghosts and Scholars* 5 (1983): 31–34.

Mason, Michael A. "On Not Letting Them Lie: Moral Significance in the Ghost Stories of M. R. James." *Studies in Short Fiction* 19 (1982): 253–260.

Pardoe, Rosemary. "The Unfinished Ghost Stories of M. R. James." *Ghosts and Scholars* 4 (1982): 37–41.

Pfaff, Richard William. *Montague Rhodes James.* London: Scholar Press, 1980.

Jansson, Tove (Marika)

Blount, Margaret. *Animal Land: The Creatures of Children's Fiction.* New York: Morrow, 1975, pp. 277–279.

Crouch, Marcus S. "Moomin-Sagas, by Tove Jansson." *Junior Bookshelf* 30 (Dec. 1966): 352–357.

Doyle, Brian. *The Who's Who of Children's Literature.* New York: Schocken, 1968, pp. 156–157.

"Finnish Twilight." *Times Literary Supplement,* October 22, 1971, pp. 1315–1316.

Fleisher, Frederic, and Fleisher, Boel. "Tove Jansson and the Moomin Family." *American-Scandinavian Review* 51 (Mar. 1963): 47–54.

Goldthwaite, John. "The Black Rabbit: Part One." *Signal* 47 (May 1985): 86–111. "Part Two." *Signal* 48 (Sept. 1985): 148–167. Reprinted in Goldthwaite's *The Natural History of Make-Believe.* London: Oxford Univ. Press, 1987.

Huse, Nancy Lyman. "Equal to Life: Tove Jansson's Moomintrolls." In *Proceedings of the Eighth Annual Conference of the Children's Literature Association.* University of Minnesota, March 1981. Ypsilanti, MI: Children's Literature Association, 1982, pp. 44–49.

Jansson, Tove. "On Winning the Andersen Award." *Top of the News* 23 (Apr. 1967): 234–239; *Bookbird* 4 (1966): 3–6.

―――. *Sculptor's Daughter.* Translated by Kingsley Hart. New York: Avon, 1969.

———. "Security and Fear in the World of Children." Translated title of her acceptance speech for the Hans Christian Andersen Medal, 1966, Finland. *Skolbiblioteket* 13, no. 3 (1967): 102–107.

The Oxford Companion to Children's Literature. Edited by Humphrey Carpenter and Mari Prichard. New York: Oxford Univ. Press, 1984, p. 356.

Searles, Baird; Meacham, Beth; and Franklin, Michael. *A Reader's Guide to Fantasy.* New York: Avon, 1982, pp. 81–82.

Third Book of Junior Authors. Edited by Doris De Montreville and Donna Hill. New York: Wilson, 1972, pp. 147–149.

Welsh, Renata. "Toffle Seen through Childish Eyes." *Bookbird* 5 (1967): 37–38.

Wilson, Anne. "Wanted—Tove Jansson's Cartoon Books!" *Signal* 52 (Jan. 1987): 12–23.

Jarrell, Randall

Adams, Charles N. *Randall Jarrell: A Bibliography.* Chapel Hill: Univ. of North Carolina Press, 1958.

Dunn, D. "Affable Misery." *Encounter* 39 (Oct. 1972): 42–48.

Ellis, Sarah. "A Second Look: *The Bat-Poet.*" *Horn Book* 57 (Aug. 1981): 453–455.

Ferguson, Suzanne. *Critical Essays on Randall Jarrell.* Boston: G. K. Hall, 1983.

Getz, Thomas. "Memory and Desire in *Fly by Night.*" In *Children's Literature,* vol. 11. New Haven, CT: Yale Univ. Press, 1983, pp. 125–134.

Griswold, Jerome Joseph. "Mother and Child in the Poetry and Children's Books of Randall Jarrell." Ph.D. dissertation, University of Connecticut, 1979.

Helbig, Alethea K., and Perkins, Agnes Regan. *Dictionary of American Children's Fiction, 1960–1984.* Westport, CT: Greenwood Press, 1986, pp. 16–17, 39, 327.

Holtze, Sally Holmes. "A Second Look: *The Animal Family.*" *Horn Book* 61 (Nov.–Dec. 1985): 714–716.

Horn, Bernard. " 'The Tongue of Gods and Children': Blakean Innocence in Randall Jarrell's Poetry." *Children's Literature,* Vol. 2. Storrs, CT: Journal of the Modern Language Association, 1973, pp. 148–151.

Howell, Pamela R. "Voice Is Voice Whether a Bat or a Poet: Randall Jarrell's *The Bat-Poet.*" In *Proceedings of the Ninth Annual Conference of the Children's Literature Association.* University of Florida, March 1982. Ypsilanti, MI: Children's Literature Association, 1983, pp. 71–76.

Jarrell, Randall. *Randall Jarrell's Letters: An Autobiography and Literary Selection.* Edited by Mary Jarrell. Boston: Houghton Mifflin, 1985.

Lovell, Barbara. "Randall Jarrell." In *American Writers for Children since 1960: Fiction. Dictionary of Literary Biography,* vol. 52. Detroit: Gale, 1986, pp. 209–213.

Lowell, Robert, ed. *Randall Jarrell, 1914–1965.* New York: Farrar, 1968.

Moore, M. "Randall Jarrell." *Atlantic Monthly* 220 (Sept. 1967): 96–98.

Neumeyer, Peter F. "Randall Jarrell's *The Animal Family:* New Land and Old." In *Proceedings of the Seventh Annual Conference of the Children's Literature Association.* Baylor University, March 1980. Ypsilanti, MI: Children's Literature Association, 1982, pp. 139–145.

———. "Randall Jarrell's *The Bat-Poet:* An Introduction to the Craft." *Children's Literature Association Quarterly* 9 (Summer 1984): 51–54.

Pflieger, Pat, and Hill, Helen M. *A Reference Guide to Modern Fantasy for Children.* Westport, CT: Greenwood Press, 1984, pp. 15–16, 268–270.

Roginski, Jim, ed. *Newbery and Caldecott Medalists and Honor Book Winners.* Littleton, CO: Libraries Unlimited, 1982, pp. 147–148.

Rosenthal, Marie. *Randall Jarrell.* Minneapolis: Univ. of Minnesota Press, 1972.

Sale, Roger. *Fairy Tales and After.* Cambridge, MA: Harvard Univ. Press, 1978, pp. 84–90.

Shapiro, Karl. *Randall Jarrell: A Lecture with a Bibliography of Jarrell Materials in the Library of Congress.* Washington, DC: Library of Congress, 1967.

Third Book of Junior Authors. Edited by Doris De Montreville and Donna Hill. New York: Wilson, 1972, pp. 140–150.

Travers, P. L. "A Kind of Visitation." In *Randall Jarrell, 1914–1965.* Edited by Robert Lowell. New York: Farrar, 1967, pp. 253–256. Reprinted from *New York Times Book Review,* Nov. 21, 1965.

Twentieth Century Children's Writers. 2nd ed. Edited by D. L. Kirkpatrick. New York: St. Martin's Press, 1983, pp. 405–406.

Updike, John. *"Fly by Night." New York Times Book Review,* Nov. 14, 1976, Children's Books Section, pp. 25, 36.

Viguers, Ruth Hill. *"The Animal Family,* a Review." *Horn Book* 42 (Feb. 1966): 45–46.

Wilson, Robert A., comp. "Randall Jarrell: A Bibliographic Checklist." *American Book Collector* 3 (May–June 1982): 32–40.

Zanderer, Leo. "Randall Jarrell: About and for Children." *The Lion and the Unicorn* 2 (Spring 1978): 73–93.

Jeffries, (John) Richard

Carpenter, Humphrey. "Bevis, the Pioneer." In Carpenter. *Secret Gardens: A Study of the Golden Age of Children's Literature.* Boston: Houghton Mifflin, 1985, pp. 103–114.

Jackson, Brian. *"Bevis:* A Lost Classic." *Use of English* 24 (Autumn 1972): 3–10.

Stoate, Graham. "The Unconscious Teaching of the Country—A Rereading of *Bevis: The Story of a Boy." Children's Literature in Education* 8 (Spring 1977): 30–38.

Twentieth Century Children's Writers. 2nd ed. Edited by D. L. Kirkpatrick. New York: St. Martin's Press, 1983, pp. 874–875.

Johnson, Crockett (pseud. of David Johnson Leisk)

Bader, Barbara. "Crockett Johnson." In *American Picturebooks from Noah's Ark to the Beast Within.* New York: Macmillan, 1976, pp. 434–442.

Third Book of Junior Authors. Edited by Doris De Montreville and Donna Hill. New York: Wilson, 1972, pp. 152–153.

Twentieth Century Children's Writers. 2nd ed. Edited by D. L. Kirkpatrick. New York: St. Martin's Press, 1983, pp. 411–412.

Johnston, Johanna

Fourth Book of Junior Authors and Illustrators. Edited by Doris De Montreville and Elizabeth D. Crawford. New York: Wilson, 1978, pp. 201–202.

Johnston, Norma

Fifth Book of Junior Authors and Illustrators. Edited by Sally Holmes Holtze. New York: Wilson, 1983, pp. 162–164.

Jones, Adrienne

Fifth Book of Junior Authors and Illustrators. Edited by Sally Holmes Holtze. New York: Wilson, 1983, pp. 164–166.

Jones, Adrienne. "And All for the Want of a Horseshoe-Nail: The Dilemma of a Writer—And of Us All." *VOYA* 6 (Feb. 1984): 316–319.

Jones, Diana Wynne

Antczak, Janice. *Science Fiction: The Mythos of a New Romance*. New York: Neal-Schuman, 1985, pp. 187–189.

Cart, Michael. "A Light in the Darkness: Humor Returns to Children's Fantasy." *School Library Journal* 33 (Apr. 1987): 48–49.

Fifth Book of Junior Authors and Illustrators. Edited by Sally Holmes Holtze. New York: Wilson, 1983, pp. 166–167.

The Oxford Companion to Children's Literature. Edited by Humphrey Carpenter and Mari Prichard. New York: Oxford Univ. Press, 1984, pp. 281–282.

Searles, Baird; Meacham, Beth; and Franklin, Michael. *A Reader's Guide to Fantasy*. New York: Avon, 1982, pp. 82–84.

Spraggs, Gillian. "True Dreams: The Fantasy Fiction of Diana Wynne Jones." *Use of English* 34 (Summer 1983): 17–22.

Twentieth Century Children's Writers. 2nd ed. Edited by D. L. Kirkpatrick. New York: St. Martin's Press, 1983, pp. 412–413.

Jones, Elizabeth Orton

Duff, Annis. "Our Miss Jones." *Horn Book* 21 (July 1945): 281–288.

Helbig, Alethea K., and Perkins, Agnes Regan. *Dictionary of American Children's Fiction, 1859–1959*. Westport, CT: Greenwood Press, 1985, pp. 259, 539–540.

Jones, Elizabeth Orton. "The Caldecott Medal Acceptance." *Horn Book* 21 (July 1945): 289–294.

The Junior Book of Authors. 2nd ed. rev. Edited by Stanley J. Kunitz and Howard Haycraft. New York: Wilson, 1951, pp. 173–174.

Roginski, Jim, ed. *Newbery and Caldecott Medalists and Honor Book Winners*. Littleton, CO: Libraries Unlimited, 1982, p. 152.

Jones, McClure

Antczak, Janice. *Science Fiction: The Mythos of a New Romance*. New York: Neal-Schuman, 1985, pp. 96–97, 179–181.

Juster, Norton

Doyle, Brian. *The Who's Who of Children's Literature*. New York: Schocken, 1968, p. 160.

Fourth Book of Junior Authors and Illustrators. Edited by Doris De Montreville and Elizabeth D. Crawford. New York: Wilson, 1978, pp. 205–206.

Helbig, Alethea K., and Perkins, Agnes Regan. *Dictionary of American Children's Fiction, 1960–1984*. Westport, CT: Greenwood Press, 1986, pp. 346, 511–512.

The Oxford Companion to Children's Literature. Edited by Humphrey Carpenter and Mari Prichard. New York: Oxford Univ. Press, 1984, p. 409.

Ragsdale, W. "Presentation of the Seventh Recognition of Merit to Norton Juster for *The Phantom Tollbooth*." *Claremont Reading Conference Yearbook* 35 (1971): 37–40.

Swinfen, Ann. *In Defense of Fantasy*. London: Routledge, 1984, pp. 118–122.

Twentieth Century Children's Writers. 2nd ed. Edited by D. L. Kirkpatrick. New York: St. Martin's Press, 1983, pp. 415–416.

Karazin, Nikolai Nikolaevich

Whitney, Elinor. *"Cranes Flying South." Horn Book* 7 (Aug. 1931): 237–239.

Kästner, Erich

Doyle, Brian. *The Who's Who of Children's Literature.* New York: Schocken, 1968, pp. 160–161.
Kästner, Erich. "The Natural History of the Author of Children's Books." *Bookbird* 2 (1965): 3–8.
Third Book of Junior Authors. Edited by Doris De Montreville and Donna Hill. New York: Wilson, 1972, pp. 157–158.
Weiss, Gerhard H. "Erich Kästner." In *Writers for Children; Critical Studies of Major Authors since the Seventeenth Century.* Edited by Jane M. Bingham. New York: Scribner, 1988, pp. 317–322.

Kemp, Gene (Rushton)

Cross, Gillian. "Children Are Real People: The Stories of Gene Kemp." *Children's Literature in Education* 10 (Autumn 1979): 131–140.
King, E. J. "Children's Writers: Gene Kemp." *School Librarian* 34 (Dec. 1986): 309–313.
The Oxford Companion to Children's Literature. Edited by Humphrey Carpenter and Mari Prichard. New York: Oxford Univ. Press, 1984, pp. 289–290.
Twentieth Century Children's Writers. 2nd ed. Edited by D. L. Kirkpatrick. New York: St. Martin's Press, 1983, pp. 425–426.

Kendall, Carol (Seeger)

Coyle, William, ed. *Ohio Authors and Their Books.* Cleveland: World, 1962.
Helbig, Alethea K., and Hill, Agnes Regan. *Dictionary of American Children's Fiction, 1859–1959.* Westport, CT: Greenwood Press, 1985, pp. 173–174, 271.
———. *Dictionary of American Children's Fiction, 1960–1984; Recent Books of Recognized Merit.* Westport, CT: Greenwood Press, 1986, pp. 353, 715.
Roginski, Jim, ed. *Newbery and Caldecott Medalists and Honor Book Winners.* Littleton, CO: Libraries Unlimited, 1982, p. 159.
Searles, Baird; Meacham, Beth; and Franklin, Michael. *A Reader's Guide to Fantasy.* New York: Avon, 1982, p. 84.
Swinfen, Ann. *In Defense of Fantasy.* London: Routledge, 1984, pp. 78, 80, 83, 85, 89.
Third Book of Junior Authors. Edited by Doris De Montreville and Donna Hill. New York: Wilson, 1972, pp. 160–161.
Twentieth Century Children's Writers. 2nd ed. Edited by D. L. Kirkpatrick. New York: St. Martin's Press, 1983, pp. 426–427.
West, Richard C. "The Tolkinians." *Orcrist* 2 (1967): 4–15.

Kennedy, Richard (Jerome)

Fifth Book of Junior Authors and Illustrators. Edited by Sally Holmes Holtze. New York: Wilson, 1983, pp. 170–171.
Lanes, Selma G. "Richard Kennedy Aims High [When Writing Children's Books]." *Publishers Weekly* 227 (Feb. 22, 1985): 102–103.
Neumeyer, Peter F. "Introducing Richard Kennedy." *Children's Literature in Education* 15 (Summer 1984): 85–92.

Twentieth Century Children's Writers. 2nd ed. Edited by D. L. Kirkpatrick. New York: St. Martin's Press, 1983, pp. 427–428.

Udal, John. "Richard Kennedy and *Pippi Longstocking.*" *Junior Bookshelf* 42 (Apr. 1978): 75–77.

Key, Alexander (Hill)

Helbig, Alethea K., and Hill, Agnes Regan. *Dictionary of American Children's Fiction, 1960–1984.* Westport, CT: Greenwood Press, 1986, pp. 220, 335–336.

Twentieth-Century Science Fiction Writers. 2nd ed. Edited by Curtis C. Smith. Chicago: St. James Press, 1986, p. 392.

King, (David) Clive

Twentieth Century Children's Writers. 2nd ed. Edited by D. L. Kirkpatrick. New York: St. Martin's Press, 1983, pp. 430–431.

King, Stephen (Edwin)

Bleiler, Richard. "Stephen King." In *Supernatural Fiction Writers: Fantasy and Horror,* vol. 2. Edited by E. F. Bleiler. New York: Scribner, 1985, pp. 1037–1044.

Bosky, Bernadette. "Stephen King and Peter Straub: Fear and Friendship." In *Discovering Stephen King.* Edited by Darrell Schweitzer. Mercer Island, WA: Starmont, 1985.

Collings, Michael R. *The Annotated Guide to Stephen King: A Primary and Secondary Bibliography of the Works of America's Premier Horror Writer.* Mercer Island, WA: Starmont, 1986.

———. *The Many Facets of Stephen King.* Mercer Island, WA: Starmont, 1985.

Indick, Ben P. "King As a Writer for Children." In *Kingdom of Fear: The World of Stephen King.* Edited by Tim Underwood. San Francisco: Underwood-Miller, 1986.

King, Stephen. "Dr. Seuss and the Two Faces of Fantasy." *Fantasy Review* 68 (1984): 10–12.

———. "Imagery and the Third Eye." *The Writer* 93 (Oct. 1980): 11–14, 44.

Leiber, Fritz. "On Fantasy." *Fantasy Newsletter* 21 (1980): 3–4, 30.

Platt, Charles. *Dream Makers.* New York: Ungar, 1987, pp. 261–272. Interview.

Strupp, Peter. "Interview with Stephen King." *Science Fiction Review* 56 (1985): 32.

Tymn, Marshall B. "Stephen King: A Bibliography." In *Discovering Stephen King.* Edited by Darrell Schweitzer. Mercer Island, WA: Starmont, 1985.

Winter, Douglas E. "Some Words with Stephen King." *Fantasy Newsletter* 56 (1983): 11–14.

———. *Stephen King: The Art of Darkness.* New York: Signet, 1986. Updated and expanded from the NAL, 1984 edition.

King-Smith, Dick

Twentieth Century Children's Writers. 2nd ed. Edited by D. L. Kirkpatrick. New York: St. Martin's Press, 1983, pp. 431–432.

Kingsley, Charles

Alderson, Brian, ed. *Children's Books in England.* 3rd ed. New York: Cambridge Univ. Press, 1982, pp. 252–255.

Avery, Gillian. "Charles Kingsley." In *Writers for Children; Critical Studies of Major*

Authors since the Seventeenth Century. Edited by Jane M. Bingham. New York: Scribner, 1988, pp. 323–328.

Baker, Richard; Connolly, John J.; and Zudeck, Ronald. "Notes on Chesterton's Notre Dame Lectures on Victorian Literature." *The Chesterton Review* 4 (1978): 115–143, 285–301.

Barry, James D. "Charles Kingsley." In George H. Ford. *Victorian Fiction: A Second Guide to Research.* Storrs, CT: Modern Language Association of America, 1978, pp. 219–222.

Buckley, Jerome Hamilton. "The Pattern of Conversion." In *The Victorian Temper: A Study in Literary Culture.* Cambridge, MA: Harvard Univ. Press, 1951, pp. 87–108.

Campbell, Robert A. "Charles Kingsley: A Bibliography of Secondary Studies." Pt. I and II. *Bulletin of Bibliographies* 33 (1976): 78–91, 104, 127–130.

Carpenter, Humphrey. "Parson Lot Takes a Cold Bath: Charles Kingsley and *The Water-Babies.*" In Carpenter. *Secret Gardens: A Study of the Golden Age of Children's Literature.* Boston: Houghton Mifflin, 1985, pp. 23–43.

Chitty, Susan. *The Beast and the Monk: A Life of Charles Kingsley.* London: Mason/ Charter, 1975.

Coleman, Dorothy. "Rabelais and *The Water-Babies.*" *Modern Language Review* 66, no. 3 (July 1971): 511–521.

Colloms, Brenda. *Charles Kingsley.* Totowa, NJ: Barnes and Noble, 1975.

Cunningham, V. "Soiled Fairy: *The Water-Babies* in Its Time." *Essays in Criticism* 35 (Apr. 1985): 121–148.

Doyle, Brian. *The Who's Who of Children's Literature.* New York: Schocken, 1968, pp. 161–163.

Harris, Styron. *Charles Kingsley: A Reference Guide.* Boston: G. K. Hall, 1981.

Ison, Mary M. "Things Nobody Ever Heard of: Jessie Willcox Smith Draws *The Water-Babies.*" *Quarterly Journal of the Library of Congress* 39 (Spring 1982): 90–101.

Jackson, Rosemary. *Fantasy: The Literature of Subversion.* New York: Methuen, 1980.

Johnston, Arthur. "*The Water-Babies:* Kingsley's Debt to Darwin." *English* 12, 7 (Autumn 1959): 215–219.

Kingsley, Frances Eliza, ed. *Charles Kingsley: His Letters and Memoirs of His Life, Edited by His Wife.* 2 vols. London: King, 1877.

Leavis, Q. D. "*The Water-Babies.*" *Children's Literature in Education* 23 (Winter 1976): 155–163.

Manlove, C(olin) N(icholas). *Modern Fantasy: Five Studies.* New York: Cambridge Univ. Press, 1975.

Martin, R. B. *The Dust of Combat: The Life & Work of Charles Kingsley.* London: Faber, 1959.

The Oxford Companion to Children's Literature. Edited by Humphrey Carpenter and Mari Prichard. New York: Oxford Univ. Press, 1984, pp. 294–295, 561–563.

Pfeiffer, John R. "*The Water-Babies.*" In *Survey of Modern Fantasy Literature,* vol. 5. Edited by Frank N. Magill. Englewood Cliffs, NJ: Salem Press, 1983, pp. 2074–2078.

Pflieger, Pat, and Hill, Helen M. *A Reference Guide to Modern Fantasy for Children.* Westport, CT: Greenwood Press, 1984, pp. xiv, xv, 285–287, 579–581.

Pope-Hennessy, Una. *Canon Charles Kingsley: A Biography.* London: Chatto, 1948.

Prickett, Stephen. "Religious Fantasy in the Nineteenth Century." In *Survey of Modern Fantasy Literature,* vol. 5. Edited by Frank N. Magill. Englewood Cliffs, NJ: Salem Press, 1983, pp. 2369–2382.

———. *Victorian Fantasy.* Bloomington: Indiana Univ. Press, 1979.

Stolzenbach, Mary M. "*The Water-Babies:* An Appreciation." *Mythlore* 8, 28 (Summer 1981): 20.

Tanner, Tony. "Mountains and Depths—An Approach to Nineteenth Century Dualism." *Review of English Literature* 3, no. 4 (Oct. 1962): 51–61.

Twentieth Century Children's Writers. 2nd ed. Edited by D. L. Kirkpatrick. New York: St. Martin's Press, 1983, pp. 875–876.

Uffelman, Larry K. "An Evolutionary Fantasy: *The Water-Babies.*" In *Charles Kingsley.* Boston: Twayne, 1979, pp. 67–81.

Kinsella, W(illiam) P(atrick)

Randall, N. "*Shoeless Joe:* Fantasy and the Humor of Fellow-Feeling." *Modern Fiction Studies* 33 (Spring 1987): 173–182.

Kipling, (Joseph) Rudyard

Alderson, Brian, ed. *Children's Books in England.* 3rd ed. New York: Cambridge Univ. Press, 1982, pp. 305–308.

Amis, Kingsley. *Rudyard Kipling and His World.* New York: Scribner, 1976.

Anderson, Celia Catlett. "Kipling's Mowgli and *Just So Stories:* The Vine of Fact and Fantasy." In *Touchstones.* Edited by Perry Nodelman. West Lafayette, IN: Children's Literature Association Publications, 1985, pp. 113–122.

———. " 'O Best Beloved': Kipling's Reading Instructions in *The Just So Stories.*" In *Proceedings of the Ninth Annual Conference of the Children's Literature Association.* University of Florida, March 1982. Ypsilanti, MI: Children's Literature Association, 1983, pp. 33–39.

Annan, Noel. "Kipling's Place in the History of Ideas." *Victorian Studies* 3, no. 4 (June 1960): 323–348. Reprinted in Andrew Rutherford. *Kipling's Mind and Art: Selected Critical Essays.* Stanford, CA: Stanford Univ. Press, 1964.

Birkenhead, Lord. *Rudyard Kipling.* New York: Random, 1978.

Birkenhead, Sheila. "The Kipling Mystery." *New Statesman* (May 4, 1979): 627–638.

Blackburn, William. "Rudyard Kipling." In *Writers for Children; Critical Studies of Major Authors since the Seventeenth Century.* Edited by Jane M. Bingham. New York: Scribner, 1988, pp. 329–336.

Blount, Margaret. "The Tables Turned at the Zoo: Mowgli and Stuart Little." In *Animal Land: The Creatures of Children's Fiction.* New York: Morrow, 1975, pp. 226–244.

Carrington, Charles. "The Kipling 'Mystery.' " *New Statesman* (Mar. 2, 1979): 298–299.

———. *Rudyard Kipling: His Life and Work.* 3rd rev. ed. London: Macmillan, 1978. Originally published 1955.

Chambers, Aidan. "Letter from England: *Just So.*" *Horn Book* 58 (Dec. 1982): 565–570.

Colvin, I. D. "This Bore Fruit Afterwards: Kipling's Childhood Reading." *National Review* 110 (Feb. 1938): 215–221.

Cushing, David. "Kipling and 'The White Seal.' " *Arlington Quarterly* 3, no. 1 (1970–1971): 171–182.

Davie, Donald. "A Puritan's Empire: The Case of Kipling." *Sewanee Review* 87 (1979): 34–48.

Doyle, Brian. *The Who's Who of Children's Literature.* New York: Schocken, 1968, pp. 164–166.

Fido, Martin. *Rudyard Kipling: An Illustrated Biography.* New York: Bedrick; dist. by Harper and Row, 1986.

Gerould, Katherine Fullerton. "The Remarkable Rightness of Rudyard Kipling." *Atlantic Monthly* 123 (Jan. 1919): 12–21.

Gilbert, Elliot L. "Three Criticisms of *The Jungle Books.*" *Kipling Journal* 33 (Dec. 1966): 6–10.

Goldthwaite, John. "The Black Rabbit: Part One." *Signal* 47 (May 1985): 86–111. "Part Two." *Signal* 48 (Sept. 1985): 148–167. Reprinted in Goldthwaite. *The Natural History of Make-Believe.* London: Oxford Univ. Press, 1987.

Green, Roger Lancelyn. *Kipling and the Children.* London: Elek Books, 1965.

———. "Rudyard Kipling." *Junior Bookshelf* 20 (Dec. 1956): 312–319.

———, ed. *Kipling: The Critical Heritage.* Totowa, NJ: Barnes and Noble, 1971.

Haines, Helen E. "The Wisdom of Baloo: Kipling and Childhood:" *Horn Book* 12 (May–June 1936): 135–143.

Harrison, James. "Kipling's Jungle Eden." *Mosaic* 7, no. 2 (Winter 1974): 151–164.

———. *Rudyard Kipling.* Boston: Twayne, 1982.

Havholm, Peter L. "Kipling and Fantasy." In *Children's Literature,* vol. 4. Philadelphia: Temple Univ. Press, 1975, pp. 91–104.

Hedges, Ned Samuel. "The Fable and the Fabulous: The Use of Traditional Forms in Children's Literature." Ph.D. dissertation, University of Nebraska, 1968.

Hindle, Alan. "Rudyard Kipling's *Rewards and Fairies.*" *School Librarian* 21 (Dec. 1973): 295–300.

Holt, Marilyn J. "Rudyard Kipling." In *Supernatural Fiction Writers: Fantasy and Horror,* vol. 1. Edited by E. F. Bleiler. New York: Scribner, 1985, pp. 437–442.

Inglis, Fred. *The Promise of Happiness.* New York: Cambridge Univ. Press, 1981, pp. 156–162.

Islam, Shamsul. "Psychological Allegory in *The Jungle Books.*" *Kipling Journal* 40 (Mar. 1973): 9–12.

Jarrett-Kerr, M. "The Theology of Rudyard Kipling." *Kipling Journal* 43 (Sept. 1976): 4–8.

The Kipling Journal. Kipling Society, 1927– .

Kipling, Rudyard. "Author's Notes on the Names in *The Jungle Books.*" In *The Burwash Edition of the Complete Works in Prose and Verse of Rudyard Kipling.* Garden City, NY: Doubleday, 1941, pp. 427–433.

———. *Something of Myself for My Friends Known and Unknown.* Garden City, NY: Doubleday, 1937.

Laski, Marghanita. *From Palm to Pine: Rudyard Kipling Abroad and at Home.* New York: Facts on File, 1987.

Lesser, Margaret. "Kipling and His Publishers." *Horn Book* 12 (Mar. 1936): 128–129.

Lewis, C. S. "Kipling's World." In *They Asked for a Paper.* London: Bles, 1962.

Lochhead, Marion. *Renaissance of Wonder.* New York: Harper and Row, 1980, pp. 70–76.

Mason, Philip. *Kipling: The Glass, the Shadow and the Fire.* New York: Harper and Row, 1975.

Moss, Robert R. *Rudyard Kipling and the Fiction of Adolescence.* New York: St. Martin's Press, 1982, pp. 107–117.

Musgrove, P. W. "Kipling's View of Educating Children." *Australian Journal of Education* 25 (1981): 211–223.

Orvel, Harold. "Hardy, Kipling, and Haggard." *English Literature in Transition* 25 (1982): 232–248.

———, ed. *Kipling: Interviews and Recollections.* 2 vols. Totowa, NJ: Barnes and Noble, 1983.

The Oxford Companion to Children's Literature. Edited by Humphrey Carpenter and Mari Prichard. New York: Oxford Univ. Press, 1984, pp. 282–285, 296–297, 428–429, 449.

Petzold, Dieter. "Fantasy Out of Myth and Fable: Animal Stories in Rudyard Kipling and Richard Adams." *Children's Literature Association Quarterly* 12 (Spring 1987): 15–19.

Pflieger, Pat, and Hill, Helen M. *A Reference Guide to Modern Fantasy for Children.* Westport, CT: Greenwood Press, 1984, pp. xv, xvi, 275–278, 287–291.

Prickett, Stephen. *Victorian Fantasy.* Bloomington: Indiana Univ. Press, 1979.

Reid, D. M. "Rudyard Kipling." *Ontario Library Review* 45 (Aug. 1961): 157–158.

Rivet, A. L. F. "Rudyard Kipling's Roman Britain." *Kipling Journal* 45 (June 1978): 5–15.

Rogers, T. "Rudyard Kipling." *School Librarian* 10 (Dec. 1961): 503–506 ff.

"Rudyard Kipling: An Annotated Bibliography of Writings about Him." *English Fiction in Transition* 3–5 (1960): 1–74, 75–148, 149–235.

Rutherford, Andrew. "Officers and Gentlemen." In Andrew Rutherford. *Kipling's Mind and Art: Selected Critical Essays.* Stanford, CA: Stanford Univ. Press, 1964.

Sale, Roger. *Fairy Tales and After: From Snow White to E. B. White.* Cambridge, MA: Harvard Univ. Press, 1978. "Kipling's Boys," pp. 195–222.

Scott-Giles, C. W. "Historical Background of Some *Puck* Stories." *Kipling Journal* 28 (June 1961): 15–21.

Searles, Baird; Meacham, Beth; and Franklin, Michael. *A Reader's Guide to Fantasy.* New York: Avon, 1982, pp. 85–86.

Shippey, T. A. *"The Jungle Books."* In *Survey of Modern Fantasy Literature,* vol. 2. Edited by Frank N. Magill. Englewood Cliffs, NJ: Salem Press, 1983, pp. 822–826.

———. "The Short Fiction of Kipling." In *Survey of Modern Fantasy Literature,* vol. 4. Edited by Frank N. Magill. Englewood Cliffs, NJ: Salem Press, 1983, pp. 1586–1588.

Steward, J. I. M. *Rudyard Kipling.* New York: Dodd, 1966.

Stott, Jon C. *Children's Literature from A to Z.* New York: McGraw-Hill, 1984, p. 156.

Sutcliff, Rosemary. *Rudyard Kipling.* New York: Walck, 1961. Reprinted in Hugh Shelley, Rosemary Sutcliff, and Leonard Clark. *Arthur Ransome, Rudyard Kipling and Walter de la Mare.* London: Bodley Head, 1968.

Tompkins, Joyce M. S. *The Art of Rudyard Kipling.* 2nd ed. London: Methuen, 1965, pp. 55–64.

———. "Kipling and Nordic Myth and Saga." *English Studies* 52 (Apr. 1971): 147–157.

———. "Report on Discussion Meeting—12th April, 1967." *Kipling Journal* 34 (Sept. 1967): 11–17.

Twentieth Century Children's Writers. 2nd ed. Edited by D. L. Kirkpatrick. New York: St. Martin's Press, 1983, pp. 433–437.

Twentieth-Century Science Fiction Writers. 2nd ed. Edited by Curtis C. Smith. Chicago: St. James Press, 1986, pp. 399–402.

Wendelmoot, Thomas Leroy. "Masonic Allusions and Themes in the Works of Rudyard Kipling." Ph.D. dissertation, University of Southern Florida, 1980.

Wilson, Angus. *The Strange Ride of Rudyard Kipling.* New York: Viking Press, 1978, pp. 122–133.

Wright, H. "Shadows on the Down: Some Influences of Rudyard Kipling on Rosemary Sutcliff." *Children's Literature in Education* 12 (Summer 1981): 90–102.

Klaveness, Jan O'Donnell

Helbig, Alethea K., and Perkins, Agnes Regan. *Dictionary of American Children's Fiction, 1960–1984.* Westport, CT: Greenwood Press, 1986, pp. 258–259, 362.

Konigsburg, E(laine) L(obl)

Callaghan, L. W. "Consistent Focus and Recurring Elements in Books for the Young by Konigsburg, O'Dell, Singer, and Snyder." Master's thesis, University of Chicago, 1979.

Cart, Michael. "A Light in the Darkness: Humor Returns to Children's Fantasy." *School Library Journal* 33 (Apr. 1987): 48–49.

Helbig, Alethea K., and Perkins, Agnes Regan. *Dictionary of American Children's Fiction, 1960–1984.* Westport, CT: Greenwood Press, 1986, p. 364.

Hopkins, Lee Bennett. *More Books by More People.* New York: Citation Press, 1974, pp. 234–238.

Jones, L. T. "Profile: Elaine Konigsburg." *Language Arts* 63 (Feb. 1986): 177–184. Interview.

Konigsburg, David. "Elaine L. Konigsburg." *Horn Book* 44 (Aug. 1968): 396–398.

Konigsburg, E. L. "Between a Peach and the Universe." In *Innocence & Experience.* Edited by Barbara Harrison and Gregory Maguire. New York: Lothrop, 1987, pp. 464–476.

———. "The Double Image: Language as the Perimeter of Culture." *School Library Journal* 16 (Feb. 1970): 31–34. Reprinted in *Issues in Children's Book Selection.* Edited by Lillian Gerhardt. New York: Bowker, 1977, pp. 24–30.

———. "Newbery Award Acceptance." *Horn Book* 44 (Aug. 1968): 391–395.

———. "Of Ariel, Caliban, and Certain Beasts of Mine Own." *Proceedings of the Seventh Annual Conference of the Children's Literature Association,* 1980. Ypsilanti, MI: Children's Literature Association, 1981, pp. 1–16.

———. "Ruthie Brittain and Because I Can." In Betsy Hearne. *Celebrating Children's Books.* New York: Lothrop, 1981, pp. 62–72.

———. "Sprezzatura: A Kind of Excellence." *Horn Book* 52 (June 1976): 253–261.

———. "The Winner of the Newbery Medal for 1968, Says. . . ." *Instructor* 78 (Apr. 1969): 67ff.

Nodelman, Perry. "E. L. Konigsburg." In *American Writers for Children since 1960: Fiction. Dictionary of Literary Biography,* vol. 52. Detroit: Gale, 1986, pp. 214–227.

The Oxford Companion to Children's Literature. Edited by Humphrey Carpenter and Mari Prichard. New York: Oxford Univ. Press, 1984, p. 298.

Rees, David. "Your Arcane Novelist—E. L. Konigsburg: An English Viewpoint." *Horn Book* 54 (Feb. 1978): 79–85. Reprinted in *Marble in the Water.* Boston: Horn Book, 1980, pp. 14–24.

Third Book of Junior Authors. Edited by Doris De Montreville and Donna Hill. New York: Wilson, 1972, pp. 164–165.

Townsend, John Rowe. *A Sounding of Storytellers.* New York: Lippincott, 1979, pp. 111–124.

Twentieth Century Children's Writers. 2nd ed. Edited by D. L. Kirkpatrick. New York: St. Martin's Press, 1983, pp. 441–442.

Kotzwinkle, William

"1977 World Fantasy Award Winners." *Locus* 10 (Nov. 1977): 1.

Twentieth-Century Science Fiction Writers. 2nd ed. Edited by Curtis C. Smith. Chicago: St. James Press, 1986, pp. 412–413.

Krüss, James (Jacob Hinrich)

Third Book of Junior Authors. Edited by Doris De Montreville and Donna Hill. New York: Wilson, 1972, pp. 166–167.

Kurtz, Katherine

Elliot, Jeffrey M. *Fantasy Voices: Interviews with American Fantasy Writers.* San Bernardino, CA: Borgo Press, 1982.

————. "Interview: Katherine Kurtz: Tapestries of Medieval Wonder." *Fantasy Newsletter* 24 (1980): 16–21. "Part Two." *Fantasy Newsletter* 25 (1980): 12–17, 31.

An Hour with Katherine Kurtz: An Introduction to the Author and Her Work. Garden Grove, NY: Hourglass Productions, 1979. (audiocassette)

"Katherine Kurtz: To the Manor Bound." *Locus* 302 (1986): 26, 32.

Kurtz, Katherine. "The Historian as a Myth-Maker and Vice Versa." *Bulletin of the Science Fiction Writers of America* 13 (1978): 16–18.

Kurtz, Katherine, and Elliot, Jeffrey M. "Interview Essay." In *Fantasists on Fantasy.* Edited by Robert H. Boyer and Kenneth J. Zahorski. New York: Avon, 1984, pp. 235–260.

Searles, Baird; Meacham, Beth; and Franklin, Michael. *A Reader's Guide to Fantasy.* New York: Avon, 1982, pp. 87–88.

Stableford, Brian. "The Deryni Trilogy." In *Survey of Modern Fantasy Literature,* vol. 1. Edited by Frank N. Magill. Englewood Cliffs, NJ: Salem Press, 1983, pp. 360–365.

Kuttner, Henry

Blish, James. "Moskowitz on Kuttner." *Riverside Quarterly* 5 (Feb. 1972): 140–143.

Bradbury, Ray. "Kuttner Recalled." *Etchings and Odysseys* 4 (1984): 7.

Moskowitz, Sam. *Seekers of Tomorrow.* New York: Ballantine, 1967, pp. 319–334.

Myers, Walter E. "The Short Fiction of Henry Kuttner. In *Survey of Modern Fantasy Literature,* vol. 4. Edited by Frank N. Magill. Englewood Cliffs, NJ: Salem Press, 1983, pp. 1592–1596.

"Recollections of Henry Kuttner by His Friends." *Etchings and Odysseys* 4 (1984): 9–11, 38.

Twentieth-Century Science Fiction Writers. 2nd ed. Edited by Curtis C. Smith. Chicago: St. James Press, 1986, pp. 414–416.

Lagerlöf, Selma (Ottiliana Lovisa)

Afzelius, Nils. "The Scandalous Selma Lagerlöf." *Scandinavica* 5, no. 2 (Nov. 1966): 91–99.

Berendsohn, Walter A. *Selma Lagerlöf: Her Life and Work.* Translated and adapted by George F. Timpson. Preface by V. Sackville-West. Port Washington, NY: Kennikat Press, 1968. Reprinted from 1931 edition.

Doyle, Brian. *The Who's Who of Children's Literature.* New York: Schocken, 1968, pp. 170–171.

Edstrom, Vivi. *Selma Lagerlöf.* Translated by Barbara Lide. Boston: Twayne, 1984.

Lagerlöf, Selma. "The Christmas Gift Book: A Childhood Memory." *Horn Book* 35 (Dec. 1959): 459–464.

————. *Mårbacka.* Translated by Velma Swanston Howard. Garden City, NY: Doubleday, 1925; continued in *Memories of My Childhood: Further Years at Mårbacka.* Garden City, NY: Doubleday, 1934.

Lagerroth, Erland. "Selma Lagerlöf Research, 1900–1964: A Survey and an Orientation." *Scandinavian Studies* 37, no. 1 (Feb. 1965): 1–30.

Larsen, Hanna Astrup. *Selma Lagerlöf.* Garden City, NY: Doubleday, 1936.

Lindquist, Jennie D. "Selma Lagerlöf." *Horn Book* 20 (Mar. 1944): 115–122.

Maule, Harry E. *Selma Lagerlöf: The Woman, Her Work, Her Message.* 2nd ed. Garden City, NY: Doubleday, 1924.

Miller, Bertha Mahony. "Editorial: Arthur Rackham and Selma Lagerlöf." *Horn Book* 16 (May 1940): 145.
The Oxford Companion to Children's Literature. Edited by Humphrey Carpenter and Mari Prichard. New York: Oxford Univ. Press, 1984, pp. 300, 578.
Rahn, Susan. "Rediscovering *Nils.*" *The Lion and the Unicorn* 10 (1986): 158–164.
St. Andrews, Bonnie. *Forbidden Fruit: On the Relationship between Women and Knowledge in Doris Lessing, Selma Lagerlöf, Kate Chopin, Margaret Atwood.* Troy, NY: Whitston, 1986.
Sale, Roger. *Fairy Tales and After.* Cambridge, MA: Harvard Univ. Press, 1978, pp. 90–97.

Lamorisse, Albert (Emmanuel)

Fourth Book of Junior Authors and Illustrators. Edited by Doris De Montreville and Elizabeth D. Crawford. New York: Wilson, 1978, pp. 217–218.

La Motte Fouqué, Baron Friedrich de

Doyle, Brian. *The Who's Who of Children's Literature.* New York: Schocken, 1968, pp. 102–103.
Hoppe, Manfred K. E. "Baron Friedrich de La Motte Fouqué." In *Supernatural Fiction Writers: Fantasy and Horror,* vol. 1. Edited by E. F. Bleiler. New York: Scribner, 1985, pp. 77–106.
The Oxford Companion to Children's Literature. Edited by Humphrey Carpenter and Mari Prichard. New York: Oxford Univ. Press, 1984, pp. 301, 551–552.
Stableford, Brian. *"Undine."* In *Survey of Modern Fantasy Literature,* vol. 4. Edited by Frank N. Magill. Englewood Cliffs, NJ: Salem Press, pp. 1992–1994.

Lamplugh, Lois

Twentieth Century Children's Writers. 2nd ed. Edited by D. L. Kirkpatrick. New York: St. Martin's Press, 1983, pp. 451–452.

Lampman, Evelyn Sibley

Helbig, Alethea K., and Perkins, Agnes Regan. *Dictionary of American Children's Fiction, 1960–1984.* Westport, CT: Greenwood Press, 1986, pp. 367–368.
More Junior Authors. Edited by Muriel Fuller. New York: Wilson, 1963, p. 131.
Twentieth Century Children's Writers. 2nd ed. Edited by D. L. Kirkpatrick. New York: St. Martin's Press, 1983, pp. 452–453.

Lang, Andrew

Anon. "A Checklist of the Works of Andrew Lang." *Indiana University Bookman* 7 (Apr. 1965): 91–101.
———. "Descriptions from the Darlington Collection of Andrew Lang." *Indiana University Bookman* 7 (Apr. 1965): 73–90.
Burns, Marjorie Jean. "Victorian Fantasists from Ruskin to Lang: A Study in Ambivalence." Ph.D. dissertation, University of California, Berkeley, 1978.
Doyle, Brian. *The Who's Who of Children's Literature.* New York: Schocken, 1968, pp. 172–174.
Green, Roger Lancelyn. *Andrew Lang.* New York: Walck, 1962.

――――. *Andrew Lang: A Critical Biography with a Short-Title Bibliography of the Works of Andrew Lang.* Leicester: Ward, 1946.

――――. "Andrew Lang and the Fairy Tale." *Review of English Studies* 20 (July 1944): 227–231.

――――. "Andrew Lang in Fairyland." *Junior Bookshelf* 26 (Oct. 1962): 171–180. Reprinted in Egoff. *Only Connect.* New York: Oxford Univ. Press, 1969, pp. 270–278.

――――. "Andrew Lang—'The Greatest Bookman of His Age.' " *Indiana University Bookman* 7 (Apr. 1965): 10–72.

――――. "C. S. Lewis and Andrew Lang." *Notes and Queries* 22 (May 1975): 208–209.

Indiana University Bookman. Andrew Lang issue. 7 (Apr. 1965): 10–101.

Lang, Andrew. *Adventures among Books.* London: Longman, 1905, pp. 3–38.

――――. "Modern Fairy Tales." In Salway. *A Peculiar Gift.* Harmondsworth, Middlesex: Kestrel, 1976, pp. 133–136.

Levitt, Andrew. "Andrew Lang." In *Writers for Children; Critical Studies of Major Authors since the Seventeenth Century.* Edited by Jane M. Bingham. New York: Scribner, 1988, pp. 337–344.

Moss, Anita. "Crime and Punishment—Or Development—In Fairy Tales and Fantasy." *Mythlore* 8 (Spring 1981): 26–28, 42.

The Oxford Companion to Children's Literature. Edited by Humphrey Carpenter and Mari Prichard. New York: Oxford Univ. Pres, 1984, pp. 302–303, 425–426.

Repplier, Agnes. "Andrew Lang." *Catholic World* 96 (Dec. 1912): 289–297.

Stott, Jon C. *Children's Literature from A to Z.* New York: McGraw-Hill, 1984, p. 161.

Twentieth Century Children's Writers. 2nd ed. Edited by D. L. Kirkpatrick. New York: St. Martin's Press, 1983, p. 876.

Langton, Jane (Gillson)

Fifth Book of Junior Authors and Illustrators. Edited by Sally Holmes Holtze. New York: Wilson, 1983, pp. 188–190.

Helbig, Alethea K., and Perkins, Agnes Regan. *Dictionary of American Children's Fiction, 1960–1984.* Westport, CT: Greenwood Press, 1986, pp. 155–156, 215–216, 369.

Langton, Jane. "Down to the Quick: The Use of Reality in Writing Fiction." *Horn Book* 49 (Feb. 1973): 24–30.

――――. "A Hair's Breadth Aside." In *Innocence & Experience.* Edited by Barbara Harrison and Gregory Maguire. New York: Lothrop, 1987, pp. 167–169.

――――. "The Weak Place in the Cloth: A Study of Fantasy for Children." *Horn Book* 49 (Oct. 1973): 433–441, and 49 (Dec. 1973): 570–578. Reprinted in Paul Heins. *Crosscurrents of Criticism.* Boston: Horn Book, 1977, pp. 185–196; and in Boyer and Zahorski. *Fantasists on Fantasy.* New York: Avon, 1984, pp. 163–180.

Rees, David. "Real and Transcendental—Jane Langton." In *Painted Desert, Green Shade.* Boston: Horn Book, 1984, pp. 75–88.

Twentieth Century Children's Writers. 2nd ed. Edited by D. L. Kirkpatrick. New York: St. Martin's Press, 1983, pp. 453–454.

Lanier, Sterling E(dmund)

Schweitzer, Darrell. "Interview: Sterling E. Lanier." *Thrust* 24 (1986); 17–19.

Twentieth-Century Science Fiction Writers. 2nd ed. Edited by Curtis C. Smith. Chicago: St. James Press, 1986, pp. 421–422.

Lathrop, Dorothy P(ulis)

Alberghene, Janice M. "Dorothy P. Lathrop." In Cech. *American Writers for Children, 1900–1960. Dictionary of Literary Biography,* vol. 22. Detroit: Gale, 1983, pp. 222–230.

Bechtel, Louise Seaman. "Dorothy Lathrop: Artist and Author." *Library Journal,* June 15, 1938, pp. 485–487.

Helbig, Alethea K., and Perkins, Agnes Regan. *Dictionary of American Children's Fiction, 1859–1959.* Westport, CT: Greenwood Press, 1985, pp. 153–154, 284.

Hopkins, Lee Bennett. "Dorothy Lathrop." In *Books Are by People.* New York: Citation Press, 1969, pp. 125–127.

The Junior Book of Authors. 2nd ed. rev. Edited by Stanley J. Kunitz and Howard Haycraft. New York: Wilson, 1951, pp. 186–187.

Lathrop, Dorothy P. "Children, Fairies, and Animals." *Horn Book* 11 (May–June 1935): 135–142.

———. "A Hunt Breakfast—Authors' Symposium." *Horn Book* 2 (Nov. 1926): 38.

———. "Illustrating De La Mare." *Horn Book* 18 (May 1942): 188–196.

———. "A Test of *Hitty*'s Pegs and Patience." *Horn Book* 6 (Feb. 1930): 27–30.

Mahony, Bertha. "Artist's Triumph." *Horn Book* 14 (July 1938): 201–208.

Renwick, Stephen Lee. "Dorothy P. Lathrop, Author and Illustrator of Children's Books." *American Artist* 6 (Oct. 1942): 12–15ff.

Roginski, Jim, ed. *Newbery and Caldecott Medalists and Honor Book Winners.* Littleton, CO: Libraries Unlimited, 1982, pp. 164–165.

Lauber, Patricia (Grace)

Third Book of Junior Authors. Edited by Doris De Montreville and Donna Hill. New York: Wilson, 1972, pp. 173–174.

Laumer, (John) Keith

Platt, Charles. *Dream Makers.* New York: Ungar, 1987, pp. 231–240. Interview.

Twentieth-Century Science Fiction Writers. 2nd ed. Edited by Curtis C. Smith. Chicago: St. James Press, 1986, pp. 425–426.

Walker, Paul. *Speaking of Science Fiction.* Oradell, NJ: Luna Publications, 1978. Interview.

Laurence, (Jean) Margaret (Wemyss)

Letson, D. R. "Mother of Manawaka: Margaret Laurence as Author of Children's Stories." *Canadian Children's Literature* 21 (1981): 17–24.

Lawrence, Ann (Margaret)

Ray, Sheila G. B. "Children's Writers: Ann Lawrence." *School Librarian* 30 (Sept. 1982): 196–199.

Twentieth Century Children's Writers. 2nd ed. Edited by D. L. Kirkpatrick. New York: St. Martin's Press, 1983, 457–458.

Lawrence, Louise (pseud. of Elizabeth Rhoda Holden)

Antczak, Janice. *Science Fiction: The Mythos of a New Romance.* New York: Neal-Schuman, 1985, pp. 186–187.

Twentieth Century Children's Writers. 2nd ed. Edited by D. L. Kirkpatrick. New York: St. Martin's Press, 1983, pp. 458–459.

Lawson, John S(hults)

Helbig, Alethea K., and Perkins, Agnes Regan. *Dictionary of American Children's Fiction, 1960–1984; Recent Books of Recognized Merit.* Westport, CT: Greenwood Press, 1986, pp. 373, 622–623.

Lawson, Robert

Avi. "Robert Lawson." In *Writers for Children; Critical Studies of Major Authors since the Seventeenth Century.* Edited by Jane M. Bingham. New York: Scribner, 1988, pp. 345–350.

Bader, Barbara. *American Picturebooks from Noah's Ark to The Beast Within.* New York: Macmillan, 1976, pp. 143–147.

Burns, Mary Mehlman. " 'There Is Enough for All': Robert Lawson's America." *Horn Book* 48 (Feb. 1972): 24–32; 48 (Apr. 1972): 120–128; and 48 (June 1972): 295–305.

Cornell, Robert W. "Robert Lawson: For All Children." *Elementary English* 50 (May 1973): 718–725, 738.

Fish, Helen Dean. "Robert Lawson, Illustrator in the Great Tradition." *Horn Book* 16 (Jan.–Feb. 1940): 17–26.

Gardner, Frederick R. *Robert Lawson on My Shelves.* Philadelphia: Free Library of Philadelphia, 1977.

Helbig, Alethea K., and Perkins, Agnes Regan. *Dictionary of American Children's Fiction, 1859–1959.* Westport, CT: Greenwood Press, 1985, pp. 42–43, 286, 361–362, 421–422, 529–530.

Inman, Sue Lile. "Robert Lawson." In Cech. *American Writers for Children, 1900–1960. Dictionary of Literary Biography,* vol. 22. Detroit: Gale, 1983, pp. 231–240.

Jones, Helen L., ed. *Robert Lawson, Illustrator: A Selection of His Characteristic Illustrations.* Boston: Little, Brown, 1972.

The Junior Book of Authors. 2nd ed. rev. Edited by Stanley J. Kunitz and Howard Haycraft. New York: Wilson, 1951, pp. 189–190.

Kurth, Ruth Justine. "Realism in Children's Books of Fantasy." *California Librarian* 39 (July 1978): 39–40.

Lawson, Marie A. "Master of *Rabbit Hill:* Robert Lawson." *Horn Book* 21 (July–Aug. 1945): 239–242.

Lawson, Robert. *At That Time.* New York: Viking Press, 1947.

———. "Caldecott Acceptance Speech." *Horn Book* 17 (July 1941): 273–284.

———. "The Genius of Arthur Rackham." *Horn Book* 16 (May 1940): 147–152.

———. "Lo, the Poor Illustrator." *Publishers Weekly* 128 (Dec. 17, 1935): 2091.

———. "Make Me a Child Again." *Horn Book* 16 (Nov.–Dec. 1940): 447–456.

———. "The Newbery Medal Acceptance." *Horn Book* 21 (July 1945): 233–238.

———. *They Were Strong and Good.* New York: Viking Press, 1940.

Lindquist, Jennie D. "The Master of *Rabbit Hill.*" *Horn Book* 33 (Aug. 1957): 273.

Madsen, Valden. "Classic Americana: Themes and Values in the Tales of Robert Lawson." *The Lion and the Unicorn* 3 (Spring 1979): 89–106.

Miller, Bertha Mahony, and Field, Elinor Whitney, eds. *Newbery Medal Books: 1922–1955.* Boston: Horn Book, 1957, pp. 255–267.

The Oxford Companion to Children's Literature. Edited by Humphrey Carpenter and Mari Prichard. New York: Oxford Univ. Press, 1984, pp. 305, 437.

Pflieger, Pat, and Hill, Helen M. *A Reference Guide to Modern Fantasy for Children.*

Westport, CT: Greenwood Press, 1984, pp. xv, xvi, 52–53, 179–180, 297–300, 370–372, 467–468, 545–546.

"Robert Lawson: Biographical Sketch." *Horn Book* 17 (July 1941): 285–288.

"The Robert Lawson Collection of the Rare Book Department of the Free Library of Philadelphia." *Horn Book* 48 (June 1972): 318.

Roginski, Jim, ed. *Newbery and Caldecott Medalists and Honor Book Winners.* Littleton, CO: Libraries Unlimited, 1982, pp. 165–168.

Salway, Lance, and Chambers, Nancy. "Book Post." *Signal* 26 (May 1978): 99–107.

Searles, Baird; Meacham, Beth; and Franklin, Michael. *A Reader's Guide to Fantasy.* New York: Avon, 1982, pp. 89–90.

Sicherman, Ruth. "An Appreciation of Robert Lawson." *Elementary English* 44 (Dec. 1967): 866–869.

Stott, Jon C. *Children's Literature from A to Z.* New York: McGraw-Hill, 1984, p. 163.

Twentieth Century Children's Writers. 2nd ed. Edited by D. L. Kirkpatrick. New York: St. Martin's Press, 1983, 459–460.

Weston, Annette H. "Robert Lawson: Author and Illustrator." *Elementary English* 47 (Jan. 1970): 74–84. Reprinted in Miriam Hoffman and Eva Samuels. *Authors and Illustrators of Children's Books.* New York: Bowker, 1972, pp. 256–267.

Leach, (Alice Mary) Maria (Doanne)

Fourth Book of Junior Authors and Illustrators. Edited by Doris De Montreville and Elizabeth D. Crawford. New York: Wilson, 1978, pp. 220–221.

Lee, Tanith

Ashley, Mike. "The Tanith Lee Bibliography." *Fantasy Macabre* 4 (1983): 27–35.

Collings, Michael R. "Words and Worlds: The Creation of a Fantasy Universe in Zelazny, Lee and Anthony." In *The Scope of the Fantastic—Theory, Technique, Major Authors.* Edited by Robert A. Collins and Howard D. Pearce. Westport, CT: Greenwood Press, 1985, pp. 173–182.

Holding, Deanne. "A Pen in Her Own Country: Tanith Lee." *Space Voyager* 13 (1985): 16–18.

Kemp, Geoff. "Tanith Lee." *Quartz* 4 (1983): 12–16. Interview.

Saunders, Charles R.; De Lint, Charles; and Elflandsson, Galad. "The Fiction of Tanith Lee: 1971–1983." *Dragonfields* 4 (1983): 21–25.

Schuyler, William M., Jr. "Recent Developments in Spell Construction." In *The Aesthetics of Fantasy Literature and Art.* Edited by Roger C. Schlobin. Notre Dame, IN: Univ. of Notre Dame Press, 1982, pp. 237–248.

Schweitzer, Darrell. "Interview: Tanith Lee." *Fantasy Newsletter* 42 (1981): 12–15.

Searles, Baird; Meacham, Beth; and Franklin, Michael. *A Reader's Guide to Fantasy.* New York: Avon, 1982, pp. 90–91.

Twentieth-Century Science Fiction Writers. 2nd ed. Edited by Curtis C. Smith. Chicago: St. James Press, 1986, pp. 427–428.

Waggoner, Diana. "Tanith Lee." In *Supernatural Fiction Writers: Fantasy and Horror,* vol. 2. Edited by E. F. Bleiler. New York: Scribner, 1985, pp. 1053–1058.

Weinkauf, Mary S. "So Much for the Gentle Sex." *Extrapolation* 26 (1985): 231–239.

Leeson, Robert (Arthur)

Twentieth Century Children's Writers. 2nd ed. Edited by D. L. Kirkpatrick. New York: St. Martin's Press, 1983, pp. 463–464.

Le Grand (Henderson)

The Junior Book of Authors. 2nd ed. rev. Edited by Stanley J. Kunitz and Howard Haycraft. New York: Wilson, 1951, pp. 192–193.

Le Guin, Ursula K(roeber)

Algeo, John. "Magic Names: Onomastics in the Fantasies of Ursula Le Guin." *American Name Society* 30, no. 2 (1982): 59–67.
Attebery, Brian. *"The Beginning Place:* Le Guin's Metafantasy." In *Children's Literature,* vol. 10. New Haven, CT: Yale Univ. Press, 1982, pp. 113–123. Reprinted in *Ursula K. Le Guin.* Edited by Harold Bloom. New York: Chelsea House, 1986.
———. "On a Far Shore: The Myth of *Earthsea.*" *Extrapolation* 21 (1980): 268–277.
———. "Women's Coming of Age in Fantasy." *Extrapolation* 28 (Spring 1987): 10–22.
Bailey, E. C., Jr. "Shadows in *Earthsea:* Le Guin's Use of a Jungian Archetype." *Extrapolation* 21 (Fall 1980): 254–261.
Bain, Dena C. "The *Tao Te Ching* as Background to the Novels of Ursula K. Le Guin." *Extrapolation* 21 (1980): 209–222. Reprinted in *Ursula K. Le Guin.* Edited by Harold Bloom. New York: Chelsea House, 1986.
Barbour, Douglas. "On Ursula Le Guin's *A Wizard of Earthsea.*" *Riverside Quarterly* 6 (Apr. 1974): 119–123.
———. "Patterns of Meaning in the Science Fiction Novels of Ursula K. Le Guin, Joanna Russ and Samuel R. Delany, 1962–1972. Ph.D. dissertation, Queen's University (Ontario, Canada), 1976.
———. "Wholeness and Balance." In *Ursula K. Le Guin.* Edited by Harold Bloom. New York: Chelsea House, 1986.
Berkley, Miriam. "Ursula K. Le Guin." *Publishers Weekly,* May 23, 1986, p. 72.
Bisenieks, Dainis. "Children, Magic and Choices." *Mythlore* 6 (Winter 1979): 13–16.
———. "Tales from the 'Perilous Realm': Good News for the Modern Child." *Christian Century,* June 5, 1974, pp. 617–620.
Bittner, James W. *Approaches to the Fiction of Ursula K. Le Guin.* Ann Arbor: Univ. of Michigan Research Press, 1984.
———. "Approaches to the Fiction of Ursula Le Guin." Ph.D. dissertation, University of Wisconsin-Madison, 1979.
Bloom, Harold, ed. *Ursula K. Le Guin.* New York: Chelsea House, 1986.
Bradbury, Margaret. "What's in a Name? Ursula Le Guin's *Earthsea* Trilogy." *School Librarian* 31 (Sept. 1983): 205–210.
Braswell, Laurel. "The Visionary Voyage in Science Fiction and Medieval Allegory." *Mosaic* 14 (Winter 1981): 125–142.
Brigg, Peter. *"The Beginning Place."* In *Survey of Modern Fantasy Literature,* vol. 1. Edited by Frank N. Magill. Englewood Cliffs, NJ: Salem Press, 1983, pp. 81–83.
Bucknall, Barbara J. *Ursula K. Le Guin.* New York: Ungar, 1981.
Cameron, Eleanor. "High Fantasy: *A Wizard of Earthsea.*" *Horn Book* 47 (Apr. 1971): 129–138. Reprinted in Paul Heins. *Crosscurrents of Criticism.* Boston: Horn Book, 1977, pp. 333–341. Revised for publication in Gerard Senick. *Children's Literature Review,* vol. 3. Detroit: Gale, 1978, pp. 124–125.
Cogell, Elizabeth Cummins. "The Metaphor of Turning and Returning in the Novels of Ursula K. Le Guin, 1968–1974." Ph.D. dissertation, University of Illinois, 1985.
———. *Ursula K. Le Guin: A Primary and Secondary Bibliography.* Boston: G. K. Hall, 1983.
Cunneen, Sheila. "Earthseans and Earthteens." *English Journal* 74 (Feb. 1985): 68–69.
Davis, Boyd H. "Childe Reader and the Saussurean Paradox." *Children's Literature Association Quarterly* 7 (Fall 1981): 36–38.

Dean, John. "Uses of the Occult in the *Earthsea* Trilogy." *Fantasy Commentator* 5 (1984): 116–121.

De Bolt, Joe, ed. *Ursula K. Le Guin: Voyager to Inner Lands and to Outer Space.* Port Washington, NY: Kennikat Press, 1979.

Dooley, Patricia. "Earthsea Patterns." *Children's Literature Association Quarterly* 4 (Summer 1979): 1–4. Reprinted in Dooley. *The First Steps.* West Lafayette, IN: Children's Literature Association Publications, 1984, pp. 14–15.

———. "Magic and Art in Ursula Le Guin's *Earthsea Trilogy.*" In *Children's Literature,* vol. 8. New Haven, CT: Yale Univ. Press, 1980, pp. 103–110.

Dunn, Margaret M. "In Defense of Dragons: Imagination as Experience in the *Earthsea Trilogy.*" In *Proceedings of the Ninth Annual Conference of the Children's Literature Association.* University of Florida, March 1982. Ypsilanti, MI: Children's Literature Association, 1983, pp. 54–60.

Edwards, Malcolm, and Holdstock, Robert. "Earthsea." In *Realms of Fantasy.* Garden City, NY: Doubleday, 1983, pp. 87–97.

Erlich, Richard D. "The Earthsea Trilogy." In *Survey of Modern Fantasy Literature,* vol. 1. Edited by Frank N. Magill. Englewood Cliffs, NJ: Salem Press, 1983, pp. 447–459.

Esmonde, Margaret P. "The Master Pattern: The Psychological Journey in *The Earthsea Trilogy.*" In Joseph Olander and Martin Greenberg. *Ursula K. Le Guin.* New York: Taplinger, 1979, pp. 15–35.

Extrapolation. Special issue. 2 (Fall 1980): 195–304.

Fantastes. "Enchantress of Earthsea." *Cambridge Review: Fantasy in Literature,* Nov. 23, 1973, pp. 43–45.

Finch, Sheila. "Oath of Fealty: No Thud, Some Blunders." *Science Fiction Review* 57 (1985): 28–30.

———. "Paradise Lost: The Prison at the Heart of Le Guin's Utopia." *Extrapolation* 26 (1985): 240–248.

Fourth Book of Junior Authors and Illustrators. Edited by Doris De Montreville and Elizabeth D. Crawford. New York: Wilson, 1978, pp. 221–223.

Fox, Geoff. "Notes on Teaching *A Wizard of Earthsea.*" *Children's Literature in Education* 11 (May 1973): 58–67. Reprinted in Geoff Fox. *Writers, Critics and Children.* New York: Agathon Press, 1976, pp. 211–223.

Galbreath, R. "Taoist Magic in *The Earthsea Trilogy.*" *Extrapolation* 21 (Fall 1980): 262–268.

Gordon, Andrew. "Ursula K. Le Guin." In *American Writers for Children since 1960: Fiction. Dictionary of Literary Biography,* vol. 52. Detroit: Gale, 1986, pp. 233–240.

Hare, Delmas Edwin. "*In This Land There Be Dragons:* Carl G. Jung, Ursula K. Le Guin, and Narrative Prose Fantasy." Ph.D. dissertation, Emory University, 1982.

Haselkorn, Mark P. "An Interview with Ursula K. Le Guin." *Science Fiction Review* 7 (May 1978): 72–74.

Hassler, Donald M. "The Touching of Love and Death in Ursula Le Guin with Comparisons to Jane Austin." *University of Mississippi Studies in English* (1983): 168–177.

Helbig, Alethea K., and Perkins, Agnes Regan. *Dictionary of American Children's Fiction, 1960–1984; Recent Books of Recognized Merit.* Westport, CT: Greenwood Press, 1986, pp. 180–181, 207–208, 375, 666–667, 736–737.

Hoxmier, Kelly. "A Positive Alternative: The Novels of Ursula K. Le Guin." *ALAN Review* 10 (Fall 1982): 3–7.

Huntington, John. "Public and Private Imperatives in Le Guin's Novels." *Science-Fiction Studies* 2 (1975): 237–243.

Inglis, Fred. *The Promise of Happiness.* New York: Cambridge Univ. Press, 1981, pp. 245–247.

————. "Spellbinding and Anthropology: The Work of Richard Adams and Ursula Le Guin." In Dennis Butts. *Good Writers for Young Readers*. St. Albans, England: Hart-Davis, 1977, pp. 114–128.

Jackson, Rosemary. *Fantasy: The Literature of Subversion*. New York: Methuen, 1980.

Jago, Wendy. "*A Wizard of Earthsea* and the Charge of Escapism." *Children's Literature in Education* 8 (July 1972): 21–29.

Jameson, Fredric. "World-Reduction in Le Guin: The Emergence of Utopian Narrative." In *Ursula K. Le Guin*. Edited by Harold Bloom. New York: Chelsea House, 1986.

Jenkins, Sue. "Growing Up in Earthsea." *Children's Literature in Education* 16 (Spring 1985): 21–31.

Kemball-Cook, Jessica. "Earthsea and Others." *New Society* (Nov. 11, 1976): 314–315.

Kuznets, Lois R. " 'High Fantasy' in America: Alexander, Le Guin and Cooper." An unpublished paper delivered at the Conference on Fantasy and Social Values in German and American Children's Literature, Humanities Institute of Brooklyn College, March 1984.

La Bar, M. "Slipping the Truth in Edgewise (Taoist Themes in Fantasies of U. K. Le Guin)." *Christianity Today,* March 27, 1981, pp. 38–39.

Le Guin, Ursula K. "The Child and the Shadow." *Quarterly Journal of the Library of Congress* 32 (Apr. 1975): 139–148. Reprinted in Ursula K. Le Guin. *The Language of the Night*. New York: Putnam, 1979, pp. 59–71; and in *The Openhearted Audience*. Washington, DC: Library of Congress, 1980, pp. 100–113.

————. "The Creative Spirit and Children's Literature: A Symposium." *Wilson Library Bulletin* 53 (Oct. 1978): 166–169.

————. "Dreams Must Explain Themselves." *Algol,* no. 21 (Nov. 1973). Reprinted in *Dreams Must Explain Themselves*. New York: Algol Press, 1975, pp. 5–13; *Signal* 19 (Jan. 1976): 3–11; Ursula K. Le Guin. *The Language of the Night*. New York: Putnam, 1979, pp. 47–56; and in Boyer and Zahorski. *Fantasists on Fantasy*. New York: Avon, 1984, pp. 181–194.

————. "Fantasy, Like Poetry, Speaks the Language of the Night." *San Francisco Sunday Examiner and Chronicle,* "World," Nov. 21, 1976.

————. *From Elfland to Poughkeepsie*. New York: Pendragon Press, 1973. Reprinted in Ursula K. Le Guin. *The Language of the Night*. New York: Putnam, 1979, pp. 83–96; and in Boyer and Zahorski. *Fantasists on Fantasy*. New York: Avon, 1984, pp. 195–210.

————. "In Defense of Fantasy." Excerpts from the acceptance remarks of Ursula Le Guin on receiving the National Book Award in Children's Books for *The Farthest Shore*. *Horn Book* 49 (June 1973): 239. Reprinted in Paul Heins. *Crosscurrents of Criticism*. Boston: Horn Book, 1977, p. 169.

————. *The Language of the Night: Essays on Fantasy and Science Fiction*. New York: Putnam, 1979.

————. "Mapping Imaginary Countries." In David Wingrove. *The Science Fiction Source Book*. New York: Van Nostrand Reinhold, 1984, pp. 77–79.

————. "On Writing Science Fiction." In *The Writer's Handbook*. Edited by Sylvia K. Burack. Boston: The Writer, 1985.

————. "Science Fiction and Mrs. Brown." In *Science Fiction at Large: A Collection of Essays*. Edited by Peter Nicholls. New York: Harper and Row, 1976, pp. 13–34.

————. "Why Are Americans Afraid of Dragons?" *Pacific North West Library Association Quarterly* 38 (Feb. 1974): 14–18. Reprinted in Ursula K. Le Guin. *The Language of the Night*. New York: Putnam, 1979, pp. 39–46; and in Edward Blishen. *The Thorny Paradise*. Boston: Horn Book, 1975, pp. 87–92, entitled "This Fear of Dragons."

Levin, Jeff. "Ursula K. Le Guin: A Select Bibliography." *Science-Fiction Studies* 2 (1975): 204–208.
Littlefield, Ralph Emerson. "Characters and Language in Eight Novels by Ursula K. Le Guin and Samuel R. Delany." Ph.D. dissertation, Florida State University, 1984.
McCaffrey, Larry, and Gregory, Sinda. "An Interview with Ursula Le Guin." *Missouri Review* 7 (1984): 64–85.
McGuire, Patrick L. "The Short Fiction of Ursula K. Le Guin." In *Survey of Modern Fantasy Literature*, vol. 4. Edited by Frank N. Magill. Englewood Cliffs, NJ: Salem Press, 1983, pp. 1607–1610.
McLean, Susan. "*The Beginning Place:* An Interpretation." *Extrapolation* 24 (Summer 1983): 130–142.
Manlove, C. N. "Conservatism in the Fantasy of Ursula Le Guin." *Extrapolation* 21 (Fall 1980): 287–297. Revised for inclusion in C. N. Manlove. *The Impulse of Fantasy Literature*. Kent, OH: Kent State Univ. Press, 1982, pp. 31–44.
Molson, Francis J. "*The Earthsea Trilogy:* Ethical Fantasy for Children." In Joe De Bolt. *Ursula K. Le Guin: Voyager to Inner Lands and Outer Space*. Port Washington, NY: Kennikat Press, 1979.
Moylan, T. "Beyond Negation: The Critical Utopias of Ursula K. Le Guin and Samuel R. Delany." *Extrapolation* 21 (Fall 1980): 236–253.
Nudelman, Rafail. "An Approach to the Structure of Le Guin's Science Fiction." *Science-Fiction Studies* 2 (1975): 210–220.
Olander, Joseph D., and Greenberg, Martin Harry, eds. *Ursula K. Le Guin*. New York: Taplinger, 1979.
The Oxford Companion to Children's Literature. Edited by Humphrey Carpenter and Mari Prichard. New York: Oxford Univ. Press, 1984, pp. 162, 308.
Parish, Margaret. "Fantasy." *English Journal* 66 (Nov. 1977): 90–93.
Patterson, Richard F. "Le Guin's Earthsea Trilogy: The Psychology of Fantasy." In *The Scope of the Fantastic—Culture, Biography, Themes, Children's Literature*. Edited by Robert A. Collins and Howard D. Pearce. Westport, CT: Greenwood Press, 1985, pp. 239–248.
Paxon, Diana. "The Tolkien Tradition." *Mythlore* 39 (1984): 23–27, 37.
Pflieger, Pat, and Hill, Helen M. *A Reference Guide to Modern Fantasy for Children*. Westport, CT: Greenwood Press, 1984, pp. xii–xvi, 181–182, 301–304, 541–542, 611–612.
Plank, Robert. "Ursula K. Le Guin and the Decline of Romantic Love." *Science-Fiction Studies* 3 (1976): 36–43.
Porter, David L. "The Politics of Le Guin's Opus." *Science-Fiction Studies* 2 (1975): 243–248.
Rabkin, Eric S. "Metalinguistics and Science Fiction." *Critical Inquiry* 6 (1979): 79–97.
Rees, David. "*Earthsea* Revisited: Ursula K. Le Guin." In *Marble in the Water*. Boston: Horn Book, 1980, pp. 78–89.
Remington, T. J. "A Time to Live and a Time to Die: Cyclical Renewal in *The Earthsea Trilogy*." *Extrapolation* 21 (Fall 1980): 278–286.
Roginski, Jim, ed. *Newbery and Caldecott Medalists and Honor Book Winners*. Littleton, CO: Libraries Unlimited, 1982, p. 168.
Rollin, Lucy W. "Exploring Earthsea: A Sixth Grade Literature Project." *Children's Literature in Education* 16 (Winter 1985): 195–202.
Samuelson, David N. "Ursula Le Guin." In *Science Fiction Writers*. Edited by E. F. Bleiler. New York: Scribner, 1982, pp. 409–418.
———. "Ursula Le Guin." In *Supernatural Fiction Writers: Fantasy and Horror*, vol. 1. Edited by E. F. Bleiler. New York: Scribner, 1985, pp. 1059–1066.
Schlobin, Roger C. "Preparing for Life's Passages: How Fantasy Literature Can Help." *Media and Methods* 16 (Nov. 1979): 26–27, 29, 50–51.

Scholes, Robert. "The Good Witch of the West." *Hollins Critic* 11, no. 2 (1974): 1–12. Revised for inclusion in *Structural Fabulation: An Essay on Fiction of the Future*. Notre Dame, IN: Univ. of Notre Dame Press, 1975, pp. 79–87. Reprinted in *Ursula K. Le Guin*. Edited by Harold Bloom. New York: Chelsea House, 1986.

Schuyler, William M., Jr. "Recent Developments in Spell Construction." In *The Aesthetics of Fantasy Literature and Art*. Edited by Roger C. Schlobin. Notre Dame, IN: Univ. of Notre Dame Press, 1982, pp. 237–248.

Searles, Baird; Meacham, Beth; and Franklin, Michael. *A Reader's Guide to Fantasy*. New York: Avon, 1982, pp. 92–94.

Sherman, Cordelia. "The Princess and the Wizard: The Fantasy Worlds of Ursula K. Le Guin and George MacDonald." *Children's Literature Association Quarterly* 12 (Spring 1987): 24–28.

Shippey, Tom. "The Golden Bough and the Incorporation of Magic in Science Fiction." *Foundation* 11/12 (1977): 119–134.

———. "The Magic Art and the Evolution of Words: Usula Le Guin's *Earthsea Trilogy*." *Mosaic* 10, no. 2 (Winter 1976–1977): 147–163. Reprinted in *Ursula K. Le Guin*. Edited by Harold Bloom. New York: Chelsea House, 1986.

Slethaug, Gordon E. "The Paradoxical Double in Le Guin's *A Wizard of Earthsea*." *Extrapolation* 27 (1986): 326–333.

Slusser, George Edgar. *The Farthest Shores of Ursula K. Le Guin*. San Bernardino, CA: Borgo Press, 1976. "*The Earthsea Trilogy*," pp. 31–46. Reprinted in *Ursula K. Le Guin*. Edited by Harold Bloom. New York: Chelsea House, 1986.

Spivak, Charlotte. *Ursula K. Le Guin*. Boston: Twayne, 1984.

Stott, Jon C. *Children's Literature from A to Z*. New York: McGraw-Hill, 1984, p. 168.

Swinfen, Ann. *In Defense of Fantasy*. London: Routledge, 1984. Discusses *The Earthsea Trilogy*, pp. 79, 82, 83, 87–88, 90, 95, 168–189, 232–233.

Taormina, Agatha. "The Hero, the Double, and the Outsider: Images of Three Archetypes in Science Fiction." Ph.D. dissertation, Carnegie-Mellon University, 1980.

Taylor, Angus. "The Politics of Space, Time, and Entropy." *Foundation* 10 (1976): 34–44.

Timmerman, John H. *Other Worlds: The Fantasy Genre*. Bowling Green, OH: Bowling Green Univ. Press, 1983. Discusses *The Wizard of Earthsea*, pp. 81–90.

Townsend, John Rowe. Guest Essay, "Heights of Fantasy." In *Children's Literature Review*, vol. 5. Detroit: Gale, 1983, pp. 10–11.

Twentieth Century Children's Writers. 2nd ed. Edited by D. L. Kirkpatrick. New York: St. Martin's Press, 1983, pp. 466–467.

Twentieth-Century Science Fiction Writers. 2nd ed. Edited by Curtis C. Smith. Chicago: St. James Press, 1986, 428–431.

Tymn, Marshall B. "Ursula K. Le Guin: A Bibliography." In Joseph Olander and Martin Greenberg. *Ursula K. Le Guin*. New York: Taplinger, 1979.

Ursula Le Guin: Woman of Science Fiction. North Hollywood, CA: Center for Cassette Studies, 1973. (audiocassette)

Walker, Jeanne Murray. "Rites of Passage Today: The Cultural Significance of *A Wizard of Earthsea*." *Mosaic* 13 (1980): 179–191.

Walker, Paul. "Ursula Le Guin: An Interview." *Luna Monthly* 63 (1976): 1–7. Reprinted in Walker. *Speaking of Science Fiction*. Oradell, NJ: Luna Publications, 1978, pp. 24–36.

Ward, Jonathon. "Ursula K. Le Guin." *Algol* 12, no. 2 (1975): 7–10.

White, Virginia L. "Bright the Hawk's Flight: The Journey of the Hero in Ursula K. Le Guin's *Earthsea Trilogy*." *Ball State University Forum* 20, no. 4 (1979): 34–45.

Wickes, George, and Westling, Louise. "Dialogue with Ursula K. Le Guin." *Northwest Review* 20 (1982): 147–159.

Wood, Susan. "Discovering Worlds: The Fiction of Ursula K. Le Guin." In *Voices for the Future: Essays on Major Science Fiction Writers,* vol. 2. Edited by Thomas D. Clareson. Bowling Green, OH: Bowling Green Univ. Press, 1979. Reprinted in *Ursula K. Le Guin.* Edited by Harold Bloom. New York: Chelsea House, 1986.

Wytenbroek, Jacqueline. "Science Fiction and Fantasy." *Extrapolation* 23 (1982): 321–332.

L'Engle, Madeleine

Carter, M. L. "The Cosmic Gospel: Lewis and L'Engle." *Mythlore* 8 (1982): 10–12.

Franklin, Hugh. "Madeleine L'Engle." *Horn Book* 39 (Aug. 1963): 356–360.

Glass, Rona. "*A Wrinkle in Time* and *The High King:* Two Couples, Two Perspectives." *Children's Literature Association Quarterly* 6 (Fall 1981): 15–18. Reprinted in Patricia Dooley. *The First Steps.* West Lafayette, IN: Children's Literature Association Publications, 1984, pp. 119–121.

Helbig, Alethea K., and Perkins, Agnes Regan. *Dictionary of American Children's Fiction, 1960–1984.* Westport, CT: Greenwood Press, 1986, pp. 375–376.

Hopkins, Lee Bennett. *More Books by More People.* New York: Citation Press, 1974, pp. 257–266.

Jones, K. "A Pentaperceptual Analysis of Social and Philosophical Commentary in *A Wrinkle in Time* by Madeleine L'Engle." Ph.D dissertation, University of Mississippi, 1977.

L'Engle, Madeleine. "Before Babel." *Horn Book* 42 (Dec. 1966): 661–670.

———. "The Centipede and the Creative Spirit." *Horn Book* 45 (Aug. 1969): 373–376.

———. "Childlike Wonder and the Truths of Science Fiction." *Children's Literature,* vol. 10. New Haven, CT: Yale Univ. Press, 1982, pp. 102–110.

———. *A Circle of Quiet.* New York: Farrar, 1972.

———. "The Danger of Wearing Glass Slippers." *Elementary English* 41 (Feb. 1964): 105–111ff.

———. "Do I Dare Disturb the Universe?" *Horn Book* 59 (Dec. 1983): 673–682.

———. "The Expanding Universe: Newbery Award Acceptance." *Horn Book* 39 (Aug. 1963): 351–355.

———. "The Key, the Door, the Road." *Horn Book* 40 (June 1964): 260–268.

———. "A Sense of Wonder." *Advocate* 2 (Winter 1983): 69–80.

"Madeleine L'Engle: Out of the Pigeonhole." *Locus* 294 (1985): 4ff.

Parker, Marygail G. "Madeleine L'Engle." In *American Writers for Children since 1960: Fiction. Dictionary of Literary Biography,* vol. 52. Detroit: Gale, 1986, pp. 241–248.

Patterson, Nancy-Lou. "Angel and Psycho-Pomp in Madeleine L'Engle's *Wind* Trilogy." *Children's Literature in Education* 14 (Winter 1983): 195–203.

Perry, Barbara. "Profile: Madeleine L'Engle: A Real Person." *Language Arts* 54 (Oct. 1977): 812–816.

Samuels, L. A. "Profile: Madeleine L'Engle." *Language Arts* 58 (Sept. 1981): 704–712.

Thompson, Hillary. "Doorways to Fantasy." *Canadian Children's Literature* 21 (1981): 8–16.

Townsend, John Rowe. *A Sense of Story.* Philadelphia: Lippincott, 1971, pp. 120–129.

Twentieth-Century Science Fiction Writers. 2nd ed. Edited by Curtis C. Smith. Chicago: St. James Press, 1986, pp. 436–437.

Wintle, Justin, and Fisher, Emma. *The Pied Pipers.* New York: Two Continents, 1975, pp. 249–262.

Levin, Betty (Lowenthal)

Levin, Betty. "The Universe and Old MacDonald." In *Innocence & Experience*. Edited by Barbara Harrison and Gregory Maguire. New York: Lothrop, 1987, pp. 102–115.
Twentieth Century Children's Writers. 2nd ed. Edited by D. L. Kirkpatrick. New York: St. Martin's Press, 1983, pp. 472–473.

Levy, Elizabeth

Fifth Book of Junior Authors and Illustrators. Edited by Sally Holmes Holtze. New York: Wilson, 1983, pp. 193–195.

Lewis, C(live) S(taples)

Arnott, Anne. *The Secret Country of C. S. Lewis*. Grand Rapids, MI: Eerdmans, 1974.
Aveling, Helan A. "The Need for Belief in the 'Narnian Chronicles.' " *CSL: The Bulletin of the New York C. S. Lewis Society* 15 (Sept. 1984): 16–17.
Aymard, E. "On C. S. Lewis and the *Narnian Chronicles*." *Caliban* 5 (1968): 129–145.
Bailey, Mark. "The Honour and Glory of a Mouse: Reepicheep of Narnia." *Mythlore* 5, 18 (Autumn 1978): 35–36, 46.
Bakke, Jeannette A. "The Lion, the Lamb and the Child. Christian Childhood Education through *The Chronicles of Narnia*." Ph.D. dissertation, University of Minnesota, 1975.
Becker, Joan Quall. "Patterns of Guilt and Grace in the Development and Function of Character in C. S. Lewis's Romances." Ph.D. dissertation, University of Washington, 1981.
Bell, Albert A., Jr. "Origin of the Name 'Narnia.' " *Mythlore* 7, no. 24 (1980): 29.
Berman, Ruth. "Dragons for Tolkien and Lewis." *Mythlore* 39 (1984): 53–58.
Bisenieks, Dainis. "Children, Magic and Choices." *Mythlore* 6, no. 19 (Winter 1979): 13–16.
Blount, Margaret. "Fallen and Redeemed: Animals in the Novels of C. S. Lewis." In *Animal Land: The Creatures of Children's Fiction*. New York: Morrow, 1975, pp. 284–306.
Brady, Charles A. "Finding God in Narnia." *America*, Oct. 27, 1956, pp. 103–105. Reprinted in Mary Lou White. *Children's Literature*. Columbus, OH: Merrill, 1976, pp. 126–130.
Brown, Carol Ann. "Once upon a Narnia." *CSL: The Bulletin of the New York C. S. Lewis Society* 8, no. 8 (1977): 1–4.
Burgess, Andrew J. "The Concept of Eden." In *The Transcendent Adventure: Studies of Religion in Science Fiction/Fantasy*. Edited by Robert Reilly. Westport, CT: Greenwood Press, 1985.
Carnell, Corbin S. "C. S. Lewis: An Appraisal." *Mythlore* 1, no. 4 (1974).
Carpenter, Humphrey. *The Inklings: C. S. Lewis, J. R. R. Tolkien, Charles Williams, and Their Friends*. Boston: Houghton Mifflin, 1979.
Carter, Margaret L. "A Note on Moral Concepts in Lewis' Fiction." *Mythlore* 5 (1978): 35.
Cassell, George F. *Clive Staples Lewis*. Chicago: Chicago Literary Club, 1950.
Chapman, Ed. "Images of the Numinous in T. H. White and C. S. Lewis." *Mythlore* 4, no. 16 (June 1978): 3–10.
Christopher, Joe R. "An Inklings Bibliography." (2) *Mythlore* 4, no. 1 (1976): 33–38; (3) *Mythlore* 4, no. 2 (1976): 33–38; (4) *Mythlore* 4 (Mar. 1977): 33–38; (5) *Mythlore*

4 (June 1977): 40–46; (6) *Mythlore* 5 (May 1978): 40–46; (7) *Mythlore* 5 (Autumn 1978): 43–46; (8) *Mythlore* 6 (Winter 1979): 46–47; (9) *Mythlore* 6 (Spring 1979): 40–46; (10) *Mythlore* 6 (Summer 1979): 38–45; (11) *Mythlore* 6 (Fall 1979): 44–47; (12) *Mythlore* 23 (1980): 41–45; (13) *Mythlore* 24 (1980): 42–47; (14) *Mythlore* 25 (1980): 43–47; (15) *Mythlore* 26 (1981): 42–46; (16) *Mythlore* 27 (1981): 43–47; (17) *Mythlore* 28 (1981): 43–47; (18) *Mythlore* 29 (1981): 43–47; (19) *Mythlore* 30 (1982): 43–47; (20) *Mythlore* 31 (1982): 37–41; (21) *Mythlore* 32 (1982): 42–46; (22) *Mythlore* 33 (1982): 42–46; (23) *Mythlore* 34 (1983): 51–55; (24) *Mythlore* 35 (1983): 51–55; (25) *Mythlore* 36 (1983): 51–55; (26) *Mythlore* 37 (1984): 51–55; (27) *Mythlore* 38 (1984): 58–63; (28) *Mythlore* 39 (1984): 59–63; (29) *Mythlore* 46 (1986): 57–59; (30) *Mythlore* 47 (1986): 51–54.

———. "An Introduction to Narnia." *Mythlore* 2, 6–8 (1975) and 3, 9 (1976). (In 4 parts)

———. "The World of Narnia." *Niekas* 32 (Winter 1983): 46–57.

Christopher, Joe R., and Ostling, Joan K. "C. S. Lewis: A Bibliographic Supplement." *CSL: The Bulletin of the New York C. S. Lewis Society* 5, no. 8 (1974): 4–6.

———. *C. S. Lewis: An Annotated Checklist of Writings about Him and His Works.* Kent, OH: Kent State Univ. Press, 1973.

Clute, John. "C. S. Lewis." In *Science Fiction Writers.* Edited by E. F. Bleiler. New York: Scribner, 1982, pp. 243–249.

———. "C. S. Lewis." In *Supernatural Fiction Writers: Fantasy and Horror,* vol. 2. Edited by E. F. Bleiler. New York: Scribner, 1985, pp. 661–666.

Colbath, Mary Lou. "Worlds as They Should Be: Middle Earth, Narnia and Prydain." *Elementary English* 48 (Dec. 1971): 937–945.

Collings, Michael R. "Of Lions and Lamp-Posts: C. S. Lewis's *The Lion, the Witch, and the Wardrobe* as Response to Olaf Stapledon's *Sirius.*" *Christianity and Literature* 34 (Summer 1983): 33–38.

Como, James T., ed. *C. S. Lewis at the Breakfast Table and Other Reminiscences.* New York: Macmillan, 1979; Collier, 1985.

Como, James T. "A Look into Narnia." *CSL: The Bulletin of the New York C. S. Lewis Society* 15 (July 1984): 1–6.

———. "Mediating Illusions: Three Studies of Narnia." *Children's Literature,* vol. 10. New Haven, CT: Yale Univ. Press, 1982, pp. 102–110.

Cox, John D. "Epistemological Release in *The Silver Chair.*" In Peter J. Schakel. *The Longing for Form: Essays on the Fiction of C. S. Lewis.* Kent, OH: Kent State Univ. Press, 1977.

Crouch, Marcus. "Chronicles of Narnia." *Junior Bookshelf* 20 (Nov. 1956): 245–253.

CSL: The Bulletin of the New York C. S. Lewis Society. New York: C. S. Lewis Society, 1969– .

Dockery, C. "The Myth of the Shadow in the Fantasies of Williams, Lewis and Tolkien." Ph.D. dissertation, Auburn University, 1975.

Doyle, Brian. *The Who's Who of Children's Literature.* New York: Schocken, 1968, pp. 178–179.

Edwards, Bruce L., Jr. "A Rhetoric of Reading: A Study of C. S. Lewis's Approach to the Written Text." Ph.D. dissertation, University of Texas at Austin, 1981.

———. "Toward a Rhetoric of Fantasy Criticism: C. S. Lewis's Readings of MacDonald and Morris." *Literature and Belief* 3 (Mar. 1983): 63–73.

Elgin, Don D. *The Comedy of the Fantastic: Ecological Perspectives on the Fantasy Novel.* Westport, CT: Greenwood Press, 1985.

Evans, Murray. "C. S. Lewis' Narnia Books: The Reader in the Myth." In *Touchstones.* Edited by Perry Nodelman. West Lafayette, IN: Children's Literature Association Publications, 1985, pp. 132–145.

"An Evening with Walter Hooper." *CSL: The Bulletin of the New York C. S. Lewis Society* 6, no. 9 (1975): 1–7.

Fitzgerald, Dorothy Hobson. "C. S. Lewis' Images." *CSL: The Bulletin of the New York C. S. Lewis Society* 14 (Sept. 1983): 1–7.

Forbes, Cheryl. "Narnia: Fantasy, But. . . ." *Christianity Today,* Apr. 23, 1976, pp. 6–10.

Ford, Paul. *Companion to Narnia: A Complete, Illustrated Guide to the Themes, Characters, and Events of C. S. Lewis's Imaginary World.* New York: Harper and Row, 1981; 1983. pap.

Foulon, Jacqueline. "The Theology of C. S. Lewis' Children's Books." Master's thesis, Fuller Theological Seminary, 1962.

Frost, Naomi. "Life after Death: Visions of Lewis and Williams." *CSL: The Bulletin of the New York C. S. Lewis Society* 6 (1975): 2–6.

Gibb, Jocelyn, ed. *Light on C. S. Lewis.* New York: Harcourt Brace Jovanovitch, 1966.

Gibson, Evan K. *C. S. Lewis, Spinner of Tales: A Guide to His Fiction.* Washington, DC: Christian Univ. Press, 1980.

Gilbert, Douglas, and Kilby, Clyde S. *C. S. Lewis: Images of His World.* Grand Rapids, MI: Eerdmans, 1973.

Glover, Donald E. *C. S. Lewis: The Art of Enchantment.* Athens: Ohio Univ. Press, 1981.

Goodknight, Glen. "A Cosmological Geography in the Works of J. R. R. Tolkien, C. S. Lewis, and Charles Williams." *Mythlore* 1, no. 3 (1974).

Gough, John. "C. S. Lewis and the Problem of David Holbrook." *Children's Literature in Education* 8 (Summer 1977): 51–62.

Green, David L. "Children's Literature Periodicals on Individual Authors, Dime Novels, Fantasy." *Phaedrus* 3 (1976): 22–24.

Green, Roger Lancelyn. *C. S. Lewis.* New York: Walck, 1963. Reprinted in Margery Fisher, Roger Lancelyn Green, and Marcus Crouch. *Henry Treese, C. S. Lewis and Beatrix Potter.* London: Bodley Head, 1969.

———. "C. S. Lewis and Andrew Lang." *Notes and Queries* 22 (May 1975): 208–209.

Green, Roger Lancelyn, and Hooper, Walter. *C. S. Lewis: A Biography.* London: Collins, 1974. New York: Harcourt Brace Jovanovich, 1974.

Griffin, William. *Clive Staples Lewis: The Drama of a Life.* New York: Harper and Row, 1986.

Haigh, John D. "The Fiction of C. S. Lewis." Ph.D. dissertation, University of Leeds (England), 1962.

Hanger, Nancy C. "The Excellent Absurdity: Substitution and Co-Inherence in C. S. Lewis and Charles Williams. *Mythlore* 34 (1983): 14–18.

Hannay, Margaret Patterson. *C. S. Lewis.* New York: Ungar, 1981.

———. "C. S. Lewis' Theory of Mythology." *Mythlore* 1, no. 1 (1974).

———. "'Surprised by Joy': C. S. Lewis' Changing Attitudes toward Women." *Mythlore* 4, 13 no. 1 (1977): 15–20.

Harsh, Donna J. "Aslan in Filmland: The Animation of Narnia." In Douglas Street. *Children's Novels and the Movies.* New York: Ungar, 1983, pp. 163–170.

Hart, Dabney Adams. *Through the Open Door: A New Look at C. S. Lewis.* Birmingham: Univ. of Alabama Press, 1984.

Hartt, Walter F. "Godly Influences: The Theology of J. R. R. Tolkien and C. S. Lewis." *Studies in the Literary Imagination* 14 (Fall 1981): 21–29.

Henthorne, Susan Cassandra. "The Image of Woman in the Fiction of C. S. Lewis." Ph.D. dissertation, State University of New York at Buffalo, 1985.

Higgins, James Edward. "Five Authors of Mystical Fancy for Children: A Critical Study." Ed.D. dissertation, Columbia University, 1965.

———. "A Letter from C. S. Lewis." *Horn Book* 42 (Dec. 1966): 533–539. Reprinted in Elinor Field. *Horn Book Reflections*. Boston: Horn Book, 1969, pp. 230–237; and in Margaret Meek. *The Cool Web*. New York: Atheneum, 1976, pp. 157–158.

Hillegas, Mark Robert, ed. *Shadows of the Imagination: The Fantasies of C. S. Lewis, J. R. R. Tolkien and Charles Williams*. Carbondale: Southern Illinois Univ. Press, 1969.

Holbrook, David. "The Problem of C. S. Lewis." *Children's Literature in Education* 10 (Mar. 1973): 3–25. Reprinted in Geoff Fox. *Writers, Critics and Children*. New York: Agathon Press, 1976, pp. 116–124.

Hollindale, P. "The Image of the Beast: C. S. Lewis's *Chronicles of Narnia*." *Use of English* 28 (Spring 1977): 16–21.

Hooper, Walter. "Narnia: The Author, the Critics, and the Tale." *Children's Literature,* vol. 3. Storrs, CT: Journal of the Modern Language Association, 1974, pp. 12–22. Reprinted in Peter J. Schakel. *The Longing for a Form*. Kent, OH: Kent State Univ. Press, 1977; and in *Reflections on Literature for Children*. Edited by Francelia Butler and Richard Rotert. Hamden, CT: Shoe String Press, 1984, pp. 247–259.

———. *Past Watchful Dragons: The Narnia Chronicles of C. S. Lewis*. New York: Macmillan, 1979.

———. "Reminiscences." *Mythlore* 3, no. 12 (1976).

———. *Through Joy and Beyond: A Pictorial Biography of C. S. Lewis*. New York: Macmillan, 1982.

Howard, Thomas. *The Achievement of C. S. Lewis*. Wheaton, IL: Harold Shaw, 1980.

———. "The 'Moral Mythology' of C. S. Lewis." *Modern Age* 22 (1978): 384–392.

Huttar, Charles A. "C. S. Lewis's Narnia and the 'Grand Design.' " In Peter J. Schakel. *The Longing for a Form*. Kent, OH: Kent State Univ. Press, 1977.

Hutton, M. "Writers for Children: C. S. Lewis." *School Librarian* 12 (July 1964): 124–126 ff.

Jenkins, Sue. "Love, Loss, and Seeking: Material Deprivation and the Quest." *Children's Literature in Education* 15 (Summer 1984): 73–84.

Johnson, William G., and Houtman, Marcia K. "Platonic Shadows in C. S. Lewis' Narnia Chronicles." *Studies in Modern Fiction* 32 (Spring 1986): 75–87.

José, Pilar San, and Starkey, Gregory. "Tolkien's Influence on C. S. Lewis." *Mallorn* 17 (1981): 23–28.

Karimipour, Zahra. "A Descriptive Bibliography of C. S. Lewis's Fiction: 1938–1981." Ph.D. dissertation, Oklahoma State University, 1985.

Karkainen, Paul A. *Narnia Explored*. Old Tappan, NJ: Revell, 1979.

Keefe, Carolyn. "Narnia Tales: A Refracting of Pictures." Ann Arbor, MI: ERIC Educational Document Reprint Service, 1978.

King, Don. "The Childlike in George MacDonald and C. S. Lewis." *Mythlore* 46 (1986): 17–22, 26.

———. "Narnia and the Seven Deadly Sins." *Mythlore* 38 (1984): 14–19.

Kirk, Tim. "A Map of Narnia." *Mythlore* 2, no. 7 (1975).

Kirkpatrick, Hope. "Hierarchy in C. S. Lewis." *CSL: The Bulletin of the New York C. S. Lewis Society* 6, no. 4 (1975): 1–6.

Kirkpatrick, Mary. "An Introduction to the Curdie Books by George MacDonald, including Parallels between Them and the Narnia Chronicles." *CSL: The Bulletin of the New York C. S. Lewis Society* 5, no. 5 (1974): 1–6.

———. "Lewis and MacDonald." *CSL: The Bulletin of the New York C. S. Lewis Society* 5, no. 7 (1974): 2–4.

Koelb, Clayton. *The Incredulous Reader: Literature and the Function of Disbelief*. Ithaca, NY: Cornell Univ. Press, 1984.

Kolbe, Martha Emily. "Three Oxford Dons as Creators of Other Worlds for Children: Lewis Carroll, C. S. Lewis and J. R. R. Tolkien." Ph.D. dissertation, University of Virginia, 1981.

Kotzin, Michael C. "C. S. Lewis and George MacDonald: *The Silver Chair* and the *Princess* Books." *Mythlore* 8, no. 27 (Spring 1981): 5–15.

———. "Mrs. Moore as the Queen of Underland." *Mythlore* 6 (Summer 1979): 46.

"The Last Battle." In M. Crouch and A. Ellis. *Chosen for Children.* 3rd ed. London: The Library Association, 1977, pp. 83–90.

Lewis, C. S. *C. S. Lewis's Letters to Children.* Edited by Lyle W. Dorsett and Marjorie Lamp. New York: Macmillan, 1985.

———. "The Dethronement of Power." *Time and Tide* 36 (Oct. 22, 1955): 1373–1374.

———. *The Discarded Image.* New York: Cambridge Univ. Press, 1964, 1967.

———. *An Experiment in Criticism.* New York: Cambridge Univ. Press, 1961. "On Myth," "The Meaning of Fantasy," "On Realism," pp. 40–49, 50–56, 70–73.

———. "The Gods Return to Earth." *Time and Tide* 35 (Aug. 1954): 1083.

———. *Of Other Worlds: Essays and Stories.* Edited by Walter Hooper. New York: Harcourt Brace Jovanovich, 1967.

———. "On Stories." In *Of Other Worlds: Essays and Stories.* New York: Harcourt Brace Jovanovich, 1967, pp. 247–259. Reprinted in *Essays Presented to Charles Williams.* Freeport, NY: Books for Libraries Press, 1972, pp. 90–105; and in Margaret Meek. *The Cool Web.* New York: Atheneum, 1978, pp. 76–90.

———. "On Three Ways of Writing for Children." *Horn Book* 39 (Oct. 1963): 459–469 (written in 1952). Reprinted in C. S. Lewis. *Of Other Worlds: Essays and Stories.* Edited by Walter Hooper. New York: Harcourt Brace Jovanovich, 1967, pp. 22–34; in Virginia Haviland. *Children and Literature.* Glenview, IL: Scott, Foresman, 1973, pp. 231–240; and in Sheila A. Egoff. *Only Connect.* New York: Oxford Univ. Press, 1980, pp. 207–220.

———. "A Preface to *Paradise Lost.*" New York: Oxford Univ. Press, 1942.

———. "Sometimes Fairy Stories May Say Best What's to Be Said." *New York Times Book Review.* Pt. II. Nov. 18, 1956, p. 3. Reprinted in C. S. Lewis. *Of Other Worlds: Essays and Stories.* New York: Harcourt Brace Jovanovich, 1967, pp. 35–38, and in Boyer and Zahorski. *Fantasists on Fantasy.* New York: Avon, 1984, pp. 111–118.

———. *Surprised by Joy: The Shape of My Early Life.* New York: Harcourt Brace Jovanovich, 1955.

———. *They Asked for a Paper.* London: Bles, 1955.

Lindskoog, Kathryn. "The First Chronicle of Narnia: The Restoring of Names." *Mythlore* 46 (1986): 43–46, 63.

———. *The Lion of Judah in Never-Never Land: The Theology of C. S. Lewis Expressed in His Fantasies for Children.* Grand Rapids, MI: Eerdmans, 1973.

Lively, Penelope. "The Wrath of God: An Opinion of the Narnia Books." *The Use of English* 20, no. 2 (Winter 1968): 126–129.

Lochhead, Marion. *Renaissance of Wonder.* New York: Harper and Row, 1980.

Loney, John Douglas. "Reality, Truth and Perspective in the Fiction of C. S. Lewis." Ph.D. dissertation, McMaster University (Canada), 1983.

Lowentrout, Peter. "The Rags of Lordship: Science Fiction, Fantasy, and the Reenchantment of the World." *Mythlore* 41 (1985): 47–51, 57.

McKenzie, Patricia Alice. "*The Last Battle:* Violence and Theology in the Novels of C. S. Lewis." Ph.D. dissertation, University of Florida, 1974.

Manlove, C. N. *Modern Fantasy: Five Studies.* New York: Cambridge Univ. Press, 1975.

Manna, Anthony L. " 'Borrowing' C. S. Lewis: Aurand Harris's Dramatization of *The*

Magician's Nephew." Children's Literature Association Quarterly 11 (Fall 1986): 148–150.

Matthews, Kenneth Ernest. "C. S. Lewis and the Modern World." Ph.D. dissertation, University of California, Los Angeles, 1983.

Meileander, Gilbert, Jr. "The Social and Ethical Thought of C. S. Lewis." Ph.D. dissertation, Princeton University, 1976.

——. *The Taste for the Other: The Social and Ethical Thought of C. S. Lewis.* Grand Rapids, MI: Eerdmans, 1978.

Montgomery, John W. "The Chronicles of Narnia and the Adolescent Reader." *Religious Education* 54 (Sept. 1959): 418–428. Reprinted in Miriam Hoffman and Eva Samuels. *Authors and Illustrators of Children's Books.* New York: Bowker, 1972, pp. 280–296.

——, ed. *Myth, Allegory and Gospel: An Interpretation of J. R. R. Tolkien, C. S. Lewis, G. K. Chesterton, and Charles Williams.* Minneapolis: Bethany, 1974.

Moorman, Charles. " 'Now Entertain Conjectures of a Time'—The Fictive Worlds of C. S. Lewis and J. R. R. Tolkien." In *Shadows of the Imagination.* Edited by Mark R. Hillegas. Carbondale: Southern Illinois Univ. Press, 1969.

——. "Sacramentalism in Charles Williams." *Chesterton Review* 8 (1982): 35–50.

More Junior Authors. Edited by Muriel Fuller. New York: Wilson, 1963, p. 140.

Morrison, John. "The Idea of Covenant in Narnia." *CSL: The Bulletin of the New York C. S. Lewis Society* 10 (Oct. 1979): 1–7.

——. "Obedience and Surrender in Narnia." *CSL: The Bulletin of the New York C. S. Lewis Society* 7, no. 12 (1976): 2–4.

Murphy, Brian. *C. S. Lewis.* Mercer Island, WA: Starmont, 1983. (bibliography)

——. "Enchanted Rationalism: The Legacy of C. S. Lewis." *Christianity and Literature* 25 (Winter 1976): 13–29.

Murrin, Michael. "The Dialectic of Multiple Worlds: An Analysis of C. S. Lewis's Narnia Stories." *Seven: An Anglo-American Literary Review* 3 (1982).

Nardo, Anna K. "Fantasy Literature and Play: An Approach to Reader Response." *Centennial Review* 22 (1978): 201–213.

Nelson, Marie. "Non-Human Speech in the Fantasy of C. S. Lewis, J. R. R. Tolkien and Richard Adams." *Mythlore* 5, no. 17 (May 1978): 37–39.

Neuleib, Janice Witherspoon. "The Concept of Evil in the Fiction of C. S. Lewis." Ph.D. dissertation, University of Illinois, 1974.

New York C. S. Lewis Society. *Bibliography of the Works of C. S. Lewis.* New Haven, CT: New York C. S. Lewis Society, 1979.

O'Hare, C. "Charles Williams, C. S. Lewis, and J. R. R. Tolkien: Three Approaches to Religion in Modern Fiction." Ph.D. dissertation, University of Toronto, 1973.

Olsen, D. "First and Second Things: The Theoretical Criticism of C. S. Lewis." Ph.D. dissertation, Bowling Green State University, 1978.

The Oxford Companion to Children's Literature. Edited by Humphrey Carpenter and Mari Prichard. New York: Oxford Univ. Press, 1984, pp. 309–310, 370.

Patterson, Nancy-Lou. "An Appreciation of Pauline Baynes." *Mythlore* 7, no. 25 (1980).

——. "Guardaci Ben: The Visionary Woman in C. S. Lewis' *Chronicles of Narnia* and *That Hideous Strength.*" *Mythlore* 6 (Summer 1979): 6–10, and 6 (Winter 1979): 20–24.

——. "Half Like a Serpent: The Green Witch in *The Silver Chair.*" *Mythlore* 40 (1984): 37–47.

——. "The Host of Heaven, Astrological and Other Images of Divinity in the Fantasies of C. S. Lewis." *Mythlore* 7 (1980): 19–29 ff.

——. "Narnia and the North: The Symbolism of Northernness in the Fantasies of C. S. Lewis." *Mythlore* 4, no. 2 (1976): 9–16.

Pauline, Sister, C.S.M. "Secondary Worlds: Lewis and Tolkien." *CSL: The Journal of the New York C. S. Lewis Society* 12 (May 1981): 1–8.

Paxon, Diana. "The Tolkien Tradition." *Mythlore* 39 (1984): 23–27, 37.

Peters, John. *C. S. Lewis: The Man and His Achievement.* Exeter, England: Paternoster Press, 1985.

Pflieger, Pat, and Hill, Helen M. *A Reference Guide to Modern Fantasy for Children.* Westport, CT: Greenwood Press, 1984, pp. xi–xvi, 249–251, 295–297, 307–311, 313–315, 342–344, 452–454, 470–472, 490–492.

Phelps, Russ A. "*Mother Hubbard's Tale* and *The Last Battle.*" *CSL: The Bulletin of the New York C. S. Lewis Society* 11 (Apr. 1980): 9–10.

Pittenger, Norman. "C. S. Lewis: Combative in Defense." *Studies in the Literary Imagination* 14 (1981): 13–20.

Pitts, Mary Ellen. "The Motif of the Garden in the Novels of J. R. R. Tolkien, Charles Williams, and C. S. Lewis." *Mythlore* 8, no. 30 (1981).

Poskanzer, Susan Cornell. "Thoughts on C. S. Lewis and *The Chronicles of Narnia.*" *Language Arts* 53 (1976): 523–526.

Presley, Horton. "C. S. Lewis: Mythmaker." In Thomas D. Clareson and Thomas L. Wymer. *Voices for the Future,* vol. 3. Bowling Green, OH: Bowling Green Univ. Press, 1984.

Price, Meredith. " 'All Shall Love Me and Despair': The Figure of Lilith in Tolkien, Lewis, Williams, and Sayers." *Mythlore* 9 (1982): 3–7 ff.

Purtill, Richard. *Lord of Elves and Eldils: Fantasy and Philosophy in C. S. Lewis and J. R. R. Tolkien.* Grand Rapids, MI: Zondervan, 1974.

Quinn, Dennis B. "The Narnia Books of C. S. Lewis: Fantastic or Wonderful?" In *Children's Literature,* vol. 12. New Haven, CT: Yale Univ. Press, 1984, pp. 105–121.

Reddy, Albert Francis, S.J. "The Else Unspeakable: An Introduction to the Fiction of C. S. Lewis." Ph.D. dissertation, University of Massachusetts, 1972.

Rigsbee, Sally. "Fantasy Places and Imaginative Belief: *The Lion, the Witch and the Wardrobe* and *The Princess and the Goblin.*" *Children's Literature Association Quarterly* 8 (Spring 1983): 10–12.

Rogers, Deborah Champton Webster. "The Fictitious Characters of C. S. Lewis and J. R. R. Tolkien in Relation to Their Medieval Sources." Ph.D. dissertation, University of Wisconsin, 1972.

Rossi, Lee D. "The Politics of Fantasy: C. S. Lewis and J. R. R. Tolkien." Ph.D. dissertation, Cornell University, 1972.

———. *The Politics of Fantasy: C. S. Lewis and J. R. R. Tolkien.* Ann Arbor: Univ. of Michigan Research Press, 1984.

Rustin, Michael. "Narnia: An Imaginary Land as Container of Moral and Emotional Adventure." In *Narratives of Love and Loss.* London: Verso, 1987, pp. 40–58.

Sadler, Glenn Edward. "C. S. Lewis." In *Writers for Children: Critical Studies of Major Authors since the Seventeenth Century.* Edited by Jane M. Bingham. New York: Scribner, 1988, pp. 357–364.

Sammons, Martha C. *A Guide through Narnia.* Wheaton, IL: Shaw, 1979.

———. "Lewis' Influence on the New Inklings: *The Chronicles of Narnia* and John White's *Tower of Geburah* and *The Iron Sceptre.*" *CSL: The Bulletin of the New York C. S. Lewis Society* 17 (Nov. 1985): 1–7.

Sardello, Robert J. "An Empirical-Phenomenological Study of Fantasy, with a Note on J. R. R. Tolkien and C. S. Lewis." *Psycho-Cultural Review* 2 (1978): 203–220.

Sayers, Dorothy L. "The Chronicles of Narnia." *Spectator* (July 22, 1955): 123.

Schakel, Peter J. "Dance as Metaphor and Myth in Lewis, Tolkien, and Williams." *Mythlore* 45 (1986): 4–8, 23.

———. *Reading with the Heart: The Way into Narnia.* Grand Rapids, MI: Eerdmans, 1979.

————, ed. *The Longing for a Form: Essays on the Fiction of C. S. Lewis*. Kent, OH: Kent State Univ. Press, 1977.

Schofield, Stephen, ed. *In Search of C. S. Lewis*. South Plainfield, NJ: Bridge Publishers, Inc., 1983.

Searles, Baird; Meacham, Beth; and Franklin, Michael. *A Reader's Guide to Fantasy*. New York: Avon, 1982, pp. 94–95.

Shippey, Tom A. "*The Chronicles of Narnia*." In *Survey of Modern Fantasy Literature*, vol. 1. Edited by Frank N. Magill. Englewood Cliffs, NJ: Salem Press, 1983, pp. 248–255.

————. "The Golden Bough and the Incorporation of Magic in Science Fiction." *Foundation* 11/12 (1977): 119–134.

Shoemaker, S. "Beyond the Walls of the World: Practical Theology in the Fantasy Novels of C. S. Lewis." Ph.D. dissertation, Duke University, 1979.

Smith, Lillian H. "News from Narnia." *Canadian Library Association Bulletin* (July 1958). Reprinted in *Horn Book* 39 (Oct. 1963): 470–473; in Elinor Field. *Horn Book Reflections*. Boston: Horn Book, 1969, pp. 225–229; and in Sheila A. Egoff. *Only Connect*. New York: Oxford Univ. Press, 1980, pp. 170–175.

Stott, Jon C. *Children's Literature from A to Z*. New York: McGraw-Hill, 1984, p. 173.

Suthamchai, Phanida. "The Fusion of Christian and Fictional Elements in C. S. Lewis's *Chronicles of Narnia*." Ph.D. dissertation, Oklahoma State University, 1985.

Swinfen, Ann. *In Defense of Fantasy*. London: Routledge, 1984, pp. 19, 22–23, 79–83, 85–86, 90–91, 103–105, 115, 147–159, 186–189, 231–232.

Terry, June S. "To Seek and to Find: Quest Literature for Children." *School Librarian* 18 (Dec. 1970): 399–404. Reprinted in Mary Lou White. *Children's Literature*. Columbus, OH: Merrill, 1976, pp. 138–143.

Thompson, Hillary. "Doorways to Fantasy." *Canadian Children's Literature* 21 (1981): 8–16.

Timmerman, John H. "*The Magician's Nephew*: Mage and Maker." In *Other Worlds: The Fantasy Genre*. Bowling Green, OH: Bowling Green Univ. Press, 1983, pp. 75–81.

Tixier, Elaine. "Imagination Baptized, or 'Holiness' in the *Chronicles of Narnia*." In Peter J. Schakel. *The Longing for a Form: Essays on the Fiction of C. S. Lewis*. Kent, OH: Kent State Univ. Press, 1977.

Twentieth Century Children's Writers. 2nd ed. Edited by D. L. Kirkpatrick. New York: St. Martin's Press, 1983, pp. 473–476.

Twentieth-Century Science Fiction Writers. 2nd ed. Edited by Curtis C. Smith. Chicago: St. James Press, 1986, pp. 444–447.

Unrue, John C. "Beastliness in Narnia: Medieval Echoes." In *Man's "Natural Powers."* Edited by Raymond P. Tripp, Jr. London: The Society for New Language Study, 1975, pp. 9–16.

Urang, Gunnar. *Shadows of Heaven: Religion and Fantasy in the Writing of C. S. Lewis, Charles Williams and J. R. R. Tolkien*. Ph.D. dissertation, University of Chicago, 1970. New York: Pilgrim Press, 1971.

Wain, John. "C. S. Lewis." *The American Scholar* 50 (1980–1981): 73–80.

Walker, Jeanne Murray. "*The Lion, the Witch, and the Wardrobe* as Rite of Passage." *Children's Literature in Education* 16 (1985): 177–188.

Walsh, Chad. *The Literary Legacy of C. S. Lewis*. New York: Harcourt Brace Jovanovich, 1979.

Ward, Samuel Keith. "C. S. Lewis and the Nature-Grace Aesthetic." Ph.D. dissertation, University of Pittsburgh, 1977.

Watson, James Darrell. "A Reader's Guide to C. S. Lewis: His Fiction." Ed.D. dissertation, East Texas University, 1981.
Wilcox, Steven Michael. *Reality, Romanticism and Reason: Perspectives on a C. S. Lewis Pedagogy.* Ph.D. dissertation, University of Colorado at Boulder, 1982.
Wolfe, Gary Kent. "Symbolic Fantasy." *Genre* 8 (1975): 194–209.
Wood, Doreen Anderson. "Of Time and Eternity: C. S. Lewis and Charles Williams." *CSL: The Bulletin of the New York C. S. Lewis Society* 17 (1986): 1–7.
Wytenbroek, Jacqueline. "Science Fiction and Fantasy." *Extrapolation* 23 (1982): 321–332.
Yandell, Steven. "The Trans-Cosmic Journeys in *The Chronicles of Narnia.*" *Mythlore* 43 (1985): 9–23.
Ziegler, Mervin. "Imagination as a Rhetorical Factor in the Works of C. S. Lewis." Ph.D. dissertation, University of Florida, 1978.

Lewis, Hilda (Winfred)

The Oxford Companion to Children's Literature. Edited by Humphrey Carpenter and Mari Prichard. New York: Oxford Univ. Press, 1984, p. 484.
Twentieth Century Children's Writers. 2nd ed. Edited by D. L. Kirkpatrick. New York: St. Martin's Press, 1983, p. 477.

Lifton, Betty Jean (Kirschner)

Helbig, Alethea K., and Perkins, Agnes Regan. *Dictionary of American Children's Fiction, 1960–1984; Recent Books of Recognized Merit.* Westport, CT: Greenwood Press, 1986, pp. 176, 380.
Lifton, Betty Jean. "In Search of Kappas." *Horn Book* 37 (Feb. 1961): 34–41.
———. "On Children's Literature: A Runcible Symposium." *Horn Book* 46 (June 1970): 255–263.
———. "Report on a Thousand Cranes." *Horn Book* 45 (Apr. 1969): 148–151.
———. "A Thousand Cranes." *Horn Book* 39 (Apr. 1963): 211–216.
Third Book of Junior Authors. Edited by Doris De Montreville and Donna Hill. New York: Wilson, 1972, pp. 178–199.
Twentieth Century Children's Writers. 2nd ed. Edited by D. L. Kirkpatrick. New York: St. Martin's Press, 1983, pp. 479–480.

Lindbergh, Anne Morrow (Spencer)

Lindbergh, Anne Morrow. *Bring Me a Unicorn: Diaries and Letters of Anne Morrow Lindbergh, 1922–1928.* New York: Harcourt Brace Jovanovich, 1972.
———. *Hour of Gold, Hour of Lead: Diaries and Letters, 1929–1932.* New York: Harcourt Brace Jovanovich, 1973.
———. *Locked Rooms and Open Doors: Diaries and Letters, 1933–1935.* New York: Harcourt Brace Jovanovich, 1974.
———. "Thoughts in the Rabbit Hole." *The Writer* 97 (Apr. 1985): 7–10.
Mercier, J. F. "Anne Lindbergh: Author of Books for Young People." *Publishers Weekly,* July 27, 1984, pp. 147–148.

Linde, Gunnel (Geijerstam)

Fourth Book of Junior Authors and Illustrators. Edited by Doris De Montreville and Elizabeth D. Crawford. New York: Wilson, 1978, pp. 226–228.

Lindgren, Astrid

Andreadis, A. Harriette. "The Screening of Pippi Longstocking." In Douglas Street. *Children's Novels and the Movies.* New York: Ungar, 1983, pp. 151–162.

Bamberger, Richard. "Astrid Lindgren and a New Kind of Books for Children." *Bookbird* 5, no. 2 (1967): 3–12.

———. "Astrid Lindgren on the Occasion of Her 70th Birthday." *Bookbird* 15, no. 2 (1977): 17–21.

Berkley, M. "*Pippi Longstocking*—And After." *Publishers Weekly,* Feb. 22, 1985, pp. 96–97.

Cott, Jonathan. "Profiles: Astrid Lindgren: The Astonishment of Being." *The New Yorker,* Feb. 28, 1983, pp. 46–63. Reprinted in Cott. *Pipers at the Gates of Dawn.* New York: Random, 1983, pp. 137–160.

Hagliden, Sten. "Astrid Lindgren, the Swedish Writer of Children's Books." *Junior Bookshelf* 23 (July 1959): 113–121. Reprinted in Miriam Hoffman and Eva Samuels. *Authors and Illustrators of Children's Books.* New York: Bowker, 1972, pp. 297–301.

Hoffeld, Laura. "*Pippi Longstocking:* The Comedy of the Natural Girl." *The Lion and Unicorn* 1, no. 1 (Spring 1977): 47–53.

Hürlimann, Bettina. *Three Centuries of Children's Books in Europe.* Translated and edited by Brian W. Alderson. Cleveland: World, 1968, pp. 81–83.

Lindgren, Astrid. "Pippi Can Lift a Horse: The Importance of Children's Books." *Quarterly Journal of the Library of Congress* 40 (Summer 1983): 188–201.

———. "A Short Talk with a Prospective Children's Writer." *Horn Book* 49 (June 1973): 248–252. Reprinted in Paul Heins. *Crosscurrents of Criticism.* Boston: Horn Book, 1977, pp. 3–6.

Lindgren, Astrid, and Von Zweigbergk, Eva. "The Road to Sunnanang." *Bookbird* 9, no 1 (1971): 37–55.

More Junior Authors. Edited by Muriel Fuller. New York: Wilson, 1963, pp. 141–142.

The Oxford Companion to Children's Literature. Edited by Humphrey Carpenter and Mari Prichard. New York: Oxford Univ. Press, 1984, pp. 312, 414.

Reeder, Kik. "*Pippi Longstocking*—Feminist or Anti-Feminist?" *Interracial Books for Children* 5, no. 4 (1974): 1.

Slayton, Ralph. "The Love Story of Astrid Lindgren." *Scandinavian Review* 63 (Dec. 1975): 44–53.

Smaridge, Norah. *Famous Modern Storytellers for Young People.* New York: Dodd, 1969, pp. 105–109.

Söderblom, Harriette. "Astrid Lindgren." Translated by Martin Naylor. *CBC Features* (formerly *The Calendar*) 40 (June–Dec. 1986).

Udal, John. "Richard Kennedy and *Pippi Longstocking.*" *Junior Bookshelf* 42 (Apr. 1978): 75–77.

Lindsay, Norman (Alfred William)

Colebatch, Hal. "Norman Lindsay and *The Magic Pudding.*" *Westerly* 1 (Mar. 1976): 83–86.

Doyle, Brian. *The Who's Who of Children's Literature.* New York: Schocken, 1968, pp. 180–181.

Hetherington, John. *Norman Lindsay.* Melbourne: Lansdowne Press, 1961.

Lindsay, Norman. *My Mask: For What Little I Know of the Man Behind It: An Autobiography.* Sydney: Argus & Robertson, 1970.

The Oxford Companion to Children's Literature. Edited by Humphrey Carpenter and Mari Prichard. New York: Oxford Univ. Press, 1984, p. 334.

Roe, Marjorie. "Forum of Children's Books: A *Magic Pudding* from Australia." *Bookbird* 6, no. 3 (Sept. 1968): 28–33.
Twentieth Century Children's Writers. 2nd ed. Edited by D. L. Kirkpatrick. New York: St. Martin's Press, 1983, pp. 480–481.

Linklater, Eric (Robert Russell)

Doyle, Brian. *The Who's Who of Children's Literature.* New York: Schocken, 1968, pp. 181–182.
The Oxford Companion to Children's Literature. Edited by Humphrey Carpenter and Mari Prichard. New York: Oxford Univ. Press, 1984, p. 575.
Twentieth Century Children's Writers. 2nd ed. Edited by D. L. Kirkpatrick. New York: St. Martin's Press, 1983, pp. 482–484.
"*The Wind on the Moon.*" In M. Crouch and A. Ellis. *Chosen for Children.* 3rd ed. London: The Library Association, 1977, pp. 35–39.

Lively, Penelope (Margaret Low)

Abbs, Peter. "Penelope Lively, Children's Fiction and the Failure of Adult Culture." *Children's Literature in Education* 18 (Fall 1975): 118–124.
Armstrong, Judith. "Ghosts as Rhetorical Devices in Children's Fiction." *Children's Literature in Education* 29, no. 9 (Summer 1978): 59–66.
Fourth Book of Junior Authors and Illustrators. Edited by Doris De Montreville and Elizabeth D. Crawford. New York: Wilson, 1978, pp. 229–231.
"*The Ghost of Thomas Kempe.*" In M. Crouch and A. Ellis. *Chosen for Children.* 3rd ed. London: The Library Association, 1974, pp. 168–172.
Hoffman, M. "Past Mistress; Interview: Penelope Lively." *Times Educational Supplement* (London) 3216 (Jan. 21, 1977): 37.
Inglis, Fred. *The Promise of Happiness.* New York: Cambridge Univ. Press, 1981, pp. 226–229.
Lively, Penelope. "Bones in the Sand." Based on a paper given at the Simmons College Center for the Study of Children's Literature, March 14, 1981. *Horn Book* 57 (Dec. 1981): 641–651. Reprinted in *Innocence & Experience.* Edited by Barbara Harrison and Gregory Maguire. New York: Lothrop, 1987, pp. 13–21.
———. "Children and Memory." *Horn Book* 49 (Aug. 1973): 400–407. Reprinted in Paul Heins. *Crosscurrents of Criticism.* Boston: Horn Book, 1977, pp. 226–233.
———. "Children and the Art of Memory, Part I." *Horn Book* 54 (Feb. 1978): 17–23. "Part II." *Horn Book* 54 (Apr. 1978): 197–203.
———. "*The Ghost of Thomas Kempe.*" *Junior Bookshelf* 38 (June 1974): 143–145.
The Oxford Companion to Children's Literature. Edited by Humphrey Carpenter and Mari Prichard. New York: Oxford Univ. Press, 1984, pp. 261–262, 322.
Pflieger, Pat, and Hill, Helen M. *A Reference Guide to Modern Fantasy for Children.* Westport, CT: Greenwood Press, 1984, pp. xii–xvi, 157–158, 204–205, 316–319, 471–472, 569–570, 591–592, 600–601.
Rees, David. "The Narrative Art of Penelope Lively." *Horn Book* 51 (Feb. 1976): 17–25. Reprinted in Paul Heins. *Crosscurrents of Criticism.* Boston: Horn Book, 1977, pp. 342–348; and in David Rees. *The Marble in the Water.* Boston: Horn Book, 1980, pp. 185–198.
———. "Time Present and Time Past: Penelope Lively." In *Marble in the Water.* Boston: Horn Book, 1980, pp. 185–198. Revised from an article in *Horn Book* 51 (Feb. 1975): 17–25. Reprinted in Paul Heins. *Crosscurrents of Criticism.* Boston: Horn Book, 1977, pp. 342–348.
Salway, Lance, and Chambers, Nancy. "Book Post." *Signal* 26 (May 1978): 99–107.

Smith, Louisa A. "Layers of Language in Lively's *The Ghost of Thomas Kempe.*" *Children's Literature Association Quarterly* 10 (Fall 1985): 114–116.
Townsend, John Rowe. "Penelope Lively." In *A Sounding of Storytellers*. Philadelphia: Lippincott, 1979, pp. 125–138.
Twentieth Century Children's Writers. 2nd ed. Edited by D. L. Kirkpatrick. New York: St. Martin's Press, 1983, pp. 488–490.

Lockley, Ronald (Mathias)

Yolen, Jane. "The Literary Underwater World." *Language Arts* 57 (1980): 403–412.

Lofting, Hugh (John)

Blishen, Edward. "Hugh Lofting." In Edward Blishen, Margaret Meek, and Roger Lancelyn Green. *Hugh Lofting/Geoffrey Trease/J. M. Barrie*. London: Bodley Head, 1968, pp. 9–61.
Certain, C. C. "*Dr. Dolittle*, the Children, and the Droll 'Huge' Lofting." *Elementary English Review* 1, no. 3 (May 1924): 90–92.
Chambers, Dewey W. "How, Now, Dr. Dolittle?" *Elementary English* 45 (Apr. 1968): 437–439 ff.
Colwell, Eileen H. "Hugh Lofting: An Appreciation." *Junior Bookshelf* 11 (Dec. 1947): 149–154.
Doyle, Brian. *The Who's Who of Children's Literature*. New York: Schocken, 1968, pp. 182–183.
Fish, Helen Dean. "Doctor Dolittle: His Life and Works." *Horn Book* 24 (Oct. 1948): 339–346. Reprinted in Elinor Field. *Horn Book Reflections*. Boston: Horn Book, 1969, pp. 218–224.
———. "Dr. Dolittle's Creator." *Saturday Review,* Jan. 10, 1948, pp. 28–29.
Helbig, Alethea K., and Perkins, Agnes Regan. *Dictionary of American Children's Fiction, 1859–1959*. Westport, CT: Greenwood Press, 1985, pp. 308, 494–496, 552–554.
"John Dolittle, M.D." *Times Literary Supplement* (London) 23 (Nov. 1951): vii.
Jones, M. E. "Connecticut's Puddleby-on-the-Marsh: Hugh Lofting." *Horn Book* 44 (Aug. 1968): 463, 475.
The Junior Book of Authors. 2nd ed. rev. Edited by Stanley J. Kunitz and Howard Haycraft. New York: Wilson, 1951, pp. 198–200.
Lofting, Christopher. "Trouble in Puddleby-on-the-Marsh." *Life Magazine* 61 (Sept. 30, 1966): 7.
Lofting, Hugh. "Children and Internationalism." *Nation,* Feb. 13, 1924, pp. 172–173.
———. "A Hunt Breakfast—Authors' Symposium." *Horn Book* 2 (Nov. 1926): 34–35.
———. "War and Dr. Dolittle." *Junior Bookshelf* 11 (Dec. 1947): 155–158.
MacCann, Donnarae. "Hugh Lofting." In *Writers for Children; Critical Studies of Major Authors since the Seventeenth Century*. Edited by Jane M. Bingham. New York: Scribner, 1988, pp. 365–372.
Mack, Lori. "A Publisher's Perspective." *Horn Book* 64 (May–June 1988): 382–384. Discusses the *Doctor Dolittle* books.
Miller, Bertha Mahony, and Field, Elinor Whitney, eds. *Newbery Medal Books: 1922–1955*. Boston: Horn Book, 1957, pp. 17–27.
The Oxford Companion to Children's Literature. Edited by Humphrey Carpenter and Mari Prichard. New York: Oxford Univ. Press, 1984, pp. 153–155, 324.
Roginski, Jim, ed. *Newbery and Caldecott Medalists and Honor Book Winners*. Littleton, CO: Libraries Unlimited, 1982, pp. 179–180.
Schlegelmilch, W. "From Fairy Tale to Children's Novel: In Honor of *Doctor Dolittle*'s

Fiftieth Birthday." *Bookbird* 8, no. 4 (1970): 14–21. Reprinted in Margaret Meek. *The Cool Web.* New York: Atheneum, 1978, pp. 265–271.

Schmidt, Gary D. "The Craft of the Cobbler's Son: Tommy Stubbins and the Narrative Form of the *Doctor Dolittle* Series." *Children's Literature Association Quarterly* 12 (Spring 1987): 19–24.

Schmidt, Nancy J. *Children's Fiction about Africa in English.* New York: Conch Magazine, 1981, pp. 175–178.

Searles, Baird; Meacham, Beth; and Franklin, Michael. *A Reader's Guide to Fantasy.* New York: Avon, 1982, pp. 96–97.

Shackford, J. "Dealing with *Dr. Dolittle:* A New Approach to the -isms." *Language Arts* 55 (Feb. 1978): 180–187.

Shenk, Dorothy C. "Hugh Lofting: Creator of *Dr. Dolittle.*" *Elementary English* 32 (Apr. 1955): 201–208.

Smaridge, Norah. *Famous Modern Storytellers for Young People.* New York: Dodd, 1969, pp. 32–37.

Suhl, Isabelle. "The 'Real' *Doctor Dolittle.*" *Interracial Books for Children* 2, no. 1–2 (Spring–Summer 1968): 1, 5–7. Reprinted in Donnarae MacCann and Gloria Woodard. *The Black American in Books for Children.* Metuchen, NJ: Scarecrow Press, 1972, pp. 78–88.

Twentieth Century Children's Writers. 2nd ed. Edited by D. L. Kirkpatrick. New York: St. Martin's Press, 1983, pp. 494–495.

Lowrey, Janette (Sebring)

Johnston, Leah Carter. "A Texas Author." *Horn Book* 23 (Jan. 1947): 56–61.

Lunn, Janet

Gagnon, A. "Janet Lunn, Writer-In-Residence [at the Regina Public Library]." *Emergency Librarian* 11 (Nov.–Dec. 1983): 21–22.

Jones, Raymond E. "Border Crossing: Janet Lunn's *The Root Cellar.*" *Children's Literature Association Quarterly* 10 (Spring 1985): 43–44.

Lunn, Janet. "Images of a Literature at Home." Presented at the Canadian Images Canadiennes Conference. *School Libraries in Canada* 7 (Spring 1987): 36–40.

McDonough, Irma, ed. "Janet Lunn." In *Profiles.* rev. ed. Ottawa: Canadian Library Association, 1975.

Lynch, Patricia (Nora)

Crouch, Marcus. *The Nesbit Tradition.* London: Benn, 1972, pp. 182–184.

Deevy, Teresa. "Patricia Lynch: A Study." *Junior Bookshelf* 13 (Mar. 1949): 17–27.

Doyle, Brian. *The Who's Who of Children's Literature.* New York: Schocken, 1968, pp. 185–186.

Graham, Eleanor. "Patricia Lynch: An Appreciation." *Junior Bookshelf* 7 (Mar. 1943): 2–6.

Lochhead, Marion. *Renaissance of Wonder.* New York: Harper and Row, 1980, pp. 77–81.

Lynch, Patricia. *A Storyteller's Childhood.* London: Dent, 1947.

The Oxford Companion to Children's Literature. Edited by Humphrey Carpenter and Mari Prichard. New York: Oxford Univ. Press, 1984, p. 326.

Twentieth Century Children's Writers. 2nd ed. Edited by D. L. Kirkpatrick. New York: St. Martin's Press, 1983, pp. 496–498.

Van Stockum, Hilda. "A Visit with Patricia Lynch." *Horn Book* 29 (Oct. 1953): 367–

372. Reprinted in Elinor Field. *Horn Book Reflections.* Boston: Horn Book, 1969, pp. 260–264.

Lynn, Elizabeth A.

Card, Orson Scott. "Unities in Digression." *Science Fiction Review* 37 (1980): 36–39.

"1980 World Fantasy Award Winners." *Locus* 13 (Oct. 1980): 1, 4.

Notkin, Debbie. "Interview: Elizabeth A. Lynn." *Janus* 5 (Spring 1979): 18–19, 25.

Reimer, James D. "Masculinity and Feminist Fantasy Authors." *Science Fiction Fantasy Review* 66 (1984): 19–21.

Spencer, Kathleen L. "*The Chronicles of Tornor.*" In *Survey of Modern Fantasy Literature,* vol. 1. Edited by Frank N. Magill. Englewood Cliffs, NJ: Salem Press, 1983, pp. 275–281.

Twentieth-Century Science Fiction Writers. 2nd ed. Edited by Curtis C. Smith. Chicago: St. James Press, 1986, pp. 470–471.

McCaffrey, Anne (Inez)

Antczak, Janice. *Science Fiction: The Mythos of a New Romance.* New York: Neal-Schuman, 1985, pp. 69–70, 114–115, 126–134, 159–160, 184–185.

Arbur, Rosemarie. *Leigh Brackett, Marion Zimmer Bradley, Anne McCaffrey: A Primary and Secondary Bibliography.* Boston: G. K. Hall, 1981.

Barr, Marleen. "Science Fiction and the Fact of Women's Repressed Creativity: Anne McCaffrey Portrays a Female Artist." *Extrapolation* 23 (Spring 1982): 70–76.

Barrett, David V. "Fire-Lizards Is Cats; Dragons Ain't Horses: Anne McCaffrey." *Vector* 1213 (1984): 3–7.

Brizzi, Mary T. *Anne McCaffrey.* Mercer Island, WA: Starmont, 1986.

"Dearest Ms. McCaffrey: Letters from Andrew Fox." *VOYA* 1 (Oct. 1978): 5–6.

Fifth Book of Junior Authors and Illustrators. Edited by Sally Holmes Holtze. New York: Wilson, 1983, pp. 206–207.

Fonstad, Karen Wynn. *The Atlas of Pern.* New York: Ballantine, 1984.

Graham, Wendy. "Dragonlady of Pern: Anne McCaffrey." *Space Voyager* 16 (1985): 19–23.

Helbig, Alethea K., and Perkins, Agnes Regan. *Dictionary of American Children's Fiction, 1960–1984.* Westport, CT: Greenwood Press, 1986, pp. 167, 410.

Heldreth, Lillian M. "Speculations on Heterosexual Equality: Morris, McCaffrey, Le Guin." In *Erotic Universe: Sexuality and Fantastic Literature.* Edited by Donald Palumbo. Westport, CT: Greenwood Press, 1986.

Liddell, Sharon. "Recommended: Anne McCaffrey." *English Journal* 73 (Nov. 1984): 89.

McCaffrey, Anne. "On Pernography." *Algol* 16 (Winter 1979): 27–28.

———. "Romance and Glamour in Science Fiction." In *Science Fiction, Today and Tomorrow.* Edited by Reginald Bretnor. New York: Harper and Row, 1974, pp. 278–294.

Markman, Roberta Hoffman. "The Fairy Tale: An Introduction to Literature and the Creative Process." *College English* 45 (1983): 31–45.

Morgan, Chris. "Interview: Anne McCaffrey." *Science Fiction Review* 44 (1983): 20–24.

———. "Science Fiction with Dragons: An Interview with Anne McCaffrey." *Extro Science Fiction* (July–Aug. 1982): 18–22.

Mura, J. "Pern Puzzle." *VOYA* 9 (July 1986): 69; "Erratum," *VOYA* (Aug.–Oct. 1986): 133.

Naha, Ed. "Living with the Dragons: Anne McCaffrey." *Future* 6 (1978): 22–23, 74.

Twentieth-Century Science Fiction Writers. 2nd ed. Edited by Curtis C. Smith. Chicago: St. James Press, 1986, pp. 492–494.
Walker, Paul. "Anne McCaffrey: An Interview." *Luna Monthly* 56 (1974): 1–5. Reprinted in Paul Walker. *Speaking of Science Fiction.* New York: Luna Publications, 1978, pp. 253–262.

MacDonald, George

Adams, Gillian. "Student Responses to *Alice in Wonderland* and *At the Back of the North Wind.*" *Children's Literature Association Quarterly* 10 (Spring 1985): 6–9.
Auden, W. H. "Afterword." *Horn Book* 43 (Apr. 1967): 176–177. Reprinted in Meek. *The Cool Web.* London: Bodley Head, 1977, pp. 103–104; and in Auden. *Forewords and Afterwords.* New York: Random, 1973, pp. 268–273.
———. "George MacDonald." In Auden. *Forewords and Afterwords.* New York: Random, 1973, pp. 268–273.
Babbitt, Natalie. "Afterword." In George MacDonald. *The Princess and Curdie.* New York: Dell, 1987.
Bergmann, Frank. "The Roots of Tolkien's Tree: The Influence of George MacDonald and German Romanticism upon Tolkien's Essay 'On Fairy Stories.'" *Mosaic* 10 (Winter 1977): 5–14.
Burns, Marjorie Jean. "Victorian Fantasists from Ruskin to Lang: A Study in Ambivalence." Ph.D. dissertation, University of California, Berkeley, 1978.
Carpenter, Humphrey. "George MacDonald and the Tender Grandmother." In *Secret Gardens: A Study of the Golden Age of Children's Literature.* Boston: Houghton Mifflin, 1985, pp. 70–85.
Cornwell, Charles Landrum. "From Self to the Shire: Studies in Victorian Fantasy." Ph.D. dissertation, University of Virginia, 1972.
Douglass, Jane. "Dealings with the Fairies, an Appreciation of George MacDonald." *Horn Book* 37 (Aug. 1961): 327–335. Reprinted in Elinor Field. *Horn Book Reflections.* Boston: Horn Book, 1969, pp. 203–210.
Doyle, Brian. *The Who's Who of Children's Literature.* New York: Schocken, 1968, pp. 186–188.
Edwards, Bruce L., Jr. "Toward a Rhetoric of Fantasy Criticism: C. S. Lewis's Readings of MacDonald and Morris." *Literature and Belief* 3 (Mar. 1983): 63–73.
Faben, Aline Sidny. "Folklore in the Fantasies and Romances of George MacDonald." Ph.D. dissertation, State University of New York at Buffalo, 1978.
"George MacDonald: *At the Back of the North Wind.*" In *Masterworks of Children's Literature,* vol. 6. Edited by Robert L. Wolff. New York: Chelsea House, 1984, pp. 171–369.
Hein, Rolland. *The Harmony Within: The Spiritual Vision of George MacDonald.* Grand Rapids, MI: Eerdmans, 1982.
Helson, Revenna, and Proysen, Alph. "The Psychological Origins of Fantasy for Children in Mid-Victorian England." *Children's Literature,* Vol. 3. Storrs, CT: Journal of the Modern Language Association, 1974, pp. 66–75.
Higgins, James Edward. "Five Authors of Mystical Fancy for Children: A Critical Study." Ed.D. dissertation, Columbia University, 1965.
Hines, Joyce Rose. "Getting Home: A Study of Fantasy and the Spiritual Journey in the Christian Supernatural Novels of Charles Williams and George MacDonald." Ph.D. dissertation, City University of New York, 1972.
Hoffeld, Laura. "Where Magic Begins." *The Lion and the Unicorn* 3, no. 1 (Spring 1979): 4–13.
Holbrook, David. "George MacDonald and Dreams of the Other World." *Seven: An Anglo-American Literary Review* 4 (1983): 27–37.

Hutton, Muriel. "The George MacDonald Collection." *Yale University Library Gazette* 51, no. 2 (Oct. 1976): 74–85.

———. "Unfamiliar Libraries XIII: The George MacDonald Collection, Brander Library, Huntly." *Book Collector* 17, no. 1 (Spring 1968): 13–25.

———. "Writers for Children: George MacDonald." *School Librarian* 12 (Dec. 1964): 244 ff.

Jackson, Rosemary. *Fantasy: The Literature of Subversion.* New York: Methuen, 1980.

Jenkins, Sue. "Love, Loss, and Seeking: Maternal Deprivation and the Quest." *Children's Literature in Education* 15 (Summer 1984): 73–84.

King, Don. "The Childlike in George MacDonald and C. S. Lewis." *Mythlore* 46 (1986): 17–22, 26.

Kirkpatrick, Mary. "An Introduction to the Curdie Books by George MacDonald, Including Parallels between Them and the Narnia Chronicles." *CSL: The Bulletin of the New York C. S. Lewis Society* 5, no. 5 (1974): 1–6.

Kocher, Paul H. "J. R. R. Tolkien and George MacDonald." *Mythlore* 8, 29 (1981); *The Crescent* 8 (1981): 3–4.

Kotzin, Michael C. "C. S. Lewis and George MacDonald: *The Silver Chair* and the *Princess* Books." *Mythlore* 8, 27 (Spring 1981): 5–15.

Landow, George P. "And the World Became Strange: Realms of Literary Fantasy." In Diane Johnson. *Fantastic Illustration and Design in Britain, 1850–1930.* Providence: Rhode Island School of Design, 1979, pp. 9–43. Reprinted in *Georgia Review* 33 (Spring 1979): 7–42.

Lewis, C. S. "Preface." In *George MacDonald: An Anthology.* Edited by C. S. Lewis. London: Bles, 1946, pp. 10–22.

Lochhead, Marion. "George MacDonald and the World of Faery." *Seven: An Anglo-American Literary Review* 3 (1982): 63–71.

———. *Renaissance of Wonder.* New York: Harper and Row, 1980, pp. 1–51. Original title: *The Renaissance of Wonder in Children's Literature.* Edinborough, 1977.

MacDonald, George. "Fairy Tale in Education." *Contemporary* 103 (1913): 491–499; *Living Age* 277 (1913): 783–790.

———. "The Fantastic Imagination." Original publication 1893. In George MacDonald. *The Gifts of the Christ Child: Fairytales and Stories for the Childlike,* vol. 1. Grand Rapids, MI: Eerdmans, 1974, pp. 23–28. Reprinted in Boyer and Zahorski. *Fantasists on Fantasy.* New York: Avon, 1984, pp. 11–22.

MacDonald, Greville. *George MacDonald and His Wife.* New York: Johnson Reprographics Corporation, 1971. Reprinted from 1924 edition.

McGillis, Roderick F. "The Fantastic Imagination: The Prose Romances of George MacDonald." Ph.D. dissertation, University of Reading (U.K.), 1973.

———. "Fantasy as Adventure: Nineteenth Century Children's Fiction." *Children's Literature Association Quarterly* 8 (Fall 1983): 18–22.

———. "George MacDonald's *Princess* Books: High Seriousness." In *Touchstones.* Edited by Perry Nodelman. West Lafayette, IN: Children's Literature Association Publications, 1985, pp. 146–162.

———. " 'If You Call Me Grandmother, That Will Do.' " *Mythlore* 6, 21 (Summer 1979): 27–28.

———. "Language and Secret Knowledge in *At the Back of the North Wind.*" In *Proceedings of the Seventh Annual Conference of the Children's Literature Association.* Baylor University, March 1980. Ypsilanti, MI: Children's Literature Association, 1982, pp. 120–127. Reprinted in *Durham University Journal* 73 (1981): 191–198.

McGregor, D. R. "Myth and Fantasy in Some Late Victorian Novelists with Special Reference to R. L. Stevenson and George MacDonald." Ph.D. dissertation, Auckland (New Zealand), 1973.

Manlove, C. N. "Circularity in Fantasy: George MacDonald." Revised from an article in *Studies in Scottish Literature,* 1982. In C. N. Manlove. *The Impulse of Fantasy Literature.* Kent, OH: Kent State Univ. Press, 1983, pp. 70–92.

———. "George MacDonald's Fairy Tales: Their Roots in MacDonald's Thought." *Studies in Scottish Literature* 8 (Oct. 1970): 97–108.

———. *Modern Fantasy: Five Studies.* New York: Cambridge Univ. Press, 1975.

Mann, Nancy Elizabeth Dawson. "George MacDonald and the Tradition of Victorian Fantasy." Ph.D. dissertation, Stanford University, 1973.

Mendolson, Michael. "Opening Moves: The Entry into the Other World." *Extrapolation* 25 (1984): 171–179.

Moss, Anita. " 'Felicitous Space' in the Fantasies of George MacDonald and Mervyn Peake." *Mythlore* 30 (1982): 16–17, 42.

Mudhenk, Rosemary Karmelich. "Another World: The Mode of Fantasy in the Fiction of Selected Nineteenth Century Writers." Ph.D. dissertation, University of California, Los Angeles, 1972.

Norton, Andre. "Afterword." In George MacDonald. *The Princess and the Goblin.* New York: Dell, 1986.

The Oxford Companion to Children's Literature. Edited by Humphrey Carpenter and Mari Prichard. New York: Oxford Univ. Press, 1984, pp. 33–34, 211, 311, 328–329, 426–427.

Pflieger, Pat, and Hill, Helen M. *A Reference Guide to Modern Fantasy for Children.* Westport, CT: Greenwood Press, 1984, pp. xiv, 28–29, 330–333, 454–457.

Pierson, Clayton Joy. "Toward Spiritual Fulfillment: A Study of the Fantasy World of George MacDonald." Ph.D. dissertation, University of Maryland, 1978.

Prickett, Stephen. *"At the Back of the North Wind."* In *Survey of Modern Fantasy Literature,* vol. 1. Edited by Frank N. Magill. Englewood Cliffs, NJ: Salem Press, 1983, pp. 63–65.

———. *"Phantastes."* In *Survey of Modern Fantasy Literature,* vol. 3. Edited by Frank N. Magill. Englewood Cliffs, NJ: Salem Press, 1983, pp. 1241–1245.

———. "Religious Fantasy in the Nineteenth Century." In *Survey of Modern Fantasy Literature,* vol. 5. Edited by Frank N. Magill. Englewood Cliffs, NJ: Salem Press, 1983, pp. 2369–2382.

———. "The Short Fiction of George MacDonald." In *Survey of Modern Fantasy Literature,* vol. 4. Edited by Frank N. Magill. Englewood Cliffs, NJ: Salem Press, 1983, pp. 1629–1632.

———. "The Two Worlds of George MacDonald." *North Wind: The Journal of the George MacDonald Society* 2 (1983): 14–23.

———. *Victorian Fantasy.* Bloomington: Indiana Univ. Press, 1979.

Ragg, Laura M. *George MacDonald and His Household: Some Personal Recollections. English* 11, no. 62 (Summer 1956): 59–63.

Reis, Richard H. *George MacDonald.* New York: Twayne, 1972.

Rigsbee, Sally. "Fantasy Places and Imaginative Belief: *The Lion, the Witch and the Wardrobe* and *The Princess and the Goblin.*" *Children's Literature Association Quarterly* 8 (Spring 1983): 10–12.

Sadler, Glenn Edward. "George MacDonald." In *Writers for Children; Critical Studies of Major Authors since the Seventeenth Century.* Edited by Jane M. Bingham. New York: Scribner, 1988, pp. 373–380.

———. "An Unpublished Children's Story by George MacDonald." In *Children's Literature,* vol. 2. Storrs, CT: Journal of the Modern Language Association, 1973. Reprinted in *Reflections on Literature for Children.* Edited by Francelia Butler and Richard Rotert. Hamden, CT: Shoe String Press, 1984, pp. 171–181.

Searles, Baird; Meacham, Beth; and Franklin, Michael. *A Reader's Guide to Fantasy.* New York: Avon, 1982, pp. 101–103.

Sherman, Cordelia. "The Princess and the Wizard: The Fantasy Worlds of Ursula K. Le Guin and George MacDonald." *Children's Literature Association Quarterly* 12 (Spring 1987): 24–28.

Sigman, Joseph. "Death's Ecstasies: Transformation and Rebirth in George MacDonald's *Phantastes*." *English Studies in Canada* 2 (1976): 203–226.

Sparks, Elisa Kay. "*The Princess and the Goblin* and *The Princess and Curdie*." In *Survey of Modern Fantasy Literature*, vol. 3. Edited by Frank N. Magill. Englewood Cliffs, NJ: Salem Press, 1983, pp. 1280–1285.

Stott, Jon C. *Children's Literature from A to Z*. New York: McGraw-Hill, 1984, p. 190.

Tanner, Tony. "Mountains and Depths—An Approach to Nineteenth Century Dualism." *Review of English Literature* 3, no. 4 (Oct. 1962): 51–61.

Thorpe, Douglas James. "A Hidden Rime: The World View of George MacDonald." Ph.D. dissertation, University of Toronto, 1981.

Twentieth Century Children's Writers. 2nd ed. Edited by D. L. Kirkpatrick. New York: St. Martin's Press, 1983, pp. 877–878.

Willard, Nancy. "Goddess in the Belfry." *Parabola* 6 (Summer 1981): 90–94.

———. "The Nonsense of Angels: George MacDonald *At the Back of the North Wind*." In *Proceedings of the Fifth Annual Conference of the Children's Literature Association*. Harvard University, March 1978. Ypsilanti, MI: Children's Literature Association, 1979, pp. 106–112. Reprinted in Jill P. May. *Children and Their Literature: A Readings Book*. West Lafayette, IN: Children's Literature Association Publications, 1983, pp. 34–40.

Willis, Leslie. " 'Born Again': The Metamorphosis of Irene in George MacDonald's *The Princess and the Goblin*." *Scottish Literary Journal* 12 (May 1985): 24–39.

Wilson, Keith. "The Quest for 'The Truth': A Reading of George MacDonald's *Phantastes*." *Études Anglaises* 34 (1981): 41–52.

Wolfe, Gary Kent. "George MacDonald." In *Supernatural Fiction Writers: Fantasy and Horror*, vol. 1. Edited by E. F. Bleiler. New York: Scribner, 1985, pp. 239–246.

———. "Symbolic Fantasy." *Genre* 8 (1975): 194–209.

Wolff, R. L. *The Golden Key: A Study of the Fiction of George MacDonald*. New Haven, CT: Yale Univ. Press, 1961.

Yates, Elizabeth. "George MacDonald." *Horn Book* 14 (Jan. 1938): 23–29.

Zanger, Jules. "Goblins, Morlocks and Weasels: Classic Fantasy and the Industrial Revolution." *Children's Literature in Education* 27, no. 4 (1977): 154–162.

McGinley, Phyllis (Louise)

Helbig, Alethea K., and Perkins, Agnes Regan. *Dictionary of American Children's Fiction, 1859–1959*. Westport, CT: Greenwood Press, 1985, pp. 324, 407.

The Junior Book of Authors. 2nd ed. rev. Edited by Stanley J. Kunitz and Howard Haycraft. New York: Wilson, 1951, pp. 205–206.

Stone, Helen. "*The Princess* Goes to Press." *Horn Book* 22 (Jan. 1946): 31–34.

Twentieth Century Children's Writers. 2nd ed. Edited by D. L. Kirkpatrick. New York: St. Martin's Press, 1983, pp. 528–530.

Wagner, Linda W. *Phyllis McGinley*. New York: Twayne, 1971.

McGraw, Eloise Jarvis

Hanff, Peter E., and Greene, Douglas G. *Bibliographia Oziana*. Demorest, GA: International Wizard of Oz Club, 1976.

Helbig, Alethea K., and Perkins, Agnes Regan. *Dictionary of American Children's Fiction, 1859–1959*. Westport, CT: Greenwood Press, 1985, p. 334.

——. *Dictionary of American Children's Fiction, 1960–1984.* Westport, CT: Greenwood Press, 1986, p. 411.

More Junior Authors. Edited by Muriel Fuller. New York: Wilson, 1963, pp. 147–148.

Roginski, Jim, ed. *Newbery and Caldecott Medalists and Honor Book Winners.* Littleton, CO: Libraries Unlimited, 1982, pp. 185–186.

Twentieth Century Children's Writers. 2nd ed. Edited by D. L. Kirkpatrick. New York: St. Martin's Press, 1983, pp. 530–531.

McHargue, Georgess

Fifth Book of Junior Authors and Illustrators. Edited by Sally Holmes Holtze. New York: Wilson, 1983, pp. 209–211.

Kuznets, Lois R. "Games of Dark: Psychofantasy in Children's Literature." *The Lion and the Unicorn* 1, no. 2 (Fall 1977): 17–24.

Yolen, Jane. "The Literary Underwater World." *Language Arts* 57 (1980): 403–412.

McKillip, Patricia A(nne)

Attebery, Brian. "Women's Coming of Age in Fantasy." *Extrapolation* 28 (Spring 1987): 10–22.

Fifth Book of Junior Authors and Illustrators. Edited by Sally Holmes Holtze. New York: Wilson, 1983, pp. 211–212.

Haunert, Rita M. "Mythic Female Heroes in the High Fantasy Novels of Patricia McKillip." Ph.D. dissertation, Bowling Green State University, 1983.

Nicholls, Peter. "The Star-Bearer Trilogy." In *Survey of Modern Fantasy Literature,* vol. 4. Edited by Frank N. Magill. Englewood Cliffs, NJ: Salem Press, 1983, pp. 1813–1820.

Searles, Baird; Meacham, Beth; and Franklin, Michael. *A Reader's Guide to Fantasy.* New York: Avon, 1982, pp. 104–106.

Sparks, Elisa Kay. "*The Forgotten Beasts of Eld.*" In *Survey of Modern Fantasy Literature,* vol. 2. Edited by Frank N. Magill. Englewood Cliffs, NJ: Salem Press, 1983, pp. 566–570.

Wymer, Thomas L. "Patricia McKillip." In *Supernatural Fiction Writers: Fantasy and Horror,* vol. 2. Edited by E. F. Bleiler. New York: Scribner, 1985, pp. 1067–1072.

McKinley, (Jennifer Carolyn) Robin (Turrell)

Arnold, Mark Alan, and Windling, Terri. "Robin McKinley." *Horn Book* 61 (July–Aug. 1985): 406–409.

Fifth Book of Junior Authors and Illustrators. Edited by Sally Holmes Holtze. New York: Wilson, 1983, pp. 212–213.

Helbig, Alethea K., and Perkins, Agnes Regan. *Dictionary of American Children's Fiction, 1960–1984.* Westport, CT: Greenwood Press, 1986, pp. 42–43, 61–62, 412.

"*The Hero and the Crown.*" In *Newbery and Caldecott Medal Books 1976–1985.* Boston: Horn Book, 1986, pp. 136–152.

Karrenbrock, Marilyn H. "Robin McKinley." In *American Writers for Children since 1960: Fiction. Dictionary of Literary Biography,* vol. 52. Detroit: Gale, 1986, pp. 262–266.

McKinley, Robin. "1985 Newbery Acceptance Speech." *Top of the News* 41 (Summer 1985): 387–394; *Horn Book* 61 (July–Aug. 1985): 395–405.

Meek, Margaret. "Happily Ever After." *Times Literary Supplement* (London), November 25, 1983, p. 1212.

Moslander, Charlotte. "An Interview with Robin McKinley." *VOYA* 8 (Feb. 1986): 368–369.

Searles, Baird; Meacham, Beth; and Franklin, Michael. *A Reader's Guide to Fantasy.* New York: Avon, 1982, pp. 106–107.

MacLachlan, Patricia

Babbitt, Natalie. "Patricia MacLachlan: The Biography." *Horn Book* 62 (July–Aug. 1986): 414–416.

Courtney, A. "Profile: Patricia MacLachlan." *Language Arts* 62 (Nov. 1985): 783–787. Interview.

Helbig, Alethea K., and Perkins, Agnes Regan. *Dictionary of American Children's Fiction, 1960–1984.* Westport, CT: Greenwood Press, 1986, p. 393.

MacLachlan, Patricia. "1986 Newbery Award Acceptance Speech." *Horn Book* 62 (July–Aug. 1986): 407–413; *Top of the News* 42 (Summer 1986): 391–395.

MacLachlan, Robert. "A Hypothetical Dilemma." *Horn Book* 62 (July–Aug. 1986): 416–419.

Rounds, L. "Cheyenne Native Patricia MacLachlan: 1986 Newbery Winner." *Wyoming Library Roundup* 4 (Spring 1986): 22–24.

McNeill (Alexander), Janet

Fourth Book of Junior Authors and Illustrators. Edited by Doris De Montreville and Elizabeth D. Crawford. New York: Wilson, 1978, pp. 245–247.

McNeill, Janet. "Enter Fairies through a Hole in the Hedge." *Junior Bookshelf* 31 (Fall 1967): 23–27.

———. "When the Magic Has to Stop." *Horn Book* 48 (Aug. 1972): 337–342.

Moss, Elaine. " 'Go On! Go On!': Janet McNeill and *The Battle of St. George Without.*" *Signal* 6 (Sept. 1971): 96–101.

Twentieth Century Children's Writers. 2nd ed. Edited by D. L. Kirkpatrick. New York: St. Martin's Press, 1983, pp. 534–535.

Maeterlinck, Maurice

The Oxford Companion to Children's Literature. Edited by Humphrey Carpenter and Mari Prichard. New York: Oxford Univ. Press, 1984, pp. 67–68.

Maguire, Gregory

Harrison, Barbara, and Maguire, Gregory, eds. *Innocence & Experience: Essays and Conversations on Children's Literature.* New York: Lothrop, 1987.

Maguire, Gregory. "Rememory." *Horn Book* 57 (Dec. 1981): 629–631. Reprinted in *Innocence & Experience.* New York: Lothrop, 1987. Based on an introductory talk given at the Simmons College Center for the Study of Children's Literature, March 14, 1981.

Mahy, Margaret (May)

Fourth Book of Junior Authors and Illustrators. Edited by Doris De Montreville and Elizabeth D. Crawford. New York: Wilson, 1978, pp. 248–250.

Hearne, Betsy. "*The Changeover.*" *Booklist* 82 (Nov. 1, 1985): 410–412. Speech given at the 1985 Children's Books Open Forum, 1985 ALA Conference.

Hoffman, M. "The Fabulous in the Ordinary: An Interview with Margaret Mahy." *School Librarian* 34 (Sept. 1986): 212–216.

Mahy, Margaret. "Joining the Network." *Signal* 54 (Sept. 1987): 151–160.

The Oxford Companion to Children's Literature. Edited by Humphrey Carpenter and Mari Prichard. New York: Oxford Univ. Press, 1984, p. 334.

Paul, Lissa. "Enigma Variations: What Feminist Theory Knows about Children's Literature." *Signal* 54 (Sept. 1987): 186–202. Discusses *The Changeover*.

Twentieth Century Children's Writers. 2nd ed. Edited by D. L. Kirkpatrick. New York: St. Martin's Press, 1983, pp. 504–506.

Malory, Sir Thomas

Kinney, Thomas L. "Arthurian Romances." In *Supernatural Fiction Writers: Fantasy and Horror,* vol. 1. Edited by E. F. Bleiler. New York: Scribner, 1985, pp. 11–18.

Paxon, Diana. "The Holy Grail." *Mythlore* 3, no. 9 (1976).

Manning, Rosemary (Joy)

Manning, Rosemary. "Our Dreams Are Tales." *Horn Book* 41 (Feb. 1965): 25–26.

Moss, Elaine. "Rosemary Manning's *Arripay: Variation on a Theme.*" *Signal* 2 (May 1970): 31–35.

Twentieth Century Children's Writers. 2nd ed. Edited by D. L. Kirkpatrick. New York: St. Martin's Press, 1983, pp. 507–508.

Mark, Jan (pseud. of Janet Marjorie Brisland)

Fifth Book of Junior Authors and Illustrators. Edited by Sally Holmes Holtze. New York: Wilson, 1983, pp. 201–203.

Hunt, Peter. "Whatever Happened to Jan Mark?" *Signal* 31 (Jan. 1980): 11–19.

March-Penny, Robbie. "I Don't Want to Learn Things, I'd Just Rather Find Out." *Children's Literature in Education* 10 (Spring 1979): 18–24.

Mark, Jan. "Journeys." *Horn Book* 63 (Mar.–Apr. 1987): 171–180.

———. "The Short Story." *Horn Book* 64 (Jan.–Feb. 1988): 42–47.

———. "The Story of the Golem." In *Innocence & Experience*. Edited by Barbara Harrison and Gregory Maguire. New York: Lothrop, 1987, pp. 184–187.

Rees, David. "No Such Thing as Fairness—Jan Mark." In *Painted Desert, Green Shade*. Boston: Horn Book, 1984, pp. 62–74. Revised from *School Librarian*, Sept. 1981.

Twentieth Century Children's Writers. 2nd ed. Edited by D. L. Kirkpatrick. New York: St. Martin's Press, 1983, pp. 511–512.

Whitehead, Winifred. "Jan Mark." *Use of English* 33 (Spring 1982): 32–39.

Marshall, James (Edward)

Fourth Book of Junior Authors and Illustrators. Edited by Doris De Montreville and Elizabeth D. Crawford. New York: Wilson, 1978, pp. 253–254.

Twentieth Century Children's Writers. 2nd ed. Edited by D. L. Kirkpatrick. New York: St. Martin's Press, 1983, pp. 513–514.

Martin, Bill (William Ivan), Jr.

Larrick, Nancy. "Profile: Bill Martin, Jr." *Language Arts,* May 1982, pp. 490–494.

Masefield, John (Edward)

Babington Smith, Constance. *John Masefield: A Life*. London: Hamish Hamilton, 1985. Original publisher Oxford Univ. Press, 1978.

Doyle, Brian. *The Who's Who of Children's Literature*. New York: Schocken, 1968, pp. 193–194.

Fisher, Marjorie. *John Masefield*. London: Bodley Head, 1963.

Hollindale, Peter. "John Masefield." *Children's Literature in Education* 23 (Winter 1976): 187–195.

L'Engle, Madeleine. "Afterword." In John Masefield. *The Midnight Folk*. New York: Dell, 1985.

Lochhead, Marion. *Renaissance of Wonder*. New York: Harper and Row, 1980.

Masefield, John. *In the Mill*. London: Heinemann, 1941.

———. *New Chum*. London: Heinemann, 1944.

———. *So Long to Learn*. New York: Macmillan, 1952.

The Oxford Companion to Children's Literature. Edited by Humphrey Carpenter and Mari Prichard. New York: Oxford Univ. Press, 1984, pp. 77–78, 342–343, 349.

Spark, Muriel. *John Masefield*. London: Nevill, 1953.

Spernlicht, Sanford. *John Masefield*. Boston: Twayne, 1977.

Strong, L. A. G. *John Masefield*. London: Longman, 1952.

Taylor, J. "John Masefield." *Ontario Library Review* 46 (Feb. 1962): 16–19.

Twentieth Century Children's Writers. 2nd ed. Edited by D. L. Kirkpatrick. New York: St. Martin's Press, 1983, pp. 518–521.

Mason, Arthur

Mason, Arthur. "*The Wee Men*." *Horn Book* 6 (Nov. 1930): 337–339.

Mason, Miriam E(vangeline)

Burns, P. C., and Hines, R. "Miriam E. Mason: Storytelling Sister." *Elementary English* 43 (Jan. 1966): 5–9 ff.

Matheson, Richard (Burton)

Blaine, Michael. "A Richard Matheson Update." *Twilight Zone,* June 1986, pp. 22–23, 94.

———. "Richard Matheson's 'Layer-Cake' Career." *Twilight Zone,* June 1986, pp. 24–25, 94.

Lofficier, Randy, and Lofficier, Jean-Marc. "Twilight Zone Interview: Richard Matheson." *Twilight Zone,* Sept.–Oct. 1983, pp. 40–41.

Neilson, Keith. "Richard Matheson." In *Supernatural Fiction Writers: Fantasy and Horror*, vol. 2. Edited by E. F. Bleiler. New York: Scribner, 1985, pp. 1073–1080.

Nicholls, Peter. "Richard Matheson." In *Science Fiction Writers*. Edited by E. F. Bleiler. New York: Scribner, 1982, pp. 425–432.

Rathbun, Mark, and Flanagan, Graeme. *Richard Matheson: He Is Legend: An Illustrated Bio-Biography*. Chico, CA: Rathbun, 1984.

Searles, Baird; Meacham, Beth; and Franklin, Michael. *A Reader's Guide to Fantasy*. New York: Avon, 1982, p. 107.

Sharp, Roberta. "The Short Fiction of Matheson." In *Survey of Modern Fantasy Literature*, vol. 4. Edited by Frank N. Magill. Englewood Cliffs, NJ: Salem Press, 1983, pp. 1645–1651.

Watson, Christine. *"Bid Time Return."* In *Survey of Modern Fantasy Literature,* vol. 1. Edited by Frank N. Magill. Englewood Cliffs, NJ: Salem Press, 1983, pp. 90–94.

Maxwell, William

Helbig, Alethea K., and Perkins, Agnes Regan. *Dictionary of American Children's Fiction, 1859–1959.* Westport, CT: Greenwood Press, 1985, pp. 209–210, 333.

Mayer, Marianna

Fourth Book of Junior Authors and Illustrators. Edited by Doris De Montreville and Elizabeth D. Crawford. New York: Wilson, 1978, pp. 257–259.

Mayhar, Ardath

Mayhar, Ardath. "Let Us Have Stories in Verse Again!" *Fantasy Review* 76 (1985): 7–41.
Twentieth-Century Science Fiction Writers. 2nd ed. Edited by Curtis C. Smith. Chicago: St. James Press, 1986, pp. 489–490.

Mayne, William (James Carter) (a.k.a. Martin Cobalt)

Alderson, Brian. "On the Littoral: William Mayne's *The Jersey Shore.*" *Children's Literature Review* 3 (Oct. 1973): 133–135.
Antczak, Janice. *Science Fiction: The Mythos of a New Romance.* New York: Neal-Schuman, 1985.
Blishen, Edward. "Writers for Children: William Mayne." *The Use of English* 20, no. 2 (Winter 1968): 99–103. Reprinted in Dennis Butts. *Good Writers for Young Readers.* St. Albans, England: Hart-Davis, 1977, pp. 79–85.
Doyle, Brian. *The Who's Who of Children's Literature.* New York: Schocken, 1968, pp. 194–195.
"A Grass Rope." In M. Crouch and A. Ellis. *Chosen for Children.* 3rd ed. London: The Library Association, 1977, pp. 91–95.
Heins, Paul. "Off the Beaten Path." *Horn Book* 49 (Dec. 1973): 580–581.
Hunt, Peter. "The Mayne Game: An Experiment in Response." *Signal* 28 (Jan. 1979): 9–25.
Inglis, Fred. *The Promise of Happiness.* New York: Cambridge Univ. Press, 1981, pp. 12–15, 228–231, 253–257.
Kuznets, Lois R. "Games of Dark: Psychofantasy in Children's Literature." *The Lion and the Unicorn* 1, no. 2 (Fall 1977): 17–24.
Mayne, William. "A Discussion with William Mayne." *Children's Literature in Education* 2 (July 1970): 48–55.
Moon, Kenneth. "Don't Tell It, Show It: The Force of Metaphor in *A Game of Dark.*" *School Librarian* 31 (Dec. 1983): 319–327.
The Oxford Companion to Children's Literature. Edited by Humphrey Carpenter and Mari Prichard. New York: Oxford Univ. Press, 1984, pp. 345–347.
Pflieger, Pat, and Hill, Helen M. *A Reference Guide to Modern Fantasy for Children.* Westport, CT: Greenwood Press, 1984, pp. xiv, 163–165, 358–360.
Searles, Baird; Meacham, Beth; and Franklin, Michael. *A Reader's Guide to Fantasy.* New York: Avon, 1982, pp. 107–108.
Stott, Jon C. *Children's Literature from A to Z.* New York: McGraw-Hill, 1984, p. 183.
Swinfen, Ann. *In Defense of Fantasy.* London: Routledge, 1984, pp. 63–67. Discusses *A Game of Dark.*

Third Book of Junior Authors. Edited by Doris De Montreville and Donna Hill. New York: Wilson, 1972, pp. 189–190.

Thompson, Hillary. "Doorways to Fantasy." *Canadian Children's Literature* 21 (1981): 8–16.

Townsend, John Rowe. "William Mayne." In *A Sense of Story.* Philadelphia: Lippincott, 1971, pp. 130–142.

———. "William Mayne." In *A Sounding of Storytellers.* Philadelphia: Lippincott, 1979, pp. 139–152.

Twentieth Century Children's Writers. 2nd ed. Edited by D. L. Kirkpatrick. New York: St. Martin's Press, 1983, pp. 523–525.

Walker, Alastair. "Landscape as Metaphor in the Novels of William Mayne." *Children's Literature in Education* 36 (Spring 1980): 31–42.

Whitaker, Muriel A. " 'The Hollow Hills': A Celtic Motif in Modern Fantasy." *Mosaic* 13 (Spring/Summer 1980): 165–178.

———. "Swords at Sunset and Bag-Puddings: Arthur in Modern Fiction." *Children's Literature in Education* 27, no. 8 (Winter 1977): 143–153.

Mazer, Norma Fox

Fifth Book of Junior Authors and Illustrators. Edited by Sally Holmes Holtze. New York: Wilson, 1983, pp. 204–206.

Helbig, Alethea K., and Perkins, Agnes Regan. *Dictionary of American Children's Fiction, 1960–1984.* Westport, CT: Greenwood Press, 1986, pp. 409, 574–575.

Mazer, Norma Fox. "Growing Up with Stories." *Top of the News* 41 (Winter 1985): 157–168.

Meigs, Cornelia (Lynde)

"Cornelia Meigs Accepts Newbery Award." *Horn Book* 10 (July 1934): 217– 220.

Helbig, Alethea K., and Perkins, Agnes Regan. *Dictionary of American Children's Fiction, 1859–1959.* Westport, CT: Greenwood Press, 1985, pp. 339–340.

The Junior Book of Authors. 2nd ed. rev. Edited by Stanley J. Kunitz and Howard Haycraft. New York: Wilson, 1951, pp. 217–219.

Meigs, Cornelia. "Following the Sea." *Horn Book* 3 (Feb. 1927): 30–38.

———. "How *The Wonderful Locomotive* Happened." *Horn Book* 4 (Aug. 1928): 32–33.

———. "Writing for Children Today." *Horn Book* 25 (Sept. 1949): 370–374.

Murdoch, Clarissa. "Cornelia Meigs: Chronicler of the Sea." *Elementary English Review* 5 (May 1928): 148–149, 153.

Patee, Doris. "Cornelia Meigs." *Horn Book* 20 (Sept.–Oct. 1944): 356–362.

Sauer, Julia L. "The Books of Cornelia Meigs." *Horn Book* 20 (Sept.–Oct. 1944): 347–355.

Twentieth Century Children's Writers. 2nd ed. Edited by D. L. Kirkpatrick. New York: St. Martin's Press, 1983, pp. 538–539.

Viguers, Susan T. "Cornelia Meigs." In *Writers for Children: Critical Studies of Major Authors since the Seventeenth Century.* Edited by Jane M. Bingham. New York: Scribner, 1988, pp. 389–392.

Whitney, Elinor. "The Stories of Cornelia Meigs." *Horn Book* 3 (Feb. 1927): 39–40.

Mendoza, George

Third Book of Junior Authors. Edited by Doris De Montreville and Donna Hill. New York: Wilson, 1972, pp. 192–193.

Merrill, Jean (Fairbanks)

Helbig, Alethea K., and Perkins, Agnes Regan. *Dictionary of American Children's Fiction, 1960–1984.* Westport, CT: Greenwood Press, 1986, pp. 418, 529, 636.
Third Book of Junior Authors. Edited by Doris De Montreville and Donna Hill. New York: Wilson, 1972, pp. 195–196.
Twentieth Century Children's Writers. 2nd ed. Edited by D. L. Kirkpatrick. New York: St. Martin's Press, 1983, pp. 541–543.

Merritt, A(braham P.)

Bleiler, E. F. "A. Merritt." In *Supernatural Fiction Writers: Fantasy and Horror,* vol. 2. Edited by E. F. Bleiler. New York: Scribner, 1985, pp. 835–844.
De Camp, L. Sprague, ed. *The Blade of Conan.* New York: Ace, 1979.
Foust, R. E. "Monstrous Image: Theory of Fantasy Antagonists." *Genre* 13 (1981): 441–453.
Moskowitz, Sam. *A. Merritt: Reflections in the Moon Pool.* Philadelphia: Train, 1985.
Twentieth-Century Science Fiction Writers. 2nd ed. Edited by Curtis C. Smith. Chicago: St. James Press, 1986, pp. 508–509.
Yoke, Carl B. "The Ship of Ishtar." In *Survey of Modern Fantasy Literature,* vol. 3. Edited by Frank N. Magill. Englewood Cliffs, NJ: Salem Press, 1983, pp. 1407–1411.

Middleton-Murray, John, Jr. *see* Cowper, Richard

Milne, A(lan) A(lexander)

Canham, Stephen. "Reassuring Readers: *Winnie-the-Pooh.*" *Children's Literature Association Quarterly* 5 (Fall 1980): 1, 25–27.
Carpenter, Humphrey. "A. A. Milne and *Winnie-the-Pooh:* Farewell to the Enchanted Places." In *Secret Gardens: The Golden Age of Children's Literature.* Boston: Houghton Mifflin, 1985, pp. 188–209.
Cock, Geoffrey. "A. A. Milne: Sources of His Creativity." *American Imago* 34 (1977): 313–326.
Crews, Frederick C. *The Pooh Perplex: A Freshman Casebook.* New York: Dutton, 1963.
Crouch, Marcus. "Pooh Lives—O.K.?" *Junior Bookshelf* 40 (Oct. 1976): 252–255. Reprinted in *Bookbird* 15, no. 2 (1977): 14–16.
Doyle, Brian. *The Who's Who of Children's Literature.* New York: Schocken, 1968, pp. 199–201.
Farjeon, Eleanor. "A. A. Milne." *Junior Bookshelf* 20 (Mar. 1956): 51–59.
Goldthwaite, John. "The Black Rabbit: Part One." *Signal* 47 (May 1985): 86–111; "The Black Rabbit: Part Two." *Signal* 48 (Sept. 1985): 148–167. Reprinted in Goldthwaite. *The Natural History of Make-Believe.* London: Oxford Univ. Press, 1987.
Graham, Eleanor. "A. A. Milne." *Junior Bookshelf* 20 (Mar. 1956): 51–59.
Gunderson, Ethel, and Gunderson, Agnes G. "A. A. Milne and Today's 7-Year-Olds." *Elementary English* 39 (May 1962): 408–411.
Haring-Smith, Tori. *A. A. Milne: A Critical Biography.* New York: Garland, 1982.
Holmstrum, John. "Whisper Who Dares." *New Statesman* 12 (Nov. 1965): 752.
Hunt, Peter. "A. A. Milne." In *Writers for Children: Critical Studies of Major Authors since the Seventeenth Century.* Edited by Jane M. Bingham. New York: Scribner, 1988, pp. 397–406.
The Junior Book of Authors. 2nd ed. rev. Edited by Stanley J. Kunitz and Howard Haycraft. New York: Wilson, 1951, pp. 221–223.

Low, Anthony. "Religious Myth in *Winnie-the-Pooh*." *Greyfriar* 22 (1981): 13–16.

Luenn, Nancy. "A Visit to Toad Hall and Pooh Forest." *Horn Book* 62 (July–Aug. 1986): 507–508.

Lurie, Alison. "Back to Pooh Corner." In *Children's Literature,* vol. 2. Storrs, CT: Journal of the Modern Language Association, 1973, pp. 11–17. Reprinted in *Reflections on Literature for Children.* Edited by Francelia Butler and Richard Rotert. Hamden, CT: Shoe String Press, 1984, pp. 32–38.

———. "Now We Are Fifty." *New York Times Book Review,* Nov. 14, 1967, p. 27.

Milne, A. A. *Autobiography.* New York: Dutton, 1939. Original British title: *It's Too Late Now: The Autobiography of a Writer.*

———. "Children's Books." *Spectator,* December 4, 1926, p. 1011.

———. *When I Was Very Young.* New York: Fountain Press, 1930.

Milne, Christopher. *The Enchanted Places.* New York: Dutton, 1974.

———. *The Path through the Trees.* New York: Dutton, 1979.

Moss, Elaine. "A. A. Milne on 'Books for Children.' " *Signal* 44 (May 1984): 89–92.

Naumann, N. "*Winnie-the-Pooh* Week and a Half." *Teacher* 93 (Apr. 1976): 42–44.

Nesmith, Mary Ethel. "The Children's Milne." *Elementary English Review* 9 (Sept. 1932): 172–173, 192.

Norton, E. "An 'Expotition' to Christopher Robin's Home." *Top of the News* 29 (Jan. 1973): 146–150.

Novak, Barbara. "Milne's Poems: Form and Content." *Elementary English* 34 (Oct. 1957): 355–361.

O'Neill, C. "The Professor Who Lives in Toad Hall." *Chronicle of Higher Education* 17 (Sept. 18, 1978): R6–7.

The Oxford Companion to Children's Literature. Edited by Humphrey Carpenter and Mari Prichard. New York: Oxford Univ. Press, 1984, pp. 261, 350–353, 575–576.

Payne, John R. "Four Children's Books by A. A. Milne." *Studies in Bibliography* 23 (1970): 127–139.

Phifer, Kenneth W. "A Bear of Very Little Brain: A Commentary on the *Pooh* Saga." *Religious Humanism* 13 (Winter 1979): 32–38.

Sale, Roger. "Child Reading and Man Reading: Oz, Babar, and Pooh." In *Children's Literature,* vol. 1. Storrs, CT: Journal of the Modern Language Association, 1972, pp. 162–172. Reprinted in *Reflections on Literature for Children.* Edited by Francelia Butler and Richard Rotert. Hamden, CT: Shoe String Press, 1984, pp. 19–31.

———. *Fairy Tales and After.* Cambridge, MA: Harvard Univ. Press, 1978, pp. 15–18.

Shepard, E. H. *The Pooh Sketchbook.* Edited by Brian Sibley. New York: Dutton, 1984.

Siddens, L. "*Winnie-the-Pooh* Goes to School." *Instructor* 84 (Mar. 1975): 70–71.

Singer, Dorothy G . "Piglet, Pooh and Piaget." *Psychology Today* 6 (June 1972): 70–74, 96.

Smaridge, Norah. *Famous Modern Storytellers for Young People.* New York: Dodd, 1969, pp. 26–31.

Stanger, Carol A. "*Winnie the Pooh* through a Feminist Lens." *The Lion and the Unicorn* 11 (Oct. 1987): 34–50.

Sterck, Kenneth. "The Real Christopher Robin: An Appreciation of A. A. Milne's Children's Verse." *Children's Literature in Education* 37 (Summer 1980): 52–61.

Stott, Jon C. *Children's Literature from A to Z.* New York: McGraw-Hill, 1984, p. 192.

Swann, Thomas Burnett. *A. A. Milne.* Boston: Twayne, 1971.

Tremper, Ellen. " 'Instigorating' Winnie-the-Pooh." *The Lion and the Unicorn* 1, no. 1 (Spring 1977): 33–46.

Twentieth Century Children's Writers. 2nd ed. Edited by D. L. Kirkpatrick. New York: St. Martin's Press, 1983, pp. 546–549.

Von Schweinitz, Eleanor. *"Pooh* without Milne." *Children's Book News* 2 (Jan.–Feb. 1967): 5–8.
Wilson, Anita. "Milne's *Pooh* Books: The Benevolent Forest." In *Touchstones.* Edited by Perry Nodelman. West Lafayette, IN: Children's Literature Association Publications, 1985, pp. 163–172.
Woods, George A. "Winnie Was Not Pooh-Poohed." *New York Times Book Review,* June 1968, pp. 7, 28.

Mirrlees, Hope

Chapman, Edgar L. *"Lud-in-the-Mist."* In *Survey of Modern Fantasy Literature,* vol. 2. Edited by Frank N. Magill. Englewood Cliffs, NJ: Salem Press, 1983, pp. 926–931.
Gentle, Mary. "Godmakers and Worldshapers: Fantasy and Metaphysics." *Vector* 106 (1982): 8–14.
Waggoner, Diana. "Hope Mirrlees." In *Supernatural Fiction Writers: Fantasy and Horror,* vol. 2. Edited by E. F. Bleiler. New York: Scribner, 1985, pp. 603–608.

Moeri, Louise

Fifth Book of Junior Authors and Illustrators. Edited by Sally Holmes Holtze. New York: Wilson, 1983, pp. 220–221.

Molesworth, Mary Louisa (Stewart)

Baker, Margaret J. "Mary Louisa Molesworth." *Junior Bookshelf* 12 (Mar. 1948): 19–26.
Doyle, Brian. *The Who's Who of Children's Literature.* New York: Schocken, 1968, pp. 203–204.
Fox, Paula. "A Second Look: *The Cuckoo Clock." Horn Book* 63 (Sept.–Oct. 1987): 592–593.
Green, Roger Lancelyn. *Mrs. Molesworth.* London: Bodley Head, 1961.
———. "Mrs. Molesworth." *Junior Bookshelf* 21 (July 1957): 101–108.
Keenan, Hugh T. "Mary Louisa Stewart Molesworth." In *Writers for Children: Critical Studies of Major Authors since the Seventeenth Century.* Edited by Jane M. Bingham. New York: Scribner, 1988, pp. 407–414.
Laski, Marghanita. *Mrs. Ewing, Mrs. Molesworth, and Mrs. Hodgson Burnett.* New York: Oxford Univ. Press, 1951.
McGillis, Roderick. "Fantasy As Adventure: Nineteenth Century Children's Fiction." *Children's Literature Association Quarterly* 8 (Fall 1983): 18–22.
Molesworth, Mrs. "On the Art of Writing Fiction for Children." *Atalanta* (London) 6 (May 1893): 583–586.
———. "Story-Reading and Story-Writing." *Chambers' Journal* (London), Nov. 5, 1898, pp. 772–775.
The Oxford Companion to Children's Literature. Edited by Humphrey Carpenter and Mari Prichard. New York: Oxford Univ. Press, 1984, pp. 137, 355, 516.
Pflieger, Pat, and Hill, Helen M. *A Reference Guide to Modern Fantasy for Children.* Westport, CT: Greenwood Press, 1984, pp. xvi, 131–132, 374–377, 520–521.
Rosenthal, Lynne M. "Writing Her Own Story: The Integration of the Self in the Fourth Dimension of Mrs. Molesworth's *The Cuckoo Clock." Children's Literature Association Quarterly* 10 (Winter 1986): 187–192.
Sircar, Sanjay Kumar. "Victorian Children's Fantasy: A Critical Study of Two Works of Fantasy of Mrs. Molesworth." M.A. dissertation, Australian National University, 1980.

Twentieth Century Children's Writers. 2nd ed. Edited by D. L. Kirkpatrick. New York: St. Martin's Press, 1983, pp. 881–882.

Monaco, Richard

Lawler, Donald L. "The *She* Series." In *Survey of Modern Fantasy Literature,* vol. 3. Edited by Frank N. Magill. Englewood Cliffs, NJ: Salem Press, 1983, pp. 1396–1401.
Smith, Curtis C. "H. Rider Haggard." In *Supernatural Fiction Writers: Fantasy and Horror,* vol. 1. Edited by E. F. Bleiler. New York: Scribner, 1985, pp. 321–328.
Twentieth-Century Science Fiction Writers. 2nd ed. Edited by Curtis C. Smith. Chicago: St. James Press, 1986, pp. 308–310. About H. Rider Haggard.

Moon, Sheila (Elizabeth)

Helbig, Alethea K., and Perkins, Agnes Regan. *Dictionary of American Children's Fiction, 1960-1984.* Westport, CT: Greenwood Press, 1986, pp. 430–431.

Moorcock, Michael (John)

Allen, Paul C. "Of Swords and Sorcery: 5." *Fantasy Crossroads* 13 (1978): 31–40.
"Behold the Man Himself." *Quartz* (Mar. 1982): 8–11. Interview.
Bilyeu, Richard. *The Tanlorn Archives: A Primary and Secondary Bibliography of the Works of Michael Moorcock, 1949–1979.* San Bernardino, CA: Borgo Press, 1982.
Butler, Ted. "*Algol* Interviews Michael Moorcock." *Algol* 15 (Winter 1978): 29–32.
Callow, A. J. *The Chronicles of Moorcock.* UK: [privately printed], 1978. (bibliography)
Clute, John. "The Eternal Champion Series." In *Survey of Modern Fantasy Literature,* vol. 1. Edited by Frank N. Magill. Englewood Cliffs, NJ: Salem Press, 1983, pp. 489–496.
Darlington, Andrew. "The Evolution of Michael Moorcock." *Dark Horizons* 22 (1981): 4–10.
Dean, John. " 'A Curious Note in the Wind': The New Literary Genre of Heroic Fantasy." *New Mexico Humanities Review* 2 (Summer, 1979): 34–41.
"*The Eildon Tree* Interviews Michael Moorcock." *The Eildon Tree* 1, no. 2 (1976): 4–8.
Glover, David. "Utopia and Fantasy in the Late 1960s: Burroughs, Moorcock, Tolkien." In *Popular Fiction and Social Change.* Edited by Christopher Pawling. New York: St. Martin's Press, 1984.
Harper, Andrew, and McAulay, George. *Michael Moorcock: A Bibliography.* Baltimore: T-K Graphics, 1976.
Lupoff, Richard. "*Rigel* Interviews Michael Moorcock." *Rigel Science Fiction* (Spring 1983): 21–25.
McFerran, Dave. "The Celtic Incarnation." *Dark Horizons* 29 (1985): 33–37.
Moorcock, Michael. "Aspects of Fantasy." In *Exploring Fantasy Worlds.* Edited by Darrell Schweitzer. San Bernardino, CA: Borgo Press, 1985.
———. "The Heroes in Heroic Fantasy." *Dragonfields* 3 (1980): 50–61.
———. "*New Worlds:* A Personal History." *Foundation* 15 (1979): 5–18.
———. "Wit and Humor in Fantasy." In *Fantasists on Fantasy.* Edited by Robert H. Boyer and Kenneth J. Zahorski. New York: Avon, 1984, pp. 265–276. Originally published in *Foundation* 16 (1979): 16–22.
———. *Wizardry and Wild Romance.* London: Gollancz, 1987.
Nicholls, Peter. "Michael Moorcock." In *Supernatural Fiction Writers: Fantasy and Horror,* volume 2. Edited by E. F. Bleiler. New York: Scribner, 1985, pp. 1081–1090.

Platt, Charles. *Dream Makers: The Uncommon People Who Write Science Fiction.* New York: Ungar, 1987, pp. 97–104. Interview.
Powers, Richard. "Introduction." In *The Sword Trilogy* by Michael Moorcock. Boston: Gregg, 1980.
Twentieth-Century Science Fiction Writers. 2nd ed. Edited by Curtis C. Smith. Chicago: St. James Press, 1986, pp. 519–524.
Walker, Paul. "Michael Moorcock: An Interview." *Luna Monthly* 59 (1975): 5–9.
————. *Speaking of Science Fiction: The Paul Walker Interviews.* Oradell, NJ: Luna Publications, 1978, pp. 213–228.

Moore, Anne Carroll

Helbig, Alethea K., and Perkins, Agnes Regan. *Dictionary of American Children's Fiction, 1859–1959.* Westport, CT: Greenwood Press, 1985, pp. 354–355, 373.
Hogarth, Grace. "A Publisher's Perspective." *Horn Book* 58 (May–June 1987): 372–377.
The Junior Book of Authors. 2nd ed. rev. Edited by Stanley J. Kunitz and Howard Haycraft. New York: Wilson, 1951, pp. 225–226.
Twentieth Century Children's Writers. 2nd Ed. Edited by D. L. Kirkpatrick. New York: St. Martin's Press, 1983, pp. 562–563.

Morgan, Alison (Mary Raikes)

Twentieth Century Children's Writers. 2nd ed. Edited by D. L. Kirkpatrick. New York: St. Martin's Press, 1983, pp. 562–563.

Morgan, Helen (Gertrude Louise Axford)

Twentieth Century Children's Writers. 2nd ed. Edited by D. L. Kirkpatrick. New York: St. Martin's Press, 1983, p. 563.

Morris, Kenneth

Bisenieks, Dainis. "Finder of the Welsh Gods." *Mythlore* 3, no. 11 (1976).
Sullivan, Charles Williams, III. "*The Fates of the Princes of Dyfed* and *Book of the Three Dragons*." In *Survey of Modern Fantasy Literature,* vol. 2. Edited by Frank N. Magill. Englewood Cliffs, NJ: Salem Press, 1983, pp. 539–542.
————. "The Influence of Celtic Myth and Legend on Modern Imaginative Fiction." Ph.D. dissertation, University of Oregon, 1976.
Zahorski, Kenneth J., and Boyer, Robert H. *Lloyd Alexander, Evangeline Walton Ensley, Kenneth Morris: A Primary and Secondary Bibliography.* Boston: G. K. Hall, 1981.

Morris, William

Allen, Elizabeth Estelle. "The Prose Romances of William Morris." Ph.D. dissertation, Tulane University, 1975.
Bono, Barbara. "The Prose Fictions of William Morris: A Study in the Literary Aesthetic of a Victorian Social Reformer." *Victorian Poetry* 13 (1975): 43–59.
Bradley, Ian. *William Morris and His World.* New York: Scribner, 1978.
Burns, Marjorie Jean. "Victorian Fantasists from Ruskin to Lang: A Study in Ambivalence." Ph.D. dissertation, University of California, Berkeley, 1978.
Carmassi, Guido Remo. "The Expanding Vision: Changes in the Emphasis in William

Morris' Late Prose Romances." Ph.D. dissertation, University of Notre Dame, 1975.

Currie, Robert. "Had Morris Gone Soft in the Head?" *Essays in Criticism* 29 (1979): 341–356.

De Camp, L. Sprague. *Literary Swordsmen and Sorcerers: The Makers of Heroic Fantasy.* Sauk City, WI: Arkham House, 1976.

Denington, Frances Barbara. "The Complete Book: An Investigation of the Development of William Morris' Aesthetic and Literary Practice." Ph.D. dissertation, McMaster University, Hamilton, Ont., Canada, 1976.

Edwards, Bruce L. "Toward a Rhetoric of Fantasy Criticism: C. S. Lewis's Readings of MacDonald and Morris." *Literature and Belief* 3 (Mar. 1983): 63–73.

Hoare, Dorothy. *The Works of Morris and Yeats in Relation to Early Saga Literature.* New York: Cambridge Univ. Press, 1937; Norwood, PA: Norwood Editions, 1975.

Jackson, Rosemary. *Fantasy: The Literature of Subversion.* New York: Methuen, 1980, pp. 42, 44, 110–112, 153–154, 156.

Keller, Donald G. "William Morris: Dreams and the End of Dreams." *The Eildon Tree* 1 (1974): 5–7.

Kirschhoff, Frederick, ed. *Studies in the Late Prose Romances of William Morris.* New York: William Morris Society, 1976.

Landow, George P. "And the World Became Strange: Realms of Literary Fantasy." In Diane L. Johnson. *Fantastic Illustration and Design in Britain, 1850–1930.* Providence: Rhode Island School of Design, 1979, pp. 9–43. Reprinted in *Georgia Review* 33 (Spring 1979): 7–42.

McCormick, Judith Kay. "Biography and the Pattern of Degeneration in the Late Prose Romances of William Morris." Ph.D. dissertation, Kansas State University, 1980.

Manlove, C. N. *The Impulse of Fantasy Literature.* Kent, OH: Kent State Univ. Press, 1983.

Mathews, Richard. "The Well at the World's End." In *Survey of Modern Fantasy Literature,* vol. 5. Edited by Frank N. Magill. Englewood Cliffs, NJ: Salem Press, 1983, pp. 2090–2096.

———. *Worlds Beyond the World: The Fantastic Vision of William Morris.* San Bernardino, CA: Borgo Press, 1978.

Mendelson, Michael. "The Modernization of Prose Romance: The Radical Form of William Morris and George MacDonald." Ph.D. dissertation, Washington State University, 1981.

———. "Opening Moves: The Entry into the Other World." *Extrapolation.* 25 (1984): 171–179.

Munn, Nancy D. "Eros and Community in the Fiction of William Morris." *Nineteenth-Century Fiction* 34 (1979): 302–325.

Pfeiffer, John R. "William Morris." In *Supernatural Fiction Writers: Fantasy and Horror,* vol. 1. Edited by E. F. Bleiler. New York: Scribner, 1985, pp. 299–306.

Ringel, Faye Joyce. "Patterns of the Hero and the Quest: Epic, Romance, Fantasy." Ph.D. Dissertation, Brown University, 1979.

Ruby, Dona Lin. "The Late Prose Romances of William Morris." Ph.D. dissertation, Northern Illinois University, 1979.

Silver, Carole. *The Romance of William Morris.* Athens, OH: Ohio Univ. Press, 1983.

Spatt, Hartley Steven. "William Morris: The Language of History and Myth." Ph.D. dissertation, Johns Hopkins University, 1975.

Stansky, Peter. *William Morris.* New York: Oxford Univ. Press, 1983.

Taylor, Angus. "Pilgrim of Hope: William Morris on the Way to Utopia." *Foundation* 32 (1984): 15–22.

Twentieth-Century Science Fiction Writers. 2nd. ed. Edited by Curtis C. Smith. Chicago: St. James Press, 1986, pp. 863–865.

Valentine, Kristin Bervig. "Motifs from Nature in the Design Work and Prose Romances of William Morris (1876–1896)." *Victorian Poetry* 13 (1975): 83–98.

———. "A Patterned Imagination: William Morris' Use of Pattern in Decorative Design and the Last Prose Romances, 1883–1896." Ph.D. dissertation, University of Utah, 1974.

Wolfshohl, Clarence. "William Morris's *The Wood Beyond the World:* The Victorian World vs. the Mythic Eternities." *Mythlore* 6 (Summer 1979): 29–32.

Mulock, Diana (pseud. of Dinah Maria Mulock Craik)

Doyle, Brian. *The Who's Who of Children's Literature.* New York: Schocken, 1968, pp. 204–205.

McGillis, Roderick. "Fantasy as Adventure: Nineteenth Century Children's Fiction." *Children's Literature Association Quarterly* 8 (Fall 1983): 18–22.

Mitchell, Sally. *Dinah Mulock Craik.* Boston: Twayne, 1983.

Mulock, Dinah Maria. *Studies from Life.* New York: Harper, 1861.

The Oxford Companion to Children's Literature. Edited by Humphrey Carpenter and Mari Prichard. New York: Oxford Univ. Press, 1984, pp. 132, 316.

Reade, Aleyn Lyell. *The Mellards and Their Descendants . . . With Memoirs of Dinah Maria Mulock.* London: Arden Press, 1915.

Showalter, Elaine. "Dinah Mulock Craik and the Tactics of Sentiment: A Case Study in Victorian Female Authorship." *Feminist Studies* 2 (1975): 5–23.

Münchausen, Karl (Friedrich Hieronymus, Baron Von)

The Oxford Companion to Children's Literature. Edited by Humphrey Carpenter and Mari Prichard. New York: Oxford Univ. Press, 1984, p. 368.

Stableford, Brian. "*Baron Münchausen's Narrative of His Marvellous Travels and Campaigns in Russia.*" In *Survey of Modern Fantasy Literature,* vol. 1. Edited by Frank N. Magill. Englewood Cliffs, NJ: Salem Press, 1983, pp. 78–80.

Tall Stories of Baron Münchausen: A Book Accompanying the Exhibition at the Bethnal Green Museum of Childhood. London: Victoria & Albert Museum, 1985.

Mundy, Talbot

Bleiler, E. F. "Talbot Mundy." In *Supernatural Fiction Writers: Fantasy and Horror,* vol. 2. Edited by E. F. Bleiler. New York: Scribner, 1985, pp. 845–852.

Chapman, Edgar L. "Om: The Secret of Ahbor Valley." In *Survey of Modern Fantasy Literature,* vol. 3. Edited by Frank N. Magill. Englewood Cliffs, NJ: Salem Press, 1983, pp. 1142–1145.

De Camp, L. Sprague, ed. *The Blade of Conan.* New York: Ace, 1979.

Ellis, Peter Berresford. *The Last Adventurer: The Life of Talbot Mundy 1879–1940.* West Kingston, RI: Grant, 1984.

Grant, Donald M. *Talbot Mundy: Messenger of Destiny.* West Kingston, RI: Grant, 1983.

Murphy, Shirley Rousseau

Murphy, Shirley Rousseau. "The Reality of Magic." *School Media Quarterly* 2 (Fall 1973): 31–35.

Myers, John Myers

Dickinson, Mike. "*Silverlock* and *The Moon's Fire-Eating Daughter.*" In *Survey of Modern Fantasy Literature*, vol. 4. Edited by Frank N. Magill. Englewood Cliffs, NJ: Salem Press, 1983, pp. 1749–1753.

Nathan, Robert (Gruntal)

Indick, Ben. "Portrait of Nathan." In *Exploring Fantasy Worlds*. Edited by Darrell Schweitzer. San Bernardino, CA: Borgo Press, 1985.

Meyers, Julia. "Robert Nathan." In *Supernatural Fiction Writers: Fantasy and Horror*, vol. 2. Edited by E. F. Bleiler. New York: Scribner, 1985, pp. 813–820.

Stableford, Brian. "*Portrait of Jenny.*" In *Survey of Modern Fantasy Literature*, vol. 3. Edited by Frank N. Magill. Englewood Cliffs, NJ: Salem Press, 1983, pp. 1276–1279.

Naylor, Phyllis Reynolds

Helbig, Alethea K., and Perkins, Agnes Regan. *Dictionary of American Children's Fiction, 1960–1984*. Westport, CT: Greenwood Press, 1986, p. 469.

Neill, John Rea

Hanff, Peter E., and Greene, Douglas G. *Bibliographia Oziana*. Demorest, GA: International Wizard of Oz Club, 1976.

Nesbit (Bland), E(dith)

Aers, Lesley. "The Treatment of Time in Four Children's Books." *Children's Literature in Education* 2 (July 1970): 69–81.

Alexander, Lloyd. "Afterword." In E. Nesbit's *Five Children and It*. Dell, 1985.

———. "A Second Look: *Five Children and It*." *Horn Book* 61 (May–June 1985): 354–361.

Armstrong, Dennis Lee. "E. Nesbit: An Entrance to *The Magic City*." Ph.D. dissertation, Johns Hopkins University, 1974.

Bell, Anthea. *E. Nesbit*. New York: Walck, 1964. Reprinted in Roger Lancelyn Green, Anthea Bell, and Elizabeth Nesbitt. *Lewis Carroll, E. Nesbit, and Howard Pyle*. London: Bodley Head, 1968.

Briggs, Julia. *A Woman of Passion: The Life of E. Nesbit, 1858–1924*. New York: New Amsterdam/Meredith, 1987.

Buckley, Mary F. "Words of Power: Language and Reality in the Fantasy Novels of E. Nesbit and P. L. Travers." Ed.D. dissertation, East Texas State University, 1977.

Carpenter, Humphrey. "E. Nesbit: A Victorian in Disguise." In *Secret Gardens: The Golden Age of Children's Literature*. Boston: Houghton Mifflin, 1985, pp. 126–137.

Colwell, Eileen H. "E. Nesbit." *Junior Bookshelf* 8 (Nov. 1944): 85–89.

Cooper, Susan. "Afterword." In *The Phoenix and the Carpet* by E. Nesbit. New York: Dell, 1987.

Crouch, Marcus S. "E. Nesbit in Kent." *Junior Bookshelf* 19, 1 (Jan. 1955): 11–21.

———. "The Nesbit Tradition." *Junior Bookshelf* 22 (Oct. 1958): 195–198.

———. *The Nesbit Tradition: The Children's Novels in England 1845–1970*. London: Benn, 1972, p. 16.

Croxon, Mary. "The Emancipated Child in the Novels of E. Nesbit." *Signal* 14 (May 1974): 51–64.

De Alonso, Joan Evans. "E. Nesbit's Well Hall, 1915–1921: A Memoir." In *Children's*

Literature, vol. 3. Storrs, CT: Journal of the Modern Language Association, 1974, pp. 147–152. Reprinted in *Reflections on Literature for Children.* Edited by Francelia Butler and Richard Rotert. Hamden, CT: Shoe String Press, 1984, pp. 229–236.

Doyle, Brian. *The Who's Who of Children's Literature.* New York: Schocken, 1968, pp. 206–208.

Eager, Edward. "Daily Magic." *Horn Book* 34 (Oct. 1958): 349–358. Reprinted in Elinor Field. *Horn Book Reflections.* Boston: Horn Book, 1969, pp. 211–217.

Ellis, Alec. "E. Nesbit and the Poor." *Junior Bookshelf* 38 (Apr. 1974): 73–78.

Fromm, Gloria G. "E. Nesbit and the Happy Moralist." *Journal of Modern Literature* 11 (Mar. 1984): 45–65.

Graham, Eleanor. "Places of Enchantment." *Horn Book* 34 (Oct. 1958): 364–365.

Green, Roger Lancelyn. "E. Nesbit: Treasure-Seeker." *Junior Bookshelf* 22 (Oct. 1958): 175–185.

Hand, Nigel. "The Other E. Nesbit." *The Use of English* 26 (Winter 1974): 108–116.

Horn Book Magazine. E. Nesbit Special Number. "Magic and the Magician." *Horn Book* 35 (Oct. 1958): 341, 347–373.

Inglis, Fred. *The Promise of Happiness.* New York: Cambridge Univ. Press, 1981, pp. 113–117.

Jackson, Rosemary. *Fantasy: The Literature of Subversion.* New York: Methuen, 1980, 145–146, 153.

Jacobs, W. J., and Jacobs, P. L. "E. Nesbit: Storyteller and Victorian Swinger." *Record* 69 (Mar. 1968): 621–623.

Junior Bookshelf. E. Nesbit special issue 22, no. 4 (Oct. 1958).

Krensky, Stephen. "A Second Look: *The Story of the Treasure Seekers.*" *Horn Book* 54 (June 1978): 310–312.

Lansner, Helen. "The Genius of E. Nesbit." *Elementary English* 43 (Jan. 1966): 53–55.

Lochhead, Marion. *Renaissance of Wonder.* New York: Harper & Row, 1980, pp. 59–69.

Lurie, Alison. "E. Nesbit." In *Writers for Children: Critical Studies of Major Authors since the Seventeenth Century.* Edited by Jane M. Bingham. New York: Scribner, 1988, pp. 423–430.

Lynch, Patricia. "Remembering E. Nesbit." *Horn Book* 29 (Oct. 1953): 342–343.

McCaffrey, Anne. "Afterword." In E. Nesbit's *Book of Dragons.* Dell, 1985.

Manlove, C(olin) N. "Fantasy as Witty Conceit: E. Nesbit." *Mosaic* 10, no. 2 (Winter 1976–1977): 109–130.

———. "The Union of Opposites in Fantasy: E. Nesbit." In C. N. Manlove. *The Impulse of Fantasy Literature.* Kent, OH: Kent State Univ. Press, 1983, pp. 46–69. Revised from an article in *Mosaic,* 1977.

Molson, Francis J. "*The Enchanted Castle.*" In *Survey of Modern Fantasy Literature,* vol. 3. Edited by Frank N. Magill. Englewood Cliffs, NJ: Salem Press, 1983, pp. 483–485.

———. "The Psammead Trilogy." In *Survey of Modern Fantasy Literature,* vol. 3. Edited by Frank N. Magill. Englewood Cliffs, NJ: Salem Press, 1983, pp. 1297–1300.

Moore, Doris Langley. *E. Nesbit: A Biography,* rev. ed. Radnor, PA: Chilton, 1966. Originally published 1933.

More Junior Authors. Edited by Muriel Fuller. New York: Wilson, 1963, pp. 157–158.

Moss, Anita. "Makers of Meaning: A Structuralist Study of Twain's *Tom Sawyer* and Nesbit's *The Enchanted Castle.*" *Children's Literature Association Quarterly* 7 (Fall 1982): 39–44.

Nesbit, E. *Long Ago When I Was Young* (original title: *The Girl's Own.* London, 1896). New York: Watts, 1966; New York: Dial, 1988.

———. "Pirates and Explorers" *Horn Book* 42 (Feb. 1966): 87–91. An excerpt from *Long Ago When I Was Young.* New York: Watts, 1966

———. *Wings and the Child; Or, The Building of Magic Cities.* London: Hodder, 1913.

The Oxford Companion to Children's Literature. Edited by Humphrey Carpenter and Mari Prichard. New York: Oxford Univ. Press, 1984, pp. 167, 187, 238, 262, 333, 371–374, 410, 499.

Parent, L. K. "Bibliography of Edith Nesbit (Bland)." M.L.S. thesis, Catholic University of America, 1962.

Pflieger, Pat, and Hill, Helen M. *A Reference Guide to Modern Fantasy for Children.* Westport, CT: Greenwood Press, 1984, pp. xii–xvi, 63–67, 173–175, 188–190, 231–233, 251–253, 338–341, 439–442, 505–508, 589–591.

Prickett, Stephen. *Victorian Fantasy.* Bloomington: Indiana Univ. Press, 1979.

Rahn, S. "News from E. Nesbit: *The Story of The Amulet* and the Socialist Utopia." *English Literature in Transition 1880–1920* 28 (1985): 124–144.

Rustin, Michael. "Magic Wishes and the Self Explorations of Children: *Five Children and It.*" In *Narratives of Love and Loss.* London: Verso, 1987, pp. 59–83.

Searles, Baird; Meacham, Beth; and Franklin, Michael. *A Reader's Guide to Fantasy.* New York: Avon, 1982, pp. 116–119.

Smith, Barbara. "The Expression of Social Values in the Writing of E. Nesbit." In *Children's Literature,* vol. 3. Storrs, CT: Journal of the Modern Language Association, 1974, pp. 153–164.

Smith, Louisa A. "The Magician's Conjuror: E. Nesbit's Illustrator, H. R. Millar." In *Proceedings of the Ninth Annual Conference of the Children's Literature Association.* University of Florida, March 1982. Ypsilanti, MI: Children's Literature Association, 1983, pp. 130–136.

Stott, Jon C. *Children's Literature from A to Z.* New York: McGraw-Hill, 1984, p. 201.

Strange, Mavis. "E. Nesbit, As I Knew Her." *Horn Book* 34 (Oct. 1958): 359–363.

Streatfeild, Noel. *Magic and the Magician: E. Nesbit and Her Children's Books.* New York: Abelard-Schuman, 1958, pp. 90–116, 127–150.

———. "The Nesbit Influence." *Junior Bookshelf* 22 (Oct. 1958): 187–193.

———. "Oswald Bastable." *Horn Book* 34 (Oct. 1958): 366–373.

Twentieth Century Children's Writers. 2nd ed. Edited by D. L. Kirkpatrick. New York: St. Martin's Press, 1983, pp. 570–573.

Walbridge, Earle F. "E. Nesbit." *Horn Book* 29 (Oct. 1953): 335–341.

Yolen, Jane. "The Literary Underwater World." *Language Arts* 57 (1980): 403–412.

Ness, Evaline (Michelow)

Third Book of Junior Authors. Edited by Doris De Montreville and Donna Hill. New York: Wilson, 1972, pp. 206–207.

Twentieth Century Children's Writers. 2nd ed. Edited by D. L. Kirkpatrick. New York: St. Martin's Press, 1983, pp. 573–574.

Newman, Robert (Howard)

Helbig, Alethea K., and Perkins, Agnes Regan. *Dictionary of American Children's Fiction, 1960–1984.* Westport, CT: Greenwood Press, 1986, p. 471.

Twentieth Century Children's Writers. 2nd ed. Edited by D. L. Kirkpatrick. New York: St. Martin's Press, 1983, pp. 575–576.

Nichols, (Joanna) Ruth

Evans, Gwyneth. " 'Nothing Odd *Ever* Happens Here.' Landscape in Canadian Fantasy." *Canadian Children's Literature* 15–16 (1980): 15–30.

Fourth Book of Junior Authors and Illustrators. Edited by Doris De Montreville and Elizabeth D. Crawford. New York: Wilson, 1978, pp. 274–275.

McDonough, Irma, ed. "Ruth Nichols." In *Profiles,* rev. ed. Ottawa: Canadian Library Association, 1975.

Nichols, Ruth. "Fantasy: The Interior Universe." In *Proceedings of the Fifth Annual Conference of the Children's Literature Association.* Ypsilanti, MI: The Children's Literature Assn., 1980, pp. 41–47.

————. "Fantasy and Escapism." *Canadian Children's Literature* 4 (1976): 20–27.

————. "Something of Myself." In *One Ocean Touching: Papers from the First Pacific Rim Conference on Children's Literature.* Metuchen, NJ: Scarecrow Press, 1979, pp. 189–194.

"Ruth Nichols: An Interview." *Children's Literature Association Quarterly* 2 (Summer 1977): 2–4.

Store, R. E. "Ruth Nichols: An Outstanding Canadian Author." *Orana* 14 (Nov. 1978): 134–146.

Stott, Jon C. *Children's Literature from A to Z.* New York: McGraw-Hill, 1984, p. 205.

————. "An Interview with Ruth Nichols." *Canadian Children's Literature* 12 (1978): 5–19.

————. "The Nature of Fantasy: A Conversation with Ruth Nichols, Susan Cooper, and Maurice Sendak." *World of Children's Books* 3, no. 2 (Fall 1978): 32–43.

Thompson, Hillary. "Doorways to Fantasy." *Canadian Children's Literature* 21 (1981): 8–16.

Twentieth Century Children's Writers. 2nd ed. Edited by D. L. Kirkpatrick. New York: St. Martin's Press, 1983, p. 576.

Nixon, Joan Lowery

Helbig, Alethea K., and Perkins, Agnes Regan. *Dictionary of American Children's Fiction, 1960–1984.* Westport, CT: Greenwood Press, 1986, p. 475.

North, Joan

Searles, Baird; Meacham, Beth; and Franklin, Michael. *A Reader's Guide to Fantasy.* New York: Avon, 1982, pp. 120–121.

Swinfen, Ann. *In Defense of Fantasy.* London: Routledge, 1984, pp. 105–106. Discusses *The Light Maze.*

Norton, Andre (pseud. of Alice Mary Norton)

Allen, L. David. "Andre Norton." In *Supernatural Fiction Writers: Fantasy and Horror,* vol. 2. Edited by E. F. Bleiler. New York: Scribner, 1985, pp. 1091–1096.

Allen, Paul. "Of Swords and Sorcery 4." *Fantasy Crossroads* 12 (1977): 21–27.

Boss, Judith E. "Elements of Style in Science Fiction: Andre Norton Compared with Others." *Extrapolation* 26 (1985): 201–211.

Carter, Lin. "Andre Norton, a Profile by Lin Carter." Introduction to *The Sioux Spaceman* by Andre Norton. Boston: Gregg, 1978.

Crouch, Marcus. *The Nesbit Tradition.* London: Benn, 1972, pp. 54–55.

Dohner, Jan. "Literature of Change: Science Fiction and Women." *Top of the News* 34 (1978): 261–265.

Elwood, Roger, ed. *The Many Worlds of Andre Norton*. Dallas: Chilton, 1974.

Fisher, Marjorie T. "Writers for Children: Andre Norton." *School Librarian* 15 (July 1967): 141–145.

Fraser, Brian M. "Putting the Past into the Future: Interview with Andre Norton." *Fantastic Science Fiction* (Oct. 1980): 4–9.

Hensley, Charlotta Cook. "Andre Norton's Science Fiction and Fantasy, 1950–1979: An Introduction to the Topics of Philosophy, Reflection, Imaginary Voyages, and Future Prediction in Selected Books for Young Readers." Ph.D. dissertation, University of Colorado at Boulder, 1980.

Lacy, N. J. *The Arthurian Encyclopedia*. New York: Garland, 1986, p. 408.

McGhan, Barry. "Andre Norton: Why Has She Been Neglected?" *Riverside Quarterly* 4 (1970): 128–131.

Miesel, Sandra. "Introduction." In *Witch World* by Andre Norton. Boston: Gregg, 1977.

Molson, Francis J. "Andre Norton." In *American Writers for Children since 1960: Fiction. Dictionary of Literary Biography,* vol. 52. Detroit: Gale, 1986, pp. 267–277.

More Junior Authors. Edited by Muriel Fuller. New York: Wilson, 1963, pp. 159–160.

Norton, Andre. *The Book of Andre Norton*. New York: DAW, 1975. "On Writing Fantasy," pp. 71–79. Reprinted in Boyer and Zahorski. *Fantasists on Fantasy*. New York: Avon, 1984, pp. 151–162.

The Oxford Companion to Children's Literature. Edited by Humphrey Carpenter and Mari Prichard. New York: Oxford Univ. Press, 1984, p. 381.

Peters, B. D. "Bio-Bibliographical Study of Andre Norton, 1960–1971." Research paper. Kent State University, 1971.

Platt, Charles. *Dream Makers II: The Uncommon Men and Women Who Write Science Fiction*. New York: Berkley, 1983, pp. 95–102. Interview.

Ruse, Gary Alan. "Algol Profile: Andre Norton." *Algol* 14 (Summer–Fall 1977): 15–17.

Schlobin, Roger C. *Andre Norton: A Primary and Secondary Bibliography*. Boston: G. K. Hall, 1980.

———. "Andre Norton: Humanity Amid the Hardware." In *The Feminine Eye*. Edited by Tom Staicar. New York: Ungar, 1982, pp. 25–31.

———. "The *Witch World* Series." In *Survey of Modern Fantasy Literature*, vol. 5. Edited by Frank N. Magill. Englewood Cliffs, NJ: Salem Press, 1983, pp. 2139–2149.

Searles, Baird; Meacham, Beth; and Franklin, Michael. *A Reader's Guide to Fantasy*. New York: Avon, 1982, pp. 121–122.

Smith, Karen Patricia. "Claiming a Place in the Universe: The Portrayal of Minorities in Seven Works by Andre Norton." *Top of the News* 42 (Winter 1986): 165–172.

Townsend, John Rowe. *A Sense of Story*. London: Longman, 1971, pp. 143–153.

Turner, David G. *The First Editions of Andre Norton*. Menlo Park, CA: Turner, 1974.

Twentieth Century Children's Writers. 2nd ed. Edited by D. L. Kirkpatrick. New York: St. Martin's Press, 1983, pp. 580–582.

Twentieth-Century Science Fiction Writers. 2nd ed. Edited by Curtis C. Smith. Chicago: St. James Press, 1986, pp. 542–544.

Walker, Paul. "Andre Norton: An Interview." *Luna Monthly* 40 (1972): 1–4. Reprinted in Walker. *Speaking of Science Fiction*. Oradell, NJ: Luna Publications, 1978, pp. 263–270.

Wilson, Andrew J. "If It's Wednesday This Must Be Narnia: Exploring the Links between Phantasy and Reality." *Dark Horizons* 24 (1981): 19–23.

Wolf, Virginia L. "Andre Norton: Feminist Pied Piper in Science Fiction." *Children's Literature Association Quarterly* 10 (Summer 1985): 66–70.

Yoke, Carl. *Roger Zelazny and Andre Norton: Proponents of Individualism.* Columbus: State Library of Ohio, 1979.

Norton, Mary (Pearson)

"The Borrowers." In M. Crouch and A. Ellis. *Chosen for Children,* 3rd ed. London: The Library Association, 1977, pp. 66–69.

Cooper, Ilene. "Popular Reading—After *The Borrowers." Booklist* 81 (Nov. 15, 1984): 452–453. (bibliography)

Davenport, Julia. "The Narrative Framework of *The Borrowers:* Mary Norton and Emily Brontë." *Children's Literature in Education* 14 (Summer 1983): 75–79.

Doyle, Brian. *The Who's Who of Children's Literature.* New York: Schocken, 1968, pp. 210–212.

Field, C. "Mary Norton." *School Librarian* 11 (July 1963): 464–469.

Hand, Nigel. "Mary Norton and *The Borrowers." Children's Literature in Education* 7 (Mar. 1972): 38–55.

———. "Mary Norton, Fred Inglis, and the World We Have Lost." In Dennis Butts. *Good Writers for Young Readers.* St. Albans, England: Hart-Davis, 1977, pp. 86–93.

Harbage, Mary. *"The Borrowers* at Home and Afield." *Elementary English* 33 (Feb. 1956): 67–75.

Heins, Ethel. *"The Borrowers Avenged." Horn Book* 59 (Apr. 1983): 155–156. Review.

Inglis, Fred. *Ideology and Imagination.* New York: Cambridge Univ. Press, 1975.

Josipovici, G. *The World and the Book.* Boulder, CO: Paladin Press, 1973.

Kuznets, Lois R. "Mary Norton's *The Borrowers:* Diaspora in Miniature." In *Touchstones.* Edited by Perry Nodelman. West Lafayette, IN: Children's Literature Association Publications, 1985, pp. 198–203.

———. "Permutations of Frame in Mary Norton's *Borrowers* Series." *Studies in Literary Imagination* 18 (Fall 1985): 65–78.

Laslett, P. *The World We Have Lost.* London: Methuen, 1971.

Olson, Barbara V. "Mary Norton and *The Borrowers." Elementary English* 47 (Feb. 1970): 185–189.

The Oxford Companion to Children's Literature. Edited by Humphrey Carpenter and Mari Prichard. New York: Oxford Univ. Press, 1984, pp. 54, 76, 381.

Pflieger, Pat, and Hill, Helen M. *A Reference Guide to Modern Fantasy for Children.* Westport, CT: Greenwood Press, 1984, pp. xii–xvi, 23–24, 69–70, 74–79, 337–338, 401–403.

Rustin, Margaret. "Deep Structures of Fantasy in Modern British Children's Books." *The Lion and the Unicorn* 10 (1986): 60–82.

Rustin, Michael. "Who Believes in '*Borrowers*'?" In *Narratives of Love and Loss.* London: Verso, 1987, pp. 163–180.

Smaridge, Norah. *Famous Modern Storytellers for Young People.* New York: Dodd, 1969, pp. 79–85.

Stableford Vivien. *"The Borrowers* Series." In *Survey of Modern Fantasy Literature,* vol. 1. Edited by Frank N. Magill. Englewood Cliffs, NJ: Salem Press, 1983, pp. 164–165.

Stott, Jon C. "Anatomy of a Masterpiece: *The Borrowers." Language Arts* 53, no. 5 (May 1976): 538–544.

———. *Children's Literature from A to Z.* New York: McGraw-Hill, 1984, p. 206.

Swinfen, Ann. *In Defense of Fantasy.* London: Routledge, 1984, pp. 127, 130–131, 191.

Third Book of Junior Authors. Edited by Doris De Montreville and Donna Hill. New York: Wilson, 1972, pp. 211–212.

Toomey, Philippa. "Reluctant Writer: Mary Norton." *Children's Book Review* 5 (Autumn/Winter 1975): 85–86.
Townsend, John Rowe. "Mary Norton." In *A Sense of Story*. Philadelphia: Lippincott, 1971, pp. 143–153.
Twentieth Century Children's Writers. 2nd ed. Edited by D. L. Kirkpatrick. New York: St. Martin's Press, 1983, p. 583.
Ulman, Ruth. "WLB Biography: Mary Norton." *Wilson Library Bulletin* 36 (May 1962): 767. Reprinted in Miriam Hoffman and Eva Samuels. *Authors and Illustrators of Children's Books*. New York: Bowker, 1972, pp. 340–342.

Nöstlinger, Christine

Fetz, Nancy Tillman. "Christine Nöstlinger's Emancipatory Fantasies." *The Lion and the Unicorn* 10 (1986): 40–53.
Fifth Book of Junior Authors and Illustrators. Edited by Sally Holmes Holtze. New York: Wilson, 1983, p. 231.

Nye, Robert

Twentieth Century Children's Writers. 2nd ed. Edited by D. L. Kirkpatrick. New York: St. Martin's Press, 1983, pp. 584–585.

Oakley, Graham

Fifth Book of Junior Authors and Illustrators. Edited by Sally Holmes Holtze. New York: Wilson, 1983, pp. 232–233.
Twentieth Century Children's Writers. 2nd ed. Edited by D. L. Kirkpatrick. New York: St. Martin's Press, 1983, pp. 585–586.

O'Brien, Robert C. (pseud. of Robert Leslie Conly)

Boulanger, Susan. "A Second Look: *The Silver Crown*." *Horn Book* 61 (Jan.–Feb. 1984): 95–98.
Fourth Book of Junior Authors and Illustrators. Edited by Doris De Montreville and Elizabeth D. Crawford. New York: Wilson, 1978, pp. 275–278.
Getting Hooked on Science Fiction. White Plains, NY: Guidance Associates, 1976. Includes *Mrs. Frisby and the Rats of NIMH*. (filmstrip and audiocassette)
Helbig, Alethea K. "Robert C. O'Brien's *Mrs. Frisby and the Rats of NIMH*: Through the Eyes of Small Animals." In *Touchstones*. Edited by Perry Nodelman. West Lafayette, IN: Children's Literature Association Publications, 1985, pp. 204–211.
Helbig, Alethea K., and Perkins, Agnes Regan. *Dictionary of American Children's Fiction, 1960–1984*. Westport, CT: Greenwood Press, 1986, pp. 441–442, 481.
Henke, James T. "Growing Up as Epic Adventure: The Biblical Collage in *Z for Zachariah*." *Children's Literature in Education* 13 (Summer 1982): 87–94.
Morse, Brian. "The Novels of Robert C. O'Brien." *Signal* 40 (Jan. 1983): 30–36.
"*Mrs. Frisby and the Rats of NIMH*." In Lee Kingman. *Newbery and Caldecott Medal Books: 1966–1975*. Boston: Horn Book, 1975, pp. 79–92.
O'Brien, Robert C. "Newbery Award Acceptance." *Horn Book* 48 (Aug. 1972): 343–348.
O'Brien, Sally M. "Robert C. O'Brien." *Horn Book* 48 (Aug. 1972): 349–351.

The Oxford Companion to Children's Literature. Edited by Humphrey Carpenter and Mari Prichard. New York: Oxford Univ. Press, 1984, p. 385.

Pflieger, Pat, and Hill, Helen M. *A Reference Guide to Modern Fantasy for Children.* Westport, CT: Greenwood Press, 1984, pp. xi, xv, 387–388, 405–406.

Roginski, Jim, ed. *Newbery and Caldecott Medalists and Honor Book Winners.* Littleton, CO: Libraries Unlimited, 1982, p. 204.

Stott, Jon C. *Children's Literature from A to Z.* New York: McGraw-Hill, 1984, p. 210.

Swinfen, Ann. *In Defense of Fantasy.* London: Routledge, 1984, pp. 36–37.

Twentieth Century Children's Writers. 2nd ed. Edited by D. L. Kirkpatrick. New York: St. Martin's Press, 1983, pp. 586–587.

Ormondroyd, Edward

Helbig, Alethea K., and Perkins, Agnes Regan. *Dictionary of American Children's Fiction, 1960–1984.* Westport, CT: Greenwood Press, 1986, pp. 492, 662–663.

Twentieth Century Children's Writers. 2nd ed. Edited by D. L. Kirkpatrick. New York: St. Martin's Press, 1983, pp. 592–593.

Orwell, George (pseud. of Eric Hugh Blair)

Asker, David Harry Desmond. "The Modern Bestiary: Animal Fiction from Hardy to Orwell." Dissertation, University of British Columbia, 1978.

Buckley, David Patrick. "The Novels of George Orwell." Ph.D. dissertation, Columbia University, 1962.

Burger, Douglas A. "*Animal Farm.*" In *Survey of Modern Fantasy Literature,* Vol. 1. Edited by Frank N. Magill. Englewood Cliffs, NJ: Salem Press, 1983, pp. 45–47.

Byrne, Katherine. "A Different-Looking Orwell." *Commonweal* 11 (Mar. 1983): 149–151.

Concannon, Gerald J. "The Development of George Orwell's Art." Ph.D. dissertation, University of Denver, 1973.

Connelly, Mark. "The Diminished Self: The Loss of Individual Autonomy in Orwell's Novels." Ph.D. dissertation, University of Wisconsin-Milwaukee, 1984.

Coppard, Audrey, and Crick, Bernard, eds. *Orwell Remembered.* New York: Facts on File, 1984.

Crick, Bernard. *George Orwell: A Life.* New York: Little, Brown, 1981; Penguin, 1982. Originally published by Secker and Warburg, 1980.

Duffey, Paula. "Form and Meaning in the Novels of George Orwell." Ph.D. dissertation, University of Pennsylvania, 1967.

Edrich, Emmanuel. "Literature, Technology, and Social Temper in the Fiction of George Orwell." Ph.D. dissertation, University of Wisconsin, 1960.

Elkins, Charles L. "George Orwell." In *Science Fiction Writers.* Edited by E. F. Bleiler. New York: Scribner, 1985, pp. 233–242.

Fiderer, Gerald Lionel. "A Psychoanalytic Study of the Novels of George Orwell." Ph.D. dissertation, University of Oklahoma, 1967.

Fink, H. K. "George Orwell's Novels in Relation to His Social and Literary Theory." Ph.D. dissertation, London University (U.K.), 1968.

Fyvel, T. R. *George Orwell: A Personal Memoir.* New York: Macmillan, 1982.

George Orwell. Maltoon, IL: Spectrum Educational Media, 1984. (audiocassette)

George Orwell. Peoria, IL: Thomas S. Klise, 1985. (filmstrip and audiocassette)

Hunter, Jefferson Estock. "George Orwell and the Uses of Literature." Ph.D. dissertation, Yale University, 1973.

Kearse, Lee Andrew, Jr. "George Orwell: Romantic Utopian." Ph.D. dissertation, Brown University, 1973.

Knapp, John V. "Dance to a Creepy Minuet: Orwell's *Burmese Days,* Precursor of *Animal Farm.*" *Modern Fiction Studies* 21 (1979): 11–29.

Mellichamp, Leslie R., Jr. "A Study of George Orwell: The Man, His Import and His Outlook." Ph.D. dissertation, Emory University, 1968.

Meyers, Jeffrey. "George Orwell: A Bibliography." *Bulletin of Bibliography* 31 (1974): 117–121.

———. "George Orwell: A Selected Checklist." *Modern Fiction Studies* 21 (1975); 133–136.

———. *A Reader's Guide to George Orwell.* London: Thames, 1975.

———, ed. *George Orwell: The Critical Heritage.* Boston: Routledge, 1975.

Meyers, Jeffrey, and Meyers, Valerie. *George Orwell: An Annotated Bibliography of Criticism.* New York: Garland, 1977.

Reilly, Patrick. *George Orwell: The Age's Adversary.* New York: St. Martin's Press, 1986.

Small, Christopher. *The Road to Miniluv: George Orwell, the State, and God.* Pittsburgh: Univ. of Pittsburgh Press, 1976.

Smith, David, and Mosher, Michael. *Orwell for Beginners.* London: Writers and Readers Publishing Cooperative, 1984.

Smyer, Richard Ingram. "Structure and Meaning in the Works of George Orwell." Ph.D. dissertation, Stanford University, 1968.

Snyder, Phillip John. "Doing the Necessary Task: The Bourgeois Humanism of George Orwell." Ph.D. dissertation, Case Western Reserve University, 1964.

Stevenson, Lionel. "Purveyors of Myth and Magic." In *Yesterday and After: The History of the English Novel.* Totowa, NJ: Barnes and Noble, 1967, pp. 111–154.

Thompson, John. *Orwell's London.* New York: Schocken, 1985.

Trambling, Victor R. S. "Following in the Footsteps of Jack London: George Orwell, Writer and Critic." *Jack London Newsletter* 11 (1978): 63–70.

Twentieth-Century Science Fiction Writers. 2nd. ed. Edited by Curtis C. Smith. Chicago: St. James Press, 1986, pp. 554–556.

The Unexpected: Stories of Humor and Fantasy. Pleasantville, NY: Educational Audio-Visual, 1979. (filmstrip and audiocassette)

Van Dellen, Robert J. "Politics in Orwell's Fiction." Ph.D. dissertation, Indiana University, 1973.

Voohees, Richard Joseph. "The Paradox of George Orwell." Ph.D. dissertation, Indiana University, 1958.

Wain, John. "Dear George Orwell: A Personal Letter." *American Scholar* 52 (Winter 1982–1983): 21–37.

Williams, Raymond. *George Orwell.* New York: Columbia Univ. Press, 1981. Originally published by Viking, 1971.

———, ed. *George Orwell: A Collection of Critical Essays.* Englewood Cliffs, NJ: Prentice-Hall, 1974.

Woodcock, George. *The Crystal Spirit: A Study of George Orwell.* New York: Schocken, 1984. Originally published by Little, Brown, 1966.

Zehr, David Morgan. "George Orwell: The Novelist's Dilemma." Ph.D. dissertation, Indiana University, 1977.

O'Shea, Pat

Cart, Michael. "A Light in the Darkness: Humor Returns to Children's Fantasy." *School Library Journal* 33 (Apr. 1987): 48–49.

Ouida (pseud. of Marie Louise de la Ramée)

Chang, Charity. *"The Nürnberg Stove* as an Artistic Fairy Tale." In *Children's Literature*, vol. 5. Philadelphia: Temple Univ. Press, 1976, pp. 148–156.
The Oxford Companion to Children's Literature. Edited by Humphrey Carpenter and Mari Prichard. New York: Oxford Univ. Press, 1984, p. 390.

Paget, (Reverend) F(rances) E(dward) (used the pseud. William Churne of Staffordshire)

The Oxford Companion to Children's Literature. Edited by Humphrey Carpenter and Mari Prichard. New York: Oxford Univ. Press, 1984, p. 393.

Paine, Albert Bigelow

Kunitz, S. J., ed. *Twentieth Century Authors.* New York: Wilson, 1942, p. 1067.

Park, (Rosina) Ruth (Lucia)

Twentieth Century Children's Writers. 2nd ed. Edited by D. L. Kirkpatrick. New York: St. Martin's Press, 1983, pp. 598–599.

Parker, (James) Edgar, (Jr.)

Third Book of Junior Authors. Edited by Doris De Montreville and Donna Hill. New York: Wilson, 1972, p. 219.

Parker, Richard

Twentieth Century Children's Writers. 2nd ed. Edited by D. L. Kirkpatrick. New York: St. Martin's Press, 1983, pp. 599–600.

Parrish (Tizell), Anne

"Anne Parrish Tizell: With a Catalog of Her Drawings and Paintings She Collected." *Wadsworth Atheneum Bulletin* (Winter, 1958).
Davis, Lavinia R. "Anne Parrish as a Writer of Children's Books." *Horn Book* 36 (Feb. 1960): 63–67.
Helbig, Alethea K., and Perkins, Agnes Regan. *Dictionary of American Children's Fiction, 1859–1959.* Westport, CT: Greenwood Press, 1985, pp. 138–139, 165, 395, 493–494.
Miller, Bertha E. Mahony. "Anne Parrish's Memorable Nonsense Story." *Horn Book* 27 (Jan.–Feb. 1951): 20–22.
———. "The Honey Heart of Earth in the Books of Anne and Dillwyn Parrish." *Horn Book* 7 (Feb. 1931): 61–67. Reprinted in Norma Fryatt. *A Horn Book Sampler.* Boston: Horn Book, 1959, pp. 4–7.
Parrish, Anne. "Do You Remember?" *Horn Book* 23 (Jan.–Feb. 1949): 26–32.
———. "For Dillwyn Parrish." *Horn Book* 36 (Feb. 1960): 68.
———. "Writing for Children." *Horn Book* 27 (Mar.–Apr. 1951): 85–89.
Roginski, Jim, ed. *Newbery and Caldecott Medalists and Honor Book Winners.* Littleton, CO: Libraries Unlimited, 1982, pp. 209–210.
Twentieth Century Children's Writers. 2nd ed. Edited by D. L. Kirkpatrick. New York: St. Martin's Press, 1983, pp. 600–601.

Parrish, (George) Dillwyn

Helbig, Alethea K., and Perkins, Agnes Regan. *Dictionary of American Children's Fiction, 1859–1959*. Westport, CT: Greenwood Press, 1985, p. 395.

Miller, Bertha E. Mahony. " 'The Honey Heart of Earth' in the Books of Anne and Dillwyn Parrish." *Horn Book* 7 (Mar. 1931): 61–67.

Parrish, Anne. "For Dillwyn Parrish." *Horn Book* 36 (Feb. 1960): 68.

Pascal, Francine

Fifth Book of Junior Authors and Illustrators. Edited by Sally Holmes Holtze. New York: Wilson, 1983, pp. 235–236.

Paton Walsh, Jill (Gillian Bliss)

Crago, Hugh. "The Readers in the Reader: An Experiment in Personal Response and Literary Criticism." *Signal* 39 (Sept. 1982): 172–182. Discusses *A Chance Child*.

Fourth Book of Junior Authors and Illustrators. Edited by Doris De Montreville and Elizabeth D. Crawford. New York: Wilson, 1978, pp. 284–285.

The Oxford Companion to Children's Literature. Edited by Humphrey Carpenter and Mari Prichard. New York: Oxford Univ. Press, 1984, pp. 560–561. (Listed under Walsh.)

Paton Walsh, Jill. "Disturbing the Universe." In *Innocence & Experience*. Edited by Barbara Harrison and Gregory Maguire. New York: Lothrop, 1987, pp. 156–164.

———. "History Is Fiction." *Horn Book* 48 (Feb. 1972): 17–23.

———. "The Lords of Time." *Quarterly Journal of the Library of Congress* 36 (Spring 1979): 96–113.

———. "Seeing Green." In Edward Blishen. *The Thorny Paradise*. Boston: Horn Book, 1975, pp. 58–61.

———. "The Writers in the Writer: A Reply to Hugh Crago." *Signal* 40 (Jan. 1983): 3–11.

———. "The Writer's Responsibility." *Children's Literature in Education* 10 (Mar. 1973): 30–36.

Pflieger, Pat, and Hill, Helen M. *A Reference Guide to Modern Fantasy for Children*. Westport, CT: Greenwood Press, 1984, pp. xii–xvi, 103–105, 425–426.

Rees, David. "Types of Ambiguity: Jill Paton Walsh." In *Marble in the Water*. Boston: Horn Book, 1980, pp. 141–154.

Townsend, John Rowe. "Jill Paton Walsh." In *A Sounding of Storytellers*. Philadelphia: Lippincott, 1979, pp. 153–165.

Twentieth Century Children's Writers. 2nd ed. Edited by D. L. Kirkpatrick. New York: St. Martin's Press, 1983, pp. 604–606.

"Writers and Critics: A Dialogue Between Jill Paton Walsh and John Rowe Townsend, Part I." *Horn Book* 58 (Oct. 1982): 498–504; "Part II." *Horn Book* 58 (Dec. 1982): 680–685.

Patten, Brian

Twentieth Century Children's Writers. 2nd ed. Edited by D. L. Kirkpatrick. New York: St. Martin's Press, 1983, pp. 606–607.

Paxon, Diana L.

Paxon, Diana. "The Holy Grail." *Mythlore* 3, no. 9 (1976).

———. "The Tolkien Tradition." *Mythlore* 39 (1984): 23–27, 37.
———. "Why Write Fantasy?" *Mythlore* 10 (Sept. 1984): 23–27.

Payne, Joan Balfour (Dicks)

Payne, Joan Balfour. "Another King for Christmas." *Horn Book* 37 (Dec. 1961): 569–585.

Pearce (Christie), (Ann) Philippa

Aers, Lesley. "The Treatment of Time in Four Children's Books." *Children's Literature in Education* 2 (July 1970): 69–81.

Billman, Carol. "Young and Old Alike: The Place of Old Women in Two Recent Novels for Children." *Children's Literature Association Quarterly* 8 (Spring 1983): 6–8, 31.

Chambers, Aidan. "Letter from England: Reaching Through a Window." *Horn Book* 57 (Apr. 1981): 229–233.

Crouch, Marcus. *The Nesbit Tradition*. London: Benn, 1972, pp. 198–200.

Doyle, Brian. *The Who's Who of Children's Literature*. New York: Schocken, 1968, pp. 214–215.

Evans, David. "The Making of *The Children of the House*." In *Further Approaches to Research in Children's Literature*. Edited by Peter Hunt. Cardiff: Univ. of Wales, 1982, pp. 51–56.

Inglis, Fred. *The Promise of Happiness*. New York: Cambridge Univ. Press, 1981, pp. 257–267.

Jackson, Brian. "Philippa Pearce in the Golden Age of Children's Literature." *The Use of English* 21, no. 3 (Spring 1970): 195–203, 207. Reprinted in Margaret Meek. *The Cool Web*. New York: Atheneum, 1978, pp. 314–324; and in Dennis Butts. *Good Writers for Young Readers*. St. Albans, England: Hart-Davis, 1977, pp. 94–103.

Jones, Raymond E. "Philippa Pearce's *Tom's Midnight Garden:* Finding and Losing Eden." In *Touchstones*. Edited by Perry Nodelman. West Lafayette, IN: Children's Literature Association Publications, 1985, pp. 212–220.

The Oxford Companion to Children's Literature. Edited by Humphrey Carpenter and Mari Prichard. New York: Oxford Univ. Press, 1984, pp. 155, 398, 534.

Pearce, Philippa. "Guest Review." *Puffin Post* (London) 14 (Spring 1980): 22–23.

———. "*Robin Hood and His Merry Men:* A Re-Reading." *Children's Literature in Education* 16 (Autumn 1985): 159–164.

———. "The Writer's View of Childhood." *Horn Book* 38 (Feb. 1962): 74–78. Reprinted in Elinor Field. *Horn Book Reflections*. Boston: Horn Book, 1969, pp. 49–53.

———. "Writing a Book: *A Dog So Small*." *Listening and Writing* (London). BBC Booklet for Schools (Autumn 1962). Reprinted in Margaret Meek. *The Cool Web*. New York: Atheneum, 1978, pp. 182–187; in *Horn Book* 43 (June 1967): 317–321; and in Edward Blishen. *The Thorny Paradise*. Boston: Horn Book, 1975, pp. 140–145.

Pflieger, Pat, and Hill, Helen M. *A Reference Guide to Modern Fantasy for Children*. Westport, CT: Greenwood Press, 1984, pp. xiii, 427–429, 543–544.

Philip, Neil. "*Tom's Midnight Garden* and the Vision of Eden." *Signal* 37 (Jan. 1982): 21–25.

Rees, David. "The Novels of Philippa Pearce." *Children's Literature in Education* 4 (Mar. 1971): 40–53. Reprinted in David Rees. *The Marble in the Water*. Boston: Horn Book, 1980, pp. 36–55, entitled "Achieving One's Heart's Desires."

Royds, Pam. "Meet Your Author—Philippa Pearce." *Puffin Post* (London) 12, no. 2 (1978): 8–9.

Rustin, Michael. "Animals in Reality and Fantasy: Two Stories by Philippa Pearce." In *Narratives of Love and Loss*. London: Verso, 1987, pp. 119–145.

————. "Loneliness, Dreaming and Discovery: *Tom's Midnight Garden.*" In *Narratives of Love and Loss*. London: Verso, 1987, pp. 27–39.

Snyder, Zilpha Keatley. "Afterword." In Philippa Pearce's *Tom's Midnight Garden*. Dell, 1985.

Swinfen, Ann. *In Defense of Fantasy*. London: Routledge, 1984, pp. 52, 58–61. Discusses *Tom's Midnight Garden*.

Third Book of Junior Authors. Edited by Doris De Montreville and Donna Hill. New York: Wilson, 1972, pp. 221–222.

"*Tom's Midnight Garden.*" In M. Crouch and A. Ellis. *Chosen for Children*, 3rd ed. London: The Library Association, 1977, pp. 96–99.

Townsend, John Rowe. "Philippa Pearce." In *A Sense of Story*. Philadelphia: Lippincott, 1971, pp. 163–171.

Twentieth Century Children's Writers. 2nd ed. Edited by D. L. Kirkpatrick. New York: St. Martin's Press, 1983, pp. 608–609.

Wolf, Virginia L. "Belief in *Tom's Midnight Garden.*" In *Proceedings of the Ninth Annual Conference of the Children's Literature Association*. University of Florida, March 1982. Ypsilanti, MI: Children's Literature Association, 1983, pp. 142–146.

Pease, (Clarence) Howard

Jennings, Shirley May. "A Study of the Creative Genesis of the Twenty-two Published Children's Novels by Howard Pease." Ed.D. dissertation, University of the Pacific, 1969.

Jennings, Shirley May, and Chambers, Dewey. "The Real Ted Moran." *Elementary English* 46 (Apr. 1969): 488–491. Reprinted in *Children's Literature: Criticism and Response*. Edited by Mary Lou White. Columbus, OH: Merrill, 1976, pp. 19–25.

The Junior Book of Authors. 2nd rev. ed. Edited by Stanley J. Kunitz and Howard Haycraft. New York: Wilson, 1951, pp. 239–240.

Twentieth Century Children's Writers. 2nd ed. Edited by D. L. Kirkpatrick. New York: St. Martin's Press, 1983, pp. 609–610.

Peck, Richard (Wayne)

Blackburn, William. "The Quest for Values in Contemporary Adolescent Fiction." Ann Arbor, MI: ERIC Educational Document Reprint Service, 1982.

Crew, Hilary. "Blossom Culp and Her Ilk: The Independent Female in Richard Peck's Young Adult Fiction." *Top of the News* 43 (Spring 1987): 297–302.

Fifth Book of Junior Authors and Illustrators. Edited by Sally Holmes Holtze. New York: Wilson, 1983, pp. 238–240.

Helbig, Alethea K., and Perkins, Agnes Regan. *Dictionary of American Children's Fiction, 1960–1984*. Westport, CT: Greenwood Press, 1986, pp. 503–504.

Peck, Richard. "Coming Full Circle: From Lesson Plans to Young Adult Novels." *Horn Book* 59 (Apr. 1983): 208–215.

————. "Communicating With a New Generation: A Challenge to Writers and Teachers." *Illinois Libraries* 57 (May 1975): 305–312.

————. "In the Country of Teenage Fiction." *American Libraries* 4 (Apr. 1973): 204–207. Reprinted in *Young Adult Literature in the Seventies*. Edited by Jana Varlejs. Metuchen, NJ: Scarecrow Press, 1978, pp. 97–105.

————. "The Invention of Adolescence and Other Thoughts on Youth." *Top of the News* 39 (Winter 1983): 182–190.

———. "People of the Word: A Look at Today's Young Adults, and Their Needs." *School Library Media Quarterly* 10 (Fall 1981): 16–21.

———. "Writing for the Young Adult." *Texas Library Journal* 51 (Winter 1975): 191–196.

Twentieth Century Children's Writers. 2nd ed. Edited by D. L. Kirkpatrick. New York: St. Martin's Press, 1983, pp. 610–611.

Peet, Bill (William Bartlett)

Bader, Barbara. *American Picturebooks from Noah's Ark to the Beast Within.* New York: Macmillan, 1976, pp. 38–42.

Twentieth Century Children's Writers. 2nd ed. Edited by D. L. Kirkpatrick. New York: St. Martin's Press, 1983, pp. 612–613.

Petersham, Maud (Fuller), and Petersham, Miska

Bader, Barbara. "Maud and Miska Petersham." In *American Picturebooks from Noah's Ark to the Beast Within.* New York: Macmillan, 1976, pp. 38–42.

The Junior Book of Authors. 2nd rev. ed. Edited by Stanley J. Kunitz and Howard Haycraft. New York: Wilson, 1951, pp. 243–244.

Peyton, K. M. (pseud. of Kathleen Wendy Peyton)

Butts, Dennis. "Writers for Children: K. M. Peyton." *The Use of English* 23 (Spring 1972): 195–202. Reprinted in Dennis Butts. *Good Writers for Young Readers.* St. Albans, England: Hart-Davis, 1977, pp. 104–113.

Crouch, Marcus. *The Nesbit Tradition.* London: Benn, 1972, pp. 152–153, 177–179.

———. "Streets Ahead in Experience." *Junior Bookshelf* 33 (June 1969): 153–159.

Hibbard, Dominic. "The Flambards Trilogy: Objections to a Winner." *Children's Literature in Education* 8 (July 1972): 5–15. Reprinted in Fox. *Writers, Critics and Children.* New York: Agathon, 1976, pp. 125–137. For response, see Ray, below.

Inglis, Fred. *The Promise of Happiness.* New York: Cambridge Univ. Press, 1981, pp. 221–224.

Jones, Cornelia, and Way, Olivia R. "K. M. Peyton." In *British Children's Authors.* Chicago: American Library Association, 1976, pp. 127–136.

Looker, Ann. "Children's Writers: K. M. Peyton." *School Librarian* 25 (Summer 1977): 223–228.

The Oxford Companion to Children's Literature. Edited by Humphrey Carpenter and Mari Prichard. New York: Oxford Univ. Press, 1984, pp. 408–409.

Peyton, K. M. "The Carnegie Medal—A Speech of Acceptance." *Junior Bookshelf* 34 (Oct. 1970): 269–271.

———. "On Not Writing a Proper Book." In Edward Blishen. *The Thorny Paradise.* Boston: Horn Book, 1975, pp. 123–127.

Ray, Colin. "*The Edge of the Cloud*—A Reply to Dominic Hibbard." *Children's Literature in Education* 9 (Nov. 1972): 5–6.

Third Book of Junior Authors. Edited by Doris De Montreville and Donna Hill. New York: Wilson, 1972, pp. 224–226.

Townsend, John Rowe. "K. M. Peyton." In *A Sense of Story.* Philadelphia: Lippincott, 1971, pp. 172–181.

———. "K. M. Peyton." In *A Sounding of Storytellers.* Philadelphia: Lippincott, 1979, pp. 166–178.

———. "A Second Look: *A Pattern of Roses.*" *Horn Book* 60 (June 1984): 361–364.

Twentieth Century Children's Writers. 2nd ed. Edited by D. L. Kirkpatrick. New York: St. Martin's Press, 1983, pp. 616–617.

Wintle, Justin, and Fisher, Emma. "K. M. Peyton." In *The Pied Pipers.* New York: Paddington Press, 1974, pp. 263–276.

Phillips, Ethel Calvert

The Junior Book of Authors, 2nd rev. ed. Edited by Stanley J. Kunitz and Howard Haycraft. New York: Wilson, 1951, pp. 244–245.

Phillips, Ethel Calvert. "A Hunt Breakfast—Authors' Symposium." *Horn Book* 2 (Nov. 1926): 36.

Phipson, Joan (pseud. of Joan Margaret Fitzhardinge)

McVitty, Walter. "Joan Phipson: Archetypal Australian Children's Books." In *Innocence and Experience.* Melborne, Australia: Nelson, 1981, pp. 37–65.

Third Book of Junior Authors. Edited by Doris De Montreville and Donna Hill. New York: Wilson, 1972, pp. 226–227.

Twentieth Century Children's Writers. 2nd ed. Edited by D. L. Kirkpatrick. New York: St. Martin's Press, 1983, pp. 617–618.

Picard, Barbara Leonie

Crouch, Marcus. *The Nesbit Tradition.* London: Benn, 1972, pp. 74–75.

Jones, Cornelia, and Way, Olivia R. "Barbara Leonie Picard." In *British Children's Authors.* Chicago: American Library Association, 1976, pp. 137–145.

Third Book of Junior Authors. Edited by Doris De Montreville and Donna Hill. New York: Wilson, 1972, p. 228.

Twentieth Century Children's Writers. 2nd ed. Edited by D. L. Kirkpatrick. New York: St. Martin's Press, 1983, pp. 618–619.

Pierce, Meredith Ann

Helbig, Alethea K., and Perkins, Agnes Regan. *Dictionary of American Children's Fiction, 1960–1984.* Westport, CT: Greenwood Press, 1986, pp. 142–143, 514.

Pierce, Meredith Ann. "A Lion in the Room." *Horn Book* 64 (Jan.–Feb. 1988): 35–41.

Pinkwater, D(aniel) Manus

Antczak, Janice. *Science Fiction: The Mythos of a New Romance.* New York: Neal-Schuman, 1985, pp. 174–178.

Fifth Book of Junior Authors and Illustrators. Edited by Sally Holmes Holtze. New York: Wilson, 1983, pp. 246–247.

Plunkett, Edward John Morton Drax *see* Dunsany, Lord

Polland, Madeleine A(ngela Cahill)

Third Book of Junior Authors. Edited by Doris De Montreville and Donna Hill. New York: Wilson, 1972, pp. 229–230.

Twentieth Century Children's Writers. 2nd ed. Edited by D. L. Kirkpatrick. New York: St. Martin's Press, 1983, pp. 620–621.

Pope, Elizabeth Marie

Fifth Book of Junior Authors and Illustrators. Edited by Sally Holmes Holtze. New York: Wilson, 1983, pp. 250–251.

Heins, Ethel L. "A Second Look: *The Sherwood Ring.*" *Horn Book* 21 (Dec. 1975): 613.

Helbig, Alethea K., and Perkins, Agnes Regan. *Dictionary of American Children's Fiction, 1859–1959.* Westport, CT: Greenwood Press, 1985, pp. 408, 466–467.

———. *Dictionary of American Children's Fiction, 1960–1984.* Westport, CT: Greenwood Press, 1986, pp. 115–116, 506–507, 522.

Pope, Elizabeth Marie. "The Attic of Faerie." *Mythlore* 9 (Spring 1982): 8–10.

Postma, Lidia

Thiel-Schoonebeek, Joke. "Lidia Postma—Fantasy as Atmosphere." *Bookbird* 1 (1980): 62–64.

Potter, (Helen) Beatrix (Heelis)

Alderson, Brian. "*The Tailor of Gloucester.*" *Children's Book News* 4 (Nov.–Dec. 1969): 309–312.

Anderson, Celia Catlett. "The Ancient Lineage of Beatrix Potter's *Mr. Todd.*" *Proceedings of the Children's Literature Association* 7 (1980): 84–90. Reprinted in *Festschrift.* Edited by Nodelman and May. West Lafayette, IN: Children's Literature Association Publications, 1983, pp. 45–47.

Banner, D. "Portrait." *Illustrated London News* 243 (Oct. 9, 1948): 394.

Boultbee, Winifred W. "Some Personal Recollections of Beatrix Potter." *Horn Book* 47 (Dec. 1971): 586–588.

Brandenburger, Barbara. "Leslie Linder." *Horn Book* 42 (Dec. 1966): 686–689.

Cameron, Eleanor. "Why Not for Children?" *Horn Book* 42 (Feb. 1966): 21–23.

Campbell, A. K. D. "The Stories of Beatrix Potter: A Suggested Order for Reading." *Children's Literature in Education* 5 (July 1971): 12–19.

Carpenter, Humphrey. "Beatrix Potter: The Ironist in Arcadia." In *Secret Gardens: The Golden Age of Children's Literature.* Boston: Houghton Mifflin, 1985, pp. 138–150.

"Centenary of Beatrix Potter's Birth Marked by Publications and Exhibits." *Library Journal* 91 (Sept. 15, 1966): 4240–4241.

Children's Literature Association Newsletter. Special Issue 2 (Winter 1978).

Clark, Keith. "The Linder Collection of the Works and Drawings of Beatrix Potter." *Horn Book* 47 (Oct. 1971): 554–555.

Coolidge, Henry P. "A Visit to Beatrix Potter." *Horn Book* 4 (Feb. 1928): 48–53.

Cott, Jonathan. "Peter Rabbit and Friends." *New York Times Book Review* (May 1, 1977): 25, 38.

Crouch, Marcus E. *Beatrix Potter.* London: Bodley Head, 1960.

———. "Leslie Linder: He Knew More About Beatrix Than She Knew Herself." *Junior Bookshelf* 37 (Oct. 1973): 301–303.

Dalphin, Marcus. "The Tale of Beatrix Potter." *Horn Book* 22 (July–Aug. 1946): 431–437.

Dohm, J. H. "My Beatrix Potter." *Junior Bookshelf* 30 (Aug. 1966): 233 ff.

Doyle, Brian. *The Who's Who of Children's Literature*. New York: Schocken, 1968, pp. 220–223.

"Free Library of Philadelphia Named Recipient of the Collamore Collection of Beatrix Potter." *Wilson Library Bulletin* 42 (Jan. 1968): 450.

Frey, Charles. "Victors and Victims in the Tales of *Peter Rabbit* and *Squirrel Nutkin*." *Children's Literature in Education* 18 (Summer 1987): 105–112.

Gilpatrick, Naomi. "The Secret Life of Beatrix Potter." *National History* 81 (Oct. 1972): 38.

Godden, Rumer. "Beatrix Potter." *Horn Book* 42 (Aug. 1966): 390–398.

———. "An Imaginary Correspondence." *Horn Book* 39 (Aug. 1963): 369–375. Reprinted in Haviland. *Children and Literature*. Glenview, IL: Scott, Foresman, 1973; and in Egoff. *Only Connect*. 1st ed. Toronto: Oxford Univ. Press, 1969, pp. 62–69.

Goldthwaite, John. "The Black Rabbit: Part One." *Signal* 47 (May 1985): 86–111; "The Black Rabbit: Part Two." *Signal* 48 (Sept. 1985): 148–167. Reprinted in Goldthwaite. *The Natural History of Make-Believe*. London: Oxford Univ. Press, 1987.

———. "Sis Beatrix (Part One)." *Signal* 53 (May 1987): 117–137; "Sis Beatrix (Part Two)." *Signal* 54 (Sept. 1987): 161–177. Reprinted in Goldthwaite. *The Natural History of Make-Believe*. New York: Oxford Univ. Press, 1987.

Grahame, Eleanor. "Beatrix Potter." *Junior Bookshelf* 3 (1939): 171–175.

Greene, Graham. "Beatrix Potter." In *The Lost Childhood and Other Essays*. New York: Viking, 1952. Reprinted in Egoff. *Only Connect*. 2nd ed. New York: Oxford Univ. Press, 1980, pp. 258–268.

———. "Beatrix Potter: A Critical Estimate." *London Mercury* 27 (Jan. 1933): 241–245.

Hale, Robert D. "Musings." *Horn Book* 64 (Jan.–Feb. 1988): 100–101.

Hamer, D. "Journal of Beatrix Potter: Some Corrections." *Notes and Queries* 16 (July 1969): 221.

Hearn, Michael Patrick. "A Second Look: *Peter Rabbit* Redux." *Horn Book* 53 (Oct. 1977): 563–566.

Hodges, Margaret. "A Second Look: *The Tailor of Gloucester*." *Horn Book* 54 (Dec. 1978): 659–664.

Hough, Richard. "The Tailors of Gloucester." *Signal* 42 (Sept. 1983): 150–154.

Hurwitz, Johanna. "Will the Real *Peter Rabbit* Please Stand Up?" *Library Journal* 94 (Apr. 15, 1969): 1687–1688.

Inglis, Fred. *The Promise of Happiness*. New York: Cambridge Univ. Press, 1981, pp. 109–111.

Jordan, Alice M. "*The Fairy Caravan* by Beatrix Potter." *Horn Book* 5 (Nov. 1929): 9–11.

The Junior Book of Authors. 2nd ed. rev. Edited by Stanley J. Kunitz and Howard Haycraft. New York: Wilson, 1951, pp. 247–249.

Junior Bookshelf. Special Issue 30 (Aug. 1966).

Lane, Margaret. "The Art of Beatrix Potter." *New Statesman and Nation* 27 (Jan. 8, 1944): 23–24.

———. *The Magic Years of Beatrix Potter*. New York: Warne, 1978.

———. "On the Writing of Beatrix Potter's Life Story." *Horn Book* 22 (Nov.–Dec. 1946): 438–445.

———. *The Tale of Beatrix Potter: A Biography*. Originally published, 1946. New York: Warne, 1968; Penguin, 1986.

Lathrop, Dorothy P. "*The Art of Beatrix Potter*." *Horn Book* 31 (Oct. 1955): 331–337.

Linder, Leslie. "*The Art of Beatrix Potter* and How It Came to Be." *Horn Book* 31 (Oct. 1955): 338–356.

──────. "The Beatrix Potter Centenary Exhibit: 1866–1966." *Top of the News* 22 (June 1966): 367–375.

──────. "Beatrix Potter's Code Writing." *Horn Book* 39 (Apr. 1963): 141–155.

──────, comp. *History of the Writings of Beatrix Potter*. New York: Warne, 1971.

Linder, Leslie, and Herring, W. A., comps. *The Art of Beatrix Potter*. New York: Warne, 1972. Originally edited by Leslie Linder and Enid Linder, 1955.

MacDonald, Ruth K. *Beatrix Potter*. Boston: Twayne, 1986.

──────. "Beatrix Potter." In *Writers for Children: Critical Studies of Major Authors Since the Seventeenth Century*. Edited by Jane M. Bingham. New York: Scribner, 1988, pp. 439–446.

──────. "Why This Is Still 1893: *The Tale of Peter Rabbit* and Beatrix Potter's Manipulations of Timelessness." *Children's Literature Association Quarterly* 10 (Winter 1986): 185–187.

McKillop, A. "Beatrix Potter Centenary, 1866–1966." *Canadian Library* 23 (Jan. 1967): 277–280.

Maloney, Margaret Crawford, ed. *Dear Ivy, Dear June: Letters from Beatrix Potter*. Toronto: Other Press, 1977.

Mayer, A. M. "Authors are People: Beatrix Potter, Author, Artist, Farmer." *Instructor* 82 (Nov. 1972): 60–61.

Messer, Persis B. "Beatrix Potter: Classic Novelist of the Nursery: A Bibliographic Essay." *Elementary English* 45 (Mar. 1968): 325–333.

Miller, Bertha Mahony. "Beatrix Potter and Her Art." *Horn Book* 31 (Oct. 1955): 329.

──────. "Beatrix Potter and Her Nursery Classics." *Horn Book* 17 (May 1941): 230–238. Reprinted in Fryatt. *Horn Book Sampler*. Boston: Horn Book, 1959, pp. 228–233.

──────. "Beatrix Potter in Letters." *Horn Book* 20 (May 1944): 214–224.

Morse, Jane Crowell, ed. *Beatrix Potter's Americans: Selected Letters*. Boston: Horn Book, 1982.

Naumann, Nancy. "Beatrix Potter: Childhood Magic for Now and September." *Learning* 11 (Aug. 1982): 32–34.

The Oxford Companion to Children's Literature. Edited by Humphrey Carpenter and Mari Prichard. New York: Oxford Univ. Press, 1984, pp. 176–177, 420–424, 514.

Potter, Beatrix. *The History of the Tale of Peter Rabbit*. New York: Warne, 1877.

──────. *Journal of Beatrix Potter from 1881–1897: Transcribed from Her Code Writing by Leslie Linder*. New York: Warne, 1966.

──────. "The Lonely Hills." *Horn Book* 18 (May 1942): 153–156.

──────. "Over the Hills and Far Away." *Horn Book* 5 (Feb. 1929): 3–10.

──────. "The 'Roots' of the Peter Rabbit Tales." *Horn Book* 5 (May 1929): 69–72. Reprinted in Meek. *The Cool Web*. London: Bodley Head, 1977, pp. 188–191.

──────. "The Strength That Comes from the Hills." *Horn Book* 20 (Mar.–Apr. 1944): 77. Reprinted in Fryatt. *Horn Book Sampler*. Boston: Horn Book, 1959, pp. 28–29.

──────. "*The Tale of the Faithful Dove*." *Horn Book* 31 (Dec. 1955): 480–492.

──────. "Wag-by-Wall." *Horn Book* 20 (May 1944): 199–202.

Pritchard, Jane, and Riddle, Brian, eds. *Beatrix Potter Studies, I*. London: Beatrix Potter Society, 1986.

Pritchett, V. S. "Fur and Freedom." *New Statesman* 72 (July 22, 1966): 131–132.

Quinby, Jane. *Beatrix Potter: A Bibliographic Check List*. London: Sawyer, 1954.

Rahn, Suzanne. "Tailpiece: *The Tale of Two Bad Mice*." *Children's Literature*, vol. 12. New Haven, CT: Yale Univ. Press, 1984, pp. 78–91.

Richardson, Patrick. "Miss Potter and the Little Rubbish." *New Society* (July 7, 1966). Reprinted in Tucker. *Suitable for Children?* London: Chatto, 1976, pp. 173–178.

Robinson, Lolly. "Beatrix Potter: Artist and Storyteller." *Horn Book* 64 (May–June 1988): 408.

Sale, Roger. "Beatrix Potter." In *Fairy Tales and After*. Cambridge, MA: Harvard Univ. Press, 1978, pp. 82–83, 126–163.

Sendak, Maurice. "The Aliveness of Peter Rabbit." *Wilson Library Bulletin* 40 (Dec. 1965): 345–348.

Shaffer, Ellen. "Beatrix Potter Lives in the Philadelphia Free Library." *Horn Book* 42 (Aug. 1966): 401–405.

Sicroff, Seth. "Prickles under the Frock: The Art of Beatrix Potter." In *Children's Literature*, vol. 2. Storrs, CT: Journal of the Modern Language Association, 1973. Reprinted in *Reflections on Literature for Children*. Edited by Francelia Butler and Richard Rotert. Hamden, CT: Shoe String Press, 1984, pp. 39–44.

Stevens, Elizabeth H. "A Visit to Mrs. Tiggywinkle." *Horn Book* 34 (Apr. 1958): 131–136.

Stott, Jon C. *Children's Literature from A to Z*. New York: McGraw-Hill, 1984, p. 228.

"The Tailor of Gloucester." *Times Literary Supplement* (London), Jan. 8, 1944, p. 15.

Taylor, Judy. *Beatrix Potter: Artist, Storyteller and Countrywoman*. New York: Viking Press, 1987.

Tucker, Nicholas. *The Child and the Book*. New York: Cambridge Univ. Press, 1981, pp. 57–66.

Twentieth Century Children's Writers. 2nd ed. Edited by D. L. Kirkpatrick. New York: St. Martin's Press, 1983, pp. 624–626.

Weiner, R. W. "Beatrix Potter: Mrs. William Heelis." *Ontario Library Review* 41 (Aug. 1957): 202–204.

Yoshida, Shin-Ichi. "The World of Beatrix Potter as Seen Through the Eyes of a Japanese Visitor." *International Library Review* 5 (Apr. 1973): 225–228.

Pratt, (Murray) Fletcher

De Camp, L. Sprague. *Literary Swordsmen and Sorcerers: The Makers of Heroic Fantasy*. Sauk City, WI: Arkham House, 1976.

Pratt, Fletcher. "A Critique of Science Fiction." In *Modern Science Fiction*. 2nd ed. Edited by Reginal Bretnor. Chicago: Advent, 1979 pp. 73–90.

Schuyler, William M., Jr. "Recent Developments in Spell Construction." In *The Aesthetics of Fantasy Literature and Art*. Edited by Roger C. Schlobin. South Bend, IN: Notre Dame Univ. Press, 1982, pp. 237–248.

Stableford, Brian M. "L. Sprague de Camp and Fletcher Pratt." In *Supernatural Fiction Writers: Fantasy and Horror*, vol. 2. Edited by E. F. Bleiler. New York: Scribner, 1985, pp. 925–932.

Twentieth-Century Science Fiction Writers. 2nd ed. Edited by Curtis C. Smith. Chicago: St. James Press, 1986, pp. 577–579.

Watson, Christine. *"The Well of the Unicorn."* In *Survey of Modern Fantasy Literature*, vol. 5. Edited by Frank N. Magill. Englewood Cliffs, NJ: Salem Press, 1983, pp. 2097–2101.

Preussler, Otfried

Fourth Book of Junior Authors and Illustrators. Edited by Doris De Montreville and Elizabeth D. Crawford. New York: Wilson, 1978, pp. 290–291.

Preussler, Otfried. "My Partner and I." *Bookbird* 10, no. 4 (1972): 22–23.

———. "What You Write for Children: Diversity and Limitations of Children's Literature." *Bookbird* 13, no. 4 (1975): 3–5.

Price, Susan

Twentieth Century Children's Writers. 2nd ed. Edited by D. L. Kirkpatrick. New York: St. Martin's Press, 1983, p. 629.

Provensen, Alice, and Provensen, Martin

"The Provensens: Book Artists for Children." *Publishers Weekly* 186 (July 13, 1964): 111–112.
Third Book of Junior Authors. Edited by Doris De Montreville and Donna Hill. New York: Wilson, 1972, pp. 231–232.

Pushkin, Alexander Sergeevich

The Oxford Companion to Children's Literature. Edited by Humphrey Carpenter and Mari Prichard. New York: Oxford Univ. Press, 1984, p. 432.

Pyle, Howard

Abbott, Charles D. *Howard Pyle: A Chronicle.* New York: Harper & Row, 1925.
Doyle, Brian. *The Who's Who of Children's Literature.* New York: Schocken, 1968, pp. 225–227.
Elzea, Rowland. "Howard Pyle's Manuscripts: The Delaware Art Museum." *Children's Literature Association Quarterly* 8 (Summer 1983): 10.
Helbig, Alethea K., and Perkins, Agnes Regan. *Dictionary of American Children's Fiction, 1859–1959.* Westport, CT: Greenwood Press, 1985, pp. 415–416.
Kirkus, Virginia. "Howard Pyle: A Backwards Glance." *Horn Book* 5 (Nov. 1929): 37–39.
May, Jill P. "Howard Pyle." In *American Writers for Children before 1900. Dictionary of Literary Biography,* vol. 42. Detroit: Gale, 1985, pp. 295–307.
———. "Howard Pyle." In *Writers for Children: Critical Studies of Major Authors since the Seventeenth Century.* Edited by Jane M. Bingham. New York: Scribner, 1988, pp. 447–454.
———. "Pyle's Fairy Tales: Folklore Remade." *Children's Literature Association Quarterly* 8 (Summer 1983): 19–21.
———. "Special Section: Howard Pyle Commemorative." *Children's Literature Association Quarterly* 8 (Summer 1983): 9–34.
Morse, Willard S., and Brincklé, Gertrude, comps. *Howard Pyle: A Record of His Illustrations and Writings* (reproduction of 1921 ed.). Detroit: Singing Tree Press, 1969.
Nesbitt, Elizabeth. *Howard Pyle.* New York: Walck, 1966. Reprinted in Roger Lancelyn Green, Anthea Bell, and Elizabeth Nesbitt. *Lewis Carroll, E. Nesbit, and Howard Pyle.* London: Bodley Head, 1968.
Nodelman, Perry. "Pyle's Sweet, Thin, Clear Tune: *The Garden behind the Moon.*" *Children's Literature Association Quarterly* 8 (Summer 1983): 22–25.
Oakley, Thornton. "Howard Pyle." *Horn Book* 7 (May 1931): 91–97.
The Oxford Companion to Children's Literature. Edited by Humphrey Carpenter and Mari Prichard. New York: Oxford Univ. Press, 1984, pp. 433–435.
Pitz, Henry C. *Howard Pyle: Writer, Illustrator, Founder of the Brandywine School.* New York: Potter, 1975.
Pyle, Howard. "When I Was a Little Boy." *Woman's Home Companion* 39 (Apr. 1912): 5. Reprinted in Phyllis Reid Fenner. *Something Shared: Children and Books.* New York: John Day, 1959, pp. 6–12.

Stott, Jon C. *Children's Literature from A to Z.* New York: McGraw-Hill, 1984, p. 232.
Twentieth Century Children's Writers. 2nd ed. Edited by D. L. Kirkpatrick. New York: St. Martin's Press, 1983, p. 883.
Yitz, Robert. "Howard Pyle's America." *Children's Literature Association Quarterly* 8 (Summer 1983): 15–16, 34.

Pyle, Katharine

The Junior Book of Authors. 2nd ed. rev. Edited by Stanley J. Kunitz and Howard Haycraft. New York: Wilson, 1951, pp. 251–252.

Quackenbush, Robert M(ead)

Fourth Book of Junior Authors and Illustrators. Edited by Doris De Montreville and Elizabeth D. Crawford. New York: Wilson, 1978, pp. 293–294.

Raskin, Ellen

Bach, Alice. "Ellen Raskin: Some Clues About Her Life." *Horn Book* 61 (Mar.–Apr. 1985): 162–167.
Flanagan, Dennis. "The Raskin Conglomerate." *Horn Book* 55 (Aug. 1979): 392–395.
Helbig, Alethea K., and Perkins, Agnes Regan. *Dictionary of American Children's Fiction, 1960–1984.* Westport, CT: Greenwood Press, 1986, pp. 212, 648.
Herman, Gertrude. "A Picture Is Worth Several Hundred Words." *Horn Book* 62 (July–Aug. 1986): 479. Discusses *Figgs and Phantoms.*
Hieatt, Constance B. "The Mystery of *Figgs and Phantoms.*" In *Children's Literature,* vol. 13. New Haven, CT: Yale Univ. Press, 1985, pp. 128–138.
Hopkins, Lee Bennet. "Ellen Raskin." In *Books Are by People.* New York: Citation Press, 1969, pp. 226–229.
Karrenbrock, Marilyn H. "Ellen Raskin." In *American Writers for Children since 1960: Fiction. Dictionary of Literary Biography,* vol. 52. Detroit: Gale, 1986, pp. 314–324.
Raskin, Ellen. "Characters and Other Clues." *Horn Book* 54 (Dec. 1978): 620–625.
———. "The Creative Spirit and Children's Literature: A Literary Symposium." *Wilson Library Bulletin* 53 (Oct. 1978): 152–154.
———. "Me and Blake, Blake and Me." In *Innocence & Experience.* Edited by Barbara Harrison and Gregory Maguire. New York: Lothrop, 1987, pp. 347–353.
———. "Newbery Award Acceptance." *Horn Book* 55 (Aug. 1979): 385–391.
———. "Profile of an Author: Ellen Raskin." *Top of the News* 28 (June 1972): 394–398.
Roginski, Jim. *Behind the Covers: Interviews with Authors and Illustrators of Books for Children and Young Adults.* Littleton, CO: Libraries Unlimited, 1985, pp. 167–176.
———, ed. *Newbery and Caldecott Medalists and Honor Book Winners.* Littleton, CO: Libraries Unlimited, 1982, pp. 215–216.
Stott, Jon C. *Children's Literature from A to Z.* New York: McGraw-Hill, 1984, p. 236.
Third Book of Junior Authors. Edited by Doris De Montreville and Donna Hill. New York: Wilson, 1972, pp. 235–236.
Twentieth Century Children's Writers. 2nd ed. Edited by D. L. Kirkpatrick. New York: St. Martin's Press, 1983, pp. 639–640.

Rawlings (Baskin), Marjorie Kinnan

Bellman, Samuel I. *Marjorie Kinnan Rawlings*. Boston: Twayne, 1974.

————. "Writing Literature for Young People: Marjorie Kinnan Rawlings's 'Secret River' of the Imagination." *Costerus* 9 (1973): 19–27.

Bigelow, Gordon E. *Frontier Eden: The Literary Career of Marjorie Kinnan Rawlings*. Gainesville: Univ. of Florida, 1966.

————. "Marjorie Kinnan Rawlings's Wilderness." *Sewanee Review* 73 (Spring 1965): 299–310.

Cech, John. "Marjorie Kinnan Rawlings's *The Secret River: A Fairy Tale, a Place, a Life.*" *Southern Studies* 19 (1977): 29–58.

Galbraith, Lachlan N. "Marjorie Kinnan Rawlings's *The Secret River*." *Elementary English* 52 (Apr. 1975): 455–459.

Helbig, Alethea K., and Perkins, Agnes Regan. *Dictionary of American Children's Fiction, 1859–1959*. Westport, CT: Greenwood Press, 1985, p. 425.

Kilgo, Reese Danley. "Marjorie Kinnan Rawlings." In Cech. *American Writers for Children, 1900–1960. Dictionary of Literary Biography*, vol. 22. Detroit: Gale, 1983, pp. 282–285.

Nichols, L. "Talk with Mrs. Rawlings." *New York Times Book Review*, Sect. 7, Feb. 1, 1953, p. 1.

Perkins, Agnes Regan. "Marjorie Kinnan Rawlings." In *Writers for Children: Critical Studies of Major Authors since the Seventeenth Century*. Edited by Jane M. Bingham. New York: Scribner, 1988, pp. 463–468.

Roginski, Jim, ed. *Newbery and Caldecott Medalists and Honor Book Winners*. Littleton, CO: Libraries Unlimited, 1982, pp. 216–217.

Third Book of Junior Authors. Edited by Doris De Montreville and Donna Hill. New York: Wilson, 1972, pp. 237–239.

Twentieth Century Children's Writers. 2nd ed. Edited by D. L. Kirkpatrick. New York: St. Martin's Press, 1983, p. 640.

Williams, William Carlos. "To the Ghost of Marjorie Kinnan Rawlings." *Virginia Quarterly Review* 36 (Fall 1960): 579–580.

York, Lamar. "Marjorie Kinnan Rawlings's Rivers." *Southern Literary Journal* 9 (Spring 1977): 91–107.

Ray, Mary (Eva Pedder)

Twentieth Century Children's Writers. 2nd ed. Edited by D. L. Kirkpatrick. New York: St. Martin's Press, 1983, pp. 640–642.

Rayner, Mary (Yorna, née Grigson)

Fifth Book of Junior Authors and Illustrators. Edited by Sally Holmes Holtze. New York: Wilson, 1983, pp. 254–255.

Twentieth Century Children's Writers. 2nd ed. Edited by D. L. Kirkpatrick. New York: St. Martin's Press, 1983, p. 642.

Reeves, James (pseud. of John Morris Reeves)

Butts, Dennis. "James Reeves: The Truthful Poet." *Junior Bookshelf* 30 (Dec. 1966): 358–363.

Hutton, M. "Writers for Children: James Reeves." *School Librarian* 14 (July 1966): 139–146.

The Oxford Companion to Children's Literature. Edited by Humphrey Carpenter and Mari Prichard. New York: Oxford Univ. Press, 1984, pp. 445–446.
Robbins, Sidney. "Interpreting in Sharing—James Reeves: *The Cold Flame.*" *Children's Literature in Education* 2 (July 1970): 7–14.
Third Book of Junior Authors. Edited by Doris De Montreville and Donna Hill. New York: Wilson, 1972, pp. 240–241.
Twentieth Century Children's Writers. 2nd ed. Edited by D. L. Kirkpatrick. New York: St. Martin's Press, 1983, pp. 646–649.

Reid Banks, Lynne

Rustin, Michael. "The Maternal Capacities of a Small Boy: *The Indian in the Cupboard.*" In *Narratives of Love and Loss.* London: Verso, 1987, pp. 104–118.
Twentieth Century Children's Writers. 2nd ed. Edited by D. L. Kirkpatrick. New York: St. Martin's Press, 1983, pp. 650–651.

Rhys, Mimpsy

Seaman, Louise H. "Mimpsy Rhys." *Horn Book* 5 (Nov. 1929): 95–99.

Richler, Mordecai

Nodelman, Perry. "*Jacob Two-Two* and the Satisfactions of Paranoia." *Canadian Children's Literature* 15–16 (1980): 31–37.
Parr, John. "Richler Rejuvenated." *Canadian Children's Literature* 1 (Autumn 1975): 96–102.
Richler, Mordecai. "Writing *Jacob Two-Two.*" *Canadian Children's Literature* 78 (Autumn 1978): 6–8.
Stott, Jon C. "Midsummer Night's Dreams: Fantasy and Self-Realization in Children's Fiction." *The Lion and the Unicorn* 1, no. 2 (Fall 1977): 25–39.

Rinkoff, Barbara (Jean)

Helbig, Alethea K., and Perkins, Agnes Regan. *Dictionary of American Children's Fiction, 1960–1984.* Westport, CT: Greenwood Press, 1986, p. 554.

Robbins, Ruth

Third Book of Junior Authors. Edited by Doris De Montreville and Donna Hill. New York: Wilson, 1972, pp. 241–242.

Roberts, Keith (John Kingston)

Hurst, L. J. "A Timeless Dance: Keith Roberts' *Pavane* Re-Examined." *Vector* 124/125 (1985): 17–19.
Kincaid, Paul. "A Mosaic of Worlds." *Vector* 132 (1986): 2–5.
Peek, Bernie. "Exercises in Landscape: An Overview of the Work of Keith Roberts." *Vector* 132 (1986): 12–13.
Roberts, Keith. "The Chalk Giant." *Vector* 132 (1986): 6–8.

Robinson, Joan (Mary) G(ale Thomas)

Crouch, Marcus. *The Nesbit Tradition.* London: Benn, 1972, pp. 208–210.

Doyle, Brian. *The Who's Who of Children's Literature.* New York: Schocken, 1968, pp. 234–235.

Twentieth Century Children's Writers. 2nd ed. Edited by D. L. Kirkpatrick. New York: St. Martin's Press, 1983, pp. 663–664.

Rodgers (Guettel), Mary

Fifth Book of Junior Authors and Illustrators. Edited by Sally Holmes Holtze. New York: Wilson, 1983, pp. 267–269.

Helbig, Alethea K., and Perkins, Agnes Regan. *Dictionary of American Children's Fiction, 1960–1984.* Westport, CT: Greenwood Press, 1986, pp. 53–54, 223–224, 558–559.

Hopkins, Lee Bennett. "*Freaky Friday* from Book to Film." *Teacher* 95 (Oct. 1977): 80–82.

Kaye, M. J. "Mary Rodgers: An Interview." *Top of the News* 40 (Winter 1984): 155–162.

Twentieth Century Children's Writers. 2nd ed. Edited by D. L. Kirkpatrick. New York: St. Martin's Press, p. 664.

Rounds, Glen (Harold)

Bader, Barbara. *American Picturebooks from Noah's Ark to the Beast Within.* New York: Macmillan, 1976, pp. 147–151.

Freeman, Russell. "Glen Rounds and Holiday House." *Horn Book* 61 (Mar.–Apr. 1985): 222–225.

The Junior Book of Authors. 2nd ed. rev. Edited by Stanley J. Kunitz and Howard Haycraft. New York: Wilson, 1951, pp. 261–262.

Twentieth Century Children's Writers. 2nd ed. Edited by D. L. Kirkpatrick. New York: St. Martin's Press, 1983, pp. 668–670.

Ruskin, John

Burns, Marjorie Jean. "Victorian Fantasists from Ruskin to Lang: A Study in Ambivalence." Ph.D. dissertation, University of California, Berkeley, 1978.

Butler, Francelia. "From Fantasy to Reality: Ruskin's *King of the Golden River,* St. George's Guild and Ruskin, Tennessee." In *Children's Literature,* vol. 1. Storrs, CT: Journal of the Modern Language Association, 1972, pp. 62–73.

Coyle, William. "Ruskin's *King of the Golden River:* A Victorian Fairy Tale." In *The Scope of the Fantastic—Culture, Biography, Themes, Children's Literature.* Edited by Robert A. Collins and Howard D. Pearce. Westport, CT: Greenwood Press, 1985, pp. 85–90.

Doyle, Brian. *The Who's Who of Children's Literature.* New York: Schocken, 1968, pp. 235–236.

Filstrup, James Merrill. "Thirst for Enchanted Views in Ruskin's *The King of the Golden River.*" In *Children's Literature,* vol. 8. New Haven, CT: Yale Univ. Press, 1980, pp. 68–79.

Hearn, Michael Patrick. "Mr. Ruskin and Miss Greenaway." *Children's Literature* 8 (1980): 22–34. Reprinted in *Reflections on Literature for Children.* Edited by Francelia Butler and Richard Rotert. Hamden, CT: Shoe String Press, 1984, pp. 182–190.

Helson, Ravenna, and Proysen, Alf. "The Psychological Origins of Fantasy for Children in Mid-Victorian England." *Children's Literature,* vol. 3. Storrs, CT: Journal of the Modern Language Association, 1974, pp. 67–76.

Knoepflmacher, U. C. "The Return to Childhood through Fairy Tale in Ruskin's *King of the Golden River.*" In *Children's Literature,* vol. 13. New Haven, CT: Yale Univ. Press, 1985, pp. 3–30.

Landow, George P. "And the World Became Strange: Realms of Literary Fantasy." In Diane L. Johnson. *Fantastic Illustration and Design in Britain, 1850–1930.* Providence: Rhode Island School of Design, 1979, pp. 9–43. Reprinted in *Georgia Review* 33 (Spring 1979): 7–42.

―――. *"The King of the Golden River."* In *Survey of Modern Fantasy Literature,* vol. 2. Edited by Frank N. Magill. Englewood Cliffs, NJ: Salem Press, 1983, pp. 852–854.

Leland, Lowell P. "John Ruskin." In *Writers for Children: Critical Studies of Major Authors since the Seventeenth Century.* Edited by Jane M. Bingham. New York: Scribner, 1988, pp. 493–496.

Miller, Patricia. "The Importance of Being Earnest: The Fairy Tale in 19th Century England." *Children's Literature Association Quarterly* 7 (Summer 1982): 11–14.

The Oxford Companion to Children's Literature. Edited by Humphrey Carpenter and Mari Prichard. New York: Oxford Univ. Press, 1984, pp. 293–294, 464.

Ruskin, John. "Fairy Land: Mrs. Allingham and Kate Greenaway." In *The Library Edition of the Works of John Ruskin,* vol. 53. Edited by E. T. Cook and Alexander Wedderburn. London: Longman, 1903–1912, pp. 327–349.

―――. "Fairy Stories." In *The Library Edition of the Works of Ruskin,* vol. 19. Edited by E. T. Cook and Alexander Wedderburn. London: Longman, 1903–1912, pp. 233–239. Reprinted in *Signal* 8 (May 1972): 81–86, by Lance Salway; Lance Salway. *A Peculiar Gift.* Harmondsworth, Middlesex: Kestrel, 1976, pp. 127–132; *Masterworks of Children's Literature,* vol. 6. New York: Stonehill/Chelsea House, 1984, pp. 163–169.

―――. *"The King of the Golden River; or The Black Brothers."* In *Masterworks of Children's Literature,* vol. 6. New York: Stonehill/Chelsea House, 1984, pp. 1–25.

―――. "Praeterita." In *The Library Edition of the Works of John Ruskin,* vol. 35. Edited by E. T. Cook and Alexander Wedderburn. London: Longman, 1903–1912.

Saberhagen, Fred (Thomas)

Twentieth-Century Science Fiction Writers. 2nd ed. Edited by Curtis C. Smith. Chicago: St. James Press, 1986, pp. 621–623.

Wilgus, Neal. "An Interview with Fred Saberhagen." *Science Fiction Review* 35 (1980): 15–16.

Saint-Exupéry, Antoine (Jean Baptiste Marie Roger), de

Arnold, James W. "Musical Fantasy: *The Little Prince.*" In *Shadows of the Magic Lamp: Fantasy and Science Fiction in Film.* Edited by George Slusser and Eric S. Rabkin. Carbondale: Southern Illinois Univ. Press, 1985.

Brand, Patricia Petrus. "The Modern French Fairy Tale: Aspects of 'Le Merveilleux' in Aymé, Supervielle, Saint-Exupéry and Sabatier." Ph.D. dissertation, University of Colorado at Boulder, 1983.

Breaux, Adele. *Saint-Exupéry in America, 1942–1943: A Memoir.* Rutherford, NJ: Fairleigh Dickinson Univ. Press, 1971.

Cate, Curtis. *Antoine de Saint-Exupéry: His Life and Times.* New York: G. P. Putnam, 1970.

Dodd, Anne W. *"The Little Prince:* A Study for Seventh Grade in Interpretation of Literature." *Elementary English* 46 (Oct. 1969): 772–776.

Fourth Book of Junior Authors and Illustrators. Edited by Doris De Montreville and Elizabeth D. Crawford. New York: Wilson, 1978, pp. 300–302.

Gagnon, Laurence. "Webs of Concern: Heidegger, *The Little Prince,* and *Charlotte's Web.*" In *Children's Literature,* vol. 2. Storrs, CT: Journal of the Modern Language Association, 1973, pp. 61–66.

Higgins, James Edward. "Five Authors of Mystical Fancy for Children: A Critical Study." Ed.D. dissertation, Columbia University, 1965.

————. "*The Little Prince:* A Legacy." *Elementary English* 37 (Dec. 1960): 514–515, 572.

Hürlimann, Bettina. "*The Little Prince* from Outer Space: An Attempt to Describe Antoine de Saint-Exupéry's *Le Petit Prince.*" In *Three Centuries of Children's Books in Europe.* Cleveland: World, 1968, pp. 93–98.

Mooney, Philip. "*The Little Prince,* a Story for Our Time." *America* 121 (Dec. 20, 1969): 610–611, 614.

The Oxford Companion to Children's Literature. Edited by Humphrey Carpenter and Mari Prichard. New York: Oxford Univ. Press, 1984, pp. 318–319.

Robinson, Joy D. Marie. *Antoine de Saint-Exupéry.* Boston: Twayne, 1984.

Smith, Louisa A. "*The Little Prince.*" In *Survey of Modern Fantasy Literature,* vol. 2. Edited by Frank N. Magill. Englewood Cliffs, NJ: Salem Press, 1983, pp. 891–893.

Sánchez-Silva, José Mariá

Hürlimann, Bettina. *Three Centuries of Children's Books in Europe.* Cleveland: World, 1968, pp. 86–87.

Third Book of Junior Authors. Edited by Doris De Montreville and Donna Hill. New York: Wilson, 1972, pp. 244–246.

Sandburg, Carl (August)

Lynn, Joanne L. "Hyacinths and Biscuits in the Village of Liver and Onions: Sandburg's *Rootabaga Stories.*" In *Children's Literature,* vol. 8. New Haven, CT: Yale Univ. Press, 1980, pp. 118–132.

Massee, May. "Carl Sandburg as a Writer for Children." *Elementary English Review* 5 (Feb. 1928): 40–42.

Mitgang, Herbert, ed. *The Letters of Carl Sandburg.* New York: Harcourt Brace Jovanovich, 1968.

The Oxford Companion to Children's Literature. Edited by Humphrey Carpenter and Mari Prichard. New York: Oxford Univ. Press, 1984, p. 460.

Perkins, Agnes Regan. "Carl Sandburg." In *Writers for Children: Critical Studies of Major Authors since the Seventeenth Century.* Edited by Jane M. Bingham. New York: Scribner, 1988, pp. 503–510.

Sandburg, Carl. *Always the Young Strangers.* New York: Harcourt Brace Jovanovich, 1952.

Sayers, Frances Clark. "Rootabaga Processional." *Horn Book* 8 (May 1932): 124–130.

Sauer, Julia L(ina)

Elleman, Barbara. "A Second Look: *Fog Magic.*" *Horn Book* 56 (Oct. 1980): 548–551.

Helbig, Alethea K., and Perkins, Agnes Regan. *Dictionary of American Children's Fiction, 1859–1959.* Westport, CT: Greenwood Press, 1985, pp. 166, 454.

More Junior Authors. Edited by Muriel Fuller. New York: Wilson, 1963, pp. 174–175.

Roginski, Jim, ed. *Newbery and Caldecott Medalists and Honor Book Winners.* Littleton, CO: Libraries Unlimited, 1982, p. 224.

Sauer, Julia L. "Making the World Safe for the Janey Larkins." In Robinson. *Readings about Children's Literature.* New York: McKay, 1966, pp. 318–327.

———. "So Close to the Gulls." *Horn Book* 25 (Sept.–Oct. 1949): 361–369.

Twentieth Century Children's Writers. 2nd ed. Edited by D. L. Kirkpatrick. New York: St. Martin's Press, 1983, p. 673.

Sawyer (Durand), Ruth

Cecile, Mother Mary, S. H. C. J. "Regina Medal Presentation." *Horn Book* 41 (Oct. 1965): 477.

Haviland, Virginia. *Ruth Sawyer.* New York: Walck, 1985.

Helbig, Alethea K. "Ruth Sawyer." In *Writers for Children: Critical Studies of Major Authors since the Seventeenth Century.* Edited by Jane M. Bingham. New York: Scribner, 1988, pp. 511–518.

Helbig, Alethea K., and Perkins, Agnes Regan. *Dictionary of American Children's Fiction, 1859–1959.* Westport, CT: Greenwood Press, 1985, pp. 148, 454–455.

Horn Book 41 (Oct. 1965): 463, 474–486. Special issue.

Jewett, E. "Ruth Sawyer Durand." *Catholic Library World* 36 (Feb. 1965): 355–357.

The Junior Book of Authors. 2nd ed. rev. Edited by Stanley J. Kunitz and Howard Haycraft. New York: Wilson, 1951, pp. 266–267.

McCloskey, Margaret Durand. "Our Fair Lady!" *Horn Book* 41 (Oct. 1965): 481–486.

Moore, Anne Carroll. "Ruth Sawyer, Storyteller." *Horn Book* 12 (Jan. 1936): 34–38.

Mulholland, Marion J. "Ruth Sawyer." In Cech. *American Writers for Children, 1900–1960. Dictionary of Literary Biography,* vol. 22. Detroit: Gale, 1983, pp. 294–298.

Newbery Medal Books: 1922–1955. Edited by Bertha Mahony Miller and Elinor Whitney Field. Boston: Horn Book, 1957, pp. 145–156.

Overton, Jacqueline. *"This Way to Christmas* with Ruth Sawyer." *Horn Book* 20 (Nov.–Dec. 1944): 447–460.

The Oxford Companion to Children's Literature. Edited by Humphrey Carpenter and Mari Prichard. New York: Oxford Univ. Press, 1984, p. 469.

Robinson, Beryl Y. "Editorial: Ruth Sawyer, 1880–1970." *Horn Book* 46 (Aug. 1970): 347.

———. "To Ruth Sawyer." *Horn Book* 41 (Oct. 1965): 478–480.

Roginski, Jim, ed. *Newbery and Caldecott Medalists and Honor Book Winners.* Littleton, CO: Libraries Unlimited, 1982, pp. 224–226.

"Ruth Sawyer Durand: A Checklist of Her *Horn Book* Articles, Editorials, Stories, and Poems; Articles and Editorials About Her." *Horn Book* 46 (Aug. 1970): 431.

Sawyer, Ruth. "Editorial: The Miracle of the Story Hour." *Horn Book* 34 (Feb. 1958): 15.

———. "The Laura Ingalls Wilder Award Acceptance." *Horn Book* 41 (Oct. 1965): 474–476.

———. "Newbery Medal Acceptance." *Horn Book* 13 (Sept. 1937): 251–255.

———. "On Reading the Bible Aloud." *Horn Book* 21 (Mar.–Apr. 1945): 99–107.

———. "Remarks Upon Receiving the Newbery Award." *ALA Bulletin* 31 (Oct. 15, 1937): 872–874.

———. "Sharers of a Heritage." *Catholic Library World* 37 (Sept. 1965): 15–17. Regina Award Acceptance Speech.

———. "Wee Meg Barnileg and the Fairies." *Horn Book* 15 (Sept. 1939): 310–318.

Sullivan, Frances. "The Laura Ingalls Wilder Award Presentation." *Horn Book* 41 (Oct. 1965): 474.

Sullivan, Sheila R. "Fairy Gold in a Storyteller's Yarns." *Elementary English* 35 (Dec. 1958): 502–507.

Twentieth Century Children's Writers. 2nd ed. Edited by D. L. Kirkpatrick. New York: St. Martin's Press, 1983, pp. 674–676.
Viguers, Ruth Hill. "Editorial: For Ruth Sawyer." *Horn Book* 37 (Dec. 1961): 521.

Sayers, Frances Clarke

Helbig, Alethea K., and Perkins, Agnes Regan. *Dictionary of American Children's Fiction, 1859–1959.* Westport, CT: Greenwood Press, 1985, pp. 362–363, 455.
The Junior Book of Authors. 2nd ed. rev. Edited by Stanley J. Kunitz and Howard Haycraft. New York: Wilson, 1951, pp. 267–268.
Sayers, Frances Clarke. "Of Memory and Muchness." *Horn Book* 20 (May 1944): 153–163.
———. "A Skimming of Memory." *Horn Book* 52 (June 1976): 270–275.
———. "A Time to Begin." *Horn Book* 50 (Dec. 1974): 674–678.
———. "Walt Disney Accused: An Interview with Frances Clarke Sayers." *Horn Book* 41 (Dec. 1965): 602–611.

Scarborough, Elizabeth Ann

Sullivan, C.W., III. "Traditional Ballads and Modern Children's Fantasy: Some Comments on Structure and Intent." *Children's Literature Association Quarterly* 11 (Fall 1986): 145–147.

Schlein, Miriam

More Junior Authors. Edited by Muriel Fuller. New York: Wilson, 1963, pp. 175–176.

Schrank, Joseph

Ward, Martha E., and Marquardt, Dorothy A. *Authors of Books for Young People.* 2nd ed. Metuchen, NJ: Scarecrow Press, 1971, pp. 455–456.

Scott, Evelyn

"Witch Perkins: A Symposium." *Horn Book* 5 (Nov. 1929): 30–32.

Sefton, Catherine (pseud. of Martin Waddell)

Twentieth Century Children's Writers. 2nd ed. Edited by D. L. Kirkpatrick. New York: St. Martin's Press, 1983, pp. 683–684.

Sègur, Comtesse de

Aiken, Joan. "The Comtesse de Sègur: 1799–1874." *Horn Book* 52 (Dec. 1976): 583–600.
Petrini, E. "Countess of Sègur." *Bookbird* 12, no. 3 (1974): 50–51.

Selden (Thompson), George

Fourth Book of Junior Authors and Illustrators. Edited by Doris De Montreville and Elizabeth D. Crawford. New York: Wilson, 1978, pp. 313–314.
Helbig, Alethea K., and Perkins, Agnes Regan. *Dictionary of American Children's*

Fiction, 1960–1984. Westport, CT: Greenwood Press, 1986, pp. 134, 233, 586–587, 679–680.

Hopkins, Lee Bennett. "George Selden." In *More Books by More People*. New York: Citation Press, 1974, pp. 303–307.

Potts, Lesley S. "George Selden." In *American Writers for Children since 1960: Fiction. Dictionary of Literary Biography*, vol. 52. Detroit: Gale, 1986, pp. 325–333.

Twentieth Century Children's Writers. 2nd ed. Edited by D. L. Kirkpatrick. New York: St. Martin's Press, 1983, pp. 684–685.

Sendak, Maurice (Bernard)

Bell, Anthea. "An Affectionate Analysis of *Higglety Pigglety Pop!*" *Horn Book* 44 (Apr. 1968): 151–154.

Braun, Saul. "Sendak Raises the Shade on Childhood." *New York Times Magazine*, June 7, 1970, p. 34.

Cech, John. "Maurice Sendak: Off the Page." *Horn Book* 62 (May–June, 1986): 305–313.

Chambers, Aidan. "Letter from England: Sendak on Show." *Horn Book* 52 (June 1976): 323–326.

Cott, Jonathan. "Maurice Sendak: King of All the Wild Things." In *Pipers at the Gates of Dawn*. New York: Random, 1983, pp. 41–87. Revised version of an interview in *Rolling Stone* 229 (Dec. 30, 1976): 55, 59.

De Luca, Geraldine. "Exploring the Levels of Childhood: The Allegorical Sensibility of Maurice Sendak." In *Children's Literature*, vol. 12. New Haven: Yale Univ. Press, 1984, pp. 3–24.

———. "Progression Through Contraries: The Triumphs of the Spirit in the Work of Maurice Sendak." In *Triumphs of the Spirit in Children's Literature*. Edited by Francelia Butler and Richard Rotert. Hamden, CT: Shoe String Press, 1986, pp. 142–149.

Dohm, J. H. "Twentieth Century Illustrators: Maurice Sendak." *Junior Bookshelf* 30 (Apr. 1966): 103–111.

Dooley, Patricia. " 'Fantasy Is the Core . . . ?'—Sendak." *Children's Literature Association Quarterly Newsletter* 1 (Autumn 1976): 1–4.

Ford, Roger H. " 'Let the Wild Rumpus Start!' " *Language Arts* 56, 4 (Apr. 1979): 386–393.

Galvin, Dallas. "Maurice Sendak Observes Children's Literature." *Harper's Bazaar* 106 (Dec. 1972): 102–103.

Griffin-Beale, Christopher. "In Search of *The Wild Things'* Pedigree." *Times Educational Supplement* (London), Jan. 30, 1976, pp. 44–45.

Harris, Muriel. "Impressions of Sendak." *Elementary English* 48, no. 7 (Nov. 1971): 825–832.

Haviland, Virginia. "Questions to an Artist Who Is Also an Author." *Quarterly Journal of the Library of Congress* 28 (Oct. 1971): 263–280. Reprinted, in part, in Miriam Hoffman and Eva Samuels. *Authors and Illustrators of Children's Books*. New York: Bowker, 1972, pp. 364–377; The Library of Congress, Washington, DC, 1972.

Hentoff, Nat. "Among the Wild Things." *New Yorker* 41 (Jan. 22, 1966): 39–40 ff. Reprinted in Egoff. *Only Connect*. 1st ed. New York: Oxford Univ. Press, 1969, pp. 323–345.

Hopkins, Lee Bennett. "Maurice Sendak." In *Books Are by People*. New York: Citation Press, 1969, pp. 250–254.

Hürlimann, Benita. "Maurice Sendak." *Graphis* 25 (1969–1970): 252–263 ff.

Lanes, Selma G. *The Art of Maurice Sendak*. New York: Abrams, 1980.

———. "The Art of Maurice Sendak: A Diversity of Influences Inform an Art for Children." *Artforum* 9 (May 1971): 70–73.

———. "Sendak at Fifty." *New York Times Book Review,* Apr. 29, 1979, pp. 23, 48–49.

"Maurice Sendak: Doctor of Fine Arts." *Horn Book* 60 (Aug. 1984): 515.

May, Jill P. "Sendak's American Hero." *Journal of Popular Culture* 12 (1978): 30–35.

More Junior Authors. Edited by Muriel Fuller. New York: Wilson, 1963, pp. 181–182.

Newbery and Caldecott Medal Books: 1966–1975. Edited by Lee Kingman. Boston: Horn Book, 1975, pp. 246–257.

Nordstrom, Ursula. "Maurice Sendak." *Library Journal,* Mar. 15, 1964, pp. 92–94.

O'Doherty, B. "Portrait of the Artist as a Young Alchemist." *New York Times Book Review,* sect. VII, pt. 2, May 12, 1963, p.3.

The Oxford Companion to Children's Literature. Edited by Humphrey Carpenter and Mari Prichard. New York: Oxford Univ. Press, 1984, pp. 474–477.

Roginski, Jim, ed. *Newbery and Caldecott Medalists and Honor Book Winners.* Littleton, CO: Libraries Unlimited, 1982, pp. 228–231.

Sendak, Maurice. "[Hans Christian Andersen Award] Acceptance Speech." *Bookbird* 8, no. 2 (1970): 6–7; *Times Literary Supplement,* July 2, 1970, p. 709.

———. "Caldecott Award Acceptance." *Horn Book* 40 (Aug. 1964): 345–351.

———. "Enamored of the Mystery." In *Innocence & Experience.* Edited by Barbara Harrison and Gregory Maguire. New York: Lothrop, 1986, pp. 362–374.

———. "I Don't Write Children's Books—I Just Know What Is in My Head." *Yale Alumni Review* (May 1972).

———. "1983 Laura Ingalls Wilder Award Acceptance Speech." *Top of the News* 39 (Summer 1983): 367–369; *Horn Book* 59 (Aug. 1983): 474–477.

———. "On the Importance of Imagination." *Claremont Reading Conference Yearbook* 29 (1965): 53–58.

———. "The Shape of Music." *New York Herald Tribune.* "Book Week Fall Children's Issue." Nov. 1, 1964, p. 1.

Shaw, Spencer G. "Laura Ingalls Wilder Award Presentation." *Horn Book* 59 (Aug. 1983): 471–473.

Steig, Michael. "Reading *Outside Over There.*" *Children's Literature,* vol. 13. New Haven, CT: Yale Univ. Press, 1985, pp. 139–153.

Stott, Jon C. *Children's Literature from A to Z.* New York: McGraw-Hill, 1984, p. 246.

———. "The Nature of Fantasy: A Conversation with Ruth Nichols, Susan Cooper, and Maurice Sendak." *World of Children's Books* 3, no. 2 (Fall 1978): 32–43.

Taylor, Mary-Agnes. "In Defense of *The Wild Things.*" *Horn Book* 46 (Dec. 1970): 642–646.

———. "Which Way to Castle Yonder?" *Children's Literature Association Quarterly* 12 (Fall 1987): 142–144. Discusses *Higglety Pigglety Pop!*

Twentieth Century Children's Writers. 2nd ed. Edited by D. L. Kirkpatrick. New York: St. Martin's Press, 1983, pp. 685–687.

Waller, Jennifer R. "Maurice Sendak and the Blakean Vision of Childhood." In *Children's Literature,* vol. 6. Philadelphia: Temple Univ. Press, 1977, pp. 130–140. Reprinted in *Reflections on Literature for Children.* Edited by Francelia Butler and Richard Rotert. Hamden, CT: Shoe String Press, 1984, pp. 260–268.

White, David E. "A Conversation with Maurice Sendak." *Horn Book* 56 (Apr. 1980): 145–155.

Wintle, Justin. "Where the *Wild Things* Come From: Interview: Maurice Sendak." *Times Educational Supplement* 3131 (May 30, 1975): 17.

Wintle, Justin, and Fisher, Emma. "Maurice Sendak." In *The Pied Pipers.* New York: Paddington Press, 1974, pp. 20–34.

Wolfe, Leo. "Maurice Sendak." *Horn Book* 40 (Aug. 1964): 351–354.

Seredy, Kate

Helbig, Alethea K. "Kate Seredy." In *Writers for Children: Critical Studies of Major Authors since the Seventeenth Century.* Edited by Jane M. Bingham. New York: Scribner, 1988, pp. 519–524.

Helbig, Alethea K., and Perkins, Agnes Regan. *Dictionary of American Children's Fiction, 1859–1959.* Westport, CT: Greenwood Press, 1985, pp. 461–462.

Higgins, James E. "Kate Seredy: Storyteller." *Horn Book* 44 (Apr. 1968): 162–168.

The Junior Book of Authors. 2nd ed. rev. Edited by Stanley J. Kunitz and Howard Haycraft. New York: Wilson, 1951, pp. 270–271.

Kassen, Aileen M. "Kate Seredy: A Person Worth Knowing." *Elementary English* 45 (Mar. 1968): 303–315. Reprinted in Miriam Hoffman and Eva Samuels. *Authors and Illustrators of Children's Books.* New York: Bowker, 1972, pp. 378–393.

"Kate Seredy." *Horn Book* 11 (July–Aug. 1935): 230–235.

Markey, Lois R. "Kate Seredy's World." *Elementary English* 29 (Dec. 1952): 451–457.

Piehl, Kathy. "Kate Seredy." In Cech. *American Writers for Children, 1900–1960. Dictionary of Literary Biography,* vol. 22. Detroit: Gale, 1985, pp. 299–306.

Roginski, Jim, ed. *Newbery and Caldecott Medalists and Honor Book Winners.* Littleton, CO: Libraries Unlimited, 1982, pp. 231–232.

Seredy, Kate. "The Country of *The Good Master.*" *Elementary English Review* 13 (May 1936): 167–168.

———. "Kate Seredy: A Letter about Her Books and Her Life." *Horn Book* (July–Aug. 1935): 239–235.

———. "Newbery Medal Acceptance." *Horn Book* 14 (July 1938): 226–229.

———. "A Small Eternal Flame." *Horn Book* 33 (Feb. 1957): 59–60.

Sutor, Peggy M. "Kate Seredy: A Bio-Bibliography." Master's thesis, Florida State University, 1955.

Thompson, B. J. "Kate Seredy." *Junior Bookshelf* 10 (July 1946): 49–52.

Twentieth Century Children's Writers. 2nd ed. Edited by D. L. Kirkpatrick. New York: St. Martin's Press, 1983, pp. 687–688.

"The White Stag." In Bertha Mahony Miller and Elinor Field. *Newbery Medal Books: 1922–1955.* Boston: Horn Book, 1957, pp. 157–165.

Serraillier, Ian (Lucien)

Third Book of Junior Authors. Edited by Doris De Montreville and Donna Hill. New York: Wilson, 1972, pp. 257–258.

Twentieth Century Children's Writers. 2nd ed. Edited by D. L. Kirkpatrick. New York: St. Martin's Press, 1983, pp. 688–690.

Seuss, Dr. (pseud. of Theodor Seuss Geisel)

Bader, Barbara. "Dr. Seuss." In *American Picturebooks from Noah's Ark to the Beast Within.* New York: Macmillan, 1976, pp. 302–312.

Bailey, John P., Jr. "Three Decades of Dr. Seuss." *Elementary English* 42 (Jan. 1965): 7–12.

Barrs, M. "Laughing Your Way Into Literacy; Dr. Seuss Books." *Times Educational Supplement* 3164 (Jan. 23, 1976): 20–21.

Cohn, R. "The Wonderful World of Dr. Seuss." *Saturday Evening Post* 230 (July 6, 1957): 17–19 ff.

Cott, Jonathan. "The Good Dr. Seuss." In *Pipers at the Gates of Dawn.* New York: Random, 1983, pp. 3–40.

Dempsey, D. "The Signature of Dr. Seuss." *The New York Times Book Review,* section 7, May 11, 1958, p. 2.

"Dr. Seuss' Success; Writing for Children." *Times Educational Supplement,* Oct. 19, 1962, pp. 2474–2489.

Dohm, Janice H. "The Curious Case of Dr. Seuss: A Minority Report from America." *Junior Bookshelf* 27, no. 6 (Dec. 1963): 323–329. Reprinted in *Top of the News* 21 (Jan. 1965): 151–155.

Doyle, Brian. *The Who's Who of Children's Literature.* New York: Schocken, 1968, pp. 241–243.

Estes, Glenn E. "Laura Ingalls Wilder Award Presentation." *Horn Book* 56 (Aug. 1980): 388–389.

Fadiman, Clifford. "A Party of One." *Holiday* 25 (Apr. 1959): 11 ff.

———. "Professionals and Confessionals: Dr. Seuss and Kenneth Grahame." In Egoff. *Only Connect.* 2nd ed. New York: Oxford Univ. Press, 1980, pp. 277–283.

Freeman, Donald. "Who Thunk You Up, Dr. Seuss?" *San Jose Mercury News.* "Parade" sect., June 15, 1969, pp. 12–13. Reprinted in Miriam Hoffman and Eva Samuels. *Authors and Illustrators of Children's Books.* New York: Bowker, 1972, pp. 165–171.

Hopkins, Lee Bennett. "Dr. Seuss." In *Books Are by People.* New York: Citation Press, 1969, pp. 255–258.

Jennings, C. R. "Dr. Seuss: What Am I Doing Here?" *Saturday Evening Post* 238 (Oct. 23, 1965): 105–109.

Kann, E. J., Jr. "Profiles: Children's Friend." *New Yorker* 36 (Dec. 17, 1960): 47–48 ff.

Kasindorf, M. "A Happy Accident." *Newsweek* 79 (Feb. 21, 1972): 100 ff.

King, Stephen. "Dr. Seuss and the Two Faces of Fantasy." *Fantasy Review* 68 (1984): 10–12.

Kuskin, Karla. "Seuss at Seventy-Five." *New York Times Book Review,* Apr. 29, 1979, pp. 23, 41–42.

Lanes, Selma. "Seuss for the Goose is Seuss for the Gander." In *Down the Rabbit Hole.* New York: Atheneum, 1971, pp. 79–89.

"The Logical Insanity of Dr. Seuss." *Time* 90 (Aug. 11, 1967): 58–59.

Lystad, M. "The World According to Dr. Seuss." *Childhood Today* 13 (May–June 1984): 19–22.

More Junior Authors. Edited by Muriel Fuller. New York: Wilson, 1963, pp. 182–183.

"Name—Ted Geisel." *Newsweek* 55 (June 20, 1960): 114–115.

Ort, Lorrene Love. "Theodor Seuss Geisel—The Children's Dr. Seuss." *Elementary English* 32 (Mar. 1955): 135–142.

The Oxford Companion to Children's Literature. Edited by Humphrey Carpenter and Mari Prichard. New York: Oxford Univ. Press, 1984, pp. 477–478.

Roginski, Jim, ed. *Newbery and Caldecott Medalists and Honor Book Winners.* Littleton, CO: Libraries Unlimited, 1982, pp. 233–236.

Sale, Roger. *Fairy Tales and After.* Cambridge, MA: Harvard Univ. Press, 1978, pp. 8–12.

Seuss, Dr. "1980 Laura Ingalls Wilder Award Acceptance Speech." *Top of the News* 36 (Summer 1980): 397–399; *Horn Book* 56 (Aug. 1980): 390–391.

Stewart-Gordon, J. "Dr. Seuss: Fanciful Sage of Childhood." *Reader's Digest* 100 (Apr. 1972): 141–145.

Stott, Jon C. *Children's Literature from A to Z.* New York: McGraw-Hill, 1984, p. 250.

Twentieth Century Children's Writers. 2nd ed. Edited by D. L. Kirkpatrick. New York: St. Martin's Press, 1983, pp. 692–694.

"The Wacky World of Dr. Seuss." *Life Magazine* 46 (April 6, 1959): 107–108 ff.
Wintle, Justin, and Fisher, Emma. "Dr. Seuss." In *The Pied Pipers*. New York: Paddington Press, 1974, pp. 113–123.

Severn, David (pseud. of David S[torr] Unwin)

The Oxford Companion to Children's Literature. Edited by Humphrey Carpenter and Mari Prichard. New York: Oxford Univ. Press, 1984, p. 479.
Twentieth Century Children's Writers. 2nd ed. Edited by D. L. Kirkpatrick. New York: St. Martin's Press, 1983, pp. 694–695.

Shannon (Wing), Monica

The Junior Book of Authors. 2nd ed. rev. Edited by Stanley J. Kunitz and Howard Haycraft. New York: Wilson, 1951, pp. 272–273.
Miller, Elizabeth Cleveland. "Monica Shannon: An Appreciation." *Horn Book* 11 (Mar. 1935): 73–81.
Roginski, Jim, ed. *Newbery and Caldecott Medalists and Honor Book Winners.* Littleton, CO: Libraries Unlimited, 1982, p. 238.
Shannon, Monica. "The Goat Who Owned Me." *Horn Book* 10 (Mar. 1934): 117–119.
———. "A Hunt Breakfast-Authors' Symposium." *Horn Book* 2 (Nov. 1926): 37–38.
Twentieth Century Children's Writers. 2nd ed. Edited by D. L. Kirkpatrick. New York: St. Martin's Press, 1983, pp. 696–697.

Shapiro, Irwin

The Junior Book of Authors. 2nd ed. rev. Edited by Stanley J. Kunitz and Howard Haycraft. New York: Wilson, 1951, pp. 273–274.

Sharmat, Marjorie Weinman

Fifth Book of Junior Authors and Illustrators. Edited by Sally Holmes Holtze. New York: Wilson, 1983, pp. 282–283.
Twentieth Century Children's Writers. 2nd ed. Edited by D. L. Kirkpatrick. New York: St. Martin's Press, 1983, pp. 697–698.

Sharp (Castle), Margery

Blount, Margaret. *Animal Land: The Creatures of Children's Fiction.* New York: Morrow, 1975, pp. 163–169.
Smith, Louisa A. "The *Miss Bianca* Series." In *Survey of Modern Fantasy Literature,* vol. 3. Edited by Frank N. Magill. Englewood Cliffs, NJ: Salem Press, 1983, pp. 1037–1039.
Third Book of Junior Authors. Edited by Doris De Montreville and Donna Hill. New York: Wilson, 1972, pp. 258–259.
Twentieth Century Children's Writers. 2nd ed. Edited by D. L. Kirkpatrick. New York: St. Martin's Press, 1983, pp. 698–700.

Shecter, Ben

Third Book of Junior Authors. Edited by Doris De Montreville and Donna Hill. New York: Wilson, 1972, pp. 259–260.

Sherburne, Zoa (Morin)

Fourth Book of Junior Authors and Illustrators. Edited by Doris De Montreville and Elizabeth D. Crawford. New York: Wilson, 1978, pp. 314–315.

Shulevitz, Uri

K, Marjorie Zaum. "Uri Shulevitz." *Horn Book* 45 (Aug. 1969): 389–391.
Shulevitz, Uri. "Caldecott Award Acceptance." *Horn Book* 45 (Aug. 1969): 385–388.
———. "Writing with Pictures." *Horn Book* 58 (Feb. 1982): 17–22.
Third Book of Junior Authors. Edited by Doris De Montreville and Donna Hill. New York: Wilson, 1972, pp. 263–264.

Shura, Mary Francis (pseud. of Mary Francis Craig)

Third Book of Junior Authors. Edited by Doris De Montreville and Donna Hill. New York: Wilson, 1972, pp. 264–265.
Toothaker, R. "Profile: Mary Frances Shura; Why She Writes." *Language Arts* 57 (Feb. 1980): 193–198.

Silverberg, Robert

Aldiss, Brian W., and Harrison, Harry, eds. *Hell's Cartographers: Some Personal Histories of Science Fiction Writers.* New York: Harper and Row, 1976, pp. 7–45.
Canary, Robert H. "Science Fiction as Fictive History." *Extrapolation* 16 (1974): 81–95.
Clareson, Thomas D. "The Fictions of Robert Silverberg." In *Voices for the Future,* vol. 2. Bowling Green, OH: Bowling Green Univ. Press, 1979.
———. *A Reader's Guide to Robert Silverberg.* Mercer Island, WA: Starmont, 1983.
———. *Robert Silverberg: A Primary and Secondary Bibliography.* Boston: G. K. Hall, 1983.
———. "Whose Castle? Speculation as to the Parameters of Science Fiction." *Essays in Arts and Sciences* 9 (1980): 139–143.
Edwards, Malcolm. "Robert Silverberg." In *Science Fiction Writers.* Edited by E. F. Bleiler. New York: Scribner, 1982, pp. 505–512.
Elliot, Jeffrey M. "Robert Silverberg—Next Stop: *Lord Valentine's Castle.*" *P*S*F*Q** 5 (1981): 18–24.
———. "Robert Silverberg Returns." *Future Life* 12 (1979): 25–27.
———. *Science Fiction Voices #2.* San Bernardino, CA: Borgo Press, 1979.
Fredericks, Casey. *The Future of Eternity: Mythologies of Science Fiction and Fantasy.* Bloomington, IN: Indiana Univ. Press, 1982.
Hall, Melissa Mia. "Interview: Robert Silverberg." *Fantasy Newsletter* 60 (1983): 16–17, 46.
Harrison, Harry. "Benford, Wolfe, Silverberg . . . and Literature." *Fantasy Review* 81 (1985): 33.
Klein, Jay Kay. "Robert Silverberg." *Analog,* Mar. 1983, p. 88.
Kroitor, Harry P. "The Special Demands of Points of View in Science Fiction." *Extrapolation* 17 (1976): 153–159.
Letson, Russell. "Falling Through Many Trapdoors: Robert Silverberg." *Extrapolation* 20 (1979): 109–117.
Platt, Charles. *Dream Makers: The Uncommon People Who Write Science Fiction.* New York: Berkley, 1980, pp. 261–268. Interview.
Robert Silverberg. North Hollywood, CA: Center for Cassette Studies, 1974. (Audiocassette)

"Robert Silverberg: Up, Up, and Away." *Locus* 289 (1985): 1.

Schweitzer, Darrell, ed. *Science Fiction Voices*. Baltimore: T-K Graphics, 1976. Interview.

Searles, Baird; Meacham, Beth, and Franklin, Michael. *A Reader's Guide to Fantasy*. New York: Avon, 1982, p. 134.

Silverberg, Robert. "Amazing, Astounding Journeys into the Unknown and Back." *Horizon* 16 (1974): 47–48.

———. "Opinion." *Amazing Stories*, July 1981, pp. 6–7.

———. "Opinion." *Amazing Stories*, May 1985, pp. 4–6.

———. "Opinion." *Amazing Stories*, Sept. 1985, p. 4.

———. "The Profession of Science Fiction: IX: Sounding Brass, Tinkling Cymbal." *Foundation* 7/8 (1975): 6–37; *Algol* 13 (1976): 7–18. Reprinted in *Hell's Cartographers: Some Personal Histories of Science Fiction Writers*. Edited by Brian Aldis and Harry Harrison. New York: Harper and Row, 1975.

———. "The Silverberg Papers." *Starship* 37 (1980): 17–21.

———. "The Silverberg Papers." *Science Fiction Chronicle* 64 (1985): 22.

———. "The Silverberg Papers: Part 2." *Starship* 38 (1980): 25–30.

———. "The Silverberg Papers: Part 3." *Starship* 39 (1980): 15–17.

———. "The Silverberg That Was." *Science Fiction Review* 6 (Nov. 1977): 8–16.

———. "Thirty Years of Writing." In David Wingrove. *The Science Fiction Source Book*. New York: Van Nostrand Reinhold, 1984, pp. 80–82.

Stableford, Brian M. "The Metamorphosis of Robert Silverberg." In Brian M. Stableford. *Masters of Science Fiction*. San Bernardino, CA: Borgo Press, 1981, pp. 32–42.

Third Book of Junior Authors. Edited by Doris De Montreville and Donna Hill. New York: Wilson, 1972, pp. 265–266.

Tuck, Donald H. "Robert Silverberg: Bibliography." *Fantasy and Science Fiction* 46 (Apr. 1974): 81–88.

Twentieth-Century Science Fiction Writers. 2nd ed. Edited by Curtis C. Smith. Chicago: St. James Press, 1986, pp. 661–666.

Walker, Paul. *Speaking of Science Fiction: The Paul Walker Interviews*. Oradell, NJ: Luna Publications, 1978, pp. 281–290.

Silverstein, Shel(by)

Fifth Book of Junior Authors and Illustrators. Edited by Sally Holmes Holtze. New York: Wilson, 1983, pp. 288–289.

Twentieth Century Children's Writers. 2nd ed. Edited by D. L. Kirkpatrick. New York: St. Martin's Press, 1983, pp. 702–703.

Simak, Clifford D(onald)

Aiken, Arnold. "An Age Without An Aim?" *Crystal Ship* 7 (1983): 5–19.

Becker, Muriel R. *Clifford D. Simak: A Primary and Secondary Bibliography*. Boston: G. K. Hall, 1980.

A Career in Science Fiction: An Interview With Clifford Simak. Lawrence, KS: Univ. of Kansas, 1975. (Film)

Chapman, Edgar L. "The Fellowship of the Talisman." In *Survey of Modern Fantasy Literature*, vol. 2. Edited by Frank N. Magill. Englewood Cliffs, NJ: Salem Press, 1983, pp. 549–552.

Clareson, Thomas D. "Clifford D. Simak: The Inhabited Universe." In *Voices for the Future: Essays on Major Science Fiction Writers*, vol. 1. Bowling Green, OH: Bowling Green Univ. Press, 1976.

Kroitor, Harry P. "The Special Demands of Point of View in Science Fiction." *Extrapolation* 17 (1976): 153–159.

Lake, Ken. "City in Ashes." *Vector* 129 (1985): 8.

Moskowitz, Sam. *Seekers of Tomorrow: Masters of Modern Science Fiction.* New York: Ballantine, 1967, pp. 266–282.

Pringle, David. "Aliens for Neighbors: A Reassessment of Clifford D. Simak." *Foundation* 11/12 (1979): 15–29.

Schweitzer, Darrell. "Clifford Simak." In *Science Fiction Voices #5.* Edited by Darrell Schweitzer. San Bernardino, CA: Borgo Press, 1981, pp. 48–55.

Simak, Clifford. " 'Room Enough for All of Us.' " *Extrapolation* 13 (1972): 102–105.

Tweet, Roald D. "Clifford D. Simak." In *Science Fiction Writers.* New York: Scribner, 1982, pp. 513–518.

Twentieth-Century Science Fiction Writers. 2nd ed. Edited by Curtis C. Smith. Chicago: St. James Press, 1986, pp. 666–668.

Walker, Paul. *Speaking of Science Fiction: The Paul Walker Interviews.* Oradell, NJ: Luna Publications, 1978, pp. 56–67. Originally published in *Luna Monthly* 57 (1975): 1–6.

Simont, Marc

More Junior Authors. Edited by Muriel Fuller. New York: Wilson, 1963, pp. 186–187.

Singer, Isaac Bashevis

Allentuck, Marcia, ed. *The Achievements of Isaac Bashevis Singer.* Carbondale: Southern Illinois Univ. Press, 1969.

Berkley, Miriam. "Isaac Bashevis Singer, His Great Success in Writing Children's Books." *Publishers Weekly* 223 (Feb. 18, 1983): 65–66.

Bernheim, Mark A. "Five Hundred Reasons of Isaac Singer." *Bookbird* 20, nos. 1–2 (1982): 31–36.

Blocker, J., and Elman, R. "Interview with Isaac Bashevis Singer." *Commentary* 36 (Nov. 1963): 364–372; 37(Mar. 1964): 20.

Bluchen, Irving H. *Isaac Bashevis Singer and the Eternal Past.* New York: New York Univ. Press, 1968.

Burgin, R. "From Conversations with Isaac Bashevis Singer: Interview." *Hudson Review* 31 (Winter 1978): 621–630.

Calaghan, L. W. "Consistent Focus and Recurring Elements in Books for the Young by Konigsburg, O'Dell, Singer, and Snyder." Master's thesis, University of Chicago, 1979.

Deitch, Gene. "Filming 'Zlateh the Goat.' " *Horn Book* 51 (June 1975): 241–249.

Flender, H. "Isaac Bashevis Singer, Interview." *Paris Review,* Fall 1968.

Haiblum, Isidore. "Isaac Bashevis Singer: Portrait of a Magician." *The Twilight Zone Magazine,* Jan.–Feb. 1984, pp. 24–27.

———. "*Twilight Zone Magazine* Interview: 'These Hidden Powers are Everywhere.' " *The Twilight Zone Magazine,* Jan.–Feb. 1984, pp. 28–29.

Hernández, Frances. "Isaac Bashevis Singer and the Supernatural." *CEA Critic* 40 (Jan. 1978): 28–32.

Hopkins, Lee Bennett. "Isaac Bashevis Singer." In *More Books by More People.* New York: Citation Press, 1974, pp. 312–317.

Iskander, Sylvia W. "Isaac Bashevis Singer." In *American Writers for Children since 1960: Fiction. Dictionary of Literary Biography,* vol. 52. Detroit: Gale, 1986, pp. 334–352.

Kimmel, Eric. "I. B. Singer's *Alone in the Wild Forest:* A Kabbalistic Parable." *Children's Literature in Education* 18 (Fall 1975): 147–158.

———. "The Wise Men of Chelm." *Horn Book* 50 (Feb. 1974): 78–82.

Kresh, Paul. *Isaac Bashevis Singer: The Magician of West 86th Street.* New York: Dial Press, 1979.

———. *Isaac Bashevis Singer: The Story of a Storyteller.* New York: Dutton/Lodestar, 1984.

Leventhal, Naomi Susan. "Storytelling in the Works of Isaac Bashevis Singer." Ph.D. dissertation, Ohio State University, 1978.

Lottman, H. "Isaac Bashevis Singer, Storyteller." *New York Times Book Review,* sect. 7, Jan. 25, 1972, p. 5.

Malin, Irving. *Critical Views of Isaac Bashevis Singer.* New York: New York Univ. Press, 1969.

———. *Isaac Bashevis Singer.* New York: Ungar, 1972.

Menashe, A. "Demons by Choice: An Interview with Isaac Bashevis Singer." *Parabola* 6, no. 4 (Fall 1981): 69–74.

Morse, Naomi S. "Values for Children in the Stories of Isaac Bashevis Singer." In MacLeod. *Children's Literature.* College Park: Univ. of Maryland, 1977.

"A Note on Isaac Bashevis Singer." *Children's Literature in Education* 6 (Fall 1975): 134–135.

The Oxford Companion to Children's Literature. Edited by Humphrey Carpenter and Mari Prichard. New York: Oxford Univ. Press, 1984, pp. 485–486.

Patterson, Sylvia W. "Isaac Singer: Writer for Children." In *Proceedings of the Eighth Annual Conference of the Children's Literature Association.* University of Minnesota, March 1981. Ypsilanti, MI: Children's Literature Association, 1982, pp. 69–76.

Pinsker, S. "Isaac Bashevis Singer: An Interview." *Critique* 11, no. 2 (1969): 16–25.

Pondrom, C. N. "Isaac Bashevis Singer." *Contemporary Literature* 10 (Winter 1969): 1–32; 10 (Summer 1964): 332–351.

Reicheck, M. "Storyteller." *New York Times Magazine,* sect. 6, Mar. 23, 1975, p. 16.

Roginski, Jim, ed. *Newbery and Caldecott Medalists and Honor Book Winners.* Littleton, CO: Libraries Unlimited, 1982, pp. 241–243.

Rubinstein, Esther Levin. "The Grotesque: Aesthetics of Pictorial Disorder in the Writings of Edgar Allan Poe and Isaac Bashevis Singer." Ph.D. dissertation, State University of New York at Albany, 1984.

Siegel, Ben. *Isaac Bashevis Singer.* Minneapolis: Univ. of Minnesota Press, 1969.

Siegel, Mark. "The Short Fiction of Isaac Bashevis Singer." In *Survey of Modern Fantasy Literature,* vol. 4. Edited by Frank N. Magill. Englewood Cliffs, NJ: Salem Press, 1983, pp. 1686–1691.

Sinclair, C. "Conversation with Isaac Bashevis Singer: Interview." *Encounter* 52 (Feb. 1979): 21–28.

Singer, Isaac Bashevis. "Are Children the Ultimate Literary Critics?" *Top of the News* 29 (Nov. 1972): 32–36.

———. " 'I See the Child as a Last Refuge.' " *New York Times Book Review,* pt. II, Nov. 9, 1969, pp. 1, 66. Reprinted in Robert Bator. *Signposts to Criticism of Children's Literature.* Chicago: American Library Association, 1983, pp. 50–53.

———. "Isaac Bashevis Singer: Interview." In Butler. *Sharing Literature With Children.* New York: McKay, 1977, pp. 155–160.

———. "Isaac Bashevis Singer on Writing for Children." In *Children's Literature,* vol. 6. Philadelphia: Temple Univ. Press, 1977, pp. 9–16. Reprinted in *Reflections on Literature for Children.* Edited by Francelia Butler and Richard Rotert. Hamden, CT: Shoe String Press, 1984, pp. 51–57.

———. *A Little Boy in Search of God: Mysticism in a Personal Light.* Garden City,

NY: Doubleday, 1976. Followed by *A Young Man in Search of Love,* Doubleday, 1978; and *Lost in America,* Doubleday, 1978.

————. " 'Our Children Are a Menace to Literature.' " *Horn Book* 50 (Dec. 1974): 679.

————. "Ten More Reasons for Loving Children." *Horn Book* 49 (Dec. 1973): 579.

Third Book of Junior Authors. Edited by Doris De Montreville and Donna Hill. New York: Wilson, 1972, pp. 266–268.

Twentieth Century Children's Writers. 2nd ed. Edited by D. L. Kirkpatrick. New York: St. Martin's Press, 1983, pp. 703–705.

Wolf, H. R. "Singer's Children's Stories and *In My Father's Court:* Universalism and the Rankian Hero." In *The Achievement of Isaac Bashevis Singer.* Edited by Allentuck. Carbondale: Southern Illinois Univ. Press, 1969, pp. 145–158.

Wolkstein, Diane. "The Stories behind the Stories: An Interview with Isaac Bashevis Singer." *Children's Literature in Education* 18 (Fall 1975): 136–146.

Singer, Marilyn

Roginski, Jim. *Behind the Covers: Interviews with Authors and Illustrators of Books for Children and Young Adults.* Littleton, CO: Libraries Unlimited, 1985, pp. 186–193.

Skurzynski, Gloria (Joan)

Fifth Book of Junior Authors and Illustrators. Edited by Sally Holmes Holtze. New York: Wilson, 1983, pp. 294–295.

Helbig, Alethea K., and Perkins, Agnes Regan. *Dictionary of American Children's Fiction, 1960–1984.* Westport, CT: Greenwood Press, 1986, pp. 602, 710.

Sleator, William (Warner III)

Fifth Book of Junior Authors and Illustrators. Edited by Sally Holmes Holtze. New York: Wilson, 1983, pp. 295–296.

Roginski, Jim. *Behind the Covers: Interviews with Authors and Illustrators of Books for Children and Young Adults.* Littleton, CO: Libraries Unlimited, 1985, pp. 194–205.

Sleigh, Barbara (de Riemer)

Doyle, Brian. *The Who's Who of Children's Literature.* New York: Schocken, 1968, pp. 247–248.

Moss, Elaine. "*Signal* Interview: Barbara Sleigh: The Voice of Magic." In *Part of the Pattern.* New York: Greenwillow, 1986, pp. 70–74. Reprinted from *Signal* 8 (May 1972): 43–48.

Twentieth Century Children's Writers. 2nd ed. Edited by D. L. Kirkpatrick. New York: St. Martin's Press, 1983, pp. 705–706.

Slobodkin, Louis

Estes, Eleanor. "Louis Slobodkin." *Horn Book* 20 (July–Aug. 1944): 299–306.

Hopkins, Lee Bennett. *More Books by More People: Interviews with Sixty-five Authors of Books for Children.* New York: Citation Press, 1974, pp. 270–272.

Roginski, Jim, ed. *Newbery and Caldecott Medalists and Honor Book Winners.* Littleton, CO: Libraries Unlimited, 1982, pp. 245–246.

Slobodkin, Louis. "The Caldecott Medal Acceptance." *Horn Book* 20 (July–Aug. 1944): 307–317.

———. "Notes on a Sculptor's Life." *Magazine of Art* 32 (June 1939): 336–338.

Twentieth Century Children's Writers. 2nd ed. Edited by D. L. Kirkpatrick. New York: St. Martin's Press, 1983, pp. 706–707.

Slote, Alfred

Fifth Book of Junior Authors and Illustrators. Edited by Sally Holmes Holtze. New York: Wilson, 1983, pp. 298–299.

Smith, Agnes

Helbig, Alethea K., and Perkins, Agnes Regan. *Dictionary of American Children's Fiction, 1859–1959*. Westport, CT: Greenwood Press, 1985, pp. 143–144, 477.

Smith, Dodie (Dorothy Gladys)

Twentieth Century Children's Writers. 2nd ed. Edited by D. L. Kirkpatrick. New York: St. Martin's Press, 1983, pp. 709–710.

Smith, Emma

Twentieth Century Children's Writers. 2nd ed. Edited by D. L. Kirkpatrick. New York: St. Martin's Press, 1983, pp. 710–711.

Smith, Thorne

Goldin, Stephen. "*Topper* and *Topper Takes a Trip*." In *Survey of Modern Fantasy Literature,* vol. 4. Edited by Frank N. Magill. Englewood Cliffs, NJ: Salem Press, 1983, pp. 1958–1962.

Neilson, Keith. "Thorne Smith." In *Supernatural Fiction Writers: Fantasy and Horror,* vol. 2. Edited by E. F. Bleiler. New York: Scribner, 1985, pp. 805–812.

Stewart, Robert. "Filmedia: Of Human Badinage." *Starship* 4 (1980): 36–37.

Snow, Jack

Hanff, Peter E., and Greene, Douglas G. *Bibliographia Oziana*. Demorest, GA: International Wizard of Oz Club, 1976.

Snyder, Zilpha Keatley

Calaghan, L. W. "Consistent Focus and Recurring Elements in Books for the Young by Konigsburg, O'Dell, Singer and Snyder." Master's thesis, University of Chicago, 1979.

Helbig, Alethea K., and Perkins, Agnes Regan. *Dictionary of American Children's Fiction, 1960–1984; Recent Books of Recognized Merit*. Westport, CT: Greenwood Press, 1986, pp. 609–610.

Hopkins, Lee Bennett. "Zilpha Keatly Snyder." In *More Books by More People*. New York: Citation Press, 1974, pp. 318–322.

Karl, Jean. "Zilpha Keatley Snyder." *Elementary English* 51 (Sept. 1974): 784–789.

Roginski, Jim, ed. *Newbery and Caldecott Medalists and Honor Book Winners*. Littleton, CO: Libraries Unlimited, 1982, pp. 247–248.

Snyder, Zilpha Keatley. "Alternate Worlds." In *Innocence & Experience*. Edited by Barbara Harrison and Gregory Maguire. New York: Lothrop, 1987, pp. 189–190.
———. "The Uses of Magic." *Catholic Library World* 44 (July 1972): 49–56.
Third Book of Junior Authors. Edited by Doris De Montreville and Donna Hill. New York: Wilson, 1972, pp. 270–271.
Twentieth Century Children's Writers. 2nd ed. Edited by D. L. Kirkpatrick. New York: St. Martin's Press, 1983, pp. 714–716.

Springer, Nancy

Paxon, Diana. "The Tolkien Tradition." *Mythlore* 39 (1984): 23–27, 37.

Steele, Mary Q(uintard Govan) (a.k.a. Wilson Gage)

Helbig, Alethea K., and Perkins, Agnes Regan. *Dictionary of American Children's Fiction, 1960–1984*. Westport, CT: Greenwood Press, 1986, pp. 341, 426–427, 624.
Roginski, Jim, ed. *Newbery and Caldecott Medalists and Honor Book Winners*. Littleton, CO: Libraries Unlimited, 1982, pp. 252–253.
Steele, Mary Q. "As Far As You Can Bear to See: Excellence in Children's Literature." *Horn Book* 51 (June 1975): 250–255.
———. "Realism, Truth, and Honesty." *Horn Book* 47 (Feb. 1971): 17–27.
Third Book of Junior Authors. Edited by Doris De Montreville and Donna Hill. New York: Wilson, 1972, p. 97.
Twentieth Century Children's Writers. 2nd ed. Edited by D. L. Kirkpatrick. New York: St. Martin's Press, 1983, pp. 723–724.

Steele, William O(wen)

Burns, P. C., and Hines, R. "Tennessee's Teller of Tall Tales: William O. Steele." *Elementary English* 38 (Dec. 1961): 545–548.
Helbig, Alethea K., and Perkins, Agnes Regan. *Dictionary of American Children's Fiction, 1859–1959*. Westport, CT: Greenwood Press, 1985, p. 487.
More Junior Authors. Edited by Muriel Fuller. New York: Wilson, 1963, pp. 192–193.
Steele, William O. "The Last Buffalo Killed in Tennessee." *Horn Book* 45 (Apr. 1969): 196–199.
———. "The Long Hunter and the Tall Tale." *Horn Book* 34 (Feb. 1958): 54–62.
Twentieth Century Children's Writers. 2nd ed. Edited by D. L. Kirkpatrick. New York: St. Martin's Press, 1983, pp. 724–726.

Steig, William

Abrahamson, Richard F. "Classroom Uses for the Books of William Steig." *Reading Teacher* 32 (Dec. 1978): 307–311.
Alberghene, Janice Marie. "From Alcott to *Abel's Island*: The Image of the Artist in American Children's Literature." Ph.D. dissertation, Brown University, 1980.
Allender, D. "William Steig at 80." *Publishers Weekly*, July 24, 1987, pp. 116–118.
Bader, Barbara. *American Picturebooks from Noah's Ark to the Beast Within*. New York: Macmillan, 1976, pp. 563–564.
Bottner, Barbara. "William Steig: The Two Legacies." *The Lion and the Unicorn* 2, no. 1 (Spring 1978): 4–16.
Cott, Jonathan. "William Steig and His Path." In *Pipers at the Gates of Dawn*. New York: Random, 1983, pp. 87–136.

Hearn, Michael Patrick. "Drawing Out William Steig." *Bookbird* 3–4 (1982): 61–65. Interview.

Helbig, Alethea K., and Regan, Agnes Perkins. *Dictionary of American Children's Fiction, 1960–1984*. Westport, CT: Greenwood Press, 1986, pp. 1–2, 162, 545–546, 625.

Higgins, James E. "William Steig: Champion for Romance." *Children's Literature in Education* 28, no. 1 (1978): 3–16.

Kingman, Lee, ed. *Newbery and Caldecott Medal Books: 1966–1975*. Boston: Horn Book, 1975, pp. 66–75.

Kraus, Robert. "William Steig." *Horn Book* 46 (Aug. 1970): 361–362.

Kuskin, Karla. " . . . and William Steig." *New York Times Book Review*, Nov. 14, 1976, pp. 24, 34.

Lanes, Selma G. "Books: A Reformed Masochist Writes a Sunlit Children's Classic." *Harper's* 245 (Oct. 1972): 122–126. Discusses *Dominic*.

Moss, Anita. "The Spear and the Piccolo: Heroic and Pastoral Dimensions of William Steig's *Dominic* and *Abel's Island*." In *Children's Literature*, vol. 10. New Haven, CT: Yale Univ. Press, 1982, pp. 124–140.

Roginski, Jim, ed. *Newbery and Caldecott Medalists and Honor Book Winners*. Littleton, CO: Libraries Unlimited, 1982, pp. 254–255.

Steig, William. "Caldecott Award Acceptance." *Horn Book* 46 (Aug. 1970): 359–360.

Stott, Jon C. *Children's Literature from A to Z*. New York: McGraw-Hill, 1984, p. 260.

Third Book of Junior Authors. Edited by Doris De Montreville and Donna Hill. New York: Wilson, 1972, pp. 276–277.

Twentieth Century Children's Writers. 2nd ed. Edited by D. L. Kirkpatrick. New York: St. Martin's Press, 1983, pp. 726–727.

"William Steig in Three Parts." *American Artist* 7 (Mar. 1943): 17–19.

Stein, Gertrude

Bechtel, Louise Seaman. "Gertrude Stein for Children." *Horn Book* 15 (Sept. 1939): 287–290. Reprinted in Fryatt. *Horn Book Sampler*. Boston: Horn Book, 1959, pp. 128–132.

Hoffeld, Laura. "Gertrude Stein's Unmentionables." *The Lion and the Unicorn* 2 (Spring 1978): 48–55.

O'Hara, J. D. "Gertrude Stein's *The World Is Round*." In Francelia Butler. *Sharing Literature With Children*. New York: McKay, 1977, pp. 446–449.

Stephens, James

Brown, M. "Leprechaun Out of Costume." *Sewanee Review* 84 (Winter 1976): 190–195.

Clute, John. "*The Crock of Gold*." In *Survey of Modern Fantasy Literature*, vol. 1. Edited by Frank N. Magill. Englewood Cliffs, NJ: Salem Press, 1983, pp. 324–327.

Craig, P. "Rounding Up the Strays." *Times Literary Supplement* 4217 (Jan. 27, 1984): 81.

Davison, Edward L. "Three Irish Poets: A. E., W. B. Yeats, and James Stephens." *English Journal* 15 (May 1926): 327–336.

Douglas, Aileen. "James Stephens." In *Supernatural Fiction Writers: Fantasy and Horror*, vol. 1. Edited by E. F. Bleiler. New York: Scribner, 1985, pp. 485–490.

Lochhead, Marion. *Renaissance of Wonder*. New York: Harper and Row, 1980, pp. 77–81.

Marshall, H. P. "James Stephens." *London Mercury* 12 (Sept. 1925): 500–510.

"A Minstrel Comes from Ireland." *Our World Weekly* 2 (Mar. 16, 1925): 107.

Morris, L. R. "Four Irish Poets." *Columbia University Quarterly* 18 (Sept. 1916): 332–344.

Peake, M. "Portrait." *London Mercury* 38 (May 1938): 606.

"Portrait." *Bookman* 78 (Aug. 1930): 316; 82 (Sept. 1932): 280.

Schley, Margaret Anne. "The Elfin Craft: Fairytale Elements in James Stephens' Prose." Ph.D. dissertation, University of North Carolina at Chapel Hill, 1982.

Searles, Baird; Meacham, Beth; and Franklin, Michael. *A Reader's Guide to Fantasy.* New York: Avon, 1982, pp. 138–139.

Stevenson, James

Fifth Book of Junior Authors and Illustrators. Edited by Sally Holmes Holtze. New York: Wilson, 1983, pp. 303–304.

Stevenson, Robert Louis (Balfour)

Brown, Douglas. "Robert Louis Stevenson: Inspiration and Industry." In *Young Writers, Young Readers.* Edited by Boris Ford. London: Hutchinson, 1960, pp. 123–129.

Butts, Dennis. *Robert Louis Stevenson.* New York: Walck, 1966.

Daiches, David. *Robert Louis Stevenson: The Makers of Modern Literature.* Norfolk, CT: New Directions Books, 1947, pp. 32–73.

Doyle, Brian. *The Who's Who of Children's Literature.* New York: Schocken, 1968, pp. 251–253.

McGregor, D. R. "Myth and Fantasy in Some Late Victorian Novels with Special Reference to Robert Louis Stevenson and George MacDonald." Ph.D. dissertation, Auckland (New Zealand), 1973.

Noble, Andrew, ed. *Robert Louis Stevenson.* Totowa, NJ: Barnes and Noble, 1983.

The Oxford Companion to Children's Literature. Edited by Humphrey Carpenter and Mari Prichard. New York: Oxford Univ. Press, 1984, pp. 496–497.

Smith, Curtis C. "Robert Louis Stevenson." In *Supernatural Fiction Writers: Fantasy and Horror,* vol. 1. Edited by E. F. Bleiler. New York: Scribner, 1985, pp. 307–315.

Svilpis, J. E. "The Short Fiction of Stevenson." In *Survey of Modern Fantasy Literature,* vol. 4. Edited by Frank N. Magill. Englewood Cliffs, NJ: Salem Press, 1983, pp. 1698–1702.

Twentieth Century Children's Writers. 2nd ed. Edited by D. L. Kirkpatrick. New York: St. Martin's Press, 1983, pp. 885–886.

Stewart, Mary (Florence Elinor)

Fries, Maureen. "The Rationalization of the Arthurian Matter in T. H. White and Mary Stewart." *Philological Quarterly* 56 (1977): 258–265.

Herman, Harold J. "The Women in Mary Stewart's Merlin Trilogy." *Interpretations* 15 (Spring 1984): 101–114.

Myers, W. E. "The Merlin Trilogy." In *Survey of Modern Fantasy Literature,* vol. 2. Englewood Cliffs, NJ: Salem Press, 1983, pp. 1010–1014.

The Oxford Companion to Children's Literature. Edited by Humphrey Carpenter and Mari Prichard. New York: Oxford Univ. Press, 1984, p. 497.

Reaves, Monetha Roberta. "The Popular Fiction Tradition and the Novels of Mary Stewart." Ph.D. dissertation, Middle Tennessee State University, 1978.

Searles, Baird; Meacham, Beth; and Franklin, Michael. *A Reader's Guide to Fantasy.* New York: Avon, 1982, p. 139.

Whitaker, Muriel A. " 'The Hollow Hills': A Celtic Motif in Modern Fantasy." *Mosaic* 13 (Spring-Summer 1980): 165–178.

Stockton, Frank (Francis) R(ichard)

Bell, Joseph. *A Bibliographical List of the Writings of Mr. Stockton.* Toronto: Soft Books, 1986.

Candill, Alma. "The Juvenile Literature of Frank R. Stockton." Master's thesis, George Peabody College for Teachers, 1930.

Eliason, Norman E. "Frank R. Stockton: A Critical Study." Master's thesis, University of Iowa, 1931.

Golemba, Henry L. *Frank R. Stockton.* Boston: Twayne, 1981.

Griffin, Martin I. J. *Frank R. Stockton: A Critical Biography.* Philadelphia: Univ. of Pennsylvania, 1939.

Hearn, Michael Patrick. "Frank R. Stockton." In *Writers for Children; Critical Studies of Major Authors Since the Seventeenth Century.* Edited by Jane M. Bingham. New York: Scribner, 1988, pp. 545–554.

Helbig, Alethea K., and Perkins, Agnes Regan. *Dictionary of American Children's Fiction, 1859–1959.* Westport, CT: Greenwood Press, 1985, pp. 196, 490.

May, Jill P. "Frank R. Stockton." In *American Writers for Children before 1900. Dictionary of Literary Biography,* vol. 42. Detroit: Gale, 1985, pp. 332–337.

The Oxford Companion to Children's Literature. Edited by Humphrey Carpenter and Mari Prichard. New York: Oxford Univ. Press, 1984, p. 497.

Twentieth Century Children's Writers. 2nd ed. Edited by D. L. Kirkpatrick. New York: St. Martin's Press, 1983, pp. 886–887.

Twentieth-Century Science Fiction Writers. 2nd ed. Edited by Curtis C. Smith. Chicago: St. James Press, 1986, pp. 701–703.

Waggoner, Diana. "Frank R. Stockton." In *Supernatural Fiction Writers: Fantasy and Horror,* vol. 2. Edited by E. F. Bleiler. New York: Scribner, 1985, pp. 753–760.

Stoddard, Sandol *see* Warburg, Sandol Stoddard

Stolz, Mary (Slattery)

Haviland, Virginia. "*Cat in the Mirror,* a Review." *Horn Book* 51 (Dec. 1975): 597–601.

Helbig, Alethea K., and Perkins, Agnes Regan. *Dictionary of American Children's Fiction, 1859–1959.* Westport, CT: Greenwood Press, 1985, pp. 490–491.

———. *Dictionary of American Children's Fiction, 1960–1984.* Westport, CT: Greenwood Press, 1986, pp. 47, 100, 626–627.

Hopkins, Lee Bennett. "Mary Stolz." In *More Books by More People.* New York: Citation Press, 1974, pp. 343–350.

Jenkins, R. "A Bio-Bibliographical Study of Mary Stolz." Research paper, Kent State University, 1974.

Kaser, Billie F. "The Literary Value and Adolescent Appeal of Mary Stolz's Novels." *Arizona English Bulletin* 14 (April 1972): 14–19.

More Junior Authors. Edited by Muriel Fuller. New York: Wilson, 1963, pp. 195–196.

The Oxford Companion to Children's Literature. Edited by Humphrey Carpenter and Mari Prichard. New York: Oxford Univ. Press, 1984, pp. 497–498.

Robinson, J. L. "Presentation of the Recognition of Merit Award to Mary Stolz." *Claremont Reading Conference Yearbook* 46 (1982): 83–87.

Roginski, Jim, ed. *Newbery and Caldecott Medalists and Honor Book Winners.* Littleton, CO: Libraries Unlimited, 1982, pp. 255–256.

Stolz, Mary. "Children's Books, According to an Ex-Child Who Not Only Remembers But Writes Them." *Claremont Reading Conference Yearbook* 31 (1967): 244–249.

———. "An Honorable Profession." *Saturday Review,* Nov. 7, 1964, pp. 45–46. Re-

printed in Robert Bator. *Signposts to Criticism of Children's Literature*. Chicago: American Library Association, 1983, pp. 46–49.
Twentieth Century Children's Writers. 2nd ed. Edited by D. L. Kirkpatrick. New York: St. Martin's Press, 1983, pp. 728–729.

Stong, Phil(ip Duffield)

Helbig, Alethea K., and Perkins, Agnes Regan. *Dictionary of American Children's Fiction, 1859–1959*. Westport, CT: Greenwood Press, 1985, pp. 491–492.
More Junior Authors. Edited by Muriel Fuller. New York: Wilson, 1963, pp. 197–198.
The Oxford Companion to Children's Literature. Edited by Humphrey Carpenter and Mari Prichard. New York: Oxford Univ. Press, 1984, p. 258.
Roginski, Jim, ed. *Newbery and Caldecott Medalists and Honor Book Winners*. Littleton, CO: Libraries Unlimited, 1982, pp. 257–258.
Twentieth Century Children's Writers. 2nd ed. Edited by D. L. Kirkpatrick. New York: St. Martin's Press, 1983, pp. 729–731.

Storr, Catherine (Cole)

Farmer, Penelope. " 'Jorinda and Jorindel' and Other Stories." *Children's Literature in Education* 7 (Mar. 1972): 23–37. Reprinted in Fox. *Writers, Critics, and Children*. New York: Agathon Press, 1976, pp. 55–72.
The Oxford Companion to Children's Literature. Edited by Humphrey Carpenter and Mari Prichard. New York: Oxford Univ. Press, 1984, p. 498.
Storr, Catherine. "Folk and Fairy Tales." *Children's Literature in Education* 17 (Spring 1986): 63–70. Paper given at the Fourth *Bookquest* Conference, Brighton Polytechnic, Spring, 1984.
———. "Things That Go Bump in the Night." *Sunday Times Magazine* (London), March 7, 1971. Reprinted in Margaret Meek. *The Cool Web*. New York: Atheneum, 1978, pp. 120–128.
———. "Why Folk Tales and Fairy Stories Live Forever." *Where* 53 (1971): 8–11. Reprinted in Robert Bator. *Signposts to Criticism of Children's Literature*. Chicago: American Library Association, 1983, pp. 177–184.
———. "Why Write? Why Write for Children?" In Edward Blishen. *The Thorny Paradise*. Boston: Horn Book, 1975, pp. 25–33.
Twentieth Century Children's Writers. 2nd ed. Edited by D. L. Kirkpatrick. New York: St. Martin's Press, 1983, pp. 731–733.

Stranger, Joyce (pseud. of Joyce Muriel Judson Wilson)

The Oxford Companion to Children's Literature. Edited by Humphrey Carpenter and Mari Prichard. New York: Oxford Univ. Press, 1984, p. 500.
Twentieth Century Children's Writers. 2nd ed. Edited by D. L. Kirkpatrick. New York: St. Martin's Press, 1983, pp. 736–738.

Straub, Peter (Francis)

Bosky, Bernadette. "Stephen King, and Peter Straub: Fear and Friendship." In *Discovering Stephen King*. Mercer Island, WA: Starmont, 1985.
Grant, Charles L. "Many Years Ago, When We All Lived in the Forest . . . " In *Shadowings*. Edited by Douglas E. Winter. Mercer Island, WA: Starmont, 1983, pp. 30–32.

Winter, Douglas E. *Faces of Fear: Encounters with the Creators of Modern Horror.* New York: Berkley, 1985.

Strugatskii, Arkadii Natanovich, and Strugatskii, Boris Natanovich

Csicery-Ronay, Istuan, Jr. "Towards the Last Fairy Tale: On the Fairy-Tale Paradigm in the Strugatsky's Science Fiction, 1963–1972." *Science-Fiction Studies* 13 (1986): 1–41.

Kuczka, Petor. "Fifty Questions: An Interview with the Strugatsky Brothers." *Foundation* 34 (1985): 16–21.

McGuire, Patrick L. "Future History, Soviet Style: The Work of the Strugatsky Brothers." In *Critical Encounters II.* Edited by Tom Staicar. New York: Ungar, 1982, pp. 104–124.

Myers, Alan. "Some Developments in Soviet Science Fiction Since 1966." *Foundation* 19 (1980): 38–47.

Salvestroni, Simonetta. "The Ambiguous Miracle in Three Novels by the Strugatsky Brothers." *Science-Fiction Studies* 11 (1984): 291–303.

Twentieth-Century Science Fiction Writers. 2nd ed. Edited by Curtis C. Smith. Chicago: St. James Press, 1986, pp. 850–852.

Sucharitkul, Somtow

"Interview: Somtow Sucharitkul." *Thrust* 18 (1982): 20–24.
"Somtow Sucharitkul: Clown Prince of Science Fiction." *Locus* 291 (1985): 1 ff.
Twentieth-Century Science Fiction Writers. 2nd ed. Edited by Curtis C. Smith. Chicago: St. James Press, 1986, pp. 706–707.

Sudbery, Rodie (Tutton)

Rees, David. "Middle of the Way: Rodie Sudbery and Beverly Cleary." In *Marble in the Water.* Boston: Horn Book, 1980, pp. 90–103.

Twentieth Century Children's Writers. 2nd ed. Edited by D. L. Kirkpatrick. New York: St. Martin's Press, 1983, p. 743.

Sutcliff, Rosemary

Adamson, Lynda Gossett. "A Content Analysis of Values in Rosemary Sutcliff's Historical Fiction for Children." Ph.D. dissertation, University of Maryland, 1981.

Colwell, Eileen H. "Rosemary Sutcliff—Lantern Bearer." *Horn Book* 36 (Jan. 1960): 200–205.

Crouch, Marcus. *The Nesbit Tradition.* London: Benn, 1972, pp. 63–66.

Inglis, Fred. *The Promise of Happiness.* New York: Cambridge Univ. Press, 1981, pp. 217–221.

———. "Reading Children's Novels: Private Culture and the Politics of Literature." *Children's Literature in Education* 5 (July 1971): 60–75. Reprinted in Fox. *Writers, Critics and Children.* New York: Agathon Press, 1976, pp. 157–173.

Jones, Cornelia, and Way, Olivia R. *British Children's Authors: Interviews at Home.* Chicago: American Library Association, 1976, pp. 146–154.

Meek, Margaret. *Rosemary Sutcliff.* New York: Walck, 1962.

More Junior Authors. Edited by Muriel Fuller. New York: Wilson, 1963, pp. 200–201.

Moss, Elaine. "Rosemary Sutcliff, a Love of Legend." In *Part of the Pattern*. New York: Greenwillow, 1986, pp. 17–19.

Potter, Joyce Elizabeth. "Eternal Relic: A Study of Setting in Rosemary Sutcliff's *Dragon Slayer*." *Children's Literature Association Quarterly* 10 (Fall 1985): 108–112.

Ryan, J. S. "Romance Blighted but Pain Vanquished: Or, the Making of Rosemary Sutcliff." *Orana* 19 (Aug. 1983): 61–67.

"Search for Selfhood: The Historical Novels of Rosemary Sutcliff." *Times Literary Supplement*, June 17, 1965, p. 498. Reprinted in Egoff. *Only Connect*. 1st ed. New York: Oxford Univ. Press, 1969, pp. 249–255.

Sutcliff, Rosemary. "Acceptance Speech: The Phoenix Award." *Children's Literature Association Quarterly* 10 (Winter 1986): 175–176.

———. "Beginning with Beowulf." *Horn Book* 29 (Feb. 1953): 36–38.

———. *Blue Remembered Hills: A Recollection*. London: Bodley Head, 1983.

———. "Rosemary Sutcliff's Thank-You Address to the Children's Literature Association in Ann Arbor, MI, 19th May, 1985, Upon Receipt of the Phoenix Award." *Children's Literature Association Quarterly* 10 (Winter 1986): 176–177.

Townsend, John Rowe. *A Sense of Story*. London: Longman, 1971, pp. 193–203.

Twentieth Century Children's Writers. 2nd ed. Edited by D. L. Kirkpatrick. New York: St. Martin's Press, 1983, pp. 744–746.

Wintle, Justin, and Fisher, Emma. *The Pied Pipers*. New York: Paddington Press, 1974, pp. 182–191.

Wright, Hilary. "Shadows on the Downs: Some Influences of Rudyard Kipling on Rosemary Sutcliff." *Children's Literature in Education* 12 (Summer 1981): 90–102.

Young, Carol C. "Goodbye to Camelot." *English Journal* 74 (Feb. 1985): 54–58.

Swift, Jonathan

Bator, Robert. "Jonathan Swift." In *Writers for Children: Critical Studies of Major Authors since the Seventeenth Century*. Edited by Jane M. Bingham. New York: Scribner, 1988, pp. 555–560.

Billingsley, Dale B. "Gulliver, Mandeville and Capital Crime." *Notes and Queries* 30 (1983): 32–33.

Bryant, D. C. "Persuasive Uses of Imaginary Literature in Certain Satires of Jonathan Swift." *Southern Speech and Communications Journal* 46 (Winter 1981): 175–183.

Case, A. E. *Four Essays on Gulliver's Travels*. Princeton, NJ: Princeton Univ. Press, 1945.

Danchin, Pierre. "The Text of *Gulliver's Travels*." *Texas Studies in Literature and Language* 2 (1960): 233–250.

Doyle, Brian. *The Who's Who of Children's Literature*. New York: Schocken, 1968, pp. 261–262.

Greenacre, Phyllis. *Swift and Carroll: A Psychoanalytic Study of Two Lives*. New York: International Universities Press, 1955.

Hazard, Paul. *Books, Children, and Men*. Boston: Horn Book, 1960, pp. 61–69.

Hubbard, Lucius. *Contributions toward a Bibliography of Gulliver's Travels*. Chicago: Hill, 1922.

Koch, Robert Allen. "Gulliver and Dr. Swift: The Issue of the Satirist's Identity." Ph.D. dissertation, Rice University, 1982.

Mortenson, Robert. "A Note on the Revision of *Gulliver's Travels*." *University of Pennsylvania Library Chronicle* 28 (Winter 1962): 26–28.

The Oxford Companion to Children's Literature. Edited by Humphrey Carpenter and Mari Prichard. New York: Oxford Univ. Press, 1984, pp. 232, 311.

Pickering, S. F. "Gulliver and the Lilliputians." *A. B. Bookman's Weekly* 73 (Jan. 9, 1984): 175 ff.

Sullivan, Evelin Elisabeth. *"Gulliver's Travels:* A Study in Meaning." Ph.D. dissertation, University of California, San Diego, 1981.

Taylor, Sheila. "The 'Secret Pocket': Private Vision and Communal Identity in *Gulliver's Travels." Studies in the Humanities* 6 (1978): 5–11.

Tilton, John W. "Gulliver's Travels as a Work of Art." *Bucknell Review* 8, no. 4: 246–254.

Washington, E. "The Habsburgs and *Gulliver's Travels." American Notes and Queries* 16 (1977–78): 83–85.

Williams, Harold. *The Text of Gulliver's Travels.* New York: Cambridge Univ. Press, 1952.

Tarn, Sir William Woodthrope

Dalphin, Marcia. "I Give You the End of a Golden String." *Horn Book* 14 (May 1938): 143–149. Reprinted in Norma Fryatt. *A Horn Book Sampler.* Boston: Horn Book, 1959, pp. 133–139.

Searles, Baird; Meacham, Beth; and Franklin, Michael. *A Reader's Guide to Fantasy.* New York: Avon, 1982, p. 143.

Yates, Elizabeth. *"The Isle of Mist." Horn Book* 14 (May 1938): 150–152.

Thackeray, William Makepeace

Burns, Marjorie Jean. "Victorian Fantasists from Ruskin to Lang: A Study in Ambivalence." Ph.D. dissertation, University of California, Berkeley, 1978.

Doyle, Brian. *The Who's Who of Children's Literature.* New York: Schocken, 1968, p. 264.

McMaster, Juliet. *"The Rose and the Ring:* Quintessential Thackeray." *Mosaic* 9, no. 4 (Summer 1976): pp. 157–165.

Manlove, C. N. "Comments on Thackeray's *The Rose and the Ring."* In C. N. Manlove. *The Impulse of Fantasy Literature.* Kent, OH: Kent State Univ. Press, 1983, pp. 7–14.

The Oxford Companion to Children's Literature. Edited by Humphrey Carpenter and Mari Prichard. New York: Oxford Univ. Press, 1984, pp. 460–461.

Ritchie, Lady. *Blackstick Papers.* New York: G. P. Putnam, 1908.

Thackeray, William Makepeace. *"The Rose and the Ring."* In *Masterworks of Children's Literature,* vol. 6. New York: Stonehill/Chelsea House, 1984, pp. 63–136.

Tremper, Ellen. "Commitment and Escape: The Fairy Tales of Thackeray, Dickens, and Wilde." *The Lion and the Unicorn* 2 (Spring 1978): 38–47.

Zanger, Jules. *"The Rose and the Ring."* In *Survey of Modern Fantasy Literature,* vol. 3. Edited by Frank N. Magill. Englewood Cliffs, NJ: Salem Press, 1983, pp. 1135–1137.

Theroux, Paul

Wright, Ann. "Paul Theroux's Christmas Tales." *Children's Literature in Education* 15 (Autumn 1984): 141–146.

Thompson, Ruth Plumly

Doyle, Brian. *The Who's Who of Children's Literature.* New York: Schocken, 1968, pp. 264–265.

Hanff, Peter E., and Greene, Douglas G. *Bibliographia Oziana.* Demorest, GA: International Wizard of Oz Club, 1976.

Hearn, Michael Patrick. "Ruth Plumly Thompson." In Cech. *American Writers for Children, 1900–1960. Dictionary of Literary Biography,* vol. 22. Detroit: Gale, 1983, pp. 307–314.

Searles, Baird; Meacham, Beth; and Franklin, Michael. *A Reader's Guide to Fantasy.* New York: Avon, 1982, pp. 143–144.

Thurber, James (Grover)

Bernstein, Burton. *Thurber: A Biography.* New York: Dodd, 1975.

Bowden, Edwin T. *James Thurber: A Bibliography.* Columbus: Ohio State Univ. Press, 1968.

Ewing, J. "Sharing Thurber with Children." *Elementary English* 32 (Feb. 1955): 99–100.

Helbig, Alethea K., and Perkins, Agnes Regan. *Dictionary of American Children's Fiction, 1859–1959.* Westport, CT: Greenwood Press, 1985, pp. 194–195, 518, 523.

Hildebrand, Ann M. "A New Phase of James Thurber's *Many Moons.*" *Children's Literature in Education* 15 (1984): 147–156.

Holmes, Charles S. *The Clocks of Columbus: The Literary Career of James Thurber.* New York: Atheneum, 1972.

————. "James Thurber and the Art of Fantasy." *Yale Review* 55 (Oct. 1965): 17–33.

More Junior Authors. Edited by Muriel Fuller. New York: Wilson, 1963, pp. 204–205.

Morsberger, Robert E. "The Short Fiction of James Thurber." In *Survey of Modern Fantasy Literature,* vol. 4. Edited by Frank N. Magill. Englewood Cliffs, NJ: Salem Press, 1983, pp. 1712–1717.

————. "The Thirteen Clocks." In *Survey of Modern Fantasy Literature,* vol. 4. Edited by Frank N. Magill. Englewood Cliffs, NJ: Salem Press, 1983, pp. 1904–1907.

————. "The White Deer." In *Survey of Modern Fantasy Literature,* vol. 5. Edited by Frank N. Magill. Englewood Cliffs, NJ: Salem Press, 1983, pp. 2118–2121.

————. "The Wonderful O." In *Survey of Modern Fantasy Literature,* vol. 5. Edited by Frank N. Magill. Englewood Cliffs, NJ: Salem Press, 1983, pp. 2159–2161.

Rupprecht, Erich S. "James Thurber." In *Supernatural Fiction Writers: Fantasy and Horror,* vol. 2. Edited by E. F. Bleiler. New York: Scribner, 1985, pp. 827–834.

Searles, Baird; Meacham, Beth; and Franklin, Michael. *A Reader's Guide to Fantasy.* New York: Avon, 1982, pp. 144–145.

Twentieth Century Children's Writers. 2nd ed. Edited by D. L. Kirkpatrick. New York: St. Martin's Press, 1983, pp. 760–761.

Vousden, E. Charles. "James Thurber." In Cech. *American Writers for Children, 1900–1960. Dictionary of Literary Biography,* vol. 22. Detroit: Gale, 1985, pp. 315–320.

Titus, Eve

Third Book of Junior Authors. Edited by Doris De Montreville and Donna Hill. New York: Wilson, 1972, pp. 283–284.

Twentieth Century Children's Writers. 2nd ed. Edited by D. L. Kirkpatrick. New York: St. Martin's Press, 1983, pp. 762–763.

Todd (Bower), Barbara Euphan

Twentieth Century Children's Writers. 2nd ed. Edited by D. L. Kirkpatrick. New York: St. Martin's Press, 1983, pp. 763–764.

Todd, Ruthven

Antczak, Janice. *Science Fiction: The Mythos of a New Romance.* New York: Neal-Schuman, 1985, pp. 168, 173.
Helbig, Alethea K., and Perkins, Agnes Regan. *Dictionary of American Children's Fiction, 1859–1959.* Westport, CT: Greenwood Press, 1985, pp. 482, 524–525.
More Junior Authors. Edited by Muriel Fuller. New York: Wilson, 1963, pp. 205–206.

Tolkien, J(ohn) R(onald) R(euel)

Allan, Jim, ed. and comp. *An Introduction to Elvish, and to Other Tongues. . . . in the Published Writings of Professor John Ronald Reuel Tolkien.* Hays, Middlesex: Bran's Head Books, 1978.
Allen, Elizabeth M. "Persian Influences on J. R. R. Tolkien's *The Lord of the Rings.*" In *The Transcendent Adventure.* Edited by Robert Reilly. Westport, CT: Greenwood Press, 1985, pp. 189–206.
Ashmolean Museum. *Catalogue of an Exhibition of Drawings by J. R. R. Tolkien.* London: Ashmolean Museum and National Book League, in conjunction with Allen & Unwin, 1976.
Barber, Dorothy Elizabeth Klein. "The Structure of *The Lord of the Rings.*" Ph.D. dissertation, University of Michigan, 1965.
Barbour, Douglas. "J. R. R. Tolkien." In *Supernatural Fiction Writers: Fantasy and Horror,* vol. 2. Edited by E. F. Bleiler. New York: Scribner, 1985, pp. 675–684.
———. "The Shadow of the Past: History in Middle Earth." *University of Windsor Review* 8 (Fall 1972): 35–42.
Barkley, Christine. "Donaldson As Heir to Tolkien." *Mythlore* 38 (1984): 50–57.
———. "Predictability and Wonder: Familiarity and Recovery in Tolkien's Works." *Mythlore* 8 (Spring 1981): 16–18.
Basney, L. "Tolkien and the Ethical Function of 'Escape' Literature." *Mosaic* 13 (Winter 1980): 23–46.
Beagle, Peter S. "Tolkien's Magic Ring." *Holiday,* June 1966, pp. 128–131. Reprinted in *The Tolkien Reader.* New York: Ballantine, 1966, pp. ix–xvi; Boyer and Zahorski. *Fantasists on Fantasy.* New York: Avon, 1984.
Becker, Alida, ed. *The Tolkien Scrapbook.* Philadelphia: Running Press, 1978.
Bergmann, Frank. "The Roots of Tolkien's Tree: The Influence of George Mac-Donald and German Romanticism Upon Tolkien's Essay 'On Fairy-Stories.' " *Mosaic* 10 (Winter 1977): 5–14.
Berman, Ruth. "Dragons for Tolkien and Lewis." *Mythlore* 39 (1984): 53–58.
———. "Victorian Dragons: The Reluctant Brood." *Children's Literature in Education* 15 (Winter 1984): 220–233.
Bisenieks, Dainis. "Power and Poetry in Middle Earth." *Mythlore* 3, 10 (1976).
Boenig, Robert. "Tolkien and Old Germanic Ethics." *Mythlore* 48 (1986): 9–12, 40.
Bold, Alan. "Hobbit Verse Versus Tolkien's Poem." In *J. R. R. Tolkien: This Far Land.* Totowa, NJ: Barnes and Noble, 1984, pp. 137–153.
Bradley, Marion Zimmer. *Men, Halflings and Hero Worship.* Baltimore: T-K Graphics, 1973.
Bratman, David S. "Books about J. R. R. Tolkien and His Works." *Science Fiction Collector* 5 (1977): 26–28.
Brooks-Rose, Christine. "The Evil Ring: Realism and the Marvellous." *Poetics Today* 1, no. 4 (1980). Reprinted in Christine Brooks-Rose. *A Rhetoric of the Unreal.* New York: Cambridge Univ. Press, 1983, pp. 233–255.
Brown, G. "Pastoralism and Industrialism in *The Lord of the Rings.*" *English Studies in Africa* 19 (Sept. 1976): 83–91.

Brunsdale, Mitzi M. "Norse Mythological Elements in *The Hobbit.*" *Mythlore* 34 (1983): 49–50, 55.

Bryce, Lynn. "The Influence of Scandinavian Mythology on the Works of J. R. R. Tolkien." *Edda,* 1983, pp. 113–119.

———. "The Use of Christian Iconography in Selected Marginalia of J. R. R. Tolkien's Lothlórien Chapters." *Extrapolation* 25 (Spring 1984): 51–59.

Bullock, Richard P. "The Importance of Free Will in *The Lord of the Rings.*" *Mythlore* 41 (1985): 29 ff.

Burger, Douglas A. "Tolkien's Elvish Craft and Frodo's Mithril Coat." In *The Scope of the Fantastic—Theory, Technique, Major Authors.* Edited by Robert A. Collins and Howard D. Pearce. Westport, CT: Greenwood Press, 1985, pp. 255–262.

———. "The Uses of the Past in *The Lord of the Rings.*" *Kansas Quarterly* 16 (Summer 1984): 23–28.

Burgess, Michael W. "Of Barghest, Orc, and Ringwraith." *Amon Hen,* Sept. 1985, pp. 15–16.

———. "Orome and the Wild Hunt: The Development of a Myth." *Mallorn* 22 (1985): 5–11.

Calabrese, John. "Elements of Myth in J. R. R. Tolkien's *Lord of the Rings* and Selected Paintings of Paul Klee." Ph.D. dissertation, Ohio University, 1980.

Callahan, Patrick J. "Animism and Magic in Tolkien's *The Lord of the Rings.*" *Riverside Quarterly* 4 (1971): 240–249.

Callaway, David. "Gollum: A Misunderstood Hero." *Mythlore* 37 (1984): 14–17, 22.

Carpenter, Humphrey. *The Inklings: C. S. Lewis, J. R. R. Tolkien, Charles Williams, and Their Friends.* Boston: Houghton Mifflin, 1979.

———. *Tolkien: A Biography.* Boston: Houghton Mifflin, 1977.

Chant, Joy. "Niggle and Numenor." *Children's Literature in Education* 19 (Winter 1975): 161–171.

Chapman, Vera. "Forerunner to Tolkien? Walter de la Mare's *The Three Royal Monkeys.*" *Mythlore* 8, 28 (1981): 32–33.

Christensen, Bonniejean McGuire. "*Beowulf* and *The Hobbit:* Elegy into Fantasy in J. R. R. Tolkien's Creative Technique." Ph.D. dissertation, University of Southern California, 1969.

Christopher, Joe R. "An Inklings Bibliography." (2) *Mythlore* 4, no. 1 (1976): 33–38; (3) *Mythlore* 4, no. 2 (1976): 33–38; (4) *Mythlore* 4 (Mar. 1977): 33–38; (5) *Mythlore* 4 (June 1977): 40–46; (6) *Mythlore* 5 (May 1978): 40–46; (7) *Mythlore* 5 (Autumn 1978): 43–46; (8) *Mythlore* 6 (Winter 1979): 46–47; (9) *Mythlore* 6 (Spring 1979): 40–46; (10) *Mythlore* 6 (Summer 1979): 38–45; (11) *Mythlore* 6 (Fall 1979): 44–47; (12) *Mythlore* 22 (1980): 41–45; (13) *Mythlore* 24 (1980): 42–47; (14) *Mythlore* 25 (1980): 43–47; (15) *Mythlore* 26 (1981): 42–46; (16) *Mythlore* 27 (1981): 43–47; (17) *Mythlore* 28 (1981): 43–47; (18) *Mythlore* 29 (1981): 43–47; (19) *Mythlore* 30 (1982): 43–47; (20) *Mythlore* 31 (1982): 37–41; (21) *Mythlore* 32 (1982): 42–46; (22) *Mythlore* 33 (1982): 42–46; (23) *Mythlore* 34 (1983): 51–55; (24) *Mythlore* 35 (1983): 51–55; (25) *Mythlore* 36 (1983): 51–55; (26) *Mythlore* 37 (1984): 51–55; (27) *Mythlore* 38 (1984): 58–63; (28) *Mythlore* 39 (1984): 59–63; (29) *Mythlore* 46 (1986): 57–59; (30) *Mythlore* 47 (1986): 51–54.

Clark, Beverly Lyon. "Crossword Puzzle: *The Hobbit.*" *Children's Literature Association Quarterly* 9 (Summer 1984): 76, 95.

Clausen, Christopher. "*The Lord of the Rings* and 'The Ballad of the White Horse.' " *South Atlantic Bulletin* 39, no. 2 (1974): 10–16.

Colbath, Mary Lou. "Worlds as They Should Be: Middle Earth, Narnia, and Prydain." *Elementary English* 48 (Dec. 1971): 937–945.

Cox, John. "Tolkien's Platonic Fantasy." *Seven: An Anglo-American Literary Review* 5 (1984): 53–69.

Crabbe, Katharyn F. *J. R. R. Tolkien.* New York: Ungar, 1981.

Crossley, Robert. "A Long Day's Dying: The Elves of J. R. R. Tolkien and Sylvia Townsend Warner." In *Death and the Serpent: Immortality in Science Fiction and Fantasy.* Edited by Carl B. Yoke and Donald M. Hassler. Westport, CT: Greenwood Press, 1985, pp. 57–70.

Crouch, Marcus S. "Another Don in Wonderland." *Junior Bookshelf* 14, no. 2 (Mar. 1950): 50–53.

Crowe, Edith. "The Many Faces of Heroism in Tolkien." *Mythlore* 36 (1983): 5–8.

Curtis, Jared. "On Re-Reading *The Hobbit,* Fifteen Years Later." *Children's Literature in Education* 15 (Summer 1984): 113–120.

Davenport, Guy. " 'The Persistence of Light,' an Article on the Fantasy of J. R. R. Tolkien." *National Review,* Apr. 20, 1965, pp. 332–334.

Davey, Colin. "Missing Rings—Revisited." *Amon Hen,* Jan. 1985, pp. 18–19.

Day, David. *A Tolkien Bestiary.* Illus. by Ian Miller and others. New York: Ballantine, 1979.

de Camp, L. Sprague. *Literary Swordsmen and Sorcerers: The Makers of Heroic Fantasy.* Sauk City, WI: Arkham House, 1976.

Deyo, Steven M. "Niggle's Leaves: The Red Book of Westmarch and Related Minor Poetry of J. R. R. Tolkien." *Mythlore* 45 (1986): 28–31 ff.

Dockery, C. "The Myth of the Shadow in the Fantasies of Williams, Lewis and Tolkien." Ph.D. dissertation, Auburn University, 1975.

Donahue, Thomas S. "A Linguist Looks at Tolkien's Elvish." *Mythlore* 37 (1984): 28–34.

Downing, Angelia. "From Quenya to the Common Speech: Linguistic Diversification in J. R. R. Tolkien's *The Lord of the Rings.*" *Revista Caneria de Estudios Ingleses* 4 (Apr. 1982): 23–31.

Doxey, William S. "Culture as an Aspect of Style in Fantasy." *West Georgia College Review* 13 (May 1981): 1–7.

Doyle, Brian. *The Who's Who of Children's Literature.* New York: Schocken, 1968, pp. 266–268.

Drury, Roger. "Providence at Elrond's Council." *Mythlore* 7 (1980): 8–9.

Dubbs, Kathleen E. "Providence, Fate, and Chance: Boethian Philosophy in *The Lord of the Rings.*" *Twentieth Century Literature* 27 (1981): 34–42.

Duriez, Colin. "Leonardo, Tolkien, and Mr. Baggins." *Mythlore* 1, 2 (1974).

Edwards, Malcolm, and Holdstock, Robert. "Middle Earth." In *Realms of Fantasy.* Garden City, NY: Doubleday, 1983, pp. 11–22.

Eiseley, Loren. "The Elvish Art of Enchantment: An Essay on J. R. R. Tolkien's *Tree and Leaf,* and on Mr. Tolkien's Other Distinguished Contributions to Imaginative Literature." *Horn Book* 41 (Aug. 1965): 364–367.

Elgin, Don D. *The Comedy of the Fantastic: Ecological Perspectives on the Fantasy Novel.* Westport, CT: Greenwood Press, 1985.

Ellison, John. "From Innocence to Experience: The Naiveté of J. R. R. Tolkien." *Mallorn* 23 (1986): 10–13.

———. "Music in Relation to Tolkien: A Critique." *Amon Hen,* May 1983, pp. 10–11.

Evans, Robley. *J. R. R. Tolkien.* New York: Crowell, 1976.

Evans, W. D. Emrys. "Illusion, Tale and Epic." *School Librarian* 21 (Mar. 1973): 5–11.

———. *"The Lord of the Rings."* *School Librarian* 16, no. 3 (1968).

Fifield, M. "Fantasy in and for the Sixties; *The Lord of the Rings,* by J. R. R. Tolkien." *English Journal* 55 (Oct. 1966): 841–844.

Flieger, Verlyn Brown. "Medieval Epic and Romance Motifs in J. R. R. Tolkien's *The Lord of the Rings.*" Ph.D. dissertation, Catholic University of America, 1977.

———. "Missing Person." *Mythlore* 46 (1986): 12–15.

Fonstad, Karen Wynn. *An Atlas of Middle Earth.* Boston: Houghton Mifflin, 1981.

Forbes, Cheryl. "Frodo Decides—Or Does He?" *Christianity Today,* Dec. 19, 1975, pp. 10–13.

Foster, Robert. *The Complete Guide to Middle Earth: From "The Hobbit" to "The Silmarillion."* New York: Ballantine, 1985. Revised edition of *A Guide to Middle Earth.* Baltimore: Mirage Press, 1971.

Fry, Carrol L. "Tolkien's Middle Earth and the Fantasy Frame." *Studies in the Humanities* 7 (1978): 35–42.

Garnett, Irene. "From Genesis to Revelation in Middle Earth." *Mallorn,* Apr. 1985, p. 39.

Giddings, Robert, ed. *J. R. R. Tolkien, This Far Land: Essays on New Aspects of Middle Earth.* Totowa, NJ: Barnes and Noble, 1984.

Giddings, Robert, and Holland, Elizabeth. *J. R. R. Tolkien: The Shores of Middle-Earth.* Frederick, MD: Altheia Books, 1982.

Glover, David. "Utopia and Fantasy in the Late 1960's: Burroughs, Moorcock, Tolkien." In *Popular Fiction and Social Change.* Edited by Christopher Pawling. New York: St. Martin's Press, 1984.

Glover, Willis B. "The Christian Character of Tolkien's Invented World." *Criticism* 13 (Winter 1971): 1, 39–53.

Goodknight, Glen. "A Comparison of Cosmological Geography in the Works of J. R. R. Tolkien, C. S. Lewis, and Charles Williams." *Mythlore* 1, 3 (1974).

Goselin, Peter Damien. "Two Faces of Eve: Galdriel and Shelob as Anima Figures." *Mythlore* 6 (Spring 1979): 3–4, 28.

Gottlieb, S. "An Interpretation of Gollum." *Tolkien Journal* 4 (1970–71): 11–12.

Gray, Thomas. "Bureaucratization in *The Lord of the Rings*." *Mythlore* 24 (1980): 3–5.

Green, David L. "Children's Literature Periodicals on Individual Authors, Dime Novels, Fantasy." *Phaedrus* 3 (1976): 22–24.

Green, William Howard. "The Four Part Structure of Bilbo's Education." In *Children's Literature,* vol. 8. New Haven, CT: Yale Univ. Press, 1980, pp. 133–140.

———. *"The Hobbit* and Other Fiction by J. R. R. Tolkien: Their Roots in Medieval Heroic Literature and Language." Ph.D. dissertation, Louisiana State University, 1969.

———. "Legendary and Historical Time in Tolkien's *Farmer Giles of Ham.*" *Notes on Contemporary Literature* 5, no. 3 (1975): 14–15.

———. "The Ring at the Center: Eaca in *The Lord of the Rings.*" *Mythlore* 4 (1976): 17–19.

Grotta, Daniel. *The Biography of J. R. R. Tolkien: Architect of Middle Earth.* 2nd ed. Philadelphia: Running Press, 1978.

Hall, Robert A., Jr. "Silent Commands? Frodo and Gollum at the Cracks of Doom." *Mythlore* 37 (1984): 5–7.

———. "Tolkien's Hobbit Tetralogy as 'Anti-Nibelungen.' " *Western Humanities Review* 32 (Autumn 1979): 351–359.

———. "Who Is the Master of the 'Precious'?" *Mythlore* 41 (1985): 34–35.

Hammond, Wayne G. "Addenda to 'J. R. R. Tolkien: A Bibliography.' " *Bulletin on Bibliography and Magazine Notes* 34 (1977): 119–127.

Hannabus, C. Stuart. "Deep Down: A Thematic and Bibliographical Excursion." *Signal* 6 (Sept. 1971): 87–95.

Hardy, Gene. "More Than a Magic Ring." In Douglas Street. *Children's Novels and the Movies.* New York: Ungar, 1983, pp. 131–140.

Hargrove, Gene. "Who Is Tom Bombadil?" *Mythlore* 47 (1986): 20–24.

Harrod, Elizabeth. "Trees in Tolkien, and What Happened under Them." *Mythlore* 39 (1984): 47–52, 58.

Hartt, Walter F. "Godly Influences: The Theology of J. R. R. Tolkien and C. S. Lewis." *Studies in the Literary Imagination* 14 (Fall 1981): 21–29.

Hedges, Ned Samuel. "The Fable and the Fabulous: The Use of Traditional Forms in Children's Literature." Ph.D. dissertation, University of Nebraska, 1968.

Helms, Randel. "All Tales Need Not Come True." *Studies in the Literary Imagination* 14 (Fall 1981): 31–45.

———. *Tolkien's World* (original British title: *Myth, Magic and Meaning in Tolkien's World*. London: Thames, 1974). Boston: Houghton Mifflin, 1974.

Hennelly, Mark M., Jr. "The Road and the Ring: Solid Geometry in Tolkien's Middle-Earth." *Mythlore* 33 (1982): 3–13.

Higgins, James Edward. "Five Authors of Mystical Fancy for Children: A Critical Study." Ed.D. dissertation, Columbia University, 1965.

Hillegas, Mark Robert, ed. *Shadows of the Imagination: The Fantasies of C. S. Lewis, J. R. R. Tolkien, and Charles Williams*. Carbondale: Southern Illinois Univ. Press, 1969.

Ho, Tisa. "The Childlike Hobbit." *Mythlore* 34 (1983): 3–9.

"The Hobbit"; Reading Motivation Unit. Wilton, CT: Current Affairs, 1977. (Filmstrip and audiocassette)

Hodge, James L. "Tolkien: Formulas of the Past." *Mythlore* 8 (1981): 15–18.

Houghton, Joe; Bywater, Mike; and Mertins, Michael. "Dragons." *Amon Hen*, Feb. 1983, pp. 13–15.

Hyde, Paul Nolan. "Leaf and Key." *Mythlore* 46 (1986): 27–29, 36.

———. "Linguistic Techniques Used in Character Development in the Works of J. R. R. Tolkien. (Vols. I–III)." Ph.D. dissertation, Purdue University, 1982.

———. "Translations from the Elvish: The Lingo-Cultural Foundations of Middle Earth." *Publications of the Missouri Philological Association* 8 (1983): 11–16.

Inglis, Fred. "Gentility and Powerlessness: Tolkien and the New Class." In *J. R. R. Tolkien: This Far Land*. Totowa, NJ: Barnes and Noble, 1984, pp. 25–41.

———. *The Promise of Happiness*. New York: Cambridge Univ. Press, 1981, pp. 194–200.

Isaacs, Neil D., and Zimbardo, Rose A., eds. *Tolkien: New Critical Perspectives*. Lexington, KY: Univ. Press of Kentucky, 1981.

———. *Tolkien and the Critics: Essays on J. R. R. Tolkien's "The Lord of the Rings."* South Bend, IN: Univ. of Notre Dame, 1968.

Jeffs, Carol. "The Forest." *Mallorn* 22 (1985): 33–36.

Jenkins, Sue. "Love, Loss and Seeking: Material Deprivation and the Quest." *Children's Literature in Education* 15 (Summer 1984): 73–84.

Johnson, Janice. "The Celeblain of Celeborn and Galadriel." *Mythlore* 32 (1982): 11–19.

Johnson, Judith A. *J. R. R. Tolkien: Six Decades of Criticism*. Westport, CT: Greenwood Press, 1986.

Jones, Diana Wynne. "The Shape of the Narrative in *The Lord of the Rings*. In *J. R. R. Tolkien: This Far Land*. Totowa, NJ: Barnes and Noble, 1984, pp. 87–107.

Jones, Kathleen. " 'Frodo Lives': Long Live Frodo!" *Amon Hen*, Oct. 1983, pp. 9–10.

———. "The Use and Misuse of Fantasy." *Mallorn* 23 (1986): 5–9.

José, Pilar San, and Starkey, Gregory. "Tolkien's Influence on C. S. Lewis." *Mallorn* 17 (1981): 23–28.

King, Roger. "Recovery, Escape, Consolation: Middle Earth and the English Fairy Tale." In *J. R. R. Tolkien: This Far Land*. Totowa, NJ: Barnes and Noble, 1984, pp. 42–55.

Kobil, Daniel T. "The Elusive Appeal of the Fantastic." *Mythlore* 4 (June 1977): 17–19; *Mythlore* 8, 29 (1981).

Kocher, Paul H. *"The Hobbit."* In *Master of Middle Earth: The Achievement of J. R. R. Tolkien*. Boston: Houghton Mifflin, 1972, pp. 19–33.

———. "Iluvatar and the Secret Fire." *Mythlore* 43 (1985): 36–37.

———. "J. R. R. Tolkien and George MacDonald." *The Crescent* 8, 29 (1981): 3–4.

———. "The Tale of the Noldor." *Mythlore* 4 (Mar. 1977): 3–7.

———. "Turin Turambar." *Mythlore* 8 (Spring 1981): 22–23.

Kolbe, Martha Emily. "Three Oxford Dons as Creators of Other Worlds for Children: Lewis Carroll, C. S. Lewis, and J. R. R. Tolkien." Ph.D. dissertation, University of Virginia, 1981.

Lawler, Donald L. *"The Silmarillion."* In *Survey of Modern Fantasy Literature*, vol. 4. Edited by Frank N. Magill. Englewood Cliffs, NJ: Salem Press, 1983, pp. 1733–1743.

Lense, Edward. "Sauron Is Watching *You:* The Role of the Great Eye in *The Lord of the Rings.*" *Mythlore* 4, 13 (1976): 3–6.

Lewis, Alex. "The Moving Mountains of Merkwood." *Amon Hen,* Jan. 1985, pp. 11–12.

Little, Edmund. *The Fantasts: Studies in J. R. R. Tolkien, Lewis Carroll, Mervyn Peake, Nikolay Gogol and Kenneth Grahame.* Amersham, England: Avebury, 1984.

Lloyd, Paul M. "The Role of Warfare and Strategy in *The Lord of the Rings.*" *Mythlore* 3, 11 (1976).

Lobdell, Jared. *England and Always: Tolkien's World of the Rings.* Grand Rapids, MI: Eerdmans, 1982.

———, ed. *A Tolkien Compass: Including J. R. R. Tolkien's Guide to the Names in 'The Lord of the Rings.'* New York: Ballantine, 1980. (Orig. pub. LaSalle, IL: Open Court, 1975.)

Lochhead, Marion. *Renaissance of Wonder.* New York: Harper and Row, 1980, pp. 101–125.

Lowentrout, Peter. "The Evocation of Good in Tolkien." *Mythlore* 38 (1984): 32–33.

Lynch, James. "The Literary Banquet and the Eucharistic Feast: Tradition in Tolkien." *Mythlore* 5 (1978): 13–14.

McGeehon, C. " 'I Have Read Everything by Tolkien.' " *Unabashed Librarian* 50 (1984): 25. (bibliography)

MacIntyre, Jean. " 'Time Shall Run Back': Tolkien's *The Hobbit.*" *Children's Literature Association Quarterly* 13 (Spring 1988): 12–16.

Mack, H. C. "A Parametric Analysis of Antithetical Conflict and Irony: Tolkien's *The Lord of the Rings.*" *Word* 31 (1981): 121–149.

McKenzie, Sister Elizabeth. "Above All Shadows Rides the Sun." *Mythlore* 2, 5 (1975).

McKinley, Robin. "J. R. R. Tolkien." In *Writers for Children: Critical Studies of Major Authors since the Seventeenth Century.* Edited by Jane M. Bingham. New York: Scribner, 1988, pp. 561–572.

McLaughlin, F. *"The Lord of the Rings;* a Fantasy Film." *Media and Methods* 15 (Nov. 1978): 14–17.

McLeish, Kenneth. "The Rippingest Yarn of All." In *J. R. R. Tolkien: This Far Land.* Totowa, NJ: Barnes and Noble, 1984, pp. 125–136.

Manlove, C. N. *Modern Fantasy: Five Studies.* New York: Cambridge Univ. Press, 1975.

Marchesani, Diane. "Tolkien's Lore: The Songs of Middle Earth." *Mythlore* 23 (1980): 3–5.

Mathews, Richard. *Lightning from a Clear Sky: Tolkien, the Trilogy, and 'The Silmarillion.'* San Bernardino, CA: Borgo Press, 1978.

———. *"The Lord of the Rings."* In *Survey of Modern Fantasy Literature*, vol. 2. Edited by Frank N. Magill. Englewood Cliffs, NJ: Salem Press, 1983, pp. 897–915.

Mende, Lisa Anne. "Gondolin, Minas Tirith and the Eucatastrophe." *Mythlore* 48 (1986): 37–40.

Mendelson, M. "Opening Moves: The Entry into the Other World." *Extrapolation* 25 (Summer 1984): 171–179.

Menzies, Janet. "Middle Earth and the Adolescent." In *J. R. R. Tolkien: This Far Land*. Totowa, NJ: Barnes and Noble, 1984, pp. 56–72.

Miesel, Sandra. *Myth, Symbol and Religion in 'The Lord of the Rings.'* Baltimore: T-K Graphics, 1973.

Miller, Miriam Youngerman. "The Green Sun: A Study of Color in J. R. R. Tolkien's *The Lord of the Rings." Mythlore* 7, 26 (1980).

———. *"The Hobbit, or There and Back Again."* In *Survey of Modern Fantasy Literature*, vol. 3. Edited by Frank N. Magill. Englewood Cliffs, NJ: Salem Press, 1983, pp. 732–739.

Miller, Stephen O. *Middle Earth: A World in Conflict*. London: T-K Graphics, 1975.

———. *Mithrandir*. Baltimore: T-K Graphics, 1974.

Milward, Peter. "Perchance to Touch: Tolkien as Scholar." *Mythlore* 22 (1979): 31–32.

Montgomery, John Warwick, ed. *Myth, Allegory and Gospel: An Interpretation of J. R. R. Tolkien/C. S. Lewis/G. K. Chesterton/Charles Williams*. Minneapolis: Bethany Fellowship, 1974.

Moorman, Charles W. "Heroism in *The Lord of the Rings." Southern Quarterly* 11 (1972): 29–39.

———. " 'Now Entertain Conjecture of a Time'—The Fictive Worlds of C. S. Lewis and J. R. R. Tolkien." In Mark R. Hillegas, ed. *Shadows of the Imagination*. Carbondale: Univ. of Southern Illinois, 1969.

More Junior Authors. Edited by Muriel Fuller. New York: Wilson, 1963, pp. 206–207.

Morgan, Gwyneth. "The Origin of the Arkenstone." *Amon Hen*, Dec. 1983, pp. 15–16.

Morris, John S. "Fantasy in a Mythless Age." In *Children's Literature*, vol. 2. Storrs, CT: Journal of the Modern Language Association, 1973, pp. 77–86.

Morrison, Louise D. *J. R. R. Tolkien's 'The Fellowship of the Ring': A Critical Commentary*. New York: Monarch Press, 1976.

Morse, Robert E. "Rings of Power in Plato and Tolkien." *Mythlore* 7 (1980): 38.

Moss, Elaine. "Smith of Wooton Major." In *Part of the Pattern*. New York: Greenwillow, 1986, p. 28.

Murphy, Paul. "The Dwarfs of the Fourth Age." *Amon Hen,* May 1984, pp. 7–8.

Nardo, Anna K. "Fantasy Literature and Play: An Approach to Reader Response." *Centennial Review* 22 (1978): 201–213.

Nelson, Marie. "Non-Human Speech in the Fantasy of C. S. Lewis, J. R. R. Tolkien and Richard Adams." *Mythlore* 5, 17 (May 1978): 37–39.

Nitzsche, Jane Chance. "The King under the Mountain: Tolkien's *Hobbit." North Dakota Quarterly* 47 (Winter 1979): 5–18.

———. *Tolkien's Art: A Mythology for England*. New York: St. Martin's Press, 1979.

Nodelman, Perry. "A Tolkien Bibliography." *Children's Literature Association Quarterly* 4 (Summer 1979): 17–18.

Noel, Ruth S. *The Languages of Tolkien's Middle Earth*. Boston: Houghton Mifflin, 1980.

———. *The Mythology of Middle Earth*. Boston: Houghton Mifflin, 1977.

Nored, Gary. *"The Lord of the Rings*—A Textual Inquiry." *Papers of the Bibliographical Society of America* 68 (Jan. 1974): 71–74.

Norman, Philip. "The Prevalence of Hobbits." *New York Times Magazine,* Jan. 15, 1967, pp. 30–31 ff.

O'Connor, Gerard W. "The Many Ways to Read an 'Old' Book." *Extrapolation* 15 (1973): 72–74.

———. "Why Tolkien's *The Lord of the Rings* Should *Not* Be Popular Culture." *Extrapolation* 13 (Dec. 1971): 48–55.

O'Hare, Coleman. "Charles Williams, C. S. Lewis, and J. R. R. Tolkien: Three

Approaches to Religion in Modern Fiction." Ph.D. dissertation, University of Toronto, 1973.

———. "On Reading an 'Old' Book." *Extrapolation* 14 (1972): 59–63.

O'Neill, Timothy R. *The Individuated Hobbit: Jung, Tolkien and the Archetypes.* Boston: Houghton Mifflin, 1979.

The Oxford Companion to Children's Literature. Edited by Humphrey Carpenter and Mari Prichard. New York: Oxford Univ. Press, 1984, pp. 254–255, 325, 529–531.

Pace, David Paul. "The Influence of Vergil's *Aeneid* on *The Lord of the Rings.*" *Mythlore* 6 (Spring 1979): 37–38.

Parker, Douglass. "Hwaet We Holbytla." *Hudson Review* 9 (1956–57): 598–609.

Partridge, Brenda. "No Sex Please—We're Hobbits: The Construction of Female Sexuality in *The Lord of the Rings.*" In *J. R. R. Tolkien: This Far Land.* Totowa, NJ: Barnes and Noble, 1984, pp. 179–198.

Pauline, Sister, CSM. "Secondary Worlds: Lewis and Tolkien." *CSL* 12 (May 1981): 1–8.

Pawling, Christopher, ed. *Popular Fiction and Social Change.* New York: St. Martin's Press, 1984.

Paxon, Diana. "The Tolkien Tradition." *Mythlore* 39 (1984): 23–27, 37.

Perret, Marion. "Rings Off Their Fingers: Hands in *The Lord of the Rings.*" *Ariel* 6 (Oct. 1975): 52–66.

Petty, Anne C. *One Ring to Bind Them All: Tolkien's Mythology.* Tuscaloosa: Univ. of Alabama Press, 1979.

Pflieger, Pat, and Hill, Helen M. *A Reference Guide to Modern Fantasy for Children.* Westport, CT: Greenwood Press, 1984, pp. xii–xvi, 243–245, 537–540.

Pitts, Mary Ellen. "The Motif of the Garden in the Novels of J. R. R. Tolkien, Charles Williams, and C. S. Lewis." *Mythlore* 8, 30 (1981).

Plimmer, Charlotte, and Plimmer, Denis. "The Man Who Understands Hobbits." *Daily Telegraph Magazine* 181 (Mar. 22, 1968): 31–32, 35.

Price, Meredith. " 'All Shall Love Me and Despair': The Figure of Lilith in Tolkien, Lewis, Williams, and Sayers." *Mythlore* 9 (1982): 3–7 ff.

Pugh, Dylan. "Atlantis and Middle Earth." *Amon Hen,* July 1984, pp. 11–12.

Purtill, Richard L. "Heaven and Other Perilous Realms." *Mythlore* 22 (1979): 3–6.

———. *Lord of Elves and Eldils: Fantasy and Philosophy in C. S. Lewis and J. R. R. Tolkien.* Grand Rapids, MI: Zondervan, 1974.

Rateliff, John D. " 'And Something Yet Remains to Be Said': Tolkien and Williams." *Mythlore* 45 (1986): 48–54.

———. "*She* and Tolkien." *Mythlore* 8 (1981): 6–8.

Rawls, Melanie. "Arwen, Shadow Bride." *Mythlore* 43 (1985): 24–25, 37.

———. "The Feminine Principle in Tolkien." *Mythlore* 38 (1984): 5–13.

———. "The Rings of Power." *Mythlore* 40 (1984): 29–32.

Ready, William. *Understanding Tolkien and 'The Lord of the Rings.'* New York: Warner Books, 1969.

Reed, A. K. "The Greatest Problem Is What Lies Ahead. Problems in Media and Mythology—An Analysis of the Rankin/Bass Production of Tolkien's *The Hobbit.*" *Journal of Popular Culture* 17 (Spring 1984): 138–146.

Ringel, Faye Joyce. "Patterns of the Hero and the Quest: Epic, Romance, Fantasy." Ph.D. dissertation, Brown University, 1979.

Robinson, Derek. "The Hasty Stroke Goes Oft Astray: Tolkien and Humour." In *J. R. R. Tolkien: This Far Land.* Totowa, NJ: Barnes and Noble, 1984, pp. 108–124.

Rockow, Karen. *Funeral Customs in Tolkien's Trilogy.* Baltimore: T-K Graphics, 1973.

Rogers, Deborah Webster. "The Fictitious Characters of C. S. Lewis and J. R. R.

Tolkien in Relation to Their Medieval Sources." Ph.D. dissertation, University of Wisconsin, 1972.

Rogers, Deborah Webster, and Rogers, Ivor A. *J. R. R. Tolkien.* Boston: Twayne, 1980.

Roos, R. "Middle Earth in the Classroom: Studying J. R. R. Tolkien." *English Journal* 58 (Nov. 1969): 1175–1180.

Rosenberg, Jerome. "The Humanity of Sam Gamgee." *Mythlore* 5, 17 (Mar. 1978): 10–11.

Rossi, Lee D. "Politics of Fantasy: C. S. Lewis and J. R. R. Tolkien." Ph.D. dissertation, Cornell University, 1972.

———. *The Politics of Fantasy: C. S. Lewis and J. R. R. Tolkien.* Ann Arbor, MI: UMI Research Press, 1984.

Rottensteiner, Franz. *The Fantasy Book: An Illustrated History from Dracula to Tolkien.* New York: Macmillan, 1978, pp. 96–98.

Russell, Mariann. " 'The Northern Literature' and the Ring Trilogy." *Mythlore* 5 (Autumn 1978): 41–42.

Ryan, J. S. "The Barghest as Possible Source for Tolkien's Goblins and Ringwraiths." *Amon Hen,* May 1985, pp. 10–11.

———. "Cultural Name Association: A Tolkien Example from Gilgamesh." *Mallorn* 22 (1985): 21–23.

———. "Entrance to a Smial!" *Amon Hen,* May 1983, pp. 12–13.

———. "Frothi, Frodo—and Dodo and Odo." *Orana* 16 (May 1980): 35–38.

———. "Gollum and the Golem: A Neglected Tolkien Association With Jewish Thought." *Orana* 18 (Aug. 1983): 110–113.

———. "Origin of the Name 'Wetwang.' " *Amon Hen,* Aug. 1983, pp. 10–13.

———. "Saruman, 'Sharkey' and Suruman: Analogous Figures of Eastern Ingenuity and Cunning." *Mythlore* 43 (1985): 43–44, 57.

———. *Tolkien: Cult or Culture?* Armidale, New South Wales: Univ. of New England, 1969.

———. "Warg, Wearg, Earg and Werewolf: A Note on a Speculative Tolkien Etymology." *Mallorn* 23 (1986): 25–29.

———. "Woses: Wild Men or 'Remnants of an Older Time'?" *Amon Hen,* Dec. 1983, pp. 7–12.

St. Clair, Gloriana. "*The Lord of the Rings* as Saga." *Mythlore* 6 (Spring 1979): 11–16.

Salu, Mary, and Farrell, Robert T, eds. *J. R. R. Tolkien, Scholar and Storyteller: Essays in Memorium.* Ithaca, NY: Cornell Univ. Press, 1979.

Sammons, Margaret. "Tolkien on Fantasy in *Smith of Wooton Major.*" *Mythlore* 43 (1985): 3–7, 37.

Sams, Edwin Boyer. "Studies in Experimental Fantasy." *Teaching English in the Two-Year College* 5 (1979): 235–237.

Sanders, Joseph Lee. "Fantasy in the 20th Century British Novel." Ph.D. dissertation, Indiana University, 1972.

Sardello, Robert J. "An Empirical-Phenomenological Study of Fantasy, With a Note on J. R. R. Tolkien and C. S. Lewis." *Psycho-Cultural Review* 2 (1978): 203–220.

Savater, Fernando. *Childhood Regained: The Art of the Storyteller.* New York: Columbia Univ. Press, 1982.

Scafella, Frank. "Tolkien, the Gospel, and the Fairy Story." *Soundings* 64 (1981): 310–325.

Schakel, Peter. "Dance as Metaphor and Myth in Lewis, Tolkien, and Williams." *Mythlore* 45 (1986): 4–8, 23.

Schmiel, Mary Eileen. "In the Forge of Los: Tolkien and the Art of Creative Fantasy." *Mythlore* 35 (1983): 17–22.

Schorr, Karl. "The Nature of Dreams in *The Lord of the Rings.*" *Mythlore* 36 (1983): 21, 46.

Science Fiction and Time Fiction. Tarrytown, NY: Prentice-Hall Media, 1977. (Filmstrip and audiocassette)

Scott, N. C. "War and Pacifism in *The Lord of the Rings.*" *Tolkien Journal* 15 (Summer 1972): 23–25, 27–30.

Scull, Chris. "The Fairy-Tale Tradition." *Mallorn* 23 (1986): 30–36.

Searles, Baird; Meacham, Beth; and Franklin, Michael. *A Reader's Guide to Fantasy.* New York: Avon, 1982, pp. 145–147.

Shippley, T. A. *The Road to Middle Earth.* Boston: Houghton Mifflin, 1983.

Shoemaker, D. "A Savvy Animator Finds Perils on the Paths of Middle Earth." *Chronicle of Higher Education* 17 (Nov. 27, 1978): 18–20.

Sirridge, Mary. "J. R. R. Tolkien and the Fairy Tale Truth." *The British Journal of Aesthetics* 15 (1975): 81–92.

Sklar, Robert. "Tolkien and Hesse: Tops of the Pops." *Nation* 204 (May 8, 1967): 598–601. Reprinted in Lenz. *Young Adult Literature.* Chicago: American Library Association, 1980, pp. 422–424.

Speth, Lee. "Cavalier Treatment." *Mythlore* 6 (Summer 1979): 18, 38.

———. "Cavalier Treatment: Once More Round the Cauldron." *Mythlore* 24 (1980): 14–15.

Stevens, C. "High Fantasy Versus Low Comedy: Humor in J. R. R. Tolkien." *Extrapolation* 21 (Summer 1980): 122–129.

———. "The Sound Systems of the Third Age of Middle Earth." *Quarterly Journal of Speech* 54 (Oct. 1968): 232–240.

Stevens, David. "The Short Fiction of J. R. R. Tolkien." In *Survey of Modern Fantasy Literature,* vol. 4. Edited by Frank N. Magill. Englewood Cliffs, NJ: Salem Press, 1983, pp. 1724–1728.

———. "Trolls and Dragons versus Pocket Handkerchiefs and 'Polite Nothings': Elements of the Fantastic and the Prosaic in *The Hobbit.*" In *The Scope of the Fantastic—Culture, Biography, Themes, Children's Literature.* Edited by Robert A. Collins and Howard D. Pearce. Westport, CT: Greenwood Press, 1985, pp. 249–256.

Stevenson, Jeff. "Life After Life." *Amon Hen,* May 1984, pp. 10–11.

Stoddard, William. "A Critical Approach to Fantasy with Application to *The Lord of the Rings.*" *Mythlore* 37 (1984): 8–13.

Stott, Jon C. *Children's Literature from A to Z.* New York: McGraw-Hill, 1984, p. 270.

Strachey, Barbara. *Journeys of Frodo: An Atlas of J. R. R. Tolkien's "The Lord of the Rings."* New York: Ballantine, 1981.

Sturch, Richard. "The Theology of *The Book of Lost Tales.*" *Amon Hen,* May 1984, pp. 9–10.

Sullivan, Charles Williams, III. "J. R. R. Tolkien's *The Hobbit:* The Magic of Words." In *Touchstones.* Edited by Perry Nodelman. West Lafayette, IN: Children's Literature Association Publications, 1985, pp. 253–261.

———. "Name and Lineage Patterns: Aragorn and *Beowulf.*" *Extrapolation* 25 (Fall 1984): 239–246.

Swinfen, Ann. *In Defense of Fantasy.* London: Routledge, 1984, pp. 78, 80–81, 84–87, 89, 93–94.

Taylor, W. L. "Frodo Lives; J. R. R. Tolkien's *The Lord of the Rings.*" *English Journal* 56 (Sept. 1967): 818–821; Reply: R. M. Stein. *English Journal* 57 (Feb. 1968): 252–253.

Terry, June S. "To Seek and to Find: Quest Literature for Children." *School Librarian*

18 (December 1970): 399–404. Reprinted in Mary Lou White. *Children's Literature.* Columbus, OH: Merrill, 1976, pp. 138–143.

Thompson, George H. "Early Review[s] of Books by J. R. R. Tolkien." *Mythlore* 41 (1985): 59–63.

"A Tolkien Bibliography." *Children's Literature Association Quarterly* 4 (Summer 1979): 17–18.

Tolkien, Christopher. "J. R. R. Tolkien: A Bibliography." *Bulletin of Bibliography* 27 (1970).

Tolkien, J. R. R. "Beowulf: The Monsters and the Critics." *Proceedings of the British Academy* 22 (1936): 248–295.

———. *The Book of Lost Tales,* vol. 1. Edited by Christopher Tolkien. Boston: Houghton Mifflin, 1984 (c. 1983), 1986.

———. *The Book of Lost Tales,* vol. 2. Edited by Christopher Tolkien. Boston: Houghton Mifflin, 1984.

———. *"The Hobbit." Horn Book* 14 (May 1938): 184–188.

———. *The Lays of Beleriad* (The History of Middle Earth, vol. 3). Edited by Christopher Tolkien. Boston: Houghton Mifflin, 1985.

———. *The Letters of J. R. R. Tolkien.* Edited and selected by Humphrey Carpenter and Christopher Tolkien. Boston: Houghton Mifflin, 1981. Excerpt entitled "To W. H. Auden" reprinted in Boyer and Zahorski. *Fantasists on Fantasy.* New York: Avon, 1984, pp. 85–94.

———. *The Monsters and the Critics, and Other Essays.* Edited by Christopher Tolkien. Boston: Houghton Mifflin, 1984 (c. 1983).

———. "On Fairy Tales. In *Essays Presented to Charles Williams* (original publication 1947). Freeport, NY: Books for Libraries Press, 1972, pp. 38–90. Reprinted in *Horn Book* 39 (1963):457, entitled "Editorial: On Fairy-Stories"; also in J. R. R. Tolkien. *Tree and Leaf.* Boston: Houghton Mifflin, 1965, pp. 3–84, entitled "On Fairy-Stories"; in *The Tolkien Reader.* New York: Ballantine, 1966, 1974, pp. 3–84, entitled "On Fairy Stories"; and in Sheila A. Egoff. *Only Connect.* New York: Oxford Univ. Press, 1980, pp. 111–120, entitled "Children and Fairy Stories." An excerpt entitled "Fantasy" has been reprinted in Boyer and Zahorski. *Fantasists on Fantasy.* New York: Avon, 1984, pp. 75–84.

———. *The Shaping of Middle Earth: The Quenta, the Ambrakanta, and the Annals.* (The History of Middle Earth, vol. 4). Edited by Christopher Tolkien. Boston: Houghton Mifflin, 1986.

———. *Unfinished Tales of Numenor and Middle Earth.* Edited by Christopher Tolkien. Boston: Houghton Mifflin, 1980, 1982.

Twentieth Century Children's Writers. 2nd ed. Edited by D. L. Kirkpatrick. New York: St. Martin's Press, 1983, pp. 765–767.

Twentieth-Century Science Fiction Writers. 2nd ed. Edited by Curtis C. Smith. Chicago: St. James Press, 1986, pp. 865–867.

Tyler, J. E. A. *The New Tolkien Companion* (originally published London: Macmillan, 1976), rev. ed. New York: St. Martin's Press, 1980.

Urang, Gunnar. "Shadows of Heaven: Religion and Fantasy in the Writing of C. S. Lewis, Charles Williams and J. R. R. Tolkien." Ph.D. dissertation, University of Chicago, 1970. New York: Pilgrim Press, 1971.

Walker, R. C. "The Little Kingdom: Some Considerations and a Map." *Mythlore* 37 (1984): 47–48.

Walker, Steven Charles. "The Making of a Hobbit, Tolkien's Tantalizing Narrative Technique." *Mythlore* 7 (1980): 6–7 ff.

———. "Narrative Technique in the Fiction of J. R. R. Tolkien." Ph.D. dissertation, Harvard University, 1973.

———. "Super Natural Supernatural: Tolkien as Realist." In *Proceedings of the Fifth Annual Conference of the Children's Literature Association.* Harvard University, Mar. 1978. Ypsilanti, MI: Children's Literature Association Publications, 1979, pp. 100–105.

———. "The War of the Rings Trilogy: An Elegy for Lost Innocence and Wonder." *Mythlore* 5 (May 1978): 3–5.

Wells, Andrew. "Armor in the Third Age." *Amon Hen,* July 1984, pp. 16–17.

West, Richard C. "An Annotated Bibliography of Tolkien Criticism." *Extrapolation* 10 (Dec. 1968): 17–49.

———. "The Status of Tolkien Scholarship." *Tolkien Journal* 15 (Summer 1972): 21.

———. *Tolkien Criticism: An Annotated Checklist,* rev. ed. Kent, OH: Kent State Univ. Press, 1981. Originally published in *Tolkien Journal* 4 (1970–1971): 14–31.

Wilson, Colin. "J. R. R. Tolkien." In *The Strength to Dream: Literature and the Imagination,* rev. ed. Westport, CT: Greenwood Press, 1973, pp. 145–148.

———. *Tree by Tolkien.* Santa Barbara, CA: Capra Press, 1974.

Wilson, Edmund. "Oo, Those Awful Orcs." *Nation* 182 (Apr. 14, 1956): 312–313.

Wood, Denis. "Growing Up Among the Stars." *Literary/Film Quarterly* 6 (1978): 327–341.

Wood, Michael. "Tolkien's Fictions." In Nicholas Tucker. *Suitable for Children? Controversies in Children's Literature.* Berkeley: Univ. of California Press, 1976, pp. 165–172. Originally published in *New Society,* Mar. 27, 1969.

Zimmerman, Manfred. "Rendering of Tolkien's Alliterative Verse." *Mythlore* 8 (1981): 21.

Zipes, Jack. *Breaking the Magic Spell: Radical Theories of Folk and Fairy Tales.* New York: Methuen, 1984.

Tomalin, Ruth

Twentieth Century Children's Writers. 2nd ed. Edited by D. L. Kirkpatrick. New York: St. Martin's Press, 1983, pp. 767–768.

Torrey, Marjorie

More Junior Authors. Edited by Muriel Fuller. New York: Wilson, 1963, pp. 207–208.

Townsend, John Rowe

Barnes, Ron. "John Rowe Townsend's Novels of Adolescence." *Children's Literature in Education* 19 (Winter 1975): 178–190.

Crouch, Marcus. *The Nesbit Tradition.* London: Benn, 1972, pp. 206–208.

Fourth Book of Junior Authors and Illustrators. Edited by Doris De Montreville and Elizabeth D. Crawford. New York: Wilson, 1978, pp. 328–330.

Hansen, Carol A. "Recommended: John Rowe Townsend." *English Journal* 73 (Mar. 1984): 89–90.

The Oxford Companion to Children's Literature. Edited by Humphrey Carpenter and Mari Prichard. New York: Oxford Univ. Press, 1984, pp. 536–537.

Rees, David. "Children's Writers: John Rowe Townsend." *School Librarian* 31 (Mar. 1983): 4–11.

———. "A Sense of Story—John Rowe Townsend." In *Painted Desert, Green Shade.* Boston: Horn Book, 1984, pp. 102–114.

Townsend, John Rowe. "Didacticism in Modern Dress." *Horn Book* 43 (Apr. 1967): 159–163.
———. "An Elusive Border." *Horn Book* 50 (Oct. 1974): 33–42.
———. "Heights of Fantasy." In *Children's Literature Review,* vol. 5. Detroit: Gale, 1983, pp. 7–12. Guest essay.
———. "In Literary Terms." *Horn Book* 47 (Aug. 1971): 347–353.
———. "The Life Journey." In *Innocence & Experience.* Edited by Barbara Harrison and Gregory Maguire. New York: Lothrop, 1987, pp. 138–147.
———. "The Now Child." *Horn Book* 49 (June 1973): 241–247.
———. "Under Two Hats." *Quarterly Journal of Library of Congress* 34 (Apr. 1977): 116–128. Reprinted in Haviland. *The Openhearted Audience.* Washington, DC: Library of Congress, 1980, pp. 133–151.
———. "A Wholly Pragmatic Definition [of Children's Literature]." In Robert Bator. *Signposts to Criticism of Children's Literature.* Chicago: American Library Association, 1983, pp. 19–20. Excerpted from "Standards of Criticism for Children's Literature." In Zena Sutherland's *The Arbuthnot Lectures, 1970–1979.* Chicago: American Library Association, 1980, pp. 26–27.
Twentieth Century Children's Writers. 2nd ed. Edited by D. L. Kirkpatrick. New York: St. Martin's Press, 1983, pp. 770–772.
Wintle, Justin, and Fisher, Emma. "John Rowe Townsend." In *The Pied Pipers.* New York: Paddington Press, 1974, pp. 236–248.
"Writers and Critics: A Dialogue Between Jill Paton Walsh and John Rowe Townsend; Part I." *Horn Book* 58 (Oct. 1982): 498–504; "Part II." *Horn Book* 58 (Dec. 1982): 680–685.

Travers, P(amela) L(yndon)

"Authors and Editors." *Publishers Weekly,* Dec. 13, 1971, pp. 7–9.
Bart, Peter, and Bart, Dorothy. "As Told and Sold by Disney." *New York Times Book Review,* May 9, 1965, pp. 2, 32–34.
Bergsten, Staffan. *Mary Poppins and Myth.* Stockholm: Almqvist and Wiksell International, 1978.
Buckley, M. "Words of Power: Language and Reality in the Fantasy Novels of E. Nesbit and P. L. Travers." Ed.D. dissertation, East Texas State University, 1977.
Burness, E., and Griswold, J. "The Art of Fiction; P. L. Travers." *Paris Review* 24 (Winter 1982): 211–229. Interview.
Cott, Jonathan. "The Wisdom of Mary Poppins: Afternoon Tea with P. L. Travers." In *Pipers at the Gate of Dawn.* New York: Random, 1983, pp. 195–240.
Doyle, Brian. *The Who's Who of Children's Literature.* New York: Schocken, 1968, pp. 268–269.
"Elusive Author Expansive with Children." *Library Journal* 91 (Mar. 15, 1966): 1640.
Field, M. "Reminiscing with P. L. Travers. *Publishers Weekly,* Mar. 21, 1986, pp. 40–41.
Frankel, Haskel. "A Rose for Mary Poppins." *Saturday Review,* Nov. 7, 1964, pp. 24–25.
Hearn, Michael Patrick. "P. L. Travers in Fantasy Land." *Children's Literature,* vol. 6. Philadelphia: Temple Univ. Press, 1977, pp. 221–224.
Hoffeld, Laura. "Where Magic Begins." *The Lion and the Unicorn* 3, no. 1 (Spring 1979): 4–13.
Hopkins, Lee Bennett. "P. L. Travers." In *More Books by More People.* New York: Citation Press, 1974, pp. 355–362.
The Junior Book of Authors. 2nd ed. rev. Edited by Stanley J. Kunitz and Howard Haycraft. New York: Wilson, 1951, pp. 287–288.

Lingeman, Richard R. "A Visit with Mary Poppins and P. L. Travers." *New York Times Magazine,* Dec. 25, 1966, pp. 12–13.

Moore, Anne Carroll. *"Mary Poppins." Horn Book* 11 (Jan.–Feb. 1936): 6–7.

Moore, Robert B. *"Mary Poppins:* A Letter from a Critic." In *Children's Literature,* vol. 10. New Haven, CT: Yale Univ. Press, 1982, pp. 211–213.

The Oxford Companion to Children's Literature. Edited by Humphrey Carpenter and Mari Prichard. New York: Oxford Univ. Press, 1984, pp. 342, 540.

Pflieger, Pat, and Hill, Helen M. *A Reference Guide to Modern Fantasy for Children.* Westport, CT: Greenwood Press, 1984, pp. xiv, 351–357, 548–551.

Roddy, Joseph. "A Visit with the Real Mary Poppins: Interview with P. L. Travers." *Look,* December 13, 1966, pp. 84 ff.

Schwartz, Albert V. "Mary Poppins Revised: An Interview with P. L. Travers." *Interracial Books for Children Bulletin* 5, no. 3 (1974): 1, 3–5. Reprinted in Donnarae MacCann and Gloria Woodard. *Cultural Conformity in Books for Children.* Metuchen, NJ: Scarecrow Press, 1977, pp. 134–140; and in White. *Children's Literature.* Columbus, OH: Merrill, 1976, pp. 75–77.

Searles, Baird; Meacham, Beth; and Franklin, Michael. *A Reader's Guide to Fantasy.* New York: Avon, 1982, pp. 147–148.

Smaridge, Norah. *Famous Modern Storytellers for Young People.* New York: Dodd, 1969, pp. 92–97.

Stone, Kay F. "Re-Awakening the Sleeping Beauty: P. L. Travers' Literary Folktale." *Proceedings of the Eighth Annual Conference of the Children's Literature Association.* Ypsilanti, MI: Children's Literature Association, 1982 pp. 84–90.

Travers, P. L. *About Sleeping Beauty.* New York: McGraw-Hill, 1975.

———. "The Black Sheep." *New York Times Book Review,* pt. II. Nov. 7, 1965, pp. 1, 61.

———. "Grimm's Women." *New York Times Book Review,* Nov. 16, 1975, p. 59.

———. "The Heroes of Childhood, A Note on Nannies." *Horn Book* 11 (May–June 1935): 147–155.

———. "I Never Wrote for Children." *New York Times Magazine,* July 2, 1978, pp. 16–18, 30.

———. "Mary Poppins: A Letter from the Author." In *Children's Literature,* vol. 10. New Haven, CT: Yale Univ. Press, 1982, pp. 214–217.

———. "My Childhood Bends Beside Me." *New Statesman* 44 (Nov. 29, 1952): 639.

———. "On Not Writing for Children." *Bookbird* 6, no. 4 (1967): 7–8. Reprinted in *Children's Literature,* vol. 4. Philadelphia: Temple University Press, 1975, pp. 15–22; *Reflections on Literature for Children.* Edited by Francelia Butler and Richard Rotert. Hamden, CT: Shoe String Press, 1984, pp. 58–65.

———. "Once I Saw a Fox Dancing Alone." *New York Herald Tribune Book Week,* May 9, 1965, p. 2.

———. "Only Connect." *Quarterly Journal of the Library of Congress* 24 (Oct. 1967): 232–248. Reprinted in Sheila A. Egoff. *Only Connect.* New York: Oxford Univ. Press, 1980, pp. 182–206; and in *The Openhearted Audience.* Washington, DC: Library of Congress, 1980, pp. 2–23.

———. "A Radical Innocence." *New York Times Book Review,* pt. II, *Children's Book Section,* May 9, 1965, pp. 38–39.

———. "Where Did She Come From, Why Did She Go?" *Saturday Evening Post,* Nov. 7, 1964, pp. 76–77.

———. "Where Do Ideas Come From?" *Bookbird* 5, no. 4 (1967): 7–8.

———. "Who Is Mary Poppins?" *Junior Bookshelf* 18 (Mar. 1964): 45–50.

———. "World Beyond World." *Chicago Sun Times Book Week,* Spring Children's Issue, May 7, 1965, pp. 4–5. Reprinted in Virginia Haviland. *Children and Literature.* Glenview, IL: Scott, Foresman, 1973, pp. 246–249.

Twentieth Century Children's Writers. 2nd ed. Edited by D. L. Kirkpatrick. New York: St. Martin's Press, 1983, pp. 772–773.

Ziner, Feenie. "Mary Poppins as a Zen Monk." *New York Times Book Review,* May 7, 1982, pp. 2, 22.

Tregarthen, Enys (pseud. of Nelie Sloggett)

Wright, Harriet S. "A Visit with Enys Tregarthen." *Horn Book* 26 (May 1950): 205–206.

Yates, Elizabeth. "Enys Tregarthen, 1851–1923." *Horn Book* 25 (May–June 1949): 231–238.

———. "How Enys Tregarthen's Cornish Legends Came to Light." *Horn Book* 16 (Sept. 1940): 334–337.

Turkle, Brinton (Cassaday)

Hopkins, Lee Bennett. "Brinton Turkle." In *Books Are by People.* New York: Citation Press, 1969, pp. 289–291.

Roginski, Jim, ed. *Newbery and Caldecott Medalists and Honor Book Winners.* Littleton, CO: Libraries Unlimited, 1982, pp. 263–265.

Third Book of Junior Authors. Edited by Doris De Montreville and Donna Hill. New York: Wilson, 1972, pp. 288–289.

Turkle, Brinton. "Confessions of a Leprechaun: An Author and Illustrator of Children's Books." *Publishers Weekly,* July 14, 1969, pp. 33–35.

Twentieth Century Children's Writers. 2nd ed. Edited by D. L. Kirkpatrick. New York: St. Martin's Press, 1983, p. 784.

Twain, Mark (pseud. of Samuel Langhorne Clemens)

Bloom, Harold, ed. *Mark Twain.* Edgemont, PA: Chelsea House, 1986.

Briden, E. F. "Advertising in 'A Connecticut Yankee.' " *American Notes and Queries* 21 (Jan.–Feb. 1983): 74.

Budd, Louis J., ed. *Critical Essays on Mark Twain, 1867–1910.* Boston: G. K. Hall, 1982.

Clareson, Thomas D. "Mark Twain." In *Supernatural Fiction Writers: Fantasy and Horror,* vol. 2. Edited by E. F. Bleiler. New York: Scribner, 1985, pp. 761–768.

Clemens, Susy. *Papa: An Intimate Biography of Mark Twain.* New York: Doubleday, 1985.

Collins, W. J. "Hank Morgan in the Garden of Forking Paths: *A Connecticut Yankee in King Arthur's Court* as Alternative History." *Modern Fiction Studies* 32 (Spring 1986): 109–114.

Doyle, Brian. *The Who's Who of Children's Literature.* New York: Schocken, 1968, pp. 274–275.

Fienberg, Lorne. "Twain's *Connecticut Yankee:* The Entrepreneur as a Daimonic Hero." *Modern Fiction Studies* 28 (Summer 1982): 155–167.

Hearn, Michael Patrick. "Mark Twain." In *Writers for Children: Critical Studies of Major Authors since the Seventeenth Century.* Edited by Jane M. Bingham. New York: Scribner, 1988, pp. 573–582.

Helbig, Alethea K., and Perkins, Agnes Regan. *Dictionary of American Children's Fiction, 1859–1959.* Westport, CT: Greenwood Press, 1985, pp. 537–538.

Kaplan, Justin. *Mr. Clemens and Mark Twain: A Biography.* New York: Simon & Schuster, 1983.

Ketterer, David. "Power Fantasy in the 'Science Fiction' of Mark Twain." In Slusser,

Rabkin, and Scholes. *Bridges to Fantasy*. Carbondale: Southern Illinois Univ. Press, 1982, pp. 130–141.

———, ed. *The Science Fiction of Mark Twain*. Hamden, CT: Archon Books, 1984.

Klass, Philip. "An Innocent in Time: Mark Twain in King Arthur's Court." *Extrapolation* 16 (1974): 17–32.

Neider, Charles, ed. *The Selected Letters of Mark Twain*. New York: Harper and Row, 1982.

The Oxford Companion to Children's Literature. Edited by Humphrey Carpenter and Mari Prichard. New York: Oxford Univ. Press, 1984, p. 546.

Stableford, Brian. *"A Connecticut Yankee in King Arthur's Court."* In *Survey of Modern Fantasy Literature*, vol. 1. Edited by Frank N. Magill. Englewood Cliffs, NJ: Salem Press, 1983, pp. 319–323.

Stott, Jon C. *Children's Literature from A to Z*. New York: McGraw-Hill, 1984, p. 275.

Tenney, Thomas Asa. *Mark Twain: A Reference Guide*. Boston: G. K. Hall, 1977.

———. "Mark Twain: A Reference Guide. 5th Annual Supplement." *American Literary Realism* 14 (1981): 157–194.

Twain, Mark. *Mark Twain's Autobiography*. 2 vols. New York: Harper and Row, 1924.

Twentieth Century Children's Writers. 2nd ed. Edited by D. L. Kirkpatrick. New York: St. Martin's Press, 1983, pp. 887–888.

Twentieth-Century Science Fiction Writers. 2nd ed. Edited by Curtis C. Smith. Chicago: St. James Press, 1986, pp. 736–741.

Winters, Donald E. "The Utopianism of Survival: Bellamy's *Looking Backward* and Twain's *A Connecticut Yankee*." *American Studies* 21 (1980): 23–28.

Zall, Paul M., ed. *Mark Twain Laughing: Humorous Anecdotes by and about Samuel L. Clemens*. Knoxville: Univ. of Tennessee, 1985.

Unwin, Nora S(picer)

More Junior Authors. Edited by Muriel Fuller. New York: Wilson, 1963, p. 216.

Unwin, Nora S. "The Artist in England, 1929–1945." *Horn Book* 23 (Mar. 1947): 121–124.

———. "With Small Victories a Lesson Is Crowned." *Horn Book* 36 (Oct. 1960): 378–385.

Yates, Elizabeth. "Portrait of an Artist." *Horn Book* 26 (Mar. 1950): 134–143.

Uttley, Alison (pseud. of Alice Jane Taylor Uttley)

Aers, Lesley. "The Treatment of Time in Four Children's Books." *Children's Literature in Education* 2 (July 1970): 69–81.

Colwell, Eileen. "Dreams and Memories: A Tribute to Alison Uttley for Her 85th Birthday." *Junior Bookshelf* 34 (Feb. 1970): 13–17.

Doyle, Brian. *The Who's Who of Children's Literature*. New York: Schocken, 1968, pp. 277–278.

Graham, Eleanor. "Alison Uttley: An Appreciation." *Junior Bookshelf* 5 (Dec. 1941): 115–120.

The Oxford Companion to Children's Literature. Edited by Humphrey Carpenter and Mari Prichard. New York: Oxford Univ. Press, 1984, p. 555.

Pflieger, Pat, and Hill, Helen M. *A Reference Guide to Modern Fantasy for Children*. Westport, CT: Greenwood Press, 1984, pp. xiii, 546–548, 564–566.

Saintsbury, Elizabeth. *The World of Alison Uttley: A Biography*. London: Baker, 1980.

Twentieth Century Children's Writers. 2nd ed. Edited by D. L. Kirkpatrick. New York: St. Martin's Press, 1983, pp. 791–793.

Uttley, Alison. *Country World: Memories of Childhood.* Selected by Lucy Meredith. London: Faber, 1984.

Van Allsburg, Chris

Fifth Book of Junior Authors and Illustrators. Edited by Sally Holmes Holtze. New York: Wilson, 1983, pp. 316–317.

Gardner, John. "Fun and Games and Dark Imaginings." *New York Times Book Review*, Apr. 26, 1981, pp. 49, 64.

"Jumanji." In *Newbery and Caldecott Medal Books: 1976–1985.* Edited by Lee Kingman. Boston: Horn Book, 1986, pp. 229–237.

Kiefer, B. "Profile: Chris Van Allsburg in Three Dimensions." *Language Arts* 64 (Oct. 1987): 664–673.

Macaulay, David. "Chris Van Allsburg." *Horn Book* 58 (Aug. 1982): 385–387.

———. "Chris Van Allsburg." *Horn Book* 62 (July–Aug. 1986): 425–429.

MacCann, Donnarae, and Richard, Olga. "Picture Books for Children." *Wilson Library Bulletin* 56 (Nov. 1981): 212–213.

McKee, Barbara. "Van Allsburg: From a Different Perspective." *Horn Book* 62 (Sept.–Oct. 1986): 566–571.

The Oxford Companion to Children's Literature. Edited by Humphrey Carpenter and Mari Prichard. New York: Oxford Univ. Press, 1984, pp. 204–207.

Van Allsburg, Chris. "1986 Caldecott Acceptance Speech." *Horn Book* 62 (July–Aug. 1986): 420–424; also in *Top of the News* 42 (Summer 1986): 396–400.

Van Leeuwen, Jean

Fifth Book of Junior Authors and Illustrators. Edited by Sally Holmes Holtze. New York: Wilson, 1983, pp. 317–318.

Van Stockum (Marlin), Hilda (Gerarda)

Coblentz, Catherine Cate. "Birthdays in an Artist's Family." *Horn Book* 20 (Nov. 1944): 461–468.

The Junior Book of Authors. 2nd ed. rev. Edited by Stanley J. Kunitz and Howard Haycraft. New York: Wilson, 1951, pp. 289–290.

Roginski, Jim, ed. *Newbery and Caldecott Medalists and Honor Book Winners.* Littleton, CO: Libraries Unlimited, 1982, pp. 268–269.

Twentieth Century Children's Writers. 2nd ed. Edited by D. L. Kirkpatrick. New York: St. Martin's Press, 1983, pp. 793–794.

Van Stockum, Hilda. "Holland During Invasion." *Horn Book* 22 (Jan. 1946): 50–54.

———. "Storytelling in the Family." *Horn Book* 37 (June 1961): 246–252.

———. "Through an Illustrator's Eyes." *Horn Book* 20 (May 1944): 176–184.

Vance, Jack (pseud. of John Holbrook Vance)

Allen, Paul C. "Of Swords and Sorcery." *Fantasy Crossroads* 9 (1976): 25–27.

Chandler, A. Bertram. "An Appreciation of Jack Vance." *Science Fiction* 4 (June 1982): 53–54.

Close, Peter. "An Interview with Jack Vance." *Science Fiction Review* 6 (Nov. 1977): 36–42.

Dean, John. "The Uses of Wilderness in American Science Fiction." *Science Fiction Studies* 9 (1982): 68–81.

Dirda, Michael. "Jack Vance." In *Supernatural Fiction Writers: Fantasy and Horror,* vol. 2. Edited by E. F. Bleiler. New York: Scribner, 1985, pp. 1105–1111.

Dowling, Terry. "A Xenographical Postscript." *Science Fiction* 2 (1980): 243–250.

Edwards, Malcolm. "Jack Vance." In *Science Fiction Writers*. Edited by E. F. Bleiler. New York: Scribner, 1982, pp. 543–550.

Letson, Russell, ed. *Jack Vance: Light from a Lone Star*. Cambridge, MA: NESFA Press, 1985.

Levack, Daniel J. H. "Jack Vance: A Bibliography." *Science Fiction* 4 (June 1982): 82–84.

Levack, Daniel J. H., and Underwood, Tim. *Fantasms: A Bibliography of the Literature of Jack Vance*. San Francisco: Underwood-Miller, 1978.

McFerran, Dave. "The Magic of *The Dying Earth*." *Anduril* 6 (1976): 35–38.

Platt, Charles. *Dream Makers II*. New York: Berkley, 1983, pp. 159–166. Interview.

Rawline, Jack P. "Linear Man: Jack Vance and the Value of Plot in Science Fiction." *Extrapolation* 24 (1983): 356–369.

Schuyler, William M., Jr. "Recent Developments in Spell Construction." In *The Aesthetics of Fantasy Literature and Art*. Edited by Roger C. Schlobin. Notre Dame, IN: Univ. of Notre Dame, 1982, pp. 237–248.

Silverberg, Robert. "Introduction." In Jack Vance. *Eyes of the Overworld*. Boston: Gregg, 1977.

Spinrad, Norman. "Introduction." In Jack Vance. *The Dragon Masters*. Boston: Gregg, 1976.

Twentieth-Century Science Fiction Writers. 2nd ed. Edited by Curtis C. Smith. Chicago: St. James Press, 1986, pp. 742–744.

Underwood, Tim, and Miller, Chuck, eds. *Jack Vance*. New York: Taplinger, 1980.

Watson, Christine. "*The Dying Earth* and *The Eyes of the Overworld*." In *Survey of Modern Fantasy Literature,* vol. 1. Edited by Frank N. Magill. Englewood Cliffs, NJ: Salem Press, 1983, pp. 441–446.

Vaughan, Agnes Carr

Vaughan, Agnes Carr. "Lucian and His True Story." *Horn Book* 6 (May 1930): 127–130.

Vinge, Joan D(ennison)

Barr, Marleen S., et al. *Reader's Guide to Suzy McKee Charnas, Octavia Butler and Joan Vinge*. Mercer Island, WA: Starmont, 1985.

Frazier, Robert. "Interview: Joan Vinge." *Thrust* 16 (1980): 6–9.

Law, Richard. "Science Fiction Women: Victims, Rebels, Heroes." In *Patterns of the Fantastic*. Mercer Island, WA: Starmont, 1983, pp. 11–20.

Platt, Charles. *Dream Makers II: The Uncommon Men and Women Who Write Science Fiction*. New York: Berkley, 1983, pp. 211–218. Interview.

Schweitzer, Darrell. "An Interview with Joan D. Vinge." *Science Fiction Review* 8 (Mar.–Apr. 1979): 8–12.

Thompson, William B. "Interview: Joan D. Vinge." *Starship* 43 (1983): 15–18.

Twentieth-Century Science Fiction Writers. 2nd ed. Edited by Curtis C. Smith. Chicago: St. James Press, 1986, pp. 755–757.

Yoke, Carl B. "From Alienation to Personal Triumph: The Science Fiction of Joan D.

Vinge." *In the Feminine Eye.* Edited by Tom Staicar. New York: Ungar, 1982, pp. 103–130.

———. "Vinge and Vegetation." *Fantasy Newsletter* 53 (1982): 24–26.

Voigt, Cynthia

Fifth Book of Junior Authors and Illustrators. Edited by Sally Holmes Holtze. New York: Wilson, 1983, pp. 320–321.

Helbig, Alethea K., and Perkins, Agnes Regan. *Dictionary of American Children's Fiction, 1960–1984.* Westport, CT: Greenwood Press, 1986, p. 700.

Henke, James T. "Dicey, Odysseus, and Hansel and Gretel: The Lost Children in Voigt's *Homecoming.*" *Children's Literature in Education* 16 (Spring 1985): 45–52.

Irving, Elsie K. "Cynthia Voigt." *Horn Book* 59 (Aug. 1983): 410–412.

Kauffman, D. "Profile: Cynthia Voigt." *Language Arts* 62 (Dec. 1985): 876–880.

Voigt, Cynthia. "Newbery Medal Acceptance." *Horn Book* 59 (Aug. 1983): 401–409.

Voigt, Jessica. "Cynthia Voigt." *Horn Book* 59 (Aug. 1983): 413.

Waber, Bernard

Bader, Barbara. *American Picturebooks from Noah's Ark to the Beast Within.* New York: Macmillan, 1976, pp. 480–483.

Harmon, Mary K. "Bernard Waber." *Elementary English* 51 (Sept. 1974): 773–776.

Third Book of Junior Authors. Edited by Doris De Montreville and Donna Hill. New York: Wilson, 1972, pp. 293–295.

Twentieth Century Children's Writers. 2nd ed. Edited by D. L. Kirkpatrick. New York: St. Martin's Press, 1983, pp. 799–800.

Wagner, Lauren McGraw

Hanff, Peter E., and Greene, Douglas G. *Bibliographia Oziana.* Demorest, GA: International Wizard of Oz Club, 1976.

Wahl, Jan (Boyer)

Third Book of Junior Authors. Edited by Doris De Montreville and Donna Hill. New York: Wilson, 1972, pp. 295–296.

Twentieth Century Children's Writers. 2nd ed. Edited by D. L. Kirkpatrick. New York: St. Martin's Press, 1983, pp. 800–802.

Walton, Evangeline (pseud. of Evangeline Ensley)

Dowdy, David A. "The Figure of Taliesin." *Mythlore* 6, no. 23 (1979).

Evans, W. D. Emrys. "The Welsh Mabinogion: Tellings and Retellings." *Children's Literature in Education* 9 (Spring 1978): 17–33.

Herman, John. "Recommended: Evangeline Walton." *English Journal* 74 (Apr. 1985): 75–76.

Spencer, Paul. "Evangeline Walton: An Interview." *Fantasy Review* 77 (1985): 7–10.

Sullivan, Charles Williams, III. "Evangeline Walton and the Welsh Mythos." *Fantasy Review* 77 (1985): 35–36, 42.

———. "The Influence of Celtic Myth and Legend on Modern Imaginative Fiction." Ph.D. dissertation, University of Oregon, 1976.

———. "The Mabinogion Tetralogy." In *Survey of Modern Fantasy Literature,* vol. 2. Edited by Frank N. Magill. Englewood Cliffs, NJ: Salem Press, 1983, pp. 932–937.

Walton, Evangeline. "Celtic Myth in the 20th Century." *Mythlore* 3 (1976): 19–22.
Zahorski, Kenneth J., and Boyer, Robert H. *Lloyd Alexander, Evangeline Walton Ensley, Kenneth Morris: A Primary and Secondary Bibliography.* Boston: G. K. Hall, 1981.

Wangerin, Walter

Burger, Douglas A. *"The Book of the Dun Cow."* In *Survey of Modern Fantasy Literature,* vol. 1. Edited by Frank N. Magill. Englewood Cliffs, NJ: Salem Press, 1983, pp. 149–153.

Warburg, Sandol Stoddard (pseud. of Sandol Stoddard)

Hopkins, Lee Bennett. "Sandol Warburg." In *Books Are by People.* New York: Citation Press, 1969, pp. 299–302.

Warner, Sylvia Townsend

Crossley, Robert. "A Long Day's Dying: The Elves of J. R. R. Tolkien and Sylvia Townsend Warner." In *Death and the Serpent: Immortality in Science Fiction and Fantasy.* Edited by Carl B. Yoke and Donald M. Hassler. Westport, CT: Greenwood Press, 1985, pp. 57–70.
Morgan, Chris. *"Kingdoms of Elfin."* In *Survey of Modern Fantasy Literature,* vol. 2. Englewood Cliffs, NJ: Salem Press, 1984, pp. 855–858.

Weir, Rosemary (Green)

Twentieth Century Children's Writers. 2nd ed. Edited by D. L. Kirkpatrick. New York: St. Martin's Press, 1983, pp. 808–809.

Welch, Ronald (pseud. of Ronald Oliver Felton)

Aers, Lesley. "The Treatment of Time in Four Children's Books." *Children's Literature in Education* 2 (July 1970): 69–81.
Crouch, Marcus. *The Nesbit Tradition.* London: Benn, 1972, pp. 72–74.
Doyle, Brian. *The Who's Who of Children's Literature.* New York: Schocken, 1968, pp. 287–288.
Twentieth Century Children's Writers. 2nd ed. Edited by D. L. Kirkpatrick. New York: St. Martin's Press, 1983, pp. 809–810.
Welch, Ronald. "Attention to Detail: The Workbooks of Ronald Welch." *Children's Literature in Education* 8 (Summer 1972): 30–38.

Wellman, Manly Wade

Benson, Gordon, Jr. *Manly Wade Wellman: The Gentleman from Chapel Hill.* Albuquerque: Benson, 1986.
Coulson, Robert. "The Recent Fantasies of Manly Wade Wellman." In *Discovering Modern Horror Fiction.* Edited by Darrell Schweitzer. Mercer Island, WA: Starmont, 1985.
Elliot, Jeffrey M. *Fantasy Voices: Interviews with American Fantasy Writers.* San Bernardino, CA: Borgo Press, 1982.
———. "Interview: Manly Wade Wellman—Better Things Waiting." *Fantasy Newsletter* 22 (1980): 16–25.

Meyers, Walter E. "Manly Wade Wellman." In *Supernatural Fiction Writers: Fantasy and Horror,* vol. 2. Edited by E. F. Bleiler. New York: Scribner, 1985, pp. 947–954.
———. "The Silver John Stories." In *Survey of Modern Fantasy Literature,* vol. 4. Edited by Frank N. Magill. Englewood Cliffs, NJ: Salem Press, 1983, pp. 1744–1748.
More Junior Authors. Edited by Muriel Fuller. New York: Wilson, 1963, pp. 222–223.
Schweitzer, Darrell. "*Amazing* Interview: An Interview With Manly Wade Wellman." *Amazing Stories,* Mar. 1981, pp. 122–126.
Searles, Baird; Meacham, Beth; and Franklin, Michael. *A Reader's Guide to Fantasy.* New York: Avon, 1982, pp 149–150.
Twentieth-Century Science Fiction Writers. 2nd ed. Edited by Curtis C. Smith. Chicago: St. James Press, 1986, pp. 777–779.
Waggoner, Diana. "Go Tell It on the Mountain: The Achievement of Manly Wade Wellman." *Fantasy Review* 90 (1986): 17–19, 50.
Wagner, Karl Edward. "Manly Wade Wellman: A Biography." *August Darleth Society Newsletter* 4 (1980): 4–9.
———. "The Old Captain Goes Home: Manly Wade Wellman, 1903–1986." *Fantasy Review* 90 (1986): 15–16, 34.

Wells, H(erbert) G(eorge)

Cook, Monte. "Tips for Time Travel." In *Philosophers Look at Science Fiction.* Edited by Nicholas D. Smith. Chicago: Nelson, 1982, pp. 47–55.
Costa, Richard Hauer. *H. G. Wells.* rev. ed. Boston: Twayne, 1985.
Crosley, Robert. *H. G. Wells.* Mercer Island, WA: Starmont, 1986.
Ferrell, Keith. *H. G. Wells: First Citizen of the Future.* New York: Evans, 1983.
Gardner, Martin. "H. G. Wells." In *Supernatural Fiction Writers: Fantasy and Horror,* vol. 1. Edited by E. F. Bleiler. New York: Scribner, 1985, pp. 397–402.
H. G. Wells. Maltoon, IL: Spectrum Educational Media, 1984. (Audiocassette)
H. G. Wells. Hawthorne, NJ: Peller, 1985. (Filmstrip-audiocassette)
H. G. Wells Society. *H. G. Wells: A Comprehensive Bibliography.* London: Polytechnic of North London, 1986.
Hammond, J. R. *Herbert George Wells: An Annotated Bibliography of His Works.* New York: Garland, 1977.
Hampson, R. G. "H. G. Wells and *The Arabian Nights.*" *The Wellsian* 6 (1983): 30–34.
Neilson, Keith. "The Short Fiction of H. G. Wells." In *Survey of Modern Fantasy Literature,* vol. 4. Edited by Frank N. Magill. Englewood Cliffs, NJ: Salem Press, 1983, pp. 1729–1932.
Parrinder, Patrick, ed. *H. G. Wells: The Critical Heritage.* New York: Routledge, 1985.
Reed, John R. *The Natural History of H. G. Wells.* Athens: Ohio Univ. Press, 1982.
Twentieth-Century Science Fiction Writers. 2nd ed. Edited by Curtis C. Smith. Chicago: St. James Press, 1986, pp. 779–783.
West, Anthony. *H. G. Wells: Aspects of a Life.* New York: Random, 1984; NAL/Meridian, 1985.
Zanger, Jules. "Goblins, Morlocks and Weasels: Classic Fantasy and the Industrial Revolution." *Children's Literature in Education* 8 (Winter 1977): 154–162.

Wells, Rosemary

Fourth Book of Junior Authors and Illustrators. Edited by Doris De Montreville and Elizabeth D. Crawford. New York: Wilson, 1978, pp. 343–345.
Mercier, Jean F. "Rosemary Wells." *Publishers Weekly* 217 (Feb. 29, 1980): 72–73.

Twentieth Century Children's Writers. 2nd ed. Edited by D. L. Kirkpatrick. New York: St. Martin's Press, 1983, pp. 810–811.

Wersba, Barbara

Cunningham, Julia. "Notes for Another's Music." *Horn Book* 47 (Dec. 1971): 617. Discusses *Let Me Fall Before I Fly*.

Third Book of Junior Authors. Edited by Doris De Montreville and Donna Hill. New York: Wilson, 1972, pp. 298–299.

Twentieth Century Children's Writers. 2nd ed. Edited by D. L. Kirkpatrick. New York: St. Martin's Press, 1983, pp. 811–812.

Vandergrift, Kay E. "Barbara Wersba." In *American Authors for Children since 1960: Fiction. Dictionary of Literary Biography,* vol. 52. Detroit: Gale, 1986, pp. 374–379.

Westall, Robert (Atkinson)

Chambers, Aidan. "Letter from England: Children at War." *Horn Book* 52 (Aug. 1976): 438–442.

Fifth Book of Junior Authors and Illustrators. Edited by Sally Holmes Holtze. New York: Wilson, 1983, pp. 322–324.

The Oxford Companion to Children's Literature. Edited by Humphrey Carpenter and Mari Prichard. New York: Oxford Univ. Press, 1984, p. 565.

Pflieger, Pat, and Hill, Helen M. *A Reference Guide to Modern Fantasy for Children.* Westport, CT: Greenwood Press, 1984, pp. xiii, 150–152, 574–576, 587–589, 603–605.

Rees, David. "Macho Man, British Style—Robert Westall." In *Painted Desert, Green Shade.* Boston: Horn Book, 1984, pp. 115–125.

Searles, Baird; Meacham, Beth; and Franklin, Michael. *A Reader's Guide to Fantasy.* New York: Avon, 1982, pp. 151–152.

Twentieth Century Children's Writers. 2nd ed. Edited by D. L. Kirkpatrick. New York: St. Martin's Press, 1983, pp. 812–813.

Westall, Robert. "The Hunt for Evil." *Signal* 34 (Jan. 1981): 3–13.

Weston, John (Harrison)

Blakely, W. Paul. "Growing Pains in Arizona: Youth in the Fiction of John Weston." *Arizona English Bulletin* 14 (April 1972): 44–50.

White, Anne Hitchcock

Fourth Book of Junior Authors and Illustrators. Edited by Doris De Montreville and Elizabeth D. Crawford. New York: Wilson, 1978, pp. 347–348.

Helbig, Alethea K., and Perkins, Agnes Regan. *Dictionary of American Children's Fiction, 1859–1959.* Westport, CT: Greenwood Press, 1985, pp. 265–266, 496, 561.

More Junior Authors. Edited by Muriel Fuller. New York: Wilson, 1963, pp. 224–225.

White, Anne Hitchcock. "The Animals, One by One." *Horn Book* 34 (June 1958): 211–219.

White, E(lwin) B(rooks)

Alberghene, Janice M. "Writing in *Charlotte's Web*." *Children's Literature in Education* 16 (Spring 1985): 32–44.

Anderson, Arthur James. *E. B. White: A Bibliography*. Metuchen, NJ: Scarecrow Press, 1978.

"Anne Carroll Moore Urged Withdrawal of *Stuart Little*." *Library Journal*, Apr. 15, 1966, pp. 2187–2188; *School Library Journal*, Apr. 15, 1966, pp. 71–72.

Apseloff, Marilyn. "*Charlotte's Web*: Flaws in the Weaving." In Douglas Street. *Children's Novels and the Movies*. New York: Ungar, 1983, pp. 171–181.

Benét, Laura. *Familiar English and American Essayists*. New York: Dodd, 1966.

Blount, Margaret. "The Tables Turned at the Zoo: Mowgli and Stuart Little." In *Animal Land: The Creatures of Children's Fiction*. New York: Morrow, 1975, pp. 226–244.

Breit, H. "Visit." *New York Herald Tribune Book Review*, Jan. 17, 1954.

Cameron, Eleanor. "McLuhan, Youth and Literature." *Horn Book* 48 (Dec. 1972): 572–579. Reprinted in Heins. *Crosscurrents of Criticism*. Boston: Horn Book, 1977, pp. 98–125.

Doyle, Brian. *The Who's Who of Children's Literature*. New York: Schocken, 1968, pp. 289–290.

Elledge, Scott. *E. B. White: A Biography*. New York: Norton, 1984.

Gagnon, Laurence. "Webs of Concern: Heidegger, *The Little Prince*, and *Charlotte's Web*." In *Children's Literature*, vol. 2. Storrs, CT: Journal of the Modern Language Association, 1973, pp. 61–66. Reprinted in *Reflections on Literature for Children*. Edited by Francelia Butler and Richard Rotert. Hamden, CT: Shoe String Press, 1984, pp. 66–71.

Glastonbury, Marion. "E. B. White's Unexpected Items of Enchantment." *Children's Literature in Education* 11 (May 1973): 3–12. Reprinted in Geoff Fox. *Writers, Critics and Children*. New York: Agathon Press, 1976, pp. 104–115.

Griffith, John. "*Charlotte's Web*: A Lonely Fantasy of Love." In *Children's Literature*, vol. 8. New Haven, CT: Yale Univ. Press, 1980, pp. 111–117.

Guth, Dorothy Lobrano, ed. *Letters of E. B. White*. New York: Harper and Row, 1976.

Helbig, Alethea K., and Perkins, Agnes Regan. *Dictionary of American Children's Fiction, 1859–1959*. Westport, CT: Greenwood Press, 1985, pp. 94, 500, 561–562.
———. *Dictionary of American Children's Fiction, 1960–1984*. Westport, CT: Greenwood Press, 1986, pp. 679, 716.

Hopkins, Lee Bennett. "E. B. White." In *More Books by More People*. New York: Citation Press, 1974, pp. 375–380.
———. "Profile in Memoriam: E. B. White." *Language Arts* 63 (Sept. 1986): 491–494.

Inglis, Fred. *The Promise of Happiness*. New York: Cambridge Univ. Press, 1981, pp. 178–180.

Kinghorn, Norton D. "The Real Miracle of *Charlotte's Web*." *Children's Literature Association Quarterly* 11 (Spring 1986): 4–9.

Konigsburg, E. L. "Book Remembered." *The Calendar* (now *CBC Features*) 39 (Oct. 1984–July 1985). Discusses *Charlotte's Web*.

Kurth, Ruth Justine. "Realism in Children's Books of Fantasy." *California Librarian* 39 (July 1978): 39–40.

Landes, Sonia. "E. B. White's *Charlotte's Web*: Caught in the Web." In *Touchstones*. Edited by Perry Nodelman. West Lafayette, IN: Children's Literature Association Publications, 1985, pp. 270–280.

Lukens, Rebecca J. *A Critical Handbook of Children's Literature*. 3rd ed. Glenview, IL: Scott, Foresman, 1986, pp. 95–97, 167–168.

Mason, Bobbie Ann. "Profile: The Elements of E. B. White's Style." *Language Arts* 56 (Sept. 1979): 692–696.

More Junior Authors. Edited by Muriel Fuller. New York: Wilson, 1963, pp. 225–226.

Neumeyer, Peter F. "The Creation of *Charlotte's Web:* From Drafts to Book." Pt. I. *Horn Book* 58 (Oct. 1982): 489–497; Pt. II. *Horn Book* 58 (Dec. 1982): 617–625.

———. "The Creation of E. B. White's *The Trumpet of the Swan:* The Manuscripts." *Horn Book* 61 (Jan.–Feb. 1985): 17–28. A shortened version of a paper presented at the conference of the Children's Literature Association, at the University of North Carolina, Charlotte, on May 25, 1984.

———. "E. B. White." In *American Writers for Children, 1900–1960.* Edited by John Cech. *Dictionary of Literary Biography,* vol. 22. Detroit: Gale, 1983, pp. 333–350.

———. "E. B. White: Aspects of Style." *Horn Book* 63 (Sept.–Oct. 1987): 568–591.

———. "What Makes a Good Children's Book? The Texture of *Charlotte's Web.*" *South Atlantic Bulletin* 44 (1979): 66–75.

Nodelman, Perry. "Text as Teacher: The Beginning of *Charlotte's Web.*" In *Children's Literature,* vol. 13. New Haven CT: Yale Univ. Press, 1985, pp. 109–127.

Nordstrom, Ursula. "Stuart, Wilbur, Charlotte: A Tale of Tales." *New York Times Book Review,* May 21, 1974, p. 8.

Nulton, Lucy. "Eight-Year-Olds in *Charlotte's Web.*" *Elementary English* 31 (Jan. 1954): 11–16.

The Oxford Companion to Children's Literature. Edited by Humphrey Carpenter and Mari Prichard. New York: Oxford Univ. Press, 1984, pp. 108, 568.

Paulus, P. C. "Claim to Fame and *Charlotte's Web.*" *Teacher* 96 (May–June 1979): 48–49.

Pflieger, Pat, and Hill, Helen M. *A Reference Guide to Modern Fantasy for Children.* Westport, CT: Greenwood Press, 1984, pp. xii, xv, 107–108, 508–509, 552–553, 593–595.

Ragsdale, W. "Presentation of the Sixth Recognition of Merit to E. B. White for *Charlotte's Web.*" *Claremont Reading Conference Yearbook* 34 (1970): 114–117.

Roginski, Jim, ed. *Newbery and Caldecott Medalists and Honor Book Winners.* Littleton, CO: Libraries Unlimited, 1982, pp. 279–280.

Rustin, Michael. "The Poetic Power of Ordinary Speech: E. B. White's Children's Stories." In *Narratives of Love and Loss.* London: Verso, 1987, pp. 146–162.

Sale, Roger. *Fairy Tales and After: From Snow White to E. B. White.* Cambridge, MA: Harvard Univ. Press, 1978, pp. 258–267.

Sampson, Edward C. *E. B. White.* Boston: Twayne, 1974.

Silvey, Anita. "In a Class By Himself." *Horn Book* 62 (Jan.–Feb. 1986): 17.

Singer, Dorothy G. "*Charlotte's Web:* Erickson's Life Cycle." *School Library Journal* 22 (Nov. 1975): 17–19.

Smaridge, Norah. *Famous Modern Storytellers for Young People.* New York: Dodd, 1969, pp. 110–114.

Solheim, Helene. "Magic in the Web: Time, Pigs, and E. B. White." *South Atlantic Quarterly* 80 (Autumn 1981): 391–405.

Stott, Jon C. *Children's Literature from A to Z.* New York: McGraw-Hill, 1984, p. 281.

Strunk, William, Jr. *The Elements of Style,* 3rd ed. With Revisions, an Introduction, and a New Chapter on Writing by E. B. White. New York: Macmillan, 1979.

Swinfen, Ann. *In Defense of Fantasy.* London: Routledge, 1984, pp. 24–25. Discusses *Stuart Little.*

Twentieth Century Children's Writers. 2nd ed. Edited by D. L. Kirkpatrick. New York: St. Martin's Press, 1983, pp. 816–818.

"Typewriter Man." *Newsweek* 55 (Feb. 22, 1960): 72.

Weales, Gerald. "The Designs of E. B. White." *New York Times,* sect. 7, pt. II, May 24, 1970, p. 2 ff. Reprinted in Miriam Hoffman and Eva Samuels. *Authors and Illustrators of Children's Books.* New York: Bowker, 1972, pp. 407–411.

White, E. B. "Children's Books." In *One Man's Meat,* rev. ed. New York: Harper and Row, 1944, pp. 23–29.

———. "Death of a Pig." *Atlantic Monthly* 181 (Jan. 1948): 30–33.

———. *The Essays of E. B. White.* New York: Harper and Row, 1977.

———. "Laura Ingalls Wilder Acceptance." *Horn Book* 46 (Aug. 1970): 349–351.

———. *The Letters of E. B. White.* Collected and edited by Dorothy Lobrano Guth. New York: Harper and Row, 1976.

———. "Mr. Forbush's Friends." In *Essays of E. B. White.* New York: Harper and Row, 1977.

———. "On Writing for Children." From "The Art of the Essay." *Paris Review,* no. 48 (Fall 1969). Reprinted in Virginia Haviland. *Children and Literature.* Glenview, IL: Scott, Foresman, 1973, p. 140.

———. *The Second Tree from the Corner.* New York: Harper and Row, 1954; 1978.

Wintle, Justin, and Fisher, Emma. "E. B. White." In *The Pied Pipers.* New York: Paddington Press, 1974, pp. 124–131.

White, Eliza Orne

"Eliza Orne White, Her Books for Children." *Horn Book* 1 (Jan. 1925): 3–9.

The Junior Book of Authors. 2nd ed. rev. Edited by Stanley J. Kunitz and Howard Haycraft. New York: Wilson, 1951, pp. 295–296.

Miller, Bertha Mahony. "Eliza Orne White and Her Books for Children." *Horn Book* 31 (Apr. 1955): 89–102. Reprinted in Andrews. *The Hewins Lectures, 1947–1962.* Boston: Horn Book, 1963, pp. 151–162.

Twentieth Century Children's Writers. 2nd ed. Edited by D. L. Kirkpatrick. New York: St. Martin's Press, 1983, pp. 818–819.

White, Eliza Orne. "Growing Old with the Radio." *Horn Book* 18 (Jan. 1942): 47–82.

White, Stewart Edward

Alter, Judy. *Stewart Edward White.* Boise, ID: Boise State Univ., 1975.

White, T(erence) H(anbury)

Allen, E. M. "The Fellowship of Merlin: The Role of the Sorcerer in *The Once and Future King* and *The Lord of the Rings.*" Master's thesis, Baylor University, 1978.

Chapman, Ed. "Images of the Numinous in T. H. White and C. S. Lewis." *Mythlore* 4, 16 (June 1977): 3–10.

Clute, John. "T. H. White." In *Supernatural Fiction Writers: Fantasy and Horror,* vol. 2. Edited by E. F. Bleiler. New York: Scribner, 1985, pp. 651–660.

Crane, John K. *T. H. White.* Boston: Twayne, 1974.

———. "T. H. White: The Fantasy of the Here and Now." *Mosaic* 10, no. 2 (Winter 1976–1977): 33–46.

de Camp, L. Sprague. *Literary Swordsmen and Sorcerers: The Makers of Heroic Fantasy.* Sauk City, WI: Arkham House, 1976.

———, ed. *The Blade of Conan.* New York: Ace, 1979.

Doyle, Brian. *The Who's Who of Children's Literature.* New York: Schocken, 1968, pp. 290–291.

Floyd, Barbara. "A Critique of *The Once and Future King,* Part 1: Not Any Common Earth." *Riverside Quarterly* 1 (1965): 175–180.

Foust, R. E. "*Mistress Masham's Repose.*" In *Survey of Modern Fantasy Literature,* vol. 3. Edited by Frank N. Magill. Englewood Cliffs, NJ: Salem Press, 1983, pp. 1052–1056.

Fries, Maureen. "The Rationalization of the Arthurian Matter in T. H. White and Mary Stewart." *Philological Quarterly* 56 (1977): 258–265.

Gallix, Francois. "T. H. White et la Legende du Roi Arthur." *Mosaic* 10, no. 2 (Winter 1976–1977): 47–64.

Garnett, David, ed. *The White/Garnett Letters*. London: Cape, 1968.

Irwin, W. R. "Swift and the Novelists." *Philological Quarterly* 45, no. 1 (Jan. 1966): 102–113.

Kellman, Martin Hirsch. "Arthur and Others: The Literary Career of T. H. White." Ph.D. dissertation, University of Pennsylvania, 1973.

Kertzer, Adrienne. "T. H. White's *The Sword in the Stone:* Education and the Child Reader." In *Touchstones*. Edited by Perry Nodelman. West Lafayette, IN: Children's Literature Association Publications, 1985, pp. 281–290.

Langton, Jane. "A Second Look: *Mistress Masham's Repose.*" *Horn Book* 57 (Oct. 1981): 565–570.

Lott, Herschel Woodley. "The Social and Political Ideals in the Major Writings of T. H. White." Ph.D. dissertation, University of Southern Mississippi, 1970.

Manlove, C. N. "Fantasy and Loss: T. H. White." In C. N. Manlove. *The Impulse of Fantasy Literature*. Kent, OH: Kent State Univ. Press, 1983, pp. 93–114 (revised from an article in *Mosaic,* 1979)

———. "Flight to Aleppo: T. H. White's *The Once and Future King.*" *Mosaic* 10, no. 2 (Winter 1976–1977): 65–84.

Mitchell, Judith H. "The Boy Who Would Be King." *Journal of Popular Culture* 17 (Spring 1984): 134–137.

Nellis, Marilyn K. "Anachronistic Humor in Two Arthurian Romances of Education: *To the Chapel Perilous* and *The Sword and the Stone.*" *Studies in Medievalism* 2 (Fall 1983): 57–77.

Nelson, Marie. "Bird Language in T. H. White's *The Sword in the Stone.*" *Mythlore* 8, 28 (1981).

The Oxford Companion to Children's Literature. Edited by Humphrey Carpenter and Mari Prichard. New York: Oxford Univ. Press, 1984, pp. 353–354, 386, 511, 568.

Pflieger, Pat, and Hill, Helen M. *A Reference Guide to Modern Fantasy for Children*. Westport, CT: Greenwood Press, 1984, pp. xii, xiv, 372–373, 516–518, 595–597.

Searles, Baird; Meacham, Beth; and Franklin, Michael. *A Reader's Guide to Fantasy*. New York: Avon, 1982, p. 152.

Shippey, T. A. *"The Once and Future King."* In *Survey of Modern Fantasy Literature,* vol. 3. Englewood Cliffs, NJ: Salem Press, 1983, pp. 1149–1157.

Sprague, Kurth. "From a Troubled Heart: T. H. White and Women in *The Once and Future King.*" Ph.D. dissertation, University of Texas, Austin, 1978.

Stevenson, Lionel. "Purveyors of Myth and Magic." In *Yesterday and After: The History of the English Novel*. Totowa, NJ: Barnes and Noble, 1967, pp. 111–154.

Stott, Jon C. *Children's Literature from A to Z*. New York: McGraw-Hill, 1984, p. 284.

Swanson, Donald R. "The Uses of Tradition: King Arthur in the Modern World." *CEA Critic* 36, no. 3 (1974): 19–21.

Swinfen, Ann. *In Defense of Fantasy*. London: Routledge, 1984, pp. 23–24, 26–30, 124, on *The Sword in the Stone;* pp. 125–126, 129–130, on *Mistress Masham's Repose*.

Twentieth Century Children's Writers. 2nd ed. Edited by D. L. Kirkpatrick. New York: St. Martin's Press, 1983, pp. 819–820.

Warner, Sylvia Ashton. *T. H. White: A Biography*. London: Cape, 1967.

Whitaker, Muriel. "Swords at Sunset and Bag-Puddings: Arthur in Modern Fiction." *Children's Literature in Education* 27, no. 8 (Winter 1977): 143–153.

Wood, Denis. "Growing Up Among the Stars." *Literary/Film Quarterly* 6 (1978): 327–341.

White, W(illiam) A(nthony) P(arker) *see* Boucher, Anthony

Whitney, Phyllis A(yame)

The Junior Book of Authors. 2nd ed. rev. Edited by Stanley J. Kunitz and Howard Haycraft. New York: Wilson, 1951, pp. 297–298.

Wibberley, Leonard (Patrick O'Connor)

Helbig, Alethea K., and Perkins, Agnes Regan. *Dictionary of American Children's Fiction, 1859–1959*. Westport, CT: Greenwood Press, 1985, pp. 563–564.
————. *Dictionary of American Children's Fiction, 1960–1984*. Westport, CT: Greenwood Press, 1986, p. 722.
More Junior Authors. Edited by Muriel Fuller. New York: Wilson, 1963, pp. 226–227.
Morgan, Chris. "The Quest of Excalibur." In *Survey of Modern Fantasy Literature*, vol. 3. Edited by Frank N. Magill. Englewood Cliffs, NJ: Salem Press, 1983, pp. 1301–1303.
Searles, Baird; Meacham, Beth; and Franklin, Michael. *A Reader's Guide to Fantasy*. New York: Avon, 1982, p. 154.
Twentieth Century Children's Writers. 2nd ed. Edited by D. L. Kirkpatrick. New York: St. Martin's Press, 1983, pp. 822–824.
Twentieth-Century Science Fiction Writers. 2nd ed. Edited by Curtis C. Smith. Chicago: St. James Press, 1986, pp. 789–791.
White, I. J. "The Historical Stories of Leonard Wibberley—An Appreciation." *Ontario Library Review* 47 (Aug. 1963): 95–97.
Wibberley, Leonard. "I Go There Quite Often." *Horn Book* 54 (June 1978): 249–256.

Wiggin, Kate Douglas (Smith)

Benner, Helen Frances. *Kate Douglas Wiggin's Country of Childhood*. Orono: Univ. Press of Maine, 1956.
Boutwell, Edna. "Kate Douglas Wiggin—The Lady with the Golden Key." In Siri Andrews. *The Hewins Lectures, 1947–1962*. Boston: Horn Book, 1963, pp. 297–319.
Butler, Francelia. "Kate Douglas Wiggin." In *Writers for Children: Critical Studies of Major Authors since the Seventeenth Century*. Edited by Jane M. Bingham. New York: Scribner, 1988, pp. 605–610.
Doyle, Brian. *The Who's Who of Children's Literature*. New York: Schocken, 1968, pp. 291–292.
Erisman, Fred. "Transcendentalism for American Youth: The Children's Books of Kate Douglas Wiggin." *New England Quarterly* 41, 2 (June 1968): 238–247.
Helbig, Alethea K., and Perkins, Agnes Regan. *Dictionary of American Children's Fiction, 1859–1959*. Westport, CT: Greenwood Press, 1985, p. 564.
Kingston, Carolyn T. *The Tragic Mode in Children's Literature*. New York: Teachers College Press, 1974, pp. 127–130.
Moss, Anita. "Kate Douglas Wiggin." In *American Writers for Children before 1900. Dictionary of Literary Biography*, vol. 42. Detroit: Gale, 1985, pp. 380–392.
Stebbins, Lucy Ward. "Kate Douglas Wiggin as a Child Knew Her." *Horn Book* 26 (Nov.–Dec. 1950): 447–454.
Twentieth Century Children's Writers. 2nd ed. Edited by D. L. Kirkpatrick. New York: St. Martin's Press, 1983, pp. 825–827.

Wiggin, Kate Douglas. *My Garden of Memory: An Autobiography*. Boston: Houghton Mifflin, 1923.

————. "What Shall Children Read?" *Cosmopolitan* 7 (Aug. 1889): 355–360.

Wilde, Oscar (pseud. of Fingal O'Flahertie Wills)

Bradley, Anna Y. "Oscar Wilde." In *Writers for Children: Critical Studies of Major Authors since the Seventeenth Century*. Edited by Jane M. Bingham. New York: Scribner, 1988, pp. 611–616.

Cohen, Philip K. *The Moral Vision of Oscar Wilde*. Rutherford, NJ: Fairleigh Dickinson Univ. Press, 1978.

Cornwell, Charles Landrum. "From Self to the Shire: Studies in Victorian Fantasy." Ph.D. dissertation, University of Virginia, 1972.

Doyle, Brian. *The Who's Who of Children's Literature*. New York: Schocken, 1968, p. 292.

Eisner, Greta. *"The Canterville Ghost."* In *Survey of Modern Fantasy Literature*, vol. 1. Edited by Frank N. Magill. Englewood Cliffs, NJ: Salem Press, 1983, pp. 190–192.

Elkins, Mary J. "Oscar Wilde." In *Supernatural Fiction Writers: Fantasy and Horror*, vol. 1. Edited by E. F. Bleiler. New York: Scribner, 1985, pp. 345–350.

Fido, Martin. *Oscar Wilde: An Illustrated Biography*. New York: Peter Bedrick, dist. by Harper, 1986.

Griswold, Jerome. "Sacrifice and Mercy in Wilde's *The Happy Prince*." In *Children's Literature*, vol. 3. Storrs, CT: Journal of the Modern Language Association, 1974, pp. 103–106.

Jackson, Rosemary. *Fantasy: The Literature of Subversion*. New York: Methuen, 1980, pp. 45, 108, 112–114, 180.

Kotzin, M. C. "*The Selfish Giant* as a Literary Fairy Tale." *Studies in Short Fiction* 16 (Fall 1979): 301–309.

Lawler, Donald L. *"The Picture of Dorian Gray."* In *Survey of Modern Fantasy Literature*, vol. 3. Edited by Frank N. Magill. Englewood Cliffs, NJ: Salem Press, 1983, pp. 1257–1261.

Martin, Robert K. "Oscar Wilde and the Fairy Tale: *The Happy Prince* as Self-Dramatization." *Studies in Short Fiction* 16 (Winter 1979): 74–77.

Monaghan, David M. "The Literary Fairy Tale: A Study of Oscar Wilde's *The Happy Prince* and *The Star Child*." *Canadian Review of Comparative Literature* 1, no. 2 (Spring 1974): 156–166.

Morley, Sheridan. *Oscar Wilde*. New York: Holt, 1976.

Nassaar, Christopher S. *Into the Demon Universe: A Literary Exploration of Oscar Wilde*. New Haven, CT: Yale Univ. Press, 1974.

The Oxford Companion to Children's Literature. Edited by Humphrey Carpenter and Mari Prichard. New York: Oxford Univ. Press, 1984, p. 238.

Quintus, John Allen. "The Moral Prerogative in Oscar Wilde: A Look at the Fairy Tales." *Virginia Quarterly Review* 53 (Autumn 1977): 708–717.

Searles, Baird; Meacham, Beth; and Franklin, Michael. *A Reader's Guide to Fantasy*. New York: Avon, 1982, pp. 154–155.

Shewan, Rodney. *Oscar Wilde: Art and Egotism*. New York: Harper and Row, 1977.

Spelman, Marilyn Kelly. "The Self-Realization Themes in *The Happy Prince* and *A House of Pomegranates*." Ph.D. dissertation, University of Colorado at Boulder, 1978.

Stableford, Brian. *"The Happy Prince and Other Tales* and *A House of Pomegranates."* In *Survey of Modern Fantasy Literature*, vol. 2. Edited by Frank N. Magill. Englewood Cliffs, NJ: Salem Press, 1983, pp. 687–689.

Tremper, Ellen. "Commitment and Escape: The Fairy Tales of Thackeray, Dickens and Wilde." *The Lion and the Unicorn* 2 (Spring 1978): 38–47.

Wilder, Cherry (pseud. of Cherry Barbara Lockett Grimm)

"Awards, Awards." *Locus* 11 (April 1978): 3.
Brown, E. C. "Snapshot." *Vector* 117 (Dec. 1983): 5–9, 38.
Twentieth-Century Science Fiction Writers. 2nd ed. Edited by Curtis C. Smith. Chicago: St. James Press, 1986, pp. 791–792.

Wilhelm, Kate (Katie Gertrude)

Law, Richard. "Science Fiction Women: Victims, Rebels, Heroes." In *Patterns of the Fantastic*. Edited by Donald M. Hassler. Mercer Island, WA: Starmont, 1983, pp. 11–20.
Platt, Charles. *Dream Makers*. New York: Berkley, 1980, pp. 193–204.
Twentieth-Century Science Fiction Writers. 2nd ed. Edited by Curtis C. Smith. Chicago: St. James Press, 1986, pp. 792–794.
Villani, Jim. "The Women Science Fiction Writers and the Non-Heroic Male Protagonist." In *Patterns of the Fantastic*. Edited by Donald M. Hassler. Mercer Island, WA: Starmont, 1983, pp. 21–30.
Wilhelm, Kate. "The Book of Ylin: A Trilogy." *Fantasy Newsletter* 58 (1983): 8–9, 38.
———. "Something Happens." In *Teaching Science Fiction: Education for Tomorrow*. Edited by Jack Williamson. Philadelphia: Owlswick Press, 1980, pp. 184–189.
———. "The Uncertain Edge of Reality." *Locus* 237 (1980): 7–8, 17.
Wood, Susan. "Kate Wilhelm Is a Writer." *Starship* 40 (1980): 7–16.

Wilkins, Mary Huiskamp *see* Calhoun, Mary

Willard, Nancy

Fifth Book of Junior Authors and Illustrators. Edited by Sally Holmes Holtze. New York: Wilson, 1983, pp. 326–327.
Helbig, Alethea K., and Perkins, Agnes Regan. *Dictionary of American Children's Fiction, 1960–1984*. Westport, CT: Greenwood Press, 1986, pp. 314–315, 570–571, 725.
Lucas, Barbara. "Nancy Willard." *Horn Book* 58 (Aug. 1982): 374–379.
Perkins, Agnes. "Nancy Willard: Scribe of Dreams." *Children's Literature Association Quarterly* 10 (Spring 1985): 38–40.
Twentieth Century Children's Writers. 2nd ed. Edited by D. L. Kirkpatrick. New York: St. Martin's Press, 1983, pp. 831–832.
Vousden, Charles E., and Ingram, Laura. "Nancy Willard." In *American Writers for Children since 1960: Fiction. Dictionary of Literary Biography*, vol. 52. Detroit: Gale, 1986, pp. 386–391.
Willard, Nancy. "Angel in the Parlor: The Reading and Writing of Fantasy." *Antioch Review* 35 (Fall 1977): 426–437.
———. "A Child's Star." *Horn Book* 30 (Dec. 1954): 447–454.
———. "A Drawing by Nancy Willard, Age Seventeen, Ann Arbor, Michigan." *Horn Book* 30 (June 1954): 191.
———. "Magic, Craft, and the Making of Children's Books." In *The Writer's Handbook*. Edited by Sylvia K. Burack. Boston: The Writer, 1985.
———. "Newbery Medal Acceptance Speech." *Horn Book* 58 (Aug. 1982): 369–373.

————. "The Spinning Room: Symbols and Storytellers." *Horn Book* 56 (Oct. 1980): 555–564.

————. "The Watcher." In *Innocence & Experience*. Edited by Barbara Harrison and Gregory Maguire. New York: Lothrop, 1987, pp. 422–426.

————. "The Well-Tempered Falsehood: The Art of Storytelling." *Top of the News* 39 (Fall 1982): 104–113.

————. "When By Now and Tree By Leaf: Time and Timelessness in the Reading and Making of Children's Books." *Children's Literature Association Quarterly* 10 (Winter 1986): 166–172.

Williams, Garth (Montgomery)

Friedberg, Joan Brest. "Garth Williams." In Cech. *American Writers for Children, 1900–1960. Dictionary of Literary Biography*, vol. 22. Detroit: Gale, 1983, pp. 367–376.

More Junior Authors. Edited by Muriel Fuller. New York: Wilson, 1963, p. 227.

Stott, Jon C. *Children's Literature from A to Z*. New York: McGraw-Hill, 1984, p. 292.

Williams, Garth. *Self-Portrait, Garth Williams*. Reading, MA: Addison-Wesley, 1982.

Williams, Jay

Fourth Book of Junior Authors and Illustrators. Edited by Doris De Montreville and Elizabeth D. Crawford. New York: Wilson, 1978, pp. 352–353.

Helbig, Alethea K., and Perkins, Agnes Regan. *Dictionary of American Children's Fiction, 1859–1959*. Westport, CT: Greenwood Press, 1985, p. 566.

————. *Dictionary of American Children's Fiction, 1960–1984*. Westport, CT: Greenwood Press, 1986, pp. 275, 726.

Newman, Robert. "Jay Williams, 1914–1978." *Signal* 27 (Sept. 1978): 112–118.

Twentieth Century Children's Writers. 2nd ed. Edited by D. L. Kirkpatrick. New York: St. Martin's Press, 1983, pp. 832–834.

Williams, Jay. "Looking for a Pattern." *Signal* 16 (Jan. 1975): 3–4.

————. "A Sense of Wonder." *Pacific Northwest Library Association Quarterly* 26 (Jan. 1962): 28–82; *Montana Libraries* 15 (Apr. 1962): 16–21; and in *Top of the News* 18 (Mar. 1962): 50–54.

Williams, Kit

"Kit Williams, Visual Photographer." *Locus* 17 (Sept. 1984): 4.

Williams (John), Ursula Moray

Doyle, Brian. *The Who's Who of Children's Literature*. New York: Schocken, 1968, p. 294.

Fourth Book of Junior Authors and Illustrators. Edited by Doris De Montreville and Elizabeth D. Crawford. New York: Wilson, 1978, pp. 269–271.

Moss, Elaine. "Ursula Moray Williams and *Adventures of the Little Wooden Horse*." *Signal* 5 (May 1971): 56–61. Reprinted in *Part of the Pattern*. New York: Greenwillow, 1986, pp. 53–57.

The Oxford Companion to Children's Literature. Edited by Humphrey Carpenter and Mari Prichard. New York: Oxford Univ. Press, 1984, p. 572.

Twentieth Century Children's Writers. 2nd ed. Edited by D. L. Kirkpatrick. New York: St. Martin's Press, 1983, pp. 559–561.

Wills, Fingal O'Flahertie *see* Wilde, Oscar

Wilson, Gahan

Schweitzer, Darrell, ed. *Science Fiction Voices*. Baltimore: T-K Graphics, 1976. Interview.

Wiater, Stanley. "Interview: Gahan Wilson." *Fantasy Newsletter* 6 (Oct.–Nov. 1983): 11–12, 46.

Wilson, Joyce Muriel Judson *see* Stranger, Joyce

Windsor, Patricia (Frances)

Fifth Book of Junior Authors and Illustrators. Edited by Sally Holmes Holtze. New York: Wilson, 1983, pp. 328–330.

Winterfeld, Henry

Third Book of Junior Authors. Edited by Doris De Montreville and Donna Hill. New York: Wilson, 1972, pp. 302–303.

Winthrop (Mahony), Elizabeth

Fifth Book of Junior Authors and Illustrators. Edited by Sally Holmes Holtze. New York: Wilson, 1983, pp. 330–331.

Wiseman, David

Fifth Book of Junior Authors and Illustrators. Edited by Sally Holmes Holtze. New York: Wilson, 1983, pp. 331–332.

Wolfe, Gene (Rodman)

Barker, Chris. "*The Citadel of the Autarch,* and *The New Sun.*" *Vector* 119 (1984): 35–37.

Clareson, Thomas D. "Variations and Design: The Fiction of Gene Wolfe." In *Voices for the Future: Volume Three*. Edited by Thomas D. Clareson and Thomas L. Wymer. Bowling Green, OH: Bowling Green Univ. Press, 1984, pp. 1–29.

Dickinson, Mike. "Why They're All Crying Wolfe." *Vector* 118 (1984): 13–20.

"A Few Minutes With Gene Wolfe." *American Fantasy* (Fall 1986): 20–21.

Frazier, Robert. "Interview: Gene Wolfe—'The Legerdemain of the Wolfe.' " *Thrust* 19 (1983): 5–9.

Gene Wolfe—Interview. Columbia, MO: American Audio Prose Library, 1984. (audiocassette)

Gillespie, Bruce. "Gene Wolfe's Slight of Hand." *Australian Science Fiction Review* (Mar. 1986): 12–17.

Goldman, Stephen G. "In Search of New Worlds: The John N. Campbell Memorial Award." *Science Fiction Writers Association Bulletin* 85 (1988): 8–9.

Gordon, Joan. "Interview: Gene Wolfe." *Science Fiction Review* 39 (1983): 18–22.

———. "An Interview with Gene Wolfe." *Science Fiction Review* 38 (1981): 18–22.

Gordon, Ruth. *Gene Wolfe*. Mercer Island, WA: Starmont, 1986.

Greenland, Colin. "Riding a Bicycle Backwards: An Interview with Gene Wolfe." *Foundation* 31 (1984): 37–44.

Hanna, Judith, and Nicholas, Joseph. "A Two-Foot Square of Gene Wolfe." *Vector* 118 (1984): 5–12.

Lane, Daryl; Vernon, William; and Carlson, David. *The Sound of Wonder: Interviews from "The Science Fiction Radio Show,"* vol. 2. Phoenix, AZ: Oryx Press, 1985, pp. 141–158.

Manlove, C. N. *"Terminus Non Est:* Gene Wolfe's *The Book of the New Sun." Kansas Quarterly* 16 (Summer 1984): 7–20.

Meyers, Walter E. *"The Book of the New Sun."* In *Survey of Modern Fantasy Literature,* vol. 1. Edited by Frank N. Magill. Englewood Cliffs, NJ: Salem Press, 1983, pp. 154–160.

Nelson, Chris. "Books by Gene Wolfe: A Checklist." *Science Fiction* 7 (1985): 15–17.

Schweitzer, Darrell. "Interview: Gene Wolfe." *Fantasy Newsletter* 49 (1982): 8–9, 37.

Swanson, Elliot. "Gene Wolfe." *Interzone* 17 (1986): 38–40.

Talbot, Norman. "The Audience and the Narrators in Gene Wolfe's *The Book of the New Sun."* In *Contrary Modes.* Edited by Jenny Blackford. Melbourne, Australia: Ebony Books, 1985.

Twentieth-Century Science Fiction Writers. 2nd ed. Edited by Curtis C. Smith. Chicago: St. James Press, 1986, pp. 810–813.

Wolfe, Gene. "Aussiecon Two, Guest of Honor Speech." *Science Fiction Chronicle* 73 (1985): 1.

———. "The Profession of Science Fiction: XVIII." *Foundation* 18 (1980): 5–11.

———. "The Special Problems of Science Fiction." *The Writer* 89 (May 1976): 12–14.

———. "What Do They Mean, Science Fiction?" *The Writer* 93 (Aug. 1980): 11–13, 45; *Science Fiction Writers Association Bulletin* 75 (1981): 20–25.

———. "Where I Get My Ideas." In *The Science Fiction Sourcebook.* Edited by David Wingrove. New York: Van Nostrand Reinhold, 1984, pp. 84–85.

Wood, James Playsted

Fourth Book of Junior Authors and Illustrators. Edited by Doris De Montreville and Elizabeth D. Crawford. New York: Wilson, 1978, pp. 353–355.

Wood, James Playsted. "The Honest Audience." *Horn Book* 43 (Oct. 1967): 612–615.

———. "Writers Do Not Exist." *Horn Book* 42 (Dec. 1966): 694–697.

Wright, Betty Ren

Helbig, Alethea K., and Perkins, Agnes Regan. *Dictionary of American Children's Fiction, 1960–1984.* Westport, CT: Greenwood Press, 1986, p. 740.

Wrightson, (Alice) Patricia (Furlonger)

Attebery, Brian. "Women's Coming of Age in Fantasy." *Extrapolation* 28 (Spring 1987): 10–22.

Barelli, Linnell. "Patricia Wrightson: Her Development in Style and Subject Matter." *Orana* 18 (Aug. 1982): 75–83.

Cooper, Susan. "A Second Look: *The Nargun and the Stars." Horn Book* 62 (Sept.–Oct. 1986): 572–574.

Crago, Hugh, and Crago, Maureen. "Patricia Wrightson." *Signal* 19 (Jan. 1976): 31–39.

Fisher, Marjorie T. "Writers for Children: Patricia Wrightson." *School Librarian* 17 (Mar. 1969): 22–26.

Fourth Book of Junior Authors and Illustrators. Edited by Doris De Montreville and Elizabeth D. Crawford. New York: Wilson, 1978, pp. 355–356.

Gilderdale, Betty. "The Novels of Patricia Wrightson." *Children's Literature in Education* 28, no. 1 (1978): 43–49.

McVitty, Walter. "Patricia Wrightson: At the Edge of Australian Vision." In *Innocence and Experience.* Melbourne, Australia: Nelson, 1981, pp. 99–132.

Moon, Kenneth. "The Use of the Natural World in Patricia Wrightson's *The Ice Is Coming* and *The Dark Bright Water.*" *Orana* 22 (May 1986): 102–106.

The Oxford Companion to Children's Literature. Edited by Humphrey Carpenter and Mari Prichard. New York: Oxford Univ. Press, 1984, p. 582.

Ryan, John S. *Australian Fantasy and Folklore.* Armidale, New South Wales: Univ. of New England, 1981.

———. "The Developing Lore of the Margin as Monster for Patricia Wrightson." *Orana* 22 (Aug. 1986): 123–132.

Saxby, Maurice. "The Art of Patricia Wrightson." *Bookbird* 24 (Nov. 2, 1986): 5–7.

———. "At Mrs. Tucker's House." *Horn Book* 64 (Mar.–Apr. 1988): 180–185.

Townsend, John Rowe. "Guest Essay, Heights of Fantasy." *Children's Literature Review,* vol. 5. Detroit: Gale, 1983, p. 11.

———. "Patricia Wrightson." In *A Sense of Story.* Philadelphia: Lippincott, 1971, pp. 204–214.

———. "Patricia Wrightson." In *A Sounding of Storytellers.* Philadelphia: Lippincott, 1979, pp. 194–206.

Twentieth Century Children's Writers. 2nd ed. Edited by D. L. Kirkpatrick. New York: St. Martin's Press, 1983, pp. 842–843.

Wrightson, Patricia. "Ever Since My Accident: Aboriginal Folklore and Australian Fantasy." *Horn Book* 56 (Dec. 1980): 609–617.

———. "The Fellowship of Man and Beast." *Horn Book* 61 (Jan.–Feb. 1985): 38–41.

———. "The Geranium Leaf." *Horn Book* 62 (Mar.–Apr. 1986): 176–185. Anne Carroll Moore Spring Lecture, N.Y. Public Library.

———. "The Nature of Fantasy." In *Readings in Children's Literature.* Edited by Moira Robinson. Frankston, Victoria, Australia: Frankston State College, 1975.

———. "Stones into Pools." *Top of the News* 41 (Spring 1985): 283–292. May Hill Arbuthnot Honor Lecture.

Young, Donald A. "Patricia Wrightson." *Junior Bookshelf* 45 (Dec. 1981): 234–237 ff.

Wuorio, Eva-Lis

Third Book of Junior Authors. Edited by Doris De Montreville and Donna Hill. New York: Wilson, 1972, pp. 306–307.

Wyndham, Lee (pseud. of Jane Andrews Lee Hyndman)

More Junior Authors. Edited by Muriel Fuller. New York: Wilson, 1963, pp. 229–230.

Yep, Laurence M(ichael)

Dinchak, Maria. "Recommended: Laurence Yep." *English Journal* 71 (Mar. 1982): 81–82.

Fifth Book of Junior Authors and Illustrators. Edited by Sally Holmes Holtze. New York: Wilson, 1983, pp. 339–340.

Helbig, Alethea K., and Perkins, Agnes Regan. *Dictionary of American Children's Fiction, 1960–1984.* Westport, CT: Greenwood Press, 1986, p. 747.

Stines, Joe. "Laurence Yep." In *American Writers for Children since 1960: Fiction. Dictionary of Literary Biography,* vol. 52. Detroit: Gale, 1986, pp. 392–397.

Twentieth Century Children's Writers. 2nd ed. Edited by D. L. Kirkpatrick. New York: St. Martin's Press, 1983, pp. 850–851.

Twentieth-Century Science Fiction Writers. 2nd ed. Edited by Curtis C. Smith. Chicago: St. James Press, 1986, pp. 821–822.

Yep, Laurence. "Books Remembered." *CBC Features* 41 (Sept. 1987–Apr. 1988). Formerly *The Calendar.*

———. "A Chinese Sense of Reality." In *Innocence & Experience.* Edited by Barbara Harrison and Gregory Maguire. New York: Lothrop, 1987, pp. 485–489.

———. "Fantasy and Reality." *Horn Book* 54 (Apr. 1978): 137–143.

———. "World Building." In *Innocence & Experience.* Edited by Barbara Harrison and Gregory Maguire. New York: Lothrop, 1987, pp. 182–183.

———. "Writing *Dragonwings.*" *Reading Teacher* 30 (Jan. 1977): 359–363.

Yolen (Stemple), Jane H(yatt)

Fourth Book of Junior Authors and Illustrators. Edited by Doris De Montreville and Elizabeth D. Crawford. New York: Wilson, 1978, pp. 356–358.

"An Interview with Jane Yolen." *Mythlore* 47 (1986): 34–36, 48.

Kreuger, William E. "Jane Yolen." In *American Writers for Children since 1960: Fiction. Dictionary of Literary Biography,* vol. 52. Detroit: Gale, 1986, pp. 398–404.

Raymond, A. "Jane Yolen: Creative Storyteller." *Early Years* 14 (Dec. 1983): 22–24.

Roginski, Jim. *Behind the Covers: Interviews with Authors and Illustrators of Books for Children and Young Adults.* Littleton, CO: Libraries Unlimited, 1985, pp. 224–238.

Schweitzer, Darrell. "Jane Yolen: The Pornography of Innocence." *Fantasy Newsletter* 62 (1983): 12–13, 38. Interview.

Stott, Jon C. *Children's Literature from A to Z.* New York: McGraw-Hill, 1984, p. 295.

Twentieth Century Children's Writers. 2nd ed. Edited by D. L. Kirkpatrick. New York: St. Martin's Press, 1983, pp. 851–853.

White, David E. "Profile: Jane Yolen." *Language Arts* 60 (1983): 652–660.

Wiater, Stanley. "*Thrust* Profile: Jane Yolen." *Thrust* 23 (1985): 16–17.

Yolen, Jane. "Dealing With Dragons." *Horn Book* 60 (June 1984): 380–388.

———. "[Children's Book Illustration:] The Eye and the Ear." *Children's Literature Association Quarterly* 6 (Winter 1981–82): 8–9. Excerpted from Jane Yolen. *Touch Magic.* New York: Philomel, 1981. Reprinted in Patricia Dooley. *The First Steps.* West Lafayette, IN: Children's Literature Association Publications, 1984, pp. 133–134.

———. "The Fault of the Nightingale." *California Medical and Library Educators Association Journal* 1 (Fall 1977): 8–12. Effects of fairy tales on children; speech given at Festival of Children's Books, May 1977.

———. "*The Girl*—From Where?—*Who Loved the Wind.*" *Wilson Library Bulletin* 46 (Oct. 1973): 139–161.

———. "Here There Be Dragons." *Top of the News* 39 (Fall 1982): 54–56. Reprinted from Jane Yolen. *Touch Magic.* New York: Philomel, 1981.

———. "The Literary Underwater World." *Language Arts* 57 (1980): 403–412.

———. "Magic Mirrors: Social Reflections in the Glass of Fantasy." *Children's Literature Association Quarterly* 11 (Summer 1986): 88–90.

———. "Makers of Modern Myths." *Horn Book* 51 (Oct. 1975): 496–497.

———. "Modern Mythmakers." *Language Arts* (May 1976): 491–495.

———. "Storytelling: The Oldest and Newest Art." In *The Writer's Handbook.* Edited by Sylvia K. Burack. Boston: The Writer, 1985.

———. "Strings That Touch the Sky." *The Writer* 97 (Jan. 1984): 7–8. Reprinted in *The Writer's Handbook.* Edited by Sylvia K. Burack. Boston: The Writer, 1985.

———. *Touch Magic: Fantasy, Faerie and Folklore in the Literature of Childhood.* New York: Philomel, 1981.

———. "Tough Magic." *Parent's Choice* (September 1978). Reprinted in *Top of the News* 35 (Winter 1979): 183–187; and in Jane Yolen. *Touch Magic.* New York: Philomel, 1981, pp. 69–74.

———. "Traveling the Road to Ithaca." In *Innocence & Experience.* Edited by Barbara Harrison and Gregory Maguire. New York: Lothrop, 1987, p. 188.

———. "The Voice of Fantasy." *Advocate* 3 (Fall 1983): 50–56.

———. "The Wood Between the Worlds." *Mythlore* 41 (1985): 5–7. Fifteenth Mythopoeic Conference Guest of Honor Speech, on Fantasy.

———. *Writing Books for Children.* rev. ed. Boston: The Writer, 1983.

York, Carol Beach

Fifth Book of Junior Authors and Illustrators. Edited by Sally Holmes Holtze. New York: Wilson, 1983, pp. 340–341.

Young, Ella

Colum, Padraic. "Ella Young: A Druidess." *Horn Book* 15 (May 1939): 183–188.

———. *Ella Young: An Appreciation.* London: Longman, 1931.

Eaton, Anne. "Ella Young's Unicorns and Kyelins." *Horn Book* 9 (Aug. 1933): 115–120.

Flanagan, Sylvia. "Ella Young at Home." *Horn Book* 15 (May 1939): 145–148.

Hadden, Anne. "Off the Beaten Path with Ella Young." *Horn Book* 15 (May 1939): 175–180.

Horn Book Magazine. Special Issue 15 (May 1939): 139–148, 175–188.

The Junior Book of Authors. 2nd ed. rev. Edited by Stanley J. Kunitz and Howard Haycraft. New York: Wilson, 1951, pp. 305–306.

Roginski, Jim, ed. *Newbery and Caldecott Medalists and Honor Book Winners.* Littleton, CO: Libraries Unlimited, 1982, pp. 295–296.

Sayers, Frances Clarke. "The Flowering Dusk of Ella Young." *Horn Book* 21 (May–June 1945): 214–220.

Terrill, Jane Verne. "Ella Young: How She Came to Know the Fairies." *Horn Book* 3 (May 1927): 3–5.

Whitney, Elinor. "A Draught from the Sacred Well." *Horn Book* 3 (May 1927): 6–9.

Young, Ella. "Faërie Music (Ceol Sidhe)." *Horn Book* 21 (May 1945): 211–213.

———. "The Poet's Fee." *Horn Book* 15 (May 1939): 139–144. Story.

Zelazny, Roger (Joseph Christopher)

Barbour, Douglas. "Roger Zelazny." In *Supernatural Fiction Writers: Fantasy and Horror,* vol. 2. Edited by E. F. Bleiler. New York: Scribner, 1985, pp. 1113–1120.

Brasswell, Laurel. "The Visionary Voyage in Science Fiction and Medieval Allegory." *Mosaic* 14 (Winter 1981): 125–142.

Collings, Michael R. "Words and Worlds: The Creation of a Fantasy Universe in Zelazny, Lee, and Anthony." In *The Scope of the Fantastic—Theory, Technique, Major Authors.* Edited by Robert A. Collins and Howard D. Pearce. Westport, CT: Greenwood Press, 1985, pp. 173–182.

Francavilla, Joseph V. "Promethean Bound: Heroes and Gods in Roger Zelazny's

Science Fiction." In *The Transcendent Adventure*. Edited by Robert Reilly. Westport, CT: Greenwood Press, 1985, pp. 207–224.

———. "These Immortals: An Alternative View of Immortality in Roger Zelazny's Science Fiction." *Extrapolation* 25 (1984): 20–33.

Krulik, Theodore. *Roger Zelazny*. New York: Ungar, 1986.

Levack, Daniel J. H. *"Amber" Dreams: A Roger Zelazny Bibliography*. Columbia, PA: Underwood-Miller, 1983.

Lucy, N. J. *The Arthurian Encyclopedia*. New York: Garland, 1986, p. 648.

Mayo, Clark. *"Changeling* and *Madwand."* In *Survey of Modern Fantasy Literature,* vol. 1. Englewood Cliffs, NJ: Salem Press, 1983, pp. 228–231.

———. *"Jack of Shadows."* In *Survey of Modern Fantasy Literature,* vol. 2. Englewood Cliffs, NJ: Salem Press, 1983, pp. 794–797.

Monteleone, Thomas F. "Fire and Ice—On Roger Zelazny's Short Fiction." *Algol* 13 (1976): 9–14.

Morrissey, Thomas J. "Zelazny: Mythmaker of Nuclear War." *Science Fiction Studies* 13 (1986): 182–192.

Nichols, Peter. "Roger Zelazny." In *Science Fiction Writers*. Edited by E. F. Bleiler. New York: Scribner, 1982, pp. 563–570.

Sanders, Joseph L. "Dancing on the Tightrope: Immortality in Roger Zelazny." In *Death and the Serpent*. Edited by Carl B. Yoke and Donald M. Hassler. Westport, CT: Greenwood Press, 1985, pp. 135–144.

———. *Roger Zelazny: A Primary and Secondary Bibliography*. Boston: G. K. Hall, 1980.

———. "Zelazny: Unfinished Business." In *Voices for the Future: Essays on Major Science Fiction Writers,* vol. 2. Edited by Thomas D. Clareson. Bowling Green, OH: Bowling Green Univ. Press, 1979.

———. "Zelazny's 'Dilvish' Series: Enduring Concerns." *Fantasy Newsletter* 62 (1983): 31–32.

Schlobin, Roger C. "The Fool and the Fantastic." *Fantasy Newsletter* 43 (1981): 6–9, 29.

Schuyler, William M., Jr. "Recent Developments in Spell Construction." In *The Aesthetics of Fantasy Literature and Art*. Edited by Roger C. Schlobin. Notre Dame, IN: Univ. of Notre Dame, 1982, pp. 237–248.

Searles, Baird; Meacham, Beth; and Franklin, Michael. *A Reader's Guide to Fantasy*. New York: Avon, 1982, pp. 160–161.

Thomson, W. B. "Interview: Roger Zelazny." *Future Life* 25 (1981): 40–42.

Thurston, Robert. "Introduction." In Roger Zelazny. *Today We Choose Faces*. Boston: Gregg, 1978.

Twentieth-Century Science Fiction Writers. 2nd ed. Edited by Curtis C. Smith. Chicago: St. James Press, 1986, pp. 831–834.

Vance, Michael, and Eads, Bill. "An Interview with Roger Zelazny." *Fantasy Newsletter* 55 (1983): 8–10.

Walker, Paul. *Speaking of Science Fiction: The Paul Walker Interviews*. Oradell, NJ: Luna Publications, 1978.

Wilgus, Neal. "Interview: Roger Zelazny." *Science Fiction Review* 36 (1980): 14–16.

Yoke, Carl B. *"The Amber Series."* In *Survey of Modern Fantasy Literature,* vol. 1. Englewood Cliffs, NJ: Salem Press, 1983, pp. 29–35.

———. *Roger Zelazny*. West Linn, OR: Starmont, 1979.

———. *Roger Zelazny and Andre Norton: Proponents of Individualism*. Columbus: State Library of Ohio, 1979.

———. "Roger Zelazny's Bold New Mythologies." In *Critical Encounters II: Writers and Themes in Science Fiction*. Edited by Tom Staicar. New York: Ungar, 1982.

———. "Roger Zelazny's Form and Chaos Philosophy." *Science Fiction* 2 (1979): 129–150.
Zelazny, Roger. "Constructing Science Fiction Novels." *The Writer* 97 (Oct. 1984): 9–12, 46.
———. "The Process of Composing." In *The Science Fiction Sourcebook*. Edited by David Wingrove. New York: Van Nostrand Reinhold, 1984.

Zemach, Harve (pseud. of Harvey Fischtrom)

Stott, Jon C. *Children's Literature from A to Z*. New York: McGraw-Hill, 1984, p. 296.
Third Book of Junior Authors. Edited by Doris De Montreville and Donna Hill. New York: Wilson, 1972, pp. 310–312.

Zimnik, Reiner

Chambers, Aidan. *Booktalk: Occasional Writing on Literature and Children*. New York: Harper and Row, 1986, pp. 19–24, 48, 69, 71, 148, 159.
Danischewsky, Nina. "Re-Viewing Reiner Zimnik." *Signal* 6 (Sept. 1971): 115–125.
Third Book of Junior Authors. Edited by Doris De Montreville and Donna Hill. New York: Wilson, 1972, pp. 312–313.

Zindel, Paul

Eaglen, Audrey. "Of Life, Love, Death, Kids, and Inhalation Therapy: An Interview with Paul Zindel." *Top of the News* 34 (Winter 1978): 178–185.
Fifth Book of Junior Authors and Illustrators. Edited by Sally Holmes Holtze. New York: Wilson, 1983, pp. 343–344.
Hipple, Theodore W. "Paul Zindel." In *American Writers for Children since 1960: Fiction. Dictionary of Literary Biography,* vol. 52. Detroit: Gale, 1986, pp. 405–410.
Hoffman, Stanley. "Winning, Losing, But Above All Taking Risks: A Look at the Novels of Paul Zindel." *The Lion and the Unicorn* 2 (Fall 1978): 78–88.
Janeczko, P. "Interview: Paul Zindel." *English Journal* 66 (Oct. 1977): 20–21.
The Oxford Companion to Children's Literature. Edited by Humphrey Carpenter and Mari Prichard. New York: Oxford Univ. Press, 1984, p. 587.
Twentieth Century Children's Writers. 2nd ed. Edited by D. L. Kirkpatrick. New York: St. Martin's Press, 1983, pp. 853–854.
Zindel, Paul. "Magic of Special People." *School Media Quarterly* 2 (Fall 1979): 29–32.

Zolotow, Charlotte S(hapiro)

Chapman, Karen Lenz. "Themes of Charlotte Zolotow's Books and Her Adult Development." Master's thesis, Claremont Graduate School, 1981.
Francis, Elizabeth. "Charlotte Zolotow." In *American Writers for Children since 1960: Fiction. Dictionary of Literary Biography,* vol. 52. Detroit: Gale, 1986, pp. 411–418.
More Junior Authors. Edited by Muriel Fuller. New York: Wilson, 1963, p. 235.
Wintle, Justin, and Fisher, Emma. *The Pied Pipers*. New York: Two Continents, 1975, pp. 87–100.
Zolotow, Charlotte. "Writing for the Very Young." *Horn Book* 61 (Sept. 1985): 536–540.

Author and Illustrator Index

This Author and Illustrator Index provides page references to the specific works of all authors and editors of books mentioned in Chapters 1 through 10, including out-of-print works. Variant titles, such as British or paperback titles, are included in parentheses following the main title. Illustrator entries refer to page numbers only and do not list specific works.

Title Index

This index provides page references to all titles mentioned in Chapters 1 through 10, including variant titles. The author surname appears in parentheses following the book title.

Subject Index

This Subject Index provides topical headings for many areas that children, young adults, and the librarians who serve them are interested in—series titles, historical periods, imaginary beings and worlds, and mythical creatures. Historical periods are listed in chronological order within a specific country (for example, Revolutionary War can be found under United States—Historical, Revolutionary War). General headings such as mythology, folklore, legends, and fantasy are not listed here. The user should refer to a specific chapter, folktale, or nation for a particular title or genre. All references are to page numbers within Chapters 1 through 10.

745

Lagerlöf, Selma. *The Wonderful Adventures of Nils*, 292
Lawson, Robert. *The Fabulous Flight*, 294
Lindgren, Astrid. *Karlsson-on-the-Roof*, 294
Mayne, William. *The Green Book of Hob Stories*, 297
Moore, Anne Carroll. *Nicholas: A Manhattan Christmas Story*, 298
Morgan, Helen. *Satchkin Patchkin*, 298
Norton, Mary. *The Borrowers*, 300
Otto, Margaret G. *The Tiny Man*, 92
Parrish, Anne, and Parrish, Dilwin. *Knee-High to a Grasshopper*, 302
Proysen, Alf. *Little Old Mrs. Pepperpot and Other Stories*, 303
Reid Banks, Lynne. *The Indian in the Cupboard*, 304
Steele, Mary Q. *Wish, Come True*, 306
Swift, Jonathan. *Gulliver's Travels into Several Remote Nations of the World*, 232
Tapp, Kathy Kennedy. *Moth-Kin Magic*, 306
Tolkien, J. R. R. *The Hobbit*, 182
Townsend, Ralph M. *A Journey to the Garden Gate*, 307
Wallace, Barbara Brooks. *The Barrel in the Basement*, 308
Wells, Rosemary. *Through the Hidden Door*, 232
Wersba, Barbara. *Let Me Fall Before I Fly*, 55
White, T. H. *Mistress Masham's Repose*, 309
Winterfeld, Henry. *Castaways in Lilliput*, 233
Winthrop, Elizabeth. *The Castle in the Attic*, 233
Yolen, Jane H. *The Wizard of Washington Square*, 366
Minnipins books
Kendall, Carol. *The Gammage Cup*, 169; *The Whisper of Glocken*, 169
Miss Bianca series
Sharp, Margery. *The Rescuers*, 97
Miss Mallard mysteries
Quackenbush, Robert M. *Express Train to Trouble: A Miss Mallard Mystery*, 263
Mr. Yowder series
Rounds, Glen. *The Day the Circus Came to Lone Tree*, 265
Monsters. *See also* Narguns
Babbitt, Natalie. *Kneeknock Rise*, 8
Bulla, Clyde Robert. *My Friend the Monster*, 12
Cameron, Eleanor. *The Terrible Churnadryne*, 279
Campbell, Hope. *Peter's Angel*, 74

Charnas, Suzy McKee. *The Bronze King*, 347
Easton, M. Coleman. *The Fisherman's Curse*, 164
Fry, Rosalie K. *Mungo*, 286
Grimble, Rosemary. *Jonothon and Large*, 288
Harris, Rosemary. *Sea Magic and Other Stories of Enchantment*, 119
Hayes, Geoffrey. *The Alligator and His Uncle Tooth: A Novel of the Sea*, 82
Larson, Jean. *The Silkspinners*, 35
Little, Jane. *Sneaker Hill*, 358
MacKellar, William. *The Smallest Monster in the World*, 296
McNeill, Janet. *A Monster Too Many*, 296
Mayne, William. *A Game of Dark*, 324
Mendoza, George. *Gwot! Horribly Funny Hairticklers*, 258
Monsters, Ghoulies and Creepy Creatures: Fantastic Stories and Poems, 125
Nesbit, E. *The Enchanted Castle*, 299
Nye, Robert. *Beowulf; a New Telling*, 202
Ormondroyd, Edward. *David and the Phoenix*, 301
Palmer, Mary. *The Magic Knight*, 44; *The Teaspoon Tree*, 301
Phipson, Joan. *The Way Home*, 328
Pinkwater, Daniel Manus. *The Frankenbagle Monster*, 262; *Yobgorgle: Mystery Monster of Lake Ontario*, 262
Sleigh, Barbara. *Stirabout Stories, Brewed in Her Own Cauldron*, 130
Trott, Susan. *The Sea Serpent of Horse*, 232
Warburg, Sandol Stoddard. *On the Way Home*, 54
Moomins series
Jansson, Tove. *Finn Family Moomintroll*, 168
Mordant's Need series
Donaldson, Stephen R. *The Mirror of Her Dreams*, 217
Morgaine series
Cherryh, C. J. *Exile's Gate*, 160
The Mouldiwarp
Nesbit, E. *The House of Arden*, 325
Moth-Kins
Tapp, Kathy Kennedy. *Moth-Kin Magic*, 306
Mundania
Anthony, Piers. *A Spell for Chameleon*, 158
Murry Family series
L'Engle, Madeleine. *Many Waters*, 321
Mushroom Planet books
Cameron, Eleanor. *Time and Mr. Bass: A Mushroom Planet Book*, 314
Mycetia
Cameron, Eleanor. *Time and Mr. Bass: A Mushroom Planet Book*, 314